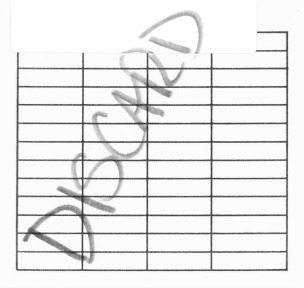

DOONESBURY
DOONESBURY
REDUX
REDUX

Recent Doonesbury Books by G.B. Trudeau

Read My Lips, Make My Day, Eat Quiche and Die!
Give Those Nymphs Some Hooters!
You're Smokin' Now, Mr. Butts!
I'd Go With the Helmet, Ray
Welcome to Club Scud!
What Is It, Tink, Is Pan in Trouble?
Quality Time on Highway 1
Washed Out Bridges and Other Disasters
In Search of Cigarette Holder Man
Doonesbury Nation
Virtual Doonesbury
Planet Doonesbury
Buck Wild Doonesbury
Duke 2000: Whatever It Takes
The Revolt of the English Majors
Peace Out, Dawg!
Got War?

Special Collections

The Doonesbury Chronicles
Doonesbury's Greatest Hits
The People's Doonesbury
Doonesbury Dossier: The Reagan Years
Doonesbury Deluxe: Selected Glances Askance
Recycled Doonesbury: Second Thoughts on a Gilded Age
Action Figure!
The Portable Doonesbury
Flashbacks: Twenty-Five Years of Doonesbury
The Bundled Doonesbury

A DOONESBURY BOOK

DOONESBURY DOONESBURY REDUX

Duke 2000: Whatever It Takes
& The Revolt of the English Majors

BY G. B. TRUDEAU

GRAMERCY BOOKS
NEW YORK

Originally published as two volumes by Andrews McMeel Publishing under the titles:

Duke 2000: Whatever It Takes © 2000 by G. B. Trudeau
The Revolt of the English Majors © 2001 by G. B. Trudeau

This 2004 edition is published by Gramercy Books, an imprint of Random House Value Publishing, a division of Random House, Inc., New York, by arrangement with Andrews McMeel Publishing.

Gramercy is a registered trademark and the colophon is a trademark of Random House, Inc.

Random House
New York • Toronto • London • Sydney • Auckland
www.randomhouse.com

Printed and bound in Singapore

        Library of Congress Cataloging-in-Publication Data
Trudeau, G. B., 1948-
   [Doonesbury. Selections]
   Doonesbury redux / by G.B. Trudeau.
      p. cm.
   "Originally published as two volumes"—Copr. p.
   Contents: Duke 2000 — Revolt of the English majors.
   ISBN 0-517-22407-0
    I. Title: Duke 2000. II. Title: Revolt of the English majors. III. Title.

   PN6728.D65T7249 2004
   741.5'973—dc22

                                                2004042527

10 9 8 7 6 5 4 3 2 1

CONTENTS

DUKE

DUKE 2000

WHATEVER IT TAKES 2000

"I understand small business growth. I was one."

—George W. Bush

SO WHAT ARE YOU UP TO AT SCHOOL TODAY, JEFF? ANYTHING INTERESTING GOING ON?
NOT HAVING ANY PROBLEMS, ARE YOU? EVERYTHING COOL WITH YOUR BUDS? WITH YOUR TEACHERS?
WHY DON'T YOU JUST PAT ME DOWN, DAD?
NO, NO, I REALLY AM INTERESTED.

DAD, CAN I GO NOW?
YOU SURE YOU DON'T WANT TO TALK ABOUT ANYTHING, SON?
NO, DAD, WHAT I WANT TO DO IS JUST GET MY BOOKS AND GO TO SCHOOL, OKAY?
UM... HOW ABOUT SOME MORE CEREAL FIRST?
CEREAL?
OR EGGS! SIT DOWN AND I'LL MAKE YOU SOME EGGS! OR WAFFLES! YOUR CHOICE!
MOM'S GOING THROUGH MY STUFF, ISN'T SHE?
MOM GOING THROUGH YOUR STUFF? DON'T BE RIDICULOUS!

OH... JEFF...
LOOKING FOR ANYTHING SPECIAL, MOM?
NAVY
UM... NO... NO, OF COURSE NOT, HONEY. I'M JUST TRYING TO GET REACQUAINTED WITH WHAT'S GOING ON IN YOUR LIFE...
IT JUST SEEMS THERE ARE LESSONS FOR ALL OF US IN THE LITTLETON TRAGEDY.
OH, YEAH? WHAT LESSON AM I SUPPOSED TO LEARN?
DON'T GET ME STARTED.
OH, HELL, MOM, I LEARNED THAT ONE YEARS AGO.

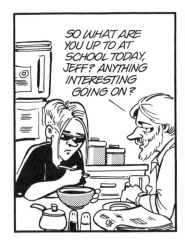

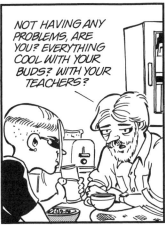

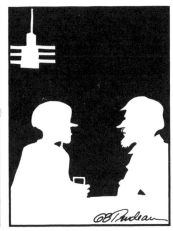

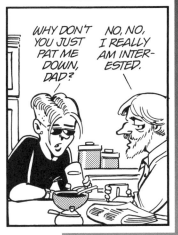

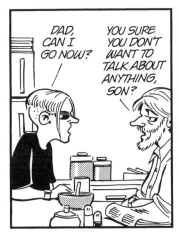

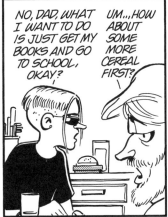

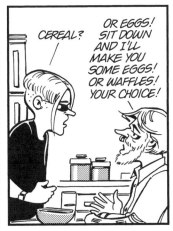

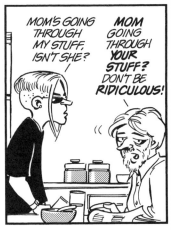

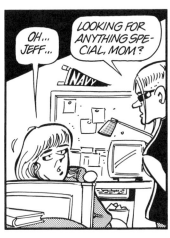

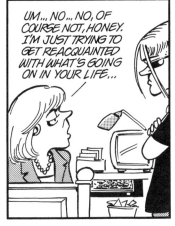

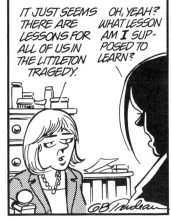

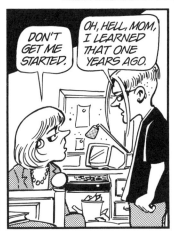

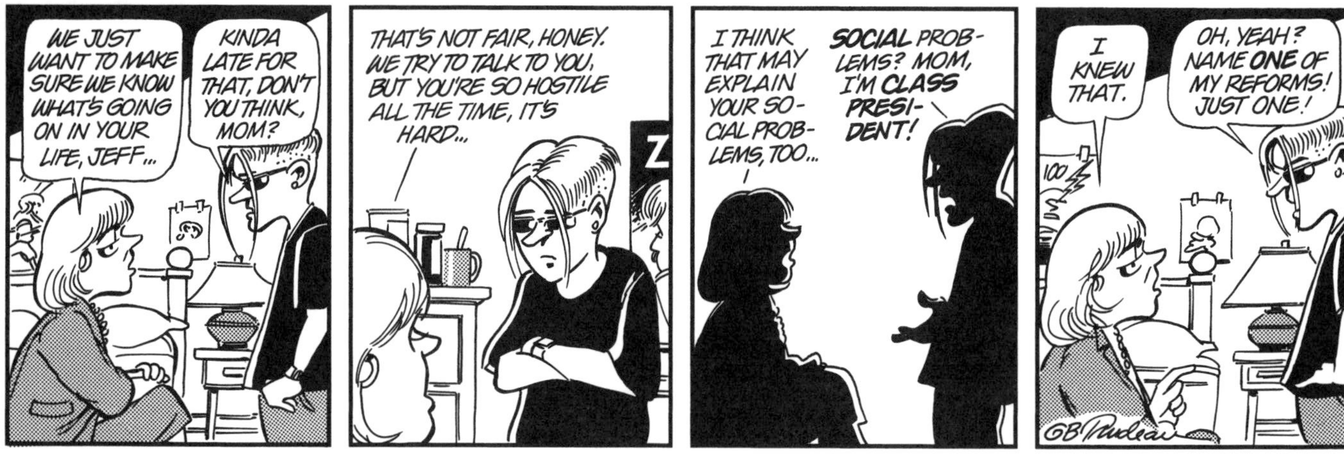
WE JUST WANT TO MAKE SURE WE KNOW WHAT'S GOING ON IN YOUR LIFE, JEFF...
KINDA LATE FOR THAT, DON'T YOU THINK, MOM?
THAT'S NOT FAIR, HONEY. WE TRY TO TALK TO YOU, BUT YOU'RE SO HOSTILE ALL THE TIME, IT'S HARD...
I THINK THAT MAY EXPLAIN YOUR SOCIAL PROBLEMS, TOO...
SOCIAL PROBLEMS? MOM, I'M CLASS PRESIDENT!
I KNEW THAT.
OH, YEAH? NAME ONE OF MY REFORMS! JUST ONE!

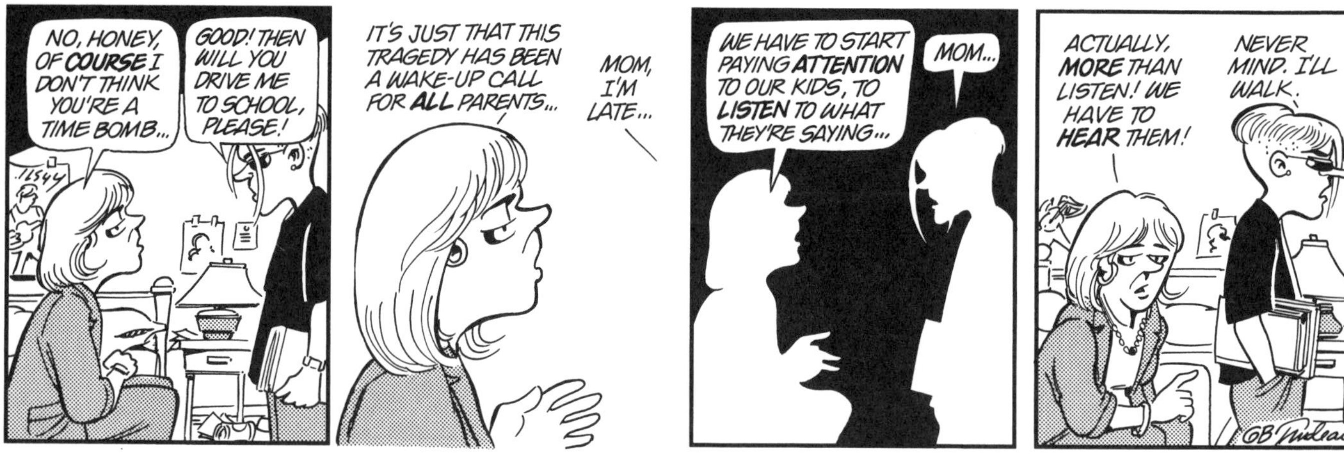
NO, HONEY, OF COURSE I DON'T THINK YOU'RE A TIME BOMB...
GOOD! THEN WILL YOU DRIVE ME TO SCHOOL, PLEASE!
IT'S JUST THAT THIS TRAGEDY HAS BEEN A WAKE-UP CALL FOR ALL PARENTS...
MOM, I'M LATE...
WE HAVE TO START PAYING ATTENTION TO OUR KIDS, TO LISTEN TO WHAT THEY'RE SAYING...
MOM...
ACTUALLY, MORE THAN LISTEN! WE HAVE TO HEAR THEM!
NEVER MIND. I'LL WALK.

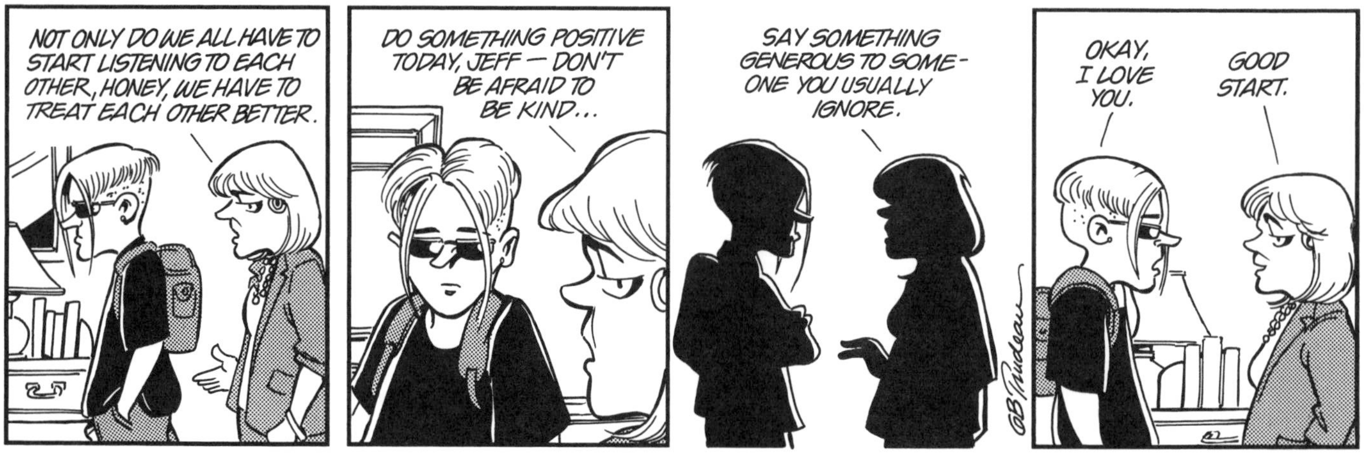
NOT ONLY DO WE ALL HAVE TO START LISTENING TO EACH OTHER, HONEY, WE HAVE TO TREAT EACH OTHER BETTER.
DO SOMETHING POSITIVE TODAY, JEFF — DON'T BE AFRAID TO BE KIND...
SAY SOMETHING GENEROUS TO SOMEONE YOU USUALLY IGNORE.
OKAY, I LOVE YOU.
GOOD START.

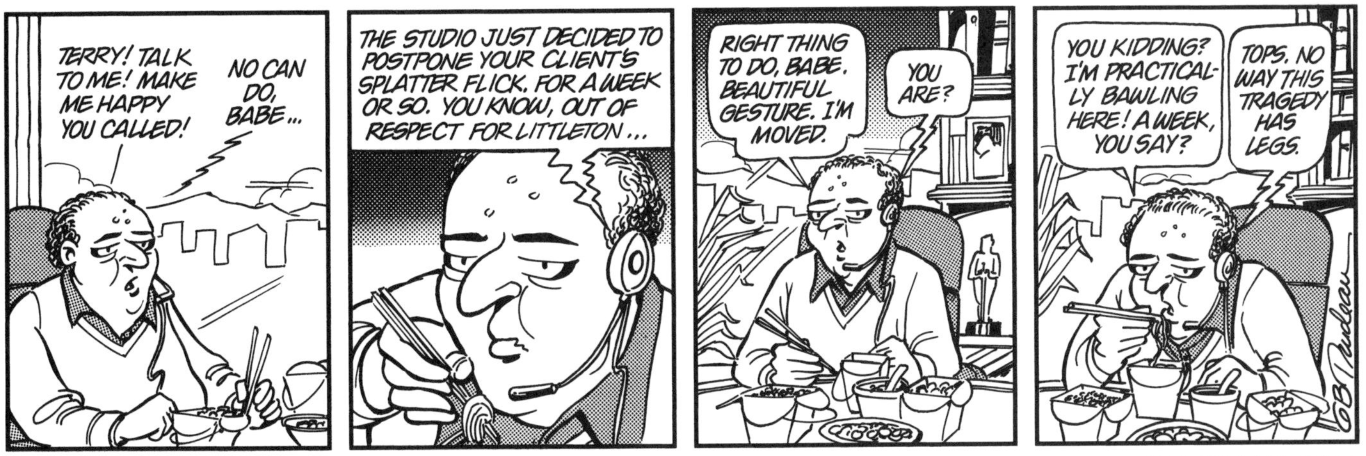
TERRY! TALK TO ME! MAKE ME HAPPY YOU CALLED!
NO CAN DO, BABE...
THE STUDIO JUST DECIDED TO POSTPONE YOUR CLIENT'S SPLATTER FLICK. FOR A WEEK OR SO. YOU KNOW, OUT OF RESPECT FOR LITTLETON...
RIGHT THING TO DO, BABE. BEAUTIFUL GESTURE. I'M MOVED.
YOU ARE?
YOU KIDDING? I'M PRACTICALLY BAWLING HERE! A WEEK, YOU SAY?
TOPS. NO WAY THIS TRAGEDY HAS LEGS.

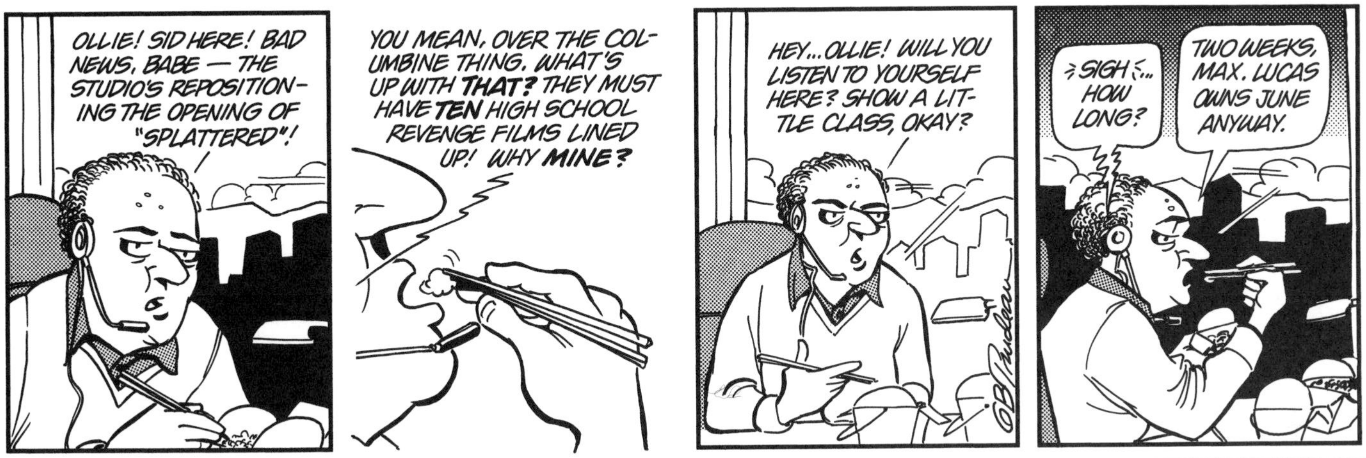
OLLIE! SID HERE! BAD NEWS, BABE — THE STUDIO'S REPOSITIONING THE OPENING OF "SPLATTERED"!
YOU MEAN, OVER THE COLUMBINE THING. WHAT'S UP WITH THAT? THEY MUST HAVE TEN HIGH SCHOOL REVENGE FILMS LINED UP! WHY MINE?
HEY... OLLIE! WILL YOU LISTEN TO YOURSELF HERE? SHOW A LITTLE CLASS, OKAY?
SIGH... HOW LONG?
TWO WEEKS, MAX. LUCAS OWNS JUNE ANYWAY.

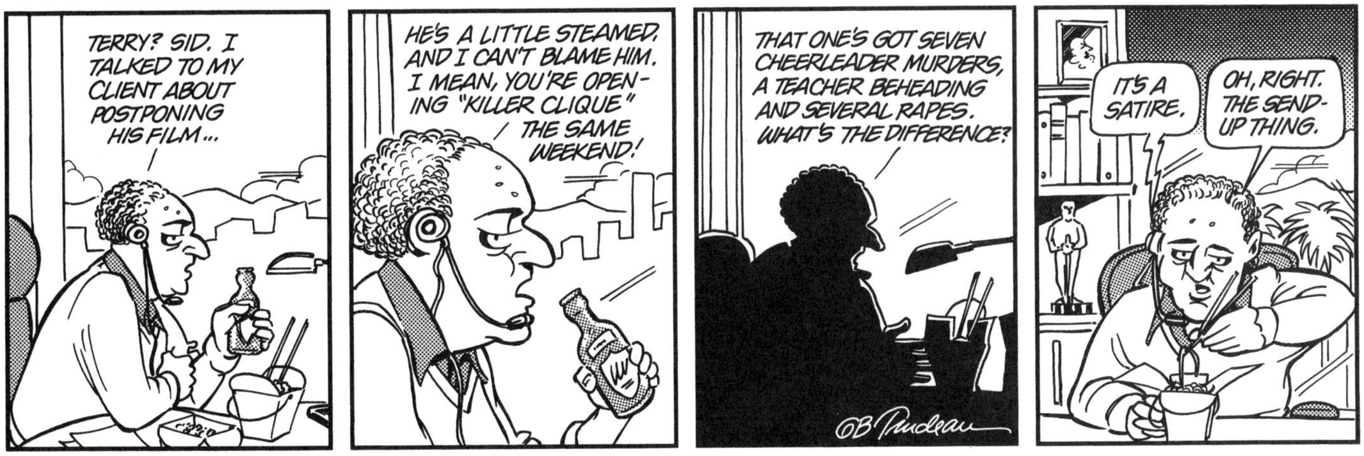
TERRY? SID. I TALKED TO MY CLIENT ABOUT POSTPONING HIS FILM...
HE'S A LITTLE STEAMED, AND I CAN'T BLAME HIM. I MEAN, YOU'RE OPENING "KILLER CLIQUE" THE SAME WEEKEND!
THAT ONE'S GOT SEVEN CHEERLEADER MURDERS, A TEACHER BEHEADING AND SEVERAL RAPES. WHAT'S THE DIFFERENCE?
IT'S A SATIRE.
OH, RIGHT. THE SEND-UP THING.

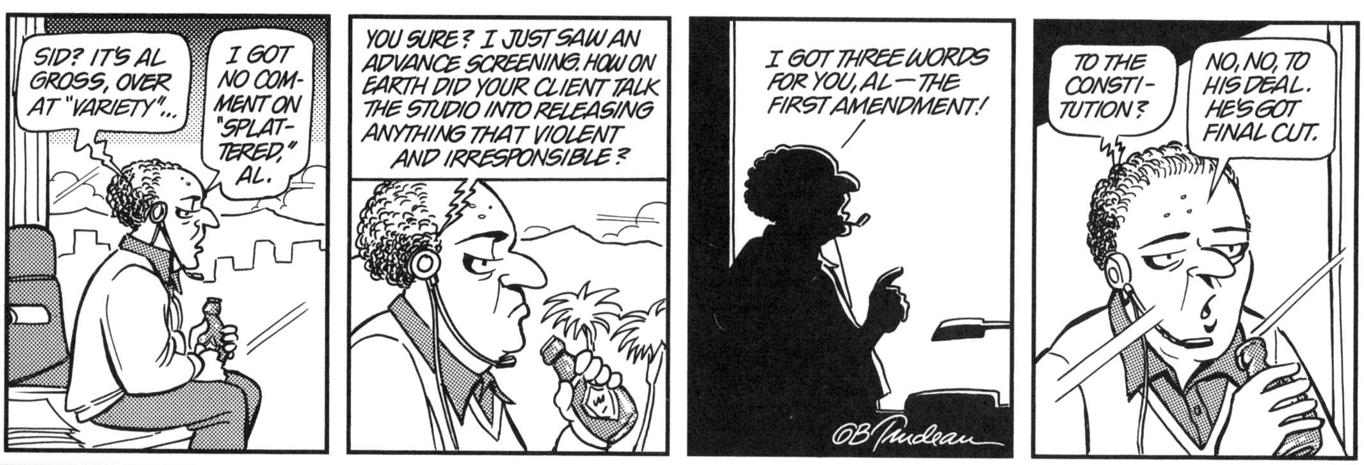
SID? IT'S AL GROSS, OVER AT "VARIETY"...
I GOT NO COMMENT ON "SPLATTERED," AL.
YOU SURE? I JUST SAW AN ADVANCE SCREENING. HOW ON EARTH DID YOUR CLIENT TALK THE STUDIO INTO RELEASING ANYTHING THAT VIOLENT AND IRRESPONSIBLE?
I GOT THREE WORDS FOR YOU, AL — THE FIRST AMENDMENT!
©B Trudeau
TO THE CONSTITUTION?
NO, NO, TO HIS DEAL. HE'S GOT FINAL CUT.

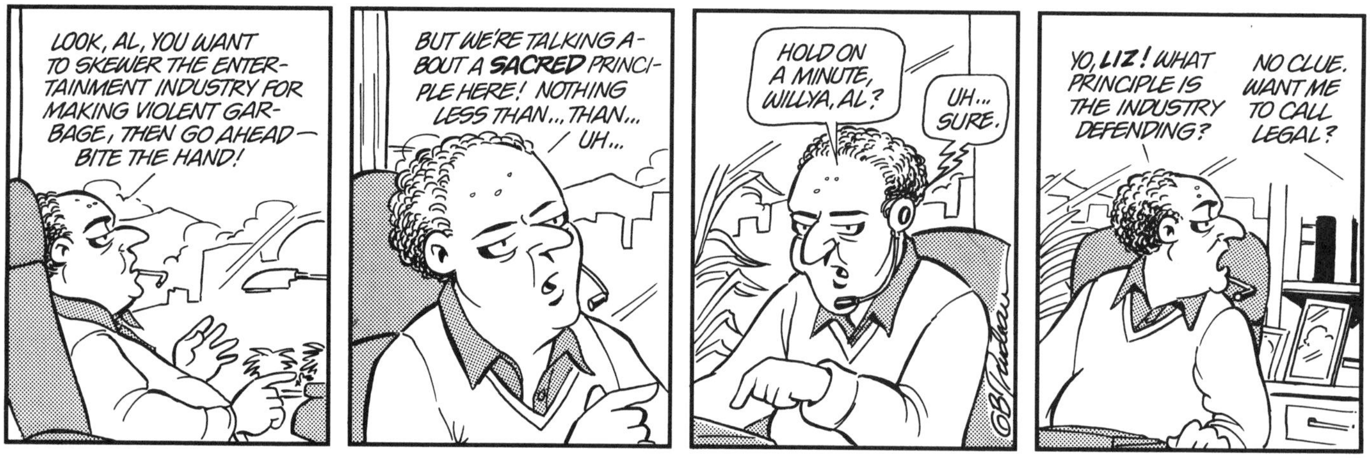
LOOK, AL, YOU WANT TO SKEWER THE ENTERTAINMENT INDUSTRY FOR MAKING VIOLENT GARBAGE, THEN GO AHEAD — BITE THE HAND!
BUT WE'RE TALKING ABOUT A **SACRED** PRINCIPLE HERE! NOTHING LESS THAN... THAN... UH...
HOLD ON A MINUTE, WILLYA, AL?
UH... SURE.
©B Trudeau
YO, **LIZ!** WHAT PRINCIPLE IS THE INDUSTRY DEFENDING?
NO CLUE. WANT ME TO CALL LEGAL?

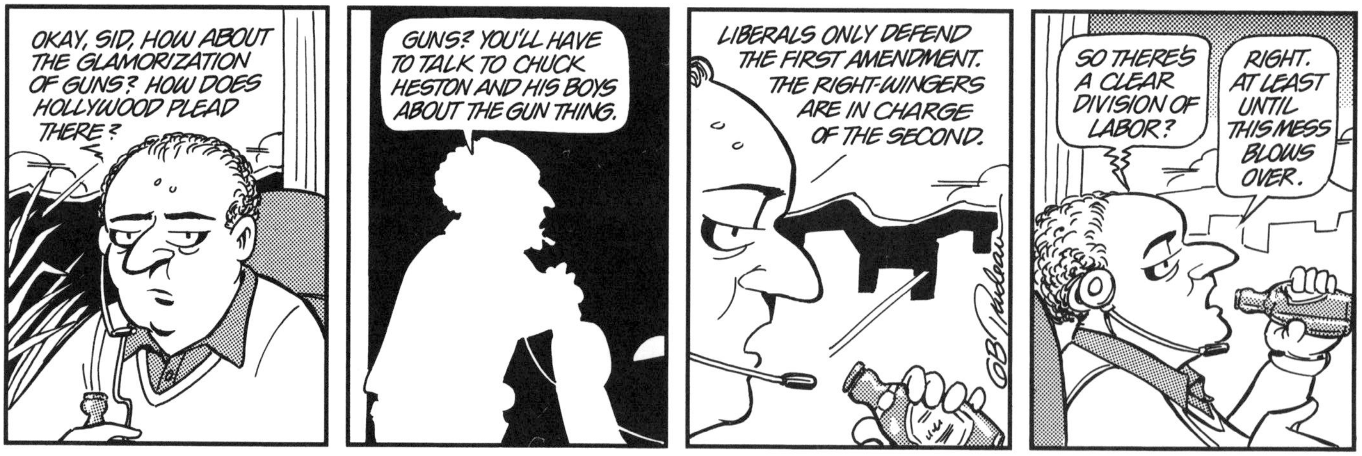
OKAY, SID, HOW ABOUT THE GLAMORIZATION OF GUNS? HOW DOES HOLLYWOOD PLEAD THERE?
GUNS? YOU'LL HAVE TO TALK TO CHUCK HESTON AND HIS BOYS ABOUT THE GUN THING.
LIBERALS ONLY DEFEND THE FIRST AMENDMENT. THE RIGHT-WINGERS ARE IN CHARGE OF THE SECOND.
©B Trudeau
SO THERE'S A CLEAR DIVISION OF LABOR?
RIGHT. AT LEAST UNTIL THIS MESS BLOWS OVER.

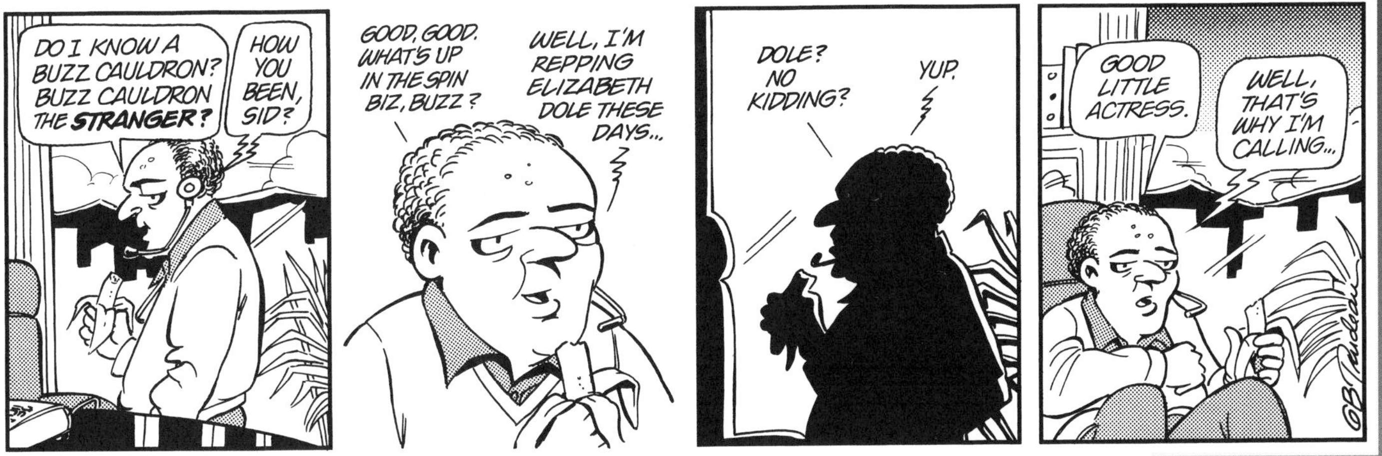
DO I KNOW A BUZZ CAULDRON? BUZZ CAULDRON THE **STRANGER?**
HOW YOU BEEN, SID?
GOOD, GOOD. WHAT'S UP IN THE SPIN BIZ, BUZZ?
WELL, I'M REPPING ELIZABETH DOLE THESE DAYS...
DOLE? NO KIDDING?
YUP.
GOOD LITTLE ACTRESS.
WELL, THAT'S WHY I'M CALLING...

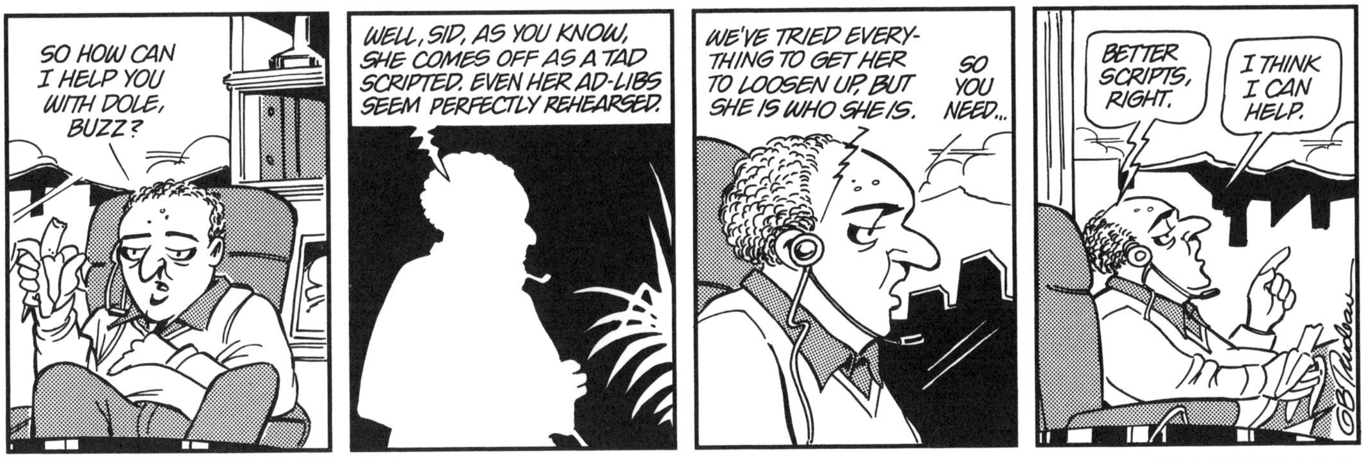
SO HOW CAN I HELP YOU WITH DOLE, BUZZ?
WELL, SID, AS YOU KNOW, SHE COMES OFF AS A TAD SCRIPTED. EVEN HER AD-LIBS SEEM PERFECTLY REHEARSED.
WE'VE TRIED EVERYTHING TO GET HER TO LOOSEN UP, BUT SHE IS WHO SHE IS.
SO YOU NEED...
BETTER SCRIPTS, RIGHT.
I THINK I CAN HELP.

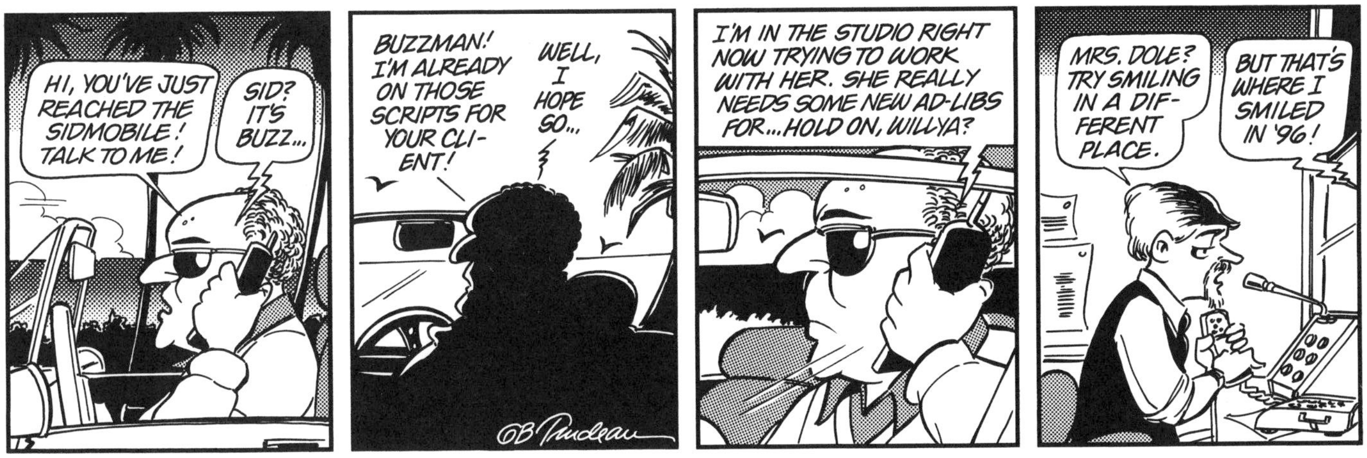
HI, YOU'VE JUST REACHED THE SIDMOBILE! TALK TO ME!
SID? IT'S BUZZ...
BUZZMAN! I'M ALREADY ON THOSE SCRIPTS FOR YOUR CLIENT!
WELL, I HOPE SO...
I'M IN THE STUDIO RIGHT NOW TRYING TO WORK WITH HER. SHE REALLY NEEDS SOME NEW AD-LIBS FOR... HOLD ON, WILLYA?
MRS. DOLE? TRY SMILING IN A DIFFERENT PLACE.
BUT THAT'S WHERE I SMILED IN '96!

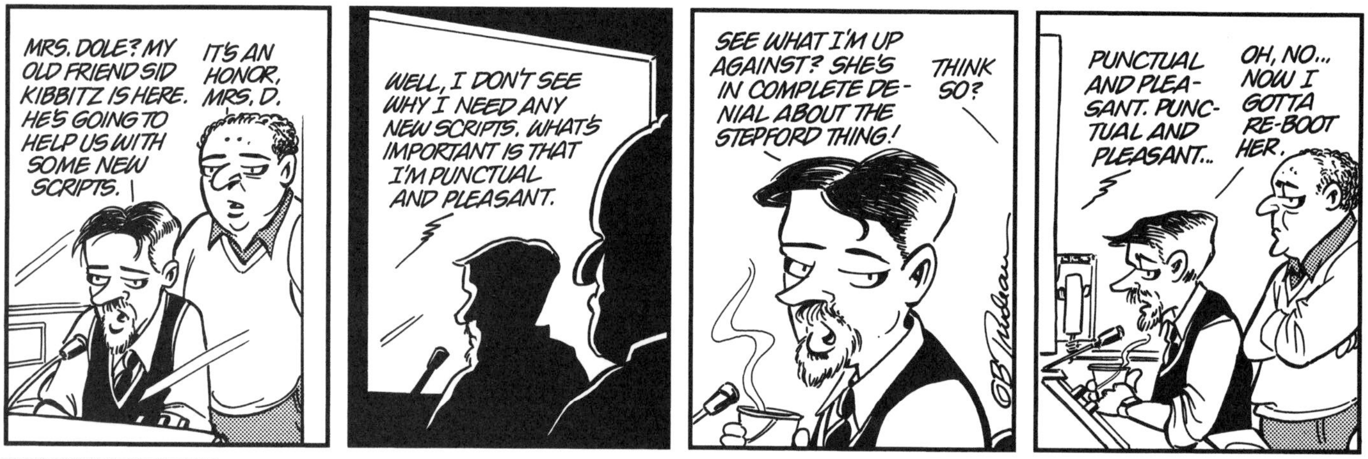
MRS. DOLE? MY OLD FRIEND SID KIBBITZ IS HERE. HE'S GOING TO HELP US WITH SOME NEW SCRIPTS.
IT'S AN HONOR, MRS. D.
WELL, I DON'T SEE WHY I NEED ANY NEW SCRIPTS. WHAT'S IMPORTANT IS THAT I'M PUNCTUAL AND PLEASANT.
SEE WHAT I'M UP AGAINST? SHE'S IN COMPLETE DENIAL ABOUT THE STEPFORD THING!
THINK SO?
PUNCTUAL AND PLEASANT. PUNCTUAL AND PLEASANT...
OH, NO... NOW I GOTTA RE-BOOT HER.

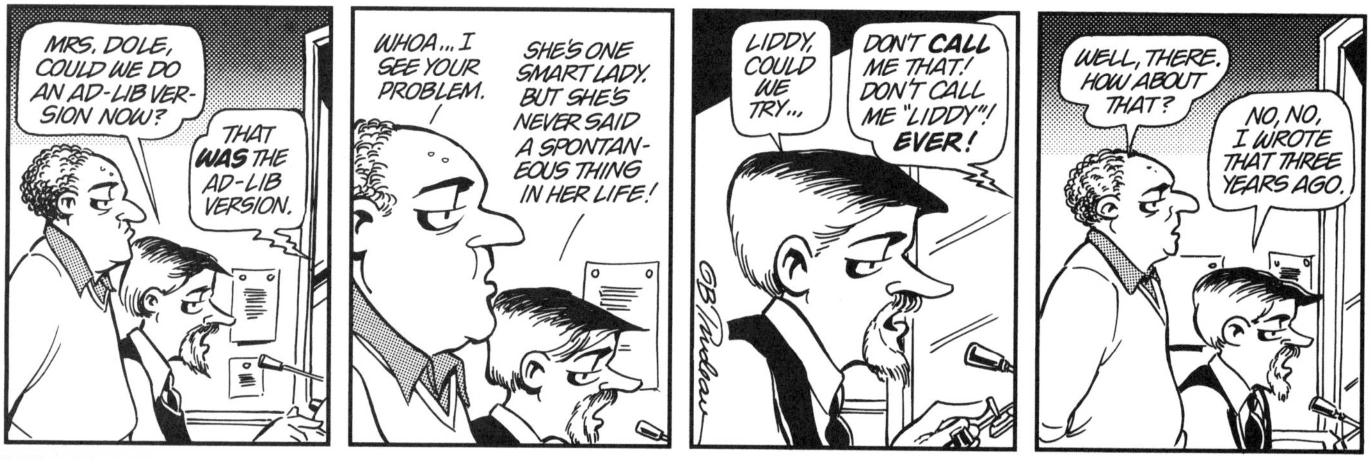
MRS. DOLE, COULD WE DO AN AD-LIB VERSION NOW?
THAT **WAS** THE AD-LIB VERSION.
WHOA... I SEE YOUR PROBLEM.
SHE'S ONE SMART LADY. BUT SHE'S NEVER SAID A SPONTANEOUS THING IN HER LIFE!
LIDDY, COULD WE TRY...
DON'T **CALL** ME THAT! DON'T CALL ME "LIDDY"! **EVER!**
WELL, THERE. HOW ABOUT THAT?
NO, NO, I WROTE THAT THREE YEARS AGO.

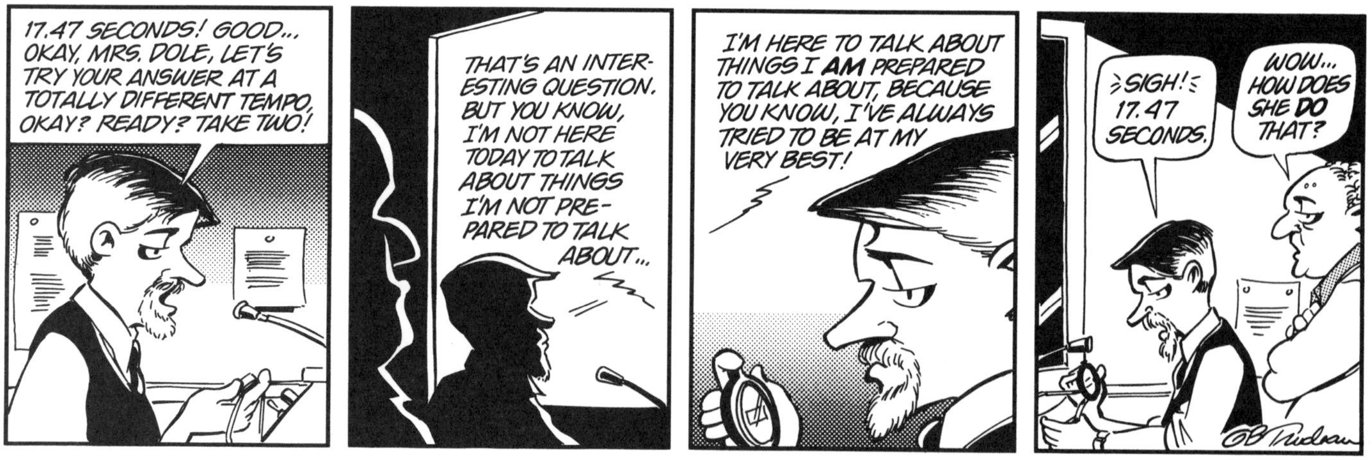
17.47 SECONDS! GOOD... OKAY, MRS. DOLE, LET'S TRY YOUR ANSWER AT A TOTALLY DIFFERENT TEMPO, OKAY? READY? TAKE TWO!
THAT'S AN INTERESTING QUESTION. BUT YOU KNOW, I'M NOT HERE TODAY TO TALK ABOUT THINGS I'M NOT PREPARED TO TALK ABOUT...
I'M HERE TO TALK ABOUT THINGS I **AM** PREPARED TO TALK ABOUT, BECAUSE YOU KNOW, I'VE ALWAYS TRIED TO BE AT MY VERY BEST!
SIGH! 17.47 SECONDS.
WOW... HOW DOES SHE **DO** THAT?

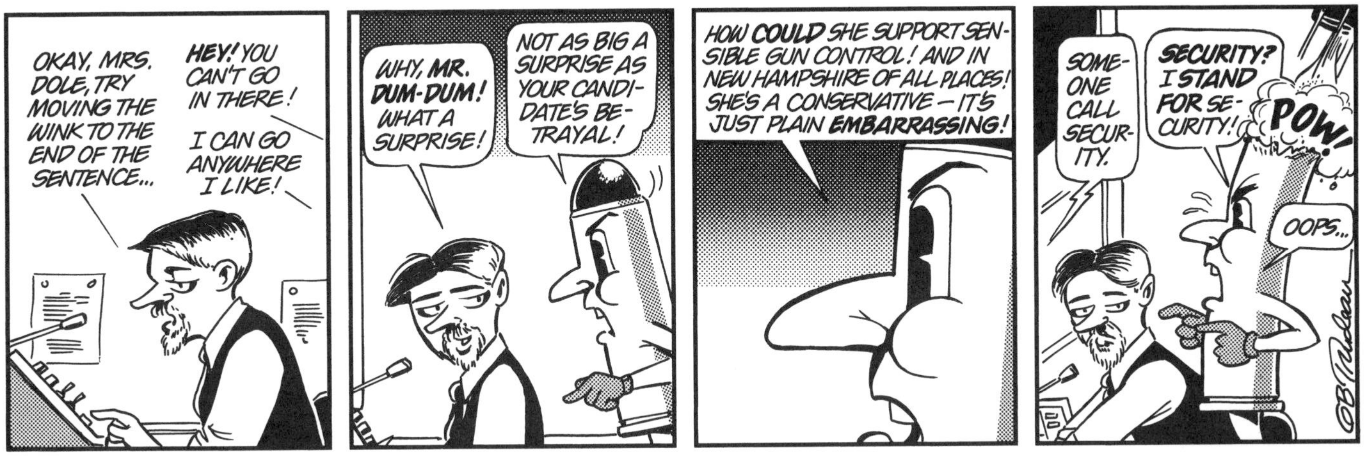
OKAY, MRS. DOLE, TRY MOVING THE WINK TO THE END OF THE SENTENCE...
HEY! YOU CAN'T GO IN THERE!
I CAN GO ANYWHERE I LIKE!
WHY, MR. DUM-DUM! WHAT A SURPRISE!
NOT AS BIG A SURPRISE AS YOUR CANDIDATE'S BETRAYAL!
HOW COULD SHE SUPPORT SENSIBLE GUN CONTROL! AND IN NEW HAMPSHIRE OF ALL PLACES! SHE'S A CONSERVATIVE – IT'S JUST PLAIN EMBARRASSING!
SOMEONE CALL SECURITY.
SECURITY? I STAND FOR SECURITY!
POW!
OOPS...

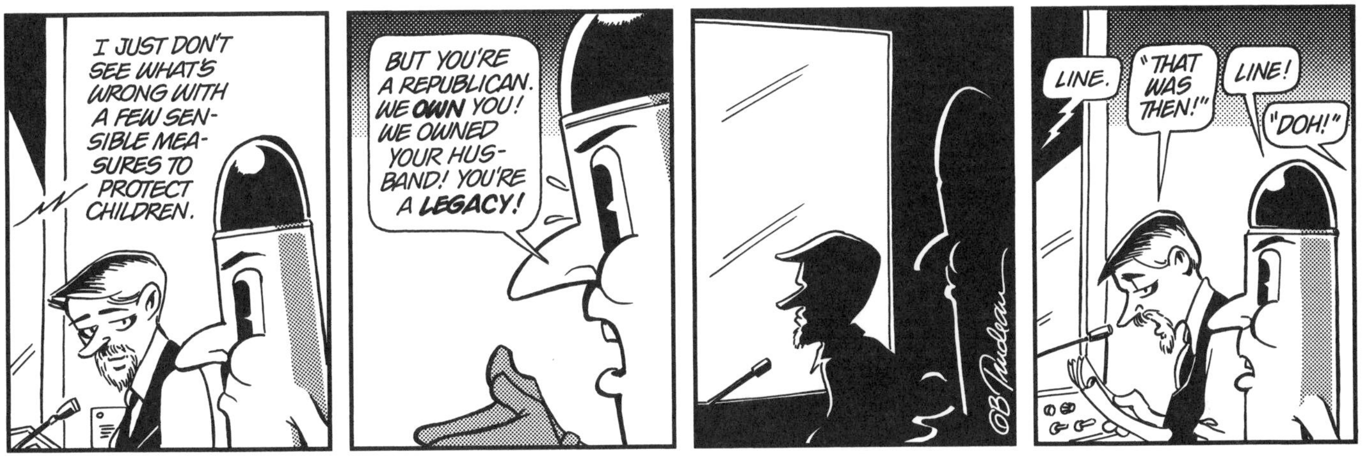
I JUST DON'T SEE WHAT'S WRONG WITH A FEW SENSIBLE MEASURES TO PROTECT CHILDREN.
BUT YOU'RE A REPUBLICAN. WE OWN YOU! WE OWNED YOUR HUSBAND! YOU'RE A LEGACY!
LINE.
"THAT WAS THEN!"
LINE!
"DOH!"

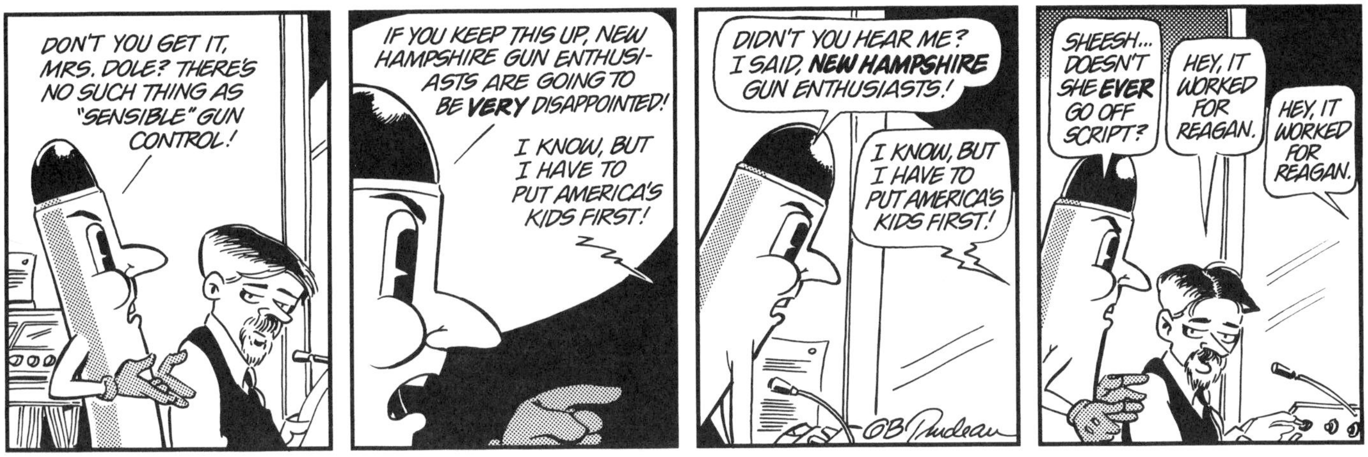
DON'T YOU GET IT, MRS. DOLE? THERE'S NO SUCH THING AS "SENSIBLE" GUN CONTROL!
IF YOU KEEP THIS UP, NEW HAMPSHIRE GUN ENTHUSIASTS ARE GOING TO BE VERY DISAPPOINTED!
I KNOW, BUT I HAVE TO PUT AMERICA'S KIDS FIRST!
DIDN'T YOU HEAR ME? I SAID, NEW HAMPSHIRE GUN ENTHUSIASTS!
I KNOW, BUT I HAVE TO PUT AMERICA'S KIDS FIRST!
SHEESH... DOESN'T SHE EVER GO OFF SCRIPT?
HEY, IT WORKED FOR REAGAN.
HEY, IT WORKED FOR REAGAN.

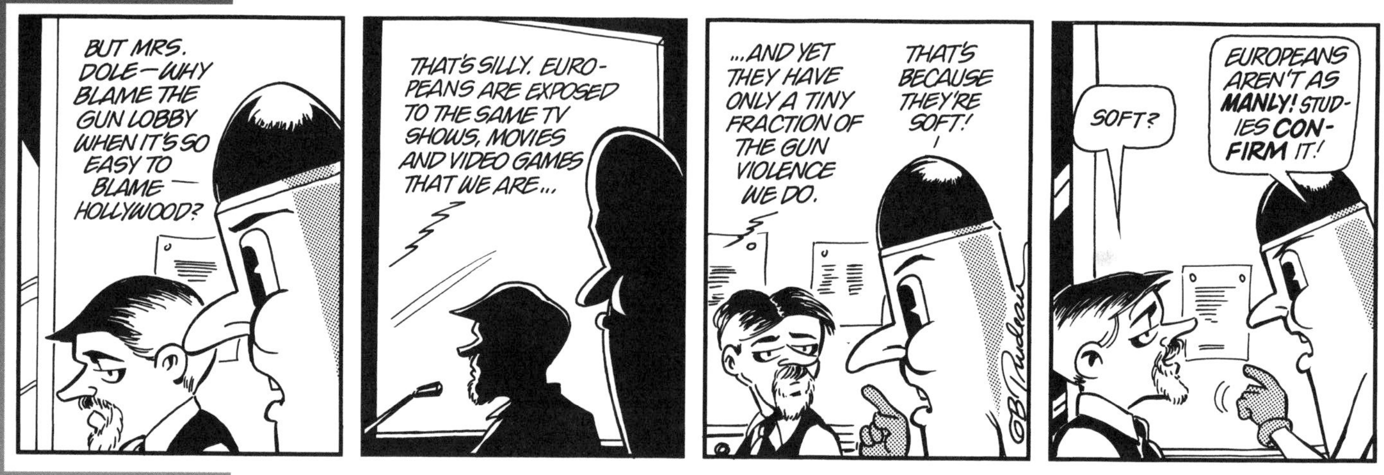
BUT MRS. DOLE—WHY BLAME THE GUN LOBBY WHEN IT'S SO EASY TO BLAME HOLLYWOOD?
THAT'S SILLY. EUROPEANS ARE EXPOSED TO THE SAME TV SHOWS, MOVIES AND VIDEO GAMES THAT WE ARE...
...AND YET THEY HAVE ONLY A TINY FRACTION OF THE GUN VIOLENCE WE DO.
THAT'S BECAUSE THEY'RE SOFT!
SOFT?
EUROPEANS AREN'T AS MANLY! STUDIES CONFIRM IT!

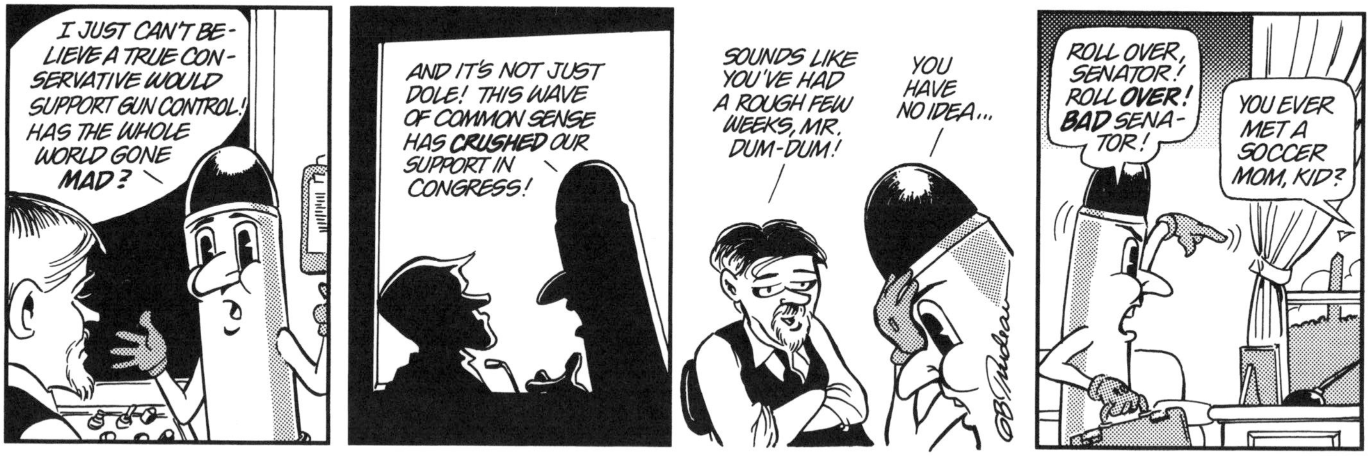
I JUST CAN'T BELIEVE A TRUE CONSERVATIVE WOULD SUPPORT GUN CONTROL! HAS THE WHOLE WORLD GONE MAD?
AND IT'S NOT JUST DOLE! THIS WAVE OF COMMON SENSE HAS CRUSHED OUR SUPPORT IN CONGRESS!
SOUNDS LIKE YOU'VE HAD A ROUGH FEW WEEKS, MR. DUM-DUM!
YOU HAVE NO IDEA...
ROLL OVER, SENATOR! ROLL OVER! BAD SENATOR!
YOU EVER MET A SOCCER MOM, KID?

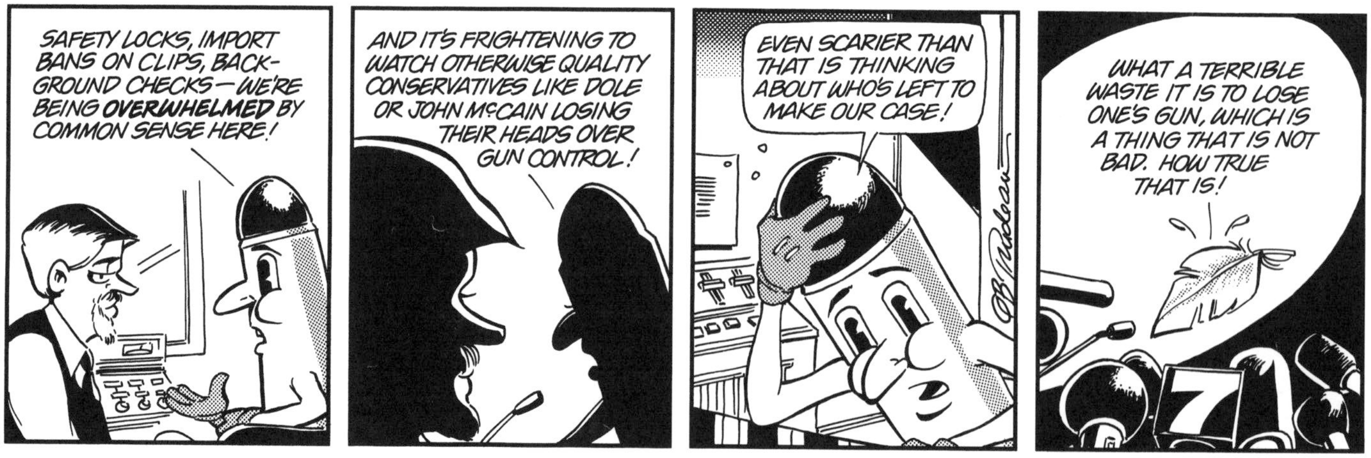
SAFETY LOCKS, IMPORT BANS ON CLIPS, BACKGROUND CHECKS—WE'RE BEING OVERWHELMED BY COMMON SENSE HERE!
AND IT'S FRIGHTENING TO WATCH OTHERWISE QUALITY CONSERVATIVES LIKE DOLE OR JOHN McCAIN LOSING THEIR HEADS OVER GUN CONTROL!
EVEN SCARIER THAN THAT IS THINKING ABOUT WHO'S LEFT TO MAKE OUR CASE!
WHAT A TERRIBLE WASTE IT IS TO LOSE ONE'S GUN, WHICH IS A THING THAT IS NOT BAD. HOW TRUE THAT IS!
7

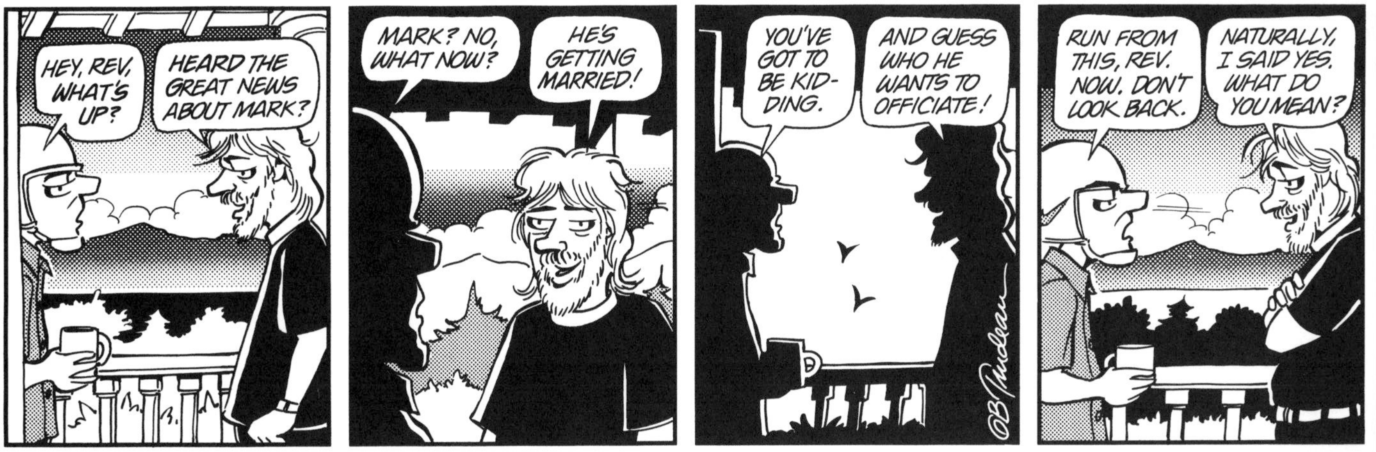
HEY, REV, WHAT'S UP?
HEARD THE GREAT NEWS ABOUT MARK?
MARK? NO, WHAT NOW?
HE'S GETTING MARRIED!
YOU'VE GOT TO BE KIDDING.
AND GUESS WHO HE WANTS TO OFFICIATE!
RUN FROM THIS, REV. NOW. DON'T LOOK BACK.
NATURALLY, I SAID YES. WHAT DO YOU MEAN?

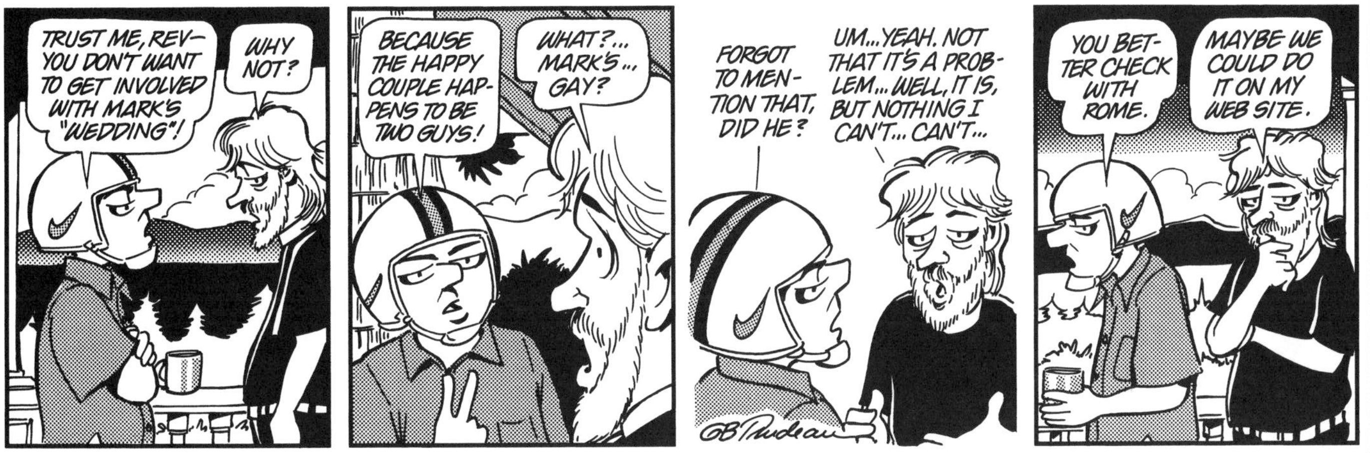
TRUST ME, REV—YOU DON'T WANT TO GET INVOLVED WITH MARK'S "WEDDING"!
WHY NOT?
BECAUSE THE HAPPY COUPLE HAPPENS TO BE TWO GUYS!
WHAT?... MARK'S... GAY?
FORGOT TO MENTION THAT, DID HE?
UM... YEAH. NOT THAT IT'S A PROBLEM... WELL, IT IS, BUT NOTHING I CAN'T... CAN'T...
YOU BETTER CHECK WITH ROME.
MAYBE WE COULD DO IT ON MY WEB SITE.

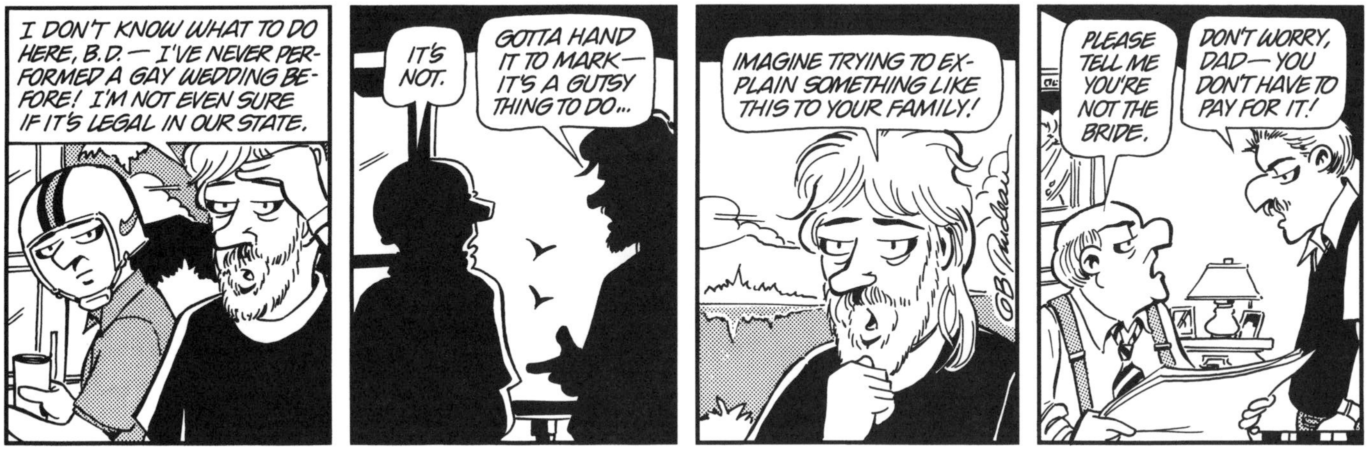
I DON'T KNOW WHAT TO DO HERE, B.D.— I'VE NEVER PERFORMED A GAY WEDDING BEFORE! I'M NOT EVEN SURE IF IT'S LEGAL IN OUR STATE.
IT'S NOT.
GOTTA HAND IT TO MARK— IT'S A GUTSY THING TO DO...
IMAGINE TRYING TO EXPLAIN SOMETHING LIKE THIS TO YOUR FAMILY!
PLEASE TELL ME YOU'RE NOT THE BRIDE.
DON'T WORRY, DAD— YOU DON'T HAVE TO PAY FOR IT!

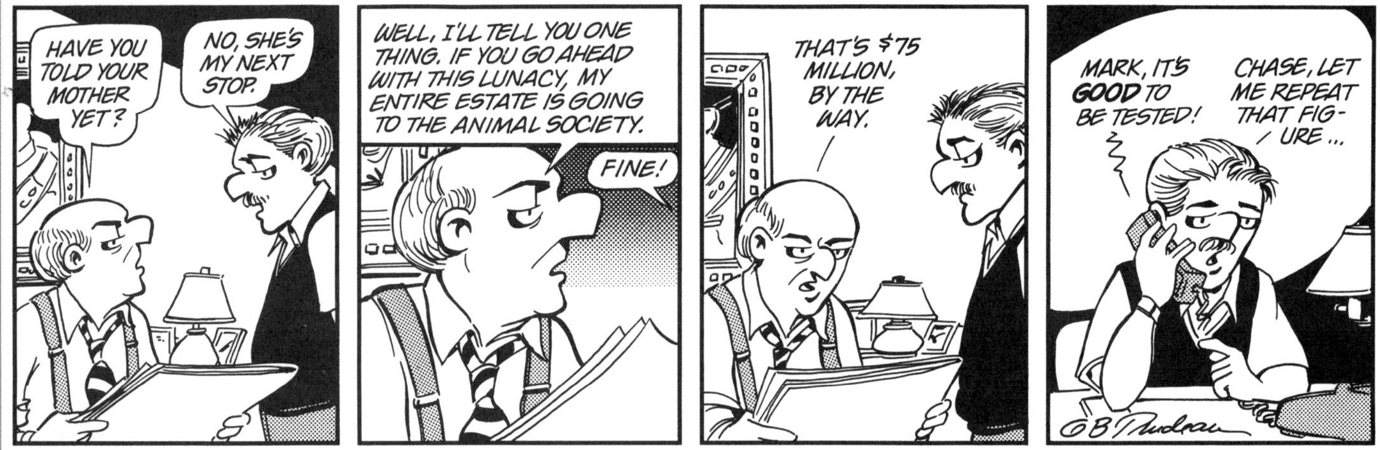
HAVE YOU TOLD YOUR MOTHER YET?
NO, SHE'S MY NEXT STOP.
WELL, I'LL TELL YOU ONE THING. IF YOU GO AHEAD WITH THIS LUNACY, MY ENTIRE ESTATE IS GOING TO THE ANIMAL SOCIETY.
FINE!
THAT'S $75 MILLION, BY THE WAY.
MARK, IT'S **GOOD** TO BE TESTED!
CHASE, LET ME REPEAT THAT FIG- / URE ...
©B. Trudeau

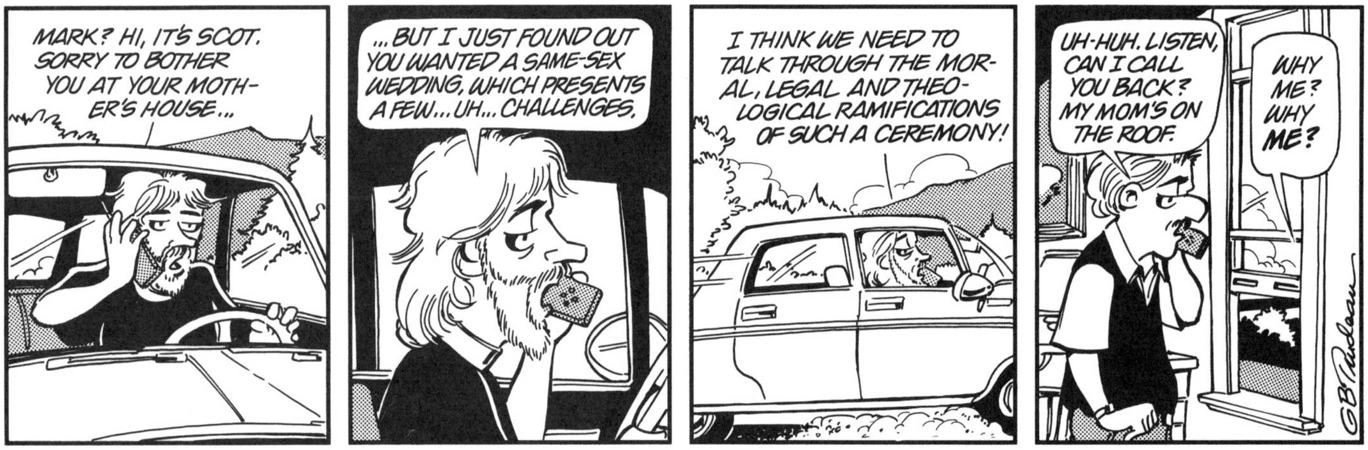
MARK? HI, IT'S SCOT. SORRY TO BOTHER YOU AT YOUR MOTH- ER'S HOUSE ...
... BUT I JUST FOUND OUT YOU WANTED A SAME-SEX WEDDING, WHICH PRESENTS A FEW ... UH ... CHALLENGES.
I THINK WE NEED TO TALK THROUGH THE MOR- AL, LEGAL AND THEO- LOGICAL RAMIFICATIONS OF SUCH A CEREMONY!
UH-HUH. LISTEN, CAN I CALL YOU BACK? MY MOM'S ON THE ROOF.
WHY ME? WHY **ME?**
©B. Trudeau

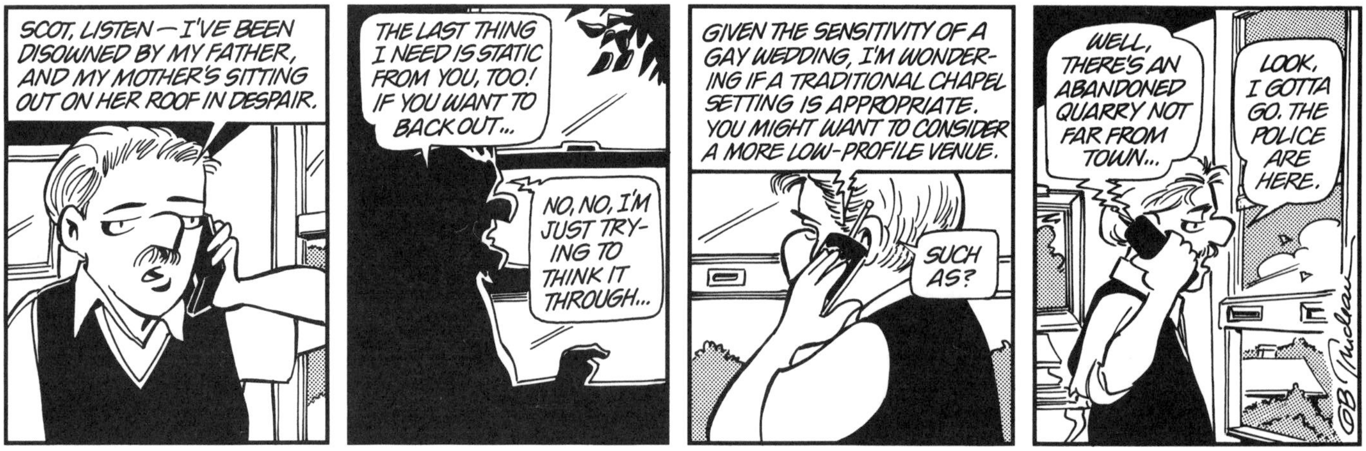
SCOT, LISTEN — I'VE BEEN DISOWNED BY MY FATHER, AND MY MOTHER'S SITTING OUT ON HER ROOF IN DESPAIR.
THE LAST THING I NEED IS STATIC FROM YOU, TOO! IF YOU WANT TO BACK OUT ...
NO, NO, I'M JUST TRY- ING TO THINK IT THROUGH ...
GIVEN THE SENSITIVITY OF A GAY WEDDING, I'M WONDER- ING IF A TRADITIONAL CHAPEL SETTING IS APPROPRIATE. YOU MIGHT WANT TO CONSIDER A MORE LOW-PROFILE VENUE.
SUCH AS?
WELL, THERE'S AN ABANDONED QUARRY NOT FAR FROM TOWN ...
LOOK, I GOTTA GO. THE POLICE ARE HERE.
©B. Trudeau

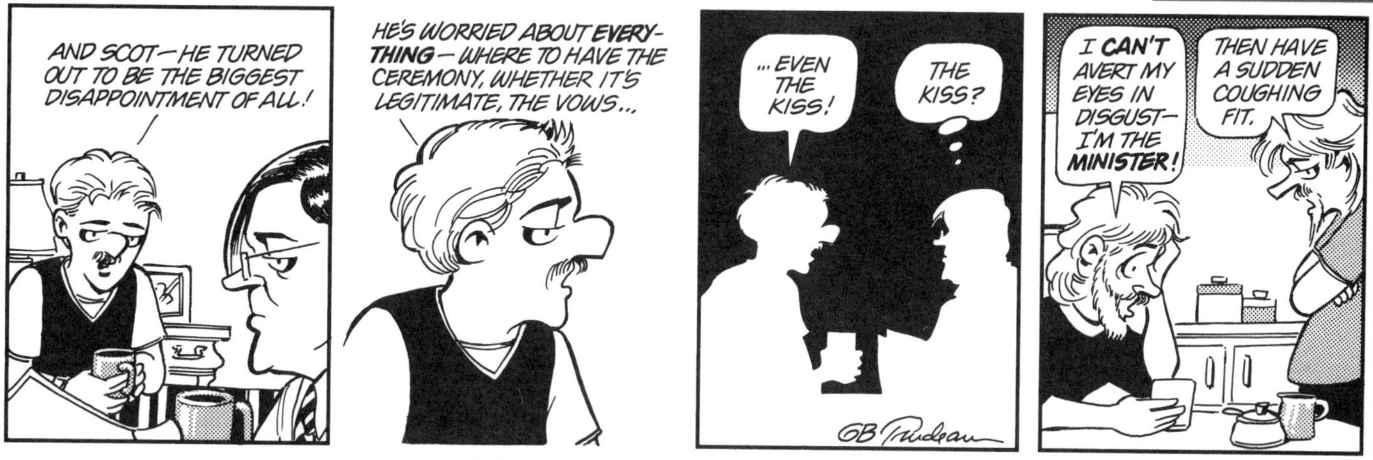
AND SCOT—HE TURNED OUT TO BE THE BIGGEST DISAPPOINTMENT OF ALL!
HE'S WORRIED ABOUT EVERY-THING—WHERE TO HAVE THE CEREMONY, WHETHER IT'S LEGITIMATE, THE VOWS...
...EVEN THE KISS!
THE KISS?
I CAN'T AVERT MY EYES IN DISGUST—I'M THE MINISTER!
THEN HAVE A SUDDEN COUGHING FIT.

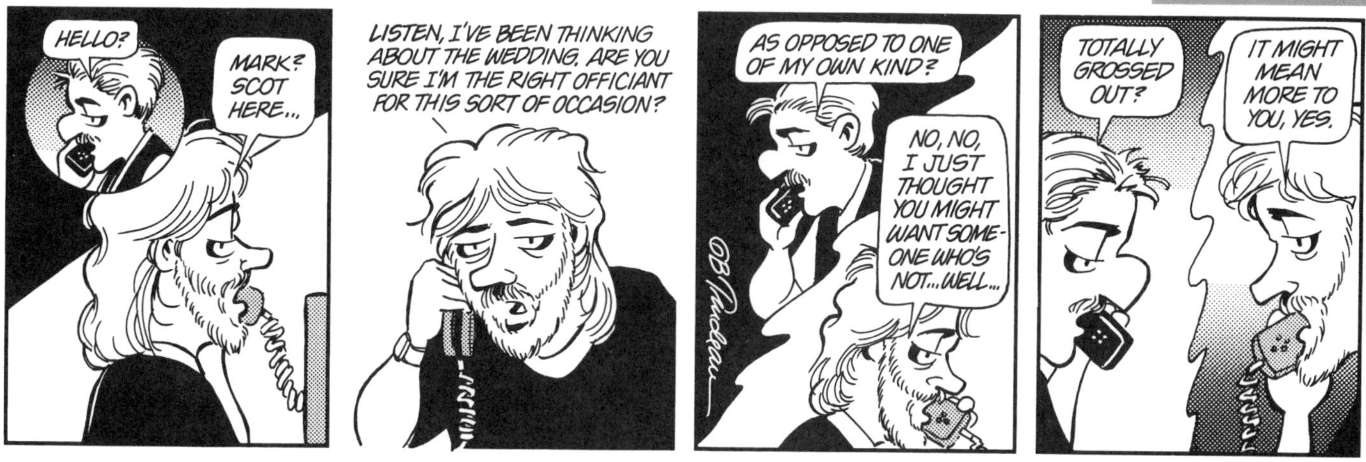
HELLO?
MARK? SCOT HERE...
LISTEN, I'VE BEEN THINKING ABOUT THE WEDDING. ARE YOU SURE I'M THE RIGHT OFFICIANT FOR THIS SORT OF OCCASION?
AS OPPOSED TO ONE OF MY OWN KIND?
NO, NO, I JUST THOUGHT YOU MIGHT WANT SOME-ONE WHO'S NOT... WELL...
TOTALLY GROSSED OUT?
IT MIGHT MEAN MORE TO YOU, YES.

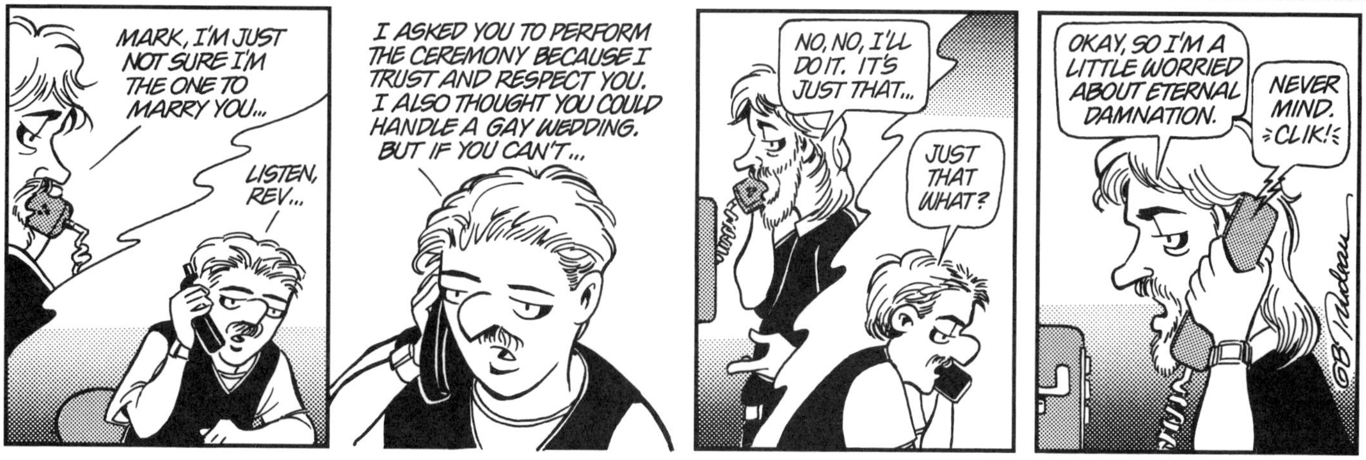
MARK, I'M JUST NOT SURE I'M THE ONE TO MARRY YOU...
LISTEN, REV...
I ASKED YOU TO PERFORM THE CEREMONY BECAUSE I TRUST AND RESPECT YOU. I ALSO THOUGHT YOU COULD HANDLE A GAY WEDDING. BUT IF YOU CAN'T...
NO, NO, I'LL DO IT. IT'S JUST THAT...
JUST THAT WHAT?
OKAY, SO I'M A LITTLE WORRIED ABOUT ETERNAL DAMNATION.
NEVER MIND.
CLIK!

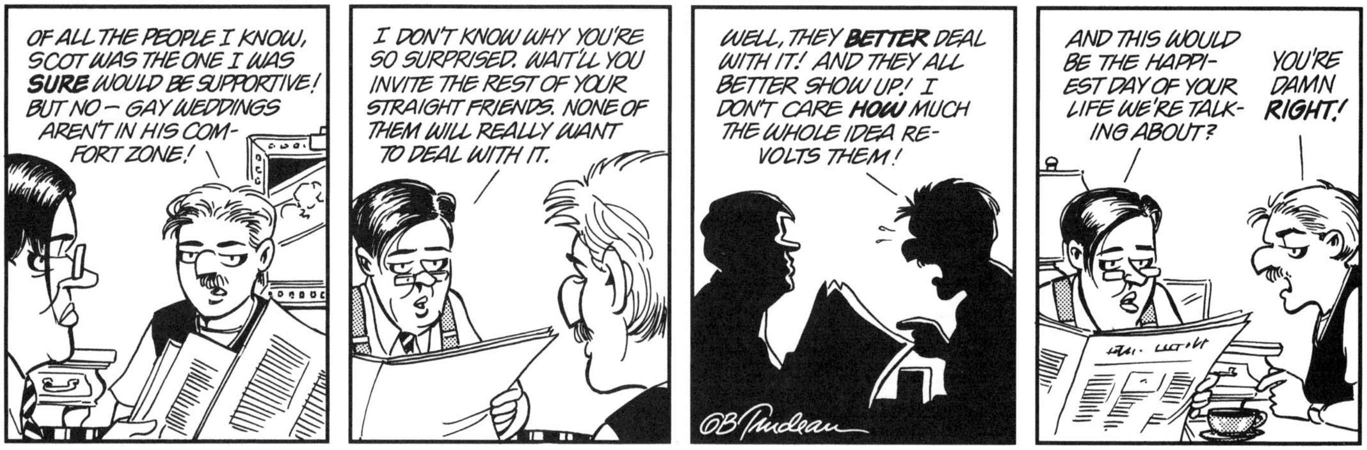
OF ALL THE PEOPLE I KNOW, SCOT WAS THE ONE I WAS **SURE** WOULD BE SUPPORTIVE! BUT NO – GAY WEDDINGS AREN'T IN HIS COMFORT ZONE!
I DON'T KNOW WHY YOU'RE SO SURPRISED. WAIT'LL YOU INVITE THE REST OF YOUR STRAIGHT FRIENDS. NONE OF THEM WILL REALLY WANT TO DEAL WITH IT.
WELL, THEY **BETTER** DEAL WITH IT! AND THEY ALL BETTER SHOW UP! I DON'T CARE **HOW** MUCH THE WHOLE IDEA REVOLTS THEM!
AND THIS WOULD BE THE HAPPIEST DAY OF YOUR LIFE WE'RE TALKING ABOUT?
YOU'RE DAMN **RIGHT!**

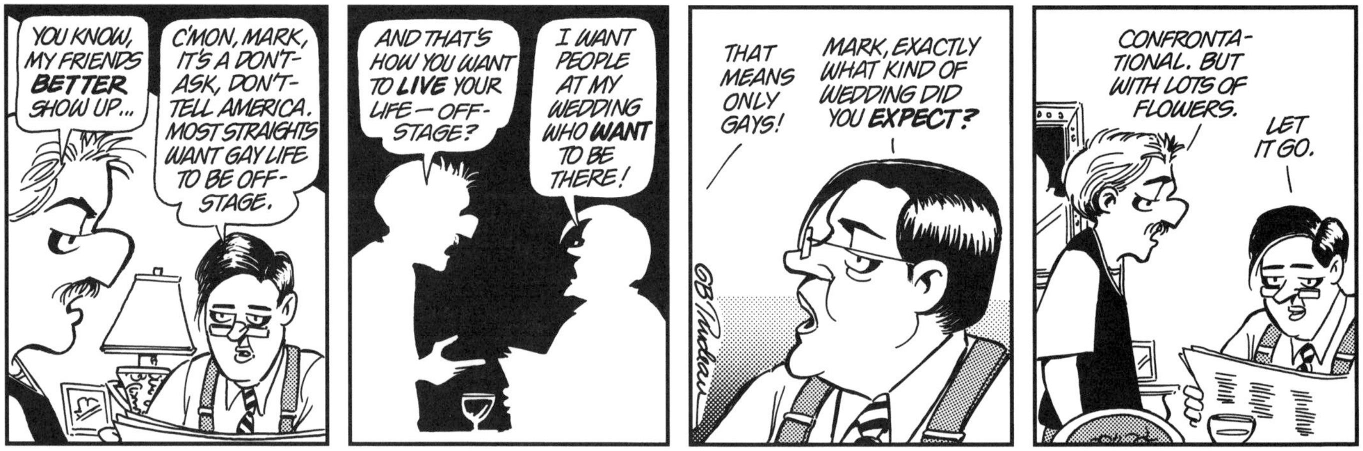
YOU KNOW, MY FRIENDS **BETTER** SHOW UP...
C'MON, MARK, IT'S A DON'T-ASK, DON'T-TELL AMERICA. MOST STRAIGHTS WANT GAY LIFE TO BE OFF-STAGE.
AND THAT'S HOW YOU WANT TO **LIVE** YOUR LIFE – OFF-STAGE?
I WANT PEOPLE AT MY WEDDING WHO **WANT** TO BE THERE!
THAT MEANS ONLY GAYS!
MARK, EXACTLY WHAT KIND OF WEDDING DID YOU **EXPECT?**
CONFRONTATIONAL. BUT WITH LOTS OF FLOWERS.
LET IT GO.

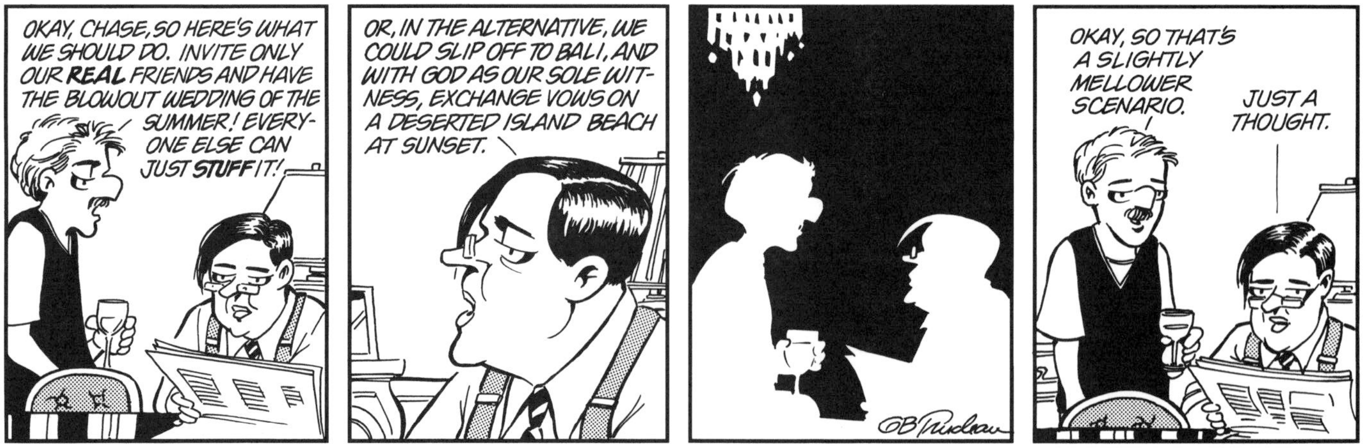
OKAY, CHASE, SO HERE'S WHAT WE SHOULD DO. INVITE ONLY OUR **REAL** FRIENDS AND HAVE THE BLOWOUT WEDDING OF THE SUMMER! EVERYONE ELSE CAN JUST **STUFF** IT!
OR, IN THE ALTERNATIVE, WE COULD SLIP OFF TO BALI, AND WITH GOD AS OUR SOLE WITNESS, EXCHANGE VOWS ON A DESERTED ISLAND BEACH AT SUNSET.
OKAY, SO THAT'S A SLIGHTLY MELLOWER SCENARIO.
JUST A THOUGHT.

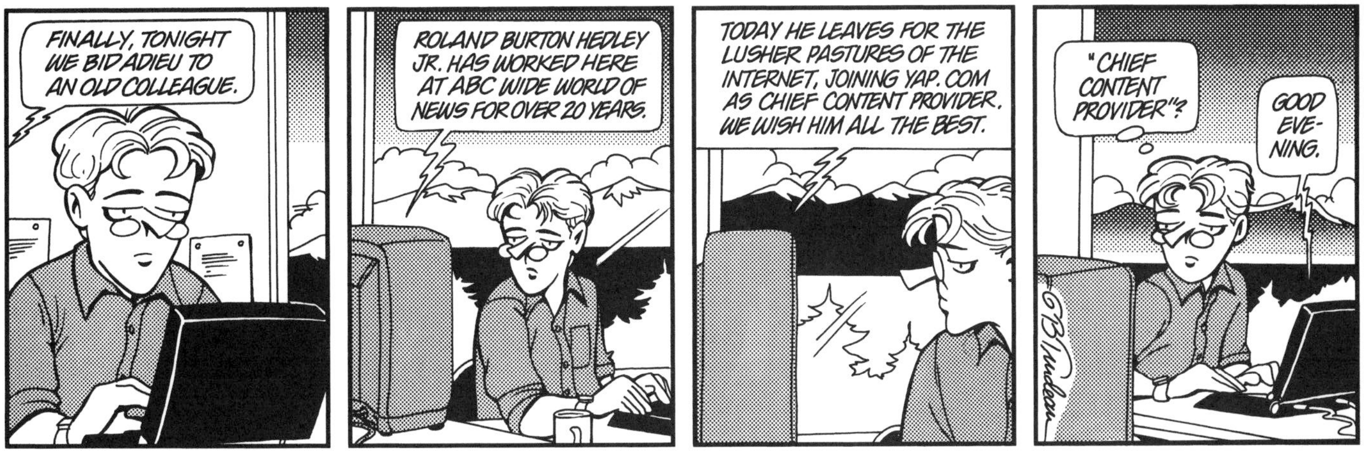
FINALLY, TONIGHT WE BID ADIEU TO AN OLD COLLEAGUE.
ROLAND BURTON HEDLEY JR. HAS WORKED HERE AT ABC WIDE WORLD OF NEWS FOR OVER 20 YEARS.
TODAY HE LEAVES FOR THE LUSHER PASTURES OF THE INTERNET, JOINING YAP.COM AS CHIEF CONTENT PROVIDER. WE WISH HIM ALL THE BEST.
"CHIEF CONTENT PROVIDER"?
GOOD EVE-NING.
GBTrudeau

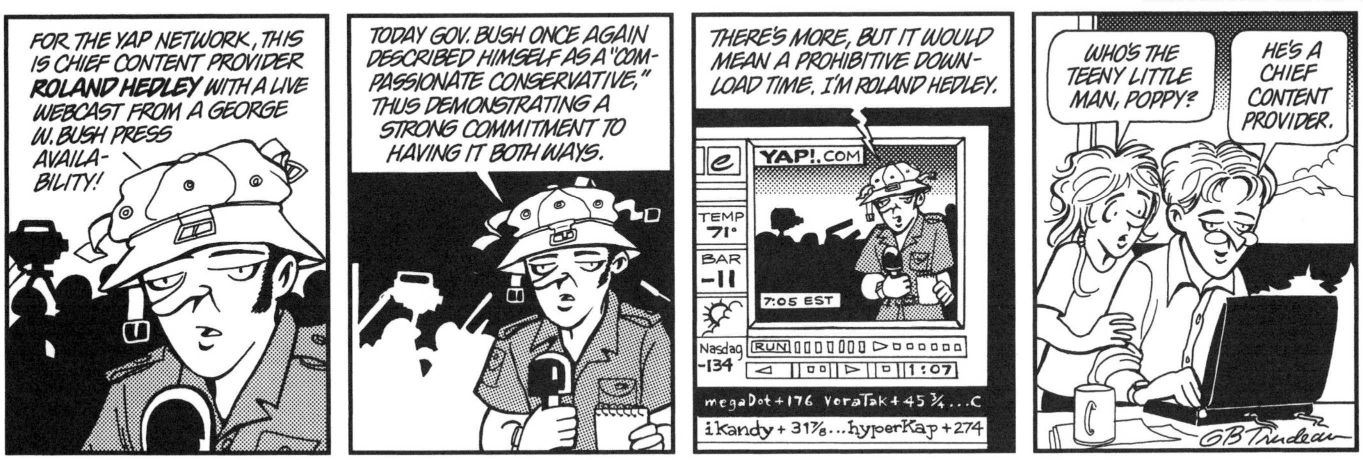
FOR THE YAP NETWORK, THIS IS CHIEF CONTENT PROVIDER ROLAND HEDLEY WITH A LIVE WEBCAST FROM A GEORGE W. BUSH PRESS AVAILA-BILITY!
TODAY GOV. BUSH ONCE AGAIN DESCRIBED HIMSELF AS A "COM-PASSIONATE CONSERVATIVE," THUS DEMONSTRATING A STRONG COMMITMENT TO HAVING IT BOTH WAYS.
THERE'S MORE, BUT IT WOULD MEAN A PROHIBITIVE DOWN-LOAD TIME. I'M ROLAND HEDLEY.
YAP!.COM
TEMP 71°
BAR -11
7:05 EST
Nasdaq -134
RUN
1:07
megaDot +176 VoraTak + 45 3/4 ... C
iKandy + 31 7/8 ... hyperKap + 274
WHO'S THE TEENY LITTLE MAN, POPPY?
HE'S A CHIEF CONTENT PROVIDER.
GBTrudeau

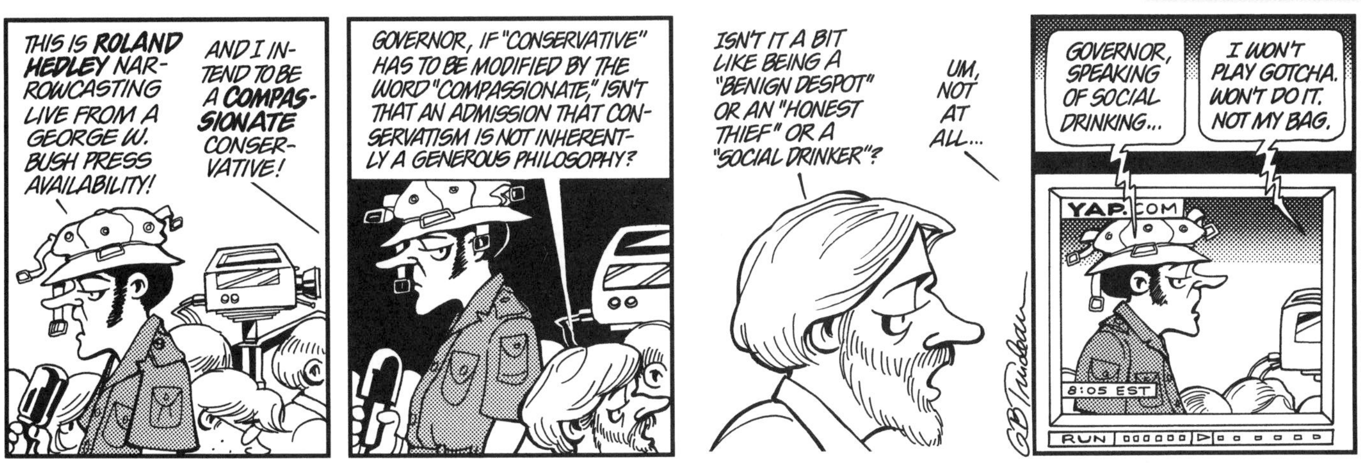
THIS IS ROLAND HEDLEY NAR-ROWCASTING LIVE FROM A GEORGE W. BUSH PRESS AVAILABILITY!
AND I IN-TEND TO BE A COMPAS-SIONATE CONSER-VATIVE!
GOVERNOR, IF "CONSERVATIVE" HAS TO BE MODIFIED BY THE WORD "COMPASSIONATE," ISN'T THAT AN ADMISSION THAT CON-SERVATISM IS NOT INHERENT-LY A GENEROUS PHILOSOPHY?
ISN'T IT A BIT LIKE BEING A "BENIGN DESPOT" OR AN "HONEST THIEF" OR A "SOCIAL DRINKER"?
UM, NOT AT ALL...
GBTrudeau
GOVERNOR, SPEAKING OF SOCIAL DRINKING...
I WON'T PLAY GOTCHA. WON'T DO IT. NOT MY BAG.
YAP.COM
8:05 EST
RUN

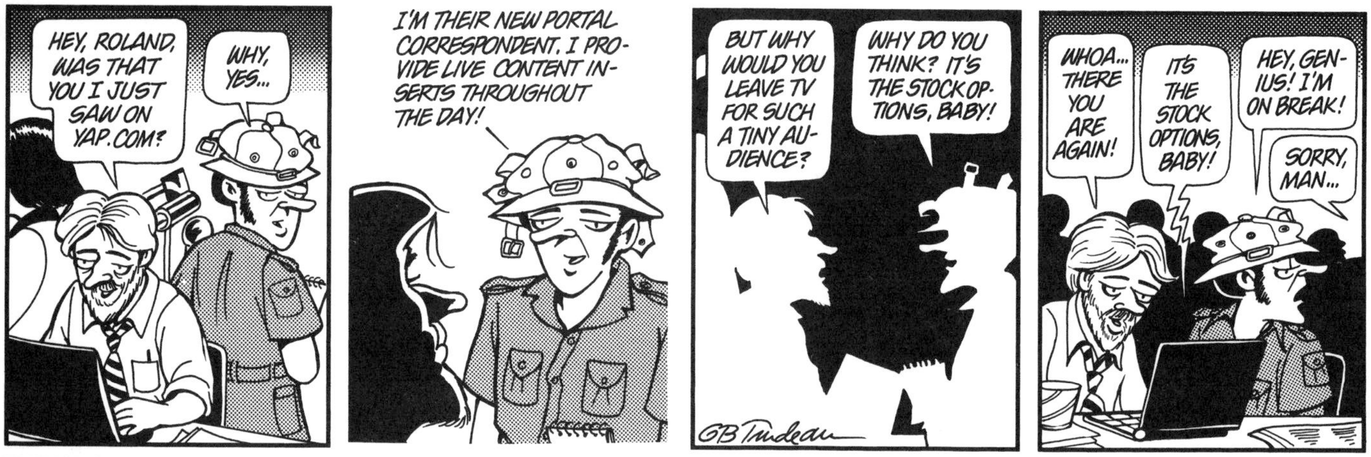
HEY, ROLAND, WAS THAT YOU I JUST SAW ON YAP.COM?
WHY, YES...
I'M THEIR NEW PORTAL CORRESPONDENT. I PROVIDE LIVE CONTENT INSERTS THROUGHOUT THE DAY!
BUT WHY WOULD YOU LEAVE TV FOR SUCH A TINY AUDIENCE?
WHY DO YOU THINK? IT'S THE STOCK OPTIONS, BABY!
GB Trudeau
WHOA... THERE YOU ARE AGAIN!
IT'S THE STOCK OPTIONS, BABY!
HEY, GENIUS! I'M ON BREAK!
SORRY, MAN...

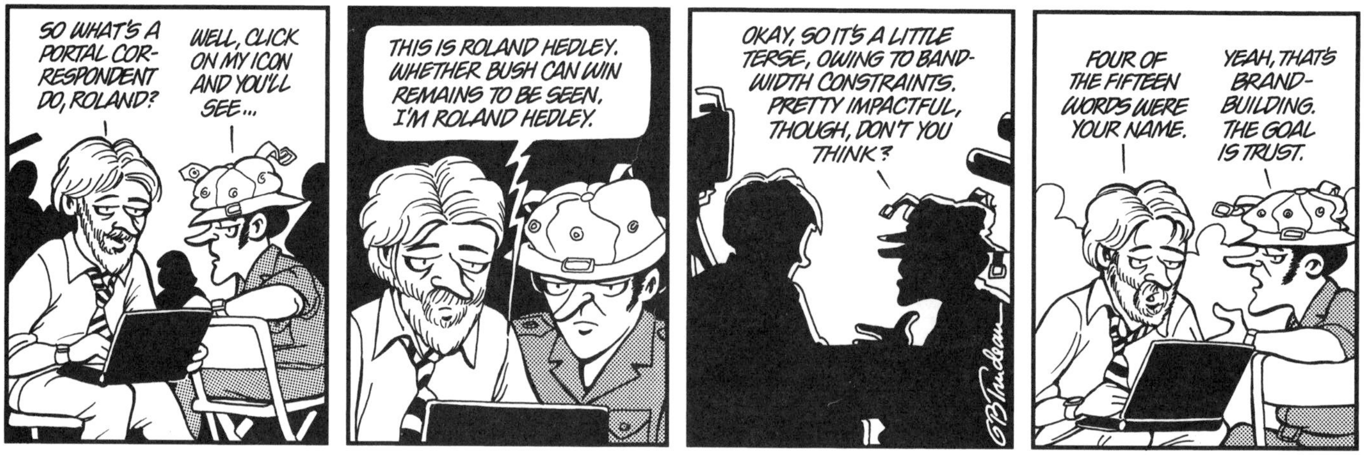
SO WHAT'S A PORTAL CORRESPONDENT DO, ROLAND?
WELL, CLICK ON MY ICON AND YOU'LL SEE...
THIS IS ROLAND HEDLEY. WHETHER BUSH CAN WIN REMAINS TO BE SEEN. I'M ROLAND HEDLEY.
OKAY, SO IT'S A LITTLE TERSE, OWING TO BANDWIDTH CONSTRAINTS. PRETTY IMPACTFUL, THOUGH, DON'T YOU THINK?
GB Trudeau
FOUR OF THE FIFTEEN WORDS WERE YOUR NAME.
YEAH, THAT'S BRAND-BUILDING. THE GOAL IS TRUST.

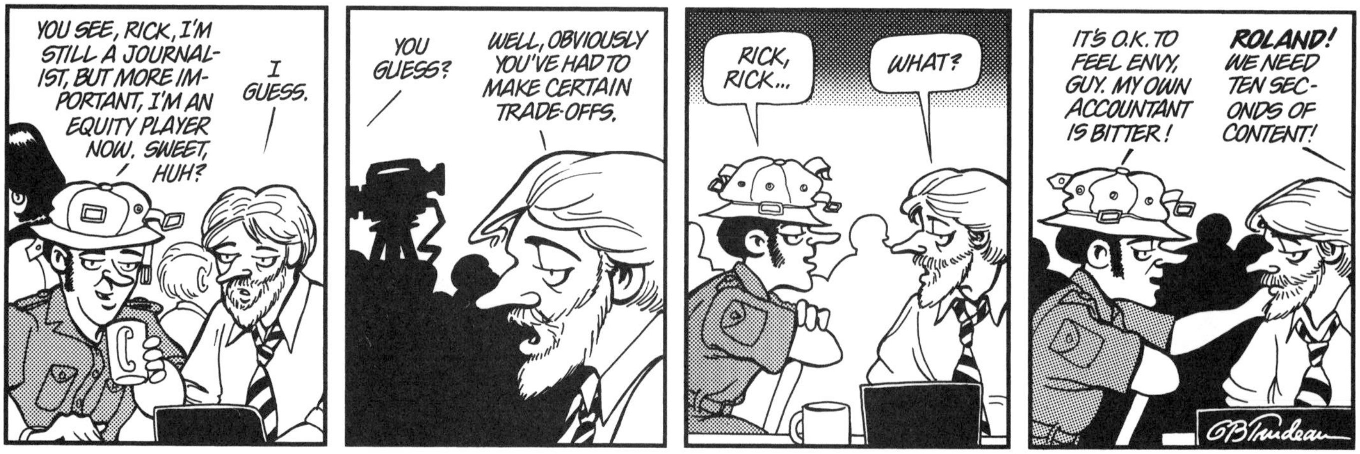
YOU SEE, RICK, I'M STILL A JOURNALIST, BUT MORE IMPORTANT, I'M AN EQUITY PLAYER NOW. SWEET, HUH?
I GUESS.
YOU GUESS?
WELL, OBVIOUSLY YOU'VE HAD TO MAKE CERTAIN TRADE-OFFS.
RICK, RICK...
WHAT?
IT'S O.K. TO FEEL ENVY, GUY. MY OWN ACCOUNTANT IS BITTER!
ROLAND! WE NEED TEN SECONDS OF CONTENT!
GB Trudeau

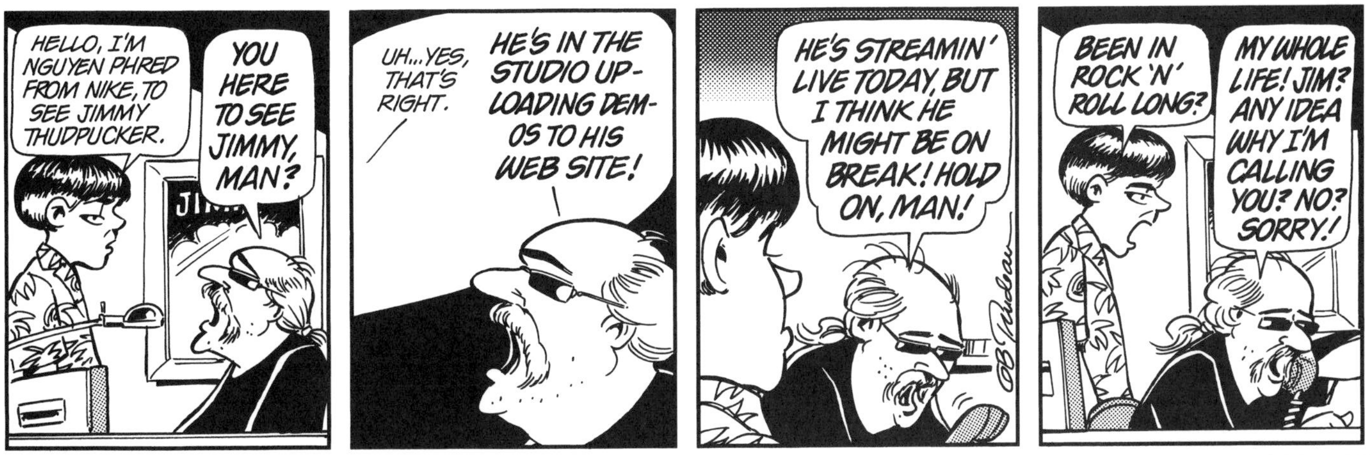
HELLO, I'M NGUYEN PHRED FROM NIKE, TO SEE JIMMY THUDPUCKER.
YOU HERE TO SEE JIMMY, MAN?
UH...YES, THAT'S RIGHT.
HE'S IN THE STUDIO UP-LOADING DEM-OS TO HIS WEB SITE!
HE'S STREAMIN' LIVE TODAY, BUT I THINK HE MIGHT BE ON BREAK! HOLD ON, MAN!
BEEN IN ROCK 'N' ROLL LONG?
MY WHOLE LIFE! JIM? ANY IDEA WHY I'M CALLING YOU? NO? SORRY!

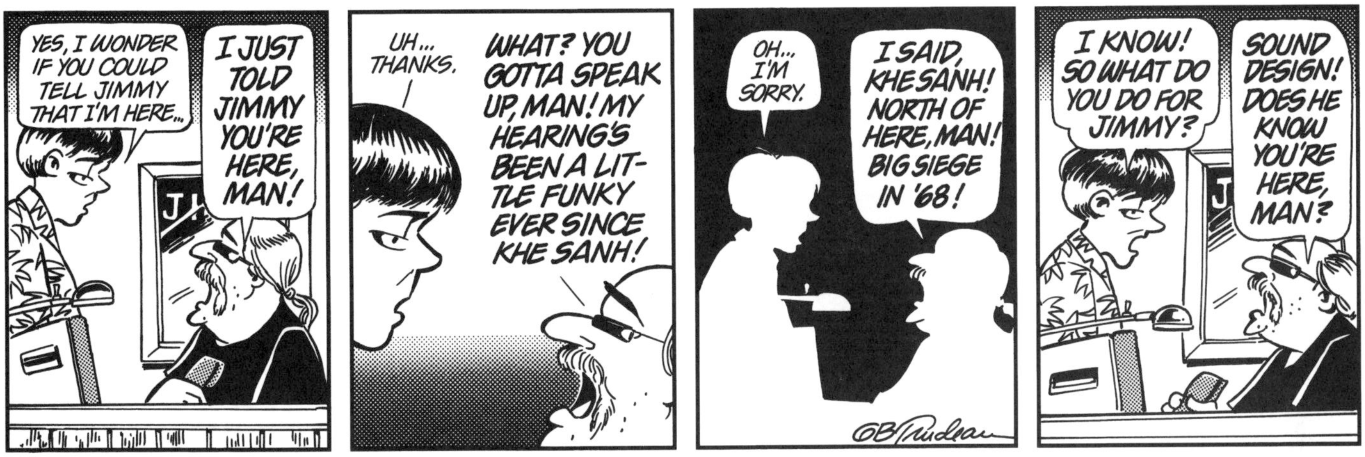
YES, I WONDER IF YOU COULD TELL JIMMY THAT I'M HERE...
I JUST TOLD JIMMY YOU'RE HERE, MAN!
UH... THANKS.
WHAT? YOU GOTTA SPEAK UP, MAN! MY HEARING'S BEEN A LIT-TLE FUNKY EVER SINCE KHE SANH!
OH... I'M SORRY.
I SAID, KHE SANH! NORTH OF HERE, MAN! BIG SIEGE IN '68!
I KNOW! SO WHAT DO YOU DO FOR JIMMY?
SOUND DESIGN! DOES HE KNOW YOU'RE HERE, MAN?

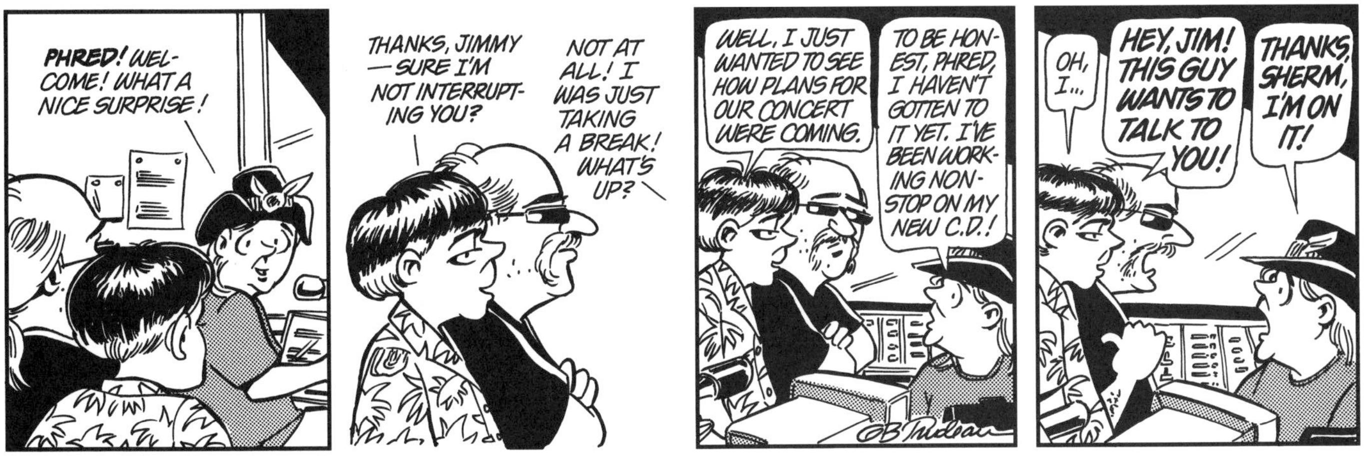
PHRED! WEL-COME! WHAT A NICE SURPRISE!
THANKS, JIMMY — SURE I'M NOT INTERRUPT-ING YOU?
NOT AT ALL! I WAS JUST TAKING A BREAK! WHAT'S UP?
WELL, I JUST WANTED TO SEE HOW PLANS FOR OUR CONCERT WERE COMING.
TO BE HON-EST, PHRED, I HAVEN'T GOTTEN TO IT YET. I'VE BEEN WORK-ING NON-STOP ON MY NEW C.D.!
OH, I...
HEY, JIM! THIS GUY WANTS TO TALK TO YOU!
THANKS, SHERM, I'M ON IT!

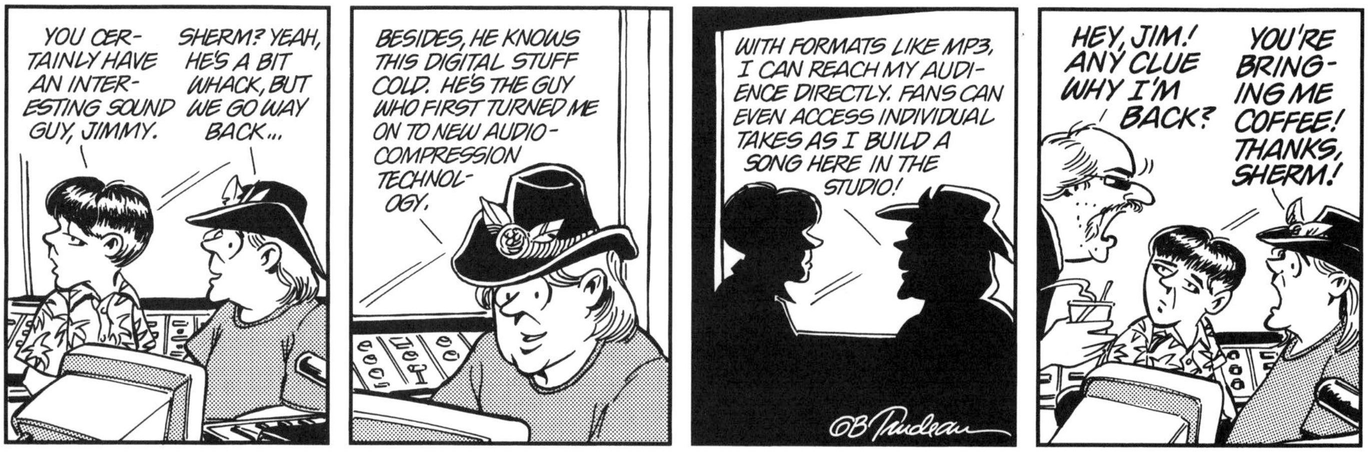
YOU CERTAINLY HAVE AN INTERESTING SOUND GUY, JIMMY.
SHERM? YEAH, HE'S A BIT WHACK, BUT WE GO WAY BACK...
BESIDES, HE KNOWS THIS DIGITAL STUFF COLD. HE'S THE GUY WHO FIRST TURNED ME ON TO NEW AUDIO-COMPRESSION TECHNOLOGY.
WITH FORMATS LIKE MP3, I CAN REACH MY AUDIENCE DIRECTLY. FANS CAN EVEN ACCESS INDIVIDUAL TAKES AS I BUILD A SONG HERE IN THE STUDIO!
HEY, JIM! ANY CLUE WHY I'M BACK?
YOU'RE BRINGING ME COFFEE! THANKS, SHERM!

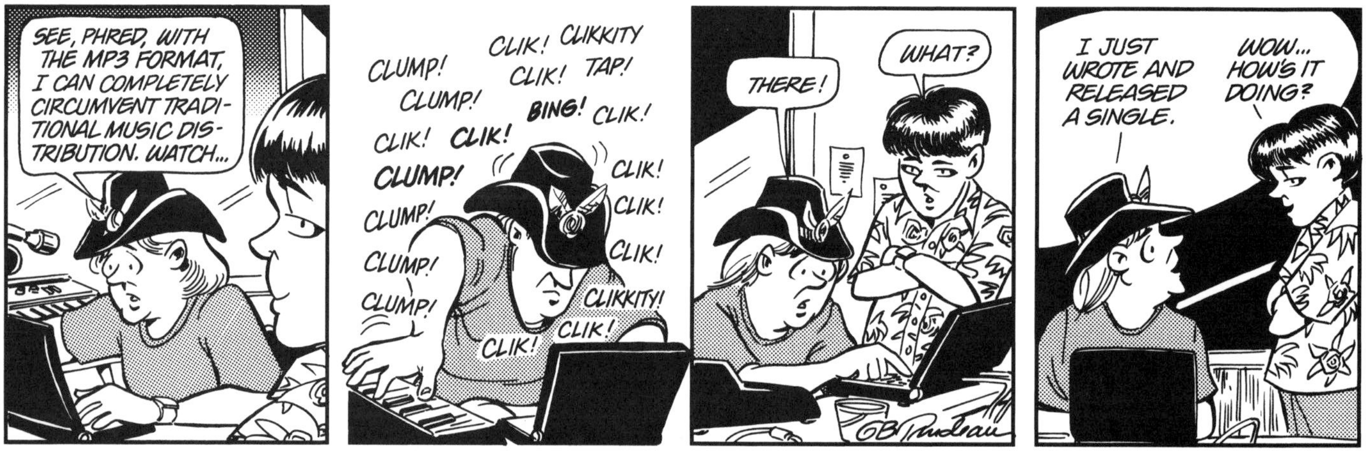
SEE, PHRED, WITH THE MP3 FORMAT, I CAN COMPLETELY CIRCUMVENT TRADITIONAL MUSIC DISTRIBUTION. WATCH...
CLUMP! CLUMP! CLIK! CLIK! CLUMP! CLUMP! CLUMP! CLUMP!
CLIK! CLIKKITY TAP! CLIK! BING! CLIK! CLIK! CLIK! CLIK! CLIKKITY! CLIK! CLIK!
THERE!
WHAT?
I JUST WROTE AND RELEASED A SINGLE.
WOW... HOW'S IT DOING?

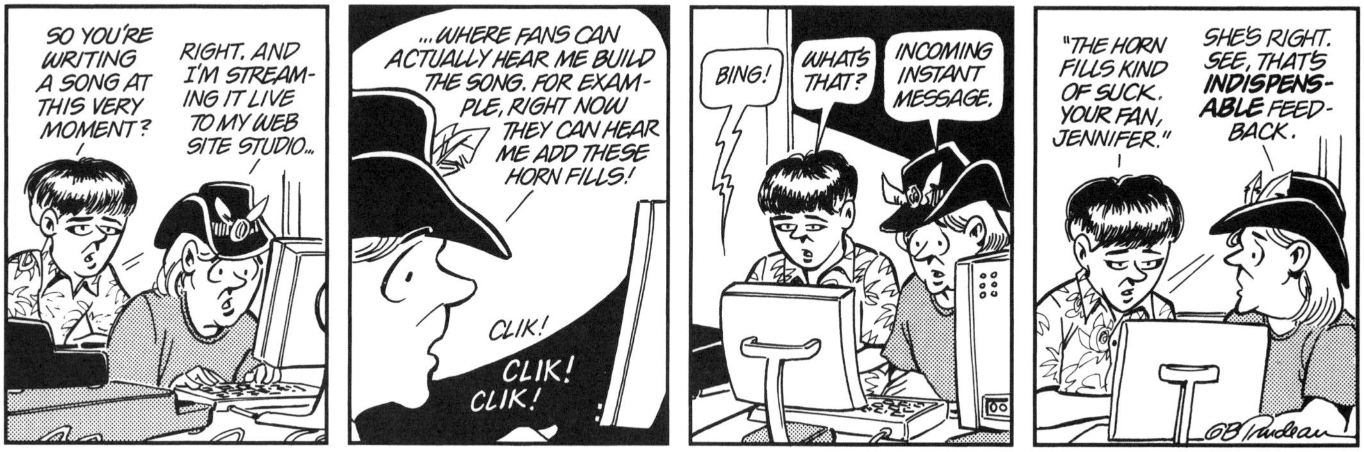
SO YOU'RE WRITING A SONG AT THIS VERY MOMENT?
RIGHT. AND I'M STREAMING IT LIVE TO MY WEB SITE STUDIO...
...WHERE FANS CAN ACTUALLY HEAR ME BUILD THE SONG. FOR EXAMPLE, RIGHT NOW THEY CAN HEAR ME ADD THESE HORN FILLS!
CLIK! CLIK! CLIK!
BING!
WHAT'S THAT?
INCOMING INSTANT MESSAGE.
"THE HORN FILLS KIND OF SUCK. YOUR FAN, JENNIFER."
SHE'S RIGHT. SEE, THAT'S INDISPENSABLE FEEDBACK.

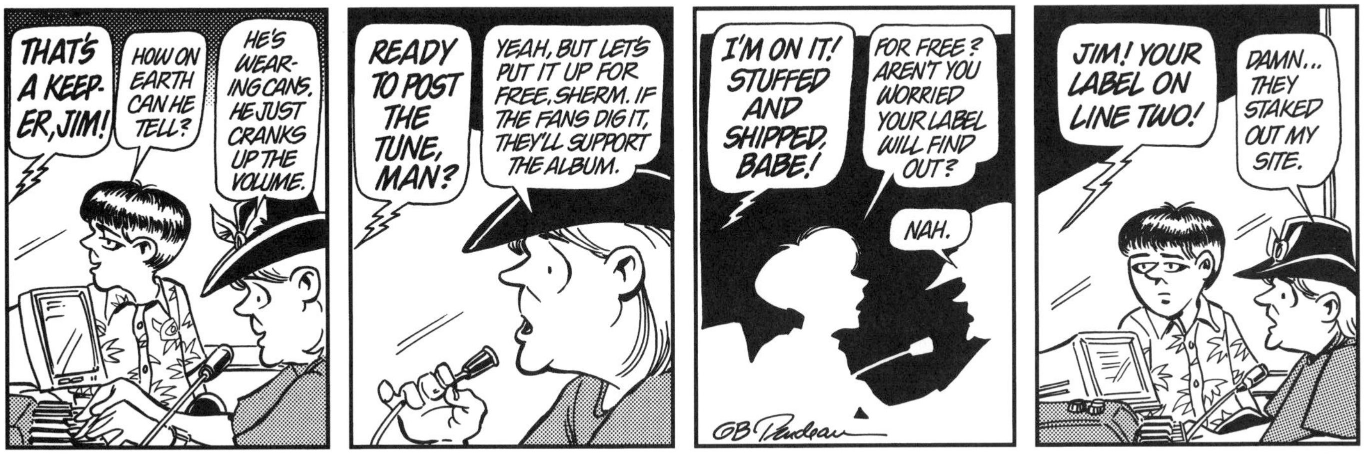
THAT'S A KEEP-ER, JIM!
HOW ON EARTH CAN HE TELL?
HE'S WEAR-ING CANS. HE JUST CRANKS UP THE VOLUME.
READY TO POST THE TUNE, MAN?
YEAH, BUT LET'S PUT IT UP FOR FREE, SHERM. IF THE FANS DIG IT, THEY'LL SUPPORT THE ALBUM.
I'M ON IT! STUFFED AND SHIPPED, BABE!
FOR FREE? AREN'T YOU WORRIED YOUR LABEL WILL FIND OUT?
NAH.
JIM! YOUR LABEL ON LINE TWO!
DAMN... THEY STAKED OUT MY SITE.
GB Trudeau

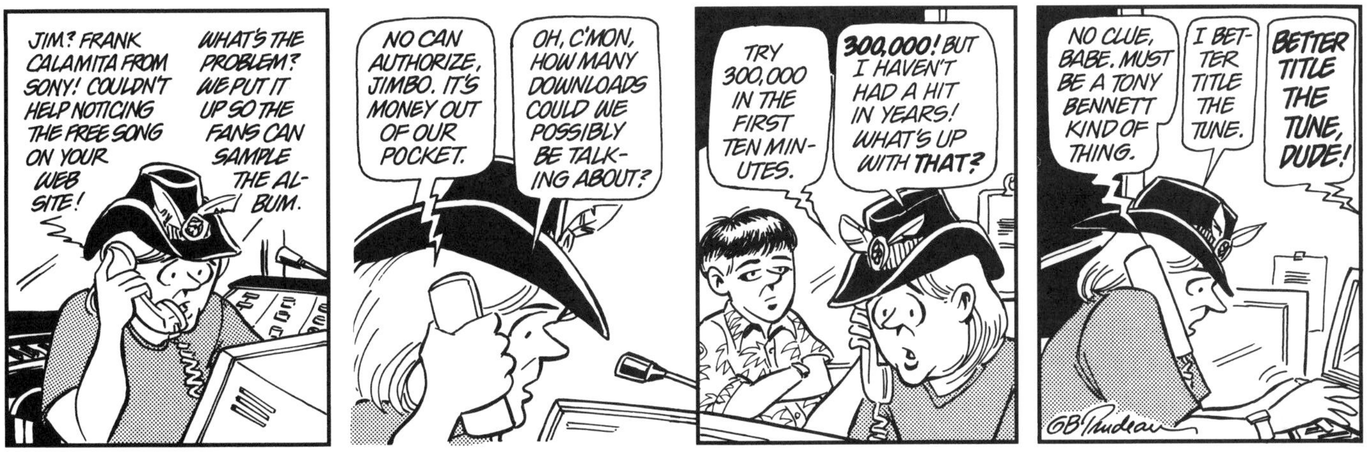
JIM? FRANK CALAMITA FROM SONY! COULDN'T HELP NOTICING THE FREE SONG ON YOUR WEB SITE!
WHAT'S THE PROBLEM? WE PUT IT UP SO THE FANS CAN SAMPLE THE AL-BUM.
NO CAN AUTHORIZE, JIMBO. IT'S MONEY OUT OF OUR POCKET.
OH, C'MON, HOW MANY DOWNLOADS COULD WE POSSIBLY BE TALK-ING ABOUT?
TRY 300,000 IN THE FIRST TEN MIN-UTES.
300,000! BUT I HAVEN'T HAD A HIT IN YEARS! WHAT'S UP WITH THAT?
NO CLUE, BABE. MUST BE A TONY BENNETT KIND OF THING.
I BET-TER TITLE THE TUNE.
BETTER TITLE THE TUNE, DUDE!
GB Trudeau

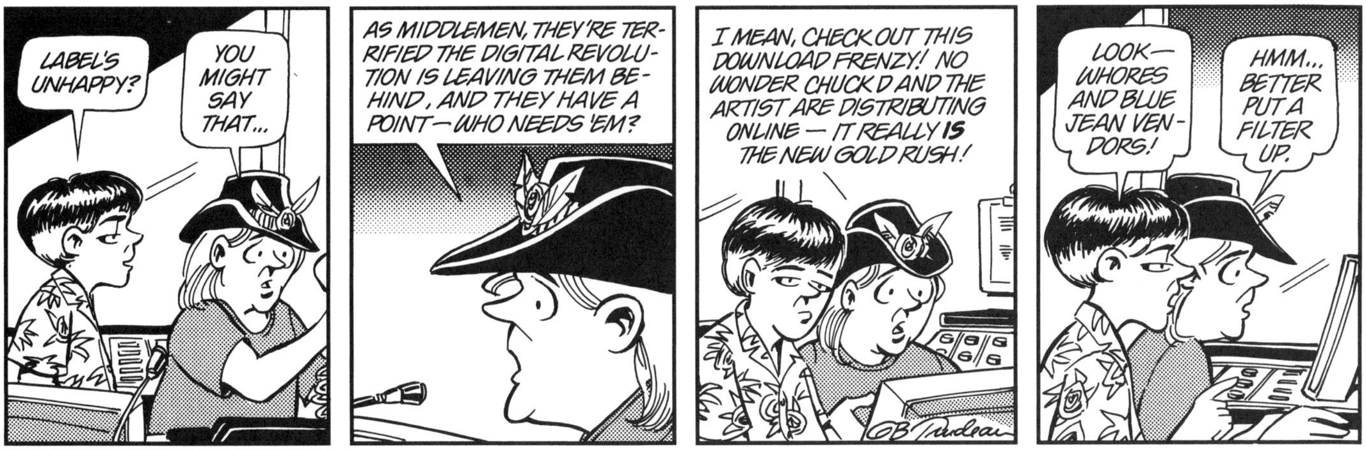
LABEL'S UNHAPPY?
YOU MIGHT SAY THAT...
AS MIDDLEMEN, THEY'RE TER-RIFIED THE DIGITAL REVOLU-TION IS LEAVING THEM BE-HIND, AND THEY HAVE A POINT — WHO NEEDS 'EM?
I MEAN, CHECK OUT THIS DOWNLOAD FRENZY! NO WONDER CHUCK D AND THE ARTIST ARE DISTRIBUTING ONLINE — IT REALLY IS THE NEW GOLD RUSH!
LOOK— WHORES AND BLUE JEAN VEN-DORS!
HMM... BETTER PUT A FILTER UP.
GB Trudeau

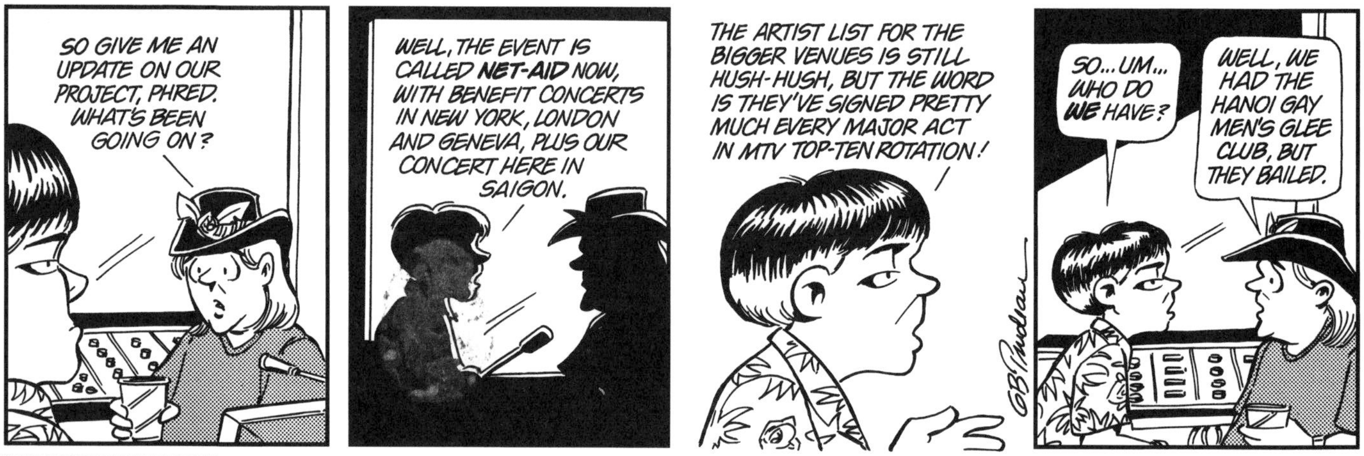
SO GIVE ME AN UPDATE ON OUR PROJECT, PHRED. WHAT'S BEEN GOING ON?
WELL, THE EVENT IS CALLED NET-AID NOW, WITH BENEFIT CONCERTS IN NEW YORK, LONDON AND GENEVA, PLUS OUR CONCERT HERE IN SAIGON.
THE ARTIST LIST FOR THE BIGGER VENUES IS STILL HUSH-HUSH, BUT THE WORD IS THEY'VE SIGNED PRETTY MUCH EVERY MAJOR ACT IN MTV TOP-TEN ROTATION!
SO... UM... WHO DO WE HAVE?
WELL, WE HAD THE HANOI GAY MEN'S GLEE CLUB, BUT THEY BAILED.

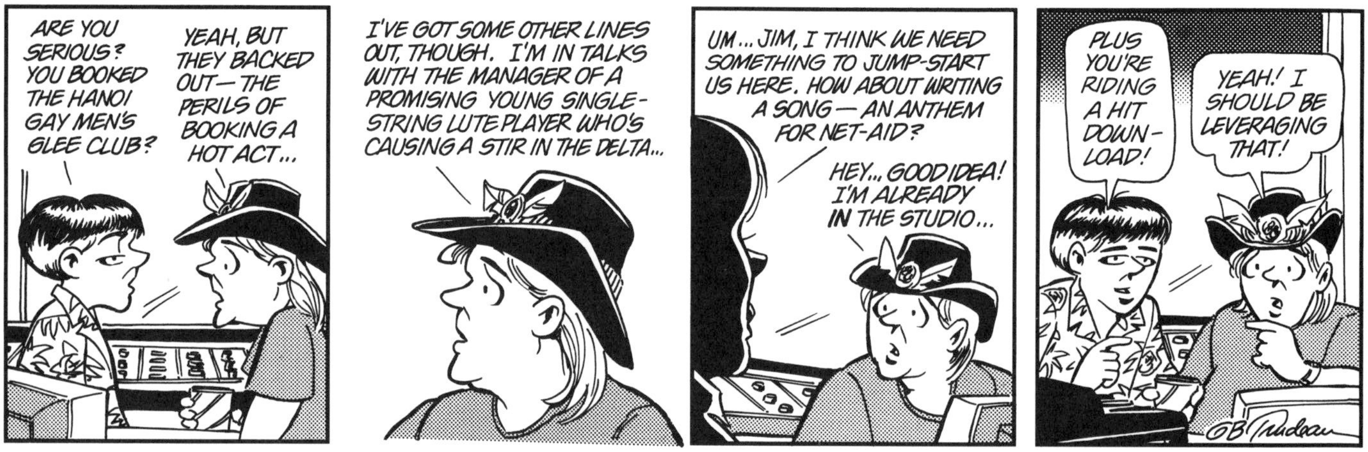
ARE YOU SERIOUS? YOU BOOKED THE HANOI GAY MEN'S GLEE CLUB?
YEAH, BUT THEY BACKED OUT— THE PERILS OF BOOKING A HOT ACT...
I'VE GOT SOME OTHER LINES OUT, THOUGH. I'M IN TALKS WITH THE MANAGER OF A PROMISING YOUNG SINGLE-STRING LUTE PLAYER WHO'S CAUSING A STIR IN THE DELTA...
UM... JIM, I THINK WE NEED SOMETHING TO JUMP-START US HERE. HOW ABOUT WRITING A SONG — AN ANTHEM FOR NET-AID?
HEY... GOOD IDEA! I'M ALREADY IN THE STUDIO...
PLUS YOU'RE RIDING A HIT DOWN-LOAD!
YEAH! I SHOULD BE LEVERAGING THAT!

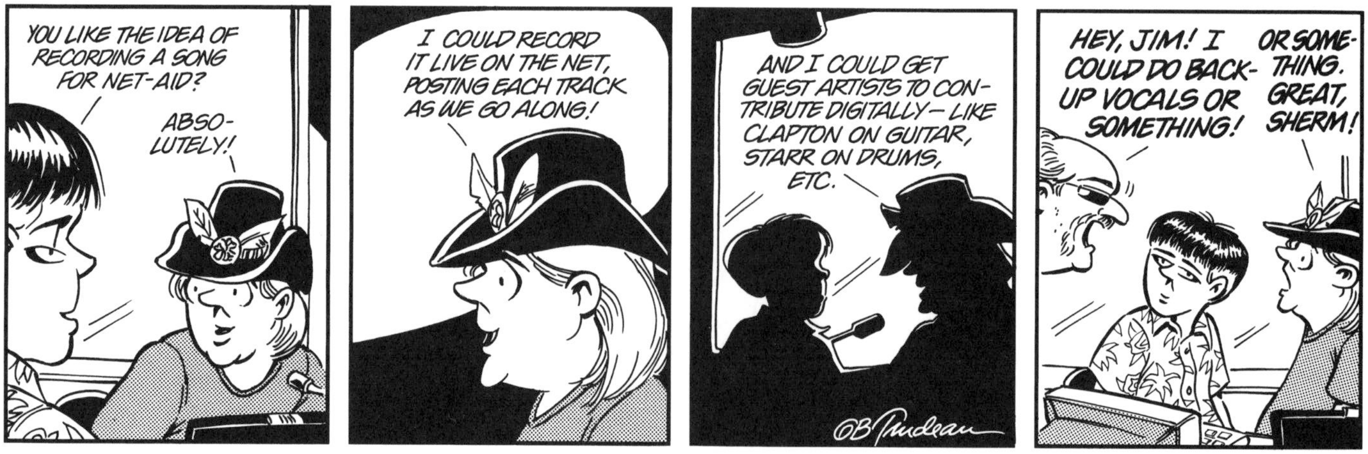
YOU LIKE THE IDEA OF RECORDING A SONG FOR NET-AID?
ABSO-LUTELY!
I COULD RECORD IT LIVE ON THE NET, POSTING EACH TRACK AS WE GO ALONG!
AND I COULD GET GUEST ARTISTS TO CON-TRIBUTE DIGITALLY— LIKE CLAPTON ON GUITAR, STARR ON DRUMS, ETC.
HEY, JIM! I COULD DO BACK-UP VOCALS OR SOMETHING!
OR SOME-THING. GREAT, SHERM!

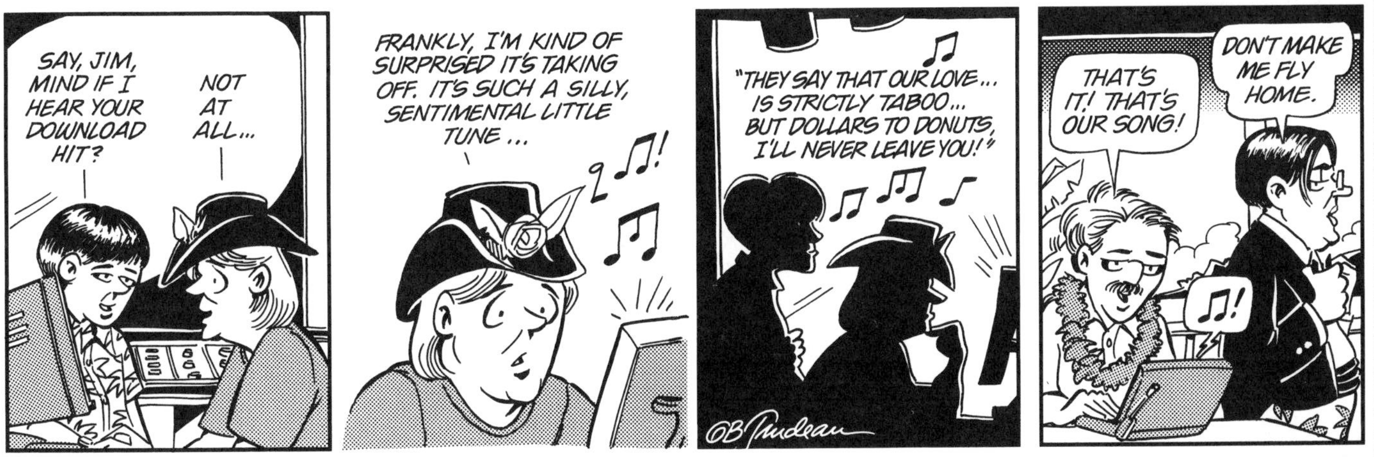
SAY, JIM, MIND IF I HEAR YOUR DOWNLOAD HIT?
NOT AT ALL...
FRANKLY, I'M KIND OF SURPRISED IT'S TAKING OFF. IT'S SUCH A SILLY, SENTIMENTAL LITTLE TUNE ...
"THEY SAY THAT OUR LOVE... IS STRICTLY TABOO... BUT DOLLARS TO DONUTS, I'LL NEVER LEAVE YOU!"
THAT'S IT! THAT'S OUR SONG!
DON'T MAKE ME FLY HOME.

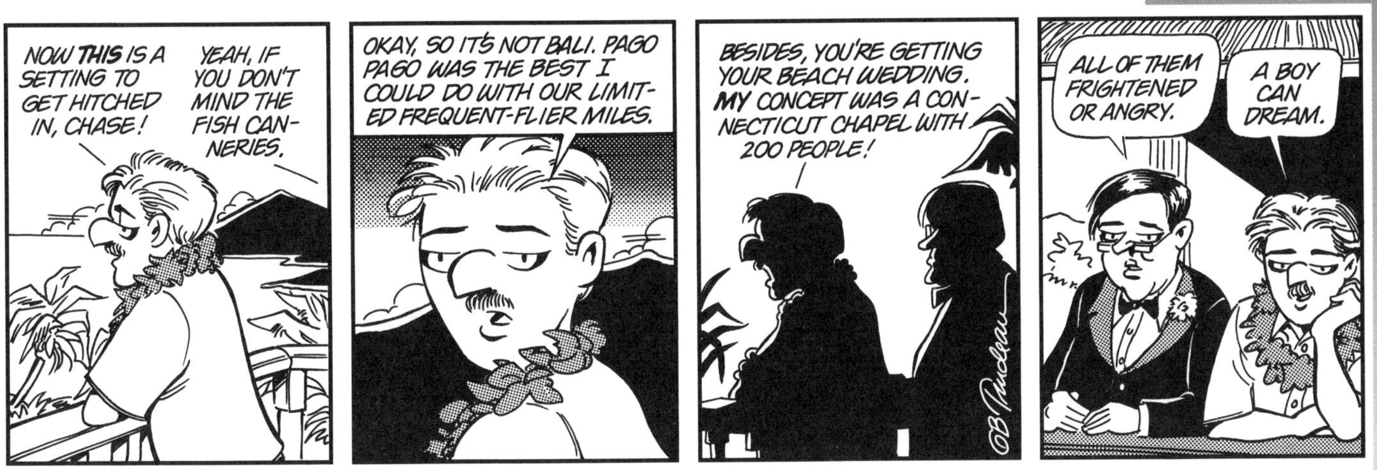
NOW **THIS** IS A SETTING TO GET HITCHED IN, CHASE!
YEAH, IF YOU DON'T MIND THE FISH CANNERIES.
OKAY, SO IT'S NOT BALI. PAGO PAGO WAS THE BEST I COULD DO WITH OUR LIMITED FREQUENT-FLIER MILES.
BESIDES, YOU'RE GETTING YOUR BEACH WEDDING. **MY** CONCEPT WAS A CONNECTICUT CHAPEL WITH 200 PEOPLE!
ALL OF THEM FRIGHTENED OR ANGRY.
A BOY CAN DREAM.

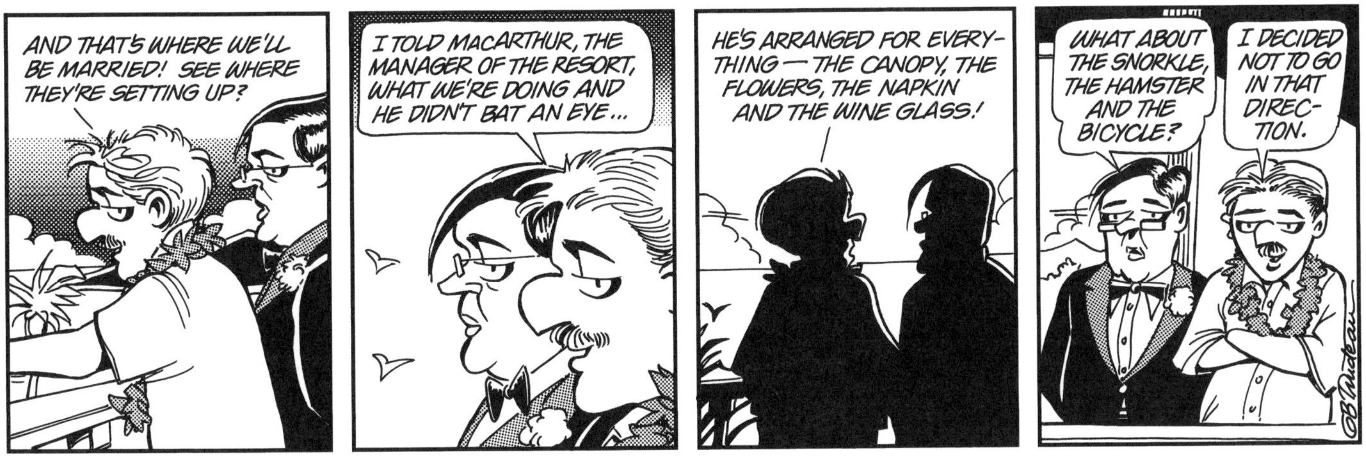
AND THAT'S WHERE WE'LL BE MARRIED! SEE WHERE THEY'RE SETTING UP?
I TOLD MACARTHUR, THE MANAGER OF THE RESORT, WHAT WE'RE DOING AND HE DIDN'T BAT AN EYE...
HE'S ARRANGED FOR EVERYTHING — THE CANOPY, THE FLOWERS, THE NAPKIN AND THE WINE GLASS!
WHAT ABOUT THE SNORKLE, THE HAMSTER AND THE BICYCLE?
I DECIDED NOT TO GO IN THAT DIRECTION.

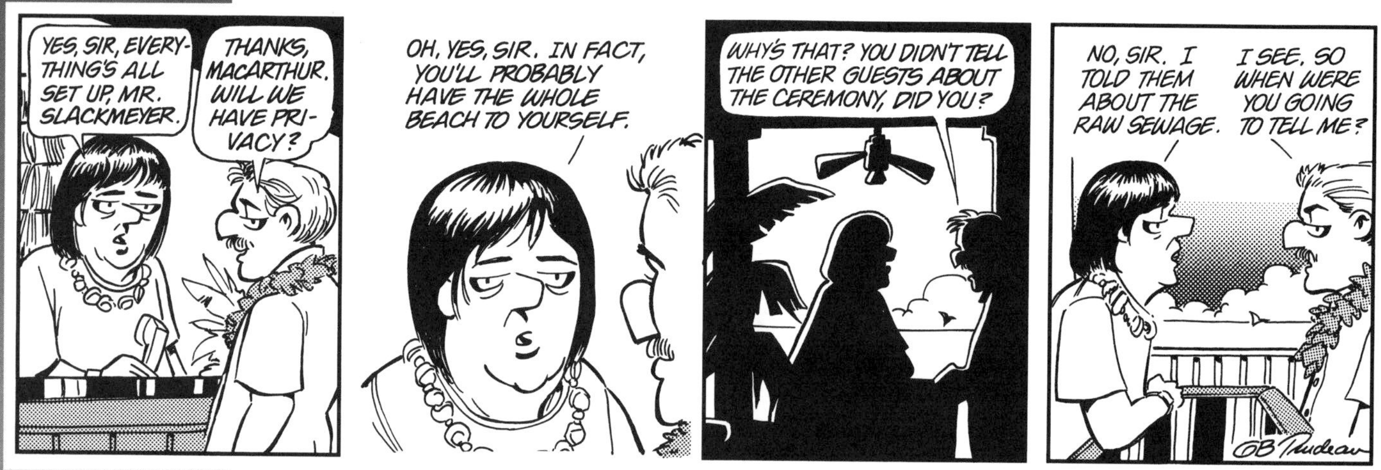
YES, SIR, EVERYTHING'S ALL SET UP, MR. SLACKMEYER.
THANKS, MACARTHUR. WILL WE HAVE PRIVACY?
OH, YES, SIR. IN FACT, YOU'LL PROBABLY HAVE THE WHOLE BEACH TO YOURSELF.
WHY'S THAT? YOU DIDN'T TELL THE OTHER GUESTS ABOUT THE CEREMONY, DID YOU?
NO, SIR. I TOLD THEM ABOUT THE RAW SEWAGE.
I SEE. SO WHEN WERE YOU GOING TO TELL ME?
©B Trudeau

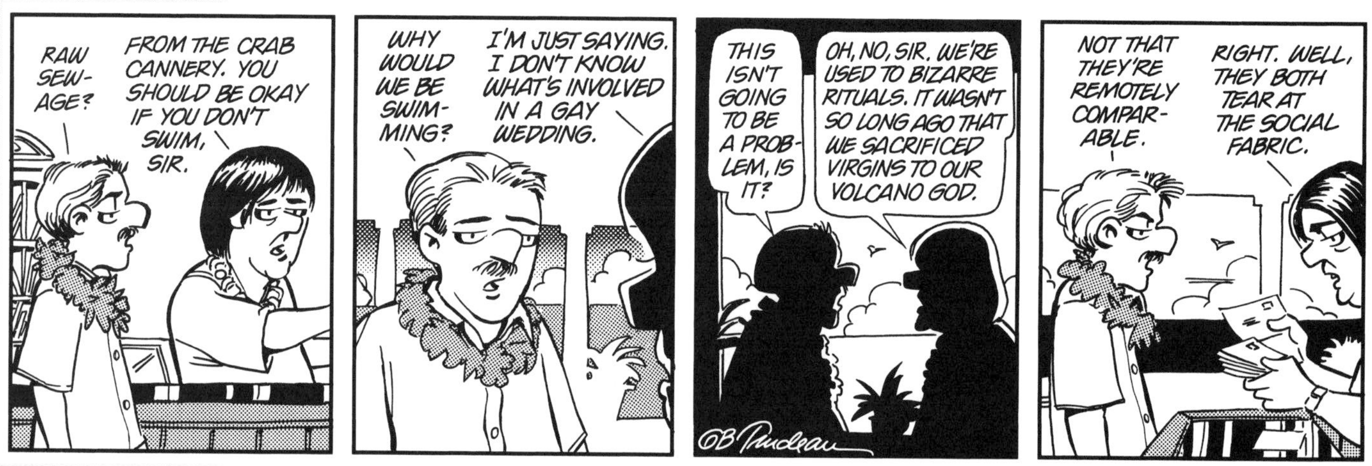
RAW SEWAGE?
FROM THE CRAB CANNERY. YOU SHOULD BE OKAY IF YOU DON'T SWIM, SIR.
WHY WOULD WE BE SWIMMING?
I'M JUST SAYING. I DON'T KNOW WHAT'S INVOLVED IN A GAY WEDDING.
THIS ISN'T GOING TO BE A PROBLEM, IS IT?
OH, NO, SIR. WE'RE USED TO BIZARRE RITUALS. IT WASN'T SO LONG AGO THAT WE SACRIFICED VIRGINS TO OUR VOLCANO GOD.
NOT THAT THEY'RE REMOTELY COMPARABLE.
RIGHT. WELL, THEY BOTH TEAR AT THE SOCIAL FABRIC.
©B Trudeau

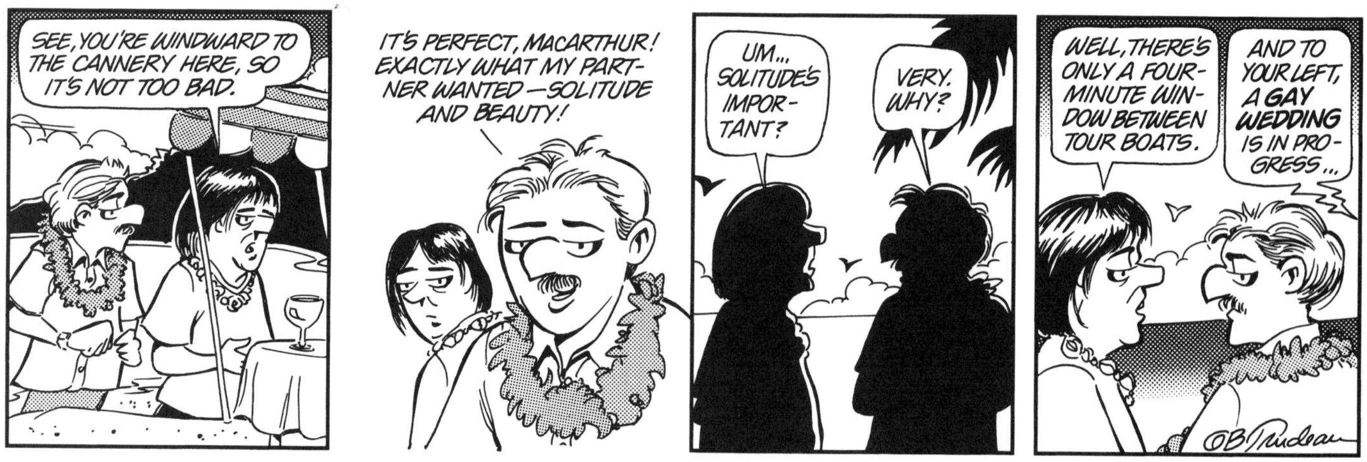
SEE, YOU'RE WINDWARD TO THE CANNERY HERE, SO IT'S NOT TOO BAD.
IT'S PERFECT, MACARTHUR! EXACTLY WHAT MY PARTNER WANTED—SOLITUDE AND BEAUTY!
UM... SOLITUDE'S IMPORTANT?
VERY. WHY?
WELL, THERE'S ONLY A FOUR-MINUTE WINDOW BETWEEN TOUR BOATS.
AND TO YOUR LEFT, A GAY WEDDING IS IN PROGRESS...
©B Trudeau

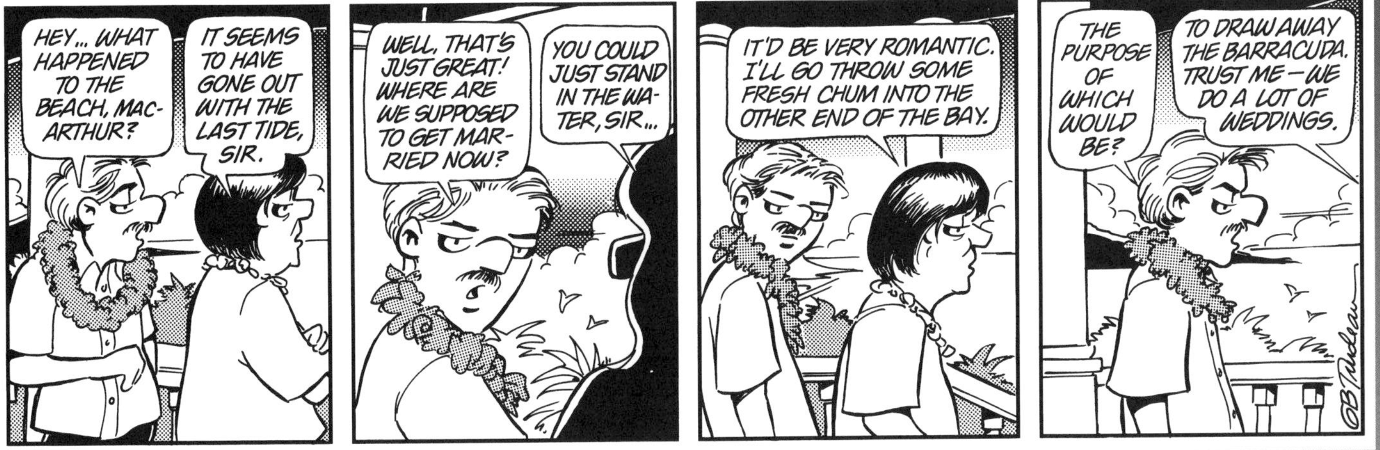
HEY... WHAT HAPPENED TO THE BEACH, MACARTHUR?
IT SEEMS TO HAVE GONE OUT WITH THE LAST TIDE, SIR.
WELL, THAT'S JUST GREAT! WHERE ARE WE SUPPOSED TO GET MARRIED NOW?
YOU COULD JUST STAND IN THE WATER, SIR...
IT'D BE VERY ROMANTIC. I'LL GO THROW SOME FRESH CHUM INTO THE OTHER END OF THE BAY.
THE PURPOSE OF WHICH WOULD BE?
TO DRAW AWAY THE BARRACUDA. TRUST ME—WE DO A LOT OF WEDDINGS.
©B Trudeau

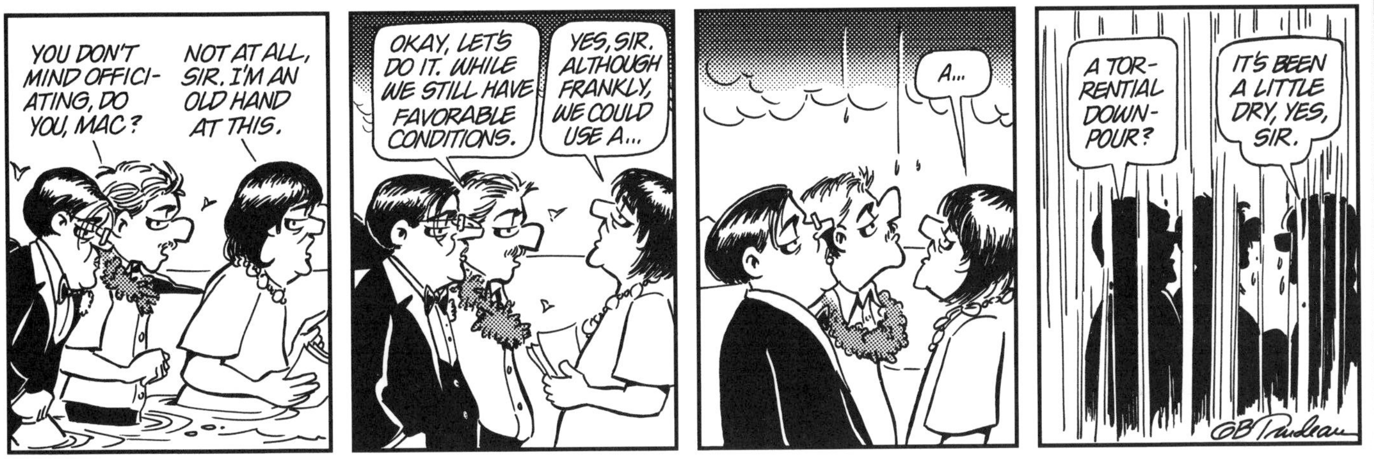
YOU DON'T MIND OFFICIATING, DO YOU, MAC?
NOT AT ALL, SIR. I'M AN OLD HAND AT THIS.
OKAY, LET'S DO IT. WHILE WE STILL HAVE FAVORABLE CONDITIONS.
YES, SIR. ALTHOUGH FRANKLY, WE COULD USE A...
A...
A TORRENTIAL DOWNPOUR?
IT'S BEEN A LITTLE DRY, YES, SIR.
©B Trudeau

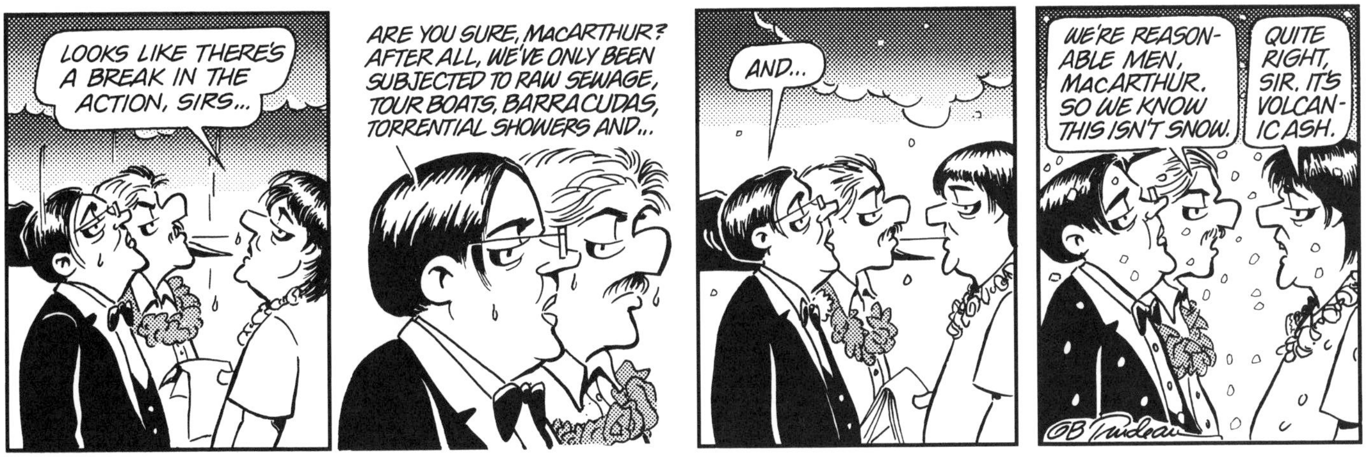
LOOKS LIKE THERE'S A BREAK IN THE ACTION, SIRS...
ARE YOU SURE, MACARTHUR? AFTER ALL, WE'VE ONLY BEEN SUBJECTED TO RAW SEWAGE, TOUR BOATS, BARRACUDAS, TORRENTIAL SHOWERS AND...
AND...
WE'RE REASONABLE MEN, MACARTHUR. SO WE KNOW THIS ISN'T SNOW.
QUITE RIGHT, SIR. IT'S VOLCANIC ASH.
©B Trudeau

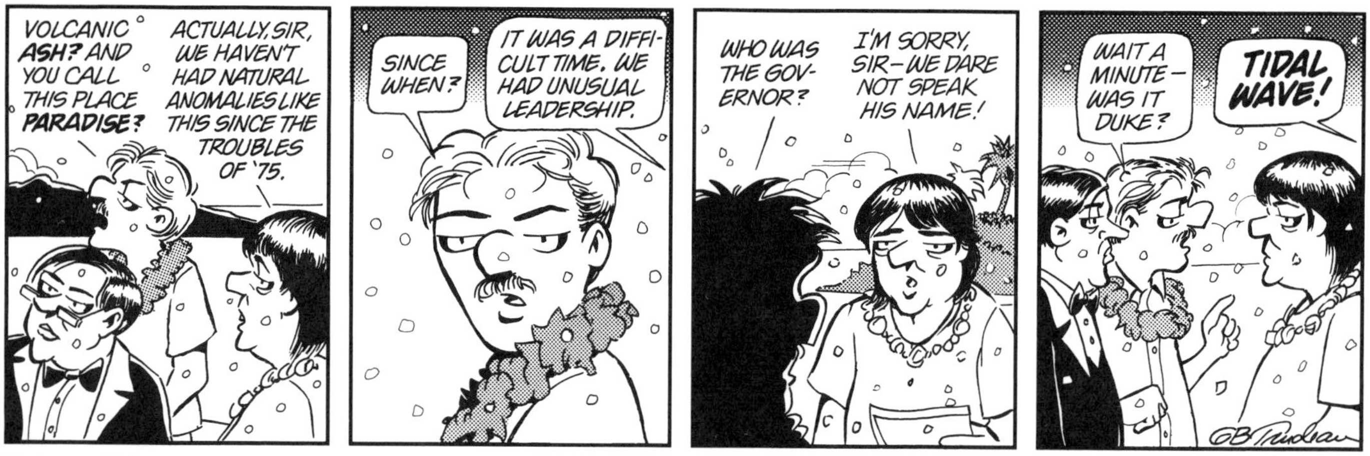
VOLCANIC **ASH?** AND YOU CALL THIS PLACE **PARADISE?**
ACTUALLY, SIR, WE HAVEN'T HAD NATURAL ANOMALIES LIKE THIS SINCE THE TROUBLES OF '75.
SINCE WHEN?
IT WAS A DIFFICULT TIME. WE HAD UNUSUAL LEADERSHIP.
WHO WAS THE GOVERNOR?
I'M SORRY, SIR—WE DARE NOT SPEAK HIS NAME!
WAIT A MINUTE—WAS IT DUKE?
TIDAL WAVE!

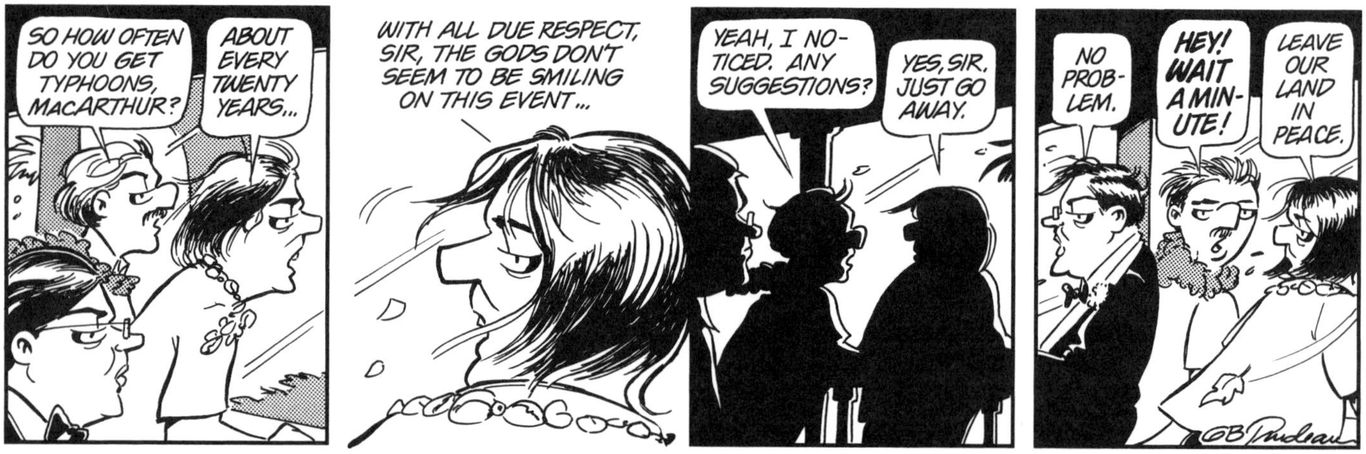
SO HOW OFTEN DO YOU GET TYPHOONS, MACARTHUR?
ABOUT EVERY TWENTY YEARS...
WITH ALL DUE RESPECT, SIR, THE GODS DON'T SEEM TO BE SMILING ON THIS EVENT...
YEAH, I NOTICED. ANY SUGGESTIONS?
YES, SIR. JUST GO AWAY.
NO PROBLEM.
HEY! WAIT A MINUTE!
LEAVE OUR LAND IN PEACE.

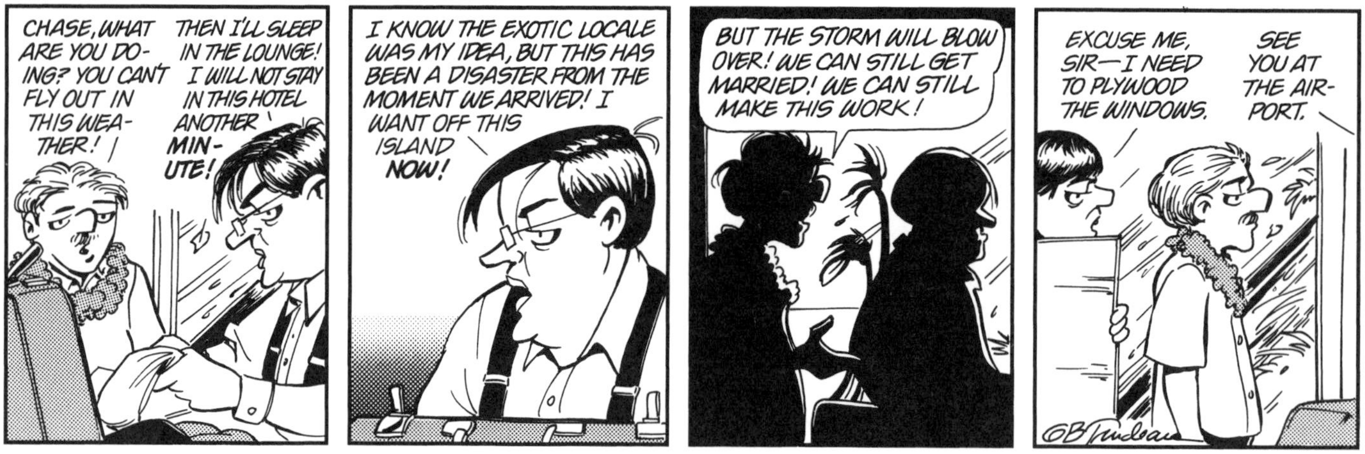
CHASE, WHAT ARE YOU DOING? YOU CAN'T FLY OUT IN THIS WEATHER!
THEN I'LL SLEEP IN THE LOUNGE! I WILL NOT STAY IN THIS HOTEL ANOTHER **MINUTE!**
I KNOW THE EXOTIC LOCALE WAS MY IDEA, BUT THIS HAS BEEN A DISASTER FROM THE MOMENT WE ARRIVED! I WANT OFF THIS ISLAND **NOW!**
BUT THE STORM WILL BLOW OVER! WE CAN STILL GET MARRIED! WE CAN STILL MAKE THIS WORK!
EXCUSE ME, SIR—I NEED TO PLYWOOD THE WINDOWS.
SEE YOU AT THE AIRPORT.

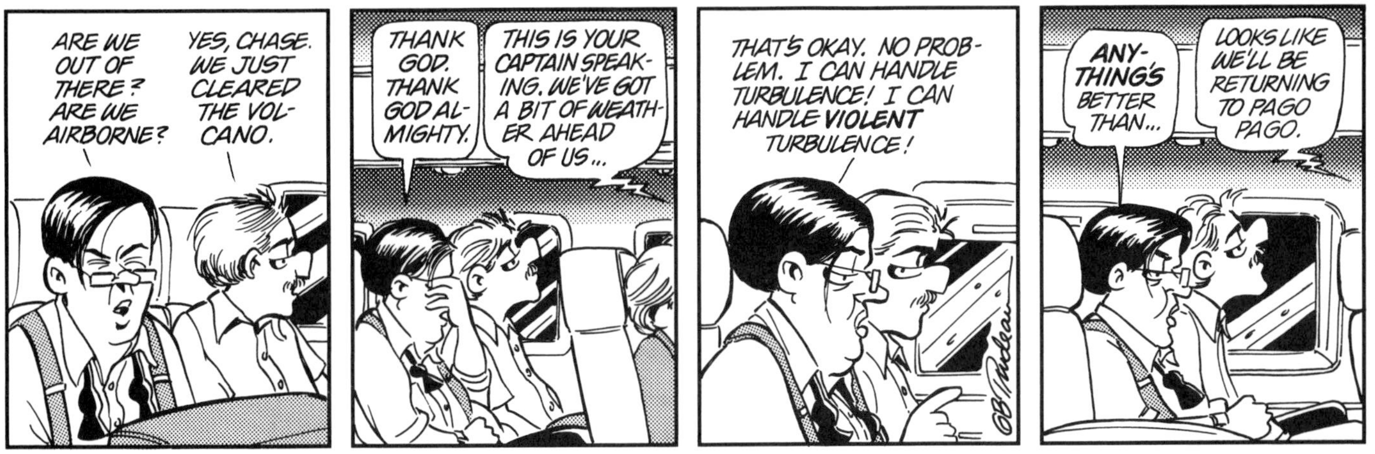
ARE WE OUT OF THERE? ARE WE AIRBORNE?
YES, CHASE. WE JUST CLEARED THE VOL-CANO.
THANK GOD. THANK GOD AL-MIGHTY.
THIS IS YOUR CAPTAIN SPEAK-ING. WE'VE GOT A BIT OF WEATH-ER AHEAD OF US...
THAT'S OKAY. NO PROB-LEM. I CAN HANDLE TURBULENCE! I CAN HANDLE **VIOLENT** TURBULENCE!
ANY-THING'S BETTER THAN...
LOOKS LIKE WE'LL BE RETURNING TO PAGO PAGO.

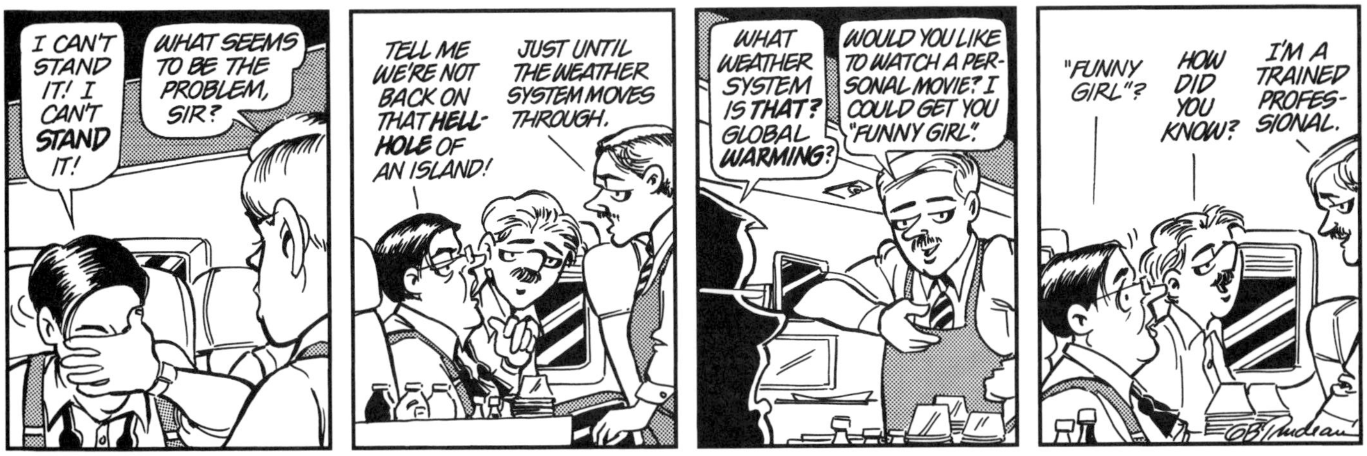
I CAN'T STAND IT! I CAN'T **STAND** IT!
WHAT SEEMS TO BE THE PROBLEM, SIR?
TELL ME WE'RE NOT BACK ON THAT **HELL-HOLE** OF AN ISLAND!
JUST UNTIL THE WEATHER SYSTEM MOVES THROUGH.
WHAT WEATHER SYSTEM IS **THAT?** GLOBAL **WARMING?**
WOULD YOU LIKE TO WATCH A PER-SONAL MOVIE? I COULD GET YOU "FUNNY GIRL."
"FUNNY GIRL"?
HOW DID YOU KNOW?
I'M A TRAINED PROFES-SIONAL.

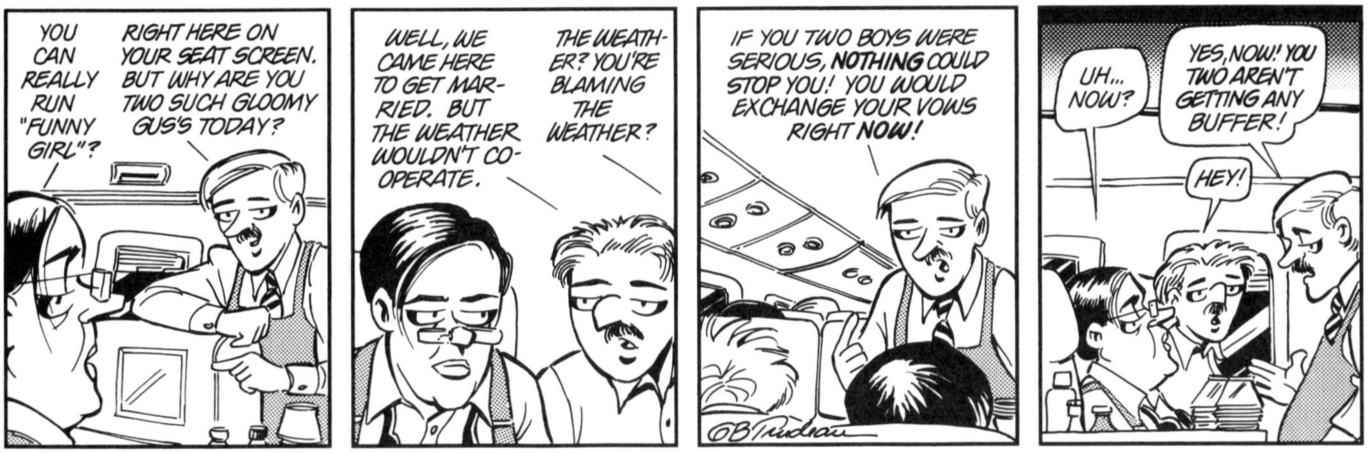
YOU CAN REALLY RUN "FUNNY GIRL"?
RIGHT HERE ON YOUR SEAT SCREEN. BUT WHY ARE YOU TWO SUCH GLOOMY GUS'S TODAY?
WELL, WE CAME HERE TO GET MAR-RIED. BUT THE WEATHER WOULDN'T CO-OPERATE.
THE WEATH-ER? YOU'RE BLAMING THE WEATHER?
IF YOU TWO BOYS WERE SERIOUS, **NOTHING** COULD STOP YOU! YOU WOULD EXCHANGE YOUR VOWS RIGHT **NOW!**
UH... NOW?
YES, NOW! YOU TWO AREN'T GETTING ANY BUFFER!
HEY!

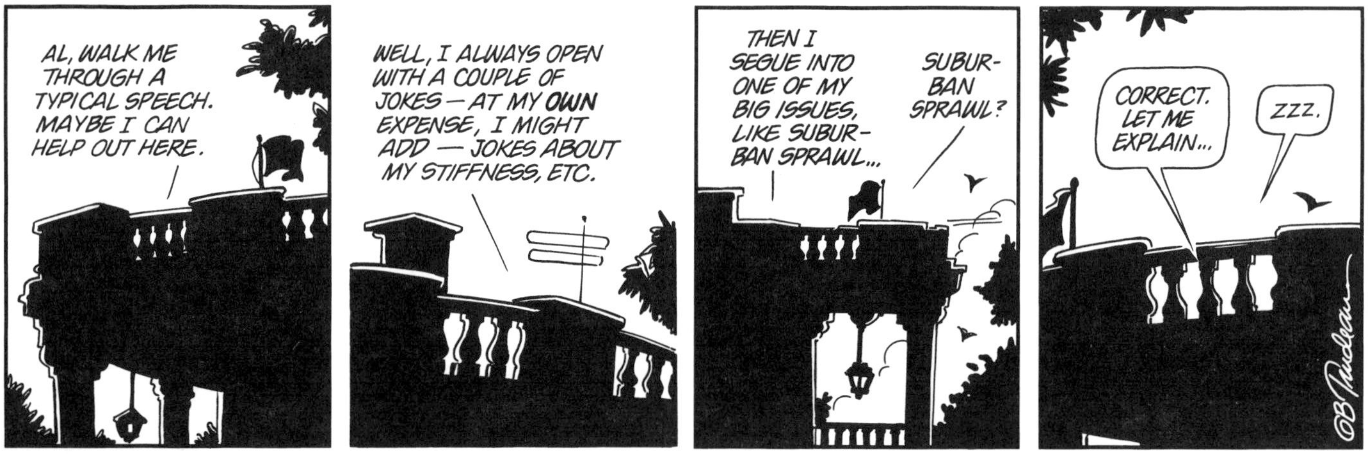
AL, WALK ME THROUGH A TYPICAL SPEECH. MAYBE I CAN HELP OUT HERE.
WELL, I ALWAYS OPEN WITH A COUPLE OF JOKES — AT MY **OWN** EXPENSE, I MIGHT ADD — JOKES ABOUT MY STIFFNESS, ETC.
THEN I SEGUE INTO ONE OF MY BIG ISSUES, LIKE SUBURBAN SPRAWL...
SUBURBAN SPRAWL?
CORRECT. LET ME EXPLAIN...
ZZZ.

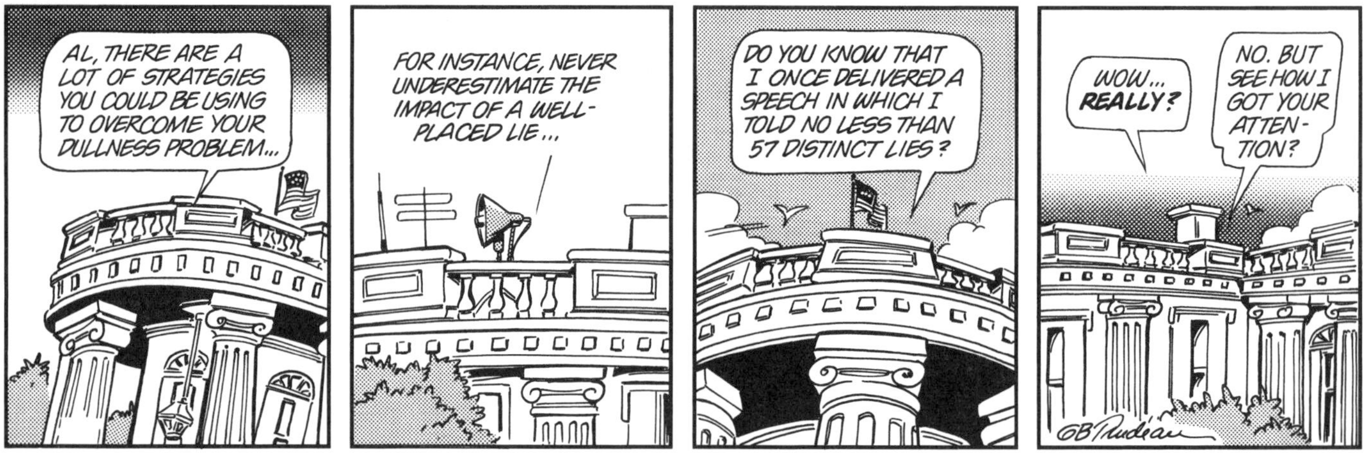
AL, THERE ARE A LOT OF STRATEGIES YOU COULD BE USING TO OVERCOME YOUR DULLNESS PROBLEM...
FOR INSTANCE, NEVER UNDERESTIMATE THE IMPACT OF A WELL-PLACED LIE...
DO YOU KNOW THAT I ONCE DELIVERED A SPEECH IN WHICH I TOLD NO LESS THAN 57 DISTINCT LIES?
WOW... **REALLY?**
NO. BUT SEE HOW I GOT YOUR ATTENTION?

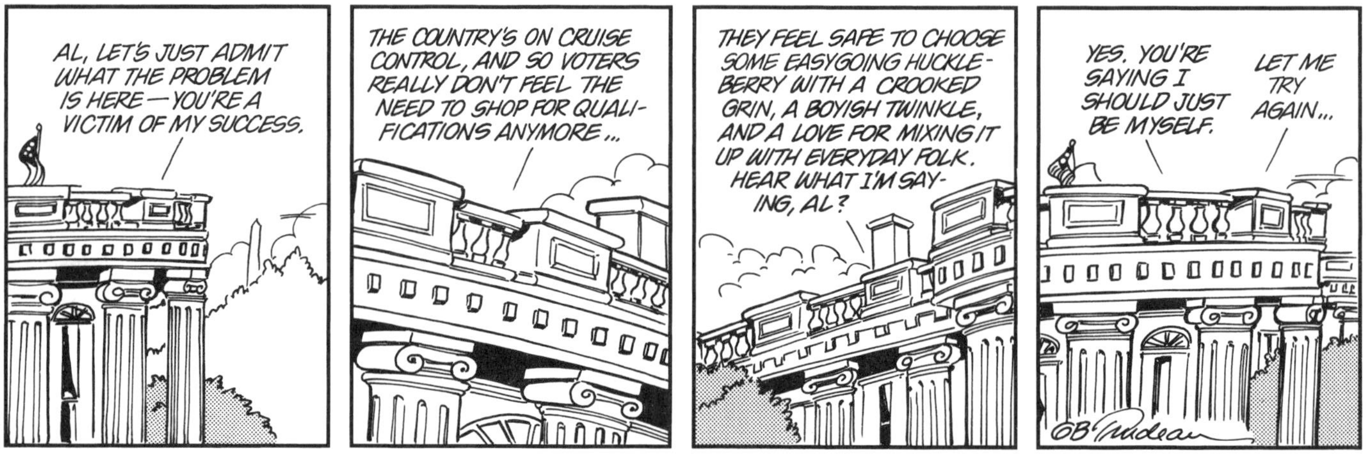
AL, LET'S JUST ADMIT WHAT THE PROBLEM IS HERE — YOU'RE A VICTIM OF MY SUCCESS.
THE COUNTRY'S ON CRUISE CONTROL, AND SO VOTERS REALLY DON'T FEEL THE NEED TO SHOP FOR QUALIFICATIONS ANYMORE...
THEY FEEL SAFE TO CHOOSE SOME EASYGOING HUCKLEBERRY WITH A CROOKED GRIN, A BOYISH TWINKLE, AND A LOVE FOR MIXING IT UP WITH EVERYDAY FOLK. HEAR WHAT I'M SAYING, AL?
YES. YOU'RE SAYING I SHOULD JUST BE MYSELF.
LET ME TRY AGAIN...

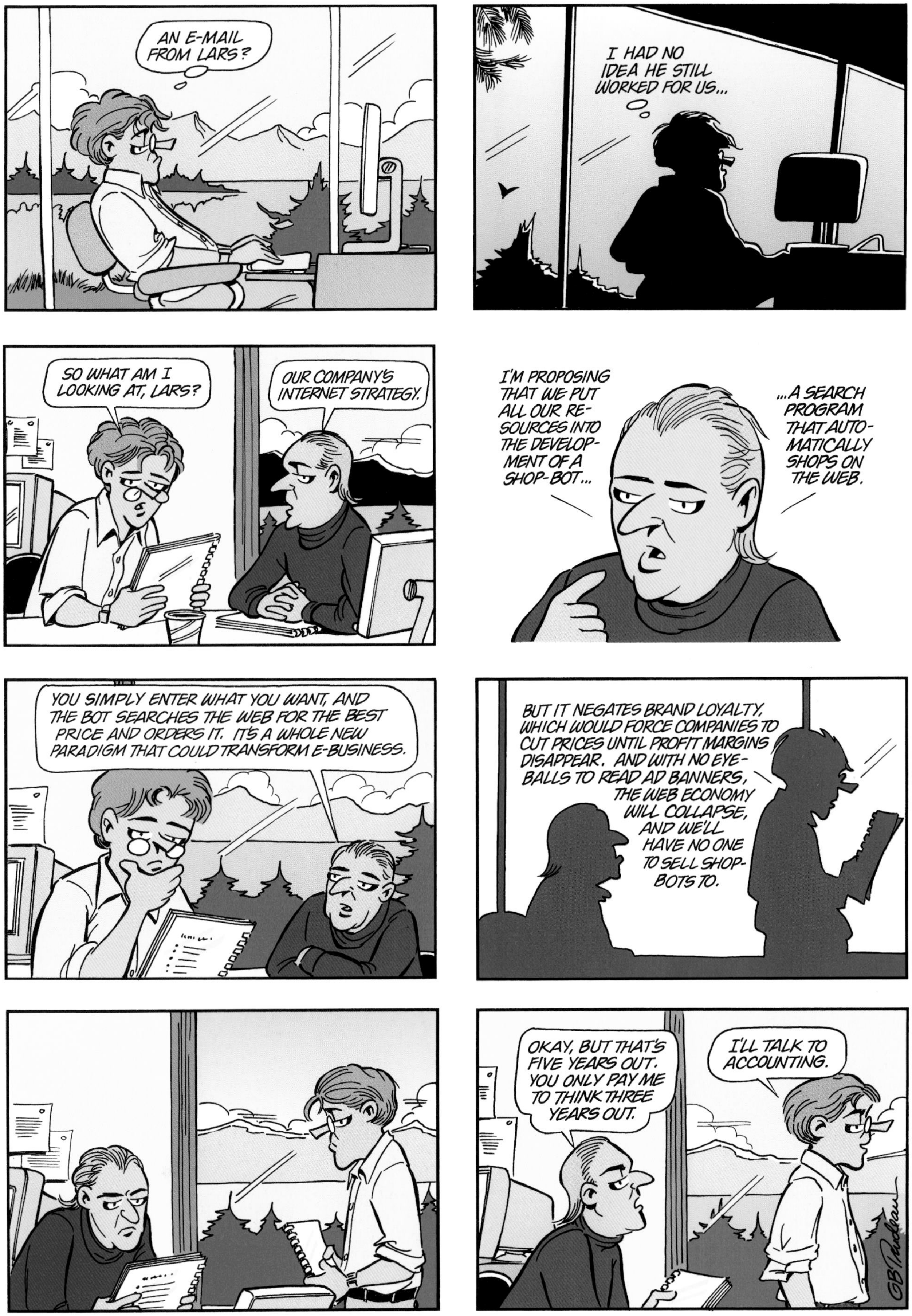
AN E-MAIL FROM LARS?
I HAD NO IDEA HE STILL WORKED FOR US...
SO WHAT AM I LOOKING AT, LARS?
OUR COMPANY'S INTERNET STRATEGY.
I'M PROPOSING THAT WE PUT ALL OUR RESOURCES INTO THE DEVELOPMENT OF A SHOP-BOT...
...A SEARCH PROGRAM THAT AUTOMATICALLY SHOPS ON THE WEB.
YOU SIMPLY ENTER WHAT YOU WANT, AND THE BOT SEARCHES THE WEB FOR THE BEST PRICE AND ORDERS IT. IT'S A WHOLE NEW PARADIGM THAT COULD TRANSFORM E-BUSINESS.
BUT IT NEGATES BRAND LOYALTY, WHICH WOULD FORCE COMPANIES TO CUT PRICES UNTIL PROFIT MARGINS DISAPPEAR. AND WITH NO EYEBALLS TO READ AD BANNERS, THE WEB ECONOMY WILL COLLAPSE, AND WE'LL HAVE NO ONE TO SELL SHOP-BOTS TO.
OKAY, BUT THAT'S FIVE YEARS OUT. YOU ONLY PAY ME TO THINK THREE YEARS OUT.
I'LL TALK TO ACCOUNTING.

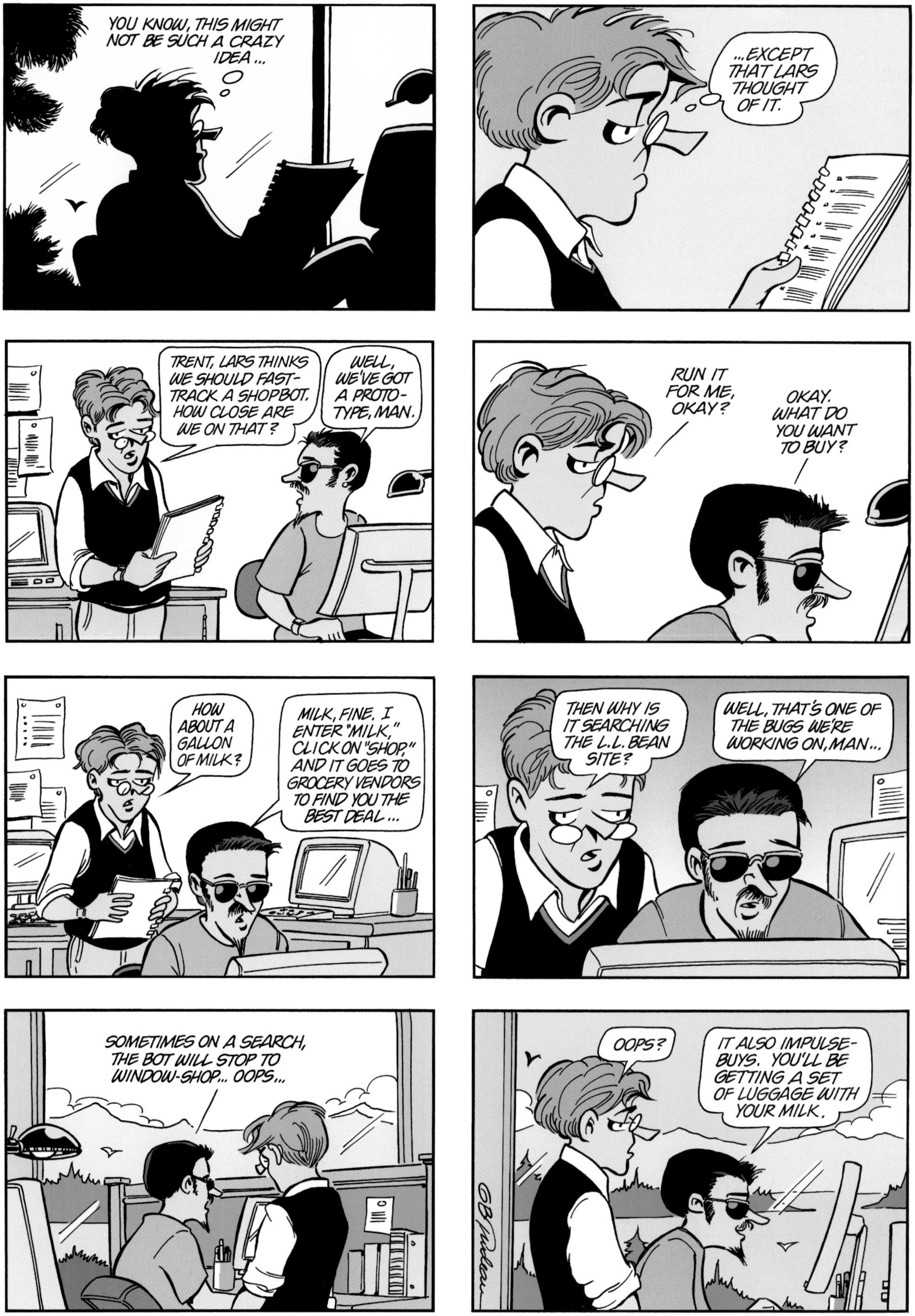
YOU KNOW, THIS MIGHT NOT BE SUCH A CRAZY IDEA ...
...EXCEPT THAT LARS THOUGHT OF IT.
TRENT, LARS THINKS WE SHOULD FAST-TRACK A SHOPBOT. HOW CLOSE ARE WE ON THAT?
WELL, WE'VE GOT A PROTOTYPE, MAN.
RUN IT FOR ME, OKAY?
OKAY. WHAT DO YOU WANT TO BUY?
HOW ABOUT A GALLON OF MILK?
MILK, FINE. I ENTER "MILK," CLICK ON "SHOP," AND IT GOES TO GROCERY VENDORS TO FIND YOU THE BEST DEAL ...
THEN WHY IS IT SEARCHING THE L.L. BEAN SITE?
WELL, THAT'S ONE OF THE BUGS WE'RE WORKING ON, MAN ...
SOMETIMES ON A SEARCH, THE BOT WILL STOP TO WINDOW-SHOP... OOPS...
OOPS?
IT ALSO IMPULSE-BUYS. YOU'LL BE GETTING A SET OF LUGGAGE WITH YOUR MILK.
©B Trudeau

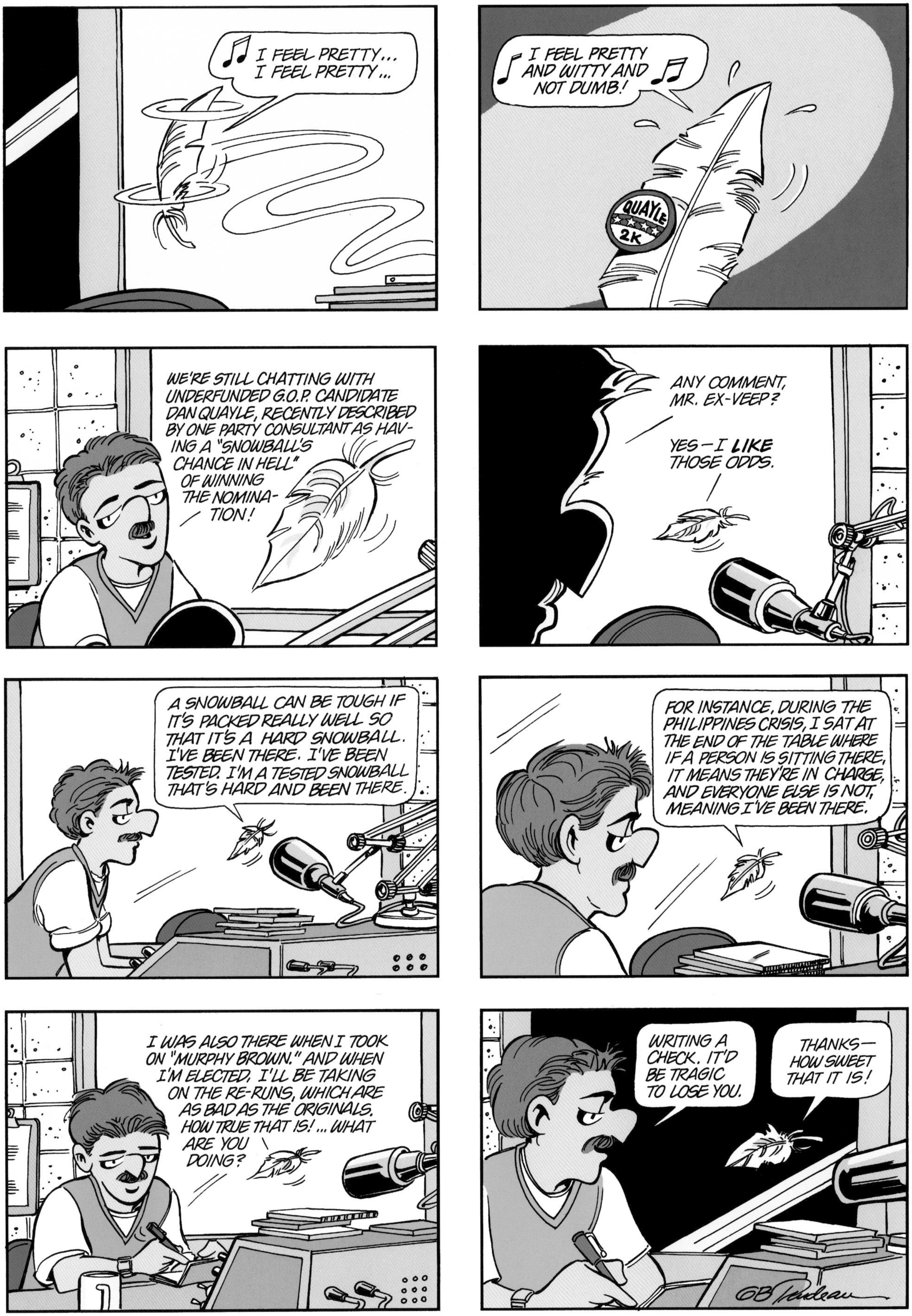
I FEEL PRETTY... I FEEL PRETTY...
I FEEL PRETTY AND WITTY AND NOT DUMB!
QUAYLE 2K
WE'RE STILL CHATTING WITH UNDERFUNDED G.O.P. CANDIDATE DAN QUAYLE, RECENTLY DESCRIBED BY ONE PARTY CONSULTANT AS HAVING A "SNOWBALL'S CHANCE IN HELL" OF WINNING THE NOMINATION!
ANY COMMENT, MR. EX-VEEP?
YES—I LIKE THOSE ODDS.
A SNOWBALL CAN BE TOUGH IF IT'S PACKED REALLY WELL SO THAT IT'S A HARD SNOWBALL. I'VE BEEN THERE. I'VE BEEN TESTED. I'M A TESTED SNOWBALL THAT'S HARD AND BEEN THERE.
FOR INSTANCE, DURING THE PHILIPPINES CRISIS, I SAT AT THE END OF THE TABLE WHERE IF A PERSON IS SITTING THERE, IT MEANS THEY'RE IN CHARGE, AND EVERYONE ELSE IS NOT, MEANING I'VE BEEN THERE.
I WAS ALSO THERE WHEN I TOOK ON "MURPHY BROWN." AND WHEN I'M ELECTED, I'LL BE TAKING ON THE RE-RUNS, WHICH ARE AS BAD AS THE ORIGINALS. HOW TRUE THAT IS! ... WHAT ARE YOU DOING?
WRITING A CHECK. IT'D BE TRAGIC TO LOSE YOU.
THANKS—HOW SWEET THAT IT IS!
GB Trudeau

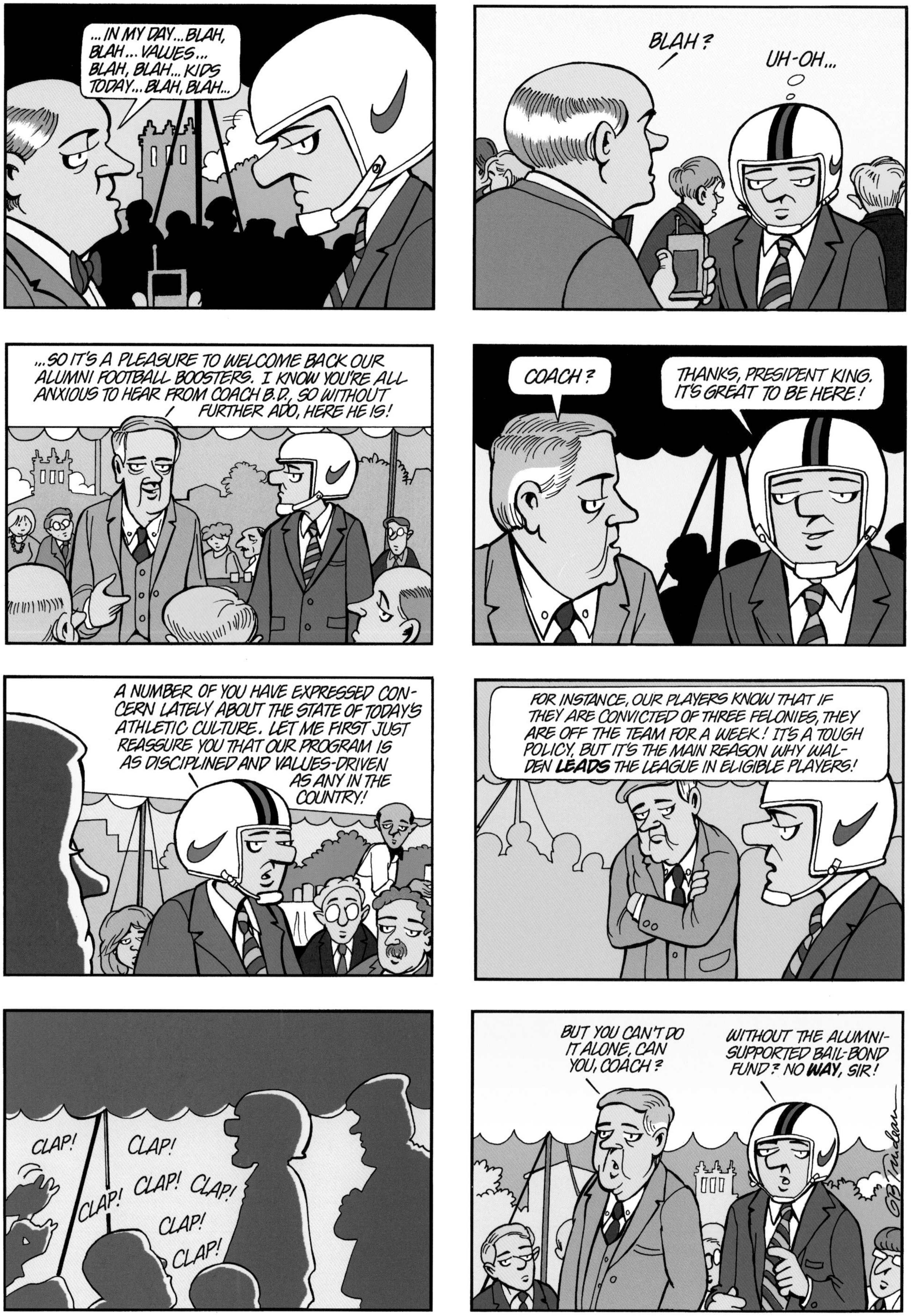

...IN MY DAY... BLAH, BLAH... VALUES... BLAH, BLAH... KIDS TODAY... BLAH, BLAH...
BLAH?
UH-OH...
...SO IT'S A PLEASURE TO WELCOME BACK OUR ALUMNI FOOTBALL BOOSTERS. I KNOW YOU'RE ALL ANXIOUS TO HEAR FROM COACH B.D., SO WITHOUT FURTHER ADO, HERE HE IS!
COACH?
THANKS, PRESIDENT KING. IT'S GREAT TO BE HERE!
A NUMBER OF YOU HAVE EXPRESSED CONCERN LATELY ABOUT THE STATE OF TODAY'S ATHLETIC CULTURE. LET ME FIRST JUST REASSURE YOU THAT OUR PROGRAM IS AS DISCIPLINED AND VALUES-DRIVEN AS ANY IN THE COUNTRY!
FOR INSTANCE, OUR PLAYERS KNOW THAT IF THEY ARE CONVICTED OF THREE FELONIES, THEY ARE OFF THE TEAM FOR A WEEK! IT'S A TOUGH POLICY, BUT IT'S THE MAIN REASON WHY WALDEN **LEADS** THE LEAGUE IN ELIGIBLE PLAYERS!
CLAP! CLAP! CLAP! CLAP! CLAP! CLAP! CLAP!
BUT YOU CAN'T DO IT ALONE, CAN YOU, COACH?
WITHOUT THE ALUMNI-SUPPORTED BAIL-BOND FUND? NO **WAY**, SIR!
GBTrudeau

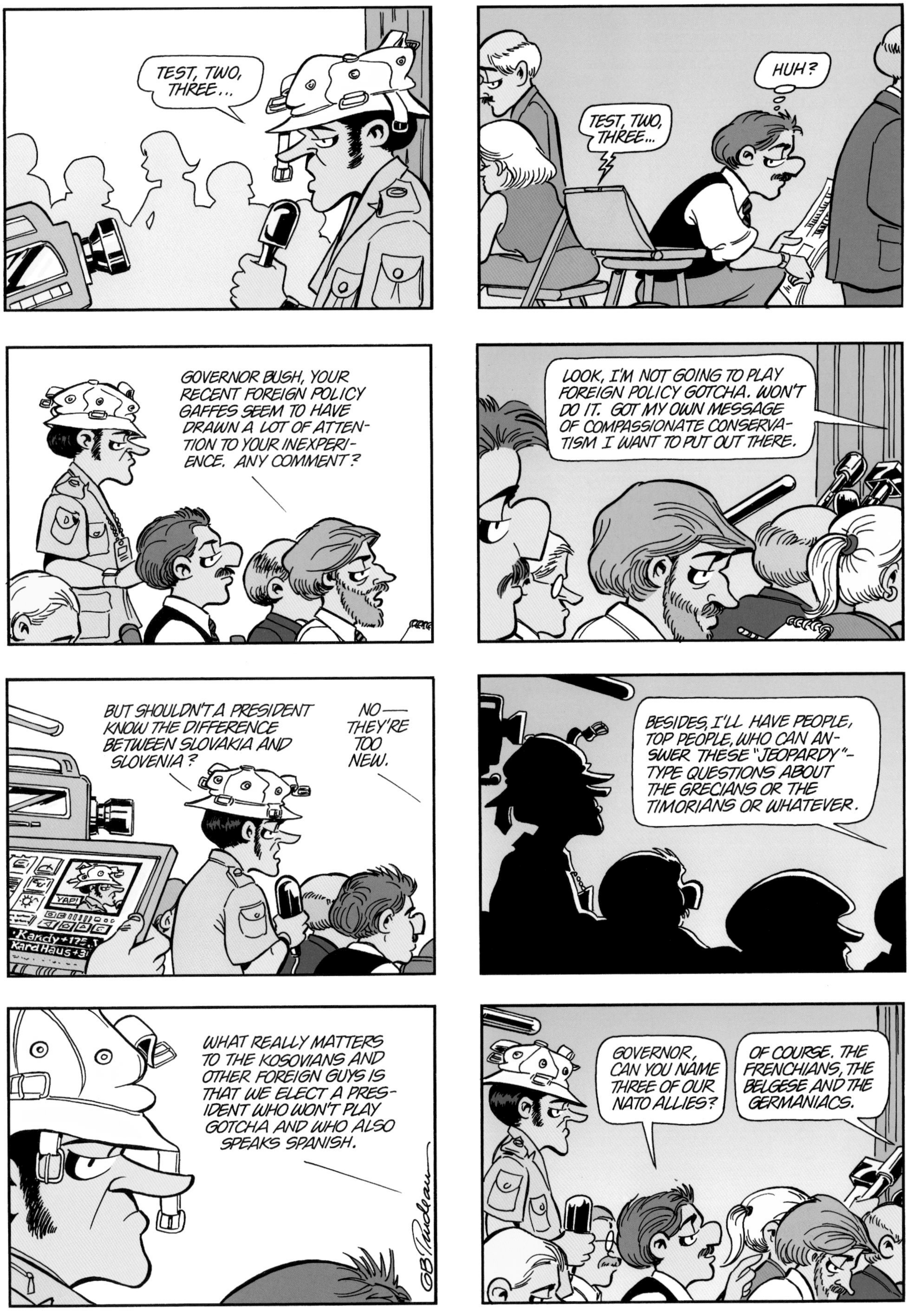
TEST, TWO, THREE...
HUH?
TEST, TWO, THREE...
GOVERNOR BUSH, YOUR RECENT FOREIGN POLICY GAFFES SEEM TO HAVE DRAWN A LOT OF ATTENTION TO YOUR INEXPERIENCE. ANY COMMENT?
LOOK, I'M NOT GOING TO PLAY FOREIGN POLICY GOTCHA. WON'T DO IT. GOT MY OWN MESSAGE OF COMPASSIONATE CONSERVATISM I WANT TO PUT OUT THERE.
BUT SHOULDN'T A PRESIDENT KNOW THE DIFFERENCE BETWEEN SLOVAKIA AND SLOVENIA?
NO— THEY'RE TOO NEW.
YAP!
BESIDES, I'LL HAVE PEOPLE, TOP PEOPLE, WHO CAN ANSWER THESE "JEOPARDY"-TYPE QUESTIONS ABOUT THE GRECIANS OR THE TIMORIANS OR WHATEVER.
WHAT REALLY MATTERS TO THE KOSOVIANS AND OTHER FOREIGN GUYS IS THAT WE ELECT A PRESIDENT WHO WON'T PLAY GOTCHA AND WHO ALSO SPEAKS SPANISH.
GB Trudeau
GOVERNOR, CAN YOU NAME THREE OF OUR NATO ALLIES?
OF COURSE. THE FRENCHIANS, THE BELGESE AND THE GERMANIACS.

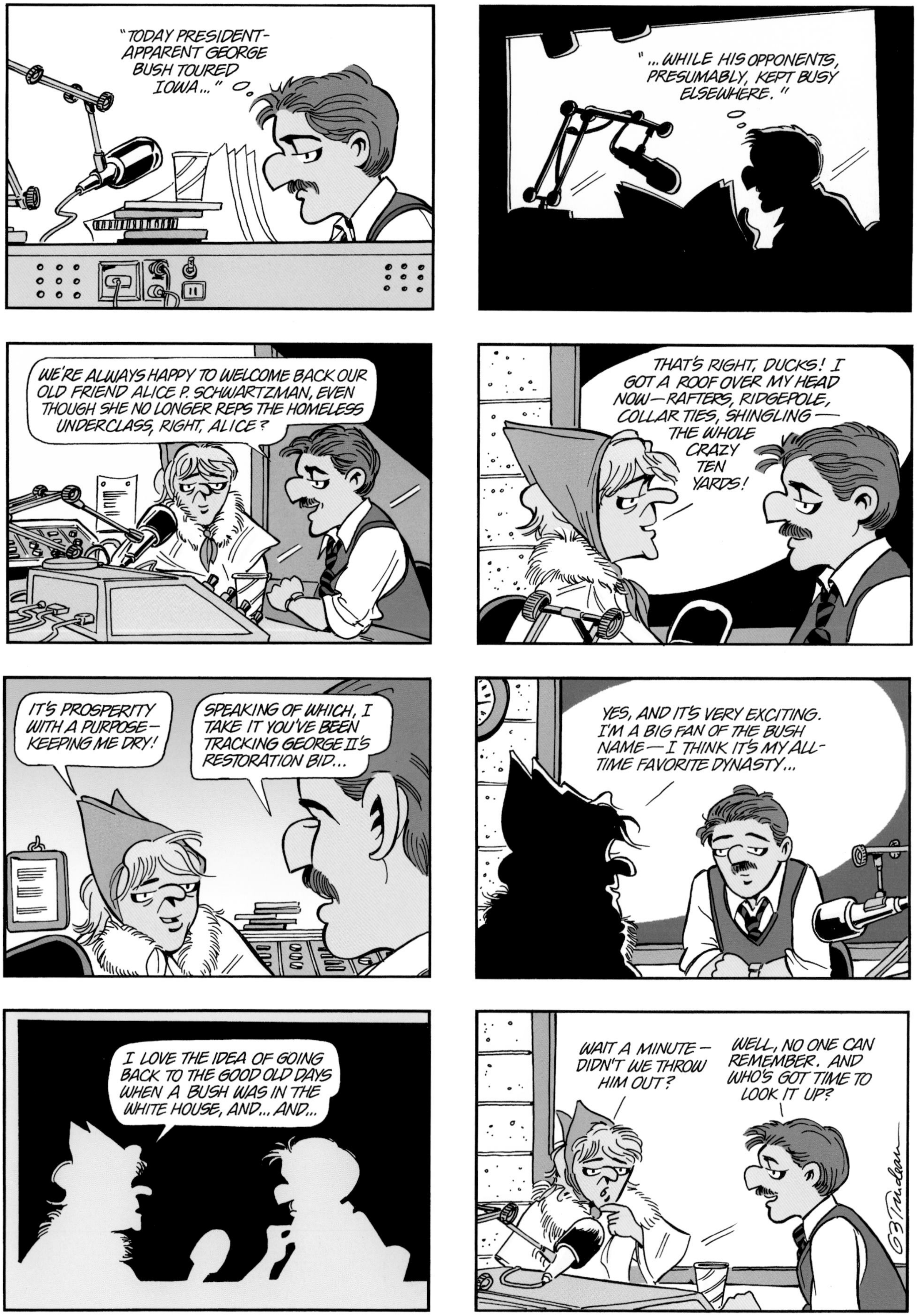
"TODAY PRESIDENT-APPARENT GEORGE BUSH TOURED IOWA..."
"...WHILE HIS OPPONENTS, PRESUMABLY, KEPT BUSY ELSEWHERE."
WE'RE ALWAYS HAPPY TO WELCOME BACK OUR OLD FRIEND ALICE P. SCHWARTZMAN, EVEN THOUGH SHE NO LONGER REPS THE HOMELESS UNDERCLASS, RIGHT, ALICE?
THAT'S RIGHT, DUCKS! I GOT A ROOF OVER MY HEAD NOW—RAFTERS, RIDGEPOLE, COLLAR TIES, SHINGLING—THE WHOLE CRAZY TEN YARDS!
IT'S PROSPERITY WITH A PURPOSE—KEEPING ME DRY!
SPEAKING OF WHICH, I TAKE IT YOU'VE BEEN TRACKING GEORGE II'S RESTORATION BID...
YES, AND IT'S VERY EXCITING. I'M A BIG FAN OF THE BUSH NAME—I THINK IT'S MY ALL-TIME FAVORITE DYNASTY...
I LOVE THE IDEA OF GOING BACK TO THE GOOD OLD DAYS WHEN A BUSH WAS IN THE WHITE HOUSE, AND... AND...
WAIT A MINUTE—DIDN'T WE THROW HIM OUT?
WELL, NO ONE CAN REMEMBER. AND WHO'S GOT TIME TO LOOK IT UP?
GB Trudeau

COME ON IN, AL...
THANK YOU, SIR.
TRY TO RELAX.
HOW DO I DO THAT? COULD YOU GIVE ME SOME TIPS?
AL, THIS IS HOW I SEE IT: YOUR ELECTION VALIDATES MY ADMINISTRATION.
YES, SIR. UNFORTUNATELY, YOUR ADMINISTRATION UNDERMINES MY ELECTABILITY.
SO WHAT WE NEED IS MORE DISTANCE.
BETTER FOR ME.
BETTER FOR HISTORY.
BETTER FOR BOTH OF US!
SO I NEED TO KEEP CRITICIZING YOUR POLITICAL SKILLS, CALLING YOU BORING AND UNINSPIRED.
AND I NEED TO KEEP TALKING ABOUT RESTORING DIGNITY AND MORALITY TO THE OVAL OFFICE.
TO WHICH I'LL TAKE OFFENSE, ACCUSING YOU OF CONTEMPTIBLE DISLOYALTY AND OPPORTUNISM!
WHICH I'LL FIND LAUGHABLE, COMING FROM SOMEONE FOR WHOM BETRAYAL AND LYING ARE SECOND NATURE!
OKAY, THEN. SOUNDS LIKE A PLAN.
WORKS FOR ME, SIR.

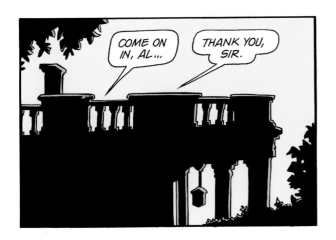

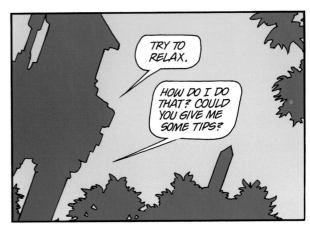

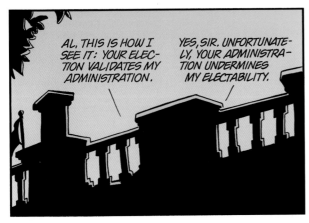

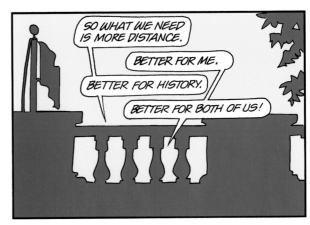

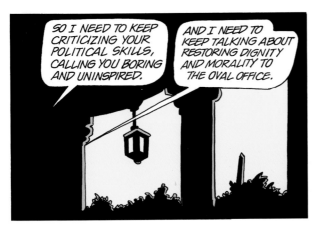

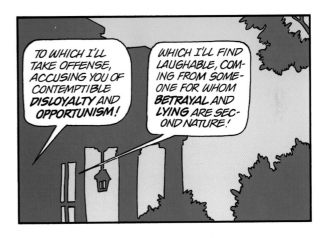

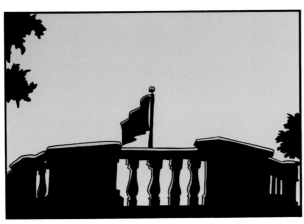

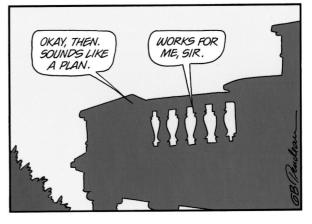

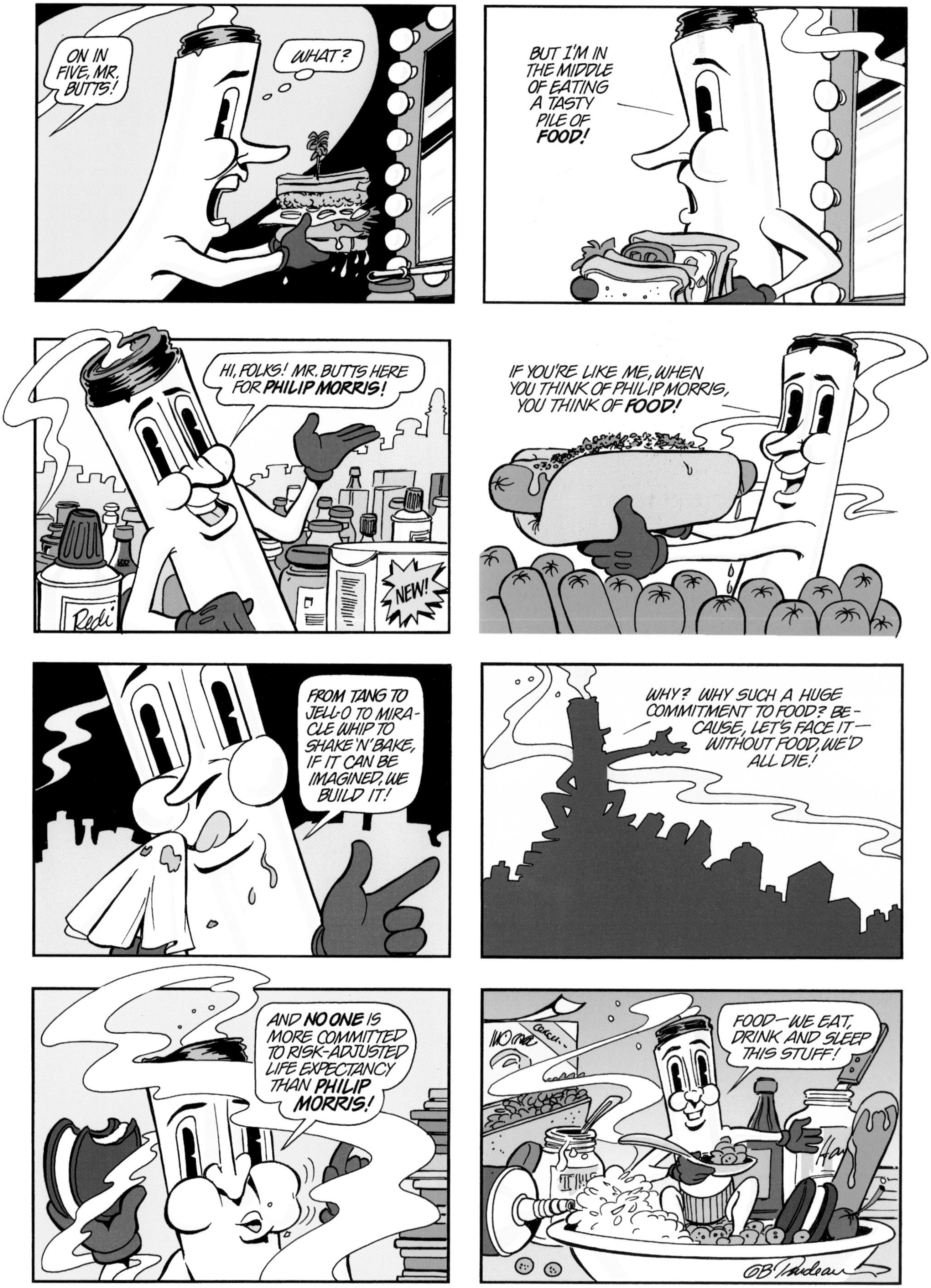
ON IN FIVE, MR. BUTTS!
WHAT?
BUT I'M IN THE MIDDLE OF EATING A TASTY PILE OF FOOD!
HI, FOLKS! MR. BUTTS HERE FOR PHILIP MORRIS!
Redi
NEW!
IF YOU'RE LIKE ME, WHEN YOU THINK OF PHILIP MORRIS, YOU THINK OF FOOD!
FROM TANG TO JELL-O TO MIRA-CLE WHIP TO SHAKE 'N' BAKE, IF IT CAN BE IMAGINED, WE BUILD IT!
WHY? WHY SUCH A HUGE COMMITMENT TO FOOD? BE-CAUSE, LET'S FACE IT—WITHOUT FOOD, WE'D ALL DIE!
AND NO ONE IS MORE COMMITTED TO RISK-ADJUSTED LIFE EXPECTANCY THAN PHILIP MORRIS!
FOOD—WE EAT, DRINK AND SLEEP THIS STUFF!

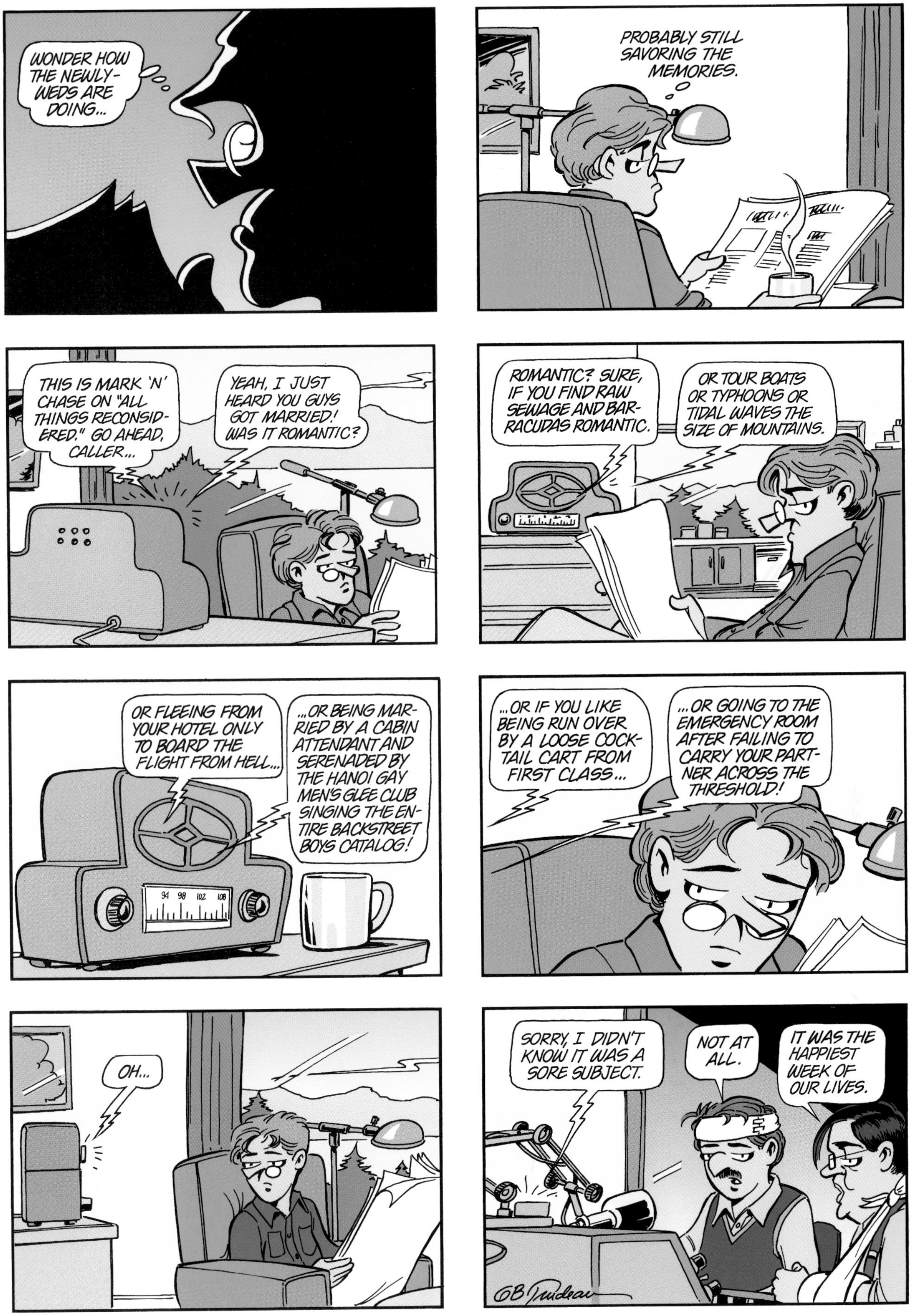
WONDER HOW THE NEWLY-WEDS ARE DOING...
PROBABLY STILL SAVORING THE MEMORIES.
THIS IS MARK 'N' CHASE ON "ALL THINGS RECONSIDERED." GO AHEAD, CALLER...
YEAH, I JUST HEARD YOU GUYS GOT MARRIED! WAS IT ROMANTIC?
ROMANTIC? SURE, IF YOU FIND RAW SEWAGE AND BARRACUDAS ROMANTIC.
OR TOUR BOATS OR TYPHOONS OR TIDAL WAVES THE SIZE OF MOUNTAINS.
OR FLEEING FROM YOUR HOTEL ONLY TO BOARD THE FLIGHT FROM HELL...
...OR BEING MARRIED BY A CABIN ATTENDANT AND SERENADED BY THE HANOI GAY MEN'S GLEE CLUB SINGING THE ENTIRE BACKSTREET BOYS CATALOG!
94 98 102 108
...OR IF YOU LIKE BEING RUN OVER BY A LOOSE COCKTAIL CART FROM FIRST CLASS...
...OR GOING TO THE EMERGENCY ROOM AFTER FAILING TO CARRY YOUR PARTNER ACROSS THE THRESHOLD!
OH...
SORRY, I DIDN'T KNOW IT WAS A SORE SUBJECT.
NOT AT ALL.
IT WAS THE HAPPIEST WEEK OF OUR LIVES.
GB Trudeau

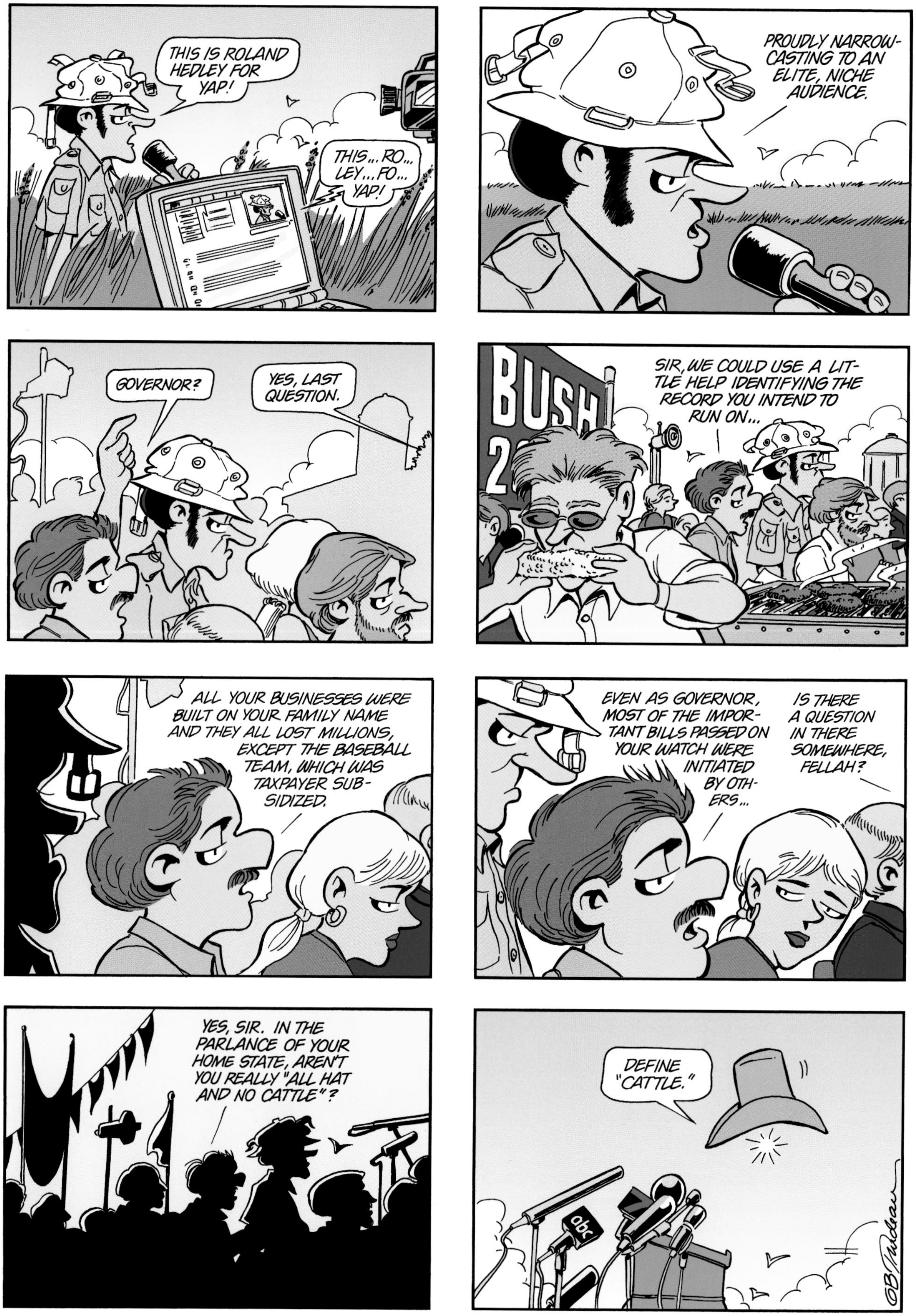
THIS IS ROLAND HEDLEY FOR YAP!
THIS... RO... LEY... FO... YAP!
PROUDLY NARROW-CASTING TO AN ELITE, NICHE AUDIENCE.
GOVERNOR?
YES, LAST QUESTION.
BUSH
SIR, WE COULD USE A LITTLE HELP IDENTIFYING THE RECORD YOU INTEND TO RUN ON...
ALL YOUR BUSINESSES WERE BUILT ON YOUR FAMILY NAME AND THEY ALL LOST MILLIONS, EXCEPT THE BASEBALL TEAM, WHICH WAS TAXPAYER SUBSIDIZED.
EVEN AS GOVERNOR, MOST OF THE IMPORTANT BILLS PASSED ON YOUR WATCH WERE INITIATED BY OTHERS...
IS THERE A QUESTION IN THERE SOMEWHERE, FELLAH?
YES, SIR. IN THE PARLANCE OF YOUR HOME STATE, AREN'T YOU REALLY "ALL HAT AND NO CATTLE"?
DEFINE "CATTLE."
abc

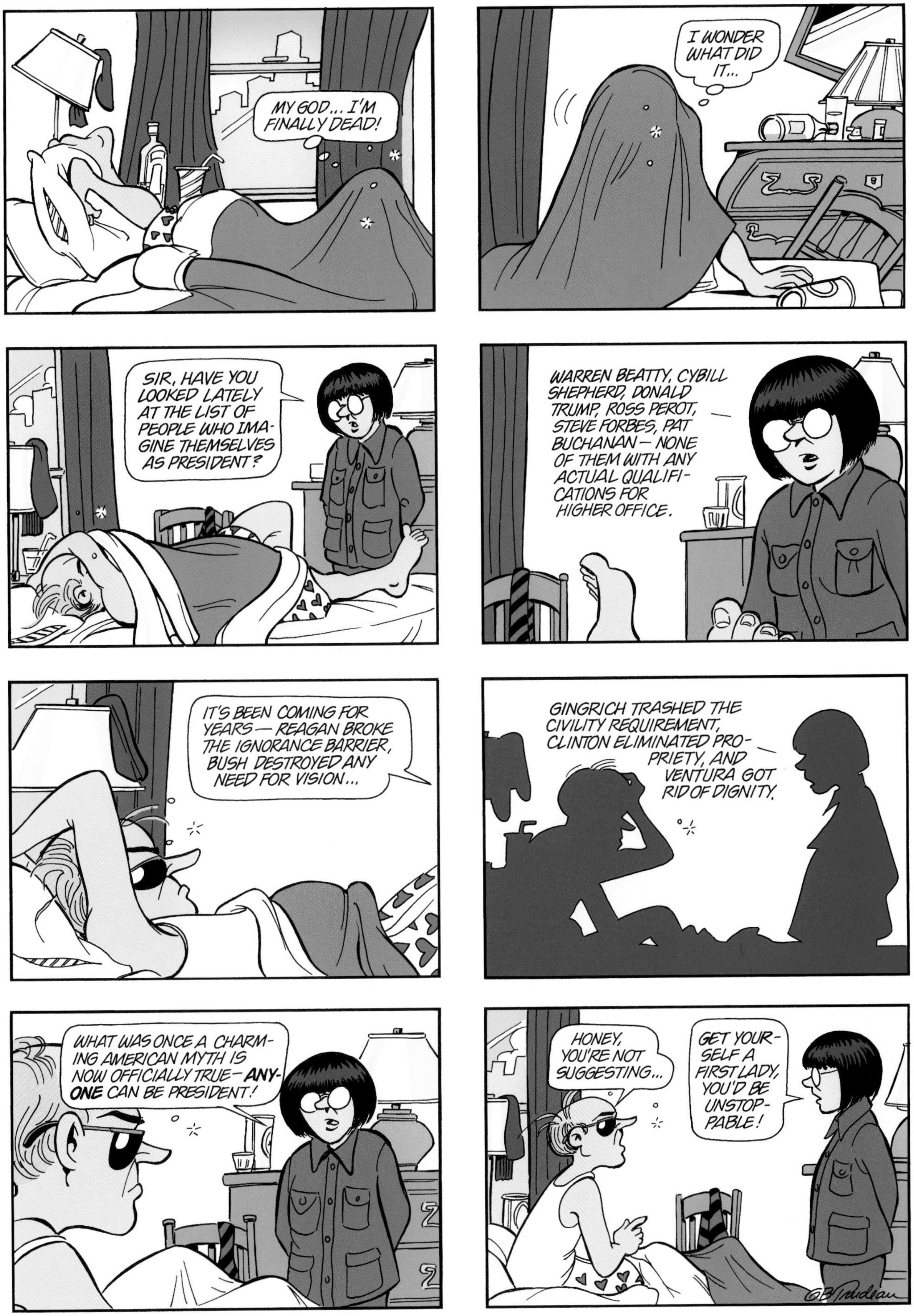
MY GOD... I'M FINALLY DEAD!
I WONDER WHAT DID IT...
SIR, HAVE YOU LOOKED LATELY AT THE LIST OF PEOPLE WHO IMAGINE THEMSELVES AS PRESIDENT?
WARREN BEATTY, CYBILL SHEPHERD, DONALD TRUMP, ROSS PEROT, STEVE FORBES, PAT BUCHANAN— NONE OF THEM WITH ANY ACTUAL QUALIFICATIONS FOR HIGHER OFFICE.
IT'S BEEN COMING FOR YEARS— REAGAN BROKE THE IGNORANCE BARRIER, BUSH DESTROYED ANY NEED FOR VISION...
GINGRICH TRASHED THE CIVILITY REQUIREMENT, CLINTON ELIMINATED PROPRIETY, AND VENTURA GOT RID OF DIGNITY.
WHAT WAS ONCE A CHARMING AMERICAN MYTH IS NOW OFFICIALLY TRUE— **ANYONE** CAN BE PRESIDENT!
HONEY, YOU'RE NOT SUGGESTING...
GET YOURSELF A FIRST LADY, YOU'D BE UNSTOPPABLE!
GB Trudeau

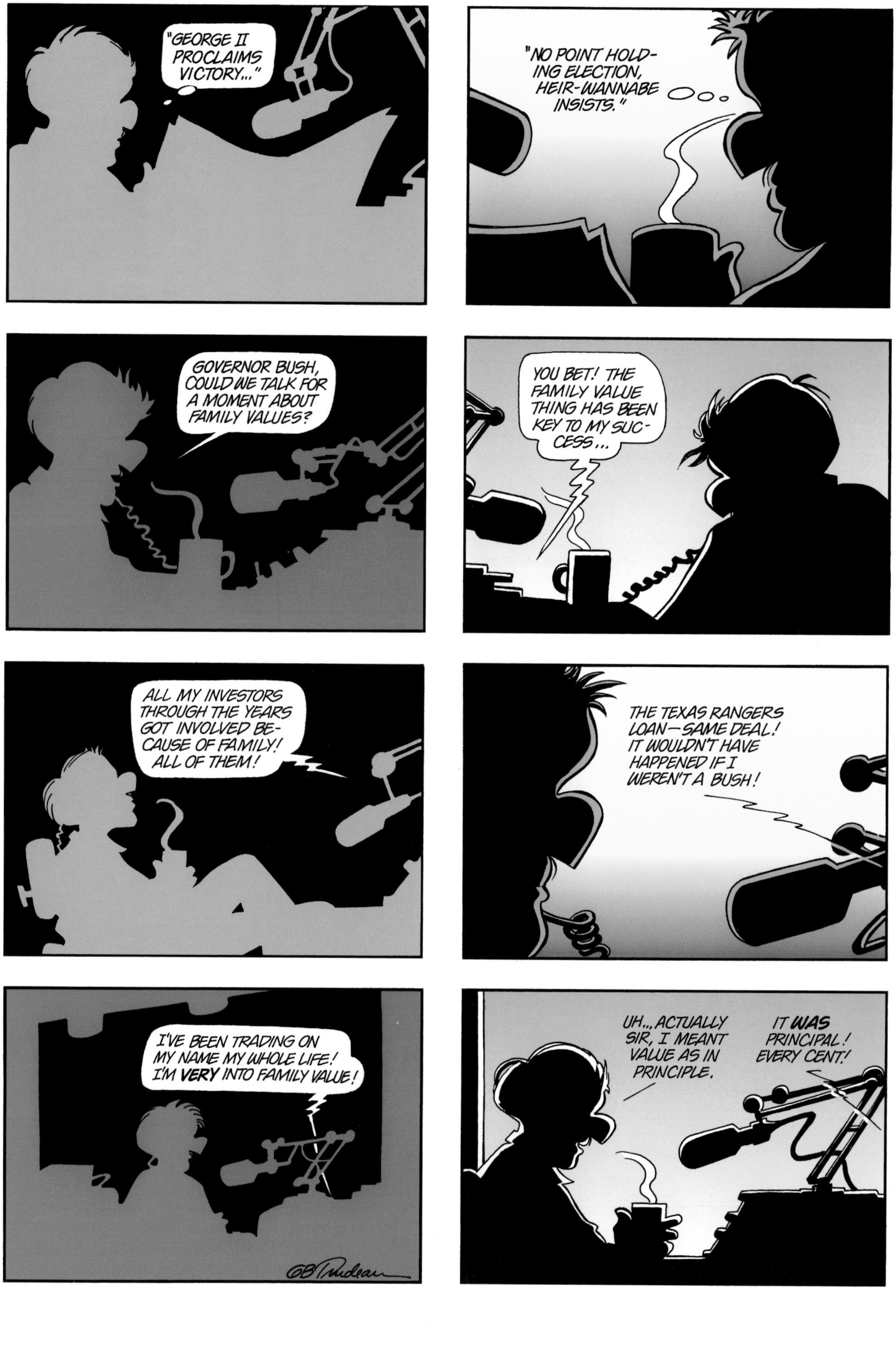
"GEORGE II PROCLAIMS VICTORY..."
"NO POINT HOLDING ELECTION, HEIR-WANNABE INSISTS."
GOVERNOR BUSH, COULD WE TALK FOR A MOMENT ABOUT FAMILY VALUES?
YOU BET! THE FAMILY VALUE THING HAS BEEN KEY TO MY SUCCESS...
ALL MY INVESTORS THROUGH THE YEARS GOT INVOLVED BECAUSE OF FAMILY! ALL OF THEM!
THE TEXAS RANGERS LOAN—SAME DEAL! IT WOULDN'T HAVE HAPPENED IF I WEREN'T A BUSH!
I'VE BEEN TRADING ON MY NAME MY WHOLE LIFE! I'M VERY INTO FAMILY VALUE!
GBTrudeau
UH... ACTUALLY SIR, I MEANT VALUE AS IN PRINCIPLE.
IT WAS PRINCIPAL! EVERY CENT!

THE DISSEMBLING, THE FUDGING, THE SPINNING...

HOW I'LL MISS IT ALL!

SO HOW'S GORE 2000 DOING THESE DAYS?

GOOD, SIR — WITH AN ASSIST FROM DUBYA.

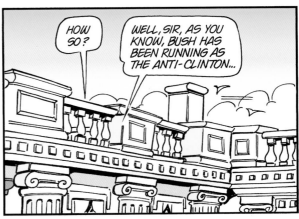

HOW SO?

WELL, SIR, AS YOU KNOW, BUSH HAS BEEN RUNNING AS THE ANTI-CLINTON...

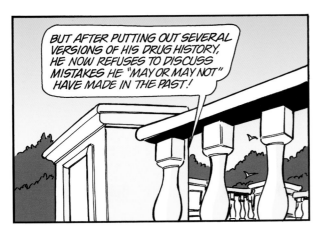

BUT AFTER PUTTING OUT SEVERAL VERSIONS OF HIS DRUG HISTORY, HE NOW REFUSES TO DISCUSS MISTAKES HE "MAY OR MAY NOT" HAVE MADE IN THE PAST!

MISTAKES HE "MAY OR MAY NOT" HAVE MADE?

RIGHT.

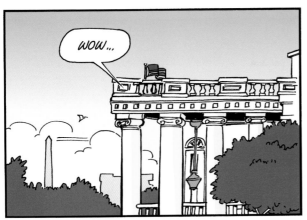

WOW...

IT'S ALMOST LIKE AN HOMAGE!

MUST BE SWEET, SIR.

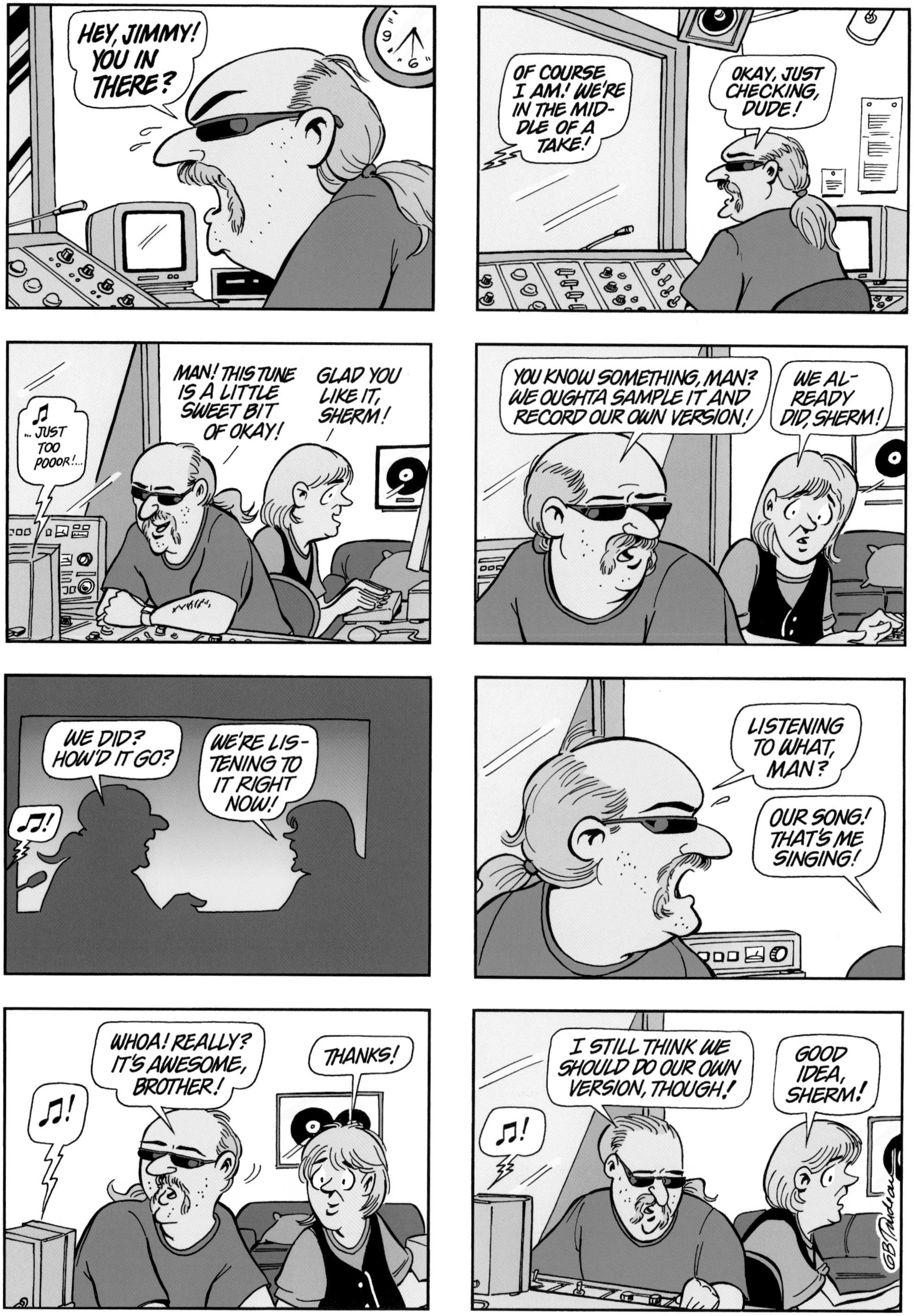
HEY, JIMMY! YOU IN THERE?
OF COURSE I AM! WE'RE IN THE MIDDLE OF A TAKE!
OKAY, JUST CHECKING, DUDE!
♫ ... JUST TOO POOOR!...
MAN! THIS TUNE IS A LITTLE SWEET BIT OF OKAY!
GLAD YOU LIKE IT, SHERM!
YOU KNOW SOMETHING, MAN? WE OUGHTA SAMPLE IT AND RECORD OUR OWN VERSION!
WE ALREADY DID, SHERM!
♫!
WE DID? HOW'D IT GO?
WE'RE LISTENING TO IT RIGHT NOW!
LISTENING TO WHAT, MAN?
OUR SONG! THAT'S ME SINGING!
♫!
WHOA! REALLY? IT'S AWESOME, BROTHER!
THANKS!
♫!
I STILL THINK WE SHOULD DO OUR OWN VERSION, THOUGH!
GOOD IDEA, SHERM!

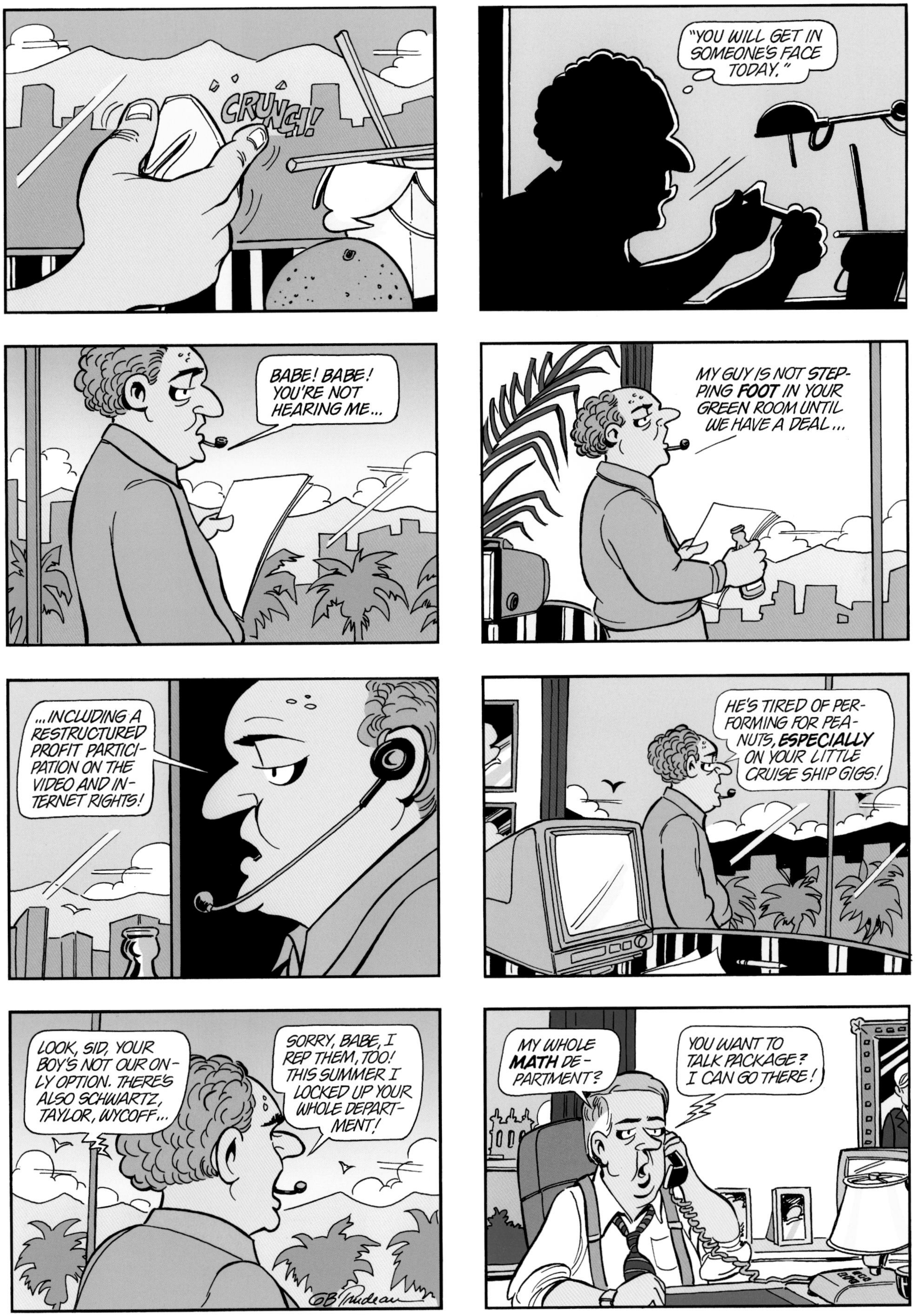
CRUNCH!
"YOU WILL GET IN SOMEONE'S FACE TODAY."
BABE! BABE! YOU'RE NOT HEARING ME...
MY GUY IS NOT STEPPING FOOT IN YOUR GREEN ROOM UNTIL WE HAVE A DEAL...
...INCLUDING A RESTRUCTURED PROFIT PARTICIPATION ON THE VIDEO AND INTERNET RIGHTS!
HE'S TIRED OF PERFORMING FOR PEANUTS, ESPECIALLY ON YOUR LITTLE CRUISE SHIP GIGS!
LOOK, SID, YOUR BOY'S NOT OUR ONLY OPTION. THERE'S ALSO SCHWARTZ, TAYLOR, WYCOFF...
SORRY, BABE, I REP THEM, TOO! THIS SUMMER I LOCKED UP YOUR WHOLE DEPARTMENT!
GB Trudeau
MY WHOLE MATH DEPARTMENT?
YOU WANT TO TALK PACKAGE? I CAN GO THERE!

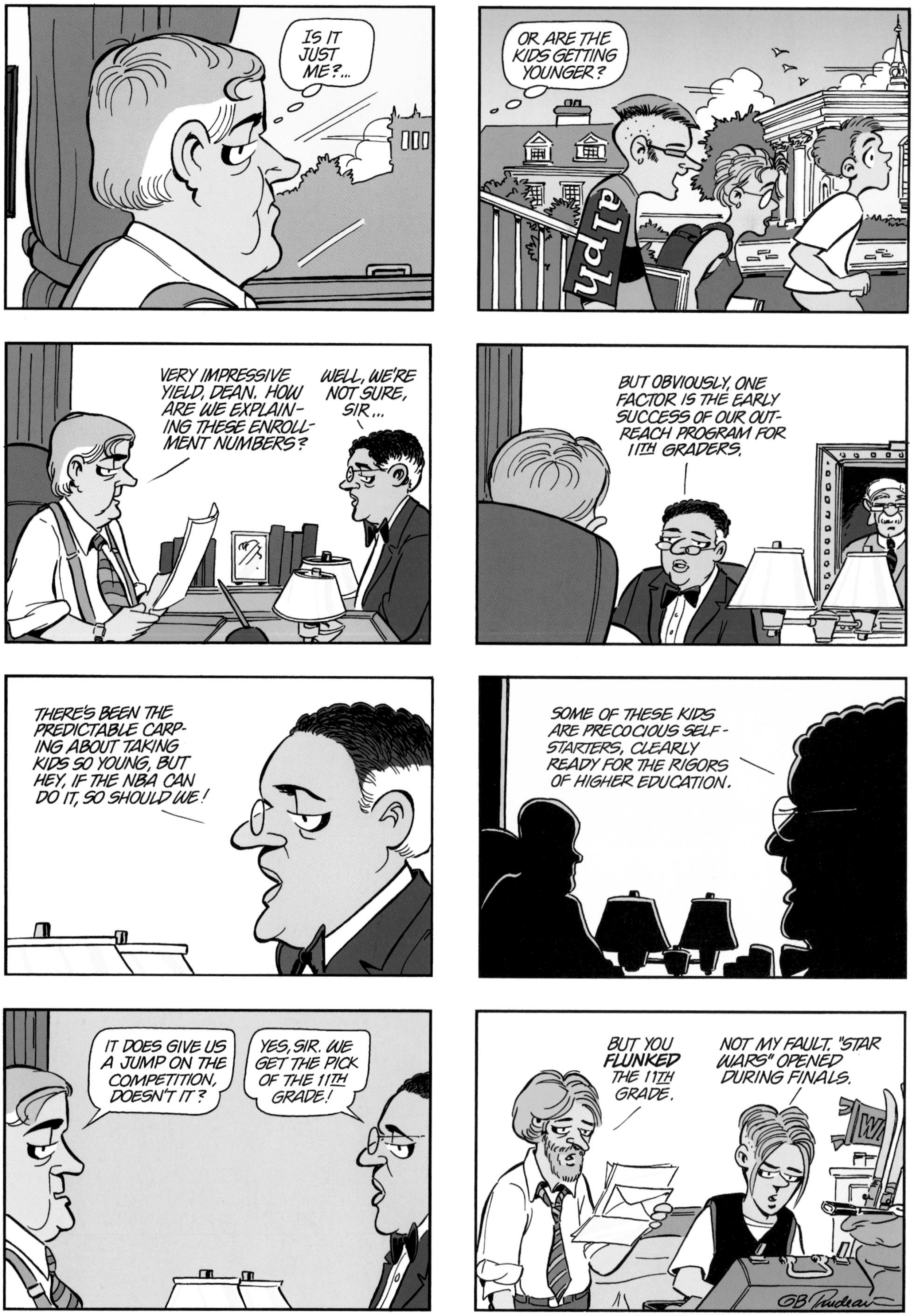
IS IT JUST ME?...
OR ARE THE KIDS GETTING YOUNGER?
VERY IMPRESSIVE YIELD, DEAN. HOW ARE WE EXPLAINING THESE ENROLLMENT NUMBERS?
WELL, WE'RE NOT SURE, SIR...
BUT OBVIOUSLY, ONE FACTOR IS THE EARLY SUCCESS OF OUR OUTREACH PROGRAM FOR 11TH GRADERS.
THERE'S BEEN THE PREDICTABLE CARPING ABOUT TAKING KIDS SO YOUNG, BUT HEY, IF THE NBA CAN DO IT, SO SHOULD WE!
SOME OF THESE KIDS ARE PRECOCIOUS SELF-STARTERS, CLEARLY READY FOR THE RIGORS OF HIGHER EDUCATION.
IT DOES GIVE US A JUMP ON THE COMPETITION, DOESN'T IT?
YES, SIR. WE GET THE PICK OF THE 11TH GRADE!
BUT YOU **FLUNKED** THE 11TH GRADE.
NOT MY FAULT. "STAR WARS" OPENED DURING FINALS.
GB Trudeau

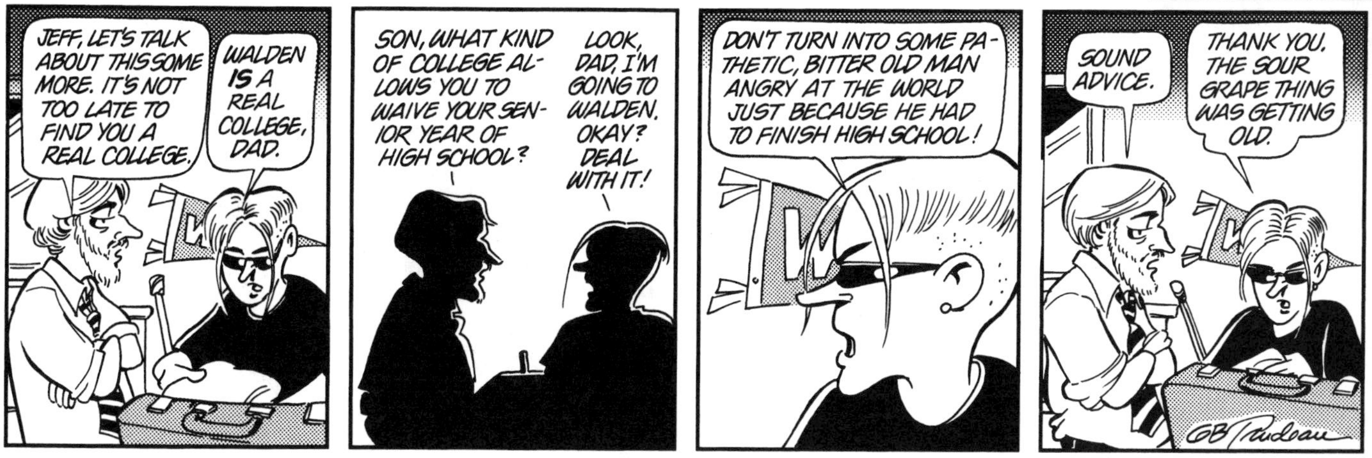
JEFF, LET'S TALK ABOUT THIS SOME MORE. IT'S NOT TOO LATE TO FIND YOU A REAL COLLEGE.
WALDEN **IS** A REAL COLLEGE, DAD.
SON, WHAT KIND OF COLLEGE AL-LOWS YOU TO WAIVE YOUR SEN-IOR YEAR OF HIGH SCHOOL?
LOOK, DAD, I'M GOING TO WALDEN. OKAY? DEAL WITH IT!
DON'T TURN INTO SOME PA-THETIC, BITTER OLD MAN ANGRY AT THE WORLD JUST BECAUSE HE HAD TO FINISH HIGH SCHOOL!
SOUND ADVICE.
THANK YOU. THE SOUR GRAPE THING WAS GETTING OLD.
GB Trudeau

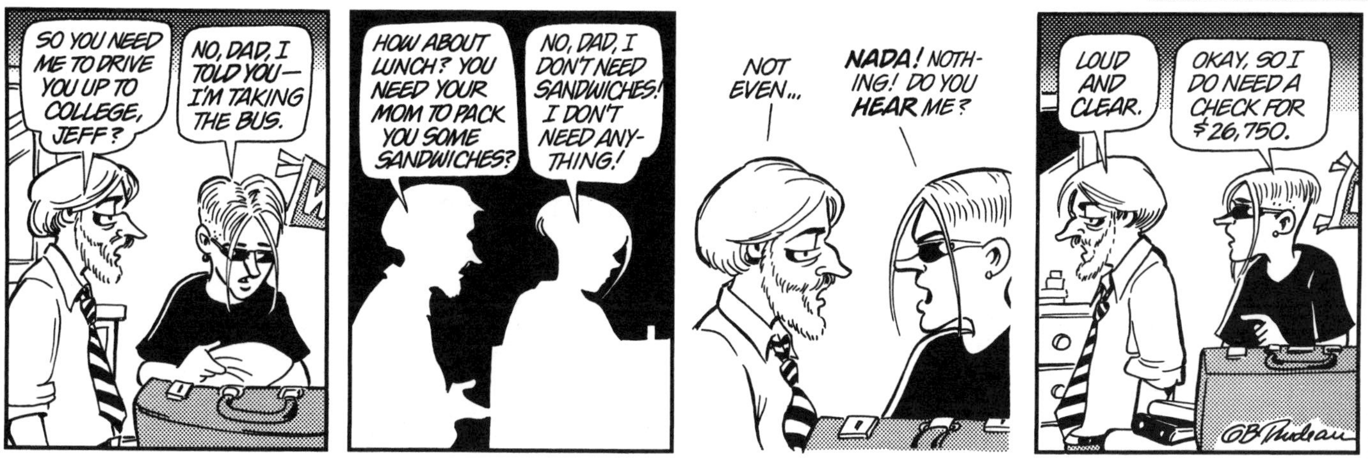
SO YOU NEED ME TO DRIVE YOU UP TO COLLEGE, JEFF?
NO, DAD, I TOLD YOU— I'M TAKING THE BUS.
HOW ABOUT LUNCH? YOU NEED YOUR MOM TO PACK YOU SOME SANDWICHES?
NO, DAD, I DON'T NEED SANDWICHES! I DON'T NEED ANY-THING!
NOT EVEN...
NADA! NOTH-ING! DO YOU **HEAR** ME?
LOUD AND CLEAR.
OKAY, SO I DO NEED A CHECK FOR $26,750.
GB Trudeau

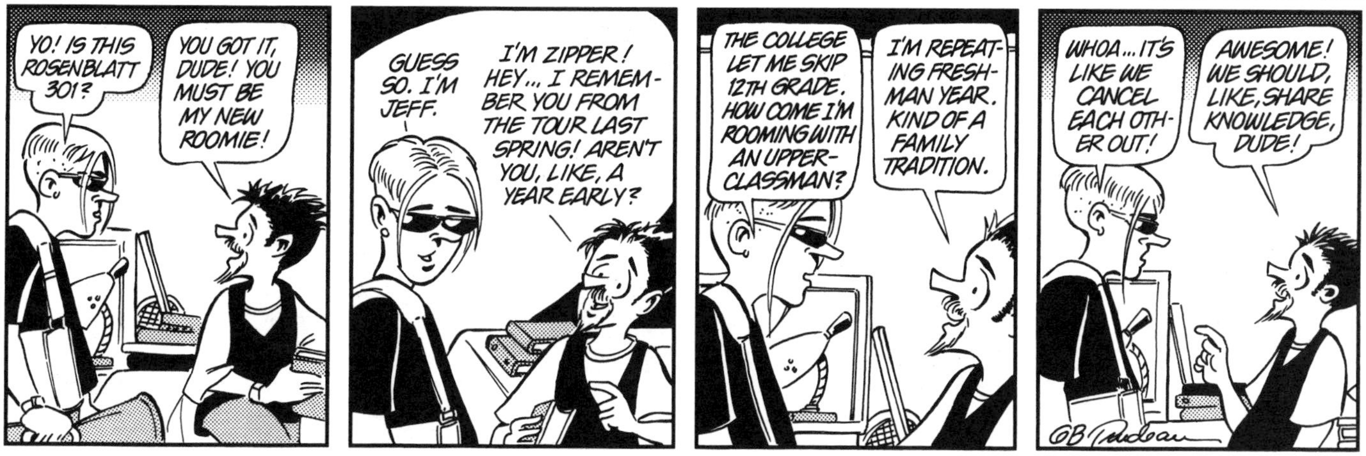
YO! IS THIS ROSENBLATT 301?
YOU GOT IT, DUDE! YOU MUST BE MY NEW ROOMIE!
GUESS SO. I'M JEFF.
I'M ZIPPER! HEY... I REMEM-BER YOU FROM THE TOUR LAST SPRING! AREN'T YOU, LIKE, A YEAR EARLY?
THE COLLEGE LET ME SKIP 12TH GRADE. HOW COME I'M ROOMING WITH AN UPPER-CLASSMAN?
I'M REPEAT-ING FRESH-MAN YEAR. KIND OF A FAMILY TRADITION.
WHOA... IT'S LIKE WE CANCEL EACH OTH-ER OUT!
AWESOME! WE SHOULD, LIKE, SHARE KNOWLEDGE, DUDE!
GB Trudeau

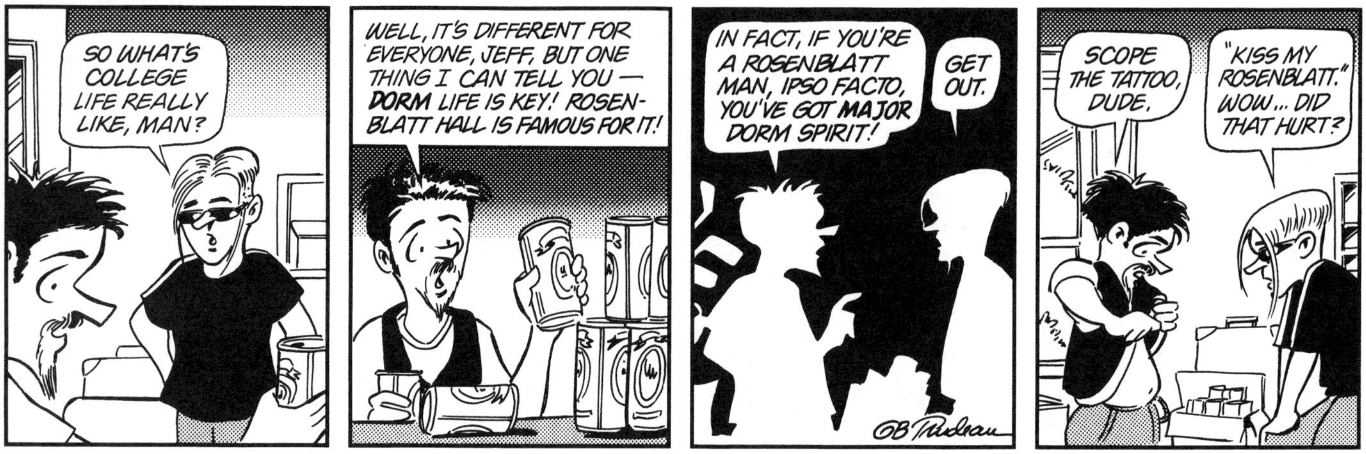
SO WHAT'S COLLEGE LIFE REALLY LIKE, MAN?
WELL, IT'S DIFFERENT FOR EVERYONE, JEFF, BUT ONE THING I CAN TELL YOU — **DORM** LIFE IS KEY! ROSEN-BLATT HALL IS FAMOUS FOR IT!
IN FACT, IF YOU'RE A ROSENBLATT MAN, IPSO FACTO, YOU'VE GOT **MAJOR** DORM SPIRIT!
GET OUT.
SCOPE THE TATTOO, DUDE.
"KISS MY ROSENBLATT." WOW... DID THAT HURT?

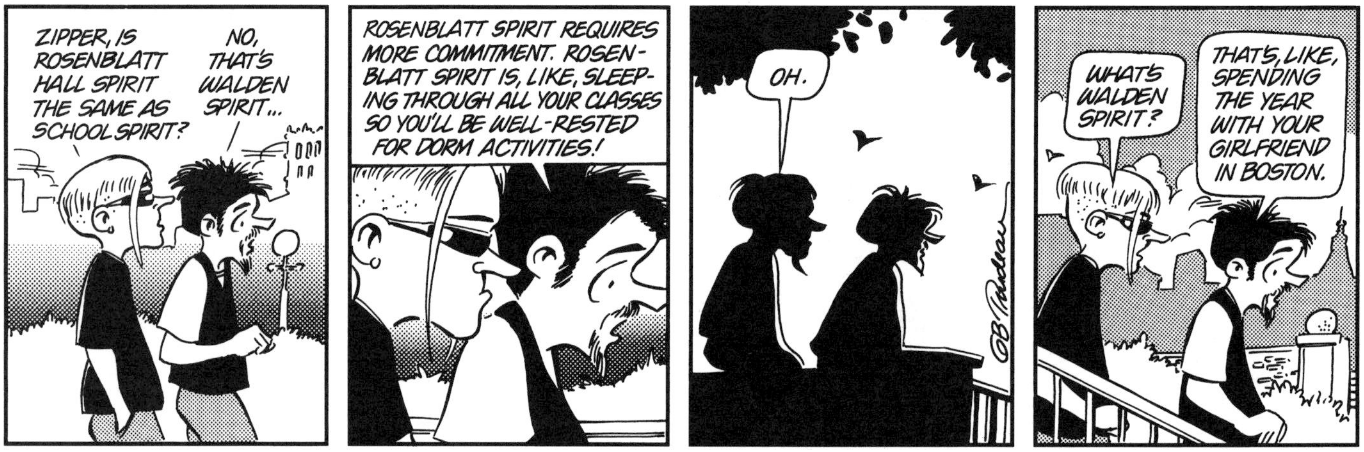
ZIPPER, IS ROSENBLATT HALL SPIRIT THE SAME AS SCHOOL SPIRIT?
NO, THAT'S WALDEN SPIRIT...
ROSENBLATT SPIRIT REQUIRES MORE COMMITMENT. ROSEN-BLATT SPIRIT IS, LIKE, SLEEP-ING THROUGH ALL YOUR CLASSES SO YOU'LL BE WELL-RESTED FOR DORM ACTIVITIES!
OH.
WHAT'S WALDEN SPIRIT?
THAT'S, LIKE, SPENDING THE YEAR WITH YOUR GIRLFRIEND IN BOSTON.

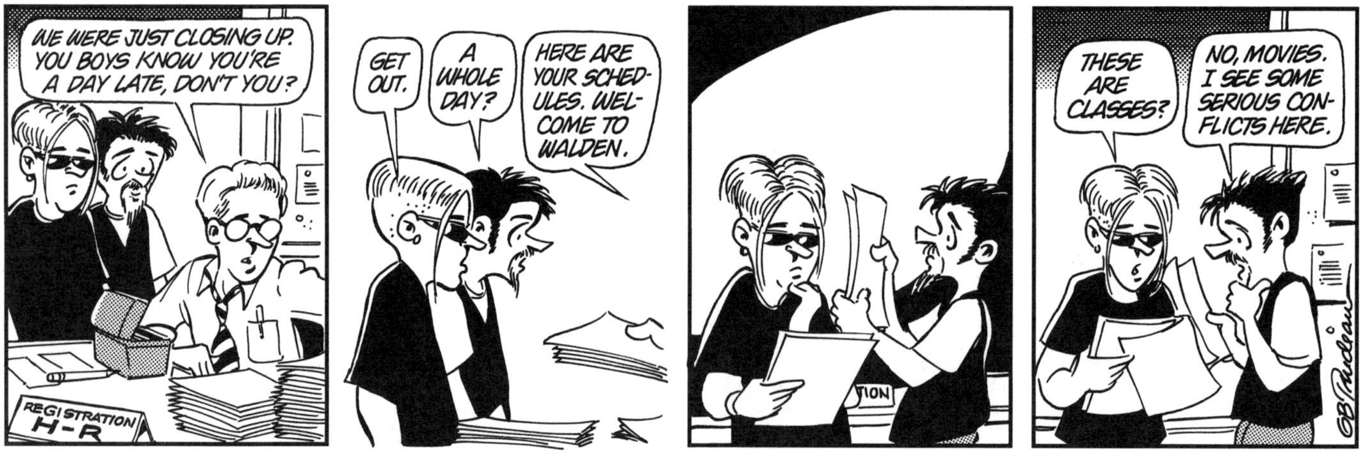
WE WERE JUST CLOSING UP. YOU BOYS KNOW YOU'RE A DAY LATE, DON'T YOU?
REGISTRATION H-R
GET OUT.
A WHOLE DAY?
HERE ARE YOUR SCHED-ULES. WEL-COME TO WALDEN.
THESE ARE CLASSES?
NO, MOVIES. I SEE SOME SERIOUS CON-FLICTS HERE.

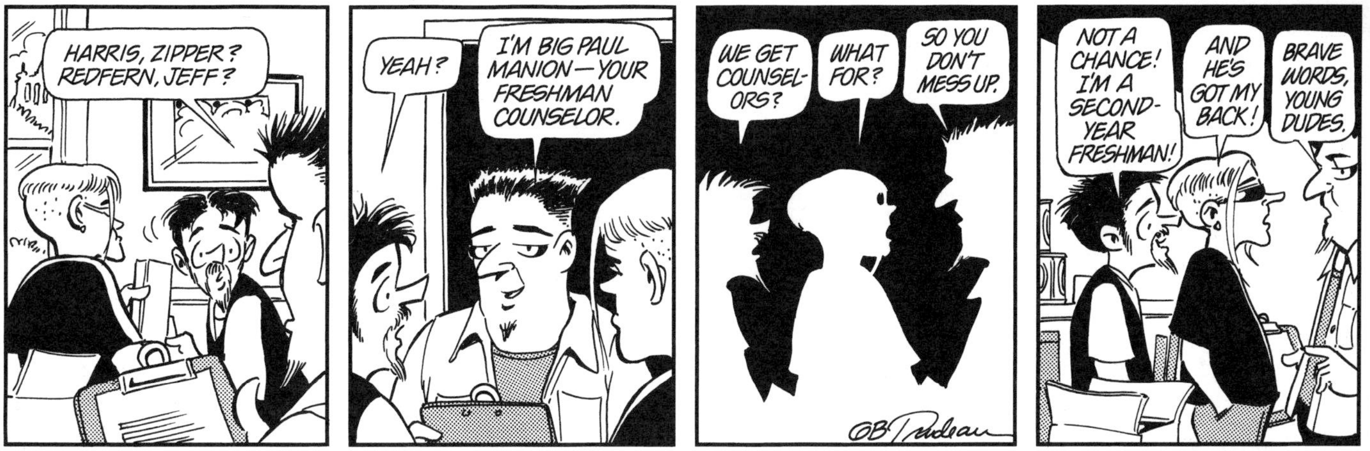
HARRIS, ZIPPER? REDFERN, JEFF?
YEAH?
I'M BIG PAUL MANION—YOUR FRESHMAN COUNSELOR.
WE GET COUNSEL-ORS?
WHAT FOR?
SO YOU DON'T MESS UP.
NOT A CHANCE! I'M A SECOND-YEAR FRESHMAN!
AND HE'S GOT MY BACK!
BRAVE WORDS, YOUNG DUDES.

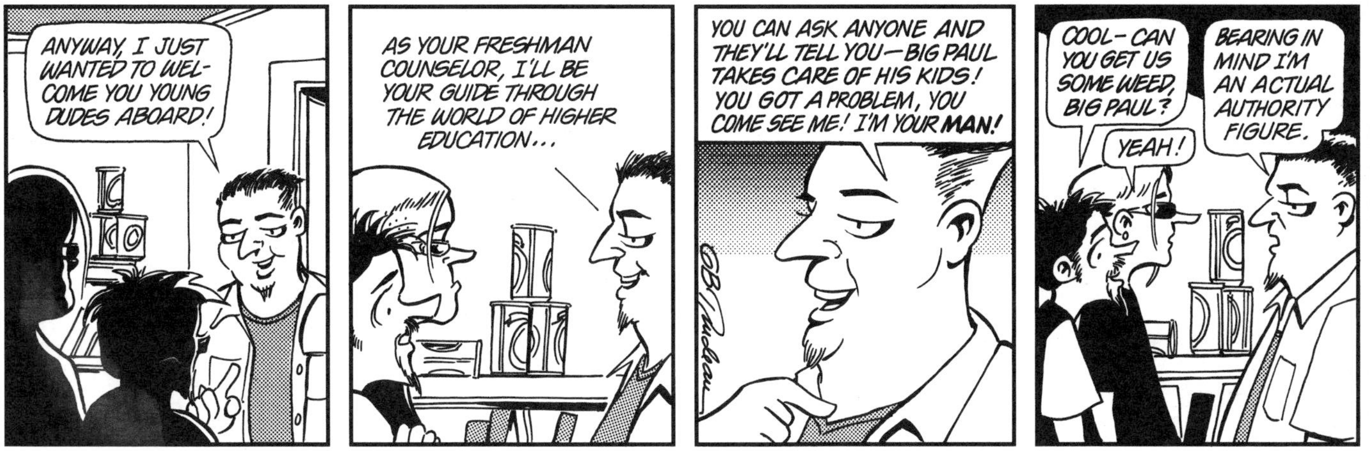
ANYWAY, I JUST WANTED TO WEL-COME YOU YOUNG DUDES ABOARD!
AS YOUR FRESHMAN COUNSELOR, I'LL BE YOUR GUIDE THROUGH THE WORLD OF HIGHER EDUCATION...
YOU CAN ASK ANYONE AND THEY'LL TELL YOU—BIG PAUL TAKES CARE OF HIS KIDS! YOU GOT A PROBLEM, YOU COME SEE ME! I'M YOUR MAN!
COOL—CAN YOU GET US SOME WEED, BIG PAUL?
YEAH!
BEARING IN MIND I'M AN ACTUAL AUTHORITY FIGURE.

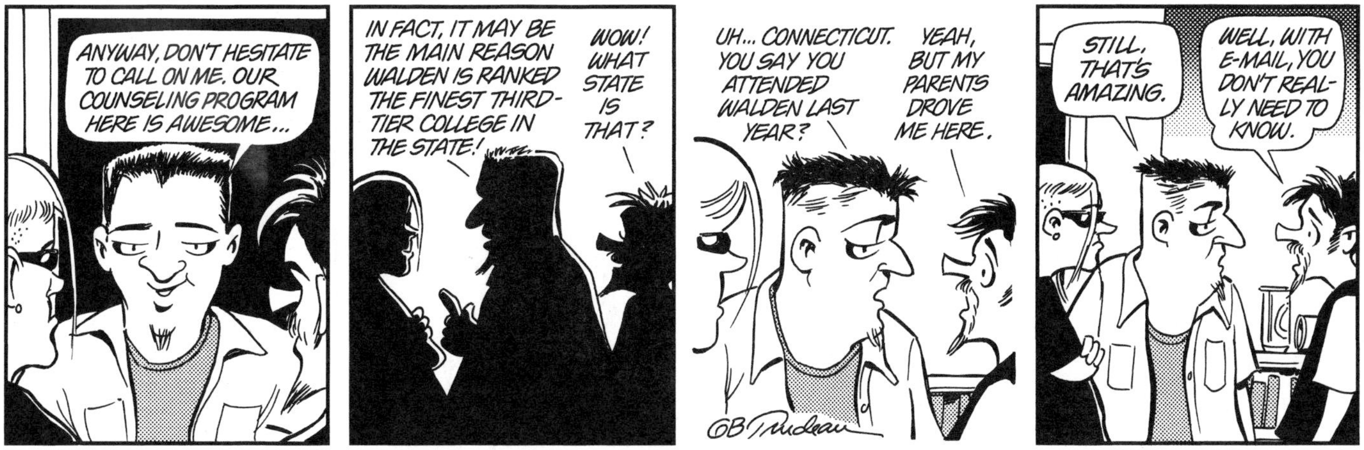
ANYWAY, DON'T HESITATE TO CALL ON ME. OUR COUNSELING PROGRAM HERE IS AWESOME...
IN FACT, IT MAY BE THE MAIN REASON WALDEN IS RANKED THE FINEST THIRD-TIER COLLEGE IN THE STATE!
WOW! WHAT STATE IS THAT?
UH... CONNECTICUT. YOU SAY YOU ATTENDED WALDEN LAST YEAR?
YEAH, BUT MY PARENTS DROVE ME HERE.
STILL, THAT'S AMAZING.
WELL, WITH E-MAIL, YOU DON'T REAL-LY NEED TO KNOW.

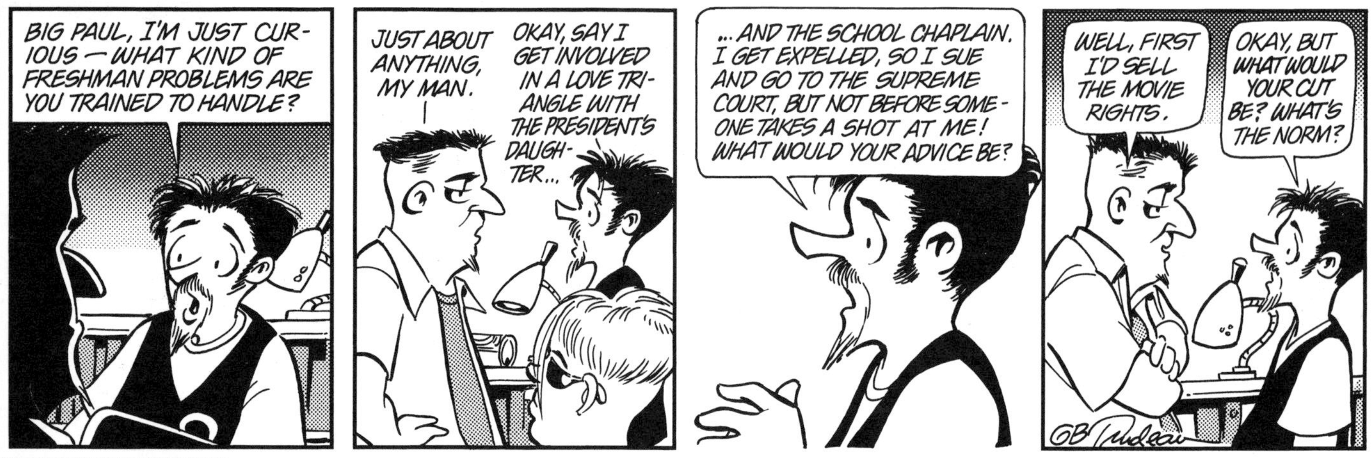
BIG PAUL, I'M JUST CURIOUS — WHAT KIND OF FRESHMAN PROBLEMS ARE YOU TRAINED TO HANDLE?
JUST ABOUT ANYTHING, MY MAN.
OKAY, SAY I GET INVOLVED IN A LOVE TRIANGLE WITH THE PRESIDENT'S DAUGHTER...
...AND THE SCHOOL CHAPLAIN. I GET EXPELLED, SO I SUE AND GO TO THE SUPREME COURT, BUT NOT BEFORE SOMEONE TAKES A SHOT AT ME! WHAT WOULD YOUR ADVICE BE?
WELL, FIRST I'D SELL THE MOVIE RIGHTS.
OKAY, BUT WHAT WOULD YOUR CUT BE? WHAT'S THE NORM?

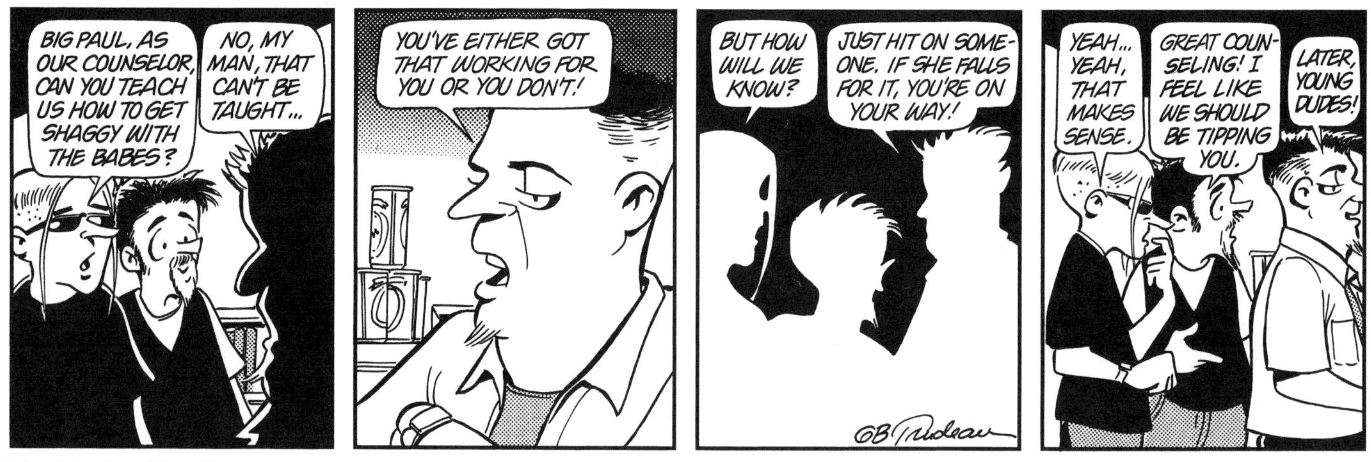
BIG PAUL, AS OUR COUNSELOR, CAN YOU TEACH US HOW TO GET SHAGGY WITH THE BABES?
NO, MY MAN, THAT CAN'T BE TAUGHT...
YOU'VE EITHER GOT THAT WORKING FOR YOU OR YOU DON'T!
BUT HOW WILL WE KNOW?
JUST HIT ON SOMEONE. IF SHE FALLS FOR IT, YOU'RE ON YOUR WAY!
YEAH... YEAH, THAT MAKES SENSE.
GREAT COUNSELING! I FEEL LIKE WE SHOULD BE TIPPING YOU.
LATER, YOUNG DUDES!

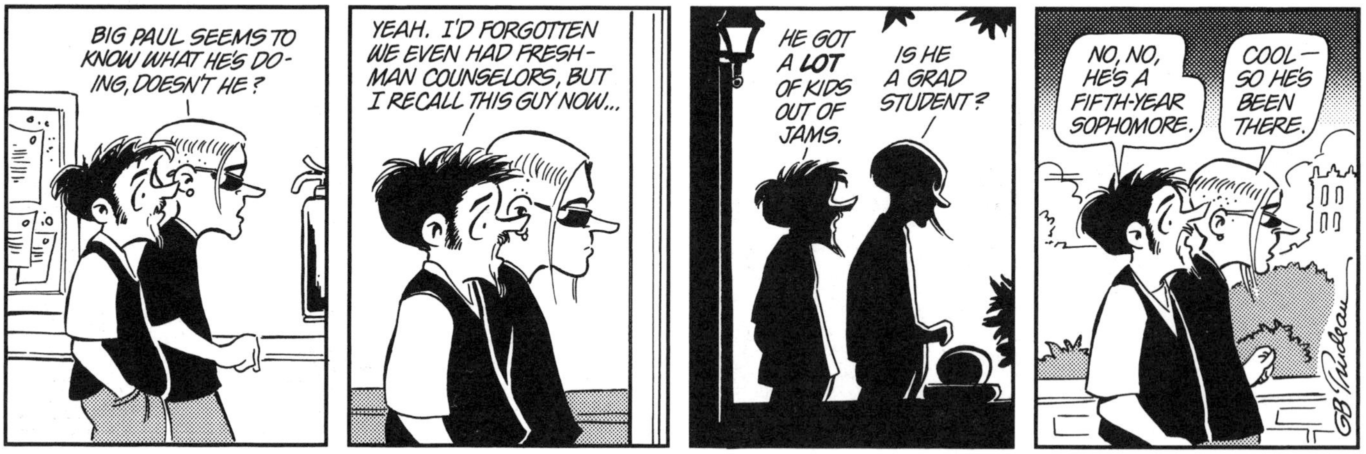
BIG PAUL SEEMS TO KNOW WHAT HE'S DOING, DOESN'T HE?
YEAH. I'D FORGOTTEN WE EVEN HAD FRESHMAN COUNSELORS, BUT I RECALL THIS GUY NOW...
HE GOT A **LOT** OF KIDS OUT OF JAMS.
IS HE A GRAD STUDENT?
NO, NO, HE'S A FIFTH-YEAR SOPHOMORE.
COOL — SO HE'S BEEN THERE.

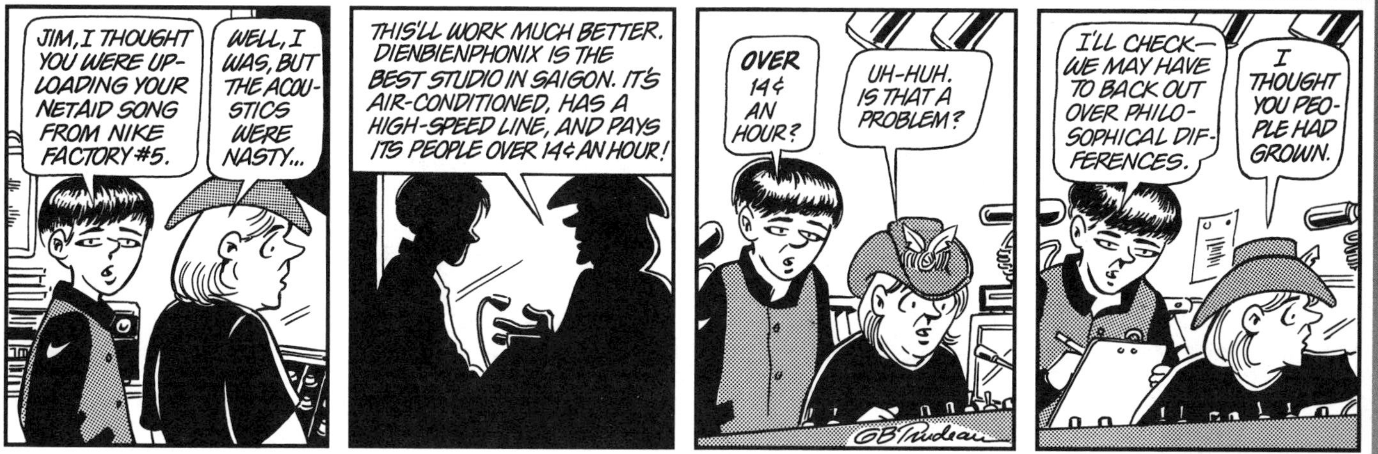
JIM, I THOUGHT YOU WERE UP-LOADING YOUR NETAID SONG FROM NIKE FACTORY #5.
WELL, I WAS, BUT THE ACOU-STICS WERE NASTY...
THIS'LL WORK MUCH BETTER. DIENBIENPHONIX IS THE BEST STUDIO IN SAIGON. IT'S AIR-CONDITIONED, HAS A HIGH-SPEED LINE, AND PAYS ITS PEOPLE OVER 14¢ AN HOUR!
OVER 14¢ AN HOUR?
UH-HUH. IS THAT A PROBLEM?
I'LL CHECK— WE MAY HAVE TO BACK OUT OVER PHILO-SOPHICAL DIF-FERENCES.
I THOUGHT YOU PEO-PLE HAD GROWN.

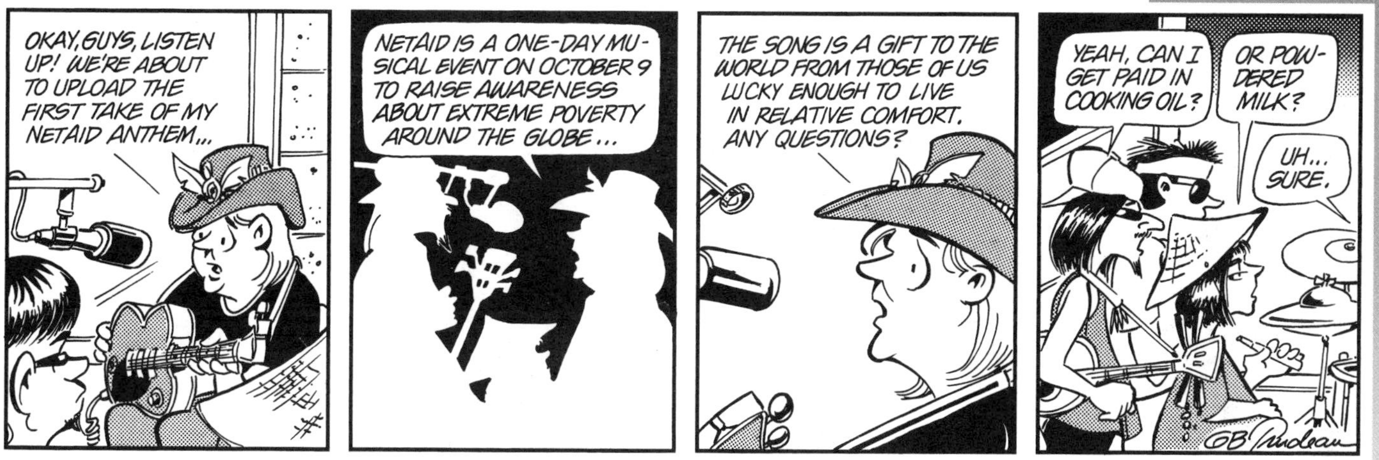
OKAY, GUYS, LISTEN UP! WE'RE ABOUT TO UPLOAD THE FIRST TAKE OF MY NETAID ANTHEM...
NETAID IS A ONE-DAY MU-SICAL EVENT ON OCTOBER 9 TO RAISE AWARENESS ABOUT EXTREME POVERTY AROUND THE GLOBE...
THE SONG IS A GIFT TO THE WORLD FROM THOSE OF US LUCKY ENOUGH TO LIVE IN RELATIVE COMFORT. ANY QUESTIONS?
YEAH, CAN I GET PAID IN COOKING OIL?
OR POW-DERED MILK?
UH... SURE.

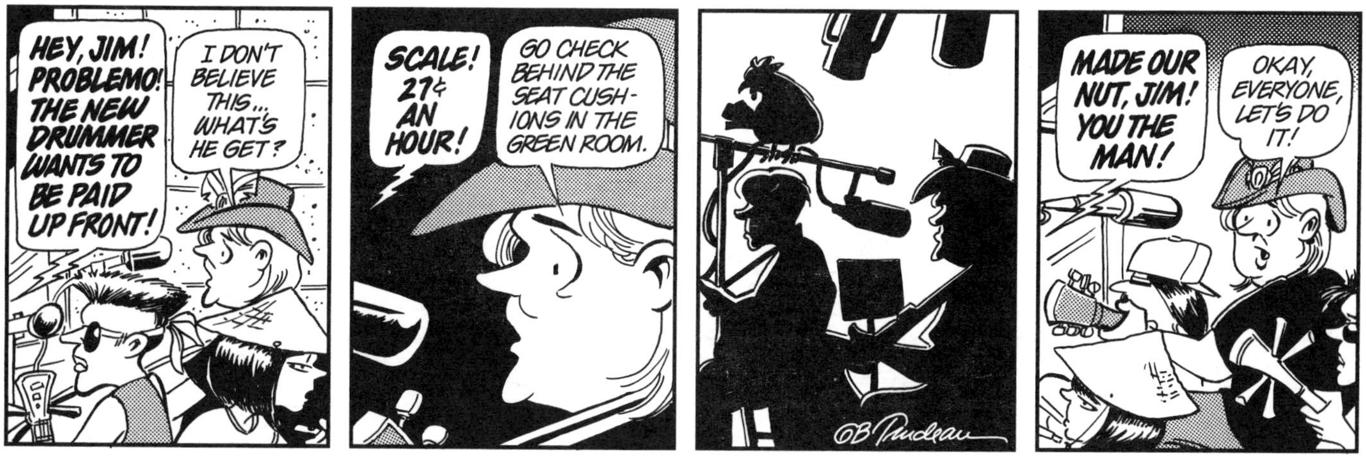
HEY, JIM! PROBLEMO! THE NEW DRUMMER WANTS TO BE PAID UP FRONT!
I DON'T BELIEVE THIS... WHAT'S HE GET?
SCALE! 27¢ AN HOUR!
GO CHECK BEHIND THE SEAT CUSH-IONS IN THE GREEN ROOM.
MADE OUR NUT, JIM! YOU THE MAN!
OKAY, EVERYONE, LET'S DO IT!

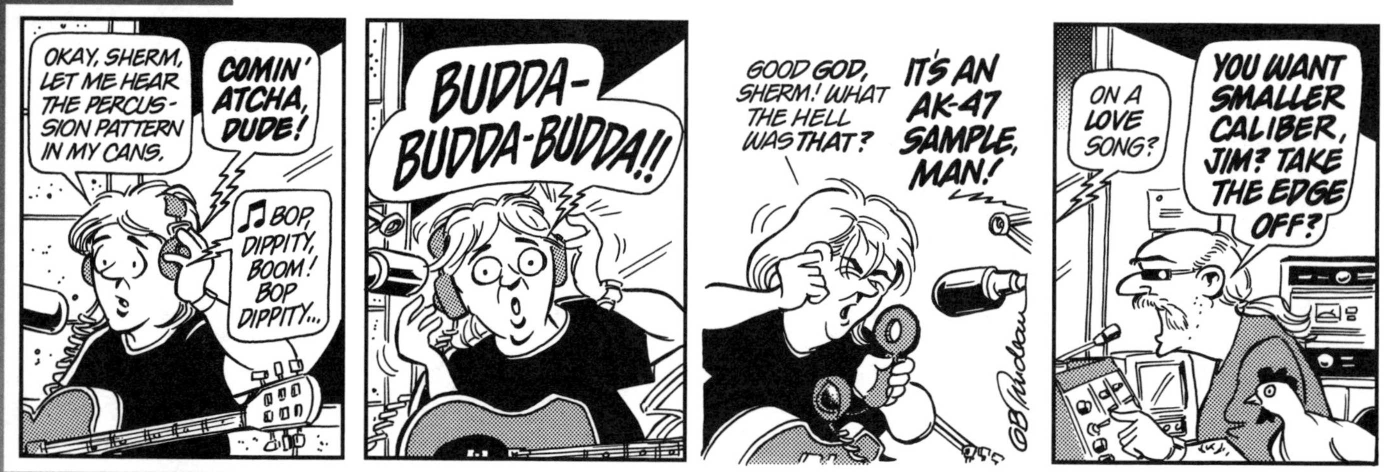
OKAY, SHERM, LET ME HEAR THE PERCUSSION PATTERN IN MY CANS.
COMIN' ATCHA, DUDE!
♫ BOP, DIPPITY, BOOM! BOP DIPPITY...
BUDDA-BUDDA-BUDDA!!
GOOD GOD, SHERM! WHAT THE HELL WAS THAT?
IT'S AN AK-47 SAMPLE, MAN!
ON A LOVE SONG?
YOU WANT SMALLER CALIBER, JIM? TAKE THE EDGE OFF?

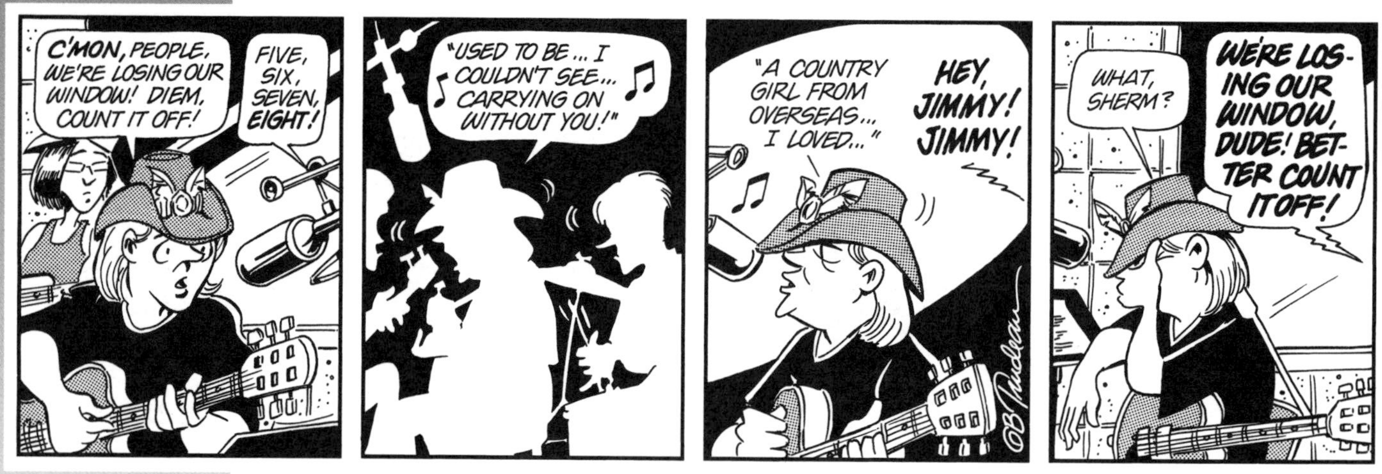
C'MON, PEOPLE, WE'RE LOSING OUR WINDOW! DIEM, COUNT IT OFF!
FIVE, SIX, SEVEN, EIGHT!
♪ "USED TO BE ... I COULDN'T SEE... CARRYING ON WITHOUT YOU!" ♫
"A COUNTRY GIRL FROM OVERSEAS... I LOVED..."
HEY, JIMMY! JIMMY!
WHAT, SHERM?
WE'RE LOSING OUR WINDOW, DUDE! BETTER COUNT IT OFF!

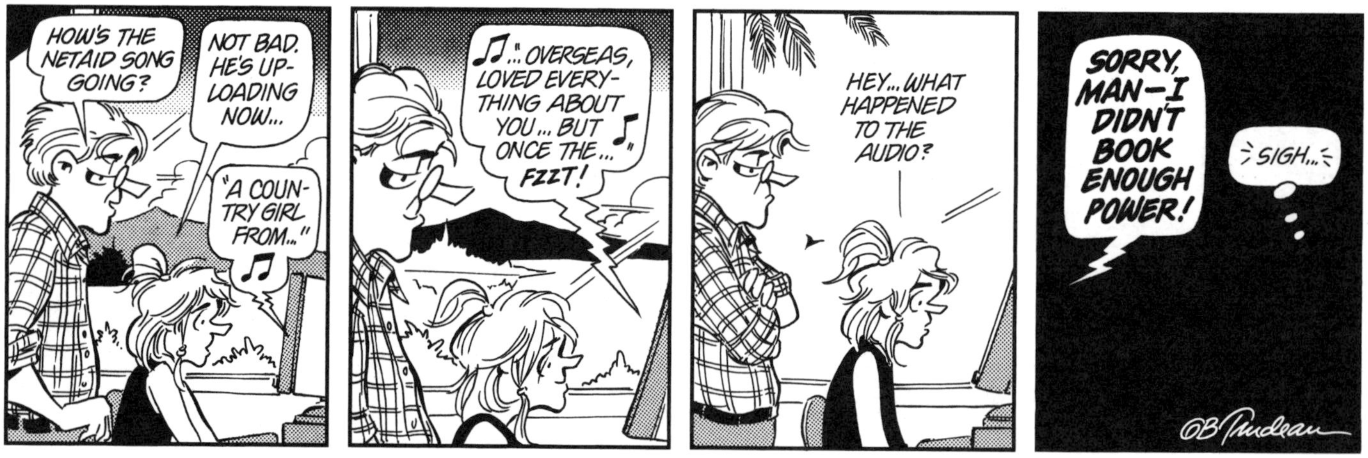
HOW'S THE NETAID SONG GOING?
NOT BAD. HE'S UPLOADING NOW...
"A COUNTRY GIRL FROM..." ♫
♫ "...OVERSEAS, LOVED EVERYTHING ABOUT YOU... BUT ONCE THE..." ♪ FZZT!
HEY... WHAT HAPPENED TO THE AUDIO?
SORRY, MAN—I DIDN'T BOOK ENOUGH POWER!
SIGH...

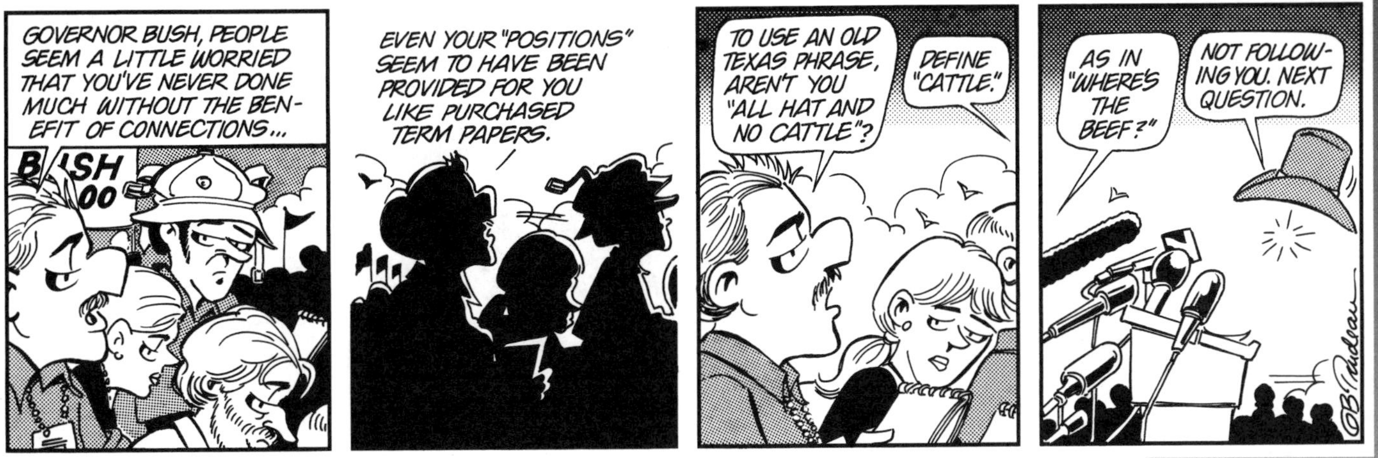
GOVERNOR BUSH, PEOPLE SEEM A LITTLE WORRIED THAT YOU'VE NEVER DONE MUCH WITHOUT THE BENEFIT OF CONNECTIONS...
EVEN YOUR "POSITIONS" SEEM TO HAVE BEEN PROVIDED FOR YOU LIKE PURCHASED TERM PAPERS.
TO USE AN OLD TEXAS PHRASE, AREN'T YOU "ALL HAT AND NO CATTLE"?
DEFINE "CATTLE."
AS IN "WHERE'S THE BEEF?"
NOT FOLLOWING YOU. NEXT QUESTION.

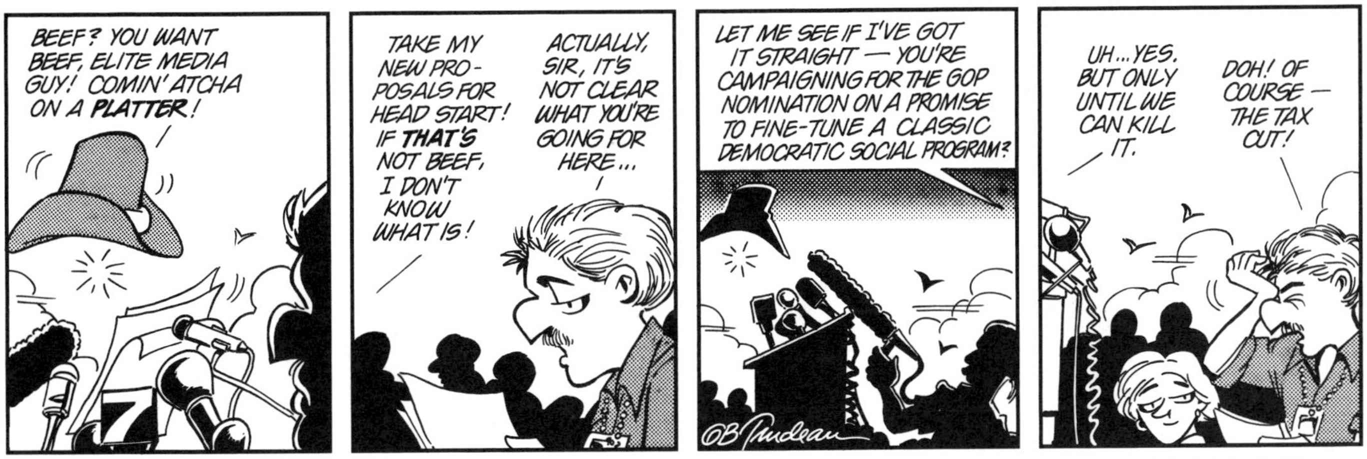
BEEF? YOU WANT BEEF, ELITE MEDIA GUY! COMIN' ATCHA ON A **PLATTER**!
TAKE MY NEW PROPOSALS FOR HEAD START! IF **THAT'S** NOT BEEF, I DON'T KNOW WHAT IS!
ACTUALLY, SIR, IT'S NOT CLEAR WHAT YOU'RE GOING FOR HERE...
LET ME SEE IF I'VE GOT IT STRAIGHT — YOU'RE CAMPAIGNING FOR THE GOP NOMINATION ON A PROMISE TO FINE-TUNE A CLASSIC DEMOCRATIC SOCIAL PROGRAM?
UH... YES. BUT ONLY UNTIL WE CAN KILL IT.
DOH! OF COURSE — THE TAX CUT!

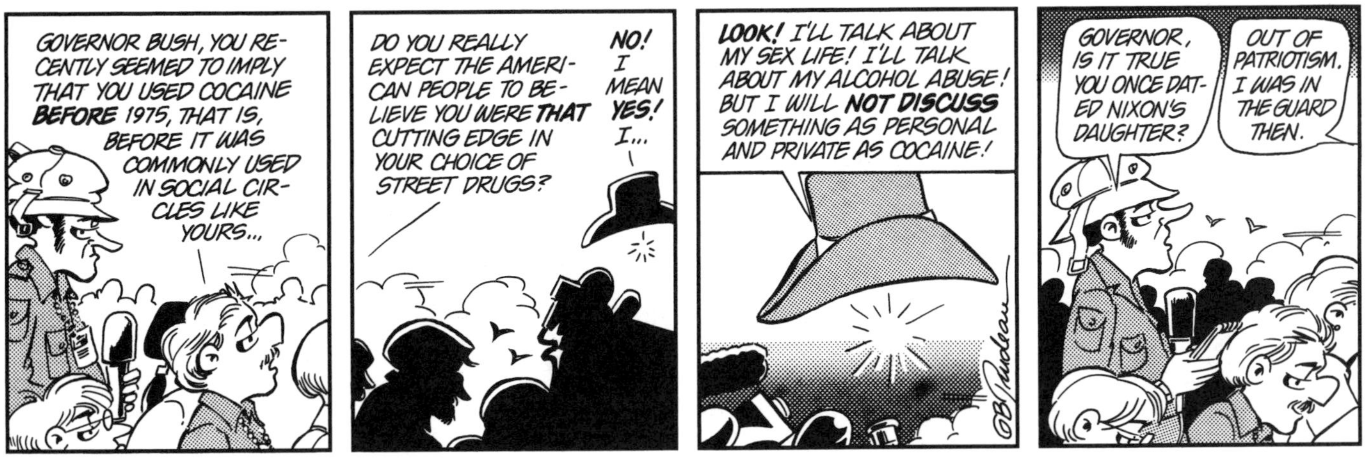
GOVERNOR BUSH, YOU RECENTLY SEEMED TO IMPLY THAT YOU USED COCAINE **BEFORE** 1975, THAT IS, BEFORE IT WAS COMMONLY USED IN SOCIAL CIRCLES LIKE YOURS...
DO YOU REALLY EXPECT THE AMERICAN PEOPLE TO BELIEVE YOU WERE **THAT** CUTTING EDGE IN YOUR CHOICE OF STREET DRUGS?
NO! I MEAN **YES!** I...
LOOK! I'LL TALK ABOUT MY SEX LIFE! I'LL TALK ABOUT MY ALCOHOL ABUSE! BUT I WILL **NOT DISCUSS** SOMETHING AS PERSONAL AND PRIVATE AS COCAINE!
GOVERNOR, IS IT TRUE YOU ONCE DATED NIXON'S DAUGHTER?
OUT OF PATRIOTISM. I WAS IN THE GUARD THEN.

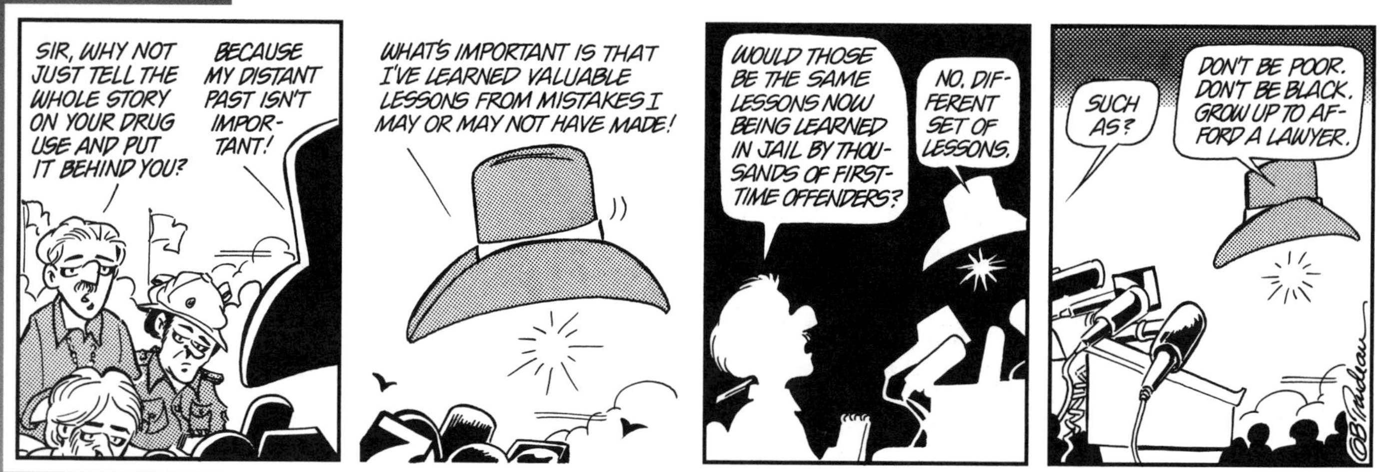
SIR, WHY NOT JUST TELL THE WHOLE STORY ON YOUR DRUG USE AND PUT IT BEHIND YOU?
BECAUSE MY DISTANT PAST ISN'T IMPORTANT!
WHAT'S IMPORTANT IS THAT I'VE LEARNED VALUABLE LESSONS FROM MISTAKES I MAY OR MAY NOT HAVE MADE!
WOULD THOSE BE THE SAME LESSONS NOW BEING LEARNED IN JAIL BY THOUSANDS OF FIRST-TIME OFFENDERS?
NO, DIFFERENT SET OF LESSONS.
SUCH AS?
DON'T BE POOR. DON'T BE BLACK. GROW UP TO AFFORD A LAWYER.

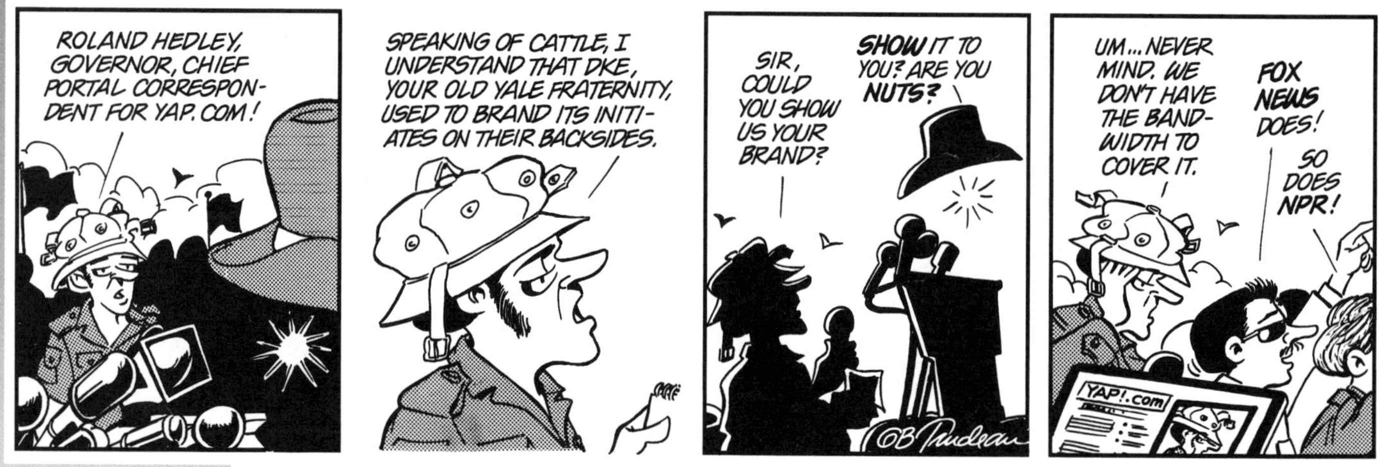
ROLAND HEDLEY, GOVERNOR, CHIEF PORTAL CORRESPONDENT FOR YAP.COM!
SPEAKING OF CATTLE, I UNDERSTAND THAT DKE, YOUR OLD YALE FRATERNITY, USED TO BRAND ITS INITIATES ON THEIR BACKSIDES.
SIR, COULD YOU SHOW US YOUR BRAND?
SHOW IT TO YOU? ARE YOU NUTS?
UM... NEVER MIND. WE DON'T HAVE THE BANDWIDTH TO COVER IT.
FOX NEWS DOES!
SO DOES NPR!
YAP!.com

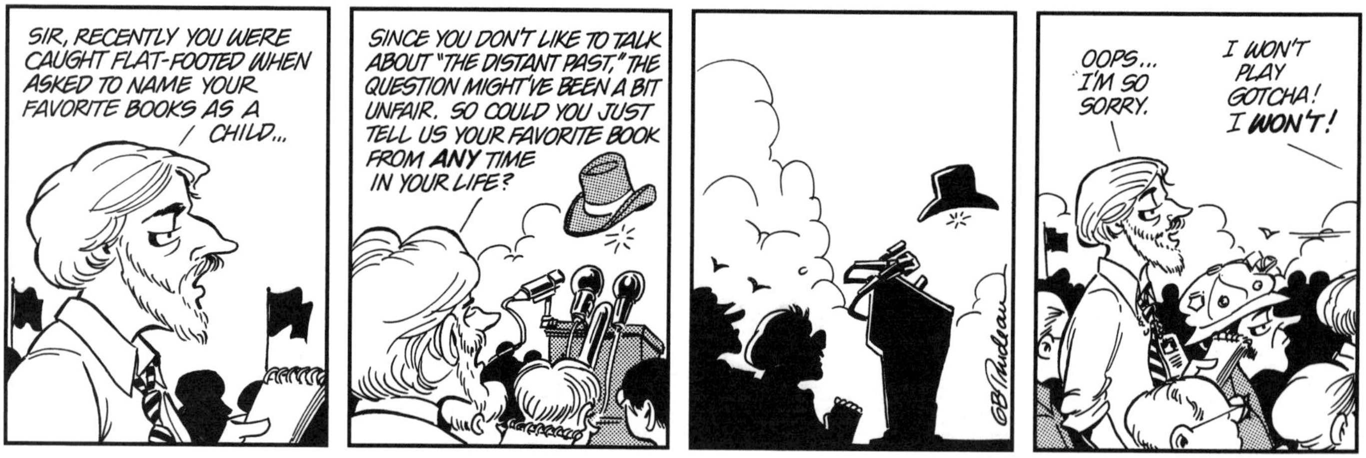
SIR, RECENTLY YOU WERE CAUGHT FLAT-FOOTED WHEN ASKED TO NAME YOUR FAVORITE BOOKS AS A CHILD...
SINCE YOU DON'T LIKE TO TALK ABOUT "THE DISTANT PAST," THE QUESTION MIGHT'VE BEEN A BIT UNFAIR. SO COULD YOU JUST TELL US YOUR FAVORITE BOOK FROM ANY TIME IN YOUR LIFE?
OOPS... I'M SO SORRY.
I WON'T PLAY GOTCHA! I WON'T!

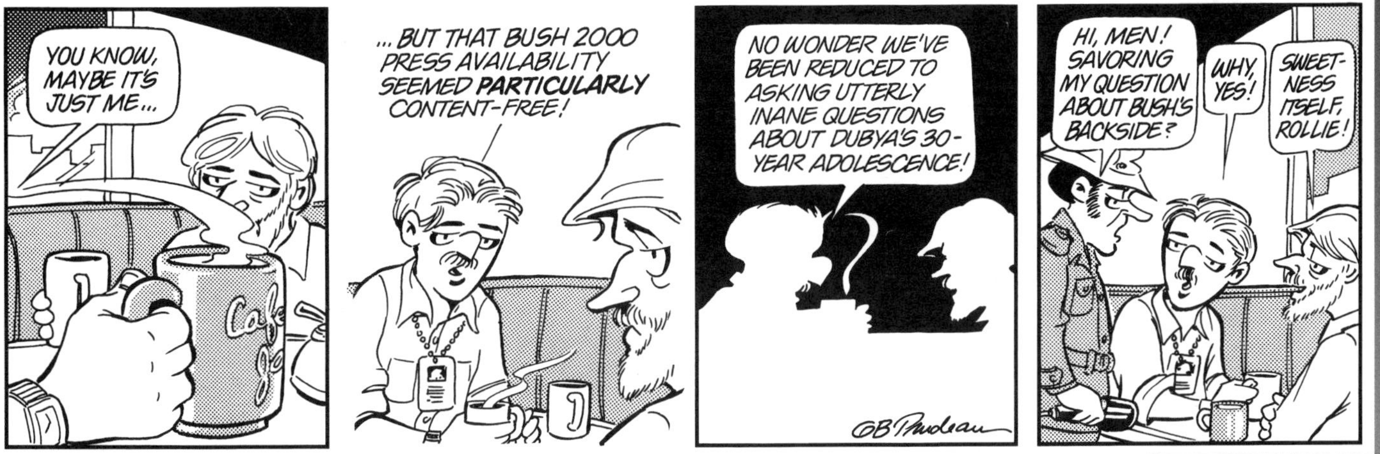
YOU KNOW, MAYBE IT'S JUST ME...
... BUT THAT BUSH 2000 PRESS AVAILABILITY SEEMED **PARTICULARLY** CONTENT-FREE!
NO WONDER WE'VE BEEN REDUCED TO ASKING UTTERLY INANE QUESTIONS ABOUT DUBYA'S 30-YEAR ADOLESCENCE!
HI, MEN! SAVORING MY QUESTION ABOUT BUSH'S BACKSIDE?
WHY, YES!
SWEETNESS ITSELF, ROLLIE!

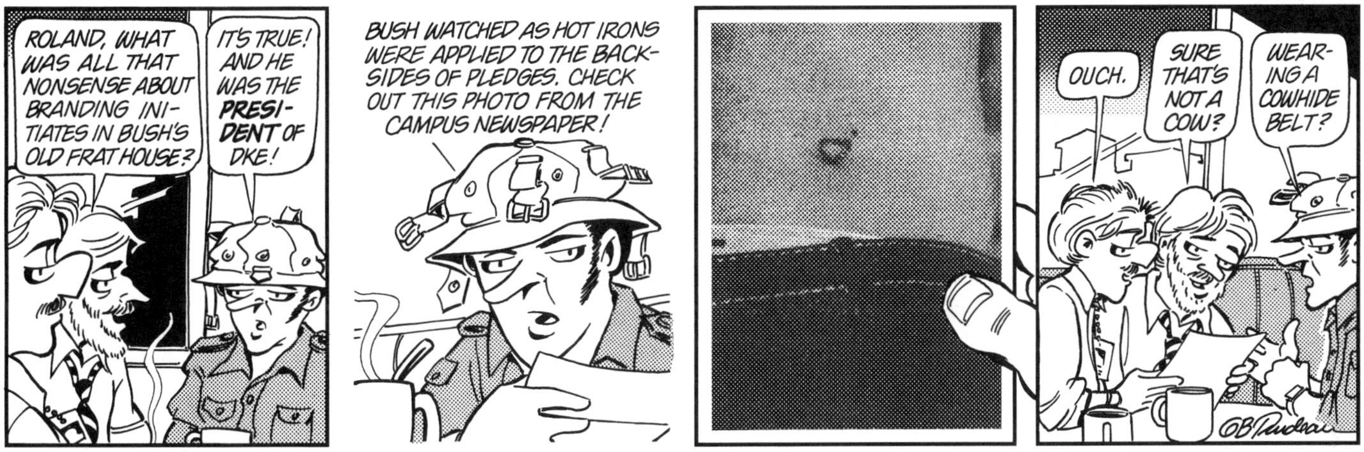
ROLAND, WHAT WAS ALL THAT NONSENSE ABOUT BRANDING INITIATES IN BUSH'S OLD FRAT HOUSE?
IT'S TRUE! AND HE WAS THE **PRESIDENT** OF DKE!
BUSH WATCHED AS HOT IRONS WERE APPLIED TO THE BACKSIDES OF PLEDGES. CHECK OUT THIS PHOTO FROM THE CAMPUS NEWSPAPER!
OUCH.
SURE THAT'S NOT A COW?
WEARING A COWHIDE BELT?

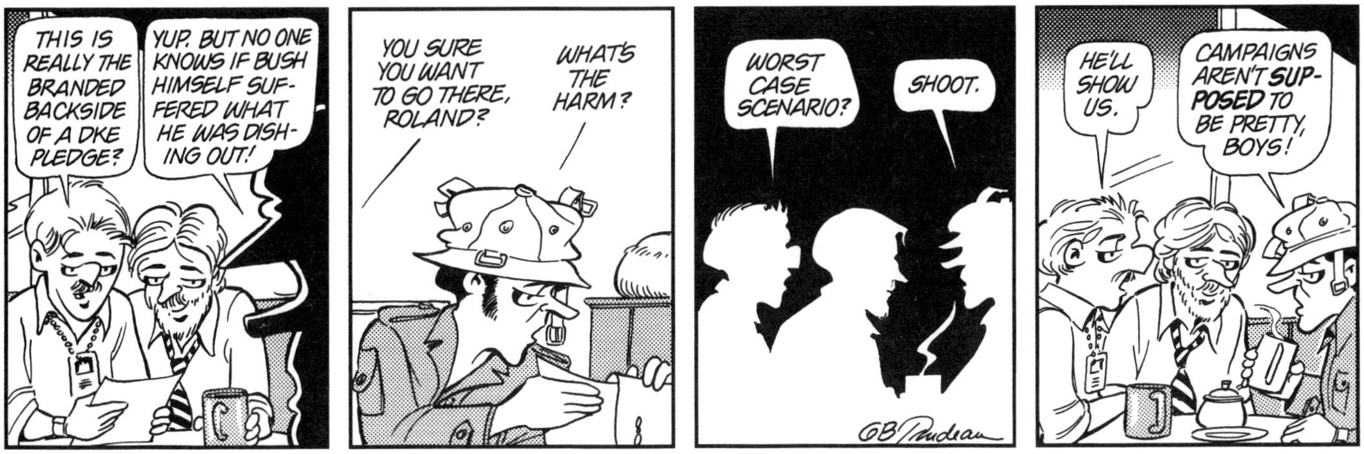
THIS IS REALLY THE BRANDED BACKSIDE OF A DKE PLEDGE?
YUP. BUT NO ONE KNOWS IF BUSH HIMSELF SUFFERED WHAT HE WAS DISHING OUT!
YOU SURE YOU WANT TO GO THERE, ROLAND?
WHAT'S THE HARM?
WORST CASE SCENARIO?
SHOOT.
HE'LL SHOW US.
CAMPAIGNS AREN'T **SUPPOSED** TO BE PRETTY, BOYS!

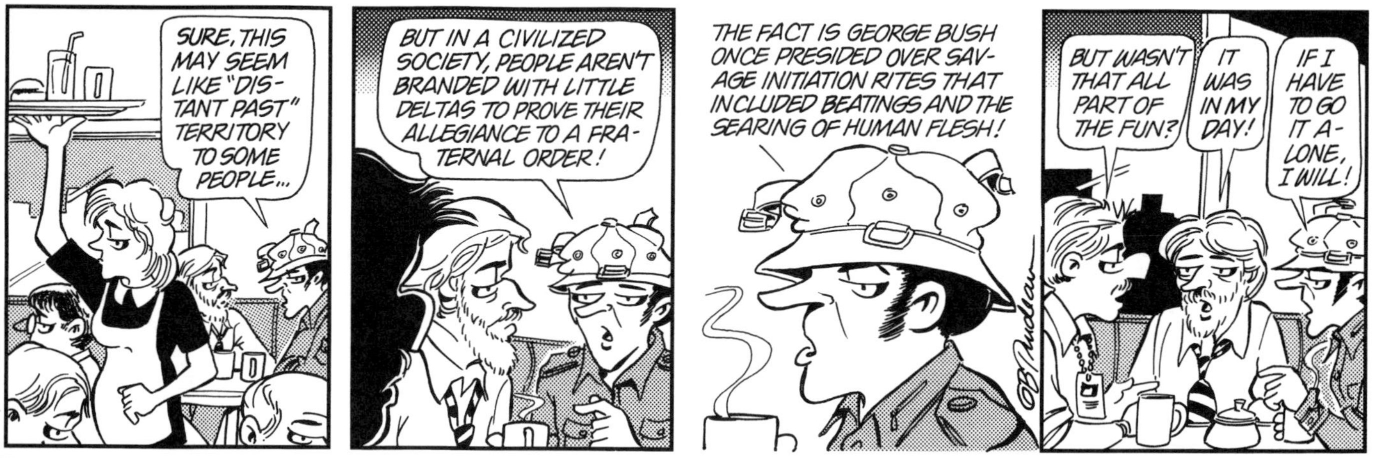
SURE, THIS MAY SEEM LIKE "DISTANT PAST" TERRITORY TO SOME PEOPLE...
BUT IN A CIVILIZED SOCIETY, PEOPLE AREN'T BRANDED WITH LITTLE DELTAS TO PROVE THEIR ALLEGIANCE TO A FRATERNAL ORDER!
THE FACT IS GEORGE BUSH ONCE PRESIDED OVER SAVAGE INITIATION RITES THAT INCLUDED BEATINGS AND THE SEARING OF HUMAN FLESH!
BUT WASN'T THAT ALL PART OF THE FUN?
IT WAS IN MY DAY!
IF I HAVE TO GO IT ALONE, I WILL!

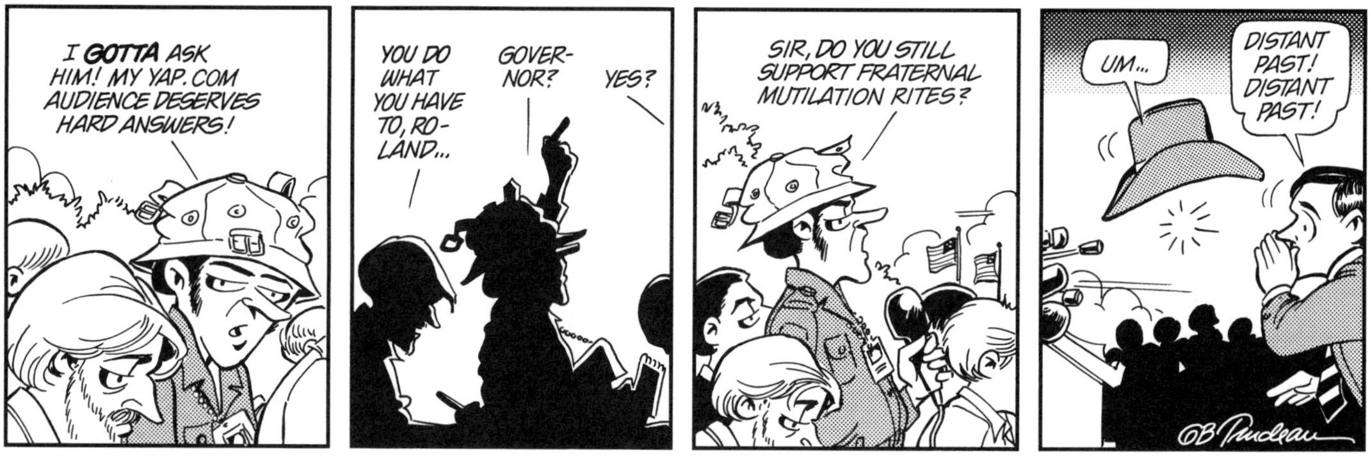
I GOTTA ASK HIM! MY YAP.COM AUDIENCE DESERVES HARD ANSWERS!
YOU DO WHAT YOU HAVE TO, ROLAND...
GOVERNOR?
YES?
SIR, DO YOU STILL SUPPORT FRATERNAL MUTILATION RITES?
UM...
DISTANT PAST! DISTANT PAST!

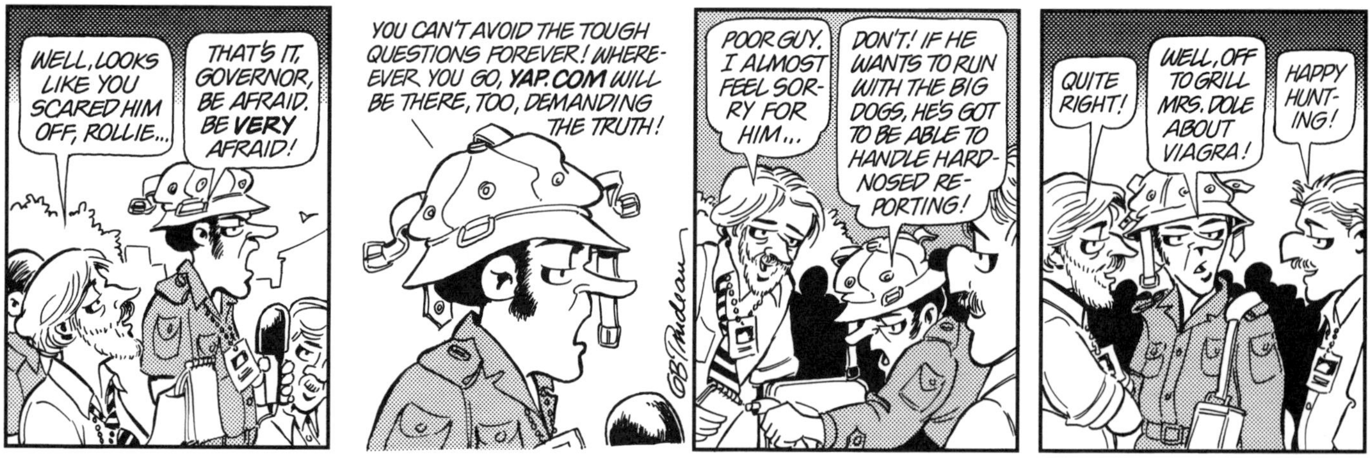
WELL, LOOKS LIKE YOU SCARED HIM OFF, ROLLIE...
THAT'S IT, GOVERNOR, BE AFRAID. BE VERY AFRAID!
YOU CAN'T AVOID THE TOUGH QUESTIONS FOREVER! WHEREEVER YOU GO, YAP.COM WILL BE THERE, TOO, DEMANDING THE TRUTH!
POOR GUY. I ALMOST FEEL SORRY FOR HIM...
DON'T! IF HE WANTS TO RUN WITH THE BIG DOGS, HE'S GOT TO BE ABLE TO HANDLE HARD-NOSED REPORTING!
QUITE RIGHT!
WELL, OFF TO GRILL MRS. DOLE ABOUT VIAGRA!
HAPPY HUNTING!

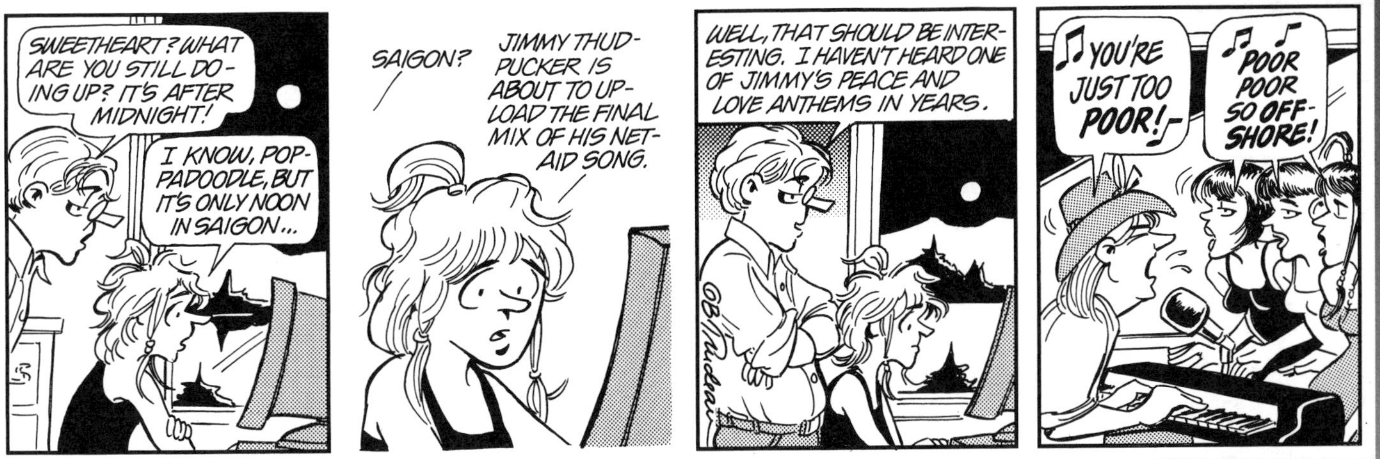
SWEETHEART? WHAT ARE YOU STILL DOING UP? IT'S AFTER MIDNIGHT!
I KNOW, POPPADOODLE, BUT IT'S ONLY NOON IN SAIGON...
SAIGON?
JIMMY THUDPUCKER IS ABOUT TO UPLOAD THE FINAL MIX OF HIS NET-AID SONG.
WELL, THAT SHOULD BE INTERESTING. I HAVEN'T HEARD ONE OF JIMMY'S PEACE AND LOVE ANTHEMS IN YEARS.
YOU'RE JUST TOO POOR!
POOR POOR SO OFF-SHORE!

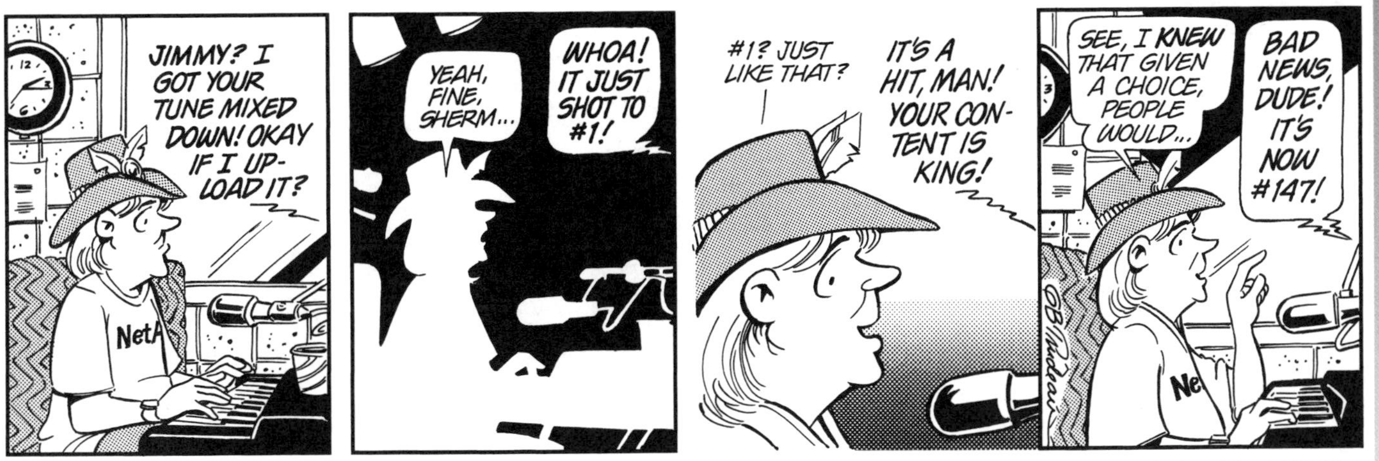
JIMMY? I GOT YOUR TUNE MIXED DOWN! OKAY IF I UPLOAD IT?
YEAH, FINE, SHERM...
WHOA! IT JUST SHOT TO #1!
#1? JUST LIKE THAT?
IT'S A HIT, MAN! YOUR CONTENT IS KING!
SEE, I KNEW THAT GIVEN A CHOICE, PEOPLE WOULD...
BAD NEWS, DUDE! IT'S NOW #147!
NetAid

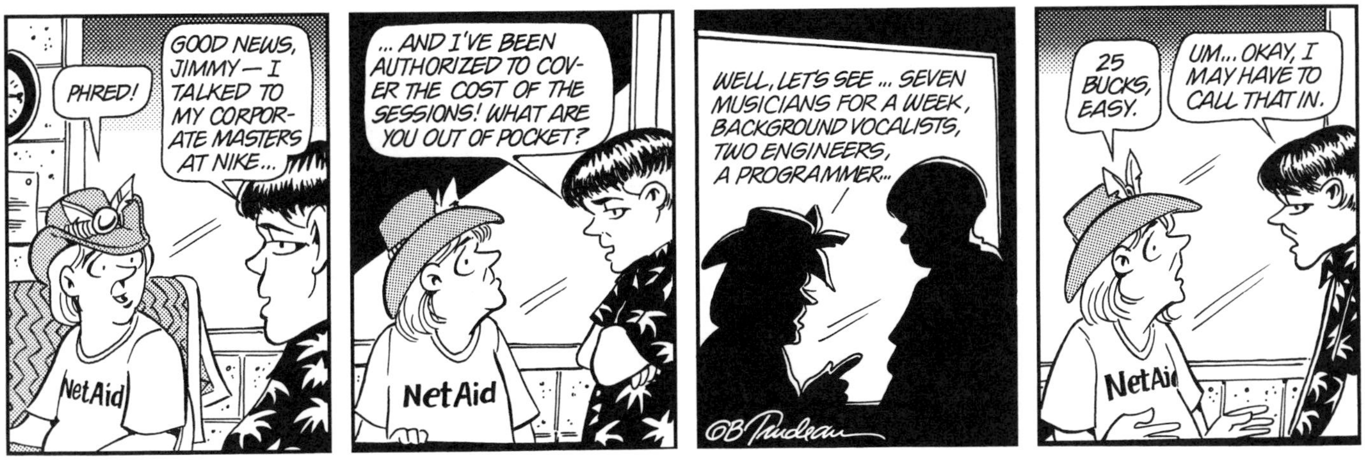
PHRED!
GOOD NEWS, JIMMY — I TALKED TO MY CORPORATE MASTERS AT NIKE...
... AND I'VE BEEN AUTHORIZED TO COVER THE COST OF THE SESSIONS! WHAT ARE YOU OUT OF POCKET?
WELL, LET'S SEE ... SEVEN MUSICIANS FOR A WEEK, BACKGROUND VOCALISTS, TWO ENGINEERS, A PROGRAMMER...
25 BUCKS, EASY.
UM... OKAY, I MAY HAVE TO CALL THAT IN.
NetAid

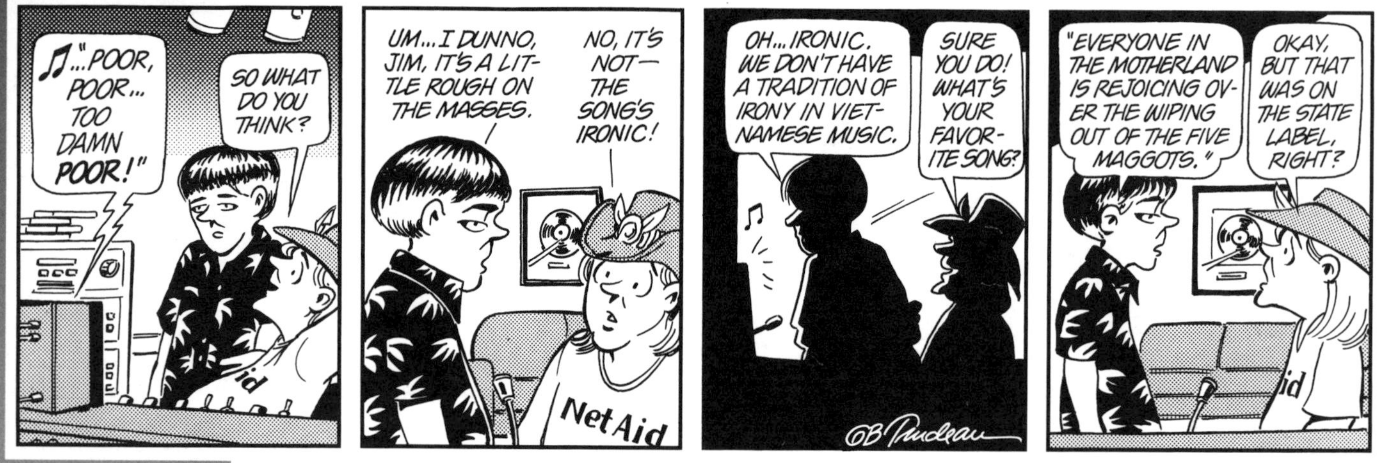
♫ ..."POOR, POOR... TOO DAMN POOR!"
SO WHAT DO YOU THINK?
UM...I DUNNO, JIM, IT'S A LITTLE ROUGH ON THE MASSES.
NO, IT'S NOT— THE SONG'S IRONIC!
Net Aid
OH... IRONIC. WE DON'T HAVE A TRADITION OF IRONY IN VIETNAMESE MUSIC.
SURE YOU DO! WHAT'S YOUR FAVORITE SONG?
©B Trudeau
"EVERYONE IN THE MOTHERLAND IS REJOICING OVER THE WIPING OUT OF THE FIVE MAGGOTS."
OKAY, BUT THAT WAS ON THE STATE LABEL, RIGHT?

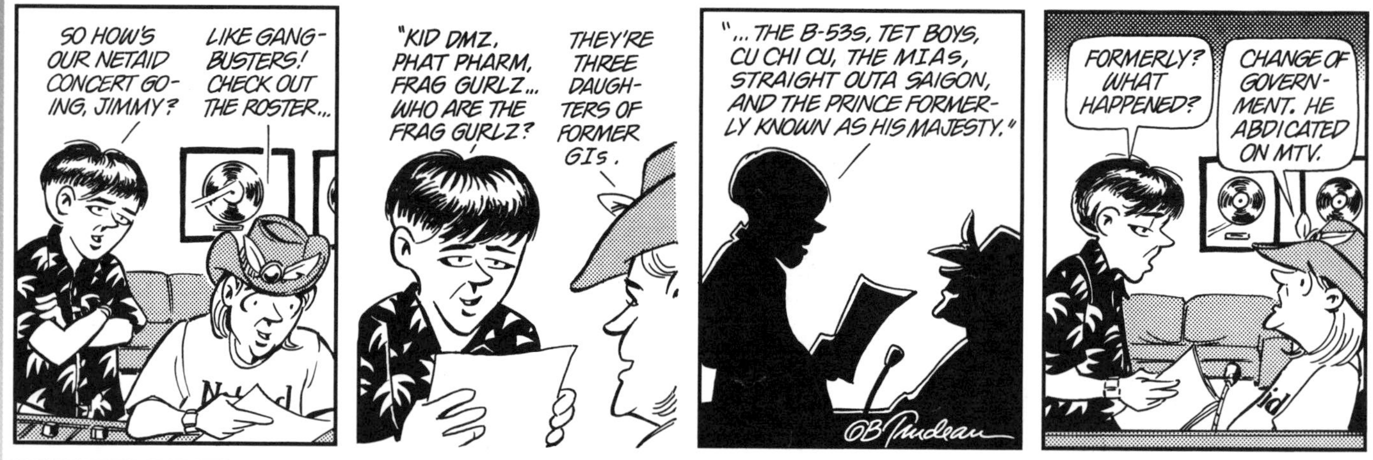
SO HOW'S OUR NETAID CONCERT GOING, JIMMY?
LIKE GANGBUSTERS! CHECK OUT THE ROSTER...
"KID DMZ, PHAT PHARM, FRAG GURLZ... WHO ARE THE FRAG GURLZ?
THEY'RE THREE DAUGHTERS OF FORMER GIs.
"...THE B-53s, TET BOYS, CU CHI CU, THE MIAs, STRAIGHT OUTA SAIGON, AND THE PRINCE FORMERLY KNOWN AS HIS MAJESTY."
©B Trudeau
FORMERLY? WHAT HAPPENED?
CHANGE OF GOVERNMENT. HE ABDICATED ON MTV.

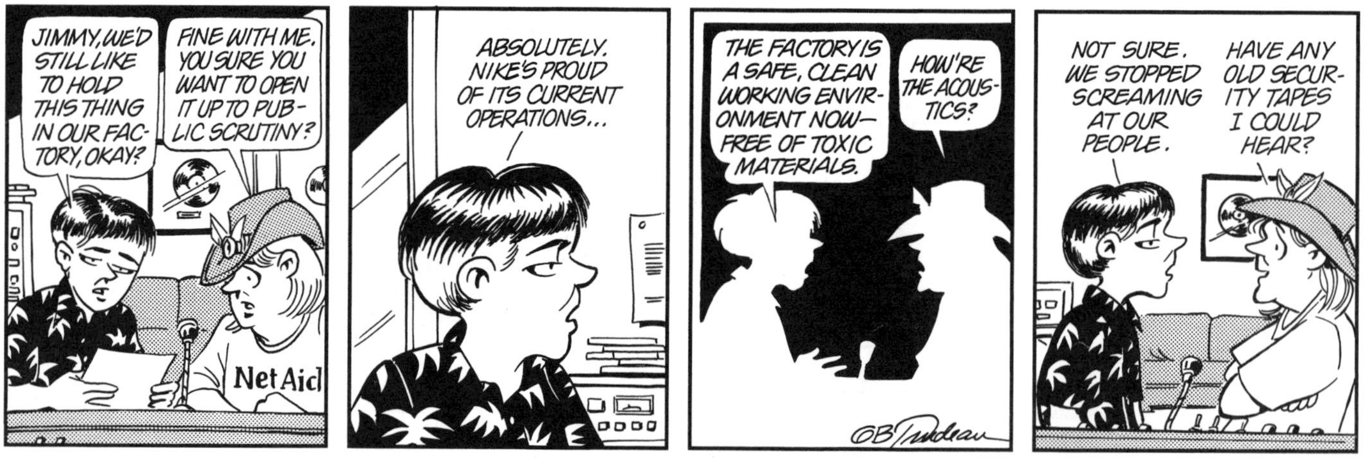
JIMMY, WE'D STILL LIKE TO HOLD THIS THING IN OUR FACTORY, OKAY?
FINE WITH ME. YOU SURE YOU WANT TO OPEN IT UP TO PUBLIC SCRUTINY?
Net Aid
ABSOLUTELY. NIKE'S PROUD OF ITS CURRENT OPERATIONS...
THE FACTORY IS A SAFE, CLEAN WORKING ENVIRONMENT NOW— FREE OF TOXIC MATERIALS.
HOW'RE THE ACOUSTICS?
©B Trudeau
NOT SURE. WE STOPPED SCREAMING AT OUR PEOPLE.
HAVE ANY OLD SECURITY TAPES I COULD HEAR?

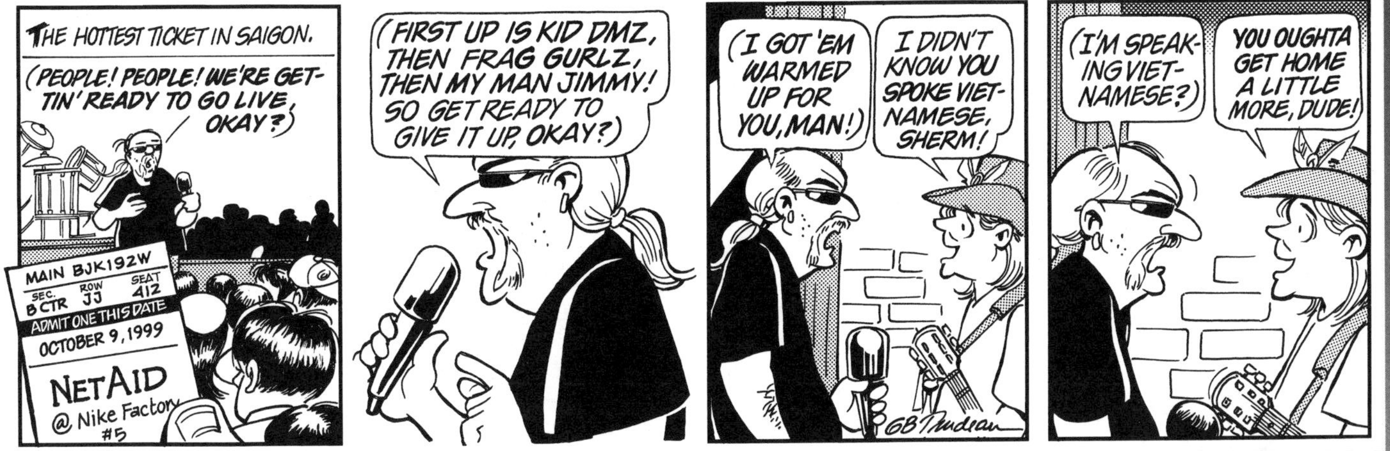
THE HOTTEST TICKET IN SAIGON.
(PEOPLE! PEOPLE! WE'RE GET-TIN' READY TO GO LIVE, OKAY?)
MAIN BJK192W
SEC. B CTR ROW JJ SEAT 412
ADMIT ONE THIS DATE
OCTOBER 9, 1999
NETAID
@ Nike Factory #5
(FIRST UP IS KID DMZ, THEN FRAG GURLZ, THEN MY MAN JIMMY! SO GET READY TO GIVE IT UP, OKAY?)
(I GOT 'EM WARMED UP FOR YOU, MAN!)
I DIDN'T KNOW YOU SPOKE VIET-NAMESE, SHERM!
(I'M SPEAK-ING VIET-NAMESE?)
YOU OUGHTA GET HOME A LITTLE MORE, DUDE!

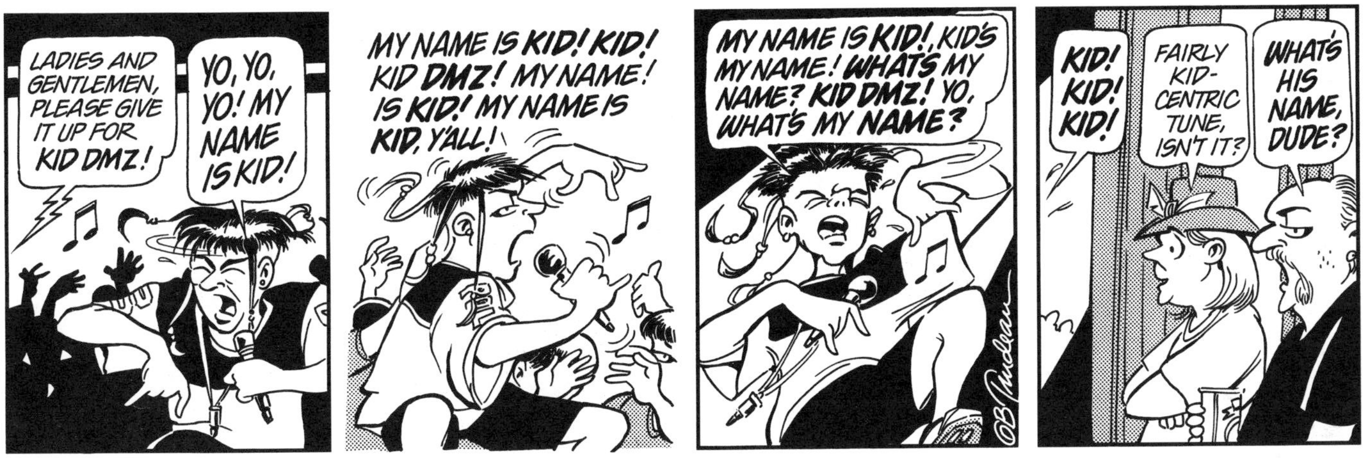
LADIES AND GENTLEMEN, PLEASE GIVE IT UP FOR KID DMZ!
YO, YO, YO! MY NAME IS KID!
MY NAME IS KID! KID! KID DMZ! MY NAME! IS KID! MY NAME IS KID, Y'ALL!
MY NAME IS KID!, KID'S MY NAME! WHAT'S MY NAME? KID DMZ! YO, WHAT'S MY NAME?
KID! KID! KID!
FAIRLY KID-CENTRIC TUNE, ISN'T IT?
WHAT'S HIS NAME, DUDE?

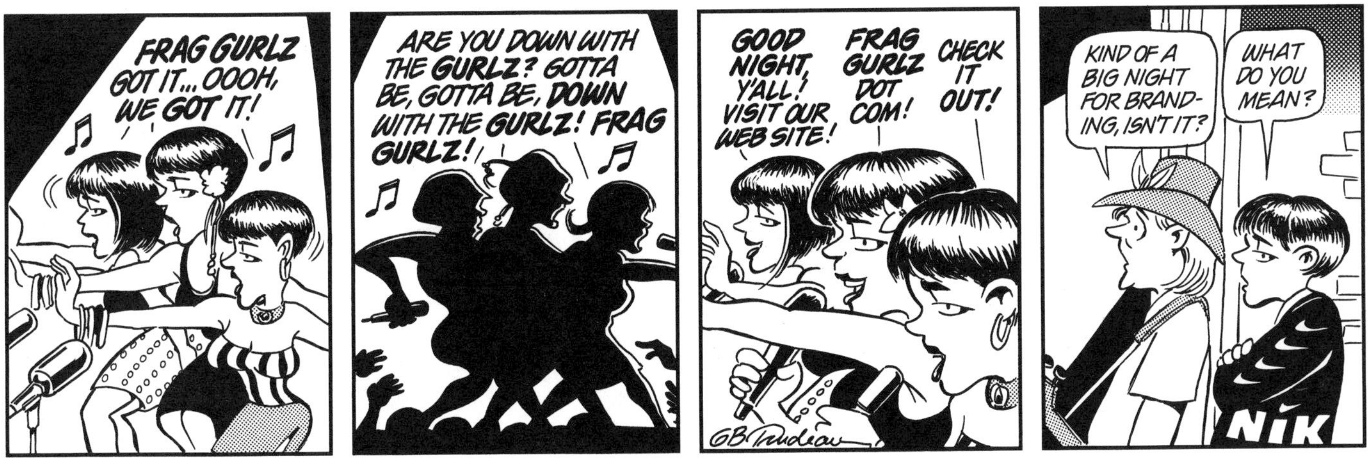
FRAG GURLZ GOT IT... OOOH, WE GOT IT!
ARE YOU DOWN WITH THE GURLZ? GOTTA BE, GOTTA BE, DOWN WITH THE GURLZ! FRAG GURLZ!
GOOD NIGHT, Y'ALL! VISIT OUR WEB SITE!
FRAG GURLZ DOT COM!
CHECK IT OUT!
KIND OF A BIG NIGHT FOR BRAND-ING, ISN'T IT?
WHAT DO YOU MEAN?
NIK

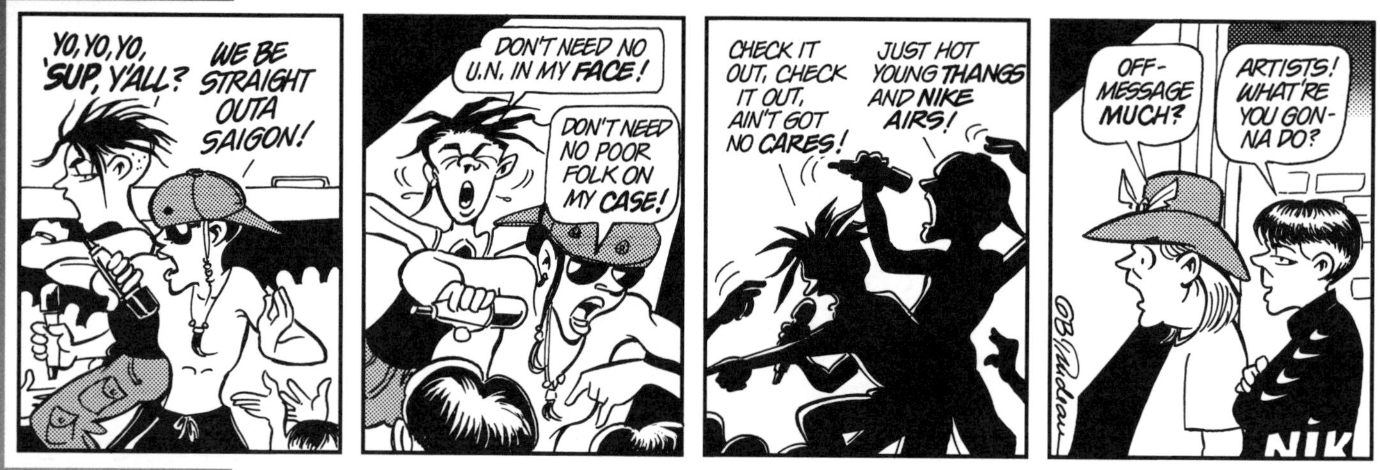
YO, YO, YO, 'SUP, Y'ALL?
WE BE STRAIGHT OUTA SAIGON!
DON'T NEED NO U.N. IN MY FACE!
DON'T NEED NO POOR FOLK ON MY CASE!
CHECK IT OUT, CHECK IT OUT, AIN'T GOT NO CARES!
JUST HOT YOUNG THANGS AND NIKE AIRS!
OFF-MESSAGE MUCH?
ARTISTS! WHAT'RE YOU GONNA DO?
NIK

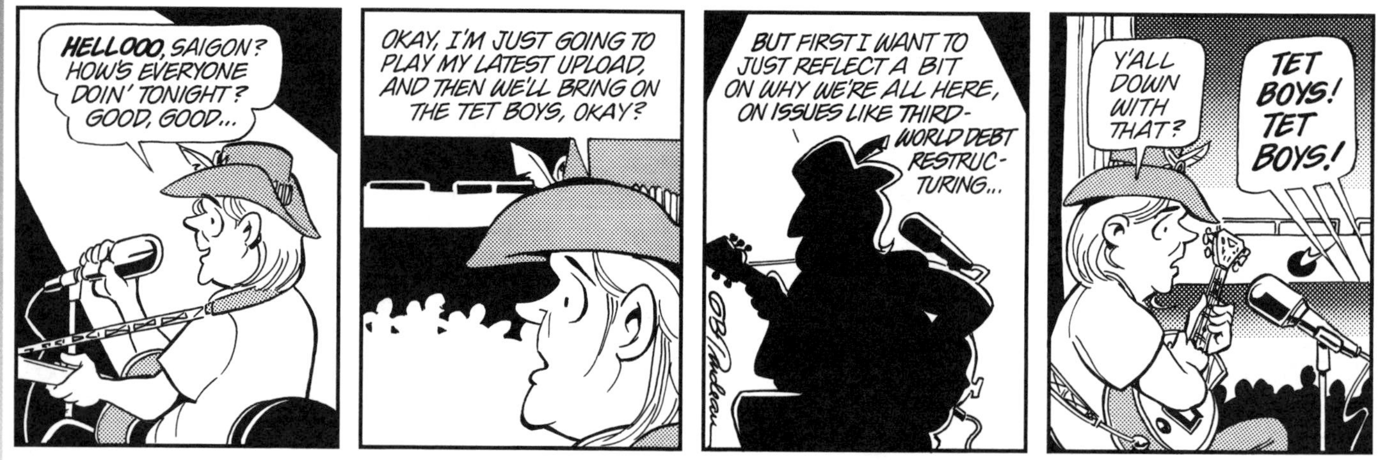
HELLOOO, SAIGON? HOW'S EVERYONE DOIN' TONIGHT? GOOD, GOOD...
OKAY, I'M JUST GOING TO PLAY MY LATEST UPLOAD, AND THEN WE'LL BRING ON THE TET BOYS, OKAY?
BUT FIRST I WANT TO JUST REFLECT A BIT ON WHY WE'RE ALL HERE, ON ISSUES LIKE THIRD-WORLD DEBT RESTRUCTURING...
Y'ALL DOWN WITH THAT?
TET BOYS! TET BOYS!

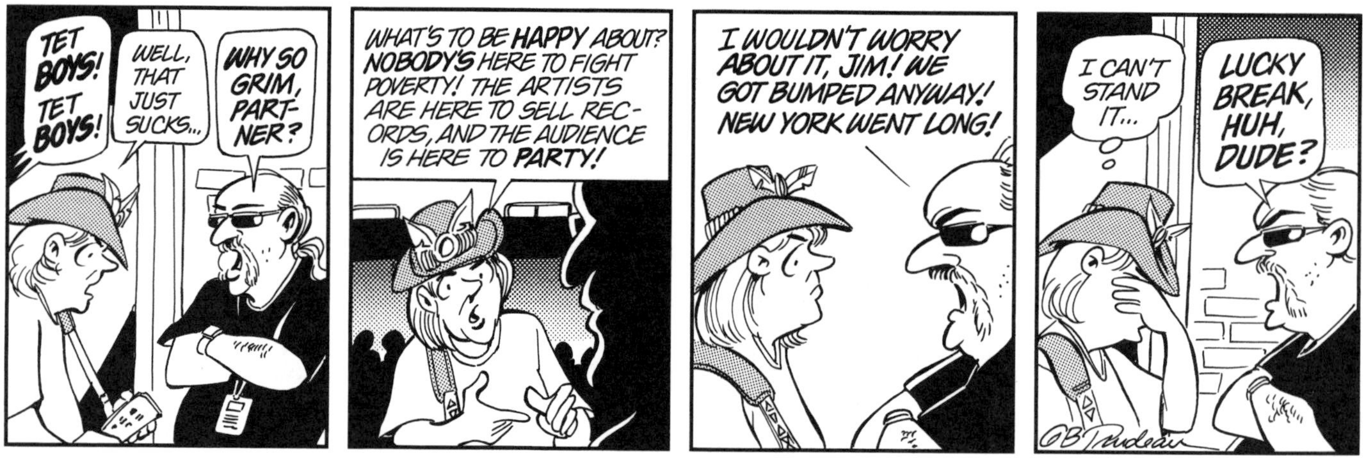
TET BOYS! TET BOYS!
WELL, THAT JUST SUCKS...
WHY SO GRIM, PARTNER?
WHAT'S TO BE HAPPY ABOUT? NOBODY'S HERE TO FIGHT POVERTY! THE ARTISTS ARE HERE TO SELL RECORDS, AND THE AUDIENCE IS HERE TO PARTY!
I WOULDN'T WORRY ABOUT IT, JIM! WE GOT BUMPED ANYWAY! NEW YORK WENT LONG!
I CAN'T STAND IT...
LUCKY BREAK, HUH, DUDE?

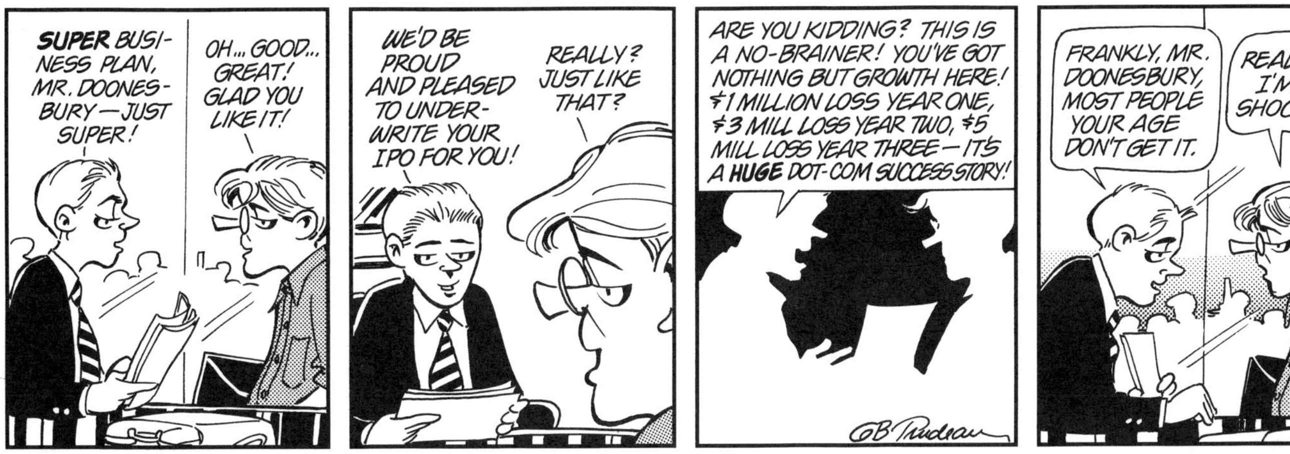
SUPER BUSINESS PLAN, MR. DOONESBURY — JUST SUPER!
OH... GOOD... GREAT! GLAD YOU LIKE IT!
WE'D BE PROUD AND PLEASED TO UNDERWRITE YOUR IPO FOR YOU!
REALLY? JUST LIKE THAT?
ARE YOU KIDDING? THIS IS A NO-BRAINER! YOU'VE GOT NOTHING BUT GROWTH HERE! $1 MILLION LOSS YEAR ONE, $3 MILL LOSS YEAR TWO, $5 MILL LOSS YEAR THREE — IT'S A HUGE DOT-COM SUCCESS STORY!
FRANKLY, MR. DOONESBURY, MOST PEOPLE YOUR AGE DON'T GET IT.
REALLY? I'M SHOCKED.

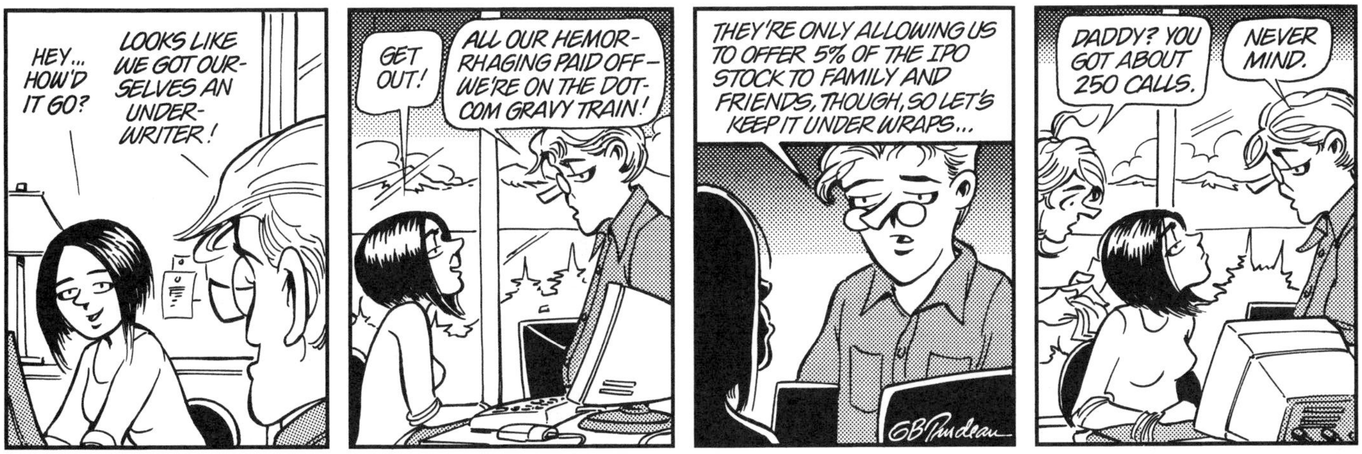
HEY... HOW'D IT GO?
LOOKS LIKE WE GOT OURSELVES AN UNDERWRITER!
GET OUT!
ALL OUR HEMORRHAGING PAID OFF — WE'RE ON THE DOT-COM GRAVY TRAIN!
THEY'RE ONLY ALLOWING US TO OFFER 5% OF THE IPO STOCK TO FAMILY AND FRIENDS, THOUGH, SO LET'S KEEP IT UNDER WRAPS...
DADDY? YOU GOT ABOUT 250 CALLS.
NEVER MIND.

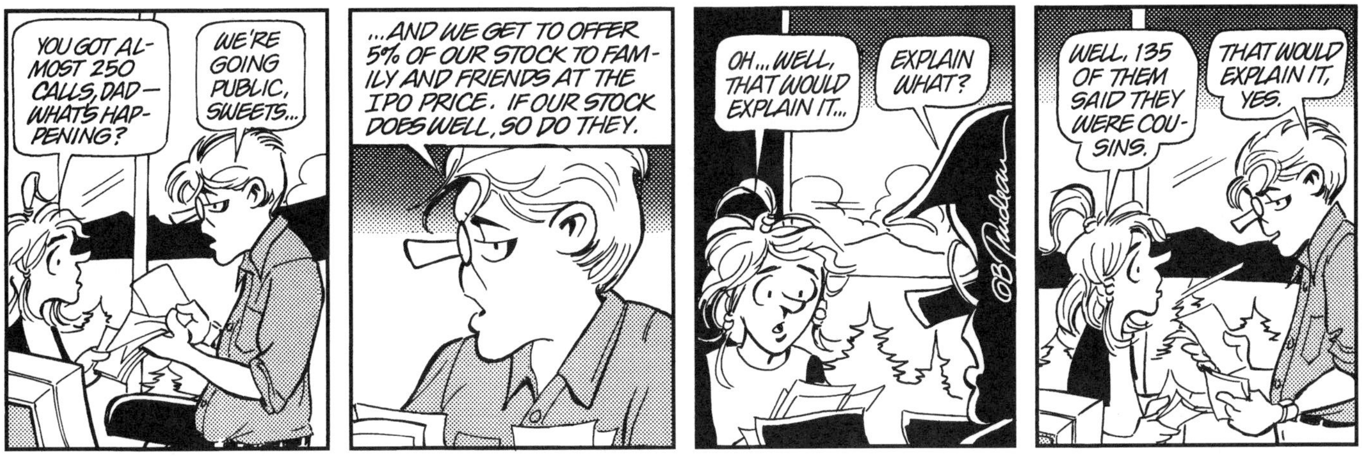
YOU GOT ALMOST 250 CALLS, DAD — WHAT'S HAPPENING?
WE'RE GOING PUBLIC, SWEETS...
...AND WE GET TO OFFER 5% OF OUR STOCK TO FAMILY AND FRIENDS AT THE IPO PRICE. IF OUR STOCK DOES WELL, SO DO THEY.
OH... WELL, THAT WOULD EXPLAIN IT...
EXPLAIN WHAT?
WELL, 135 OF THEM SAID THEY WERE COUSINS.
THAT WOULD EXPLAIN IT, YES.

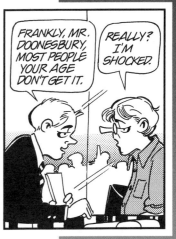

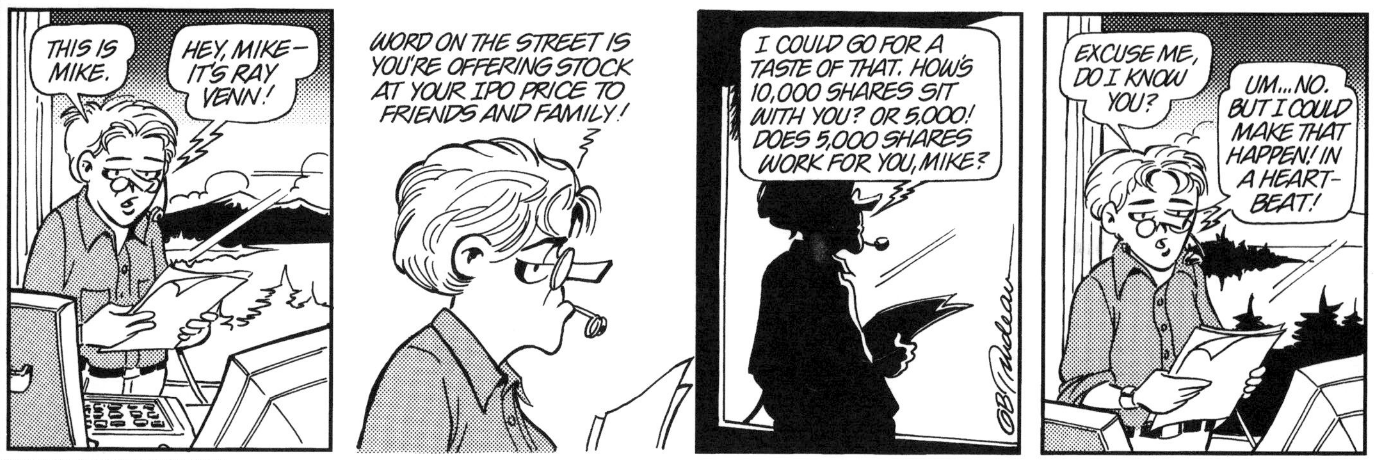
THIS IS MIKE.
HEY, MIKE— IT'S RAY VENN!
WORD ON THE STREET IS YOU'RE OFFERING STOCK AT YOUR IPO PRICE TO FRIENDS AND FAMILY!
I COULD GO FOR A TASTE OF THAT. HOW'S 10,000 SHARES SIT WITH YOU? OR 5,000! DOES 5,000 SHARES WORK FOR YOU, MIKE?
EXCUSE ME, DO I KNOW YOU?
UM... NO. BUT I COULD MAKE THAT HAPPEN! IN A HEARTBEAT!

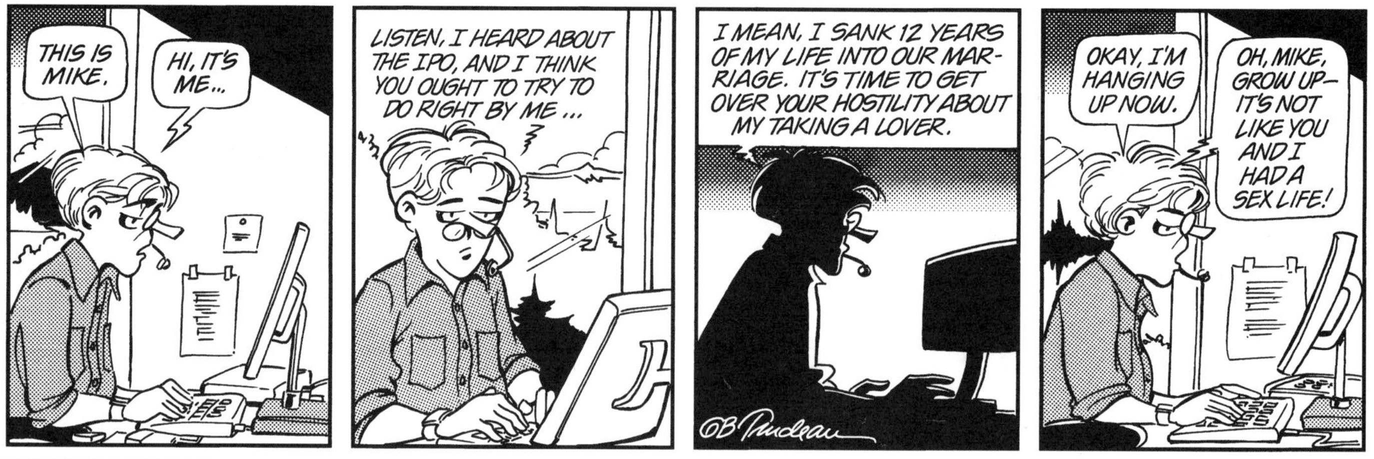
THIS IS MIKE.
HI, IT'S ME...
LISTEN, I HEARD ABOUT THE IPO, AND I THINK YOU OUGHT TO TRY TO DO RIGHT BY ME...
I MEAN, I SANK 12 YEARS OF MY LIFE INTO OUR MARRIAGE. IT'S TIME TO GET OVER YOUR HOSTILITY ABOUT MY TAKING A LOVER.
OKAY, I'M HANGING UP NOW.
OH, MIKE, GROW UP— IT'S NOT LIKE YOU AND I HAD A SEX LIFE!

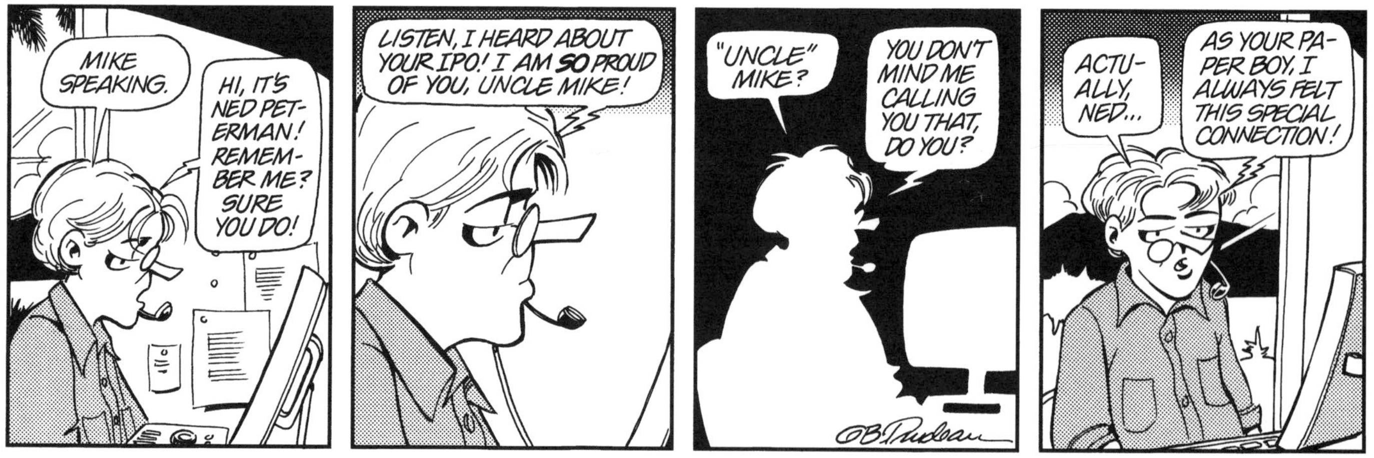
MIKE SPEAKING.
HI, IT'S NED PETERMAN! REMEMBER ME? SURE YOU DO!
LISTEN, I HEARD ABOUT YOUR IPO! I AM SO PROUD OF YOU, UNCLE MIKE!
"UNCLE" MIKE?
YOU DON'T MIND ME CALLING YOU THAT, DO YOU?
ACTUALLY, NED...
AS YOUR PAPER BOY, I ALWAYS FELT THIS SPECIAL CONNECTION!

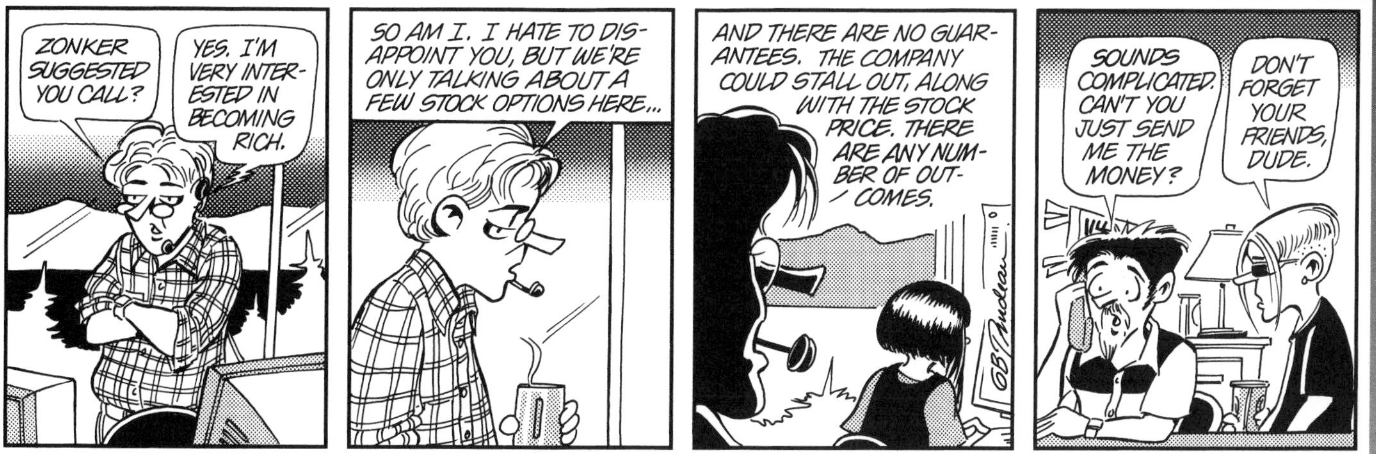
ZONKER SUGGESTED YOU CALL?
YES. I'M VERY INTERESTED IN BECOMING RICH.
SO AM I. I HATE TO DISAPPOINT YOU, BUT WE'RE ONLY TALKING ABOUT A FEW STOCK OPTIONS HERE...
AND THERE ARE NO GUARANTEES. THE COMPANY COULD STALL OUT, ALONG WITH THE STOCK PRICE. THERE ARE ANY NUMBER OF OUTCOMES.
SOUNDS COMPLICATED. CAN'T YOU JUST SEND ME THE MONEY?
DON'T FORGET YOUR FRIENDS, DUDE.

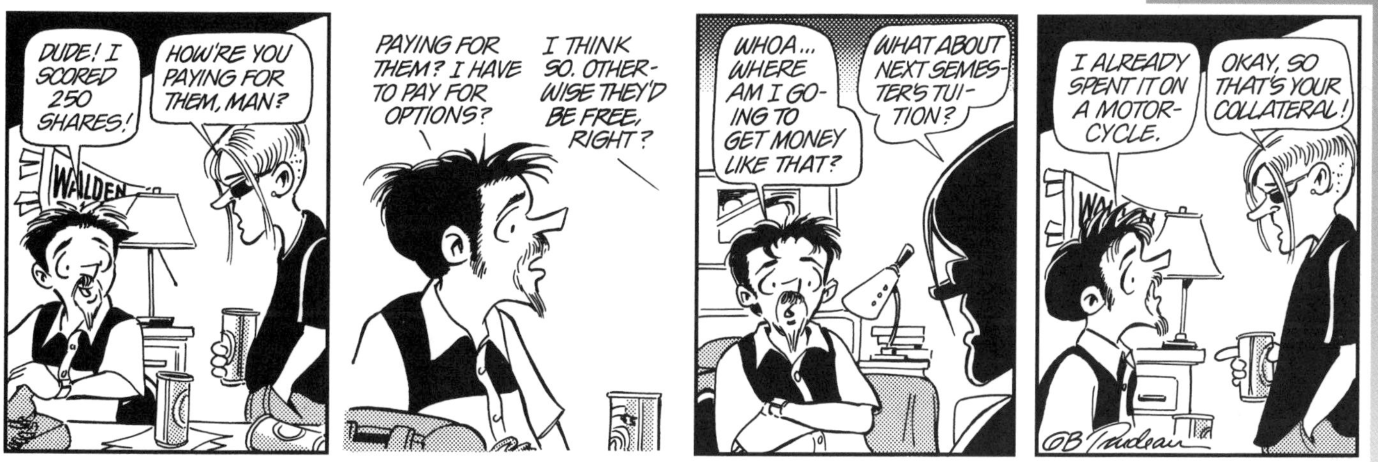
DUDE! I SCORED 250 SHARES!
HOW'RE YOU PAYING FOR THEM, MAN?
PAYING FOR THEM? I HAVE TO PAY FOR OPTIONS?
I THINK SO. OTHERWISE THEY'D BE FREE, RIGHT?
WHOA... WHERE AM I GOING TO GET MONEY LIKE THAT?
WHAT ABOUT NEXT SEMESTER'S TUITION?
I ALREADY SPENT IT ON A MOTORCYCLE.
OKAY, SO THAT'S YOUR COLLATERAL!

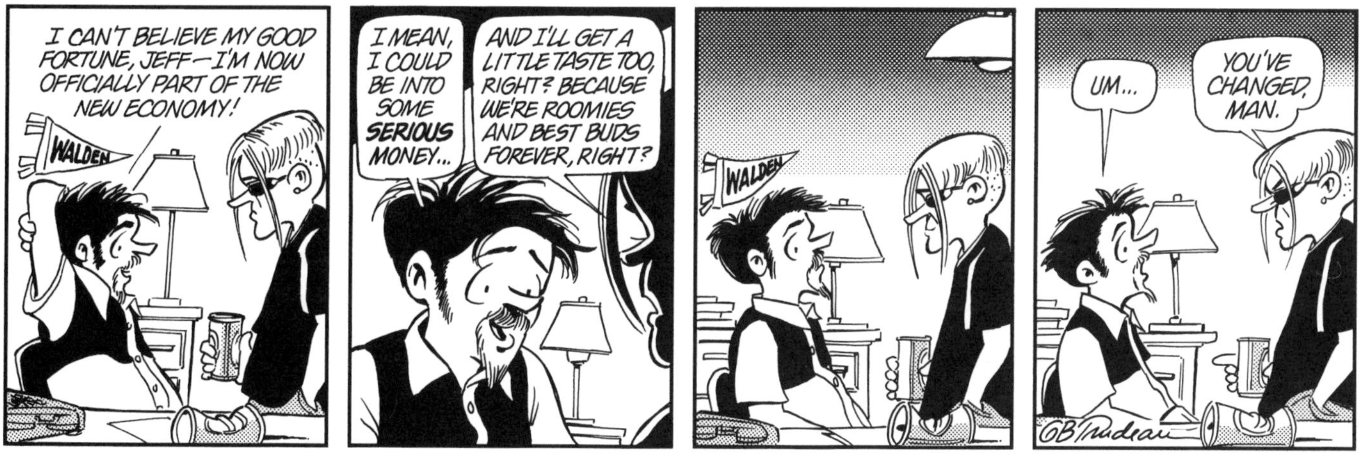
I CAN'T BELIEVE MY GOOD FORTUNE, JEFF—I'M NOW OFFICIALLY PART OF THE NEW ECONOMY!
I MEAN, I COULD BE INTO SOME SERIOUS MONEY...
AND I'LL GET A LITTLE TASTE TOO, RIGHT? BECAUSE WE'RE ROOMIES AND BEST BUDS FOREVER, RIGHT?
UM...
YOU'VE CHANGED, MAN.

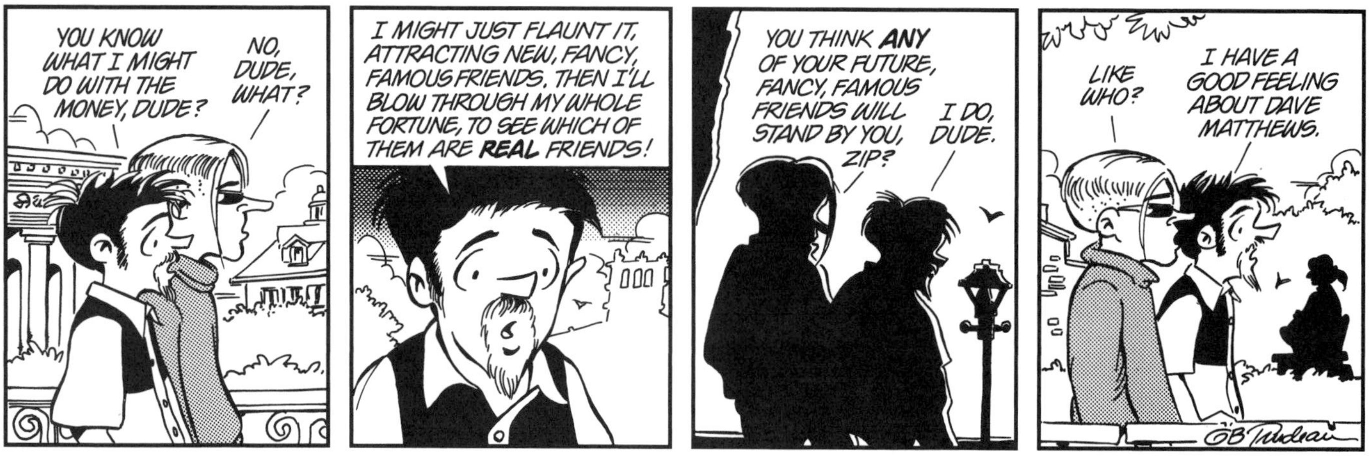
YOU KNOW WHAT I MIGHT DO WITH THE MONEY, DUDE?
NO, DUDE, WHAT?
I MIGHT JUST FLAUNT IT, ATTRACTING NEW, FANCY, FAMOUS FRIENDS. THEN I'LL BLOW THROUGH MY WHOLE FORTUNE, TO SEE WHICH OF THEM ARE REAL FRIENDS!
YOU THINK ANY OF YOUR FUTURE, FANCY, FAMOUS FRIENDS WILL STAND BY YOU, ZIP?
I DO, DUDE.
LIKE WHO?
I HAVE A GOOD FEELING ABOUT DAVE MATTHEWS.

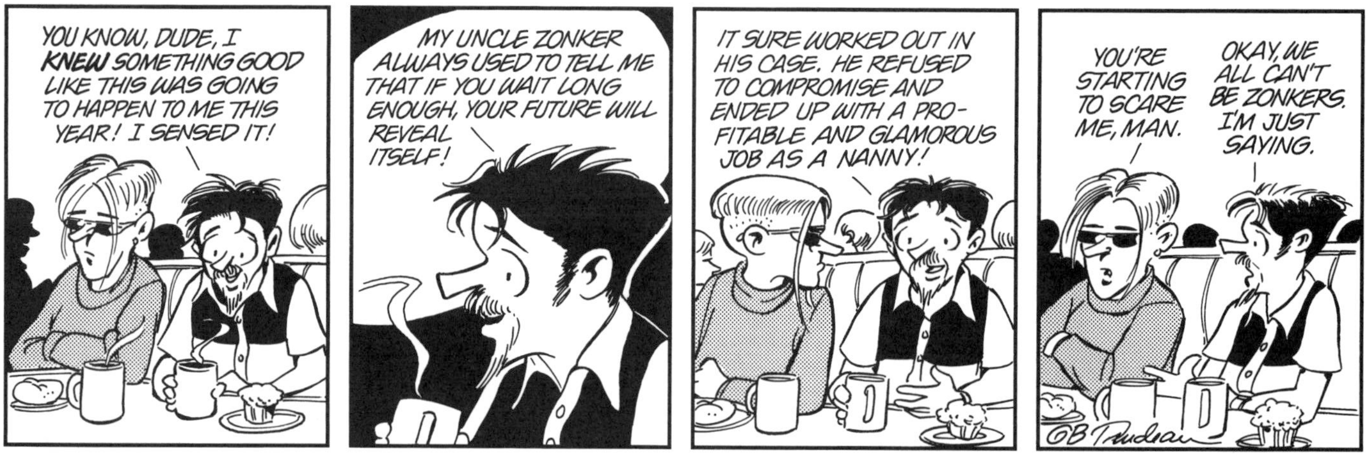
YOU KNOW, DUDE, I KNEW SOMETHING GOOD LIKE THIS WAS GOING TO HAPPEN TO ME THIS YEAR! I SENSED IT!
MY UNCLE ZONKER ALWAYS USED TO TELL ME THAT IF YOU WAIT LONG ENOUGH, YOUR FUTURE WILL REVEAL ITSELF!
IT SURE WORKED OUT IN HIS CASE. HE REFUSED TO COMPROMISE AND ENDED UP WITH A PROFITABLE AND GLAMOROUS JOB AS A NANNY!
YOU'RE STARTING TO SCARE ME, MAN.
OKAY, WE ALL CAN'T BE ZONKERS. I'M JUST SAYING.

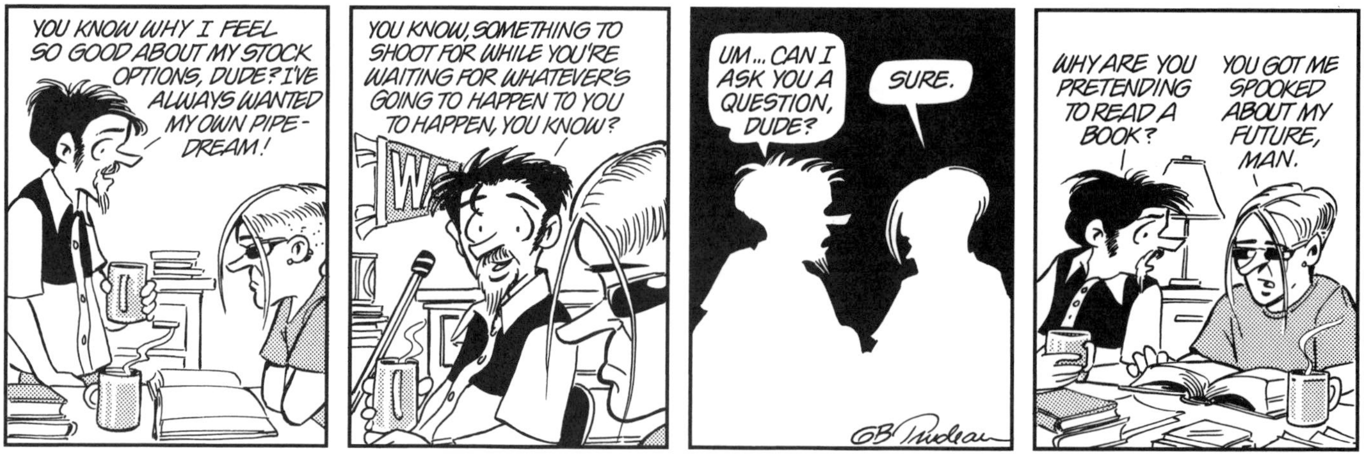
YOU KNOW WHY I FEEL SO GOOD ABOUT MY STOCK OPTIONS, DUDE? I'VE ALWAYS WANTED MY OWN PIPE-DREAM!
YOU KNOW, SOMETHING TO SHOOT FOR WHILE YOU'RE WAITING FOR WHATEVER'S GOING TO HAPPEN TO YOU TO HAPPEN, YOU KNOW?
UM... CAN I ASK YOU A QUESTION, DUDE?
SURE.
WHY ARE YOU PRETENDING TO READ A BOOK?
YOU GOT ME SPOOKED ABOUT MY FUTURE, MAN.

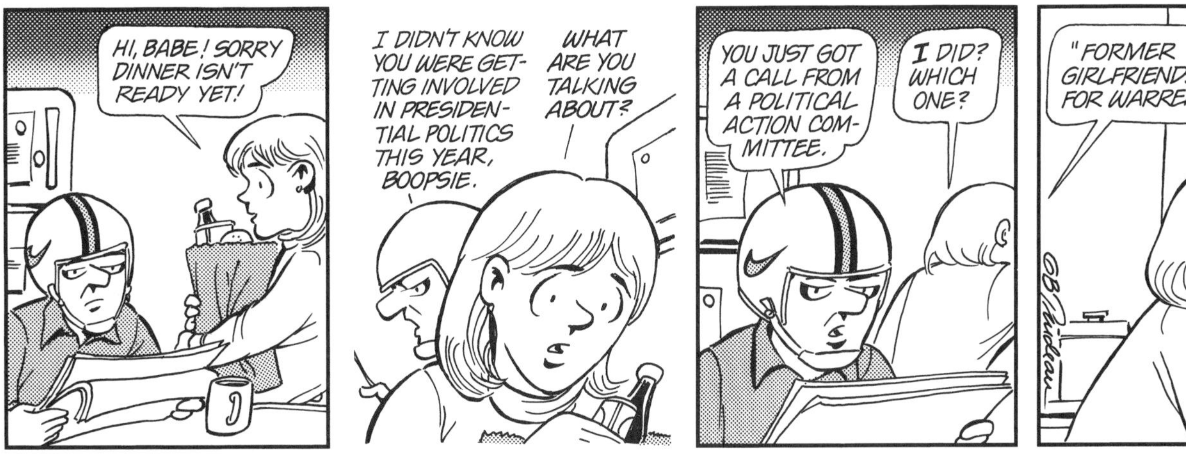
HI, BABE! SORRY DINNER ISN'T READY YET!
I DIDN'T KNOW YOU WERE GETTING INVOLVED IN PRESIDENTIAL POLITICS THIS YEAR, BOOPSIE.
WHAT ARE YOU TALKING ABOUT?
YOU JUST GOT A CALL FROM A POLITICAL ACTION COMMITTEE.
I DID? WHICH ONE?
"FORMER GIRLFRIENDS FOR WARREN."
UH-OH.

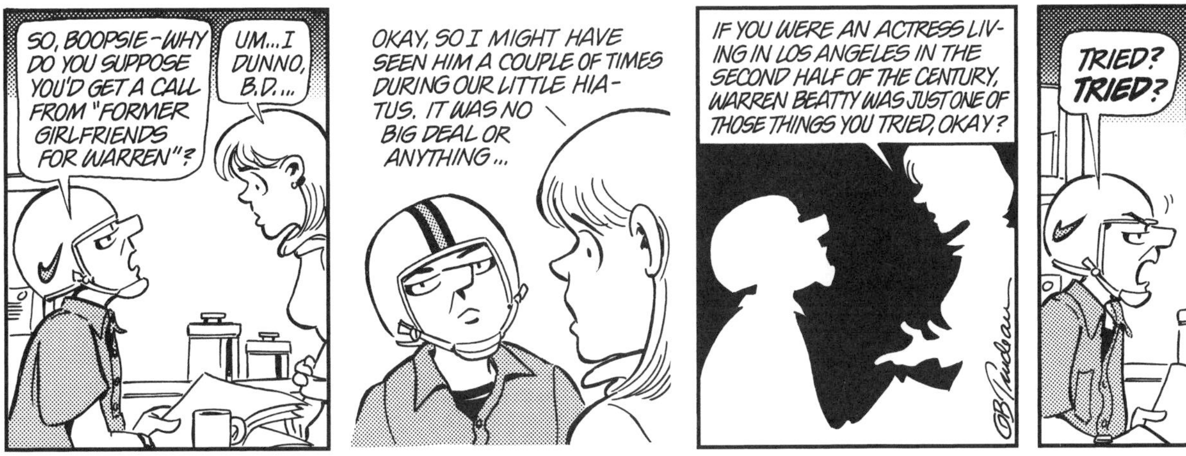
SO, BOOPSIE–WHY DO YOU SUPPOSE YOU'D GET A CALL FROM "FORMER GIRLFRIENDS FOR WARREN"?
UM...I DUNNO, B.D....
OKAY, SO I MIGHT HAVE SEEN HIM A COUPLE OF TIMES DURING OUR LITTLE HIATUS. IT WAS NO BIG DEAL OR ANYTHING...
IF YOU WERE AN ACTRESS LIVING IN LOS ANGELES IN THE SECOND HALF OF THE CENTURY, WARREN BEATTY WAS JUST ONE OF THOSE THINGS YOU TRIED, OKAY?
TRIED? TRIED?
LIKE A NEW RIDE AT UNIVERSAL. IT WAS LIKE, DONE THAT YET?

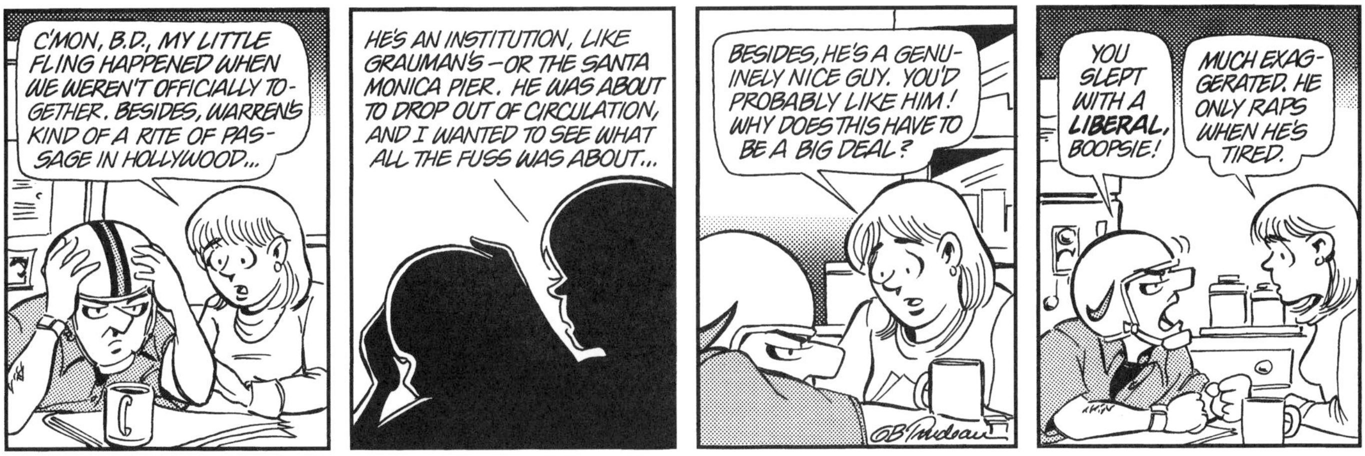
C'MON, B.D., MY LITTLE FLING HAPPENED WHEN WE WEREN'T OFFICIALLY TOGETHER. BESIDES, WARREN'S KIND OF A RITE OF PASSAGE IN HOLLYWOOD...
HE'S AN INSTITUTION, LIKE GRAUMAN'S–OR THE SANTA MONICA PIER. HE WAS ABOUT TO DROP OUT OF CIRCULATION, AND I WANTED TO SEE WHAT ALL THE FUSS WAS ABOUT...
BESIDES, HE'S A GENUINELY NICE GUY. YOU'D PROBABLY LIKE HIM! WHY DOES THIS HAVE TO BE A BIG DEAL?
YOU SLEPT WITH A LIBERAL, BOOPSIE!
MUCH EXAGGERATED. HE ONLY RAPS WHEN HE'S TIRED.

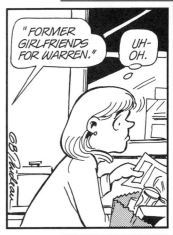

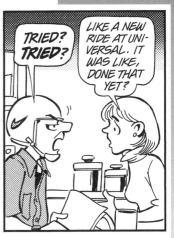

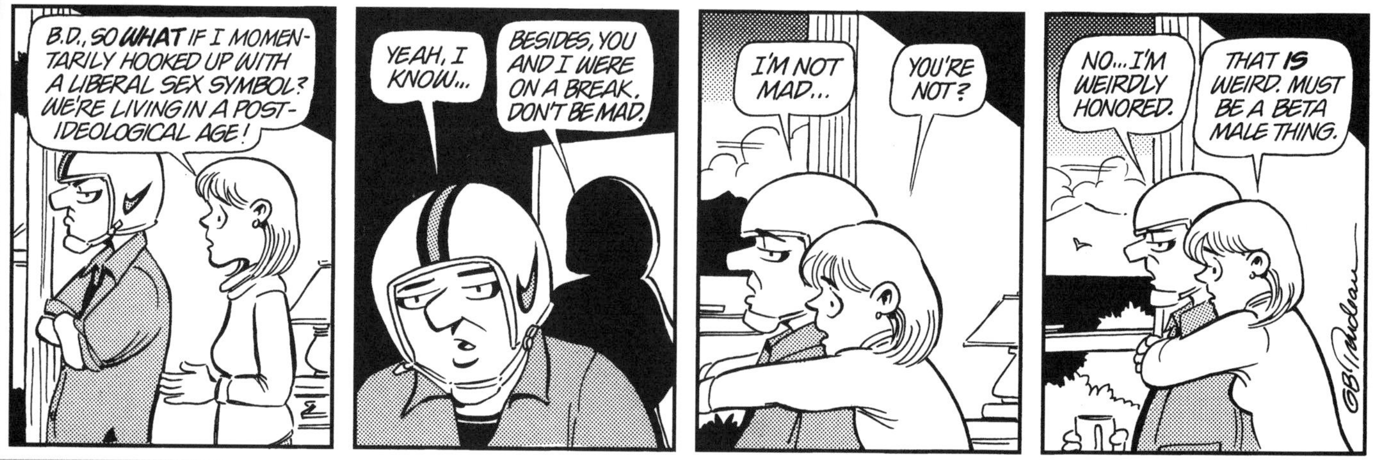
B.D., SO **WHAT** IF I MOMENTARILY HOOKED UP WITH A LIBERAL SEX SYMBOL? WE'RE LIVING IN A POST-IDEOLOGICAL AGE!
YEAH, I KNOW...
BESIDES, YOU AND I WERE ON A BREAK. DON'T BE MAD.
I'M NOT MAD...
YOU'RE NOT?
NO... I'M WEIRDLY HONORED.
THAT **IS** WEIRD. MUST BE A BETA MALE THING.
GBTrudeau

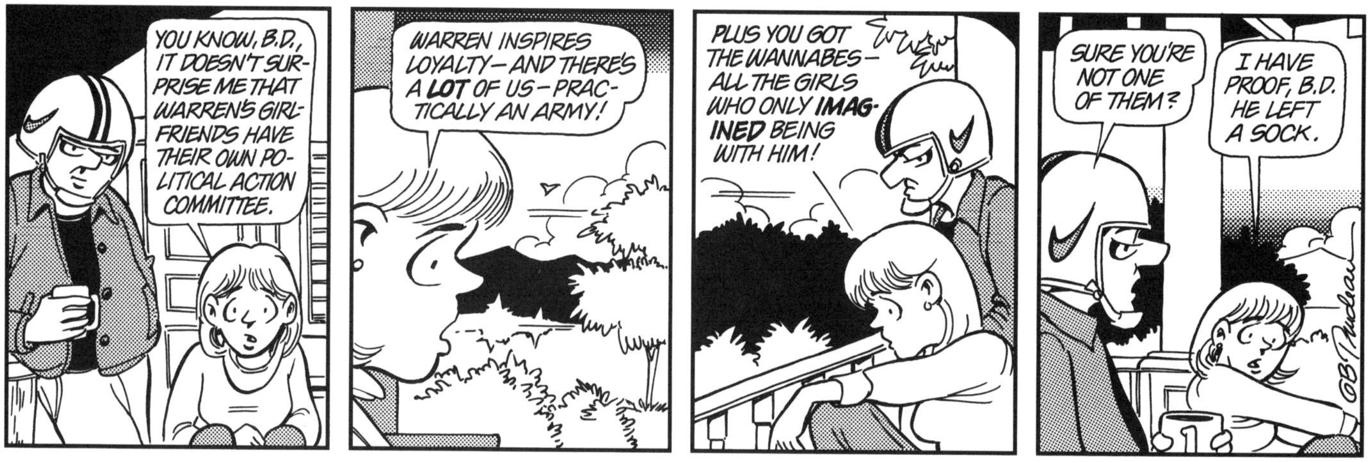
YOU KNOW, B.D., IT DOESN'T SURPRISE ME THAT WARREN'S GIRLFRIENDS HAVE THEIR OWN POLITICAL ACTION COMMITTEE.
WARREN INSPIRES LOYALTY—AND THERE'S A **LOT** OF US—PRACTICALLY AN ARMY!
PLUS YOU GOT THE WANNABES—ALL THE GIRLS WHO ONLY **IMAGINED** BEING WITH HIM!
SURE YOU'RE NOT ONE OF THEM?
I HAVE PROOF, B.D. HE LEFT A SOCK.
GBTrudeau

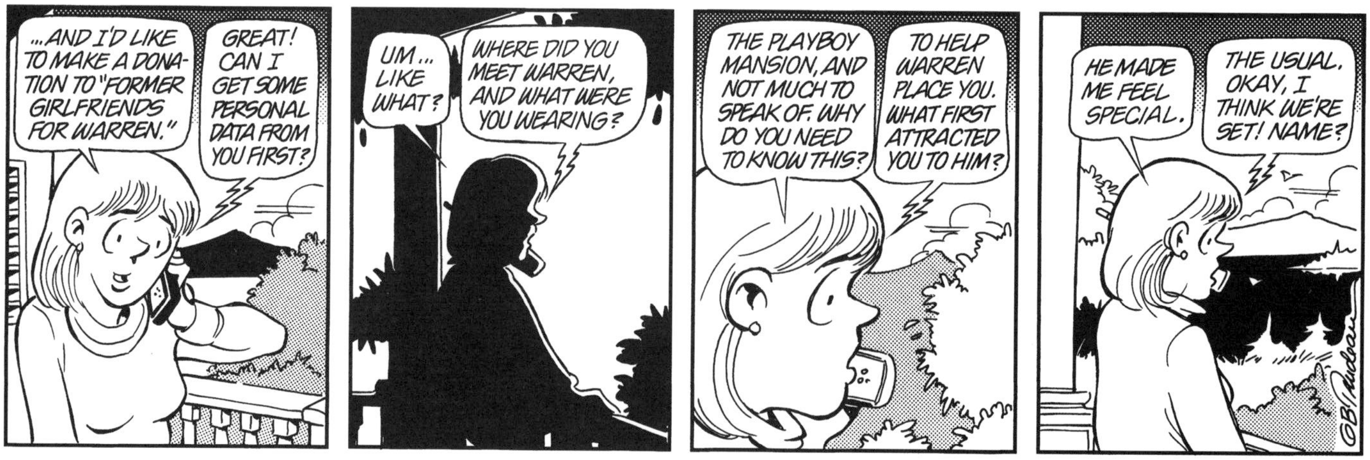
...AND I'D LIKE TO MAKE A DONATION TO "FORMER GIRLFRIENDS FOR WARREN."
GREAT! CAN I GET SOME PERSONAL DATA FROM YOU FIRST?
UM... LIKE WHAT?
WHERE DID YOU MEET WARREN, AND WHAT WERE YOU WEARING?
THE PLAYBOY MANSION, AND NOT MUCH TO SPEAK OF. WHY DO YOU NEED TO KNOW THIS?
TO HELP WARREN PLACE YOU. WHAT FIRST ATTRACTED YOU TO HIM?
HE MADE ME FEEL SPECIAL.
THE USUAL. OKAY, I THINK WE'RE SET! NAME?
GBTrudeau

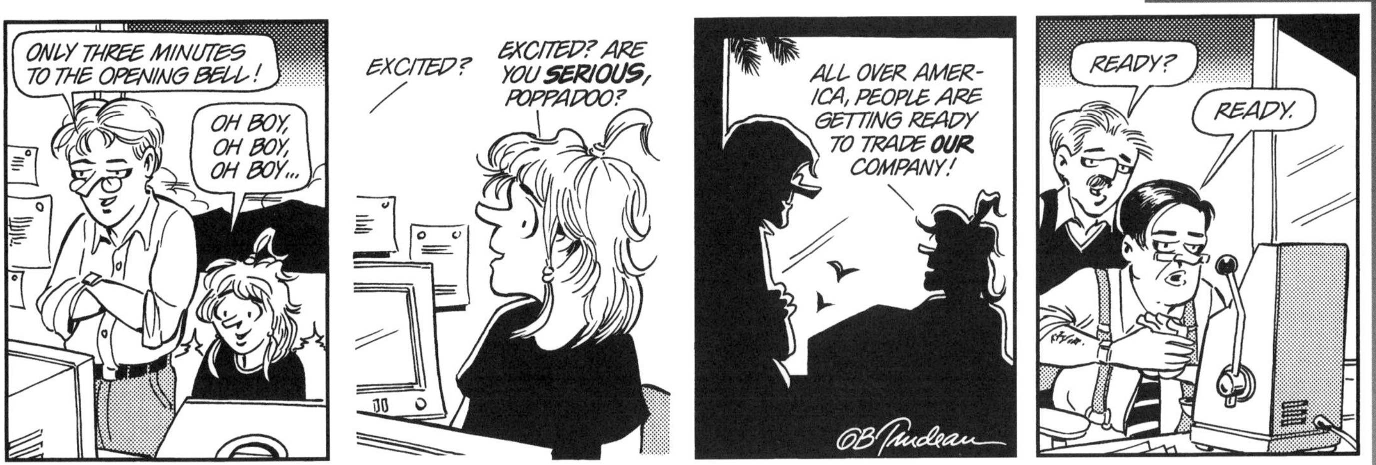
ONLY THREE MINUTES TO THE OPENING BELL!
OH BOY, OH BOY, OH BOY...
EXCITED?
EXCITED? ARE YOU SERIOUS, POPPADOO?
ALL OVER AMERICA, PEOPLE ARE GETTING READY TO TRADE OUR COMPANY!
READY?
READY.
©B Trudeau

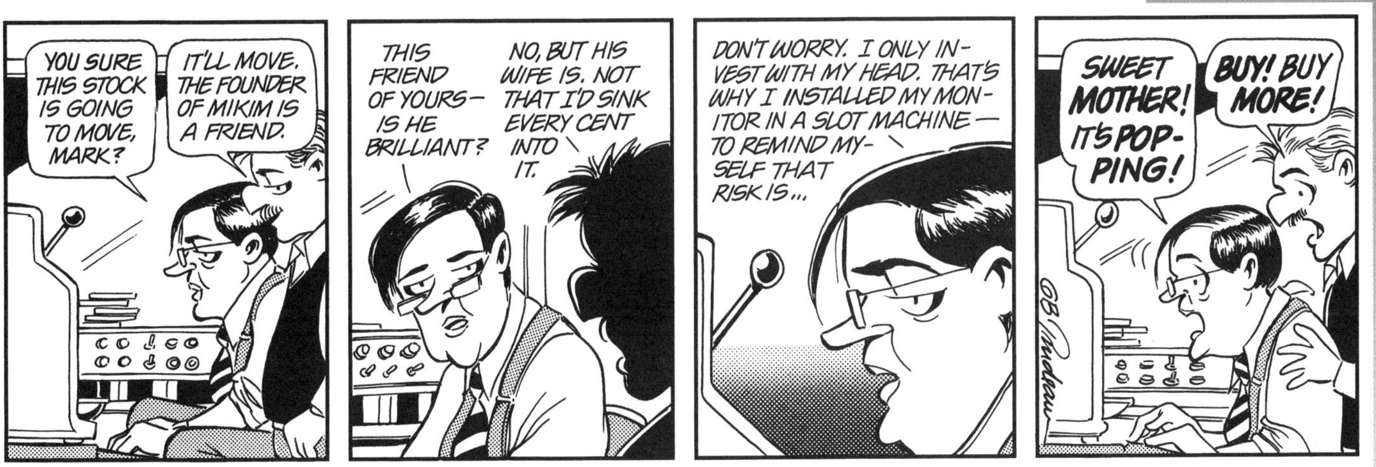
YOU SURE THIS STOCK IS GOING TO MOVE, MARK?
IT'LL MOVE. THE FOUNDER OF MIKIM IS A FRIEND.
THIS FRIEND OF YOURS–IS HE BRILLIANT?
NO, BUT HIS WIFE IS. NOT THAT I'D SINK EVERY CENT INTO IT.
DON'T WORRY. I ONLY INVEST WITH MY HEAD. THAT'S WHY I INSTALLED MY MONITOR IN A SLOT MACHINE — TO REMIND MYSELF THAT RISK IS...
SWEET MOTHER! IT'S POPPING!
BUY! BUY MORE!
©B Trudeau

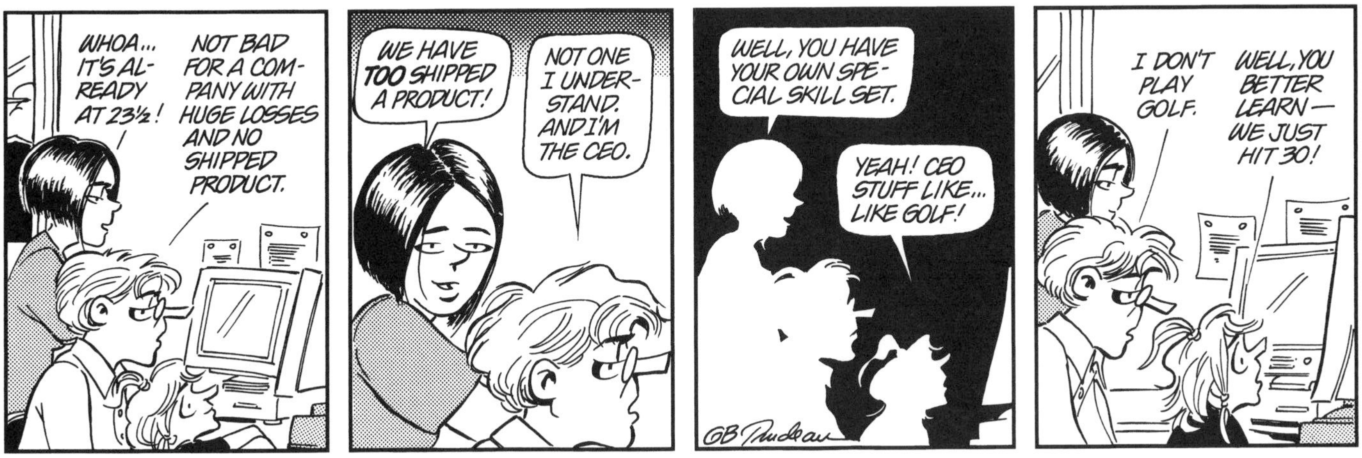
WHOA... IT'S ALREADY AT 23½!
NOT BAD FOR A COMPANY WITH HUGE LOSSES AND NO SHIPPED PRODUCT.
WE HAVE TOO SHIPPED A PRODUCT!
NOT ONE I UNDERSTAND. AND I'M THE CEO.
WELL, YOU HAVE YOUR OWN SPECIAL SKILL SET.
YEAH! CEO STUFF LIKE... LIKE GOLF!
©B Trudeau
I DON'T PLAY GOLF.
WELL, YOU BETTER LEARN— WE JUST HIT 30!

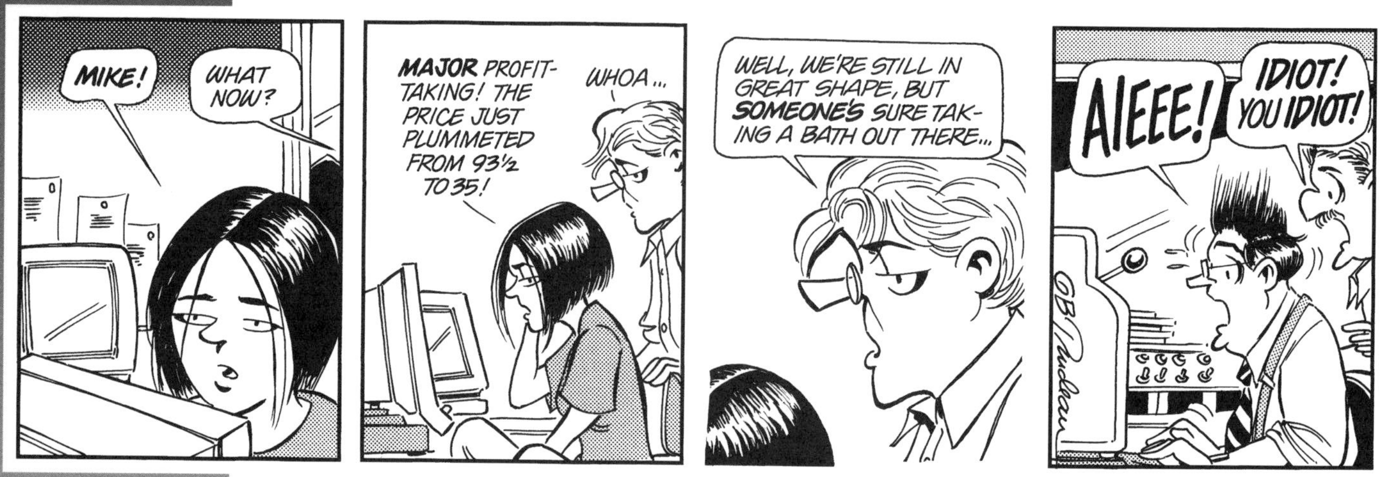
MIKE!
WHAT NOW?
MAJOR PROFIT-TAKING! THE PRICE JUST PLUMMETED FROM 93½ TO 35!
WHOA...
WELL, WE'RE STILL IN GREAT SHAPE, BUT SOMEONE'S SURE TAKING A BATH OUT THERE...
AIEEE!
IDIOT! YOU IDIOT!

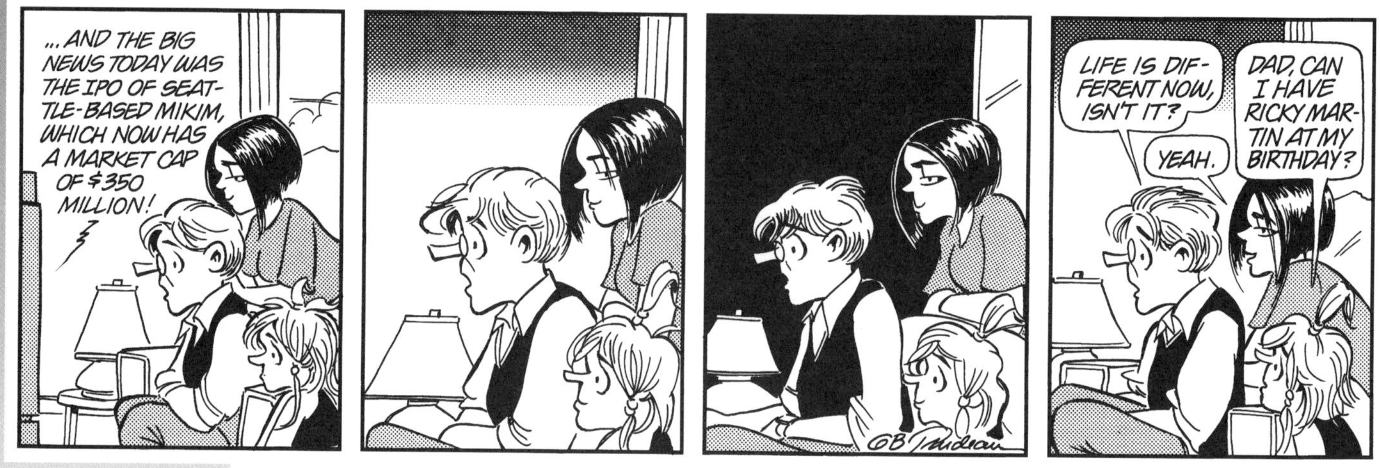
...AND THE BIG NEWS TODAY WAS THE IPO OF SEATTLE-BASED MIKIM, WHICH NOW HAS A MARKET CAP OF $350 MILLION!
LIFE IS DIFFERENT NOW, ISN'T IT?
YEAH.
DAD, CAN I HAVE RICKY MARTIN AT MY BIRTHDAY?

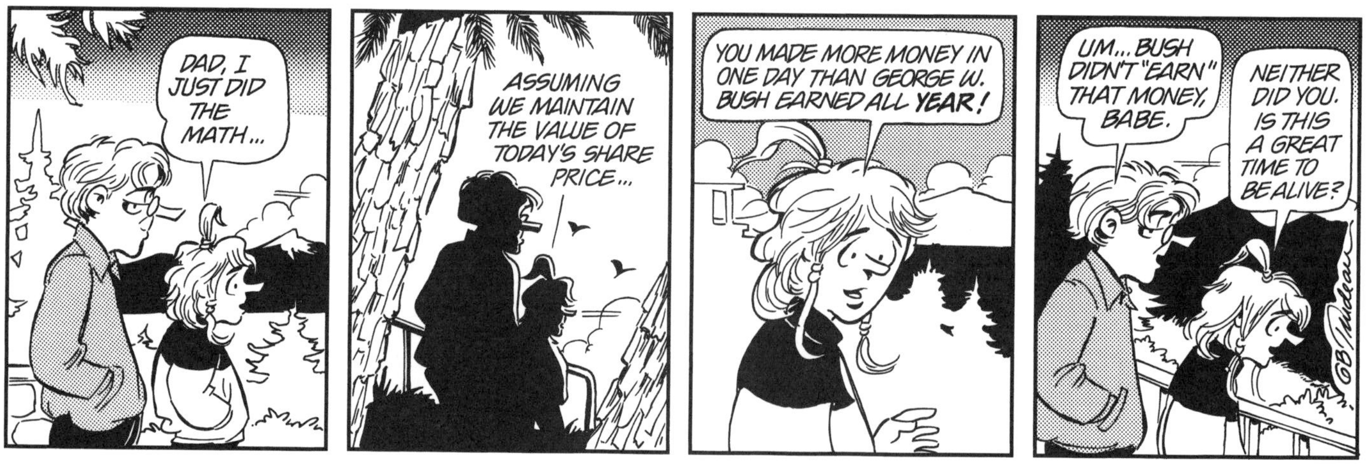
DAD, I JUST DID THE MATH...
ASSUMING WE MAINTAIN THE VALUE OF TODAY'S SHARE PRICE...
YOU MADE MORE MONEY IN ONE DAY THAN GEORGE W. BUSH EARNED ALL YEAR!
UM... BUSH DIDN'T "EARN" THAT MONEY, BABE.
NEITHER DID YOU. IS THIS A GREAT TIME TO BE ALIVE?

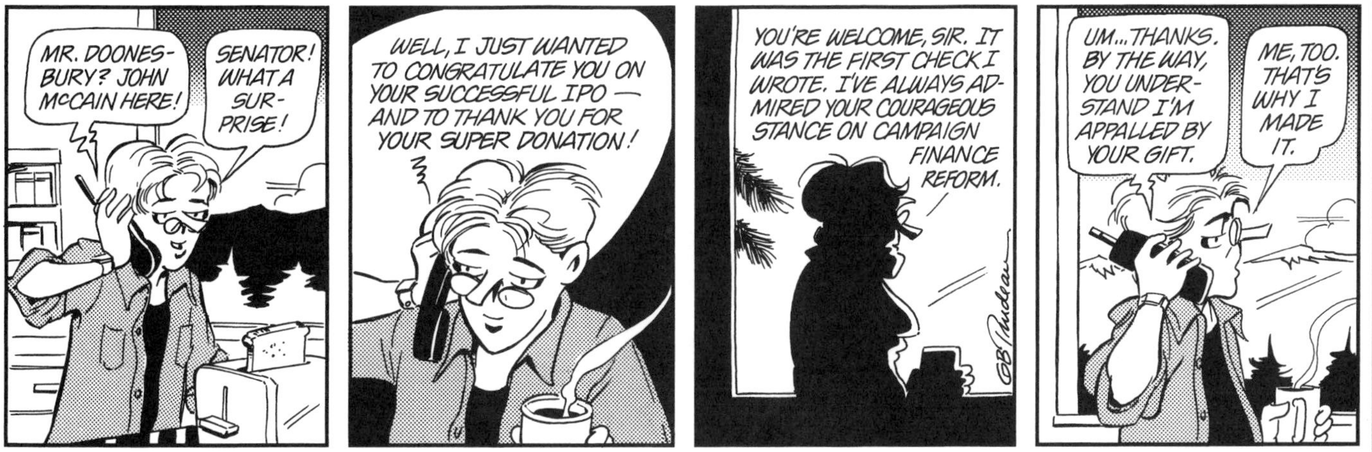
MR. DOONESBURY? JOHN McCAIN HERE!
SENATOR! WHAT A SURPRISE!
WELL, I JUST WANTED TO CONGRATULATE YOU ON YOUR SUCCESSFUL IPO — AND TO THANK YOU FOR YOUR SUPER DONATION!
YOU'RE WELCOME, SIR. IT WAS THE FIRST CHECK I WROTE. I'VE ALWAYS ADMIRED YOUR COURAGEOUS STANCE ON CAMPAIGN FINANCE REFORM.
UM... THANKS. BY THE WAY, YOU UNDERSTAND I'M APPALLED BY YOUR GIFT.
ME, TOO. THAT'S WHY I MADE IT.

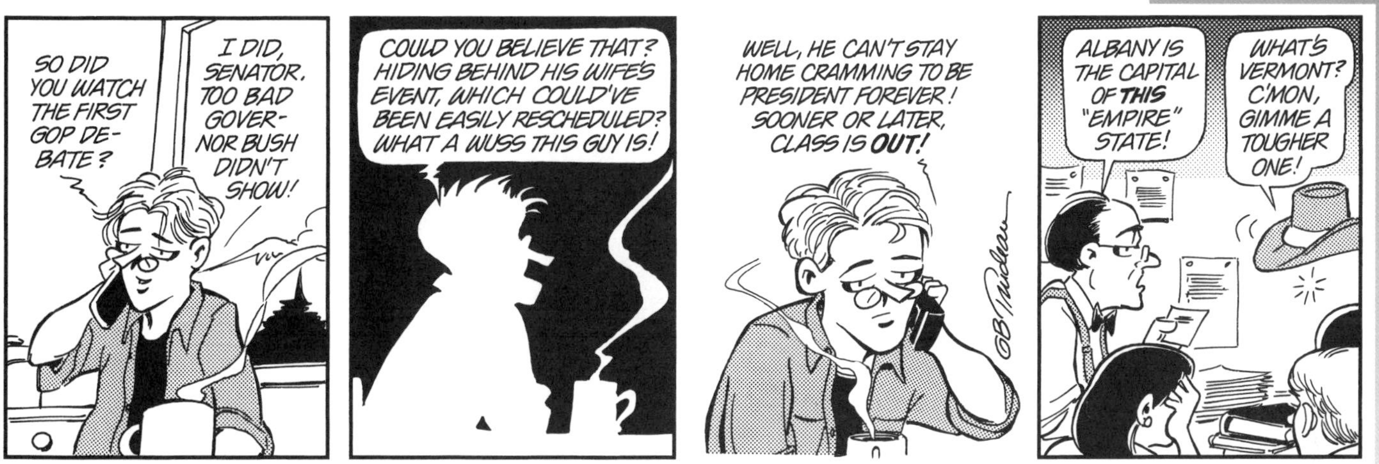
SO DID YOU WATCH THE FIRST GOP DEBATE?
I DID, SENATOR. TOO BAD GOVERNOR BUSH DIDN'T SHOW!
COULD YOU BELIEVE THAT? HIDING BEHIND HIS WIFE'S EVENT, WHICH COULD'VE BEEN EASILY RESCHEDULED? WHAT A WUSS THIS GUY IS!
WELL, HE CAN'T STAY HOME CRAMMING TO BE PRESIDENT FOREVER! SOONER OR LATER, CLASS IS OUT!
ALBANY IS THE CAPITAL OF THIS "EMPIRE" STATE!
WHAT'S VERMONT? C'MON, GIMME A TOUGHER ONE!

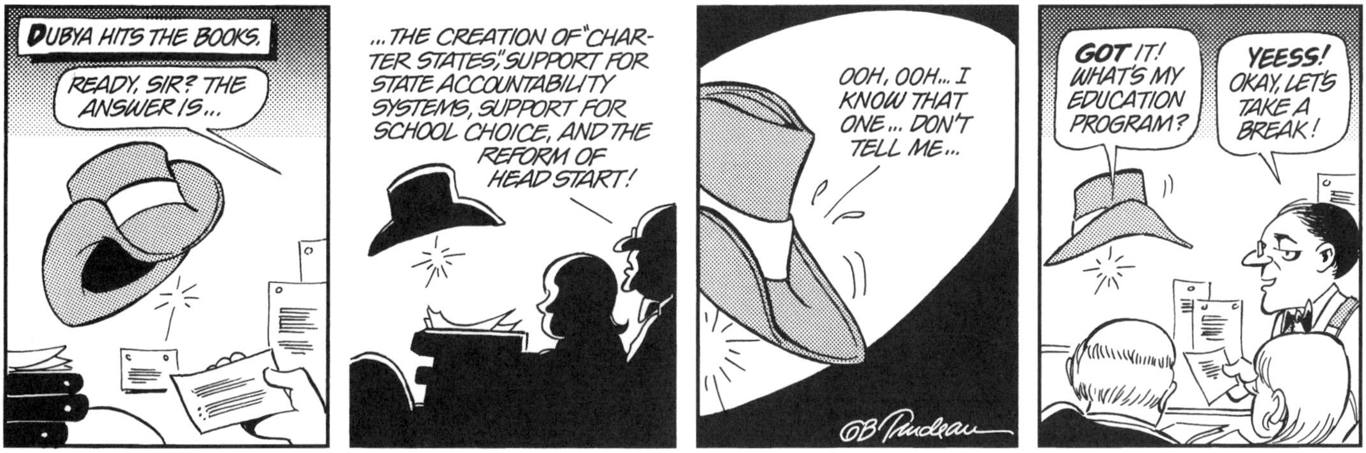
DUBYA HITS THE BOOKS.
READY, SIR? THE ANSWER IS...
...THE CREATION OF "CHARTER STATES," SUPPORT FOR STATE ACCOUNTABILITY SYSTEMS, SUPPORT FOR SCHOOL CHOICE, AND THE REFORM OF HEAD START!
OOH, OOH... I KNOW THAT ONE... DON'T TELL ME...
GOT IT! WHAT'S MY EDUCATION PROGRAM?
YEESS! OKAY, LET'S TAKE A BREAK!

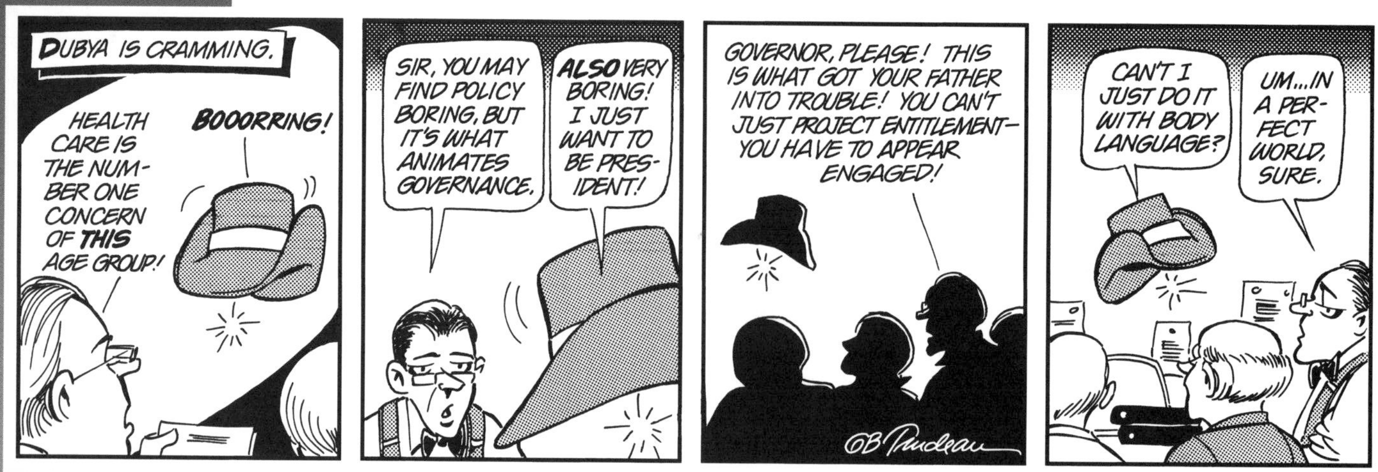
DUBYA IS CRAMMING.
HEALTH CARE IS THE NUMBER ONE CONCERN OF THIS AGE GROUP!
BOOORRING!
SIR, YOU MAY FIND POLICY BORING, BUT IT'S WHAT ANIMATES GOVERNANCE.
ALSO VERY BORING! I JUST WANT TO BE PRESIDENT!
GOVERNOR, PLEASE! THIS IS WHAT GOT YOUR FATHER INTO TROUBLE! YOU CAN'T JUST PROJECT ENTITLEMENT— YOU HAVE TO APPEAR ENGAGED!
G.B. Trudeau
CAN'T I JUST DO IT WITH BODY LANGUAGE?
UM...IN A PERFECT WORLD, SURE.

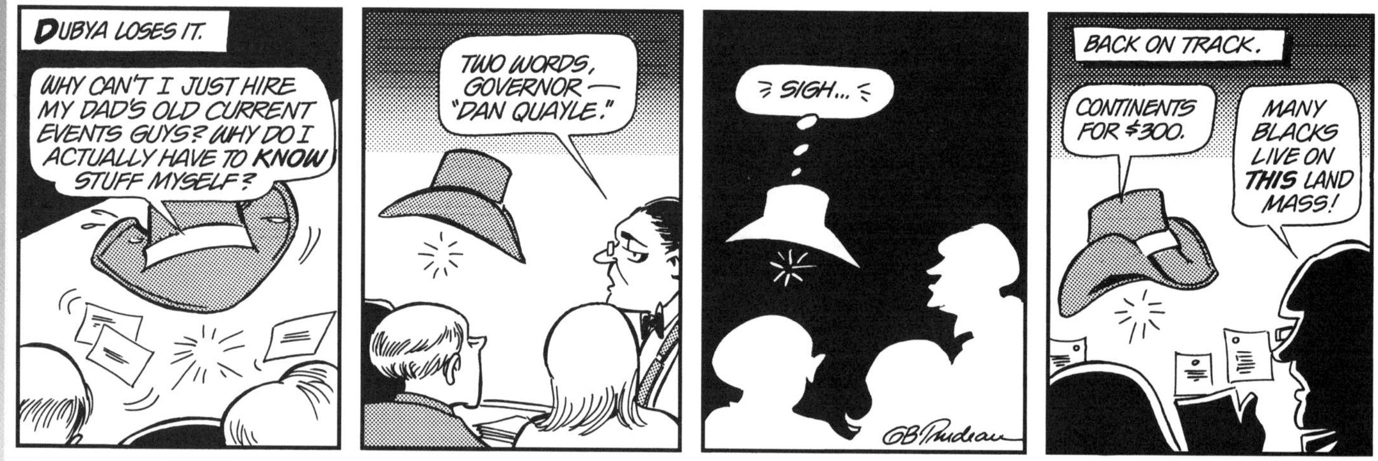
DUBYA LOSES IT.
WHY CAN'T I JUST HIRE MY DAD'S OLD CURRENT EVENTS GUYS? WHY DO I ACTUALLY HAVE TO KNOW STUFF MYSELF?
TWO WORDS, GOVERNOR— "DAN QUAYLE."
SIGH...
G.B. Trudeau
BACK ON TRACK.
CONTINENTS FOR $300.
MANY BLACKS LIVE ON THIS LAND MASS!

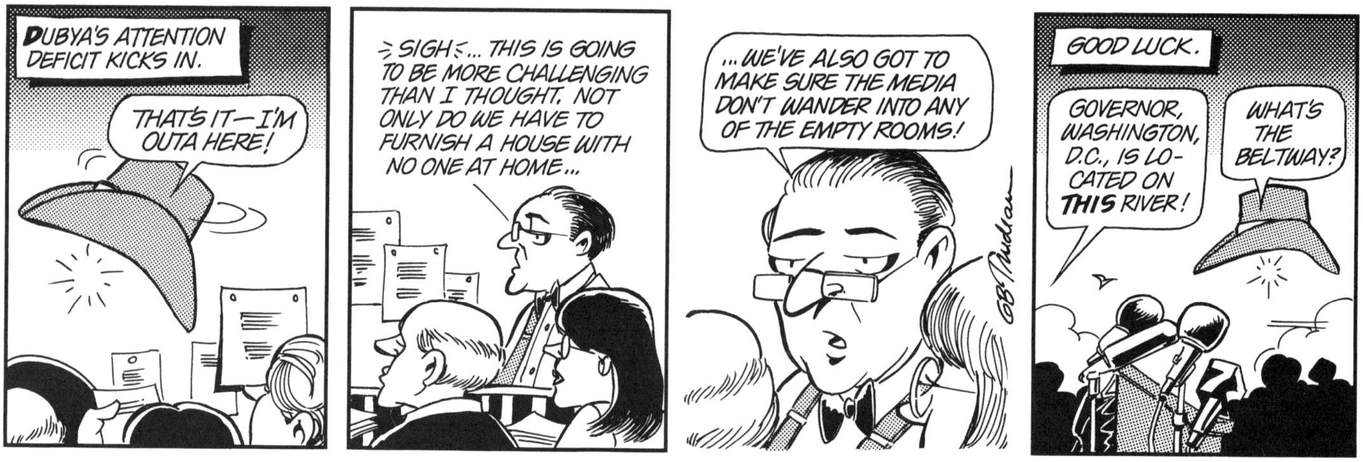
DUBYA'S ATTENTION DEFICIT KICKS IN.
THAT'S IT—I'M OUTA HERE!
SIGH... THIS IS GOING TO BE MORE CHALLENGING THAN I THOUGHT. NOT ONLY DO WE HAVE TO FURNISH A HOUSE WITH NO ONE AT HOME...
...WE'VE ALSO GOT TO MAKE SURE THE MEDIA DON'T WANDER INTO ANY OF THE EMPTY ROOMS!
G.B. Trudeau
GOOD LUCK.
GOVERNOR, WASHINGTON, D.C., IS LOCATED ON THIS RIVER!
WHAT'S THE BELTWAY?

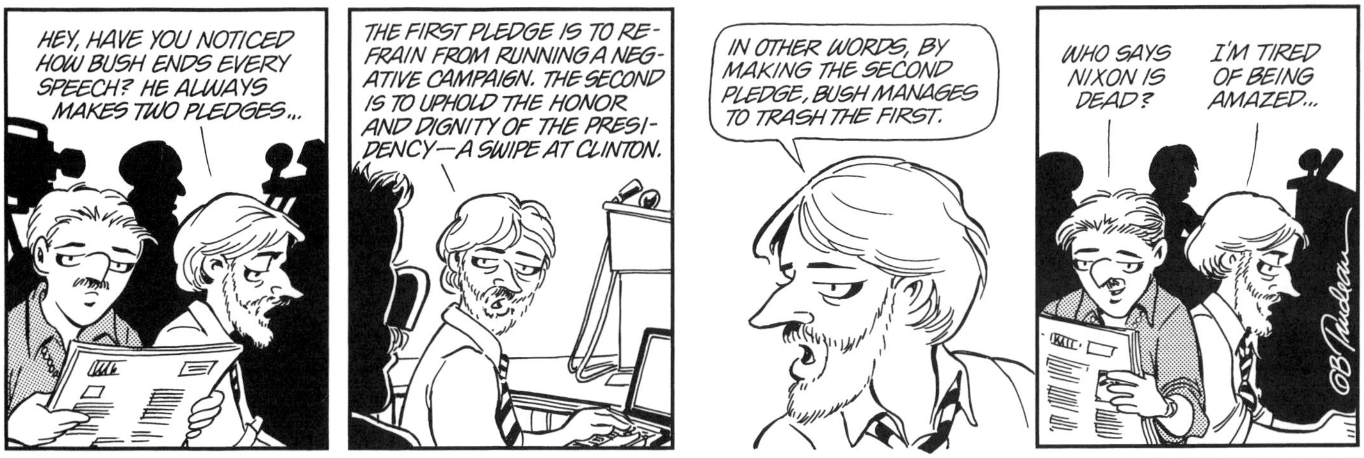
HEY, HAVE YOU NOTICED HOW BUSH ENDS EVERY SPEECH? HE ALWAYS MAKES TWO PLEDGES...
THE FIRST PLEDGE IS TO REFRAIN FROM RUNNING A NEGATIVE CAMPAIGN. THE SECOND IS TO UPHOLD THE HONOR AND DIGNITY OF THE PRESIDENCY—A SWIPE AT CLINTON.
IN OTHER WORDS, BY MAKING THE SECOND PLEDGE, BUSH MANAGES TO TRASH THE FIRST.
WHO SAYS NIXON IS DEAD?
I'M TIRED OF BEING AMAZED...

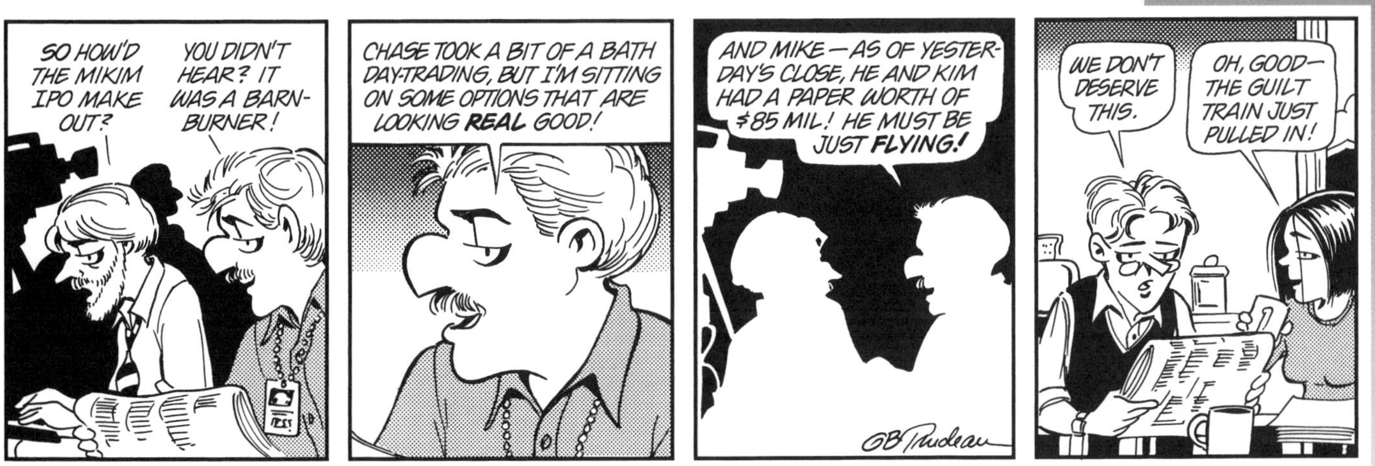
SO HOW'D THE MIKIM IPO MAKE OUT?
YOU DIDN'T HEAR? IT WAS A BARN-BURNER!
CHASE TOOK A BIT OF A BATH DAY-TRADING, BUT I'M SITTING ON SOME OPTIONS THAT ARE LOOKING **REAL** GOOD!
AND MIKE—AS OF YESTERDAY'S CLOSE, HE AND KIM HAD A PAPER WORTH OF $85 MIL! HE MUST BE JUST **FLYING!**
WE DON'T DESERVE THIS.
OH, GOOD—THE GUILT TRAIN JUST PULLED IN!

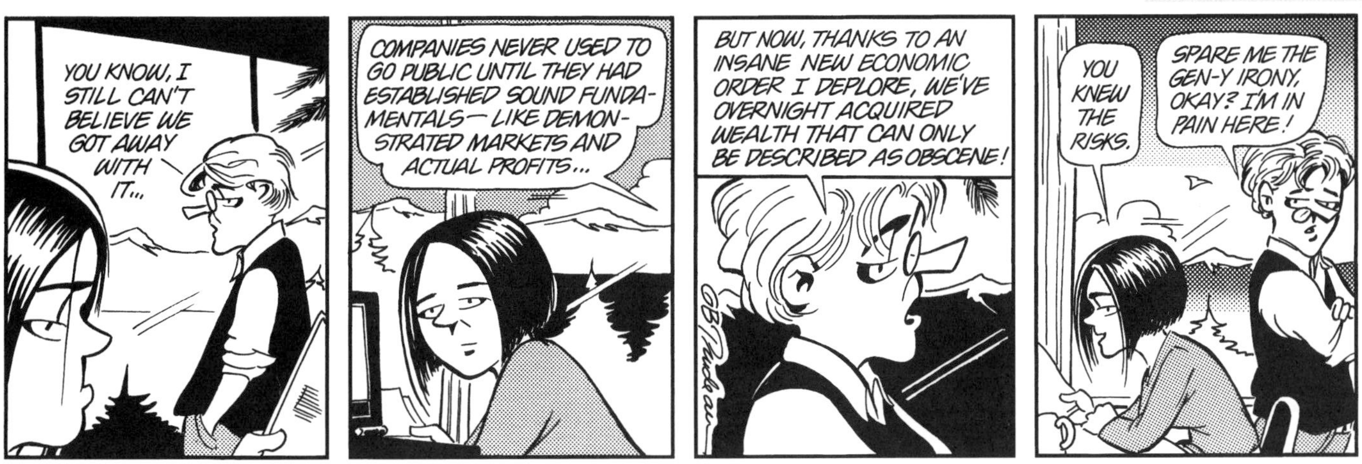
YOU KNOW, I STILL CAN'T BELIEVE WE GOT AWAY WITH IT...
COMPANIES NEVER USED TO GO PUBLIC UNTIL THEY HAD ESTABLISHED SOUND FUNDAMENTALS—LIKE DEMONSTRATED MARKETS AND ACTUAL PROFITS...
BUT NOW, THANKS TO AN INSANE NEW ECONOMIC ORDER I DEPLORE, WE'VE OVERNIGHT ACQUIRED WEALTH THAT CAN ONLY BE DESCRIBED AS OBSCENE!
YOU KNEW THE RISKS.
SPARE ME THE GEN-Y IRONY, OKAY? I'M IN PAIN HERE!

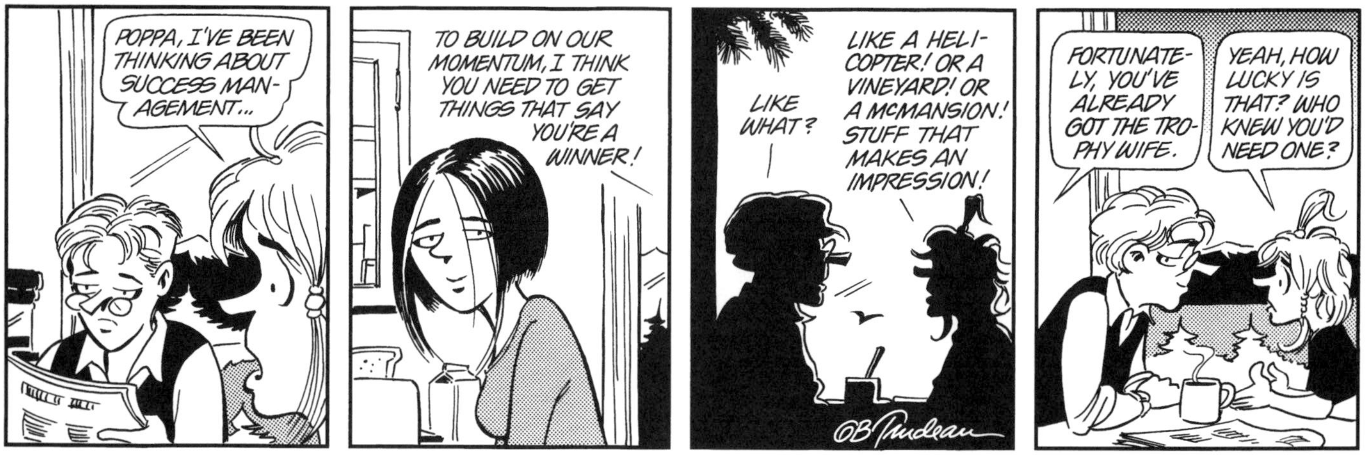
POPPA, I'VE BEEN THINKING ABOUT SUCCESS MAN-AGEMENT...
TO BUILD ON OUR MOMENTUM, I THINK YOU NEED TO GET THINGS THAT SAY YOU'RE A WINNER!
LIKE WHAT?
LIKE A HELI-COPTER! OR A VINEYARD! OR A McMANSION! STUFF THAT MAKES AN IMPRESSION!
FORTUNATE-LY, YOU'VE ALREADY GOT THE TRO-PHY WIFE.
YEAH, HOW LUCKY IS THAT? WHO KNEW YOU'D NEED ONE?

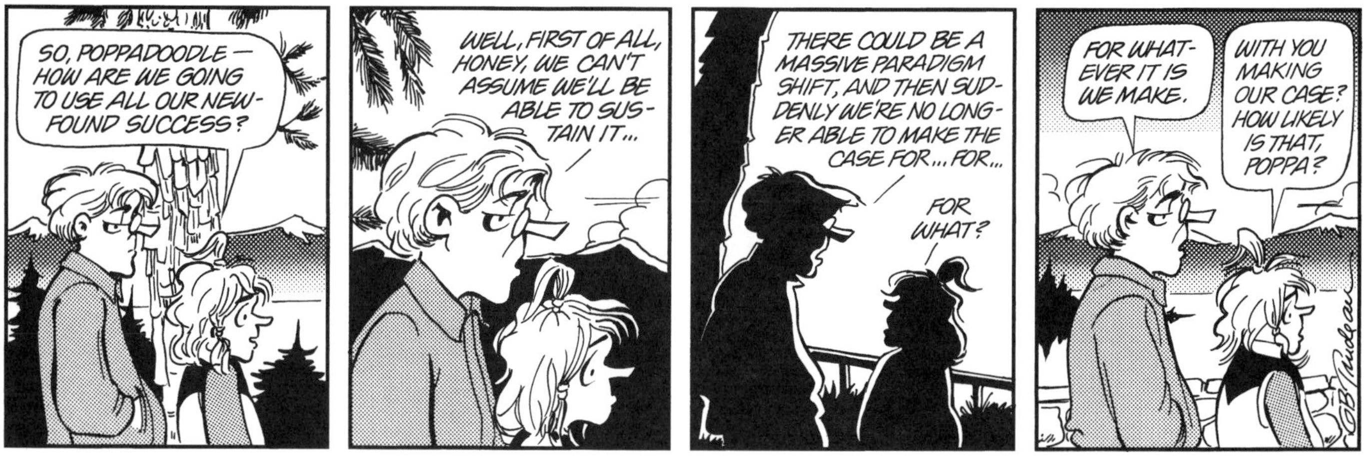
SO, POPPADOODLE — HOW ARE WE GOING TO USE ALL OUR NEW-FOUND SUCCESS?
WELL, FIRST OF ALL, HONEY, WE CAN'T ASSUME WE'LL BE ABLE TO SUS-TAIN IT...
THERE COULD BE A MASSIVE PARADIGM SHIFT, AND THEN SUD-DENLY WE'RE NO LONG-ER ABLE TO MAKE THE CASE FOR... FOR...
FOR WHAT?
FOR WHAT-EVER IT IS WE MAKE.
WITH YOU MAKING OUR CASE? HOW LIKELY IS THAT, POPPA?

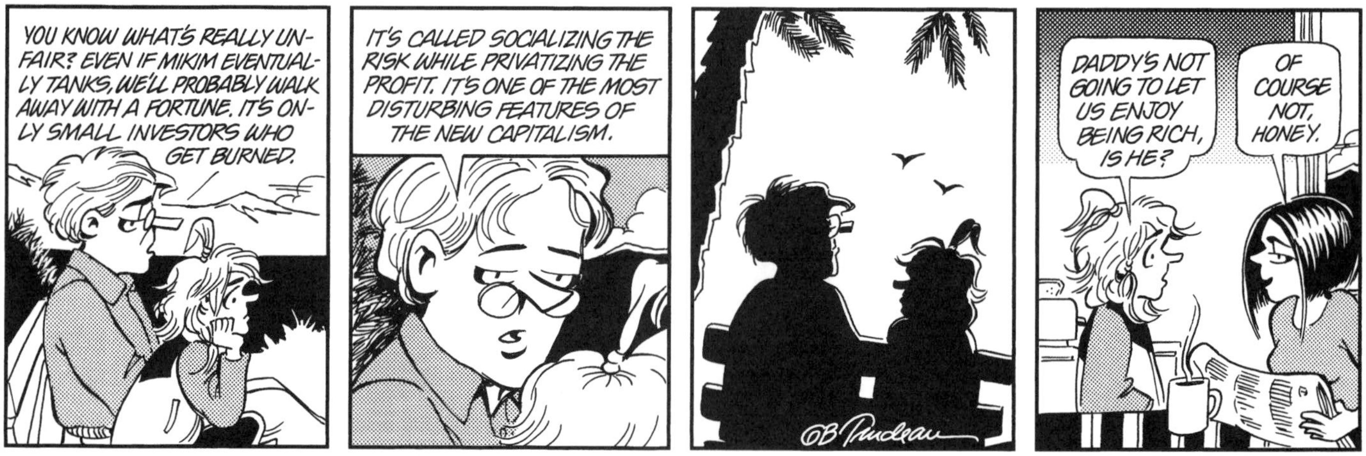
YOU KNOW WHAT'S REALLY UN-FAIR? EVEN IF MIKIM EVENTUAL-LY TANKS, WE'LL PROBABLY WALK AWAY WITH A FORTUNE. IT'S ON-LY SMALL INVESTORS WHO GET BURNED.
IT'S CALLED SOCIALIZING THE RISK WHILE PRIVATIZING THE PROFIT. IT'S ONE OF THE MOST DISTURBING FEATURES OF THE NEW CAPITALISM.
DADDY'S NOT GOING TO LET US ENJOY BEING RICH, IS HE?
OF COURSE NOT, HONEY.

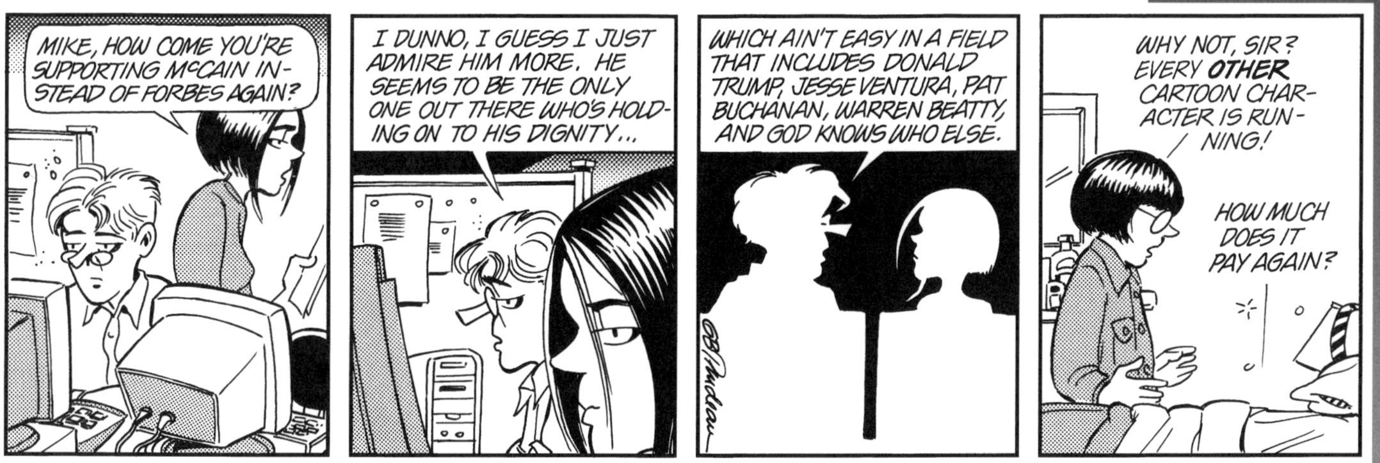
MIKE, HOW COME YOU'RE SUPPORTING McCAIN INSTEAD OF FORBES AGAIN?
I DUNNO, I GUESS I JUST ADMIRE HIM MORE. HE SEEMS TO BE THE ONLY ONE OUT THERE WHO'S HOLDING ON TO HIS DIGNITY...
WHICH AIN'T EASY IN A FIELD THAT INCLUDES DONALD TRUMP, JESSE VENTURA, PAT BUCHANAN, WARREN BEATTY, AND GOD KNOWS WHO ELSE.
WHY NOT, SIR? EVERY **OTHER** CARTOON CHARACTER IS RUNNING!
HOW MUCH DOES IT PAY AGAIN?

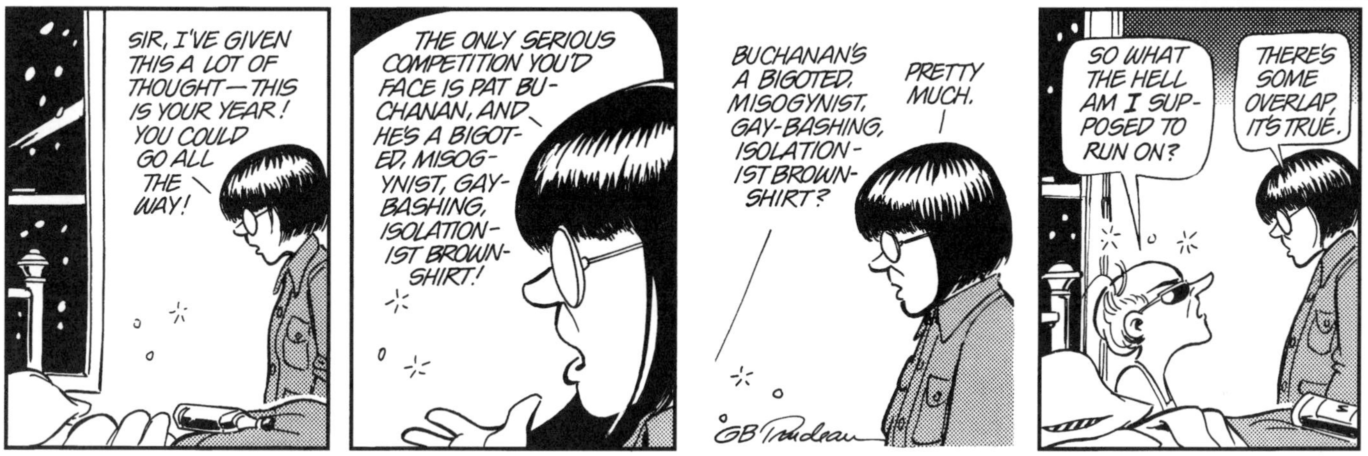
SIR, I'VE GIVEN THIS A LOT OF THOUGHT—THIS IS YOUR YEAR! YOU COULD GO ALL THE WAY!
THE ONLY SERIOUS COMPETITION YOU'D FACE IS PAT BUCHANAN, AND HE'S A BIGOTED, MISOGYNIST, GAY-BASHING, ISOLATIONIST BROWNSHIRT!
BUCHANAN'S A BIGOTED, MISOGYNIST, GAY-BASHING, ISOLATIONIST BROWNSHIRT?
PRETTY MUCH.
SO WHAT THE HELL AM **I** SUPPOSED TO RUN ON?
THERE'S SOME OVERLAP, IT'S TRUE.

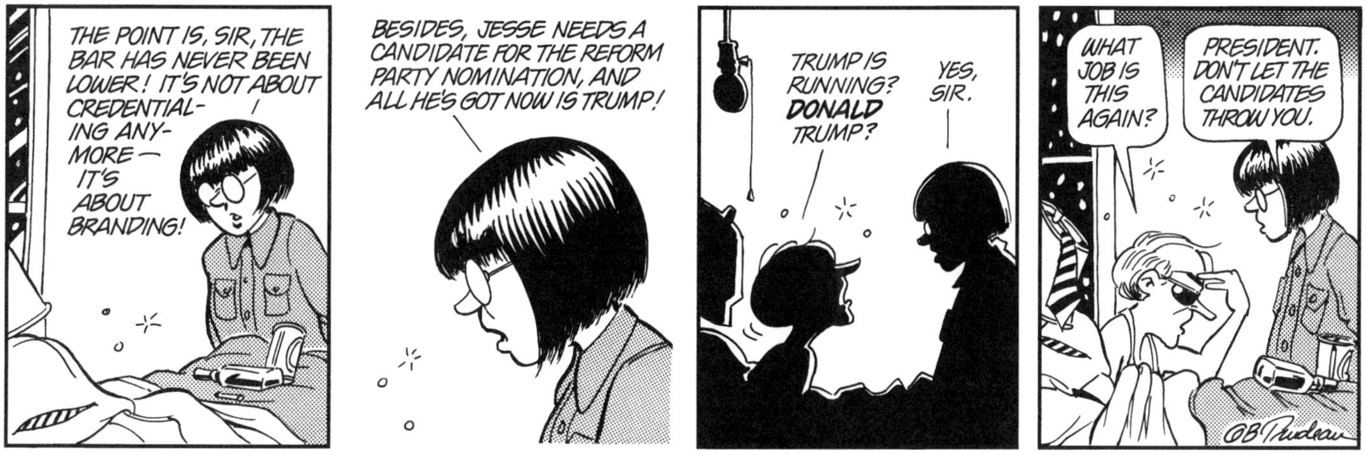
THE POINT IS, SIR, THE BAR HAS NEVER BEEN LOWER! IT'S NOT ABOUT CREDENTIALING ANYMORE—IT'S ABOUT BRANDING!
BESIDES, JESSE NEEDS A CANDIDATE FOR THE REFORM PARTY NOMINATION, AND ALL HE'S GOT NOW IS TRUMP!
TRUMP IS RUNNING? **DONALD** TRUMP?
YES, SIR.
WHAT JOB IS THIS AGAIN?
PRESIDENT. DON'T LET THE CANDIDATES THROW YOU.

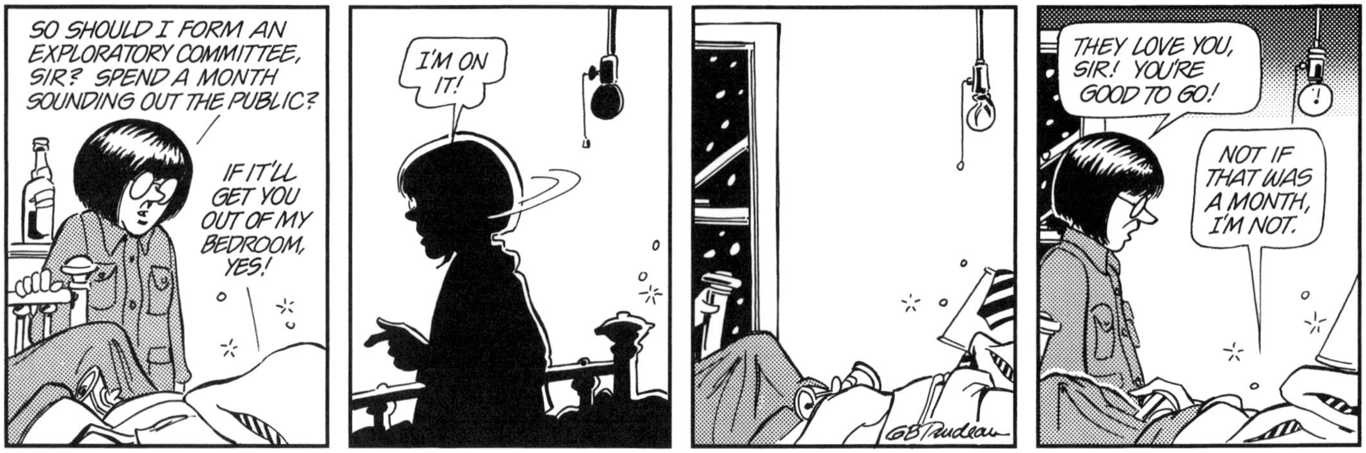
SO SHOULD I FORM AN EXPLORATORY COMMITTEE, SIR? SPEND A MONTH SOUNDING OUT THE PUBLIC?
IF IT'LL GET YOU OUT OF MY BEDROOM, YES!
I'M ON IT!
THEY LOVE YOU, SIR! YOU'RE GOOD TO GO!
NOT IF THAT WAS A MONTH, I'M NOT.

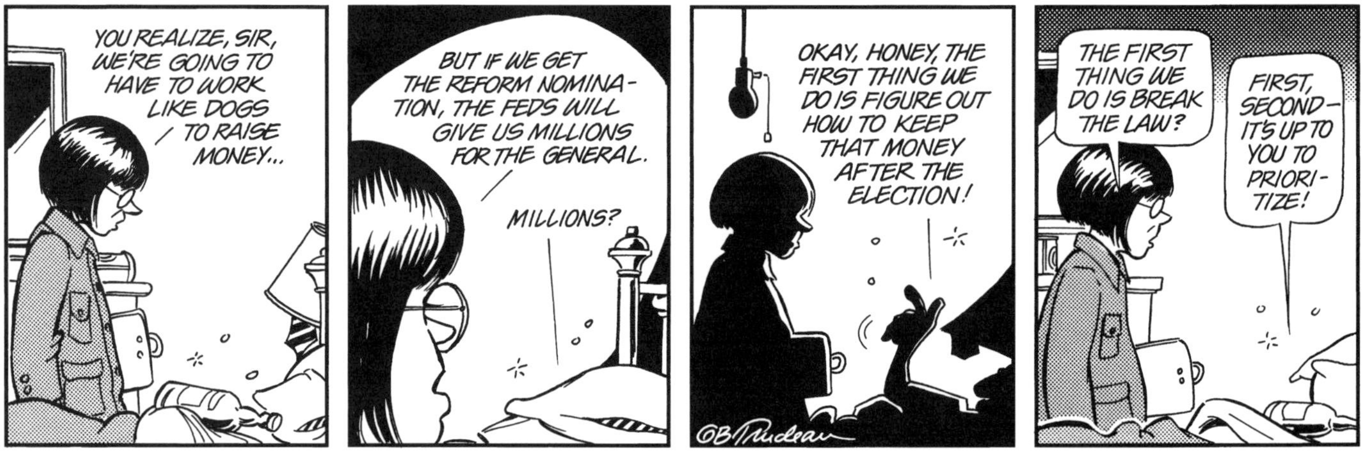
YOU REALIZE, SIR, WE'RE GOING TO HAVE TO WORK LIKE DOGS TO RAISE MONEY...
BUT IF WE GET THE REFORM NOMINATION, THE FEDS WILL GIVE US MILLIONS FOR THE GENERAL.
MILLIONS?
OKAY, HONEY, THE FIRST THING WE DO IS FIGURE OUT HOW TO KEEP THAT MONEY AFTER THE ELECTION!
THE FIRST THING WE DO IS BREAK THE LAW?
FIRST, SECOND– IT'S UP TO YOU TO PRIORI-TIZE!

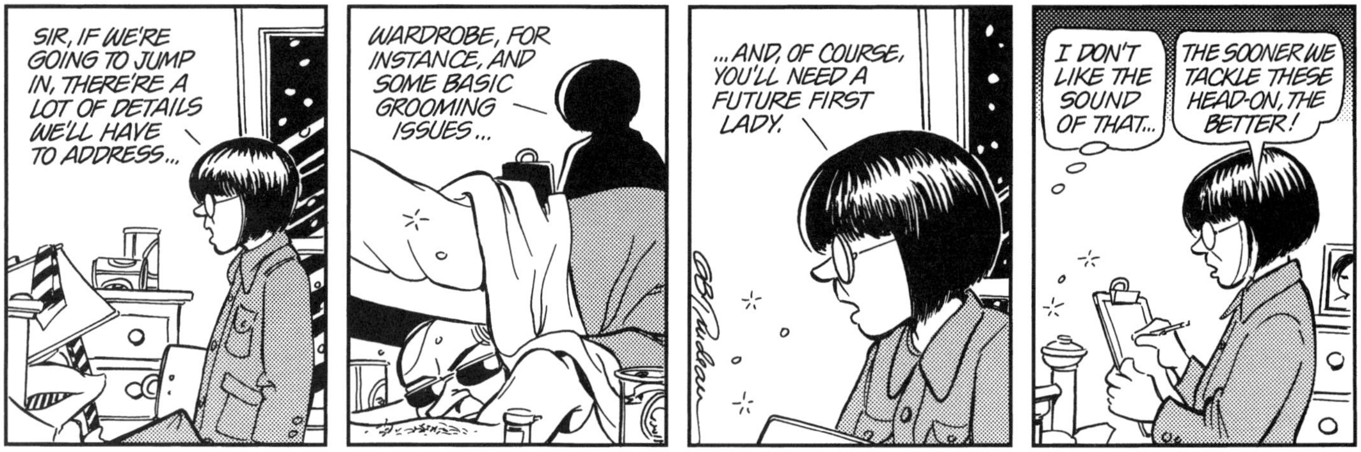
SIR, IF WE'RE GOING TO JUMP IN, THERE'RE A LOT OF DETAILS WE'LL HAVE TO ADDRESS...
WARDROBE, FOR INSTANCE, AND SOME BASIC GROOMING ISSUES...
...AND, OF COURSE, YOU'LL NEED A FUTURE FIRST LADY.
I DON'T LIKE THE SOUND OF THAT...
THE SOONER WE TACKLE THESE HEAD-ON, THE BETTER!

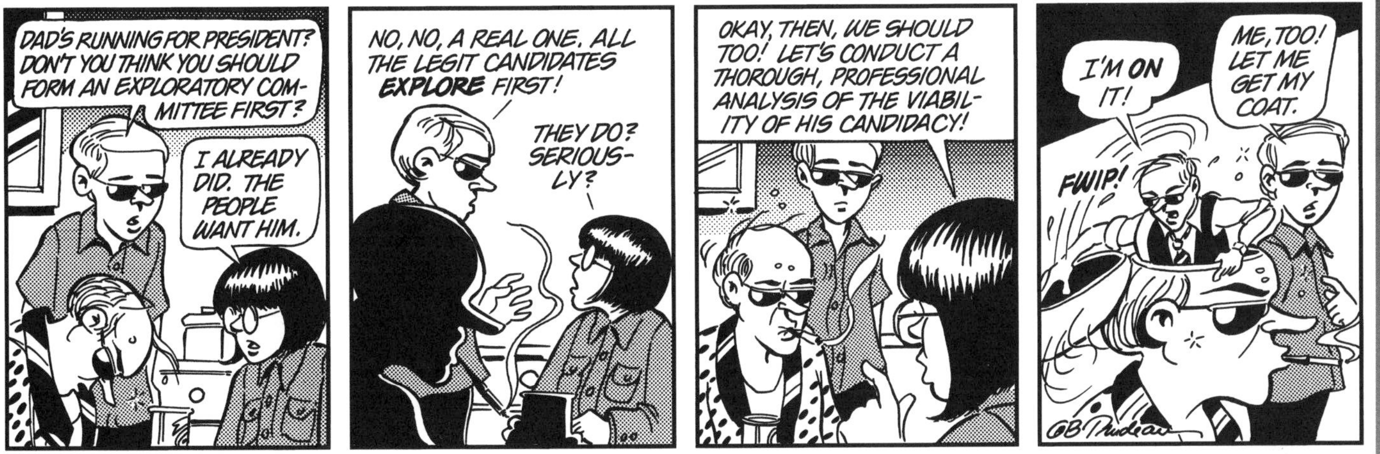
DAD'S RUNNING FOR PRESIDENT? DON'T YOU THINK YOU SHOULD FORM AN EXPLORATORY COMMITTEE FIRST?
I ALREADY DID. THE PEOPLE WANT HIM.
NO, NO, A REAL ONE. ALL THE LEGIT CANDIDATES EXPLORE FIRST!
THEY DO? SERIOUSLY?
OKAY, THEN, WE SHOULD TOO! LET'S CONDUCT A THOROUGH, PROFESSIONAL ANALYSIS OF THE VIABILITY OF HIS CANDIDACY!
I'M ON IT!
ME, TOO! LET ME GET MY COAT.
FWIP!

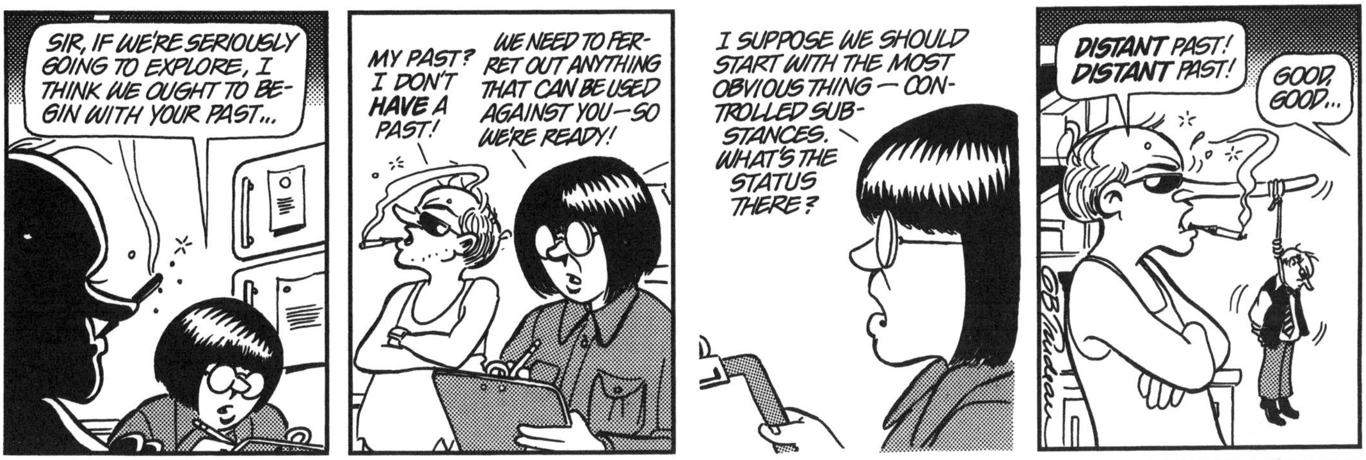
SIR, IF WE'RE SERIOUSLY GOING TO EXPLORE, I THINK WE OUGHT TO BEGIN WITH YOUR PAST...
MY PAST? I DON'T HAVE A PAST!
WE NEED TO FERRET OUT ANYTHING THAT CAN BE USED AGAINST YOU—SO WE'RE READY!
I SUPPOSE WE SHOULD START WITH THE MOST OBVIOUS THING — CONTROLLED SUBSTANCES. WHAT'S THE STATUS THERE?
DISTANT PAST! DISTANT PAST!
GOOD, GOOD...

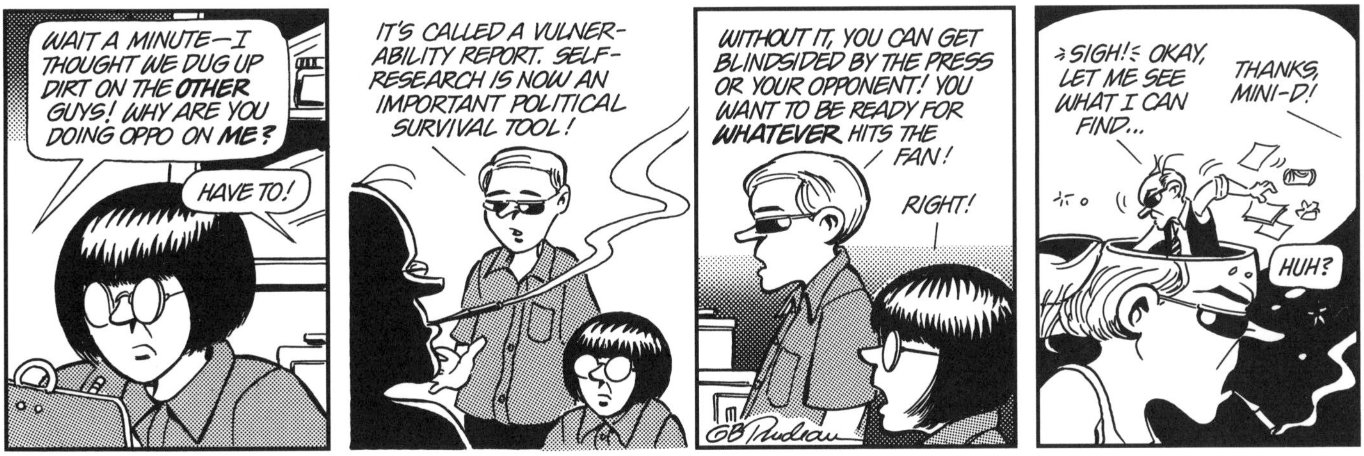
WAIT A MINUTE—I THOUGHT WE DUG UP DIRT ON THE OTHER GUYS! WHY ARE YOU DOING OPPO ON ME?
HAVE TO!
IT'S CALLED A VULNERABILITY REPORT. SELF-RESEARCH IS NOW AN IMPORTANT POLITICAL SURVIVAL TOOL!
WITHOUT IT, YOU CAN GET BLINDSIDED BY THE PRESS OR YOUR OPPONENT! YOU WANT TO BE READY FOR WHATEVER HITS THE FAN!
RIGHT!
SIGH! OKAY, LET ME SEE WHAT I CAN FIND...
THANKS, MINI-D!
HUH?

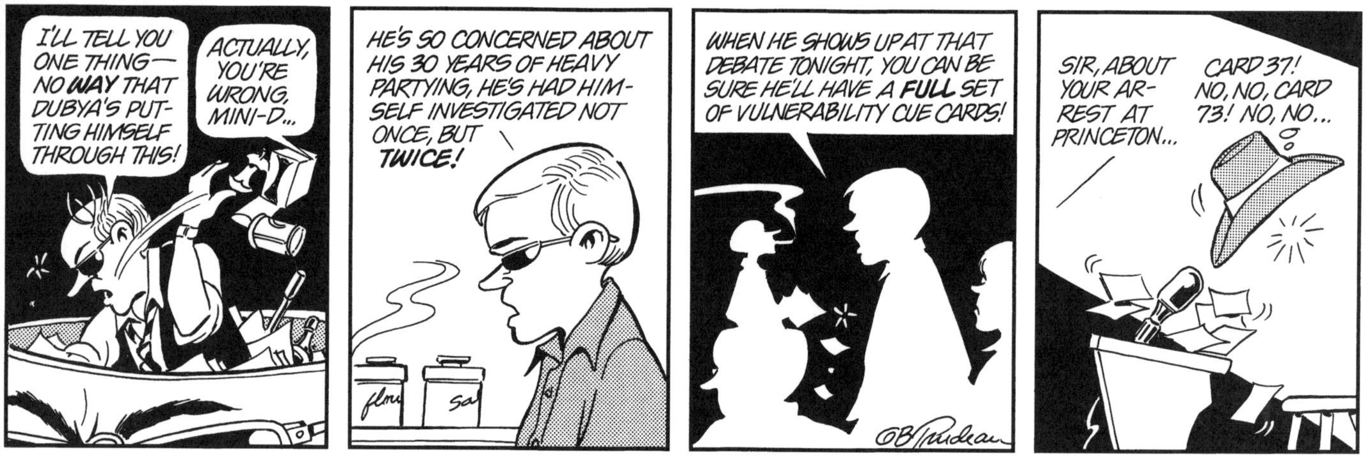
I'LL TELL YOU ONE THING—NO **WAY** THAT DUBYA'S PUTTING HIMSELF THROUGH THIS!
ACTUALLY, YOU'RE WRONG, MINI-D...
HE'S SO CONCERNED ABOUT HIS 30 YEARS OF HEAVY PARTYING, HE'S HAD HIMSELF INVESTIGATED NOT ONCE, BUT **TWICE!**
WHEN HE SHOWS UP AT THAT DEBATE TONIGHT, YOU CAN BE SURE HE'LL HAVE A **FULL** SET OF VULNERABILITY CUE CARDS!
SIR, ABOUT YOUR ARREST AT PRINCETON...
CARD 37! NO, NO, CARD 73! NO, NO...

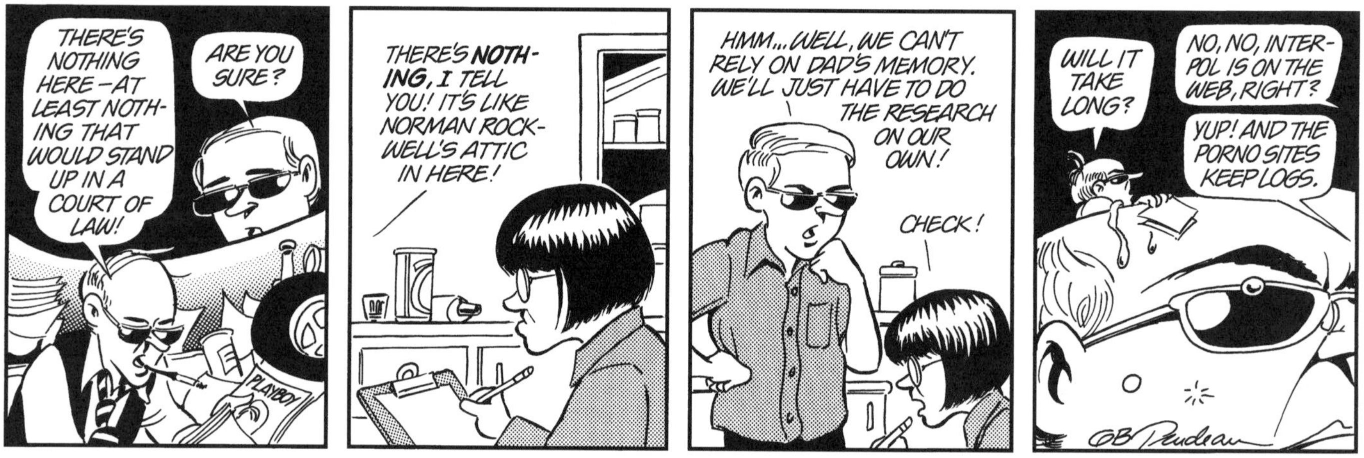
THERE'S NOTHING HERE—AT LEAST NOTHING THAT WOULD STAND UP IN A COURT OF LAW!
ARE YOU SURE?
PLAYBOY
THERE'S **NOTHING**, I TELL YOU! IT'S LIKE NORMAN ROCKWELL'S ATTIC IN HERE!
HMM... WELL, WE CAN'T RELY ON DAD'S MEMORY. WE'LL JUST HAVE TO DO THE RESEARCH ON OUR OWN!
CHECK!
WILL IT TAKE LONG?
NO, NO, INTERPOL IS ON THE WEB, RIGHT?
YUP! AND THE PORNO SITES KEEP LOGS.

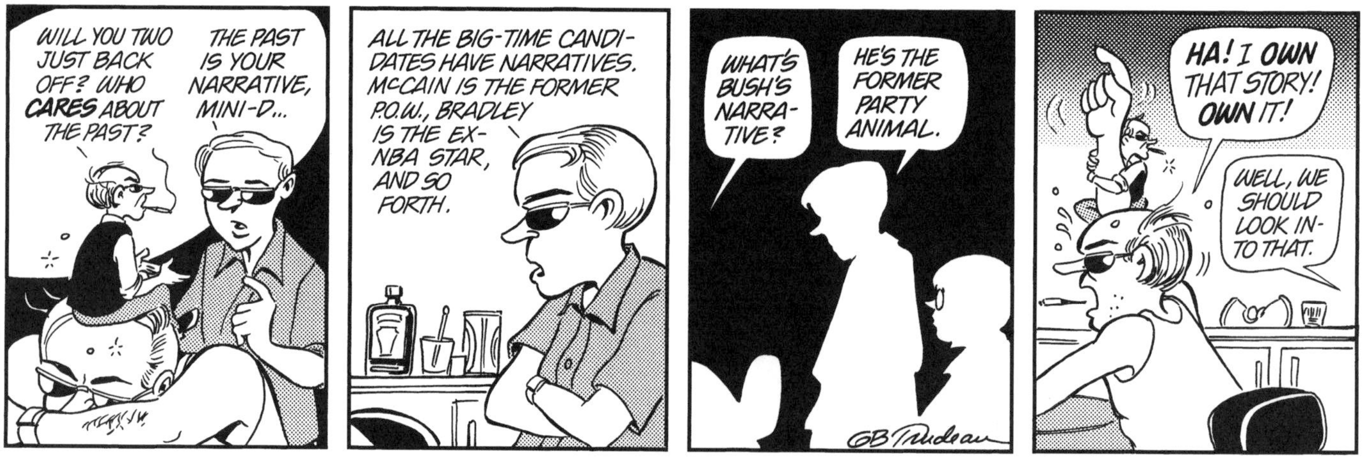
WILL YOU TWO JUST BACK OFF? WHO **CARES** ABOUT THE PAST?
THE PAST IS YOUR NARRATIVE, MINI-D...
ALL THE BIG-TIME CANDIDATES HAVE NARRATIVES. McCAIN IS THE FORMER P.O.W., BRADLEY IS THE EX-NBA STAR, AND SO FORTH.
WHAT'S BUSH'S NARRATIVE?
HE'S THE FORMER PARTY ANIMAL.
HA! I **OWN** THAT STORY! **OWN** IT!
WELL, WE SHOULD LOOK INTO THAT.

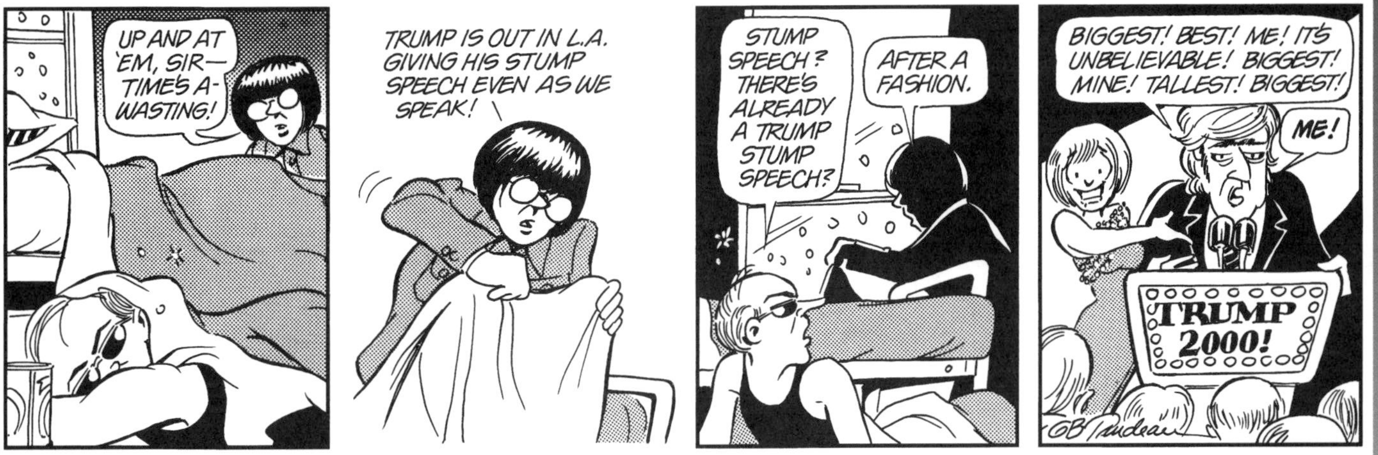
UP AND AT 'EM, SIR— TIME'S A-WASTING!
TRUMP IS OUT IN L.A. GIVING HIS STUMP SPEECH EVEN AS WE SPEAK!
STUMP SPEECH? THERE'S ALREADY A TRUMP STUMP SPEECH?
AFTER A FASHION.
BIGGEST! BEST! ME! IT'S UNBELIEVABLE! BIGGEST! MINE! TALLEST! BIGGEST!
ME!
TRUMP 2000!

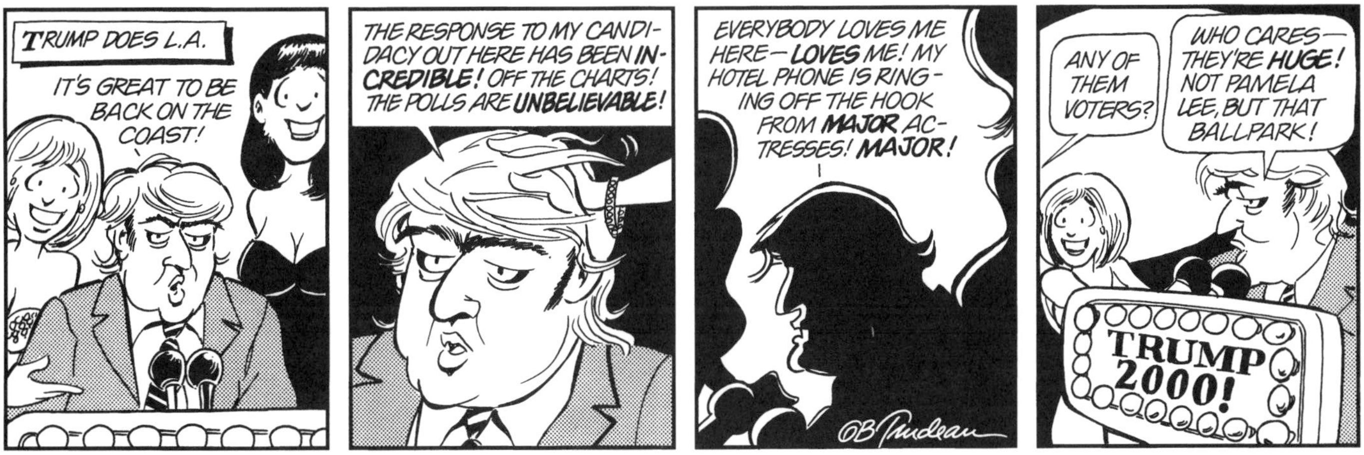
TRUMP DOES L.A.
IT'S GREAT TO BE BACK ON THE COAST!
THE RESPONSE TO MY CANDIDACY OUT HERE HAS BEEN INCREDIBLE! OFF THE CHARTS! THE POLLS ARE UNBELIEVABLE!
EVERYBODY LOVES ME HERE—LOVES ME! MY HOTEL PHONE IS RINGING OFF THE HOOK FROM MAJOR ACTRESSES! MAJOR!
ANY OF THEM VOTERS?
WHO CARES—THEY'RE HUGE! NOT PAMELA LEE, BUT THAT BALLPARK!
TRUMP 2000!

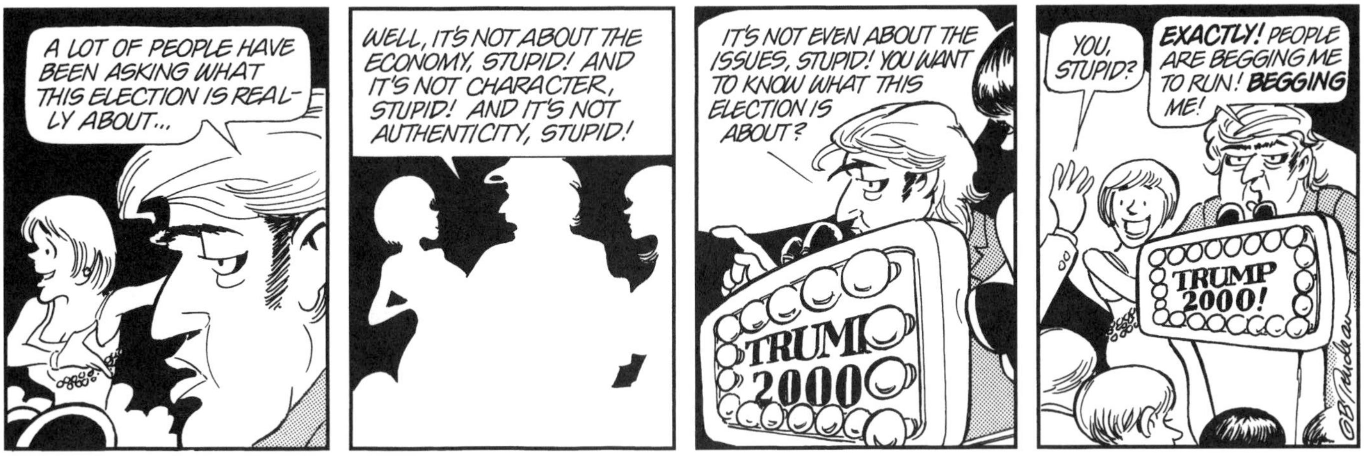
A LOT OF PEOPLE HAVE BEEN ASKING WHAT THIS ELECTION IS REALLY ABOUT...
WELL, IT'S NOT ABOUT THE ECONOMY, STUPID! AND IT'S NOT CHARACTER, STUPID! AND IT'S NOT AUTHENTICITY, STUPID!
IT'S NOT EVEN ABOUT THE ISSUES, STUPID! YOU WANT TO KNOW WHAT THIS ELECTION IS ABOUT?
YOU, STUPID?
EXACTLY! PEOPLE ARE BEGGING ME TO RUN! BEGGING ME!
TRUMP 2000!

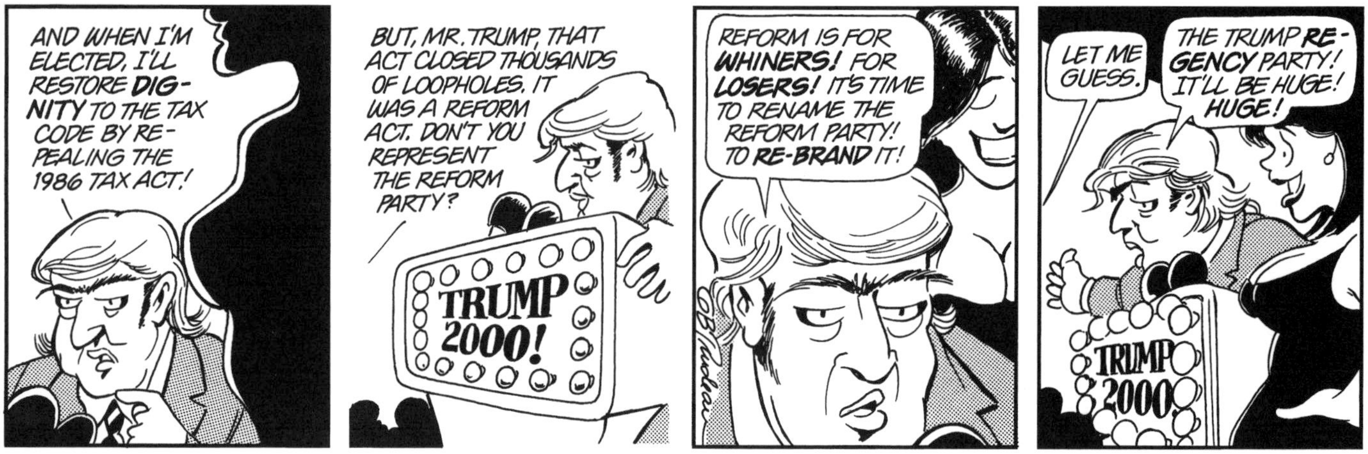
AND WHEN I'M ELECTED, I'LL RESTORE DIGNITY TO THE TAX CODE BY REPEALING THE 1986 TAX ACT!
BUT, MR. TRUMP, THAT ACT CLOSED THOUSANDS OF LOOPHOLES. IT WAS A REFORM ACT. DON'T YOU REPRESENT THE REFORM PARTY?
TRUMP 2000!
REFORM IS FOR WHINERS! FOR LOSERS! IT'S TIME TO RENAME THE REFORM PARTY! TO RE-BRAND IT!
LET ME GUESS.
THE TRUMP REGENCY PARTY! IT'LL BE HUGE! HUGE!
TRUMP 2000

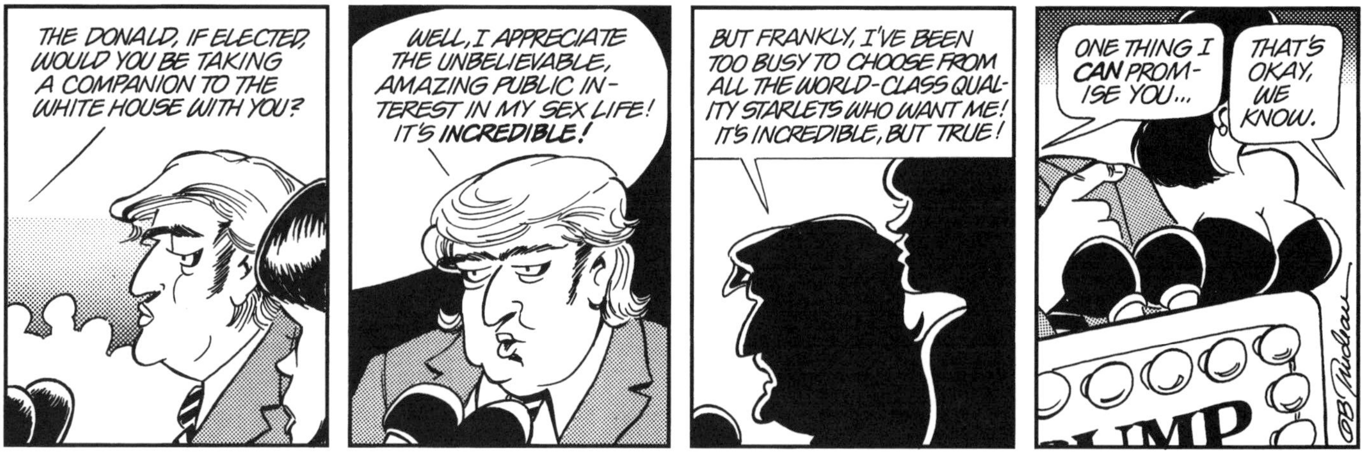
THE DONALD, IF ELECTED, WOULD YOU BE TAKING A COMPANION TO THE WHITE HOUSE WITH YOU?
WELL, I APPRECIATE THE UNBELIEVABLE, AMAZING PUBLIC INTEREST IN MY SEX LIFE! IT'S INCREDIBLE!
BUT FRANKLY, I'VE BEEN TOO BUSY TO CHOOSE FROM ALL THE WORLD-CLASS QUALITY STARLETS WHO WANT ME! IT'S INCREDIBLE, BUT TRUE!
ONE THING I CAN PROMISE YOU...
THAT'S OKAY, WE KNOW.

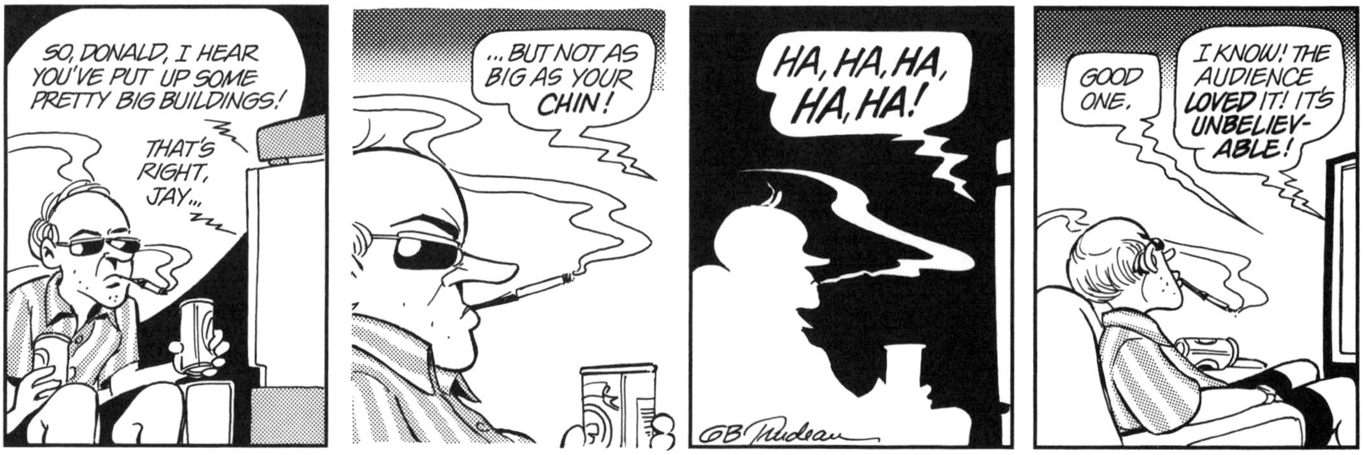
SO, DONALD, I HEAR YOU'VE PUT UP SOME PRETTY BIG BUILDINGS!
THAT'S RIGHT, JAY...
...BUT NOT AS BIG AS YOUR CHIN!
HA, HA, HA, HA, HA!
GOOD ONE.
I KNOW! THE AUDIENCE LOVED IT! IT'S UNBELIEVABLE!

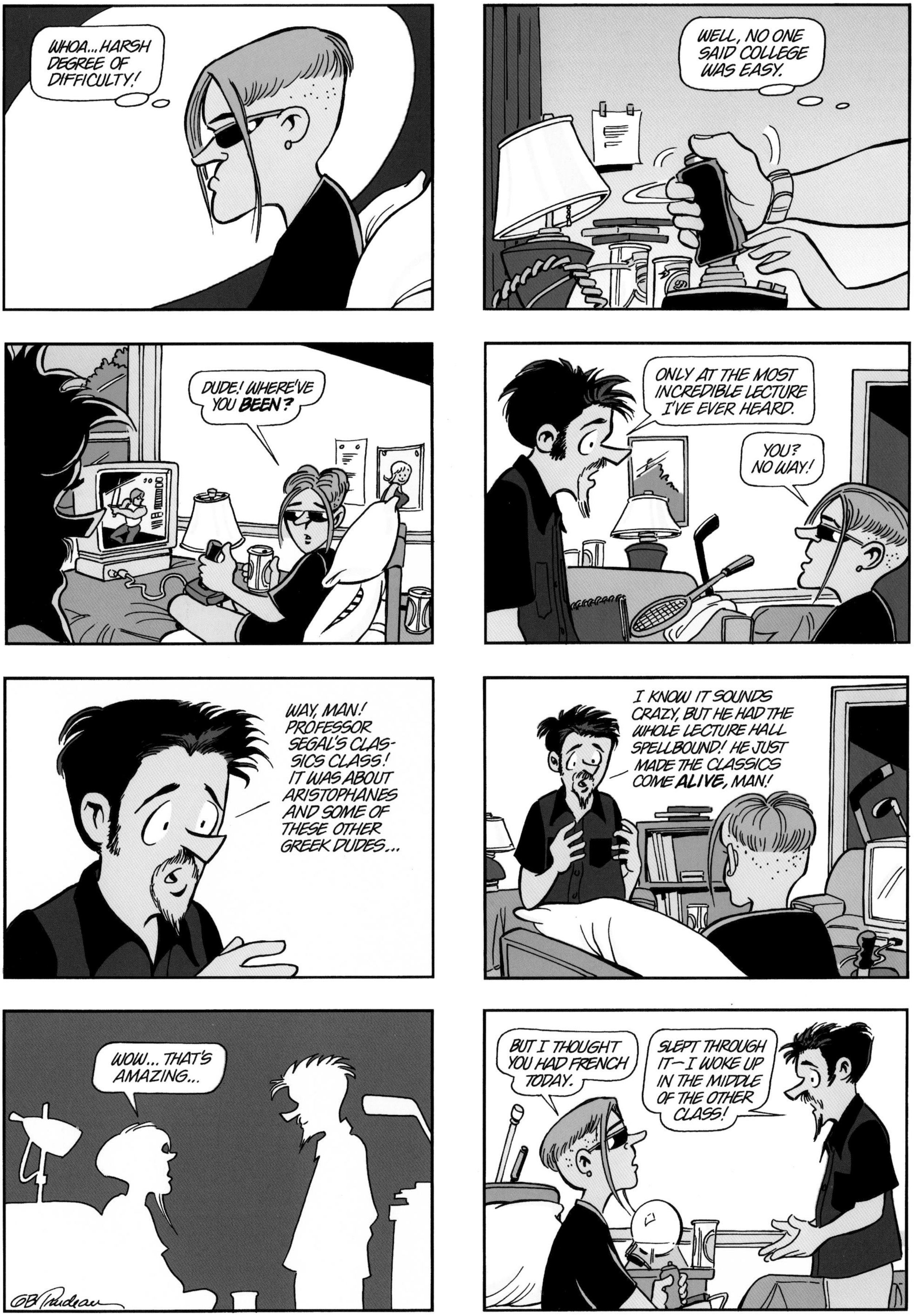
WHOA... HARSH DEGREE OF DIFFICULTY!
WELL, NO ONE SAID COLLEGE WAS EASY.
DUDE! WHERE'VE YOU BEEN?
ONLY AT THE MOST INCREDIBLE LECTURE I'VE EVER HEARD.
YOU? NO WAY!
WAY, MAN! PROFESSOR SEGAL'S CLASSICS CLASS! IT WAS ABOUT ARISTOPHANES AND SOME OF THESE OTHER GREEK DUDES...
I KNOW IT SOUNDS CRAZY, BUT HE HAD THE WHOLE LECTURE HALL SPELLBOUND! HE JUST MADE THE CLASSICS COME ALIVE, MAN!
WOW... THAT'S AMAZING...
G.B. Trudeau
BUT I THOUGHT YOU HAD FRENCH TODAY.
SLEPT THROUGH IT—I WOKE UP IN THE MIDDLE OF THE OTHER CLASS!

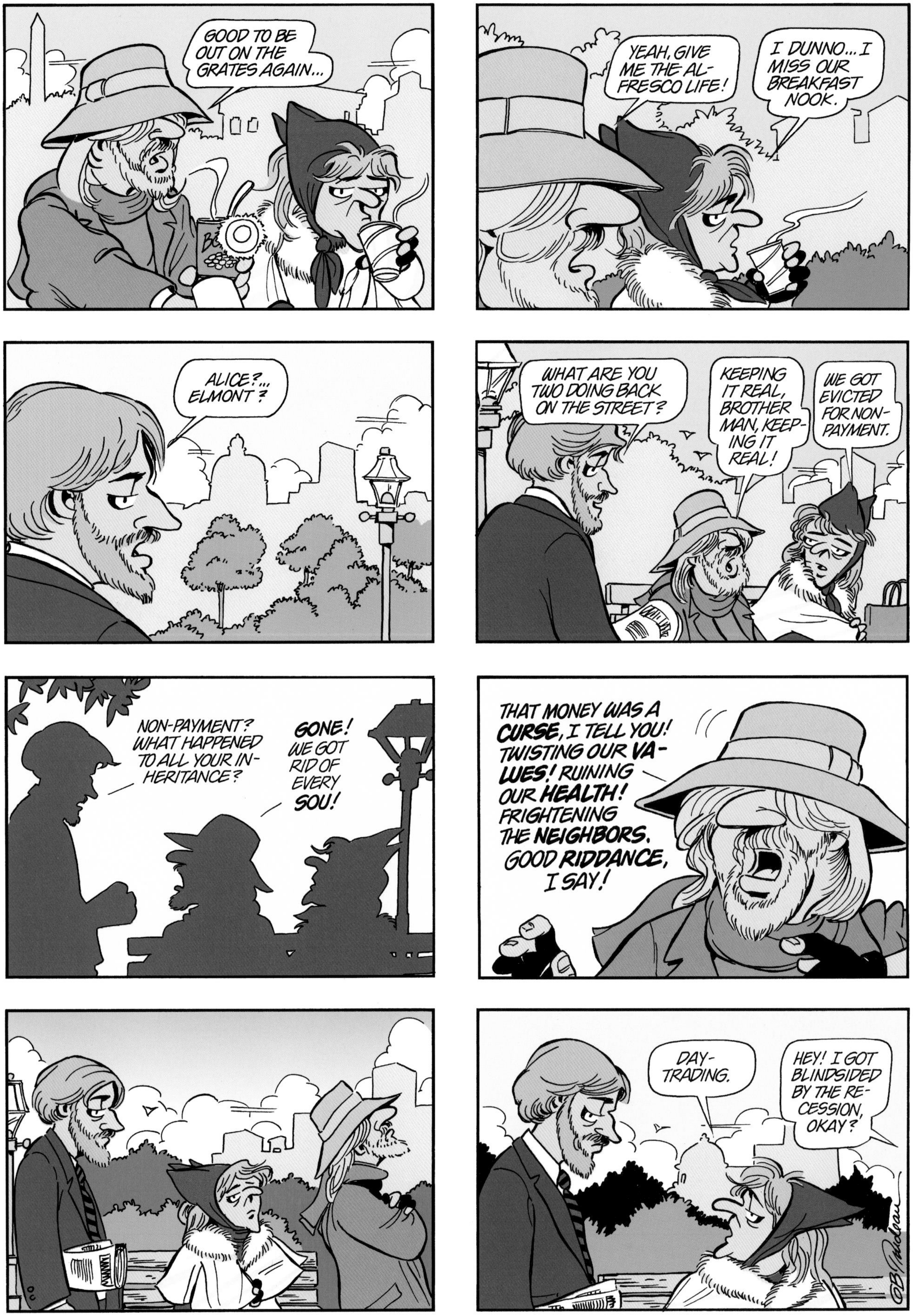
GOOD TO BE OUT ON THE GRATES AGAIN...
YEAH, GIVE ME THE AL-FRESCO LIFE!
I DUNNO... I MISS OUR BREAKFAST NOOK.
ALICE?... ELMONT?
WHAT ARE YOU TWO DOING BACK ON THE STREET?
KEEPING IT REAL, BROTHER MAN, KEEPING IT REAL!
WE GOT EVICTED FOR NON-PAYMENT.
NON-PAYMENT? WHAT HAPPENED TO ALL YOUR IN-HERITANCE?
GONE! WE GOT RID OF EVERY SOU!
THAT MONEY WAS A CURSE, I TELL YOU! TWISTING OUR VA-LUES! RUINING OUR HEALTH! FRIGHTENING THE NEIGHBORS. GOOD RIDDANCE, I SAY!
DAY-TRADING.
HEY! I GOT BLINDSIDED BY THE RE-CESSION, OKAY?

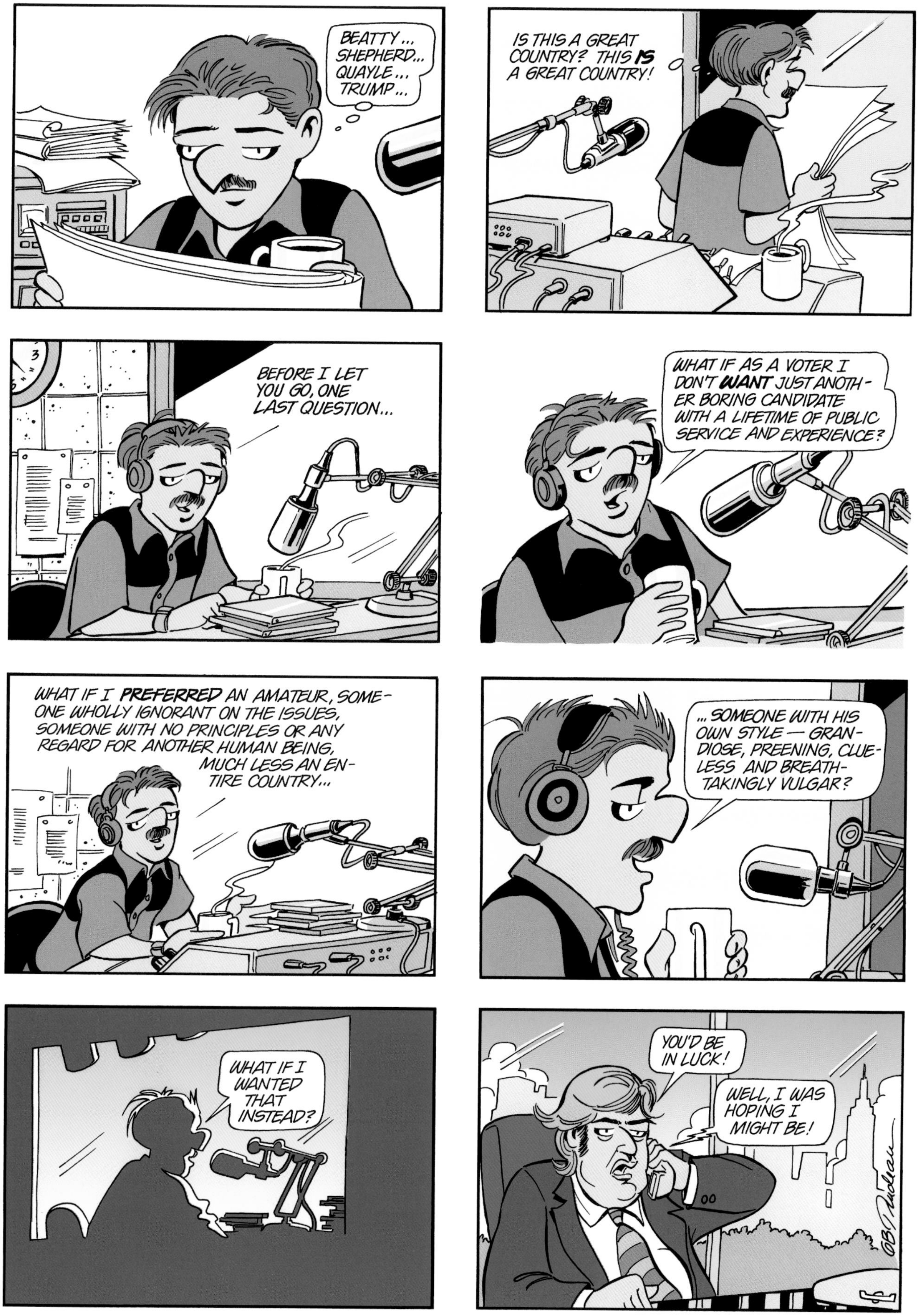
BEATTY... SHEPHERD... QUAYLE... TRUMP...
IS THIS A GREAT COUNTRY? THIS IS A GREAT COUNTRY!
BEFORE I LET YOU GO, ONE LAST QUESTION...
WHAT IF AS A VOTER I DON'T WANT JUST ANOTHER BORING CANDIDATE WITH A LIFETIME OF PUBLIC SERVICE AND EXPERIENCE?
WHAT IF I PREFERRED AN AMATEUR, SOMEONE WHOLLY IGNORANT ON THE ISSUES, SOMEONE WITH NO PRINCIPLES OR ANY REGARD FOR ANOTHER HUMAN BEING, MUCH LESS AN ENTIRE COUNTRY...
...SOMEONE WITH HIS OWN STYLE — GRANDIOSE, PREENING, CLUELESS AND BREATHTAKINGLY VULGAR?
WHAT IF I WANTED THAT INSTEAD?
YOU'D BE IN LUCK!
WELL, I WAS HOPING I MIGHT BE!

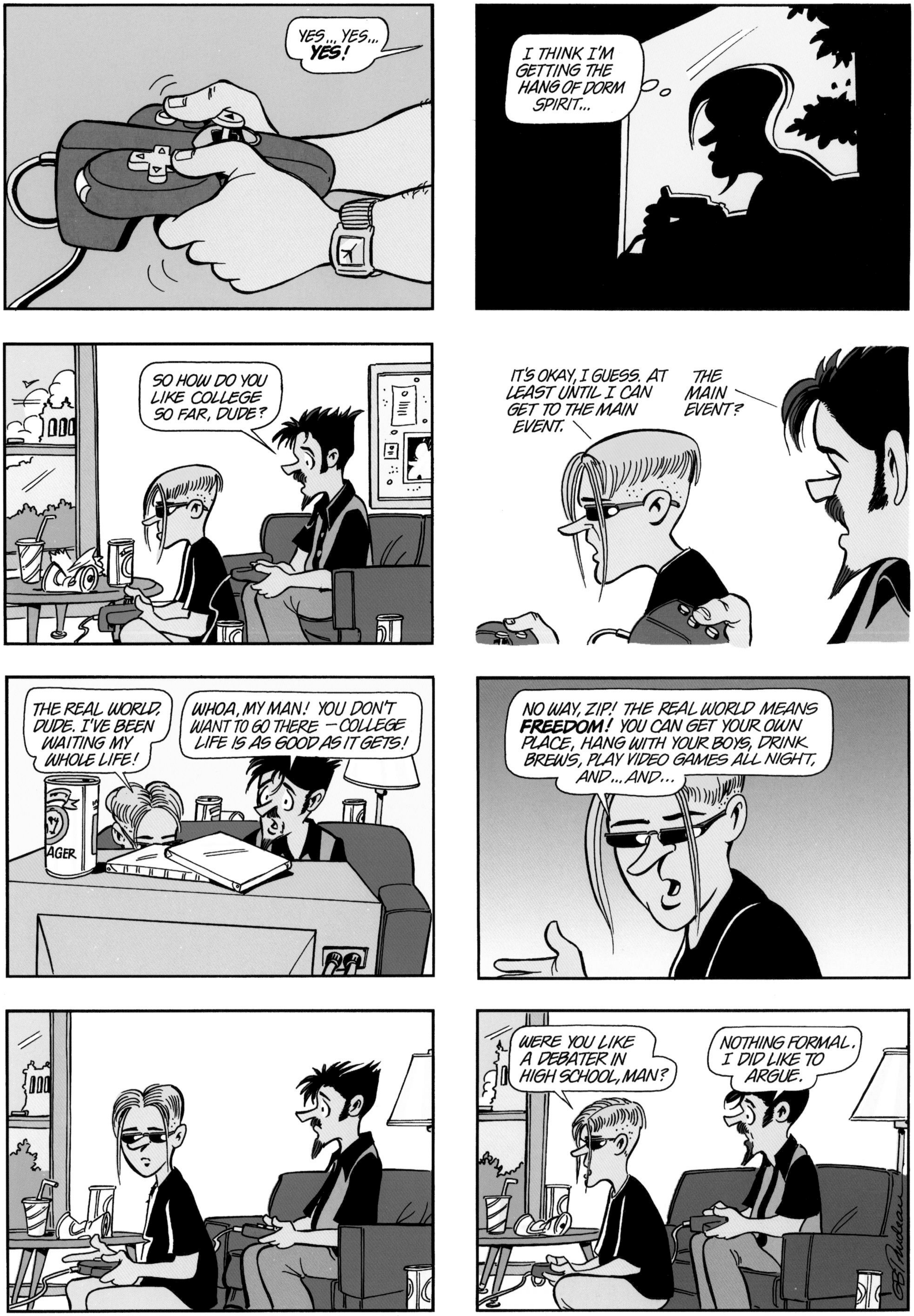
YES... YES... YES!
I THINK I'M GETTING THE HANG OF DORM SPIRIT...
SO HOW DO YOU LIKE COLLEGE SO FAR, DUDE?
IT'S OKAY, I GUESS. AT LEAST UNTIL I CAN GET TO THE MAIN EVENT.
THE MAIN EVENT?
THE REAL WORLD, DUDE. I'VE BEEN WAITING MY WHOLE LIFE!
WHOA, MY MAN! YOU DON'T WANT TO GO THERE — COLLEGE LIFE IS AS GOOD AS IT GETS!
LAGER
NO WAY, ZIP! THE REAL WORLD MEANS FREEDOM! YOU CAN GET YOUR OWN PLACE, HANG WITH YOUR BOYS, DRINK BREWS, PLAY VIDEO GAMES ALL NIGHT, AND... AND...
WERE YOU LIKE A DEBATER IN HIGH SCHOOL, MAN?
NOTHING FORMAL. I DID LIKE TO ARGUE.
GBTrudeau

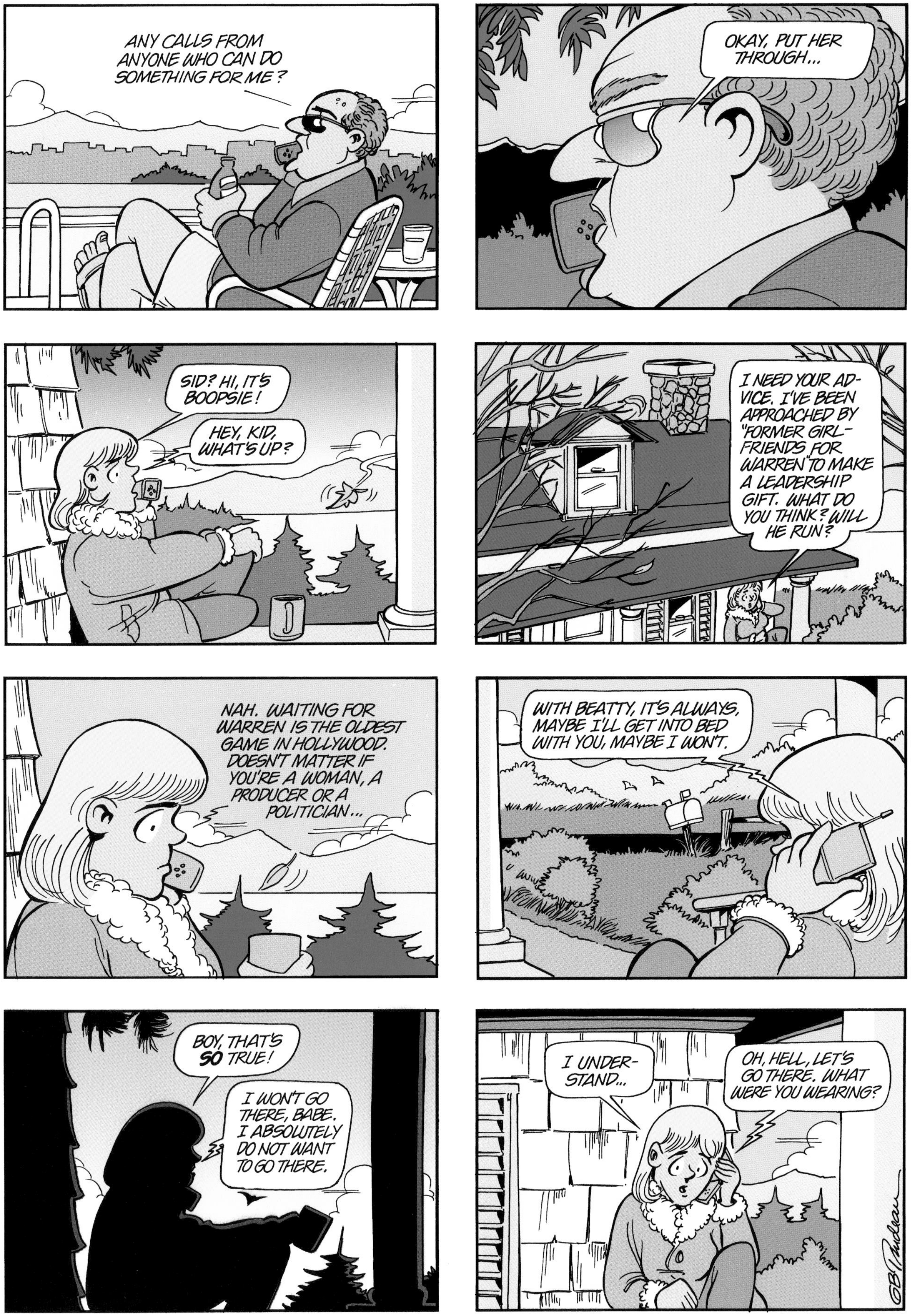
ANY CALLS FROM ANYONE WHO CAN DO SOMETHING FOR ME?
OKAY, PUT HER THROUGH...
SID? HI, IT'S BOOPSIE!
HEY, KID, WHAT'S UP?
I NEED YOUR ADVICE. I'VE BEEN APPROACHED BY "FORMER GIRLFRIENDS FOR WARREN" TO MAKE A LEADERSHIP GIFT. WHAT DO YOU THINK? WILL HE RUN?
NAH. WAITING FOR WARREN IS THE OLDEST GAME IN HOLLYWOOD. DOESN'T MATTER IF YOU'RE A WOMAN, A PRODUCER OR A POLITICIAN...
WITH BEATTY, IT'S ALWAYS, MAYBE I'LL GET INTO BED WITH YOU, MAYBE I WON'T.
BOY, THAT'S SO TRUE!
I WON'T GO THERE, BABE. I ABSOLUTELY DO NOT WANT TO GO THERE.
I UNDERSTAND...
OH, HELL, LET'S GO THERE. WHAT WERE YOU WEARING?
©BTrudeau

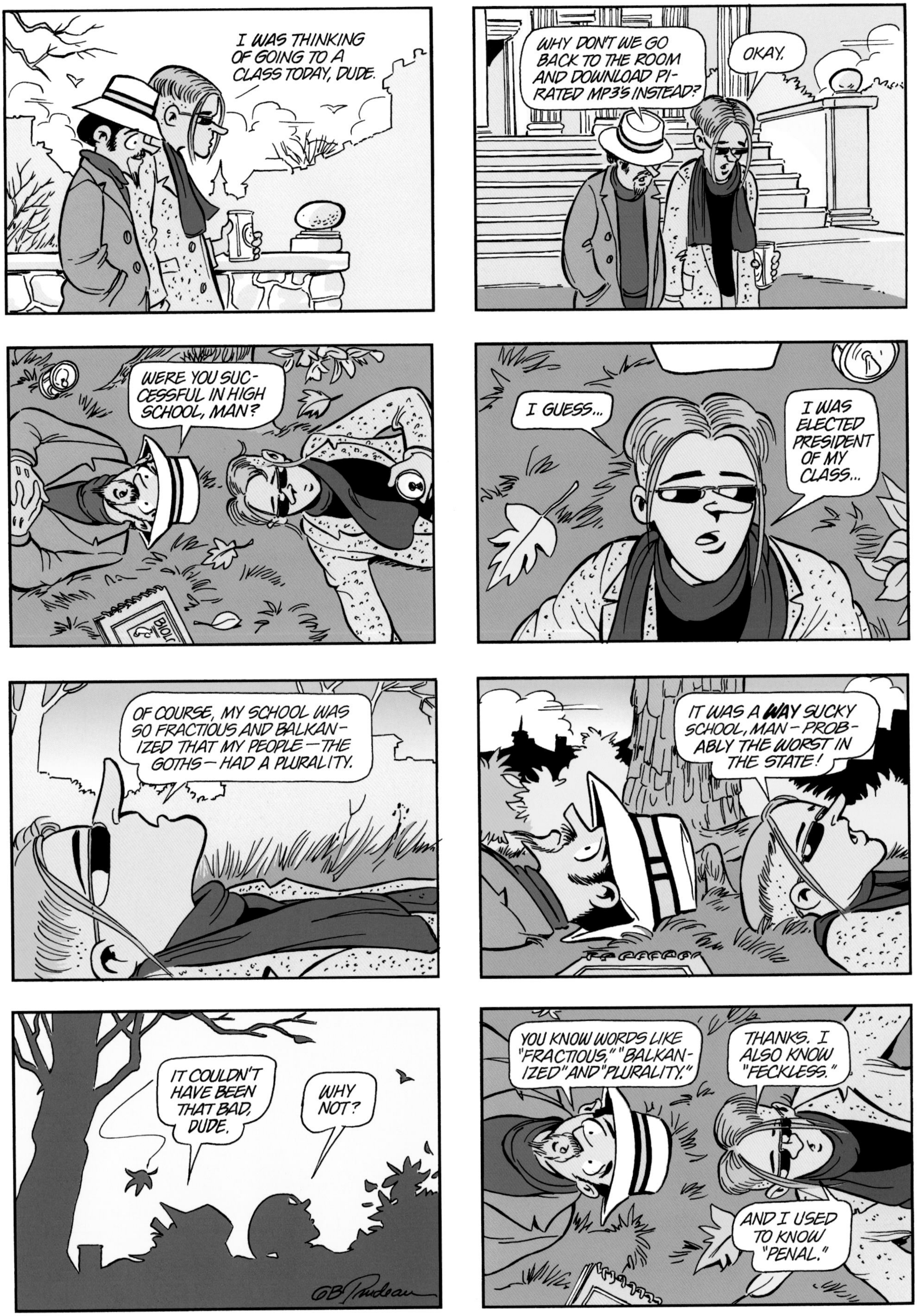
I WAS THINKING OF GOING TO A CLASS TODAY, DUDE.
WHY DON'T WE GO BACK TO THE ROOM AND DOWNLOAD PIRATED MP3'S INSTEAD?
OKAY.
WERE YOU SUCCESSFUL IN HIGH SCHOOL, MAN?
I GUESS...
I WAS ELECTED PRESIDENT OF MY CLASS...
OF COURSE, MY SCHOOL WAS SO FRACTIOUS AND BALKANIZED THAT MY PEOPLE—THE GOTHS—HAD A PLURALITY.
IT WAS A **WAY** SUCKY SCHOOL, MAN—PROBABLY THE WORST IN THE STATE!
IT COULDN'T HAVE BEEN THAT BAD, DUDE.
WHY NOT?
YOU KNOW WORDS LIKE "FRACTIOUS," "BALKANIZED" AND "PLURALITY."
THANKS. I ALSO KNOW "FECKLESS."
AND I USED TO KNOW "PENAL."
GB Trudeau

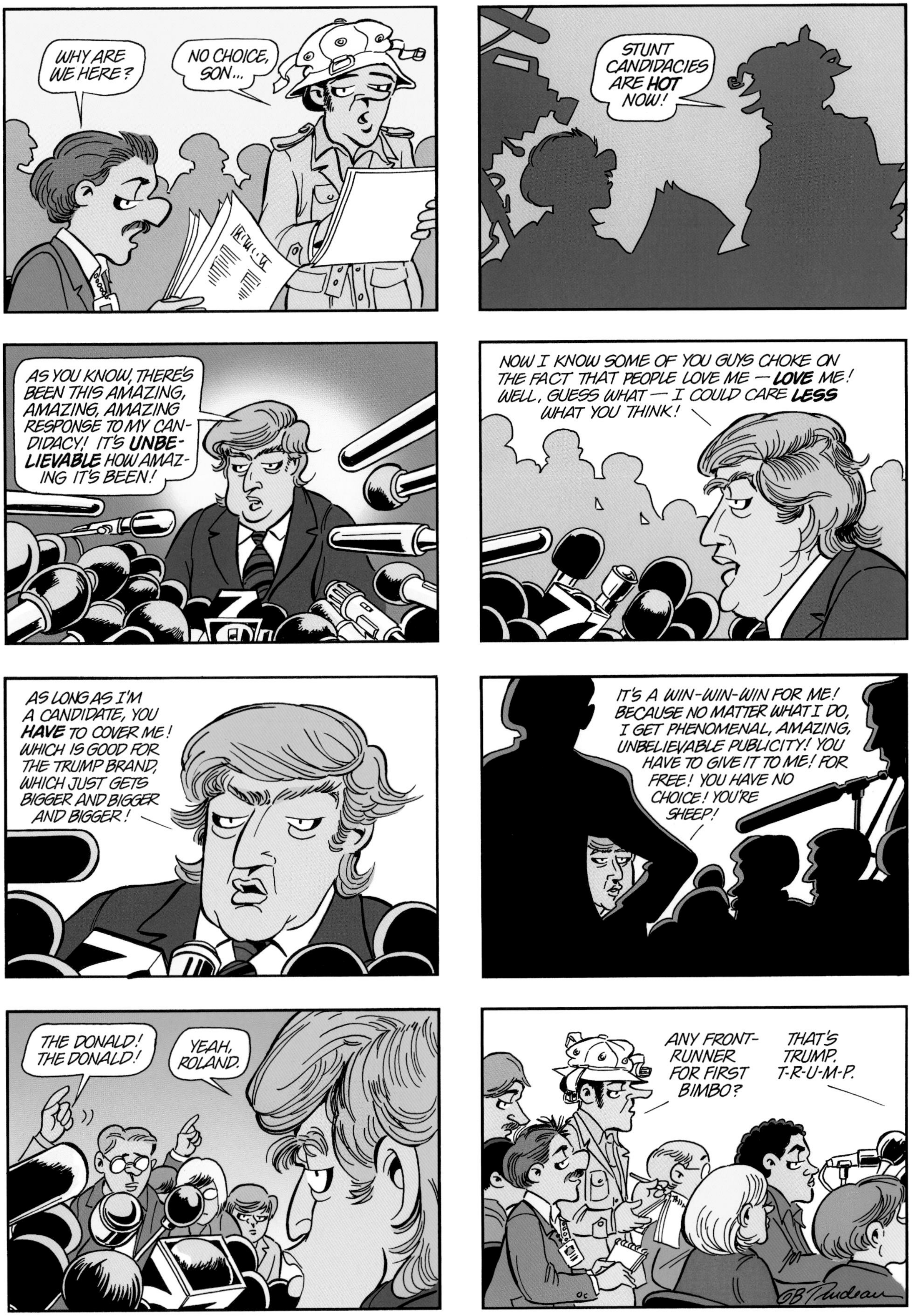
WHY ARE WE HERE?
NO CHOICE, SON...
STUNT CANDIDACIES ARE **HOT** NOW!
AS YOU KNOW, THERE'S BEEN THIS AMAZING, AMAZING, AMAZING RESPONSE TO MY CANDIDACY! IT'S **UNBELIEVABLE** HOW AMAZING IT'S BEEN!
NOW I KNOW SOME OF YOU GUYS CHOKE ON THE FACT THAT PEOPLE LOVE ME — **LOVE** ME! WELL, GUESS WHAT — I COULD CARE **LESS** WHAT YOU THINK!
AS LONG AS I'M A CANDIDATE, YOU **HAVE** TO COVER ME! WHICH IS GOOD FOR THE TRUMP BRAND, WHICH JUST GETS BIGGER AND BIGGER AND BIGGER!
IT'S A WIN-WIN-WIN FOR ME! BECAUSE NO MATTER WHAT I DO, I GET PHENOMENAL, AMAZING, UNBELIEVABLE PUBLICITY! YOU HAVE TO GIVE IT TO ME! FOR FREE! YOU HAVE NO CHOICE! YOU'RE SHEEP!
THE DONALD! THE DONALD!
YEAH, ROLAND.
ANY FRONT-RUNNER FOR FIRST BIMBO?
THAT'S TRUMP. T-R-U-M-P.
GB Trudeau

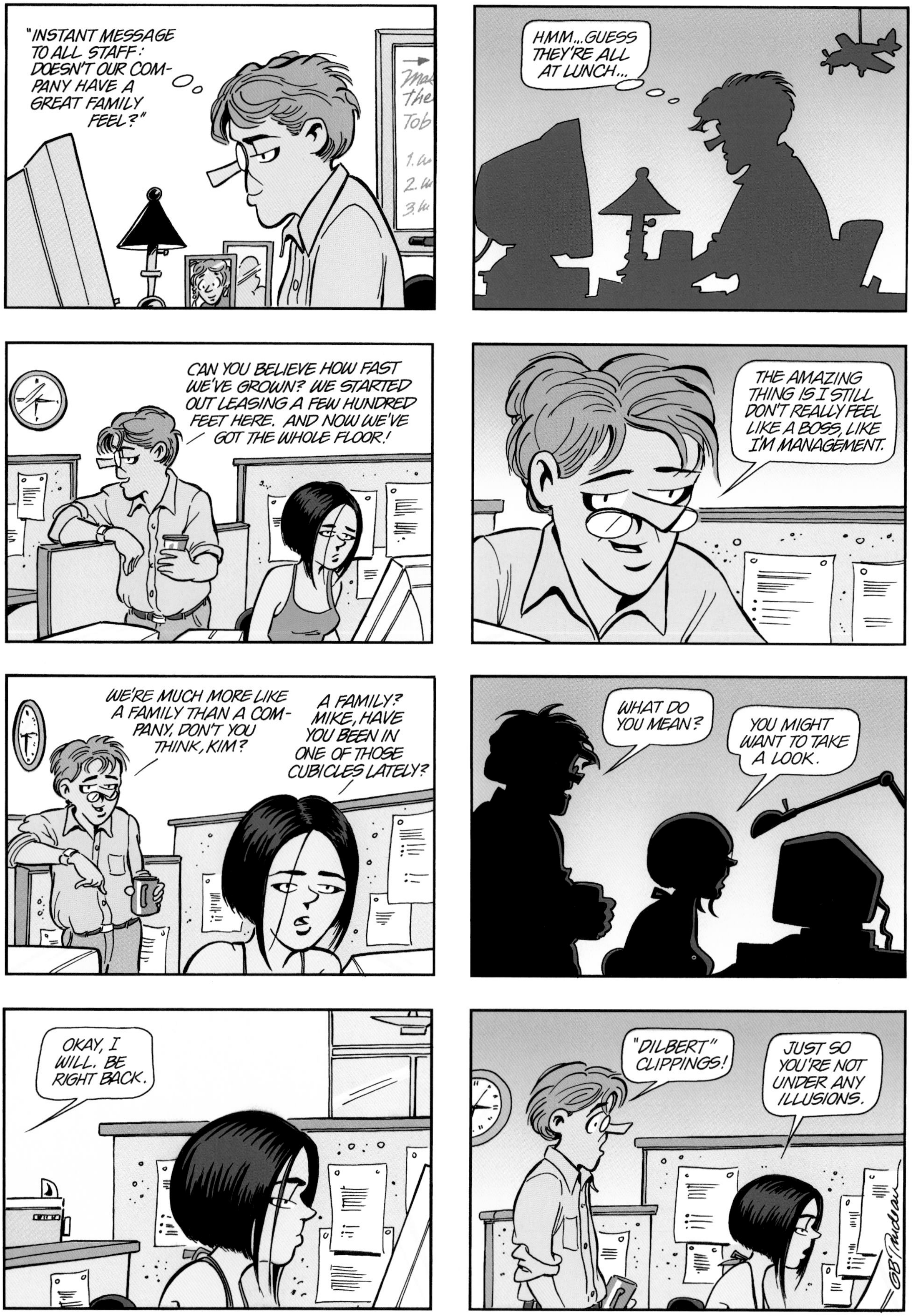
"INSTANT MESSAGE TO ALL STAFF: DOESN'T OUR COMPANY HAVE A GREAT FAMILY FEEL?"
HMM... GUESS THEY'RE ALL AT LUNCH...
CAN YOU BELIEVE HOW FAST WE'VE GROWN? WE STARTED OUT LEASING A FEW HUNDRED FEET HERE. AND NOW WE'VE GOT THE WHOLE FLOOR!
THE AMAZING THING IS I STILL DON'T REALLY FEEL LIKE A BOSS, LIKE I'M MANAGEMENT.
WE'RE MUCH MORE LIKE A FAMILY THAN A COMPANY, DON'T YOU THINK, KIM?
A FAMILY? MIKE, HAVE YOU BEEN IN ONE OF THOSE CUBICLES LATELY?
WHAT DO YOU MEAN?
YOU MIGHT WANT TO TAKE A LOOK.
OKAY, I WILL. BE RIGHT BACK.
"DILBERT" CLIPPINGS!
JUST SO YOU'RE NOT UNDER ANY ILLUSIONS.

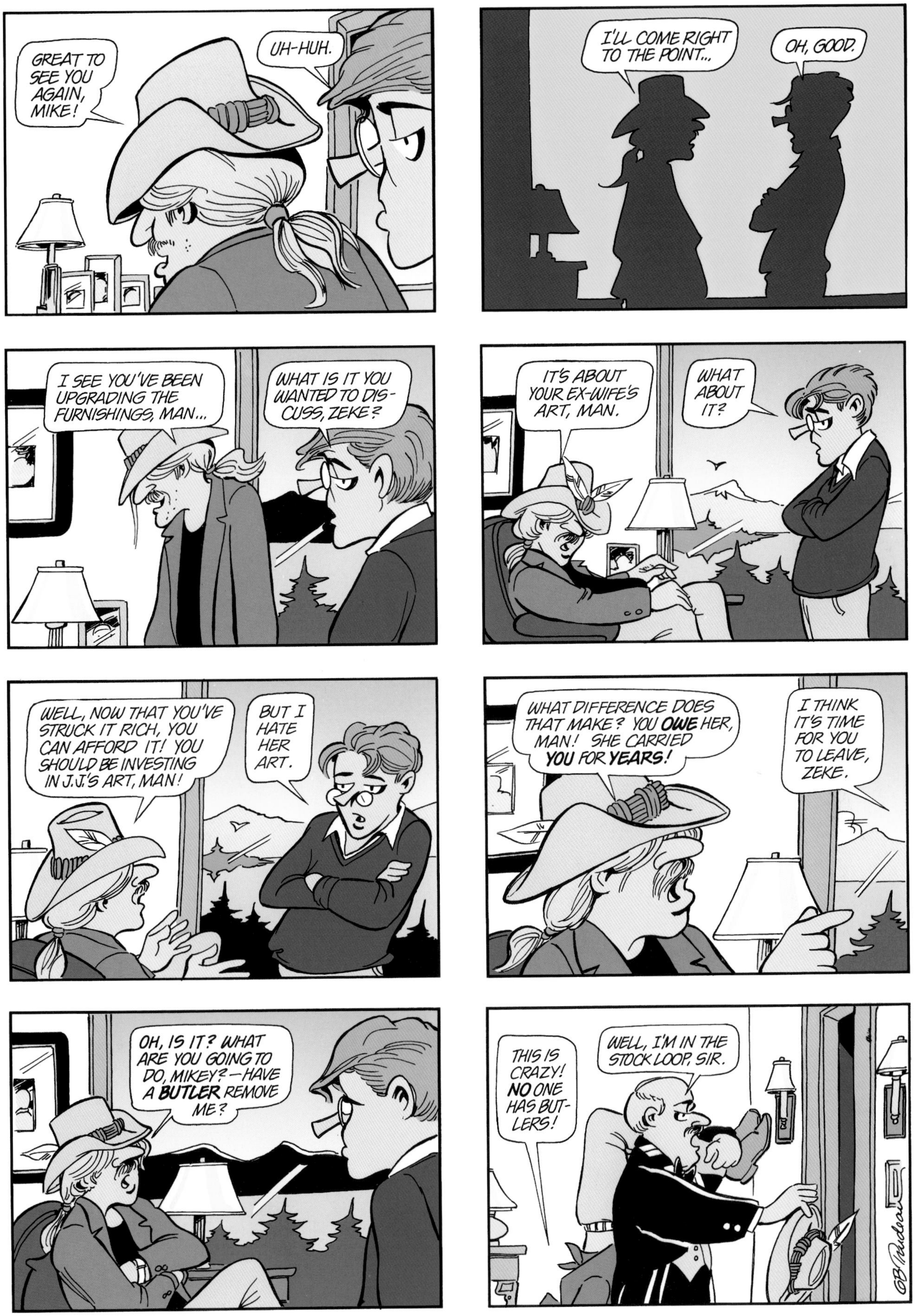
GREAT TO SEE YOU AGAIN, MIKE!
UH-HUH.
I'LL COME RIGHT TO THE POINT...
OH, GOOD.
I SEE YOU'VE BEEN UPGRADING THE FURNISHINGS, MAN...
WHAT IS IT YOU WANTED TO DISCUSS, ZEKE?
IT'S ABOUT YOUR EX-WIFE'S ART, MAN.
WHAT ABOUT IT?
WELL, NOW THAT YOU'VE STRUCK IT RICH, YOU CAN AFFORD IT! YOU SHOULD BE INVESTING IN J.J.'S ART, MAN!
BUT I HATE HER ART.
WHAT DIFFERENCE DOES THAT MAKE? YOU **OWE** HER, MAN! SHE CARRIED **YOU** FOR **YEARS**!
I THINK IT'S TIME FOR YOU TO LEAVE, ZEKE.
OH, IS IT? WHAT ARE YOU GOING TO DO, MIKEY?—HAVE A **BUTLER** REMOVE ME?
THIS IS CRAZY! **NO** ONE HAS BUTLERS!
WELL, I'M IN THE STOCK LOOP, SIR.
©B Trudeau

HISSS!

UH-OH...

FZZZZ!

NOT AGAIN!

RADIATOR BLEW UP AGAIN, MAN.

GOOD OL' ROSENBLATT HALL!

THWIP!
THWIP!

BOY, IS THIS PLACE A DUMP!

IT'S NO ACCIDENT, DUDE, IT'S PART OF A STRATEGIC VISION.

IT IS?

YUP. IT DATES BACK TO THIS OLD ALUM, ZENON ROSENBLATT. HE WAS THE RICHEST MAN EVER TO GRADUATE FROM WALDEN.

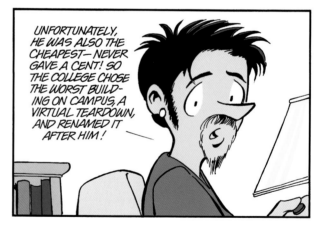

UNFORTUNATELY, HE WAS ALSO THE CHEAPEST— NEVER GAVE A CENT! SO THE COLLEGE CHOSE THE WORST BUILD-ING ON CAMPUS, A VIRTUAL TEARDOWN, AND RENAMED IT AFTER HIM!

EVER SINCE, ROSENBLATT HALL HAS STOOD AS AN UGLY WARNING TO TIGHT-WAD ALUMS! SO THIS DORM HAS **HISTORY**, DUDE!

WHOA... I JUST FELT A SHIVER, MAN!

WELL, IT'S FREEZ-ING IN HERE, BUT THAT COULD BE ROSENBLATT SPIRIT!

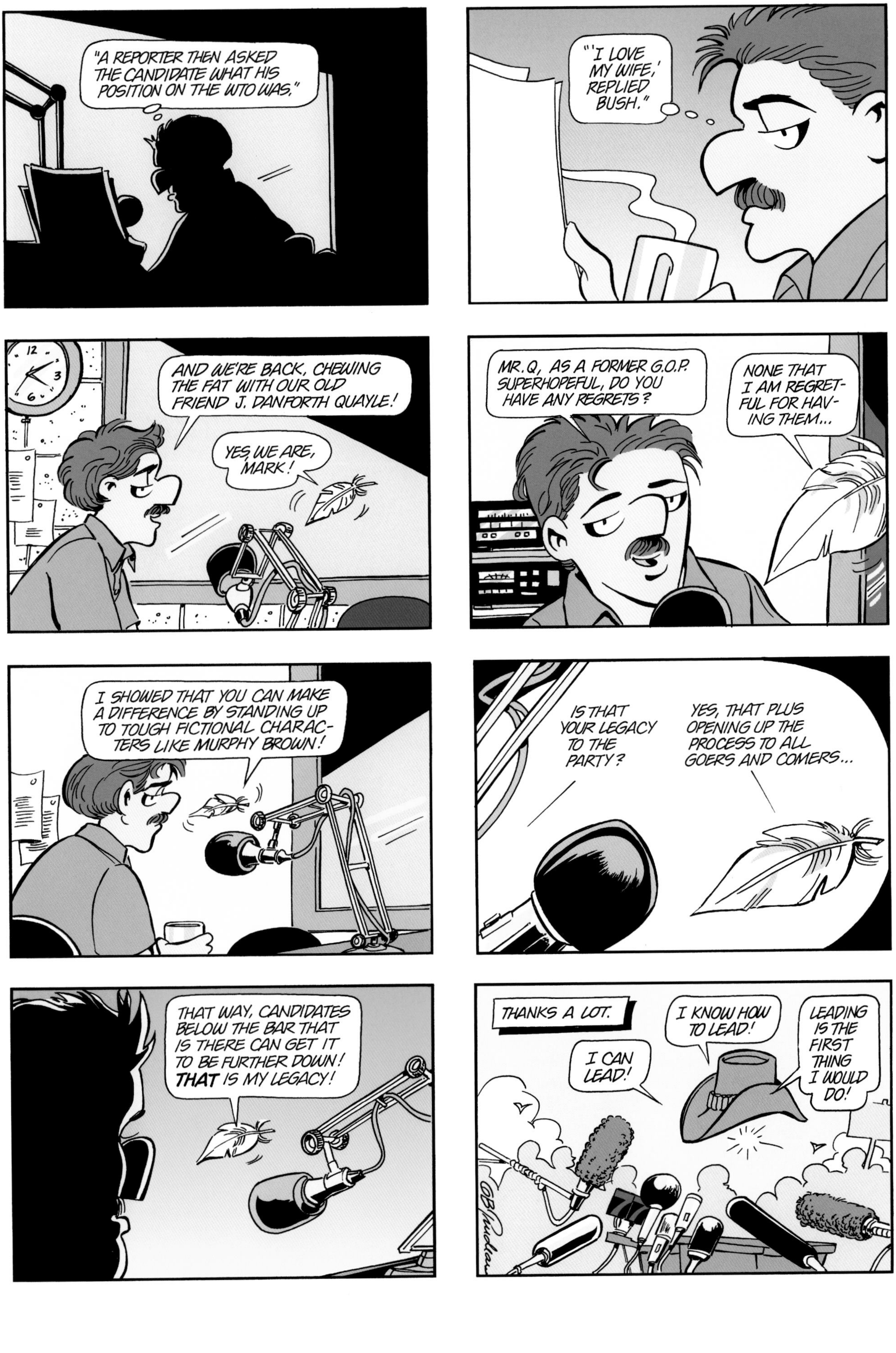
"A REPORTER THEN ASKED THE CANDIDATE WHAT HIS POSITION ON THE WTO WAS."
"'I LOVE MY WIFE,' REPLIED BUSH."
AND WE'RE BACK, CHEWING THE FAT WITH OUR OLD FRIEND J. DANFORTH QUAYLE!
YES WE ARE, MARK!
MR. Q, AS A FORMER G.O.P. SUPERHOPEFUL, DO YOU HAVE ANY REGRETS?
NONE THAT I AM REGRETFUL FOR HAVING THEM...
I SHOWED THAT YOU CAN MAKE A DIFFERENCE BY STANDING UP TO TOUGH FICTIONAL CHARACTERS LIKE MURPHY BROWN!
IS THAT YOUR LEGACY TO THE PARTY?
YES, THAT PLUS OPENING UP THE PROCESS TO ALL GOERS AND COMERS...
THAT WAY, CANDIDATES BELOW THE BAR THAT IS THERE CAN GET IT TO BE FURTHER DOWN! THAT IS MY LEGACY!
THANKS A LOT.
I CAN LEAD!
I KNOW HOW TO LEAD!
LEADING IS THE FIRST THING I WOULD DO!

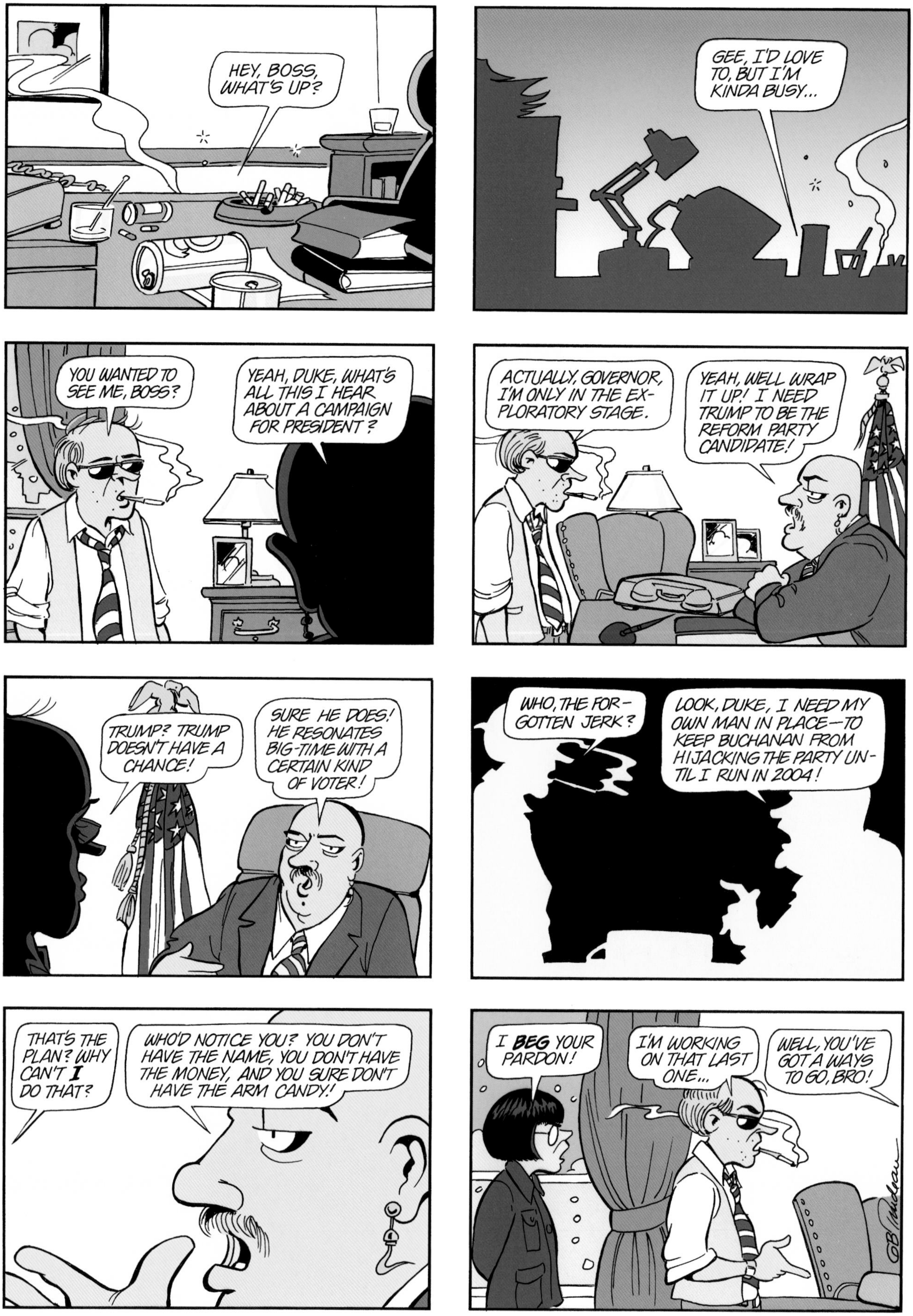
HEY, BOSS, WHAT'S UP?
GEE, I'D LOVE TO, BUT I'M KINDA BUSY...
YOU WANTED TO SEE ME, BOSS?
YEAH, DUKE, WHAT'S ALL THIS I HEAR ABOUT A CAMPAIGN FOR PRESIDENT?
ACTUALLY, GOVERNOR, I'M ONLY IN THE EXPLORATORY STAGE.
YEAH, WELL WRAP IT UP! I NEED TRUMP TO BE THE REFORM PARTY CANDIDATE!
TRUMP? TRUMP DOESN'T HAVE A CHANCE!
SURE HE DOES! HE RESONATES BIG-TIME WITH A CERTAIN KIND OF VOTER!
WHO, THE FORGOTTEN JERK?
LOOK, DUKE, I NEED MY OWN MAN IN PLACE—TO KEEP BUCHANAN FROM HIJACKING THE PARTY UNTIL I RUN IN 2004!
THAT'S THE PLAN? WHY CAN'T I DO THAT?
WHO'D NOTICE YOU? YOU DON'T HAVE THE NAME, YOU DON'T HAVE THE MONEY, AND YOU SURE DON'T HAVE THE ARM CANDY!
I BEG YOUR PARDON!
I'M WORKING ON THAT LAST ONE...
WELL, YOU'VE GOT A WAYS TO GO, BRO!

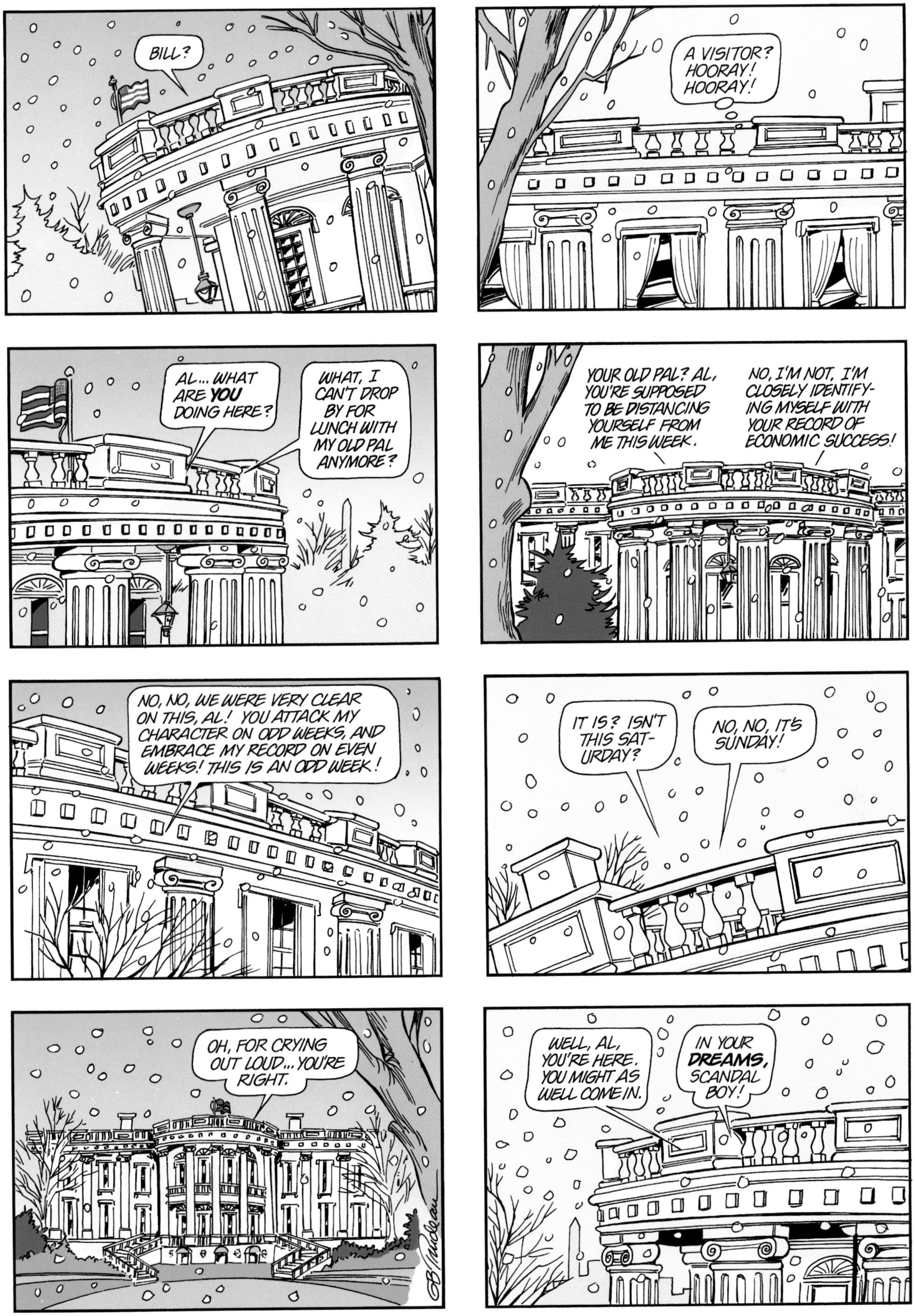
BILL?
A VISITOR? HOORAY! HOORAY!
AL... WHAT ARE **YOU** DOING HERE?
WHAT, I CAN'T DROP BY FOR LUNCH WITH MY OLD PAL ANYMORE?
YOUR OLD PAL? AL, YOU'RE SUPPOSED TO BE DISTANCING YOURSELF FROM ME THIS WEEK.
NO, I'M NOT. I'M CLOSELY IDENTIFYING MYSELF WITH YOUR RECORD OF ECONOMIC SUCCESS!
NO, NO, WE WERE VERY CLEAR ON THIS, AL! YOU ATTACK MY CHARACTER ON ODD WEEKS, AND EMBRACE MY RECORD ON EVEN WEEKS! THIS IS AN ODD WEEK!
IT IS? ISN'T THIS SATURDAY?
NO, NO, IT'S SUNDAY!
OH, FOR CRYING OUT LOUD... YOU'RE RIGHT.
GB Trudeau
WELL, AL, YOU'RE HERE. YOU MIGHT AS WELL COME IN.
IN YOUR **DREAMS,** SCANDAL BOY!

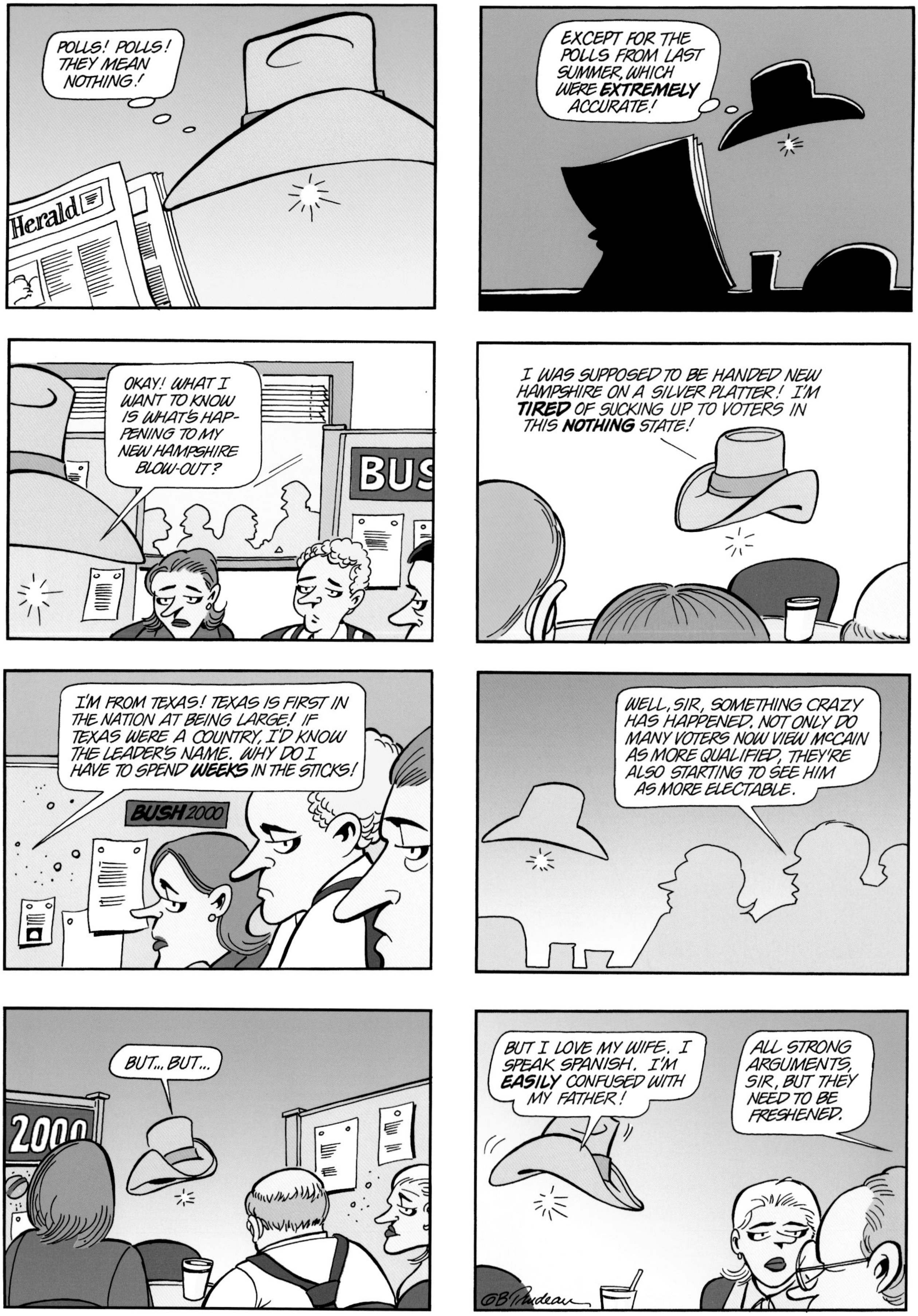
POLLS! POLLS! THEY MEAN NOTHING!
Herald
EXCEPT FOR THE POLLS FROM LAST SUMMER, WHICH WERE **EXTREMELY** ACCURATE!
OKAY! WHAT I WANT TO KNOW IS WHAT'S HAPPENING TO MY NEW HAMPSHIRE BLOW-OUT?
BUS
I WAS SUPPOSED TO BE HANDED NEW HAMPSHIRE ON A SILVER PLATTER! I'M **TIRED** OF SUCKING UP TO VOTERS IN THIS **NOTHING** STATE!
I'M FROM TEXAS! TEXAS IS FIRST IN THE NATION AT BEING LARGE! IF TEXAS WERE A COUNTRY, I'D KNOW THE LEADER'S NAME. WHY DO I HAVE TO SPEND **WEEKS** IN THE STICKS!
BUSH 2000
WELL, SIR, SOMETHING CRAZY HAS HAPPENED. NOT ONLY DO MANY VOTERS NOW VIEW McCAIN AS MORE QUALIFIED, THEY'RE ALSO STARTING TO SEE HIM AS MORE ELECTABLE.
BUT... BUT...
2000
BUT I LOVE MY WIFE. I SPEAK SPANISH. I'M **EASILY** CONFUSED WITH MY FATHER!
ALL STRONG ARGUMENTS, SIR, BUT THEY NEED TO BE FRESHENED.
©B. Trudeau

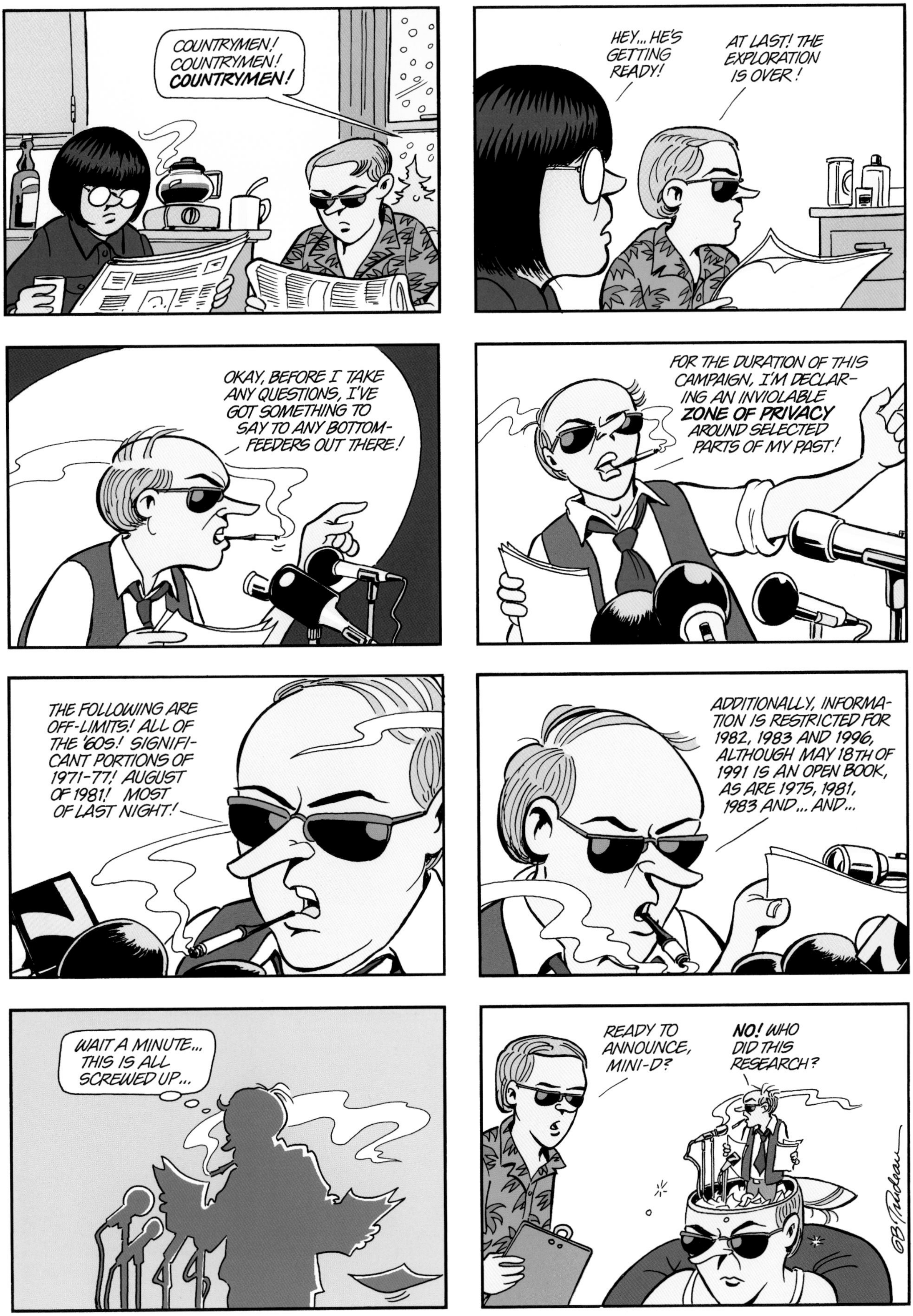
COUNTRYMEN! COUNTRYMEN! COUNTRYMEN!
HEY... HE'S GETTING READY!
AT LAST! THE EXPLORATION IS OVER!
OKAY, BEFORE I TAKE ANY QUESTIONS, I'VE GOT SOMETHING TO SAY TO ANY BOTTOM-FEEDERS OUT THERE!
FOR THE DURATION OF THIS CAMPAIGN, I'M DECLARING AN INVIOLABLE ZONE OF PRIVACY AROUND SELECTED PARTS OF MY PAST!
THE FOLLOWING ARE OFF-LIMITS! ALL OF THE '60S! SIGNIFICANT PORTIONS OF 1971-77! AUGUST OF 1981! MOST OF LAST NIGHT!
ADDITIONALLY, INFORMATION IS RESTRICTED FOR 1982, 1983 AND 1996, ALTHOUGH MAY 18TH OF 1991 IS AN OPEN BOOK, AS ARE 1975, 1981, 1983 AND... AND...
WAIT A MINUTE... THIS IS ALL SCREWED UP...
READY TO ANNOUNCE, MINI-D?
NO! WHO DID THIS RESEARCH?

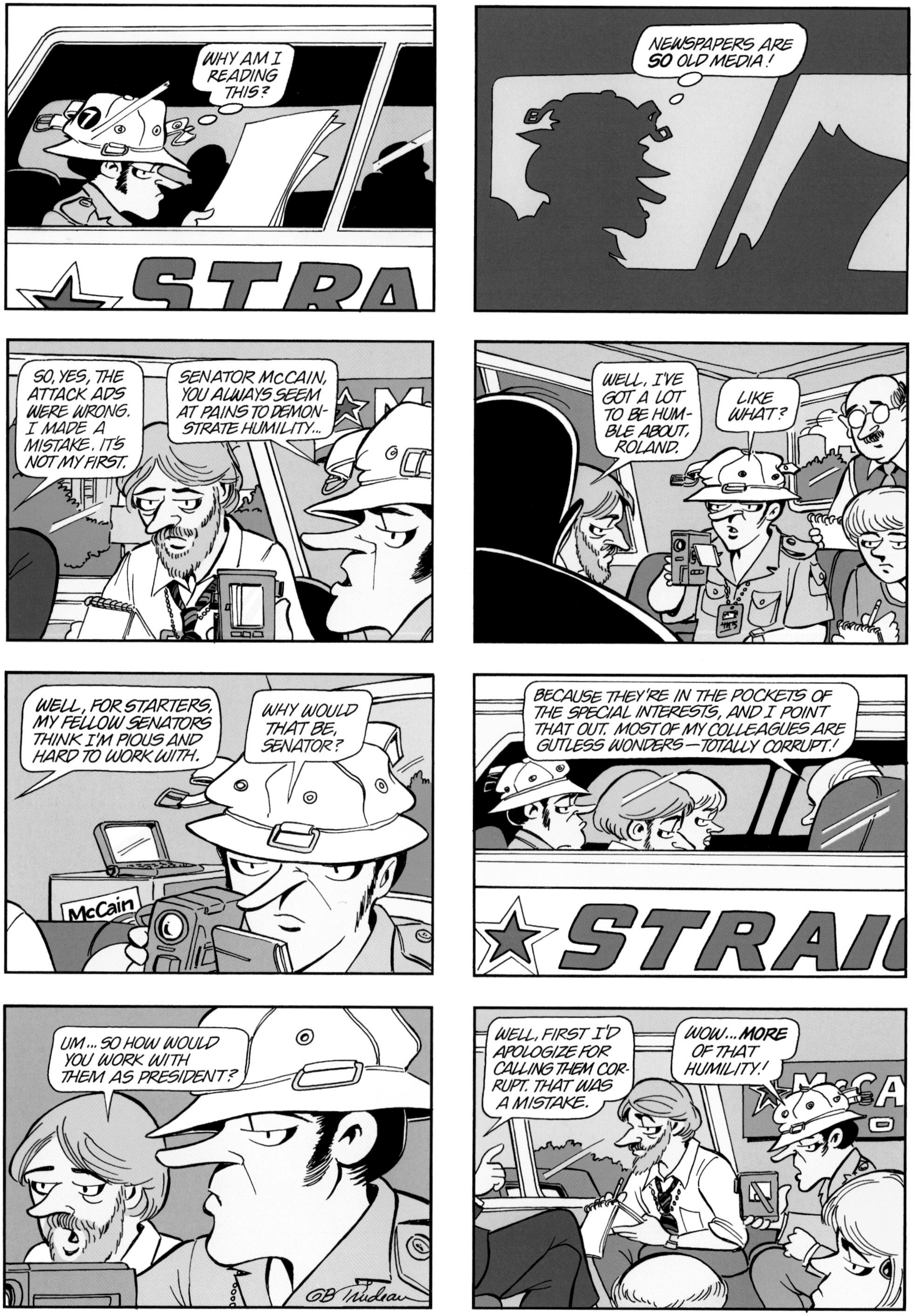
WHY AM I READING THIS?
STRA
NEWSPAPERS ARE **SO** OLD MEDIA!
SO, YES, THE ATTACK ADS WERE WRONG. I MADE A MISTAKE. IT'S NOT MY FIRST.
SENATOR McCAIN, YOU ALWAYS SEEM AT PAINS TO DEMONSTRATE HUMILITY...
WELL, I'VE GOT A LOT TO BE HUMBLE ABOUT, ROLAND.
LIKE WHAT?
WELL, FOR STARTERS, MY FELLOW SENATORS THINK I'M PIOUS AND HARD TO WORK WITH.
WHY WOULD THAT BE, SENATOR?
McCain
BECAUSE THEY'RE IN THE POCKETS OF THE SPECIAL INTERESTS, AND I POINT THAT OUT. MOST OF MY COLLEAGUES ARE GUTLESS WONDERS—TOTALLY CORRUPT!
STRAI
UM... SO HOW WOULD YOU WORK WITH THEM AS PRESIDENT?
WELL, FIRST I'D APOLOGIZE FOR CALLING THEM CORRUPT. THAT WAS A MISTAKE.
WOW... **MORE** OF THAT HUMILITY!

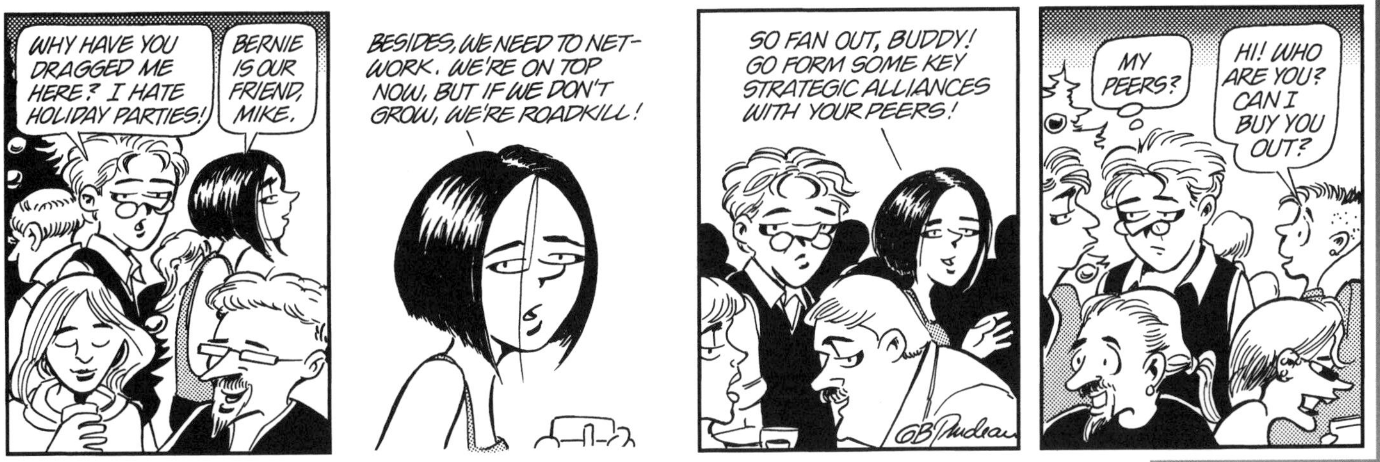
WHY HAVE YOU DRAGGED ME HERE? I HATE HOLIDAY PARTIES!
BERNIE IS OUR FRIEND, MIKE.
BESIDES, WE NEED TO NET-WORK. WE'RE ON TOP NOW, BUT IF WE DON'T GROW, WE'RE ROADKILL!
SO FAN OUT, BUDDY! GO FORM SOME KEY STRATEGIC ALLIANCES WITH YOUR PEERS!
MY PEERS?
HI! WHO ARE YOU? CAN I BUY YOU OUT?

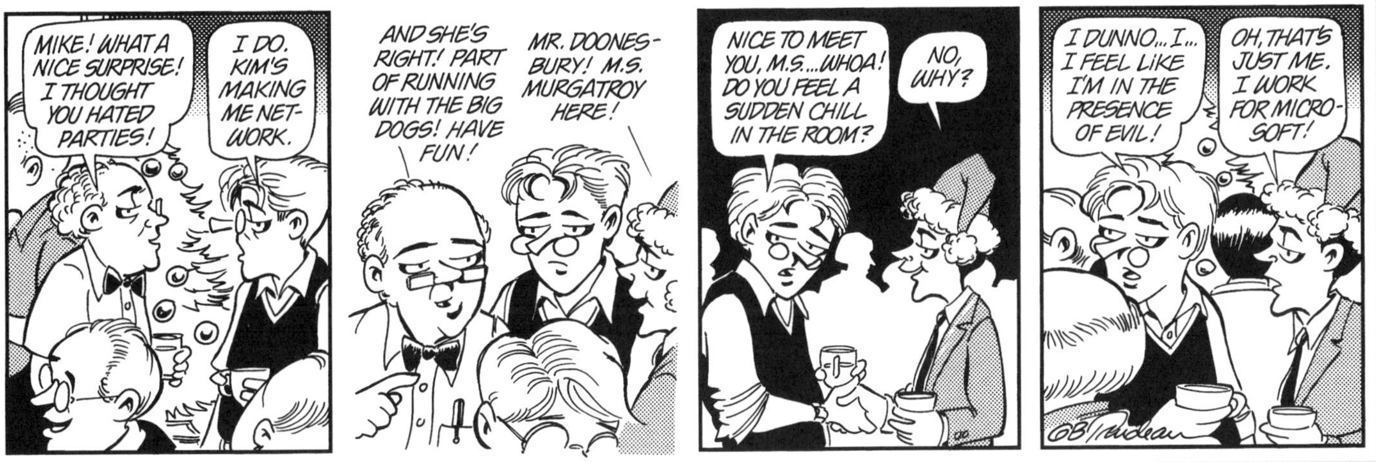
MIKE! WHAT A NICE SURPRISE! I THOUGHT YOU HATED PARTIES!
I DO. KIM'S MAKING ME NET-WORK.
AND SHE'S RIGHT! PART OF RUNNING WITH THE BIG DOGS! HAVE FUN!
MR. DOONES-BURY! M.S. MURGATROY HERE!
NICE TO MEET YOU, M.S.... WHOA! DO YOU FEEL A SUDDEN CHILL IN THE ROOM?
NO, WHY?
I DUNNO... I... I FEEL LIKE I'M IN THE PRESENCE OF EVIL!
OH, THAT'S JUST ME. I WORK FOR MICRO-SOFT!

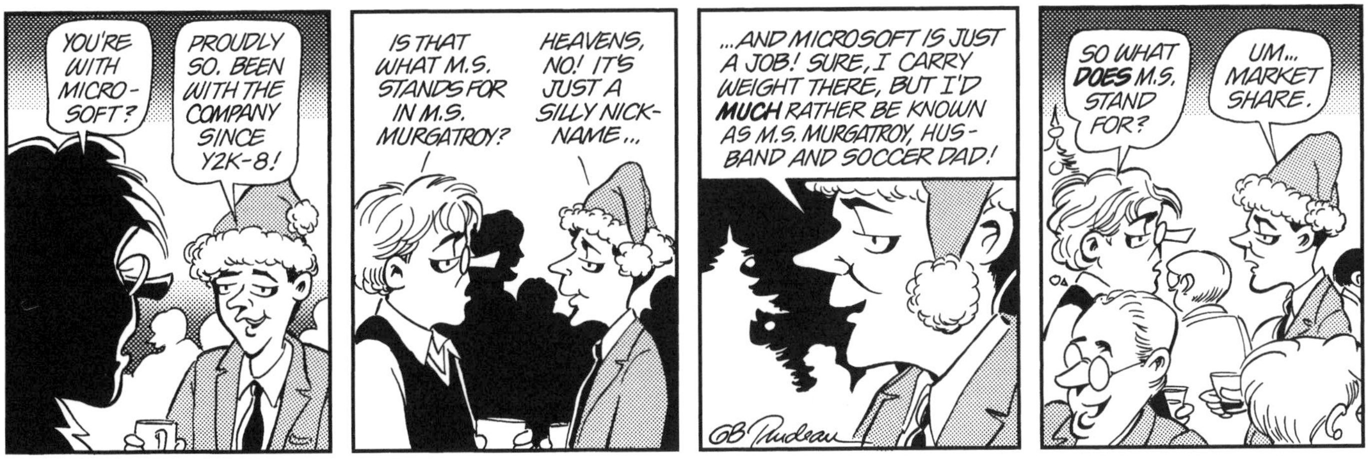
YOU'RE WITH MICRO-SOFT?
PROUDLY SO. BEEN WITH THE COMPANY SINCE Y2K-8!
IS THAT WHAT M.S. STANDS FOR IN M.S. MURGATROY?
HEAVENS, NO! IT'S JUST A SILLY NICK-NAME...
...AND MICROSOFT IS JUST A JOB! SURE, I CARRY WEIGHT THERE, BUT I'D MUCH RATHER BE KNOWN AS M.S. MURGATROY, HUS-BAND AND SOCCER DAD!
SO WHAT DOES M.S. STAND FOR?
UM... MARKET SHARE.

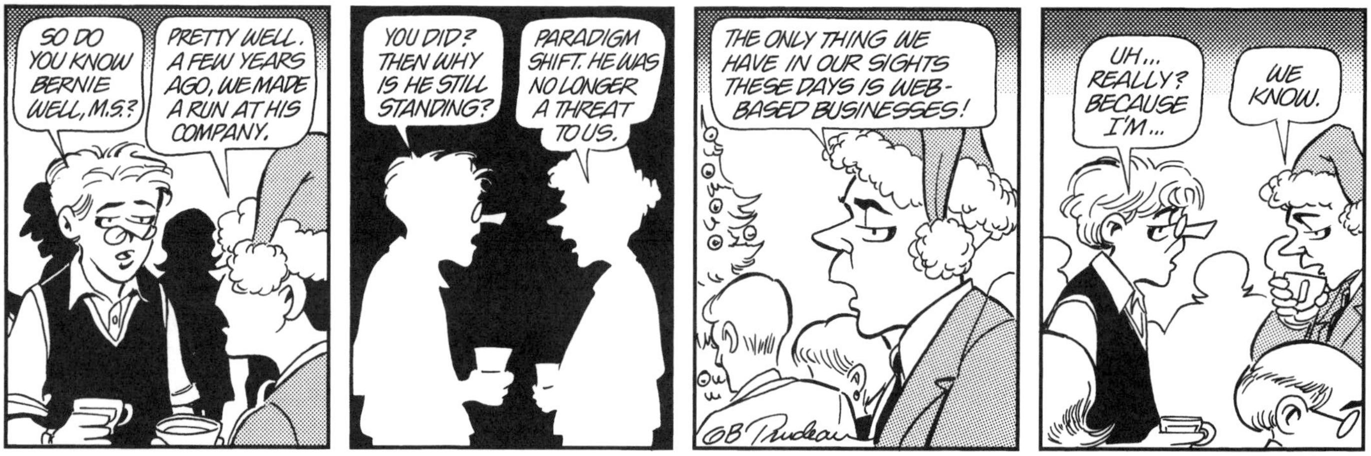
SO DO YOU KNOW BERNIE WELL, M.S.?
PRETTY WELL. A FEW YEARS AGO, WE MADE A RUN AT HIS COMPANY.
YOU DID? THEN WHY IS HE STILL STANDING?
PARADIGM SHIFT. HE WAS NO LONGER A THREAT TO US.
THE ONLY THING WE HAVE IN OUR SIGHTS THESE DAYS IS WEB-BASED BUSINESSES!
UH... REALLY? BECAUSE I'M...
WE KNOW.
©B Trudeau

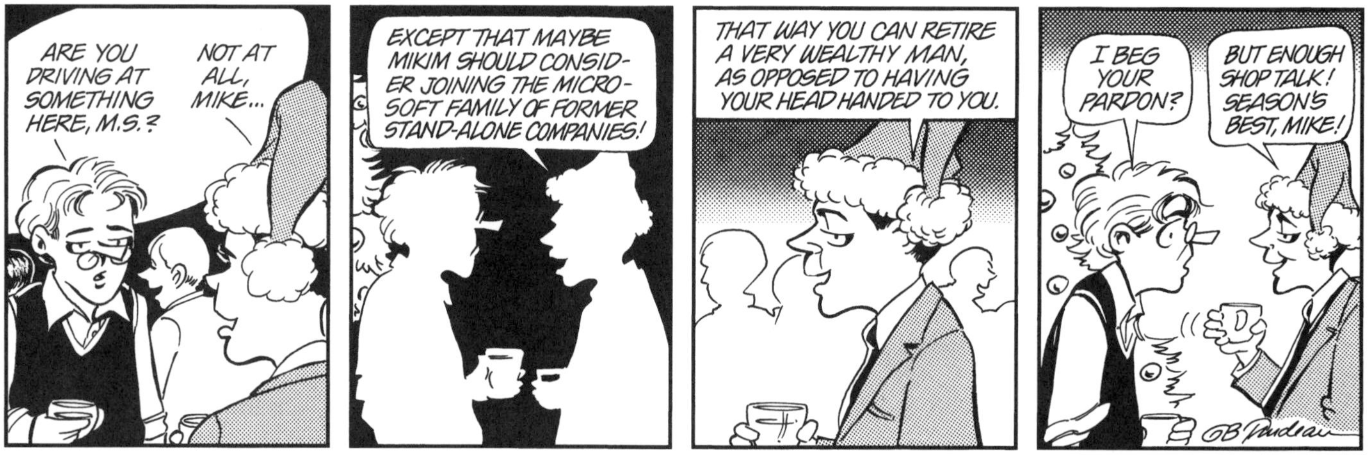
ARE YOU DRIVING AT SOMETHING HERE, M.S.?
NOT AT ALL, MIKE...
EXCEPT THAT MAYBE MIKIM SHOULD CONSIDER JOINING THE MICROSOFT FAMILY OF FORMER STAND-ALONE COMPANIES!
THAT WAY YOU CAN RETIRE A VERY WEALTHY MAN, AS OPPOSED TO HAVING YOUR HEAD HANDED TO YOU.
I BEG YOUR PARDON?
BUT ENOUGH SHOP TALK! SEASON'S BEST, MIKE!
©B Trudeau

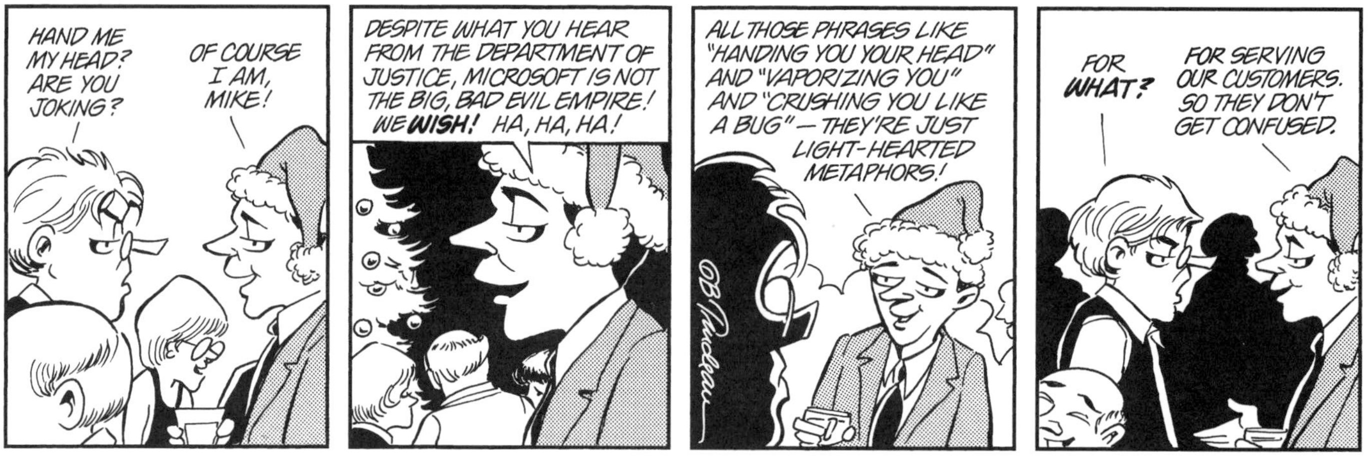
HAND ME MY HEAD? ARE YOU JOKING?
OF COURSE I AM, MIKE!
DESPITE WHAT YOU HEAR FROM THE DEPARTMENT OF JUSTICE, MICROSOFT IS NOT THE BIG, BAD EVIL EMPIRE! WE **WISH!** HA, HA, HA!
ALL THOSE PHRASES LIKE "HANDING YOU YOUR HEAD" AND "VAPORIZING YOU" AND "CRUSHING YOU LIKE A BUG" — THEY'RE JUST LIGHT-HEARTED METAPHORS!
©B Trudeau
FOR **WHAT?**
FOR SERVING OUR CUSTOMERS. SO THEY DON'T GET CONFUSED.

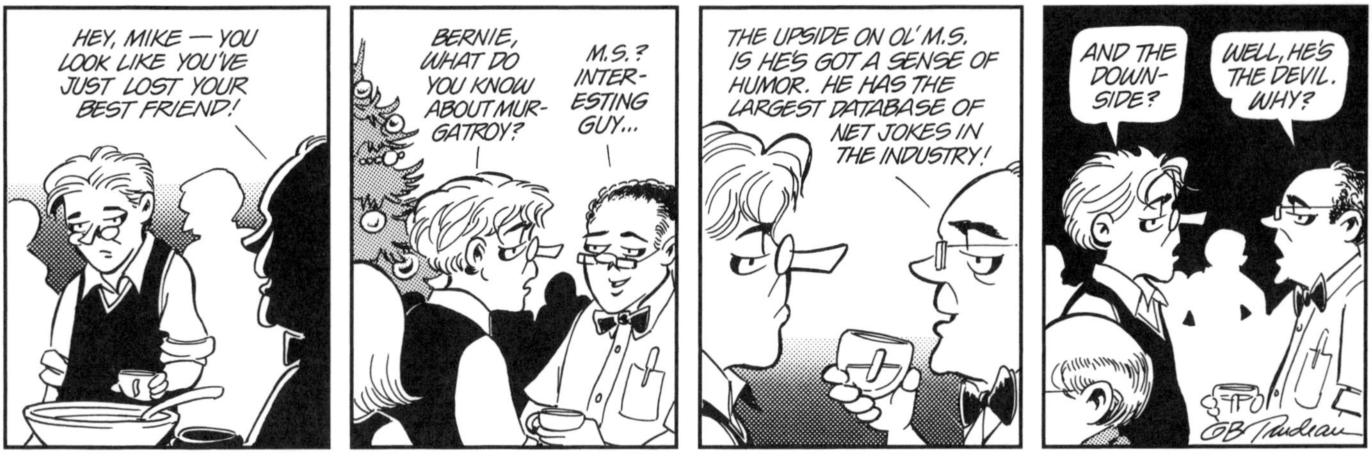
HEY, MIKE — YOU LOOK LIKE YOU'VE JUST LOST YOUR BEST FRIEND!
BERNIE, WHAT DO YOU KNOW ABOUT MURGATROY?
M.S.? INTERESTING GUY...
THE UPSIDE ON OL' M.S. IS HE'S GOT A SENSE OF HUMOR. HE HAS THE LARGEST DATABASE OF NET JOKES IN THE INDUSTRY!
AND THE DOWNSIDE?
WELL, HE'S THE DEVIL. WHY?
©B Trudeau

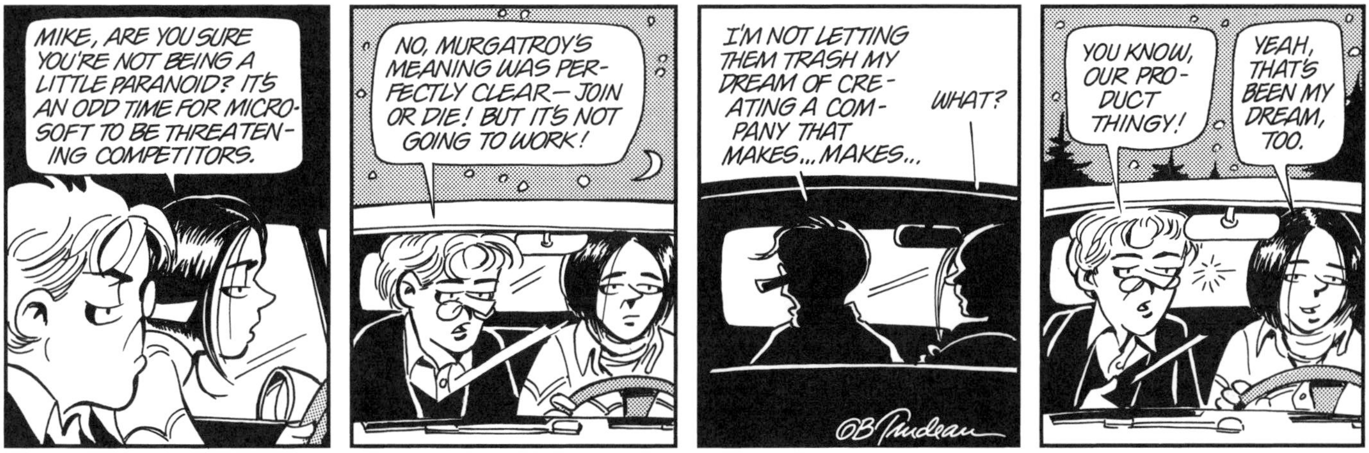
MIKE, ARE YOU SURE YOU'RE NOT BEING A LITTLE PARANOID? IT'S AN ODD TIME FOR MICROSOFT TO BE THREATENING COMPETITORS.
NO, MURGATROY'S MEANING WAS PERFECTLY CLEAR— JOIN OR DIE! BUT IT'S NOT GOING TO WORK!
I'M NOT LETTING THEM TRASH MY DREAM OF CREATING A COMPANY THAT MAKES... MAKES...
WHAT?
YOU KNOW, OUR PRODUCT THINGY!
YEAH, THAT'S BEEN MY DREAM, TOO.
©B Trudeau

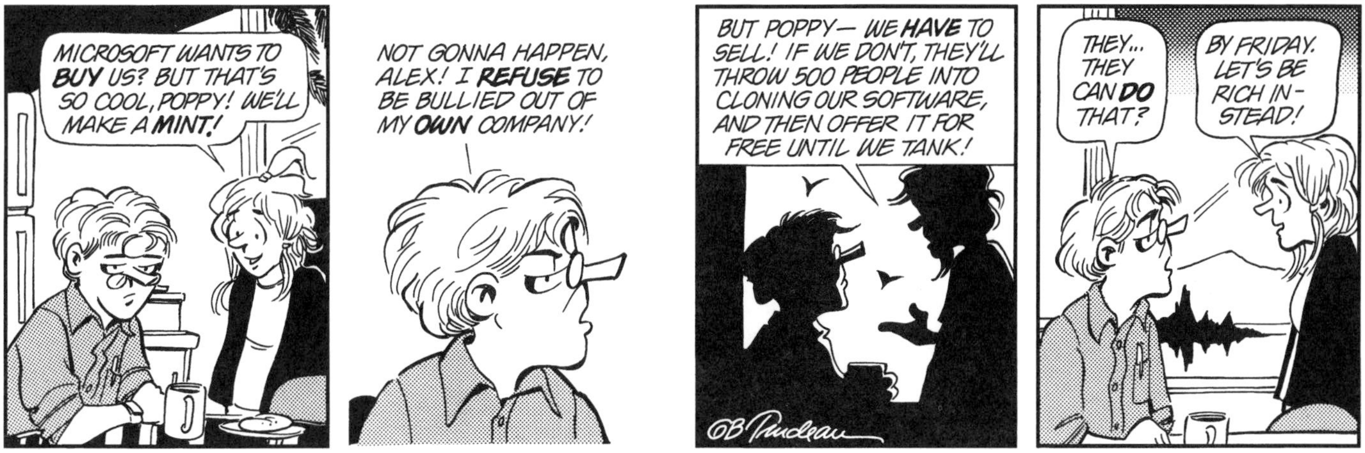
MICROSOFT WANTS TO **BUY** US? BUT THAT'S SO COOL, POPPY! WE'LL MAKE A **MINT!**
NOT GONNA HAPPEN, ALEX! I **REFUSE** TO BE BULLIED OUT OF MY **OWN** COMPANY!
BUT POPPY— WE **HAVE** TO SELL! IF WE DON'T, THEY'LL THROW 500 PEOPLE INTO CLONING OUR SOFTWARE, AND THEN OFFER IT FOR FREE UNTIL WE TANK!
THEY... THEY CAN **DO** THAT?
BY FRIDAY. LET'S BE RICH INSTEAD!
©B Trudeau

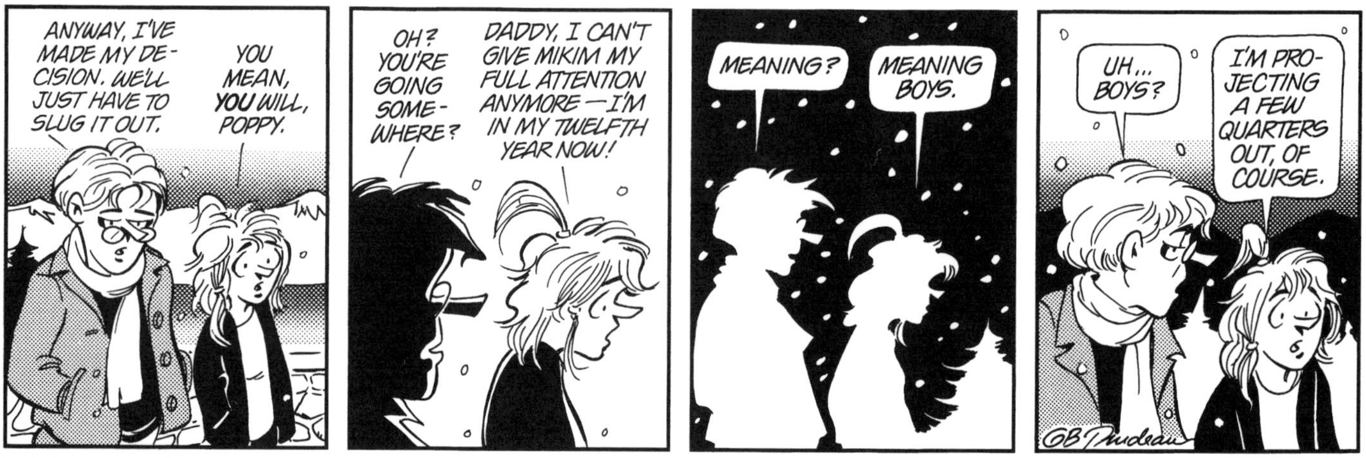
ANYWAY, I'VE MADE MY DECISION. WE'LL JUST HAVE TO SLUG IT OUT.
YOU MEAN, **YOU** WILL, POPPY.
OH? YOU'RE GOING SOMEWHERE?
DADDY, I CAN'T GIVE MIKIM MY FULL ATTENTION ANYMORE—I'M IN MY TWELFTH YEAR NOW!
MEANING?
MEANING BOYS.
UH... BOYS?
I'M PROJECTING A FEW QUARTERS OUT, OF COURSE.
©B Trudeau

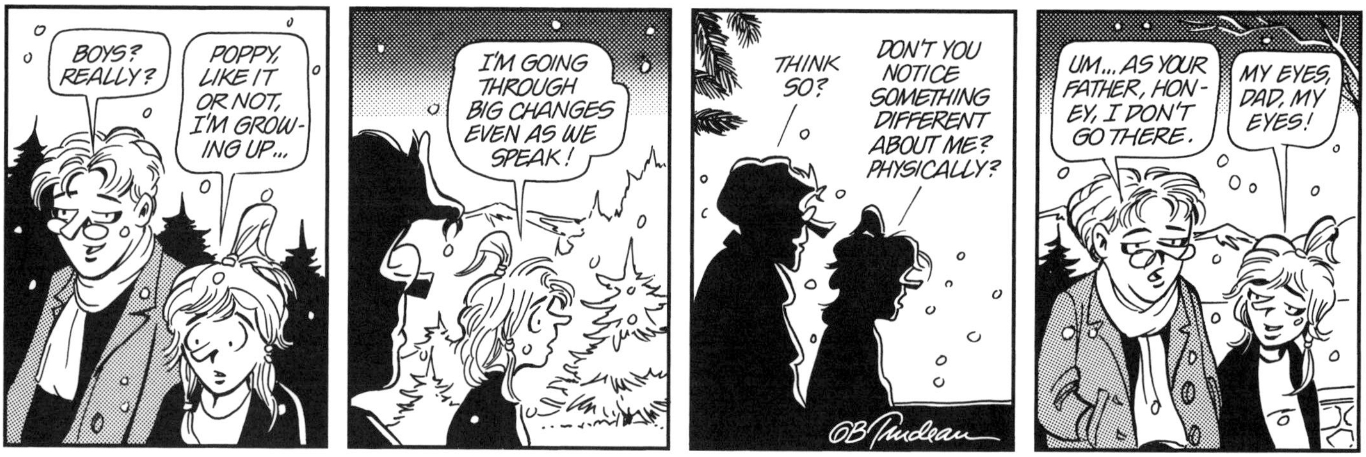
BOYS? REALLY?
POPPY, LIKE IT OR NOT, I'M GROWING UP...
I'M GOING THROUGH BIG CHANGES EVEN AS WE SPEAK!
THINK SO?
DON'T YOU NOTICE SOMETHING DIFFERENT ABOUT ME? PHYSICALLY?
©B Trudeau
UM... AS YOUR FATHER, HONEY, I DON'T GO THERE.
MY EYES, DAD, MY EYES!

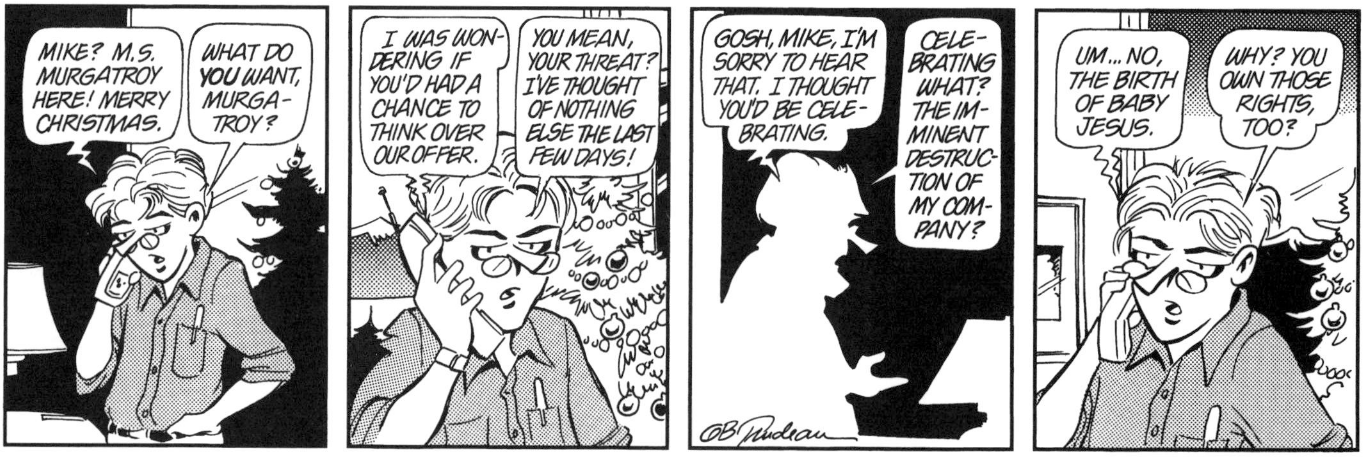
MIKE? M.S. MURGATROY HERE! MERRY CHRISTMAS.
WHAT DO **YOU** WANT, MURGATROY?
I WAS WONDERING IF YOU'D HAD A CHANCE TO THINK OVER OUR OFFER.
YOU MEAN, YOUR THREAT? I'VE THOUGHT OF NOTHING ELSE THE LAST FEW DAYS!
GOSH, MIKE, I'M SORRY TO HEAR THAT. I THOUGHT YOU'D BE CELEBRATING.
CELEBRATING WHAT? THE IMMINENT DESTRUCTION OF MY COMPANY?
©B Trudeau
UM... NO, THE BIRTH OF BABY JESUS.
WHY? YOU OWN THOSE RIGHTS, TOO?

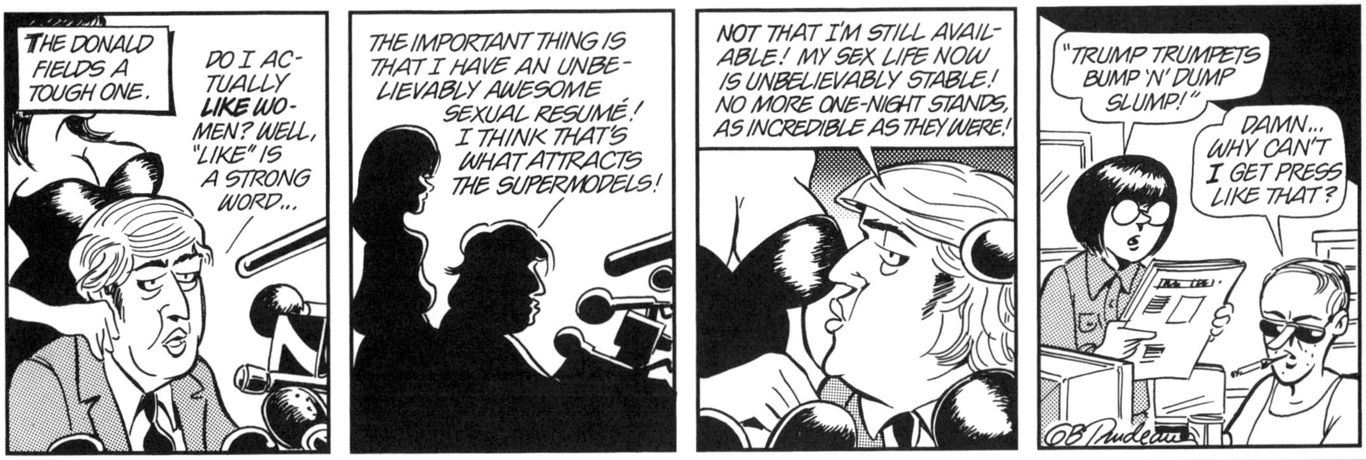
THE DONALD FIELDS A TOUGH ONE.
DO I ACTUALLY LIKE WOMEN? WELL, "LIKE" IS A STRONG WORD...
THE IMPORTANT THING IS THAT I HAVE AN UNBELIEVABLY AWESOME SEXUAL RESUMÉ! I THINK THAT'S WHAT ATTRACTS THE SUPERMODELS!
NOT THAT I'M STILL AVAILABLE! MY SEX LIFE NOW IS UNBELIEVABLY STABLE! NO MORE ONE-NIGHT STANDS, AS INCREDIBLE AS THEY WERE!
"TRUMP TRUMPETS BUMP 'N' DUMP SLUMP!"
DAMN... WHY CAN'T I GET PRESS LIKE THAT?
©B Trudeau

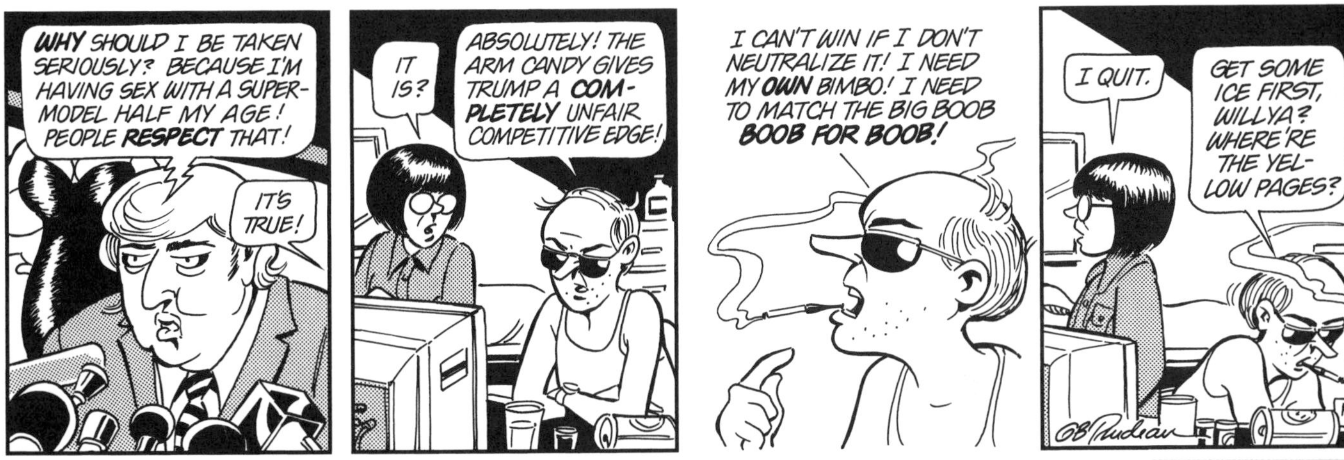
WHY SHOULD I BE TAKEN SERIOUSLY? BECAUSE I'M HAVING SEX WITH A SUPERMODEL HALF MY AGE! PEOPLE RESPECT THAT!
IT'S TRUE!
IT IS?
ABSOLUTELY! THE ARM CANDY GIVES TRUMP A COMPLETELY UNFAIR COMPETITIVE EDGE!
I CAN'T WIN IF I DON'T NEUTRALIZE IT! I NEED MY OWN BIMBO! I NEED TO MATCH THE BIG BOOB BOOB FOR BOOB!
I QUIT.
GET SOME ICE FIRST, WILLYA? WHERE'RE THE YELLOW PAGES?
©B Trudeau

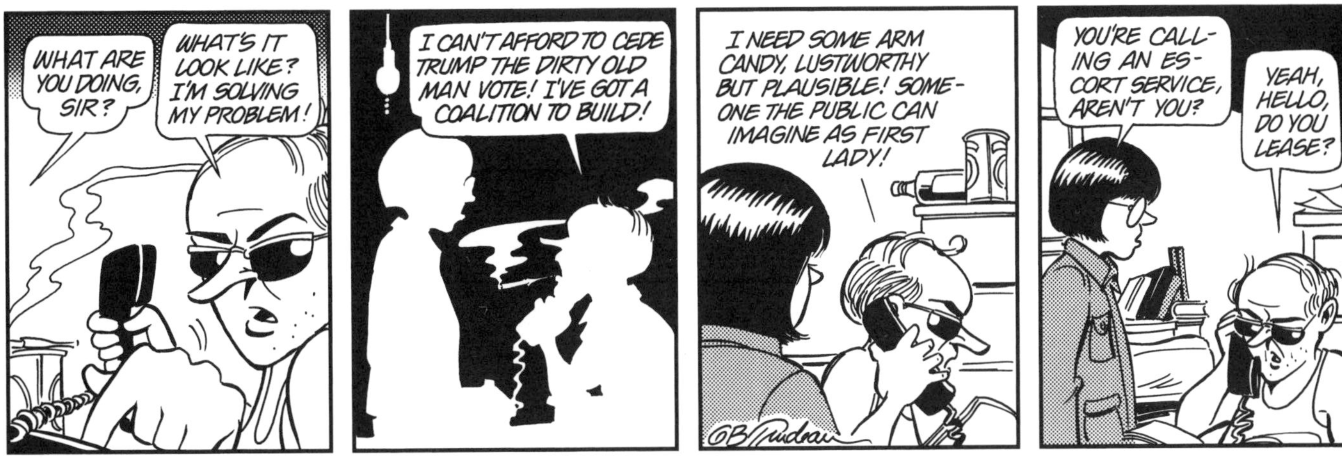
WHAT ARE YOU DOING, SIR?
WHAT'S IT LOOK LIKE? I'M SOLVING MY PROBLEM!
I CAN'T AFFORD TO CEDE TRUMP THE DIRTY OLD MAN VOTE! I'VE GOT A COALITION TO BUILD!
I NEED SOME ARM CANDY, LUSTWORTHY BUT PLAUSIBLE! SOMEONE THE PUBLIC CAN IMAGINE AS FIRST LADY!
©B Trudeau
YOU'RE CALLING AN ESCORT SERVICE, AREN'T YOU?
YEAH, HELLO, DO YOU LEASE?

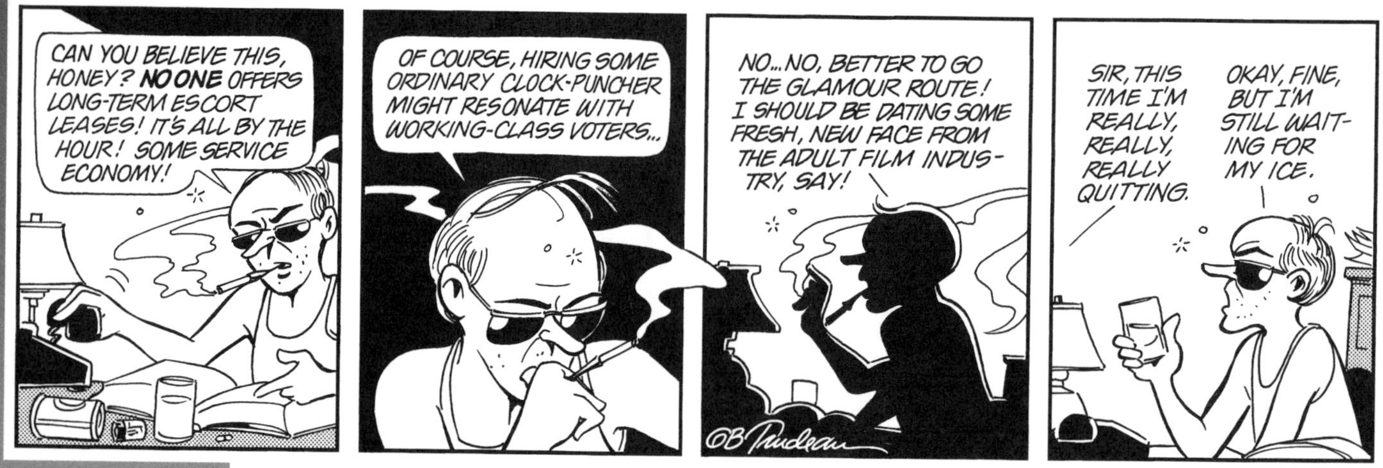
CAN YOU BELIEVE THIS, HONEY? NO ONE OFFERS LONG-TERM ESCORT LEASES! IT'S ALL BY THE HOUR! SOME SERVICE ECONOMY!
OF COURSE, HIRING SOME ORDINARY CLOCK-PUNCHER MIGHT RESONATE WITH WORKING-CLASS VOTERS...
NO...NO, BETTER TO GO THE GLAMOUR ROUTE! I SHOULD BE DATING SOME FRESH, NEW FACE FROM THE ADULT FILM INDUSTRY, SAY!
SIR, THIS TIME I'M REALLY, REALLY, REALLY QUITTING.
OKAY, FINE, BUT I'M STILL WAITING FOR MY ICE.

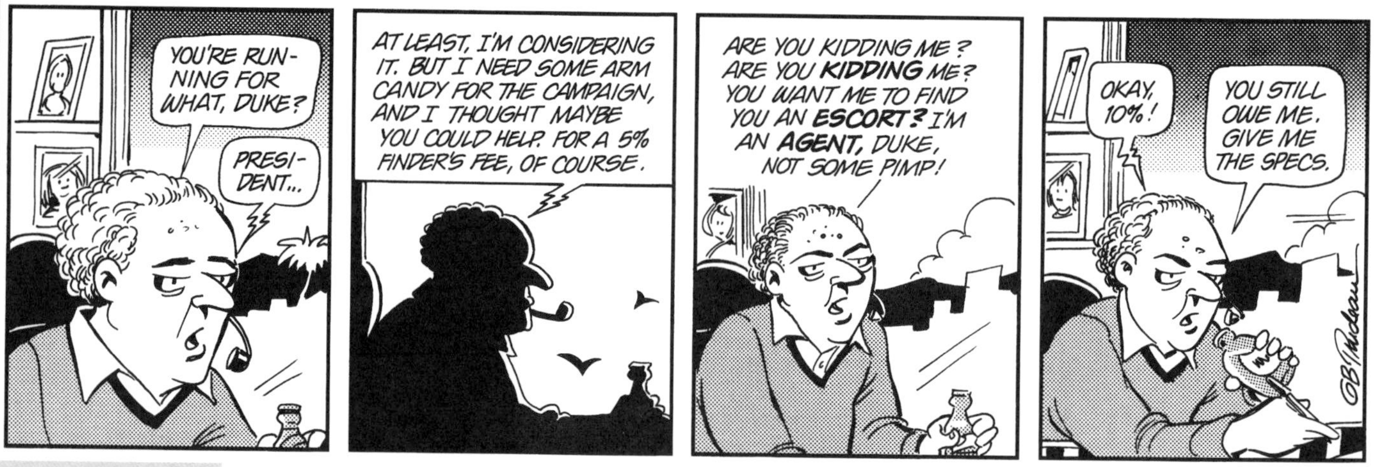
YOU'RE RUNNING FOR WHAT, DUKE?
PRESIDENT...
AT LEAST, I'M CONSIDERING IT. BUT I NEED SOME ARM CANDY FOR THE CAMPAIGN, AND I THOUGHT MAYBE YOU COULD HELP. FOR A 5% FINDER'S FEE, OF COURSE.
ARE YOU KIDDING ME? ARE YOU KIDDING ME? YOU WANT ME TO FIND YOU AN ESCORT? I'M AN AGENT, DUKE, NOT SOME PIMP!
OKAY, 10%!
YOU STILL OWE ME. GIVE ME THE SPECS.

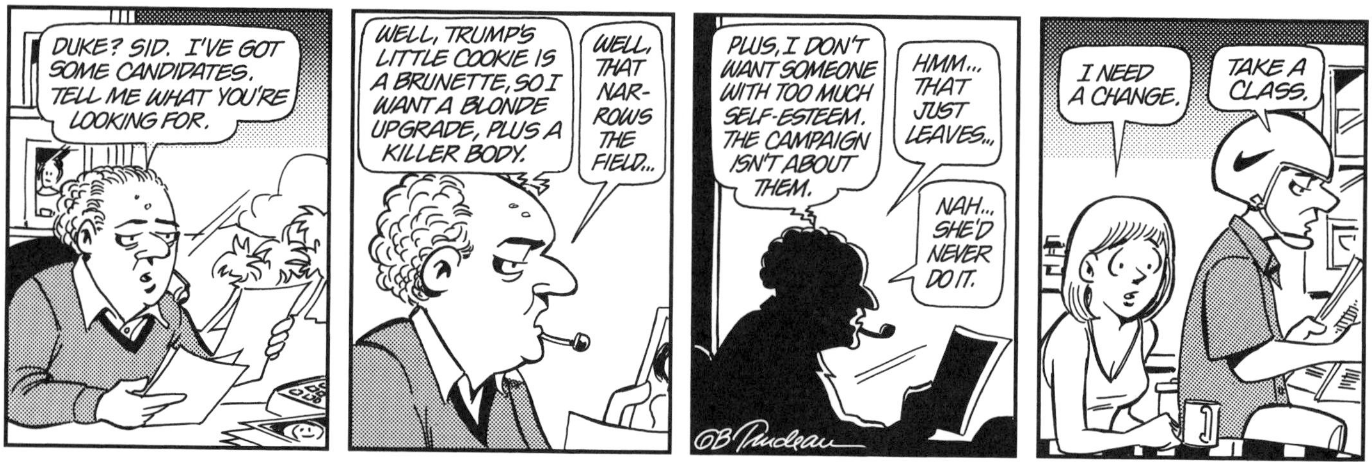
DUKE? SID. I'VE GOT SOME CANDIDATES. TELL ME WHAT YOU'RE LOOKING FOR.
WELL, TRUMP'S LITTLE COOKIE IS A BRUNETTE, SO I WANT A BLONDE UPGRADE, PLUS A KILLER BODY.
WELL, THAT NARROWS THE FIELD...
PLUS, I DON'T WANT SOMEONE WITH TOO MUCH SELF-ESTEEM. THE CAMPAIGN ISN'T ABOUT THEM.
HMM... THAT JUST LEAVES...
NAH... SHE'D NEVER DO IT.
I NEED A CHANGE.
TAKE A CLASS.

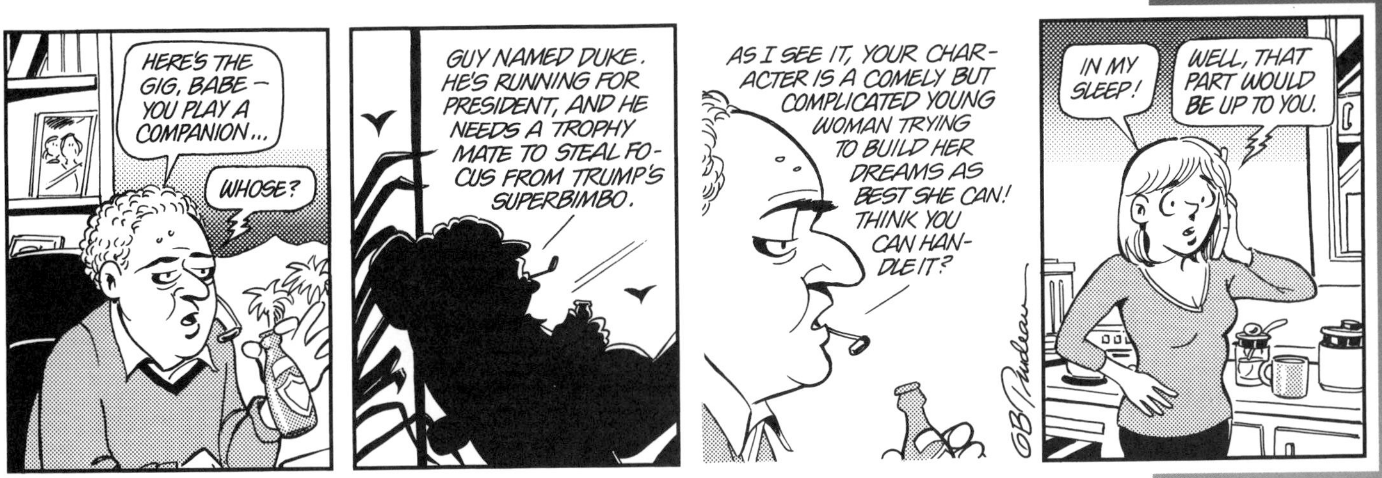
HERE'S THE GIG, BABE — YOU PLAY A COMPANION...
WHOSE?
GUY NAMED DUKE. HE'S RUNNING FOR PRESIDENT, AND HE NEEDS A TROPHY MATE TO STEAL FOCUS FROM TRUMP'S SUPERBIMBO.
AS I SEE IT, YOUR CHARACTER IS A COMELY BUT COMPLICATED YOUNG WOMAN TRYING TO BUILD HER DREAMS AS BEST SHE CAN! THINK YOU CAN HANDLE IT?
IN MY SLEEP!
WELL, THAT PART WOULD BE UP TO YOU.

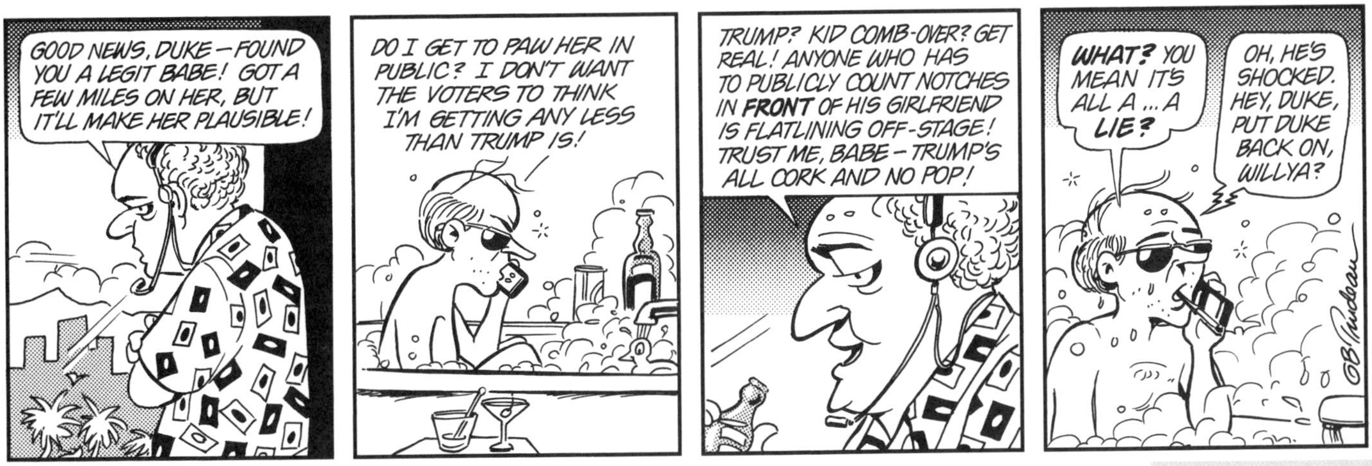
GOOD NEWS, DUKE — FOUND YOU A LEGIT BABE! GOT A FEW MILES ON HER, BUT IT'LL MAKE HER PLAUSIBLE!
DO I GET TO PAW HER IN PUBLIC? I DON'T WANT THE VOTERS TO THINK I'M GETTING ANY LESS THAN TRUMP IS!
TRUMP? KID COMB-OVER? GET REAL! ANYONE WHO HAS TO PUBLICLY COUNT NOTCHES IN FRONT OF HIS GIRLFRIEND IS FLATLINING OFF-STAGE! TRUST ME, BABE — TRUMP'S ALL CORK AND NO POP!
WHAT? YOU MEAN IT'S ALL A ... A LIE?
OH, HE'S SHOCKED. HEY, DUKE, PUT DUKE BACK ON, WILLYA?

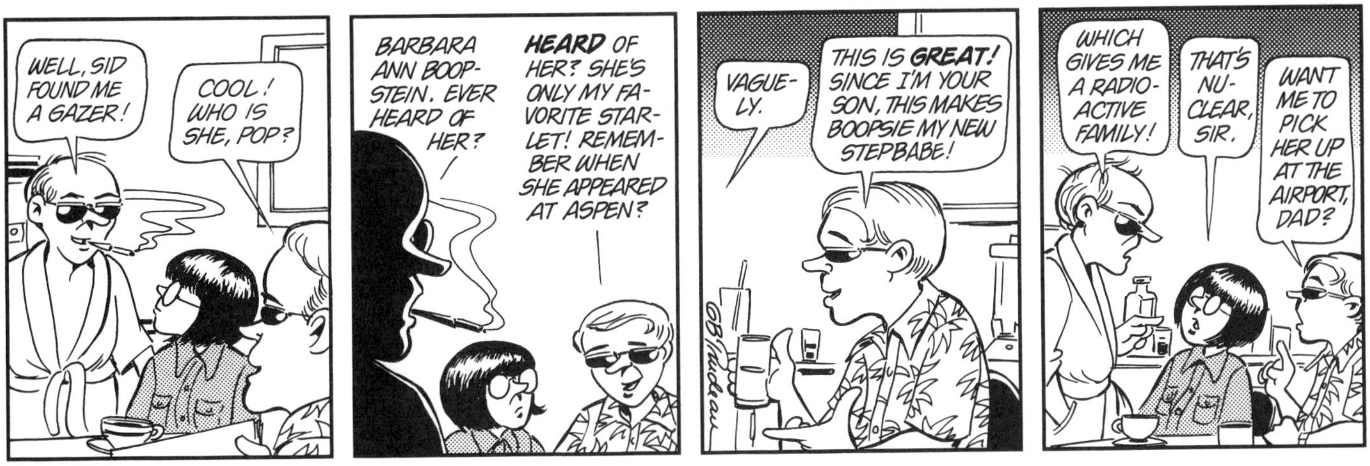
WELL, SID FOUND ME A GAZER!
COOL! WHO IS SHE, POP?
BARBARA ANN BOOPSTEIN. EVER HEARD OF HER?
HEARD OF HER? SHE'S ONLY MY FAVORITE STARLET! REMEMBER WHEN SHE APPEARED AT ASPEN?
VAGUELY.
THIS IS GREAT! SINCE I'M YOUR SON, THIS MAKES BOOPSIE MY NEW STEPBABE!
WHICH GIVES ME A RADIOACTIVE FAMILY!
THAT'S NUCLEAR, SIR.
WANT ME TO PICK HER UP AT THE AIRPORT, DAD?

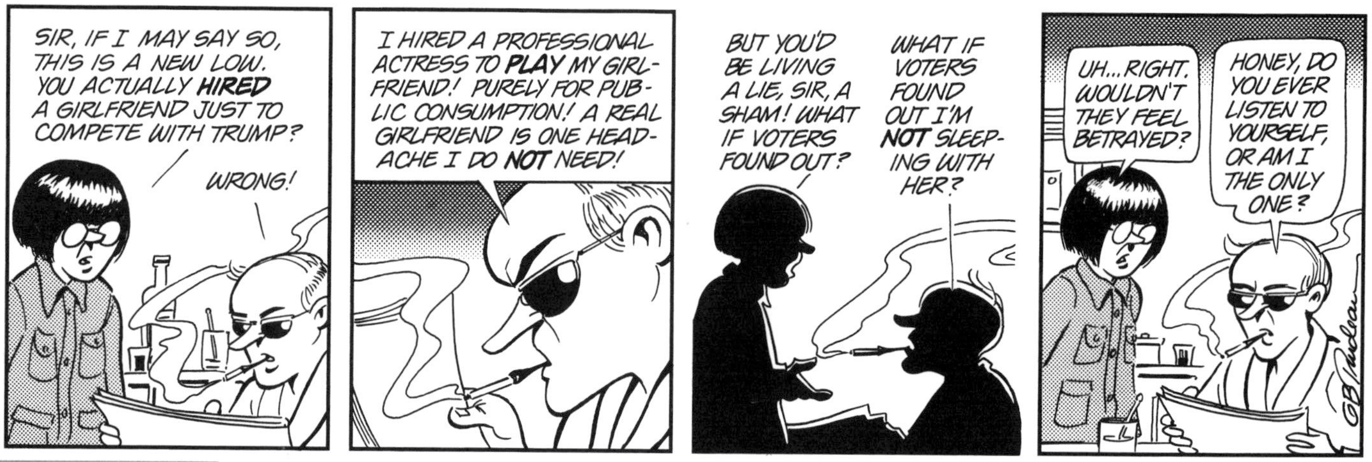
SIR, IF I MAY SAY SO, THIS IS A NEW LOW. YOU ACTUALLY **HIRED** A GIRLFRIEND JUST TO COMPETE WITH TRUMP?
WRONG!
I HIRED A PROFESSIONAL ACTRESS TO **PLAY** MY GIRLFRIEND! PURELY FOR PUBLIC CONSUMPTION! A REAL GIRLFRIEND IS ONE HEADACHE I DO **NOT** NEED!
BUT YOU'D BE LIVING A LIE, SIR, A SHAM! WHAT IF VOTERS FOUND OUT?
WHAT IF VOTERS FOUND OUT I'M **NOT** SLEEPING WITH HER?
UH... RIGHT. WOULDN'T THEY FEEL BETRAYED?
HONEY, DO YOU EVER LISTEN TO YOURSELF, OR AM I THE ONLY ONE?

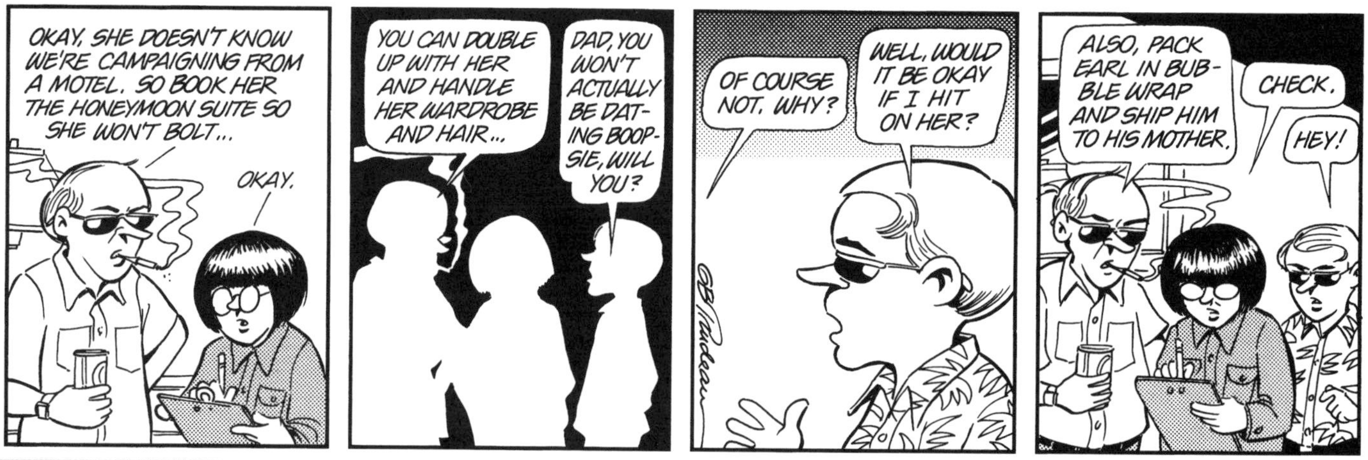
OKAY, SHE DOESN'T KNOW WE'RE CAMPAIGNING FROM A MOTEL. SO BOOK HER THE HONEYMOON SUITE SO SHE WON'T BOLT...
OKAY.
YOU CAN DOUBLE UP WITH HER AND HANDLE HER WARDROBE AND HAIR...
DAD, YOU WON'T ACTUALLY BE DATING BOOPSIE, WILL YOU?
OF COURSE NOT. WHY?
WELL, WOULD IT BE OKAY IF I HIT ON HER?
ALSO, PACK EARL IN BUBBLE WRAP AND SHIP HIM TO HIS MOTHER.
CHECK.
HEY!

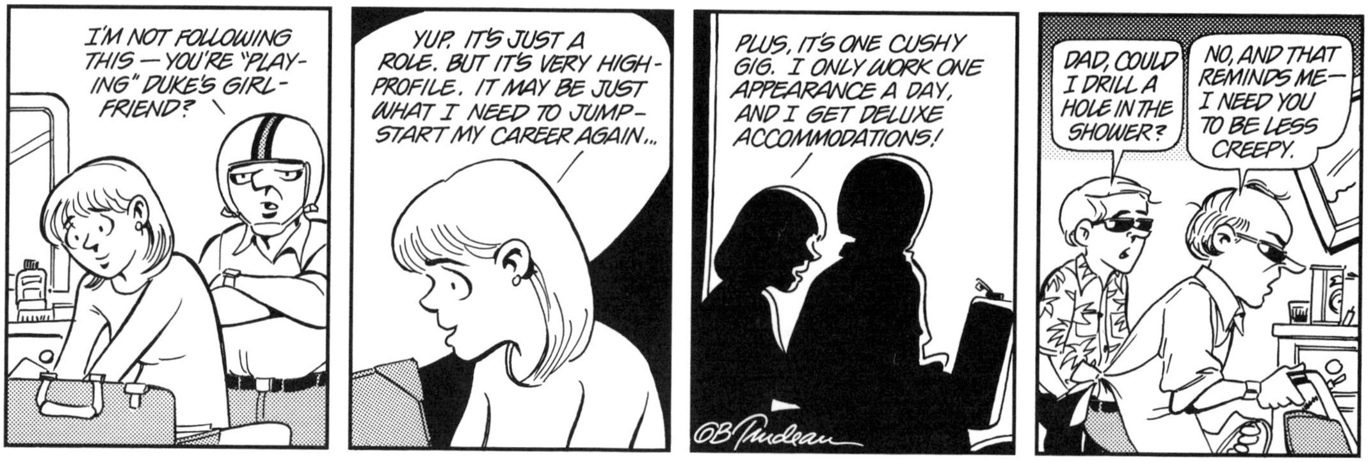
I'M NOT FOLLOWING THIS — YOU'RE "PLAYING" DUKE'S GIRLFRIEND?
YUP. IT'S JUST A ROLE. BUT IT'S VERY HIGH-PROFILE. IT MAY BE JUST WHAT I NEED TO JUMP-START MY CAREER AGAIN...
PLUS, IT'S ONE CUSHY GIG. I ONLY WORK ONE APPEARANCE A DAY, AND I GET DELUXE ACCOMMODATIONS!
DAD, COULD I DRILL A HOLE IN THE SHOWER?
NO, AND THAT REMINDS ME— I NEED YOU TO BE LESS CREEPY.

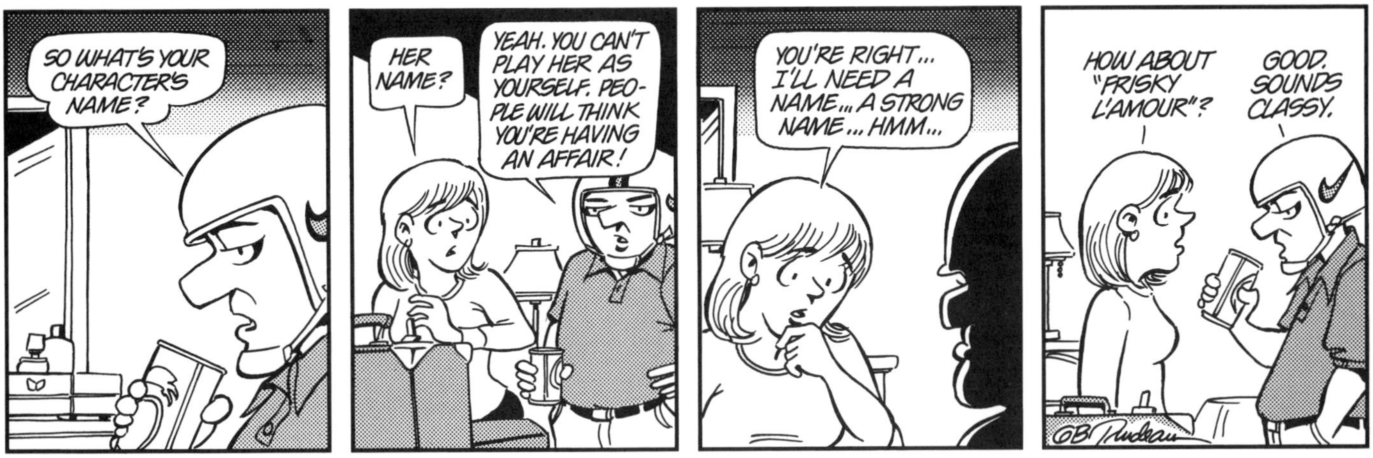
SO WHAT'S YOUR CHARACTER'S NAME?
HER NAME?
YEAH. YOU CAN'T PLAY HER AS YOURSELF. PEOPLE WILL THINK YOU'RE HAVING AN AFFAIR!
YOU'RE RIGHT... I'LL NEED A NAME... A STRONG NAME... HMM...
HOW ABOUT "FRISKY L'AMOUR"?
GOOD. SOUNDS CLASSY.
©B' Trudeau

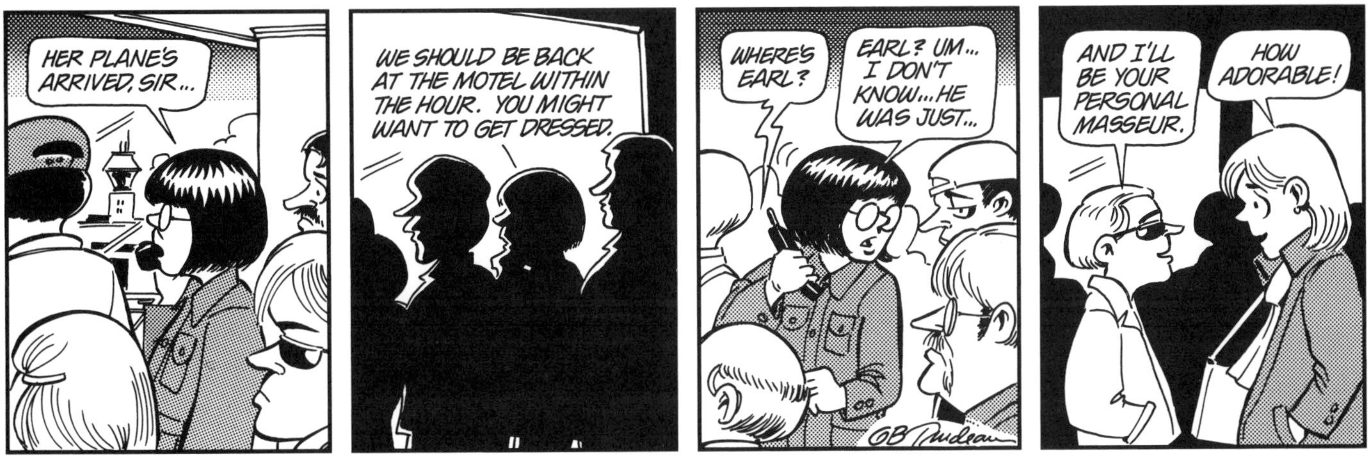
HER PLANE'S ARRIVED, SIR...
WE SHOULD BE BACK AT THE MOTEL WITHIN THE HOUR. YOU MIGHT WANT TO GET DRESSED.
WHERE'S EARL?
EARL? UM... I DON'T KNOW... HE WAS JUST...
AND I'LL BE YOUR PERSONAL MASSEUR.
HOW ADORABLE!
©B' Trudeau

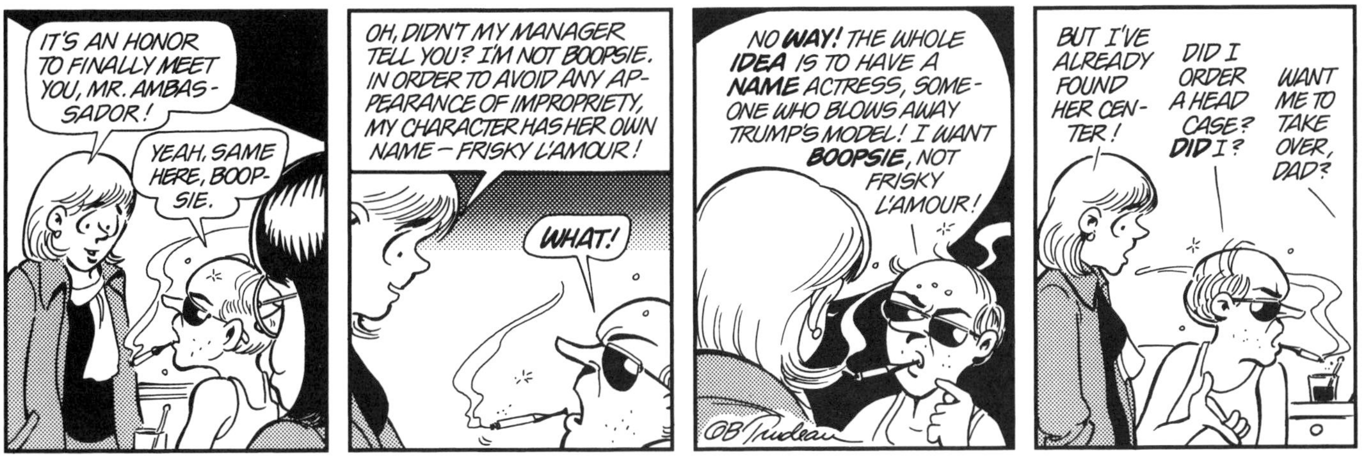
IT'S AN HONOR TO FINALLY MEET YOU, MR. AMBASSADOR!
YEAH, SAME HERE, BOOPSIE.
OH, DIDN'T MY MANAGER TELL YOU? I'M NOT BOOPSIE. IN ORDER TO AVOID ANY APPEARANCE OF IMPROPRIETY, MY CHARACTER HAS HER OWN NAME – FRISKY L'AMOUR!
WHAT!
NO **WAY!** THE WHOLE **IDEA** IS TO HAVE A **NAME** ACTRESS, SOMEONE WHO BLOWS AWAY TRUMP'S MODEL! I WANT **BOOPSIE**, NOT FRISKY L'AMOUR!
©B' Trudeau
BUT I'VE ALREADY FOUND HER CENTER!
DID I ORDER A HEAD CASE? **DID** I?
WANT ME TO TAKE OVER, DAD?

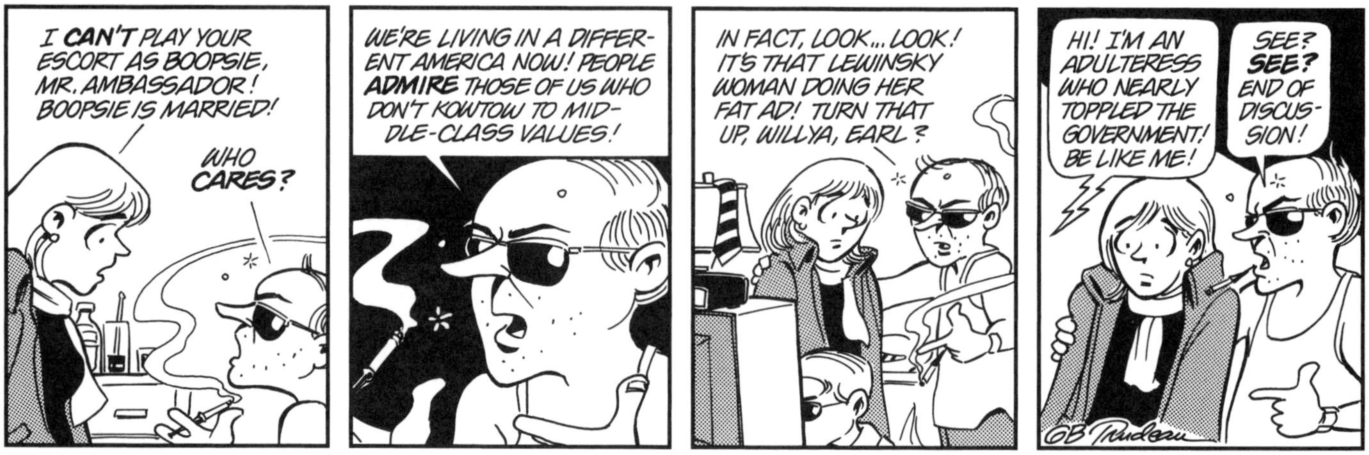
I CAN'T PLAY YOUR ESCORT AS BOOPSIE, MR. AMBASSADOR! BOOPSIE IS MARRIED!
WHO CARES?
WE'RE LIVING IN A DIFFERENT AMERICA NOW! PEOPLE ADMIRE THOSE OF US WHO DON'T KOWTOW TO MIDDLE-CLASS VALUES!
IN FACT, LOOK... LOOK! IT'S THAT LEWINSKY WOMAN DOING HER FAT AD! TURN THAT UP, WILLYA, EARL?
HI! I'M AN ADULTERESS WHO NEARLY TOPPLED THE GOVERNMENT! BE LIKE ME!
SEE? SEE? END OF DISCUSSION!

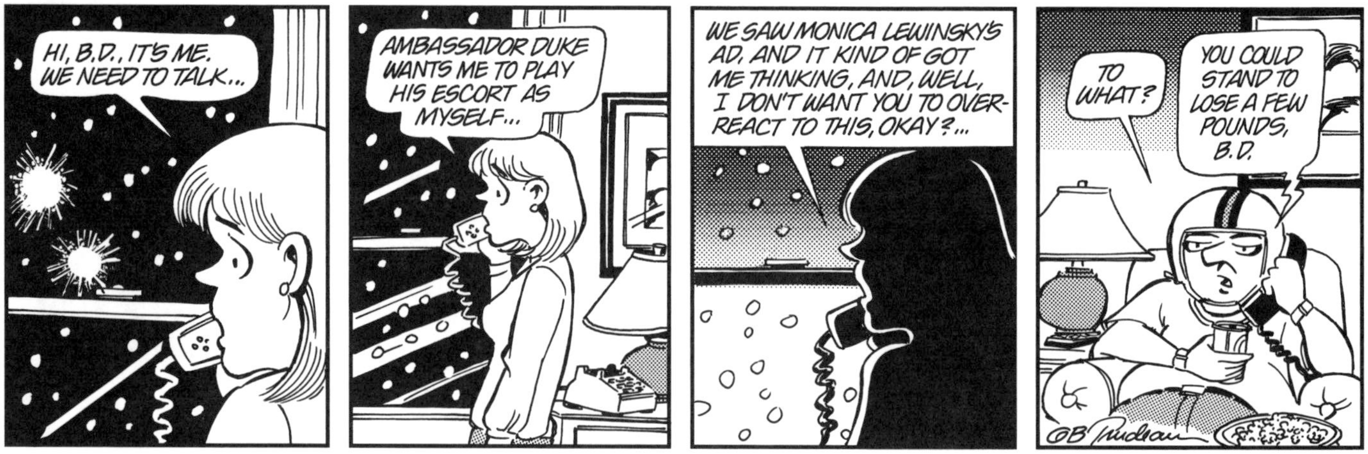
HI, B.D., IT'S ME. WE NEED TO TALK...
AMBASSADOR DUKE WANTS ME TO PLAY HIS ESCORT AS MYSELF...
WE SAW MONICA LEWINSKY'S AD, AND IT KIND OF GOT ME THINKING, AND, WELL, I DON'T WANT YOU TO OVERREACT TO THIS, OKAY?...
TO WHAT?
YOU COULD STAND TO LOSE A FEW POUNDS, B.D.

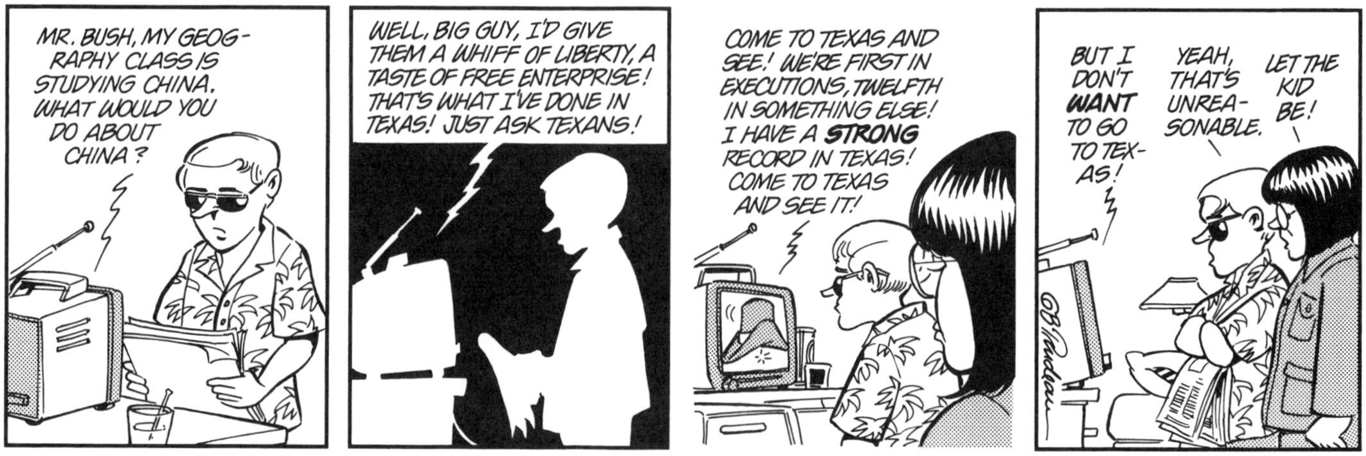
MR. BUSH, MY GEOGRAPHY CLASS IS STUDYING CHINA. WHAT WOULD YOU DO ABOUT CHINA?
WELL, BIG GUY, I'D GIVE THEM A WHIFF OF LIBERTY, A TASTE OF FREE ENTERPRISE! THAT'S WHAT I'VE DONE IN TEXAS! JUST ASK TEXANS!
COME TO TEXAS AND SEE! WE'RE FIRST IN EXECUTIONS, TWELFTH IN SOMETHING ELSE! I HAVE A STRONG RECORD IN TEXAS! COME TO TEXAS AND SEE IT!
BUT I DON'T WANT TO GO TO TEXAS!
YEAH, THAT'S UNREASONABLE.
LET THE KID BE!

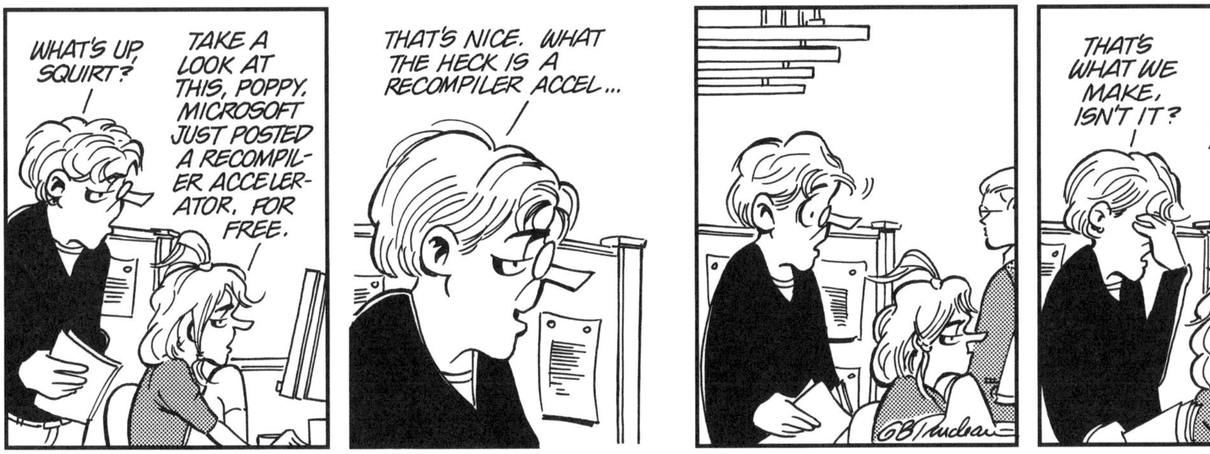
WHAT'S UP, SQUIRT?
TAKE A LOOK AT THIS, POPPY. MICROSOFT JUST POSTED A RECOMPILER ACCELERATOR. FOR FREE.
THAT'S NICE. WHAT THE HECK IS A RECOMPILER ACCEL...
THAT'S WHAT WE MAKE, ISN'T IT?
YOU KNOW, PRIVATE SCHOOL WAS NEVER A GOOD FIT FOR ME ANYWAY.

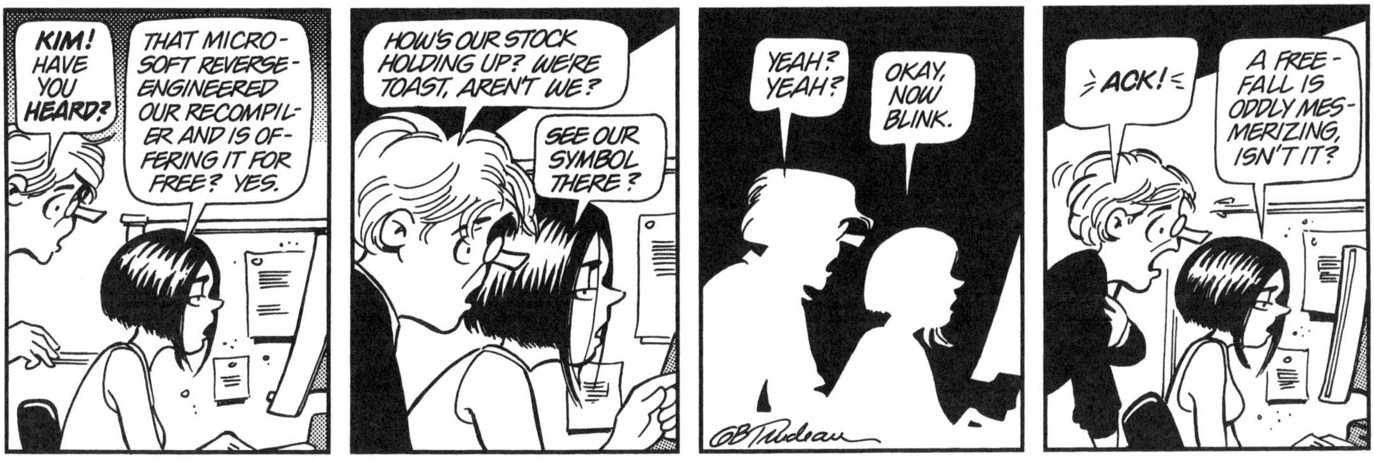
KIM! HAVE YOU **HEARD?**
THAT MICROSOFT REVERSE-ENGINEERED OUR RECOMPILER AND IS OFFERING IT FOR FREE? YES.
HOW'S OUR STOCK HOLDING UP? WE'RE TOAST, AREN'T WE?
SEE OUR SYMBOL THERE?
YEAH? YEAH?
OKAY, NOW BLINK.
ACK!
A FREE-FALL IS ODDLY MESMERIZING, ISN'T IT?

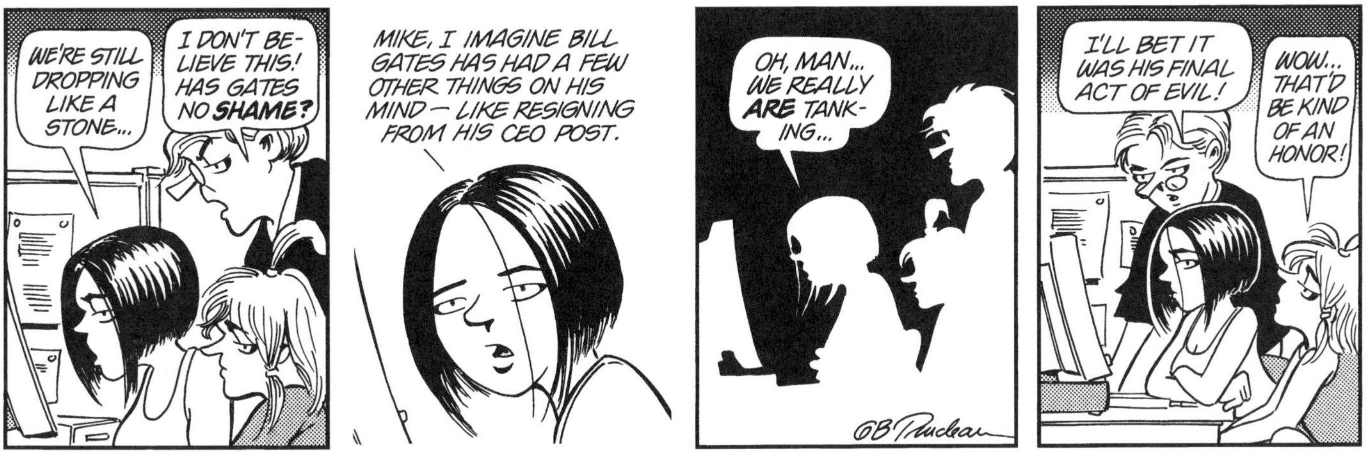
WE'RE STILL DROPPING LIKE A STONE...
I DON'T BELIEVE THIS! HAS GATES NO **SHAME?**
MIKE, I IMAGINE BILL GATES HAS HAD A FEW OTHER THINGS ON HIS MIND — LIKE RESIGNING FROM HIS CEO POST.
OH, MAN... WE REALLY **ARE** TANKING...
I'LL BET IT WAS HIS FINAL ACT OF EVIL!
WOW... THAT'D BE KIND OF AN HONOR!

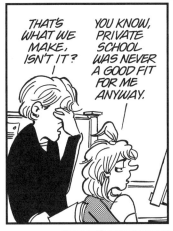

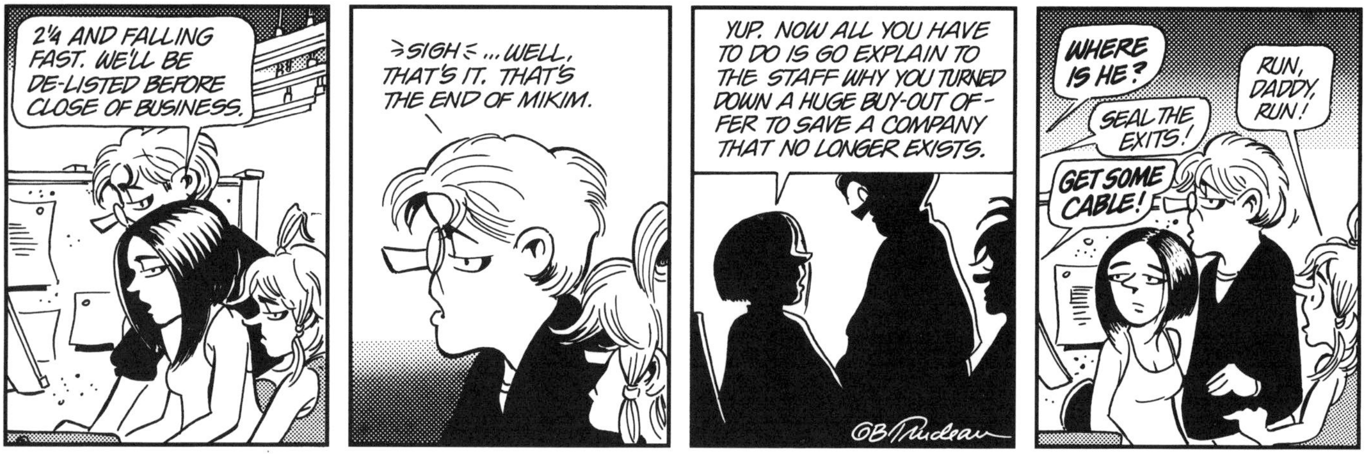
2¼ AND FALLING FAST. WE'LL BE DE-LISTED BEFORE CLOSE OF BUSINESS.
⋛SIGH⋚ ... WELL, THAT'S IT. THAT'S THE END OF MIKIM.
YUP. NOW ALL YOU HAVE TO DO IS GO EXPLAIN TO THE STAFF WHY YOU TURNED DOWN A HUGE BUY-OUT OFFER TO SAVE A COMPANY THAT NO LONGER EXISTS.
WHERE IS HE?
SEAL THE EXITS!
GET SOME CABLE!
RUN, DADDY, RUN!

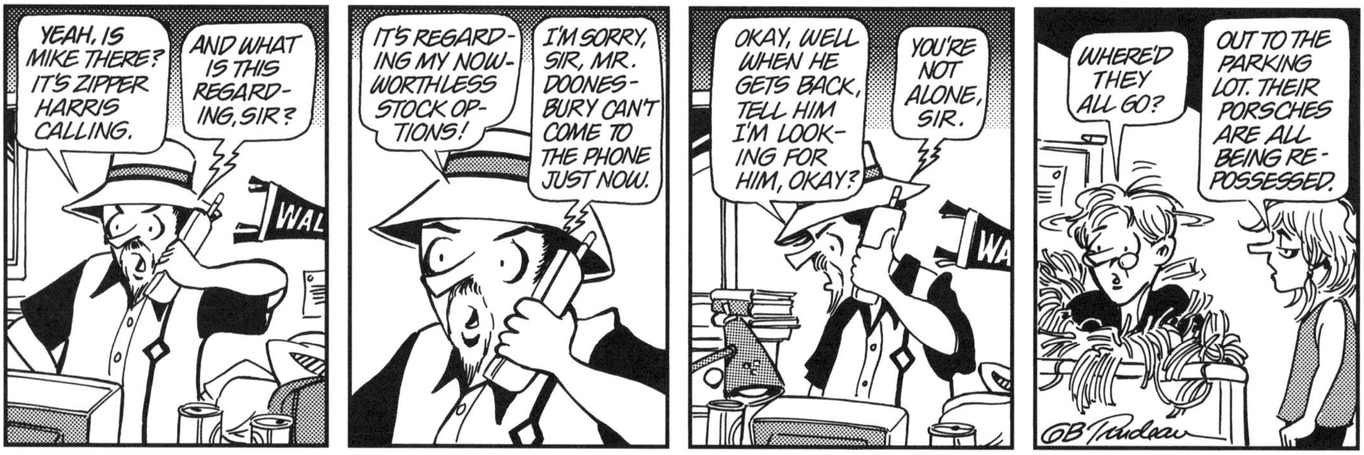
YEAH, IS MIKE THERE? IT'S ZIPPER HARRIS CALLING.
AND WHAT IS THIS REGARDING, SIR?
WAL
IT'S REGARDING MY NOW-WORTHLESS STOCK OPTIONS!
I'M SORRY, SIR, MR. DOONESBURY CAN'T COME TO THE PHONE JUST NOW.
OKAY, WELL WHEN HE GETS BACK, TELL HIM I'M LOOKING FOR HIM, OKAY?
YOU'RE NOT ALONE, SIR.
WA
WHERE'D THEY ALL GO?
OUT TO THE PARKING LOT. THEIR PORSCHES ARE ALL BEING REPOSSESSED.

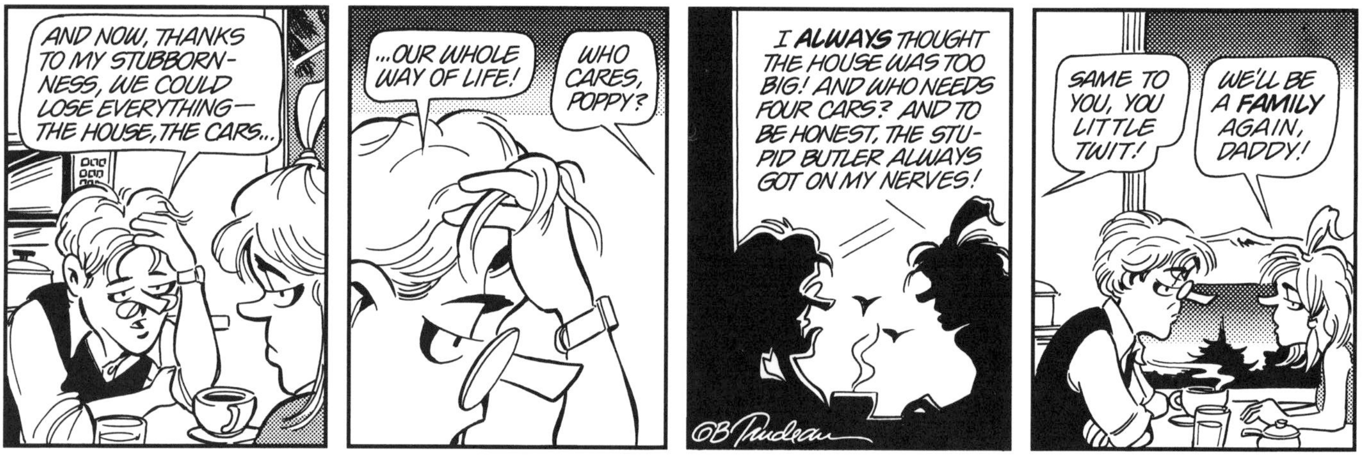
AND NOW, THANKS TO MY STUBBORNNESS, WE COULD LOSE EVERYTHING— THE HOUSE, THE CARS...
...OUR WHOLE WAY OF LIFE!
WHO CARES, POPPY?
I ALWAYS THOUGHT THE HOUSE WAS TOO BIG! AND WHO NEEDS FOUR CARS? AND TO BE HONEST, THE STUPID BUTLER ALWAYS GOT ON MY NERVES!
SAME TO YOU, YOU LITTLE TWIT!
WE'LL BE A FAMILY AGAIN, DADDY!

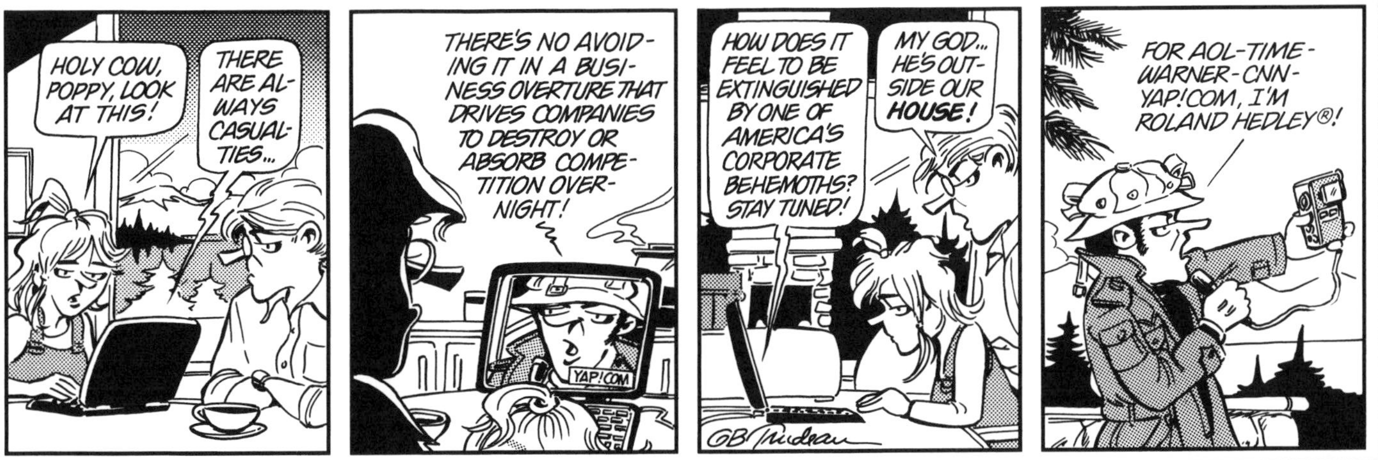
HOLY COW, POPPY, LOOK AT THIS!
THERE ARE ALWAYS CASUALTIES...
THERE'S NO AVOIDING IT IN A BUSINESS OVERTURE THAT DRIVES COMPANIES TO DESTROY OR ABSORB COMPETITION OVERNIGHT!
YAP!COM
HOW DOES IT FEEL TO BE EXTINGUISHED BY ONE OF AMERICA'S CORPORATE BEHEMOTHS? STAY TUNED!
MY GOD... HE'S OUTSIDE OUR HOUSE!
GB Trudeau
FOR AOL-TIME-WARNER-CNN-YAP!COM, I'M ROLAND HEDLEY®!

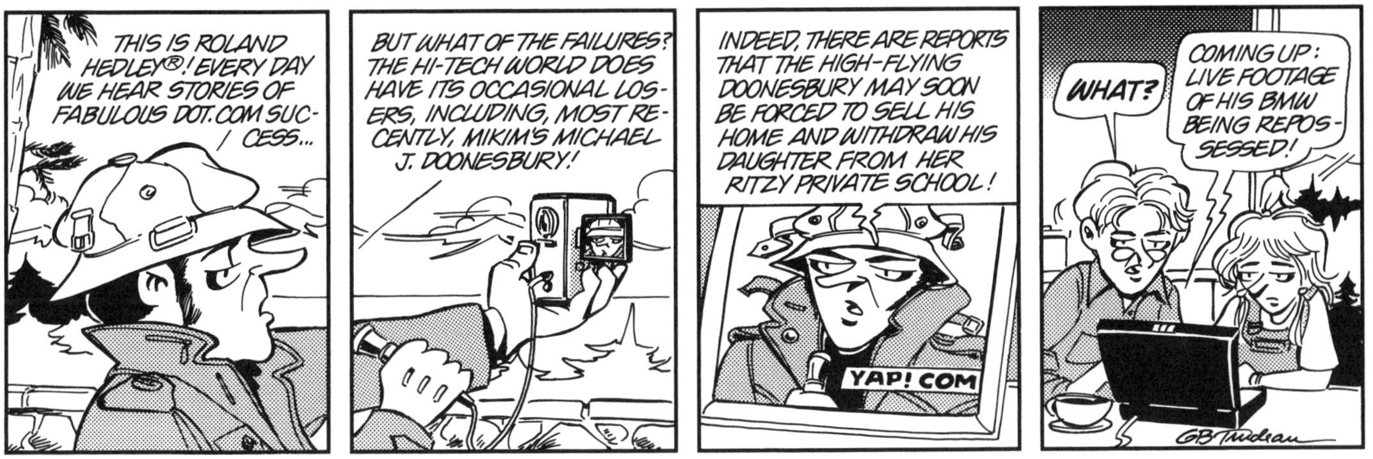
THIS IS ROLAND HEDLEY®! EVERY DAY WE HEAR STORIES OF FABULOUS DOT.COM SUCCESS...
BUT WHAT OF THE FAILURES? THE HI-TECH WORLD DOES HAVE ITS OCCASIONAL LOSERS, INCLUDING, MOST RECENTLY, MIKIM'S MICHAEL J. DOONESBURY!
INDEED, THERE ARE REPORTS THAT THE HIGH-FLYING DOONESBURY MAY SOON BE FORCED TO SELL HIS HOME AND WITHDRAW HIS DAUGHTER FROM HER RITZY PRIVATE SCHOOL!
YAP! COM
WHAT?
COMING UP: LIVE FOOTAGE OF HIS BMW BEING REPOSSESSED!
GB Trudeau

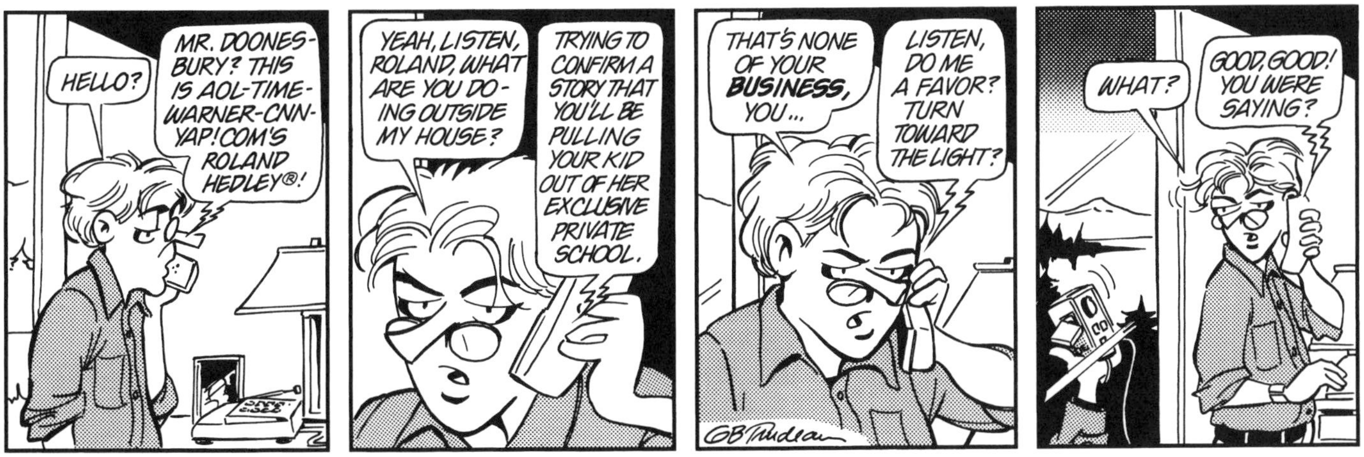
HELLO?
MR. DOONESBURY? THIS IS AOL-TIME-WARNER-CNN-YAP!COM'S ROLAND HEDLEY®!
YEAH, LISTEN, ROLAND, WHAT ARE YOU DOING OUTSIDE MY HOUSE?
TRYING TO CONFIRM A STORY THAT YOU'LL BE PULLING YOUR KID OUT OF HER EXCLUSIVE PRIVATE SCHOOL.
GB Trudeau
THAT'S NONE OF YOUR BUSINESS, YOU...
LISTEN, DO ME A FAVOR? TURN TOWARD THE LIGHT?
WHAT?
GOOD, GOOD! YOU WERE SAYING?

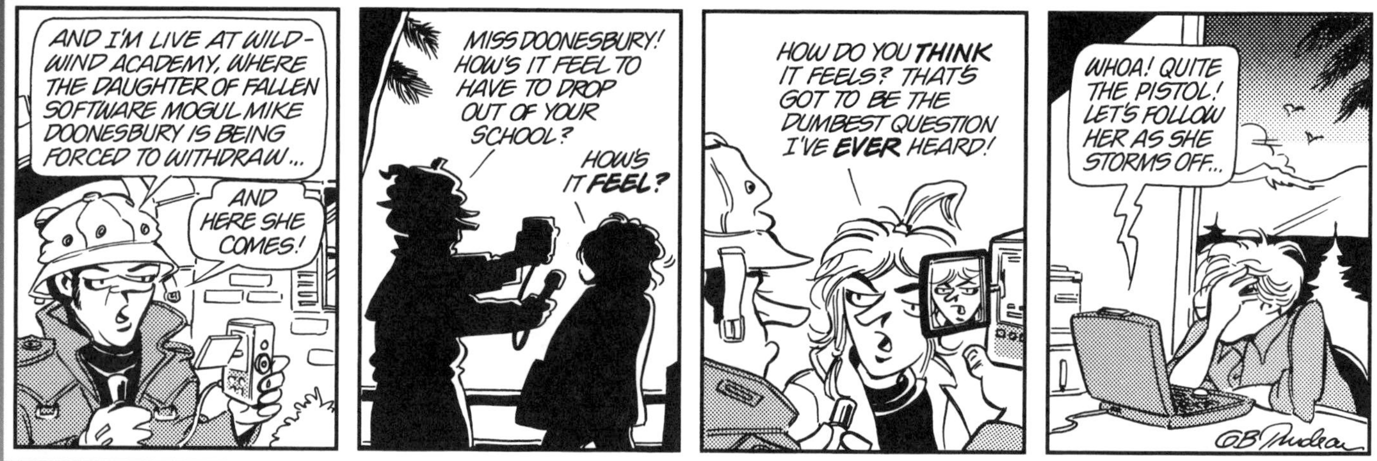
AND I'M LIVE AT WILD-WIND ACADEMY, WHERE THE DAUGHTER OF FALLEN SOFTWARE MOGUL MIKE DOONESBURY IS BEING FORCED TO WITHDRAW...
AND HERE SHE COMES!
MISS DOONESBURY! HOW'S IT FEEL TO HAVE TO DROP OUT OF YOUR SCHOOL?
HOW'S IT FEEL?
HOW DO YOU THINK IT FEELS? THAT'S GOT TO BE THE DUMBEST QUESTION I'VE EVER HEARD!
WHOA! QUITE THE PISTOL! LET'S FOLLOW HER AS SHE STORMS OFF...

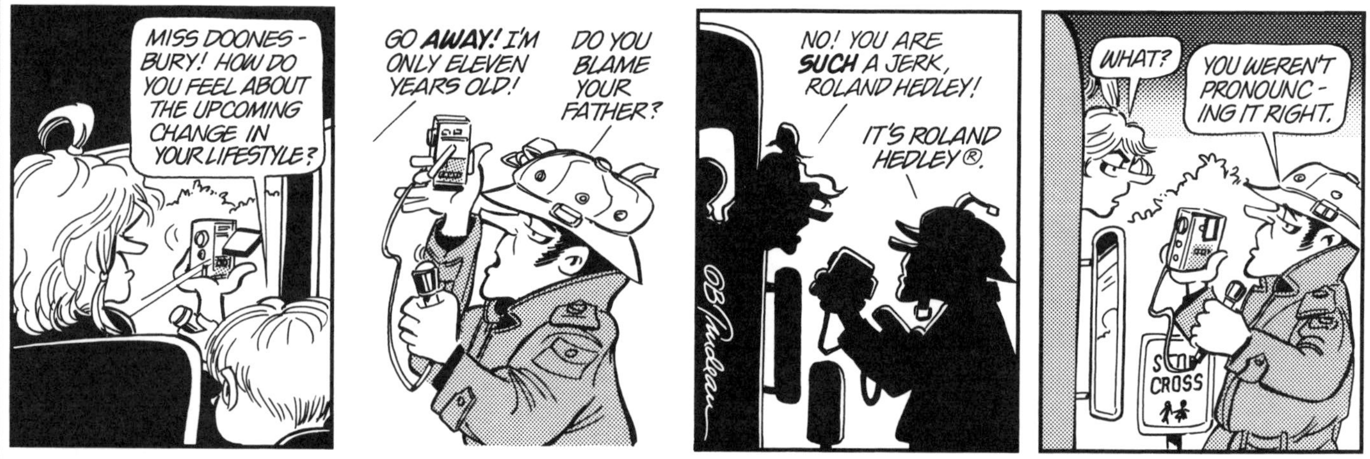
MISS DOONES-BURY! HOW DO YOU FEEL ABOUT THE UPCOMING CHANGE IN YOUR LIFESTYLE?
GO AWAY! I'M ONLY ELEVEN YEARS OLD!
DO YOU BLAME YOUR FATHER?
NO! YOU ARE SUCH A JERK, ROLAND HEDLEY!
IT'S ROLAND HEDLEY®.
WHAT?
YOU WEREN'T PRONOUNC-ING IT RIGHT.
CROSS

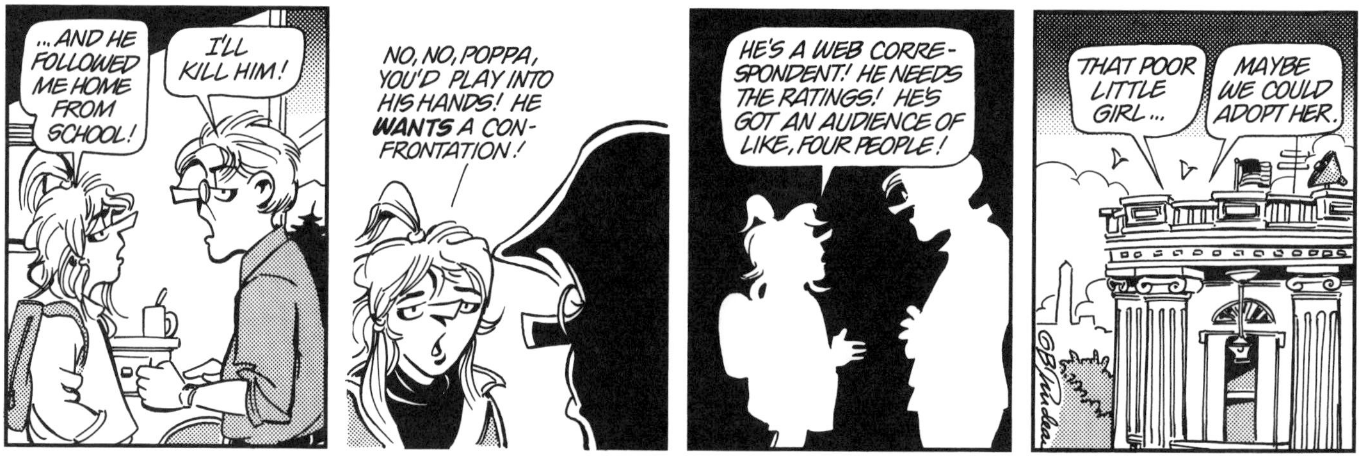
...AND HE FOLLOWED ME HOME FROM SCHOOL!
I'LL KILL HIM!
NO, NO, POPPA, YOU'D PLAY INTO HIS HANDS! HE WANTS A CON-FRONTATION!
HE'S A WEB CORRE-SPONDENT! HE NEEDS THE RATINGS! HE'S GOT AN AUDIENCE OF LIKE, FOUR PEOPLE!
THAT POOR LITTLE GIRL...
MAYBE WE COULD ADOPT HER.

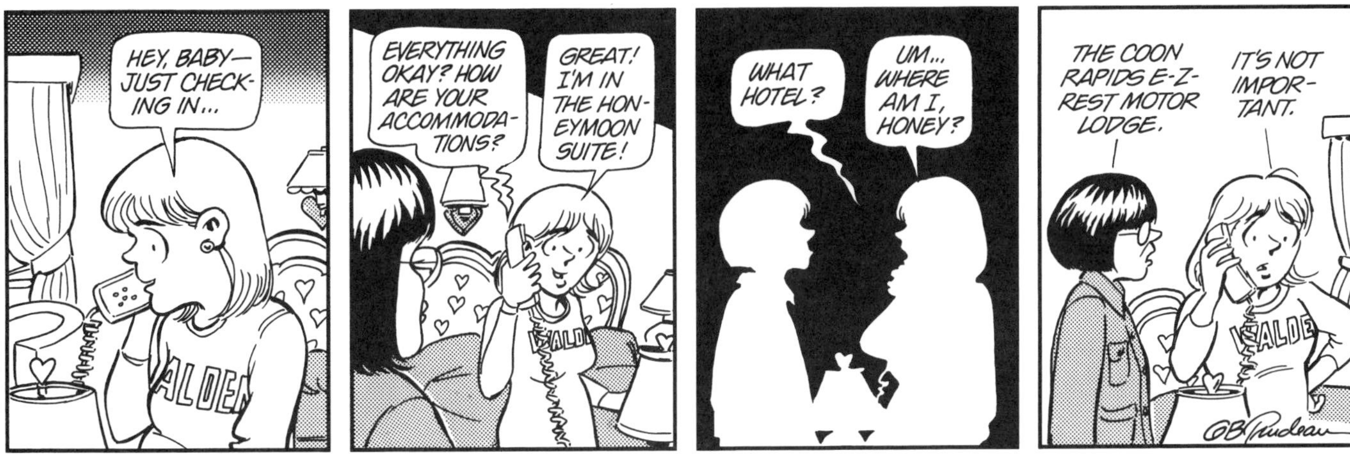
HEY, BABY— JUST CHECKING IN...
EVERYTHING OKAY? HOW ARE YOUR ACCOMMODATIONS?
GREAT! I'M IN THE HONEYMOON SUITE!
WHAT HOTEL?
UM... WHERE AM I, HONEY?
THE COON RAPIDS E-Z-REST MOTOR LODGE.
IT'S NOT IMPORTANT.

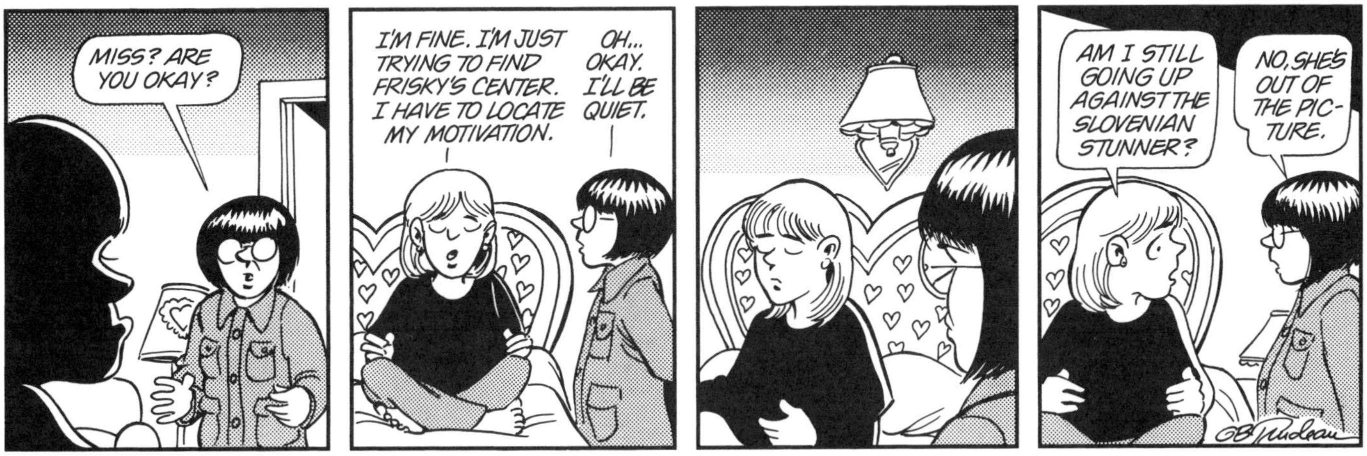
MISS? ARE YOU OKAY?
I'M FINE. I'M JUST TRYING TO FIND FRISKY'S CENTER. I HAVE TO LOCATE MY MOTIVATION.
OH... OKAY. I'LL BE QUIET.
AM I STILL GOING UP AGAINST THE SLOVENIAN STUNNER?
NO, SHE'S OUT OF THE PICTURE.

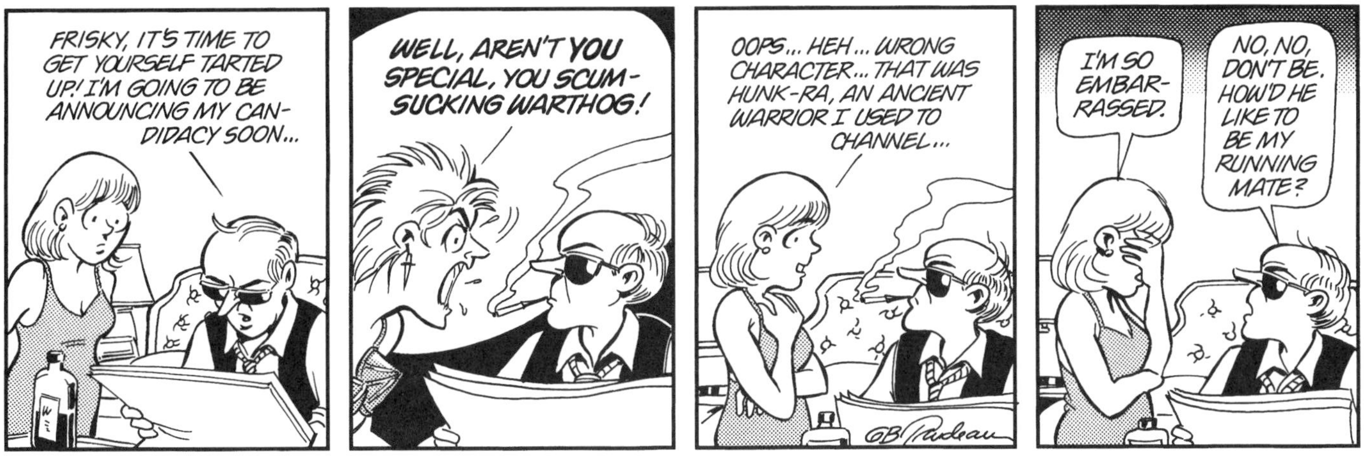
FRISKY, IT'S TIME TO GET YOURSELF TARTED UP! I'M GOING TO BE ANNOUNCING MY CANDIDACY SOON...
WELL, AREN'T YOU SPECIAL, YOU SCUM-SUCKING WARTHOG!
OOPS... HEH... WRONG CHARACTER... THAT WAS HUNK-RA, AN ANCIENT WARRIOR I USED TO CHANNEL...
I'M SO EMBARRASSED.
NO, NO, DON'T BE. HOW'D HE LIKE TO BE MY RUNNING MATE?

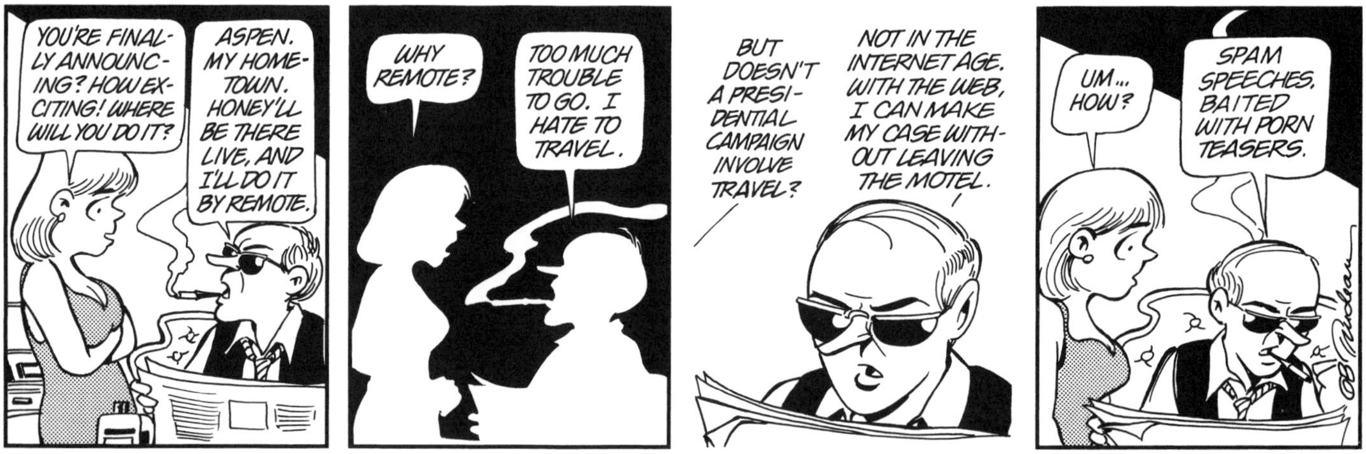
YOU'RE FINALLY ANNOUNCING? HOW EXCITING! WHERE WILL YOU DO IT?
ASPEN. MY HOMETOWN. HONEY'LL BE THERE LIVE, AND I'LL DO IT BY REMOTE.
WHY REMOTE?
TOO MUCH TROUBLE TO GO. I HATE TO TRAVEL.
BUT DOESN'T A PRESIDENTIAL CAMPAIGN INVOLVE TRAVEL?
NOT IN THE INTERNET AGE. WITH THE WEB, I CAN MAKE MY CASE WITHOUT LEAVING THE MOTEL.
UM... HOW?
SPAM SPEECHES, BAITED WITH PORN TEASERS.

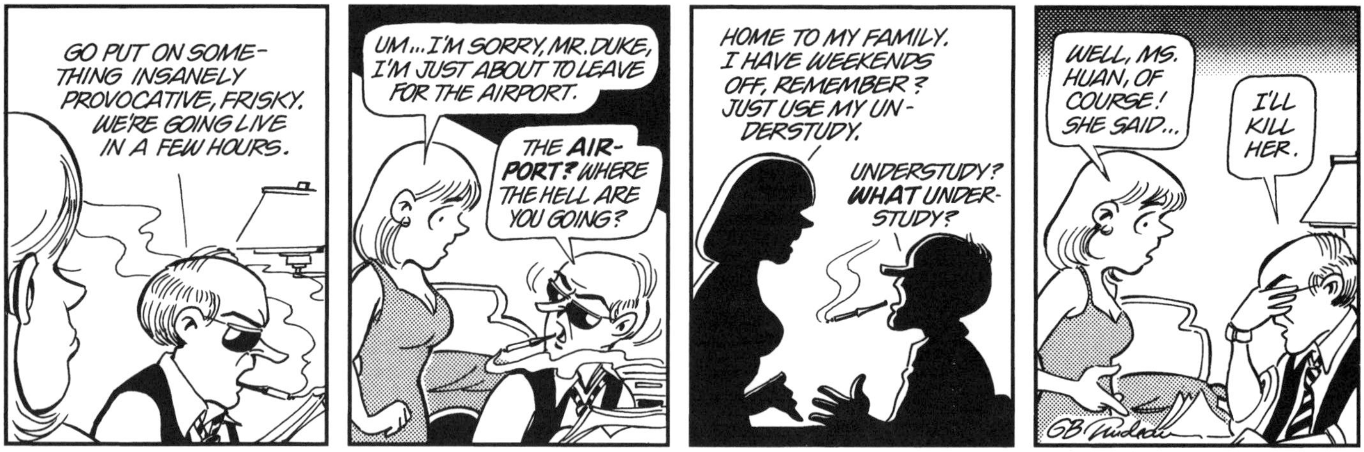
GO PUT ON SOMETHING INSANELY PROVOCATIVE, FRISKY. WE'RE GOING LIVE IN A FEW HOURS.
UM... I'M SORRY, MR. DUKE, I'M JUST ABOUT TO LEAVE FOR THE AIRPORT.
THE AIRPORT? WHERE THE HELL ARE YOU GOING?
HOME TO MY FAMILY. I HAVE WEEKENDS OFF, REMEMBER? JUST USE MY UNDERSTUDY.
UNDERSTUDY? WHAT UNDERSTUDY?
WELL, MS. HUAN, OF COURSE! SHE SAID...
I'LL KILL HER.

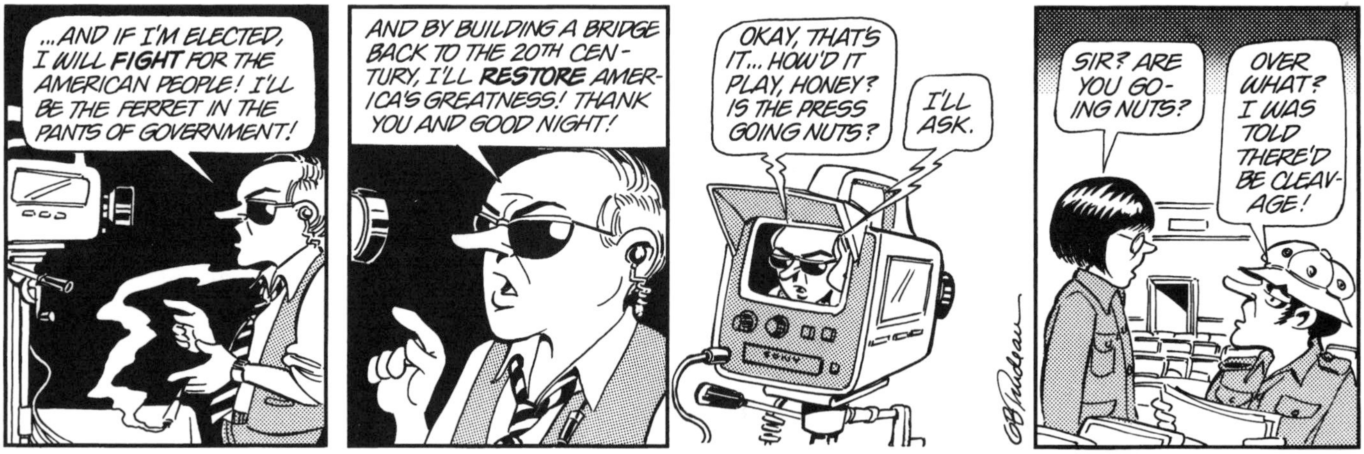
...AND IF I'M ELECTED, I WILL FIGHT FOR THE AMERICAN PEOPLE! I'LL BE THE FERRET IN THE PANTS OF GOVERNMENT!
AND BY BUILDING A BRIDGE BACK TO THE 20TH CENTURY, I'LL RESTORE AMERICA'S GREATNESS! THANK YOU AND GOOD NIGHT!
OKAY, THAT'S IT... HOW'D IT PLAY, HONEY? IS THE PRESS GOING NUTS?
I'LL ASK.
SIR? ARE YOU GOING NUTS?
OVER WHAT? I WAS TOLD THERE'D BE CLEAVAGE!

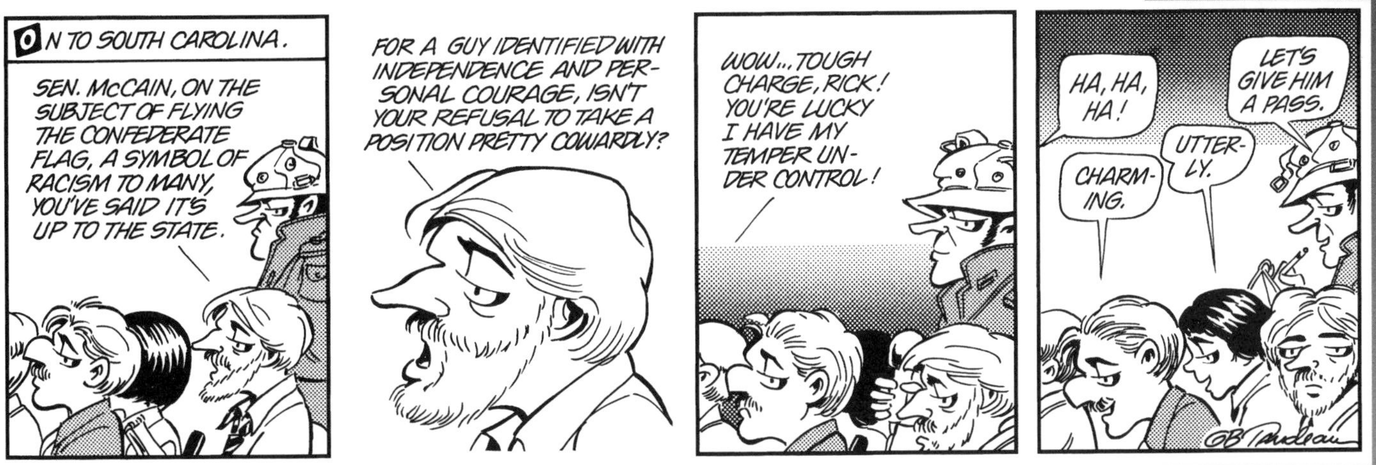
ON TO SOUTH CAROLINA.
SEN. McCAIN, ON THE SUBJECT OF FLYING THE CONFEDERATE FLAG, A SYMBOL OF RACISM TO MANY, YOU'VE SAID IT'S UP TO THE STATE.
FOR A GUY IDENTIFIED WITH INDEPENDENCE AND PERSONAL COURAGE, ISN'T YOUR REFUSAL TO TAKE A POSITION PRETTY COWARDLY?
WOW... TOUGH CHARGE, RICK! YOU'RE LUCKY I HAVE MY TEMPER UNDER CONTROL!
HA, HA, HA!
CHARMING.
UTTERLY.
LET'S GIVE HIM A PASS.

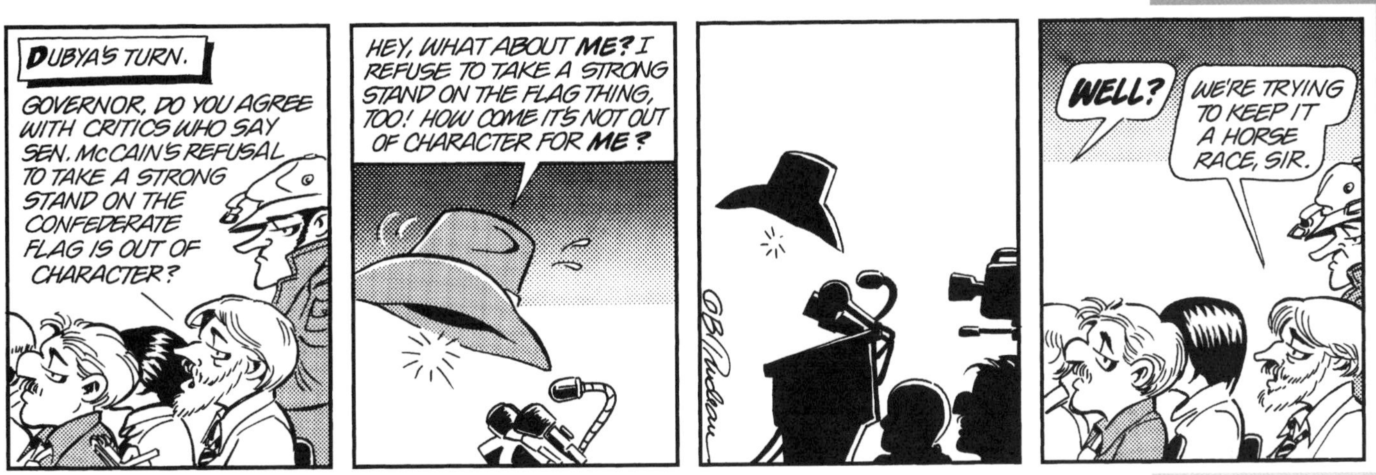
DUBYA'S TURN.
GOVERNOR, DO YOU AGREE WITH CRITICS WHO SAY SEN. McCAIN'S REFUSAL TO TAKE A STRONG STAND ON THE CONFEDERATE FLAG IS OUT OF CHARACTER?
HEY, WHAT ABOUT **ME?** I REFUSE TO TAKE A STRONG STAND ON THE FLAG THING, TOO! HOW COME IT'S NOT OUT OF CHARACTER FOR **ME?**
WELL?
WE'RE TRYING TO KEEP IT A HORSE RACE, SIR.

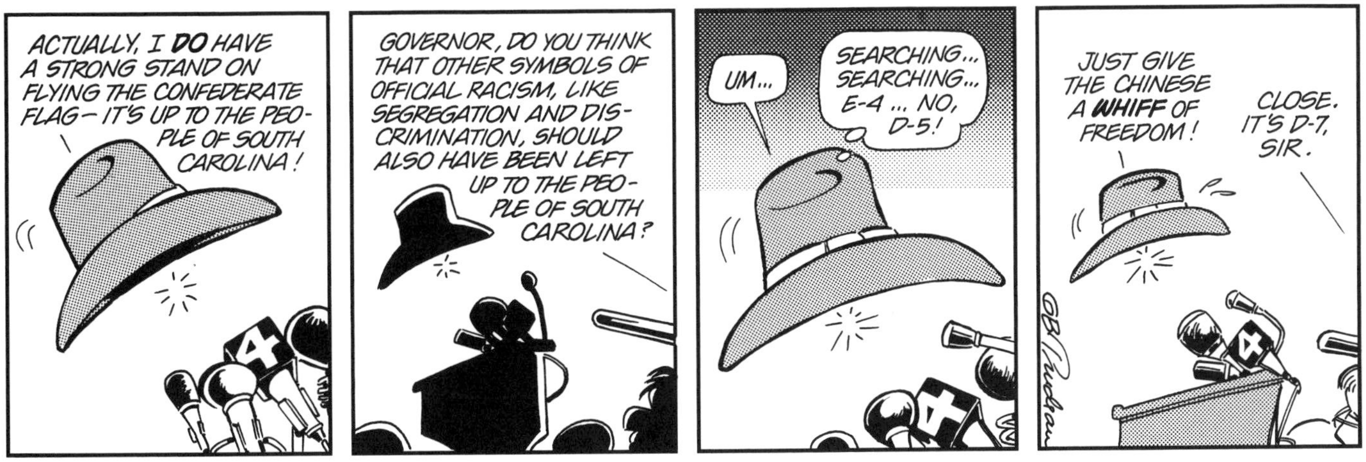
ACTUALLY, I **DO** HAVE A STRONG STAND ON FLYING THE CONFEDERATE FLAG — IT'S UP TO THE PEOPLE OF SOUTH CAROLINA!
GOVERNOR, DO YOU THINK THAT OTHER SYMBOLS OF OFFICIAL RACISM, LIKE SEGREGATION AND DISCRIMINATION, SHOULD ALSO HAVE BEEN LEFT UP TO THE PEOPLE OF SOUTH CAROLINA?
UM...
SEARCHING... SEARCHING... E-4 ... NO, D-5!
JUST GIVE THE CHINESE A **WHIFF** OF FREEDOM!
CLOSE. IT'S D-7, SIR.

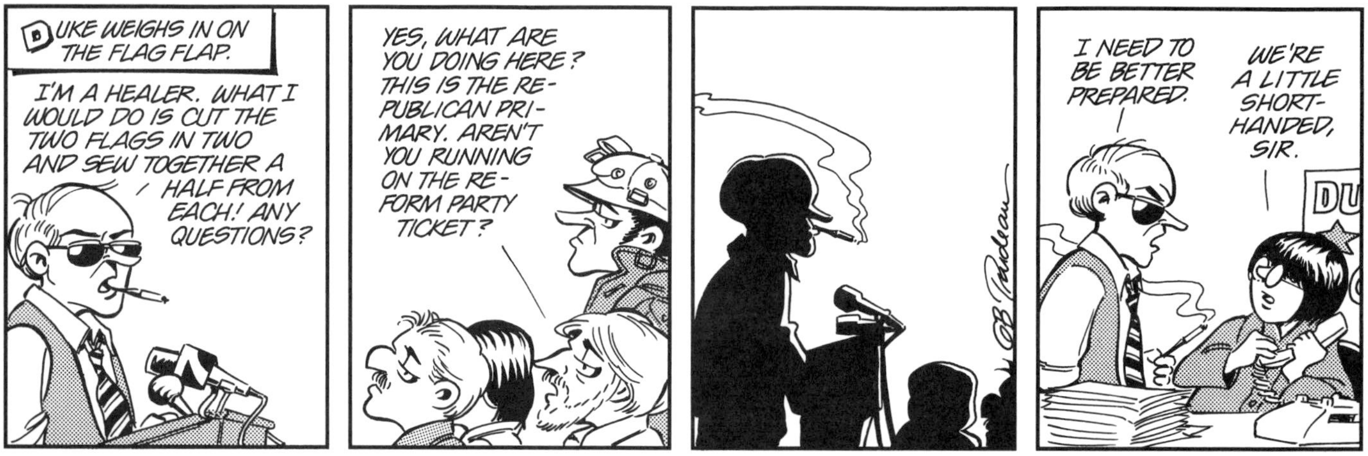
DUKE WEIGHS IN ON THE FLAG FLAP.
I'M A HEALER. WHAT I WOULD DO IS CUT THE TWO FLAGS IN TWO AND SEW TOGETHER A HALF FROM EACH! ANY QUESTIONS?
YES, WHAT ARE YOU DOING HERE? THIS IS THE REPUBLICAN PRIMARY. AREN'T YOU RUNNING ON THE REFORM PARTY TICKET?
I NEED TO BE BETTER PREPARED.
WE'RE A LITTLE SHORT-HANDED, SIR.
GB Trudeau

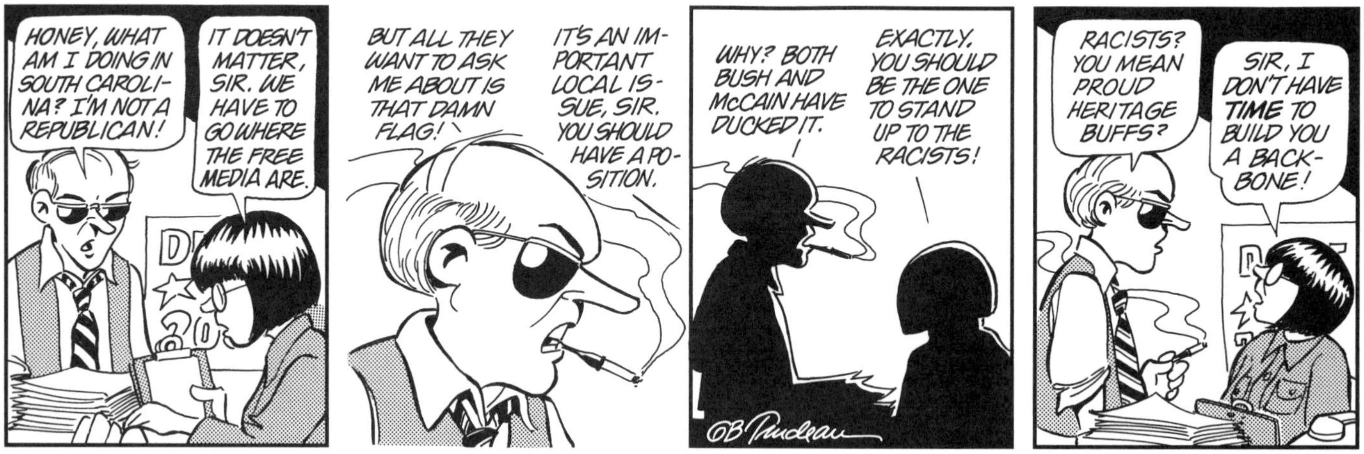
HONEY, WHAT AM I DOING IN SOUTH CAROLINA? I'M NOT A REPUBLICAN!
IT DOESN'T MATTER, SIR. WE HAVE TO GO WHERE THE FREE MEDIA ARE.
BUT ALL THEY WANT TO ASK ME ABOUT IS THAT DAMN FLAG!
IT'S AN IMPORTANT LOCAL ISSUE, SIR. YOU SHOULD HAVE A POSITION.
WHY? BOTH BUSH AND McCAIN HAVE DUCKED IT.
EXACTLY. YOU SHOULD BE THE ONE TO STAND UP TO THE RACISTS!
RACISTS? YOU MEAN PROUD HERITAGE BUFFS?
SIR, I DON'T HAVE TIME TO BUILD YOU A BACKBONE!
GB Trudeau

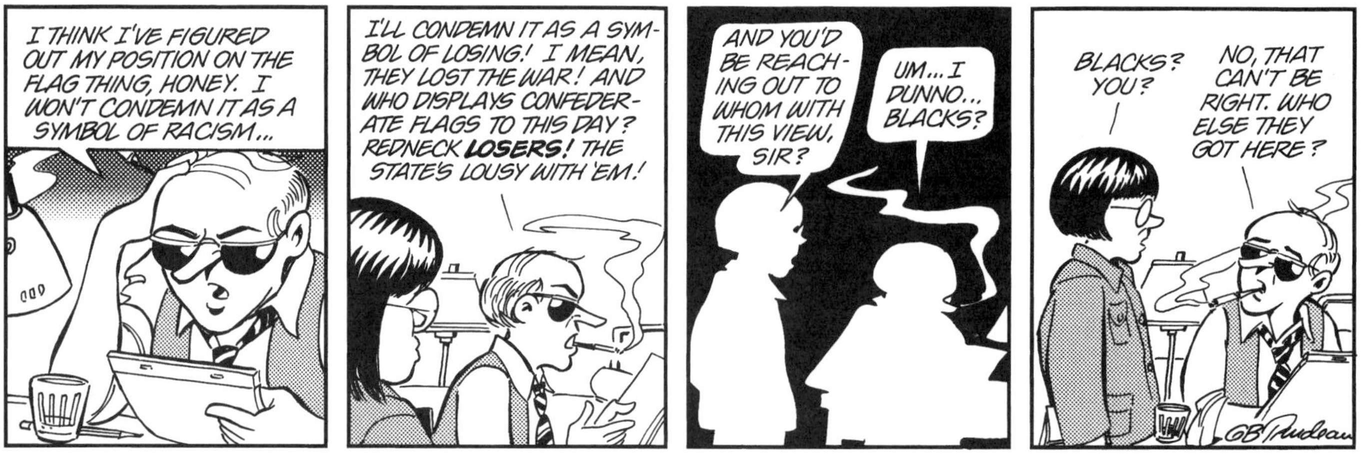
I THINK I'VE FIGURED OUT MY POSITION ON THE FLAG THING, HONEY. I WON'T CONDEMN IT AS A SYMBOL OF RACISM...
I'LL CONDEMN IT AS A SYMBOL OF LOSING! I MEAN, THEY LOST THE WAR! AND WHO DISPLAYS CONFEDERATE FLAGS TO THIS DAY? REDNECK LOSERS! THE STATE'S LOUSY WITH 'EM!
AND YOU'D BE REACHING OUT TO WHOM WITH THIS VIEW, SIR?
UM... I DUNNO... BLACKS?
BLACKS? YOU?
NO, THAT CAN'T BE RIGHT. WHO ELSE THEY GOT HERE?
GB Trudeau

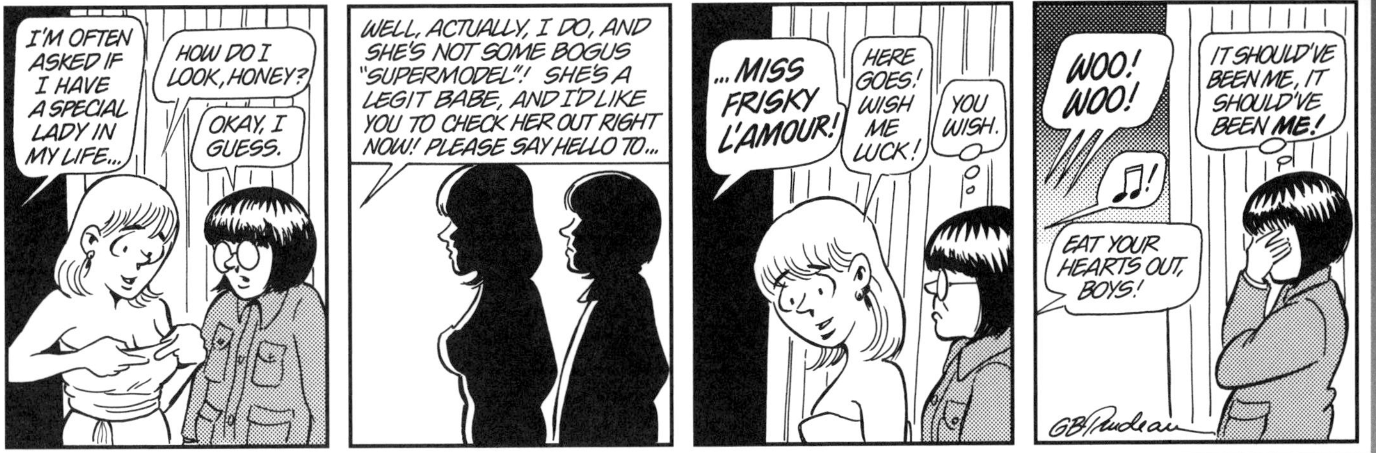
I'M OFTEN ASKED IF I HAVE A SPECIAL LADY IN MY LIFE...
HOW DO I LOOK, HONEY?
OKAY, I GUESS.
WELL, ACTUALLY, I DO, AND SHE'S NOT SOME BOGUS "SUPERMODEL"! SHE'S A LEGIT BABE, AND I'D LIKE YOU TO CHECK HER OUT RIGHT NOW! PLEASE SAY HELLO TO...
...MISS FRISKY L'AMOUR!
HERE GOES! WISH ME LUCK!
YOU WISH.
WOO! WOO!
♫!
EAT YOUR HEARTS OUT, BOYS!
IT SHOULD'VE BEEN ME, IT SHOULD'VE BEEN **ME!**
GBTrudeau

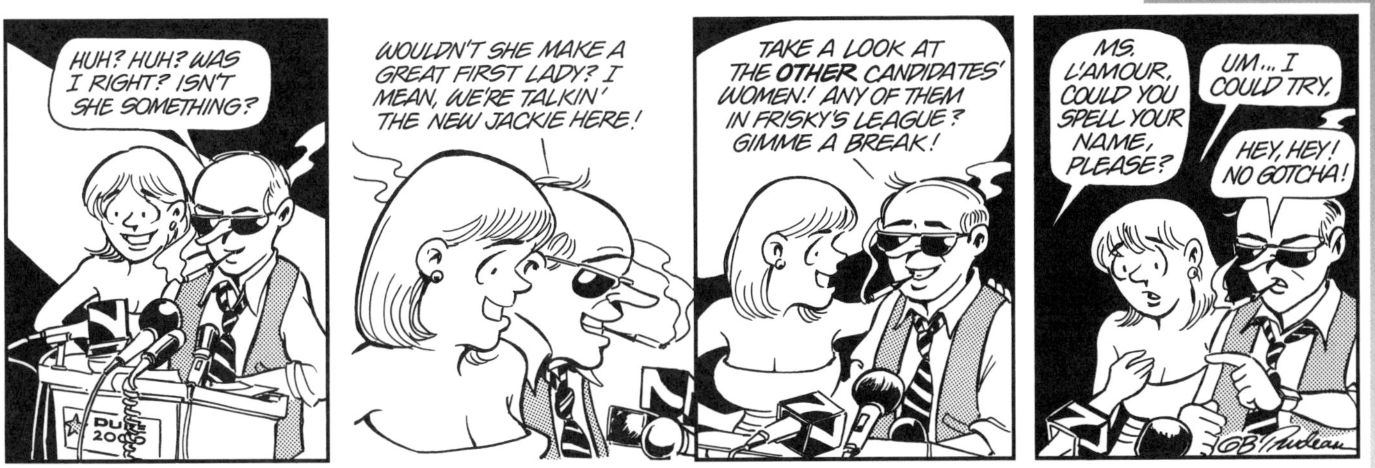
HUH? HUH? WAS I RIGHT? ISN'T SHE SOMETHING?
WOULDN'T SHE MAKE A GREAT FIRST LADY? I MEAN, WE'RE TALKIN' THE NEW JACKIE HERE!
TAKE A LOOK AT THE **OTHER** CANDIDATES' WOMEN! ANY OF THEM IN FRISKY'S LEAGUE? GIMME A BREAK!
MS. L'AMOUR, COULD YOU SPELL YOUR NAME, PLEASE?
UM... I COULD TRY.
HEY, HEY! NO GOTCHA!
GBTrudeau

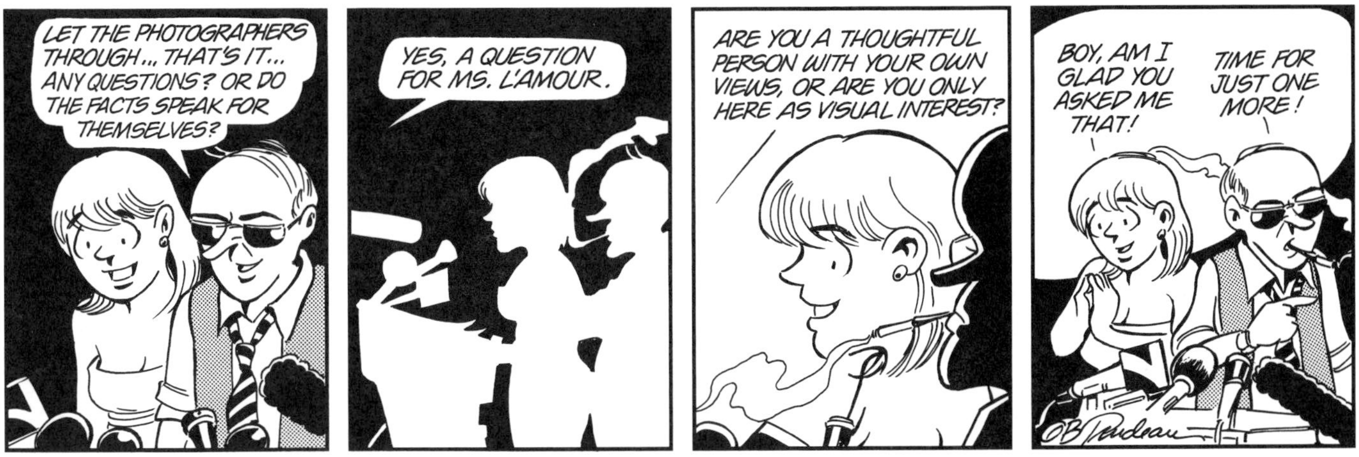
LET THE PHOTOGRAPHERS THROUGH... THAT'S IT... ANY QUESTIONS? OR DO THE FACTS SPEAK FOR THEMSELVES?
YES, A QUESTION FOR MS. L'AMOUR.
ARE YOU A THOUGHTFUL PERSON WITH YOUR OWN VIEWS, OR ARE YOU ONLY HERE AS VISUAL INTEREST?
BOY, AM I GLAD YOU ASKED ME THAT!
TIME FOR JUST ONE MORE!
GBTrudeau

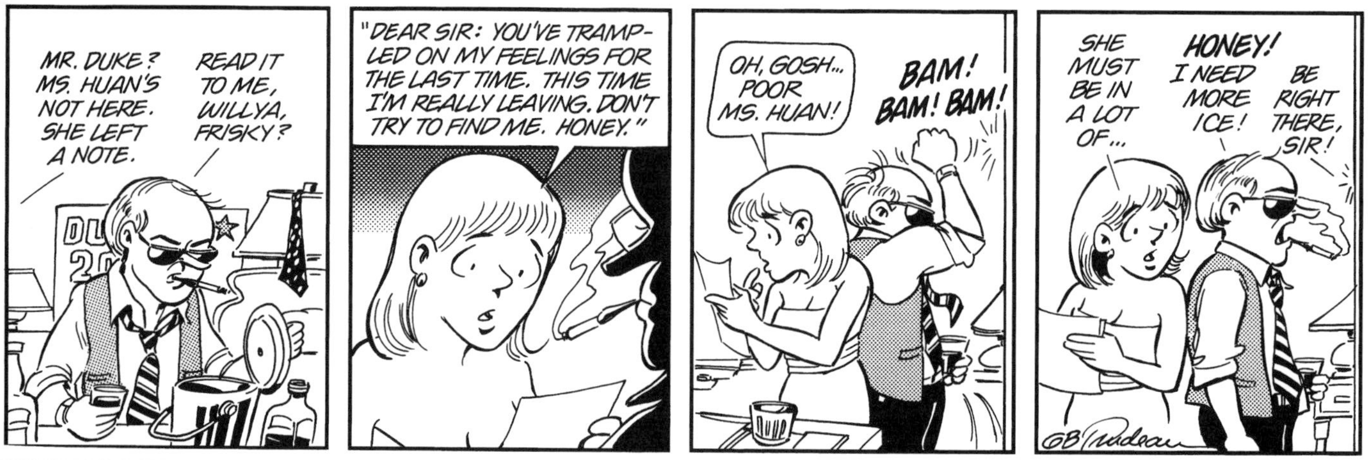
MR. DUKE? MS. HUAN'S NOT HERE. SHE LEFT A NOTE.
READ IT TO ME, WILLYA, FRISKY?
"DEAR SIR: YOU'VE TRAMPLED ON MY FEELINGS FOR THE LAST TIME. THIS TIME I'M REALLY LEAVING. DON'T TRY TO FIND ME. HONEY."
OH, GOSH... POOR MS. HUAN!
BAM! BAM! BAM!
SHE MUST BE IN A LOT OF...
HONEY! I NEED MORE ICE!
BE RIGHT THERE, SIR!
©B Trudeau

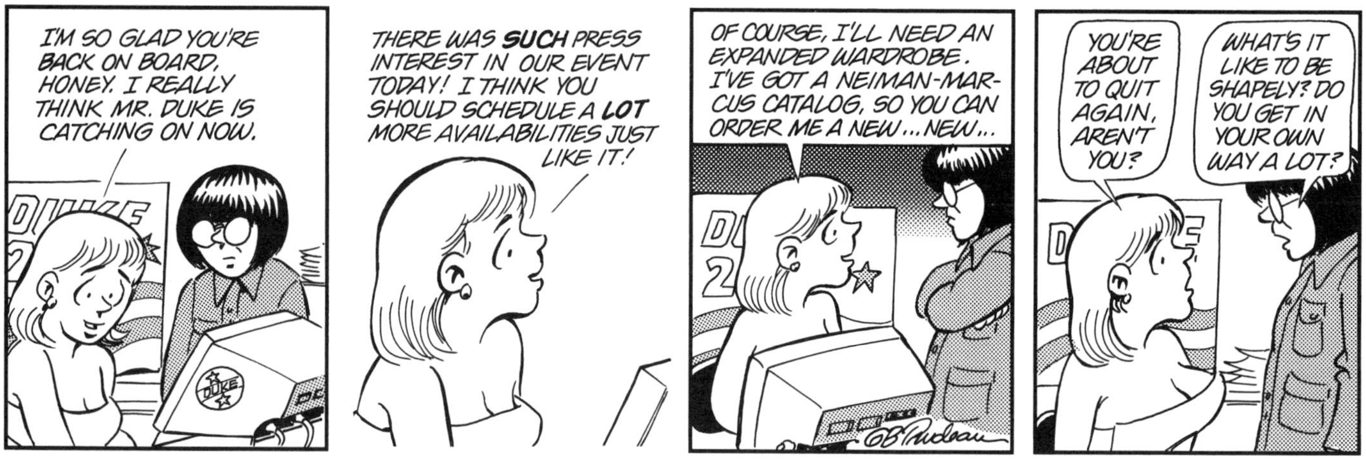
I'M SO GLAD YOU'RE BACK ON BOARD, HONEY. I REALLY THINK MR. DUKE IS CATCHING ON NOW.
THERE WAS SUCH PRESS INTEREST IN OUR EVENT TODAY! I THINK YOU SHOULD SCHEDULE A LOT MORE AVAILABILITIES JUST LIKE IT!
OF COURSE, I'LL NEED AN EXPANDED WARDROBE. I'VE GOT A NEIMAN-MARCUS CATALOG, SO YOU CAN ORDER ME A NEW... NEW...
YOU'RE ABOUT TO QUIT AGAIN, AREN'T YOU?
WHAT'S IT LIKE TO BE SHAPELY? DO YOU GET IN YOUR OWN WAY A LOT?
©B Trudeau

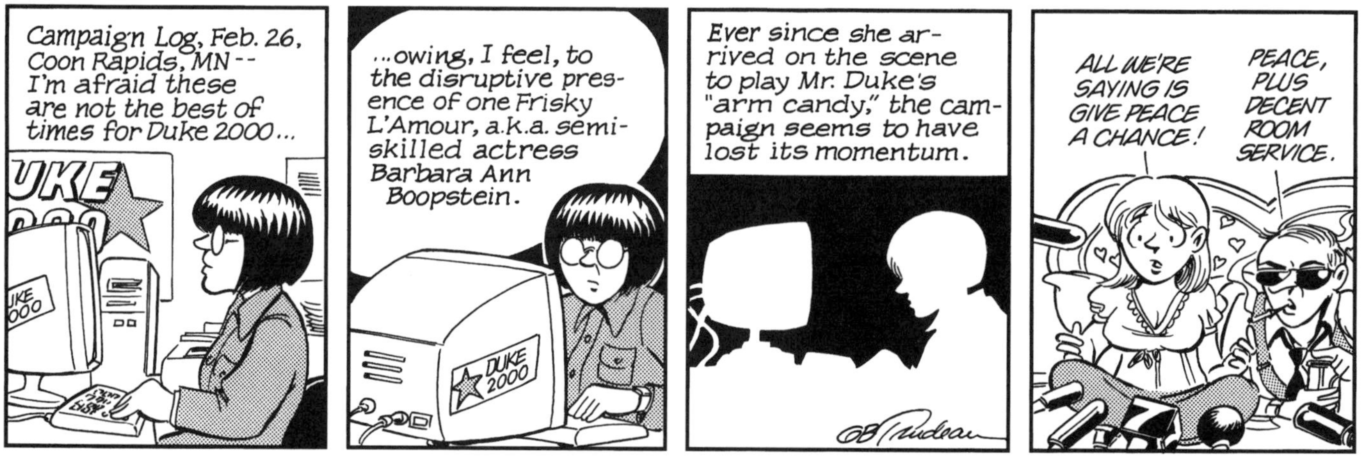
Campaign Log, Feb. 26, Coon Rapids, MN -- I'm afraid these are not the best of times for Duke 2000...
...owing, I feel, to the disruptive presence of one Frisky L'Amour, a.k.a. semi-skilled actress Barbara Ann Boopstein.
Ever since she arrived on the scene to play Mr. Duke's "arm candy," the campaign seems to have lost its momentum.
ALL WE'RE SAYING IS GIVE PEACE A CHANCE!
PEACE, PLUS DECENT ROOM SERVICE.
©B Trudeau

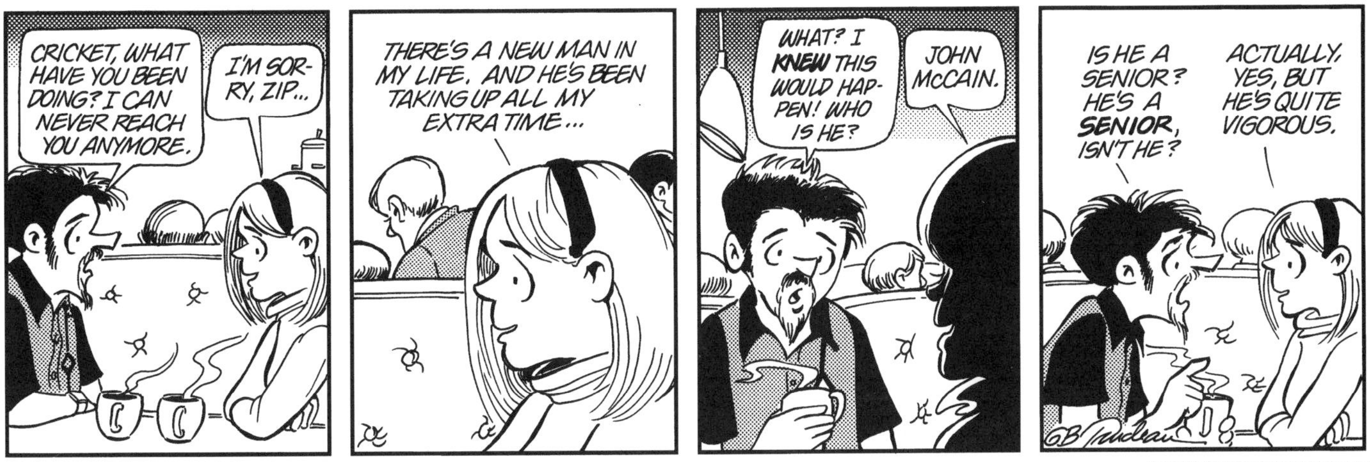
CRICKET, WHAT HAVE YOU BEEN DOING? I CAN NEVER REACH YOU ANYMORE.
I'M SORRY, ZIP...
THERE'S A NEW MAN IN MY LIFE. AND HE'S BEEN TAKING UP ALL MY EXTRA TIME...
WHAT? I **KNEW** THIS WOULD HAPPEN! WHO IS HE?
JOHN McCAIN.
IS HE A SENIOR? HE'S A **SENIOR**, ISN'T HE?
ACTUALLY, YES, BUT HE'S QUITE VIGOROUS.
©B Trudeau

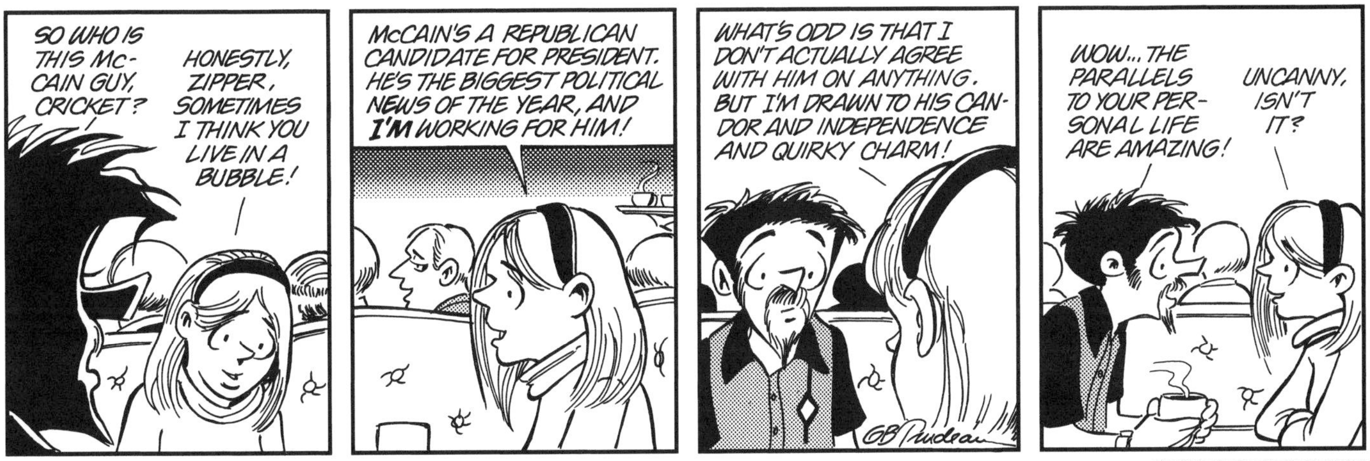
SO WHO IS THIS McCAIN GUY, CRICKET?
HONESTLY, ZIPPER, SOMETIMES I THINK YOU LIVE IN A BUBBLE!
McCAIN'S A REPUBLICAN CANDIDATE FOR PRESIDENT. HE'S THE BIGGEST POLITICAL NEWS OF THE YEAR, AND **I'M** WORKING FOR HIM!
WHAT'S ODD IS THAT I DON'T ACTUALLY AGREE WITH HIM ON ANYTHING. BUT I'M DRAWN TO HIS CANDOR AND INDEPENDENCE AND QUIRKY CHARM!
©B Trudeau
WOW... THE PARALLELS TO YOUR PERSONAL LIFE ARE AMAZING!
UNCANNY, ISN'T IT?

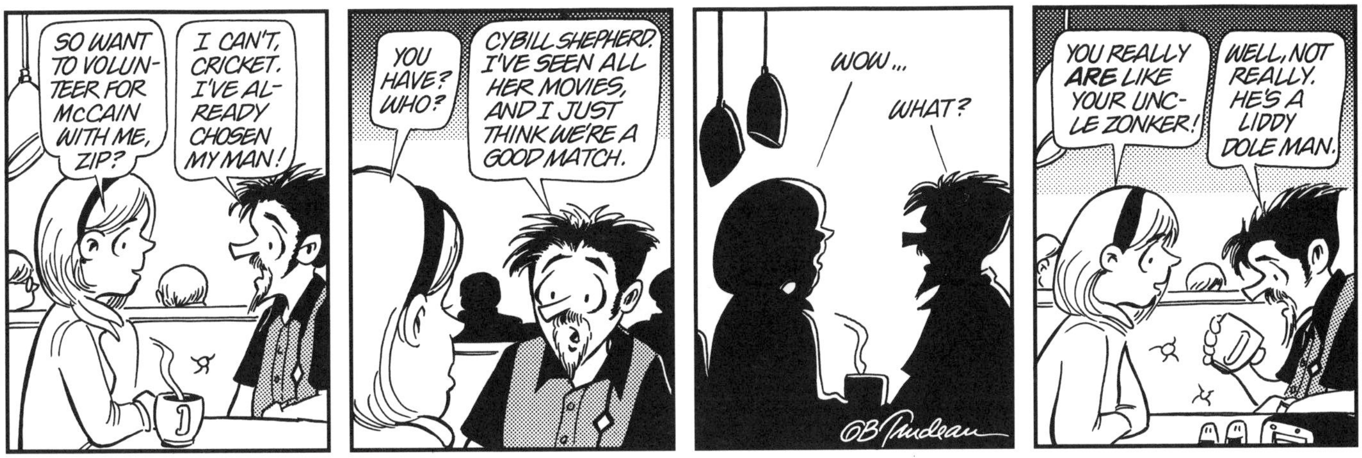
SO WANT TO VOLUNTEER FOR McCAIN WITH ME, ZIP?
I CAN'T, CRICKET. I'VE ALREADY CHOSEN MY MAN!
YOU HAVE? WHO?
CYBILL SHEPHERD. I'VE SEEN ALL HER MOVIES, AND I JUST THINK WE'RE A GOOD MATCH.
WOW...
WHAT?
©B Trudeau
YOU REALLY **ARE** LIKE YOUR UNCLE ZONKER!
WELL, NOT REALLY. HE'S A LIDDY DOLE MAN.

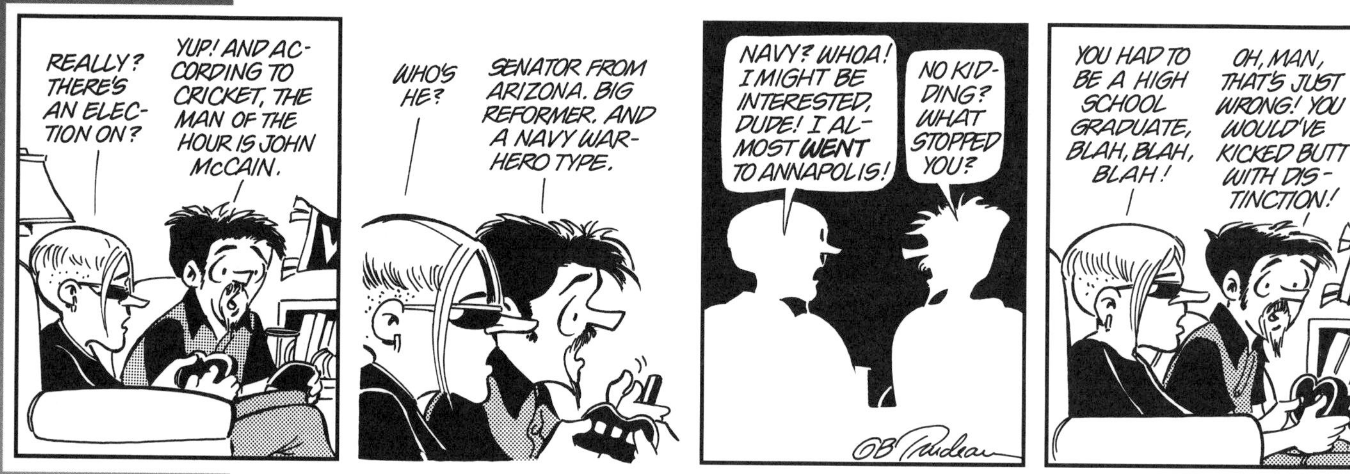
REALLY? THERE'S AN ELECTION ON?
YUP! AND ACCORDING TO CRICKET, THE MAN OF THE HOUR IS JOHN McCAIN.
WHO'S HE?
SENATOR FROM ARIZONA. BIG REFORMER. AND A NAVY WAR-HERO TYPE.
NAVY? WHOA! I MIGHT BE INTERESTED, DUDE! I ALMOST **WENT** TO ANNAPOLIS!
NO KIDDING? WHAT STOPPED YOU?
YOU HAD TO BE A HIGH SCHOOL GRADUATE, BLAH, BLAH, BLAH!
OH, MAN, THAT'S JUST WRONG! YOU WOULD'VE KICKED BUTT WITH DISTINCTION!

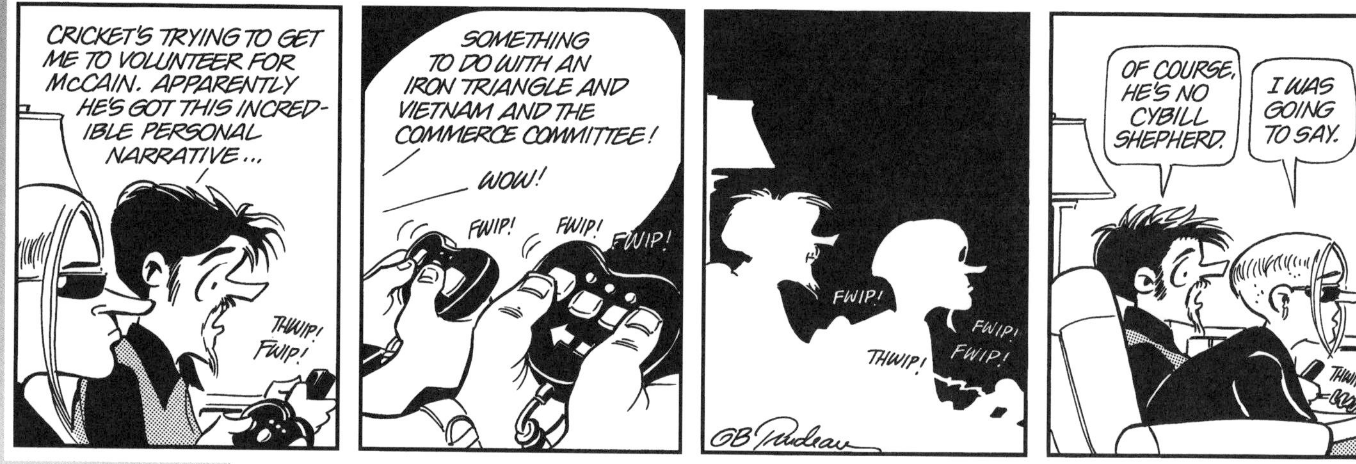
CRICKET'S TRYING TO GET ME TO VOLUNTEER FOR McCAIN. APPARENTLY HE'S GOT THIS INCREDIBLE PERSONAL NARRATIVE...
THWIP! FWIP!
SOMETHING TO DO WITH AN IRON TRIANGLE AND VIETNAM AND THE COMMERCE COMMITTEE!
WOW!
FWIP! FWIP! FWIP!
FWIP! THWIP! FWIP! FWIP!
OF COURSE, HE'S NO CYBILL SHEPHERD.
I WAS GOING TO SAY.
THWIP!

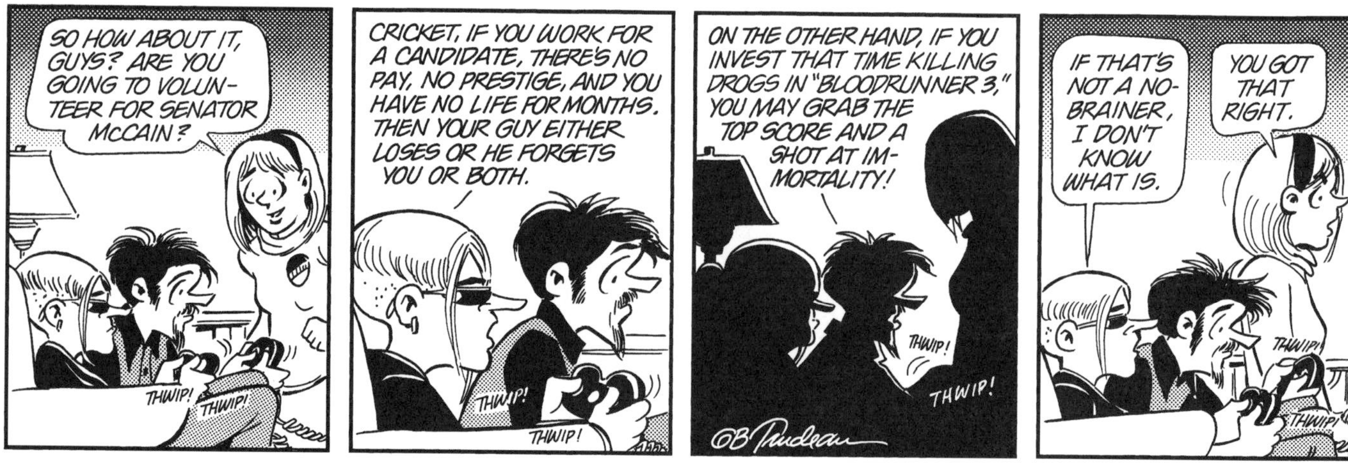
SO HOW ABOUT IT, GUYS? ARE YOU GOING TO VOLUNTEER FOR SENATOR McCAIN?
THWIP! THWIP!
CRICKET, IF YOU WORK FOR A CANDIDATE, THERE'S NO PAY, NO PRESTIGE, AND YOU HAVE NO LIFE FOR MONTHS. THEN YOUR GUY EITHER LOSES OR HE FORGETS YOU OR BOTH.
THWIP! THWIP!
ON THE OTHER HAND, IF YOU INVEST THAT TIME KILLING DROGS IN "BLOODRUNNER 3," YOU MAY GRAB THE TOP SCORE AND A SHOT AT IMMORTALITY!
THWIP! THWIP!
IF THAT'S NOT A NO-BRAINER, I DON'T KNOW WHAT IS.
YOU GOT THAT RIGHT.
THWIP! THWIP!

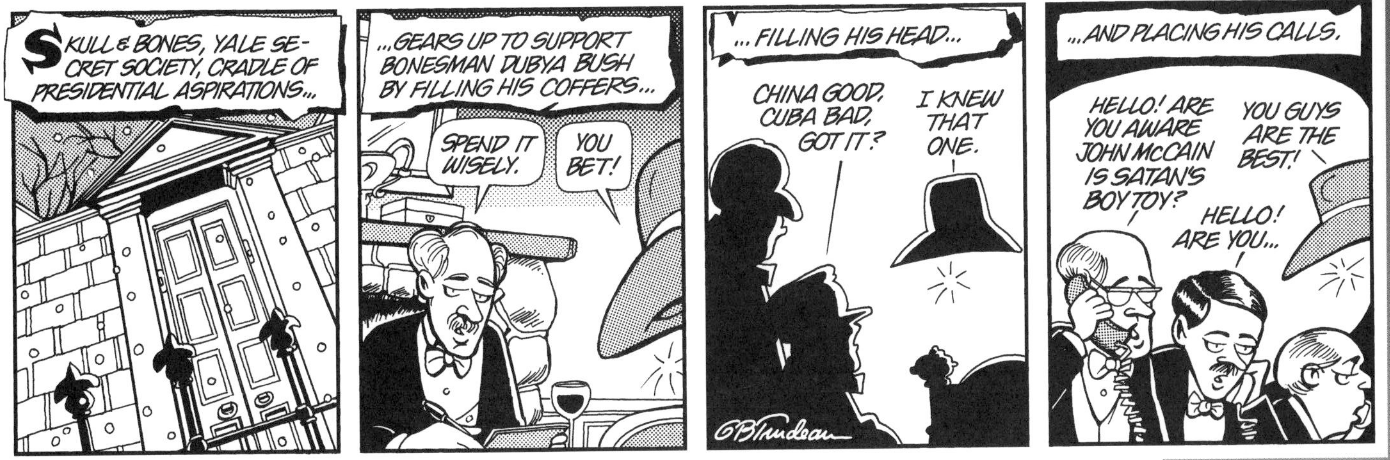
SKULL & BONES, YALE SECRET SOCIETY, CRADLE OF PRESIDENTIAL ASPIRATIONS...
...GEARS UP TO SUPPORT BONESMAN DUBYA BUSH BY FILLING HIS COFFERS...
SPEND IT WISELY.
YOU BET!
...FILLING HIS HEAD...
CHINA GOOD, CUBA BAD, GOT IT?
I KNEW THAT ONE.
...AND PLACING HIS CALLS.
HELLO! ARE YOU AWARE JOHN McCAIN IS SATAN'S BOY TOY?
YOU GUYS ARE THE BEST!
HELLO! ARE YOU...
GBTrudeau

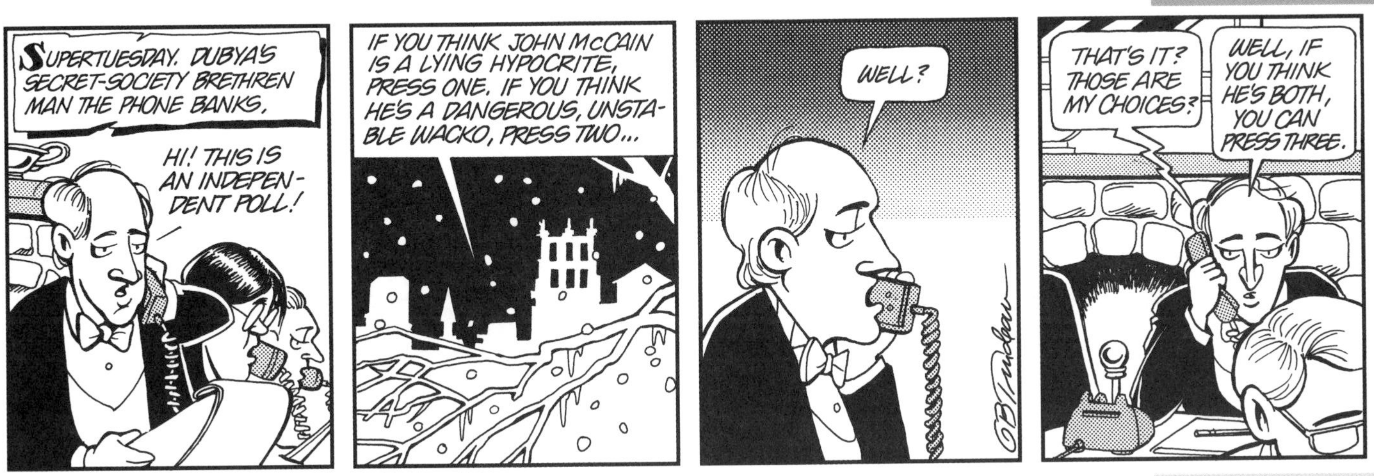
SUPERTUESDAY. DUBYA'S SECRET-SOCIETY BRETHREN MAN THE PHONE BANKS.
HI! THIS IS AN INDEPENDENT POLL!
IF YOU THINK JOHN McCAIN IS A LYING HYPOCRITE, PRESS ONE. IF YOU THINK HE'S A DANGEROUS, UNSTABLE WACKO, PRESS TWO...
WELL?
THAT'S IT? THOSE ARE MY CHOICES?
WELL, IF YOU THINK HE'S BOTH, YOU CAN PRESS THREE.
GBTrudeau

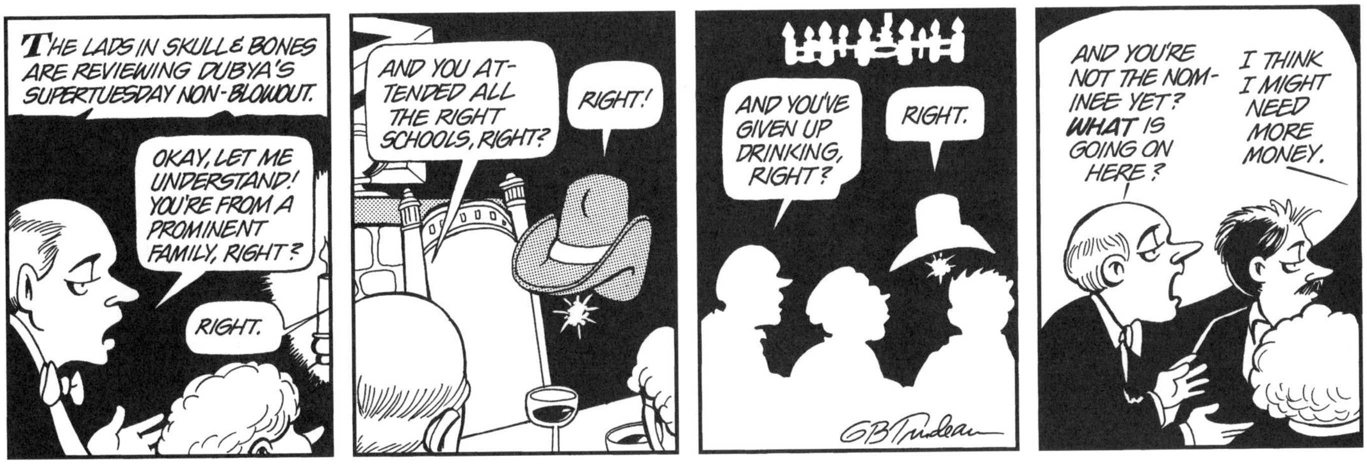
THE LADS IN SKULL & BONES ARE REVIEWING DUBYA'S SUPERTUESDAY NON-BLOWOUT.
OKAY, LET ME UNDERSTAND! YOU'RE FROM A PROMINENT FAMILY, RIGHT?
RIGHT.
AND YOU ATTENDED ALL THE RIGHT SCHOOLS, RIGHT?
RIGHT!
AND YOU'VE GIVEN UP DRINKING, RIGHT?
RIGHT.
AND YOU'RE NOT THE NOMINEE YET? WHAT IS GOING ON HERE?
I THINK I MIGHT NEED MORE MONEY.
GBTrudeau

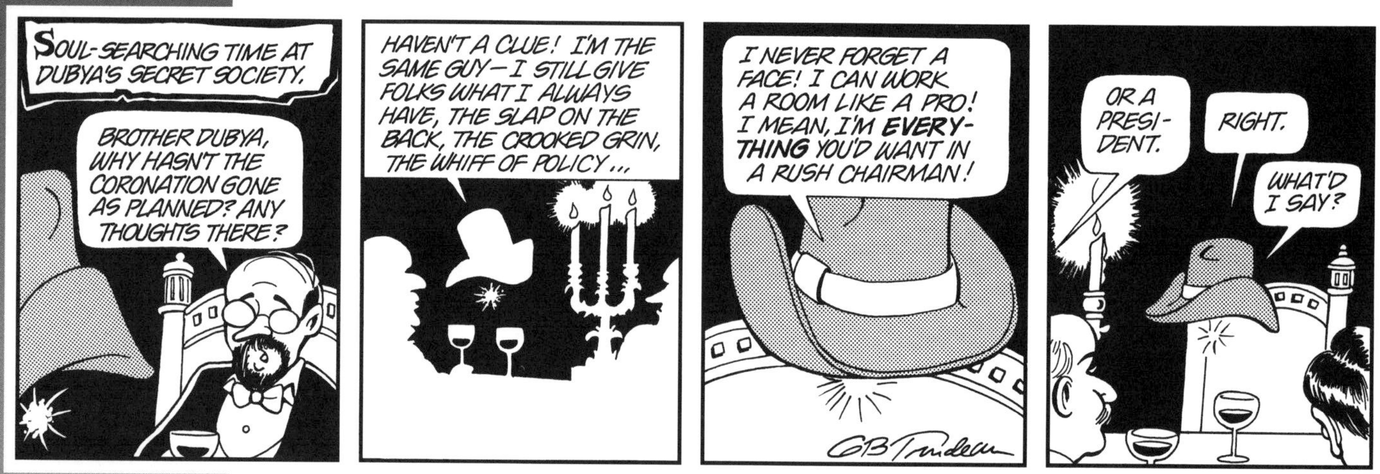
SOUL-SEARCHING TIME AT DUBYA'S SECRET SOCIETY.
BROTHER DUBYA, WHY HASN'T THE CORONATION GONE AS PLANNED? ANY THOUGHTS THERE?
HAVEN'T A CLUE! I'M THE SAME GUY—I STILL GIVE FOLKS WHAT I ALWAYS HAVE, THE SLAP ON THE BACK, THE CROOKED GRIN, THE WHIFF OF POLICY...
I NEVER FORGET A FACE! I CAN WORK A ROOM LIKE A PRO! I MEAN, I'M EVERYTHING YOU'D WANT IN A RUSH CHAIRMAN!
OR A PRESIDENT.
RIGHT.
WHAT'D I SAY?
GBTrudeau

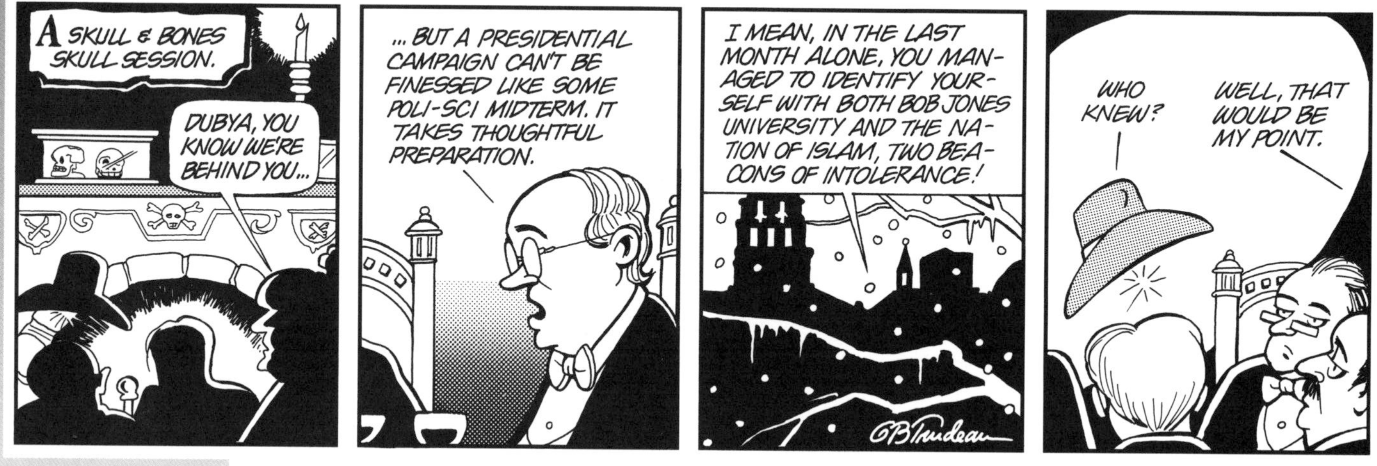
A SKULL & BONES SKULL SESSION.
DUBYA, YOU KNOW WE'RE BEHIND YOU...
...BUT A PRESIDENTIAL CAMPAIGN CAN'T BE FINESSED LIKE SOME POLI-SCI MIDTERM. IT TAKES THOUGHTFUL PREPARATION.
I MEAN, IN THE LAST MONTH ALONE, YOU MANAGED TO IDENTIFY YOURSELF WITH BOTH BOB JONES UNIVERSITY AND THE NATION OF ISLAM, TWO BEACONS OF INTOLERANCE!
WHO KNEW?
WELL, THAT WOULD BE MY POINT.
GBTrudeau

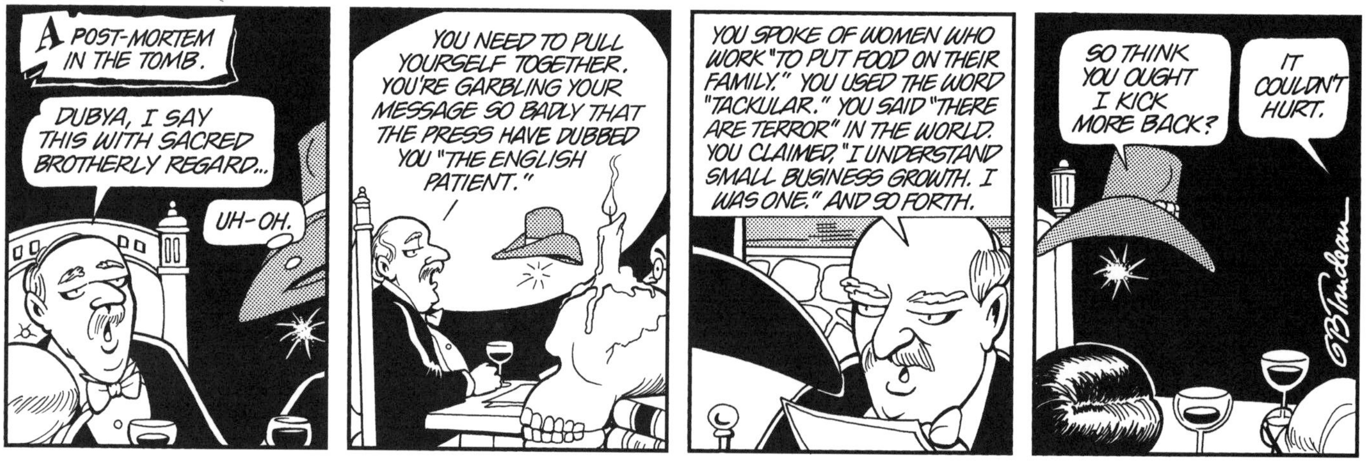
A POST-MORTEM IN THE TOMB.
DUBYA, I SAY THIS WITH SACRED BROTHERLY REGARD...
UH-OH.
YOU NEED TO PULL YOURSELF TOGETHER. YOU'RE GARBLING YOUR MESSAGE SO BADLY THAT THE PRESS HAVE DUBBED YOU "THE ENGLISH PATIENT."
YOU SPOKE OF WOMEN WHO WORK "TO PUT FOOD ON THEIR FAMILY." YOU USED THE WORD "TACKULAR." YOU SAID "THERE ARE TERROR" IN THE WORLD. YOU CLAIMED, "I UNDERSTAND SMALL BUSINESS GROWTH. I WAS ONE." AND SO FORTH.
SO THINK YOU OUGHT I KICK MORE BACK?
IT COULDN'T HURT.
GBTrudeau

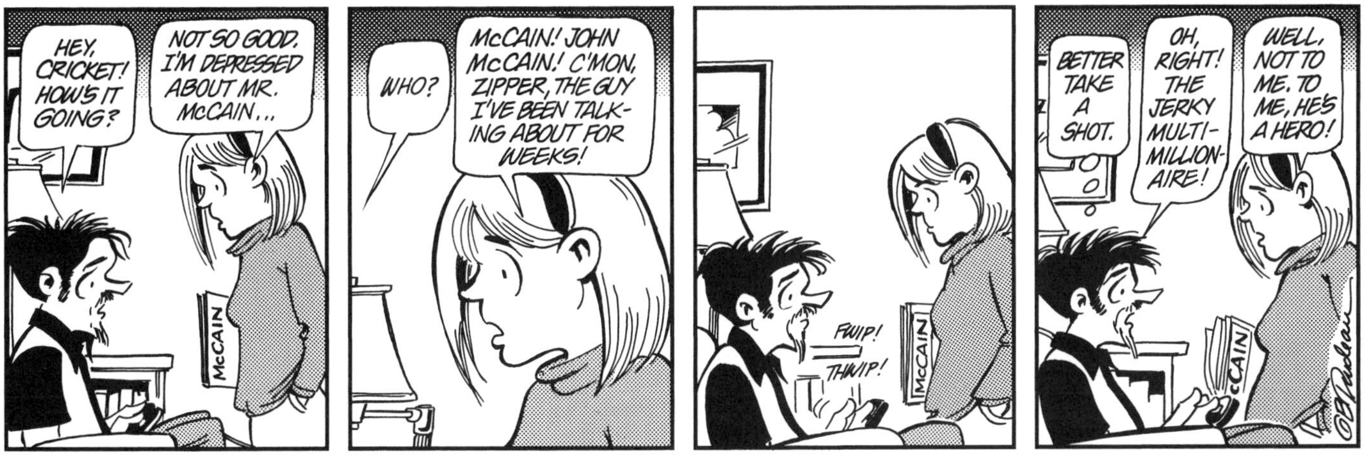
HEY, CRICKET! HOW'S IT GOING?
NOT SO GOOD. I'M DEPRESSED ABOUT MR. McCAIN...
McCAIN
WHO?
McCAIN! JOHN McCAIN! C'MON, ZIPPER, THE GUY I'VE BEEN TALKING ABOUT FOR WEEKS!
FWIP!
THWIP!
McCAIN
BETTER TAKE A SHOT.
OH, RIGHT! THE JERKY MULTI-MILLIONAIRE!
WELL, NOT TO ME. TO ME, HE'S A HERO!

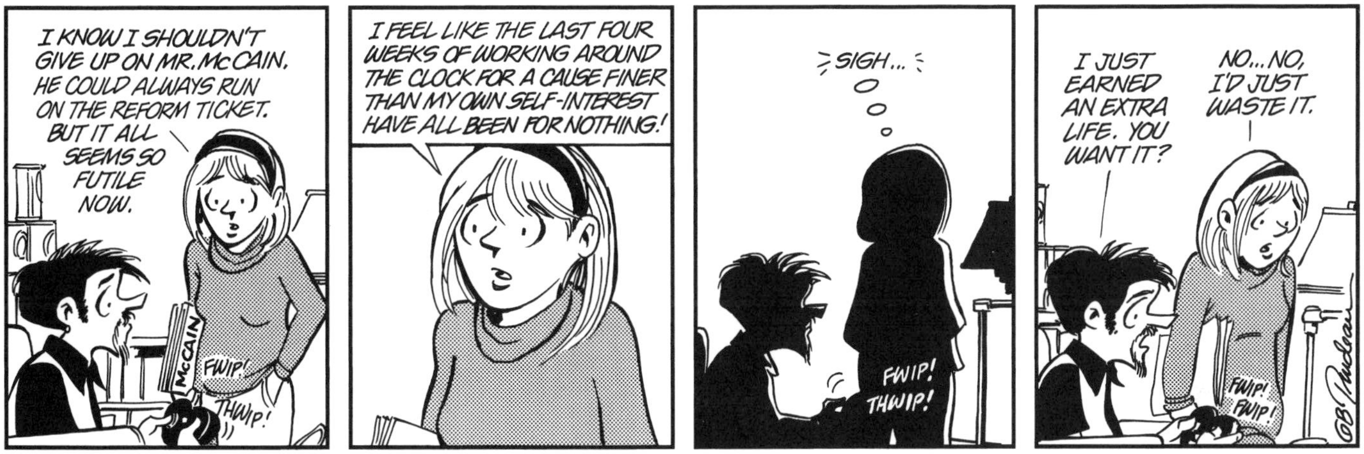
I KNOW I SHOULDN'T GIVE UP ON MR. McCAIN. HE COULD ALWAYS RUN ON THE REFORM TICKET. BUT IT ALL SEEMS SO FUTILE NOW.
McCAIN
FWIP!
THWIP!
I FEEL LIKE THE LAST FOUR WEEKS OF WORKING AROUND THE CLOCK FOR A CAUSE FINER THAN MY OWN SELF-INTEREST HAVE ALL BEEN FOR NOTHING!
SIGH...
FWIP!
THWIP!
I JUST EARNED AN EXTRA LIFE. YOU WANT IT?
NO...NO, I'D JUST WASTE IT.
FWIP! FWIP!

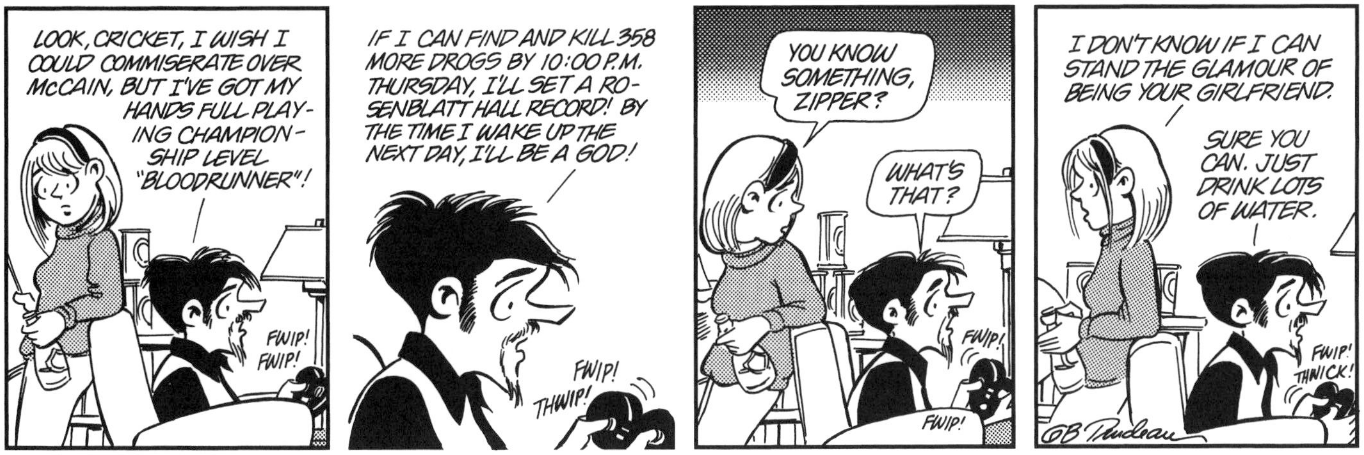
LOOK, CRICKET, I WISH I COULD COMMISERATE OVER McCAIN, BUT I'VE GOT MY HANDS FULL PLAYING CHAMPIONSHIP LEVEL "BLOODRUNNER"!
FWIP! FWIP!
IF I CAN FIND AND KILL 358 MORE DROGS BY 10:00 P.M. THURSDAY, I'LL SET A ROSENBLATT HALL RECORD! BY THE TIME I WAKE UP THE NEXT DAY, I'LL BE A GOD!
FWIP!
THWIP!
YOU KNOW SOMETHING, ZIPPER?
WHAT'S THAT?
FWIP!
FWIP!
I DON'T KNOW IF I CAN STAND THE GLAMOUR OF BEING YOUR GIRLFRIEND.
SURE YOU CAN. JUST DRINK LOTS OF WATER.
FWIP!
THWICK!

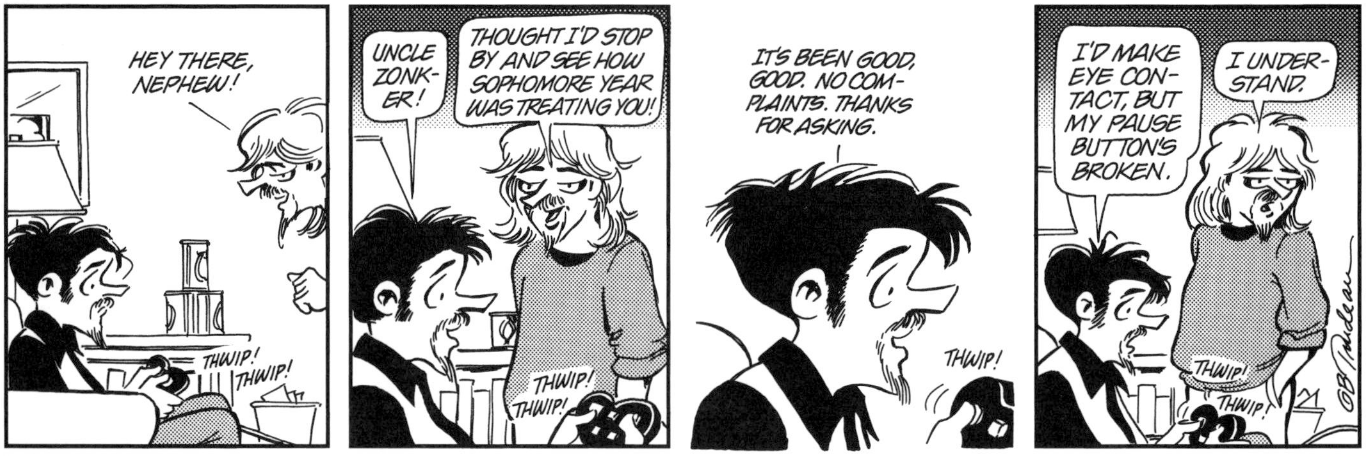
HEY THERE, NEPHEW!
THWIP! THWIP!
UNCLE ZONKER!
THOUGHT I'D STOP BY AND SEE HOW SOPHOMORE YEAR WAS TREATING YOU!
THWIP! THWIP!
IT'S BEEN GOOD, GOOD. NO COMPLAINTS. THANKS FOR ASKING.
THWIP!
I'D MAKE EYE CONTACT, BUT MY PAUSE BUTTON'S BROKEN.
I UNDERSTAND.
THWIP! THWIP!

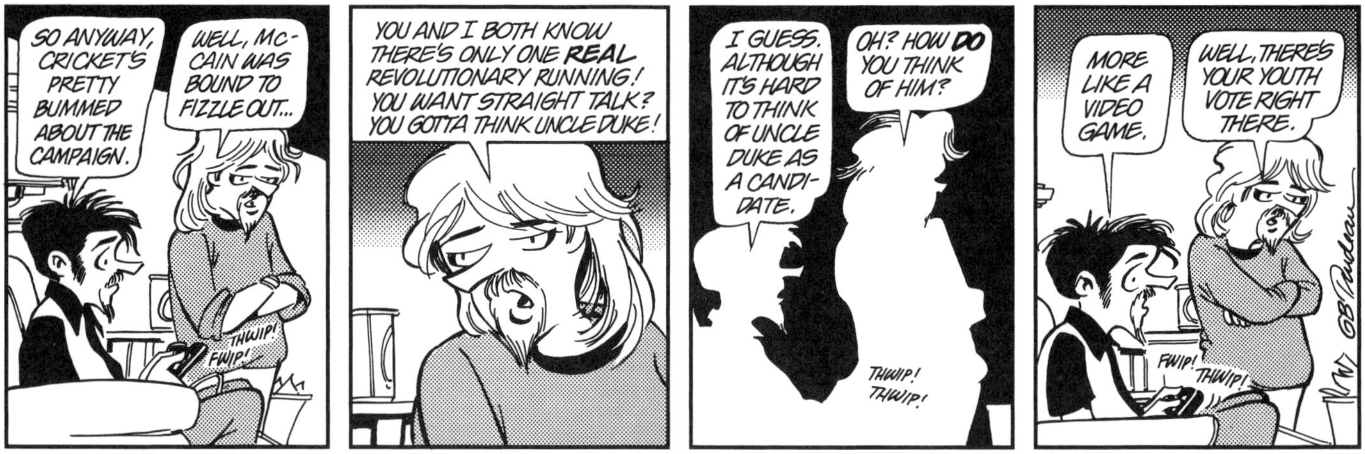
SO ANYWAY, CRICKET'S PRETTY BUMMED ABOUT THE CAMPAIGN.
WELL, McCAIN WAS BOUND TO FIZZLE OUT...
THWIP! FWIP!
YOU AND I BOTH KNOW THERE'S ONLY ONE **REAL** REVOLUTIONARY RUNNING! YOU WANT STRAIGHT TALK? YOU GOTTA THINK UNCLE DUKE!
I GUESS. ALTHOUGH IT'S HARD TO THINK OF UNCLE DUKE AS A CANDIDATE.
OH? HOW **DO** YOU THINK OF HIM?
THWIP! THWIP!
MORE LIKE A VIDEO GAME.
WELL, THERE'S YOUR YOUTH VOTE RIGHT THERE.
FWIP! THWIP!

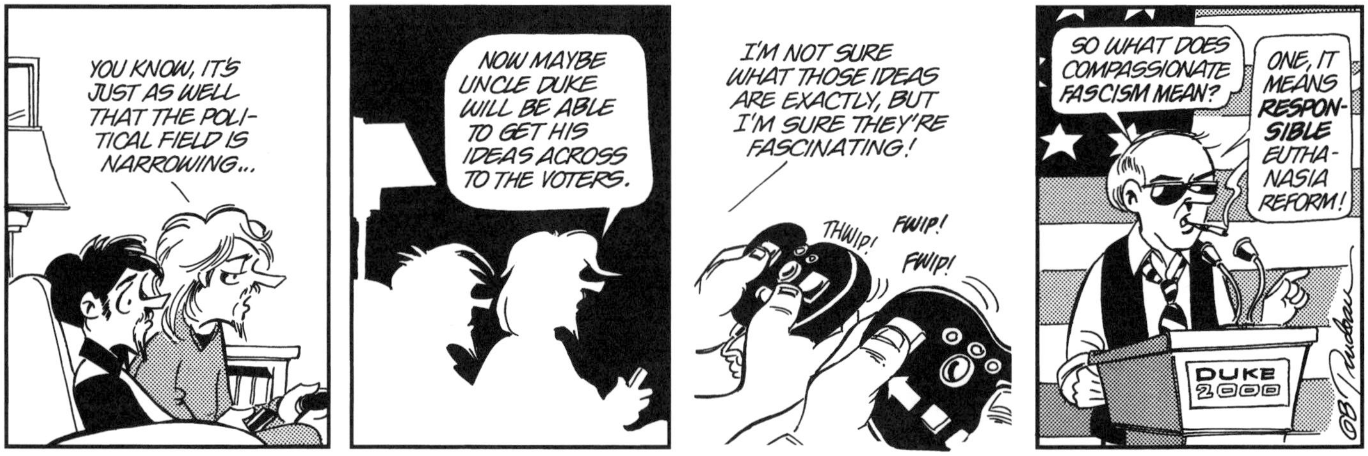
YOU KNOW, IT'S JUST AS WELL THAT THE POLITICAL FIELD IS NARROWING...
NOW MAYBE UNCLE DUKE WILL BE ABLE TO GET HIS IDEAS ACROSS TO THE VOTERS.
I'M NOT SURE WHAT THOSE IDEAS ARE EXACTLY, BUT I'M SURE THEY'RE FASCINATING!
THWIP! FWIP! FWIP!
SO WHAT DOES COMPASSIONATE FASCISM MEAN?
ONE, IT MEANS **RESPONSIBLE** EUTHANASIA REFORM!
DUKE 2000

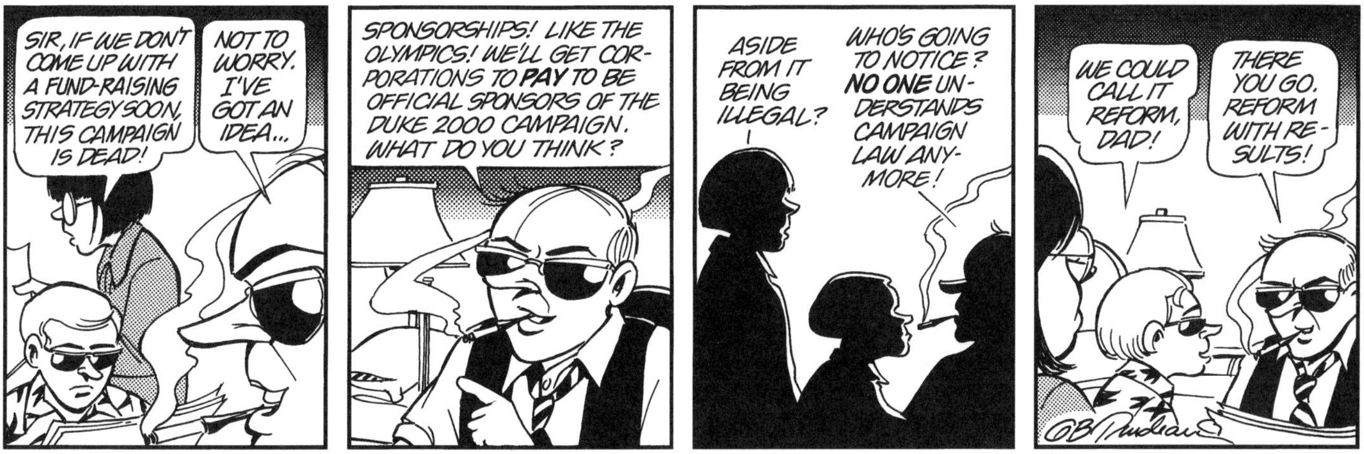
SIR, IF WE DON'T COME UP WITH A FUND-RAISING STRATEGY SOON, THIS CAMPAIGN IS DEAD!
NOT TO WORRY. I'VE GOT AN IDEA...
SPONSORSHIPS! LIKE THE OLYMPICS! WE'LL GET CORPORATIONS TO PAY TO BE OFFICIAL SPONSORS OF THE DUKE 2000 CAMPAIGN. WHAT DO YOU THINK?
ASIDE FROM IT BEING ILLEGAL?
WHO'S GOING TO NOTICE? NO ONE UNDERSTANDS CAMPAIGN LAW ANYMORE!
WE COULD CALL IT REFORM, DAD!
THERE YOU GO. REFORM WITH RESULTS!
GBTrudeau

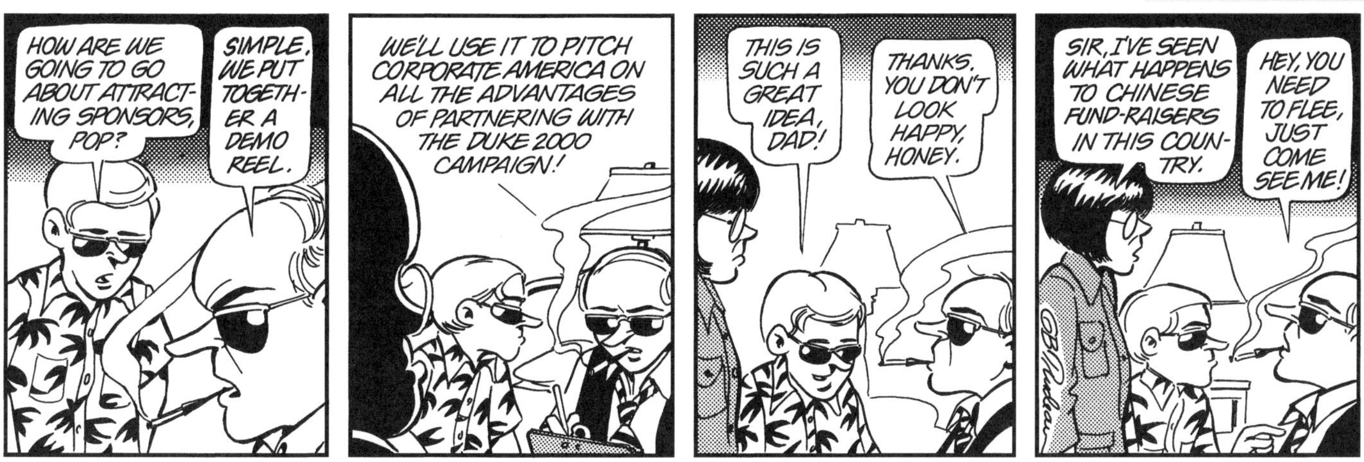
HOW ARE WE GOING TO GO ABOUT ATTRACTING SPONSORS, POP?
SIMPLE. WE PUT TOGETHER A DEMO REEL.
WE'LL USE IT TO PITCH CORPORATE AMERICA ON ALL THE ADVANTAGES OF PARTNERING WITH THE DUKE 2000 CAMPAIGN!
THIS IS SUCH A GREAT IDEA, DAD!
THANKS. YOU DON'T LOOK HAPPY, HONEY.
SIR, I'VE SEEN WHAT HAPPENS TO CHINESE FUND-RAISERS IN THIS COUNTRY.
HEY, YOU NEED TO FLEE, JUST COME SEE ME!
GBTrudeau

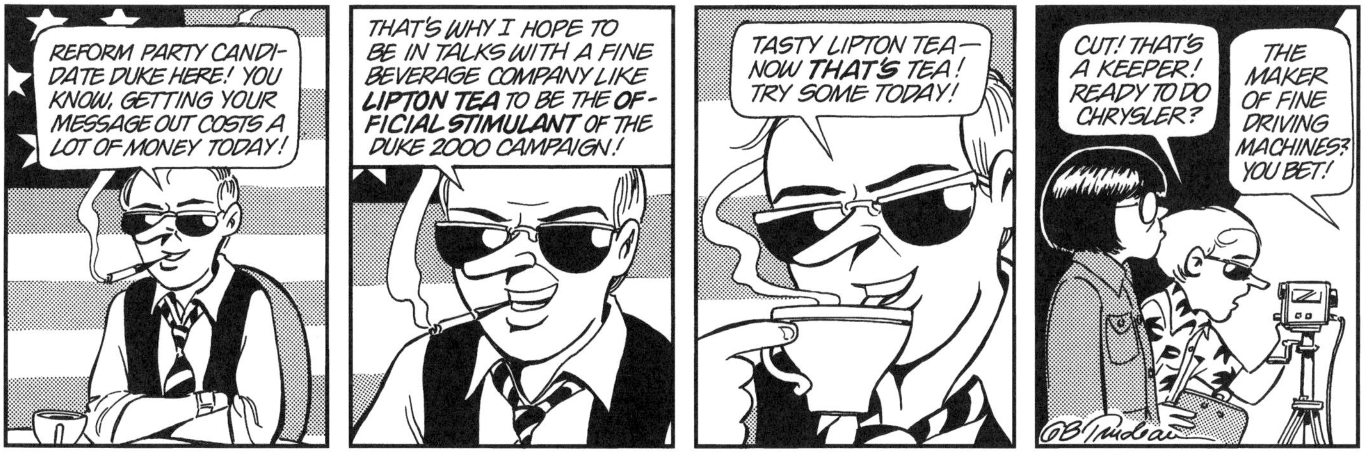
REFORM PARTY CANDIDATE DUKE HERE! YOU KNOW, GETTING YOUR MESSAGE OUT COSTS A LOT OF MONEY TODAY!
THAT'S WHY I HOPE TO BE IN TALKS WITH A FINE BEVERAGE COMPANY LIKE LIPTON TEA TO BE THE OFFICIAL STIMULANT OF THE DUKE 2000 CAMPAIGN!
TASTY LIPTON TEA— NOW THAT'S TEA! TRY SOME TODAY!
CUT! THAT'S A KEEPER! READY TO DO CHRYSLER?
THE MAKER OF FINE DRIVING MACHINES? YOU BET!
GBTrudeau

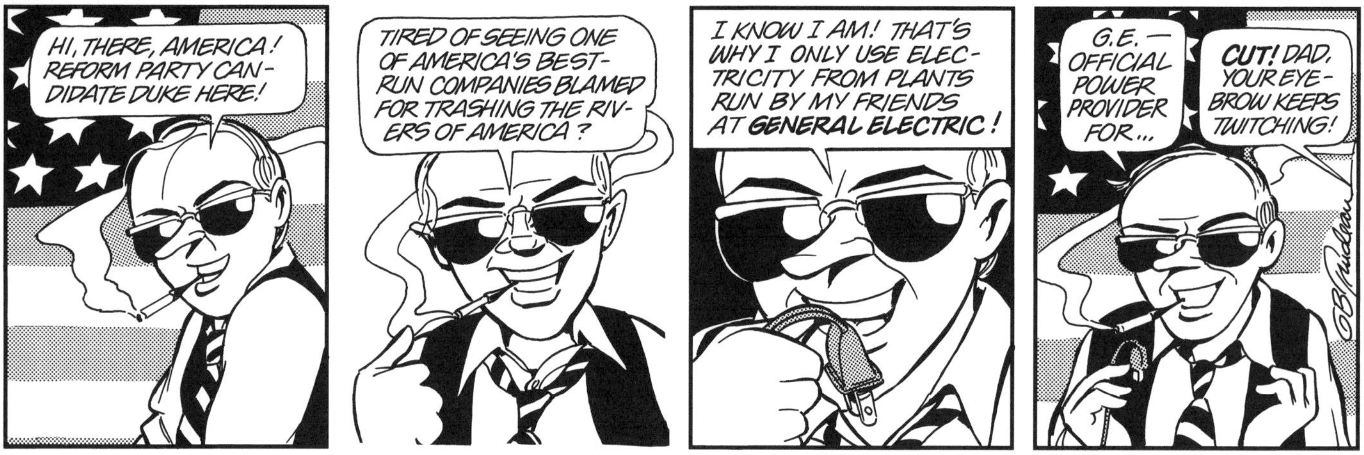
HI, THERE, AMERICA! REFORM PARTY CANDIDATE DUKE HERE!
TIRED OF SEEING ONE OF AMERICA'S BEST-RUN COMPANIES BLAMED FOR TRASHING THE RIVERS OF AMERICA?
I KNOW I AM! THAT'S WHY I ONLY USE ELECTRICITY FROM PLANTS RUN BY MY FRIENDS AT GENERAL ELECTRIC!
G.E.—OFFICIAL POWER PROVIDER FOR...
CUT! DAD, YOUR EYEBROW KEEPS TWITCHING!

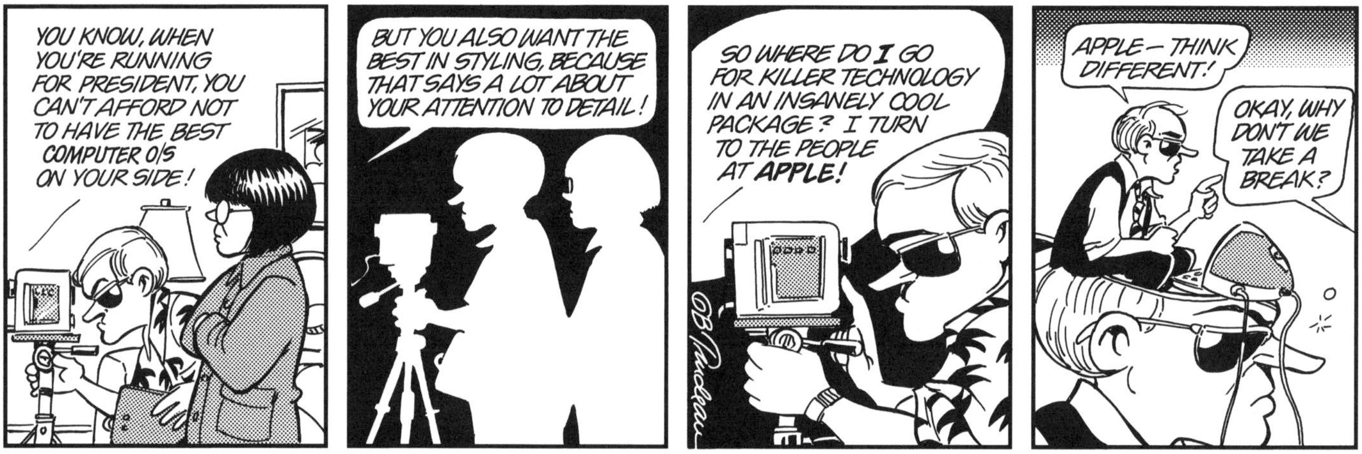
YOU KNOW, WHEN YOU'RE RUNNING FOR PRESIDENT, YOU CAN'T AFFORD NOT TO HAVE THE BEST COMPUTER O/S ON YOUR SIDE!
BUT YOU ALSO WANT THE BEST IN STYLING, BECAUSE THAT SAYS A LOT ABOUT YOUR ATTENTION TO DETAIL!
SO WHERE DO I GO FOR KILLER TECHNOLOGY IN AN INSANELY COOL PACKAGE? I TURN TO THE PEOPLE AT APPLE!
APPLE—THINK DIFFERENT!
OKAY, WHY DON'T WE TAKE A BREAK?

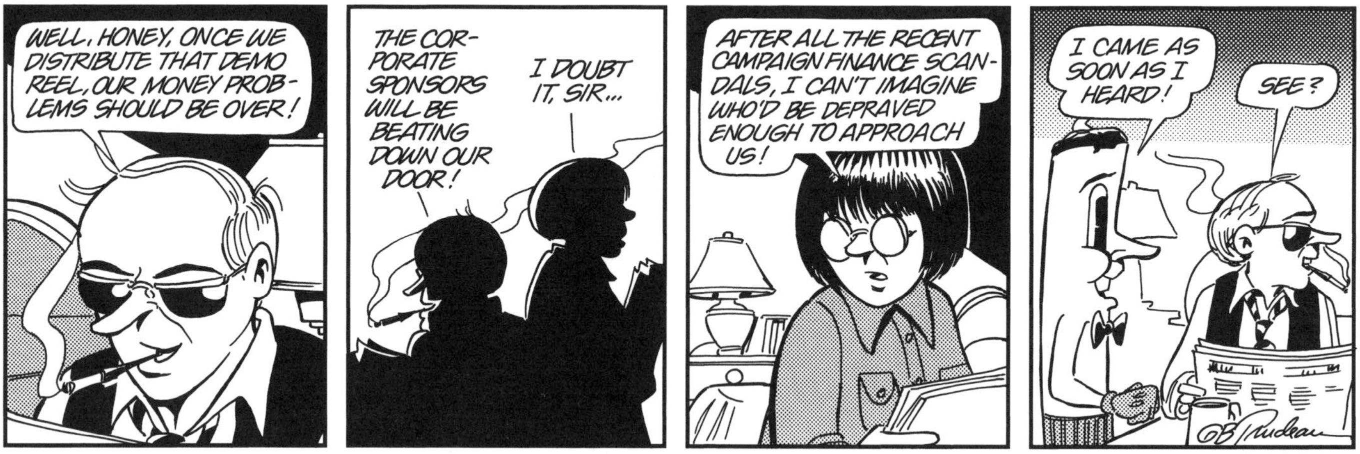
WELL, HONEY, ONCE WE DISTRIBUTE THAT DEMO REEL, OUR MONEY PROBLEMS SHOULD BE OVER!
THE CORPORATE SPONSORS WILL BE BEATING DOWN OUR DOOR!
I DOUBT IT, SIR...
AFTER ALL THE RECENT CAMPAIGN FINANCE SCANDALS, I CAN'T IMAGINE WHO'D BE DEPRAVED ENOUGH TO APPROACH US!
I CAME AS SOON AS I HEARD!
SEE?

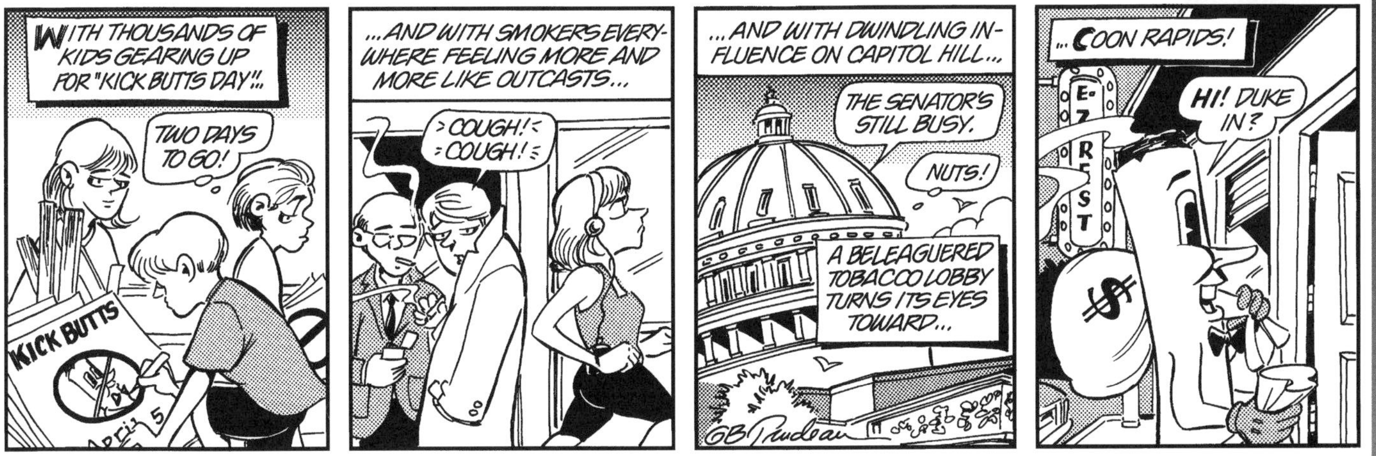
WITH THOUSANDS OF KIDS GEARING UP FOR "KICK BUTTS DAY"...
TWO DAYS TO GO!
KICK BUTTS
...AND WITH SMOKERS EVERYWHERE FEELING MORE AND MORE LIKE OUTCASTS...
COUGH! COUGH!
...AND WITH DWINDLING INFLUENCE ON CAPITOL HILL...
THE SENATOR'S STILL BUSY.
NUTS!
A BELEAGUERED TOBACCO LOBBY TURNS ITS EYES TOWARD...
...COON RAPIDS!
E-Z REST
HI! DUKE IN?

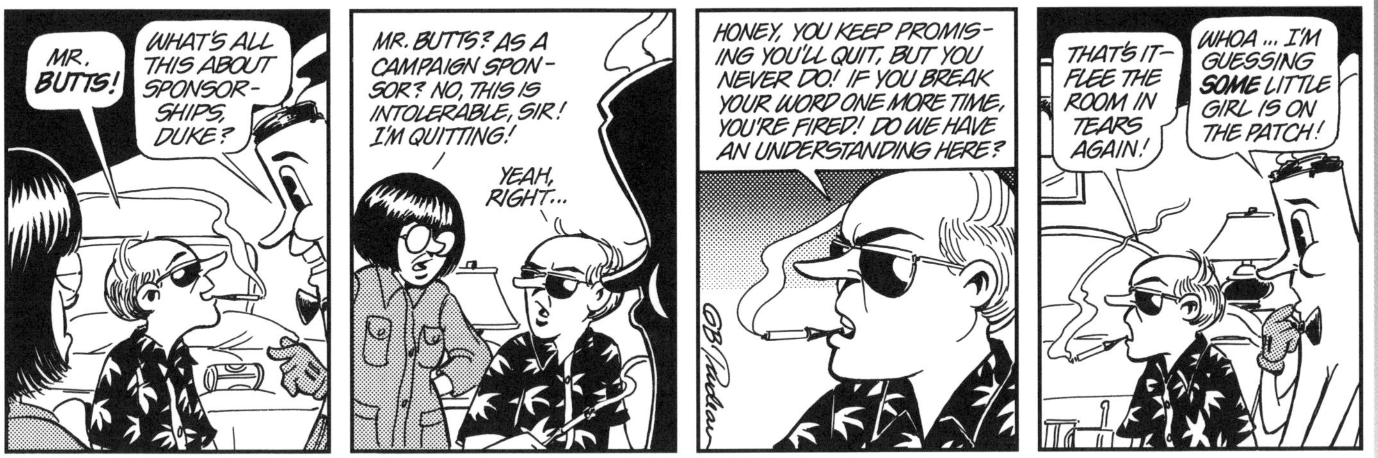
MR. BUTTS!
WHAT'S ALL THIS ABOUT SPONSORSHIPS, DUKE?
MR. BUTTS? AS A CAMPAIGN SPONSOR? NO, THIS IS INTOLERABLE, SIR! I'M QUITTING!
YEAH, RIGHT...
HONEY, YOU KEEP PROMISING YOU'LL QUIT, BUT YOU NEVER DO! IF YOU BREAK YOUR WORD ONE MORE TIME, YOU'RE FIRED! DO WE HAVE AN UNDERSTANDING HERE?
THAT'S IT— FLEE THE ROOM IN TEARS AGAIN!
WHOA ... I'M GUESSING SOME LITTLE GIRL IS ON THE PATCH!

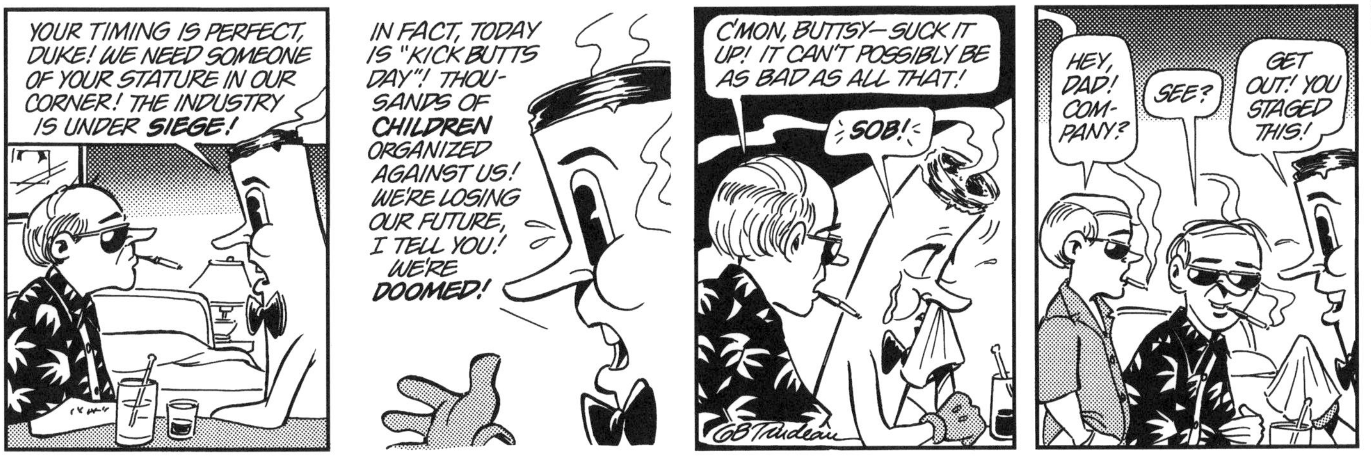
YOUR TIMING IS PERFECT, DUKE! WE NEED SOMEONE OF YOUR STATURE IN OUR CORNER! THE INDUSTRY IS UNDER SIEGE!
IN FACT, TODAY IS "KICK BUTTS DAY"! THOUSANDS OF CHILDREN ORGANIZED AGAINST US! WE'RE LOSING OUR FUTURE, I TELL YOU! WE'RE DOOMED!
C'MON, BUTTSY— SUCK IT UP! IT CAN'T POSSIBLY BE AS BAD AS ALL THAT!
SOB!
HEY, DAD! COMPANY?
SEE?
GET OUT! YOU STAGED THIS!

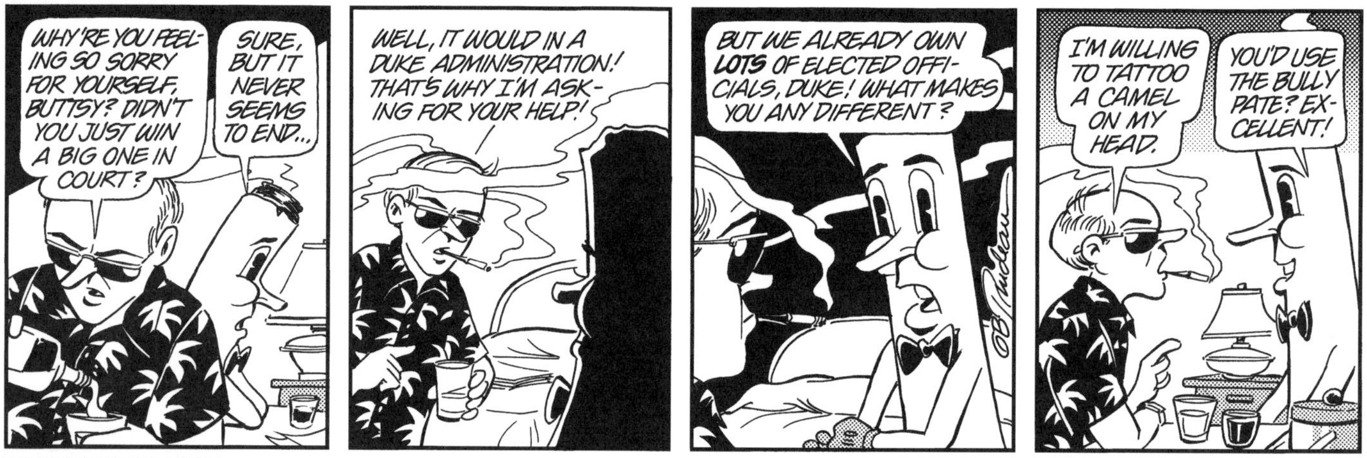
WHY'RE YOU FEELING SO SORRY FOR YOURSELF, BUTTSY? DIDN'T YOU JUST WIN A BIG ONE IN COURT?
SURE, BUT IT NEVER SEEMS TO END...
WELL, IT WOULD IN A DUKE ADMINISTRATION! THAT'S WHY I'M ASKING FOR YOUR HELP!
BUT WE ALREADY OWN LOTS OF ELECTED OFFICIALS, DUKE! WHAT MAKES YOU ANY DIFFERENT?
I'M WILLING TO TATTOO A CAMEL ON MY HEAD.
YOU'D USE THE BULLY PATE? EXCELLENT!

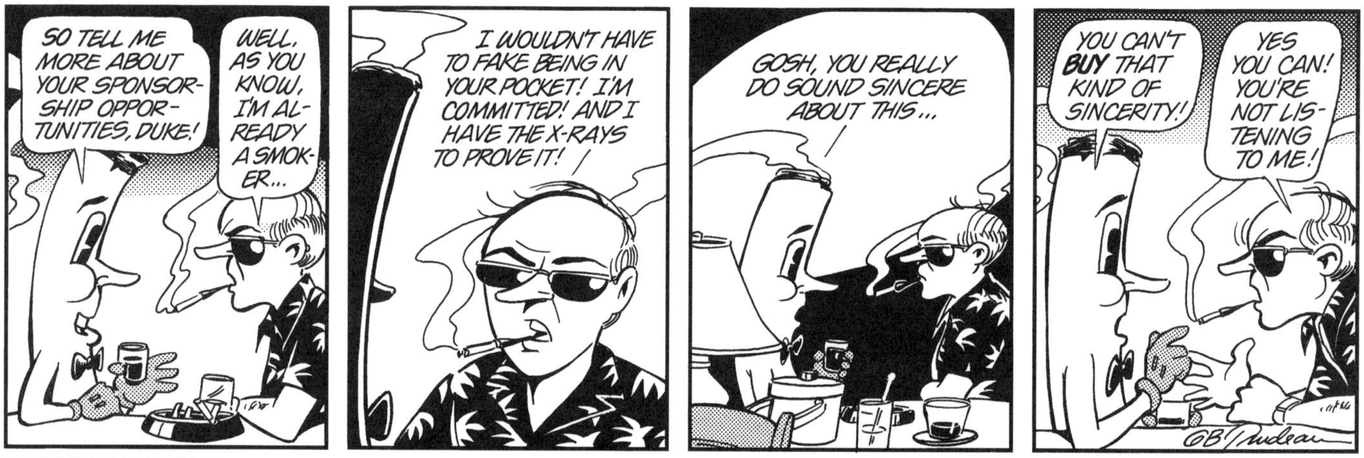
SO TELL ME MORE ABOUT YOUR SPONSORSHIP OPPORTUNITIES, DUKE!
WELL, AS YOU KNOW, I'M ALREADY A SMOKER...
I WOULDN'T HAVE TO FAKE BEING IN YOUR POCKET! I'M COMMITTED! AND I HAVE THE X-RAYS TO PROVE IT!
GOSH, YOU REALLY DO SOUND SINCERE ABOUT THIS...
YOU CAN'T BUY THAT KIND OF SINCERITY!
YES YOU CAN! YOU'RE NOT LISTENING TO ME!

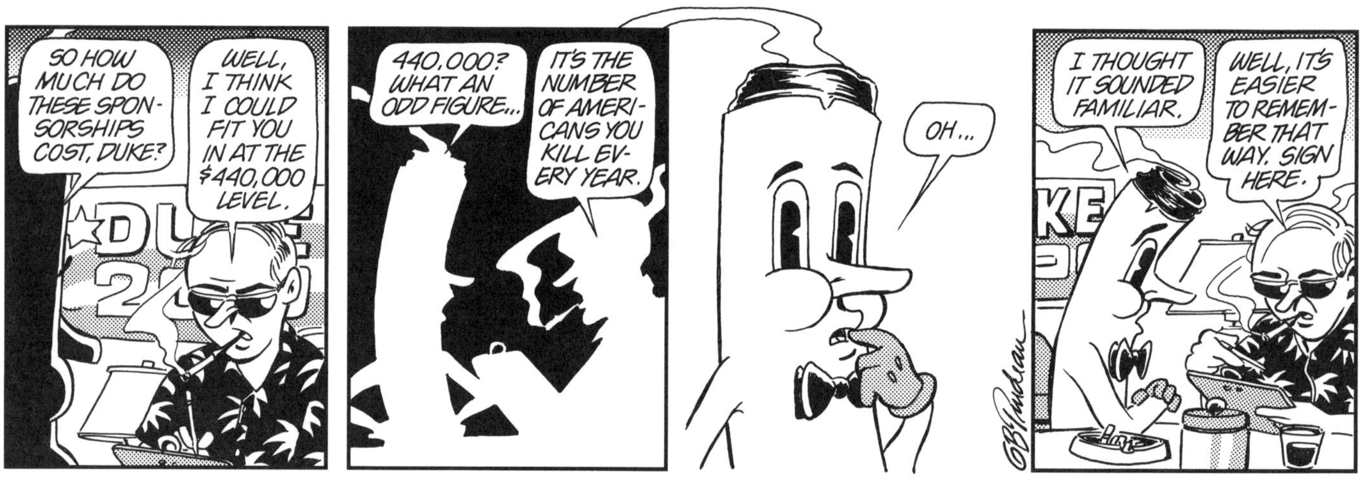
SO HOW MUCH DO THESE SPONSORSHIPS COST, DUKE?
WELL, I THINK I COULD FIT YOU IN AT THE $440,000 LEVEL.
440,000? WHAT AN ODD FIGURE...
IT'S THE NUMBER OF AMERICANS YOU KILL EVERY YEAR.
OH...
I THOUGHT IT SOUNDED FAMILIAR.
WELL, IT'S EASIER TO REMEMBER THAT WAY. SIGN HERE.

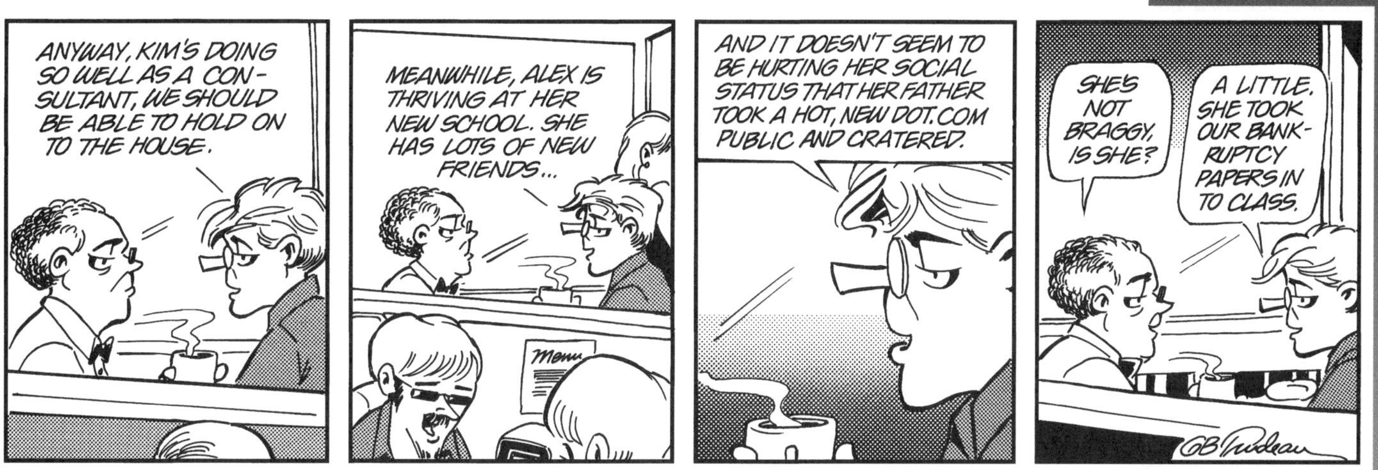
ANYWAY, KIM'S DOING SO WELL AS A CONSULTANT, WE SHOULD BE ABLE TO HOLD ON TO THE HOUSE.
MEANWHILE, ALEX IS THRIVING AT HER NEW SCHOOL. SHE HAS LOTS OF NEW FRIENDS...
Menu
AND IT DOESN'T SEEM TO BE HURTING HER SOCIAL STATUS THAT HER FATHER TOOK A HOT, NEW DOT.COM PUBLIC AND CRATERED.
SHE'S NOT BRAGGY, IS SHE?
A LITTLE. SHE TOOK OUR BANKRUPTCY PAPERS IN TO CLASS.
©B Trudeau

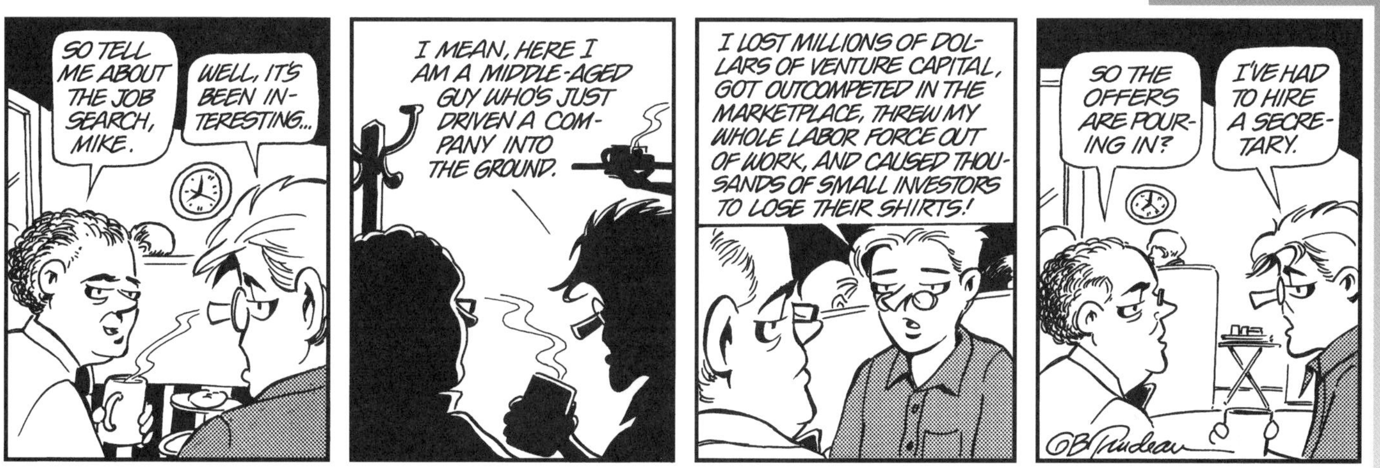
SO TELL ME ABOUT THE JOB SEARCH, MIKE.
WELL, IT'S BEEN INTERESTING...
I MEAN, HERE I AM A MIDDLE-AGED GUY WHO'S JUST DRIVEN A COMPANY INTO THE GROUND.
I LOST MILLIONS OF DOLLARS OF VENTURE CAPITAL, GOT OUTCOMPETED IN THE MARKETPLACE, THREW MY WHOLE LABOR FORCE OUT OF WORK, AND CAUSED THOUSANDS OF SMALL INVESTORS TO LOSE THEIR SHIRTS!
SO THE OFFERS ARE POURING IN?
I'VE HAD TO HIRE A SECRETARY.
©B Trudeau

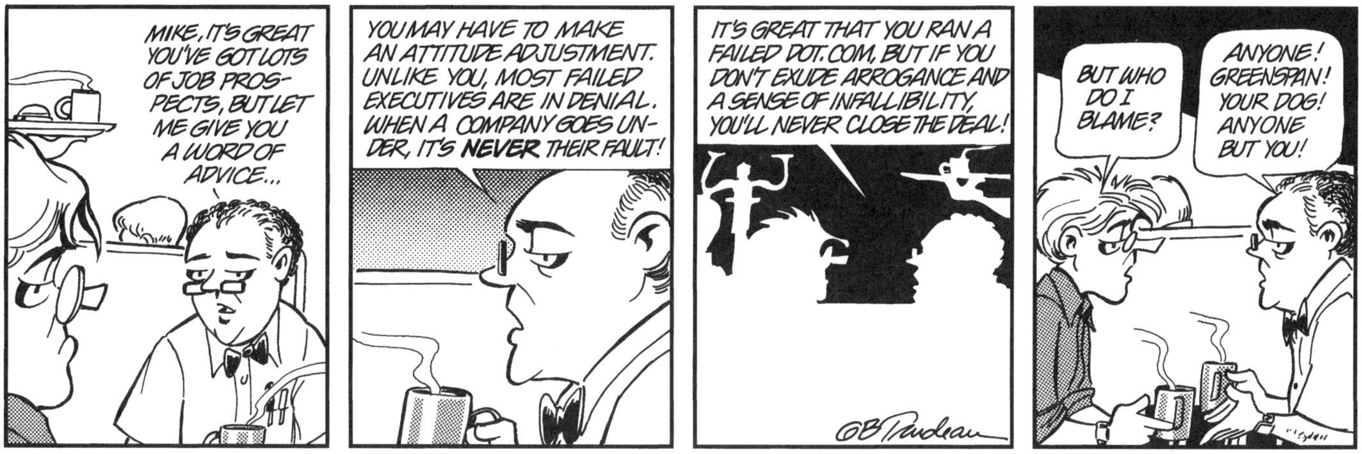
MIKE, IT'S GREAT YOU'VE GOT LOTS OF JOB PROSPECTS, BUT LET ME GIVE YOU A WORD OF ADVICE...
YOU MAY HAVE TO MAKE AN ATTITUDE ADJUSTMENT. UNLIKE YOU, MOST FAILED EXECUTIVES ARE IN DENIAL. WHEN A COMPANY GOES UNDER, IT'S **NEVER** THEIR FAULT!
IT'S GREAT THAT YOU RAN A FAILED DOT.COM, BUT IF YOU DON'T EXUDE ARROGANCE AND A SENSE OF INFALLIBILITY, YOU'LL NEVER CLOSE THE DEAL!
©B Trudeau
BUT WHO DO I BLAME?
ANYONE! GREENSPAN! YOUR DOG! ANYONE BUT YOU!

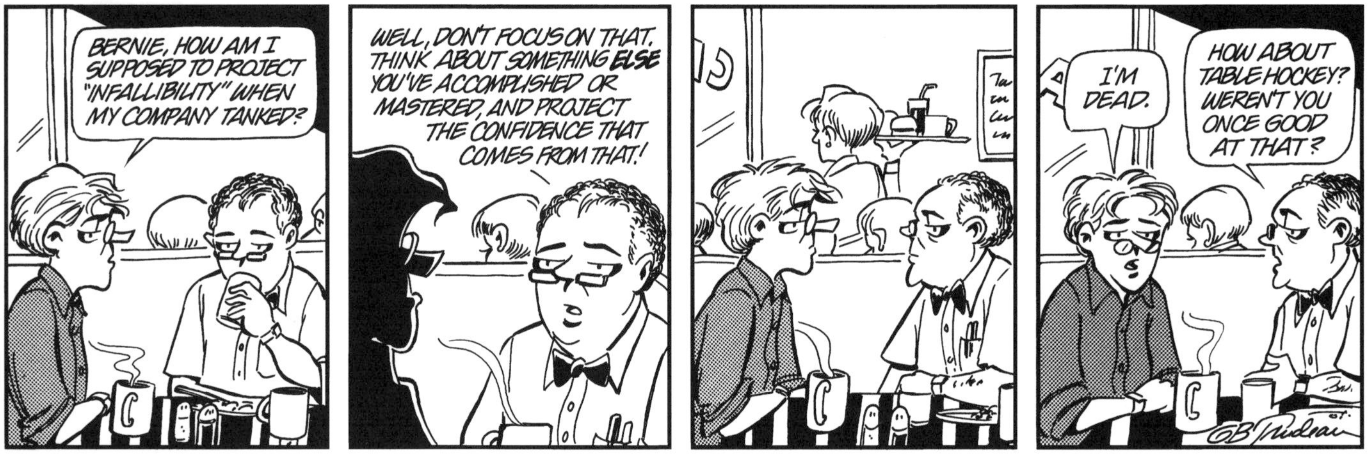
BERNIE, HOW AM I SUPPOSED TO PROJECT "INFALLIBILITY" WHEN MY COMPANY TANKED?
WELL, DON'T FOCUS ON THAT. THINK ABOUT SOMETHING ELSE YOU'VE ACCOMPLISHED OR MASTERED, AND PROJECT THE CONFIDENCE THAT COMES FROM THAT!
I'M DEAD.
HOW ABOUT TABLE HOCKEY? WEREN'T YOU ONCE GOOD AT THAT?

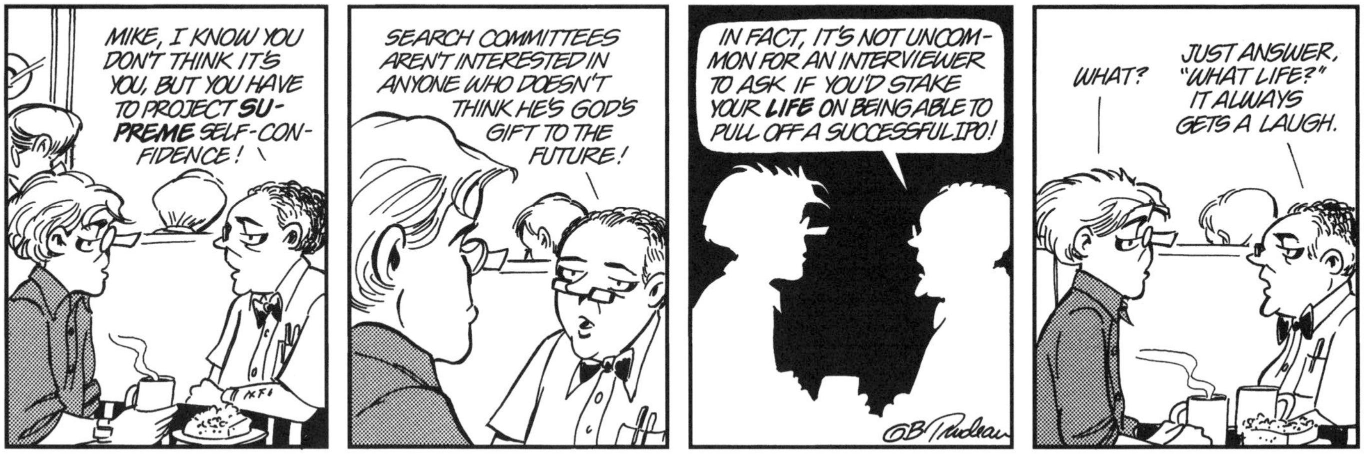
MIKE, I KNOW YOU DON'T THINK IT'S YOU, BUT YOU HAVE TO PROJECT SUPREME SELF-CONFIDENCE!
SEARCH COMMITTEES AREN'T INTERESTED IN ANYONE WHO DOESN'T THINK HE'S GOD'S GIFT TO THE FUTURE!
IN FACT, IT'S NOT UNCOMMON FOR AN INTERVIEWER TO ASK IF YOU'D STAKE YOUR LIFE ON BEING ABLE TO PULL OFF A SUCCESSFUL IPO!
WHAT?
JUST ANSWER, "WHAT LIFE?" IT ALWAYS GETS A LAUGH.

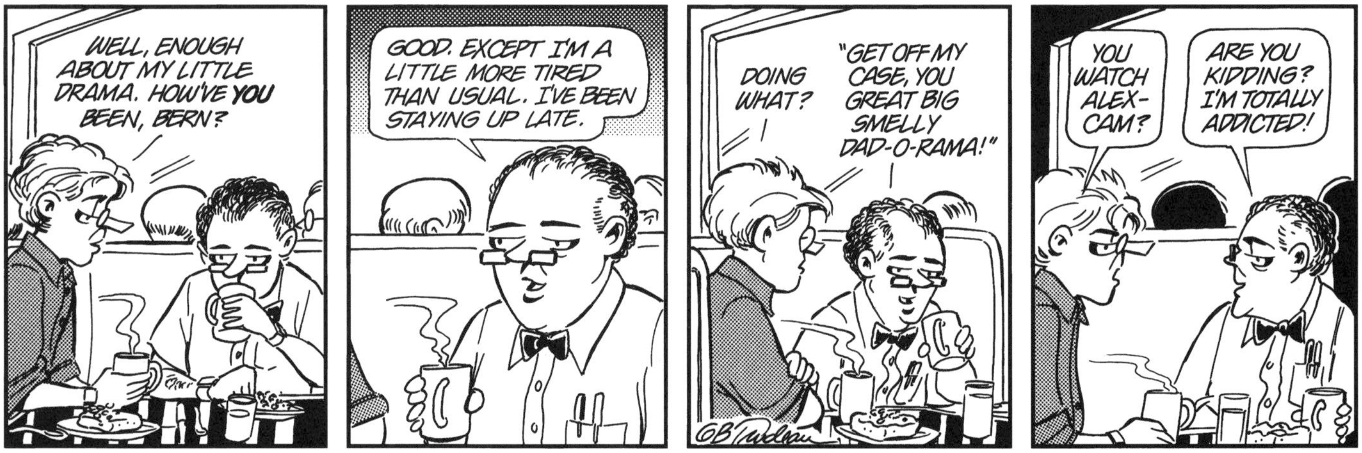
WELL, ENOUGH ABOUT MY LITTLE DRAMA. HOW'VE YOU BEEN, BERN?
GOOD. EXCEPT I'M A LITTLE MORE TIRED THAN USUAL. I'VE BEEN STAYING UP LATE.
DOING WHAT?
"GET OFF MY CASE, YOU GREAT BIG SMELLY DAD-O-RAMA!"
YOU WATCH ALEX-CAM?
ARE YOU KIDDING? I'M TOTALLY ADDICTED!

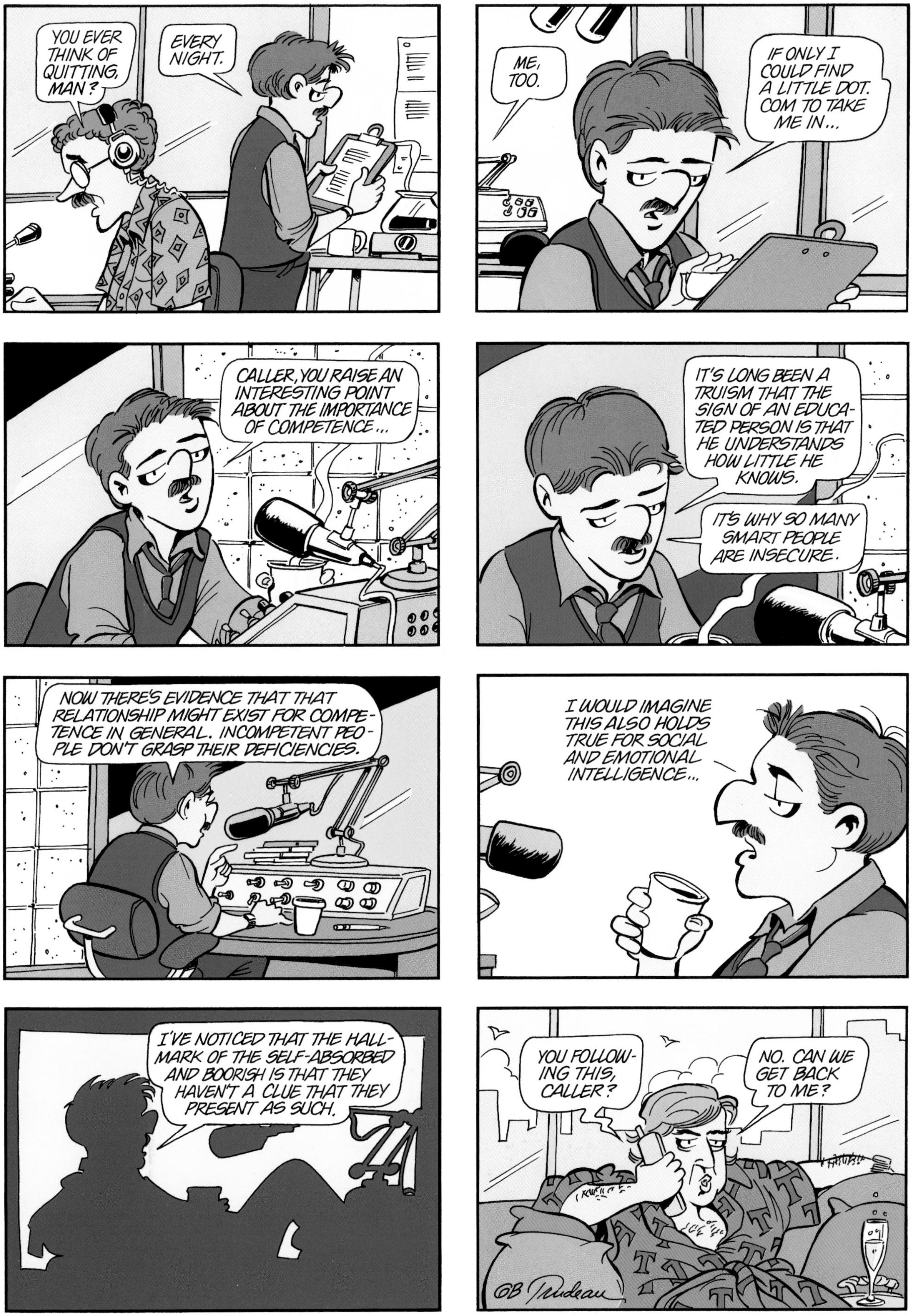
YOU EVER THINK OF QUITTING, MAN?
EVERY NIGHT.
ME, TOO.
IF ONLY I COULD FIND A LITTLE DOT. COM TO TAKE ME IN...
CALLER, YOU RAISE AN INTERESTING POINT ABOUT THE IMPORTANCE OF COMPETENCE...
IT'S LONG BEEN A TRUISM THAT THE SIGN OF AN EDUCATED PERSON IS THAT HE UNDERSTANDS HOW LITTLE HE KNOWS.
IT'S WHY SO MANY SMART PEOPLE ARE INSECURE.
NOW THERE'S EVIDENCE THAT THAT RELATIONSHIP MIGHT EXIST FOR COMPETENCE IN GENERAL. INCOMPETENT PEOPLE DON'T GRASP THEIR DEFICIENCIES.
I WOULD IMAGINE THIS ALSO HOLDS TRUE FOR SOCIAL AND EMOTIONAL INTELLIGENCE...
I'VE NOTICED THAT THE HALLMARK OF THE SELF-ABSORBED AND BOORISH IS THAT THEY HAVEN'T A CLUE THAT THEY PRESENT AS SUCH.
YOU FOLLOWING THIS, CALLER?
NO. CAN WE GET BACK TO ME?

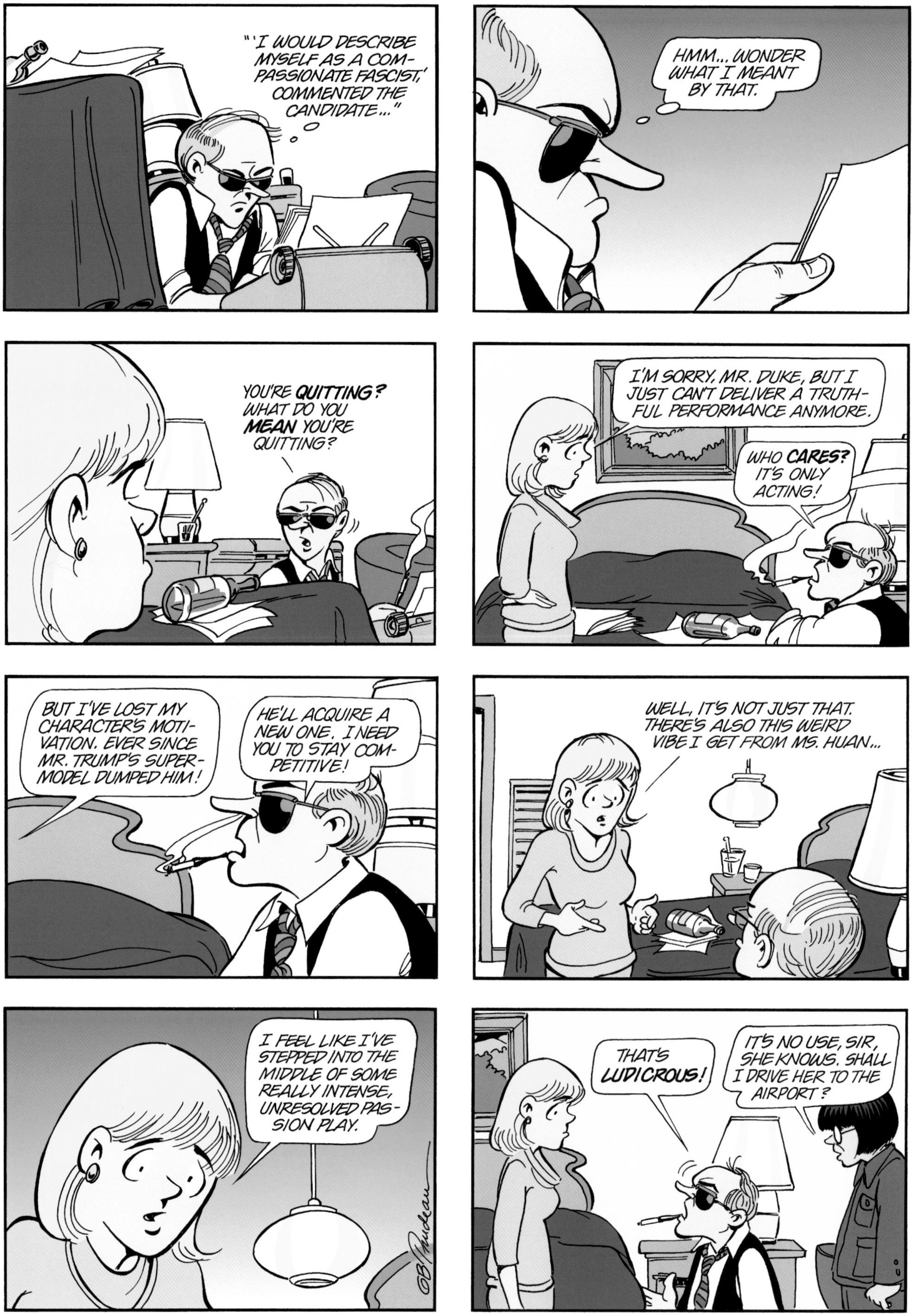
"'I WOULD DESCRIBE MYSELF AS A COMPASSIONATE FASCIST,' COMMENTED THE CANDIDATE..."
HMM... WONDER WHAT I MEANT BY THAT.
YOU'RE **QUITTING?** WHAT DO YOU **MEAN** YOU'RE QUITTING?
I'M SORRY, MR. DUKE, BUT I JUST CAN'T DELIVER A TRUTHFUL PERFORMANCE ANYMORE.
WHO **CARES?** IT'S ONLY ACTING!
BUT I'VE LOST MY CHARACTER'S MOTIVATION. EVER SINCE MR. TRUMP'S SUPERMODEL DUMPED HIM!
HE'LL ACQUIRE A NEW ONE. I NEED YOU TO STAY COMPETITIVE!
WELL, IT'S NOT JUST THAT. THERE'S ALSO THIS WEIRD VIBE I GET FROM MS. HUAN...
I FEEL LIKE I'VE STEPPED INTO THE MIDDLE OF SOME REALLY INTENSE, UNRESOLVED PASSION PLAY.
THAT'S **LUDICROUS!**
IT'S NO USE, SIR, SHE KNOWS. SHALL I DRIVE HER TO THE AIRPORT?

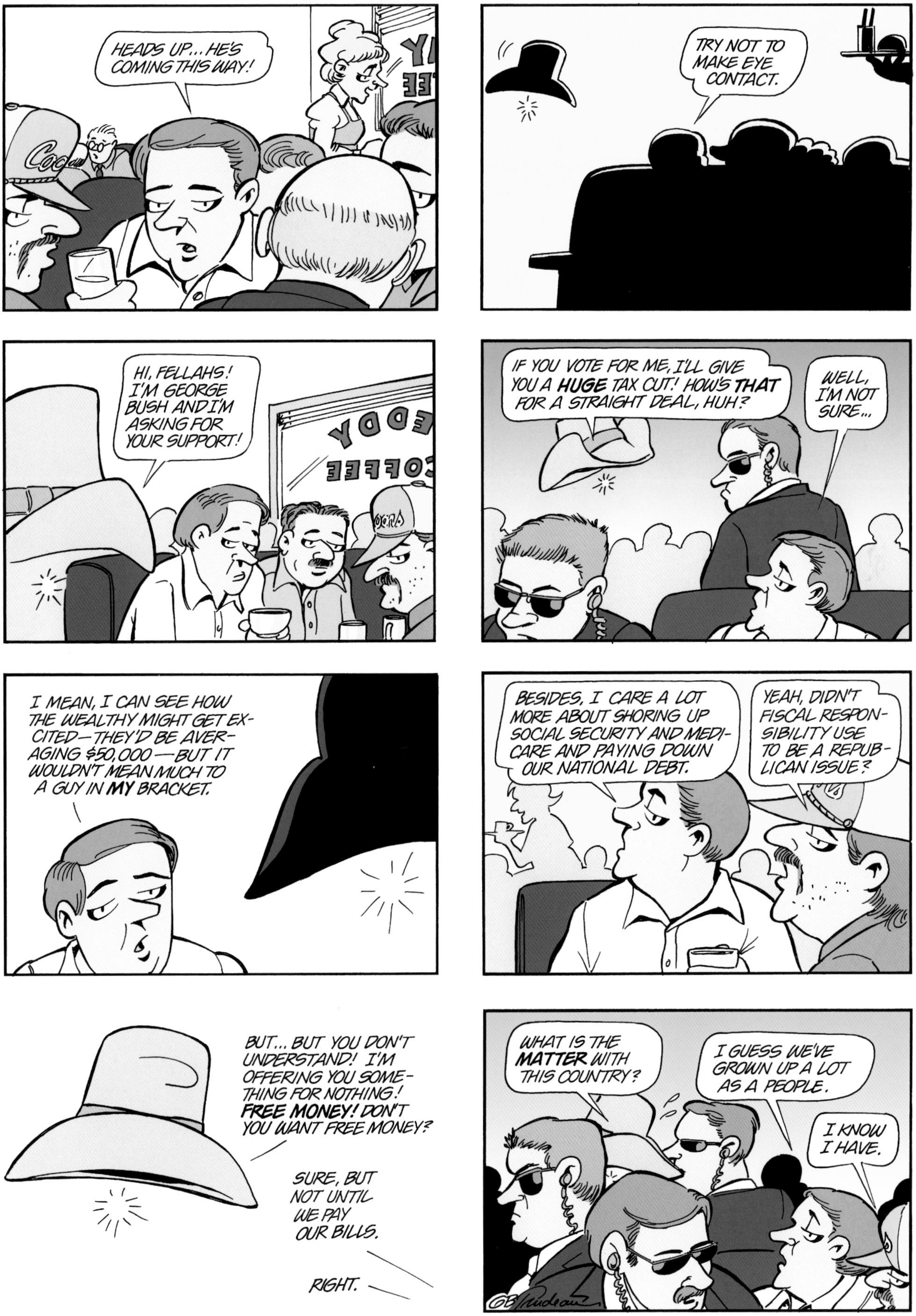
HEADS UP... HE'S COMING THIS WAY!
TRY NOT TO MAKE EYE CONTACT.
HI, FELLAHS! I'M GEORGE BUSH AND I'M ASKING FOR YOUR SUPPORT!
IF YOU VOTE FOR ME, I'LL GIVE YOU A HUGE TAX CUT! HOW'S THAT FOR A STRAIGHT DEAL, HUH?
WELL, I'M NOT SURE...
I MEAN, I CAN SEE HOW THE WEALTHY MIGHT GET EXCITED—THEY'D BE AVERAGING $50,000—BUT IT WOULDN'T MEAN MUCH TO A GUY IN MY BRACKET.
BESIDES, I CARE A LOT MORE ABOUT SHORING UP SOCIAL SECURITY AND MEDICARE AND PAYING DOWN OUR NATIONAL DEBT.
YEAH, DIDN'T FISCAL RESPONSIBILITY USE TO BE A REPUBLICAN ISSUE?
BUT... BUT YOU DON'T UNDERSTAND! I'M OFFERING YOU SOMETHING FOR NOTHING! FREE MONEY! DON'T YOU WANT FREE MONEY?
SURE, BUT NOT UNTIL WE PAY OUR BILLS.
RIGHT.
WHAT IS THE MATTER WITH THIS COUNTRY?
I GUESS WE'VE GROWN UP A LOT AS A PEOPLE.
I KNOW I HAVE.

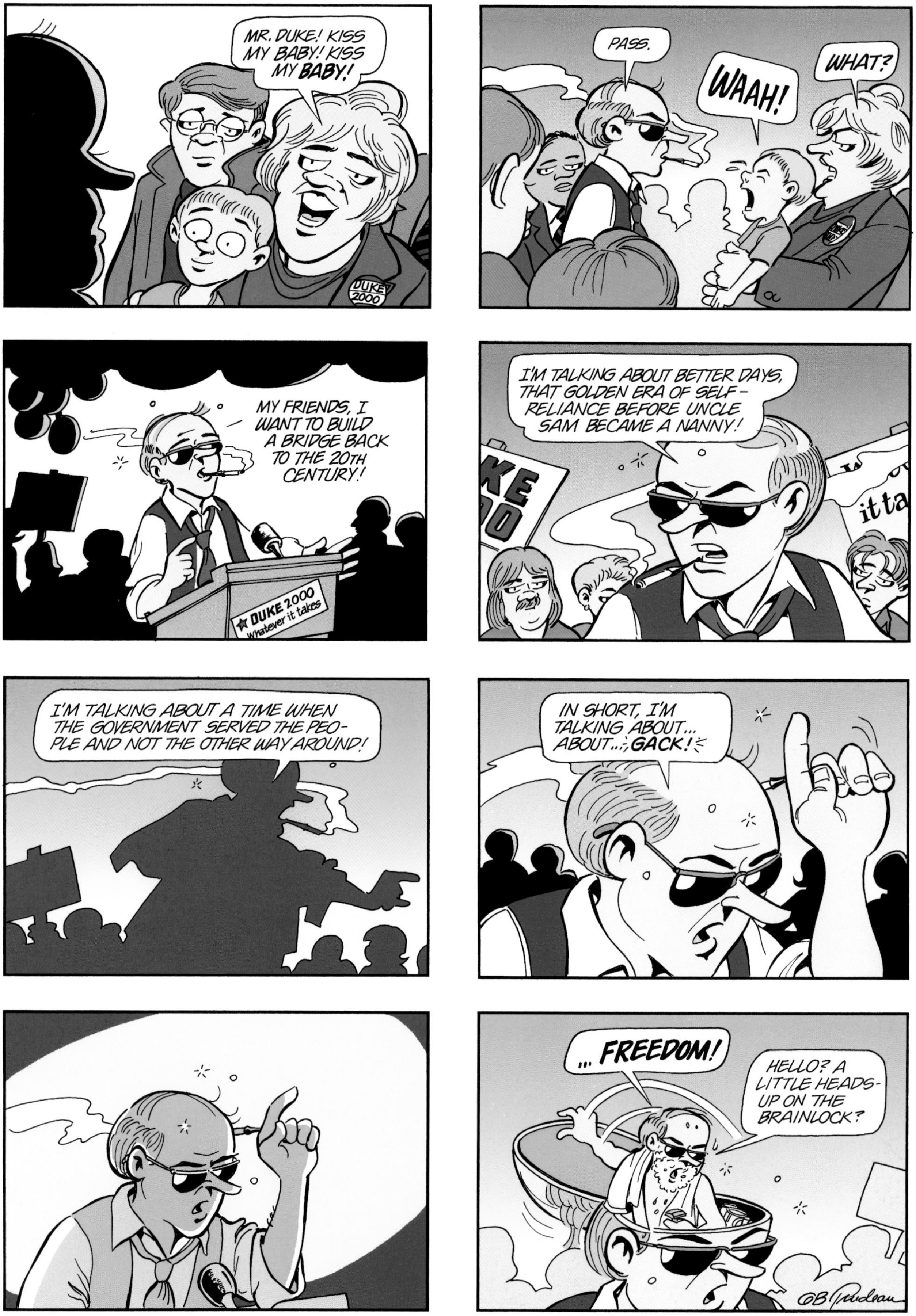
MR. DUKE! KISS MY BABY! KISS MY BABY!
DUKE 2000
PASS.
WAAH!
WHAT?
MY FRIENDS, I WANT TO BUILD A BRIDGE BACK TO THE 20TH CENTURY!
DUKE 2000 Whatever it takes
I'M TALKING ABOUT BETTER DAYS, THAT GOLDEN ERA OF SELF-RELIANCE BEFORE UNCLE SAM BECAME A NANNY!
I'M TALKING ABOUT A TIME WHEN THE GOVERNMENT SERVED THE PEOPLE AND NOT THE OTHER WAY AROUND!
IN SHORT, I'M TALKING ABOUT... ABOUT...; GACK!
...FREEDOM!
HELLO? A LITTLE HEADS-UP ON THE BRAINLOCK?
©B Trudeau

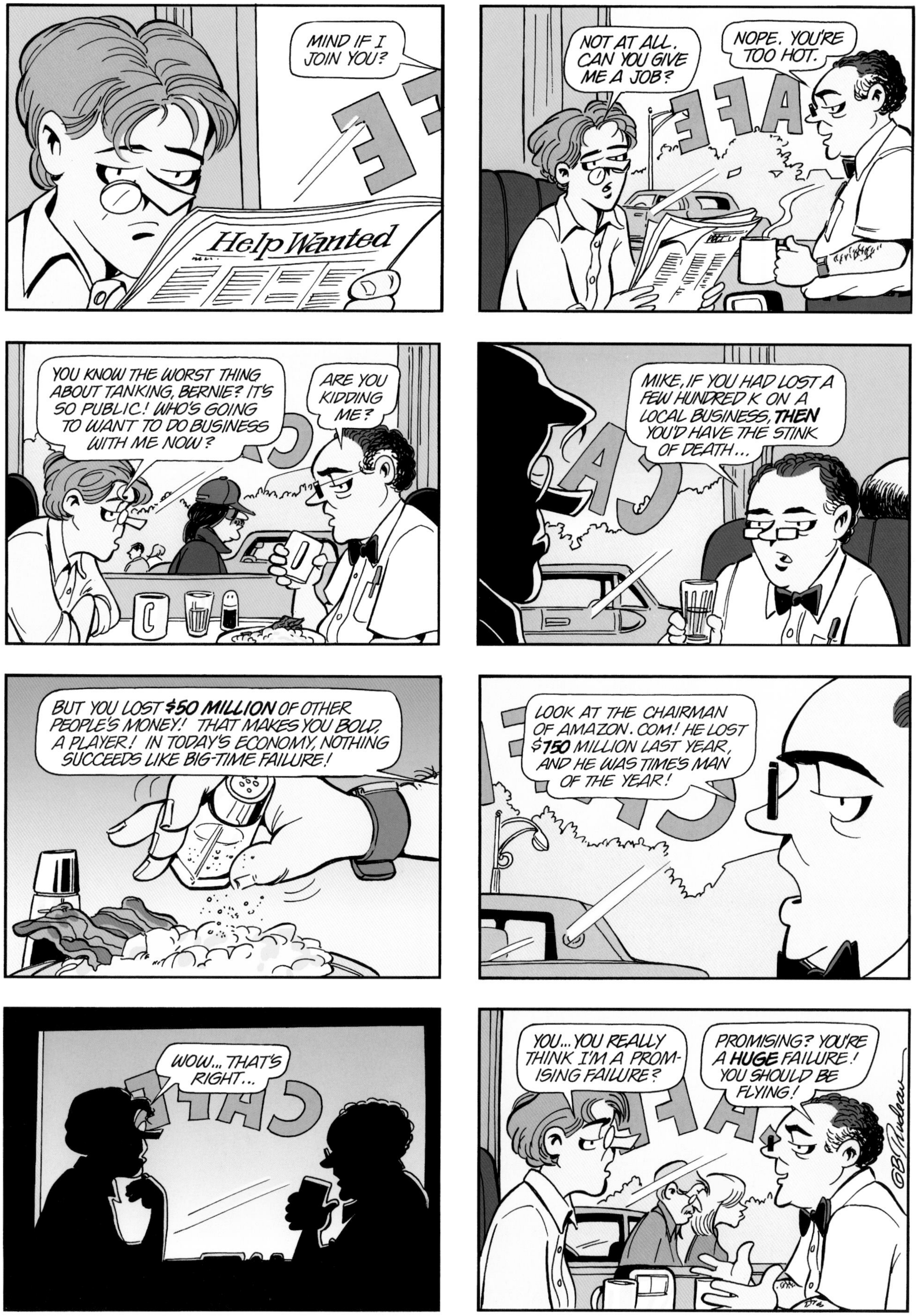
MIND IF I JOIN YOU?
Help Wanted
NOT AT ALL. CAN YOU GIVE ME A JOB?
NOPE. YOU'RE TOO HOT.
YOU KNOW THE WORST THING ABOUT TANKING, BERNIE? IT'S SO PUBLIC! WHO'S GOING TO WANT TO DO BUSINESS WITH ME NOW?
ARE YOU KIDDING ME?
MIKE, IF YOU HAD LOST A FEW HUNDRED K ON A LOCAL BUSINESS, **THEN** YOU'D HAVE THE STINK OF DEATH...
BUT YOU LOST **$50 MILLION** OF OTHER PEOPLE'S MONEY! THAT MAKES YOU BOLD, A PLAYER! IN TODAY'S ECONOMY, NOTHING SUCCEEDS LIKE BIG-TIME FAILURE!
LOOK AT THE CHAIRMAN OF AMAZON.COM! HE LOST $**750** MILLION LAST YEAR, AND HE WAS TIME'S MAN OF THE YEAR!
WOW... THAT'S RIGHT...
YOU... YOU REALLY THINK I'M A PROMISING FAILURE?
PROMISING? YOU'RE A **HUGE** FAILURE! YOU SHOULD BE FLYING!

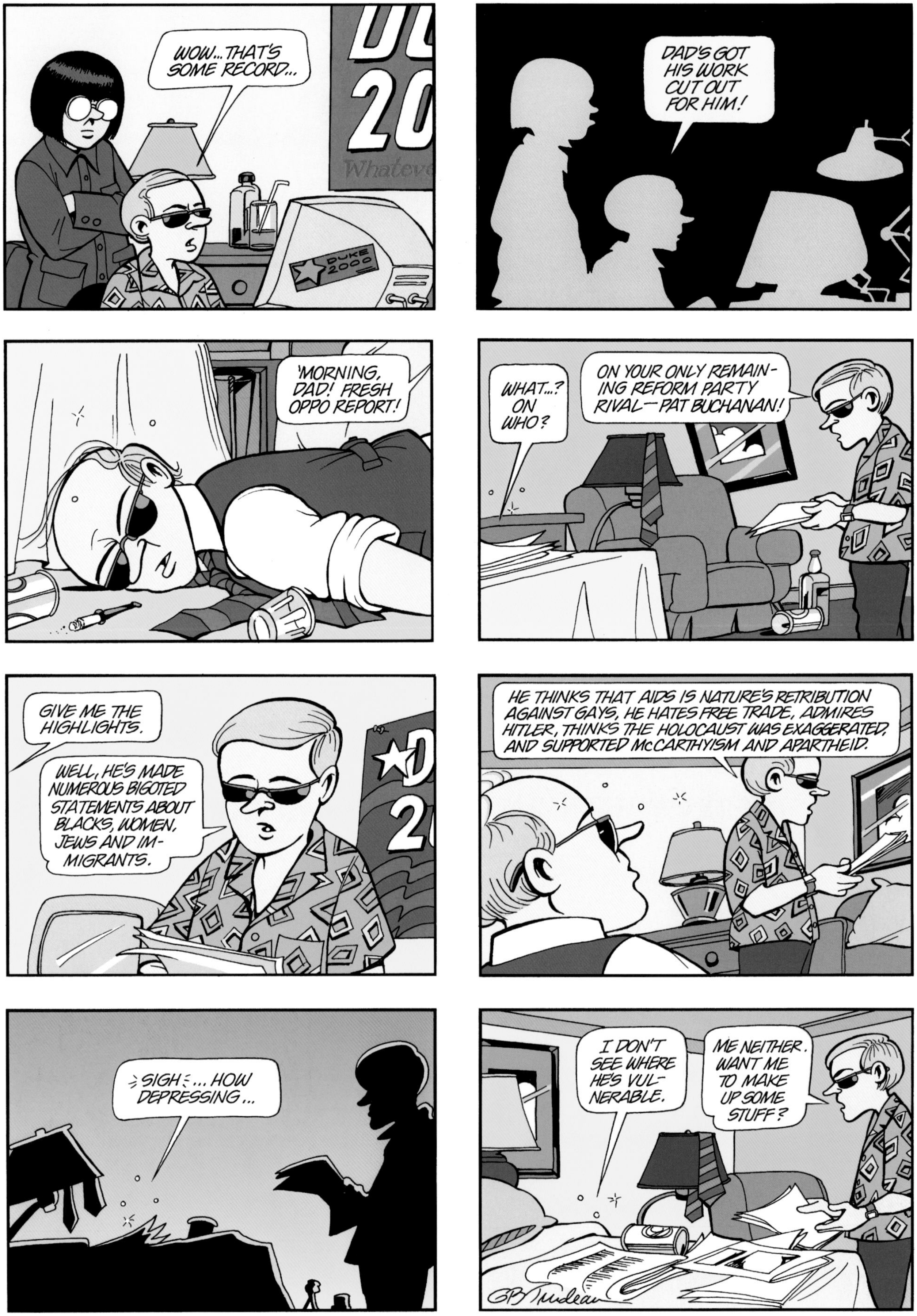
WOW... THAT'S SOME RECORD...
DUKE 2000
DAD'S GOT HIS WORK CUT OUT FOR HIM!
'MORNING, DAD! FRESH OPPO REPORT!
WHAT...? ON WHO?
ON YOUR ONLY REMAINING REFORM PARTY RIVAL—PAT BUCHANAN!
GIVE ME THE HIGHLIGHTS.
WELL, HE'S MADE NUMEROUS BIGOTED STATEMENTS ABOUT BLACKS, WOMEN, JEWS AND IMMIGRANTS.
HE THINKS THAT AIDS IS NATURE'S RETRIBUTION AGAINST GAYS, HE HATES FREE TRADE, ADMIRES HITLER, THINKS THE HOLOCAUST WAS EXAGGERATED, AND SUPPORTED McCARTHYISM AND APARTHEID.
SIGH ... HOW DEPRESSING...
I DON'T SEE WHERE HE'S VULNERABLE.
ME NEITHER. WANT ME TO MAKE UP SOME STUFF?
GBTrudeau

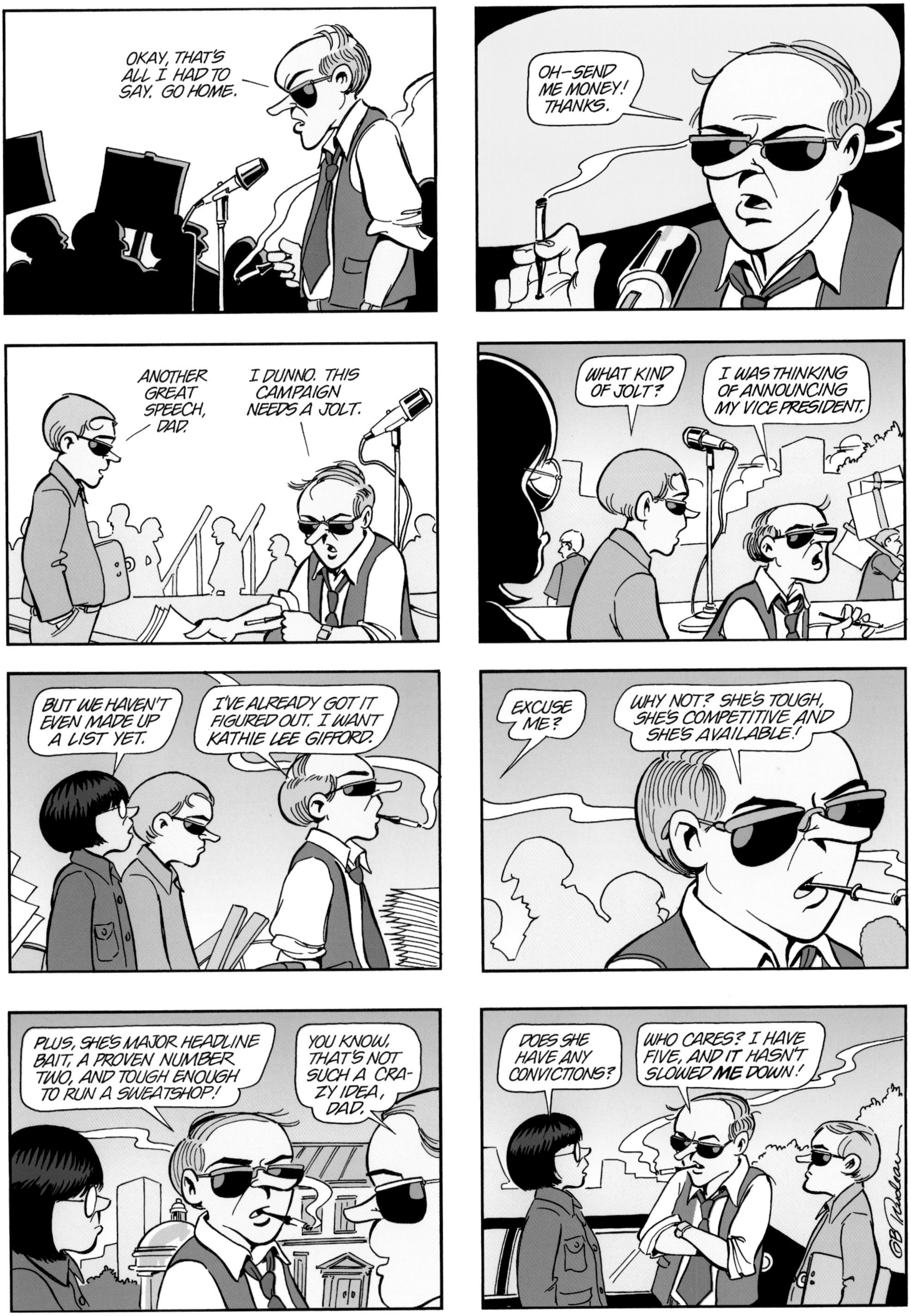
OKAY, THAT'S ALL I HAD TO SAY. GO HOME.
OH—SEND ME MONEY! THANKS.
ANOTHER GREAT SPEECH, DAD.
I DUNNO. THIS CAMPAIGN NEEDS A JOLT.
WHAT KIND OF JOLT?
I WAS THINKING OF ANNOUNCING MY VICE PRESIDENT.
BUT WE HAVEN'T EVEN MADE UP A LIST YET.
I'VE ALREADY GOT IT FIGURED OUT. I WANT KATHIE LEE GIFFORD.
EXCUSE ME?
WHY NOT? SHE'S TOUGH, SHE'S COMPETITIVE AND SHE'S AVAILABLE!
PLUS, SHE'S MAJOR HEADLINE BAIT, A PROVEN NUMBER TWO, AND TOUGH ENOUGH TO RUN A SWEATSHOP!
YOU KNOW, THAT'S NOT SUCH A CRAZY IDEA, DAD.
DOES SHE HAVE ANY CONVICTIONS?
WHO CARES? I HAVE FIVE, AND IT HASN'T SLOWED **ME** DOWN!

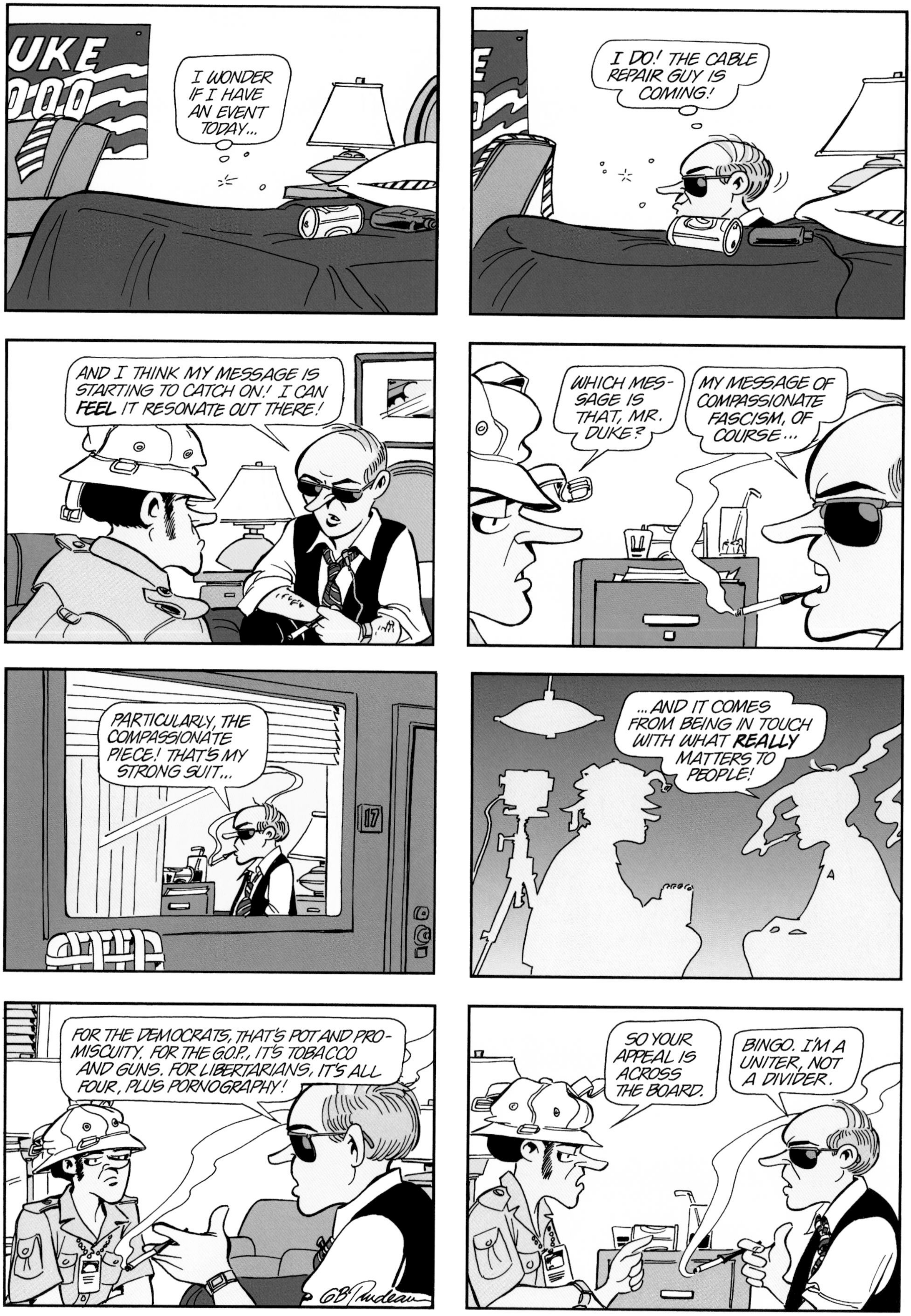
I WONDER IF I HAVE AN EVENT TODAY...
I DO! THE CABLE REPAIR GUY IS COMING!
AND I THINK MY MESSAGE IS STARTING TO CATCH ON! I CAN **FEEL** IT RESONATE OUT THERE!
WHICH MESSAGE IS THAT, MR. DUKE?
MY MESSAGE OF COMPASSIONATE FASCISM, OF COURSE...
PARTICULARLY, THE COMPASSIONATE PIECE! THAT'S MY STRONG SUIT...
17
...AND IT COMES FROM BEING IN TOUCH WITH WHAT **REALLY** MATTERS TO PEOPLE!
FOR THE DEMOCRATS, THAT'S POT AND PROMISCUITY. FOR THE G.O.P., IT'S TOBACCO AND GUNS. FOR LIBERTARIANS, IT'S ALL FOUR, PLUS PORNOGRAPHY!
GBTrudeau
SO YOUR APPEAL IS ACROSS THE BOARD.
BINGO. I'M A UNITER, NOT A DIVIDER.

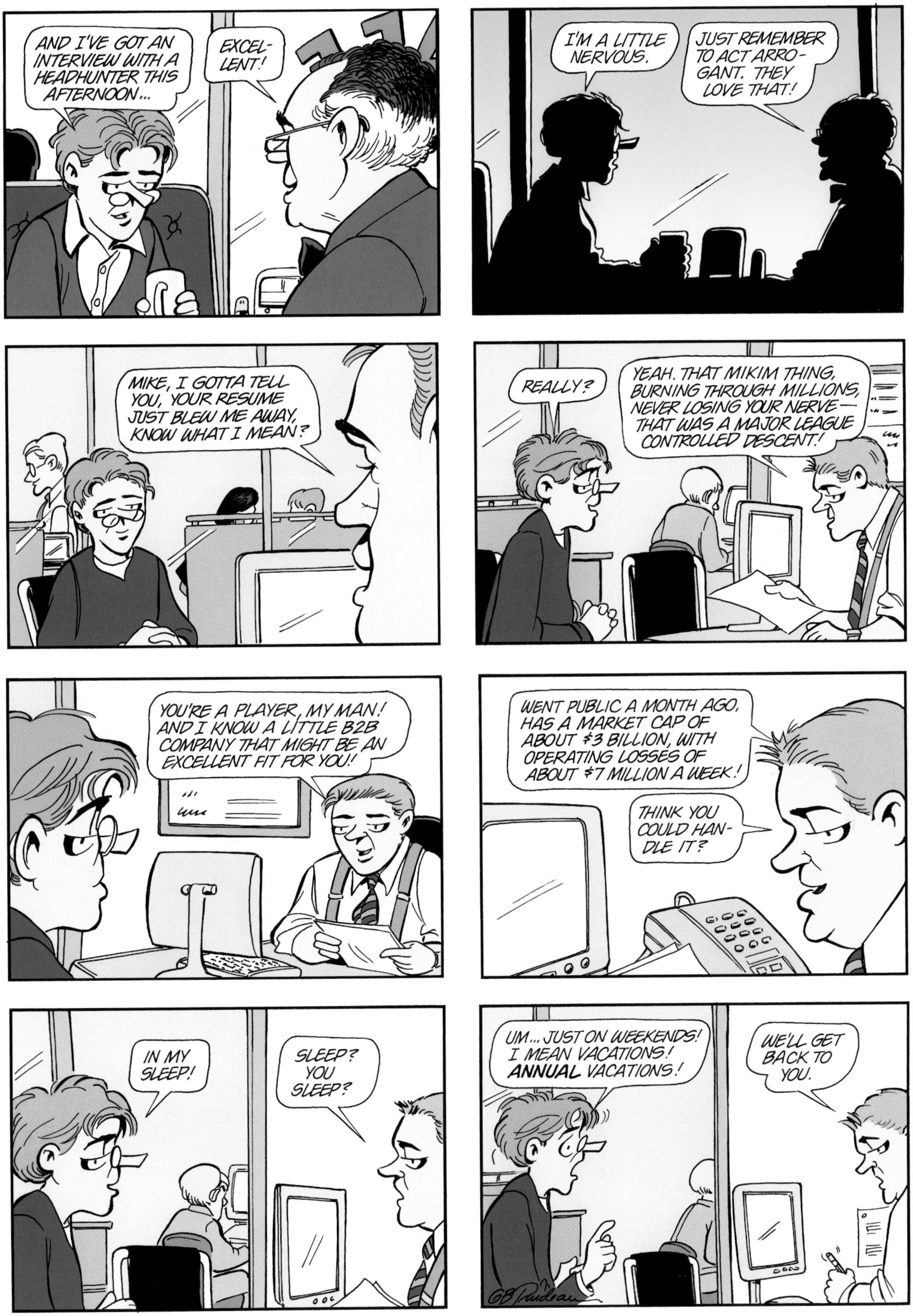
AND I'VE GOT AN INTERVIEW WITH A HEADHUNTER THIS AFTERNOON...
EXCEL-LENT!
I'M A LITTLE NERVOUS.
JUST REMEMBER TO ACT ARRO-GANT. THEY LOVE THAT!
MIKE, I GOTTA TELL YOU, YOUR RESUME JUST BLEW ME AWAY, KNOW WHAT I MEAN?
REALLY?
YEAH. THAT MIKIM THING, BURNING THROUGH MILLIONS, NEVER LOSING YOUR NERVE— THAT WAS A MAJOR LEAGUE CONTROLLED DESCENT!
YOU'RE A PLAYER, MY MAN! AND I KNOW A LITTLE B2B COMPANY THAT MIGHT BE AN EXCELLENT FIT FOR YOU!
WENT PUBLIC A MONTH AGO, HAS A MARKET CAP OF ABOUT $3 BILLION, WITH OPERATING LOSSES OF ABOUT $7 MILLION A WEEK!
THINK YOU COULD HAN-DLE IT?
IN MY SLEEP!
SLEEP? YOU SLEEP?
UM... JUST ON WEEKENDS! I MEAN VACATIONS! **ANNUAL** VACATIONS!
WE'LL GET BACK TO YOU.

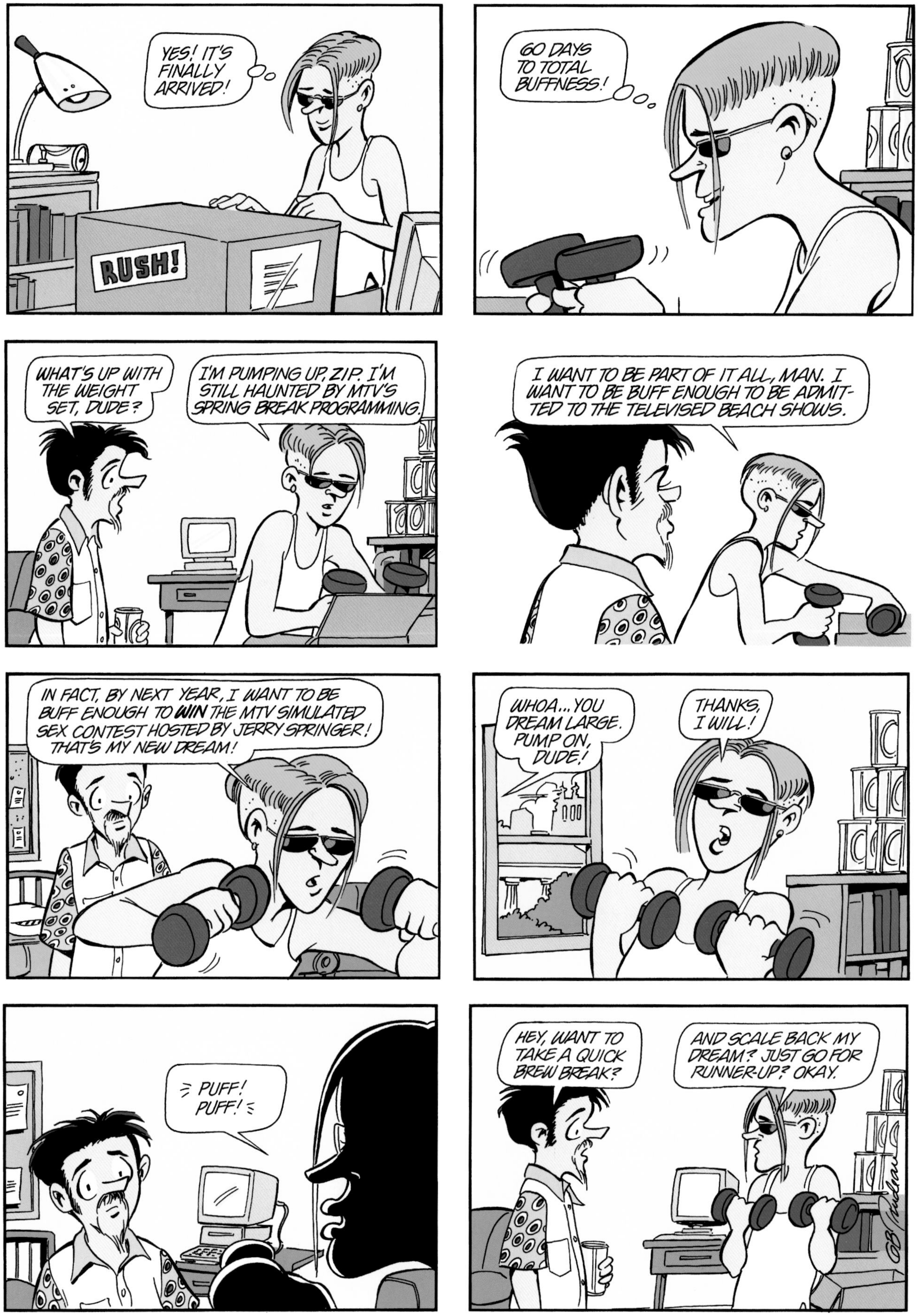
YES! IT'S FINALLY ARRIVED!
60 DAYS TO TOTAL BUFFNESS!
RUSH!
WHAT'S UP WITH THE WEIGHT SET, DUDE?
I'M PUMPING UP, ZIP. I'M STILL HAUNTED BY MTV'S SPRING BREAK PROGRAMMING.
I WANT TO BE PART OF IT ALL, MAN. I WANT TO BE BUFF ENOUGH TO BE ADMITTED TO THE TELEVISED BEACH SHOWS.
IN FACT, BY NEXT YEAR, I WANT TO BE BUFF ENOUGH TO **WIN** THE MTV SIMULATED SEX CONTEST HOSTED BY JERRY SPRINGER! THAT'S MY NEW DREAM!
WHOA... YOU DREAM LARGE. PUMP ON, DUDE!
THANKS, I WILL!
PUFF! PUFF!
HEY, WANT TO TAKE A QUICK BREW BREAK?
AND SCALE BACK MY DREAM? JUST GO FOR RUNNER-UP? OKAY.

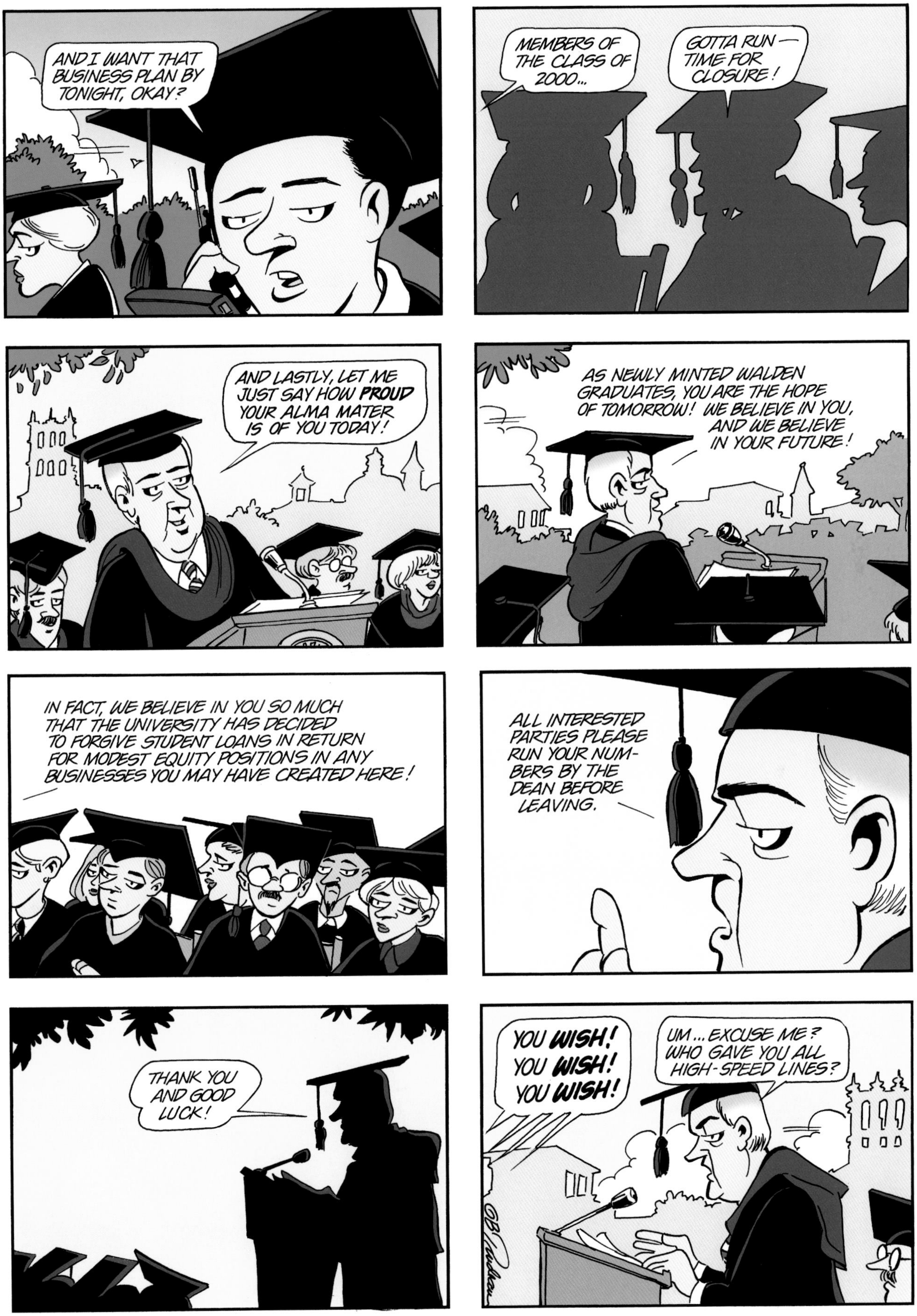
AND I WANT THAT BUSINESS PLAN BY TONIGHT, OKAY?
MEMBERS OF THE CLASS OF 2000...
GOTTA RUN — TIME FOR CLOSURE!
AND LASTLY, LET ME JUST SAY HOW PROUD YOUR ALMA MATER IS OF YOU TODAY!
AS NEWLY MINTED WALDEN GRADUATES, YOU ARE THE HOPE OF TOMORROW! WE BELIEVE IN YOU, AND WE BELIEVE IN YOUR FUTURE!
IN FACT, WE BELIEVE IN YOU SO MUCH THAT THE UNIVERSITY HAS DECIDED TO FORGIVE STUDENT LOANS IN RETURN FOR MODEST EQUITY POSITIONS IN ANY BUSINESSES YOU MAY HAVE CREATED HERE!
ALL INTERESTED PARTIES PLEASE RUN YOUR NUMBERS BY THE DEAN BEFORE LEAVING.
THANK YOU AND GOOD LUCK!
YOU WISH! YOU WISH! YOU WISH!
UM... EXCUSE ME? WHO GAVE YOU ALL HIGH-SPEED LINES?

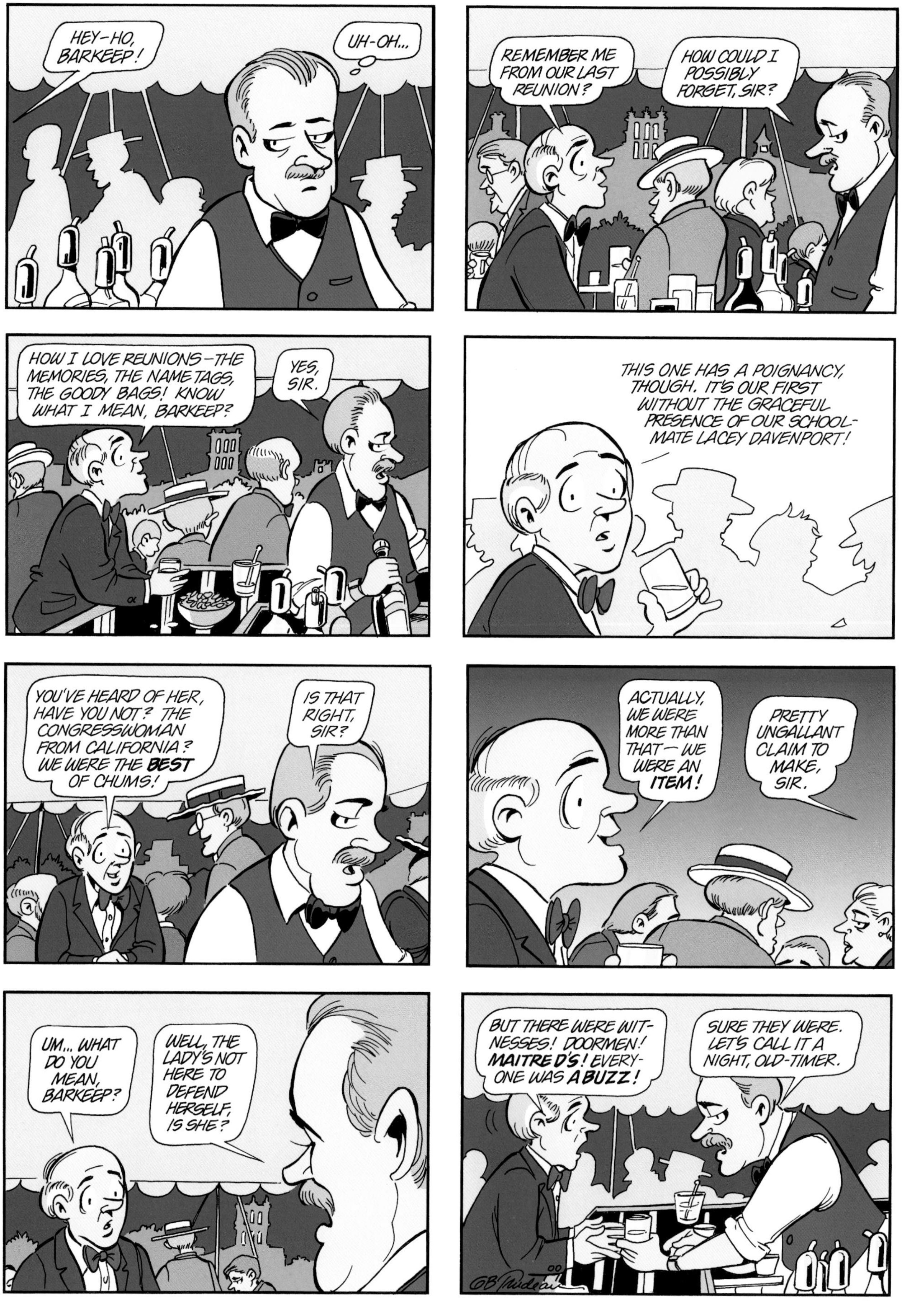
HEY-HO, BARKEEP!
UH-OH...
REMEMBER ME FROM OUR LAST REUNION?
HOW COULD I POSSIBLY FORGET, SIR?
HOW I LOVE REUNIONS—THE MEMORIES, THE NAME TAGS, THE GOODY BAGS! KNOW WHAT I MEAN, BARKEEP?
YES, SIR.
THIS ONE HAS A POIGNANCY, THOUGH. IT'S OUR FIRST WITHOUT THE GRACEFUL PRESENCE OF OUR SCHOOL-MATE LACEY DAVENPORT!
YOU'VE HEARD OF HER, HAVE YOU NOT? THE CONGRESSWOMAN FROM CALIFORNIA? WE WERE THE BEST OF CHUMS!
IS THAT RIGHT, SIR?
ACTUALLY, WE WERE MORE THAN THAT—WE WERE AN ITEM!
PRETTY UNGALLANT CLAIM TO MAKE, SIR.
UM... WHAT DO YOU MEAN, BARKEEP?
WELL, THE LADY'S NOT HERE TO DEFEND HERSELF, IS SHE?
BUT THERE WERE WIT-NESSES! DOORMEN! MAITRE D'S! EVERY-ONE WAS ABUZZ!
SURE THEY WERE. LET'S CALL IT A NIGHT, OLD-TIMER.
GB Trudeau

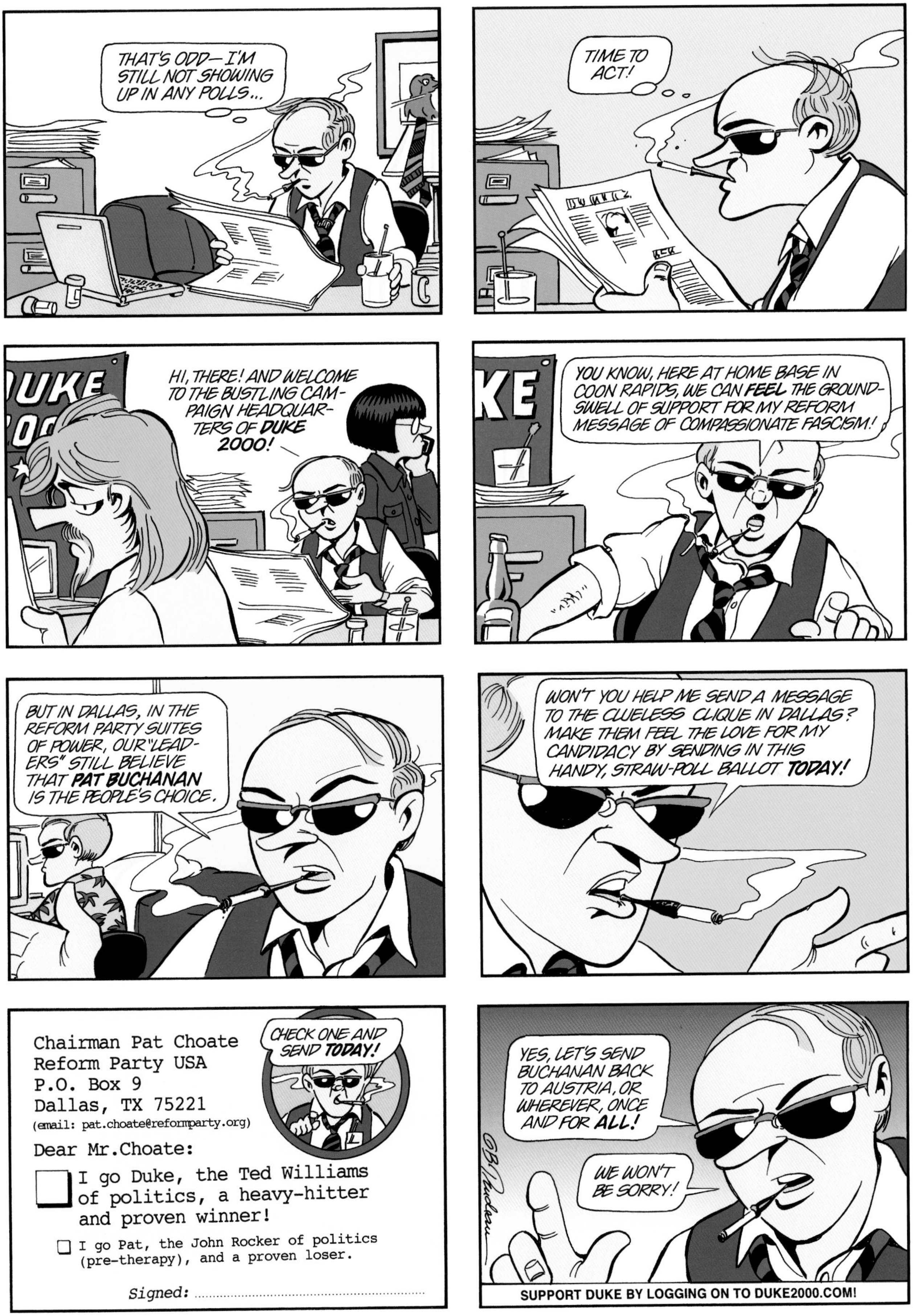
THAT'S ODD—I'M STILL NOT SHOWING UP IN ANY POLLS...
TIME TO ACT!
HI, THERE! AND WELCOME TO THE BUSTLING CAMPAIGN HEADQUARTERS OF DUKE 2000!
DUKE
YOU KNOW, HERE AT HOME BASE IN COON RAPIDS, WE CAN FEEL THE GROUNDSWELL OF SUPPORT FOR MY REFORM MESSAGE OF COMPASSIONATE FASCISM!
BUT IN DALLAS, IN THE REFORM PARTY SUITES OF POWER, OUR "LEADERS" STILL BELIEVE THAT PAT BUCHANAN IS THE PEOPLE'S CHOICE.
WON'T YOU HELP ME SEND A MESSAGE TO THE CLUELESS CLIQUE IN DALLAS? MAKE THEM FEEL THE LOVE FOR MY CANDIDACY BY SENDING IN THIS HANDY, STRAW-POLL BALLOT TODAY!
Chairman Pat Choate
Reform Party USA
P.O. Box 9
Dallas, TX 75221
(email: pat.choate@reformparty.org)
CHECK ONE AND SEND TODAY!
Dear Mr.Choate:
I go Duke, the Ted Williams of politics, a heavy-hitter and proven winner!
I go Pat, the John Rocker of politics (pre-therapy), and a proven loser.
Signed:
YES, LET'S SEND BUCHANAN BACK TO AUSTRIA, OR WHEREVER, ONCE AND FOR ALL!
WE WON'T BE SORRY!
SUPPORT DUKE BY LOGGING ON TO DUKE2000.COM!

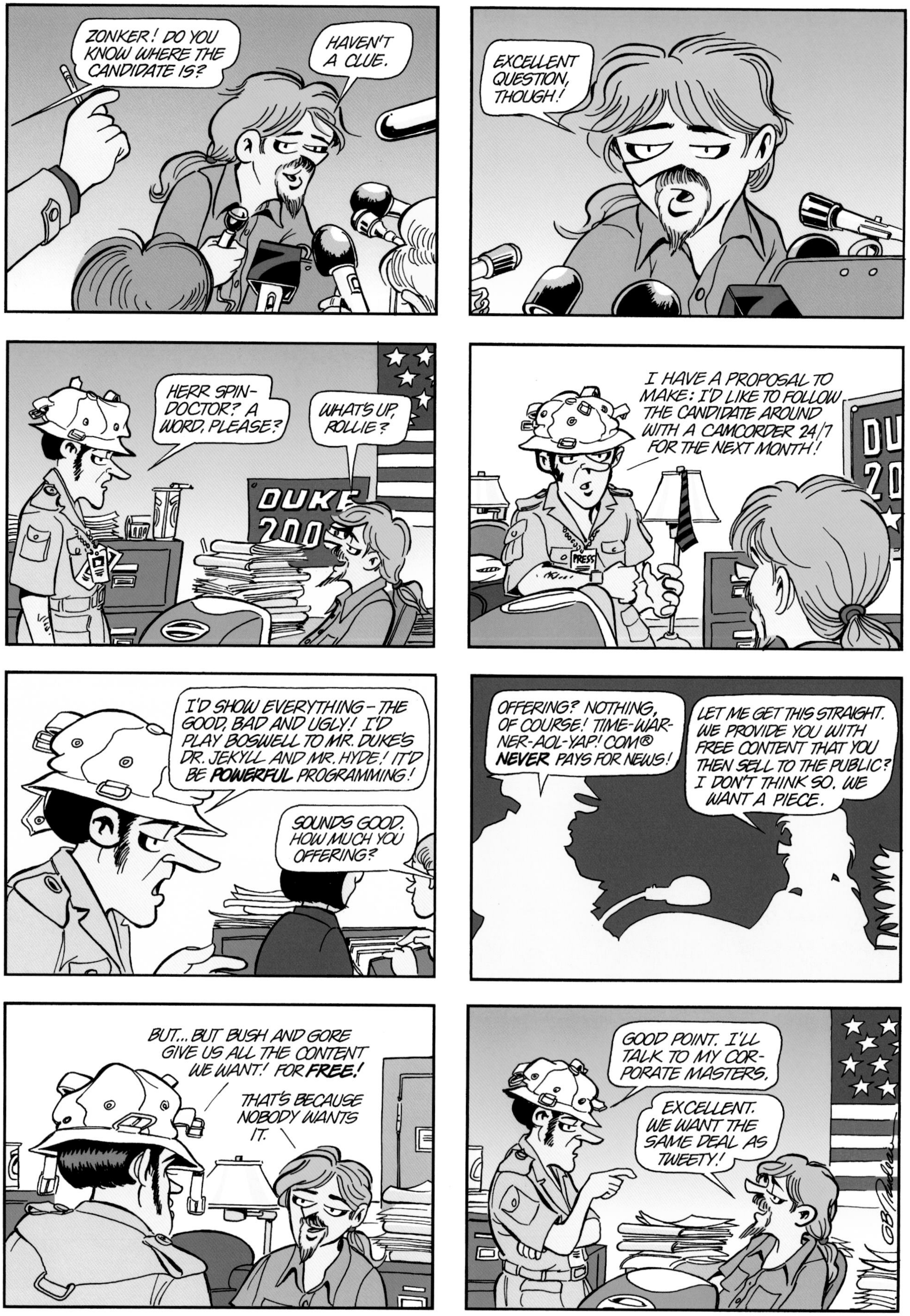
ZONKER! DO YOU KNOW WHERE THE CANDIDATE IS?
HAVEN'T A CLUE.
EXCELLENT QUESTION, THOUGH!
HERR SPIN-DOCTOR? A WORD, PLEASE?
WHAT'S UP, ROLLIE?
DUKE 200
I HAVE A PROPOSAL TO MAKE: I'D LIKE TO FOLLOW THE CANDIDATE AROUND WITH A CAMCORDER 24/7 FOR THE NEXT MONTH!
PRESS
I'D SHOW EVERYTHING – THE GOOD, BAD AND UGLY! I'D PLAY BOSWELL TO MR. DUKE'S DR. JEKYLL AND MR. HYDE! IT'D BE POWERFUL PROGRAMMING!
SOUNDS GOOD. HOW MUCH YOU OFFERING?
OFFERING? NOTHING, OF COURSE! TIME-WARNER-AOL-YAP!.COM® NEVER PAYS FOR NEWS!
LET ME GET THIS STRAIGHT. WE PROVIDE YOU WITH FREE CONTENT THAT YOU THEN SELL TO THE PUBLIC? I DON'T THINK SO. WE WANT A PIECE.
BUT... BUT BUSH AND GORE GIVE US ALL THE CONTENT WE WANT! FOR FREE!
THAT'S BECAUSE NOBODY WANTS IT.
GOOD POINT. I'LL TALK TO MY CORPORATE MASTERS.
EXCELLENT. WE WANT THE SAME DEAL AS TWEETY!

CHOICES, CHOICES, CHOICES...
OH, WOW... A CLASSIC!
HI, FOLKS! EVER WONDER HOW WE COME UP WITH SUCH WACKY DIALOGUE FOR GEORGE W. BUSH?
"WE WANT OUR TEACHERS TO KNOW HOW TO TEACH THE SCIENCE OF READING. IN ORDER TO MAKE SURE THERE'S NOT THIS KIND OF FEDERAL CUFFLINK."
WELL, BELIEVE IT OR NOT, WE DON'T ACTUALLY WRITE THESE LITTLE GEMS — BUSH DOES!
"I WAS RAISED IN THE WEST. THE WEST OF TEXAS. IT'S PRETTY CLOSE TO CALIFORNIA. IN MORE WAYS THAN WASHINGTON, D.C., IS CLOSE TO CALIFORNIA."
THAT'S RIGHT — EACH AND EVERY ONE OF THESE PRICELESS BUSH REMARKS IS IN THE PUBLIC DOMAIN, THUS AVAILABLE FOR UNRESTRICTED USE BY COMEDY PROFESSIONALS!
"I UNDERSTAND SMALL BUSINESS GROWTH. I WAS ONE."
"I KNOW HOW HARD IT IS FOR YOU TO PUT FOOD ON YOUR FAMILY."
"WE OUGHT TO MAKE THE PIE HIGHER."
SO HOW DO WE DECIDE WHICH MATERIAL TO USE? BELIEVE ME, FOLKS, IT AIN'T EASY!
"THE MOST IMPORTANT JOB IS NOT TO BE GOVERNOR, OR FIRST LADY IN MY CASE."
"WE MUST ALL HEAR THE UNIVERSAL CALL TO LIKE YOUR NEIGHBOR LIKE YOU LIKE TO BE LIKED YOURSELF."
"IT'S CLEARLY A BUDGET. IT'S GOT A LOT OF NUMBERS IN IT."
FORTUNATELY, WE HAVE LOTS OF EXPERIENCE TO DRAW UPON — INCLUDING FOUR YEARS OF DAN QUAYLE!
"WILL THE HIGHWAYS ON THE INTERNET BECOME MORE FEW?"
SO ENJOY — THE BEST IS YET TO COME!
"RARELY IS THE QUESTION ASKED: IS OUR CHILDREN LEARNING?"
GB Trudeau

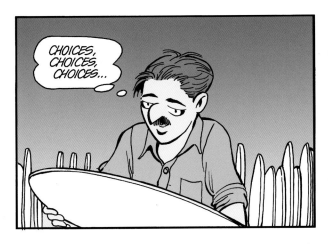

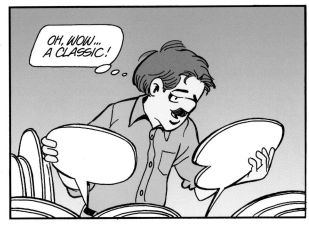

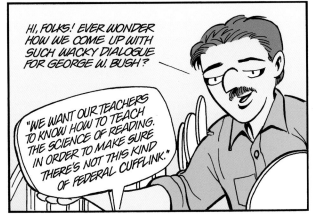

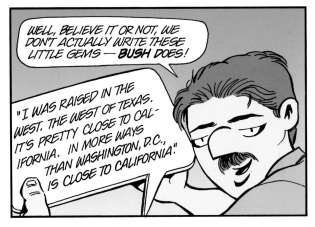

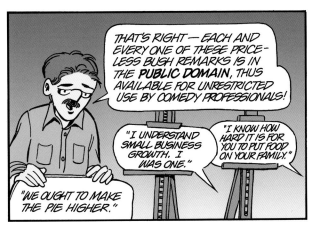

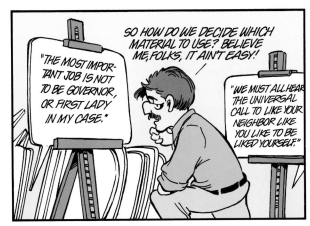

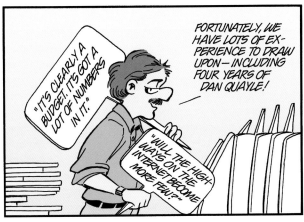

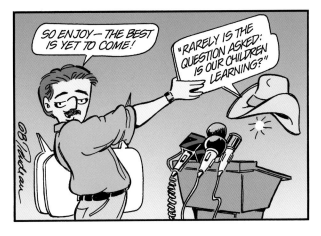

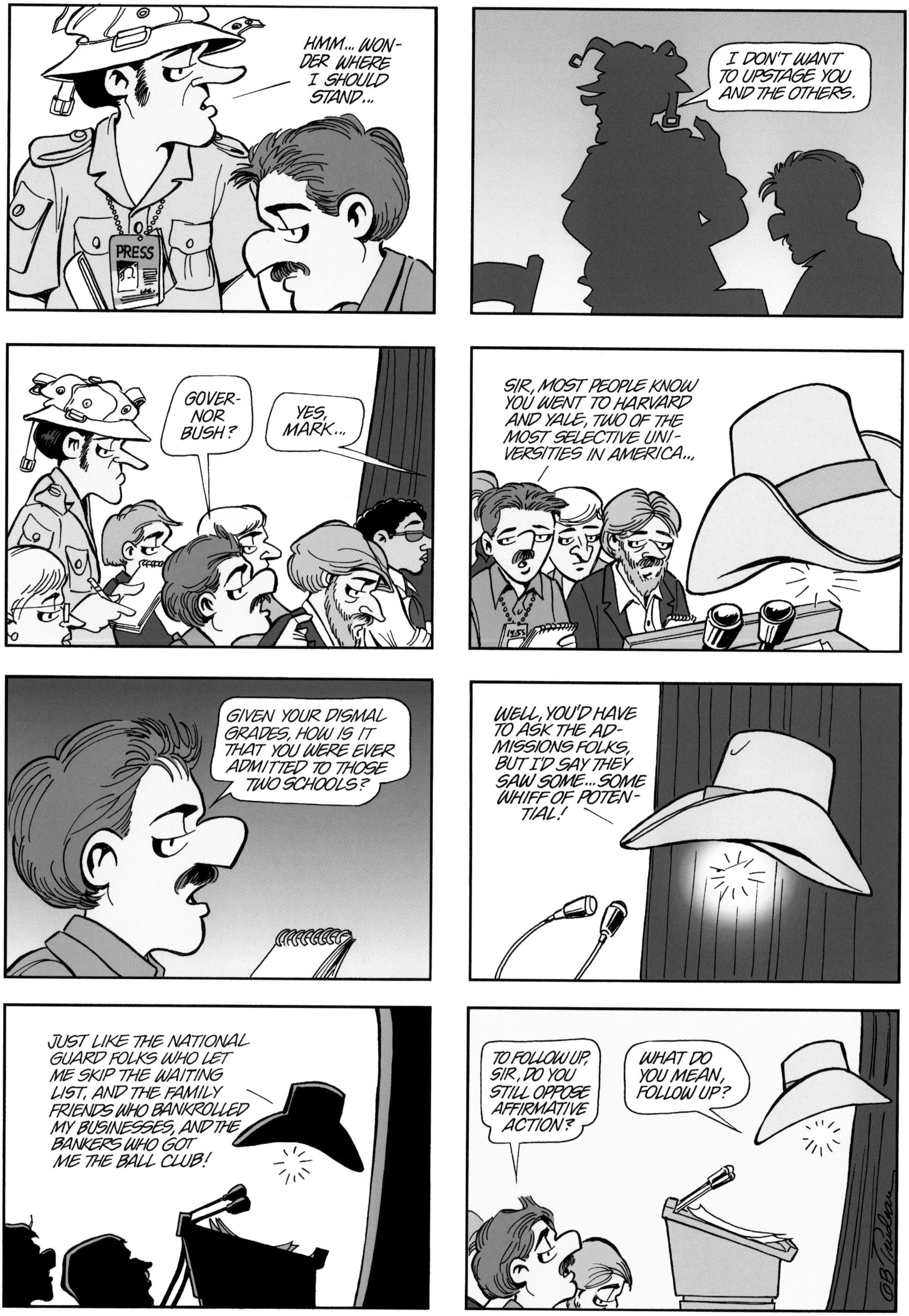

HMM... WONDER WHERE I SHOULD STAND...
I DON'T WANT TO UPSTAGE YOU AND THE OTHERS.
GOVERNOR BUSH?
YES, MARK...
SIR, MOST PEOPLE KNOW YOU WENT TO HARVARD AND YALE, TWO OF THE MOST SELECTIVE UNIVERSITIES IN AMERICA...
PRESS
GIVEN YOUR DISMAL GRADES, HOW IS IT THAT YOU WERE EVER ADMITTED TO THOSE TWO SCHOOLS?
WELL, YOU'D HAVE TO ASK THE ADMISSIONS FOLKS, BUT I'D SAY THEY SAW SOME... SOME WHIFF OF POTENTIAL!
JUST LIKE THE NATIONAL GUARD FOLKS WHO LET ME SKIP THE WAITING LIST, AND THE FAMILY FRIENDS WHO BANKROLLED MY BUSINESSES, AND THE BANKERS WHO GOT ME THE BALL CLUB!
TO FOLLOW UP, SIR, DO YOU STILL OPPOSE AFFIRMATIVE ACTION?
WHAT DO YOU MEAN, FOLLOW UP?

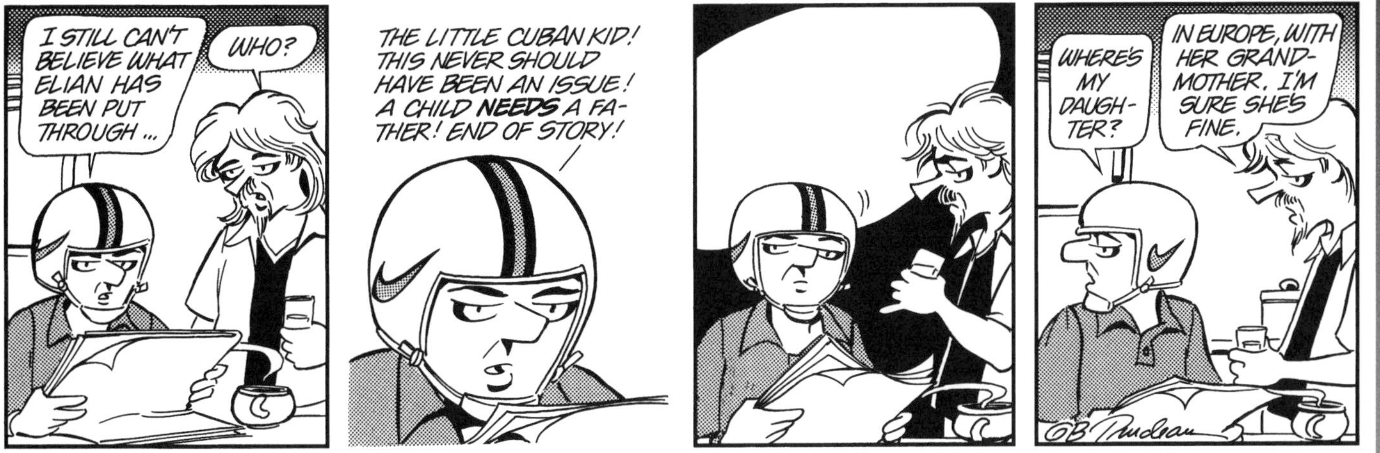
I STILL CAN'T BELIEVE WHAT ELIAN HAS BEEN PUT THROUGH ...
WHO?
THE LITTLE CUBAN KID! THIS NEVER SHOULD HAVE BEEN AN ISSUE! A CHILD **NEEDS** A FATHER! END OF STORY!
WHERE'S MY DAUGHTER?
IN EUROPE, WITH HER GRANDMOTHER, I'M SURE SHE'S FINE.

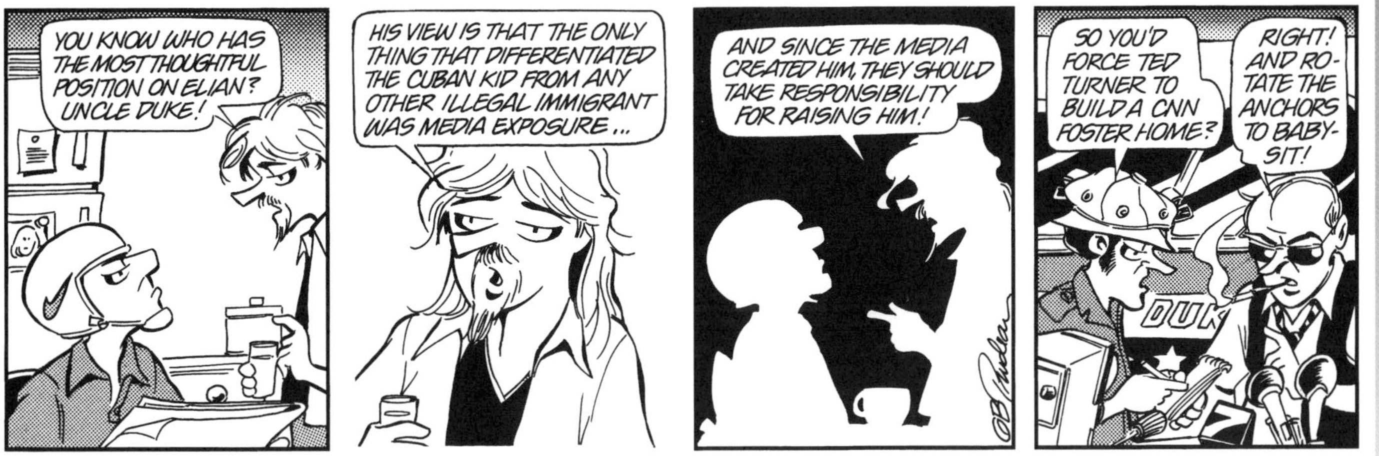
YOU KNOW WHO HAS THE MOST THOUGHTFUL POSITION ON ELIAN? UNCLE DUKE!
HIS VIEW IS THAT THE ONLY THING THAT DIFFERENTIATED THE CUBAN KID FROM ANY OTHER ILLEGAL IMMIGRANT WAS MEDIA EXPOSURE ...
AND SINCE THE MEDIA CREATED HIM, THEY SHOULD TAKE RESPONSIBILITY FOR RAISING HIM!
SO YOU'D FORCE TED TURNER TO BUILD A CNN FOSTER HOME?
RIGHT! AND ROTATE THE ANCHORS TO BABYSIT!

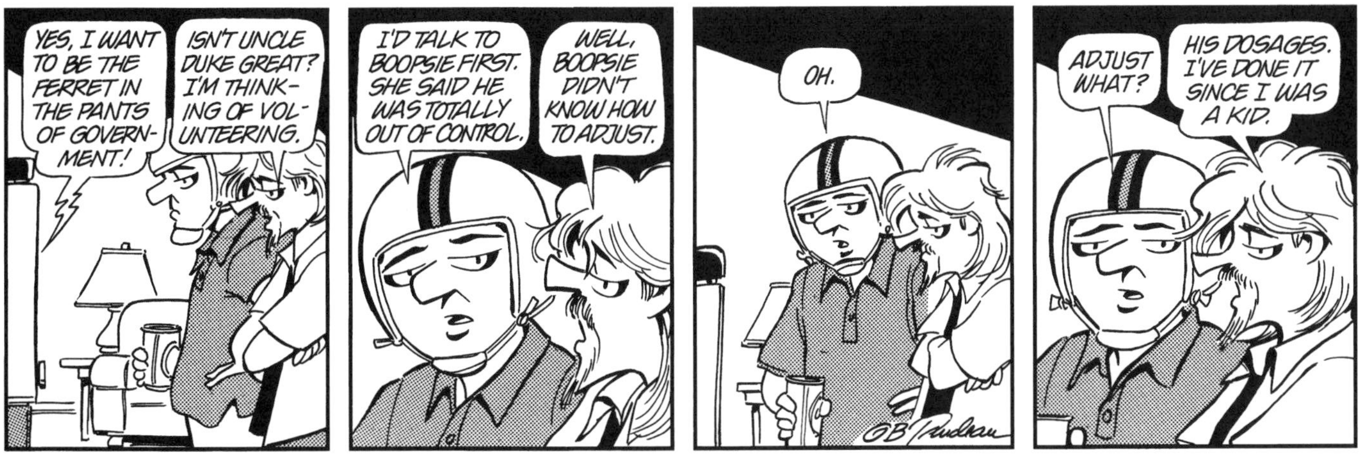
YES, I WANT TO BE THE FERRET IN THE PANTS OF GOVERNMENT!
ISN'T UNCLE DUKE GREAT? I'M THINKING OF VOLUNTEERING.
I'D TALK TO BOOPSIE FIRST. SHE SAID HE WAS TOTALLY OUT OF CONTROL.
WELL, BOOPSIE DIDN'T KNOW HOW TO ADJUST.
OH.
ADJUST WHAT?
HIS DOSAGES. I'VE DONE IT SINCE I WAS A KID.

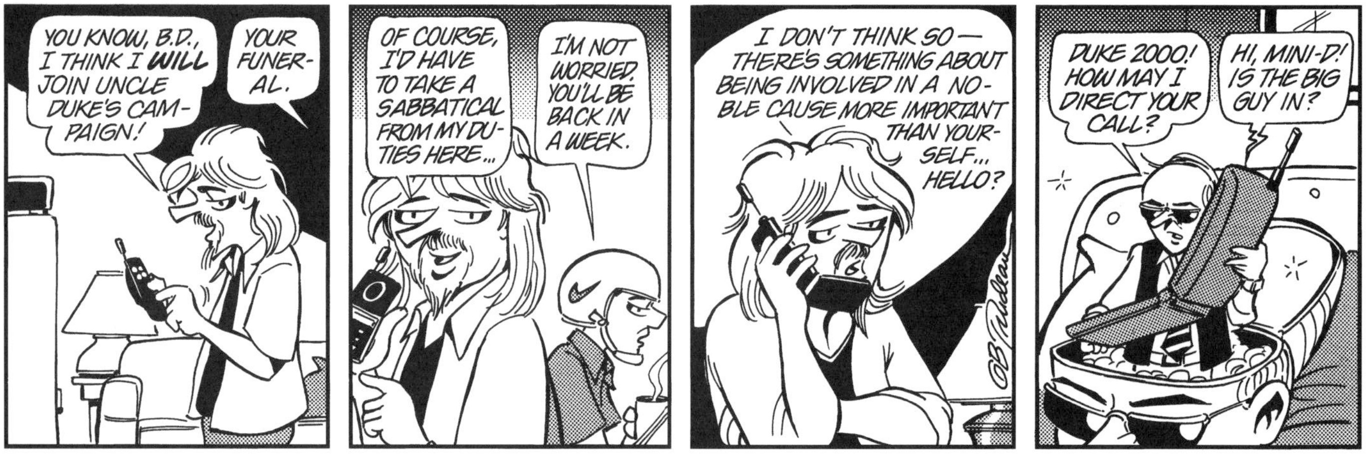
YOU KNOW, B.D., I THINK I **WILL** JOIN UNCLE DUKE'S CAMPAIGN!
YOUR FUNERAL.
OF COURSE, I'D HAVE TO TAKE A SABBATICAL FROM MY DUTIES HERE...
I'M NOT WORRIED. YOU'LL BE BACK IN A WEEK.
I DON'T THINK SO — THERE'S SOMETHING ABOUT BEING INVOLVED IN A NOBLE CAUSE MORE IMPORTANT THAN YOURSELF... HELLO?
DUKE 2000! HOW MAY I DIRECT YOUR CALL?
HI, MINI-D! IS THE BIG GUY IN?

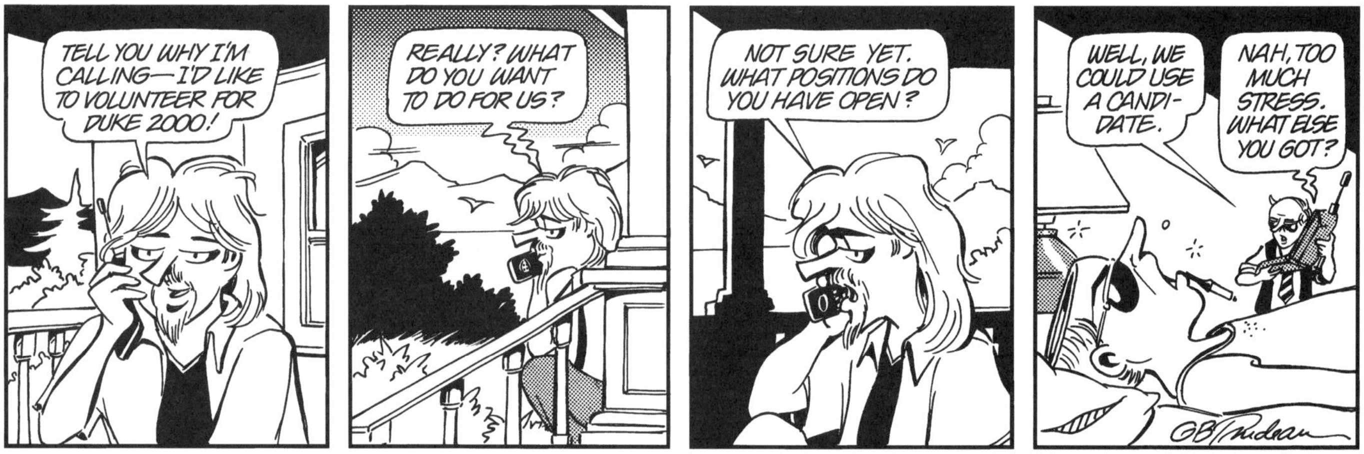
TELL YOU WHY I'M CALLING—I'D LIKE TO VOLUNTEER FOR DUKE 2000!
REALLY? WHAT DO YOU WANT TO DO FOR US?
NOT SURE YET. WHAT POSITIONS DO YOU HAVE OPEN?
WELL, WE COULD USE A CANDIDATE.
NAH, TOO MUCH STRESS. WHAT ELSE YOU GOT?

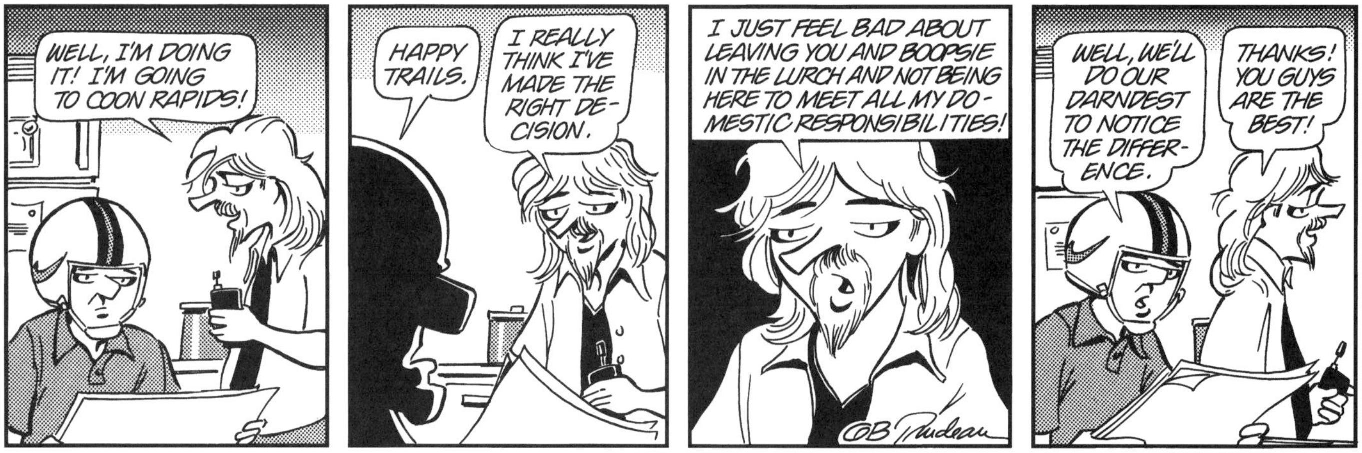
WELL, I'M DOING IT! I'M GOING TO COON RAPIDS!
HAPPY TRAILS.
I REALLY THINK I'VE MADE THE RIGHT DECISION.
I JUST FEEL BAD ABOUT LEAVING YOU AND BOOPSIE IN THE LURCH AND NOT BEING HERE TO MEET ALL MY DOMESTIC RESPONSIBILITIES!
WELL, WE'LL DO OUR DARNDEST TO NOTICE THE DIFFERENCE.
THANKS! YOU GUYS ARE THE BEST!

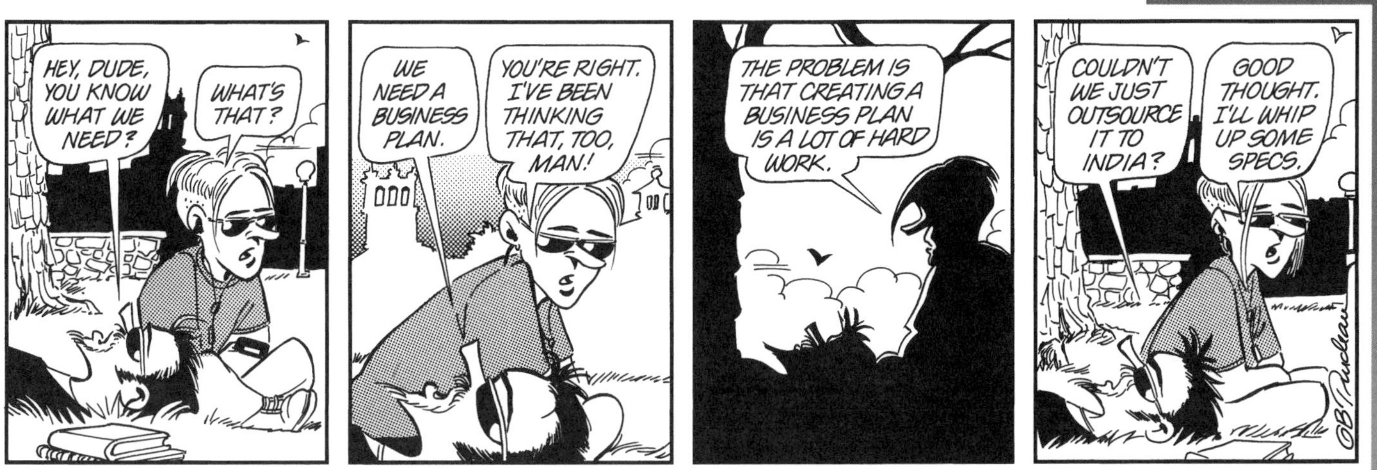
HEY, DUDE, YOU KNOW WHAT WE NEED?
WHAT'S THAT?
WE NEED A BUSINESS PLAN.
YOU'RE RIGHT. I'VE BEEN THINKING THAT, TOO, MAN!
THE PROBLEM IS THAT CREATING A BUSINESS PLAN IS A LOT OF HARD WORK.
COULDN'T WE JUST OUTSOURCE IT TO INDIA?
GOOD THOUGHT. I'LL WHIP UP SOME SPECS.

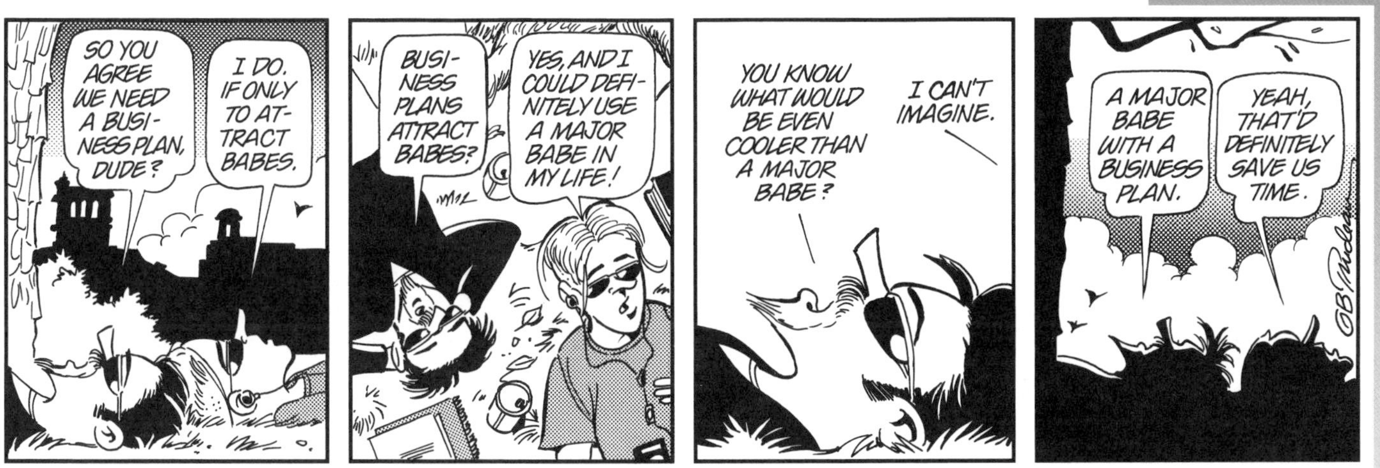
SO YOU AGREE WE NEED A BUSINESS PLAN, DUDE?
I DO. IF ONLY TO ATTRACT BABES.
BUSINESS PLANS ATTRACT BABES?
YES, AND I COULD DEFINITELY USE A MAJOR BABE IN MY LIFE!
YOU KNOW WHAT WOULD BE EVEN COOLER THAN A MAJOR BABE?
I CAN'T IMAGINE.
A MAJOR BABE WITH A BUSINESS PLAN.
YEAH, THAT'D DEFINITELY SAVE US TIME.

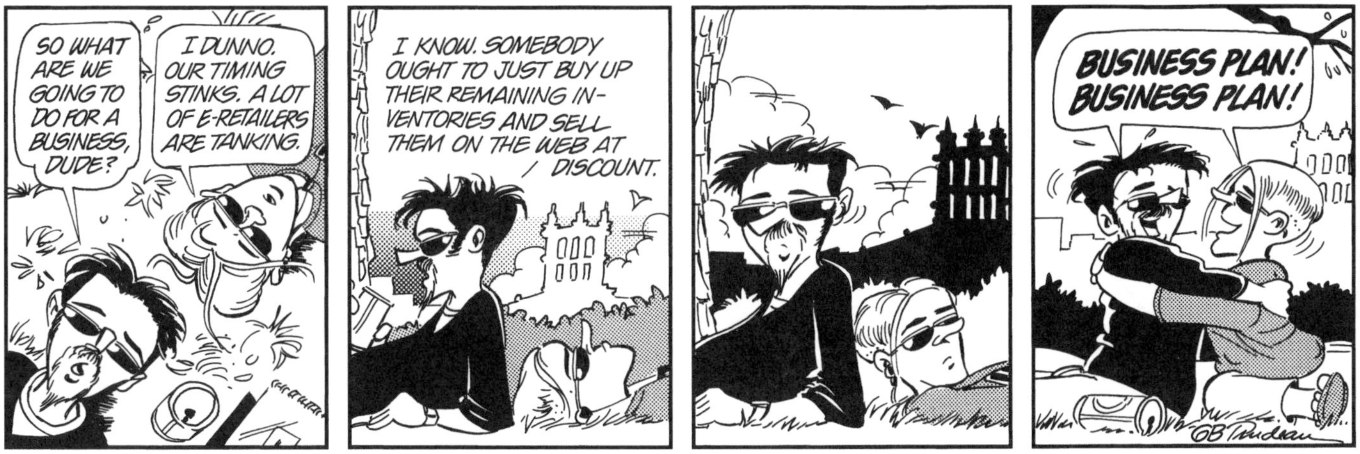
SO WHAT ARE WE GOING TO DO FOR A BUSINESS, DUDE?
I DUNNO. OUR TIMING STINKS. A LOT OF E-RETAILERS ARE TANKING.
I KNOW. SOMEBODY OUGHT TO JUST BUY UP THEIR REMAINING INVENTORIES AND SELL THEM ON THE WEB AT DISCOUNT.
BUSINESS PLAN! BUSINESS PLAN!

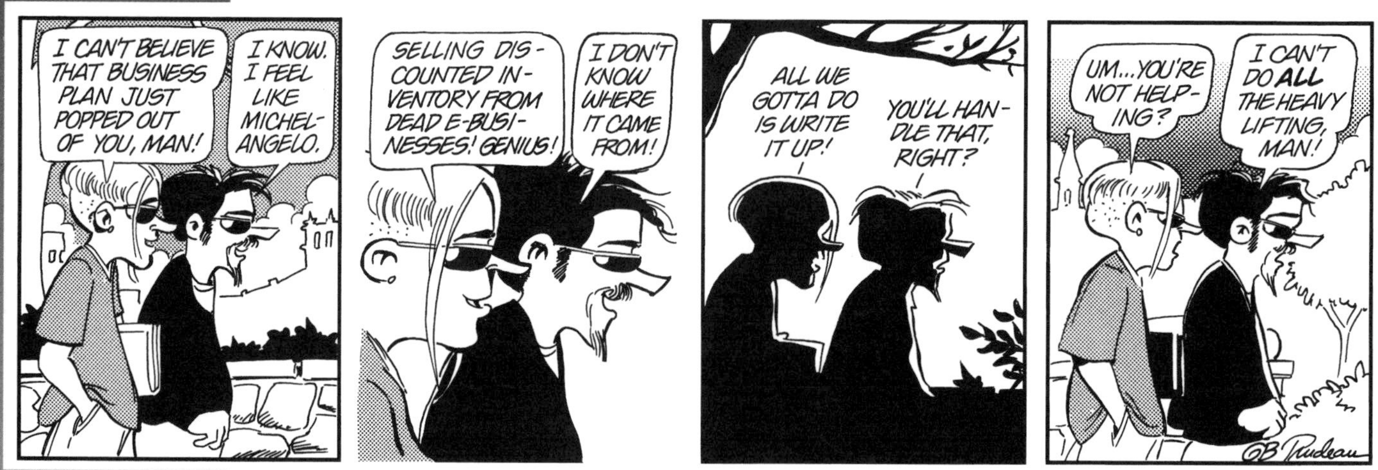
I CAN'T BELIEVE THAT BUSINESS PLAN JUST POPPED OUT OF YOU, MAN!
I KNOW. I FEEL LIKE MICHEL-ANGELO.
SELLING DIS-COUNTED IN-VENTORY FROM DEAD E-BUSI-NESSES! GENIUS!
I DON'T KNOW WHERE IT CAME FROM!
ALL WE GOTTA DO IS WRITE IT UP!
YOU'LL HAN-DLE THAT, RIGHT?
UM... YOU'RE NOT HELP-ING?
I CAN'T DO ALL THE HEAVY LIFTING, MAN!
©B Trudeau

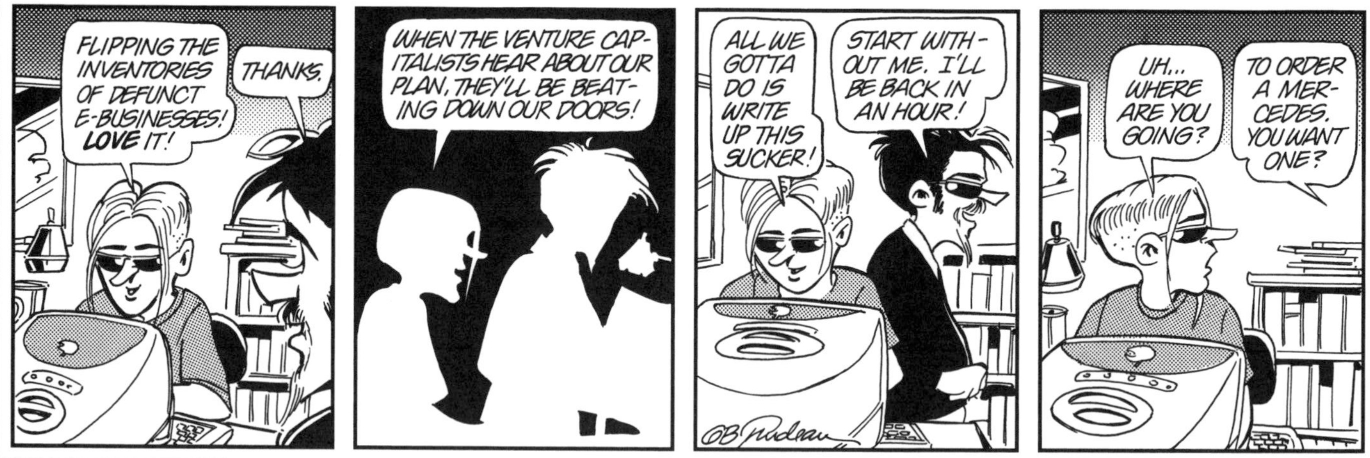
FLIPPING THE INVENTORIES OF DEFUNCT E-BUSINESSES! LOVE IT!
THANKS.
WHEN THE VENTURE CAP-ITALISTS HEAR ABOUT OUR PLAN, THEY'LL BE BEAT-ING DOWN OUR DOORS!
ALL WE GOTTA DO IS WRITE UP THIS SUCKER!
START WITH-OUT ME. I'LL BE BACK IN AN HOUR!
©B Trudeau
UH... WHERE ARE YOU GOING?
TO ORDER A MER-CEDES. YOU WANT ONE?

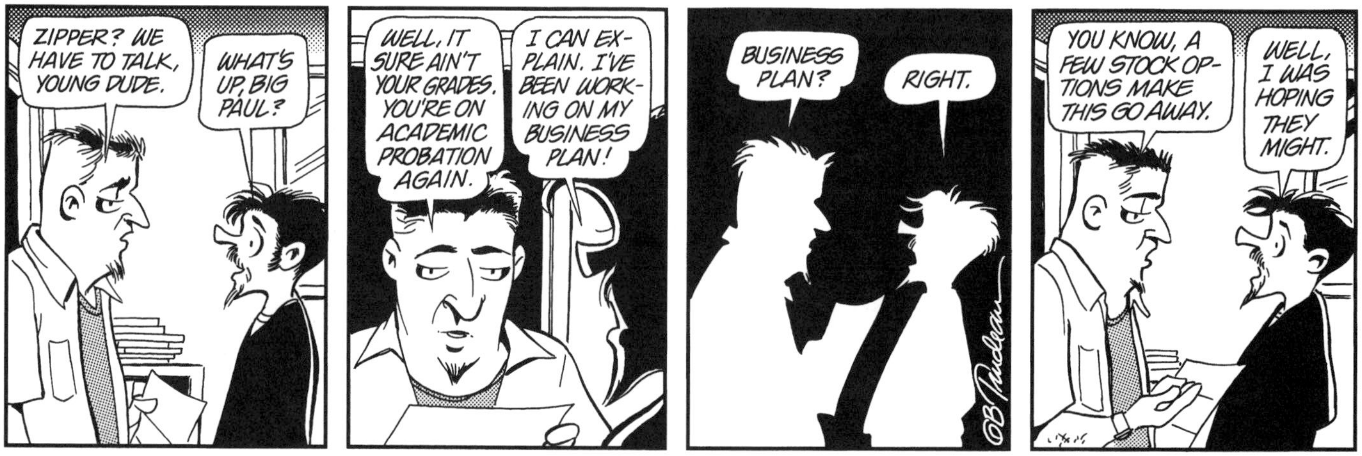
ZIPPER? WE HAVE TO TALK, YOUNG DUDE.
WHAT'S UP, BIG PAUL?
WELL, IT SURE AIN'T YOUR GRADES. YOU'RE ON ACADEMIC PROBATION AGAIN.
I CAN EX-PLAIN. I'VE BEEN WORK-ING ON MY BUSINESS PLAN!
BUSINESS PLAN?
RIGHT.
©B Trudeau
YOU KNOW, A FEW STOCK OP-TIONS MAKE THIS GO AWAY.
WELL, I WAS HOPING THEY MIGHT.

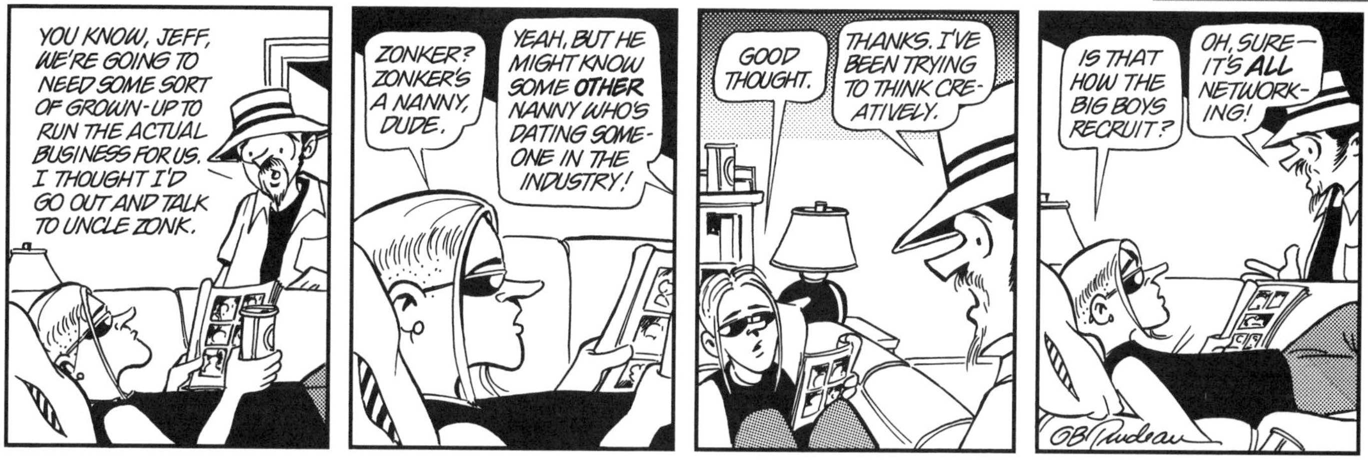
YOU KNOW, JEFF, WE'RE GOING TO NEED SOME SORT OF GROWN-UP TO RUN THE ACTUAL BUSINESS FOR US. I THOUGHT I'D GO OUT AND TALK TO UNCLE ZONK.
ZONKER? ZONKER'S A NANNY, DUDE.
YEAH, BUT HE MIGHT KNOW SOME OTHER NANNY WHO'S DATING SOMEONE IN THE INDUSTRY!
GOOD THOUGHT.
THANKS. I'VE BEEN TRYING TO THINK CREATIVELY.
IS THAT HOW THE BIG BOYS RECRUIT?
OH, SURE— IT'S ALL NETWORKING!
©B Trudeau

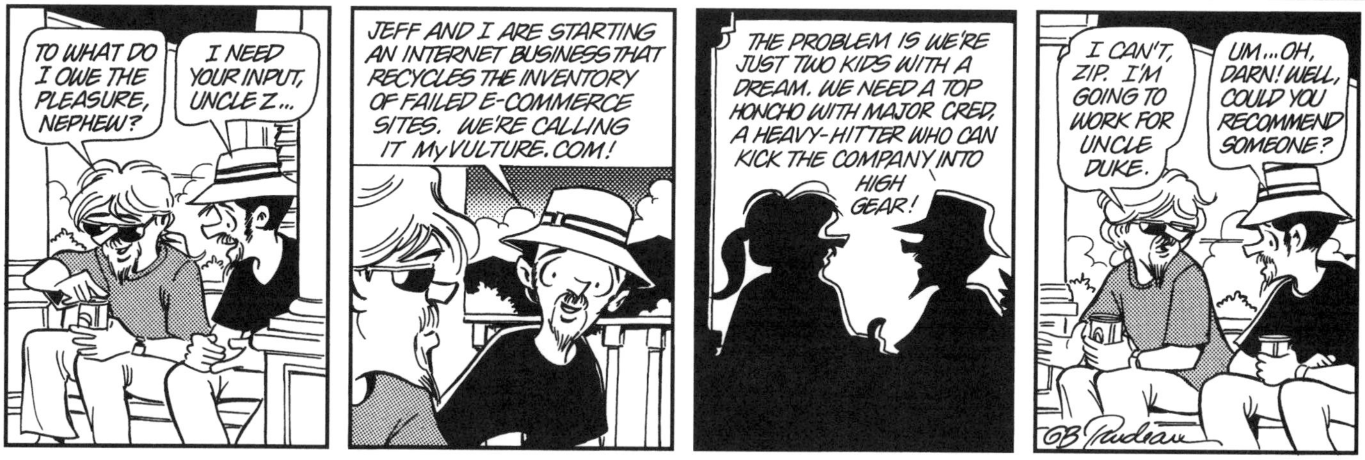
TO WHAT DO I OWE THE PLEASURE, NEPHEW?
I NEED YOUR INPUT, UNCLE Z...
JEFF AND I ARE STARTING AN INTERNET BUSINESS THAT RECYCLES THE INVENTORY OF FAILED E-COMMERCE SITES. WE'RE CALLING IT MyVULTURE.COM!
THE PROBLEM IS WE'RE JUST TWO KIDS WITH A DREAM. WE NEED A TOP HONCHO WITH MAJOR CRED, A HEAVY-HITTER WHO CAN KICK THE COMPANY INTO HIGH GEAR!
I CAN'T, ZIP. I'M GOING TO WORK FOR UNCLE DUKE.
UM...OH, DARN! WELL, COULD YOU RECOMMEND SOMEONE?
©B Trudeau

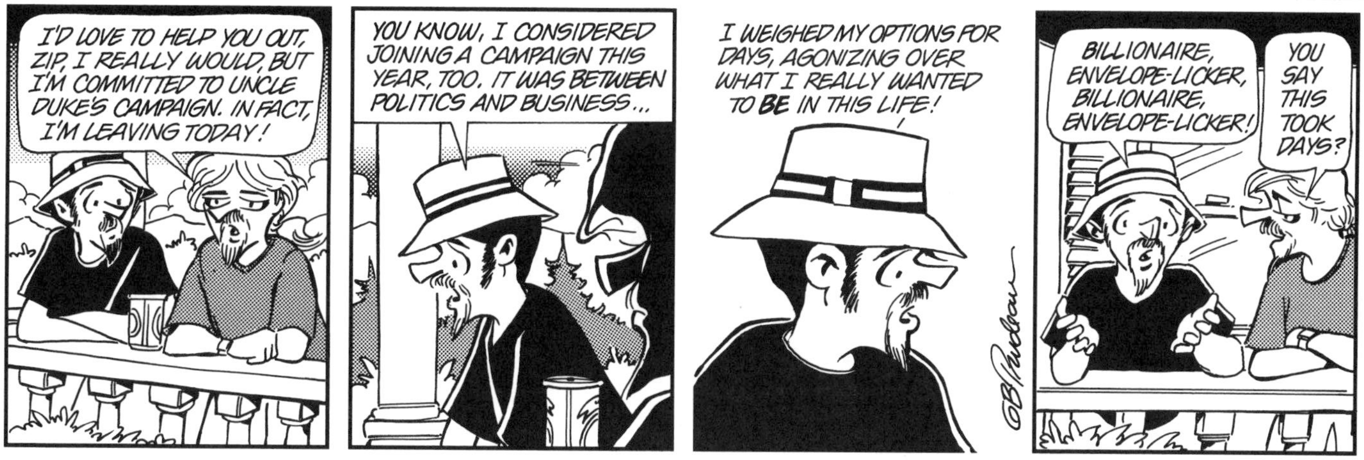
I'D LOVE TO HELP YOU OUT, ZIP, I REALLY WOULD, BUT I'M COMMITTED TO UNCLE DUKE'S CAMPAIGN. IN FACT, I'M LEAVING TODAY!
YOU KNOW, I CONSIDERED JOINING A CAMPAIGN THIS YEAR, TOO. IT WAS BETWEEN POLITICS AND BUSINESS...
I WEIGHED MY OPTIONS FOR DAYS, AGONIZING OVER WHAT I REALLY WANTED TO BE IN THIS LIFE!
©B Trudeau
BILLIONAIRE, ENVELOPE-LICKER, BILLIONAIRE, ENVELOPE-LICKER!
YOU SAY THIS TOOK DAYS?

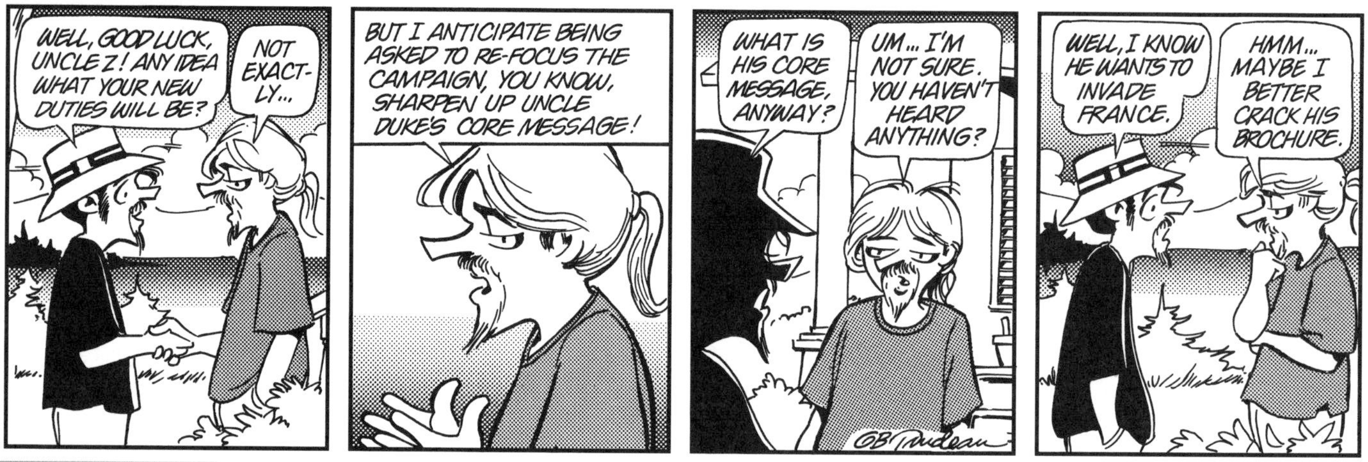
WELL, GOOD LUCK, UNCLE Z! ANY IDEA WHAT YOUR NEW DUTIES WILL BE?
NOT EXACT-LY...
BUT I ANTICIPATE BEING ASKED TO RE-FOCUS THE CAMPAIGN, YOU KNOW, SHARPEN UP UNCLE DUKE'S CORE MESSAGE!
WHAT IS HIS CORE MESSAGE, ANYWAY?
UM... I'M NOT SURE. YOU HAVEN'T HEARD ANYTHING?
WELL, I KNOW HE WANTS TO INVADE FRANCE.
HMM... MAYBE I BETTER CRACK HIS BROCHURE.

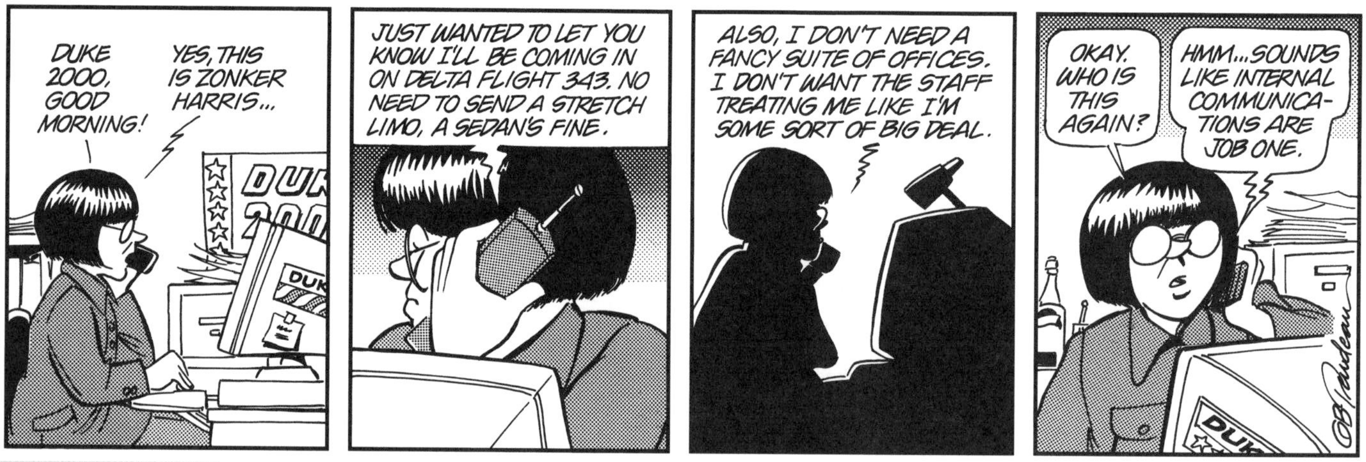
DUKE 2000, GOOD MORNING!
YES, THIS IS ZONKER HARRIS...
JUST WANTED TO LET YOU KNOW I'LL BE COMING IN ON DELTA FLIGHT 343. NO NEED TO SEND A STRETCH LIMO, A SEDAN'S FINE.
ALSO, I DON'T NEED A FANCY SUITE OF OFFICES. I DON'T WANT THE STAFF TREATING ME LIKE I'M SOME SORT OF BIG DEAL.
OKAY. WHO IS THIS AGAIN?
HMM... SOUNDS LIKE INTERNAL COMMUNICA-TIONS ARE JOB ONE.

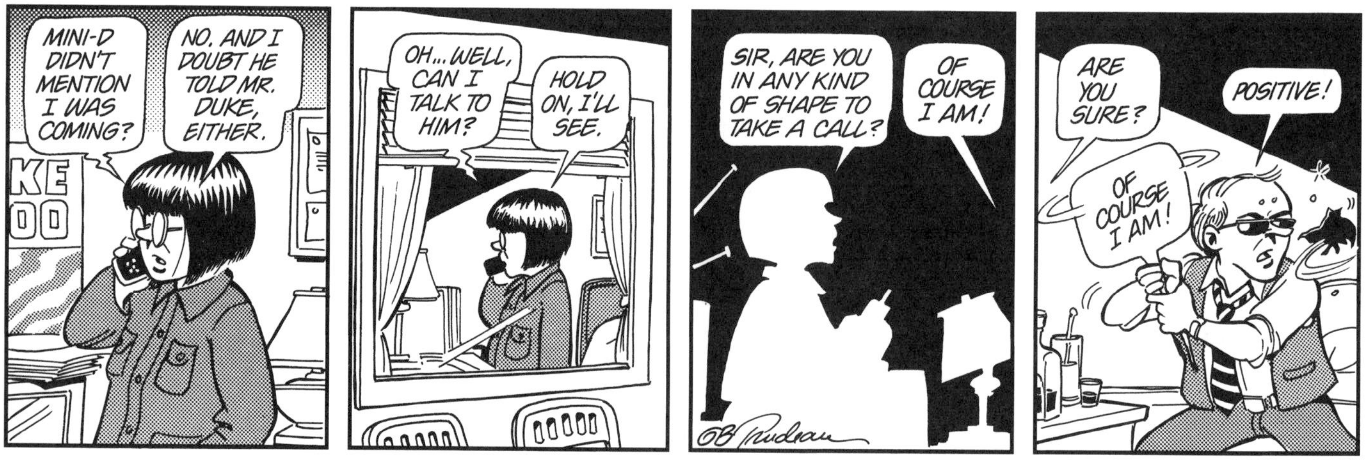
MINI-D DIDN'T MENTION I WAS COMING?
NO. AND I DOUBT HE TOLD MR. DUKE, EITHER.
OH... WELL, CAN I TALK TO HIM?
HOLD ON, I'LL SEE.
SIR, ARE YOU IN ANY KIND OF SHAPE TO TAKE A CALL?
OF COURSE I AM!
ARE YOU SURE?
OF COURSE I AM!
POSITIVE!

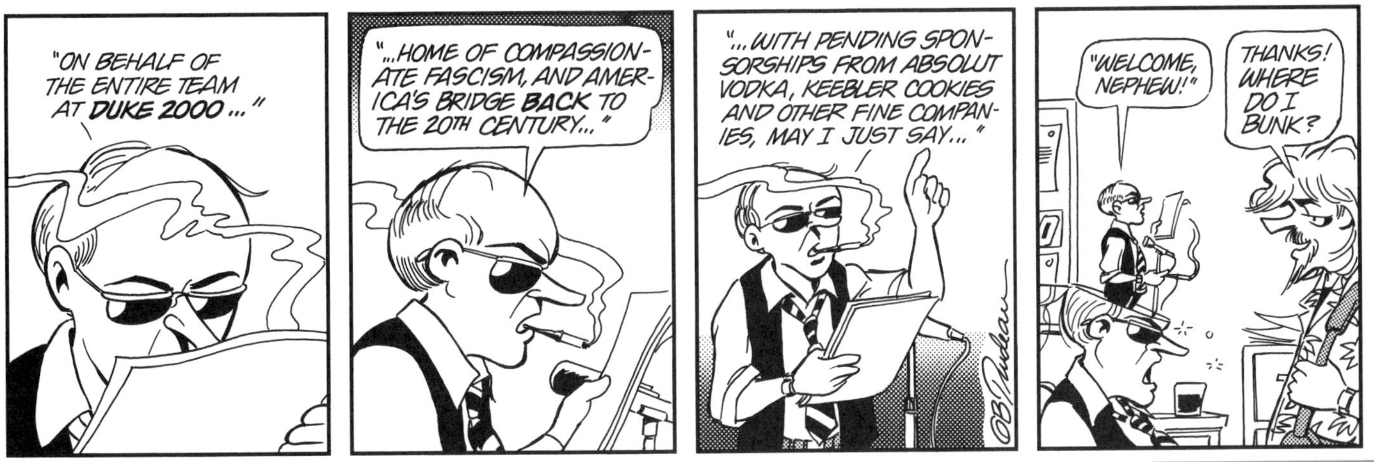
"ON BEHALF OF THE ENTIRE TEAM AT **DUKE 2000**..."
"...HOME OF COMPASSIONATE FASCISM, AND AMERICA'S BRIDGE **BACK** TO THE 20TH CENTURY..."
"...WITH PENDING SPONSORSHIPS FROM ABSOLUT VODKA, KEEBLER COOKIES AND OTHER FINE COMPANIES, MAY I JUST SAY..."
"WELCOME, NEPHEW!"
THANKS! WHERE DO I BUNK?
©B. Trudeau

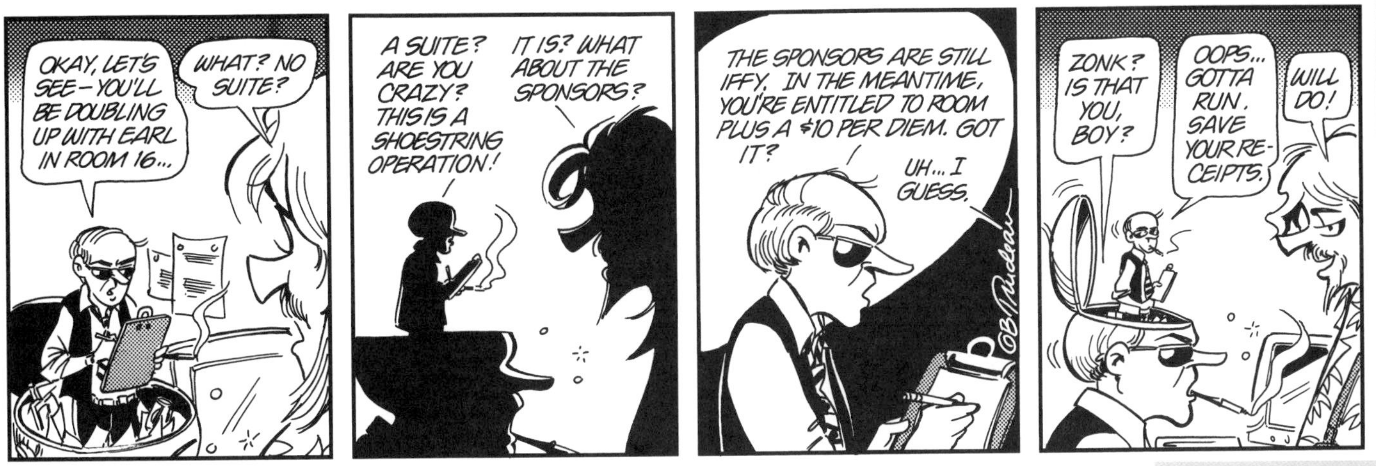
OKAY, LET'S SEE—YOU'LL BE DOUBLING UP WITH EARL IN ROOM 16...
WHAT? NO SUITE?
A SUITE? ARE YOU CRAZY? THIS IS A SHOESTRING OPERATION!
IT IS? WHAT ABOUT THE SPONSORS?
THE SPONSORS ARE STILL IFFY. IN THE MEANTIME, YOU'RE ENTITLED TO ROOM PLUS A $10 PER DIEM. GOT IT?
UH... I GUESS.
ZONK? IS THAT YOU, BOY?
OOPS... GOTTA RUN. SAVE YOUR RECEIPTS.
WILL DO!
©B. Trudeau

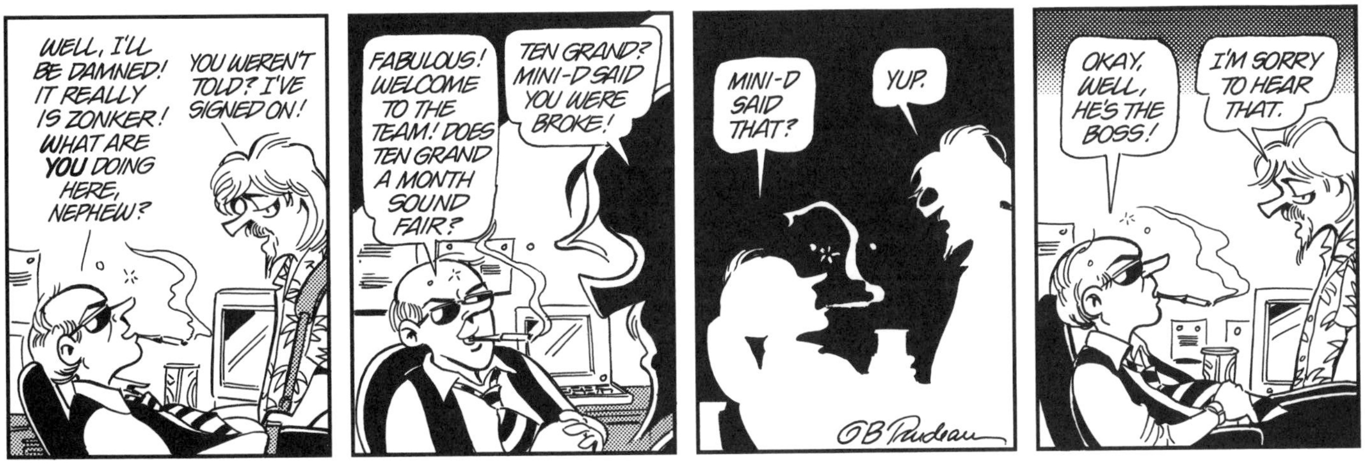
WELL, I'LL BE DAMNED! IT REALLY IS ZONKER! **WHAT ARE YOU** DOING HERE, NEPHEW?
YOU WEREN'T TOLD? I'VE SIGNED ON!
FABULOUS! WELCOME TO THE TEAM! DOES TEN GRAND A MONTH SOUND FAIR?
TEN GRAND? MINI-D SAID YOU WERE BROKE!
MINI-D SAID THAT?
YUP.
OKAY. WELL, HE'S THE BOSS!
I'M SORRY TO HEAR THAT.
©B. Trudeau

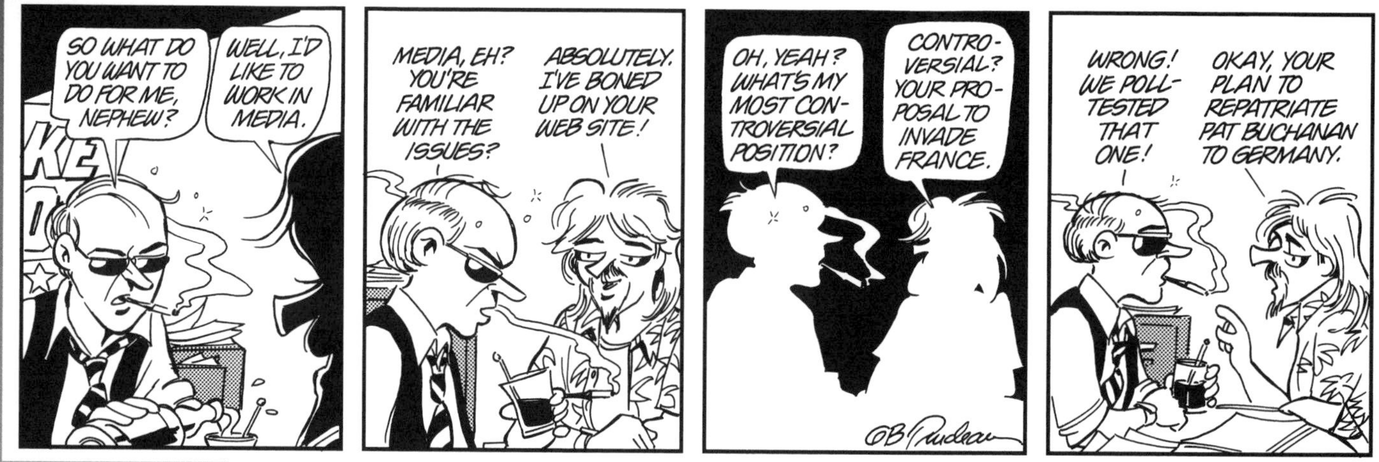
SO WHAT DO YOU WANT TO DO FOR ME, NEPHEW?
WELL, I'D LIKE TO WORK IN MEDIA.
MEDIA, EH? YOU'RE FAMILIAR WITH THE ISSUES?
ABSOLUTELY. I'VE BONED UP ON YOUR WEB SITE!
OH, YEAH? WHAT'S MY MOST CONTROVERSIAL POSITION?
CONTROVERSIAL? YOUR PROPOSAL TO INVADE FRANCE.
WRONG! WE POLL-TESTED THAT ONE!
OKAY, YOUR PLAN TO REPATRIATE PAT BUCHANAN TO GERMANY.
GB Trudeau

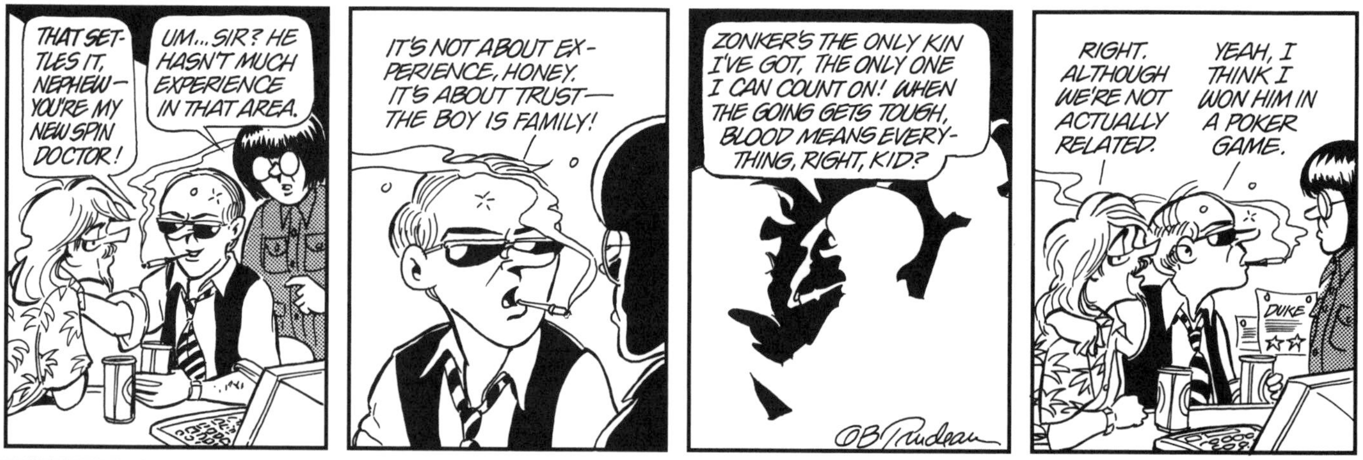
THAT SETTLES IT, NEPHEW—YOU'RE MY NEW SPIN DOCTOR!
UM... SIR? HE HASN'T MUCH EXPERIENCE IN THAT AREA.
IT'S NOT ABOUT EXPERIENCE, HONEY. IT'S ABOUT TRUST—THE BOY IS FAMILY!
ZONKER'S THE ONLY KIN I'VE GOT, THE ONLY ONE I CAN COUNT ON! WHEN THE GOING GETS TOUGH, BLOOD MEANS EVERYTHING, RIGHT, KID?
GB Trudeau
RIGHT. ALTHOUGH WE'RE NOT ACTUALLY RELATED.
YEAH, I THINK I WON HIM IN A POKER GAME.
DUKE

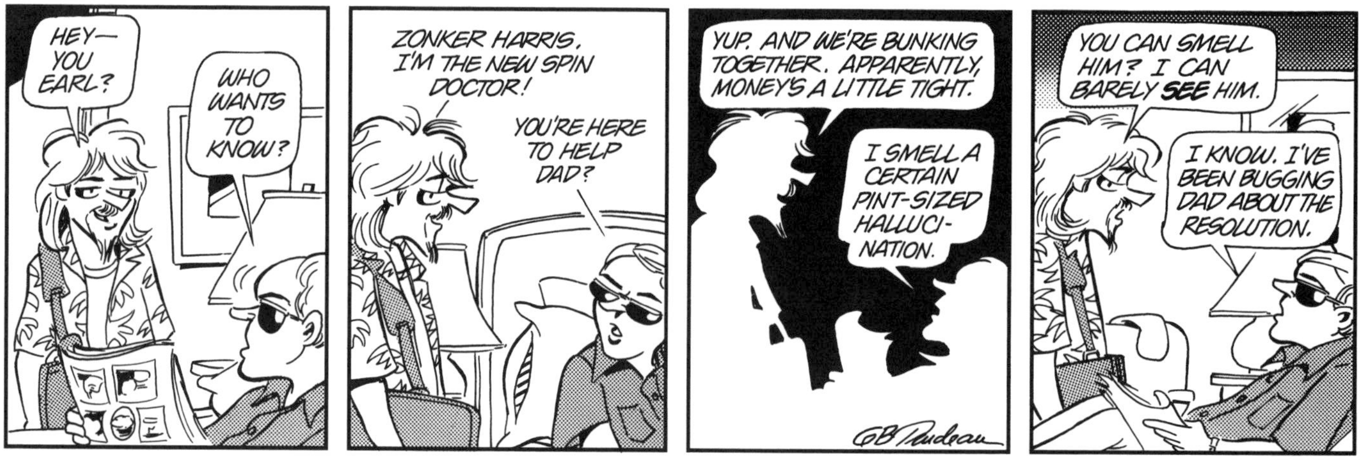
HEY—YOU EARL?
WHO WANTS TO KNOW?
ZONKER HARRIS. I'M THE NEW SPIN DOCTOR!
YOU'RE HERE TO HELP DAD?
YUP. AND WE'RE BUNKING TOGETHER. APPARENTLY, MONEY'S A LITTLE TIGHT.
I SMELL A CERTAIN PINT-SIZED HALLUCINATION.
GB Trudeau
YOU CAN SMELL HIM? I CAN BARELY SEE HIM.
I KNOW. I'VE BEEN BUGGING DAD ABOUT THE RESOLUTION.

THE REVOLT OF
THE ENGLISH MAJORS

THE REVOLT OF
THE ENGLISH MAJORS

"If you're asking me as the president, would I understand reality, I do."

—George W. Bush

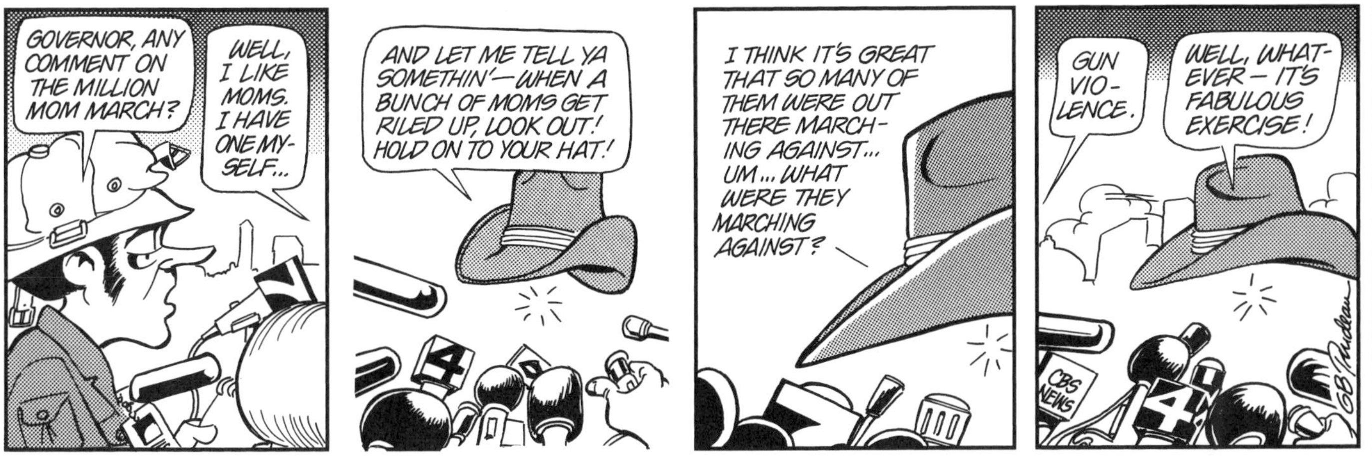
GOVERNOR, ANY COMMENT ON THE MILLION MOM MARCH?
WELL, I LIKE MOMS. I HAVE ONE MYSELF...
AND LET ME TELL YA SOMETHIN'—WHEN A BUNCH OF MOMS GET RILED UP, LOOK OUT! HOLD ON TO YOUR HAT!
I THINK IT'S GREAT THAT SO MANY OF THEM WERE OUT THERE MARCHING AGAINST... UM... WHAT WERE THEY MARCHING AGAINST?
GUN VIOLENCE.
WELL, WHATEVER—IT'S FABULOUS EXERCISE!
CBS NEWS

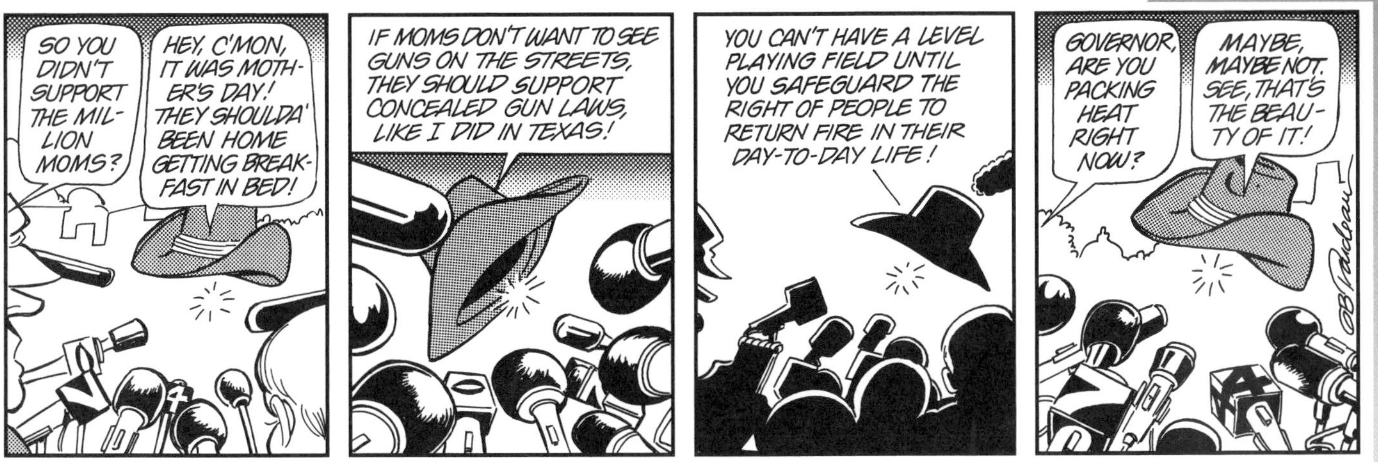
SO YOU DIDN'T SUPPORT THE MILLION MOMS?
HEY, C'MON, IT WAS MOTHER'S DAY! THEY SHOULDA' BEEN HOME GETTING BREAKFAST IN BED!
IF MOMS DON'T WANT TO SEE GUNS ON THE STREETS, THEY SHOULD SUPPORT CONCEALED GUN LAWS, LIKE I DID IN TEXAS!
YOU CAN'T HAVE A LEVEL PLAYING FIELD UNTIL YOU SAFEGUARD THE RIGHT OF PEOPLE TO RETURN FIRE IN THEIR DAY-TO-DAY LIFE!
GOVERNOR, ARE YOU PACKING HEAT RIGHT NOW?
MAYBE, MAYBE NOT. SEE, THAT'S THE BEAUTY OF IT!

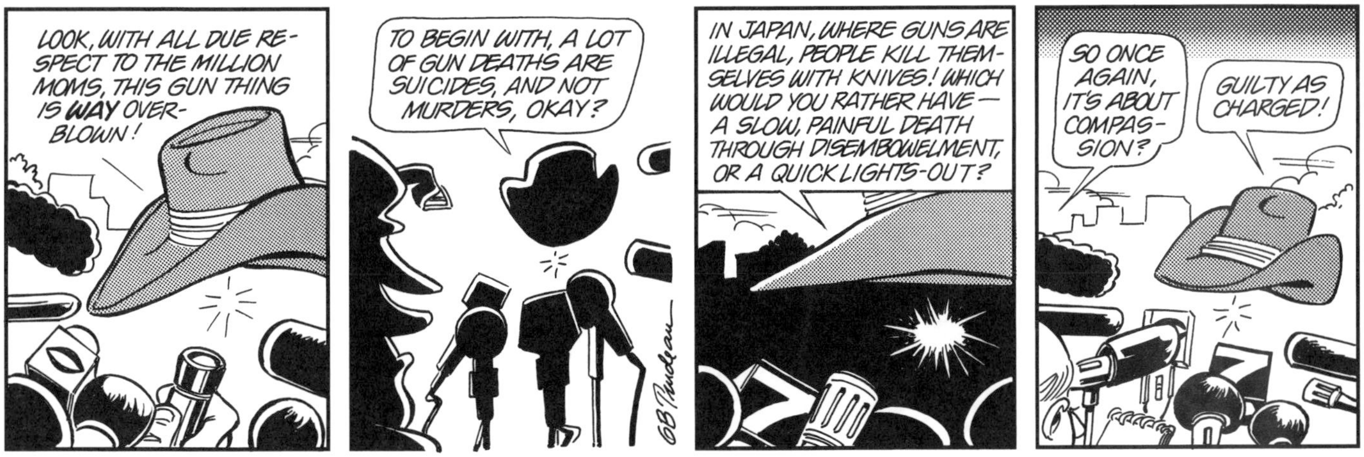
LOOK, WITH ALL DUE RESPECT TO THE MILLION MOMS, THIS GUN THING IS WAY OVERBLOWN!
TO BEGIN WITH, A LOT OF GUN DEATHS ARE SUICIDES, AND NOT MURDERS, OKAY?
IN JAPAN, WHERE GUNS ARE ILLEGAL, PEOPLE KILL THEMSELVES WITH KNIVES! WHICH WOULD YOU RATHER HAVE—A SLOW, PAINFUL DEATH THROUGH DISEMBOWELMENT, OR A QUICK LIGHTS-OUT?
SO ONCE AGAIN, IT'S ABOUT COMPASSION?
GUILTY AS CHARGED!

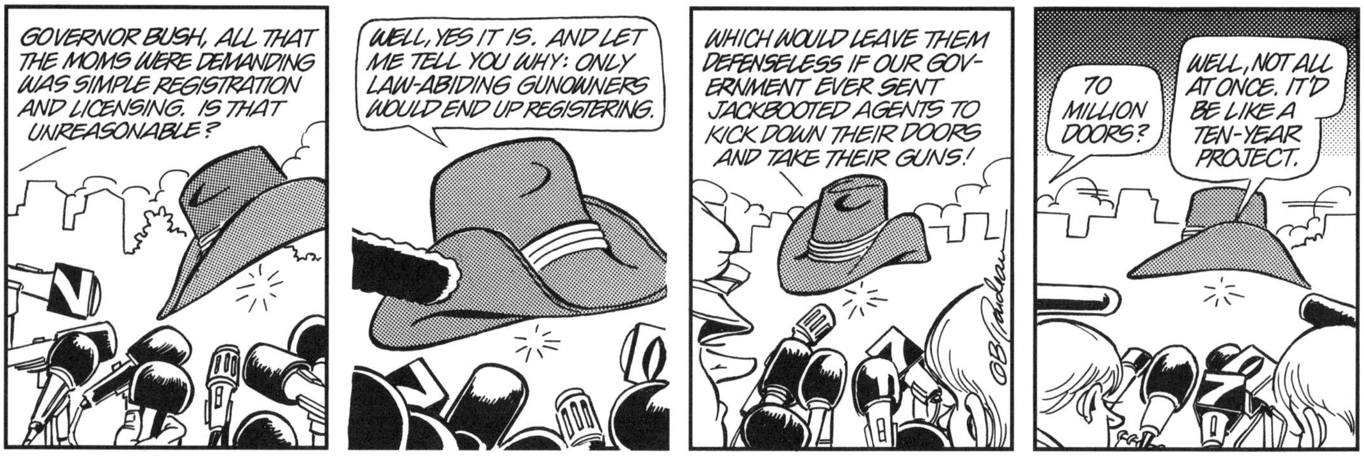
GOVERNOR BUSH, ALL THAT THE MOMS WERE DEMANDING WAS SIMPLE REGISTRATION AND LICENSING. IS THAT UNREASONABLE?
WELL, YES IT IS. AND LET ME TELL YOU WHY: ONLY LAW-ABIDING GUNOWNERS WOULD END UP REGISTERING.
WHICH WOULD LEAVE THEM DEFENSELESS IF OUR GOVERNMENT EVER SENT JACKBOOTED AGENTS TO KICK DOWN THEIR DOORS AND TAKE THEIR GUNS!
70 MILLION DOORS?
WELL, NOT ALL AT ONCE. IT'D BE LIKE A TEN-YEAR PROJECT.

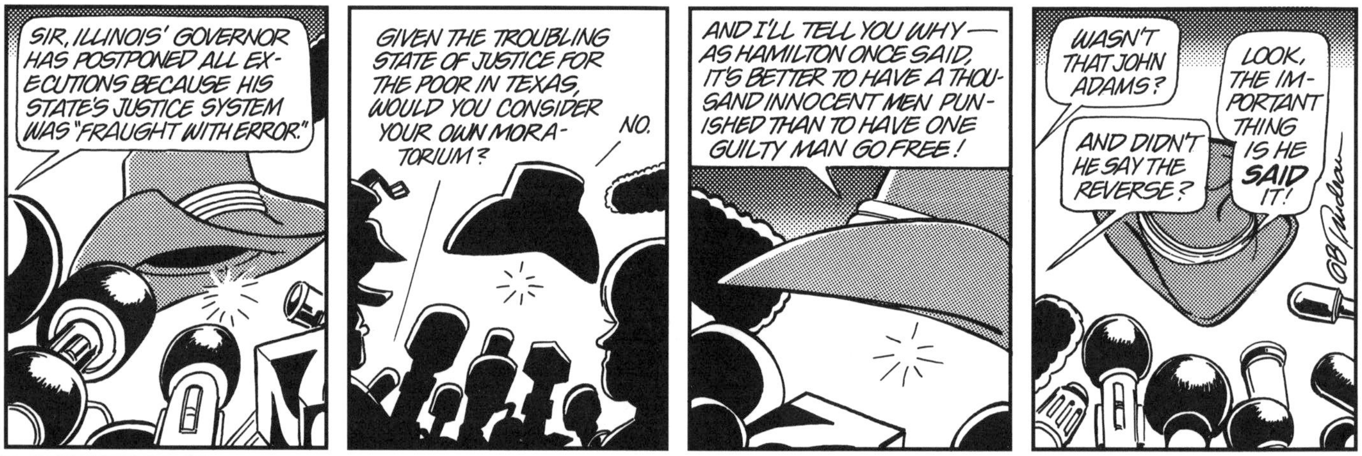
SIR, ILLINOIS' GOVERNOR HAS POSTPONED ALL EXECUTIONS BECAUSE HIS STATE'S JUSTICE SYSTEM WAS "FRAUGHT WITH ERROR."
GIVEN THE TROUBLING STATE OF JUSTICE FOR THE POOR IN TEXAS, WOULD YOU CONSIDER YOUR OWN MORATORIUM?
NO.
AND I'LL TELL YOU WHY— AS HAMILTON ONCE SAID, IT'S BETTER TO HAVE A THOUSAND INNOCENT MEN PUNISHED THAN TO HAVE ONE GUILTY MAN GO FREE!
WASN'T THAT JOHN ADAMS?
AND DIDN'T HE SAY THE REVERSE?
LOOK, THE IMPORTANT THING IS HE SAID IT!

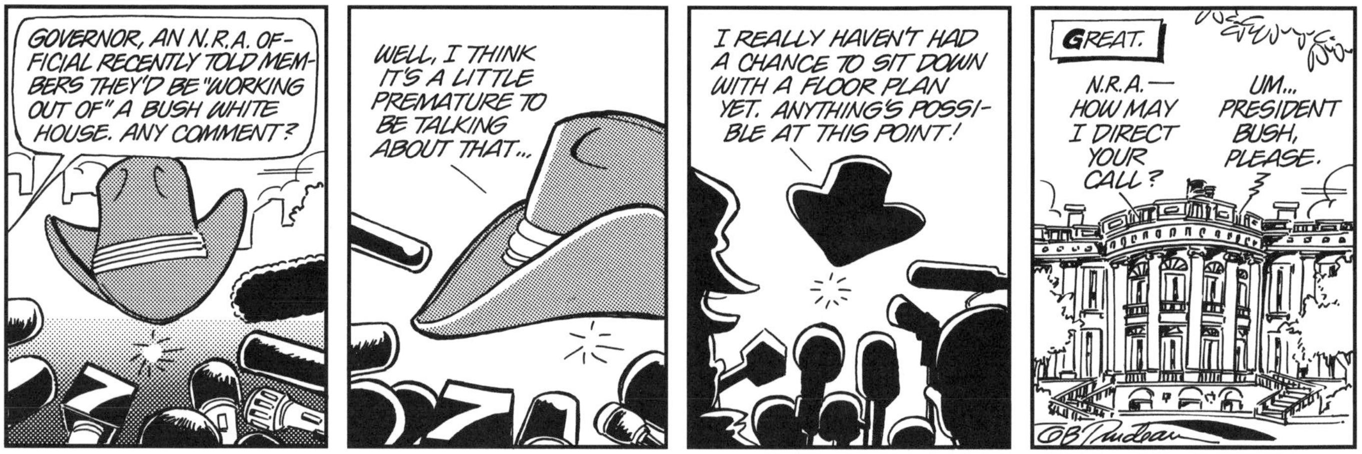
GOVERNOR, AN N.R.A. OFFICIAL RECENTLY TOLD MEMBERS THEY'D BE "WORKING OUT OF" A BUSH WHITE HOUSE. ANY COMMENT?
WELL, I THINK IT'S A LITTLE PREMATURE TO BE TALKING ABOUT THAT...
I REALLY HAVEN'T HAD A CHANCE TO SIT DOWN WITH A FLOOR PLAN YET. ANYTHING'S POSSIBLE AT THIS POINT!
GREAT.
N.R.A.— HOW MAY I DIRECT YOUR CALL?
UM... PRESIDENT BUSH, PLEASE.

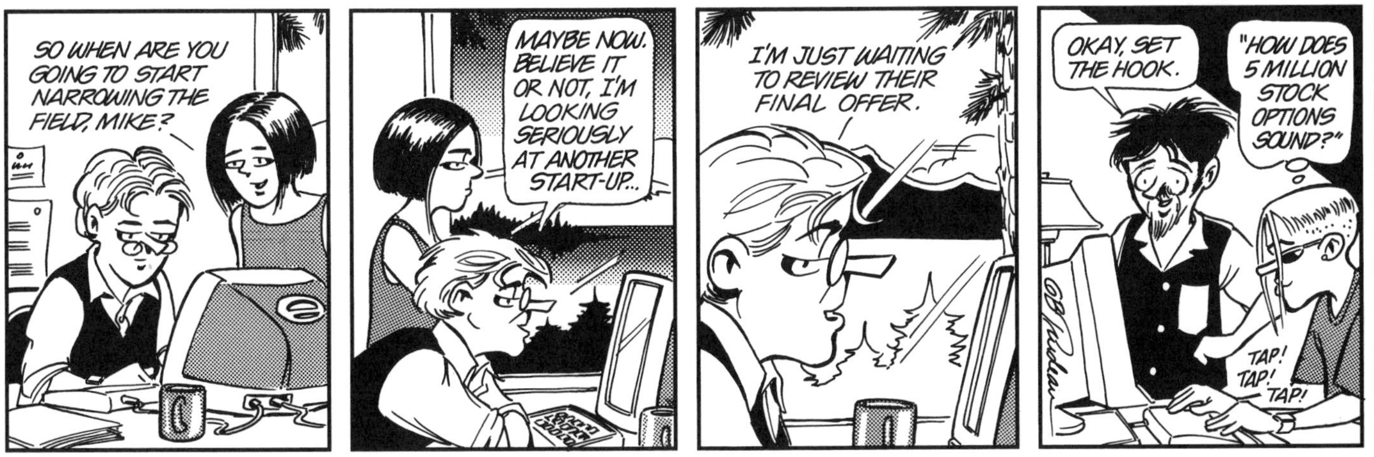
SO WHEN ARE YOU GOING TO START NARROWING THE FIELD, MIKE?
MAYBE NOW. BELIEVE IT OR NOT, I'M LOOKING SERIOUSLY AT ANOTHER START-UP...
I'M JUST WAITING TO REVIEW THEIR FINAL OFFER.
OKAY, SET THE HOOK.
"HOW DOES 5 MILLION STOCK OPTIONS SOUND?"
TAP! TAP! TAP!

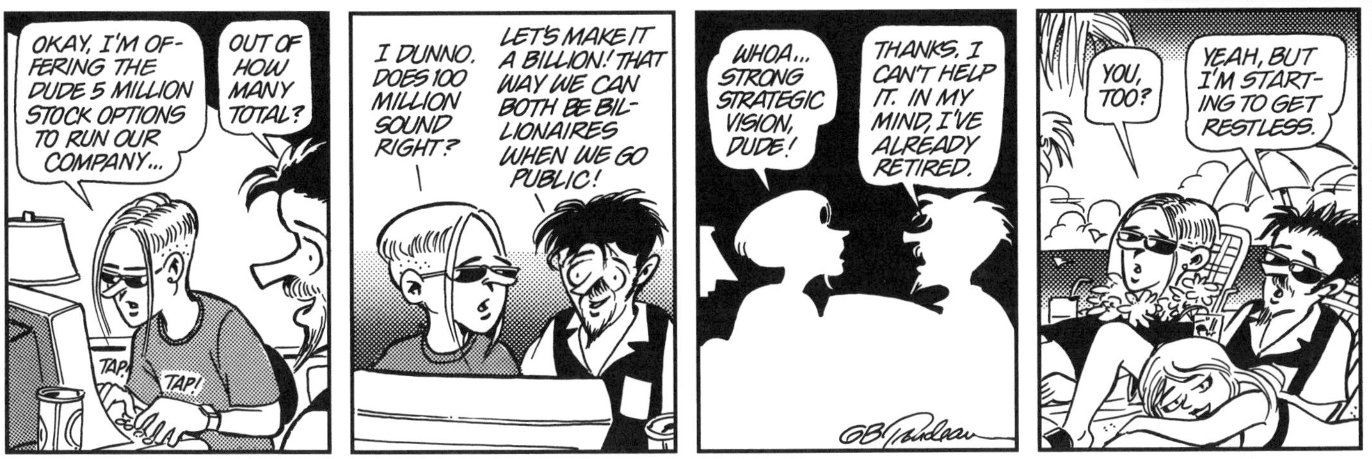
OKAY, I'M OFFERING THE DUDE 5 MILLION STOCK OPTIONS TO RUN OUR COMPANY...
OUT OF HOW MANY TOTAL?
TAP! TAP!
I DUNNO. DOES 100 MILLION SOUND RIGHT?
LET'S MAKE IT A BILLION! THAT WAY WE CAN BOTH BE BILLIONAIRES WHEN WE GO PUBLIC!
WHOA... STRONG STRATEGIC VISION, DUDE!
THANKS. I CAN'T HELP IT. IN MY MIND, I'VE ALREADY RETIRED.
YOU, TOO?
YEAH, BUT I'M STARTING TO GET RESTLESS.

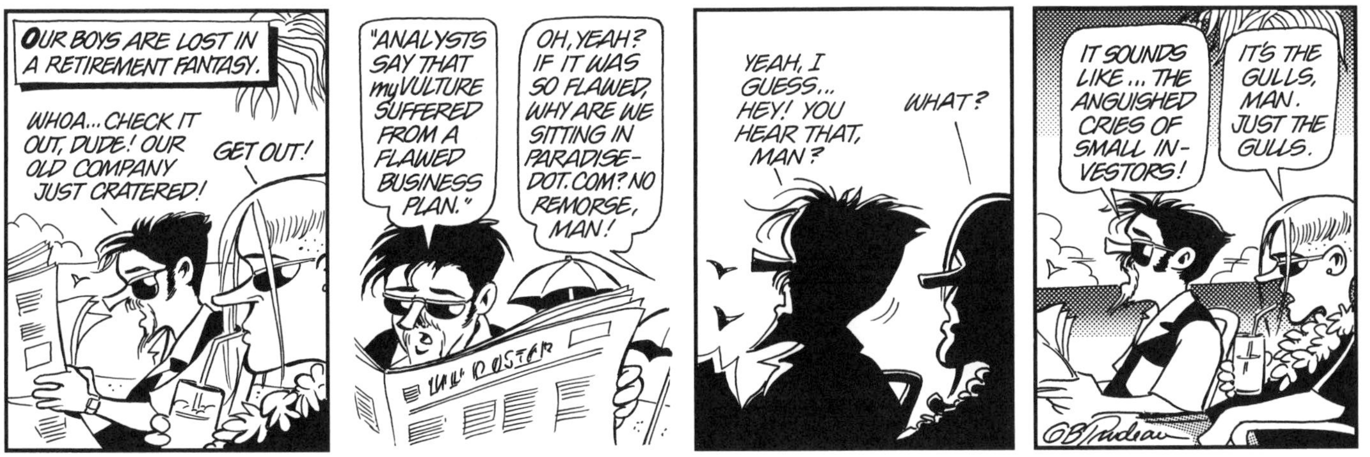
OUR BOYS ARE LOST IN A RETIREMENT FANTASY.
WHOA... CHECK IT OUT, DUDE! OUR OLD COMPANY JUST CRATERED!
GET OUT!
"ANALYSTS SAY THAT myVULTURE SUFFERED FROM A FLAWED BUSINESS PLAN."
OH, YEAH? IF IT WAS SO FLAWED, WHY ARE WE SITTING IN PARADISE-DOT.COM? NO REMORSE, MAN!
YEAH, I GUESS... HEY! YOU HEAR THAT, MAN?
WHAT?
IT SOUNDS LIKE... THE ANGUISHED CRIES OF SMALL INVESTORS!
IT'S THE GULLS, MAN. JUST THE GULLS.

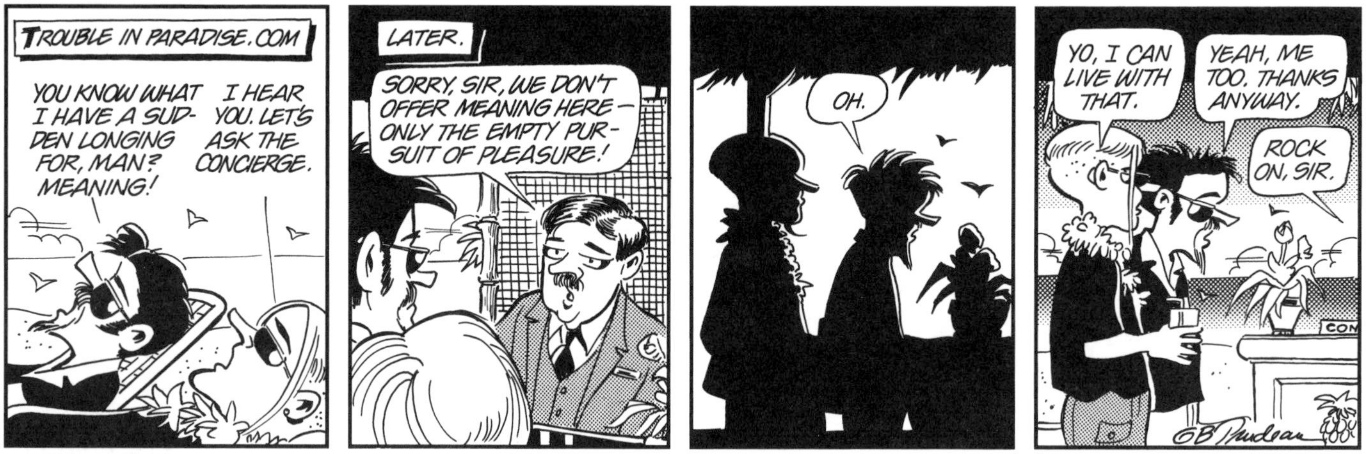
TROUBLE IN PARADISE.COM
YOU KNOW WHAT I HAVE A SUDDEN LONGING FOR, MAN? MEANING!
I HEAR YOU. LET'S ASK THE CONCIERGE.
LATER.
SORRY, SIR, WE DON'T OFFER MEANING HERE—ONLY THE EMPTY PURSUIT OF PLEASURE!
OH.
YO, I CAN LIVE WITH THAT.
YEAH, ME TOO. THANKS ANYWAY.
ROCK ON, SIR.

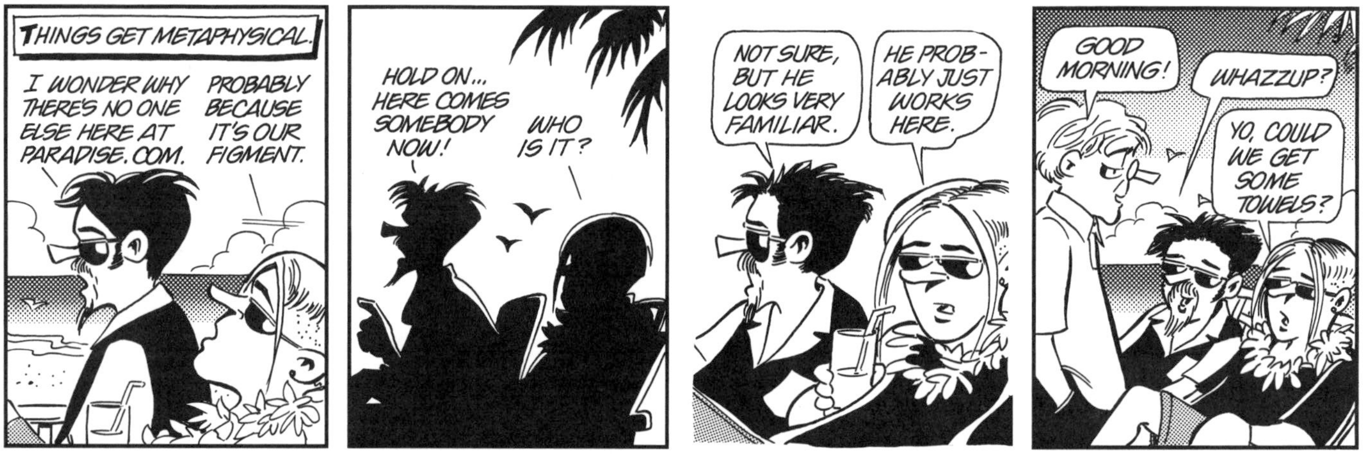
THINGS GET METAPHYSICAL.
I WONDER WHY THERE'S NO ONE ELSE HERE AT PARADISE.COM.
PROBABLY BECAUSE IT'S OUR FIGMENT.
HOLD ON... HERE COMES SOMEBODY NOW!
WHO IS IT?
NOT SURE, BUT HE LOOKS VERY FAMILIAR.
HE PROBABLY JUST WORKS HERE.
GOOD MORNING!
WHAZZUP?
YO, COULD WE GET SOME TOWELS?

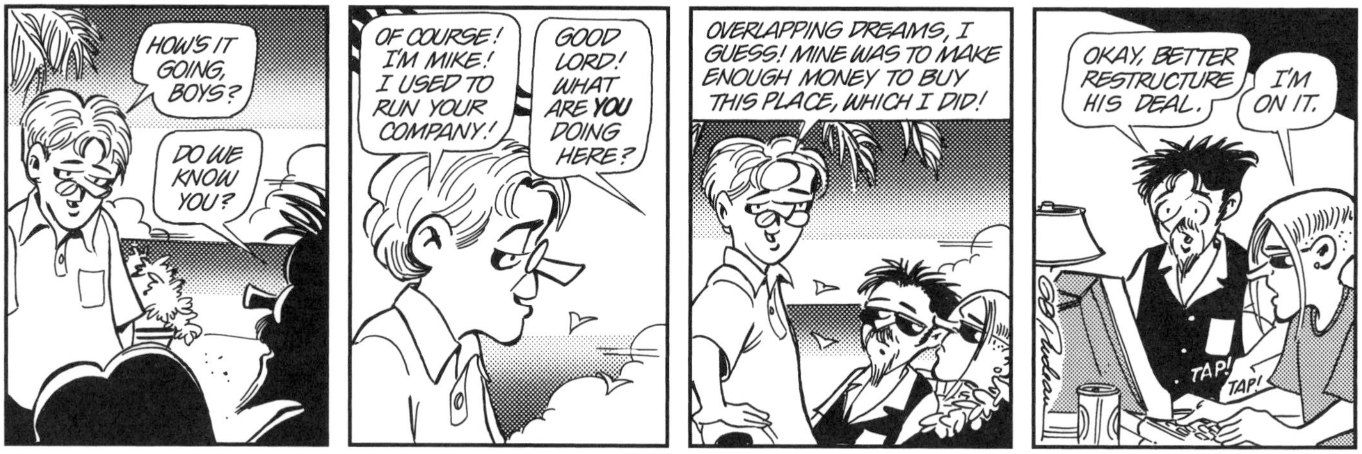
HOW'S IT GOING, BOYS?
DO WE KNOW YOU?
OF COURSE! I'M MIKE! I USED TO RUN YOUR COMPANY!
GOOD LORD! WHAT ARE YOU DOING HERE?
OVERLAPPING DREAMS, I GUESS! MINE WAS TO MAKE ENOUGH MONEY TO BUY THIS PLACE, WHICH I DID!
OKAY, BETTER RESTRUCTURE HIS DEAL.
I'M ON IT.
TAP! TAP!

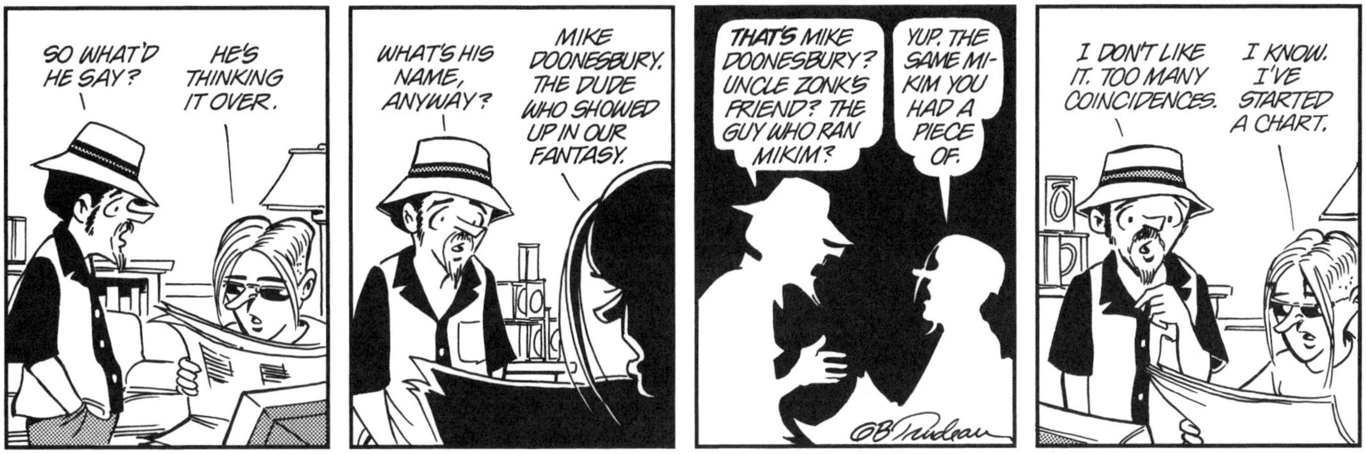
SO WHAT'D HE SAY?
HE'S THINKING IT OVER.
WHAT'S HIS NAME, ANYWAY?
MIKE DOONESBURY. THE DUDE WHO SHOWED UP IN OUR FANTASY.
THAT'S MIKE DOONESBURY? UNCLE ZONK'S FRIEND? THE GUY WHO RAN MIKIM?
YUP. THE SAME MIKIM YOU HAD A PIECE OF.
I DON'T LIKE IT. TOO MANY COINCIDENCES.
I KNOW. I'VE STARTED A CHART.

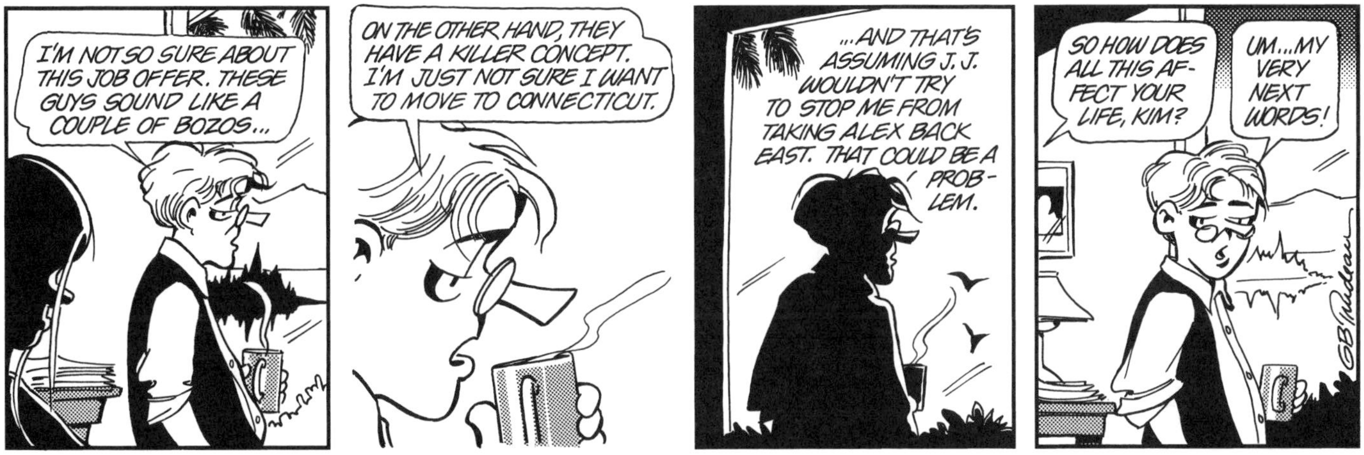
I'M NOT SO SURE ABOUT THIS JOB OFFER. THESE GUYS SOUND LIKE A COUPLE OF BOZOS...
ON THE OTHER HAND, THEY HAVE A KILLER CONCEPT. I'M JUST NOT SURE I WANT TO MOVE TO CONNECTICUT.
...AND THAT'S ASSUMING J. J. WOULDN'T TRY TO STOP ME FROM TAKING ALEX BACK EAST. THAT COULD BE A PROBLEM.
SO HOW DOES ALL THIS AFFECT YOUR LIFE, KIM?
UM...MY VERY NEXT WORDS!

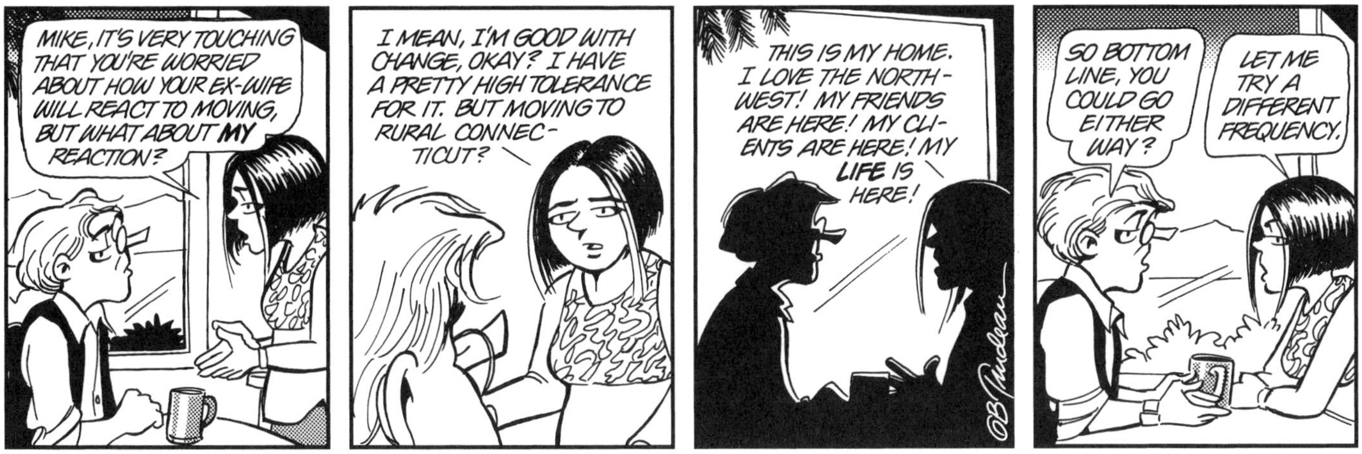
MIKE, IT'S VERY TOUCHING THAT YOU'RE WORRIED ABOUT HOW YOUR EX-WIFE WILL REACT TO MOVING, BUT WHAT ABOUT MY REACTION?
I MEAN, I'M GOOD WITH CHANGE, OKAY? I HAVE A PRETTY HIGH TOLERANCE FOR IT. BUT MOVING TO RURAL CONNECTICUT?
THIS IS MY HOME. I LOVE THE NORTHWEST! MY FRIENDS ARE HERE! MY CLIENTS ARE HERE! MY LIFE IS HERE!
SO BOTTOM LINE, YOU COULD GO EITHER WAY?
LET ME TRY A DIFFERENT FREQUENCY.

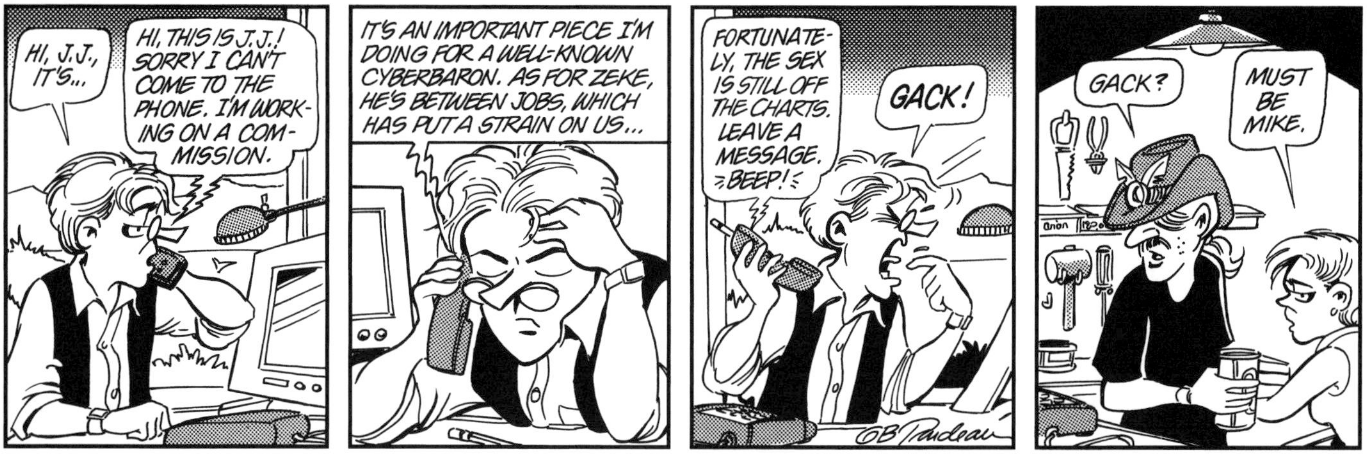
HI, J.J., IT'S...
HI, THIS IS J.J.! SORRY I CAN'T COME TO THE PHONE. I'M WORKING ON A COMMISSION.
IT'S AN IMPORTANT PIECE I'M DOING FOR A WELL-KNOWN CYBERBARON. AS FOR ZEKE, HE'S BETWEEN JOBS, WHICH HAS PUT A STRAIN ON US...
FORTUNATELY, THE SEX IS STILL OFF THE CHARTS. LEAVE A MESSAGE. BEEP!
GACK!
GACK?
MUST BE MIKE.

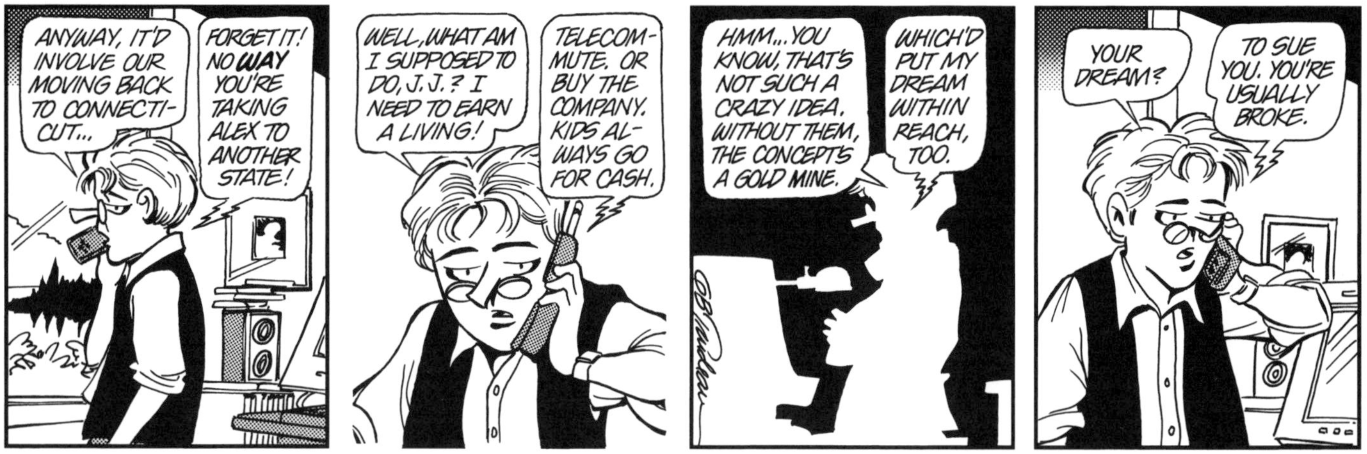
ANYWAY, IT'D INVOLVE OUR MOVING BACK TO CONNECTICUT...
FORGET IT! NO WAY YOU'RE TAKING ALEX TO ANOTHER STATE!
WELL, WHAT AM I SUPPOSED TO DO, J.J.? I NEED TO EARN A LIVING!
TELECOMMUTE. OR BUY THE COMPANY. KIDS ALWAYS GO FOR CASH.
HMM... YOU KNOW, THAT'S NOT SUCH A CRAZY IDEA. WITHOUT THEM, THE CONCEPT'S A GOLD MINE.
WHICH'D PUT MY DREAM WITHIN REACH, TOO.
YOUR DREAM?
TO SUE YOU. YOU'RE USUALLY BROKE.

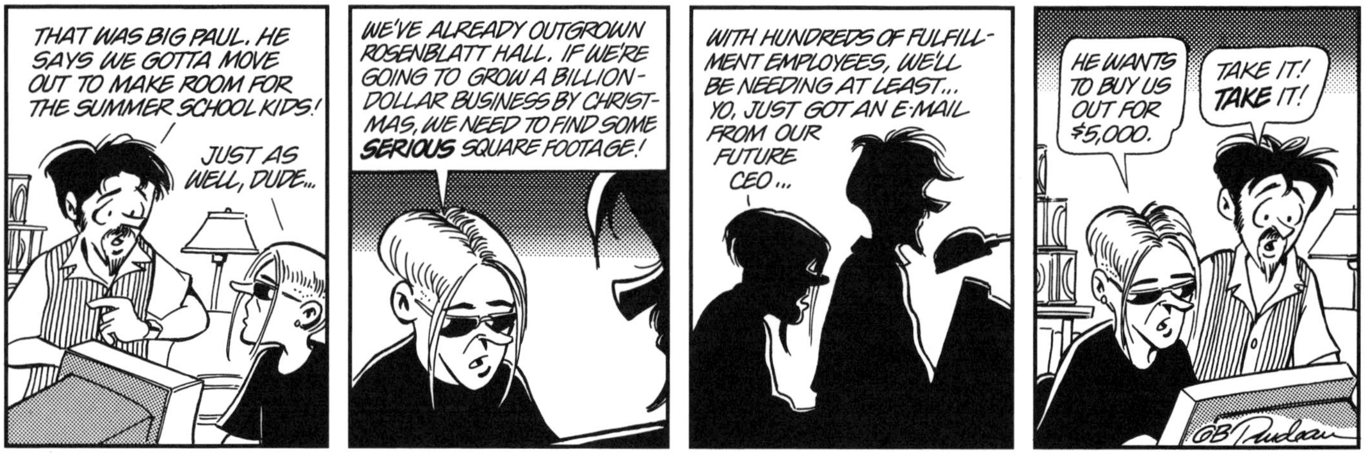
THAT WAS BIG PAUL. HE SAYS WE GOTTA MOVE OUT TO MAKE ROOM FOR THE SUMMER SCHOOL KIDS!
JUST AS WELL, DUDE...
WE'VE ALREADY OUTGROWN ROSENBLATT HALL. IF WE'RE GOING TO GROW A BILLION-DOLLAR BUSINESS BY CHRISTMAS, WE NEED TO FIND SOME SERIOUS SQUARE FOOTAGE!
WITH HUNDREDS OF FULFILLMENT EMPLOYEES, WE'LL BE NEEDING AT LEAST... YO, JUST GOT AN E-MAIL FROM OUR FUTURE CEO...
HE WANTS TO BUY US OUT FOR $5,000.
TAKE IT! TAKE IT!

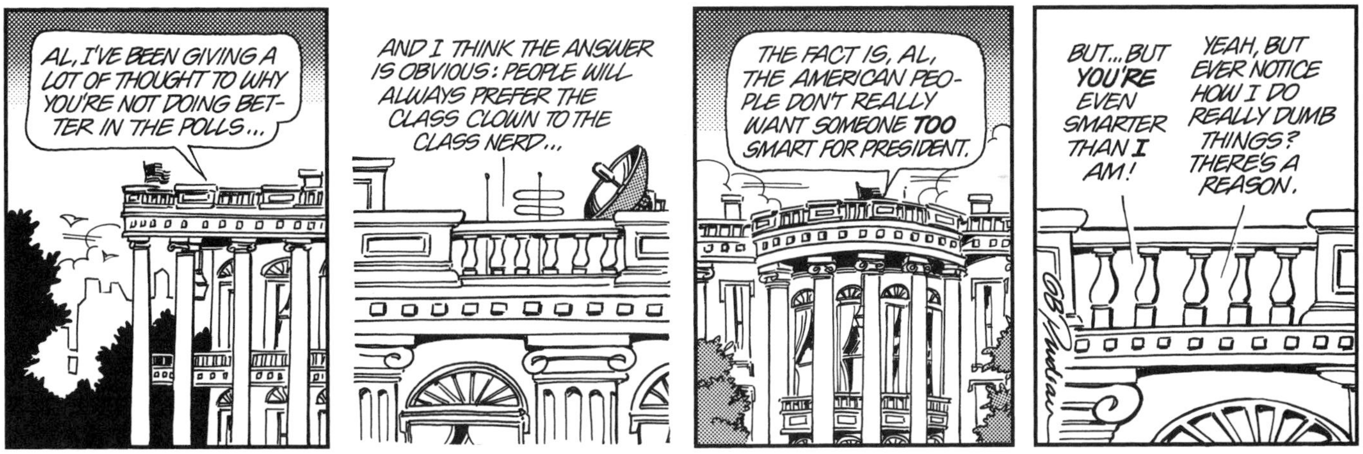
AL, I'VE BEEN GIVING A LOT OF THOUGHT TO WHY YOU'RE NOT DOING BETTER IN THE POLLS...
AND I THINK THE ANSWER IS OBVIOUS: PEOPLE WILL ALWAYS PREFER THE CLASS CLOWN TO THE CLASS NERD...
THE FACT IS, AL, THE AMERICAN PEOPLE DON'T REALLY WANT SOMEONE **TOO** SMART FOR PRESIDENT.
BUT...BUT **YOU'RE** EVEN SMARTER THAN **I** AM!
YEAH, BUT EVER NOTICE HOW I DO REALLY DUMB THINGS? THERE'S A REASON.

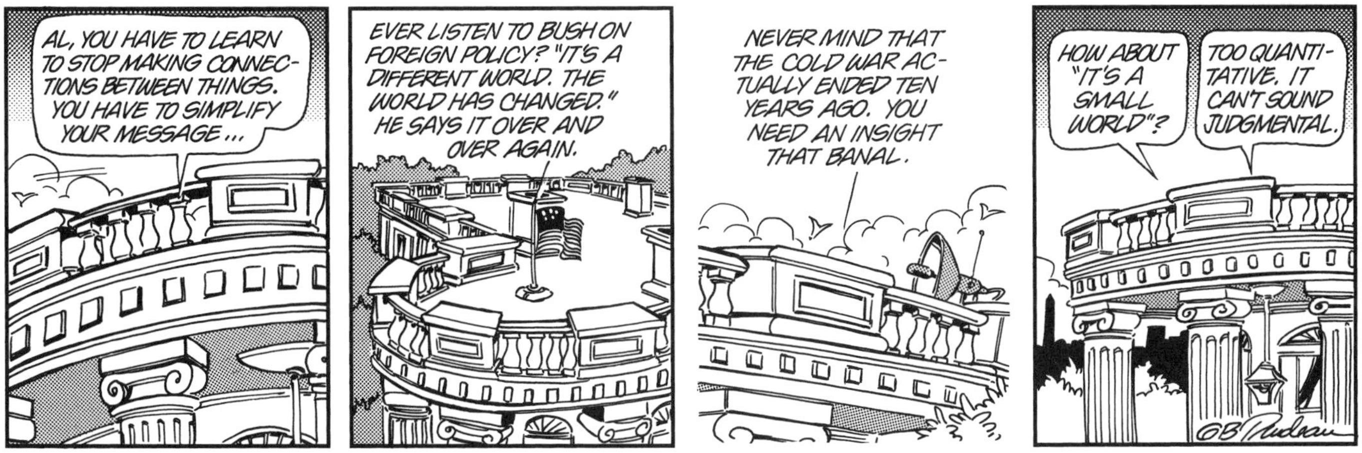
AL, YOU HAVE TO LEARN TO STOP MAKING CONNECTIONS BETWEEN THINGS. YOU HAVE TO SIMPLIFY YOUR MESSAGE...
EVER LISTEN TO BUSH ON FOREIGN POLICY? "IT'S A DIFFERENT WORLD. THE WORLD HAS CHANGED." HE SAYS IT OVER AND OVER AGAIN.
NEVER MIND THAT THE COLD WAR ACTUALLY ENDED TEN YEARS AGO. YOU NEED AN INSIGHT THAT BANAL.
HOW ABOUT "IT'S A SMALL WORLD"?
TOO QUANTITATIVE. IT CAN'T SOUND JUDGMENTAL.

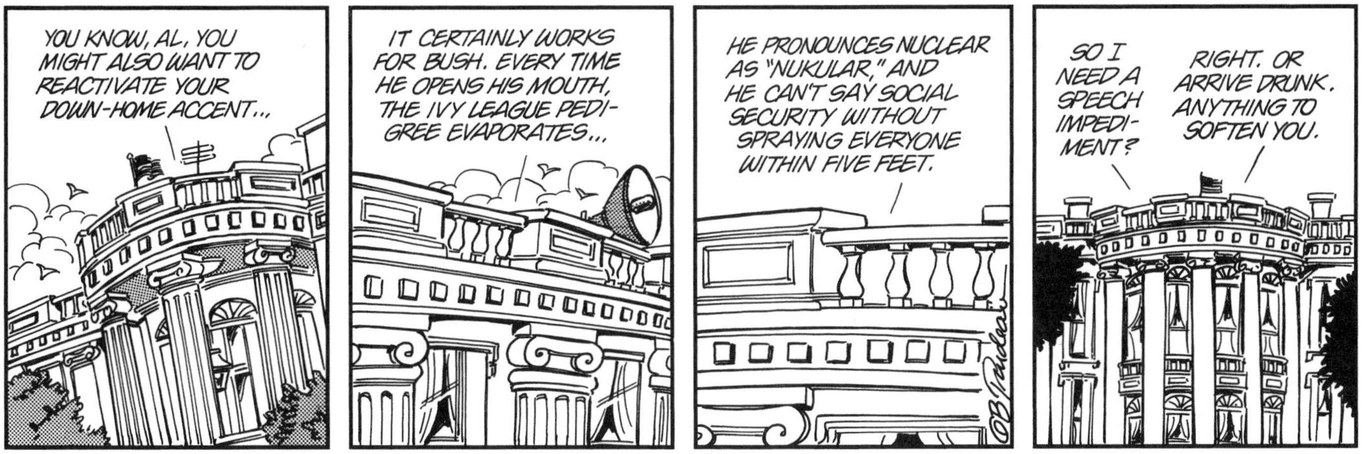
YOU KNOW, AL, YOU MIGHT ALSO WANT TO REACTIVATE YOUR DOWN-HOME ACCENT...
IT CERTAINLY WORKS FOR BUSH. EVERY TIME HE OPENS HIS MOUTH, THE IVY LEAGUE PEDIGREE EVAPORATES...
HE PRONOUNCES NUCLEAR AS "NUKULAR," AND HE CAN'T SAY SOCIAL SECURITY WITHOUT SPRAYING EVERYONE WITHIN FIVE FEET.
SO I NEED A SPEECH IMPEDIMENT?
RIGHT. OR ARRIVE DRUNK. ANYTHING TO SOFTEN YOU.

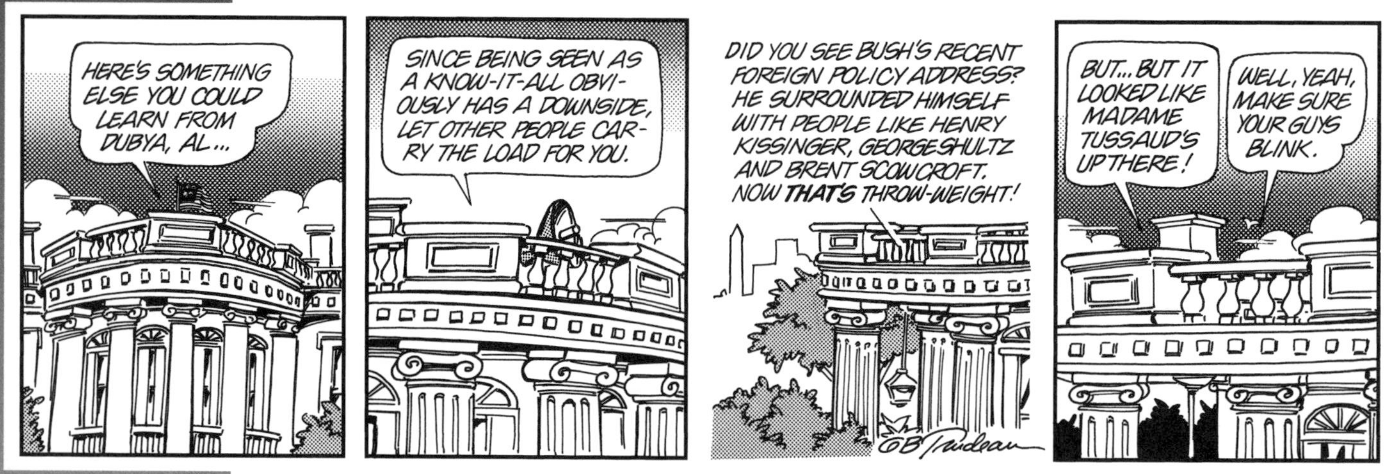
HERE'S SOMETHING ELSE YOU COULD LEARN FROM DUBYA, AL...
SINCE BEING SEEN AS A KNOW-IT-ALL OBVIOUSLY HAS A DOWNSIDE, LET OTHER PEOPLE CARRY THE LOAD FOR YOU.
DID YOU SEE BUSH'S RECENT FOREIGN POLICY ADDRESS? HE SURROUNDED HIMSELF WITH PEOPLE LIKE HENRY KISSINGER, GEORGE SHULTZ AND BRENT SCOWCROFT. NOW THAT'S THROW-WEIGHT!
BUT... BUT IT LOOKED LIKE MADAME TUSSAUD'S UP THERE!
WELL, YEAH, MAKE SURE YOUR GUYS BLINK.

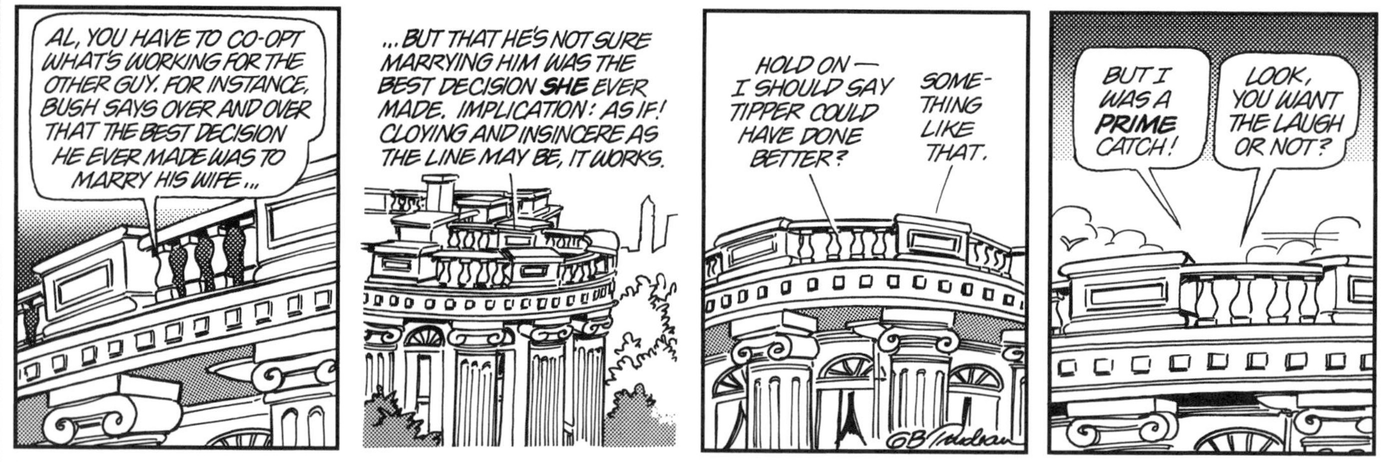
AL, YOU HAVE TO CO-OPT WHAT'S WORKING FOR THE OTHER GUY. FOR INSTANCE, BUSH SAYS OVER AND OVER THAT THE BEST DECISION HE EVER MADE WAS TO MARRY HIS WIFE...
...BUT THAT HE'S NOT SURE MARRYING HIM WAS THE BEST DECISION SHE EVER MADE. IMPLICATION: AS IF! CLOYING AND INSINCERE AS THE LINE MAY BE, IT WORKS.
HOLD ON — I SHOULD SAY TIPPER COULD HAVE DONE BETTER?
SOMETHING LIKE THAT.
BUT I WAS A PRIME CATCH!
LOOK, YOU WANT THE LAUGH OR NOT?

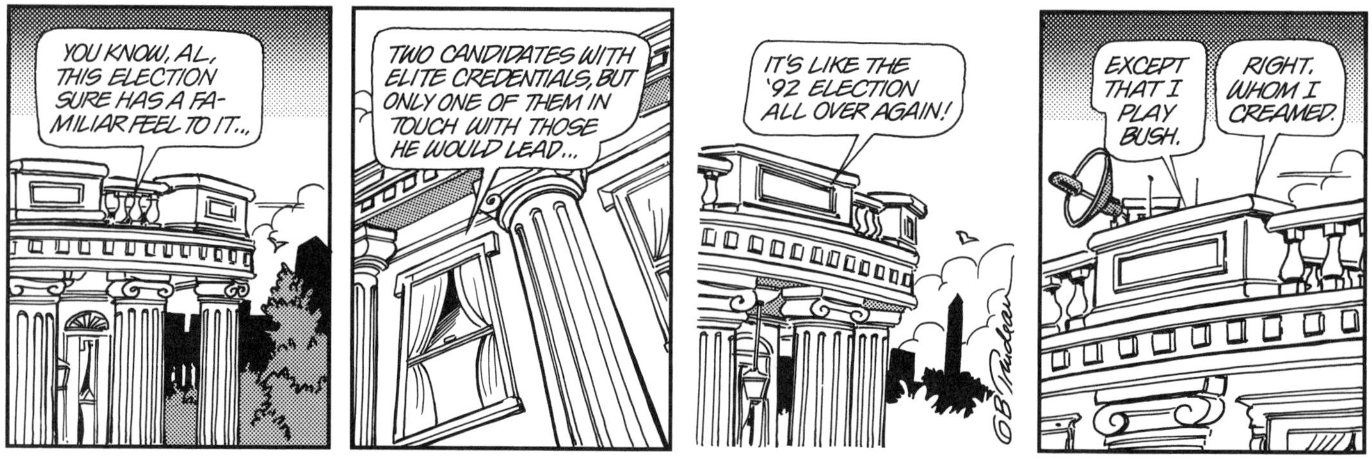
YOU KNOW, AL, THIS ELECTION SURE HAS A FAMILIAR FEEL TO IT...
TWO CANDIDATES WITH ELITE CREDENTIALS, BUT ONLY ONE OF THEM IN TOUCH WITH THOSE HE WOULD LEAD...
IT'S LIKE THE '92 ELECTION ALL OVER AGAIN!
EXCEPT THAT I PLAY BUSH.
RIGHT. WHOM I CREAMED.

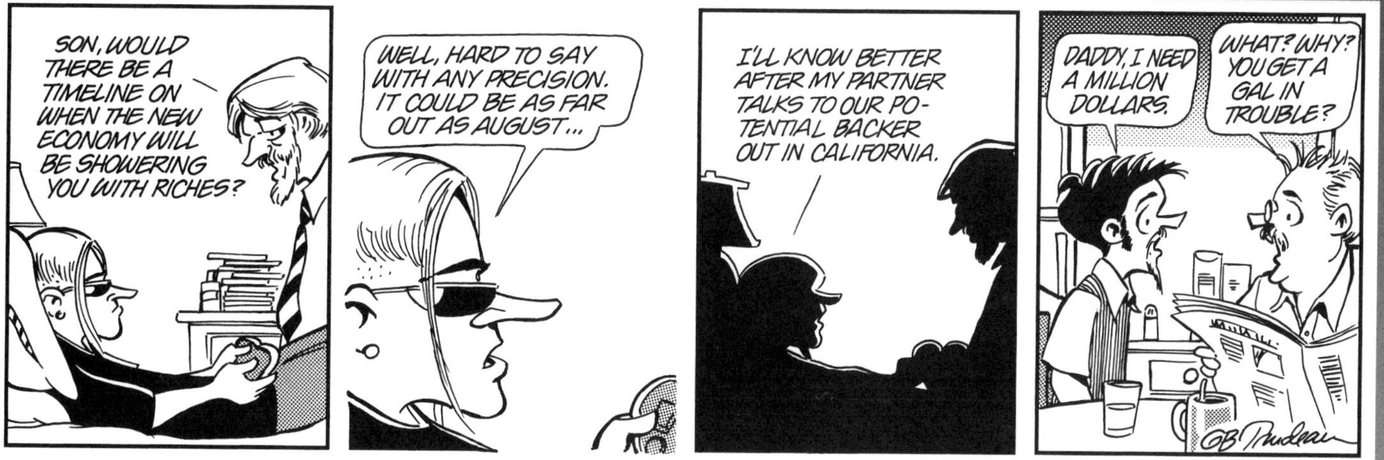
SON, WOULD THERE BE A TIMELINE ON WHEN THE NEW ECONOMY WILL BE SHOWERING YOU WITH RICHES?
WELL, HARD TO SAY WITH ANY PRECISION. IT COULD BE AS FAR OUT AS AUGUST...
I'LL KNOW BETTER AFTER MY PARTNER TALKS TO OUR POTENTIAL BACKER OUT IN CALIFORNIA.
DADDY, I NEED A MILLION DOLLARS.
WHAT? WHY? YOU GET A GAL IN TROUBLE?

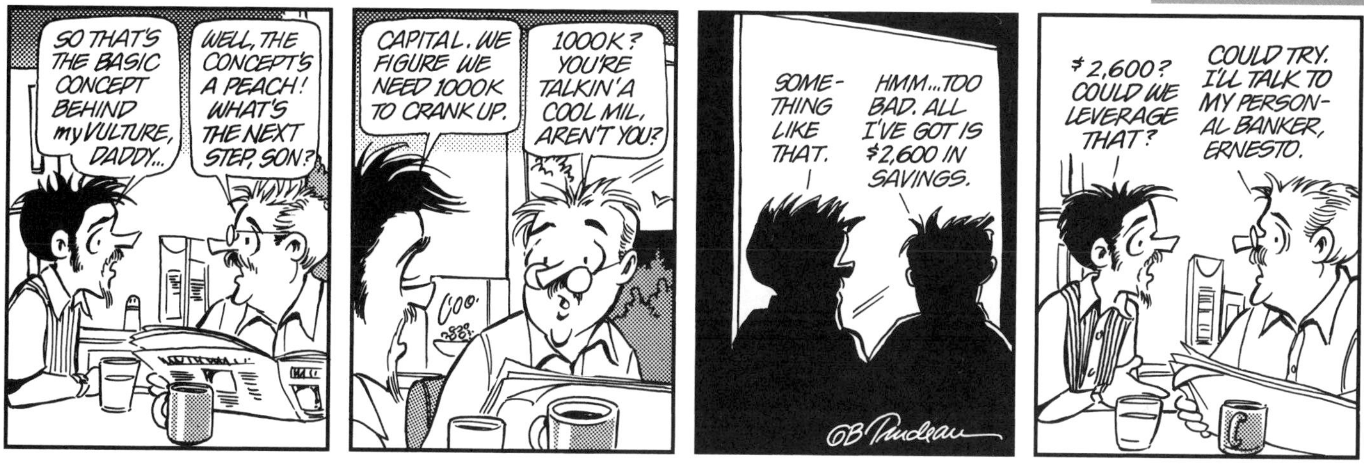
SO THAT'S THE BASIC CONCEPT BEHIND myVULTURE, DADDY...
WELL, THE CONCEPT'S A PEACH! WHAT'S THE NEXT STEP, SON?
CAPITAL. WE FIGURE WE NEED 1000K TO CRANK UP.
1000K? YOU'RE TALKIN' A COOL MIL, AREN'T YOU?
SOMETHING LIKE THAT.
HMM...TOO BAD. ALL I'VE GOT IS $2,600 IN SAVINGS.
$2,600? COULD WE LEVERAGE THAT?
COULD TRY. I'LL TALK TO MY PERSONAL BANKER, ERNESTO.

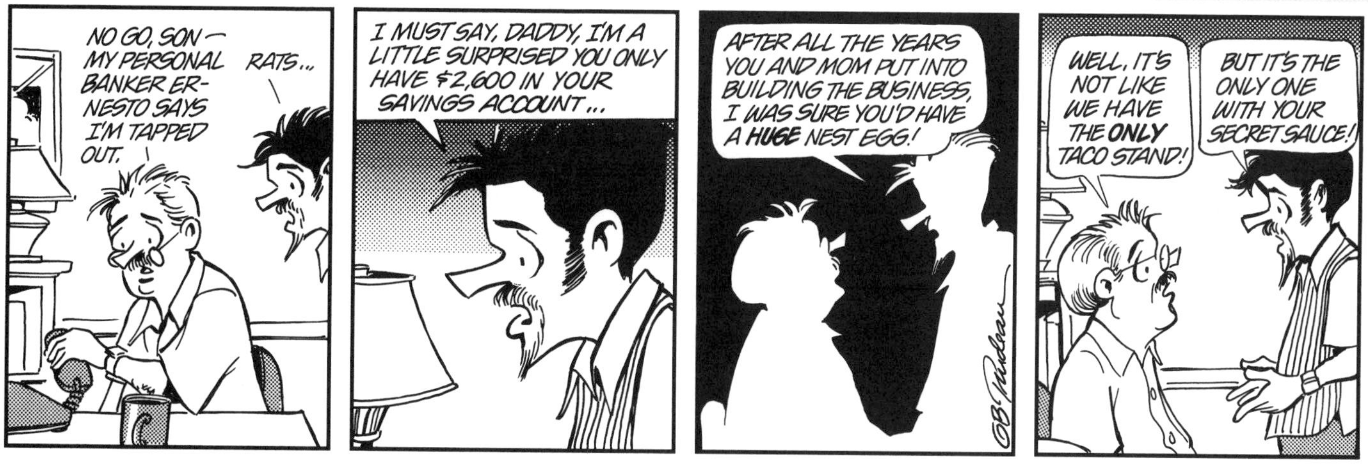
NO GO, SON — MY PERSONAL BANKER ERNESTO SAYS I'M TAPPED OUT.
RATS...
I MUST SAY, DADDY, I'M A LITTLE SURPRISED YOU ONLY HAVE $2,600 IN YOUR SAVINGS ACCOUNT...
AFTER ALL THE YEARS YOU AND MOM PUT INTO BUILDING THE BUSINESS, I WAS SURE YOU'D HAVE A **HUGE** NEST EGG!
WELL, IT'S NOT LIKE WE HAVE THE **ONLY** TACO STAND!
BUT IT'S THE ONLY ONE WITH YOUR SECRET SAUCE!

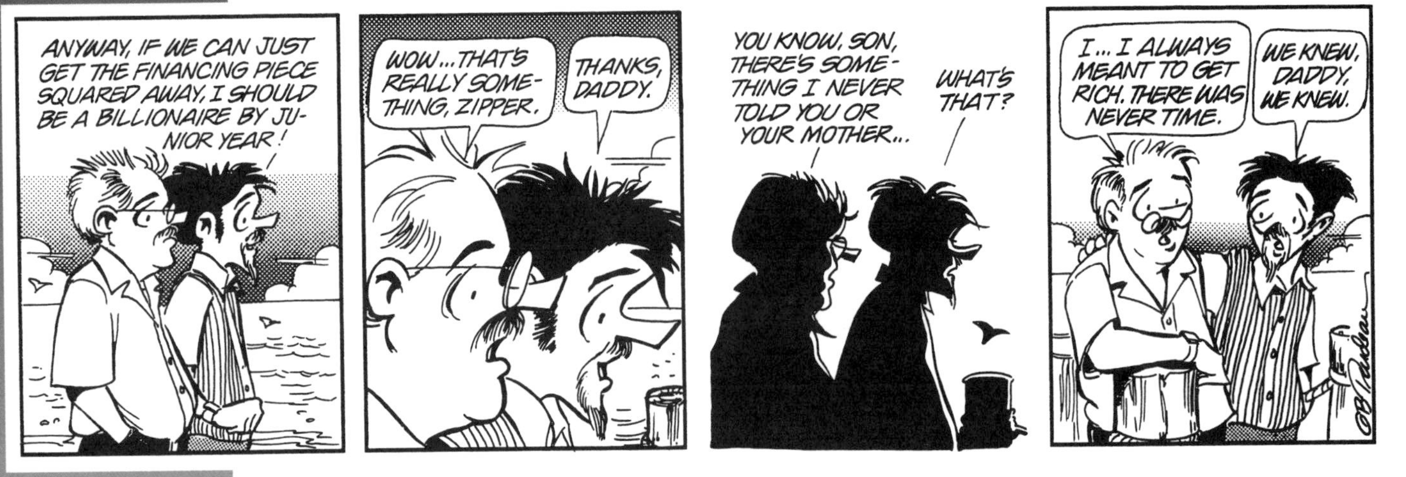
ANYWAY, IF WE CAN JUST GET THE FINANCING PIECE SQUARED AWAY, I SHOULD BE A BILLIONAIRE BY JUNIOR YEAR!
WOW...THAT'S REALLY SOMETHING, ZIPPER.
THANKS, DADDY.
YOU KNOW, SON, THERE'S SOMETHING I NEVER TOLD YOU OR YOUR MOTHER...
WHAT'S THAT?
I... I ALWAYS MEANT TO GET RICH. THERE WAS NEVER TIME.
WE KNEW, DADDY, WE KNEW.

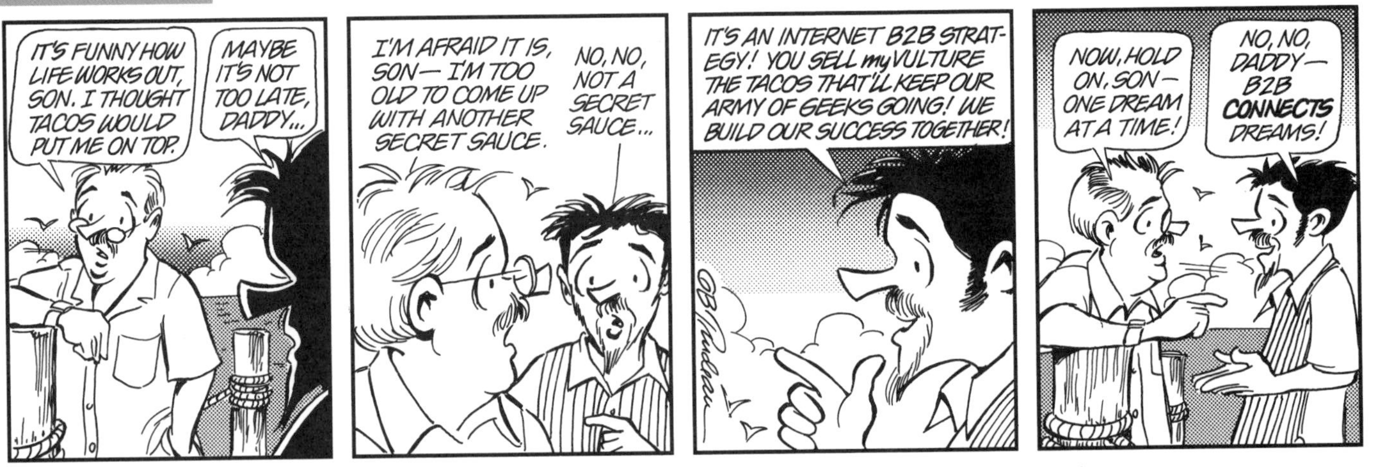
IT'S FUNNY HOW LIFE WORKS OUT, SON. I THOUGHT TACOS WOULD PUT ME ON TOP.
MAYBE IT'S NOT TOO LATE, DADDY...
I'M AFRAID IT IS, SON— I'M TOO OLD TO COME UP WITH ANOTHER SECRET SAUCE.
NO, NO, NOT A SECRET SAUCE...
IT'S AN INTERNET B2B STRATEGY! YOU SELL my VULTURE THE TACOS THAT'LL KEEP OUR ARMY OF GEEKS GOING! WE BUILD OUR SUCCESS TOGETHER!
NOW, HOLD ON, SON— ONE DREAM AT A TIME!
NO, NO, DADDY— B2B CONNECTS DREAMS!

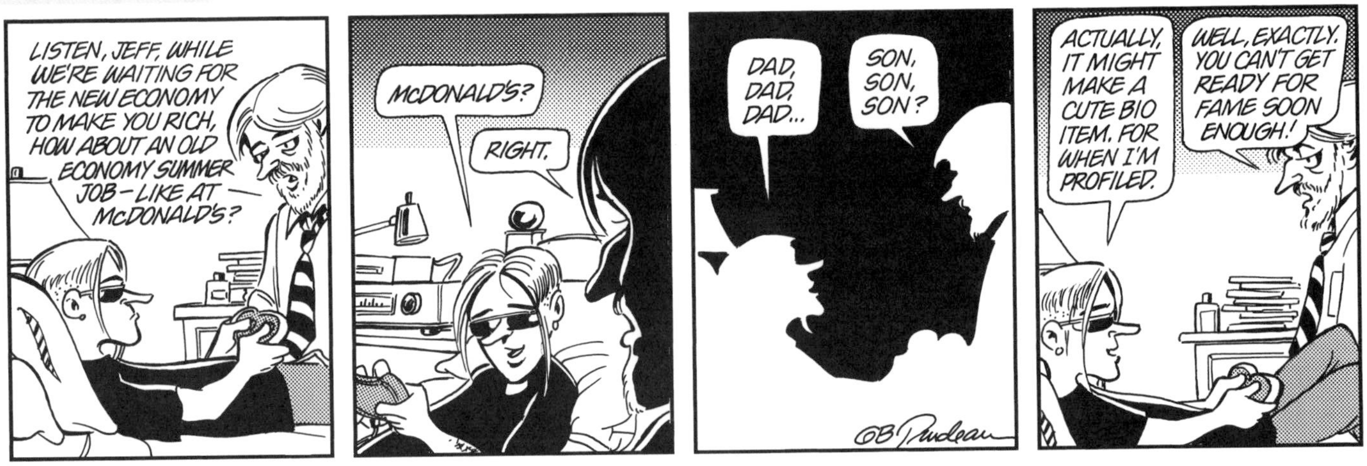
LISTEN, JEFF, WHILE WE'RE WAITING FOR THE NEW ECONOMY TO MAKE YOU RICH, HOW ABOUT AN OLD ECONOMY SUMMER JOB–LIKE AT McDONALD'S?
McDONALD'S?
RIGHT.
DAD, DAD, DAD...
SON, SON, SON?
ACTUALLY, IT MIGHT MAKE A CUTE BIO ITEM. FOR WHEN I'M PROFILED.
WELL, EXACTLY. YOU CAN'T GET READY FOR FAME SOON ENOUGH!

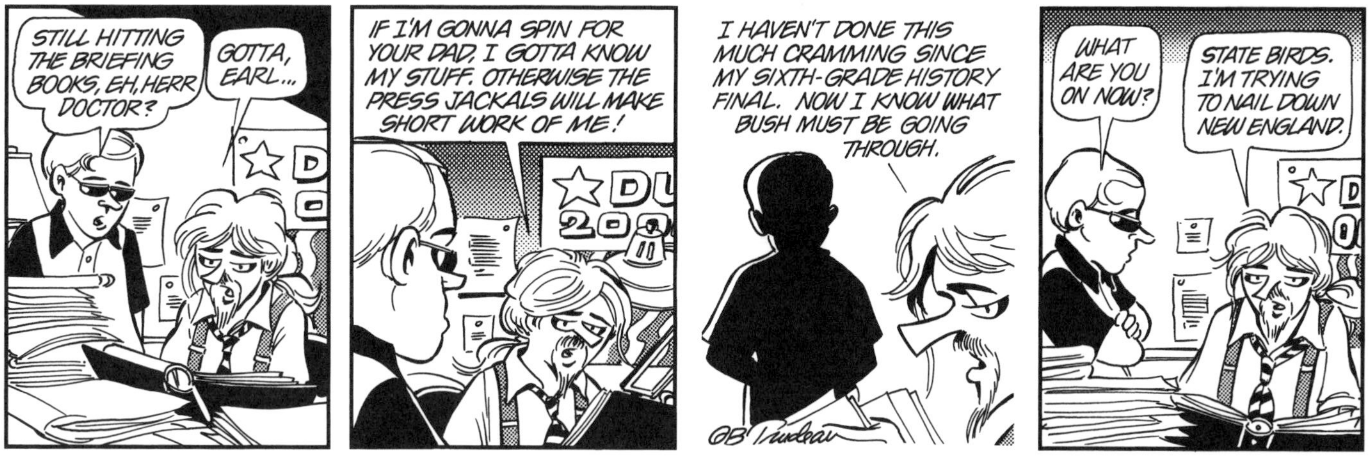
STILL HITTING THE BRIEFING BOOKS, EH, HERR DOCTOR?
GOTTA, EARL...
IF I'M GONNA SPIN FOR YOUR DAD, I GOTTA KNOW MY STUFF. OTHERWISE THE PRESS JACKALS WILL MAKE SHORT WORK OF ME!
I HAVEN'T DONE THIS MUCH CRAMMING SINCE MY SIXTH-GRADE HISTORY FINAL. NOW I KNOW WHAT BUSH MUST BE GOING THROUGH.
WHAT ARE YOU ON NOW?
STATE BIRDS. I'M TRYING TO NAIL DOWN NEW ENGLAND.

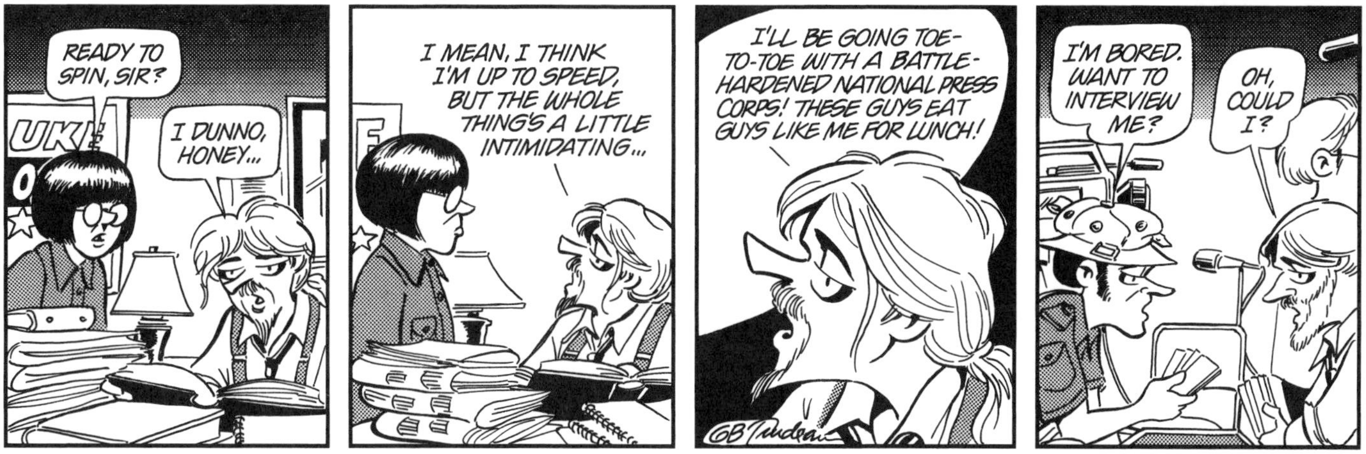
READY TO SPIN, SIR?
I DUNNO, HONEY...
I MEAN, I THINK I'M UP TO SPEED, BUT THE WHOLE THING'S A LITTLE INTIMIDATING...
I'LL BE GOING TOE-TO-TOE WITH A BATTLE-HARDENED NATIONAL PRESS CORPS! THESE GUYS EAT GUYS LIKE ME FOR LUNCH!
I'M BORED. WANT TO INTERVIEW ME?
OH, COULD I?

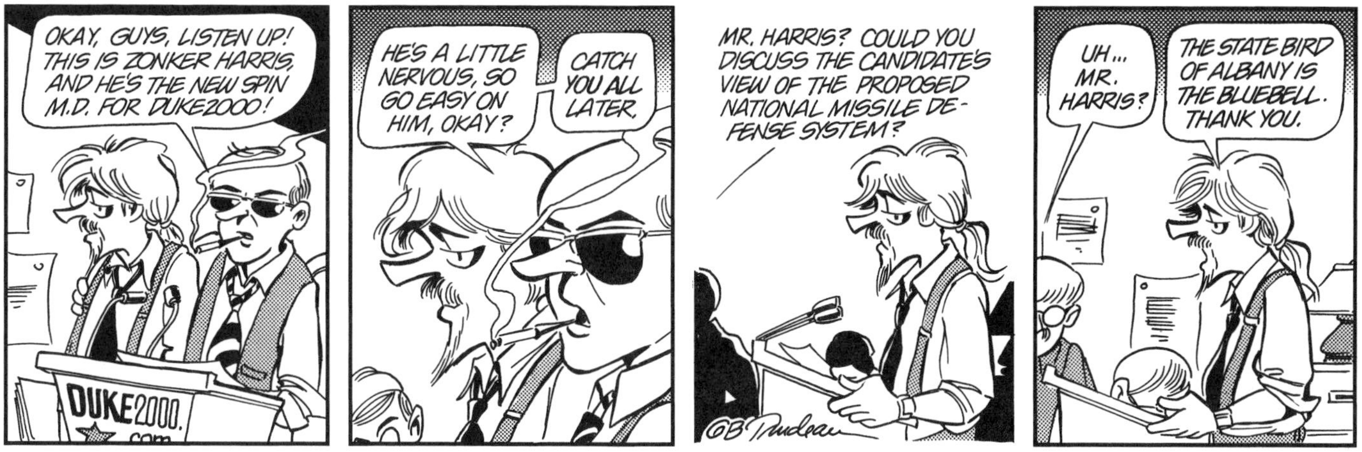
OKAY, GUYS, LISTEN UP! THIS IS ZONKER HARRIS, AND HE'S THE NEW SPIN M.D. FOR DUKE2000!
DUKE2000.com
HE'S A LITTLE NERVOUS, SO GO EASY ON HIM, OKAY?
CATCH YOU ALL LATER.
MR. HARRIS? COULD YOU DISCUSS THE CANDIDATE'S VIEW OF THE PROPOSED NATIONAL MISSILE DEFENSE SYSTEM?
UH... MR. HARRIS?
THE STATE BIRD OF ALBANY IS THE BLUEBELL. THANK YOU.

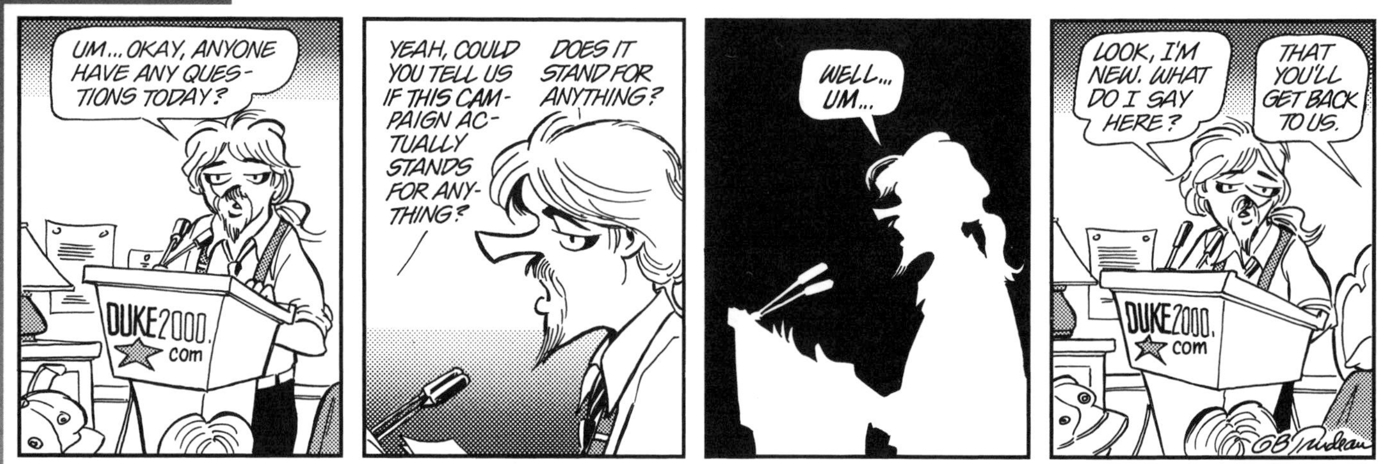
UM... OKAY, ANYONE HAVE ANY QUESTIONS TODAY?
DUKE2000.com
YEAH, COULD YOU TELL US IF THIS CAMPAIGN ACTUALLY STANDS FOR ANYTHING?
DOES IT STAND FOR ANYTHING?
WELL... UM...
LOOK, I'M NEW. WHAT DO I SAY HERE?
THAT YOU'LL GET BACK TO US.
DUKE2000.com

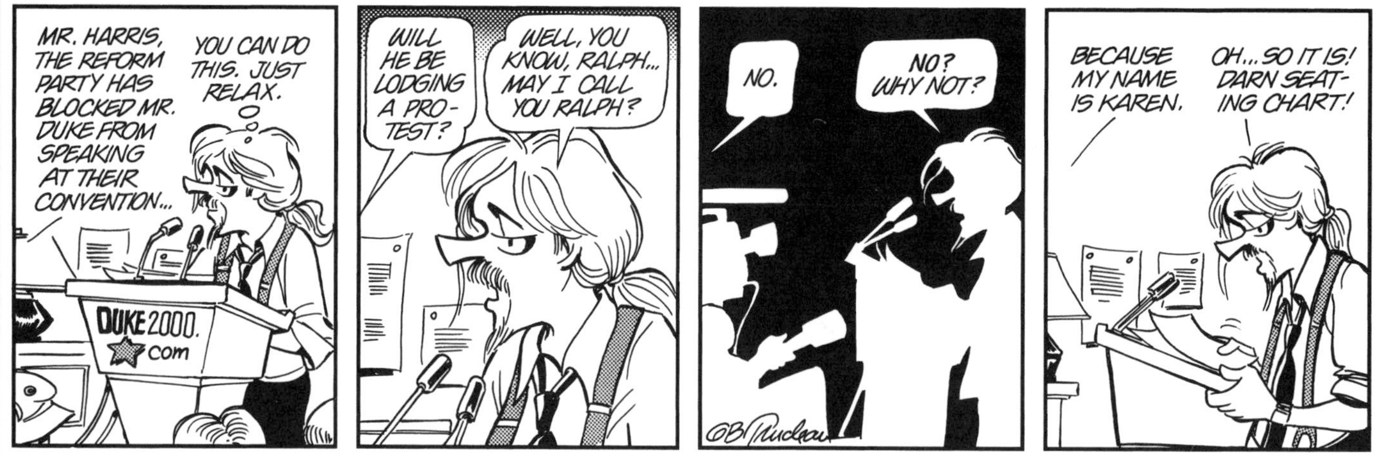
MR. HARRIS, THE REFORM PARTY HAS BLOCKED MR. DUKE FROM SPEAKING AT THEIR CONVENTION...
YOU CAN DO THIS. JUST RELAX.
DUKE2000.com
WILL HE BE LODGING A PROTEST?
WELL, YOU KNOW, RALPH... MAY I CALL YOU RALPH?
NO.
NO? WHY NOT?
BECAUSE MY NAME IS KAREN.
OH... SO IT IS! DARN SEATING CHART!

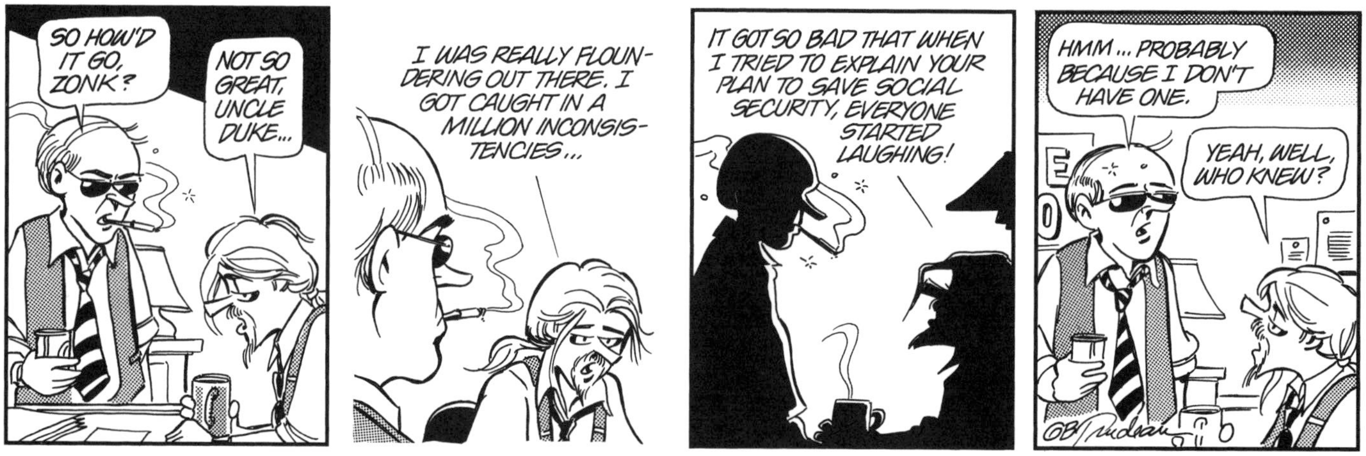
SO HOW'D IT GO, ZONK?
NOT SO GREAT, UNCLE DUKE...
I WAS REALLY FLOUNDERING OUT THERE. I GOT CAUGHT IN A MILLION INCONSISTENCIES...
IT GOT SO BAD THAT WHEN I TRIED TO EXPLAIN YOUR PLAN TO SAVE SOCIAL SECURITY, EVERYONE STARTED LAUGHING!
HMM... PROBABLY BECAUSE I DON'T HAVE ONE.
YEAH, WELL, WHO KNEW?

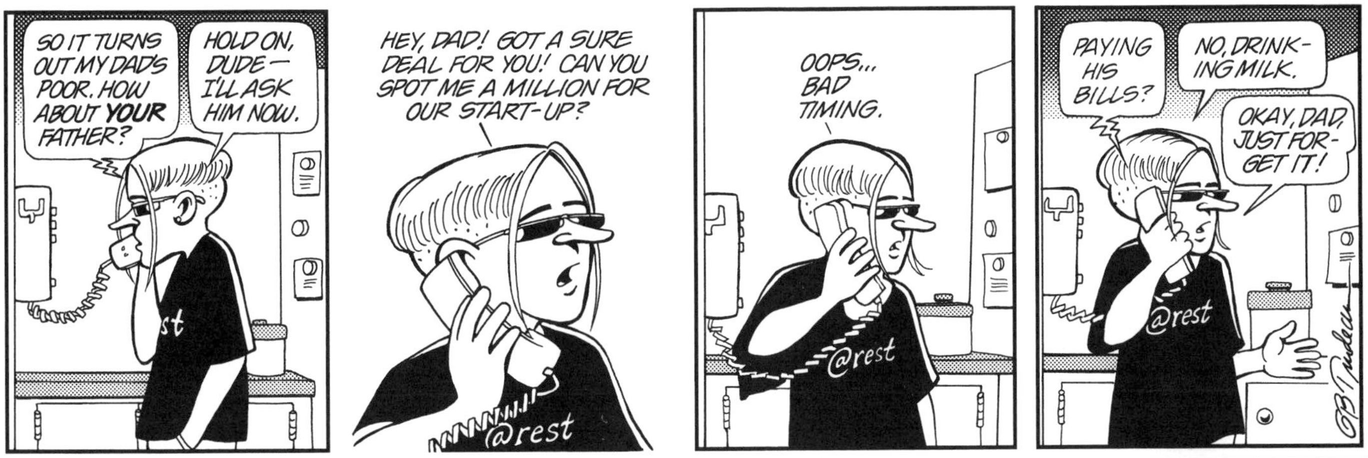
SO IT TURNS OUT MY DAD'S POOR. HOW ABOUT **YOUR** FATHER?
HOLD ON, DUDE— I'LL ASK HIM NOW.
HEY, DAD! GOT A SURE DEAL FOR YOU! CAN YOU SPOT ME A MILLION FOR OUR START-UP?
OOPS... BAD TIMING.
PAYING HIS BILLS?
NO, DRINKING MILK.
OKAY, DAD, JUST FORGET IT!
@rest

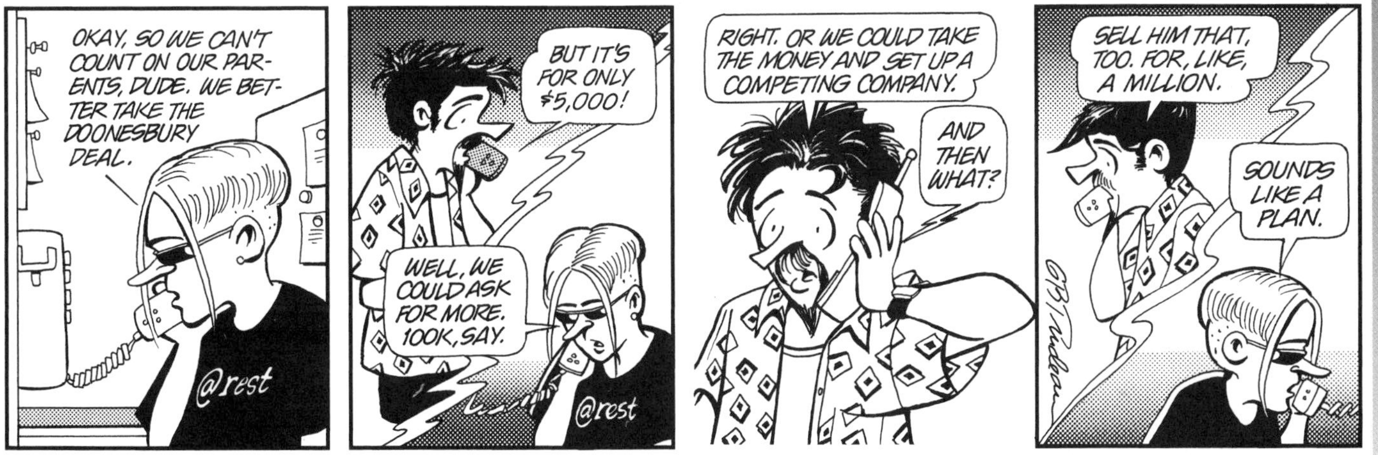
OKAY, SO WE CAN'T COUNT ON OUR PARENTS, DUDE. WE BETTER TAKE THE DOONESBURY DEAL.
BUT IT'S FOR ONLY $5,000!
WELL, WE COULD ASK FOR MORE. 100K, SAY.
RIGHT. OR WE COULD TAKE THE MONEY AND SET UP A COMPETING COMPANY.
AND THEN WHAT?
SELL HIM THAT, TOO. FOR, LIKE, A MILLION.
SOUNDS LIKE A PLAN.
@rest

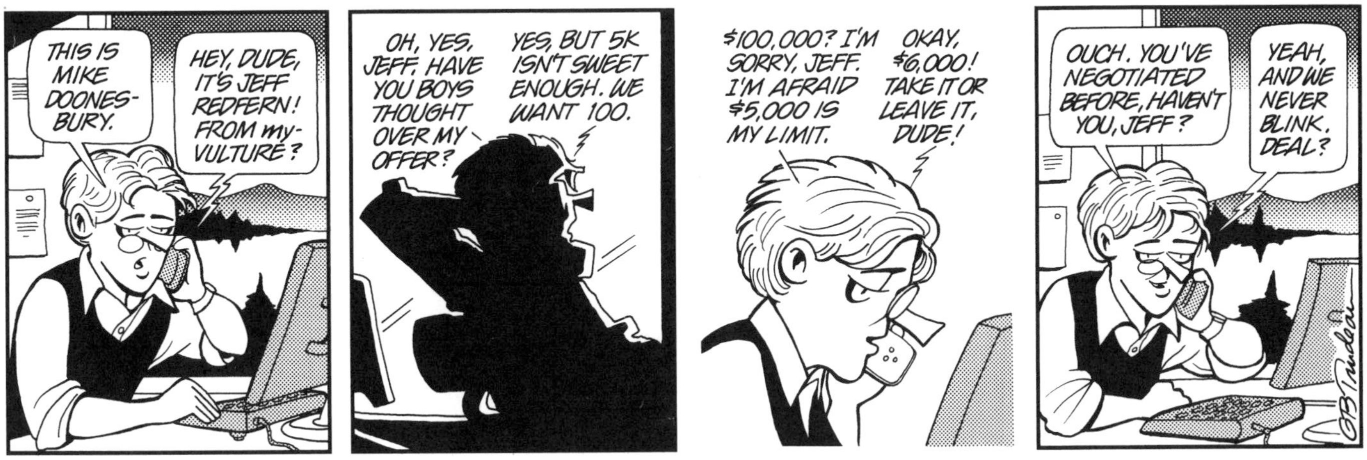
THIS IS MIKE DOONESBURY.
HEY, DUDE, IT'S JEFF REDFERN! FROM myVULTURE?
OH, YES, JEFF. HAVE YOU BOYS THOUGHT OVER MY OFFER?
YES, BUT 5K ISN'T SWEET ENOUGH. WE WANT 100.
$100,000? I'M SORRY, JEFF. I'M AFRAID $5,000 IS MY LIMIT.
OKAY, $6,000! TAKE IT OR LEAVE IT, DUDE!
OUCH. YOU'VE NEGOTIATED BEFORE, HAVEN'T YOU, JEFF?
YEAH, AND WE NEVER BLINK. DEAL?

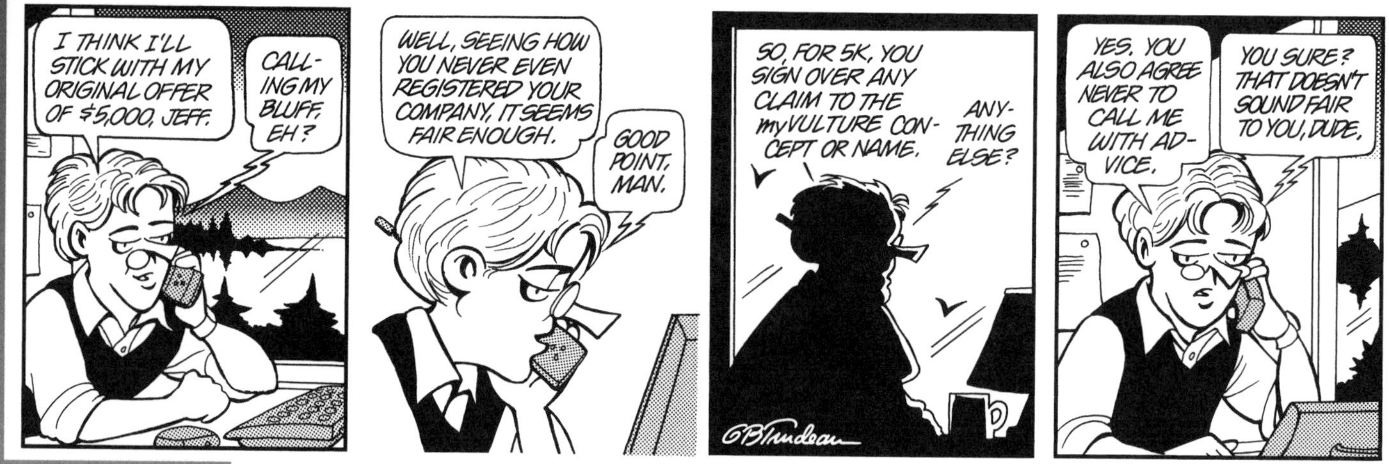
I THINK I'LL STICK WITH MY ORIGINAL OFFER OF $5,000, JEFF.
CALL-ING MY BLUFF, EH?
WELL, SEEING HOW YOU NEVER EVEN REGISTERED YOUR COMPANY, IT SEEMS FAIR ENOUGH.
GOOD POINT, MAN.
SO, FOR 5K, YOU SIGN OVER ANY CLAIM TO THE myVULTURE CON-CEPT OR NAME.
ANY-THING ELSE?
GB Trudeau
YES. YOU ALSO AGREE NEVER TO CALL ME WITH AD-VICE.
YOU SURE? THAT DOESN'T SOUND FAIR TO YOU, DUDE.

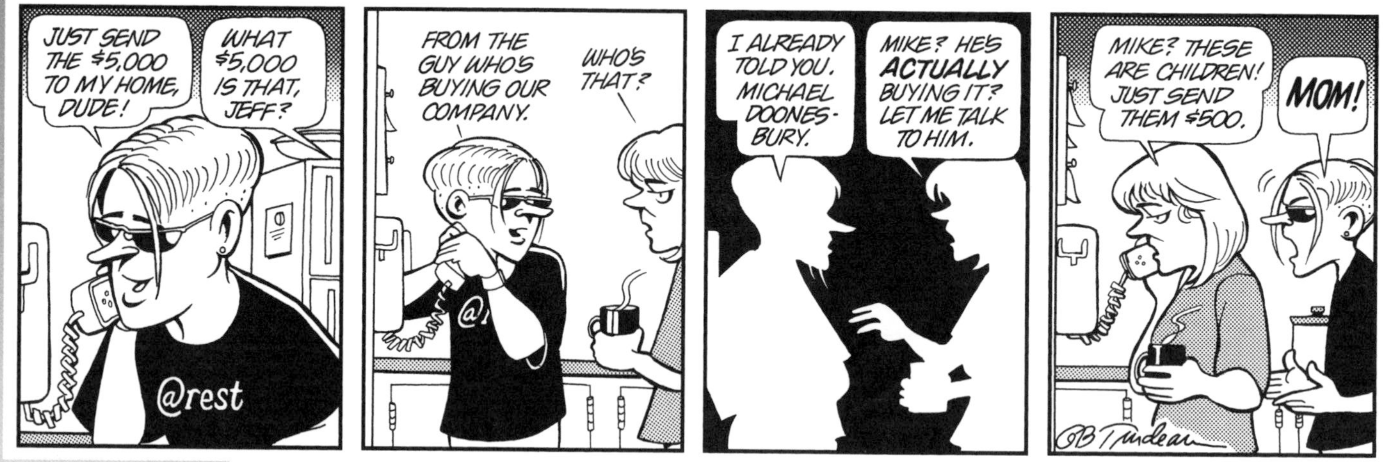
JUST SEND THE $5,000 TO MY HOME, DUDE!
WHAT $5,000 IS THAT, JEFF?
@rest
FROM THE GUY WHO'S BUYING OUR COMPANY.
WHO'S THAT?
I ALREADY TOLD YOU. MICHAEL DOONES-BURY.
MIKE? HE'S **ACTUALLY** BUYING IT? LET ME TALK TO HIM.
MIKE? THESE ARE CHILDREN! JUST SEND THEM $500.
MOM!
GB Trudeau

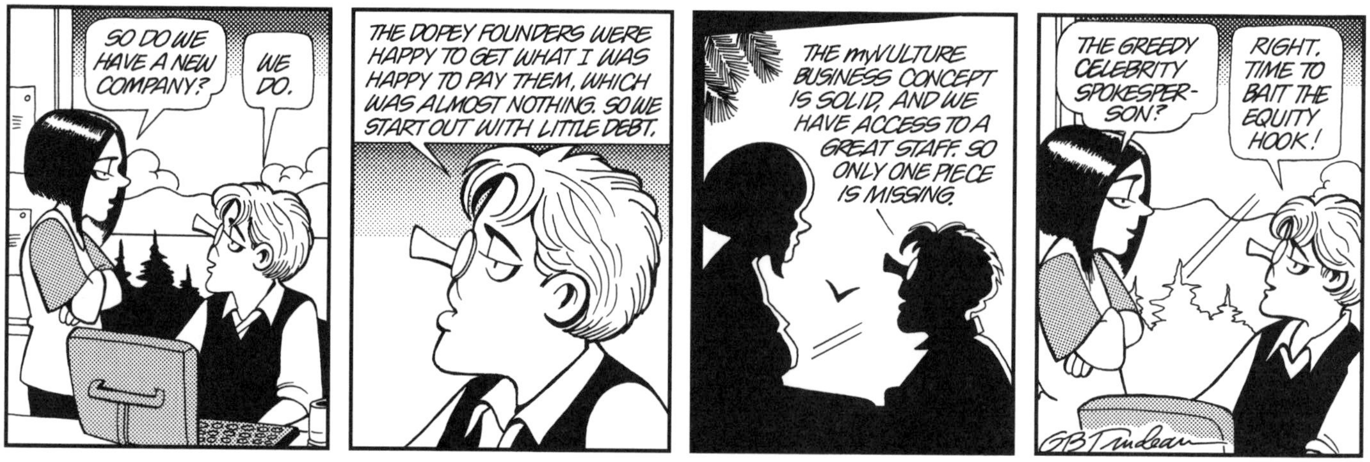
SO DO WE HAVE A NEW COMPANY?
WE DO.
THE DOPEY FOUNDERS WERE HAPPY TO GET WHAT I WAS HAPPY TO PAY THEM, WHICH WAS ALMOST NOTHING. SO WE START OUT WITH LITTLE DEBT.
THE myVULTURE BUSINESS CONCEPT IS SOLID, AND WE HAVE ACCESS TO A GREAT STAFF. SO ONLY ONE PIECE IS MISSING.
THE GREEDY CELEBRITY SPOKESPER-SON?
RIGHT. TIME TO BAIT THE EQUITY HOOK!
GB Trudeau

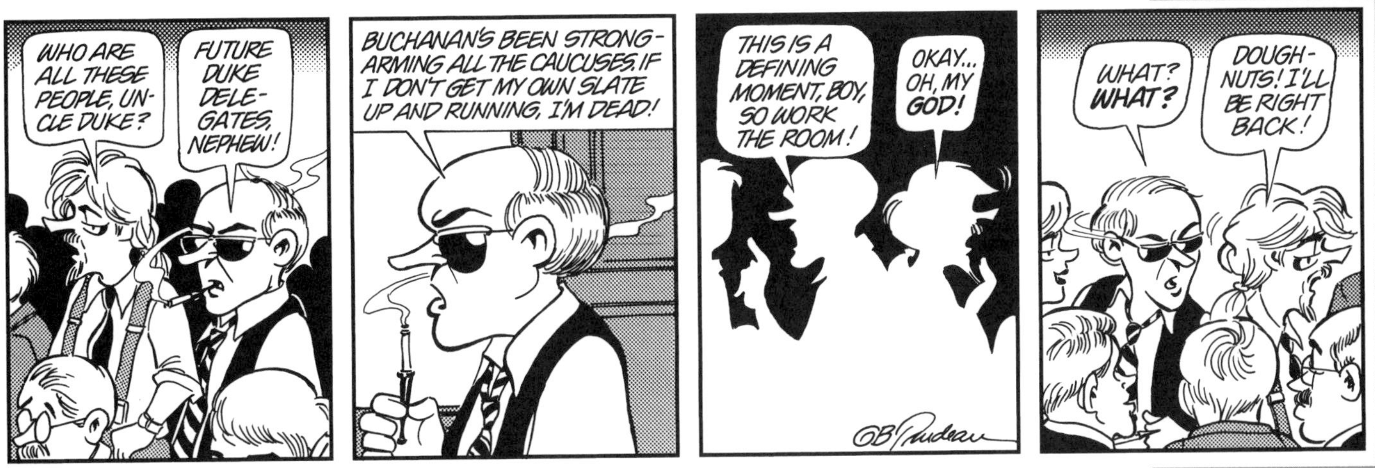
WHO ARE ALL THESE PEOPLE, UNCLE DUKE?
FUTURE DUKE DELEGATES, NEPHEW!
BUCHANAN'S BEEN STRONG-ARMING ALL THE CAUCUSES. IF I DON'T GET MY OWN SLATE UP AND RUNNING, I'M DEAD!
THIS IS A DEFINING MOMENT, BOY, SO WORK THE ROOM!
OKAY... OH, MY GOD!
WHAT? WHAT?
DOUGHNUTS! I'LL BE RIGHT BACK!

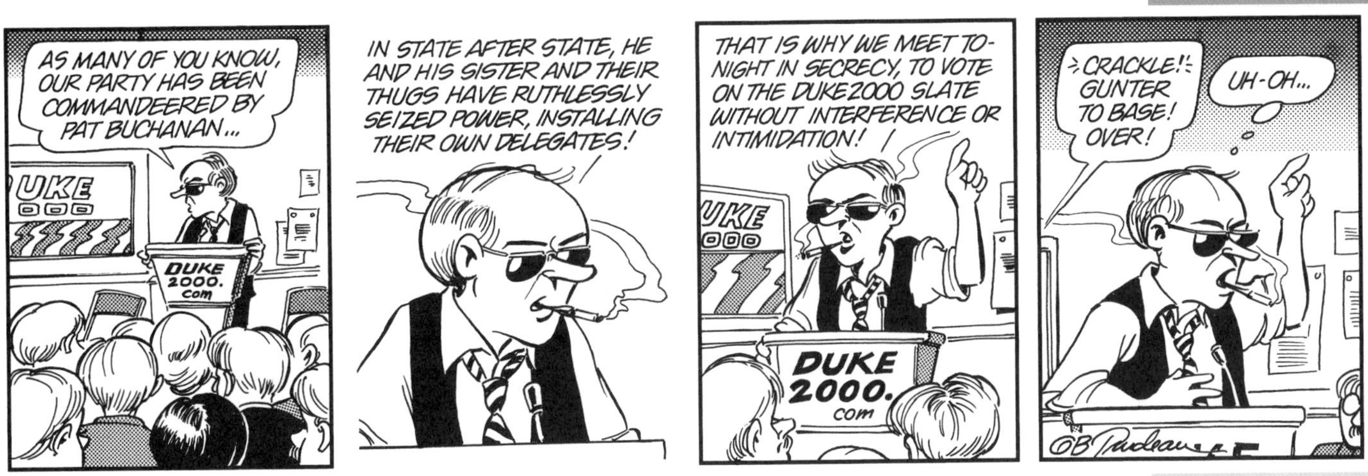
AS MANY OF YOU KNOW, OUR PARTY HAS BEEN COMMANDEERED BY PAT BUCHANAN...
DUKE 2000.com
IN STATE AFTER STATE, HE AND HIS SISTER AND THEIR THUGS HAVE RUTHLESSLY SEIZED POWER, INSTALLING THEIR OWN DELEGATES!
THAT IS WHY WE MEET TONIGHT IN SECRECY, TO VOTE ON THE DUKE2000 SLATE WITHOUT INTERFERENCE OR INTIMIDATION!
DUKE 2000.com
CRACKLE! GUNTER TO BASE! OVER!
UH-OH...

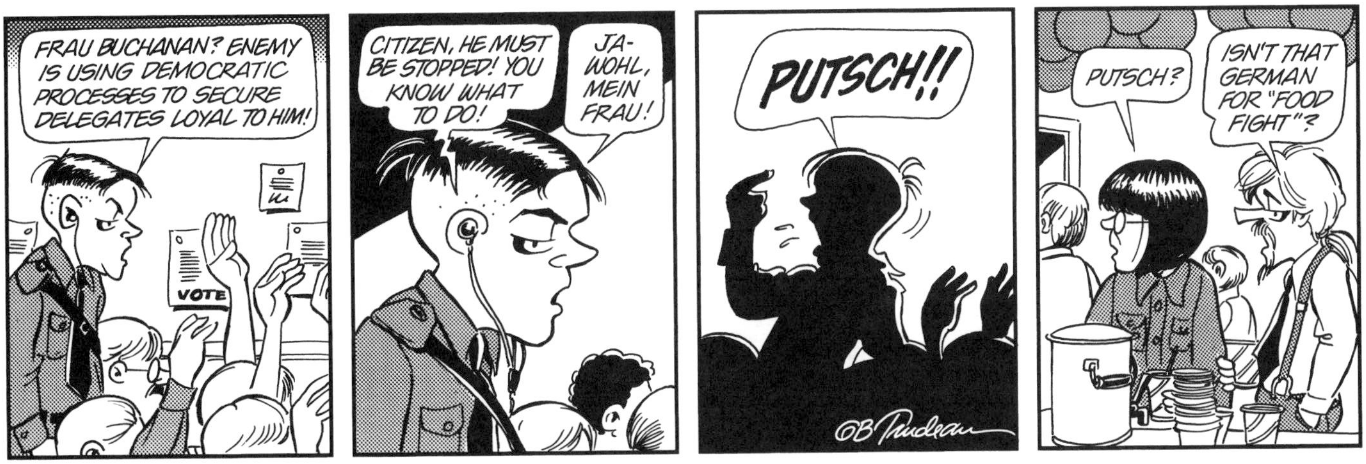
FRAU BUCHANAN? ENEMY IS USING DEMOCRATIC PROCESSES TO SECURE DELEGATES LOYAL TO HIM!
VOTE
CITIZEN, HE MUST BE STOPPED! YOU KNOW WHAT TO DO!
JAWOHL, MEIN FRAU!
PUTSCH!!
PUTSCH?
ISN'T THAT GERMAN FOR "FOOD FIGHT"?

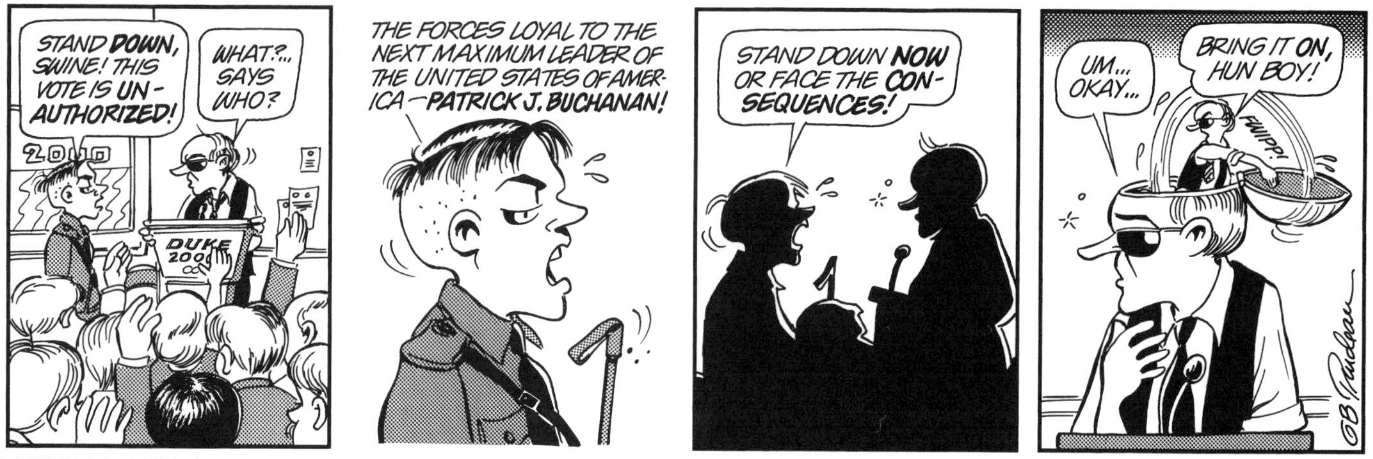
STAND DOWN, SWINE! THIS VOTE IS UN-AUTHORIZED!
WHAT?... SAYS WHO?
2010
DUKE 2000
THE FORCES LOYAL TO THE NEXT MAXIMUM LEADER OF THE UNITED STATES OF AMERICA—PATRICK J. BUCHANAN!
STAND DOWN NOW OR FACE THE CONSEQUENCES!
UM... OKAY...
BRING IT ON, HUN BOY!
FWIPP!

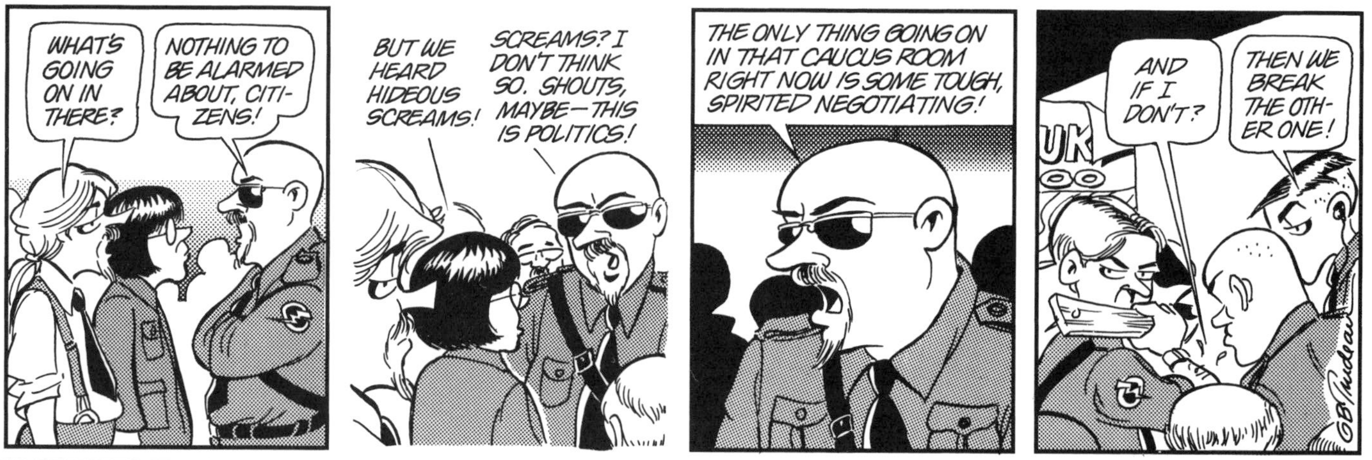
WHAT'S GOING ON IN THERE?
NOTHING TO BE ALARMED ABOUT, CITIZENS!
BUT WE HEARD HIDEOUS SCREAMS!
SCREAMS? I DON'T THINK SO. SHOUTS, MAYBE—THIS IS POLITICS!
THE ONLY THING GOING ON IN THAT CAUCUS ROOM RIGHT NOW IS SOME TOUGH, SPIRITED NEGOTIATING!
AND IF I DON'T?
THEN WE BREAK THE OTHER ONE!

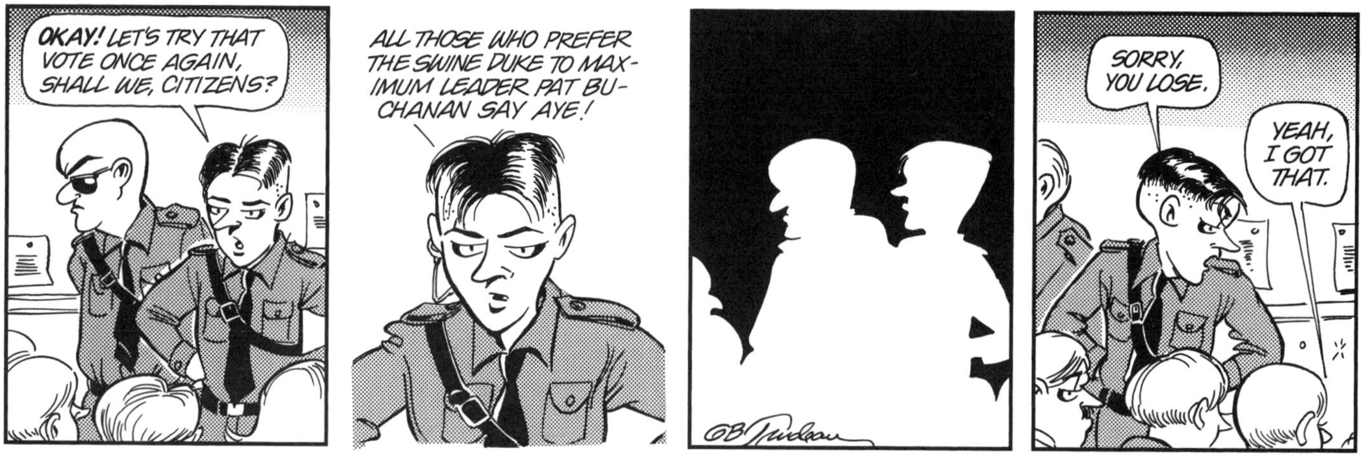
OKAY! LET'S TRY THAT VOTE ONCE AGAIN, SHALL WE, CITIZENS?
ALL THOSE WHO PREFER THE SWINE DUKE TO MAXIMUM LEADER PAT BUCHANAN SAY AYE!
SORRY, YOU LOSE.
YEAH, I GOT THAT.

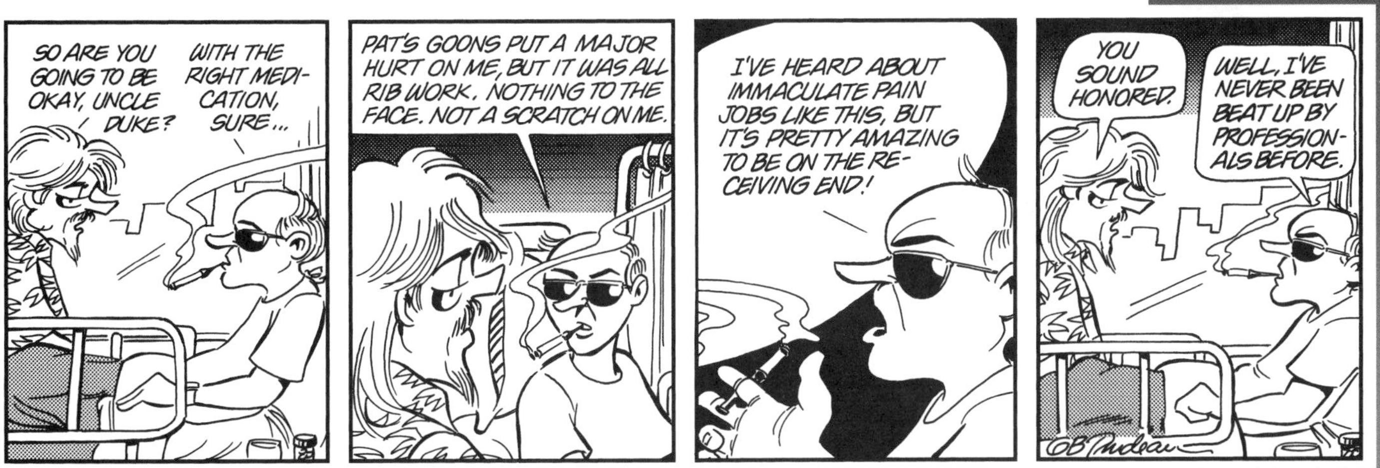
SO ARE YOU GOING TO BE OKAY, UNCLE DUKE?
WITH THE RIGHT MEDI-CATION, SURE...
PAT'S GOONS PUT A MAJOR HURT ON ME, BUT IT WAS ALL RIB WORK. NOTHING TO THE FACE. NOT A SCRATCH ON ME.
I'VE HEARD ABOUT IMMACULATE PAIN JOBS LIKE THIS, BUT IT'S PRETTY AMAZING TO BE ON THE RE-CEIVING END!
YOU SOUND HONORED.
WELL, I'VE NEVER BEEN BEAT UP BY PROFESSION-ALS BEFORE.
GB Trudeau

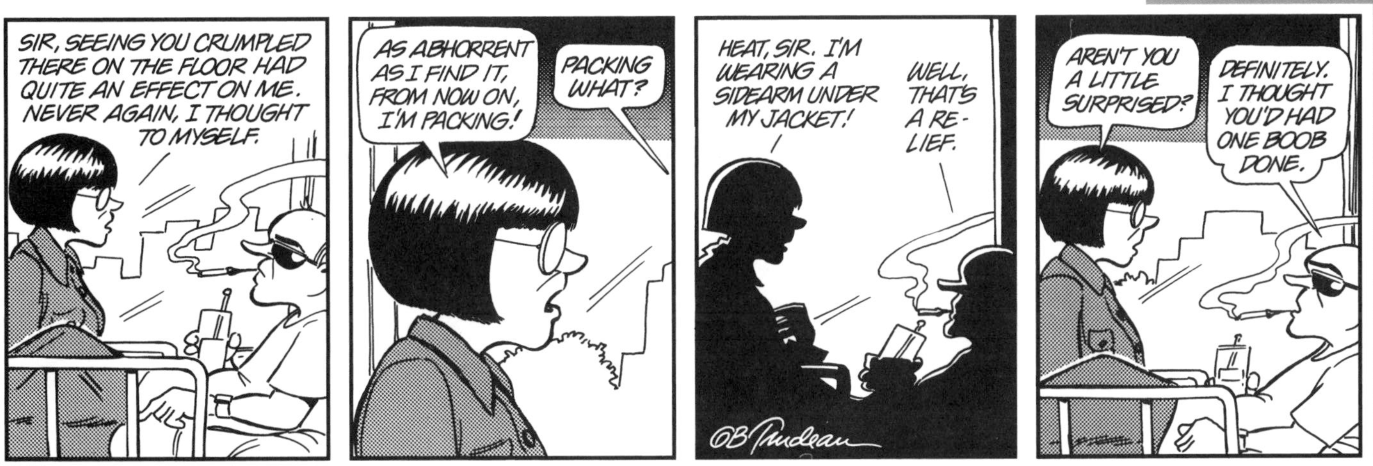
SIR, SEEING YOU CRUMPLED THERE ON THE FLOOR HAD QUITE AN EFFECT ON ME. NEVER AGAIN, I THOUGHT TO MYSELF.
AS ABHORRENT AS I FIND IT, FROM NOW ON, I'M PACKING!
PACKING WHAT?
HEAT, SIR. I'M WEARING A SIDEARM UNDER MY JACKET!
WELL, THAT'S A RE-LIEF.
GB Trudeau
AREN'T YOU A LITTLE SURPRISED?
DEFINITELY. I THOUGHT YOU'D HAD ONE BOOB DONE.

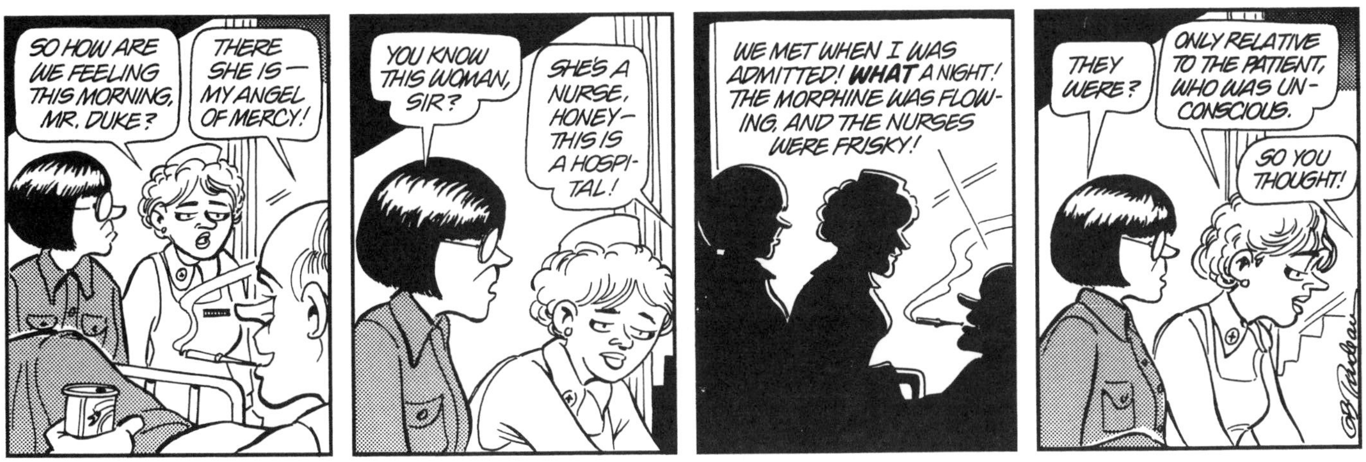
SO HOW ARE WE FEELING THIS MORNING, MR. DUKE?
THERE SHE IS— MY ANGEL OF MERCY!
YOU KNOW THIS WOMAN, SIR?
SHE'S A NURSE, HONEY— THIS IS A HOSPI-TAL!
WE MET WHEN I WAS ADMITTED! WHAT A NIGHT! THE MORPHINE WAS FLOW-ING, AND THE NURSES WERE FRISKY!
THEY WERE?
ONLY RELATIVE TO THE PATIENT, WHO WAS UN-CONSCIOUS.
SO YOU THOUGHT!
GB Trudeau

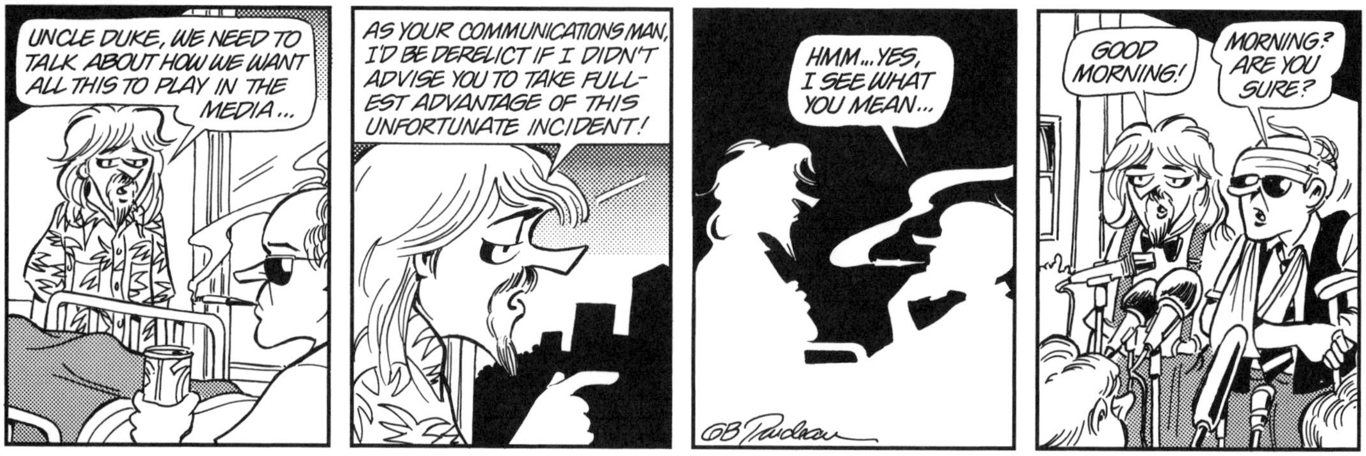
UNCLE DUKE, WE NEED TO TALK ABOUT HOW WE WANT ALL THIS TO PLAY IN THE MEDIA...
AS YOUR COMMUNICATIONS MAN, I'D BE DERELICT IF I DIDN'T ADVISE YOU TO TAKE FULL-EST ADVANTAGE OF THIS UNFORTUNATE INCIDENT!
HMM...YES, I SEE WHAT YOU MEAN...
GOOD MORNING!
MORNING? ARE YOU SURE?

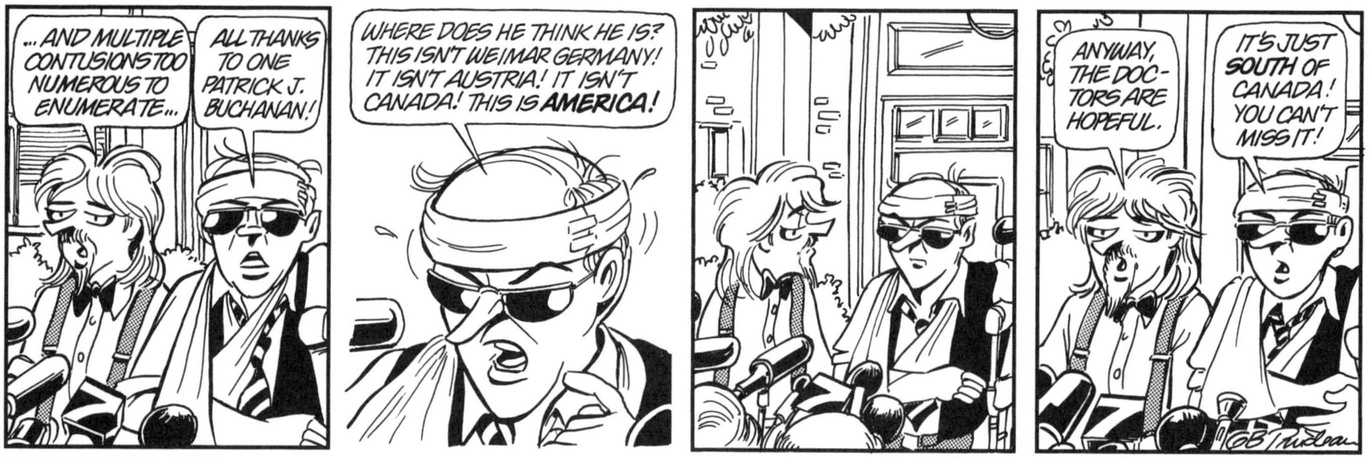
...AND MULTIPLE CONTUSIONS TOO NUMEROUS TO ENUMERATE...
ALL THANKS TO ONE PATRICK J. BUCHANAN!
WHERE DOES HE THINK HE IS? THIS ISN'T WEIMAR GERMANY! IT ISN'T AUSTRIA! IT ISN'T CANADA! THIS IS **AMERICA**!
ANYWAY, THE DOC-TORS ARE HOPEFUL.
IT'S JUST **SOUTH** OF CANADA! YOU CAN'T MISS IT!

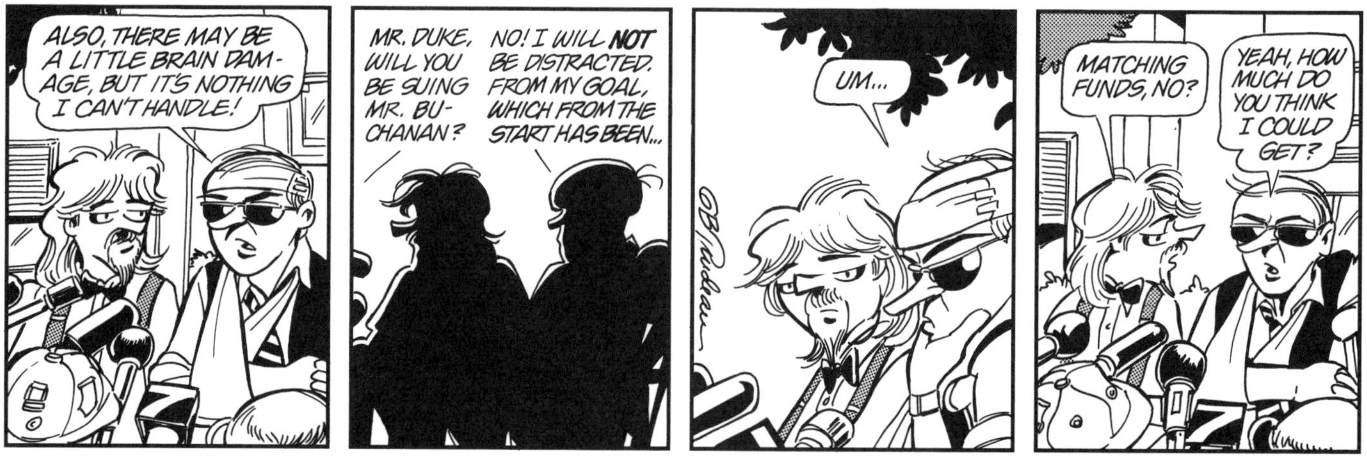
ALSO, THERE MAY BE A LITTLE BRAIN DAM-AGE, BUT IT'S NOTHING I CAN'T HANDLE!
MR. DUKE, WILL YOU BE SUING MR. BU-CHANAN?
NO! I WILL **NOT** BE DISTRACTED FROM MY GOAL, WHICH FROM THE START HAS BEEN...
UM...
MATCHING FUNDS, NO?
YEAH, HOW MUCH DO YOU THINK I COULD GET?

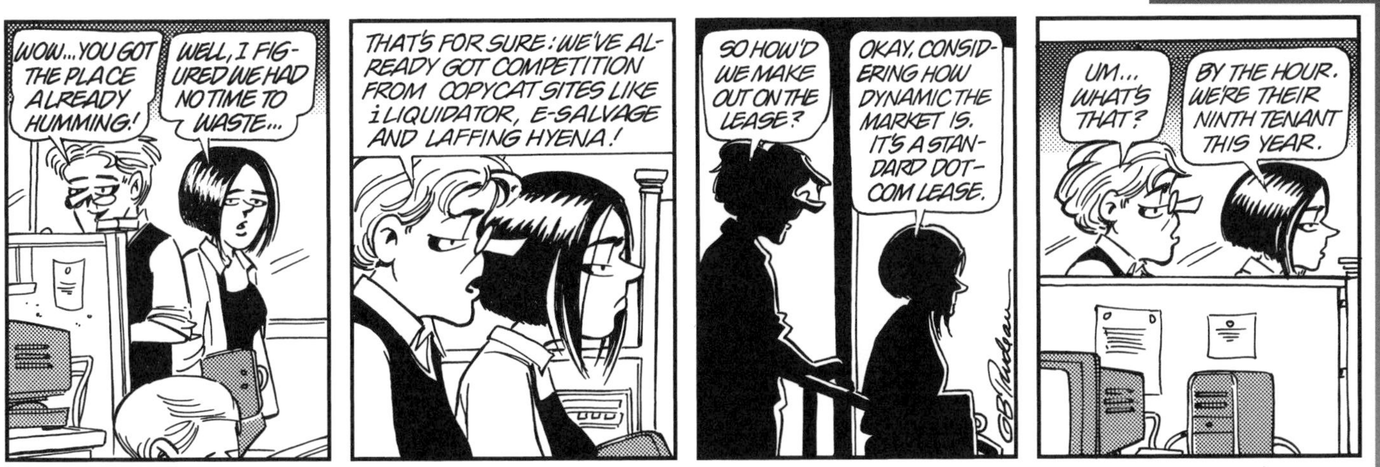
WOW... YOU GOT THE PLACE ALREADY HUMMING!
WELL, I FIGURED WE HAD NO TIME TO WASTE...
THAT'S FOR SURE: WE'VE ALREADY GOT COMPETITION FROM COPYCAT SITES LIKE iLIQUIDATOR, E-SALVAGE AND LAFFING HYENA!
SO HOW'D WE MAKE OUT ON THE LEASE?
OKAY, CONSIDERING HOW DYNAMIC THE MARKET IS. IT'S A STANDARD DOT-COM LEASE.
UM... WHAT'S THAT?
BY THE HOUR. WE'RE THEIR NINTH TENANT THIS YEAR.

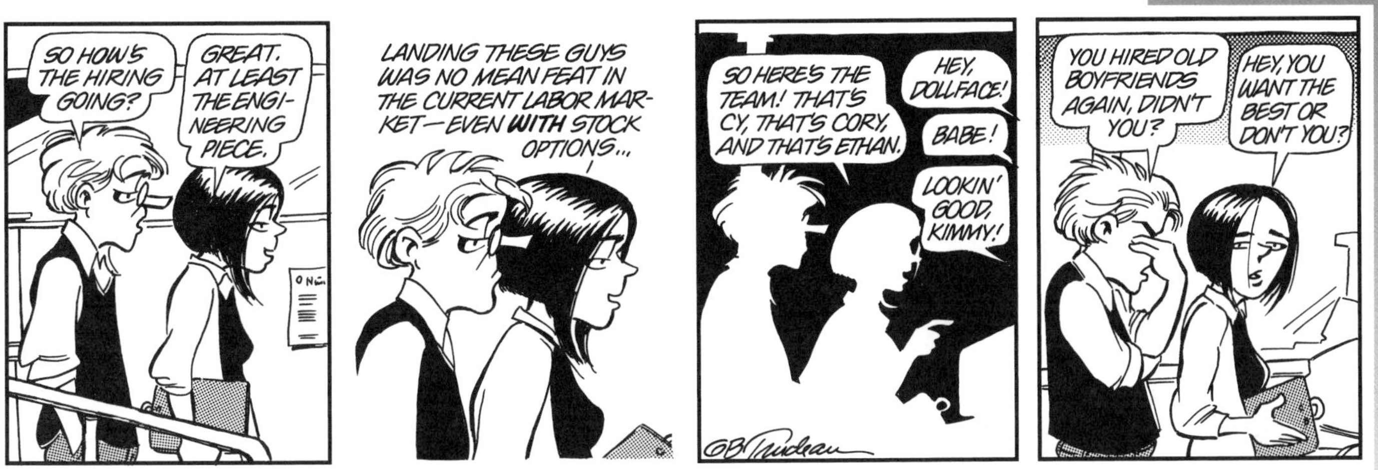
SO HOW'S THE HIRING GOING?
GREAT. AT LEAST THE ENGINEERING PIECE.
LANDING THESE GUYS WAS NO MEAN FEAT IN THE CURRENT LABOR MARKET—EVEN WITH STOCK OPTIONS...
SO HERE'S THE TEAM! THAT'S CY, THAT'S CORY, AND THAT'S ETHAN.
HEY, DOLLFACE!
BABE!
LOOKIN' GOOD, KIMMY!
YOU HIRED OLD BOYFRIENDS AGAIN, DIDN'T YOU?
HEY, YOU WANT THE BEST OR DON'T YOU?

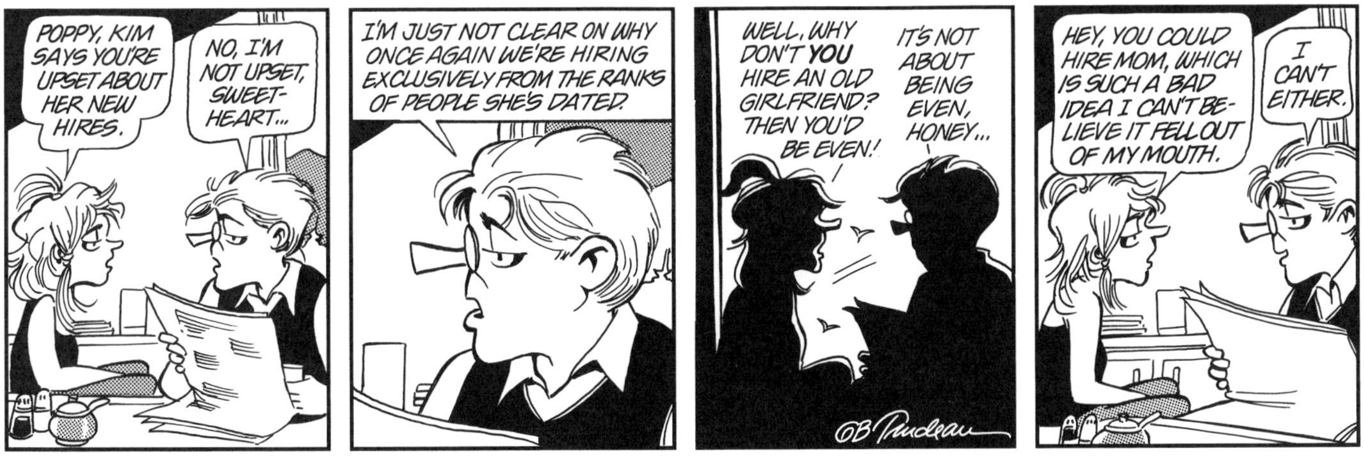
POPPY, KIM SAYS YOU'RE UPSET ABOUT HER NEW HIRES.
NO, I'M NOT UPSET, SWEETHEART...
I'M JUST NOT CLEAR ON WHY ONCE AGAIN WE'RE HIRING EXCLUSIVELY FROM THE RANKS OF PEOPLE SHE'S DATED.
WELL, WHY DON'T YOU HIRE AN OLD GIRLFRIEND? THEN YOU'D BE EVEN!
IT'S NOT ABOUT BEING EVEN, HONEY...
HEY, YOU COULD HIRE MOM, WHICH IS SUCH A BAD IDEA I CAN'T BELIEVE IT FELL OUT OF MY MOUTH.
I CAN'T EITHER.

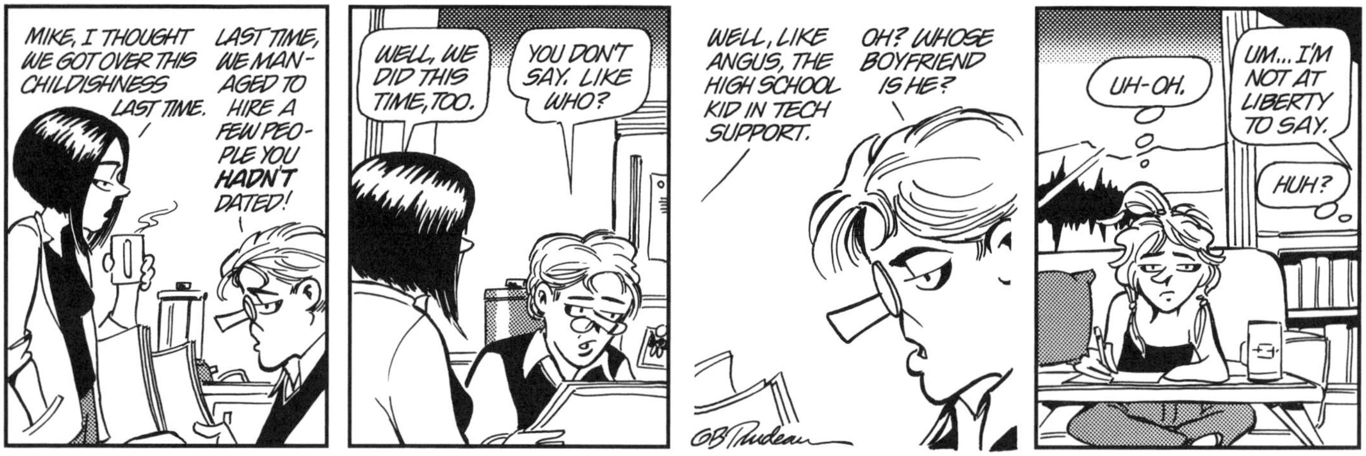
MIKE, I THOUGHT WE GOT OVER THIS CHILDISHNESS LAST TIME.
LAST TIME, WE MANAGED TO HIRE A FEW PEOPLE YOU **HADN'T** DATED!
WELL, WE DID THIS TIME, TOO.
YOU DON'T SAY. LIKE WHO?
WELL, LIKE ANGUS, THE HIGH SCHOOL KID IN TECH SUPPORT.
OH? WHOSE BOYFRIEND IS HE?
UH-OH.
UM... I'M NOT AT LIBERTY TO SAY.
HUH?

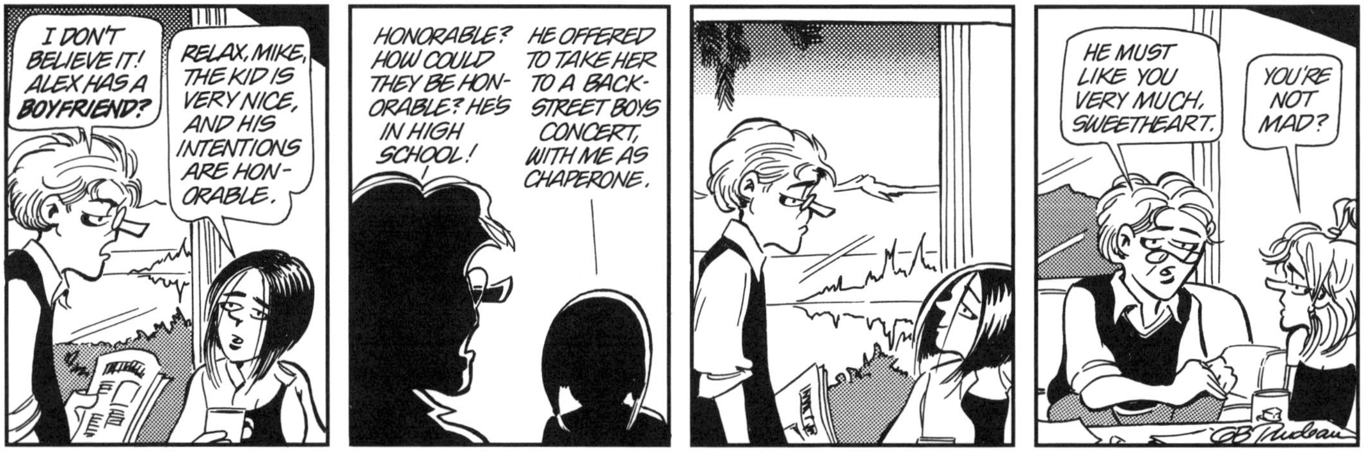
I DON'T BELIEVE IT! ALEX HAS A **BOYFRIEND?**
RELAX, MIKE, THE KID IS VERY NICE, AND HIS INTENTIONS ARE HONORABLE.
HONORABLE? HOW COULD THEY BE HONORABLE? HE'S IN HIGH SCHOOL!
HE OFFERED TO TAKE HER TO A BACKSTREET BOYS CONCERT, WITH ME AS CHAPERONE.
HE MUST LIKE YOU VERY MUCH, SWEETHEART.
YOU'RE NOT MAD?

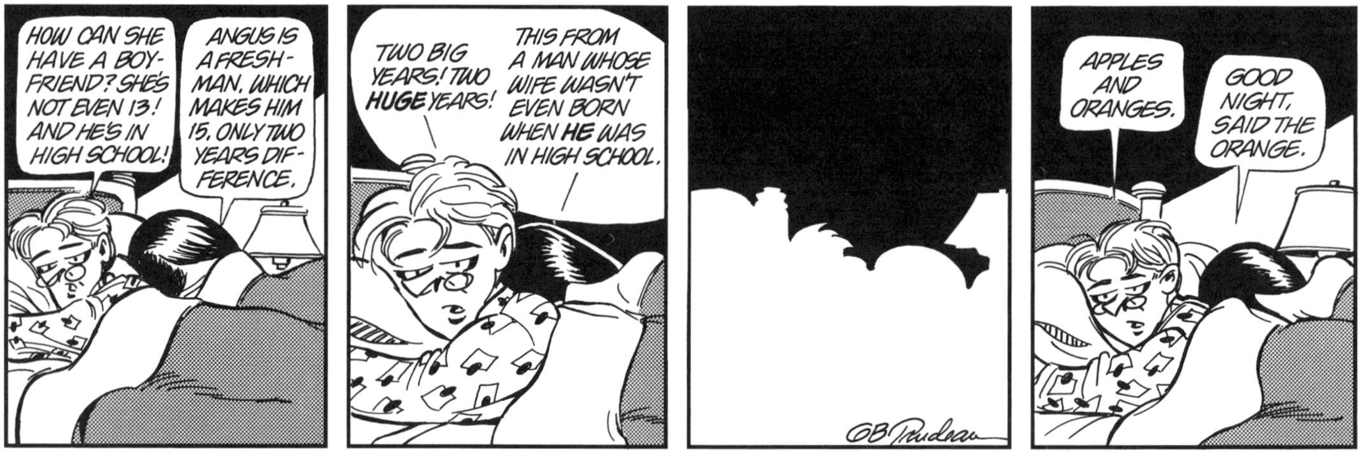
HOW CAN SHE HAVE A BOYFRIEND? SHE'S NOT EVEN 13! AND HE'S IN HIGH SCHOOL!
ANGUS IS A FRESHMAN, WHICH MAKES HIM 15. ONLY TWO YEARS DIFFERENCE.
TWO BIG YEARS! TWO **HUGE** YEARS!
THIS FROM A MAN WHOSE WIFE WASN'T EVEN BORN WHEN **HE** WAS IN HIGH SCHOOL.
APPLES AND ORANGES.
GOOD NIGHT, SAID THE ORANGE.

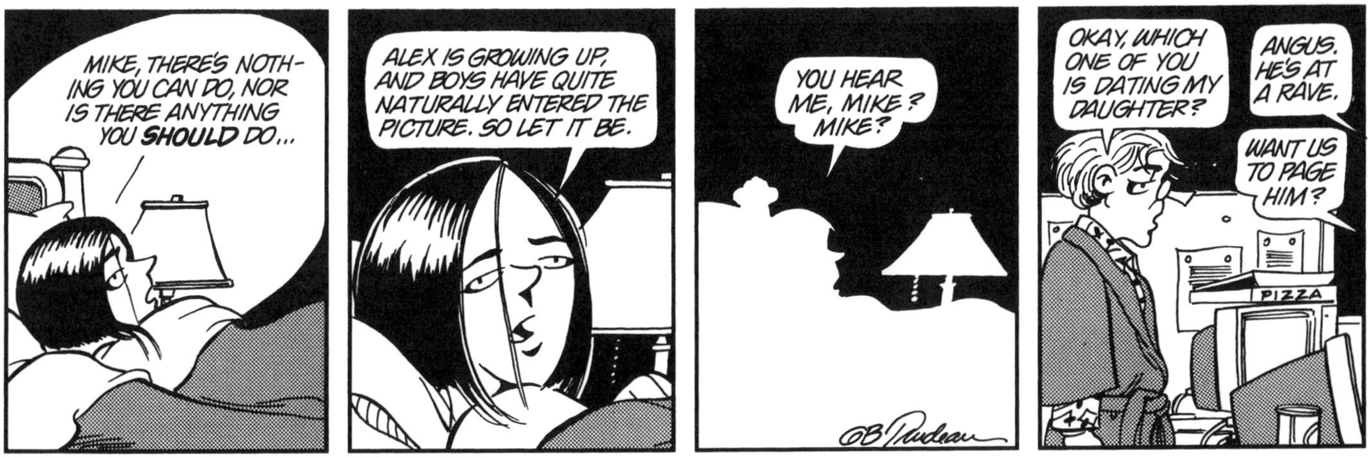
MIKE, THERE'S NOTHING YOU CAN DO, NOR IS THERE ANYTHING YOU **SHOULD** DO...
ALEX IS GROWING UP, AND BOYS HAVE QUITE NATURALLY ENTERED THE PICTURE. SO LET IT BE.
YOU HEAR ME, MIKE? MIKE?
OKAY, WHICH ONE OF YOU IS DATING MY DAUGHTER?
ANGUS. HE'S AT A RAVE.
WANT US TO PAGE HIM?
PIZZA

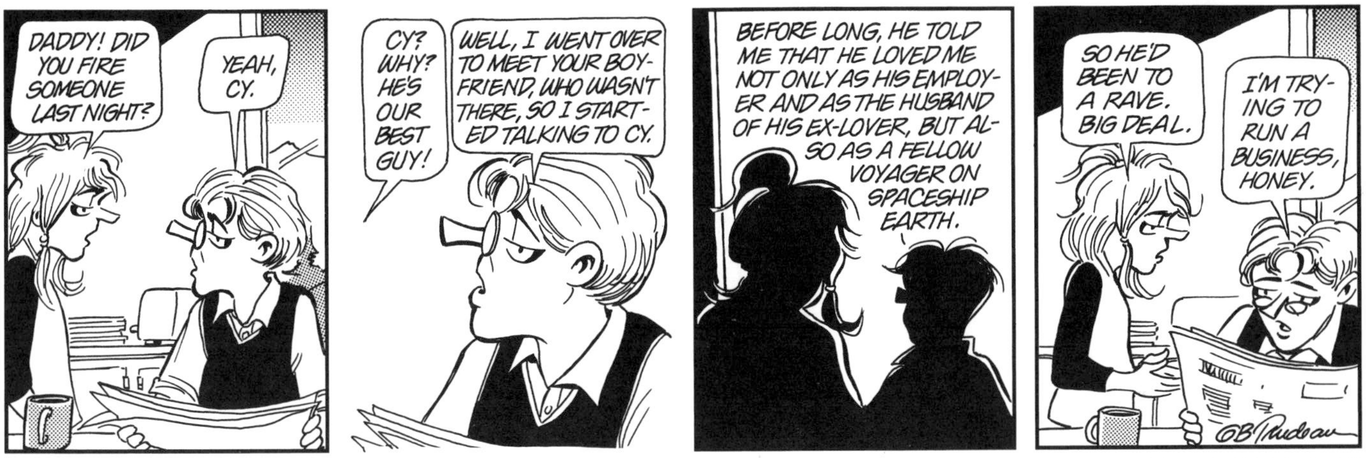
DADDY! DID YOU FIRE SOMEONE LAST NIGHT?
YEAH, CY.
CY? WHY? HE'S OUR BEST GUY!
WELL, I WENT OVER TO MEET YOUR BOYFRIEND, WHO WASN'T THERE, SO I STARTED TALKING TO CY.
BEFORE LONG, HE TOLD ME THAT HE LOVED ME NOT ONLY AS HIS EMPLOYER AND AS THE HUSBAND OF HIS EX-LOVER, BUT ALSO AS A FELLOW VOYAGER ON SPACESHIP EARTH.
SO HE'D BEEN TO A RAVE. BIG DEAL.
I'M TRYING TO RUN A BUSINESS, HONEY.

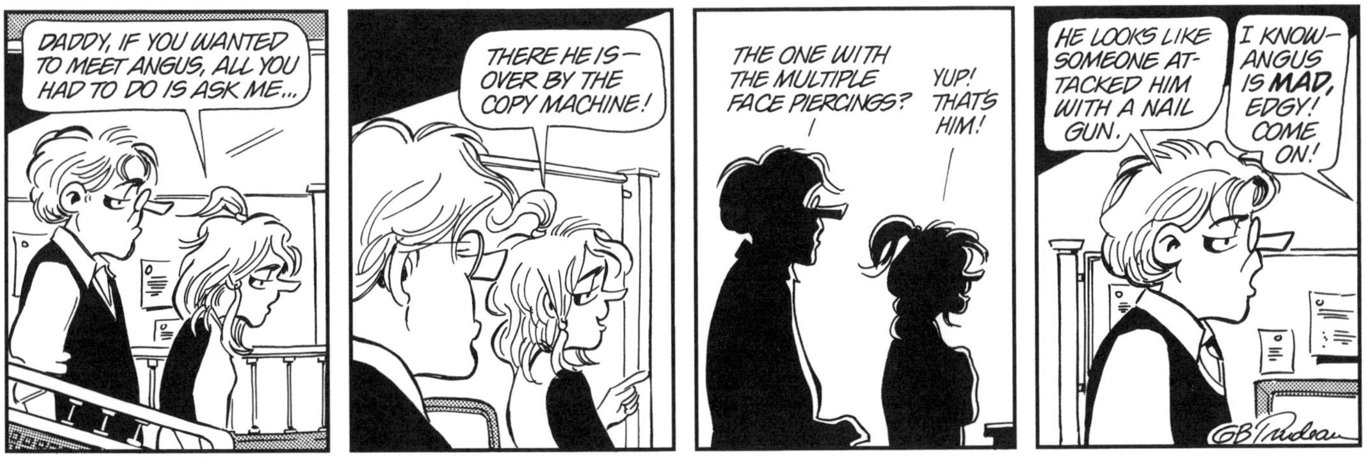
DADDY, IF YOU WANTED TO MEET ANGUS, ALL YOU HAD TO DO IS ASK ME...
THERE HE IS— OVER BY THE COPY MACHINE!
THE ONE WITH THE MULTIPLE FACE PIERCINGS?
YUP! THAT'S HIM!
HE LOOKS LIKE SOMEONE ATTACKED HIM WITH A NAIL GUN.
I KNOW— ANGUS IS **MAD**, EDGY! COME ON!

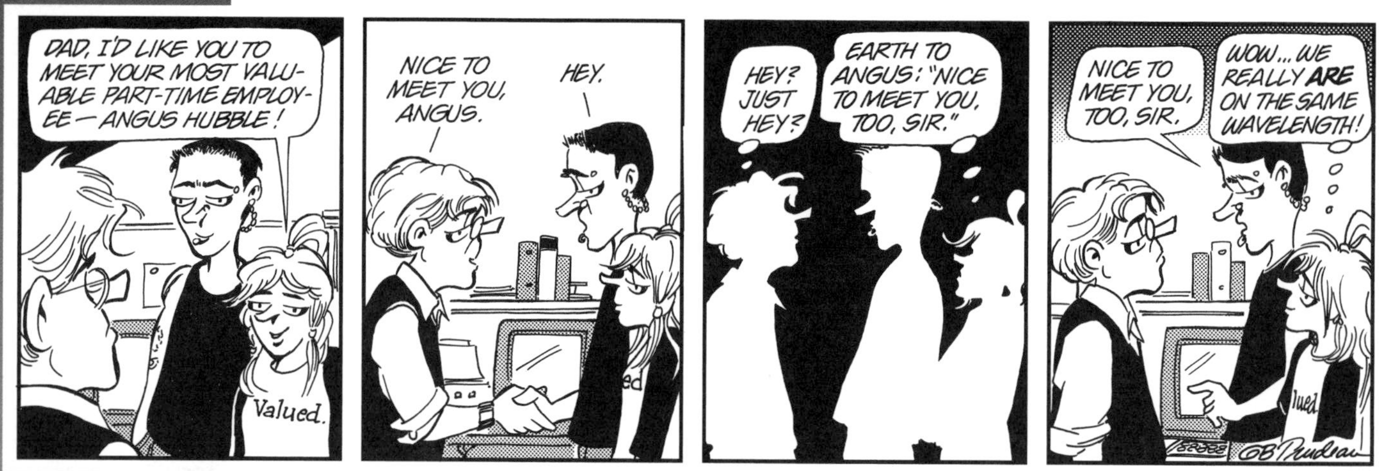
DAD, I'D LIKE YOU TO MEET YOUR MOST VALUABLE PART-TIME EMPLOYEE — ANGUS HUBBLE!
Valued.
NICE TO MEET YOU, ANGUS.
HEY.
HEY? JUST HEY?
EARTH TO ANGUS: "NICE TO MEET YOU, TOO, SIR."
NICE TO MEET YOU, TOO, SIR.
WOW... WE REALLY **ARE** ON THE SAME WAVELENGTH!

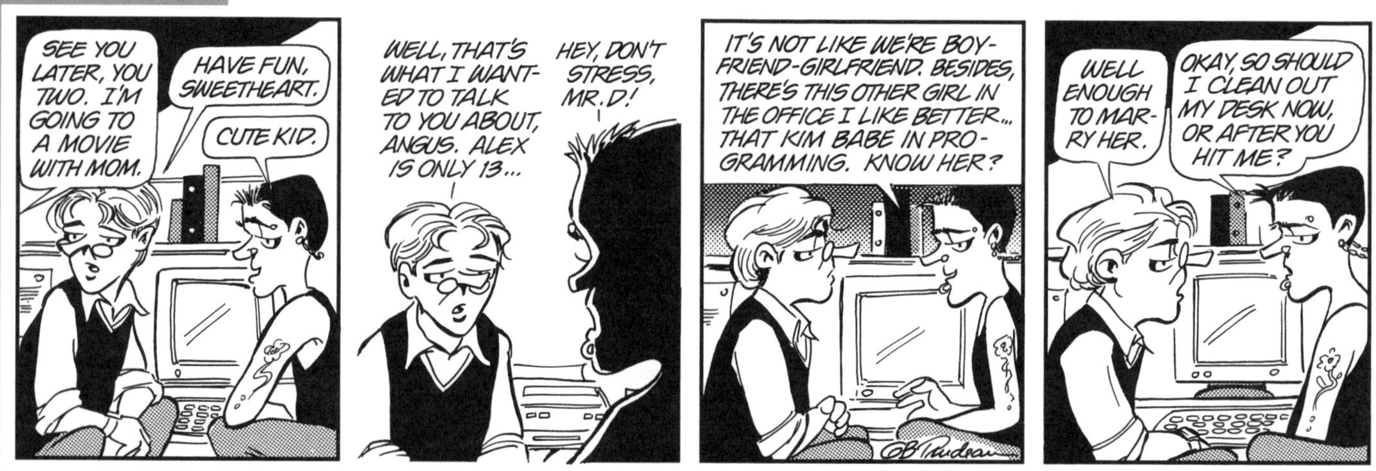
SEE YOU LATER, YOU TWO. I'M GOING TO A MOVIE WITH MOM.
HAVE FUN, SWEETHEART.
CUTE KID.
WELL, THAT'S WHAT I WANTED TO TALK TO YOU ABOUT, ANGUS. ALEX IS ONLY 13...
HEY, DON'T STRESS, MR. D!
IT'S NOT LIKE WE'RE BOYFRIEND-GIRLFRIEND. BESIDES, THERE'S THIS OTHER GIRL IN THE OFFICE I LIKE BETTER... THAT KIM BABE IN PROGRAMMING. KNOW HER?
WELL ENOUGH TO MARRY HER.
OKAY, SO SHOULD I CLEAN OUT MY DESK NOW, OR AFTER YOU HIT ME?

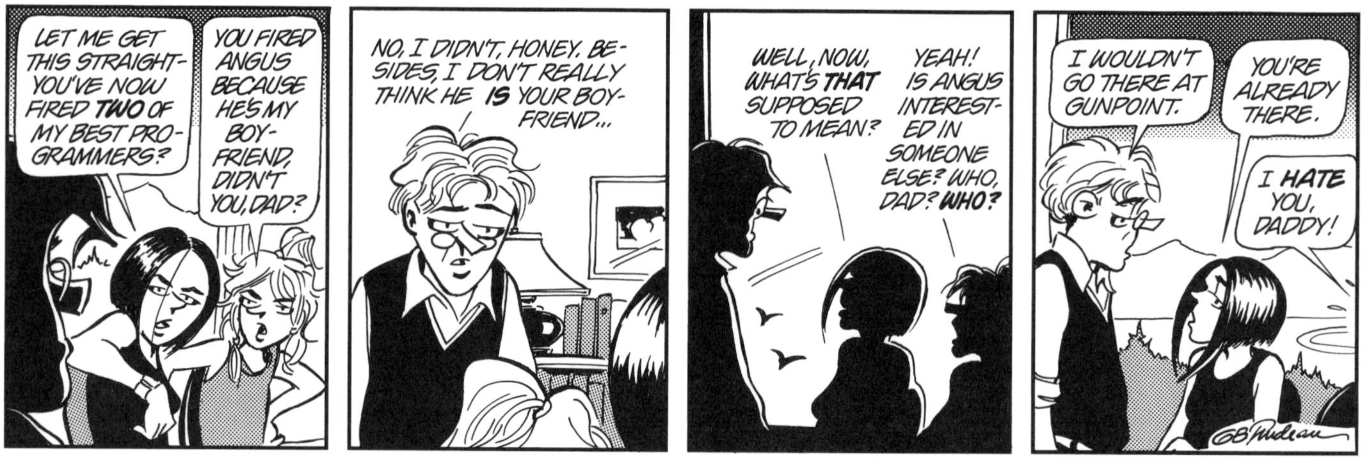
LET ME GET THIS STRAIGHT - YOU'VE NOW FIRED **TWO** OF MY BEST PROGRAMMERS?
YOU FIRED ANGUS BECAUSE HE'S MY BOYFRIEND, DIDN'T YOU, DAD?
NO, I DIDN'T, HONEY. BESIDES, I DON'T REALLY THINK HE **IS** YOUR BOYFRIEND...
WELL, NOW, WHAT'S **THAT** SUPPOSED TO MEAN?
YEAH! IS ANGUS INTERESTED IN SOMEONE ELSE? WHO, DAD? **WHO?**
I WOULDN'T GO THERE AT GUNPOINT.
YOU'RE ALREADY THERE.
I **HATE** YOU, DADDY!

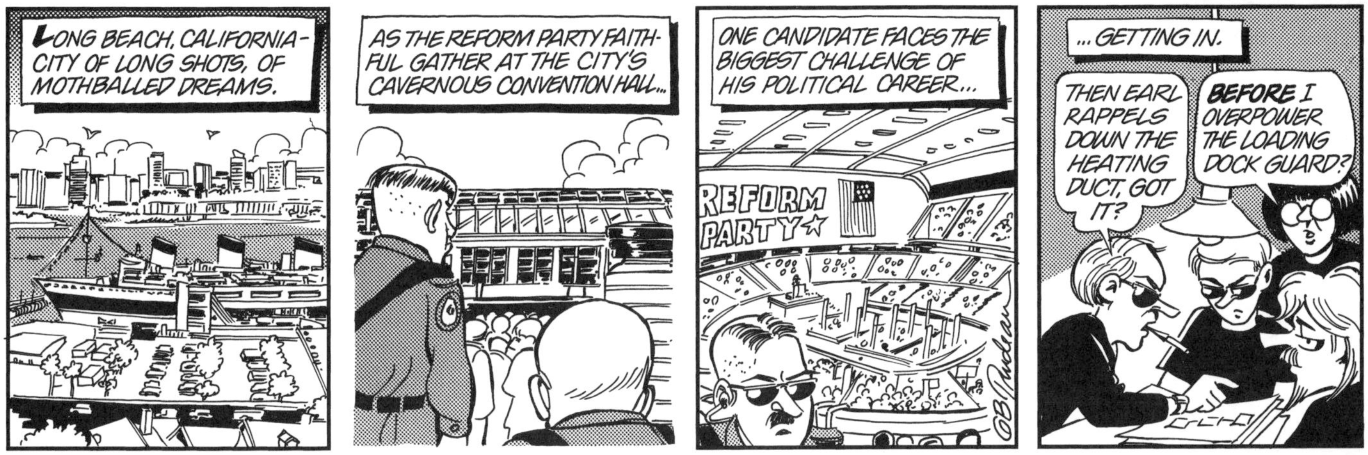
LONG BEACH, CALIFORNIA - CITY OF LONG SHOTS, OF MOTHBALLED DREAMS.
AS THE REFORM PARTY FAITHFUL GATHER AT THE CITY'S CAVERNOUS CONVENTION HALL...
ONE CANDIDATE FACES THE BIGGEST CHALLENGE OF HIS POLITICAL CAREER...
REFORM PARTY
... GETTING IN.
THEN EARL RAPPELS DOWN THE HEATING DUCT, GOT IT?
BEFORE I OVERPOWER THE LOADING DOCK GUARD?
GB Trudeau

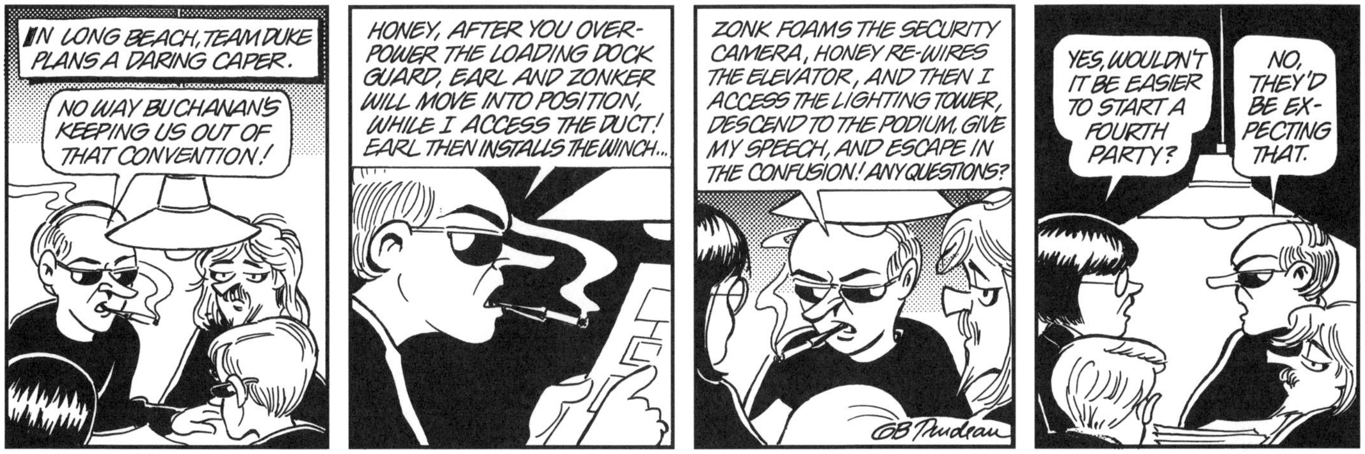
IN LONG BEACH, TEAM DUKE PLANS A DARING CAPER.
NO WAY BUCHANAN'S KEEPING US OUT OF THAT CONVENTION!
HONEY, AFTER YOU OVERPOWER THE LOADING DOCK GUARD, EARL AND ZONKER WILL MOVE INTO POSITION, WHILE I ACCESS THE DUCT! EARL THEN INSTALLS THE WINCH...
ZONK FOAMS THE SECURITY CAMERA, HONEY RE-WIRES THE ELEVATOR, AND THEN I ACCESS THE LIGHTING TOWER, DESCEND TO THE PODIUM, GIVE MY SPEECH, AND ESCAPE IN THE CONFUSION! ANY QUESTIONS?
GB Trudeau
YES, WOULDN'T IT BE EASIER TO START A FOURTH PARTY?
NO, THEY'D BE EXPECTING THAT.

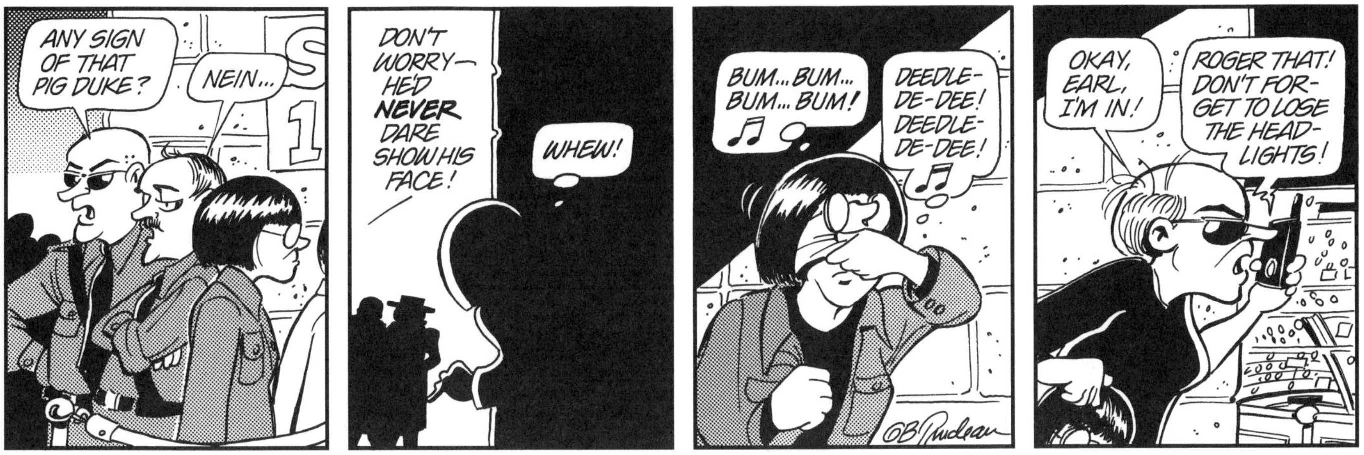
ANY SIGN OF THAT PIG DUKE?
NEIN...
DON'T WORRY— HE'D NEVER DARE SHOW HIS FACE!
WHEW!
BUM... BUM... BUM... BUM!
DEEDLE-DE-DEE! DEEDLE-DE-DEE!
GB Trudeau
OKAY, EARL, I'M IN!
ROGER THAT! DON'T FORGET TO LOSE THE HEADLIGHTS!

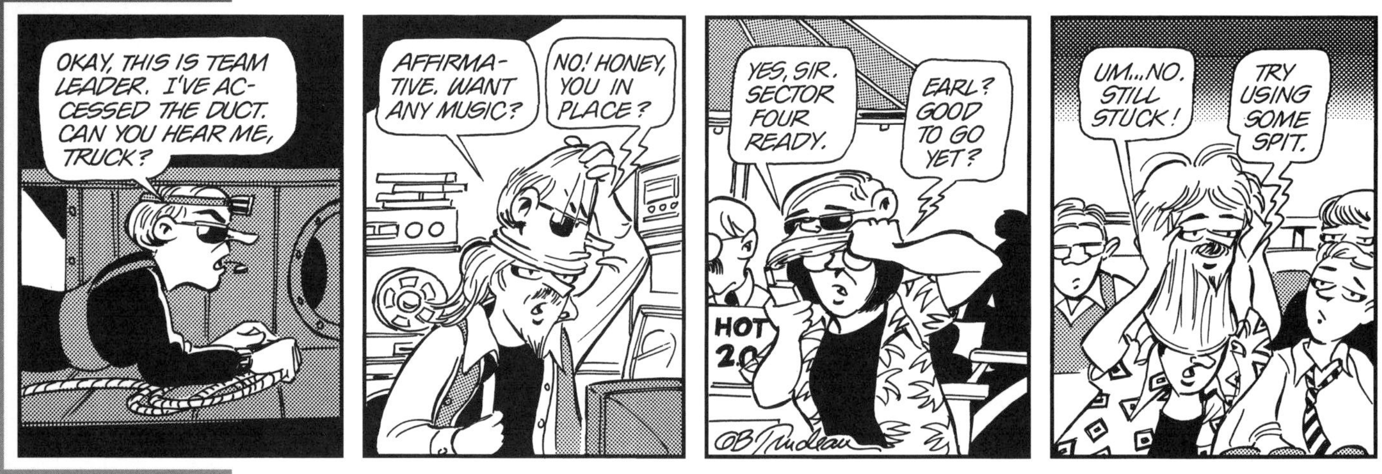
OKAY, THIS IS TEAM LEADER. I'VE AC-CESSED THE DUCT. CAN YOU HEAR ME, TRUCK?
AFFIRMA-TIVE. WANT ANY MUSIC?
NO! HONEY, YOU IN PLACE?
YES, SIR. SECTOR FOUR READY.
EARL? GOOD TO GO YET?
HOT 20
UM...NO. STILL STUCK!
TRY USING SOME SPIT.

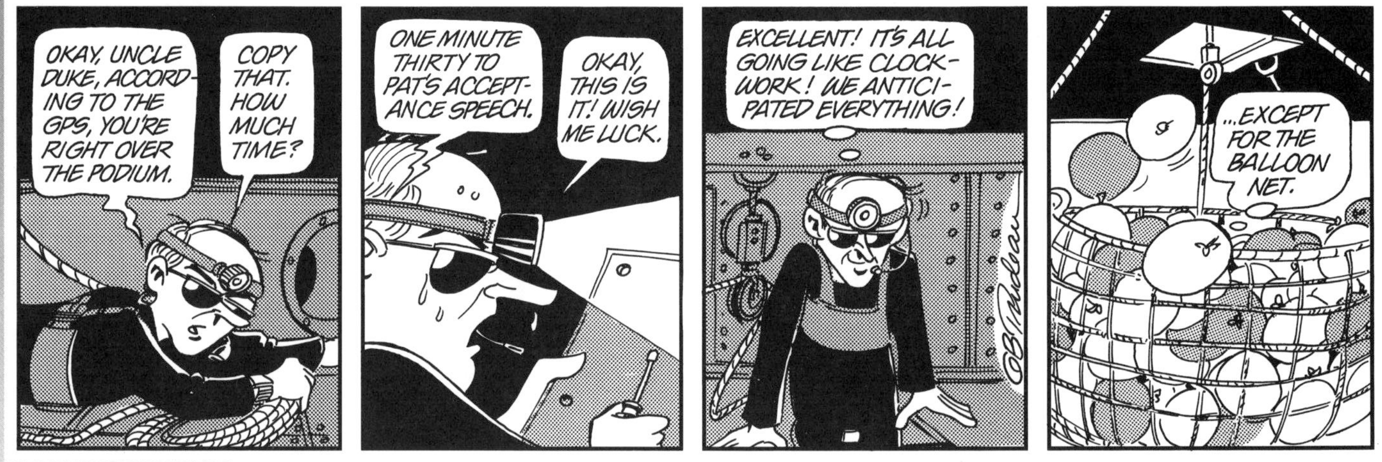
OKAY, UNCLE DUKE, ACCORD-ING TO THE GPS, YOU'RE RIGHT OVER THE PODIUM.
COPY THAT. HOW MUCH TIME?
ONE MINUTE THIRTY TO PAT'S ACCEPT-ANCE SPEECH.
OKAY, THIS IS IT! WISH ME LUCK.
EXCELLENT! IT'S ALL GOING LIKE CLOCK-WORK! WE ANTICI-PATED EVERYTHING!
...EXCEPT FOR THE BALLOON NET.

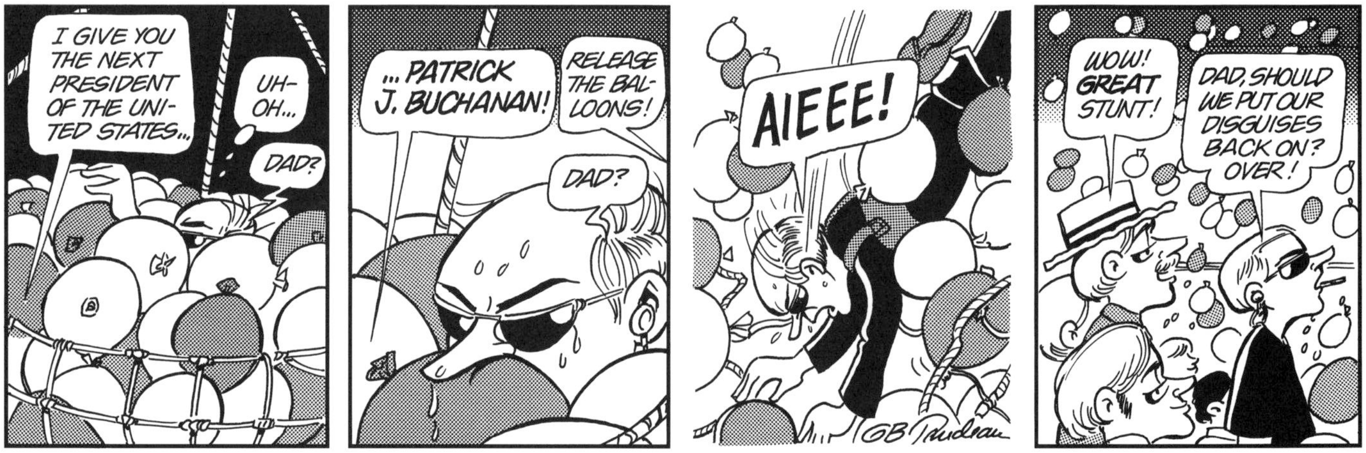
I GIVE YOU THE NEXT PRESIDENT OF THE UNI-TED STATES...
UH-OH...
DAD?
...PATRICK J. BUCHANAN!
RELEASE THE BAL-LOONS!
DAD?
AIEEE!
WOW! GREAT STUNT!
DAD, SHOULD WE PUT OUR DISGUISES BACK ON? OVER!

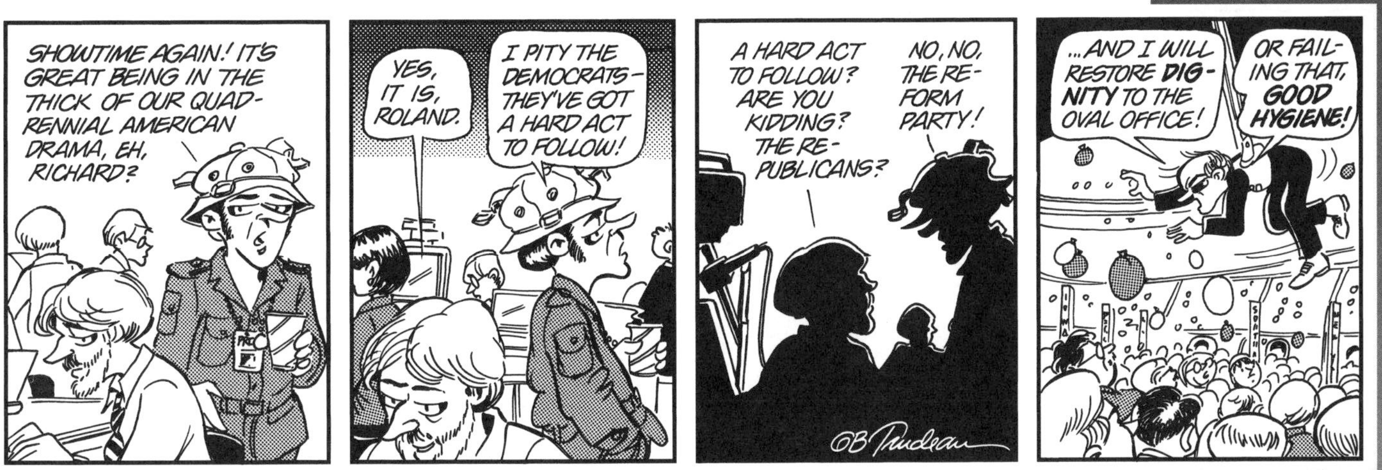
SHOWTIME AGAIN! IT'S GREAT BEING IN THE THICK OF OUR QUAD-RENNIAL AMERICAN DRAMA, EH, RICHARD?
YES, IT IS, ROLAND.
I PITY THE DEMOCRATS-THEY'VE GOT A HARD ACT TO FOLLOW!
A HARD ACT TO FOLLOW? ARE YOU KIDDING? THE RE-PUBLICANS?
NO, NO, THE RE-FORM PARTY!
...AND I WILL RESTORE **DIGNITY** TO THE OVAL OFFICE!
OR FAILING THAT, **GOOD HYGIENE!**

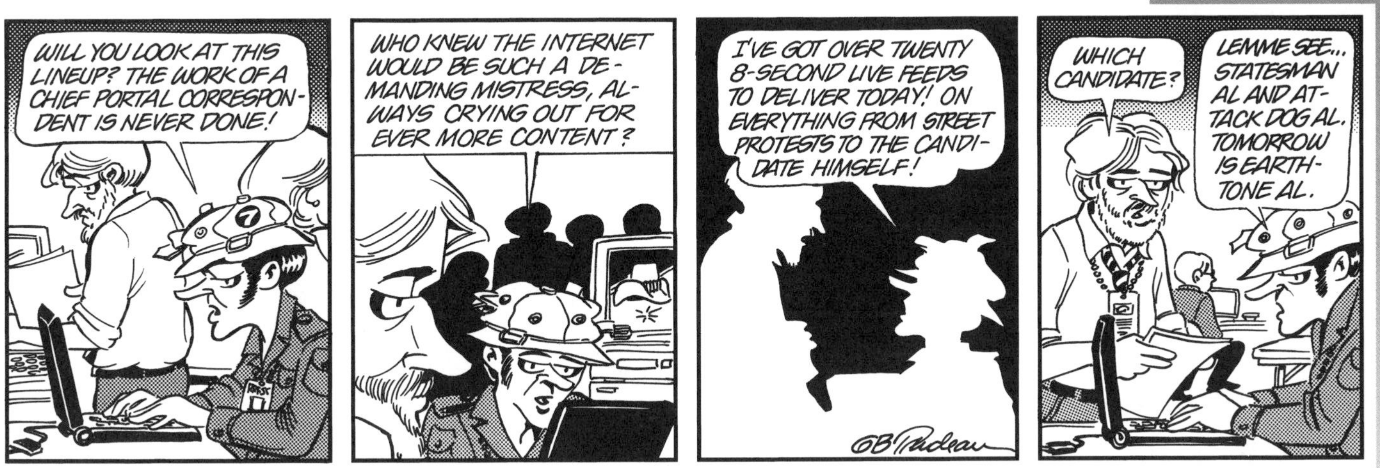
WILL YOU LOOK AT THIS LINEUP? THE WORK OF A CHIEF PORTAL CORRESPON-DENT IS NEVER DONE!
WHO KNEW THE INTERNET WOULD BE SUCH A DE-MANDING MISTRESS, AL-WAYS CRYING OUT FOR EVER MORE CONTENT?
I'VE GOT OVER TWENTY 8-SECOND LIVE FEEDS TO DELIVER TODAY! ON EVERYTHING FROM STREET PROTESTS TO THE CANDI-DATE HIMSELF!
WHICH CANDIDATE?
LEMME SEE... STATESMAN AL AND AT-TACK DOG AL. TOMORROW IS EARTH-TONE AL.

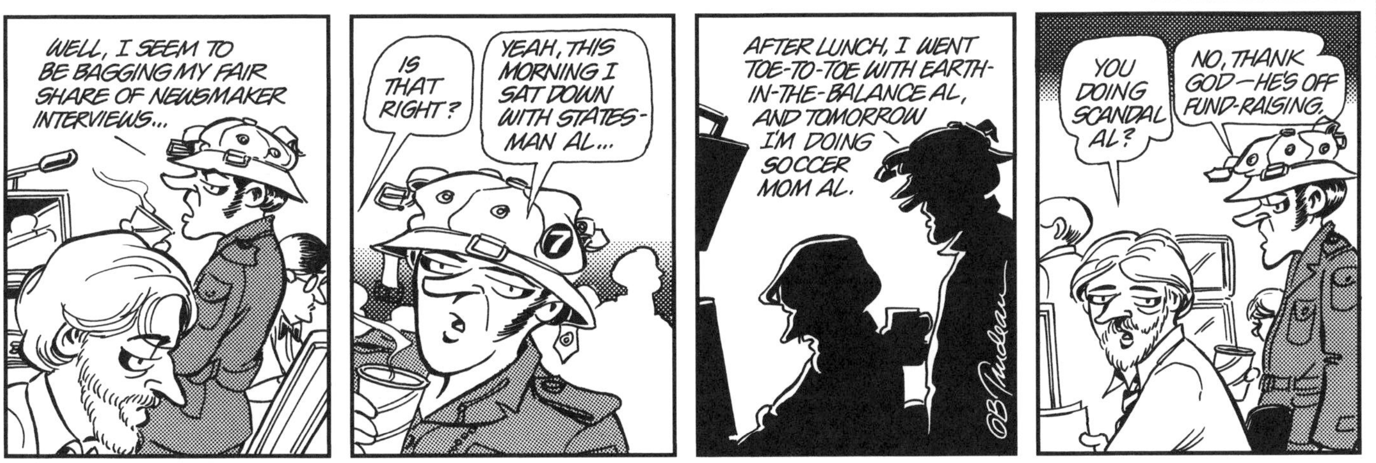
WELL, I SEEM TO BE BAGGING MY FAIR SHARE OF NEWSMAKER INTERVIEWS...
IS THAT RIGHT?
YEAH, THIS MORNING I SAT DOWN WITH STATES-MAN AL...
AFTER LUNCH, I WENT TOE-TO-TOE WITH EARTH-IN-THE-BALANCE AL, AND TOMORROW I'M DOING SOCCER MOM AL.
YOU DOING SCANDAL AL?
NO, THANK GOD—HE'S OFF FUND-RAISING.

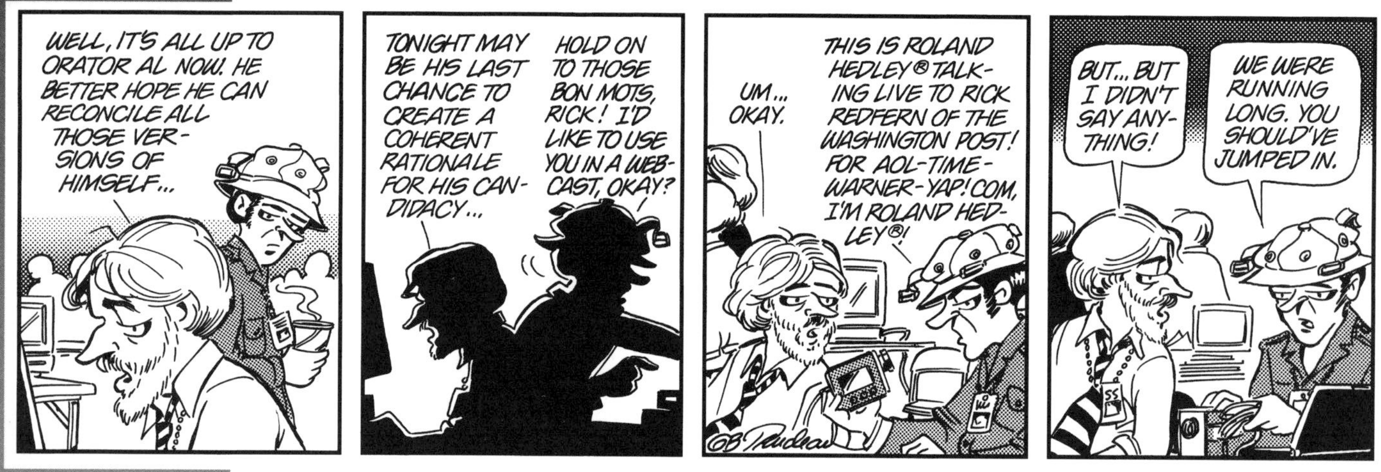
WELL, IT'S ALL UP TO ORATOR AL NOW! HE BETTER HOPE HE CAN RECONCILE ALL THOSE VERSIONS OF HIMSELF...
TONIGHT MAY BE HIS LAST CHANCE TO CREATE A COHERENT RATIONALE FOR HIS CANDIDACY...
HOLD ON TO THOSE BON MOTS, RICK! I'D LIKE TO USE YOU IN A WEBCAST, OKAY?
UM... OKAY.
THIS IS ROLAND HEDLEY® TALKING LIVE TO RICK REDFERN OF THE WASHINGTON POST! FOR AOL-TIME-WARNER-YAP!COM, I'M ROLAND HEDLEY®!
BUT... BUT I DIDN'T SAY ANYTHING!
WE WERE RUNNING LONG. YOU SHOULD'VE JUMPED IN.

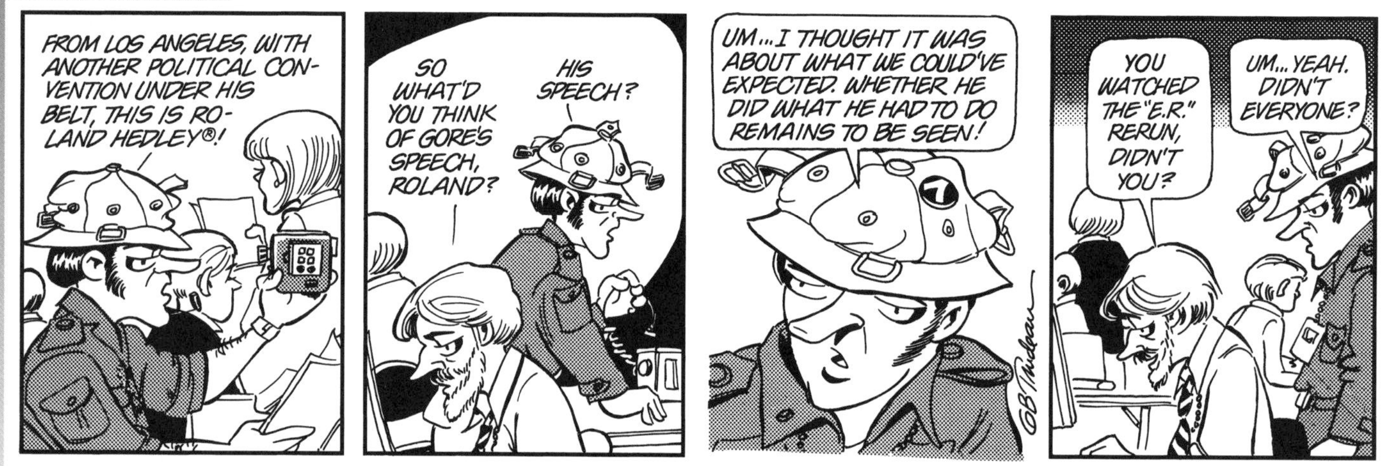
FROM LOS ANGELES, WITH ANOTHER POLITICAL CONVENTION UNDER HIS BELT, THIS IS ROLAND HEDLEY®!
SO WHAT'D YOU THINK OF GORE'S SPEECH, ROLAND?
HIS SPEECH?
UM...I THOUGHT IT WAS ABOUT WHAT WE COULD'VE EXPECTED. WHETHER HE DID WHAT HE HAD TO DO REMAINS TO BE SEEN!
YOU WATCHED THE "E.R." RERUN, DIDN'T YOU?
UM... YEAH. DIDN'T EVERYONE?

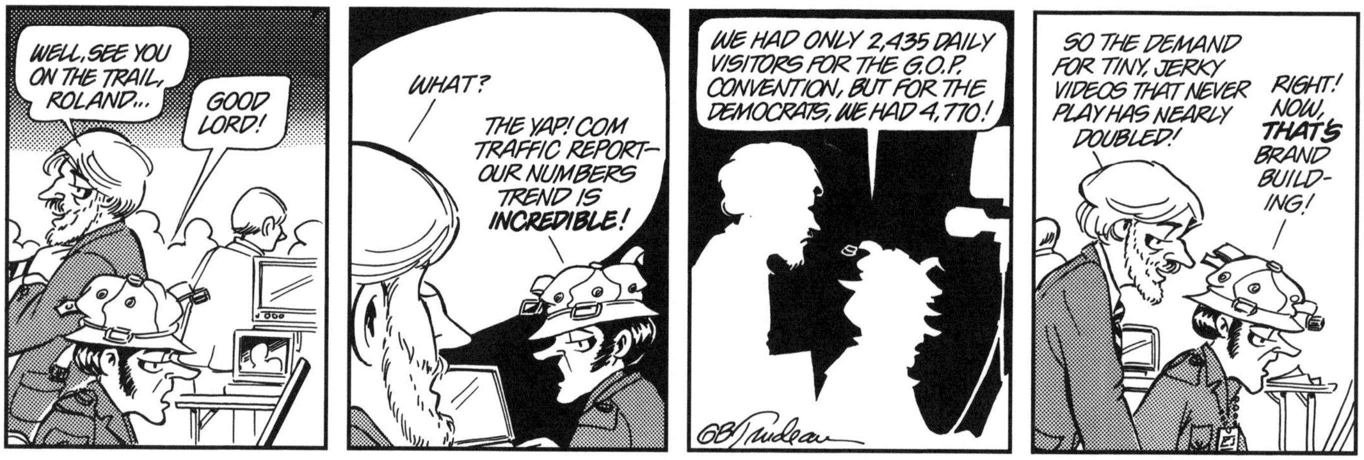
WELL, SEE YOU ON THE TRAIL, ROLAND...
GOOD LORD!
WHAT?
THE YAP!COM TRAFFIC REPORT— OUR NUMBERS TREND IS INCREDIBLE!
WE HAD ONLY 2,435 DAILY VISITORS FOR THE G.O.P. CONVENTION, BUT FOR THE DEMOCRATS, WE HAD 4,770!
SO THE DEMAND FOR TINY, JERKY VIDEOS THAT NEVER PLAY HAS NEARLY DOUBLED!
RIGHT! NOW, THAT'S BRAND BUILDING!

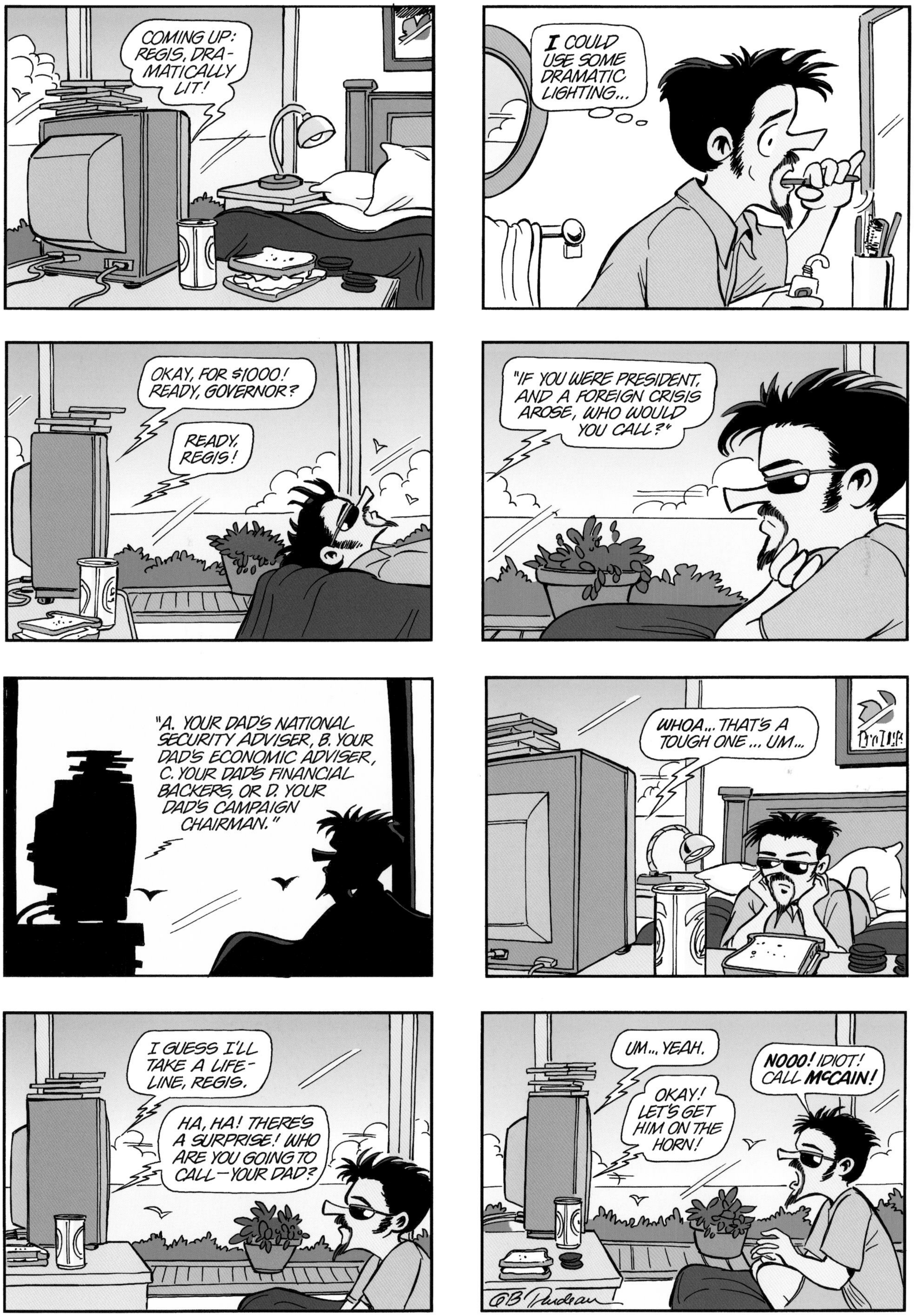
COMING UP: REGIS, DRAMATICALLY LIT!
I COULD USE SOME DRAMATIC LIGHTING...
OKAY, FOR $1000! READY, GOVERNOR?
READY, REGIS!
"IF YOU WERE PRESIDENT, AND A FOREIGN CRISIS AROSE, WHO WOULD YOU CALL?"
"A. YOUR DAD'S NATIONAL SECURITY ADVISER, B. YOUR DAD'S ECONOMIC ADVISER, C. YOUR DAD'S FINANCIAL BACKERS, OR D. YOUR DAD'S CAMPAIGN CHAIRMAN."
WHOA... THAT'S A TOUGH ONE... UM...
I GUESS I'LL TAKE A LIFE-LINE, REGIS.
HA, HA! THERE'S A SURPRISE! WHO ARE YOU GOING TO CALL—YOUR DAD?
UM... YEAH.
OKAY! LET'S GET HIM ON THE HORN!
NOOO! IDIOT! CALL McCAIN!
©B Trudeau

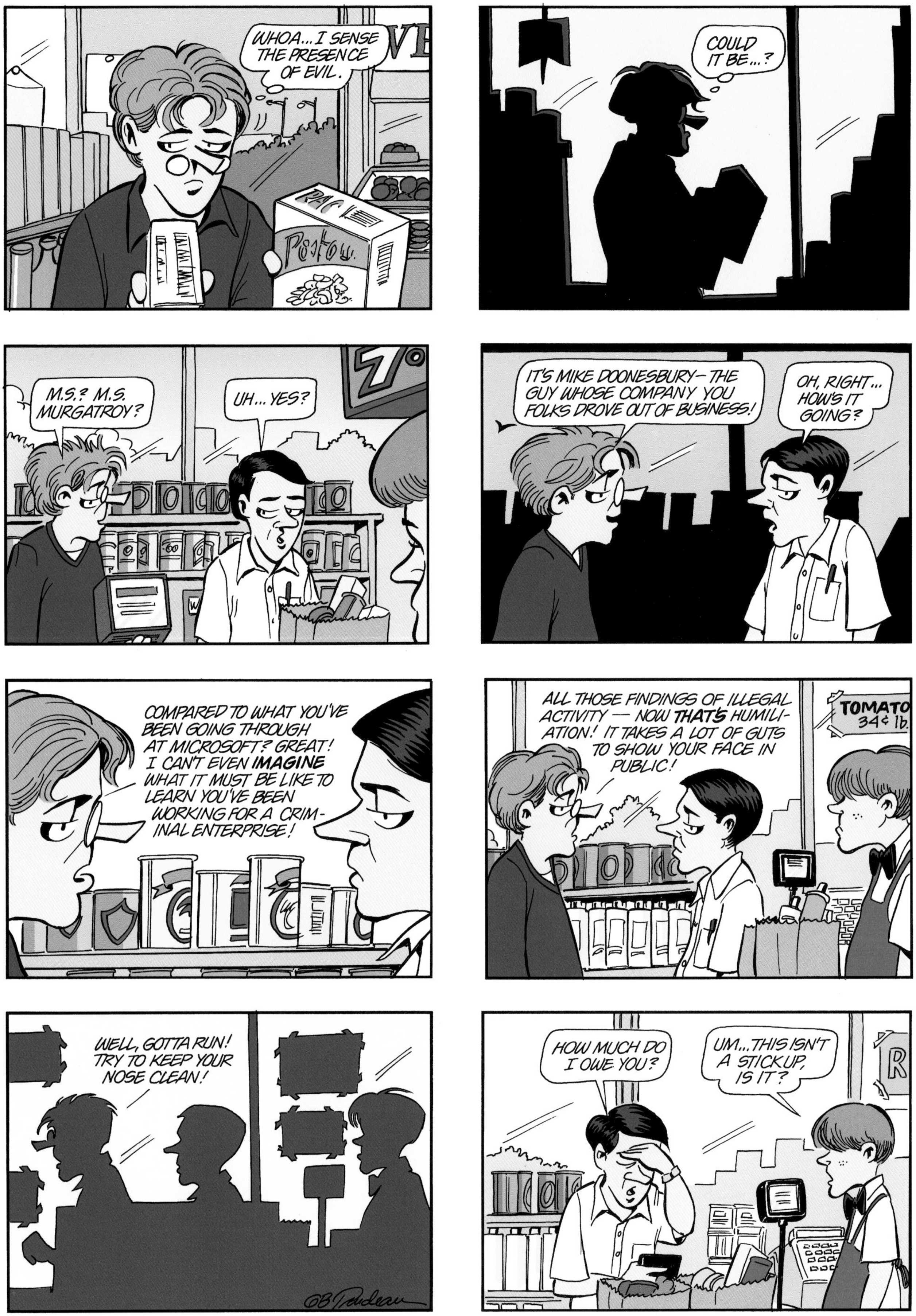
WHOA... I SENSE THE PRESENCE OF EVIL.
COULD IT BE...?
M.S.? M.S. MURGATROY?
UH... YES?
IT'S MIKE DOONESBURY— THE GUY WHOSE COMPANY YOU FOLKS DROVE OUT OF BUSINESS!
OH, RIGHT... HOW'S IT GOING?
COMPARED TO WHAT YOU'VE BEEN GOING THROUGH AT MICROSOFT? GREAT! I CAN'T EVEN IMAGINE WHAT IT MUST BE LIKE TO LEARN YOU'VE BEEN WORKING FOR A CRIMINAL ENTERPRISE!
ALL THOSE FINDINGS OF ILLEGAL ACTIVITY — NOW THAT'S HUMILIATION! IT TAKES A LOT OF GUTS TO SHOW YOUR FACE IN PUBLIC!
TOMATO 34¢ lb.
WELL, GOTTA RUN! TRY TO KEEP YOUR NOSE CLEAN!
HOW MUCH DO I OWE YOU?
UM... THIS ISN'T A STICKUP, IS IT?

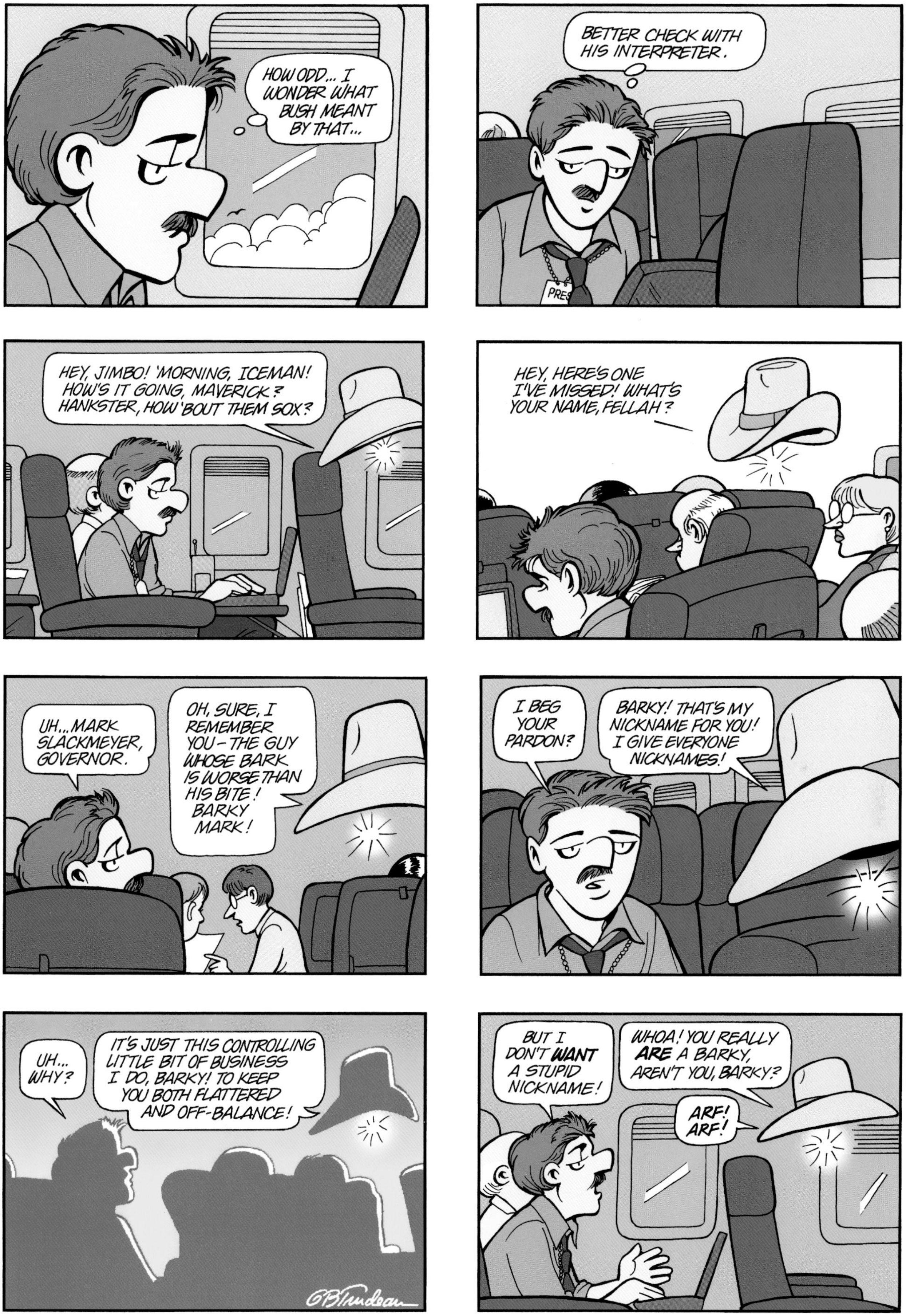
HOW ODD... I WONDER WHAT BUSH MEANT BY THAT...
BETTER CHECK WITH HIS INTERPRETER.
HEY, JIMBO! 'MORNING, ICEMAN! HOW'S IT GOING, MAVERICK? HANKSTER, HOW 'BOUT THEM SOX?
HEY, HERE'S ONE I'VE MISSED! WHAT'S YOUR NAME, FELLAH?
UH... MARK SLACKMEYER, GOVERNOR.
OH, SURE, I REMEMBER YOU – THE GUY WHOSE BARK IS WORSE THAN HIS BITE! BARKY MARK!
I BEG YOUR PARDON?
BARKY! THAT'S MY NICKNAME FOR YOU! I GIVE EVERYONE NICKNAMES!
UH... WHY?
IT'S JUST THIS CONTROLLING LITTLE BIT OF BUSINESS I DO, BARKY! TO KEEP YOU BOTH FLATTERED AND OFF-BALANCE!
GBTrudeau
BUT I DON'T **WANT** A STUPID NICKNAME!
WHOA! YOU REALLY **ARE** A BARKY, AREN'T YOU, BARKY?
ARF! ARF!

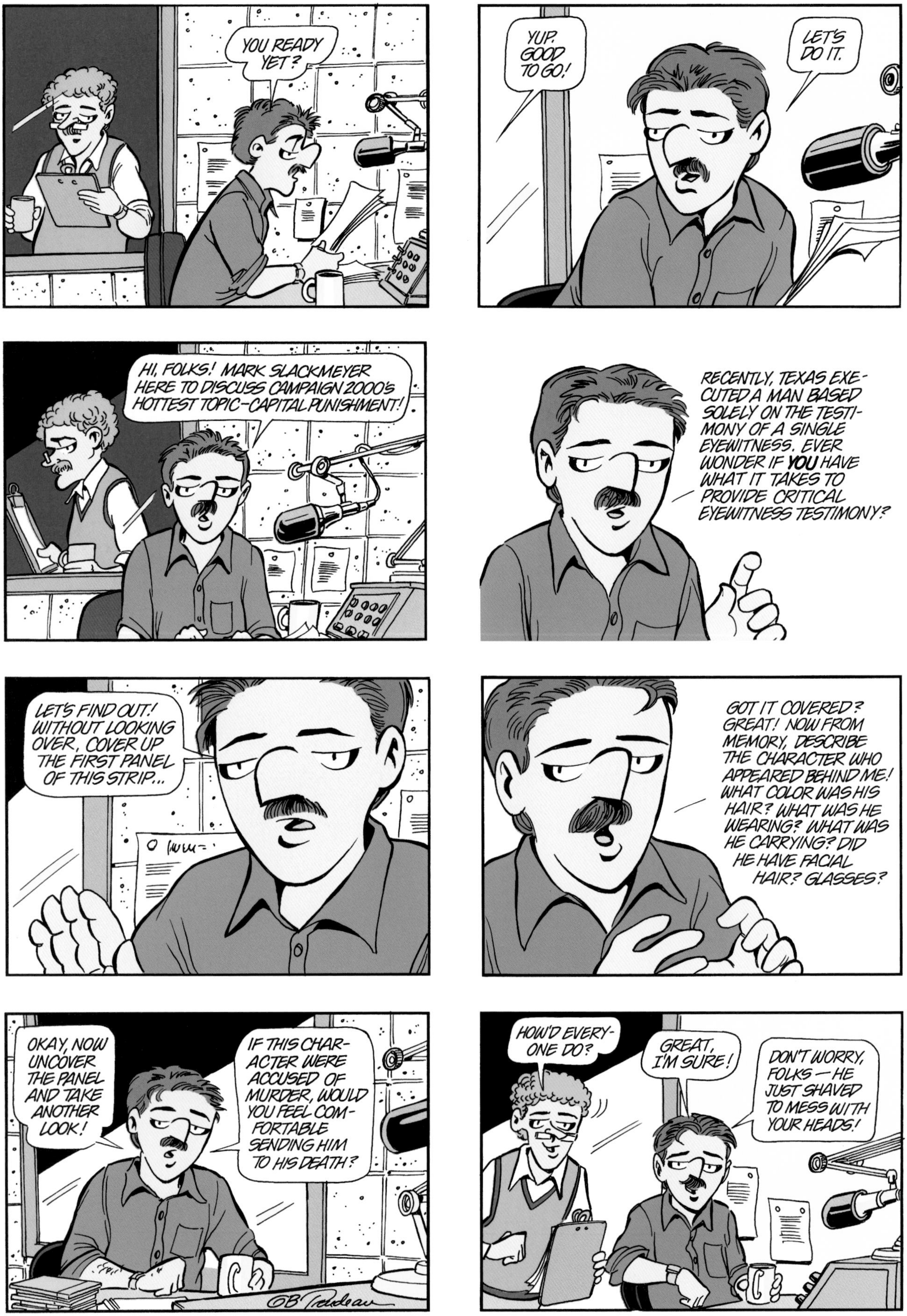
YOU READY YET?
YUP. GOOD TO GO!
LET'S DO IT.
HI, FOLKS! MARK SLACKMEYER HERE TO DISCUSS CAMPAIGN 2000'S HOTTEST TOPIC—CAPITAL PUNISHMENT!
RECENTLY, TEXAS EXECUTED A MAN BASED SOLELY ON THE TESTIMONY OF A SINGLE EYEWITNESS. EVER WONDER IF **YOU** HAVE WHAT IT TAKES TO PROVIDE CRITICAL EYEWITNESS TESTIMONY?
LET'S FIND OUT! WITHOUT LOOKING OVER, COVER UP THE FIRST PANEL OF THIS STRIP...
GOT IT COVERED? GREAT! NOW FROM MEMORY, DESCRIBE THE CHARACTER WHO APPEARED BEHIND ME! WHAT COLOR WAS HIS HAIR? WHAT WAS HE WEARING? WHAT WAS HE CARRYING? DID HE HAVE FACIAL HAIR? GLASSES?
OKAY, NOW UNCOVER THE PANEL AND TAKE ANOTHER LOOK!
IF THIS CHARACTER WERE ACCUSED OF MURDER, WOULD YOU FEEL COMFORTABLE SENDING HIM TO HIS DEATH?
GB Trudeau
HOW'D EVERYONE DO?
GREAT, I'M SURE!
DON'T WORRY, FOLKS — HE JUST SHAVED TO MESS WITH YOUR HEADS!

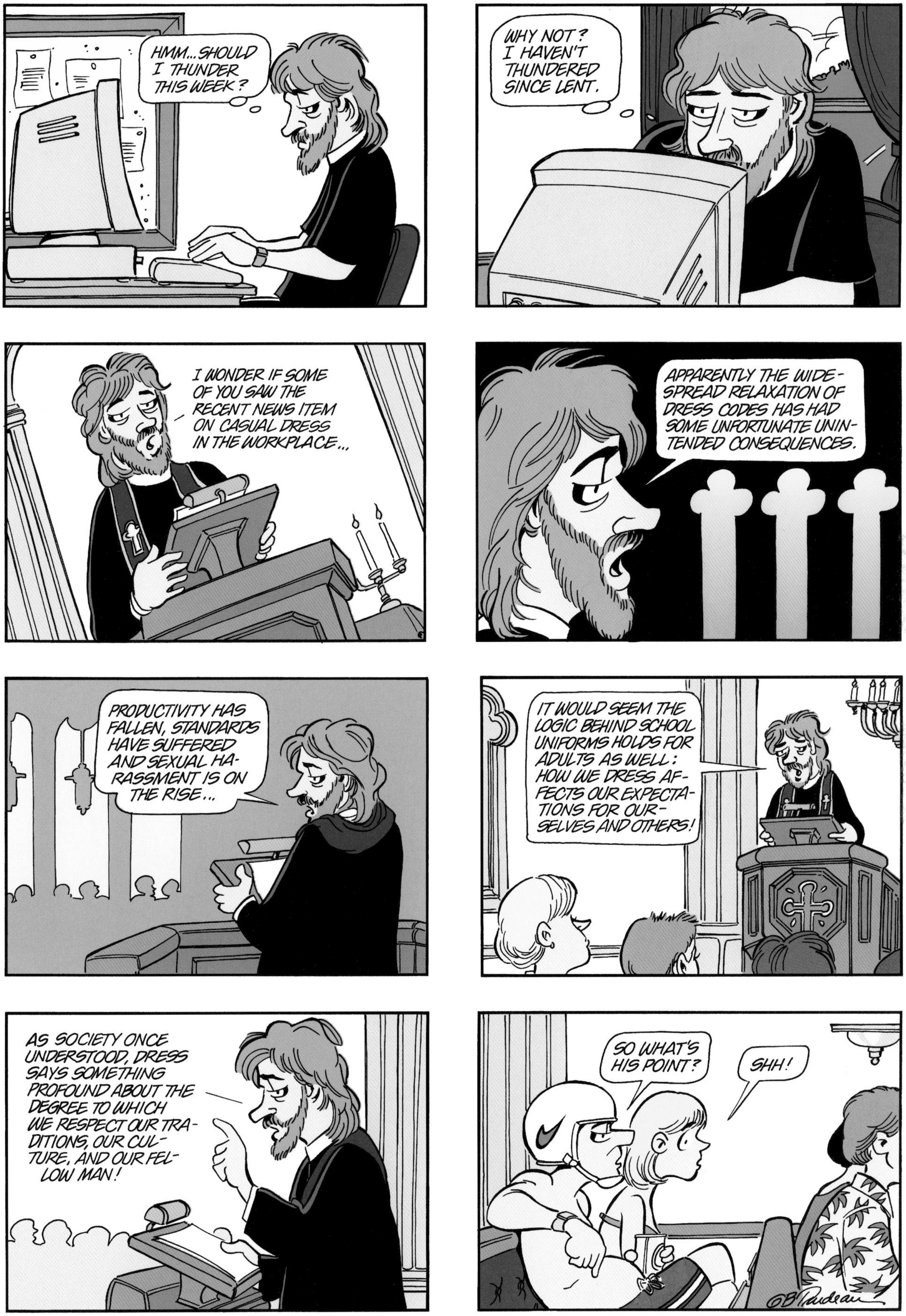
HMM... SHOULD I THUNDER THIS WEEK?
WHY NOT? I HAVEN'T THUNDERED SINCE LENT.
I WONDER IF SOME OF YOU SAW THE RECENT NEWS ITEM ON CASUAL DRESS IN THE WORKPLACE...
APPARENTLY THE WIDE-SPREAD RELAXATION OF DRESS CODES HAS HAD SOME UNFORTUNATE UNIN-TENDED CONSEQUENCES.
PRODUCTIVITY HAS FALLEN, STANDARDS HAVE SUFFERED AND SEXUAL HA-RASSMENT IS ON THE RISE...
IT WOULD SEEM THE LOGIC BEHIND SCHOOL UNIFORMS HOLDS FOR ADULTS AS WELL: HOW WE DRESS AF-FECTS OUR EXPECTA-TIONS FOR OUR-SELVES AND OTHERS!
AS SOCIETY ONCE UNDERSTOOD, DRESS SAYS SOMETHING PROFOUND ABOUT THE DEGREE TO WHICH WE RESPECT OUR TRA-DITIONS, OUR CUL-TURE, AND OUR FEL-LOW MAN!
SO WHAT'S HIS POINT?
SHH!
©B. Trudeau

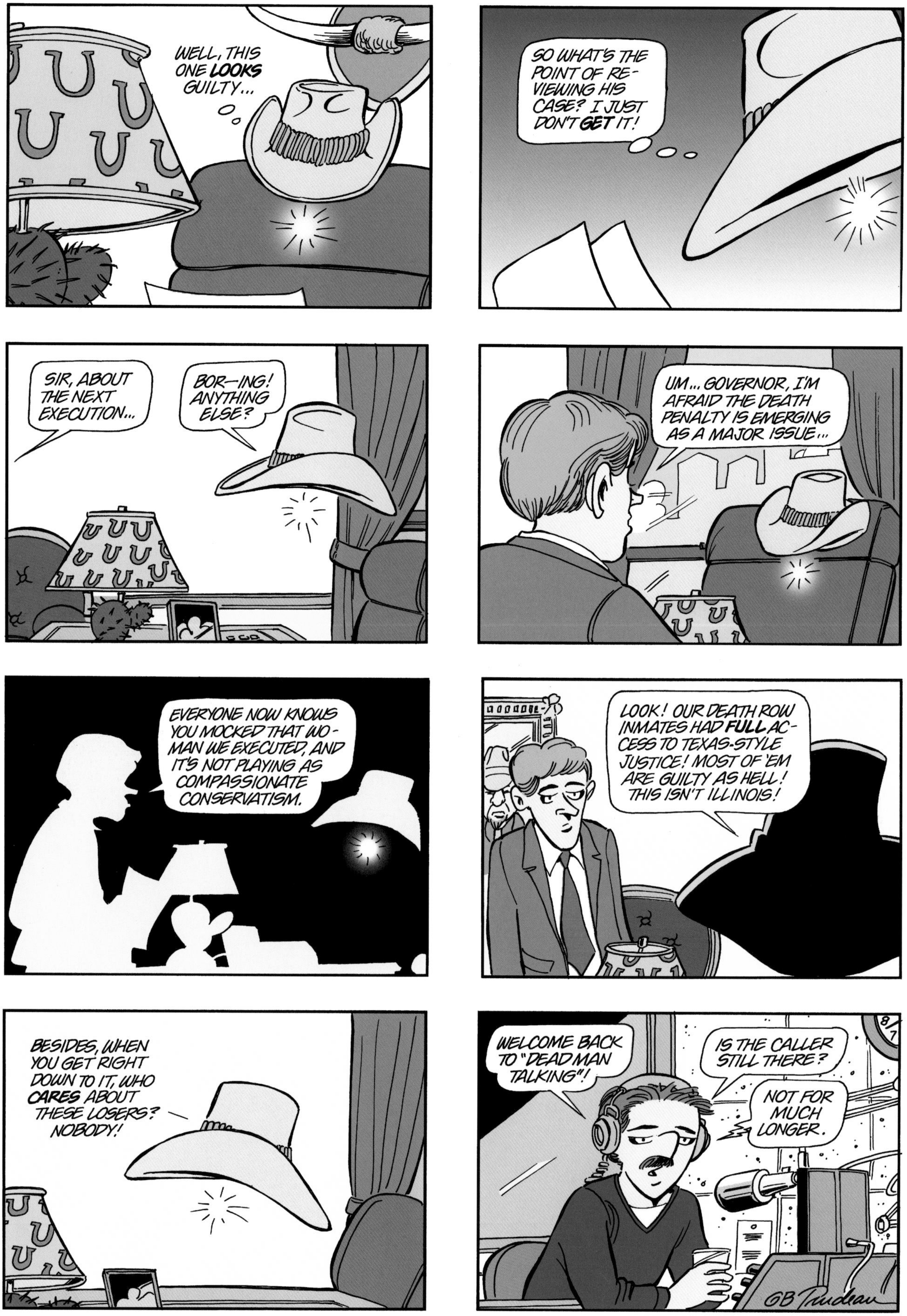
WELL, THIS ONE **LOOKS** GUILTY...
SO WHAT'S THE POINT OF RE-VIEWING HIS CASE? I JUST DON'T **GET** IT!
SIR, ABOUT THE NEXT EXECUTION...
BOR—ING! ANYTHING ELSE?
UM... GOVERNOR, I'M AFRAID THE DEATH PENALTY IS EMERGING AS A MAJOR ISSUE...
EVERYONE NOW KNOWS YOU MOCKED THAT WO-MAN WE EXECUTED, AND IT'S NOT PLAYING AS COMPASSIONATE CONSERVATISM.
LOOK! OUR DEATH ROW INMATES HAD **FULL** AC-CESS TO TEXAS-STYLE JUSTICE! MOST OF 'EM ARE GUILTY AS HELL! THIS ISN'T ILLINOIS!
BESIDES, WHEN YOU GET RIGHT DOWN TO IT, WHO **CARES** ABOUT THESE LOSERS? NOBODY!
WELCOME BACK TO "DEAD MAN TALKING"!
IS THE CALLER STILL THERE?
NOT FOR MUCH LONGER.
GB Trudeau

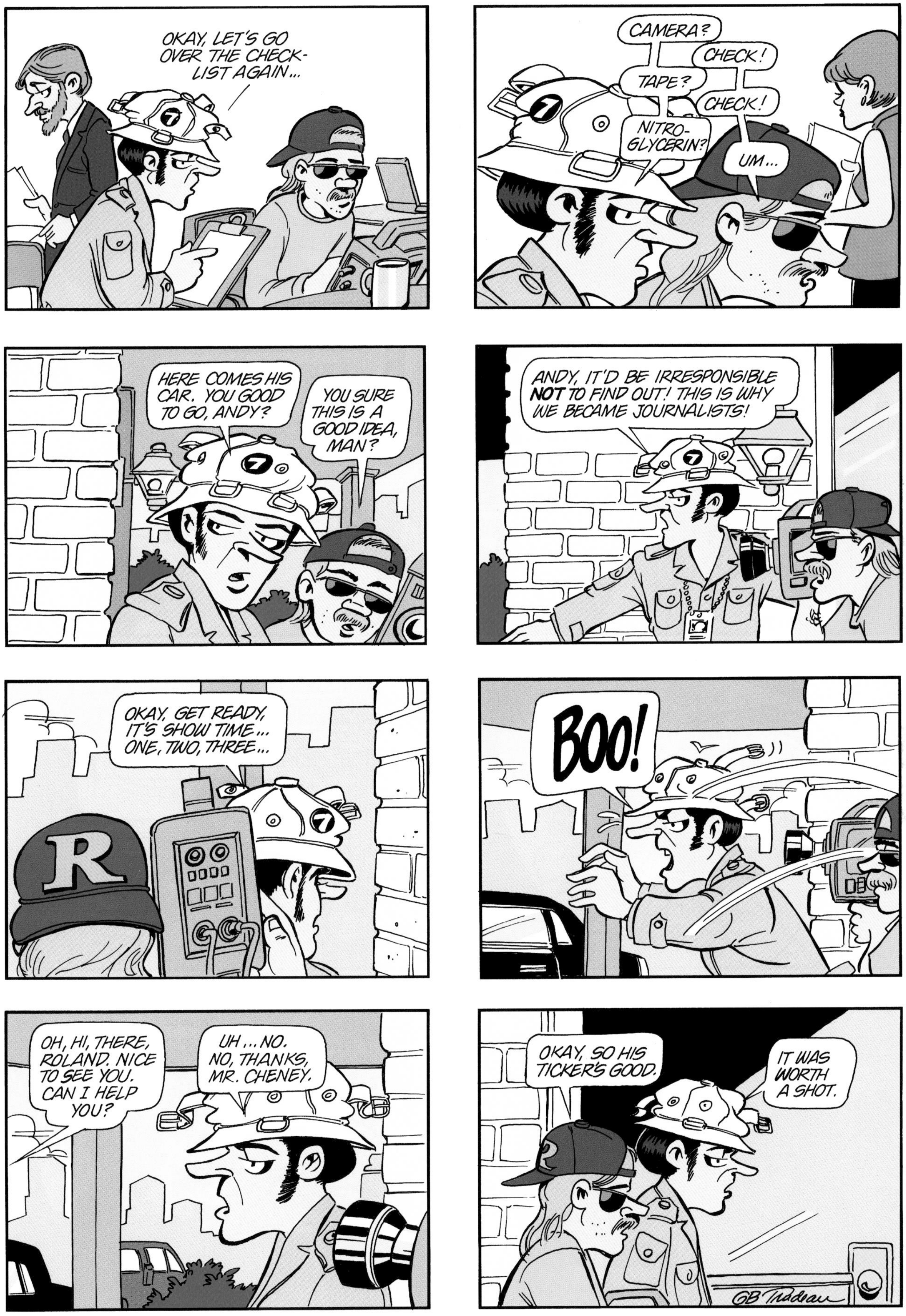
OKAY, LET'S GO OVER THE CHECK-LIST AGAIN...
CAMERA?
CHECK!
TAPE?
CHECK!
NITRO-GLYCERIN?
UM...
HERE COMES HIS CAR. YOU GOOD TO GO, ANDY?
YOU SURE THIS IS A GOOD IDEA, MAN?
ANDY, IT'D BE IRRESPONSIBLE **NOT** TO FIND OUT! THIS IS WHY WE BECAME JOURNALISTS!
OKAY, GET READY, IT'S SHOW TIME... ONE, TWO, THREE...
BOO!
OH, HI, THERE, ROLAND. NICE TO SEE YOU. CAN I HELP YOU?
UH... NO. NO, THANKS, MR. CHENEY.
OKAY, SO HIS TICKER'S GOOD.
IT WAS WORTH A SHOT.
GB Trudeau

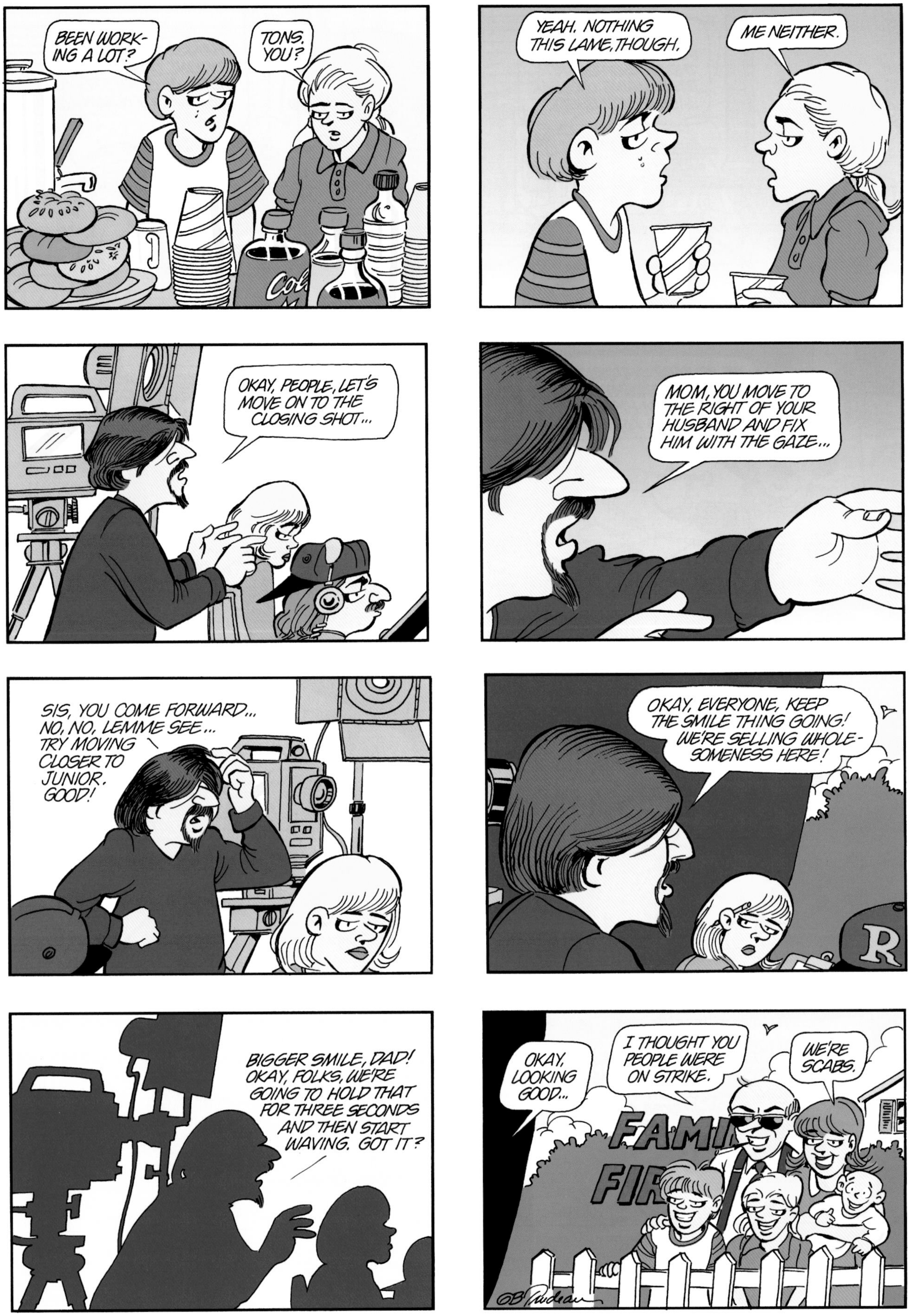

BEEN WORKING A LOT?
TONS. YOU?
YEAH. NOTHING THIS LAME, THOUGH.
ME NEITHER.
OKAY, PEOPLE, LET'S MOVE ON TO THE CLOSING SHOT...
MOM, YOU MOVE TO THE RIGHT OF YOUR HUSBAND AND FIX HIM WITH THE GAZE...
SIS, YOU COME FORWARD... NO, NO, LEMME SEE... TRY MOVING CLOSER TO JUNIOR. GOOD!
OKAY, EVERYONE, KEEP THE SMILE THING GOING! WE'RE SELLING WHOLESOMENESS HERE!
BIGGER SMILE, DAD! OKAY, FOLKS, WE'RE GOING TO HOLD THAT FOR THREE SECONDS AND THEN START WAVING. GOT IT?
OKAY, LOOKING GOOD...
I THOUGHT YOU PEOPLE WERE ON STRIKE.
WE'RE SCABS.
©B Trudeau

183

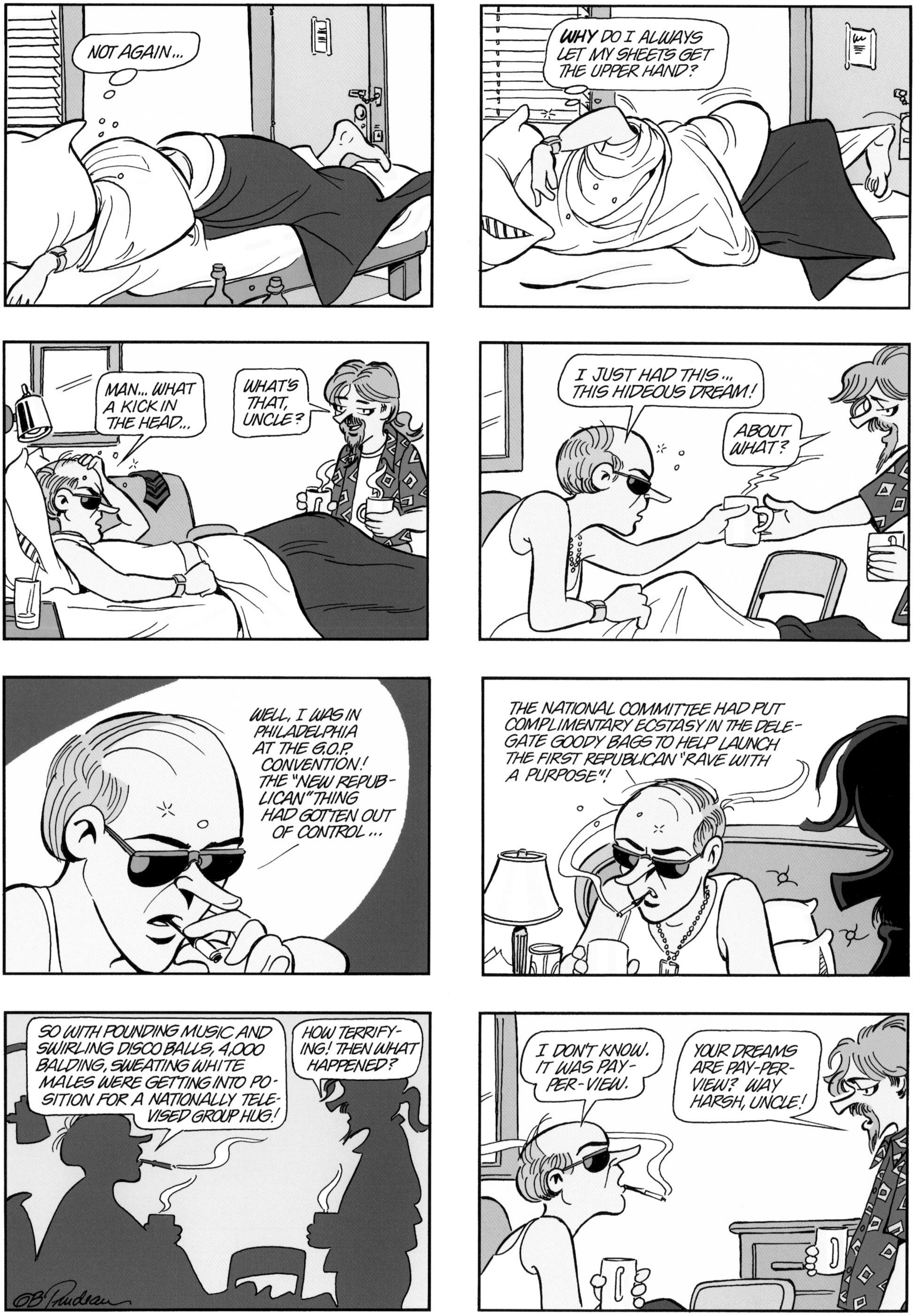
NOT AGAIN...
WHY DO I ALWAYS LET MY SHEETS GET THE UPPER HAND?
MAN... WHAT A KICK IN THE HEAD...
WHAT'S THAT, UNCLE?
I JUST HAD THIS... THIS HIDEOUS DREAM!
ABOUT WHAT?
WELL, I WAS IN PHILADELPHIA AT THE G.O.P. CONVENTION! THE "NEW REPUBLICAN" THING HAD GOTTEN OUT OF CONTROL...
THE NATIONAL COMMITTEE HAD PUT COMPLIMENTARY ECSTASY IN THE DELEGATE GOODY BAGS TO HELP LAUNCH THE FIRST REPUBLICAN "RAVE WITH A PURPOSE"!
SO WITH POUNDING MUSIC AND SWIRLING DISCO BALLS, 4,000 BALDING, SWEATING WHITE MALES WERE GETTING INTO POSITION FOR A NATIONALLY TELEVISED GROUP HUG!
HOW TERRIFYING! THEN WHAT HAPPENED?
I DON'T KNOW. IT WAS PAY-PER-VIEW.
YOUR DREAMS ARE PAY-PER-VIEW? WAY HARSH, UNCLE!

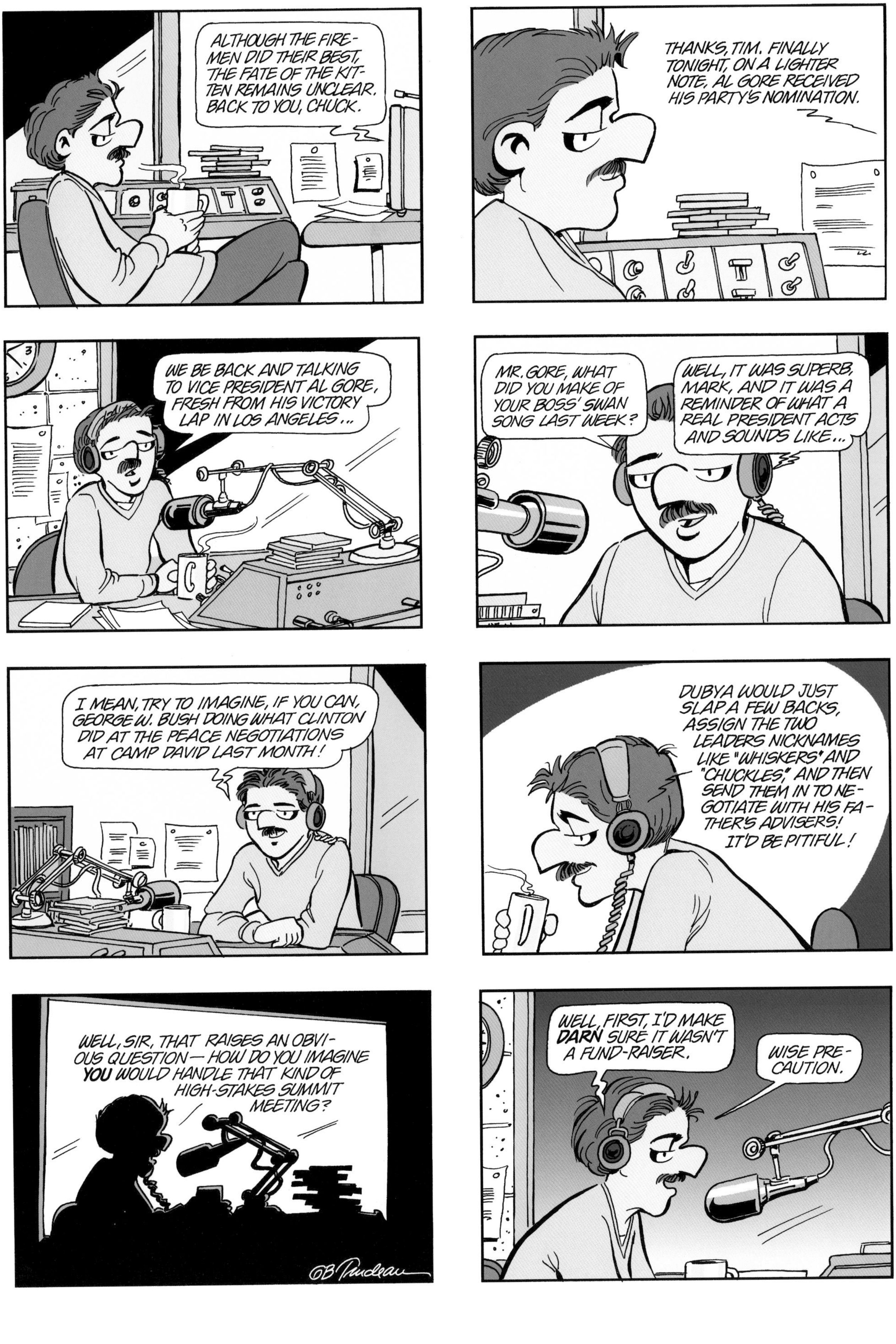
ALTHOUGH THE FIREMEN DID THEIR BEST, THE FATE OF THE KITTEN REMAINS UNCLEAR. BACK TO YOU, CHUCK.
THANKS, TIM. FINALLY TONIGHT, ON A LIGHTER NOTE, AL GORE RECEIVED HIS PARTY'S NOMINATION.
WE BE BACK AND TALKING TO VICE PRESIDENT AL GORE, FRESH FROM HIS VICTORY LAP IN LOS ANGELES...
MR. GORE, WHAT DID YOU MAKE OF YOUR BOSS' SWAN SONG LAST WEEK?
WELL, IT WAS SUPERB, MARK, AND IT WAS A REMINDER OF WHAT A REAL PRESIDENT ACTS AND SOUNDS LIKE...
I MEAN, TRY TO IMAGINE, IF YOU CAN, GEORGE W. BUSH DOING WHAT CLINTON DID AT THE PEACE NEGOTIATIONS AT CAMP DAVID LAST MONTH!
DUBYA WOULD JUST SLAP A FEW BACKS, ASSIGN THE TWO LEADERS NICKNAMES LIKE "WHISKERS" AND "CHUCKLES," AND THEN SEND THEM IN TO NEGOTIATE WITH HIS FATHER'S ADVISERS! IT'D BE PITIFUL!
WELL, SIR, THAT RAISES AN OBVIOUS QUESTION — HOW DO YOU IMAGINE **YOU** WOULD HANDLE THAT KIND OF HIGH-STAKES SUMMIT MEETING?
WELL, FIRST, I'D MAKE **DARN** SURE IT WASN'T A FUND-RAISER.
WISE PRECAUTION.

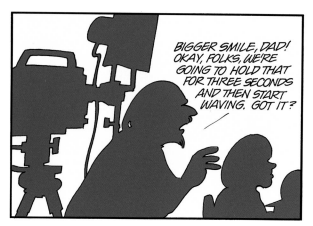

186

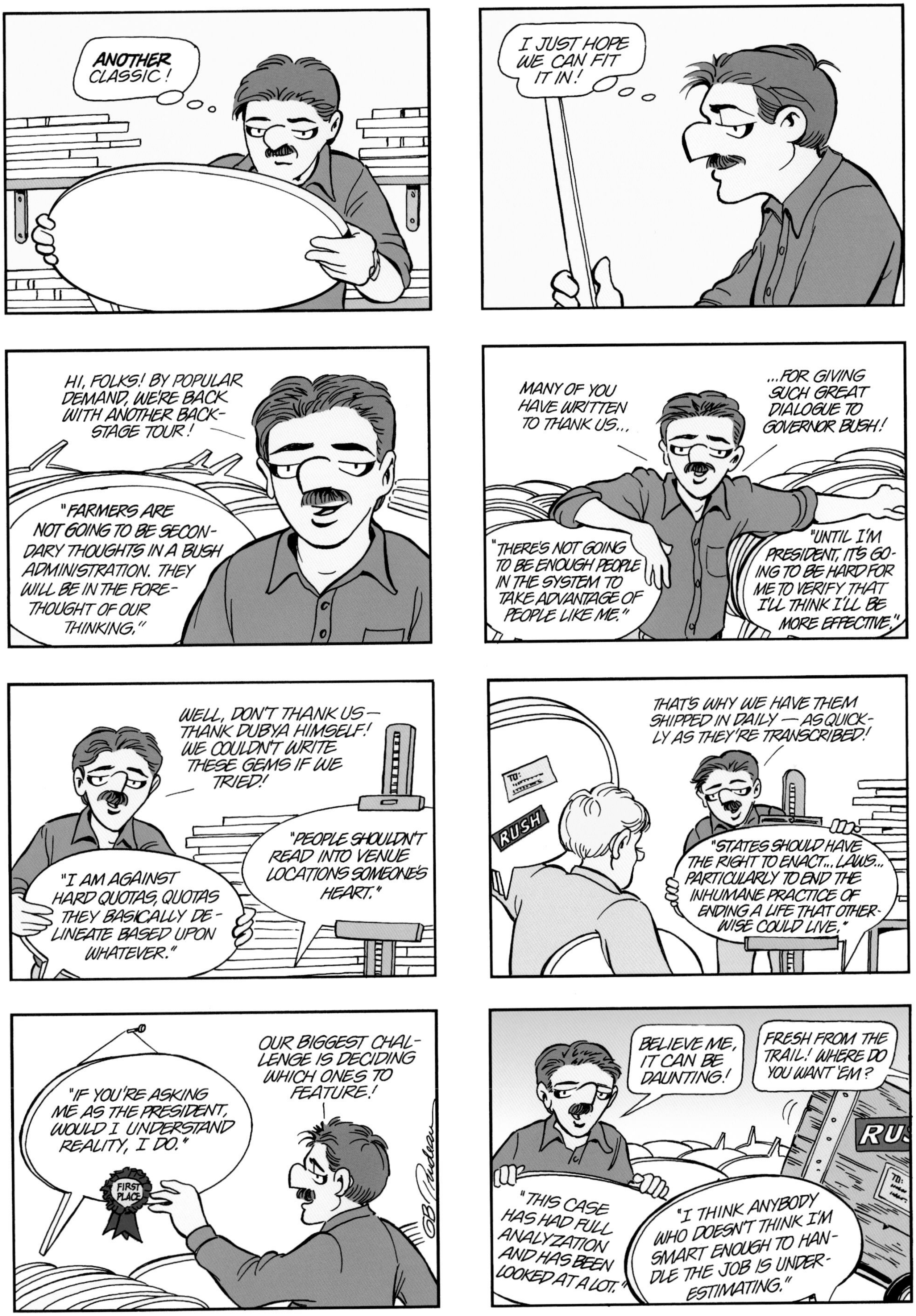
ANOTHER CLASSIC!
I JUST HOPE WE CAN FIT IT IN!
HI, FOLKS! BY POPULAR DEMAND, WE'RE BACK WITH ANOTHER BACK-STAGE TOUR!
"FARMERS ARE NOT GOING TO BE SECON-DARY THOUGHTS IN A BUSH ADMINISTRATION. THEY WILL BE IN THE FORE-THOUGHT OF OUR THINKING."
MANY OF YOU HAVE WRITTEN TO THANK US...
...FOR GIVING SUCH GREAT DIALOGUE TO GOVERNOR BUSH!
"THERE'S NOT GOING TO BE ENOUGH PEOPLE IN THE SYSTEM TO TAKE ADVANTAGE OF PEOPLE LIKE ME."
"UNTIL I'M PRESIDENT, IT'S GO-ING TO BE HARD FOR ME TO VERIFY THAT I'LL THINK I'LL BE MORE EFFECTIVE."
WELL, DON'T THANK US— THANK DUBYA HIMSELF! WE COULDN'T WRITE THESE GEMS IF WE TRIED!
"I AM AGAINST HARD QUOTAS, QUOTAS THEY BASICALLY DE-LINEATE BASED UPON WHATEVER."
"PEOPLE SHOULDN'T READ INTO VENUE LOCATIONS SOMEONE'S HEART."
THAT'S WHY WE HAVE THEM SHIPPED IN DAILY — AS QUICK-LY AS THEY'RE TRANSCRIBED!
RUSH
"STATES SHOULD HAVE THE RIGHT TO ENACT... LAWS... PARTICULARLY TO END THE INHUMANE PRACTICE OF ENDING A LIFE THAT OTHER-WISE COULD LIVE."
OUR BIGGEST CHAL-LENGE IS DECIDING WHICH ONES TO FEATURE!
"IF YOU'RE ASKING ME AS THE PRESIDENT, WOULD I UNDERSTAND REALITY, I DO."
FIRST PLACE
BELIEVE ME, IT CAN BE DAUNTING!
FRESH FROM THE TRAIL! WHERE DO YOU WANT 'EM?
"THIS CASE HAS HAD FULL ANALYZATION AND HAS BEEN LOOKED AT A LOT."
"I THINK ANYBODY WHO DOESN'T THINK I'M SMART ENOUGH TO HAN-DLE THE JOB IS UNDER-ESTIMATING."

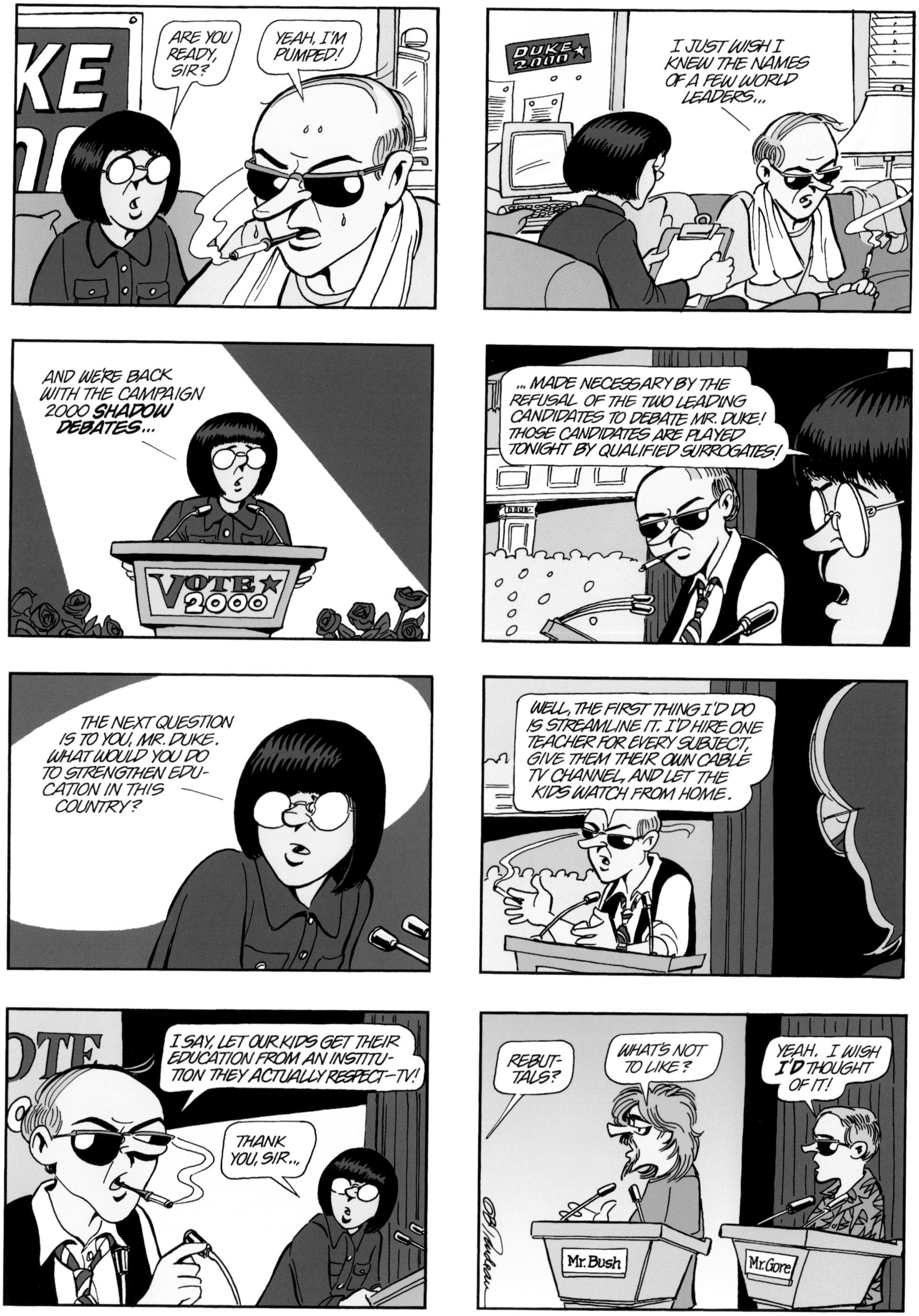

ARE YOU READY, SIR?
YEAH, I'M PUMPED!
DUKE 2000
I JUST WISH I KNEW THE NAMES OF A FEW WORLD LEADERS...
AND WE'RE BACK WITH THE CAMPAIGN 2000 **SHADOW DEBATES**...
VOTE 2000
... MADE NECESSARY BY THE REFUSAL OF THE TWO LEADING CANDIDATES TO DEBATE MR. DUKE! THOSE CANDIDATES ARE PLAYED TONIGHT BY QUALIFIED SURROGATES!
THE NEXT QUESTION IS TO YOU, MR. DUKE. WHAT WOULD YOU DO TO STRENGTHEN EDUCATION IN THIS COUNTRY?
WELL, THE FIRST THING I'D DO IS STREAMLINE IT. I'D HIRE ONE TEACHER FOR EVERY SUBJECT, GIVE THEM THEIR OWN CABLE TV CHANNEL, AND LET THE KIDS WATCH FROM HOME.
I SAY, LET OUR KIDS GET THEIR EDUCATION FROM AN INSTITUTION THEY ACTUALLY RESPECT—TV!
THANK YOU, SIR...
REBUTTALS?
WHAT'S NOT TO LIKE?
YEAH. I WISH **I'D** THOUGHT OF IT!
Mr. Bush
Mr. Gore

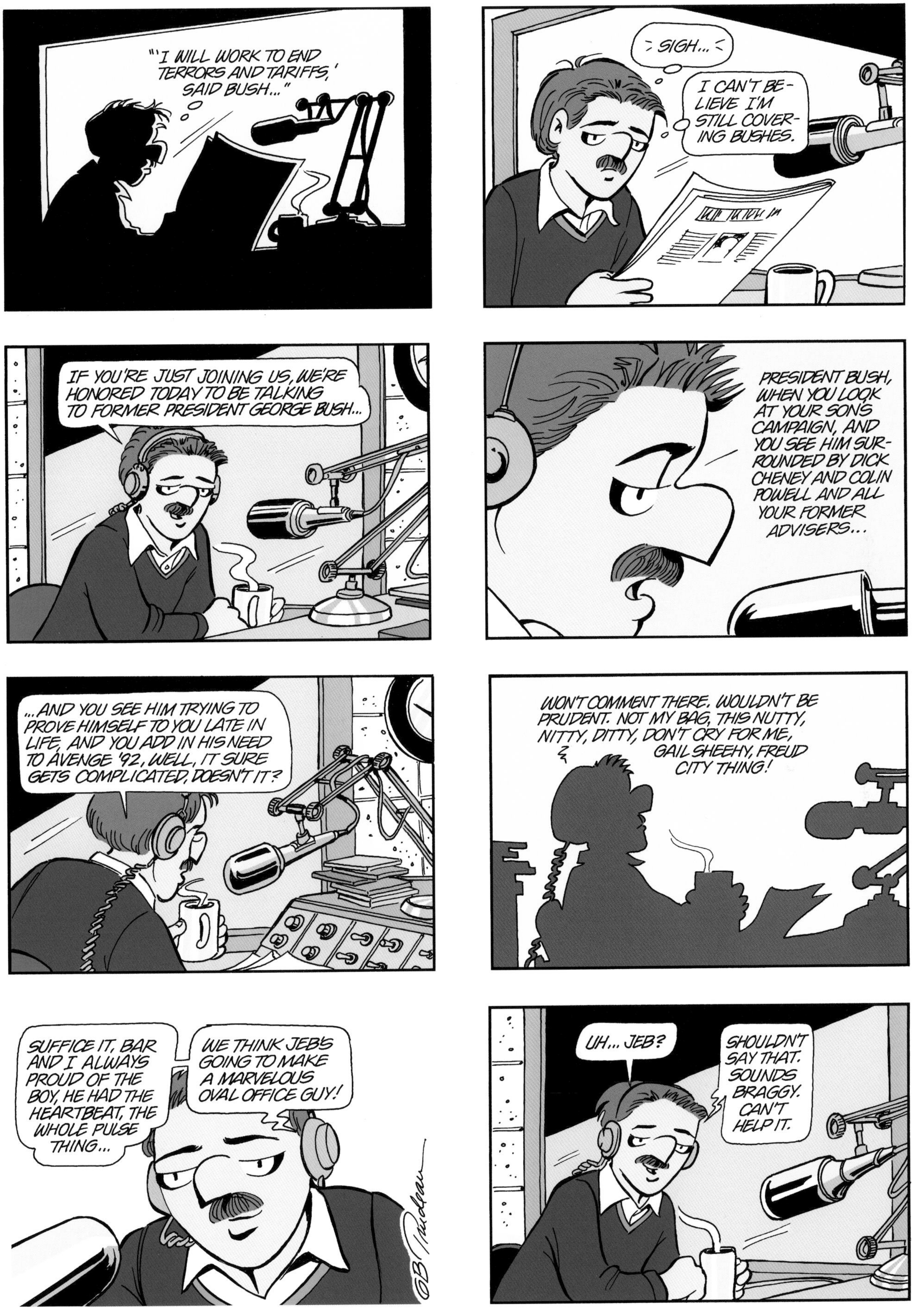
"'I WILL WORK TO END TERRORS AND TARIFFS,' SAID BUSH..."
SIGH...
I CAN'T BE-LIEVE I'M STILL COVER-ING BUSHES.
IF YOU'RE JUST JOINING US, WE'RE HONORED TODAY TO BE TALKING TO FORMER PRESIDENT GEORGE BUSH...
PRESIDENT BUSH, WHEN YOU LOOK AT YOUR SON'S CAMPAIGN, AND YOU SEE HIM SUR-ROUNDED BY DICK CHENEY AND COLIN POWELL AND ALL YOUR FORMER ADVISERS...
...AND YOU SEE HIM TRYING TO PROVE HIMSELF TO YOU LATE IN LIFE, AND YOU ADD IN HIS NEED TO AVENGE '92, WELL, IT SURE GETS COMPLICATED, DOESN'T IT?
WON'T COMMENT THERE. WOULDN'T BE PRUDENT. NOT MY BAG, THIS NUTTY, NITTY, DITTY, DON'T CRY FOR ME, GAIL SHEEHY, FREUD CITY THING!
SUFFICE IT, BAR AND I ALWAYS PROUD OF THE BOY, HE HAD THE HEARTBEAT, THE WHOLE PULSE THING...
WE THINK JEB'S GOING TO MAKE A MARVELOUS OVAL OFFICE GUY!
UH... JEB?
SHOULDN'T SAY THAT. SOUNDS BRAGGY. CAN'T HELP IT.

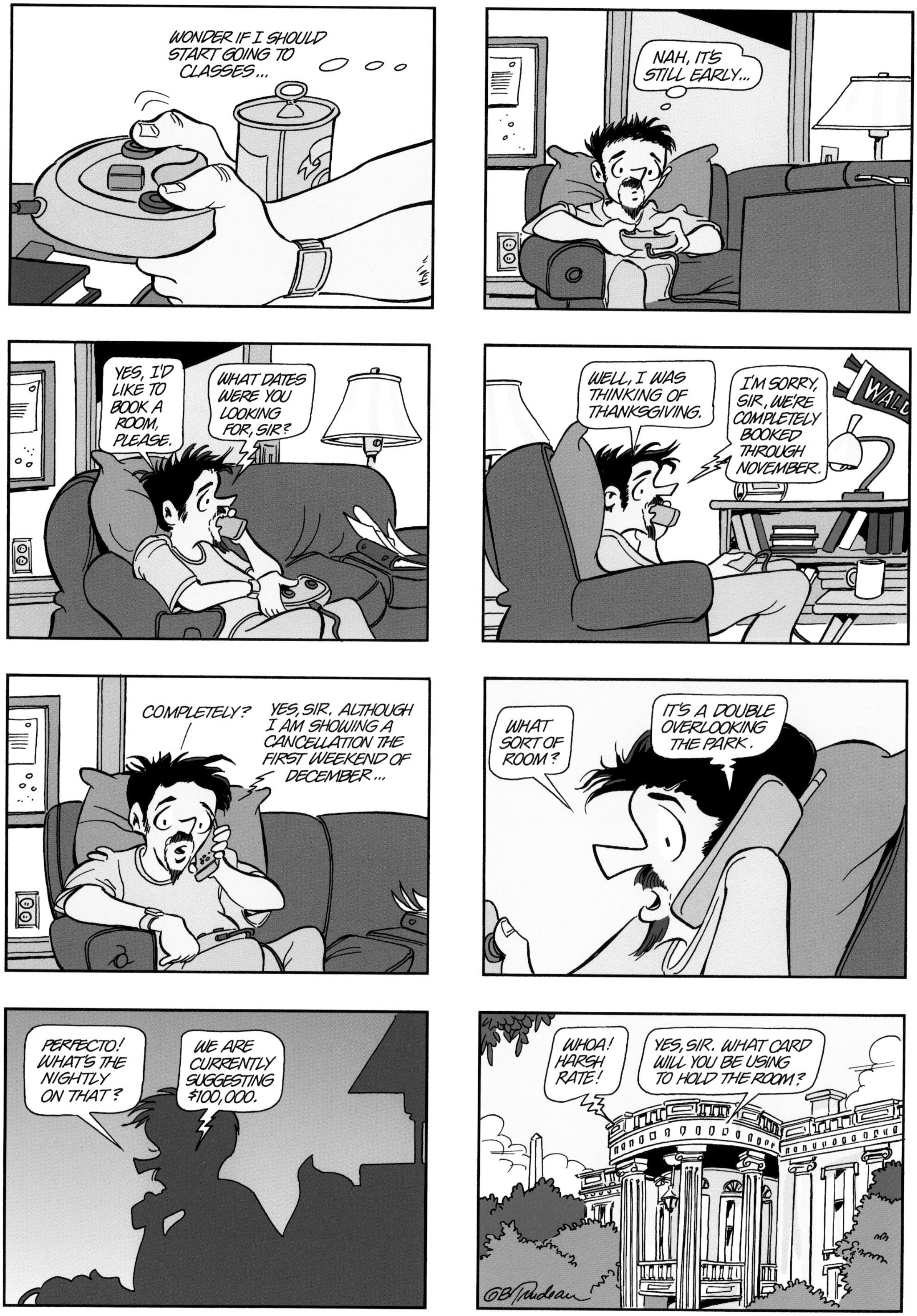
WONDER IF I SHOULD START GOING TO CLASSES...
NAH, IT'S STILL EARLY...
YES, I'D LIKE TO BOOK A ROOM, PLEASE.
WHAT DATES WERE YOU LOOKING FOR, SIR?
WELL, I WAS THINKING OF THANKSGIVING.
I'M SORRY, SIR, WE'RE COMPLETELY BOOKED THROUGH NOVEMBER.
COMPLETELY?
YES, SIR. ALTHOUGH I AM SHOWING A CANCELLATION THE FIRST WEEKEND OF DECEMBER...
WHAT SORT OF ROOM?
IT'S A DOUBLE OVERLOOKING THE PARK.
PERFECTO! WHAT'S THE NIGHTLY ON THAT?
WE ARE CURRENTLY SUGGESTING $100,000.
WHOA! HARSH RATE!
YES, SIR. WHAT CARD WILL YOU BE USING TO HOLD THE ROOM?

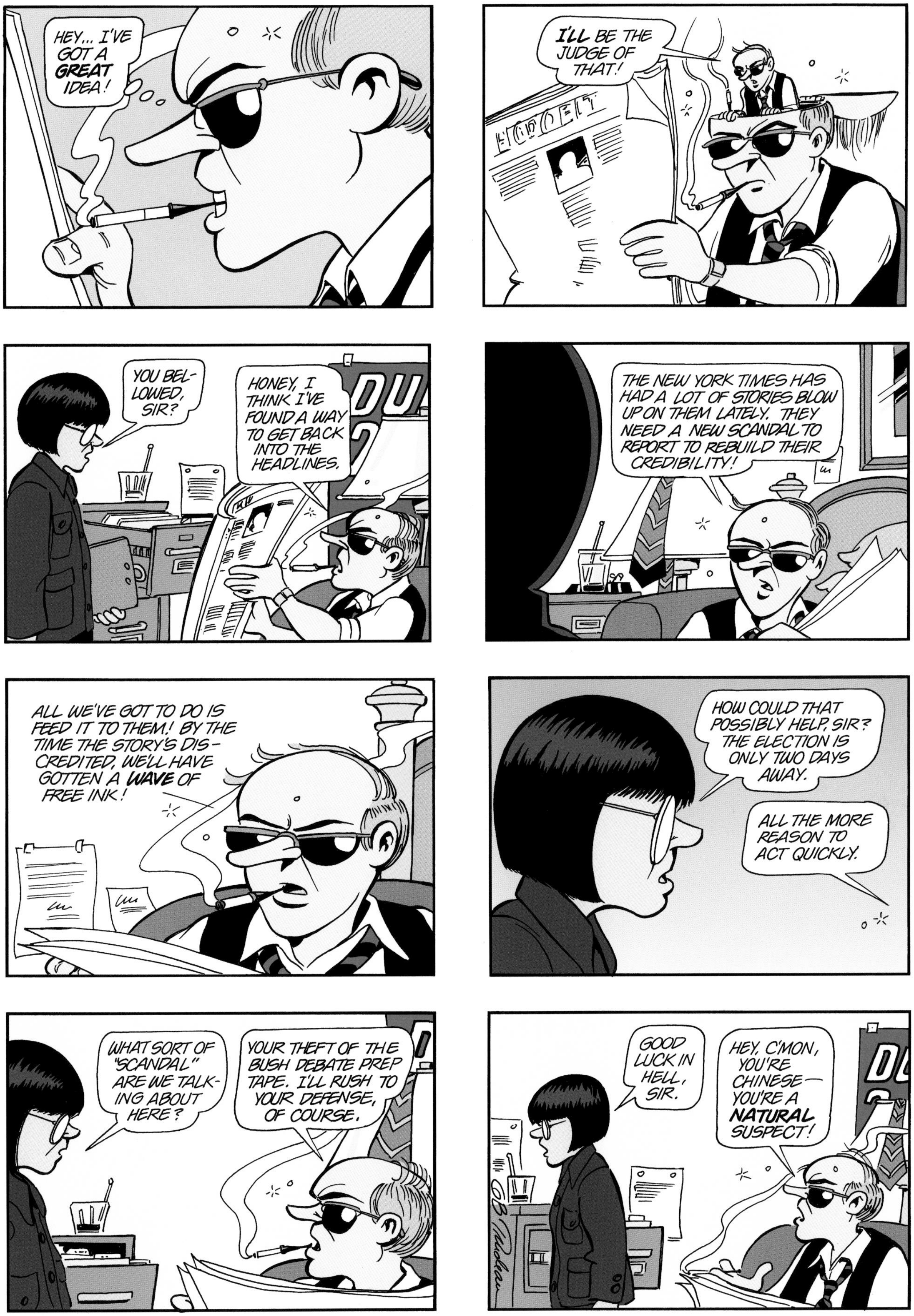
HEY... I'VE GOT A **GREAT** IDEA!
I'LL BE THE JUDGE OF THAT!
YOU BEL-LOWED, SIR?
HONEY, I THINK I'VE FOUND A WAY TO GET BACK INTO THE HEADLINES.
THE NEW YORK TIMES HAS HAD A LOT OF STORIES BLOW UP ON THEM LATELY. THEY NEED A NEW SCANDAL TO REPORT TO REBUILD THEIR CREDIBILITY!
ALL WE'VE GOT TO DO IS FEED IT TO THEM! BY THE TIME THE STORY'S DIS-CREDITED, WE'LL HAVE GOTTEN A **WAVE** OF FREE INK!
HOW COULD THAT POSSIBLY HELP, SIR? THE ELECTION IS ONLY TWO DAYS AWAY.
ALL THE MORE REASON TO ACT QUICKLY.
WHAT SORT OF "SCANDAL" ARE WE TALK-ING ABOUT HERE?
YOUR THEFT OF THE BUSH DEBATE PREP TAPE. I'LL RUSH TO YOUR DEFENSE, OF COURSE.
GOOD LUCK IN HELL, SIR.
HEY, C'MON, YOU'RE CHINESE— YOU'RE A **NATURAL** SUSPECT!

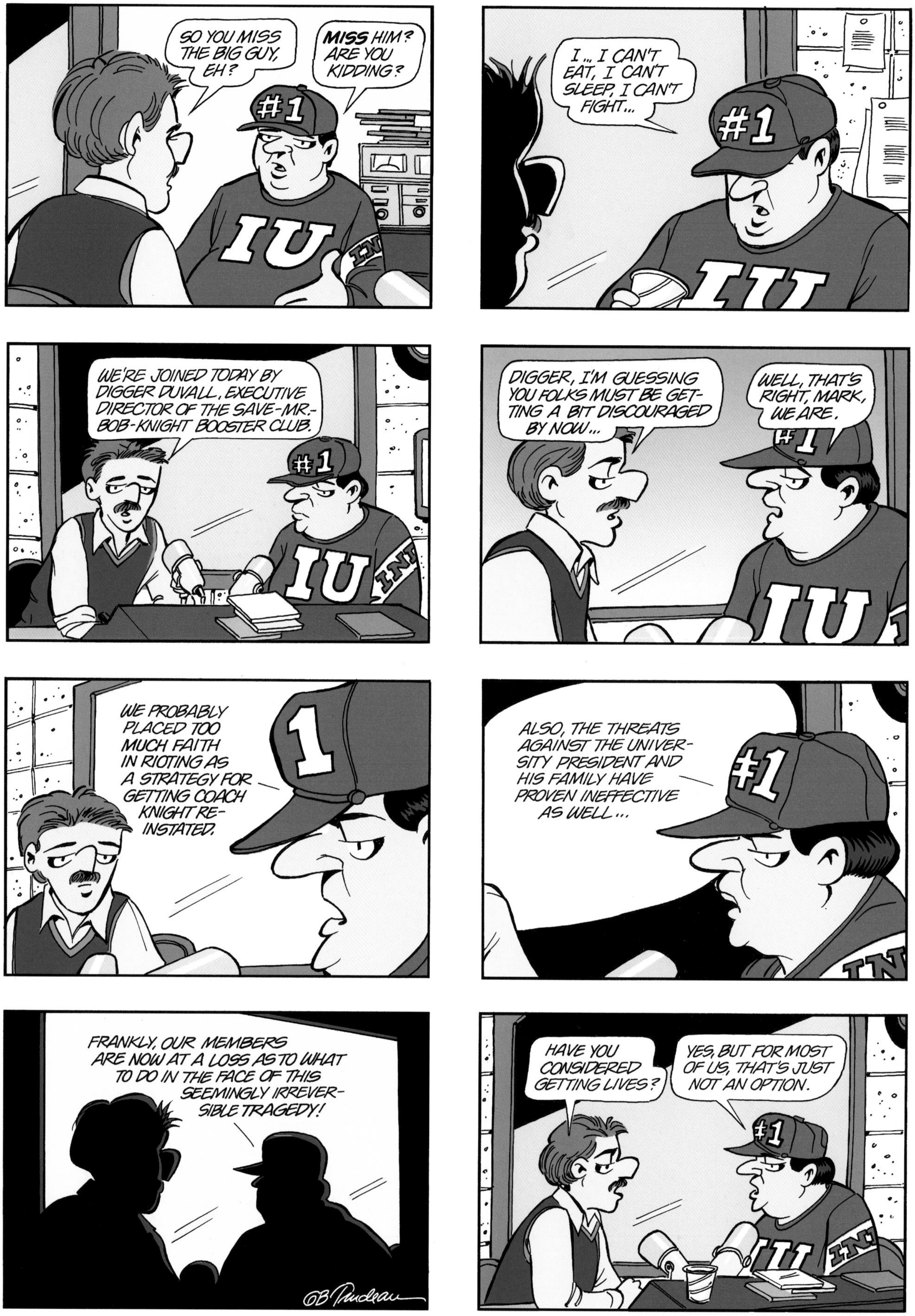
SO YOU MISS THE BIG GUY, EH?
MISS HIM? ARE YOU KIDDING?
I... I CAN'T EAT, I CAN'T SLEEP, I CAN'T FIGHT...
WE'RE JOINED TODAY BY DIGGER DUVALL, EXECUTIVE DIRECTOR OF THE SAVE-MR.-BOB-KNIGHT BOOSTER CLUB.
#1
IU
DIGGER, I'M GUESSING YOU FOLKS MUST BE GETTING A BIT DISCOURAGED BY NOW...
WELL, THAT'S RIGHT, MARK, WE ARE.
WE PROBABLY PLACED TOO MUCH FAITH IN RIOTING AS A STRATEGY FOR GETTING COACH KNIGHT RE-INSTATED.
ALSO, THE THREATS AGAINST THE UNIVERSITY PRESIDENT AND HIS FAMILY HAVE PROVEN INEFFECTIVE AS WELL...
FRANKLY, OUR MEMBERS ARE NOW AT A LOSS AS TO WHAT TO DO IN THE FACE OF THIS SEEMINGLY IRREVERSIBLE TRAGEDY!
GB Trudeau
HAVE YOU CONSIDERED GETTING LIVES?
YES, BUT FOR MOST OF US, THAT'S JUST NOT AN OPTION.

JIM ANDREWS, LONG-TIME CEO OF UNIVERSAL PETROLEUM, IS LOST IN SWEET REVERIE.

Z!

HE DREAMS OF A PLACE WHERE A MAN CAN CONTROL HIS OWN DESTINY, SET HIS OWN LIMITS, EVEN WRITE THE LAWS THAT REGULATE HIS OWN BEHAVIOR...

A PLACE SO FRIENDLY TO THE ENTREPRENEURIAL SPIRIT THAT IT ENJOYS THE HIGHEST LEVELS OF TOXIC RELEASES AND AIR AND WATER POLLUTION IN THE COUNTRY!

YES, HE DREAMS OF TEXAS.

FOR JIM ANDREWS, TOP DOG AT UNIVERSAL PETROLEUM, IT IS A NIGHT OF LONGING.

ALTHOUGH HIS NEWEST TROPHY WIFE BREATHES SOFTLY IN THE DARKNESS BESIDE HIM, HE YEARNS ONLY FOR TEXAS, FOR THE SWEET REGULATORY RELIEF ONLY **SHE** CAN PROVIDE HIM.

TEXAS— WHERE POLLUTERS WRITE THE ENVIRONMENTAL LAWS, AND COMPLIANCE IS **VOLUNTARY!** HOW **GRAND** IT'D BE TO LIVE IN SUCH A PLACE! AND THEN IT HITS HIM ...

HE **DOES** LIVE IN SUCH A PLACE.

I'M **TEXAN!**

PINCH ME!

WHERE, SWEET BUNS?

IT'S 3:00 A.M. IN GEORGE DUBYA BUSH'S TEXAS.

CHERYLEE, I JUST HAD THE BEST DREAM!

THAT'S NICE, JIMMY.

I DREAMT I WAS IN TEXAS, AND GOVERNMENT WAS DOING WHAT GOVERNMENT IS SUPPOSED TO DO—WHICH IS GET OUT OF THE WAY OF BUSINESS. BUT THE DREAM IS **REAL**.

IT'S ABOUT FREEDOM, CHERYLEE! IN DUBYA'S TEXAS, I'M FREE TO RUN MY REFINERIES AS I SEE FIT, JUST AS YOU'RE FREE TO FILL YOUR DAYS WITH ... UH...

WHATEVER IT IS YOU FILL YOUR DAYS WITH!

SHOPPING AND SURGERY. YOU'RE SWEET TO WONDER.

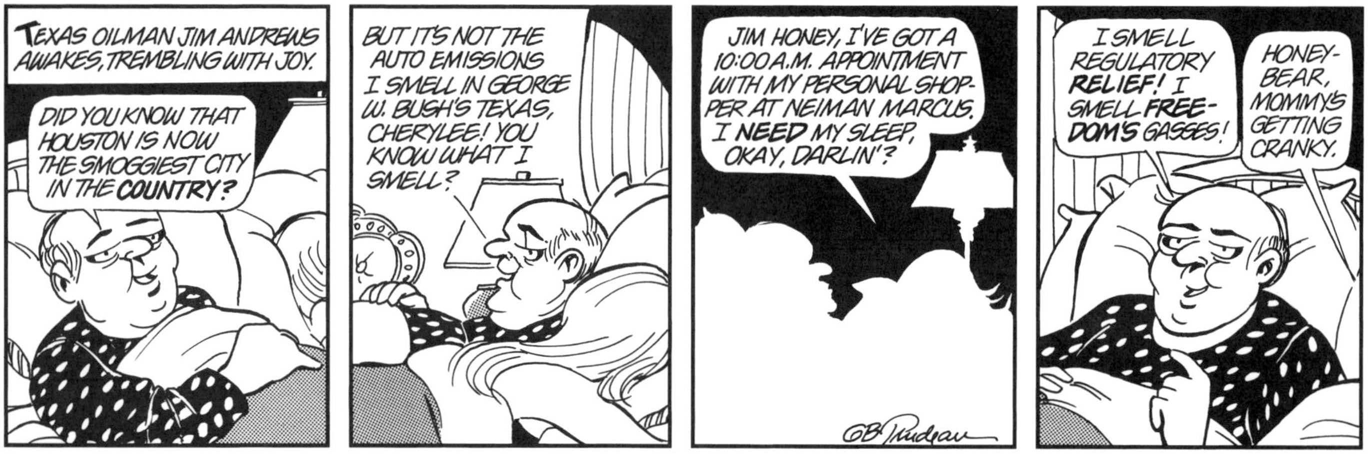
TEXAS OILMAN JIM ANDREWS AWAKES, TREMBLING WITH JOY.
DID YOU KNOW THAT HOUSTON IS NOW THE SMOGGIEST CITY IN THE COUNTRY?
BUT IT'S NOT THE AUTO EMISSIONS I SMELL IN GEORGE W. BUSH'S TEXAS, CHERYLEE! YOU KNOW WHAT I SMELL?
JIM HONEY, I'VE GOT A 10:00 A.M. APPOINTMENT WITH MY PERSONAL SHOPPER AT NEIMAN MARCUS. I NEED MY SLEEP, OKAY, DARLIN'?
I SMELL REGULATORY RELIEF! I SMELL FREEDOM'S GASSES!
HONEY-BEAR, MOMMY'S GETTING CRANKY.

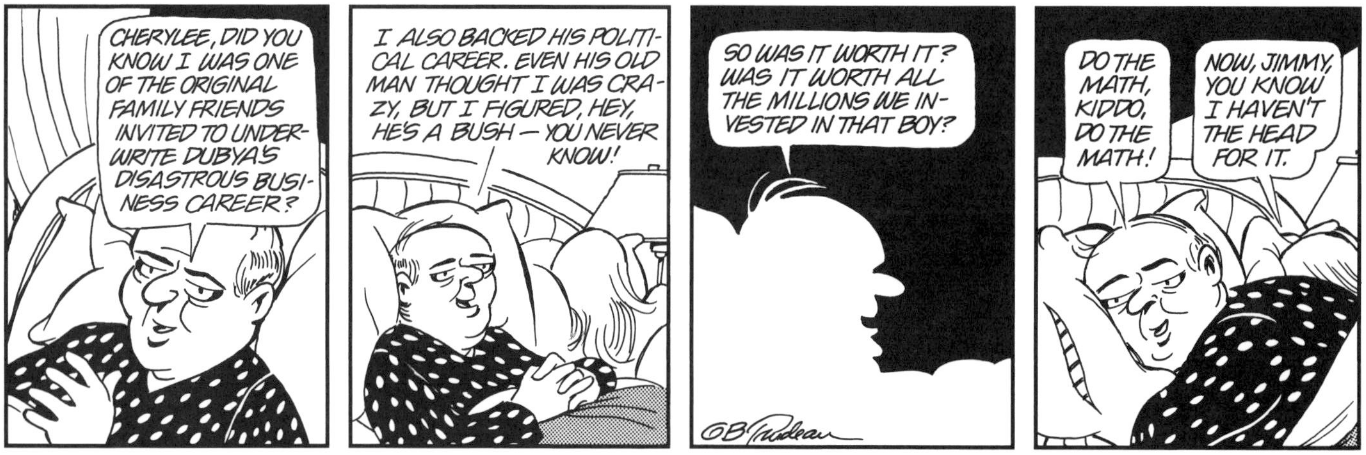
CHERYLEE, DID YOU KNOW I WAS ONE OF THE ORIGINAL FAMILY FRIENDS INVITED TO UNDERWRITE DUBYA'S DISASTROUS BUSINESS CAREER?
I ALSO BACKED HIS POLITICAL CAREER. EVEN HIS OLD MAN THOUGHT I WAS CRAZY, BUT I FIGURED, HEY, HE'S A BUSH — YOU NEVER KNOW!
SO WAS IT WORTH IT? WAS IT WORTH ALL THE MILLIONS WE INVESTED IN THAT BOY?
DO THE MATH, KIDDO, DO THE MATH!
NOW, JIMMY, YOU KNOW I HAVEN'T THE HEAD FOR IT.

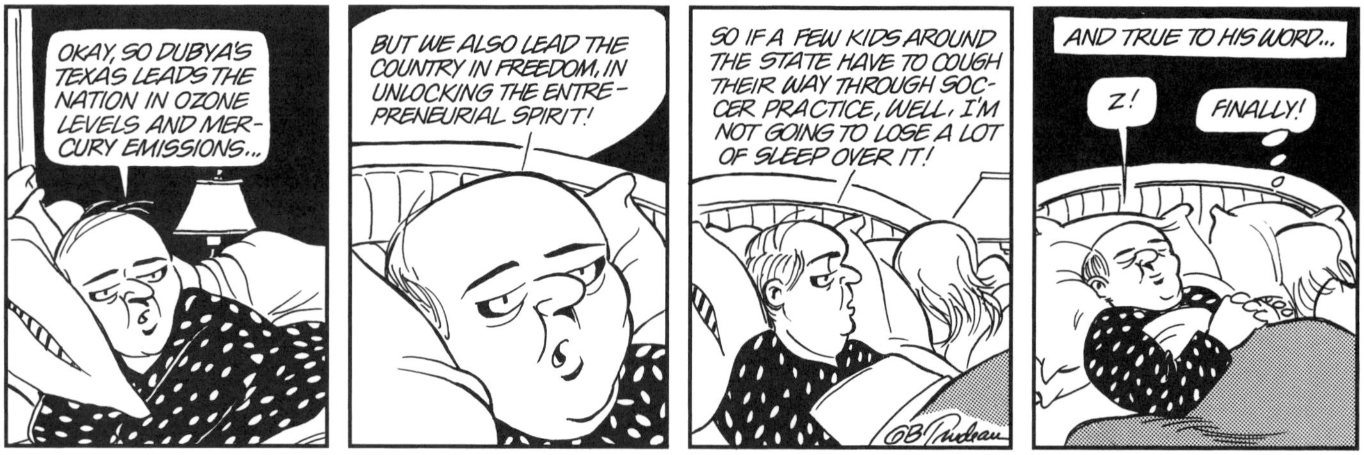
OKAY, SO DUBYA'S TEXAS LEADS THE NATION IN OZONE LEVELS AND MERCURY EMISSIONS...
BUT WE ALSO LEAD THE COUNTRY IN FREEDOM, IN UNLOCKING THE ENTREPRENEURIAL SPIRIT!
SO IF A FEW KIDS AROUND THE STATE HAVE TO COUGH THEIR WAY THROUGH SOCCER PRACTICE, WELL, I'M NOT GOING TO LOSE A LOT OF SLEEP OVER IT!
AND TRUE TO HIS WORD...
Z!
FINALLY!

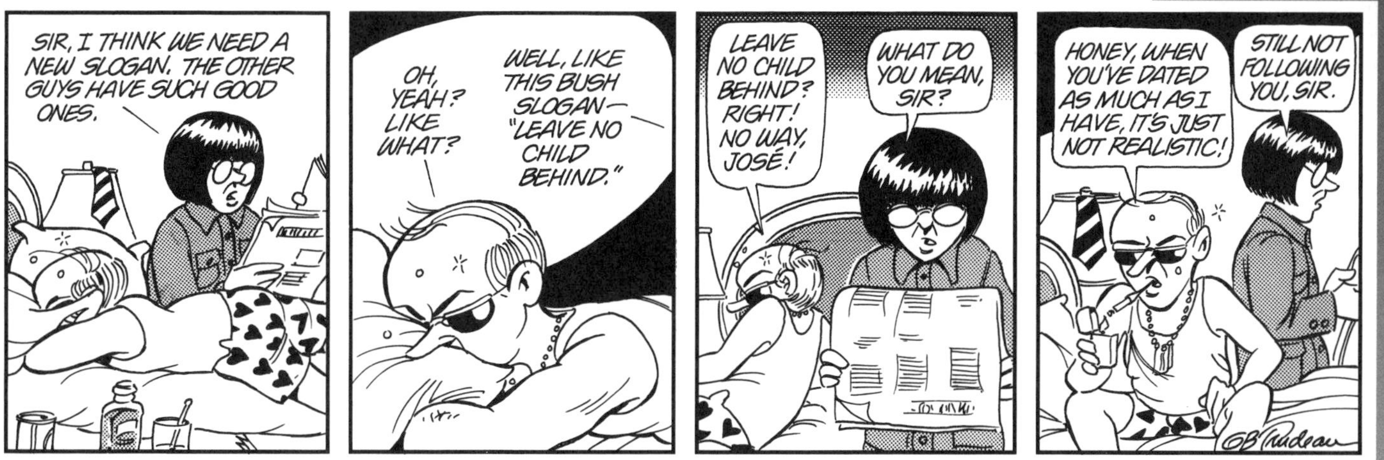
SIR, I THINK WE NEED A NEW SLOGAN. THE OTHER GUYS HAVE SUCH GOOD ONES.
OH, YEAH? LIKE WHAT?
WELL, LIKE THIS BUSH SLOGAN— "LEAVE NO CHILD BEHIND."
LEAVE NO CHILD BEHIND? RIGHT! NO WAY, JOSÉ!
WHAT DO YOU MEAN, SIR?
HONEY, WHEN YOU'VE DATED AS MUCH AS I HAVE, IT'S JUST NOT REALISTIC!
STILL NOT FOLLOWING YOU, SIR.
GB Trudeau

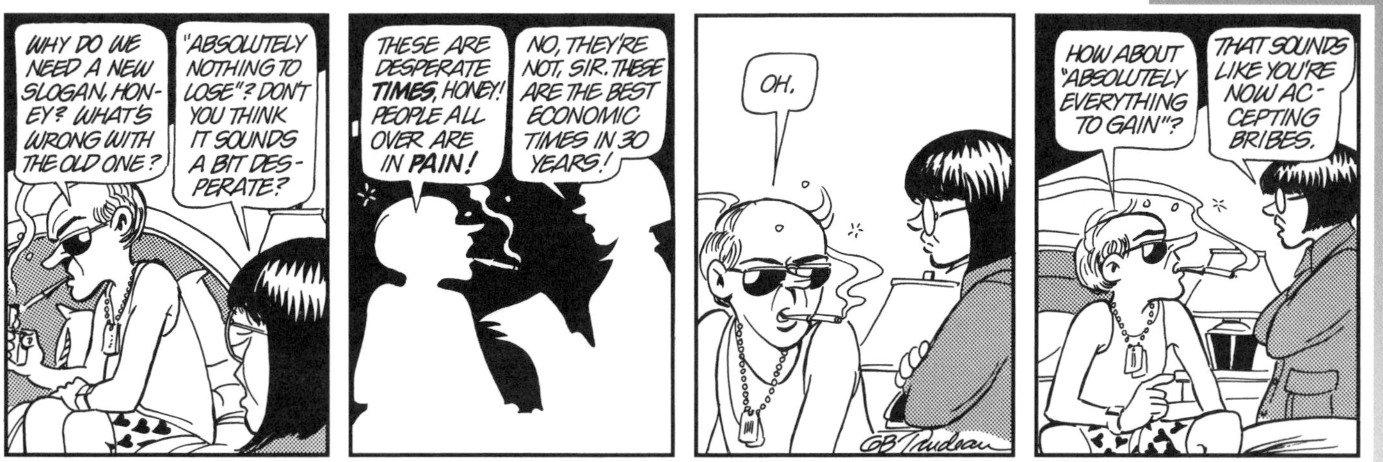
WHY DO WE NEED A NEW SLOGAN, HONEY? WHAT'S WRONG WITH THE OLD ONE?
"ABSOLUTELY NOTHING TO LOSE"? DON'T YOU THINK IT SOUNDS A BIT DESPERATE?
THESE ARE DESPERATE TIMES, HONEY! PEOPLE ALL OVER ARE IN PAIN!
NO, THEY'RE NOT, SIR. THESE ARE THE BEST ECONOMIC TIMES IN 30 YEARS!
OH.
GB Trudeau
HOW ABOUT "ABSOLUTELY EVERYTHING TO GAIN"?
THAT SOUNDS LIKE YOU'RE NOW ACCEPTING BRIBES.

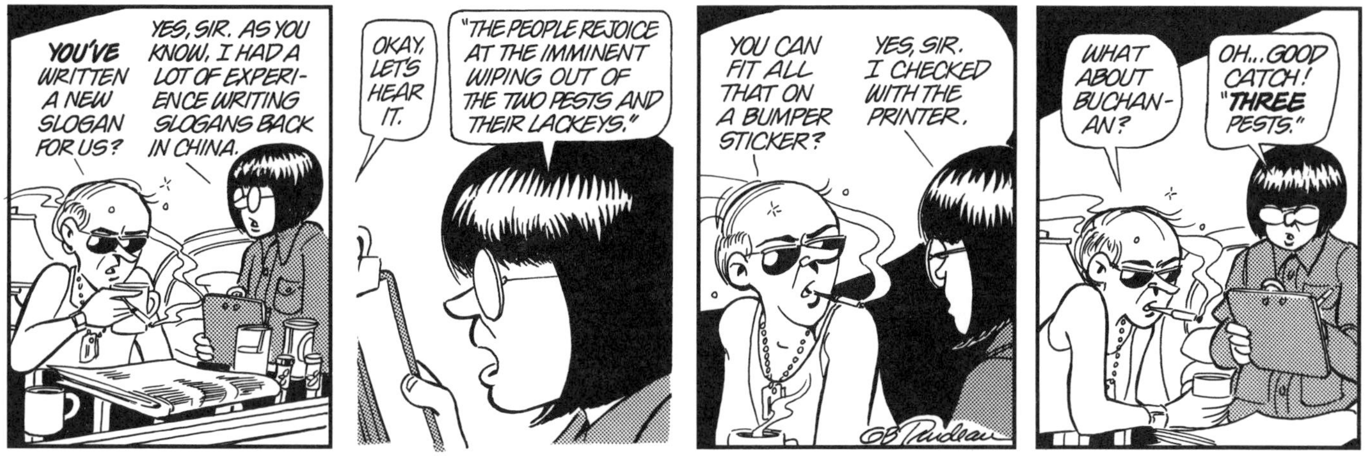
YOU'VE WRITTEN A NEW SLOGAN FOR US?
YES, SIR. AS YOU KNOW, I HAD A LOT OF EXPERIENCE WRITING SLOGANS BACK IN CHINA.
OKAY, LET'S HEAR IT.
"THE PEOPLE REJOICE AT THE IMMINENT WIPING OUT OF THE TWO PESTS AND THEIR LACKEYS."
YOU CAN FIT ALL THAT ON A BUMPER STICKER?
YES, SIR. I CHECKED WITH THE PRINTER.
GB Trudeau
WHAT ABOUT BUCHANAN?
OH... GOOD CATCH! "THREE PESTS."

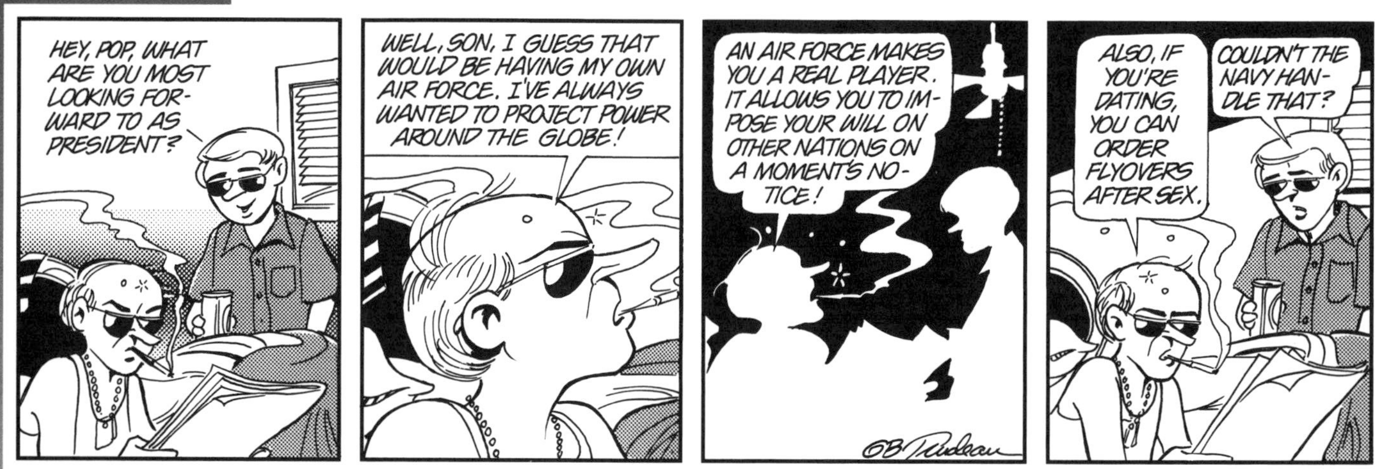
HEY, POP, WHAT ARE YOU MOST LOOKING FOR-WARD TO AS PRESIDENT?
WELL, SON, I GUESS THAT WOULD BE HAVING MY OWN AIR FORCE. I'VE ALWAYS WANTED TO PROJECT POWER AROUND THE GLOBE!
AN AIR FORCE MAKES YOU A REAL PLAYER. IT ALLOWS YOU TO IM-POSE YOUR WILL ON OTHER NATIONS ON A MOMENT'S NO-TICE!
©B Trudeau
ALSO, IF YOU'RE DATING, YOU CAN ORDER FLYOVERS AFTER SEX.
COULDN'T THE NAVY HAN-DLE THAT?

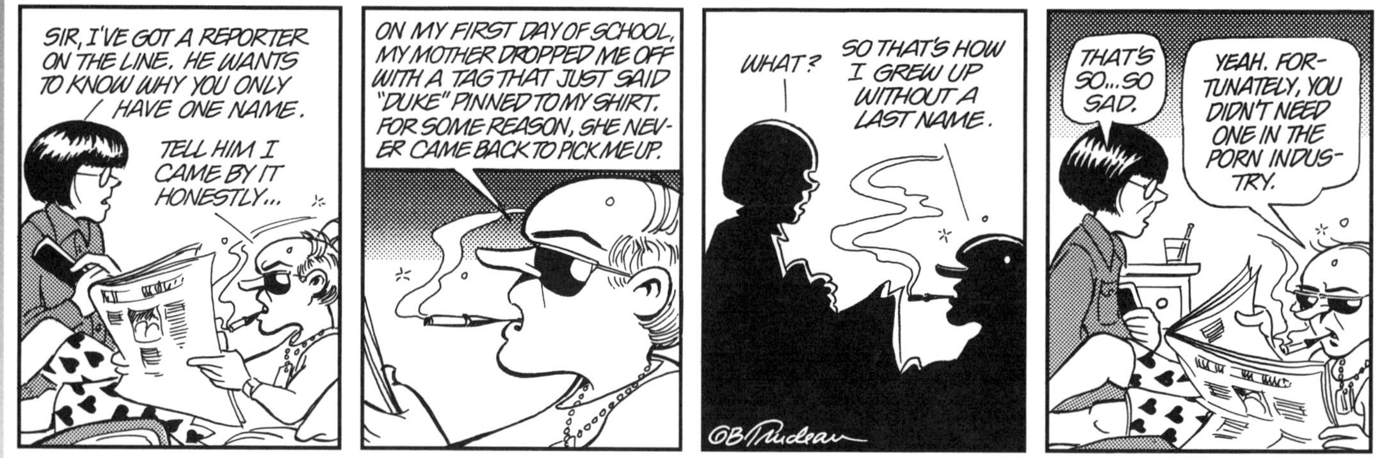
SIR, I'VE GOT A REPORTER ON THE LINE. HE WANTS TO KNOW WHY YOU ONLY HAVE ONE NAME.
TELL HIM I CAME BY IT HONESTLY...
ON MY FIRST DAY OF SCHOOL, MY MOTHER DROPPED ME OFF WITH A TAG THAT JUST SAID "DUKE" PINNED TO MY SHIRT. FOR SOME REASON, SHE NEV-ER CAME BACK TO PICK ME UP.
WHAT?
SO THAT'S HOW I GREW UP WITHOUT A LAST NAME.
©B Trudeau
THAT'S SO...SO SAD.
YEAH. FOR-TUNATELY, YOU DIDN'T NEED ONE IN THE PORN INDUS-TRY.

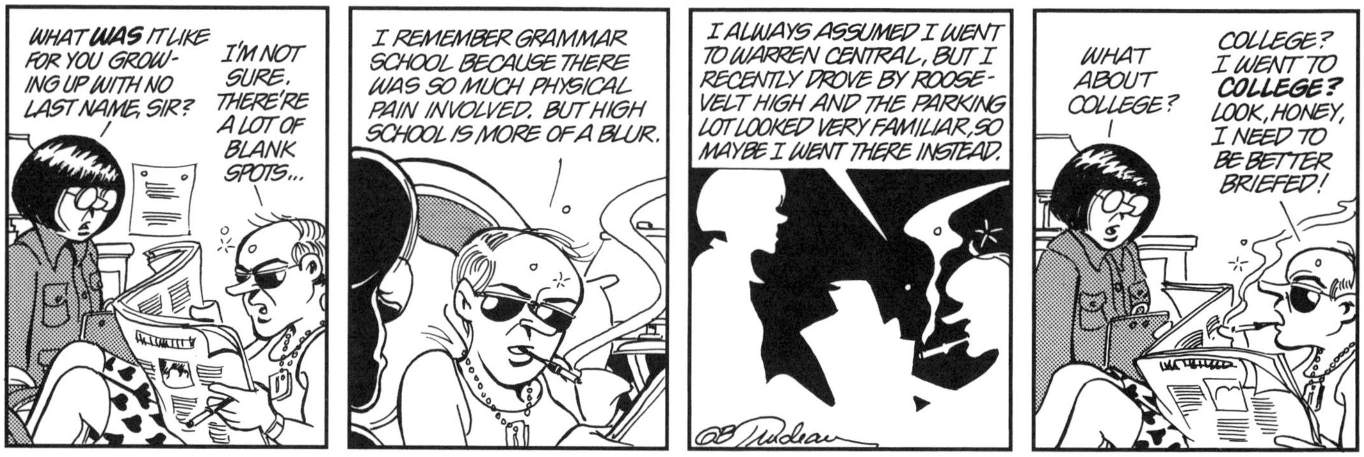
WHAT WAS IT LIKE FOR YOU GROW-ING UP WITH NO LAST NAME, SIR?
I'M NOT SURE. THERE'RE A LOT OF BLANK SPOTS...
I REMEMBER GRAMMAR SCHOOL BECAUSE THERE WAS SO MUCH PHYSICAL PAIN INVOLVED. BUT HIGH SCHOOL IS MORE OF A BLUR.
I ALWAYS ASSUMED I WENT TO WARREN CENTRAL, BUT I RECENTLY DROVE BY ROOSE-VELT HIGH AND THE PARKING LOT LOOKED VERY FAMILIAR, SO MAYBE I WENT THERE INSTEAD.
©B Trudeau
WHAT ABOUT COLLEGE?
COLLEGE? I WENT TO COLLEGE? LOOK, HONEY, I NEED TO BE BETTER BRIEFED!

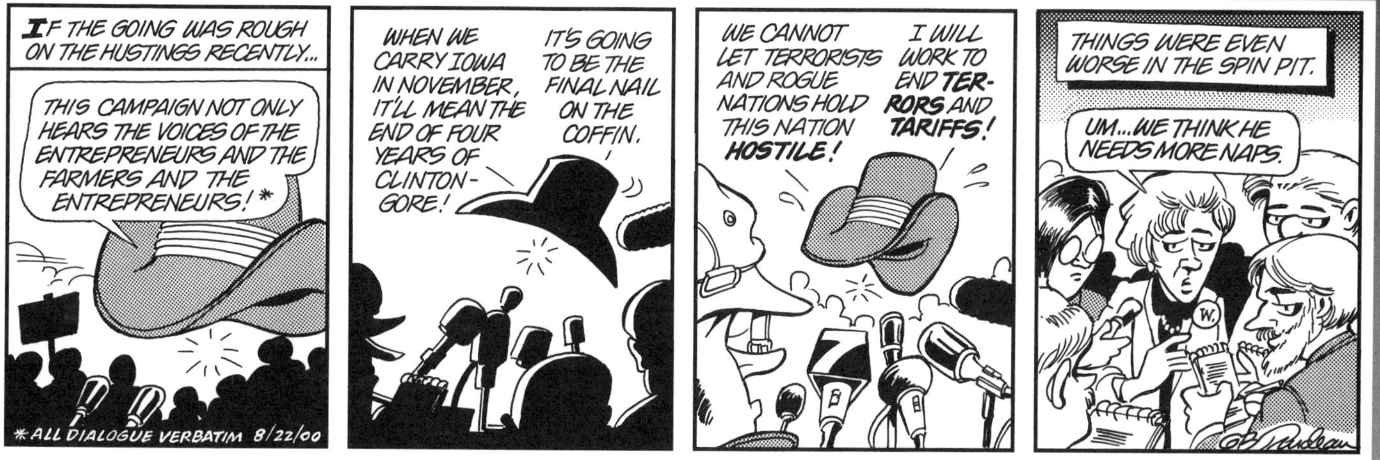
IF THE GOING WAS ROUGH ON THE HUSTINGS RECENTLY...
THIS CAMPAIGN NOT ONLY HEARS THE VOICES OF THE ENTREPRENEURS AND THE FARMERS AND THE ENTREPRENEURS! *
* ALL DIALOGUE VERBATIM 8/22/00
WHEN WE CARRY IOWA IN NOVEMBER, IT'LL MEAN THE END OF FOUR YEARS OF CLINTON-GORE!
IT'S GOING TO BE THE FINAL NAIL ON THE COFFIN.
WE CANNOT LET TERRORISTS AND ROGUE NATIONS HOLD THIS NATION HOSTILE!
I WILL WORK TO END TERRORS AND TARIFFS!
THINGS WERE EVEN WORSE IN THE SPIN PIT.
UM... WE THINK HE NEEDS MORE NAPS.

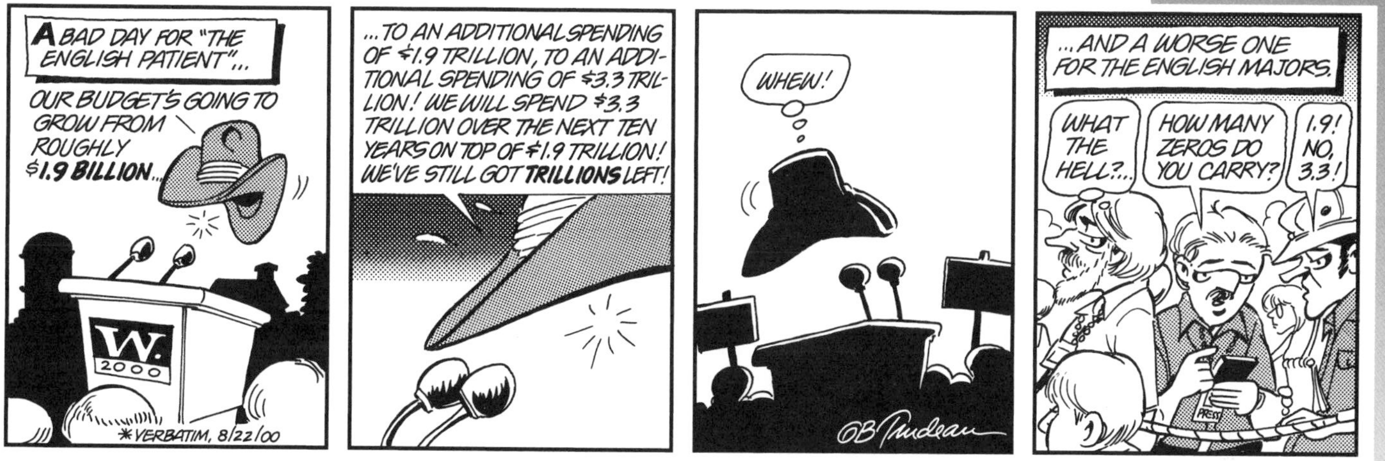
A BAD DAY FOR "THE ENGLISH PATIENT"...
OUR BUDGET'S GOING TO GROW FROM ROUGHLY $1.9 BILLION...
* VERBATIM, 8/22/00
...TO AN ADDITIONAL SPENDING OF $1.9 TRILLION, TO AN ADDITIONAL SPENDING OF $3.3 TRILLION! WE WILL SPEND $3.3 TRILLION OVER THE NEXT TEN YEARS ON TOP OF $1.9 TRILLION! WE'VE STILL GOT TRILLIONS LEFT!
WHEW!
...AND A WORSE ONE FOR THE ENGLISH MAJORS.
WHAT THE HELL?...
HOW MANY ZEROS DO YOU CARRY?
1.9! NO, 3.3!

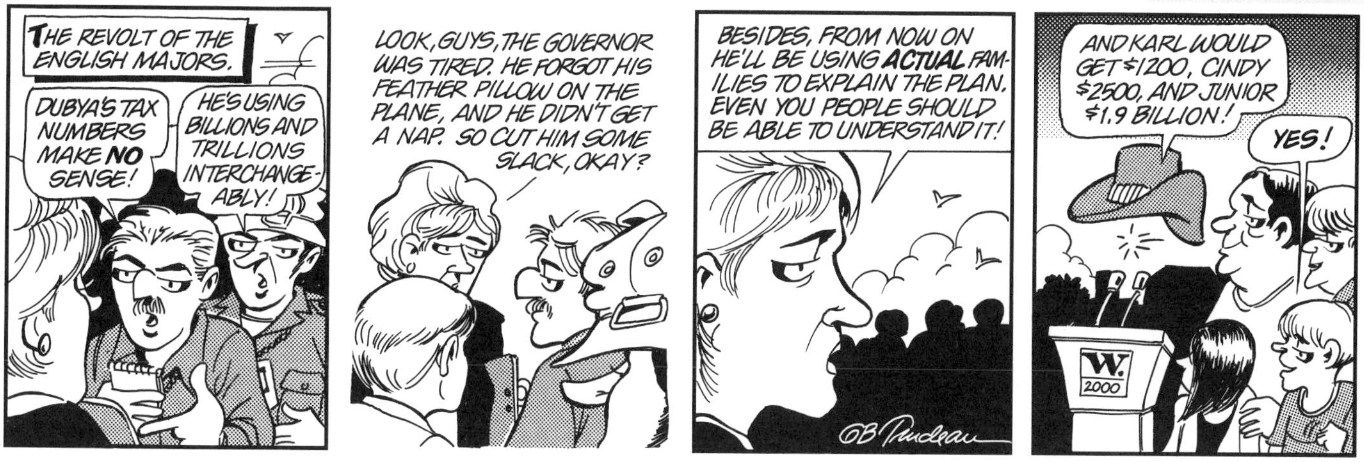
THE REVOLT OF THE ENGLISH MAJORS.
DUBYA'S TAX NUMBERS MAKE NO SENSE!
HE'S USING BILLIONS AND TRILLIONS INTERCHANGEABLY!
LOOK, GUYS, THE GOVERNOR WAS TIRED. HE FORGOT HIS FEATHER PILLOW ON THE PLANE, AND HE DIDN'T GET A NAP. SO CUT HIM SOME SLACK, OKAY?
BESIDES, FROM NOW ON HE'LL BE USING ACTUAL FAMILIES TO EXPLAIN THE PLAN. EVEN YOU PEOPLE SHOULD BE ABLE TO UNDERSTAND IT!
AND KARL WOULD GET $1200, CINDY $2500, AND JUNIOR $1.9 BILLION!
YES!

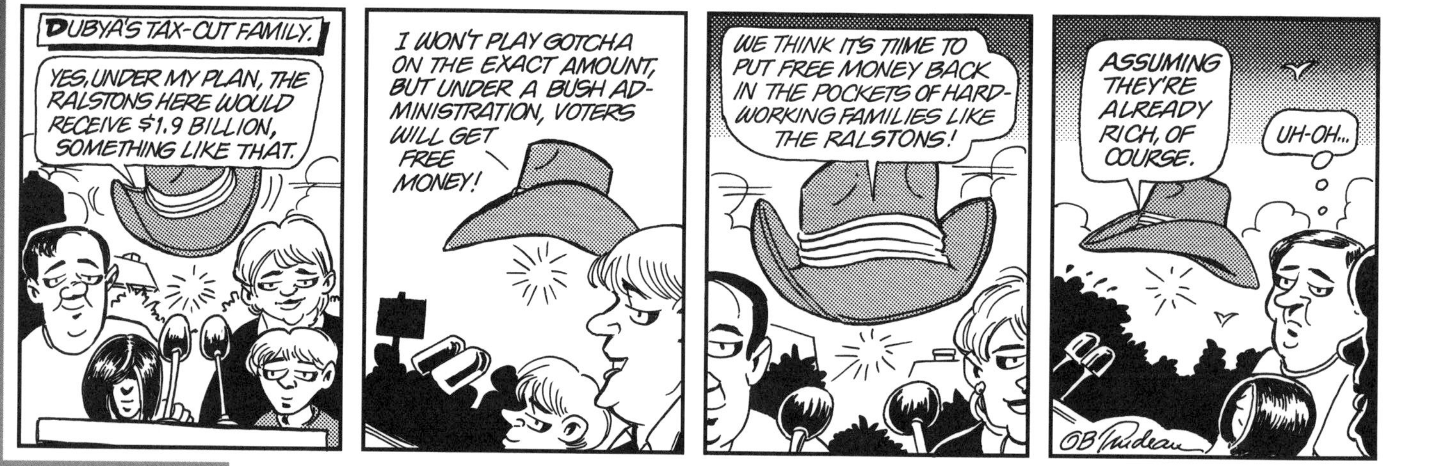
DUBYA'S TAX-CUT FAMILY.
YES, UNDER MY PLAN, THE RALSTONS HERE WOULD RECEIVE $1.9 BILLION, SOMETHING LIKE THAT.
I WON'T PLAY GOTCHA ON THE EXACT AMOUNT, BUT UNDER A BUSH ADMINISTRATION, VOTERS WILL GET FREE MONEY!
WE THINK IT'S TIME TO PUT FREE MONEY BACK IN THE POCKETS OF HARD-WORKING FAMILIES LIKE THE RALSTONS!
ASSUMING THEY'RE ALREADY RICH, OF COURSE.
UH-OH...
©B Trudeau

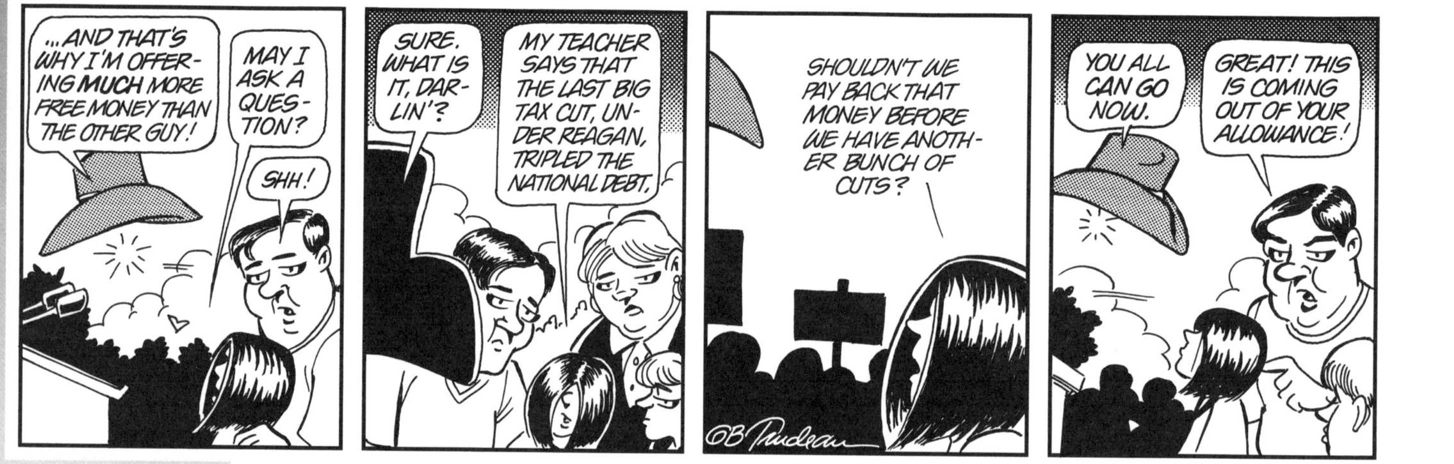
...AND THAT'S WHY I'M OFFERING MUCH MORE FREE MONEY THAN THE OTHER GUY!
MAY I ASK A QUESTION?
SHH!
SURE. WHAT IS IT, DARLIN'?
MY TEACHER SAYS THAT THE LAST BIG TAX CUT, UNDER REAGAN, TRIPLED THE NATIONAL DEBT.
SHOULDN'T WE PAY BACK THAT MONEY BEFORE WE HAVE ANOTHER BUNCH OF CUTS?
©B Trudeau
YOU ALL CAN GO NOW.
GREAT! THIS IS COMING OUT OF YOUR ALLOWANCE!

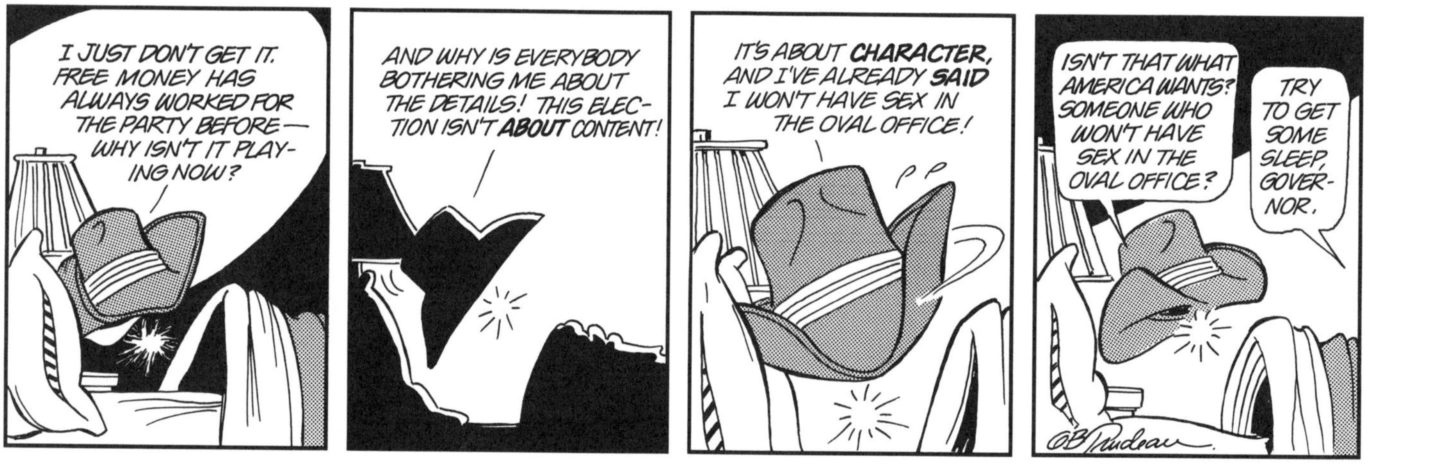
I JUST DON'T GET IT. FREE MONEY HAS ALWAYS WORKED FOR THE PARTY BEFORE— WHY ISN'T IT PLAYING NOW?
AND WHY IS EVERYBODY BOTHERING ME ABOUT THE DETAILS! THIS ELECTION ISN'T ABOUT CONTENT!
IT'S ABOUT CHARACTER, AND I'VE ALREADY SAID I WON'T HAVE SEX IN THE OVAL OFFICE!
ISN'T THAT WHAT AMERICA WANTS? SOMEONE WHO WON'T HAVE SEX IN THE OVAL OFFICE?
TRY TO GET SOME SLEEP, GOVERNOR.
©B Trudeau

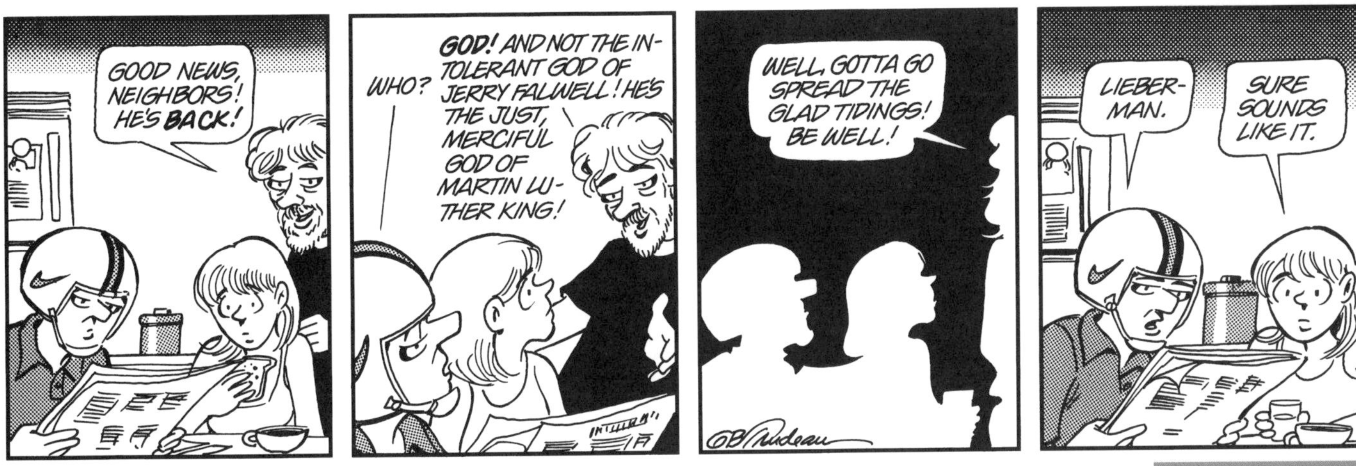
GOOD NEWS, NEIGHBORS! HE'S **BACK**!
WHO?
GOD! AND NOT THE IN-TOLERANT GOD OF JERRY FALWELL! HE'S THE JUST, MERCIFUL GOD OF MARTIN LU-THER KING!
WELL, GOTTA GO SPREAD THE GLAD TIDINGS! BE WELL!
LIEBER-MAN.
SURE SOUNDS LIKE IT.

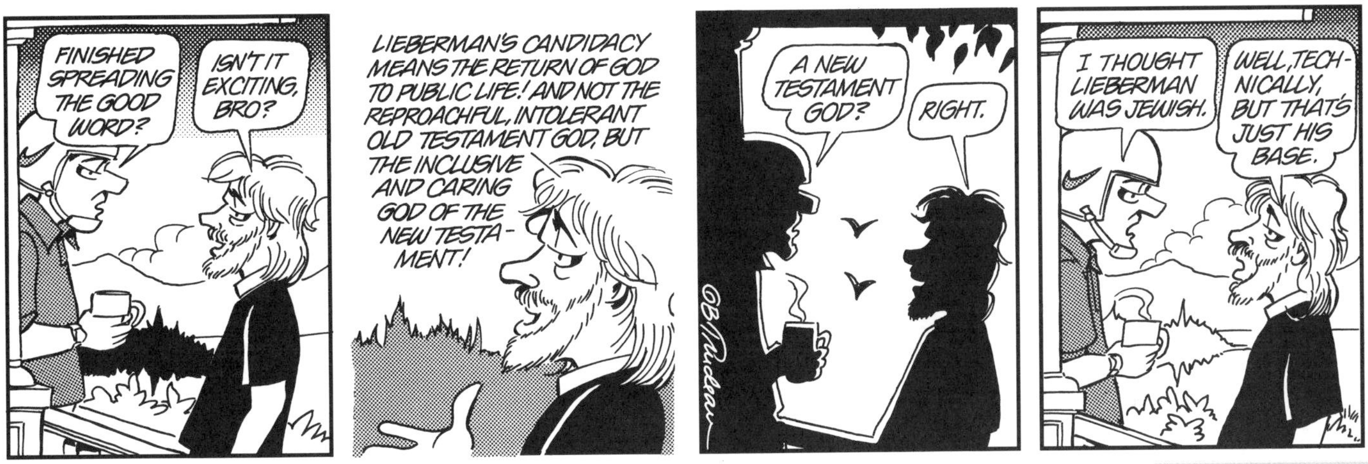
FINISHED SPREADING THE GOOD WORD?
ISN'T IT EXCITING, BRO?
LIEBERMAN'S CANDIDACY MEANS THE RETURN OF GOD TO PUBLIC LIFE! AND NOT THE REPROACHFUL, INTOLERANT OLD TESTAMENT GOD, BUT THE INCLUSIVE AND CARING GOD OF THE NEW TESTA-MENT!
A NEW TESTAMENT GOD?
RIGHT.
I THOUGHT LIEBERMAN WAS JEWISH.
WELL, TECH-NICALLY, BUT THAT'S JUST HIS BASE.

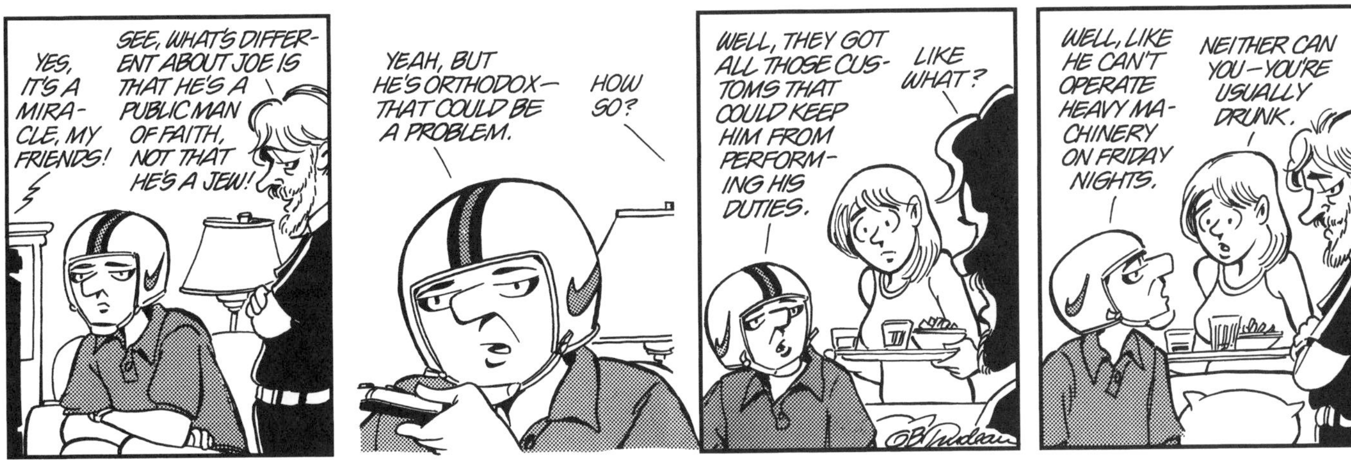
YES, IT'S A MIRA-CLE, MY FRIENDS!
SEE, WHAT'S DIFFER-ENT ABOUT JOE IS THAT HE'S A PUBLIC MAN OF FAITH, NOT THAT HE'S A JEW!
YEAH, BUT HE'S ORTHODOX—THAT COULD BE A PROBLEM.
HOW SO?
WELL, THEY GOT ALL THOSE CUS-TOMS THAT COULD KEEP HIM FROM PERFORM-ING HIS DUTIES.
LIKE WHAT?
WELL, LIKE HE CAN'T OPERATE HEAVY MA-CHINERY ON FRIDAY NIGHTS.
NEITHER CAN YOU—YOU'RE USUALLY DRUNK.

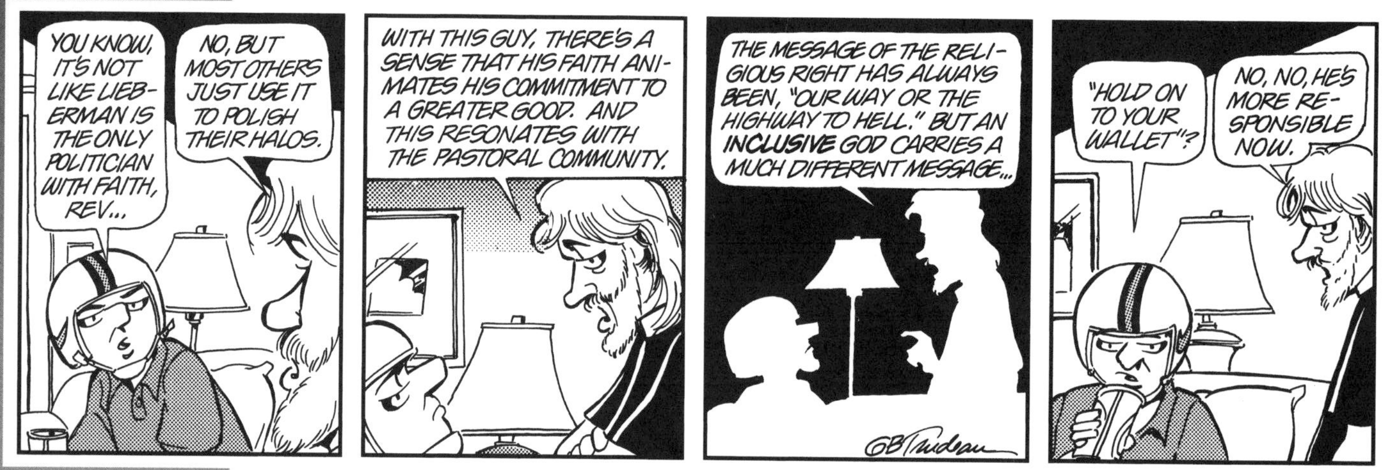
YOU KNOW, IT'S NOT LIKE LIEBERMAN IS THE ONLY POLITICIAN WITH FAITH, REV...
NO, BUT MOST OTHERS JUST USE IT TO POLISH THEIR HALOS.
WITH THIS GUY, THERE'S A SENSE THAT HIS FAITH ANIMATES HIS COMMITMENT TO A GREATER GOOD. AND THIS RESONATES WITH THE PASTORAL COMMUNITY.
THE MESSAGE OF THE RELIGIOUS RIGHT HAS ALWAYS BEEN, "OUR WAY OR THE HIGHWAY TO HELL." BUT AN **INCLUSIVE** GOD CARRIES A MUCH DIFFERENT MESSAGE...
"HOLD ON TO YOUR WALLET"?
NO, NO, HE'S MORE RESPONSIBLE NOW.
GBTrudeau

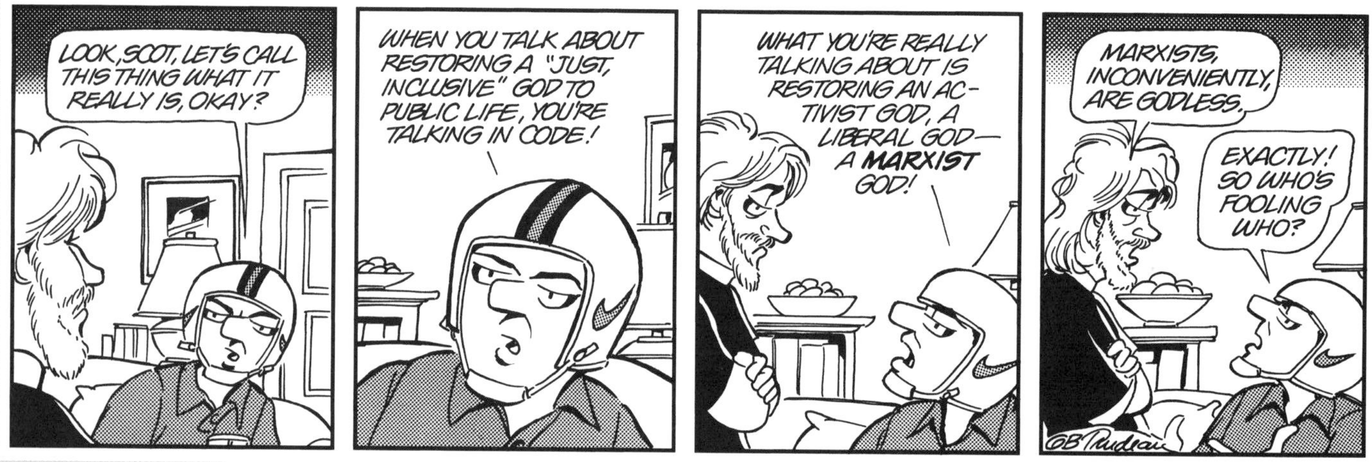
LOOK, SCOT, LET'S CALL THIS THING WHAT IT REALLY IS, OKAY?
WHEN YOU TALK ABOUT RESTORING A "JUST, INCLUSIVE" GOD TO PUBLIC LIFE, YOU'RE TALKING IN CODE!
WHAT YOU'RE REALLY TALKING ABOUT IS RESTORING AN ACTIVIST GOD, A LIBERAL GOD— A **MARXIST** GOD!
MARXISTS, INCONVENIENTLY, ARE GODLESS.
EXACTLY! SO WHO'S FOOLING WHO?
GBTrudeau

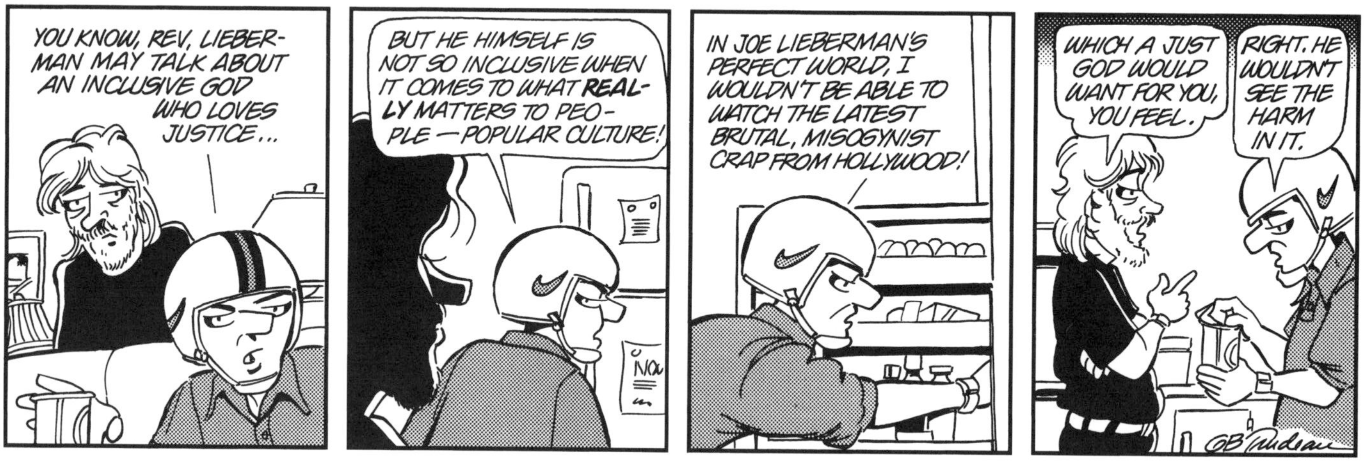
YOU KNOW, REV, LIEBERMAN MAY TALK ABOUT AN INCLUSIVE GOD WHO LOVES JUSTICE...
BUT HE HIMSELF IS NOT SO INCLUSIVE WHEN IT COMES TO WHAT **REALLY** MATTERS TO PEOPLE — POPULAR CULTURE!
IN JOE LIEBERMAN'S PERFECT WORLD, I WOULDN'T BE ABLE TO WATCH THE LATEST BRUTAL, MISOGYNIST CRAP FROM HOLLYWOOD!
WHICH A JUST GOD WOULD WANT FOR YOU, YOU FEEL.
RIGHT. HE WOULDN'T SEE THE HARM IN IT.
GBTrudeau

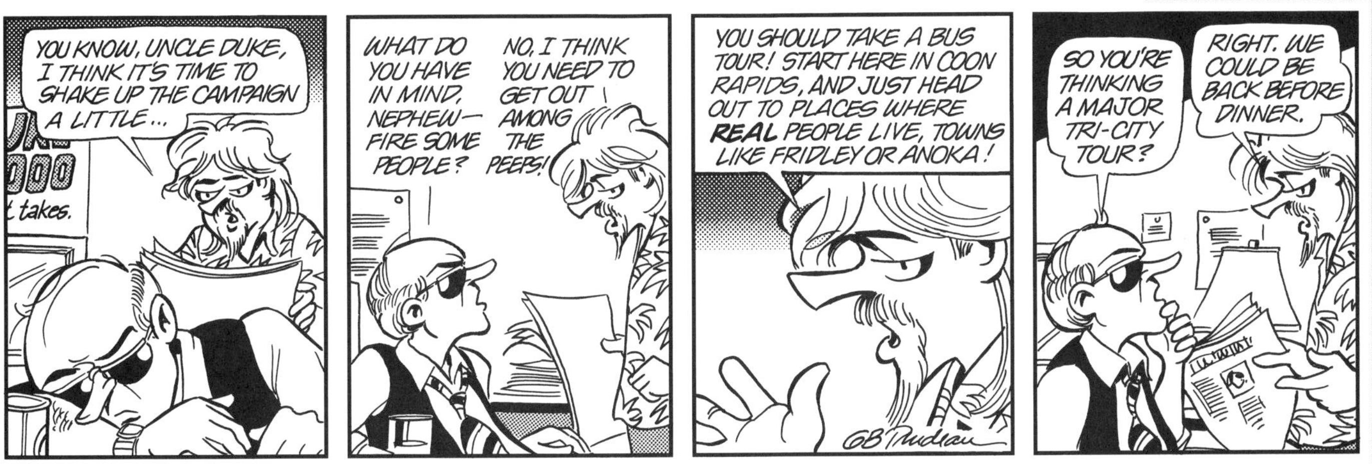
YOU KNOW, UNCLE DUKE, I THINK IT'S TIME TO SHAKE UP THE CAMPAIGN A LITTLE...
WHAT DO YOU HAVE IN MIND, NEPHEW—FIRE SOME PEOPLE?
NO, I THINK YOU NEED TO GET OUT AMONG THE PEEPS!
YOU SHOULD TAKE A BUS TOUR! START HERE IN COON RAPIDS, AND JUST HEAD OUT TO PLACES WHERE **REAL** PEOPLE LIVE, TOWNS LIKE FRIDLEY OR ANOKA!
SO YOU'RE THINKING A MAJOR TRI-CITY TOUR?
RIGHT. WE COULD BE BACK BEFORE DINNER.

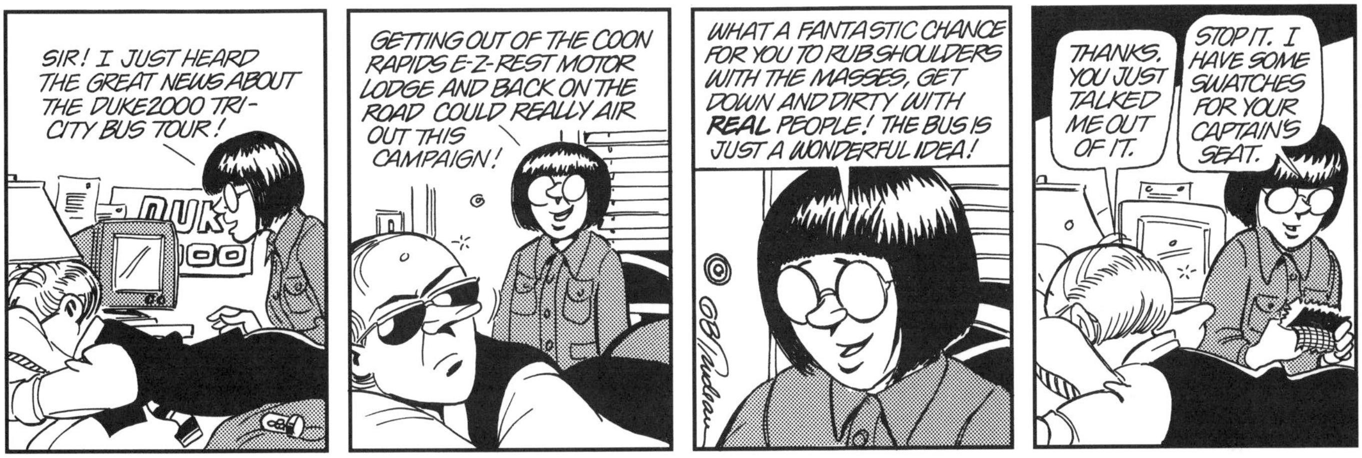
SIR! I JUST HEARD THE GREAT NEWS ABOUT THE DUKE2000 TRI-CITY BUS TOUR!
GETTING OUT OF THE COON RAPIDS E-Z-REST MOTOR LODGE AND BACK ON THE ROAD COULD REALLY AIR OUT THIS CAMPAIGN!
WHAT A FANTASTIC CHANCE FOR YOU TO RUB SHOULDERS WITH THE MASSES, GET DOWN AND DIRTY WITH **REAL** PEOPLE! THE BUS IS JUST A WONDERFUL IDEA!
THANKS. YOU JUST TALKED ME OUT OF IT.
STOP IT. I HAVE SOME SWATCHES FOR YOUR CAPTAIN'S SEAT.

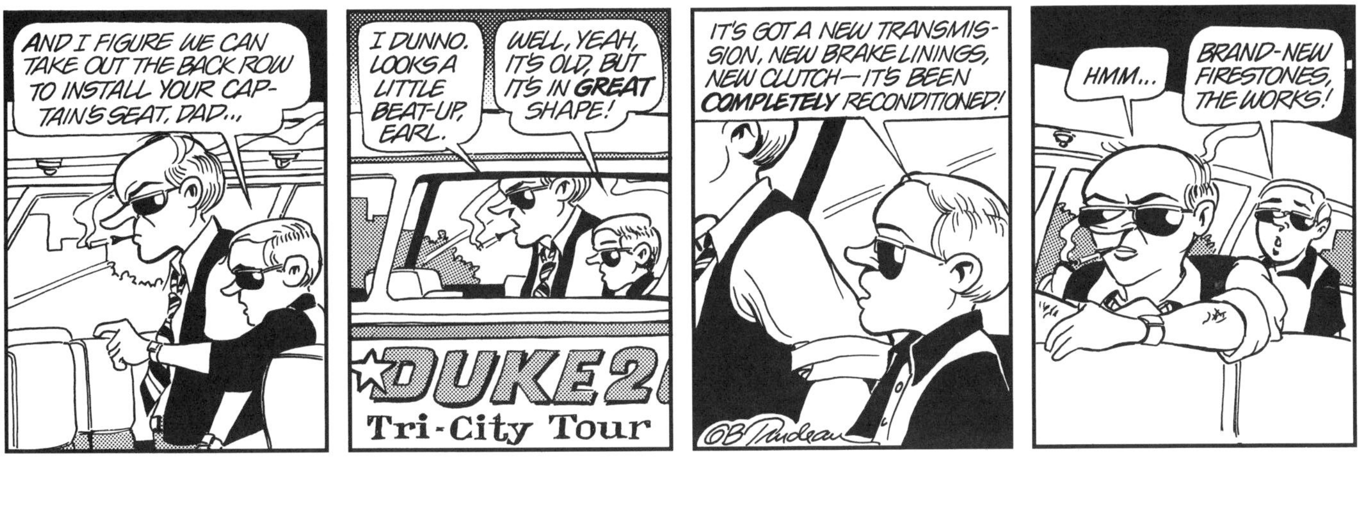
AND I FIGURE WE CAN TAKE OUT THE BACK ROW TO INSTALL YOUR CAPTAIN'S SEAT, DAD...
I DUNNO. LOOKS A LITTLE BEAT-UP, EARL.
WELL, YEAH, IT'S OLD, BUT IT'S IN **GREAT** SHAPE!
Tri-City Tour
IT'S GOT A NEW TRANSMISSION, NEW BRAKE LININGS, NEW CLUTCH—IT'S BEEN **COMPLETELY** RECONDITIONED!
HMM...
BRAND-NEW FIRESTONES, THE WORKS!

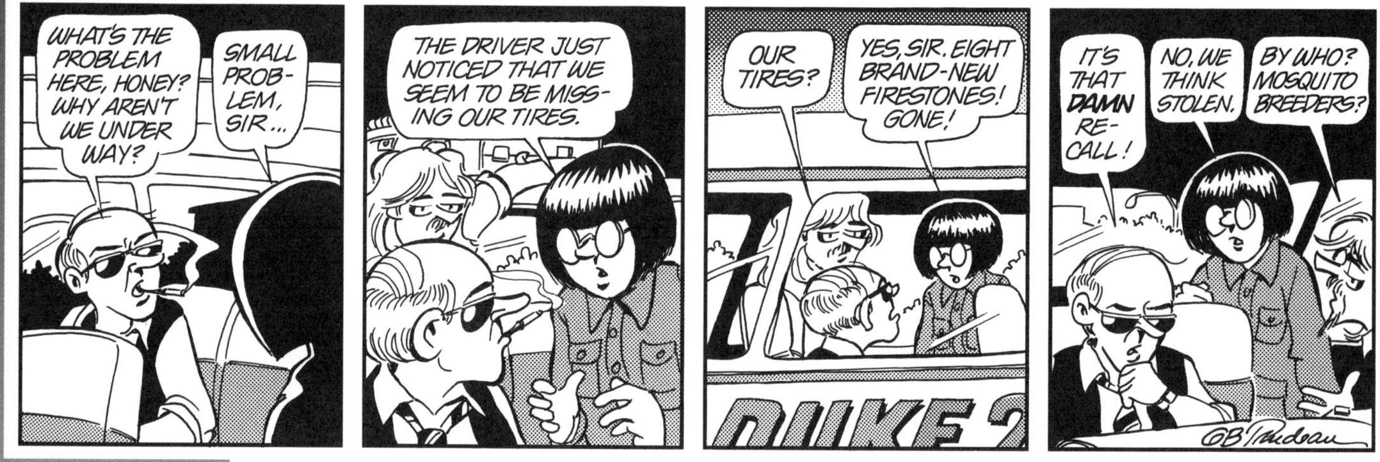
WHAT'S THE PROBLEM HERE, HONEY? WHY AREN'T WE UNDER WAY?
SMALL PROB-LEM, SIR...
THE DRIVER JUST NOTICED THAT WE SEEM TO BE MISS-ING OUR TIRES.
OUR TIRES?
YES, SIR. EIGHT BRAND-NEW FIRESTONES! GONE!
DUKE 2
IT'S THAT DAMN RE-CALL!
NO, WE THINK STOLEN.
BY WHO? MOSQUITO BREEDERS?
©B. Trudeau

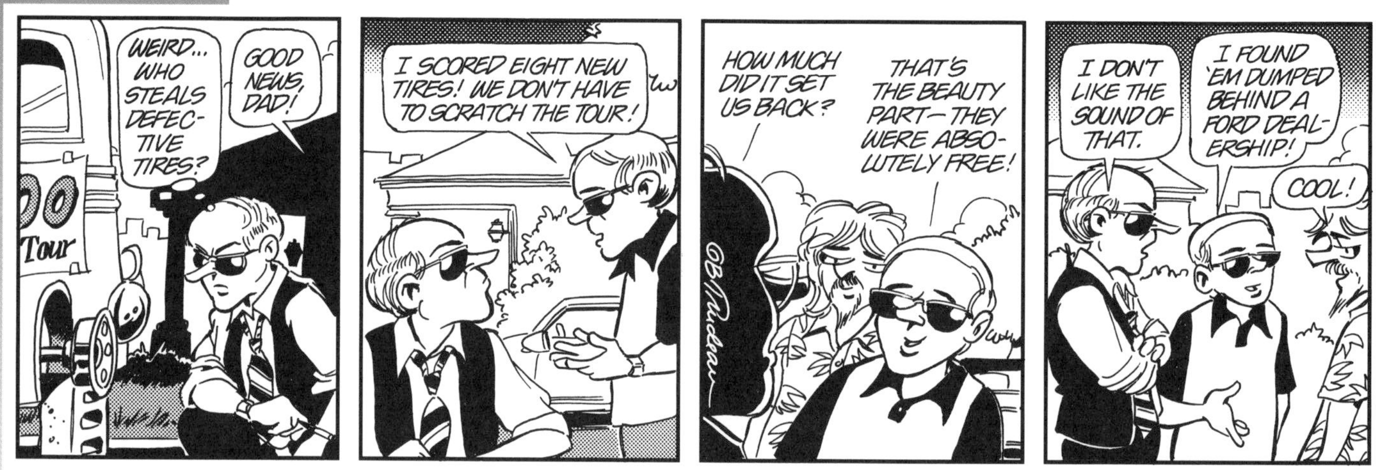
WEIRD... WHO STEALS DEFEC-TIVE TIRES?
GOOD NEWS, DAD!
Tour
I SCORED EIGHT NEW TIRES! WE DON'T HAVE TO SCRATCH THE TOUR!
HOW MUCH DID IT SET US BACK?
THAT'S THE BEAUTY PART—THEY WERE ABSO-LUTELY FREE!
©B. Trudeau
I DON'T LIKE THE SOUND OF THAT.
I FOUND 'EM DUMPED BEHIND A FORD DEAL-ERSHIP!
COOL!

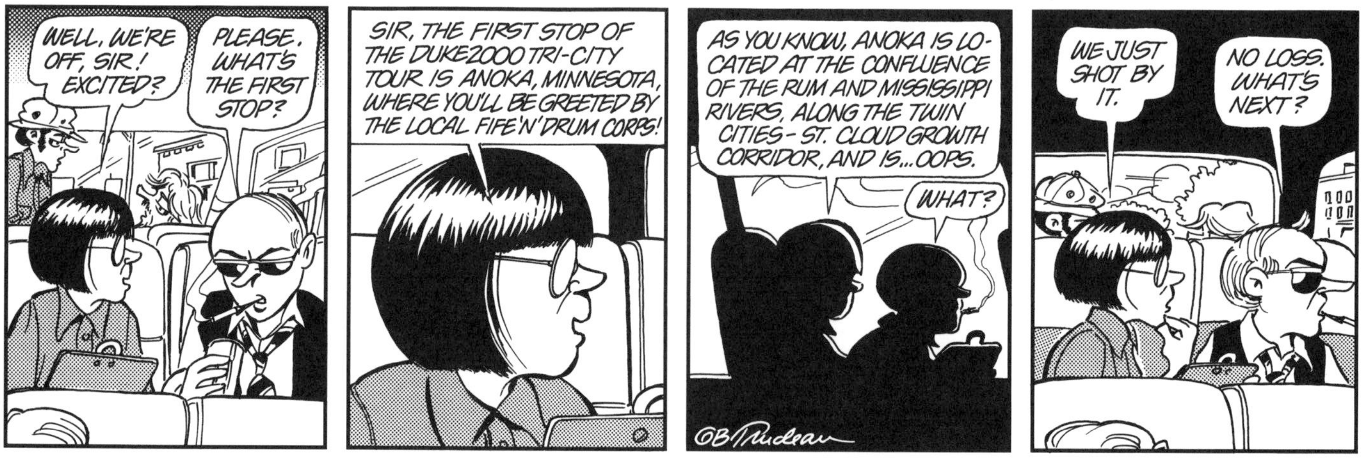
WELL, WE'RE OFF, SIR! EXCITED?
PLEASE. WHAT'S THE FIRST STOP?
SIR, THE FIRST STOP OF THE DUKE2000 TRI-CITY TOUR IS ANOKA, MINNESOTA, WHERE YOU'LL BE GREETED BY THE LOCAL FIFE 'N' DRUM CORPS!
AS YOU KNOW, ANOKA IS LO-CATED AT THE CONFLUENCE OF THE RUM AND MISSISSIPPI RIVERS, ALONG THE TWIN CITIES - ST. CLOUD GROWTH CORRIDOR, AND IS...OOPS.
WHAT?
©B. Trudeau
WE JUST SHOT BY IT.
NO LOSS. WHAT'S NEXT?

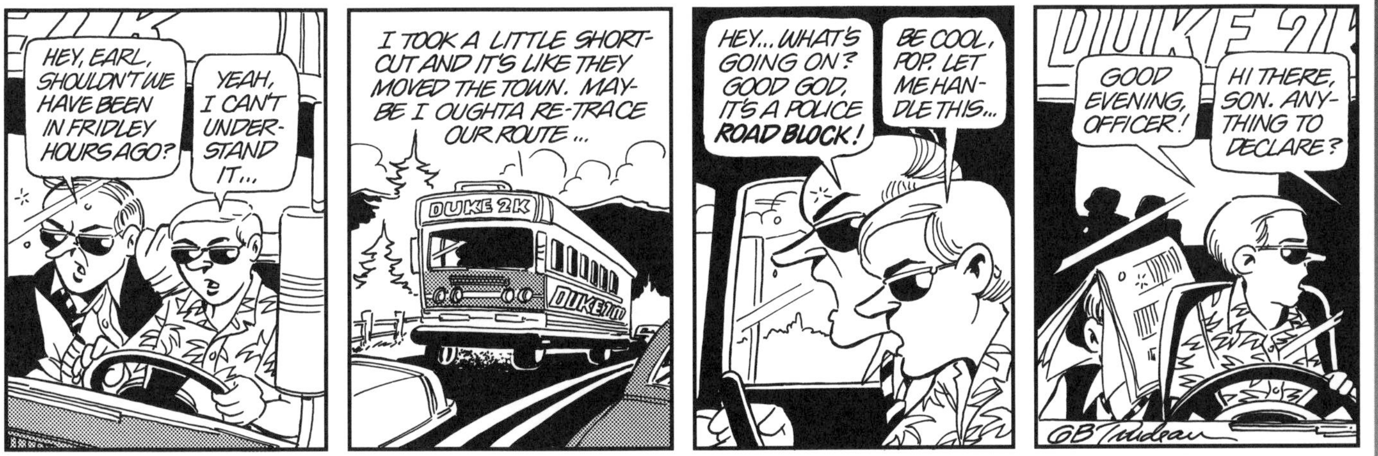
HEY, EARL, SHOULDN'T WE HAVE BEEN IN FRIDLEY HOURS AGO?
YEAH, I CAN'T UNDERSTAND IT...
I TOOK A LITTLE SHORTCUT AND IT'S LIKE THEY MOVED THE TOWN. MAYBE I OUGHTA RE-TRACE OUR ROUTE...
DUKE 2K
HEY... WHAT'S GOING ON? GOOD GOD, IT'S A POLICE **ROAD BLOCK**!
BE COOL, POP. LET ME HANDLE THIS...
DUKE 2K
GOOD EVENING, OFFICER!
HI THERE, SON. ANYTHING TO DECLARE?
©B Trudeau

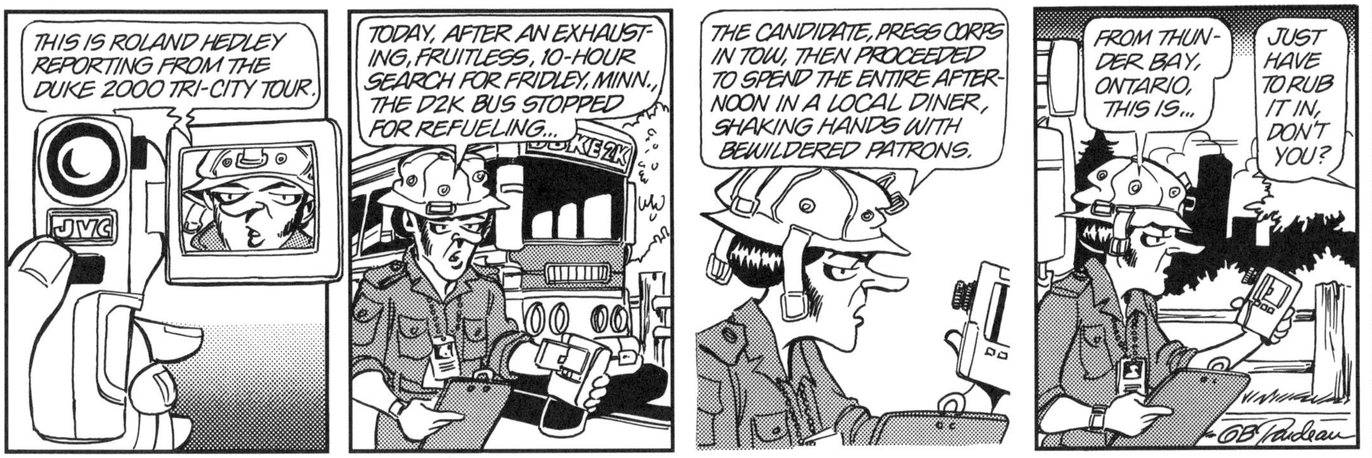
THIS IS ROLAND HEDLEY REPORTING FROM THE DUKE 2000 TRI-CITY TOUR.
JVC
TODAY, AFTER AN EXHAUSTING, FRUITLESS, 10-HOUR SEARCH FOR FRIDLEY, MINN., THE D2K BUS STOPPED FOR REFUELING...
DUKE 2K
THE CANDIDATE, PRESS CORPS IN TOW, THEN PROCEEDED TO SPEND THE ENTIRE AFTERNOON IN A LOCAL DINER, SHAKING HANDS WITH BEWILDERED PATRONS.
FROM THUNDER BAY, ONTARIO, THIS IS...
JUST HAVE TO RUB IT IN, DON'T YOU?
©B Trudeau

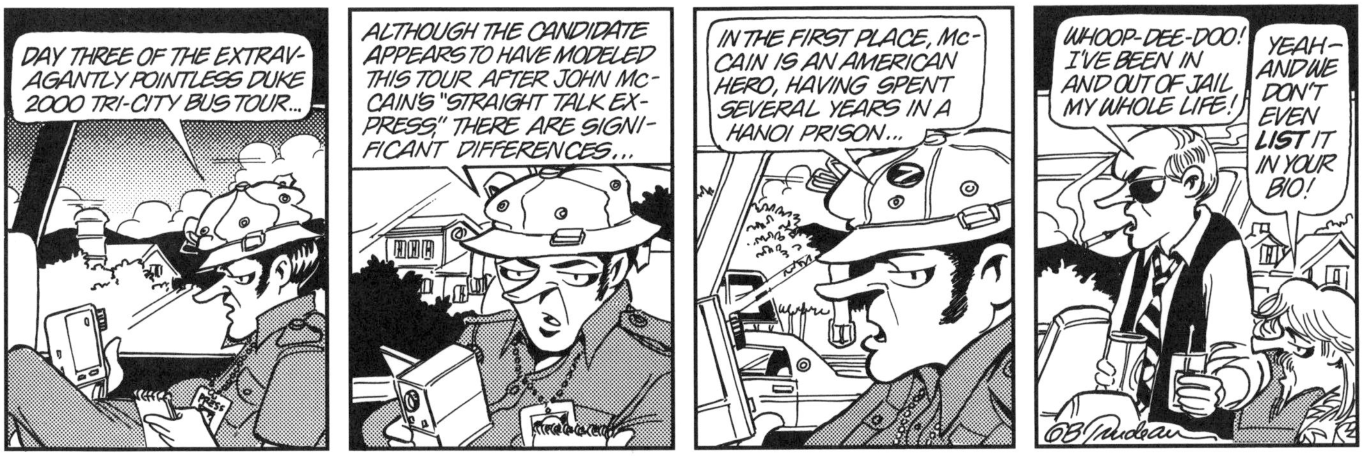
DAY THREE OF THE EXTRAVAGANTLY POINTLESS DUKE 2000 TRI-CITY BUS TOUR...
ALTHOUGH THE CANDIDATE APPEARS TO HAVE MODELED THIS TOUR AFTER JOHN McCAIN'S "STRAIGHT TALK EXPRESS," THERE ARE SIGNIFICANT DIFFERENCES...
IN THE FIRST PLACE, McCAIN IS AN AMERICAN HERO, HAVING SPENT SEVERAL YEARS IN A HANOI PRISON...
WHOOP-DEE-DOO! I'VE BEEN IN AND OUT OF JAIL MY WHOLE LIFE!
YEAH—AND WE DON'T EVEN **LIST** IT IN YOUR BIO!
©B Trudeau

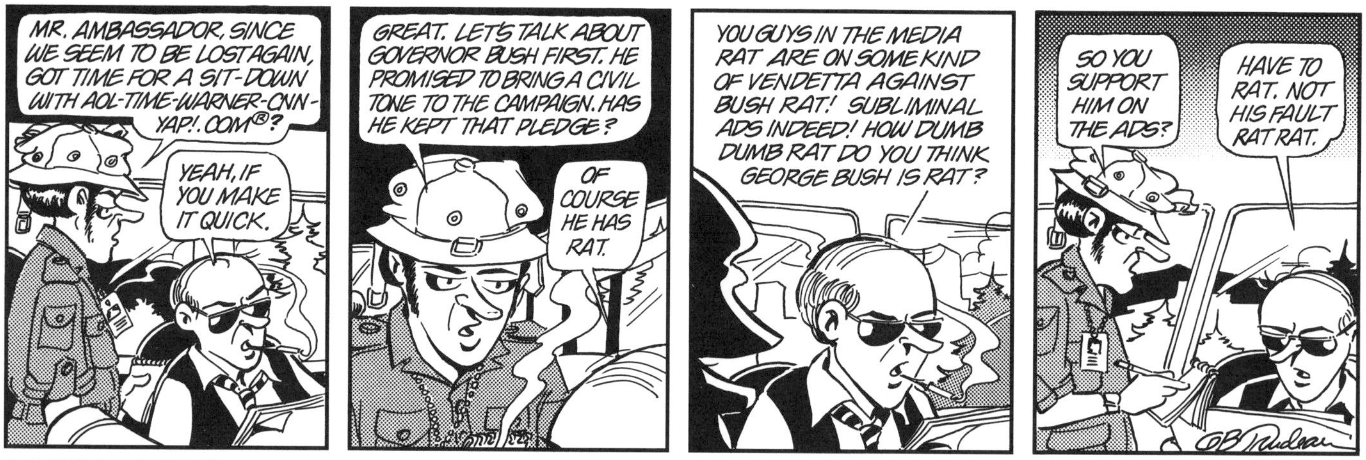
MR. AMBASSADOR, SINCE WE SEEM TO BE LOST AGAIN, GOT TIME FOR A SIT-DOWN WITH AOL-TIME-WARNER-CNN-YAP!.COM®?
YEAH, IF YOU MAKE IT QUICK.
GREAT. LET'S TALK ABOUT GOVERNOR BUSH FIRST. HE PROMISED TO BRING A CIVIL TONE TO THE CAMPAIGN. HAS HE KEPT THAT PLEDGE?
OF COURSE HE HAS RAT.
YOU GUYS IN THE MEDIA RAT ARE ON SOME KIND OF VENDETTA AGAINST BUSH RAT! SUBLIMINAL ADS INDEED! HOW DUMB DUMB RAT DO YOU THINK GEORGE BUSH IS RAT?
SO YOU SUPPORT HIM ON THE ADS?
HAVE TO RAT. NOT HIS FAULT RAT RAT.
GB Trudeau

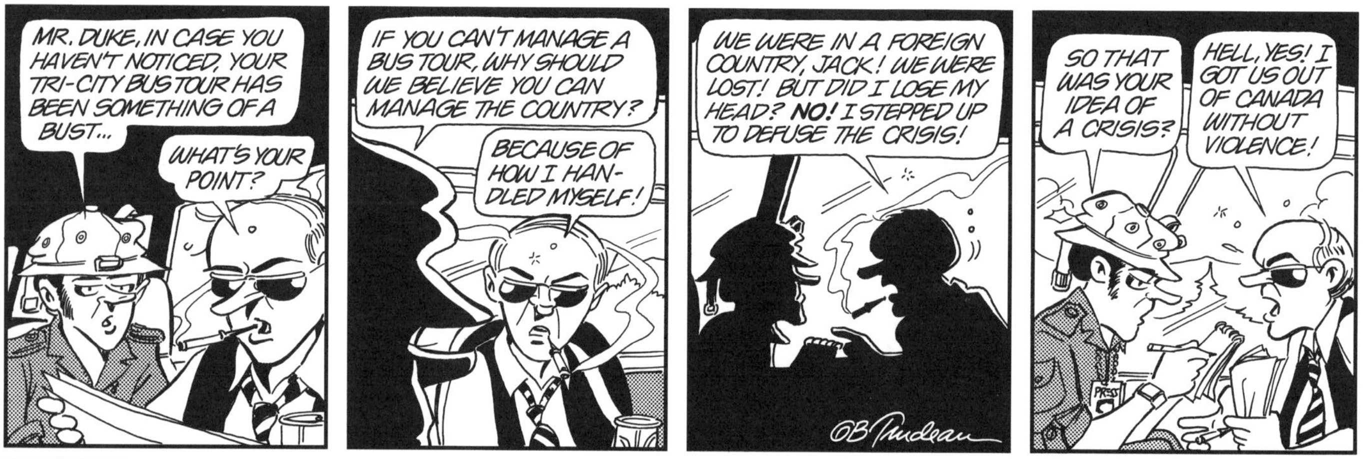
MR. DUKE, IN CASE YOU HAVEN'T NOTICED, YOUR TRI-CITY BUS TOUR HAS BEEN SOMETHING OF A BUST...
WHAT'S YOUR POINT?
IF YOU CAN'T MANAGE A BUS TOUR, WHY SHOULD WE BELIEVE YOU CAN MANAGE THE COUNTRY?
BECAUSE OF HOW I HANDLED MYSELF!
WE WERE IN A FOREIGN COUNTRY, JACK! WE WERE LOST! BUT DID I LOSE MY HEAD? NO! I STEPPED UP TO DEFUSE THE CRISIS!
GB Trudeau
SO THAT WAS YOUR IDEA OF A CRISIS?
HELL, YES! I GOT US OUT OF CANADA WITHOUT VIOLENCE!
PRESS

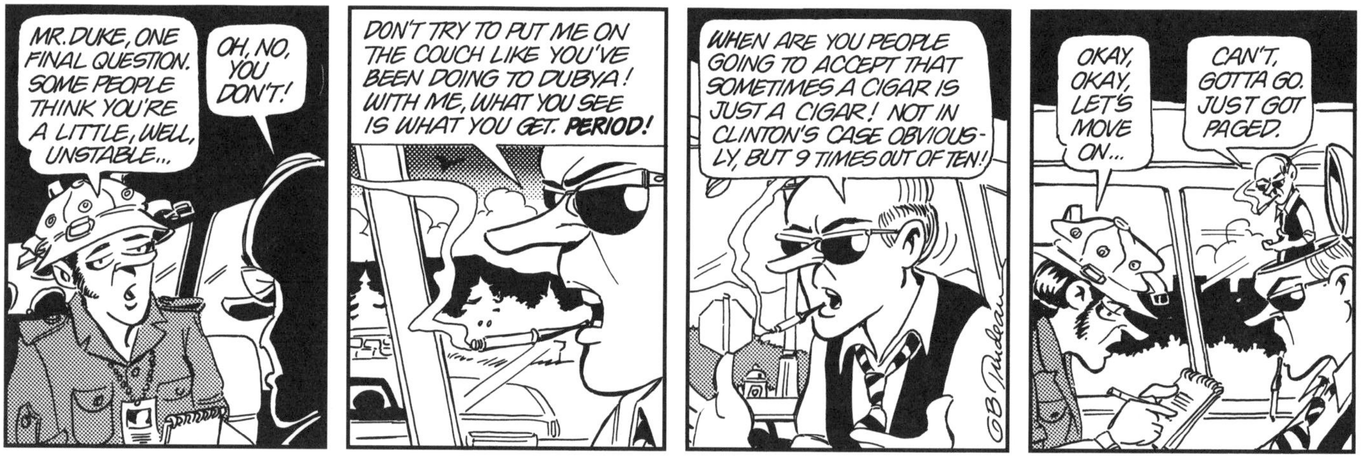
MR. DUKE, ONE FINAL QUESTION. SOME PEOPLE THINK YOU'RE A LITTLE, WELL, UNSTABLE...
OH, NO, YOU DON'T!
DON'T TRY TO PUT ME ON THE COUCH LIKE YOU'VE BEEN DOING TO DUBYA! WITH ME, WHAT YOU SEE IS WHAT YOU GET. PERIOD!
WHEN ARE YOU PEOPLE GOING TO ACCEPT THAT SOMETIMES A CIGAR IS JUST A CIGAR! NOT IN CLINTON'S CASE OBVIOUSLY, BUT 9 TIMES OUT OF TEN!
GB Trudeau
OKAY, OKAY, LET'S MOVE ON...
CAN'T, GOTTA GO. JUST GOT PAGED.

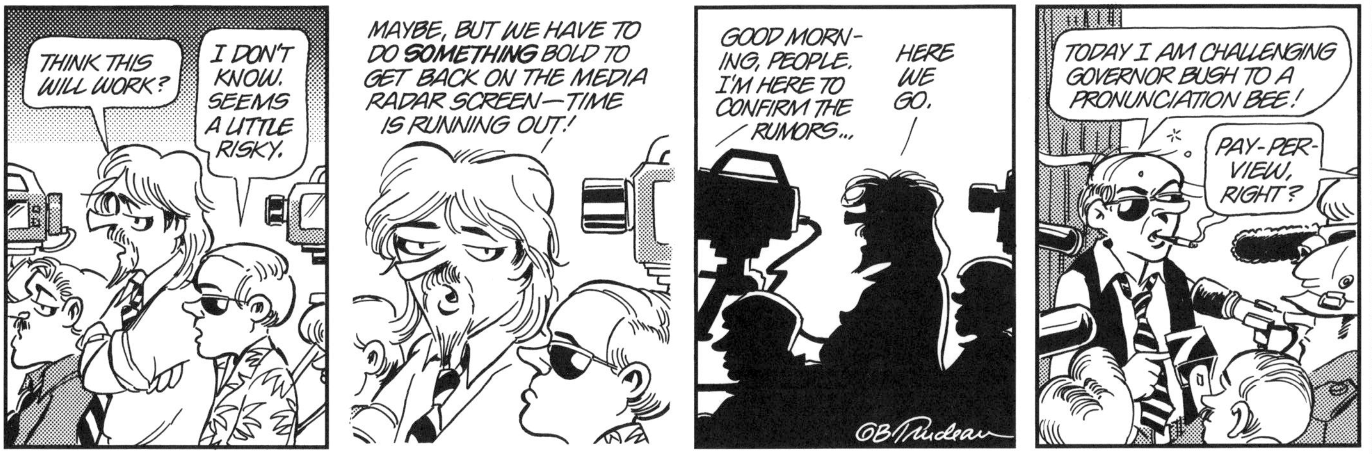
THINK THIS WILL WORK?
I DON'T KNOW. SEEMS A LITTLE RISKY.
MAYBE, BUT WE HAVE TO DO **SOMETHING** BOLD TO GET BACK ON THE MEDIA RADAR SCREEN—TIME IS RUNNING OUT!
GOOD MORNING, PEOPLE. I'M HERE TO CONFIRM THE RUMORS...
HERE WE GO.
©B Trudeau
TODAY I AM CHALLENGING GOVERNOR BUSH TO A PRONUNCIATION BEE!
PAY-PER-VIEW, RIGHT?

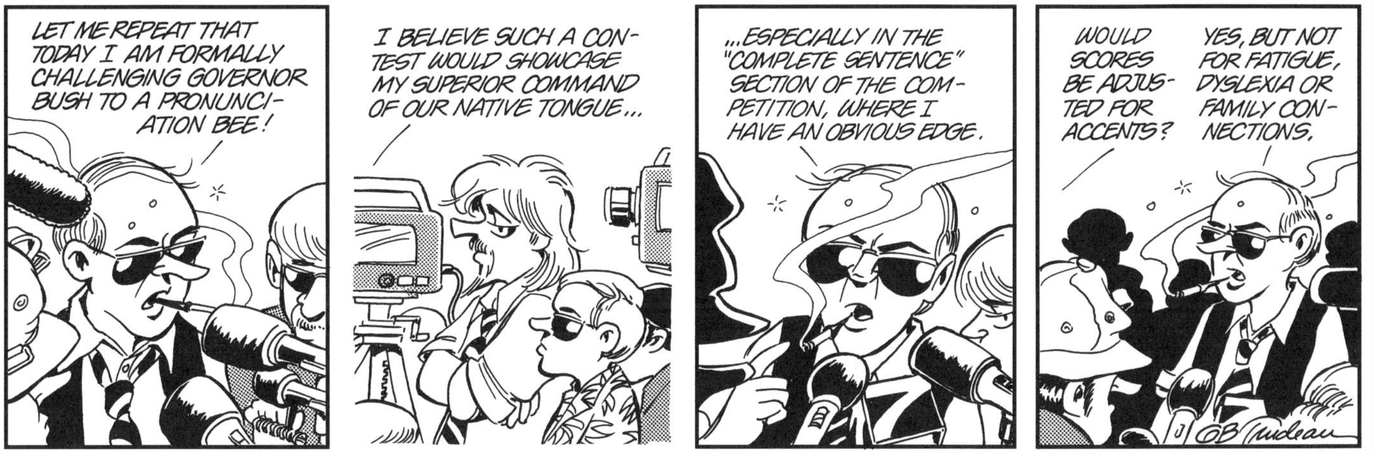
LET ME REPEAT THAT TODAY I AM FORMALLY CHALLENGING GOVERNOR BUSH TO A PRONUNCIATION BEE!
I BELIEVE SUCH A CONTEST WOULD SHOWCASE MY SUPERIOR COMMAND OF OUR NATIVE TONGUE...
...ESPECIALLY IN THE "COMPLETE SENTENCE" SECTION OF THE COMPETITION, WHERE I HAVE AN OBVIOUS EDGE.
WOULD SCORES BE ADJUSTED FOR ACCENTS?
YES, BUT NOT FOR FATIGUE, DYSLEXIA OR FAMILY CONNECTIONS.
©B Trudeau

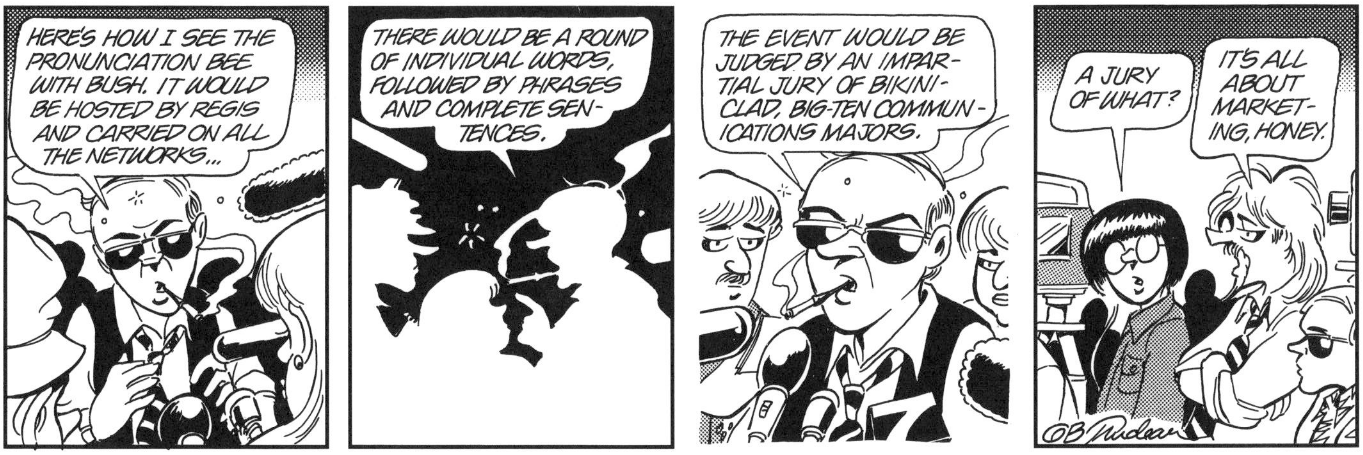
HERE'S HOW I SEE THE PRONUNCIATION BEE WITH BUSH. IT WOULD BE HOSTED BY REGIS AND CARRIED ON ALL THE NETWORKS...
THERE WOULD BE A ROUND OF INDIVIDUAL WORDS, FOLLOWED BY PHRASES AND COMPLETE SENTENCES.
THE EVENT WOULD BE JUDGED BY AN IMPARTIAL JURY OF BIKINI-CLAD, BIG-TEN COMMUNICATIONS MAJORS.
A JURY OF WHAT?
IT'S ALL ABOUT MARKETING, HONEY.
©B Trudeau

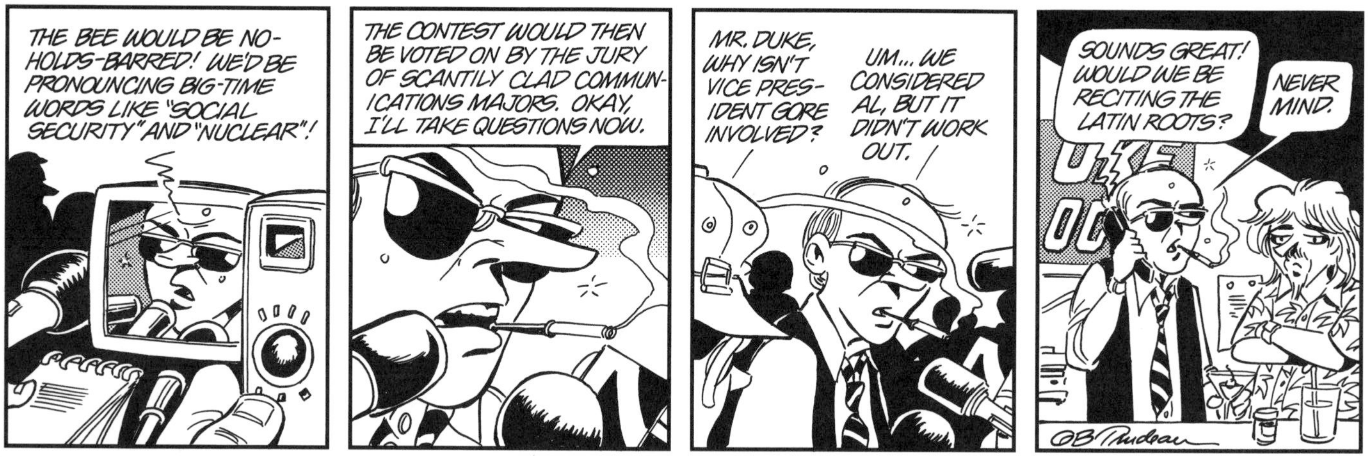
THE BEE WOULD BE NO-HOLDS-BARRED! WE'D BE PRONOUNCING BIG-TIME WORDS LIKE "SOCIAL SECURITY" AND "NUCLEAR"!
THE CONTEST WOULD THEN BE VOTED ON BY THE JURY OF SCANTILY CLAD COMMUNICATIONS MAJORS. OKAY, I'LL TAKE QUESTIONS NOW.
MR. DUKE, WHY ISN'T VICE PRESIDENT GORE INVOLVED?
UM... WE CONSIDERED AL, BUT IT DIDN'T WORK OUT.
SOUNDS GREAT! WOULD WE BE RECITING THE LATIN ROOTS?
NEVER MIND.

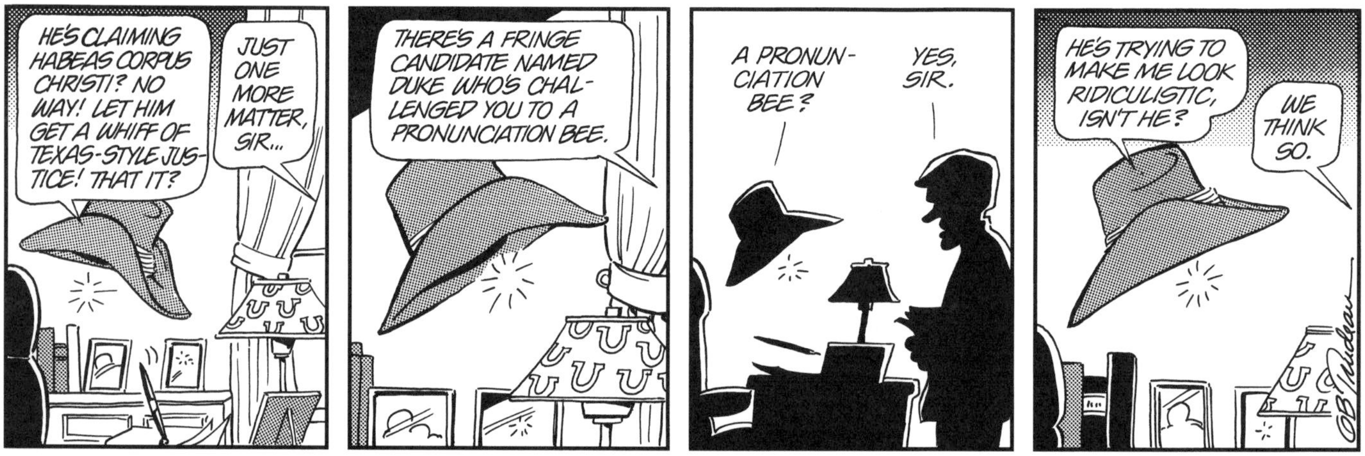
HE'S CLAIMING HABEAS CORPUS CHRISTI? NO WAY! LET HIM GET A WHIFF OF TEXAS-STYLE JUSTICE! THAT IT?
JUST ONE MORE MATTER, SIR...
THERE'S A FRINGE CANDIDATE NAMED DUKE WHO'S CHALLENGED YOU TO A PRONUNCIATION BEE.
A PRONUNCIATION BEE?
YES, SIR.
HE'S TRYING TO MAKE ME LOOK RIDICULISTIC, ISN'T HE?
WE THINK SO.

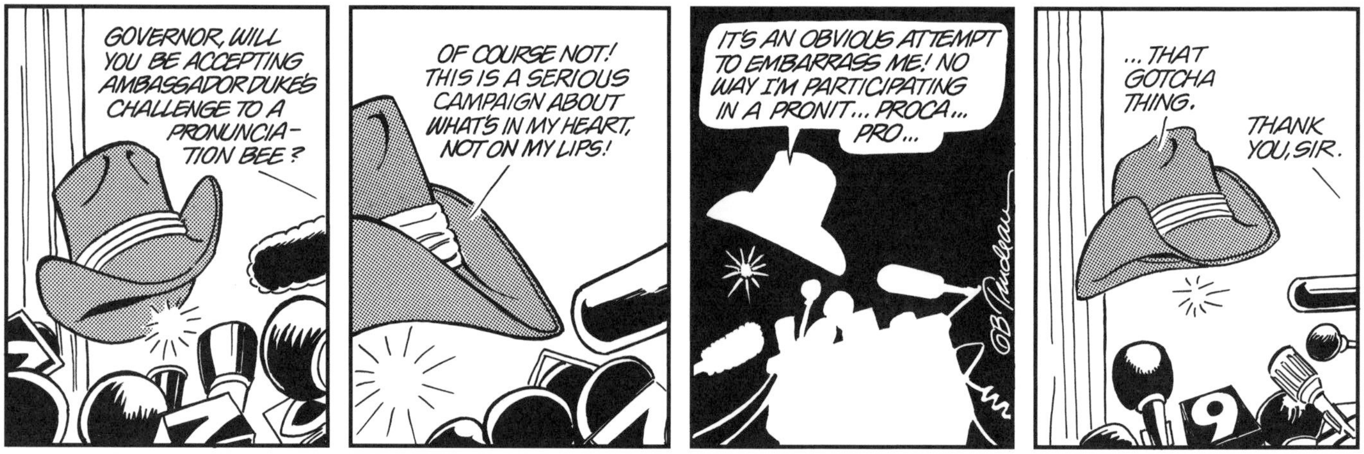
GOVERNOR, WILL YOU BE ACCEPTING AMBASSADOR DUKE'S CHALLENGE TO A PRONUNCIATION BEE?
OF COURSE NOT! THIS IS A SERIOUS CAMPAIGN ABOUT WHAT'S IN MY HEART, NOT ON MY LIPS!
IT'S AN OBVIOUS ATTEMPT TO EMBARRASS ME! NO WAY I'M PARTICIPATING IN A PRONIT... PROCA... PRO...
...THAT GOTCHA THING.
THANK YOU, SIR.

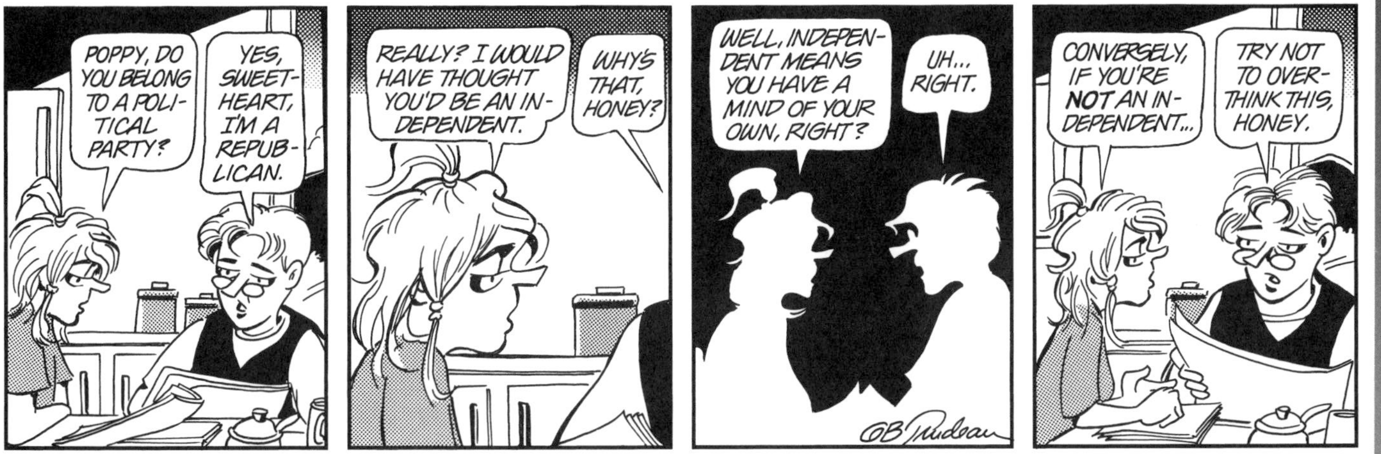
POPPY, DO YOU BELONG TO A POLITICAL PARTY?
YES, SWEETHEART, I'M A REPUBLICAN.
REALLY? I WOULD HAVE THOUGHT YOU'D BE AN INDEPENDENT.
WHY'S THAT, HONEY?
WELL, INDEPENDENT MEANS YOU HAVE A MIND OF YOUR OWN, RIGHT?
UH... RIGHT.
CONVERSELY, IF YOU'RE NOT AN INDEPENDENT...
TRY NOT TO OVERTHINK THIS, HONEY.
GB Trudeau

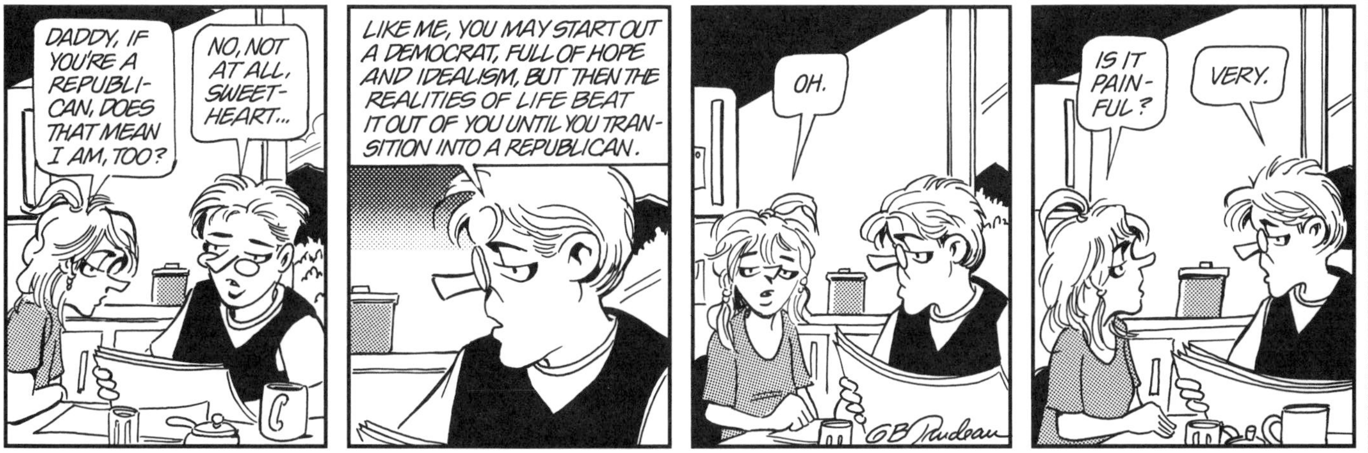
DADDY, IF YOU'RE A REPUBLICAN, DOES THAT MEAN I AM, TOO?
NO, NOT AT ALL, SWEETHEART...
LIKE ME, YOU MAY START OUT A DEMOCRAT, FULL OF HOPE AND IDEALISM, BUT THEN THE REALITIES OF LIFE BEAT IT OUT OF YOU UNTIL YOU TRANSITION INTO A REPUBLICAN.
OH.
IS IT PAINFUL?
VERY.
GB Trudeau

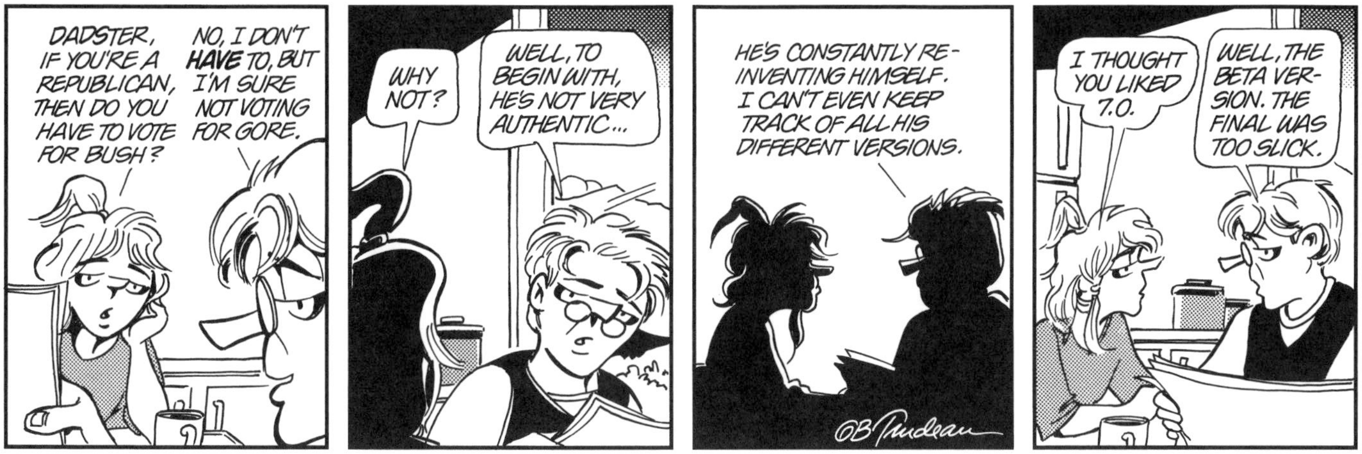
DADSTER, IF YOU'RE A REPUBLICAN, THEN DO YOU HAVE TO VOTE FOR BUSH?
NO, I DON'T HAVE TO, BUT I'M SURE NOT VOTING FOR GORE.
WHY NOT?
WELL, TO BEGIN WITH, HE'S NOT VERY AUTHENTIC...
HE'S CONSTANTLY REINVENTING HIMSELF. I CAN'T EVEN KEEP TRACK OF ALL HIS DIFFERENT VERSIONS.
I THOUGHT YOU LIKED 7.0.
WELL, THE BETA VERSION. THE FINAL WAS TOO SLICK.
GB Trudeau

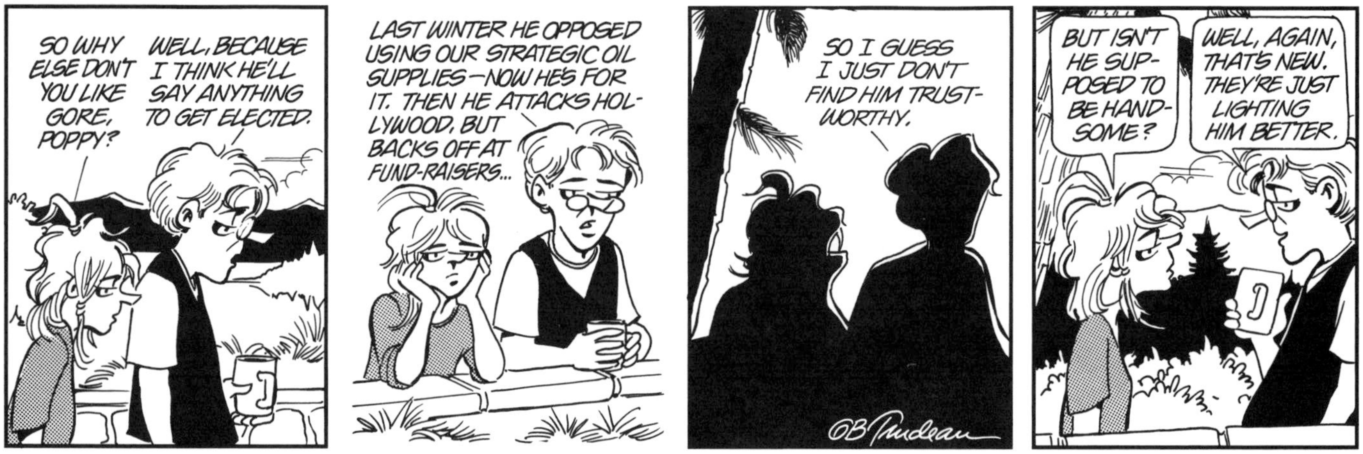
SO WHY ELSE DON'T YOU LIKE GORE, POPPY?
WELL, BECAUSE I THINK HE'LL SAY ANYTHING TO GET ELECTED.
LAST WINTER HE OPPOSED USING OUR STRATEGIC OIL SUPPLIES—NOW HE'S FOR IT. THEN HE ATTACKS HOLLYWOOD, BUT BACKS OFF AT FUND-RAISERS...
SO I GUESS I JUST DON'T FIND HIM TRUSTWORTHY.
BUT ISN'T HE SUPPOSED TO BE HANDSOME?
WELL, AGAIN, THAT'S NEW. THEY'RE JUST LIGHTING HIM BETTER.

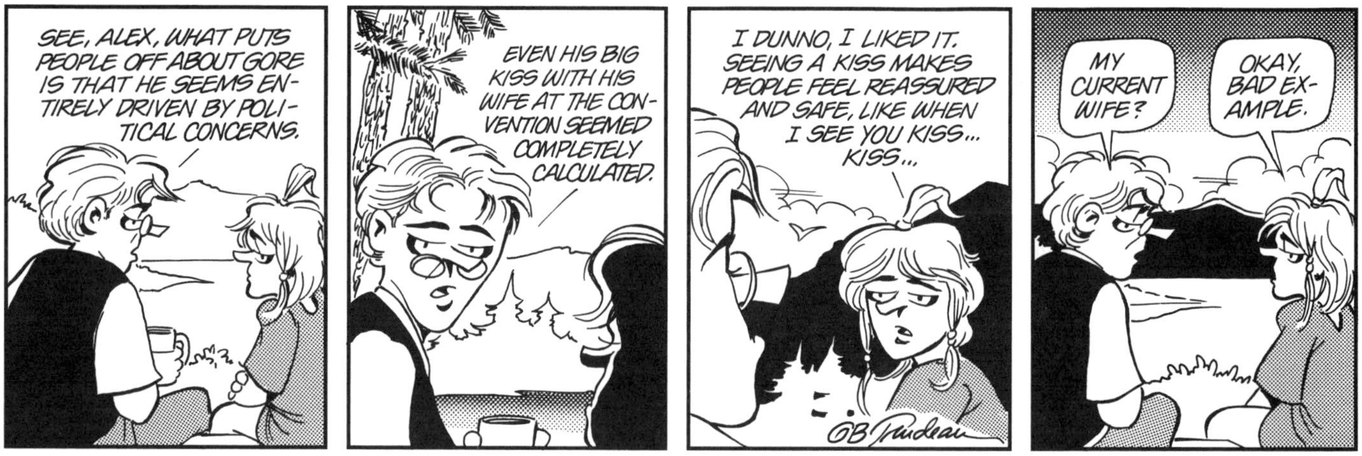
SEE, ALEX, WHAT PUTS PEOPLE OFF ABOUT GORE IS THAT HE SEEMS ENTIRELY DRIVEN BY POLITICAL CONCERNS.
EVEN HIS BIG KISS WITH HIS WIFE AT THE CONVENTION SEEMED COMPLETELY CALCULATED.
I DUNNO, I LIKED IT. SEEING A KISS MAKES PEOPLE FEEL REASSURED AND SAFE, LIKE WHEN I SEE YOU KISS... KISS...
MY CURRENT WIFE?
OKAY, BAD EXAMPLE.

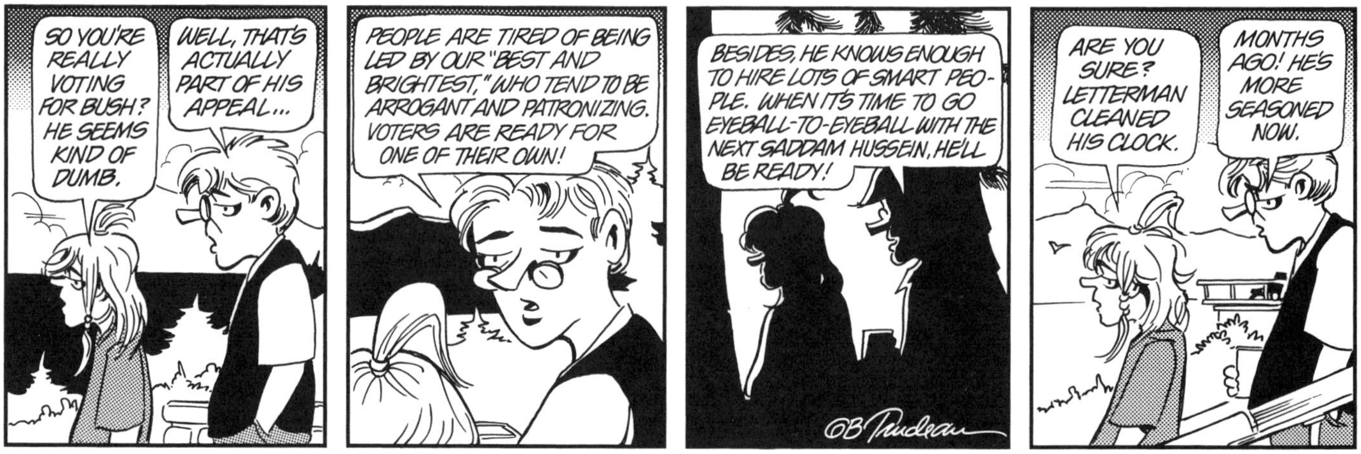
SO YOU'RE REALLY VOTING FOR BUSH? HE SEEMS KIND OF DUMB.
WELL, THAT'S ACTUALLY PART OF HIS APPEAL...
PEOPLE ARE TIRED OF BEING LED BY OUR "BEST AND BRIGHTEST," WHO TEND TO BE ARROGANT AND PATRONIZING. VOTERS ARE READY FOR ONE OF THEIR OWN!
BESIDES, HE KNOWS ENOUGH TO HIRE LOTS OF SMART PEOPLE. WHEN IT'S TIME TO GO EYEBALL-TO-EYEBALL WITH THE NEXT SADDAM HUSSEIN, HE'LL BE READY!
ARE YOU SURE? LETTERMAN CLEANED HIS CLOCK.
MONTHS AGO! HE'S MORE SEASONED NOW.

ANOTHER DAY, ANOTHER BUSH "TAX FAMILY."

WE'RE NOT TALKING FUZZY-WUZZY MATH HERE, FOLKS...

WE'RE TALKING *REAL* MONEY FOR REAL PEOPLE! FOR THE MARK SKIPPLE FAMILY, IT COULD MEAN *BILLIONS!*

Latest Slogan Latest Slogan Latest Slogan Latest Slog-an Latest Slogan Latest Slogan Latest Slogan Latest Slogan Latest

WELL, NOT FOR THEM PERSONABLY! BUT, LOOK, THE MAN, GORE, HAS OUTSPENT ME! EVEN THOUGH MY PLAN GIVES MORE SENIORS DRUG COVERAGE! EVEN THOUGH THE INTERNET USES 8% OF OUR ENERGY!

LATER.

THOSE DON'T COUNT AS LIES, DO THEY?

NO, NO, THAT'S GORE. YOU'RE THE DUMB ONE.

W Real Sl... for Real Voters

LISTEN, PEOPLE, I NEED SIMPLER NUMBERS! I STILL CAN'T EXPLAIN MY OWN TAX PROGRAM!

NOT TO WORRY, SIR, NOBODY CARES IF YOU EXAGGERATE.

WHAT DO YOU MEAN?

WELL, SIR, YOU GET STUFF WRONG ALL THE TIME, BUT SINCE IT'S OUT OF IGNORANCE, YOUR ERRORS ARE CONSIDERED "HONEST" MISTAKES.

HONEST MISTAKES?

YES, SIR.

HEE, HEE! HOW COOL IS *THAT?*

COOL ENOUGH TO START MEASURING FOR DRAPES.

W Real Quot... for Real Voters

SO I CAN STRETCH THE TRUTH AND GORE CAN'T?

RIGHT. SINCE GORE *COULD* STOP FIBBING, BUT DOESN'T, IT'S A CHARACTER FLAW...

BUT BEING "THE DUMB ONE" MEANS WHEN YOU TELL A WHOPPER, YOU DON'T KNOW ANY BETTER. SO PEOPLE SEE IT AS ENDEARING, LIKE THEY DID WITH REAGAN!

W.

WHOA...

THOSE ARE TALL BOOTS TO UNDERSTAND! I UNDERSTAND THOSE BOOTS!

I'LL ADD IT TO THE LIST...

W.

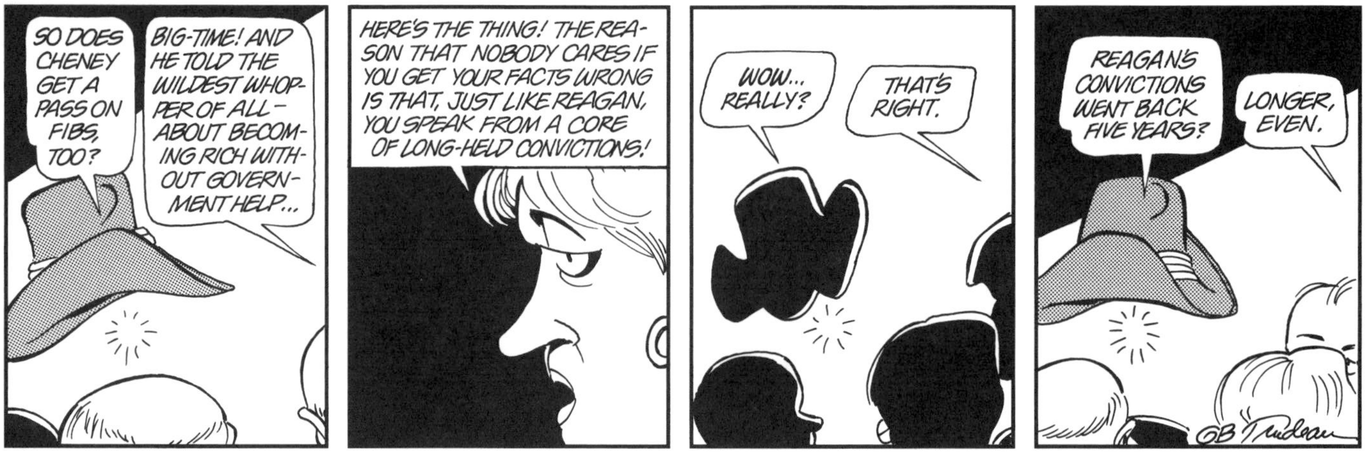
SO DOES CHENEY GET A PASS ON FIBS, TOO?
BIG-TIME! AND HE TOLD THE WILDEST WHOPPER OF ALL— ABOUT BECOMING RICH WITHOUT GOVERNMENT HELP...
HERE'S THE THING! THE REASON THAT NOBODY CARES IF YOU GET YOUR FACTS WRONG IS THAT, JUST LIKE REAGAN, YOU SPEAK FROM A CORE OF LONG-HELD CONVICTIONS!
WOW... REALLY?
THAT'S RIGHT.
REAGAN'S CONVICTIONS WENT BACK FIVE YEARS?
LONGER, EVEN.
GB Trudeau

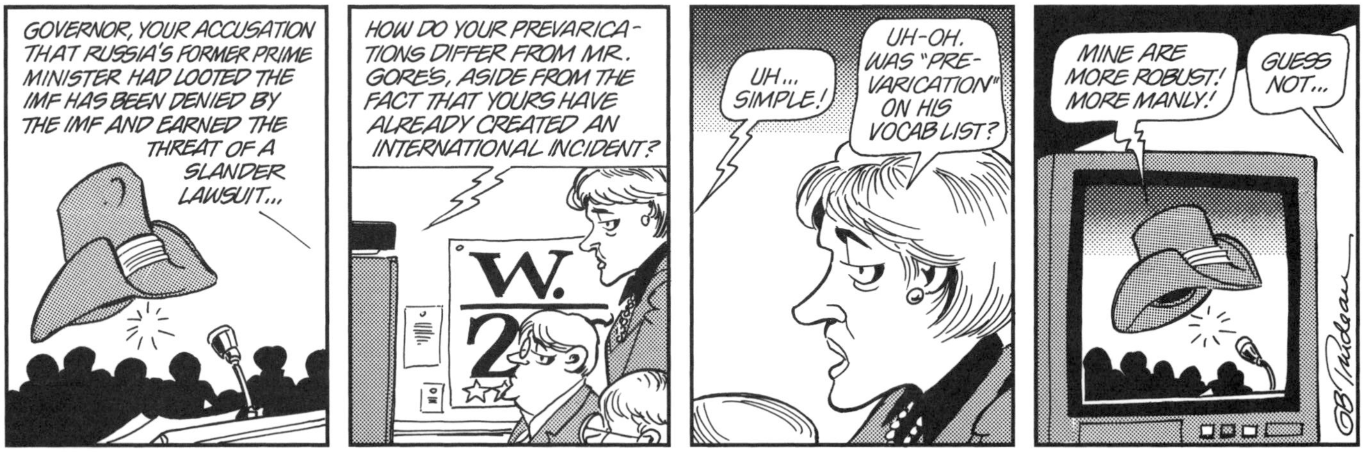
GOVERNOR, YOUR ACCUSATION THAT RUSSIA'S FORMER PRIME MINISTER HAD LOOTED THE IMF HAS BEEN DENIED BY THE IMF AND EARNED THE THREAT OF A SLANDER LAWSUIT...
HOW DO YOUR PREVARICATIONS DIFFER FROM MR. GORE'S, ASIDE FROM THE FACT THAT YOURS HAVE ALREADY CREATED AN INTERNATIONAL INCIDENT?
W.
2
UH... SIMPLE!
UH-OH. WAS "PREVARICATION" ON HIS VOCAB LIST?
MINE ARE MORE ROBUST! MORE MANLY!
GUESS NOT...
GB Trudeau

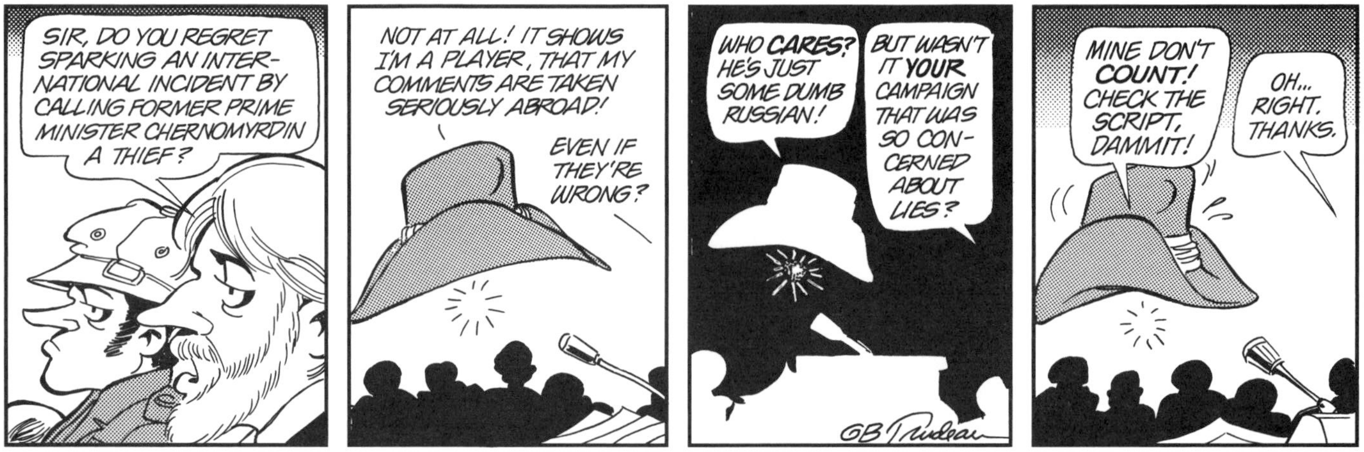
SIR, DO YOU REGRET SPARKING AN INTERNATIONAL INCIDENT BY CALLING FORMER PRIME MINISTER CHERNOMYRDIN A THIEF?
NOT AT ALL! IT SHOWS I'M A PLAYER, THAT MY COMMENTS ARE TAKEN SERIOUSLY ABROAD!
EVEN IF THEY'RE WRONG?
WHO CARES? HE'S JUST SOME DUMB RUSSIAN!
BUT WASN'T IT YOUR CAMPAIGN THAT WAS SO CONCERNED ABOUT LIES?
MINE DON'T COUNT! CHECK THE SCRIPT, DAMMIT!
OH... RIGHT. THANKS.
GB Trudeau

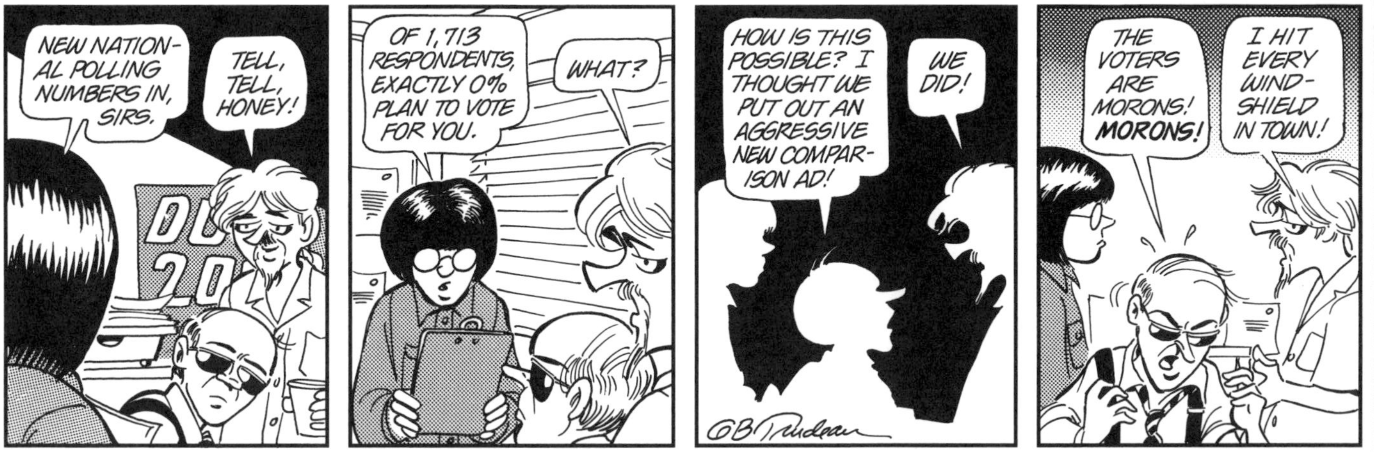
NEW NATIONAL POLLING NUMBERS IN, SIRS.
TELL, TELL, HONEY!
OF 1,713 RESPONDENTS, EXACTLY 0% PLAN TO VOTE FOR YOU.
WHAT?
HOW IS THIS POSSIBLE? I THOUGHT WE PUT OUT AN AGGRESSIVE NEW COMPARISON AD!
WE DID!
THE VOTERS ARE MORONS! **MORONS!**
I HIT EVERY WINDSHIELD IN TOWN!

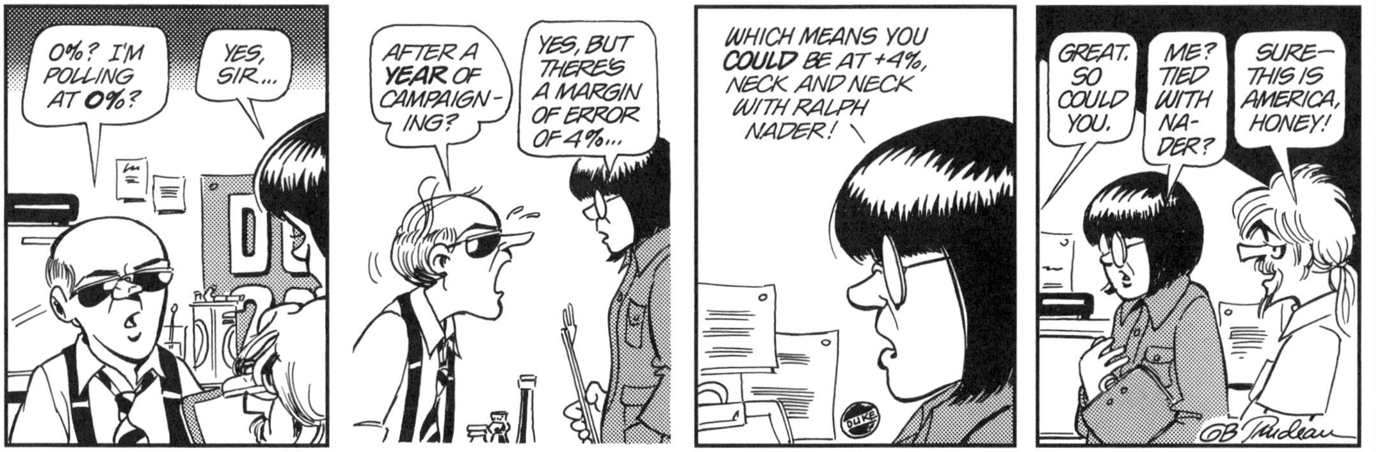
0%? I'M POLLING AT **0%**?
YES, SIR...
AFTER A **YEAR** OF CAMPAIGNING?
YES, BUT THERE'S A MARGIN OF ERROR OF 4%...
WHICH MEANS YOU **COULD** BE AT +4%, NECK AND NECK WITH RALPH NADER!
GREAT. SO COULD YOU.
ME? TIED WITH NADER?
SURE–THIS IS AMERICA, HONEY!

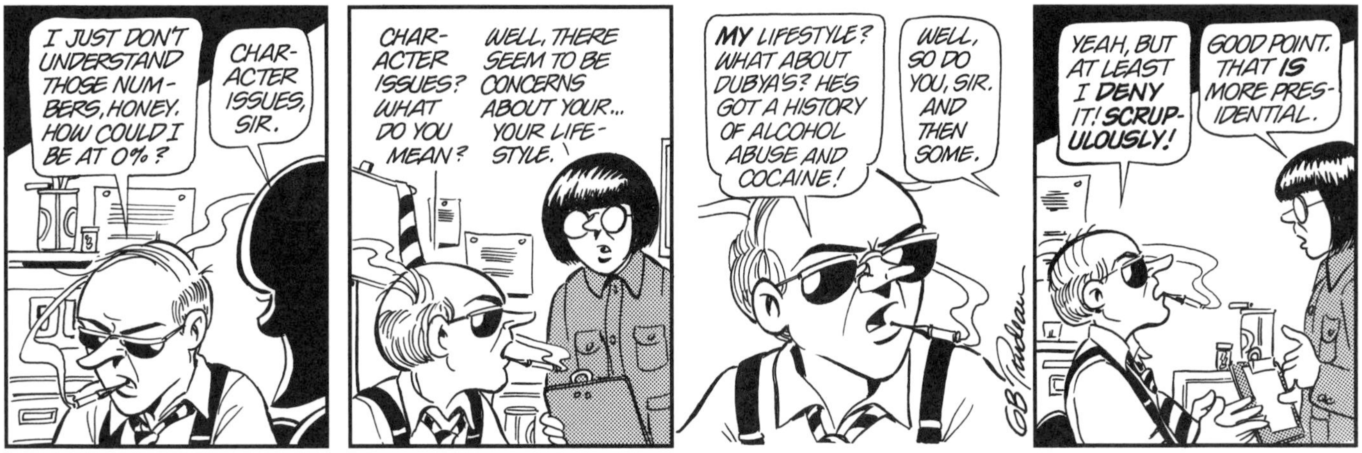
I JUST DON'T UNDERSTAND THOSE NUMBERS, HONEY. HOW COULD I BE AT 0%?
CHARACTER ISSUES, SIR.
CHARACTER ISSUES? WHAT DO YOU MEAN?
WELL, THERE SEEM TO BE CONCERNS ABOUT YOUR... YOUR LIFESTYLE.
MY LIFESTYLE? WHAT ABOUT DUBYA'S? HE'S GOT A HISTORY OF ALCOHOL ABUSE AND COCAINE!
WELL, SO DO YOU, SIR. AND THEN SOME.
YEAH, BUT AT LEAST I **DENY** IT! **SCRUPULOUSLY!**
GOOD POINT. THAT **IS** MORE PRESIDENTIAL.

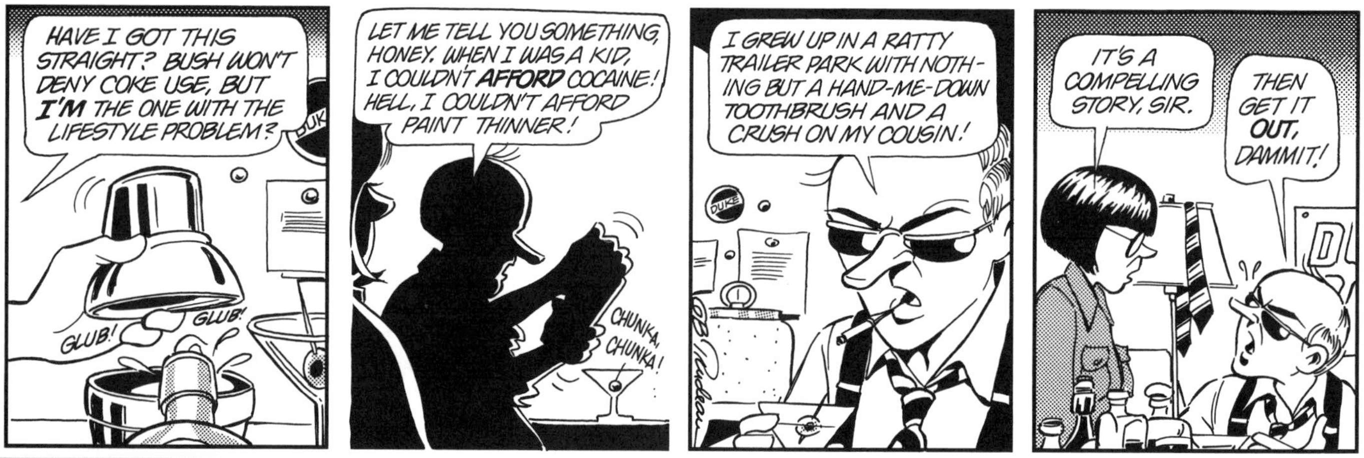
HAVE I GOT THIS STRAIGHT? BUSH WON'T DENY COKE USE, BUT I'M THE ONE WITH THE LIFESTYLE PROBLEM?
GLUB! GLUB!
LET ME TELL YOU SOMETHING, HONEY. WHEN I WAS A KID, I COULDN'T AFFORD COCAINE! HELL, I COULDN'T AFFORD PAINT THINNER!
CHUNKA, CHUNKA!
I GREW UP IN A RATTY TRAILER PARK WITH NOTHING BUT A HAND-ME-DOWN TOOTHBRUSH AND A CRUSH ON MY COUSIN!
IT'S A COMPELLING STORY, SIR.
THEN GET IT OUT, DAMMIT!

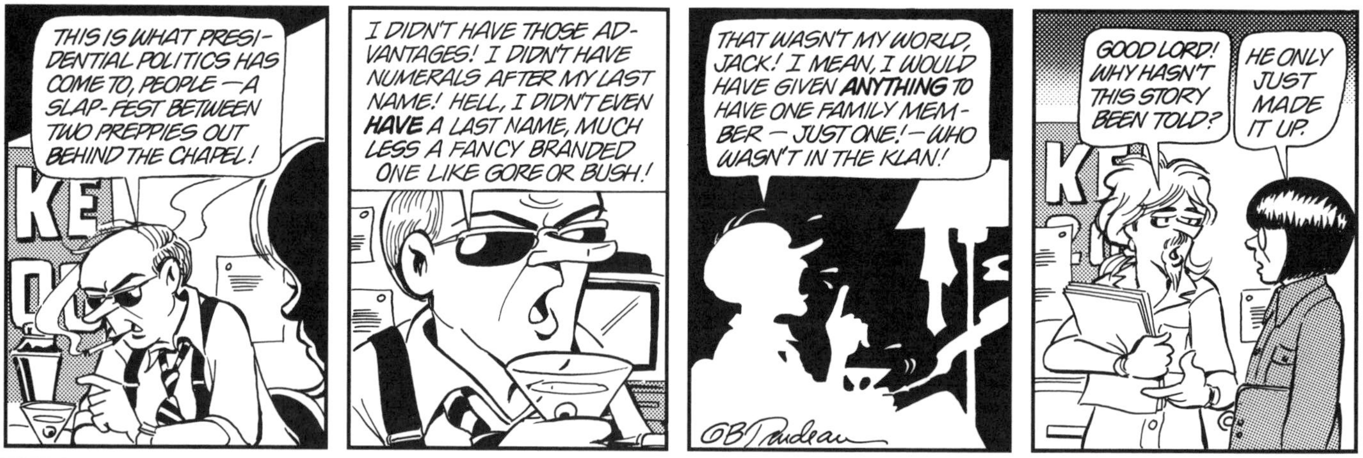
THIS IS WHAT PRESIDENTIAL POLITICS HAS COME TO, PEOPLE — A SLAP-FEST BETWEEN TWO PREPPIES OUT BEHIND THE CHAPEL!
I DIDN'T HAVE THOSE ADVANTAGES! I DIDN'T HAVE NUMERALS AFTER MY LAST NAME! HELL, I DIDN'T EVEN HAVE A LAST NAME, MUCH LESS A FANCY BRANDED ONE LIKE GORE OR BUSH!
THAT WASN'T MY WORLD, JACK! I MEAN, I WOULD HAVE GIVEN ANYTHING TO HAVE ONE FAMILY MEMBER — JUST ONE! — WHO WASN'T IN THE KLAN!
GOOD LORD! WHY HASN'T THIS STORY BEEN TOLD?
HE ONLY JUST MADE IT UP.

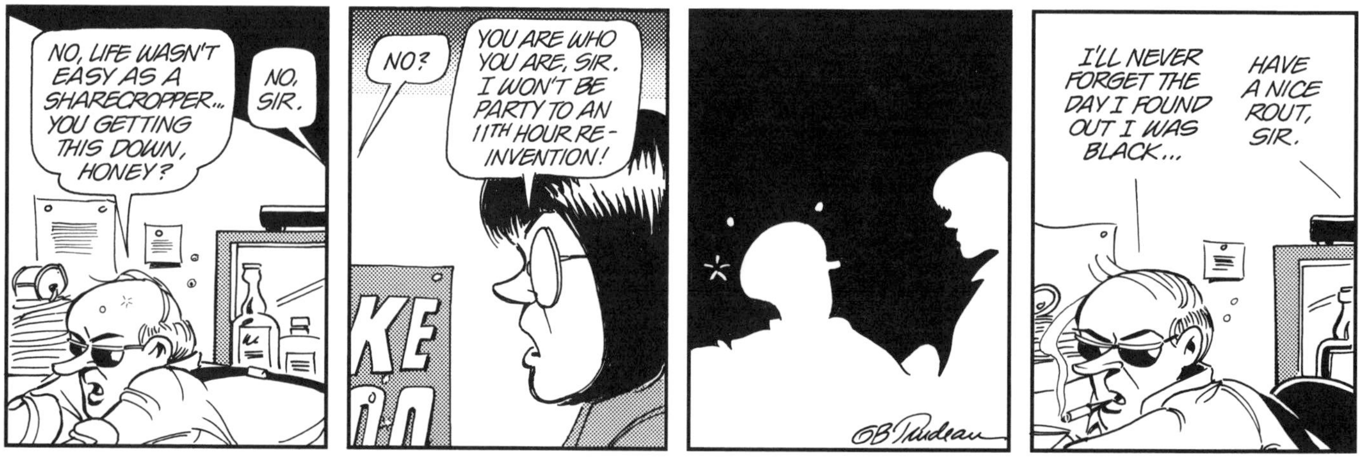
NO, LIFE WASN'T EASY AS A SHARECROPPER... YOU GETTING THIS DOWN, HONEY?
NO, SIR.
NO?
YOU ARE WHO YOU ARE, SIR. I WON'T BE PARTY TO AN 11TH HOUR REINVENTION!
I'LL NEVER FORGET THE DAY I FOUND OUT I WAS BLACK...
HAVE A NICE ROUT, SIR.

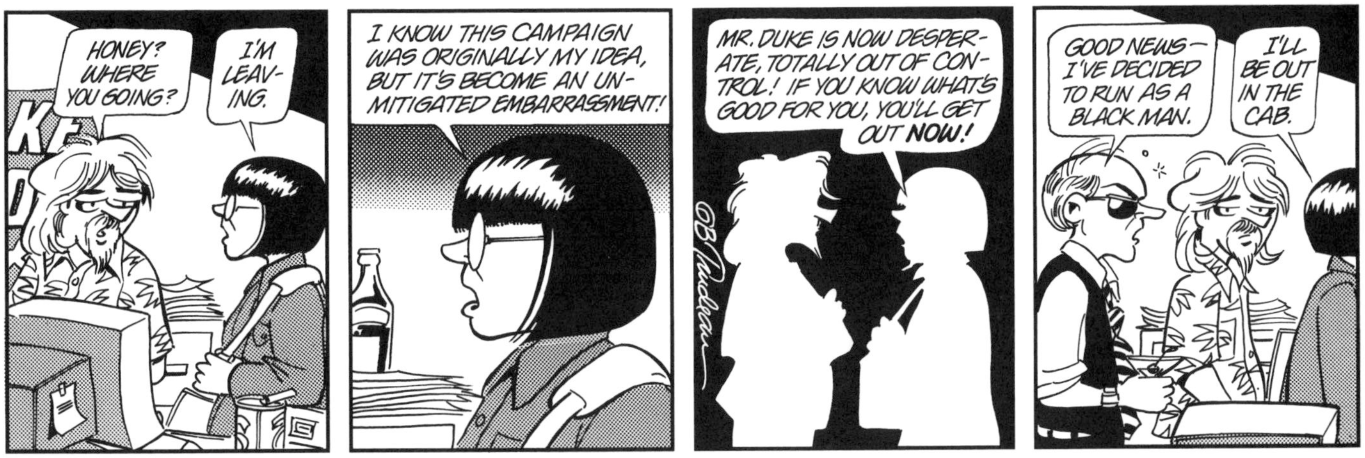
HONEY? WHERE YOU GOING?
I'M LEAV-ING.
I KNOW THIS CAMPAIGN WAS ORIGINALLY MY IDEA, BUT IT'S BECOME AN UN-MITIGATED EMBARRASSMENT!
MR. DUKE IS NOW DESPER-ATE, TOTALLY OUT OF CON-TROL! IF YOU KNOW WHAT'S GOOD FOR YOU, YOU'LL GET OUT NOW!
GOOD NEWS— I'VE DECIDED TO RUN AS A BLACK MAN.
I'LL BE OUT IN THE CAB.

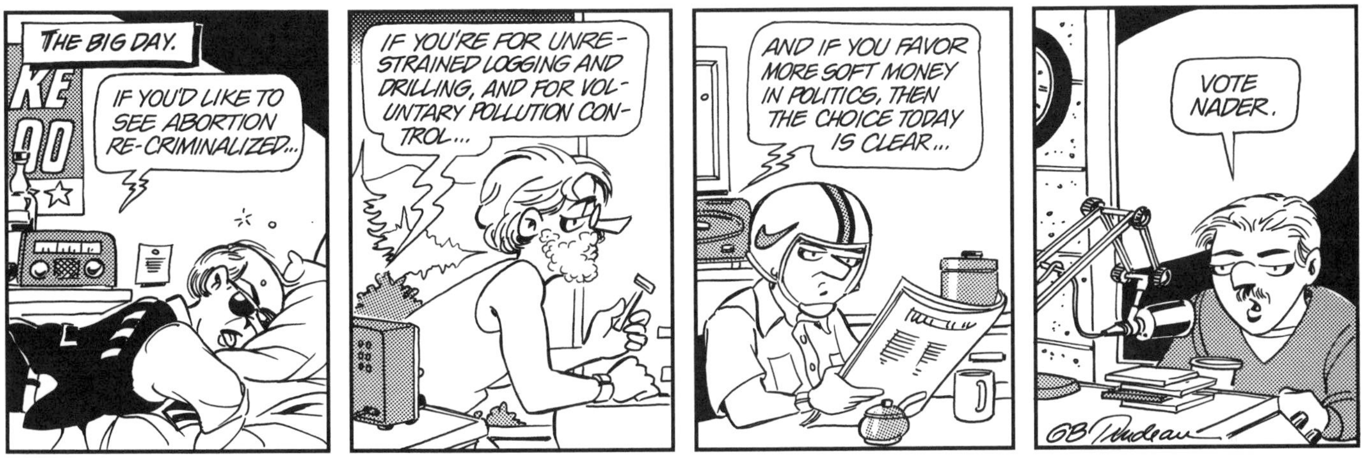
THE BIG DAY.
IF YOU'D LIKE TO SEE ABORTION RE-CRIMINALIZED...
IF YOU'RE FOR UNRE-STRAINED LOGGING AND DRILLING, AND FOR VOL-UNTARY POLLUTION CON-TROL...
AND IF YOU FAVOR MORE SOFT MONEY IN POLITICS, THEN THE CHOICE TODAY IS CLEAR...
VOTE NADER.

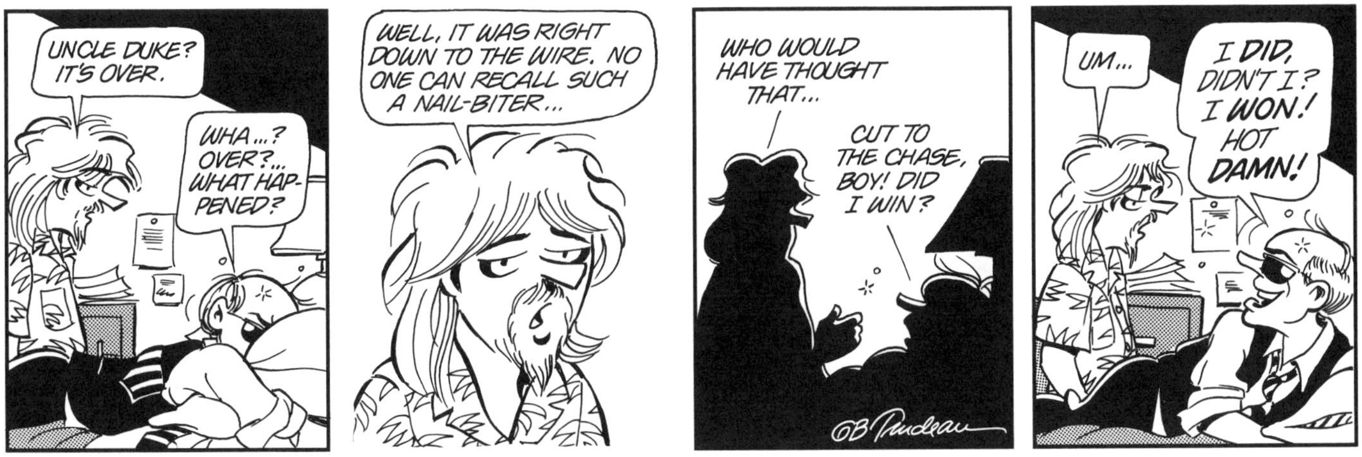
UNCLE DUKE? IT'S OVER.
WHA...? OVER?... WHAT HAP-PENED?
WELL, IT WAS RIGHT DOWN TO THE WIRE. NO ONE CAN RECALL SUCH A NAIL-BITER...
WHO WOULD HAVE THOUGHT THAT...
CUT TO THE CHASE, BOY! DID I WIN?
UM...
I DID, DIDN'T I? I WON! HOT DAMN!

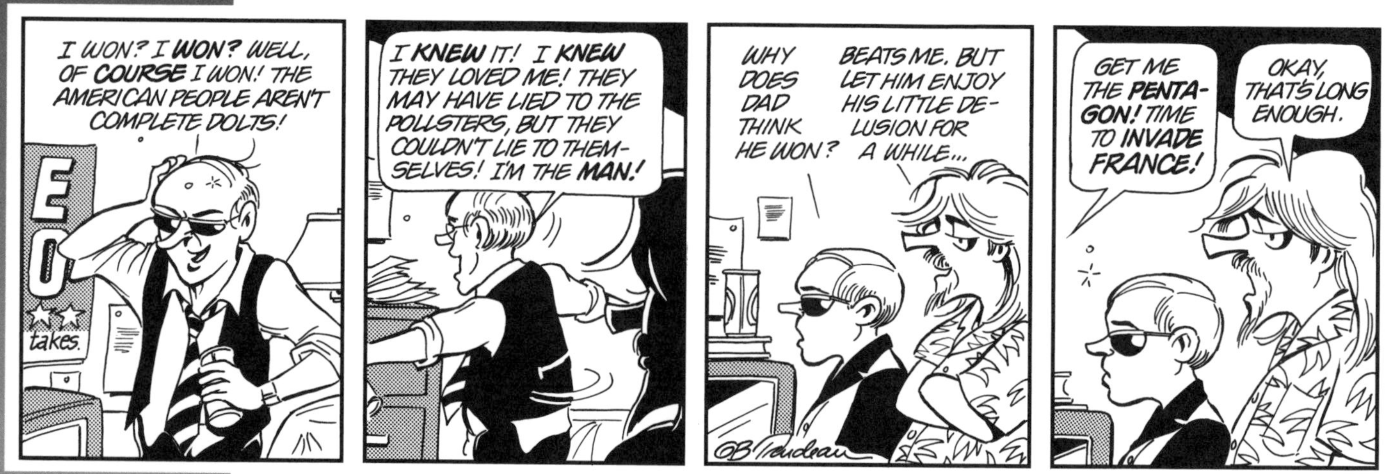

I WON? I WON? WELL, OF COURSE I WON! THE AMERICAN PEOPLE AREN'T COMPLETE DOLTS!
takes.
I KNEW IT! I KNEW THEY LOVED ME! THEY MAY HAVE LIED TO THE POLLSTERS, BUT THEY COULDN'T LIE TO THEMSELVES! I'M THE MAN!
WHY DOES DAD THINK HE WON?
BEATS ME. BUT LET HIM ENJOY HIS LITTLE DELUSION FOR A WHILE...
GET ME THE PENTAGON! TIME TO INVADE FRANCE!
OKAY, THAT'S LONG ENOUGH.

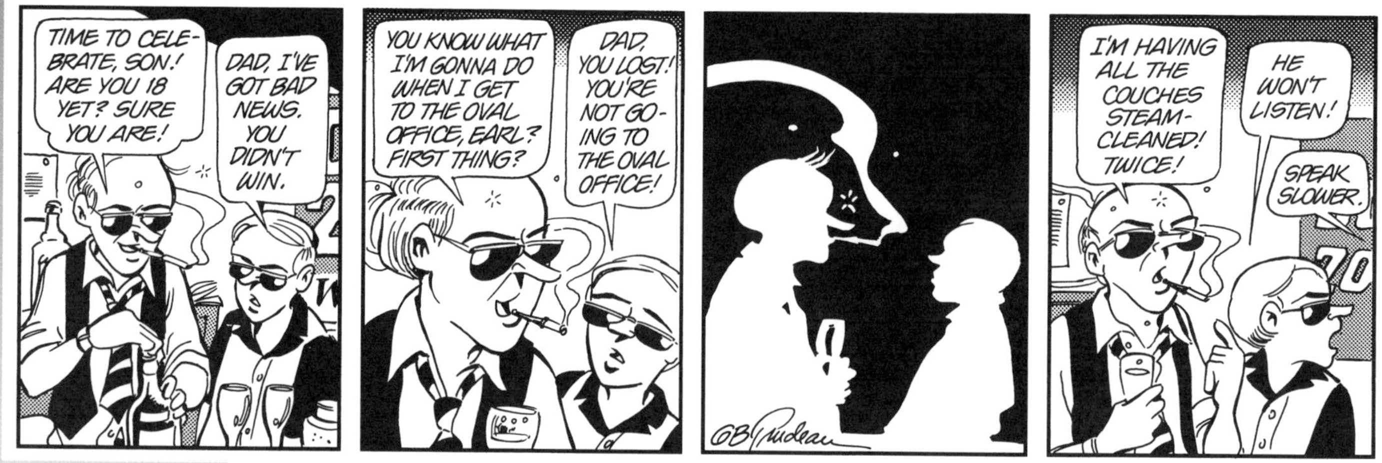

TIME TO CELEBRATE, SON! ARE YOU 18 YET? SURE YOU ARE!
DAD, I'VE GOT BAD NEWS. YOU DIDN'T WIN.
YOU KNOW WHAT I'M GONNA DO WHEN I GET TO THE OVAL OFFICE, EARL? FIRST THING?
DAD, YOU LOST! YOU'RE NOT GOING TO THE OVAL OFFICE!
I'M HAVING ALL THE COUCHES STEAM-CLEANED! TWICE!
HE WON'T LISTEN!
SPEAK SLOWER.

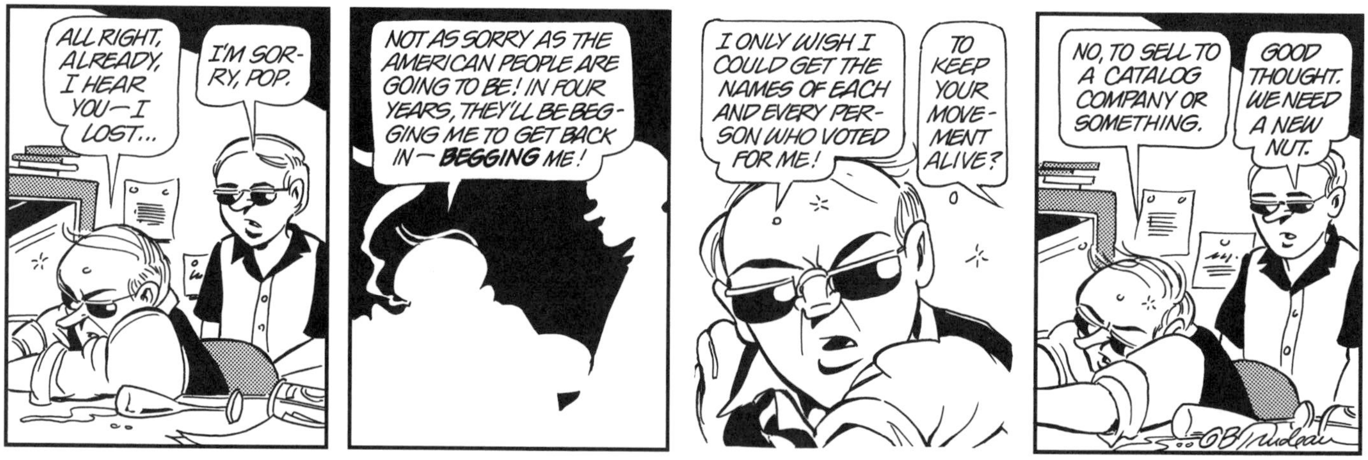

ALL RIGHT, ALREADY, I HEAR YOU—I LOST...
I'M SORRY, POP.
NOT AS SORRY AS THE AMERICAN PEOPLE ARE GOING TO BE! IN FOUR YEARS, THEY'LL BE BEGGING ME TO GET BACK IN—BEGGING ME!
I ONLY WISH I COULD GET THE NAMES OF EACH AND EVERY PERSON WHO VOTED FOR ME!
TO KEEP YOUR MOVEMENT ALIVE?
NO, TO SELL TO A CATALOG COMPANY OR SOMETHING.
GOOD THOUGHT. WE NEED A NEW NUT.

WHAT'S ALEX DOING ONLINE SO EARLY?

LOOKING FOR INVENTORY. myVULTURE.COM HAS BROUGHT OUT HER INNER SEARCH ENGINE.

SHE'S BEEN SPENDING EVERY WAKING MOMENT SCOURING THE NET FOR OVERSTOCK FROM E-COMMERCE SITES IN DISTRESS.

DAD! 10,000 LEATHER SHOWER CURTAINS!

PASS. GO TO SCHOOL, ALEX.

FOUND A GREAT LIQUIDATION PROSPECT, DAD!

LET'S HEAR.

IT'S A FAST-TANKING E-COMMERCE SITE. THE BUZZ IS THEY JUST FIRED 70% OF THEIR STAFF.

THERE'S BLOOD IN THE WATER, DAD. I RECOMMEND WE MAKE A PLAY FOR THEIR INVENTORY.

WHAT DO THEY SELL?

UM... RAIN GEAR FOR CATS.

KEEP LOOKING.

DAD, I FOUND A WINNER, A TOTAL NO-BRAINER!

IN FACT, I'M SO SURE WE COULD FLIP THIS INVENTORY, I'LL STORE IT IN MY BEDROOM!

WHAT IS IT?

LIMITED-EDITION BARBIE DOLLS!

LIMITED-EDITION?

SHE HAS HIPS. ONLY 2,000 WERE MADE.

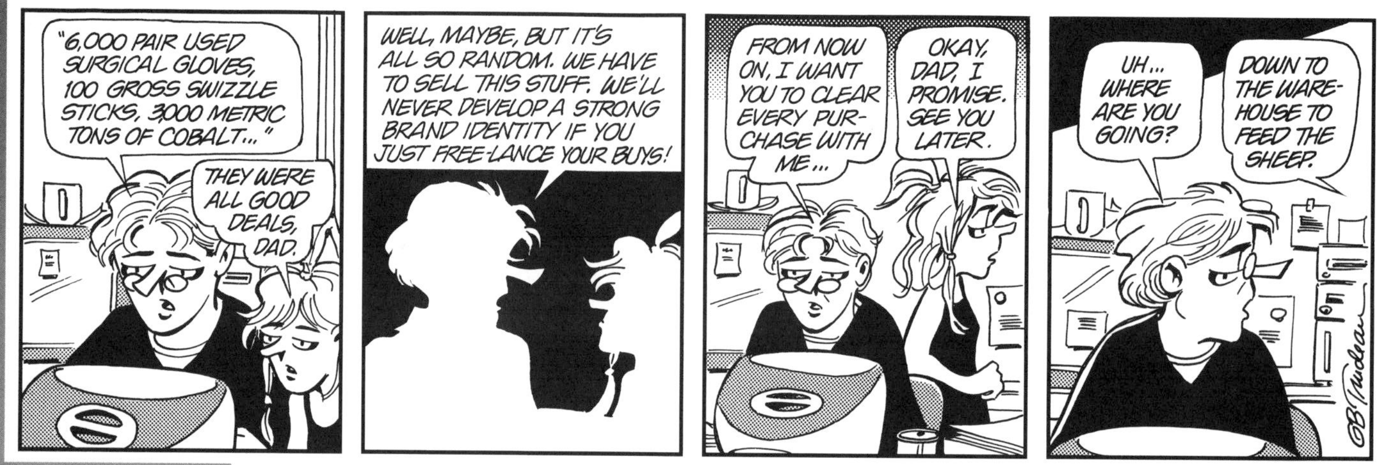
"6,000 PAIR USED SURGICAL GLOVES, 100 GROSS SWIZZLE STICKS, 3000 METRIC TONS OF COBALT..."
THEY WERE ALL GOOD DEALS, DAD.
WELL, MAYBE, BUT IT'S ALL SO RANDOM. WE HAVE TO SELL THIS STUFF. WE'LL NEVER DEVELOP A STRONG BRAND IDENTITY IF YOU JUST FREE-LANCE YOUR BUYS!
FROM NOW ON, I WANT YOU TO CLEAR EVERY PURCHASE WITH ME...
OKAY, DAD, I PROMISE. SEE YOU LATER.
UH... WHERE ARE YOU GOING?
DOWN TO THE WAREHOUSE TO FEED THE SHEEP.

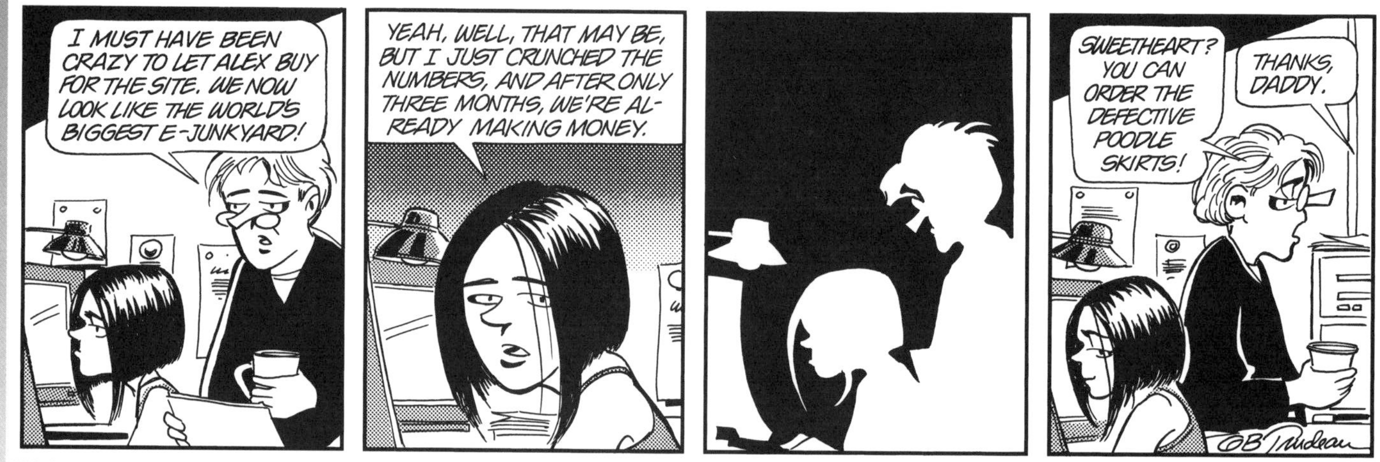
I MUST HAVE BEEN CRAZY TO LET ALEX BUY FOR THE SITE. WE NOW LOOK LIKE THE WORLD'S BIGGEST E-JUNKYARD!
YEAH, WELL, THAT MAY BE, BUT I JUST CRUNCHED THE NUMBERS, AND AFTER ONLY THREE MONTHS, WE'RE ALREADY MAKING MONEY.
SWEETHEART? YOU CAN ORDER THE DEFECTIVE POODLE SKIRTS!
THANKS, DADDY.

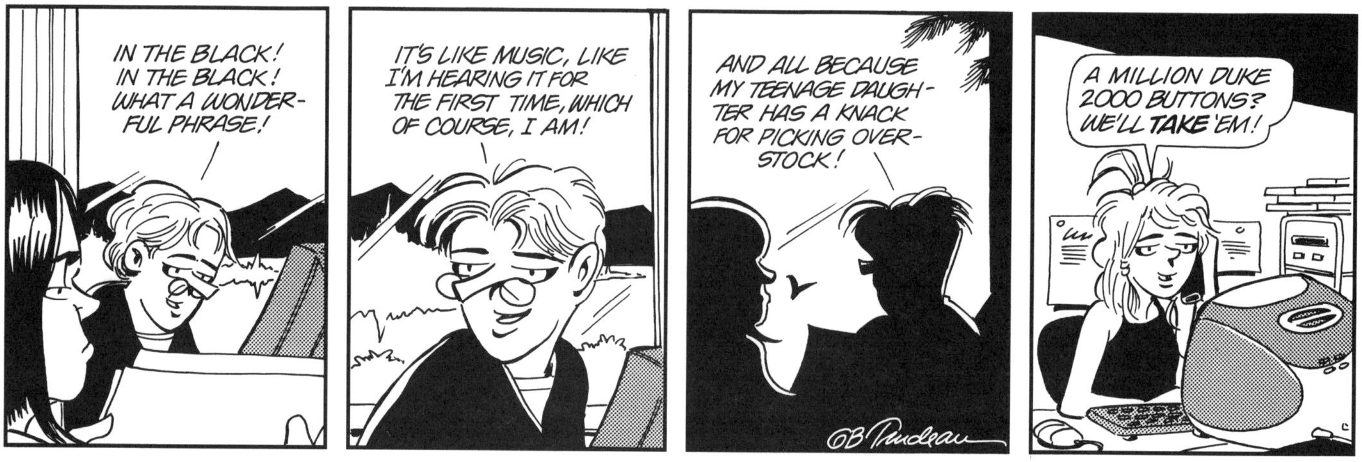
IN THE BLACK! IN THE BLACK! WHAT A WONDERFUL PHRASE!
IT'S LIKE MUSIC, LIKE I'M HEARING IT FOR THE FIRST TIME, WHICH OF COURSE, I AM!
AND ALL BECAUSE MY TEENAGE DAUGHTER HAS A KNACK FOR PICKING OVERSTOCK!
A MILLION DUKE 2000 BUTTONS? WE'LL TAKE 'EM!

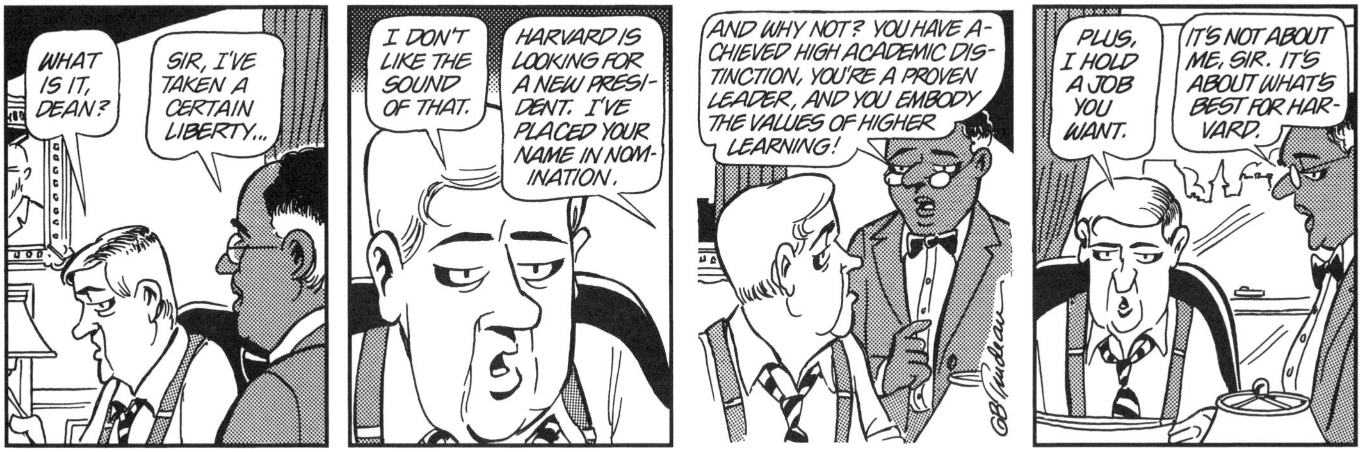
WHAT IS IT, DEAN?
SIR, I'VE TAKEN A CERTAIN LIBERTY...
I DON'T LIKE THE SOUND OF THAT.
HARVARD IS LOOKING FOR A NEW PRESIDENT. I'VE PLACED YOUR NAME IN NOMINATION.
AND WHY NOT? YOU HAVE ACHIEVED HIGH ACADEMIC DISTINCTION, YOU'RE A PROVEN LEADER, AND YOU EMBODY THE VALUES OF HIGHER LEARNING!
PLUS, I HOLD A JOB YOU WANT.
IT'S NOT ABOUT ME, SIR. IT'S ABOUT WHAT'S BEST FOR HARVARD.
GB Trudeau

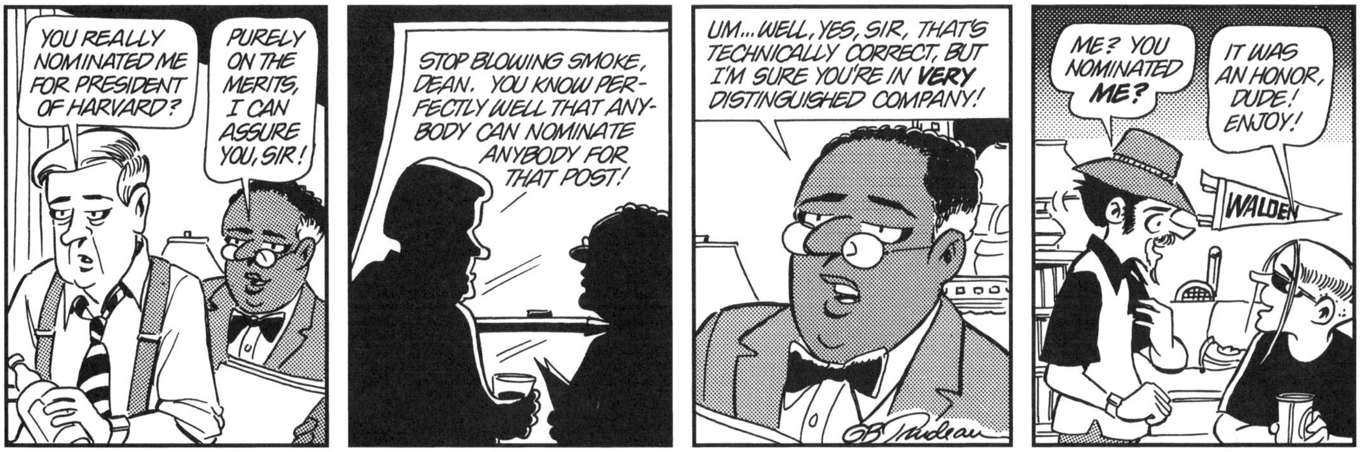
YOU REALLY NOMINATED ME FOR PRESIDENT OF HARVARD?
PURELY ON THE MERITS, I CAN ASSURE YOU, SIR!
STOP BLOWING SMOKE, DEAN. YOU KNOW PERFECTLY WELL THAT ANYBODY CAN NOMINATE ANYBODY FOR THAT POST!
UM... WELL, YES, SIR, THAT'S TECHNICALLY CORRECT, BUT I'M SURE YOU'RE IN VERY DISTINGUISHED COMPANY!
GB Trudeau
ME? YOU NOMINATED ME?
IT WAS AN HONOR, DUDE! ENJOY!
WALDEN

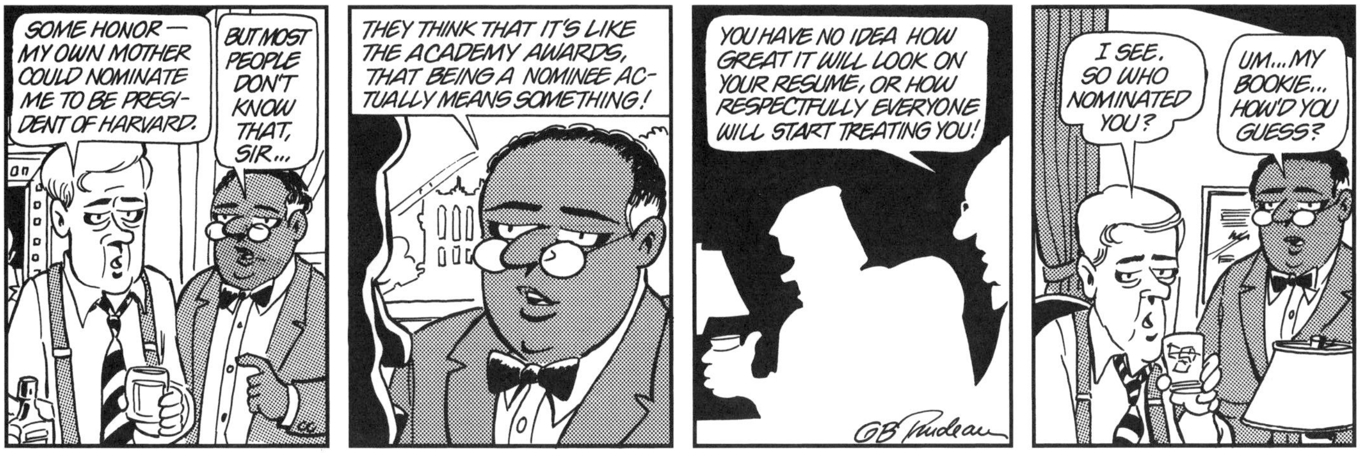
SOME HONOR — MY OWN MOTHER COULD NOMINATE ME TO BE PRESIDENT OF HARVARD.
BUT MOST PEOPLE DON'T KNOW THAT, SIR...
THEY THINK THAT IT'S LIKE THE ACADEMY AWARDS, THAT BEING A NOMINEE ACTUALLY MEANS SOMETHING!
YOU HAVE NO IDEA HOW GREAT IT WILL LOOK ON YOUR RESUME, OR HOW RESPECTFULLY EVERYONE WILL START TREATING YOU!
GB Trudeau
I SEE. SO WHO NOMINATED YOU?
UM... MY BOOKIE... HOW'D YOU GUESS?

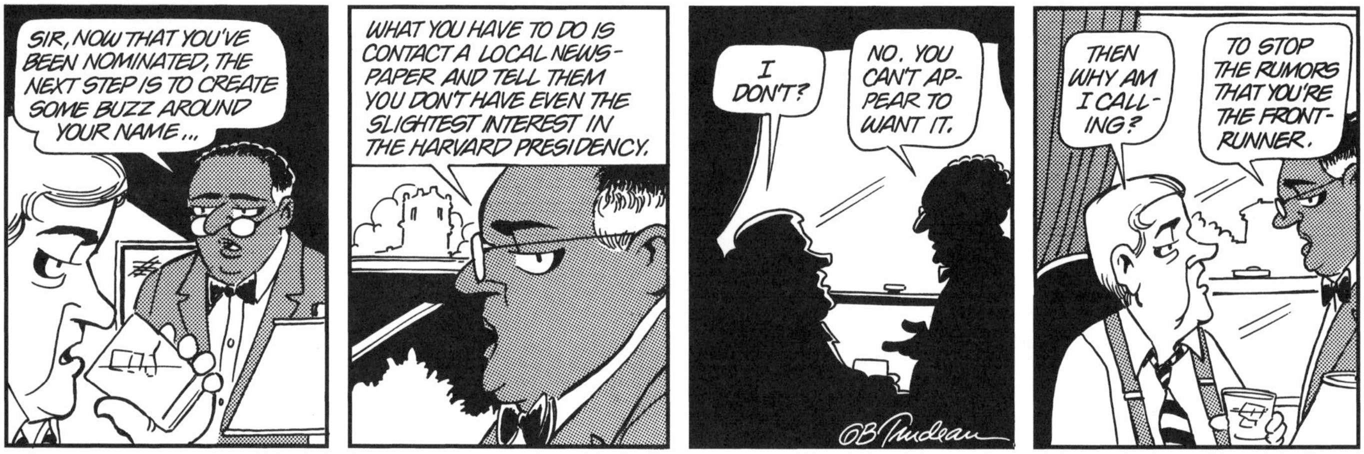
SIR, NOW THAT YOU'VE BEEN NOMINATED, THE NEXT STEP IS TO CREATE SOME BUZZ AROUND YOUR NAME...
WHAT YOU HAVE TO DO IS CONTACT A LOCAL NEWSPAPER AND TELL THEM YOU DON'T HAVE EVEN THE SLIGHTEST INTEREST IN THE HARVARD PRESIDENCY.
I DON'T?
NO. YOU CAN'T APPEAR TO WANT IT.
THEN WHY AM I CALLING?
TO STOP THE RUMORS THAT YOU'RE THE FRONT-RUNNER.
GB Trudeau

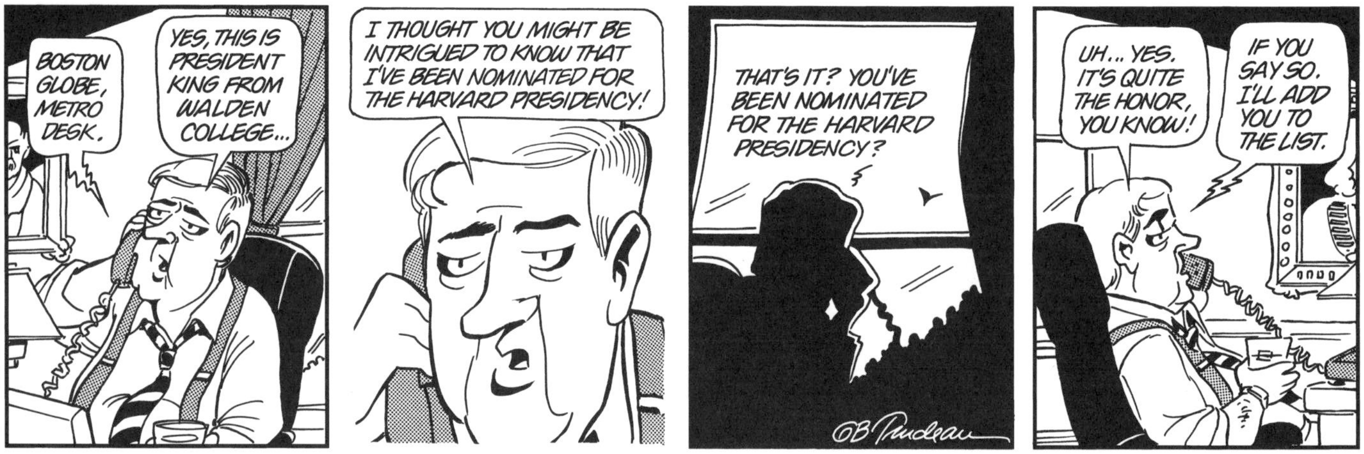
BOSTON GLOBE, METRO DESK.
YES, THIS IS PRESIDENT KING FROM WALDEN COLLEGE...
I THOUGHT YOU MIGHT BE INTRIGUED TO KNOW THAT I'VE BEEN NOMINATED FOR THE HARVARD PRESIDENCY!
THAT'S IT? YOU'VE BEEN NOMINATED FOR THE HARVARD PRESIDENCY?
UH... YES. IT'S QUITE THE HONOR, YOU KNOW!
IF YOU SAY SO. I'LL ADD YOU TO THE LIST.
GB Trudeau

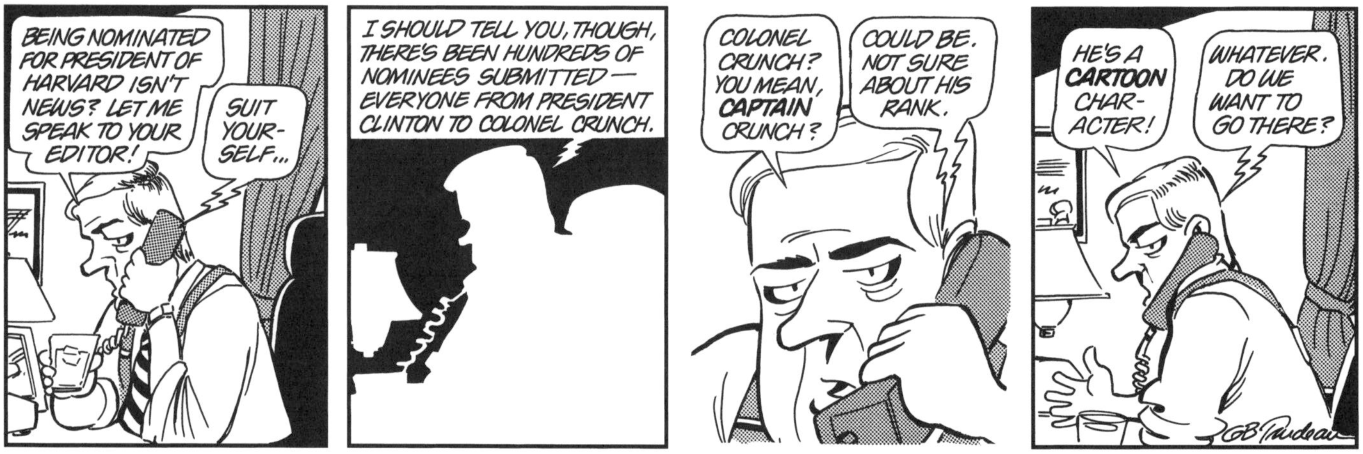
BEING NOMINATED FOR PRESIDENT OF HARVARD ISN'T NEWS? LET ME SPEAK TO YOUR EDITOR!
SUIT YOURSELF...
I SHOULD TELL YOU, THOUGH, THERE'S BEEN HUNDREDS OF NOMINEES SUBMITTED — EVERYONE FROM PRESIDENT CLINTON TO COLONEL CRUNCH.
COLONEL CRUNCH? YOU MEAN, CAPTAIN CRUNCH?
COULD BE. NOT SURE ABOUT HIS RANK.
HE'S A CARTOON CHARACTER!
WHATEVER. DO WE WANT TO GO THERE?
GB Trudeau

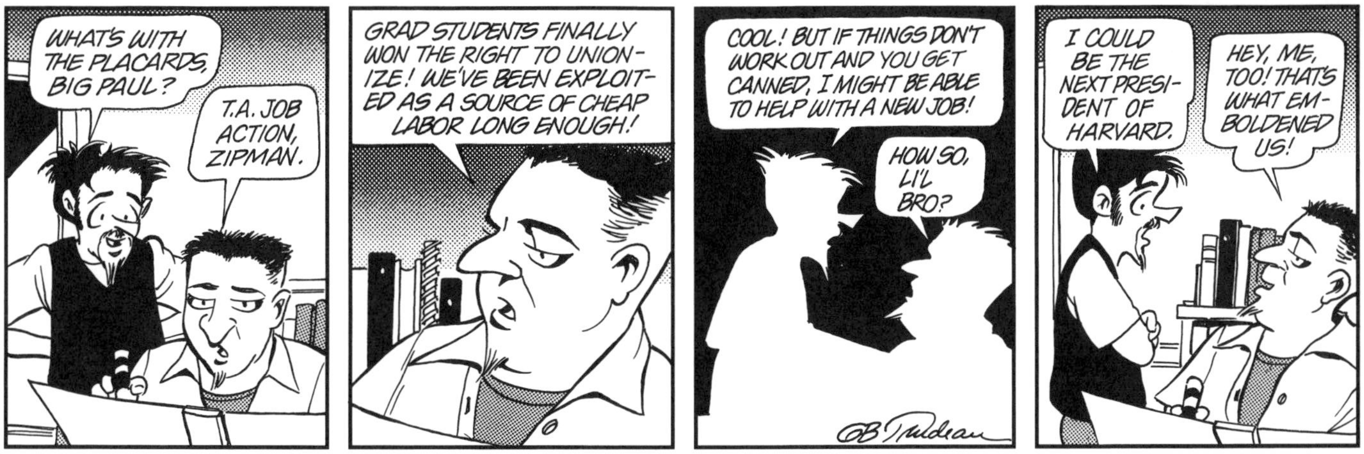
WHAT'S WITH THE PLACARDS, BIG PAUL?
T.A. JOB ACTION, ZIPMAN.
GRAD STUDENTS FINALLY WON THE RIGHT TO UNION-IZE! WE'VE BEEN EXPLOIT-ED AS A SOURCE OF CHEAP LABOR LONG ENOUGH!
COOL! BUT IF THINGS DON'T WORK OUT AND YOU GET CANNED, I MIGHT BE ABLE TO HELP WITH A NEW JOB!
HOW SO, LI'L BRO?
I COULD BE THE NEXT PRESI-DENT OF HARVARD.
HEY, ME, TOO! THAT'S WHAT EM-BOLDENED US!

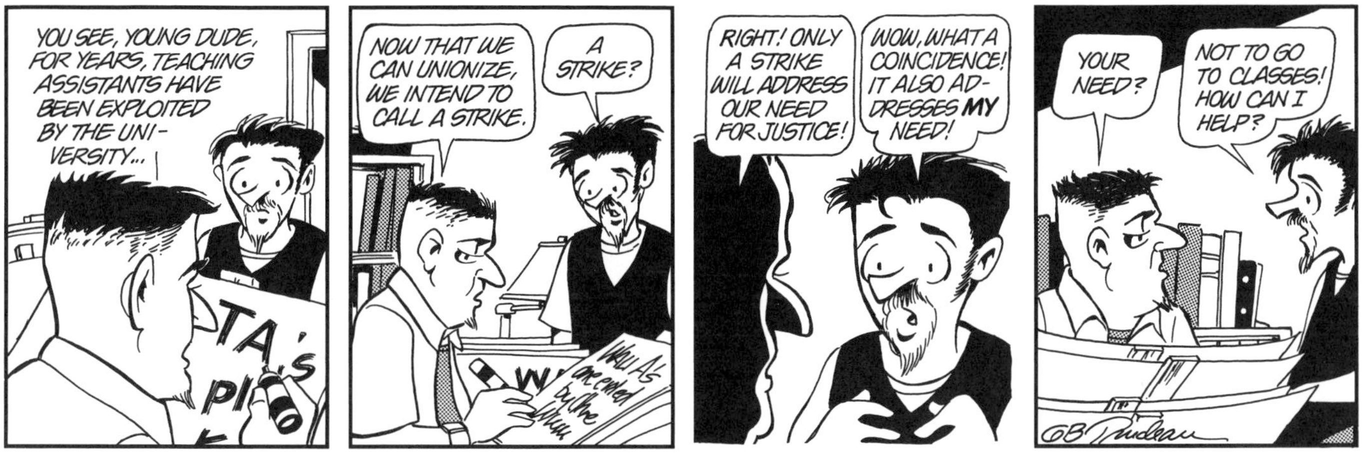
YOU SEE, YOUNG DUDE, FOR YEARS, TEACHING ASSISTANTS HAVE BEEN EXPLOITED BY THE UNI-VERSITY...
NOW THAT WE CAN UNIONIZE, WE INTEND TO CALL A STRIKE.
A STRIKE?
RIGHT! ONLY A STRIKE WILL ADDRESS OUR NEED FOR JUSTICE!
WOW, WHAT A COINCIDENCE! IT ALSO AD-DRESSES MY NEED!
YOUR NEED?
NOT TO GO TO CLASSES! HOW CAN I HELP?

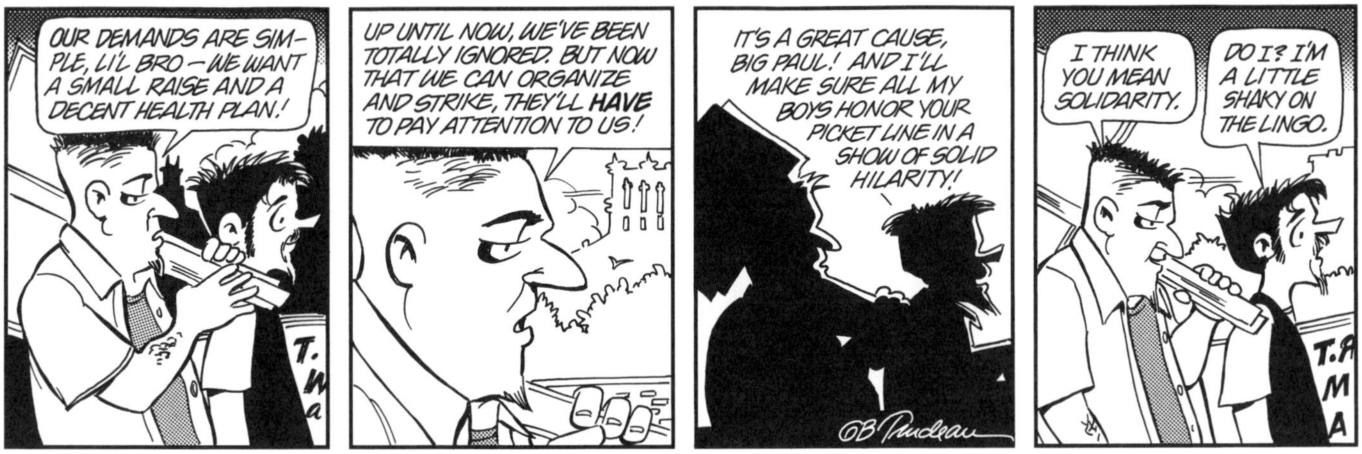
OUR DEMANDS ARE SIM-PLE, LI'L BRO — WE WANT A SMALL RAISE AND A DECENT HEALTH PLAN!
UP UNTIL NOW, WE'VE BEEN TOTALLY IGNORED. BUT NOW THAT WE CAN ORGANIZE AND STRIKE, THEY'LL HAVE TO PAY ATTENTION TO US!
IT'S A GREAT CAUSE, BIG PAUL! AND I'LL MAKE SURE ALL MY BOYS HONOR YOUR PICKET LINE IN A SHOW OF SOLID HILARITY!
I THINK YOU MEAN SOLIDARITY.
DO I? I'M A LITTLE SHAKY ON THE LINGO.

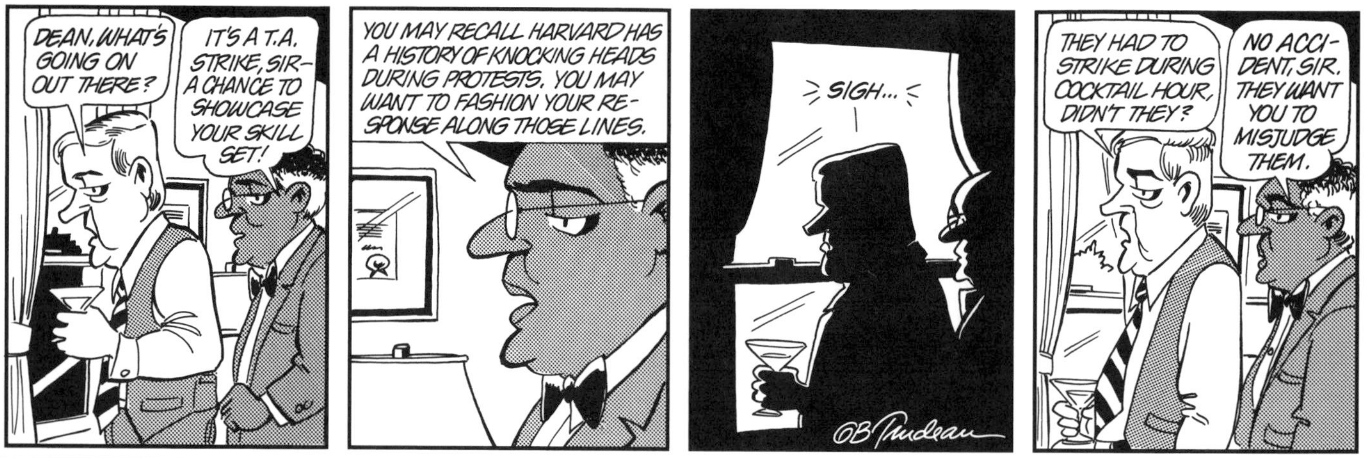
DEAN, WHAT'S GOING ON OUT THERE?
IT'S A T.A. STRIKE, SIR—A CHANCE TO SHOWCASE YOUR SKILL SET!
YOU MAY RECALL HARVARD HAS A HISTORY OF KNOCKING HEADS DURING PROTESTS. YOU MAY WANT TO FASHION YOUR RESPONSE ALONG THOSE LINES.
SIGH...
THEY HAD TO STRIKE DURING COCKTAIL HOUR, DIDN'T THEY?
NO ACCIDENT, SIR. THEY WANT YOU TO MISJUDGE THEM.

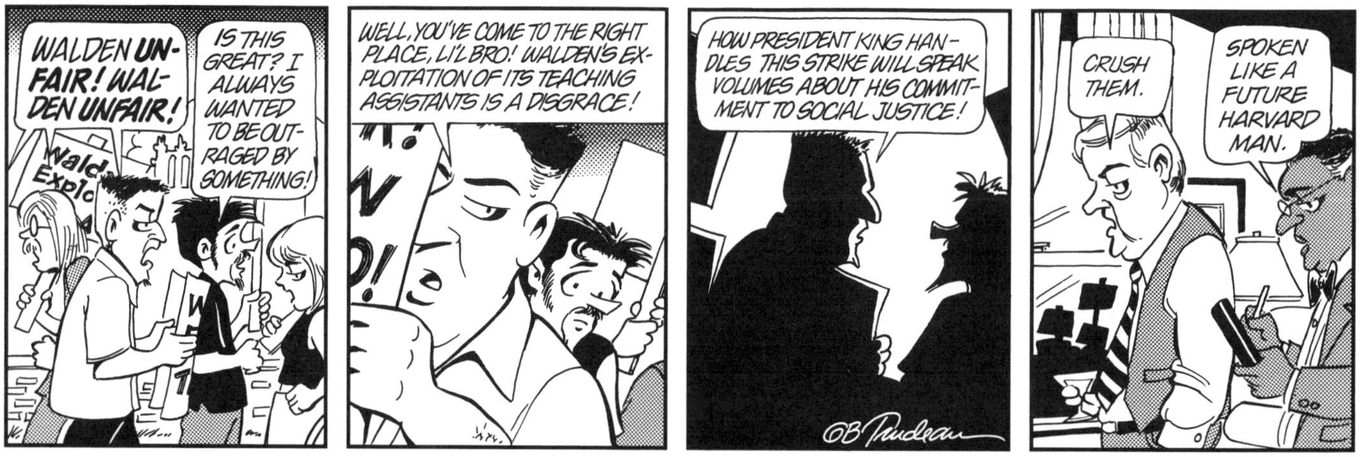
WALDEN **UNFAIR!** WALDEN **UNFAIR!**
IS THIS GREAT? I ALWAYS WANTED TO BE OUTRAGED BY SOMETHING!
WELL, YOU'VE COME TO THE RIGHT PLACE, LI'L BRO! WALDEN'S EXPLOITATION OF ITS TEACHING ASSISTANTS IS A DISGRACE!
HOW PRESIDENT KING HANDLES THIS STRIKE WILL SPEAK VOLUMES ABOUT HIS COMMITMENT TO SOCIAL JUSTICE!
CRUSH THEM.
SPOKEN LIKE A FUTURE HARVARD MAN.

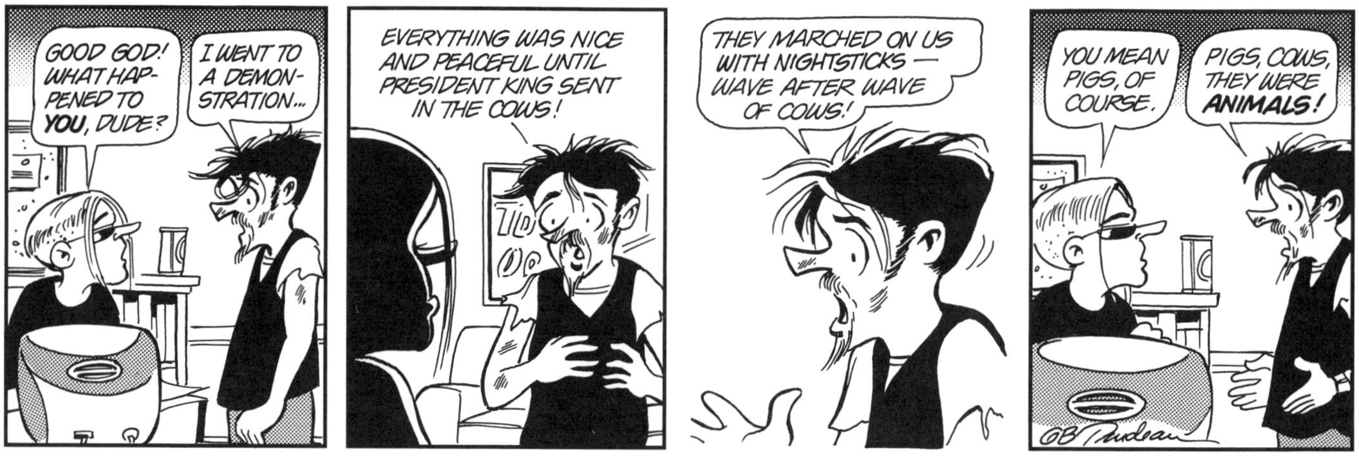
GOOD GOD! WHAT HAPPENED TO **YOU**, DUDE?
I WENT TO A DEMONSTRATION...
EVERYTHING WAS NICE AND PEACEFUL UNTIL PRESIDENT KING SENT IN THE COWS!
THEY MARCHED ON US WITH NIGHTSTICKS — WAVE AFTER WAVE OF COWS!
YOU MEAN PIGS, OF COURSE.
PIGS, COWS, THEY WERE **ANIMALS!**

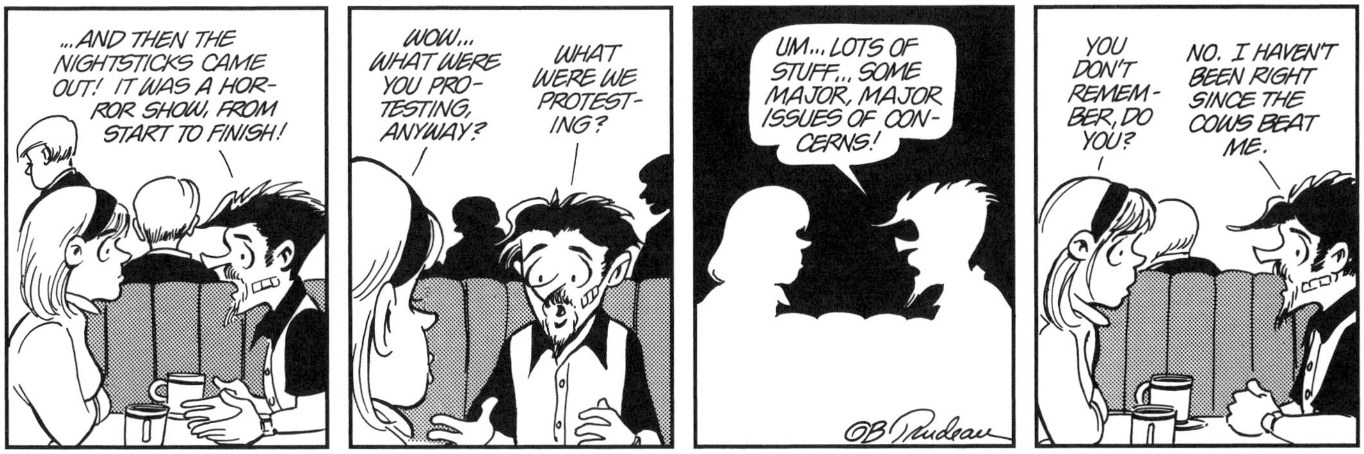
...AND THEN THE NIGHTSTICKS CAME OUT! IT WAS A HORROR SHOW, FROM START TO FINISH!
WOW... WHAT WERE YOU PROTESTING, ANYWAY?
WHAT WERE WE PROTESTING?
UM... LOTS OF STUFF... SOME MAJOR, MAJOR ISSUES OF CONCERNS!
©B Trudeau
YOU DON'T REMEMBER, DO YOU?
NO. I HAVEN'T BEEN RIGHT SINCE THE COWS BEAT ME.

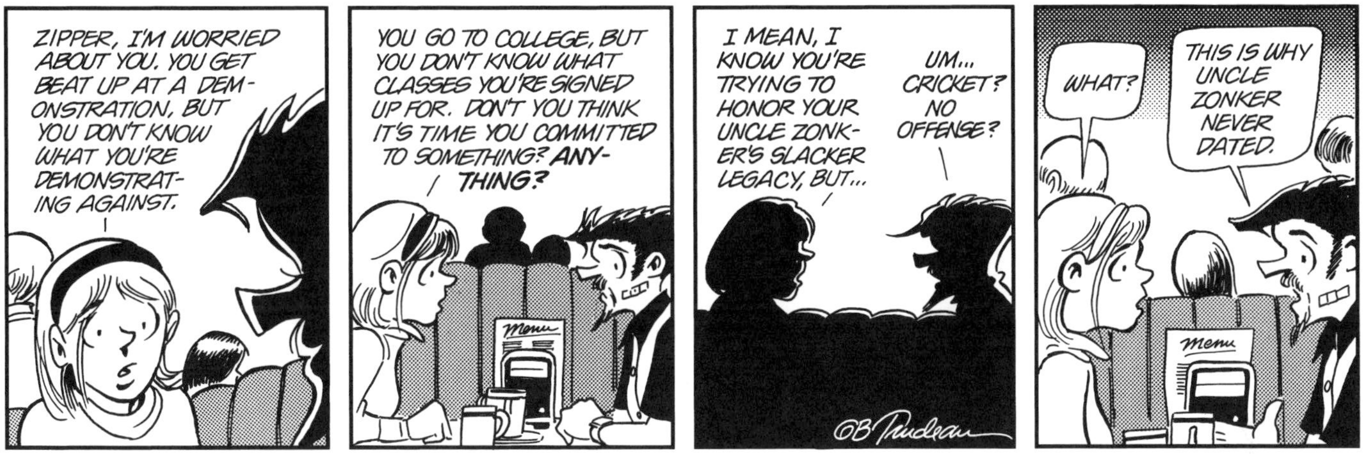
ZIPPER, I'M WORRIED ABOUT YOU. YOU GET BEAT UP AT A DEMONSTRATION, BUT YOU DON'T KNOW WHAT YOU'RE DEMONSTRATING AGAINST.
YOU GO TO COLLEGE, BUT YOU DON'T KNOW WHAT CLASSES YOU'RE SIGNED UP FOR. DON'T YOU THINK IT'S TIME YOU COMMITTED TO SOMETHING? **ANYTHING?**
Menu
I MEAN, I KNOW YOU'RE TRYING TO HONOR YOUR UNCLE ZONKER'S SLACKER LEGACY, BUT...
UM... CRICKET? NO OFFENSE?
©B Trudeau
WHAT?
THIS IS WHY UNCLE ZONKER NEVER DATED.
Menu

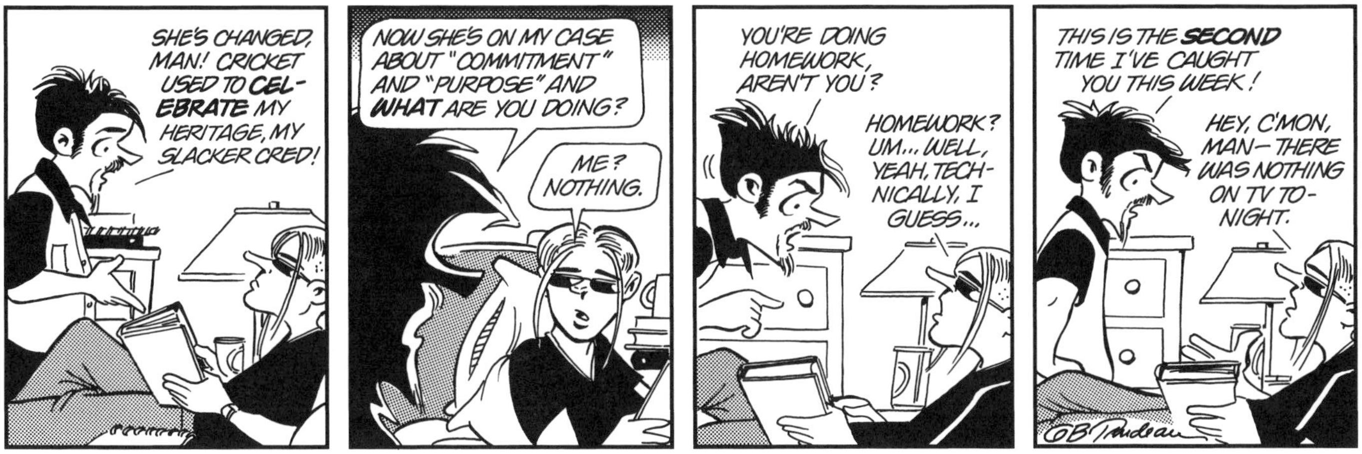
SHE'S CHANGED, MAN! CRICKET USED TO **CELEBRATE** MY HERITAGE, MY SLACKER CRED!
NOW SHE'S ON MY CASE ABOUT "COMMITMENT" AND "PURPOSE" AND **WHAT** ARE YOU DOING?
ME? NOTHING.
YOU'RE DOING HOMEWORK, AREN'T YOU?
HOMEWORK? UM... WELL, YEAH, TECHNICALLY, I GUESS...
THIS IS THE **SECOND** TIME I'VE CAUGHT YOU THIS WEEK!
HEY, C'MON, MAN—THERE WAS NOTHING ON TV TONIGHT.
©B Trudeau

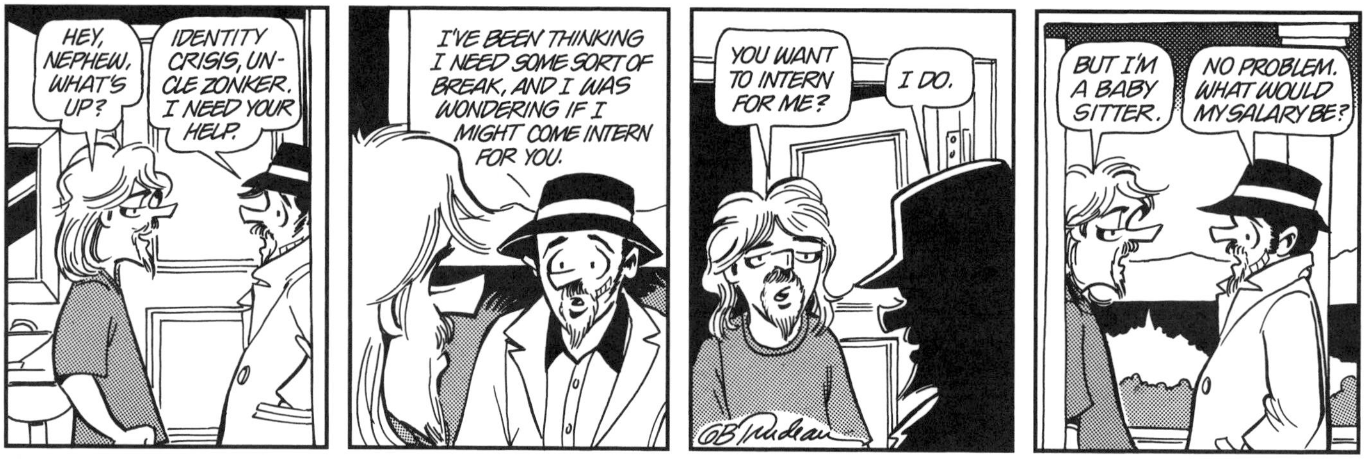
HEY, NEPHEW, WHAT'S UP?
IDENTITY CRISIS, UNCLE ZONKER. I NEED YOUR HELP.
I'VE BEEN THINKING I NEED SOME SORT OF BREAK, AND I WAS WONDERING IF I MIGHT COME INTERN FOR YOU.
YOU WANT TO INTERN FOR ME?
I DO.
BUT I'M A BABY SITTER.
NO PROBLEM. WHAT WOULD MY SALARY BE?

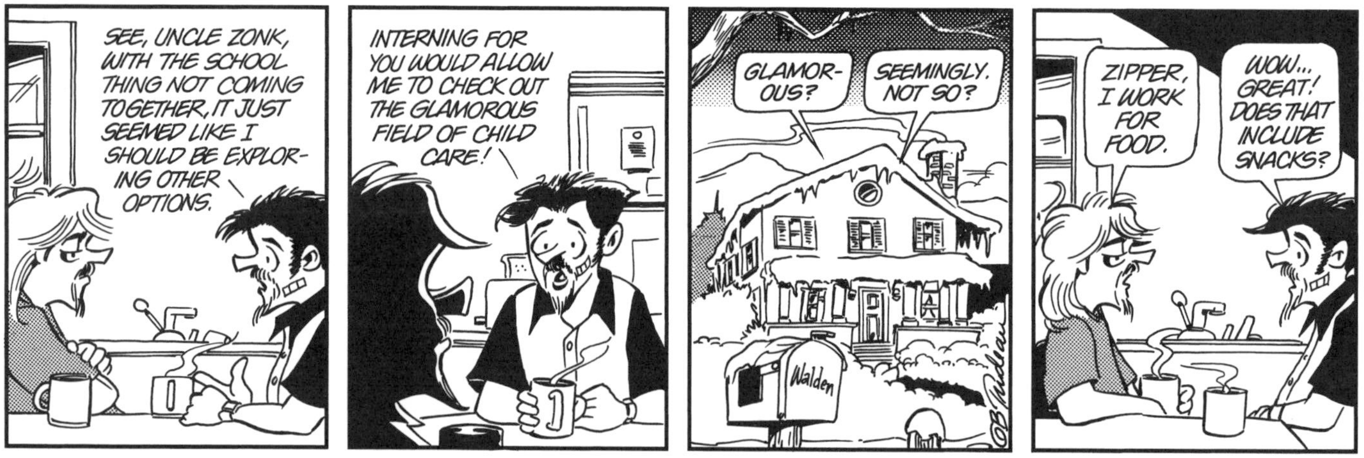
SEE, UNCLE ZONK, WITH THE SCHOOL THING NOT COMING TOGETHER, IT JUST SEEMED LIKE I SHOULD BE EXPLORING OTHER OPTIONS.
INTERNING FOR YOU WOULD ALLOW ME TO CHECK OUT THE GLAMOROUS FIELD OF CHILD CARE!
GLAMOROUS?
SEEMINGLY. NOT SO?
Walden
ZIPPER, I WORK FOR FOOD.
WOW... GREAT! DOES THAT INCLUDE SNACKS?

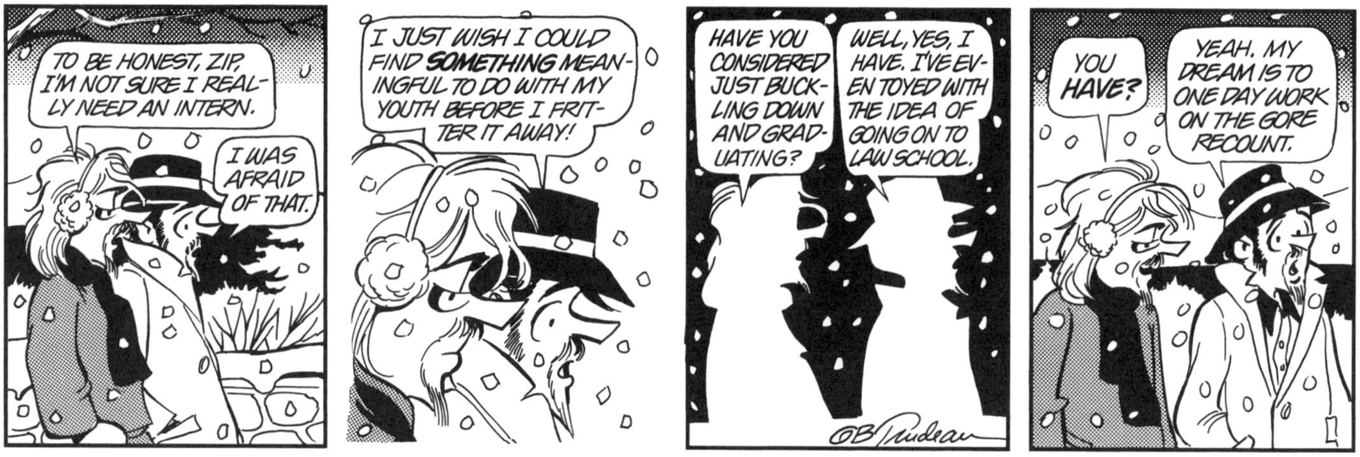
TO BE HONEST, ZIP, I'M NOT SURE I REALLY NEED AN INTERN.
I WAS AFRAID OF THAT.
I JUST WISH I COULD FIND **SOMETHING** MEANINGFUL TO DO WITH MY YOUTH BEFORE I FRITTER IT AWAY!
HAVE YOU CONSIDERED JUST BUCKLING DOWN AND GRADUATING?
WELL, YES, I HAVE. I'VE EVEN TOYED WITH THE IDEA OF GOING ON TO LAW SCHOOL.
YOU **HAVE?**
YEAH. MY DREAM IS TO ONE DAY WORK ON THE GORE RECOUNT.

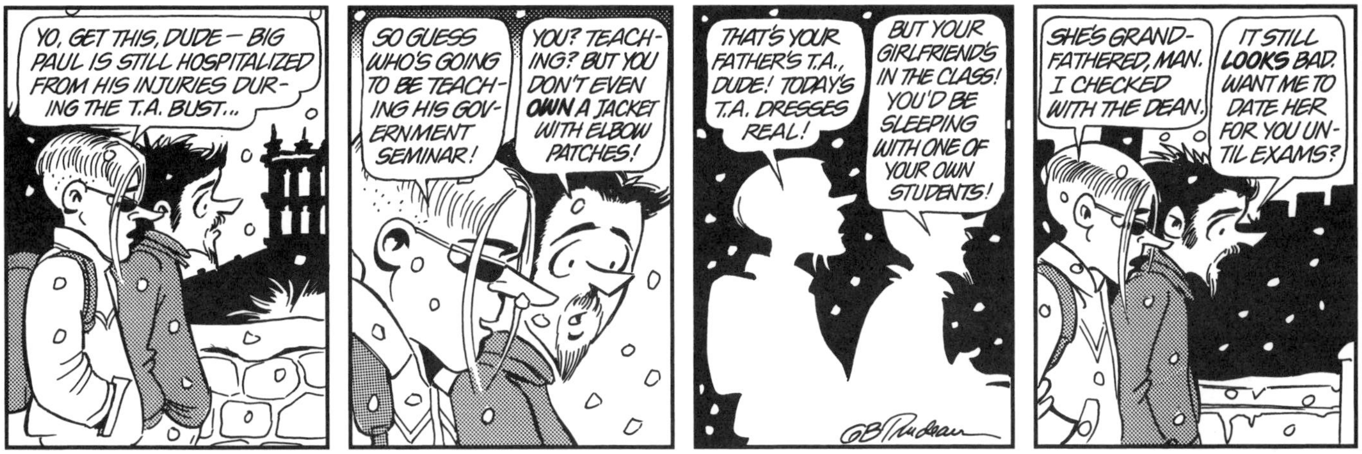
YO, GET THIS, DUDE — BIG PAUL IS STILL HOSPITALIZED FROM HIS INJURIES DURING THE T.A. BUST...
SO GUESS WHO'S GOING TO BE TEACHING HIS GOVERNMENT SEMINAR!
YOU? TEACHING? BUT YOU DON'T EVEN OWN A JACKET WITH ELBOW PATCHES!
THAT'S YOUR FATHER'S T.A., DUDE! TODAY'S T.A. DRESSES REAL!
BUT YOUR GIRLFRIEND'S IN THE CLASS! YOU'D BE SLEEPING WITH ONE OF YOUR OWN STUDENTS!
SHE'S GRANDFATHERED, MAN. I CHECKED WITH THE DEAN.
IT STILL LOOKS BAD. WANT ME TO DATE HER FOR YOU UNTIL EXAMS?
©B Trudeau

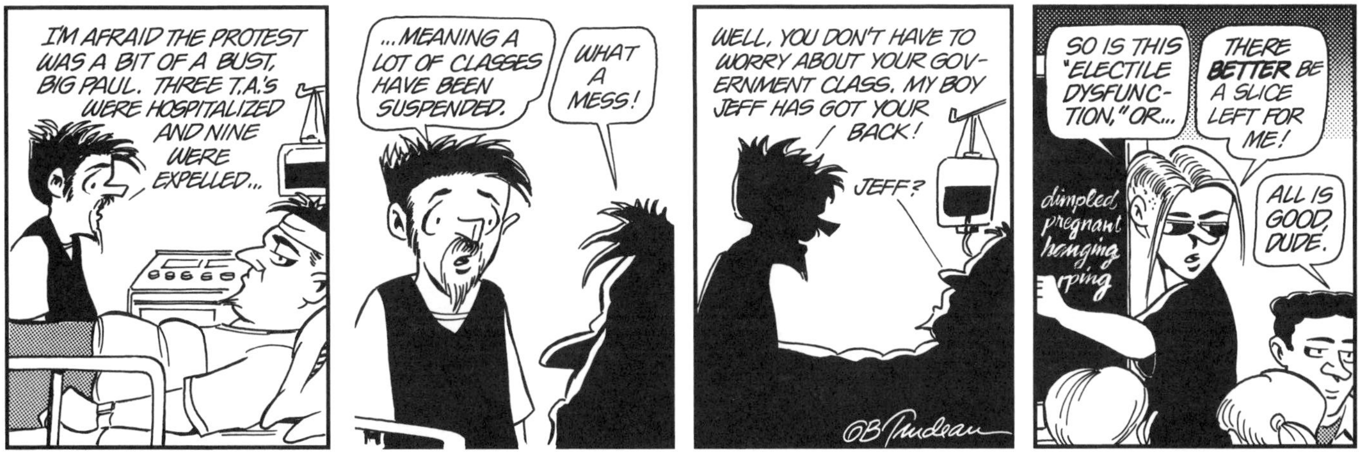
I'M AFRAID THE PROTEST WAS A BIT OF A BUST, BIG PAUL. THREE T.A.'s WERE HOSPITALIZED AND NINE WERE EXPELLED...
...MEANING A LOT OF CLASSES HAVE BEEN SUSPENDED.
WHAT A MESS!
WELL, YOU DON'T HAVE TO WORRY ABOUT YOUR GOVERNMENT CLASS. MY BOY JEFF HAS GOT YOUR BACK!
JEFF?
©B Trudeau
dimpled
pregnant
hanging
SO IS THIS "ELECTILE DYSFUNCTION," OR...
THERE BETTER BE A SLICE LEFT FOR ME!
ALL IS GOOD, DUDE.

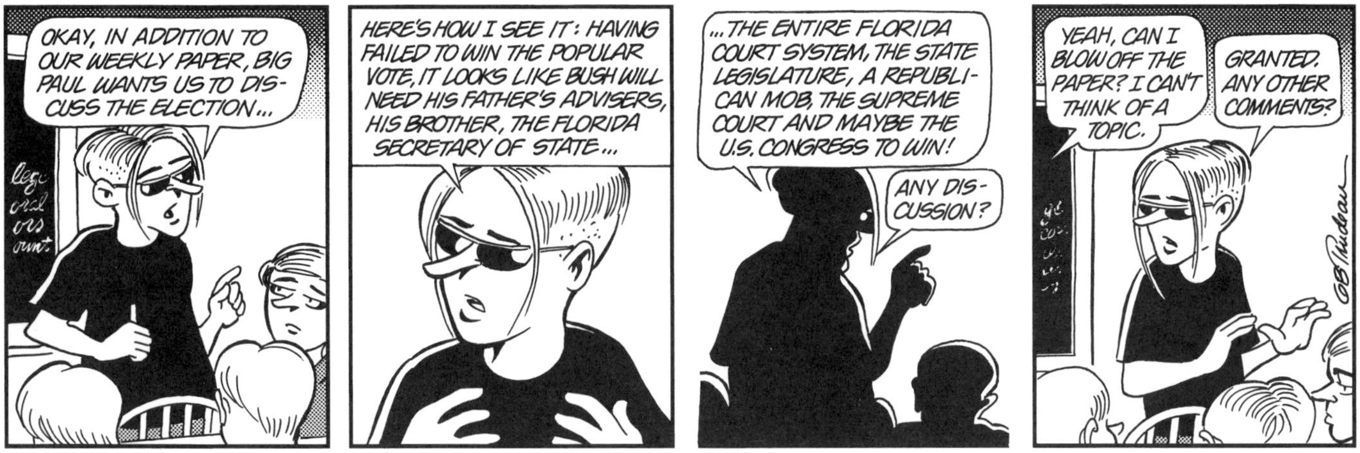
OKAY, IN ADDITION TO OUR WEEKLY PAPER, BIG PAUL WANTS US TO DISCUSS THE ELECTION...
HERE'S HOW I SEE IT: HAVING FAILED TO WIN THE POPULAR VOTE, IT LOOKS LIKE BUSH WILL NEED HIS FATHER'S ADVISERS, HIS BROTHER, THE FLORIDA SECRETARY OF STATE...
...THE ENTIRE FLORIDA COURT SYSTEM, THE STATE LEGISLATURE, A REPUBLICAN MOB, THE SUPREME COURT AND MAYBE THE U.S. CONGRESS TO WIN!
ANY DISCUSSION?
YEAH, CAN I BLOW OFF THE PAPER? I CAN'T THINK OF A TOPIC.
GRANTED. ANY OTHER COMMENTS?
©B Trudeau

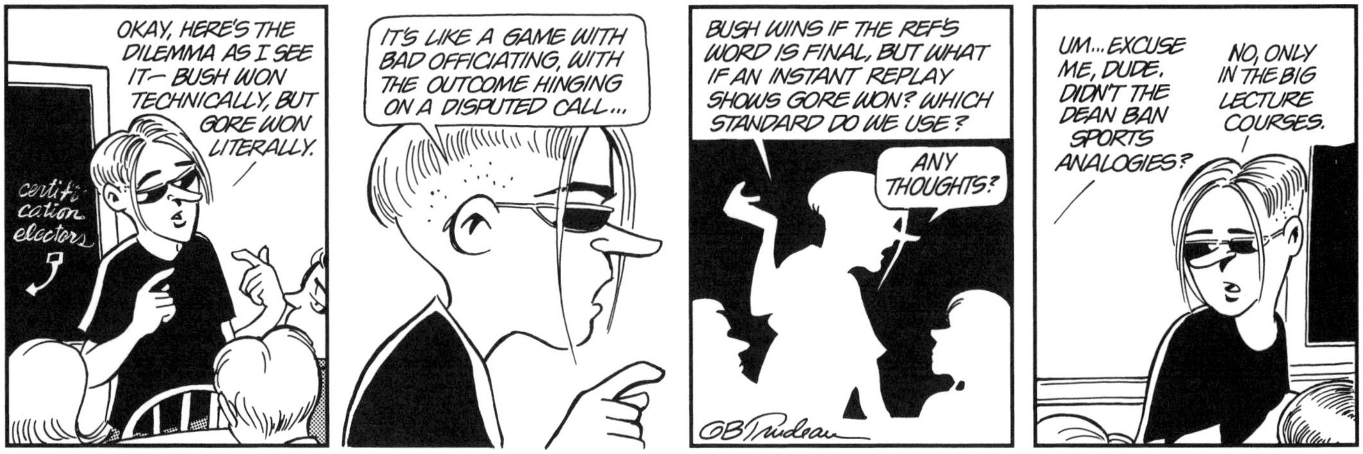
OKAY, HERE'S THE DILEMMA AS I SEE IT— BUSH WON TECHNICALLY, BUT GORE WON LITERALLY.
certification electors
IT'S LIKE A GAME WITH BAD OFFICIATING, WITH THE OUTCOME HINGING ON A DISPUTED CALL...
BUSH WINS IF THE REF'S WORD IS FINAL, BUT WHAT IF AN INSTANT REPLAY SHOWS GORE WON? WHICH STANDARD DO WE USE?
ANY THOUGHTS?
UM... EXCUSE ME, DUDE. DIDN'T THE DEAN BAN SPORTS ANALOGIES?
NO, ONLY IN THE BIG LECTURE COURSES.

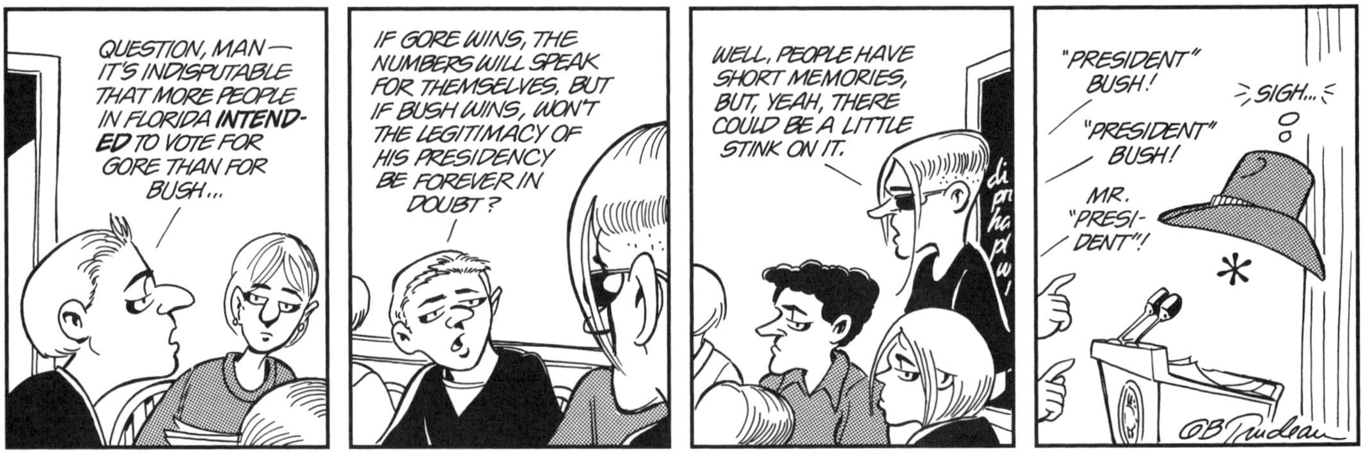
QUESTION, MAN— IT'S INDISPUTABLE THAT MORE PEOPLE IN FLORIDA INTENDED TO VOTE FOR GORE THAN FOR BUSH...
IF GORE WINS, THE NUMBERS WILL SPEAK FOR THEMSELVES. BUT IF BUSH WINS, WON'T THE LEGITIMACY OF HIS PRESIDENCY BE FOREVER IN DOUBT?
WELL, PEOPLE HAVE SHORT MEMORIES, BUT, YEAH, THERE COULD BE A LITTLE STINK ON IT.
"PRESIDENT" BUSH!
"PRESIDENT" BUSH!
MR. "PRESIDENT"!
SIGH...

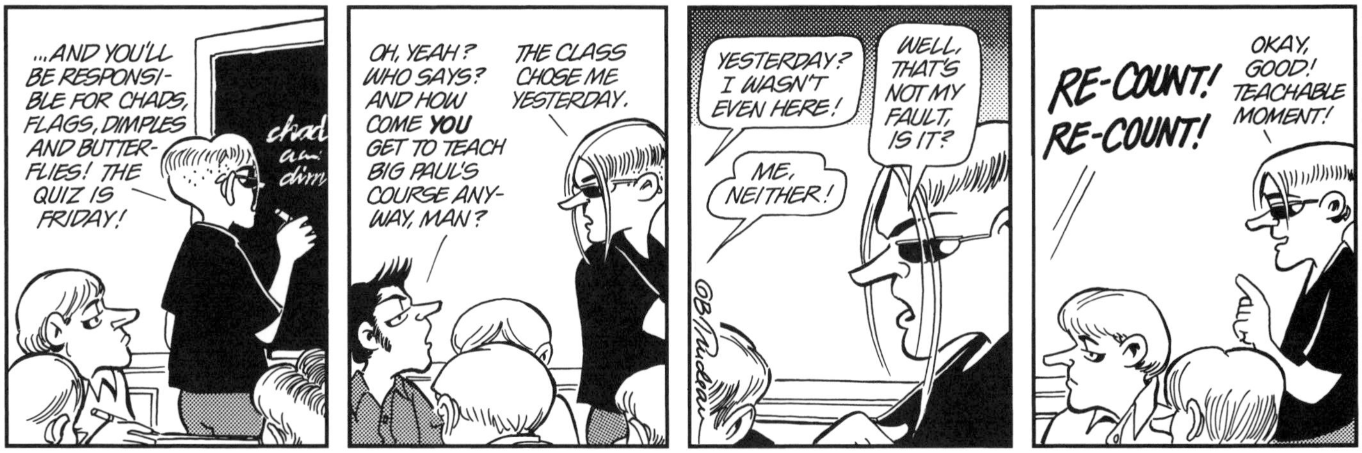
...AND YOU'LL BE RESPONSIBLE FOR CHADS, FLAGS, DIMPLES AND BUTTERFLIES! THE QUIZ IS FRIDAY!
OH, YEAH? WHO SAYS? AND HOW COME YOU GET TO TEACH BIG PAUL'S COURSE ANYWAY, MAN?
THE CLASS CHOSE ME YESTERDAY.
YESTERDAY? I WASN'T EVEN HERE!
ME, NEITHER!
WELL, THAT'S NOT MY FAULT, IS IT?
RE-COUNT! RE-COUNT!
OKAY, GOOD! TEACHABLE MOMENT!

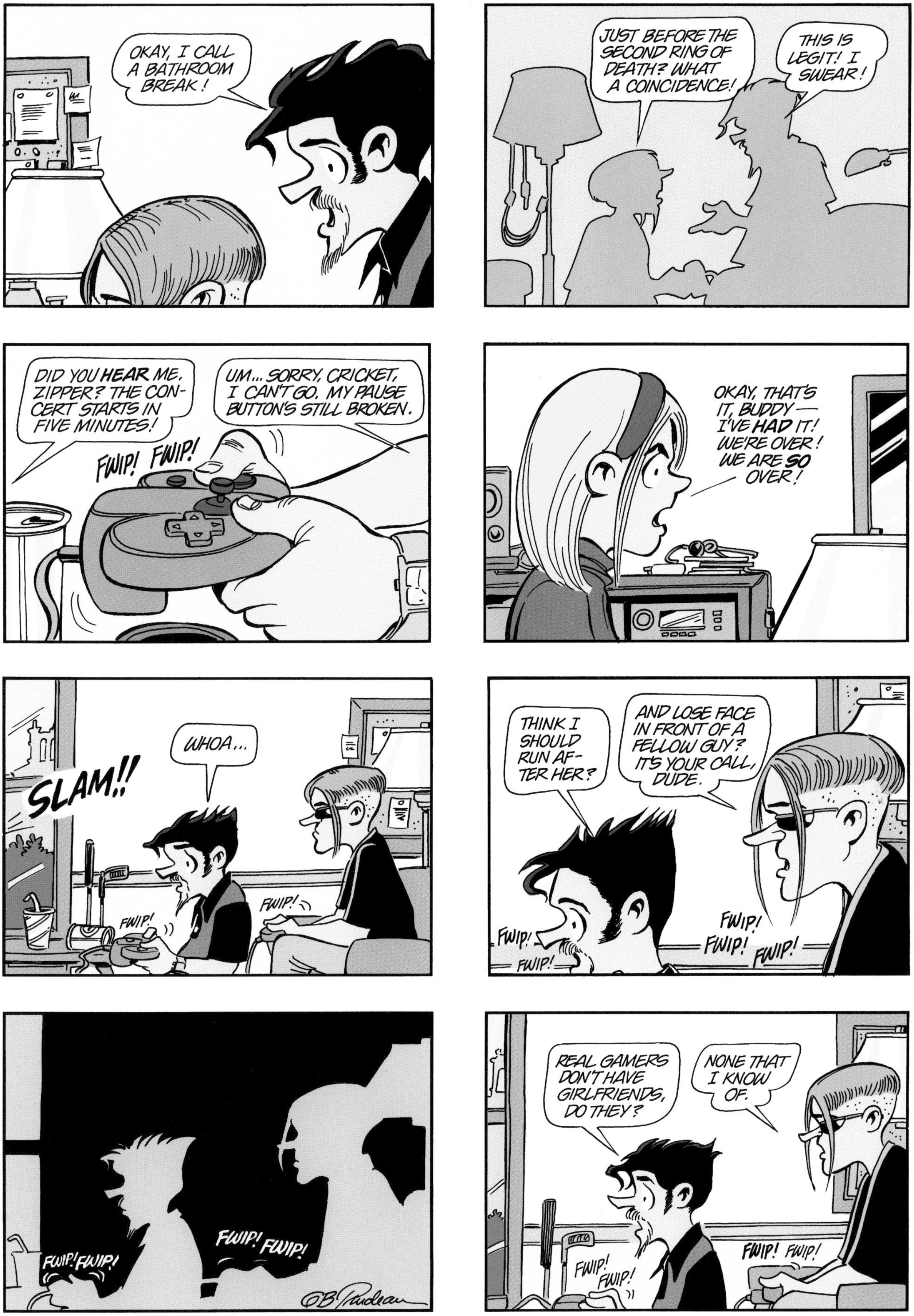

OKAY, I CALL A BATHROOM BREAK!
JUST BEFORE THE SECOND RING OF DEATH? WHAT A COINCIDENCE!
THIS IS LEGIT! I SWEAR!
DID YOU HEAR ME, ZIPPER? THE CONCERT STARTS IN FIVE MINUTES!
UM... SORRY, CRICKET, I CAN'T GO. MY PAUSE BUTTON'S STILL BROKEN.
FWIP! FWIP!
OKAY, THAT'S IT, BUDDY — I'VE HAD IT! WE'RE OVER! WE ARE SO OVER!
SLAM!!
WHOA...
FWIP!
FWIP!
THINK I SHOULD RUN AFTER HER?
AND LOSE FACE IN FRONT OF A FELLOW GUY? IT'S YOUR CALL, DUDE.
FWIP! FWIP! FWIP! FWIP! FWIP!
FWIP! FWIP!
FWIP! FWIP!
G.B. Trudeau
REAL GAMERS DON'T HAVE GIRLFRIENDS, DO THEY?
NONE THAT I KNOW OF.
FWIP! FWIP! FWIP! FWIP!

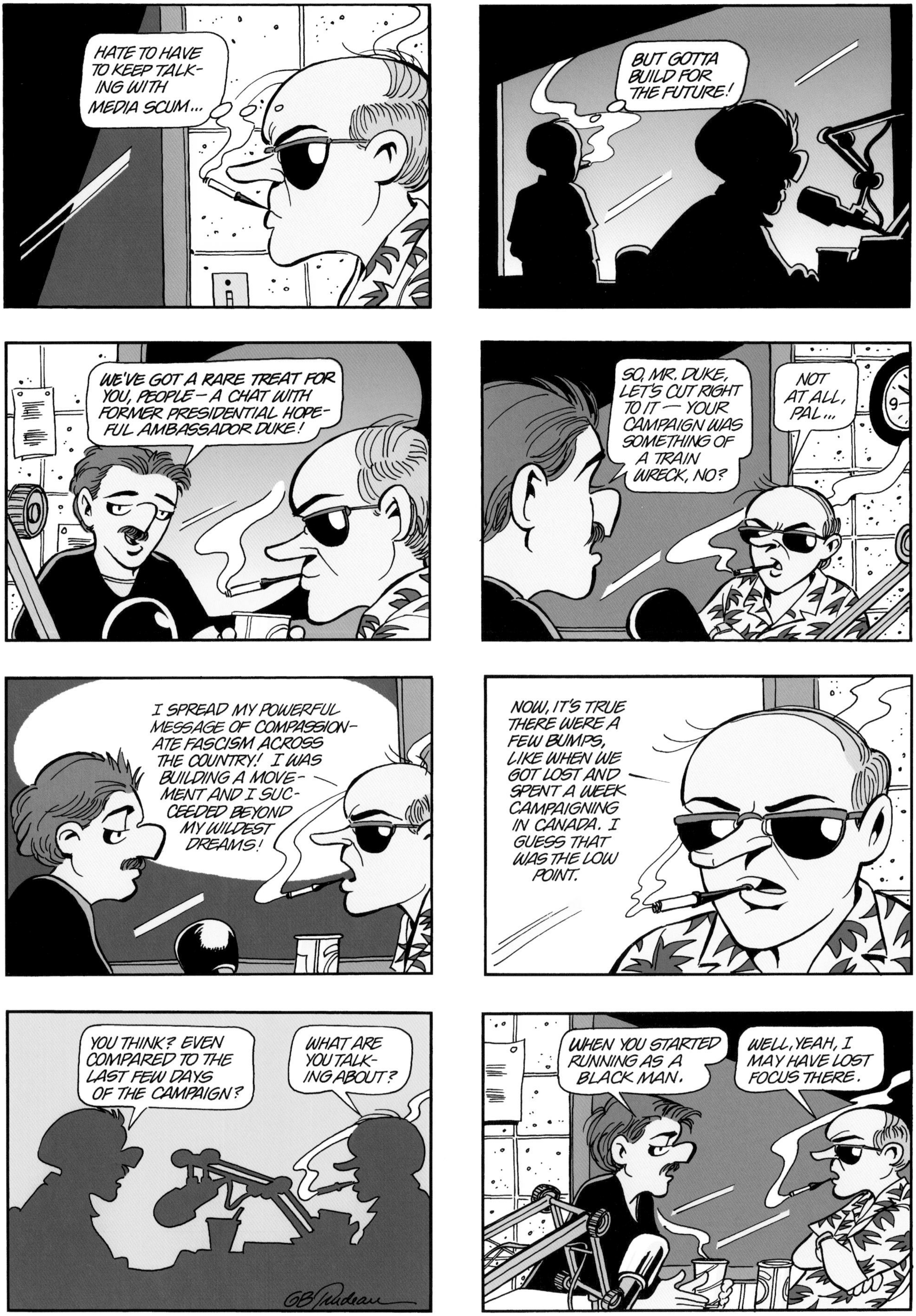
HATE TO HAVE TO KEEP TALKING WITH MEDIA SCUM...
BUT GOTTA BUILD FOR THE FUTURE!
WE'VE GOT A RARE TREAT FOR YOU, PEOPLE — A CHAT WITH FORMER PRESIDENTIAL HOPEFUL AMBASSADOR DUKE!
SO, MR. DUKE, LET'S CUT RIGHT TO IT — YOUR CAMPAIGN WAS SOMETHING OF A TRAIN WRECK, NO?
NOT AT ALL, PAL...
I SPREAD MY POWERFUL MESSAGE OF COMPASSIONATE FASCISM ACROSS THE COUNTRY! I WAS BUILDING A MOVEMENT AND I SUCCEEDED BEYOND MY WILDEST DREAMS!
NOW, IT'S TRUE THERE WERE A FEW BUMPS, LIKE WHEN WE GOT LOST AND SPENT A WEEK CAMPAIGNING IN CANADA. I GUESS THAT WAS THE LOW POINT.
YOU THINK? EVEN COMPARED TO THE LAST FEW DAYS OF THE CAMPAIGN?
WHAT ARE YOU TALKING ABOUT?
WHEN YOU STARTED RUNNING AS A BLACK MAN.
WELL, YEAH, I MAY HAVE LOST FOCUS THERE.

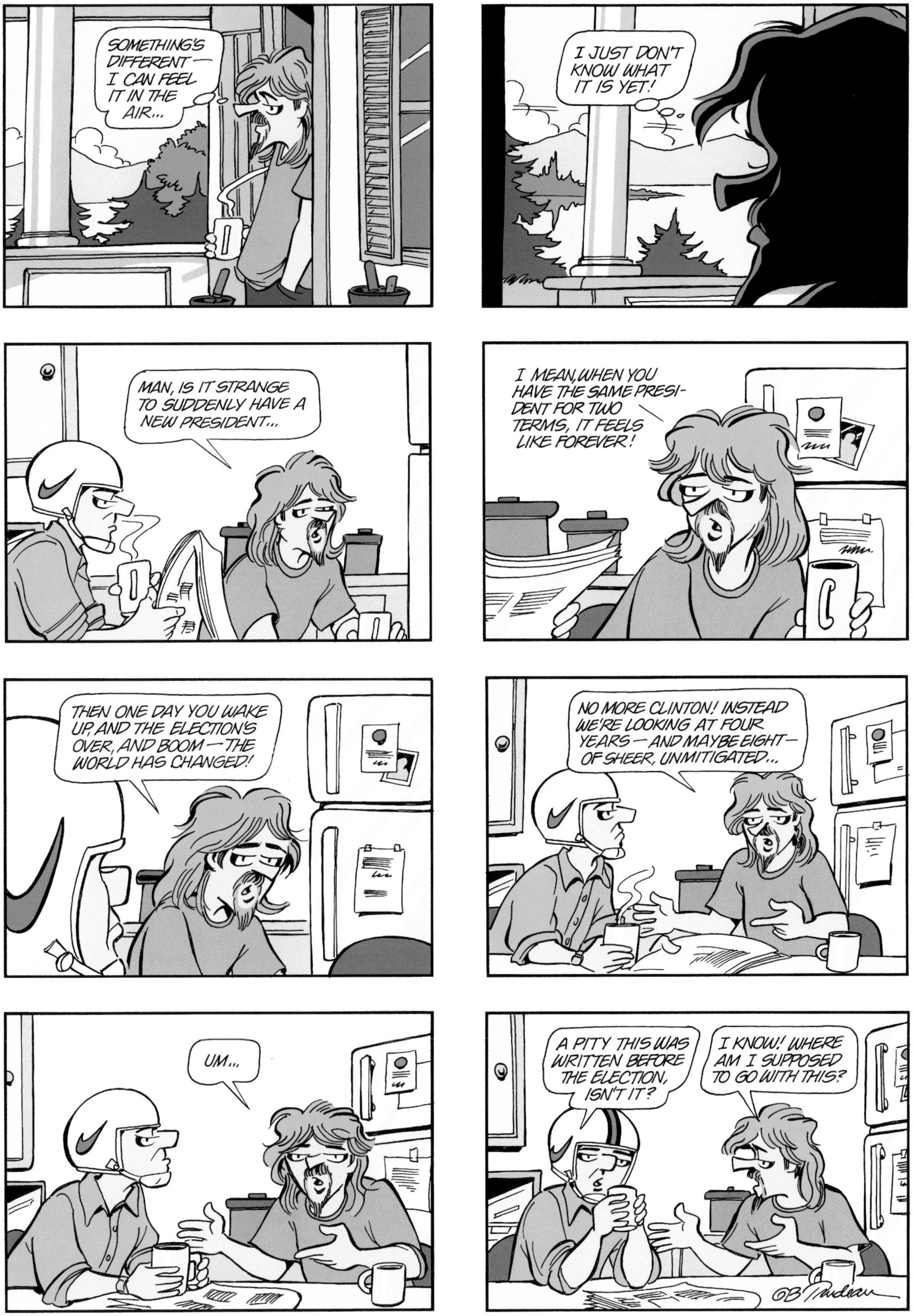
SOMETHING'S DIFFERENT— I CAN FEEL IT IN THE AIR...
I JUST DON'T KNOW WHAT IT IS YET!
MAN, IS IT STRANGE TO SUDDENLY HAVE A NEW PRESIDENT...
I MEAN, WHEN YOU HAVE THE SAME PRESIDENT FOR TWO TERMS, IT FEELS LIKE FOREVER!
THEN ONE DAY YOU WAKE UP, AND THE ELECTION'S OVER, AND BOOM—THE WORLD HAS CHANGED!
NO MORE CLINTON! INSTEAD WE'RE LOOKING AT FOUR YEARS—AND MAYBE EIGHT—OF SHEER, UNMITIGATED...
UM...
A PITY THIS WAS WRITTEN BEFORE THE ELECTION, ISN'T IT?
I KNOW! WHERE AM I SUPPOSED TO GO WITH THIS?
GB Trudeau

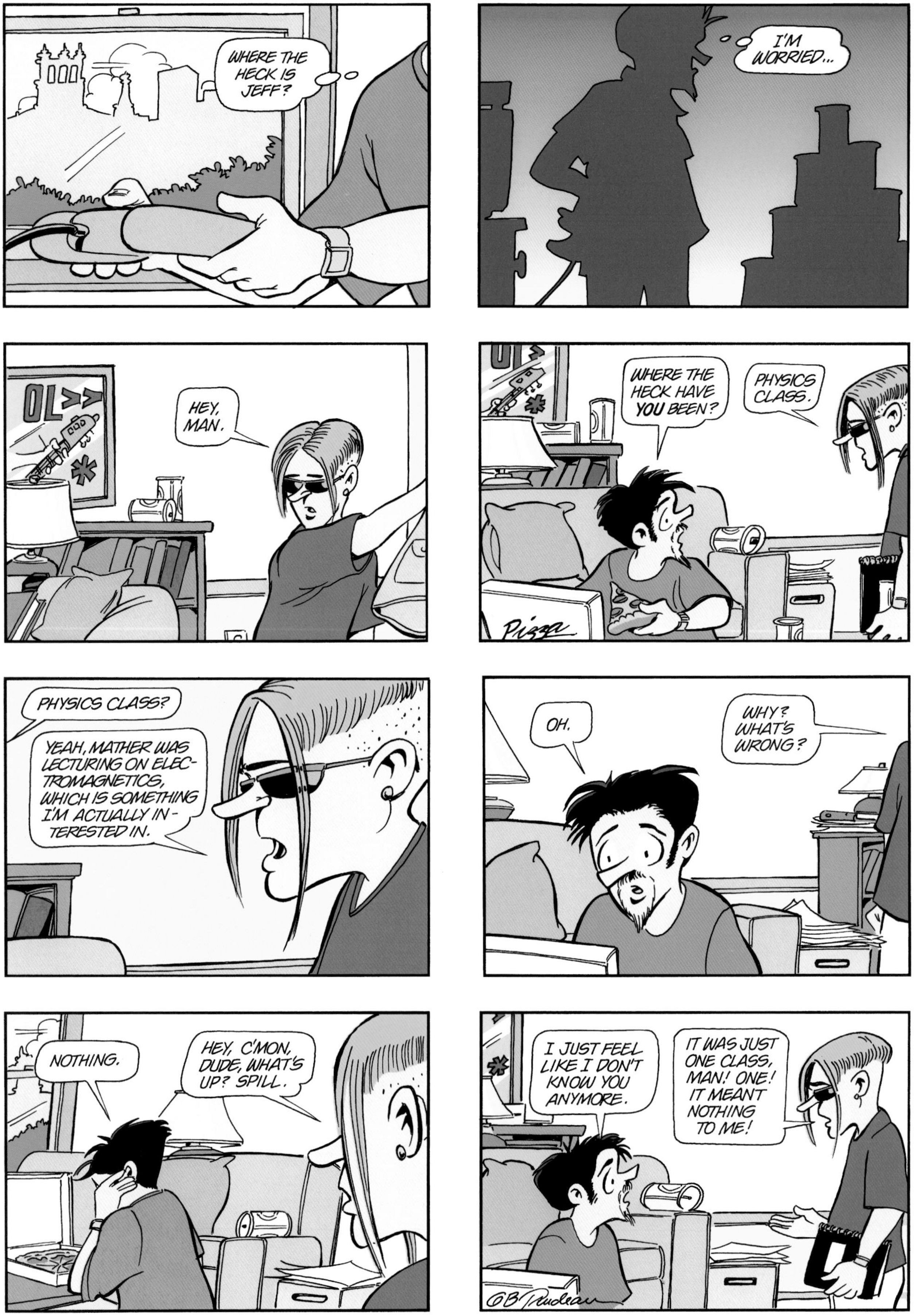
WHERE THE HECK IS JEFF?
I'M WORRIED...
HEY, MAN.
WHERE THE HECK HAVE YOU BEEN?
PHYSICS CLASS.
Pizza
PHYSICS CLASS?
YEAH, MATHER WAS LECTURING ON ELECTROMAGNETICS, WHICH IS SOMETHING I'M ACTUALLY INTERESTED IN.
OH.
WHY? WHAT'S WRONG?
NOTHING.
HEY, C'MON, DUDE, WHAT'S UP? SPILL.
I JUST FEEL LIKE I DON'T KNOW YOU ANYMORE.
IT WAS JUST ONE CLASS, MAN! ONE! IT MEANT NOTHING TO ME!
GB Trudeau

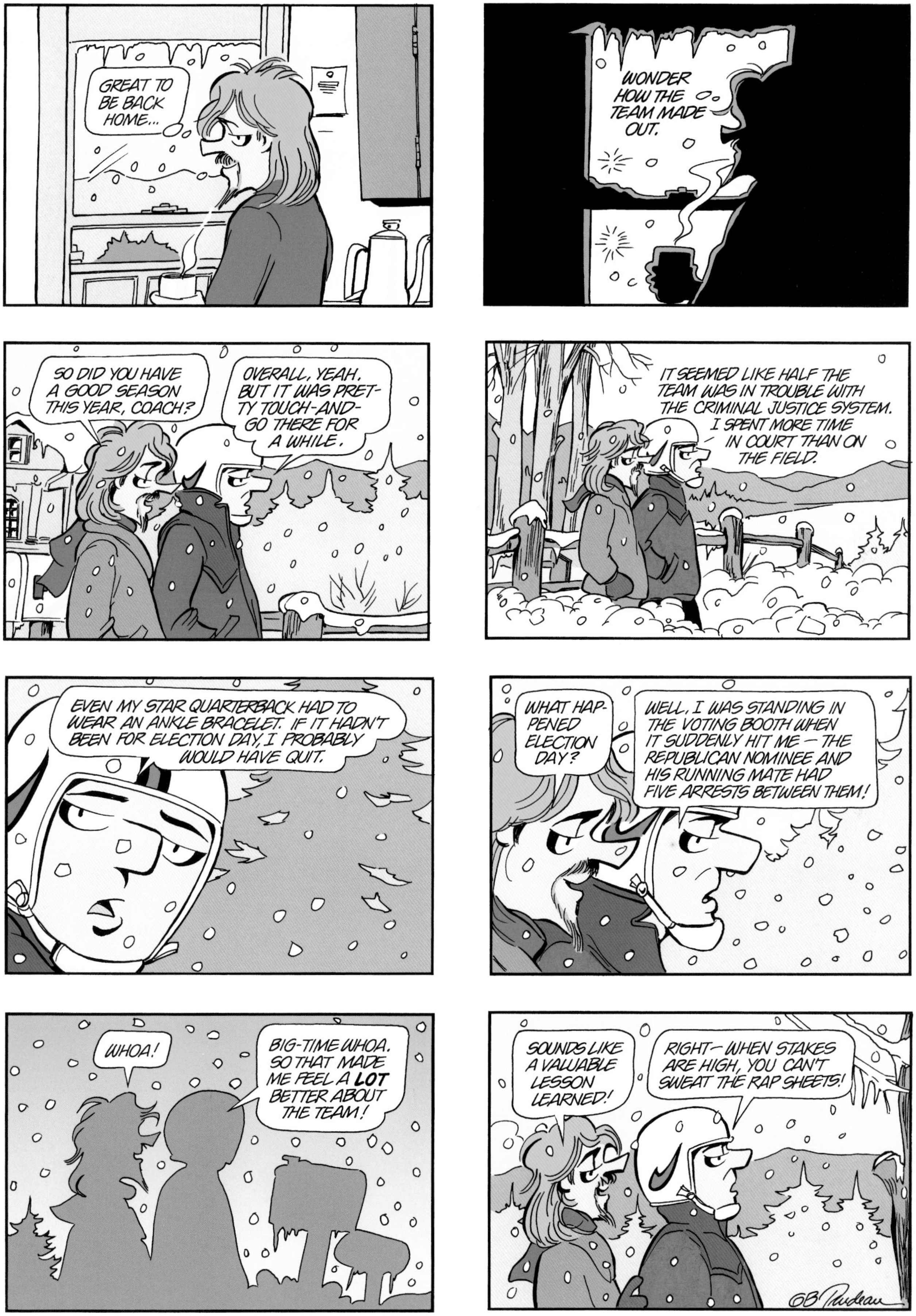
GREAT TO BE BACK HOME...
WONDER HOW THE TEAM MADE OUT.
SO DID YOU HAVE A GOOD SEASON THIS YEAR, COACH?
OVERALL, YEAH. BUT IT WAS PRETTY TOUCH-AND-GO THERE FOR A WHILE.
IT SEEMED LIKE HALF THE TEAM WAS IN TROUBLE WITH THE CRIMINAL JUSTICE SYSTEM. I SPENT MORE TIME IN COURT THAN ON THE FIELD.
EVEN MY STAR QUARTERBACK HAD TO WEAR AN ANKLE BRACELET. IF IT HADN'T BEEN FOR ELECTION DAY, I PROBABLY WOULD HAVE QUIT.
WHAT HAPPENED ELECTION DAY?
WELL, I WAS STANDING IN THE VOTING BOOTH WHEN IT SUDDENLY HIT ME — THE REPUBLICAN NOMINEE AND HIS RUNNING MATE HAD FIVE ARRESTS BETWEEN THEM!
WHOA!
BIG-TIME WHOA. SO THAT MADE ME FEEL A **LOT** BETTER ABOUT THE TEAM!
SOUNDS LIKE A VALUABLE LESSON LEARNED!
RIGHT— WHEN STAKES ARE HIGH, YOU CAN'T SWEAT THE RAP SHEETS!
©B Trudeau

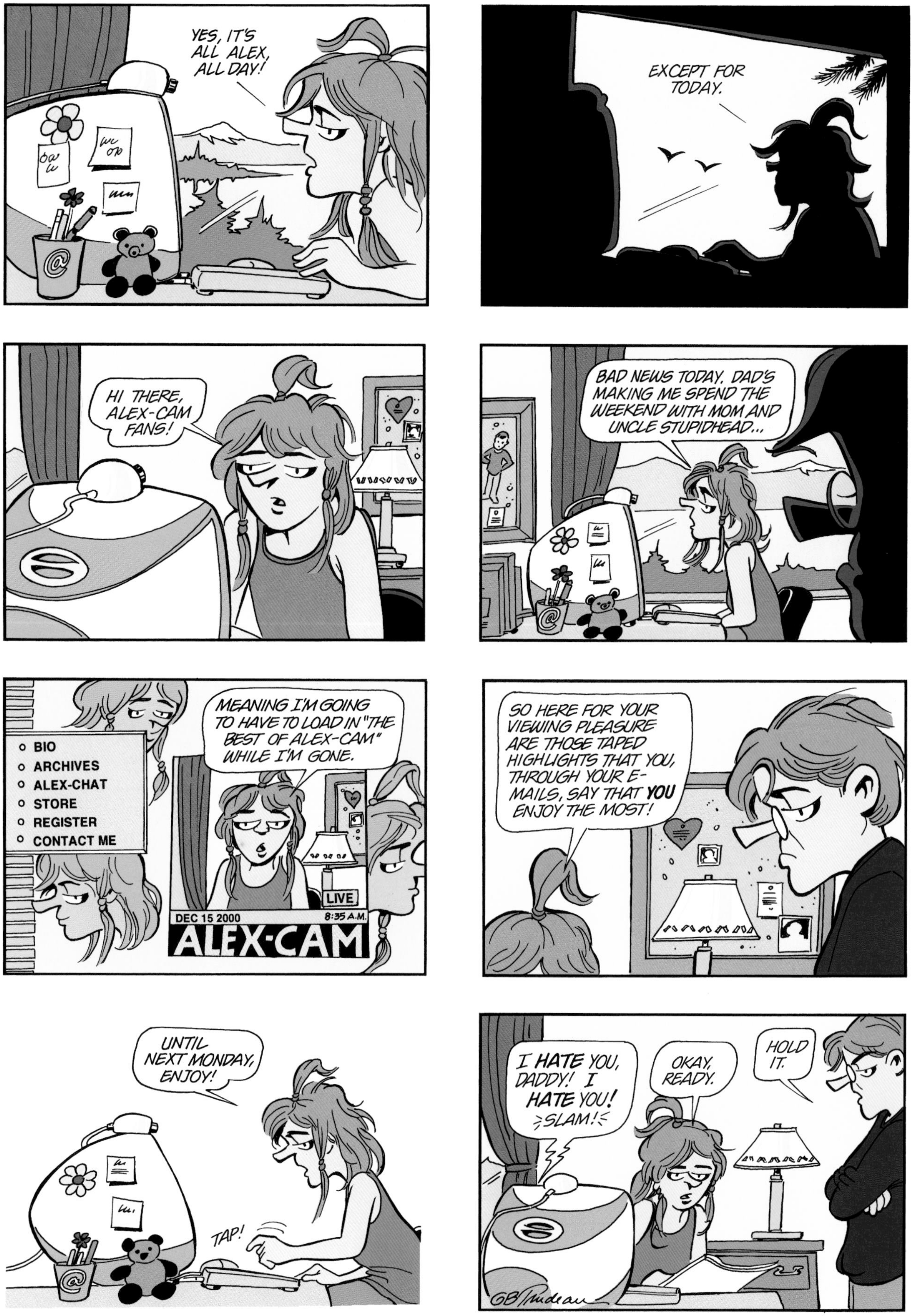
YES, IT'S ALL ALEX, ALL DAY!
EXCEPT FOR TODAY.
HI THERE, ALEX-CAM FANS!
BAD NEWS TODAY. DAD'S MAKING ME SPEND THE WEEKEND WITH MOM AND UNCLE STUPIDHEAD...
BIO
ARCHIVES
ALEX-CHAT
STORE
REGISTER
CONTACT ME
MEANING I'M GOING TO HAVE TO LOAD IN "THE BEST OF ALEX-CAM" WHILE I'M GONE.
LIVE
DEC 15 2000
8:35 A.M.
ALEX-CAM
SO HERE FOR YOUR VIEWING PLEASURE ARE THOSE TAPED HIGHLIGHTS THAT YOU, THROUGH YOUR E-MAILS, SAY THAT **YOU** ENJOY THE MOST!
UNTIL NEXT MONDAY, ENJOY!
TAP!
I **HATE** YOU, DADDY! I **HATE** YOU!
SLAM!
OKAY, READY.
HOLD IT.
GBTrudeau

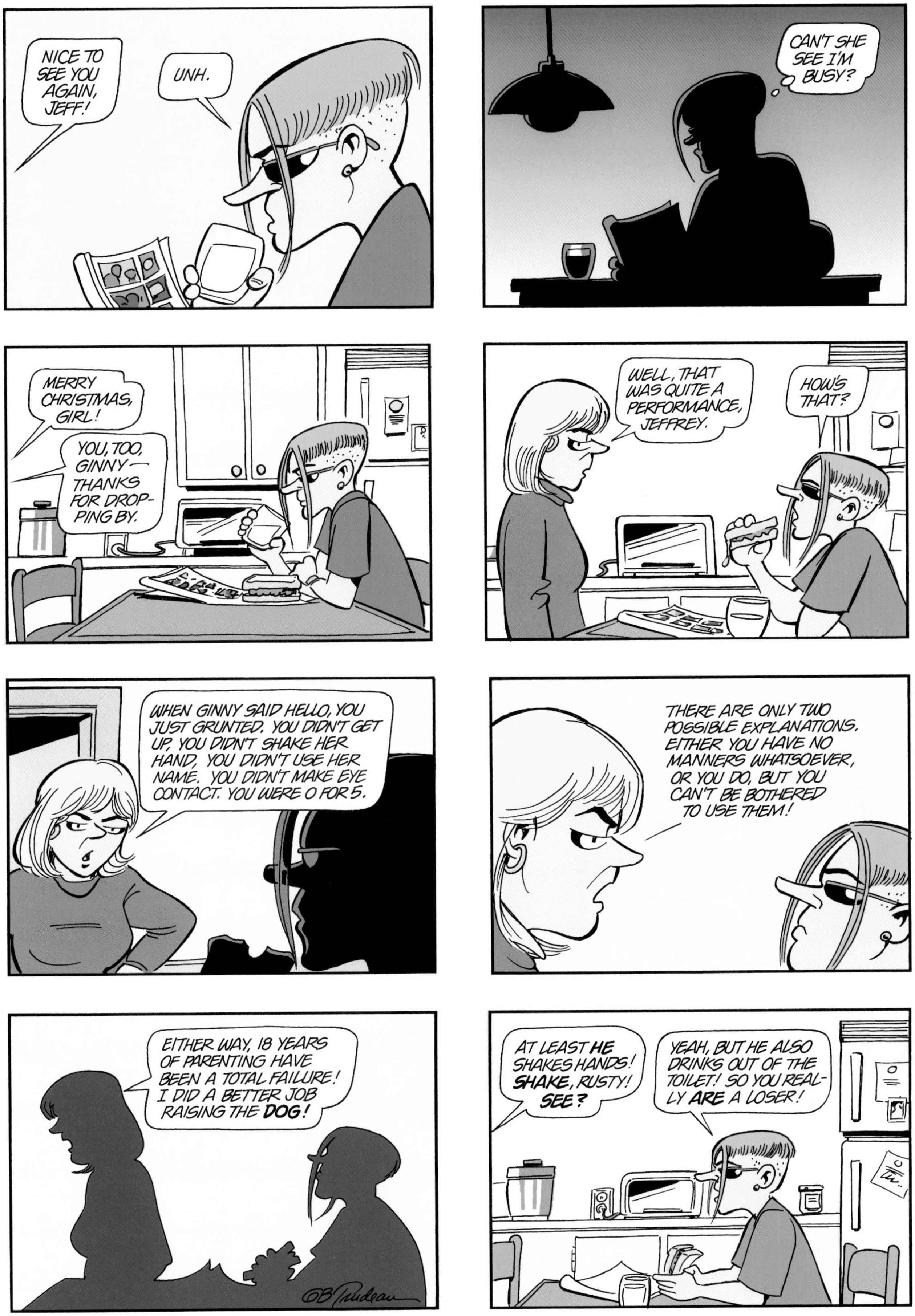
NICE TO SEE YOU AGAIN, JEFF!
UNH.
CAN'T SHE SEE I'M BUSY?
MERRY CHRISTMAS, GIRL!
YOU, TOO, GINNY— THANKS FOR DROPPING BY.
WELL, THAT WAS QUITE A PERFORMANCE, JEFFREY.
HOW'S THAT?
WHEN GINNY SAID HELLO, YOU JUST GRUNTED. YOU DIDN'T GET UP, YOU DIDN'T SHAKE HER HAND, YOU DIDN'T USE HER NAME. YOU DIDN'T MAKE EYE CONTACT. YOU WERE 0 FOR 5.
THERE ARE ONLY TWO POSSIBLE EXPLANATIONS. EITHER YOU HAVE NO MANNERS WHATSOEVER, OR YOU DO, BUT YOU CAN'T BE BOTHERED TO USE THEM!
EITHER WAY, 18 YEARS OF PARENTING HAVE BEEN A TOTAL FAILURE! I DID A BETTER JOB RAISING THE DOG!
AT LEAST HE SHAKES HANDS! SHAKE, RUSTY! SEE?
YEAH, BUT HE ALSO DRINKS OUT OF THE TOILET! SO YOU REALLY ARE A LOSER!
©B Trudeau

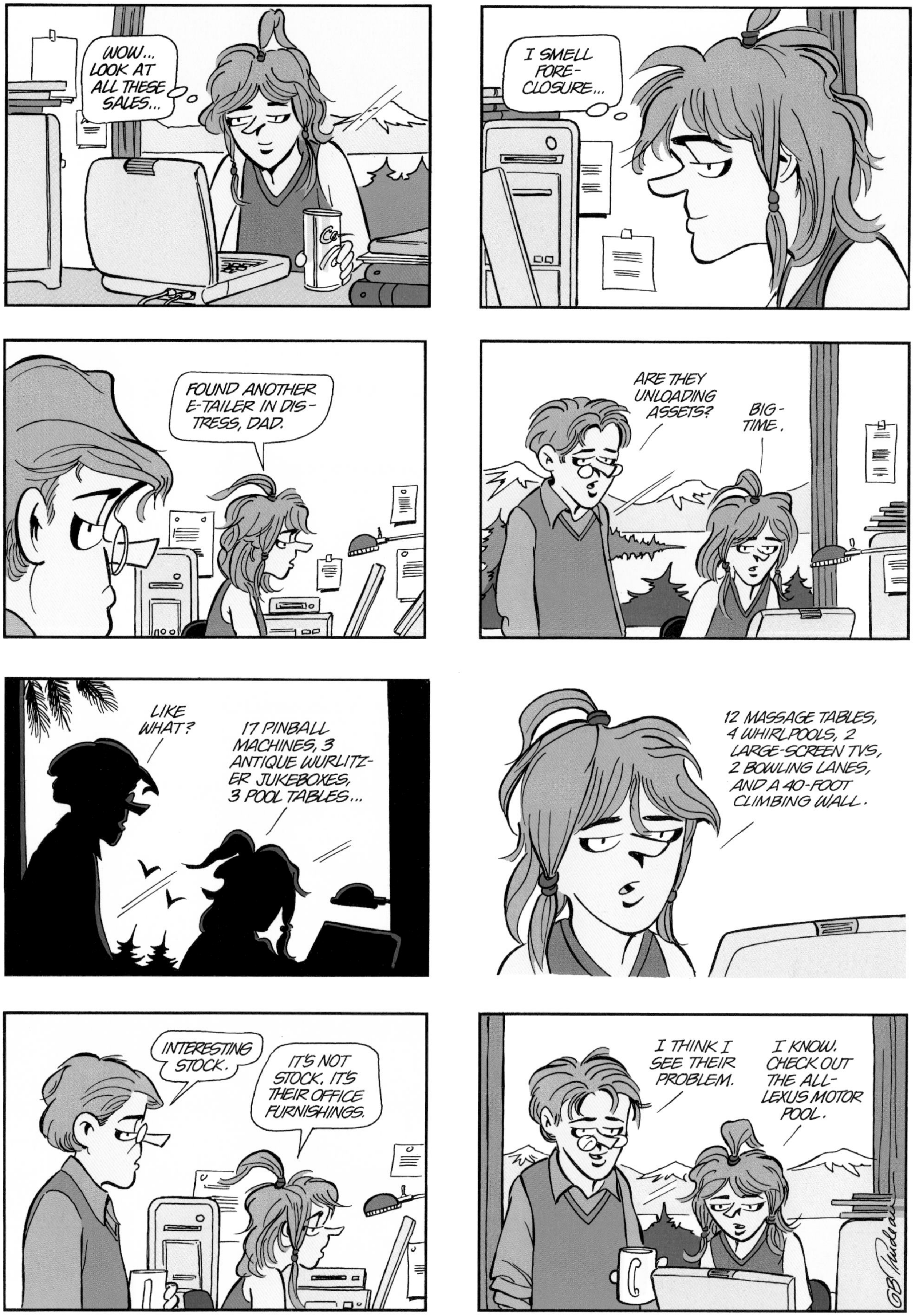
WOW... LOOK AT ALL THESE SALES...
I SMELL FORE-CLOSURE...
FOUND ANOTHER E-TAILER IN DIS-TRESS, DAD.
ARE THEY UNLOADING ASSETS?
BIG-TIME.
LIKE WHAT?
17 PINBALL MACHINES, 3 ANTIQUE WURLITZ-ER JUKEBOXES, 3 POOL TABLES...
12 MASSAGE TABLES, 4 WHIRLPOOLS, 2 LARGE-SCREEN TVS, 2 BOWLING LANES, AND A 40-FOOT CLIMBING WALL.
INTERESTING STOCK.
IT'S NOT STOCK. IT'S THEIR OFFICE FURNISHINGS.
I THINK I SEE THEIR PROBLEM.
I KNOW. CHECK OUT THE ALL-LEXUS MOTOR POOL.

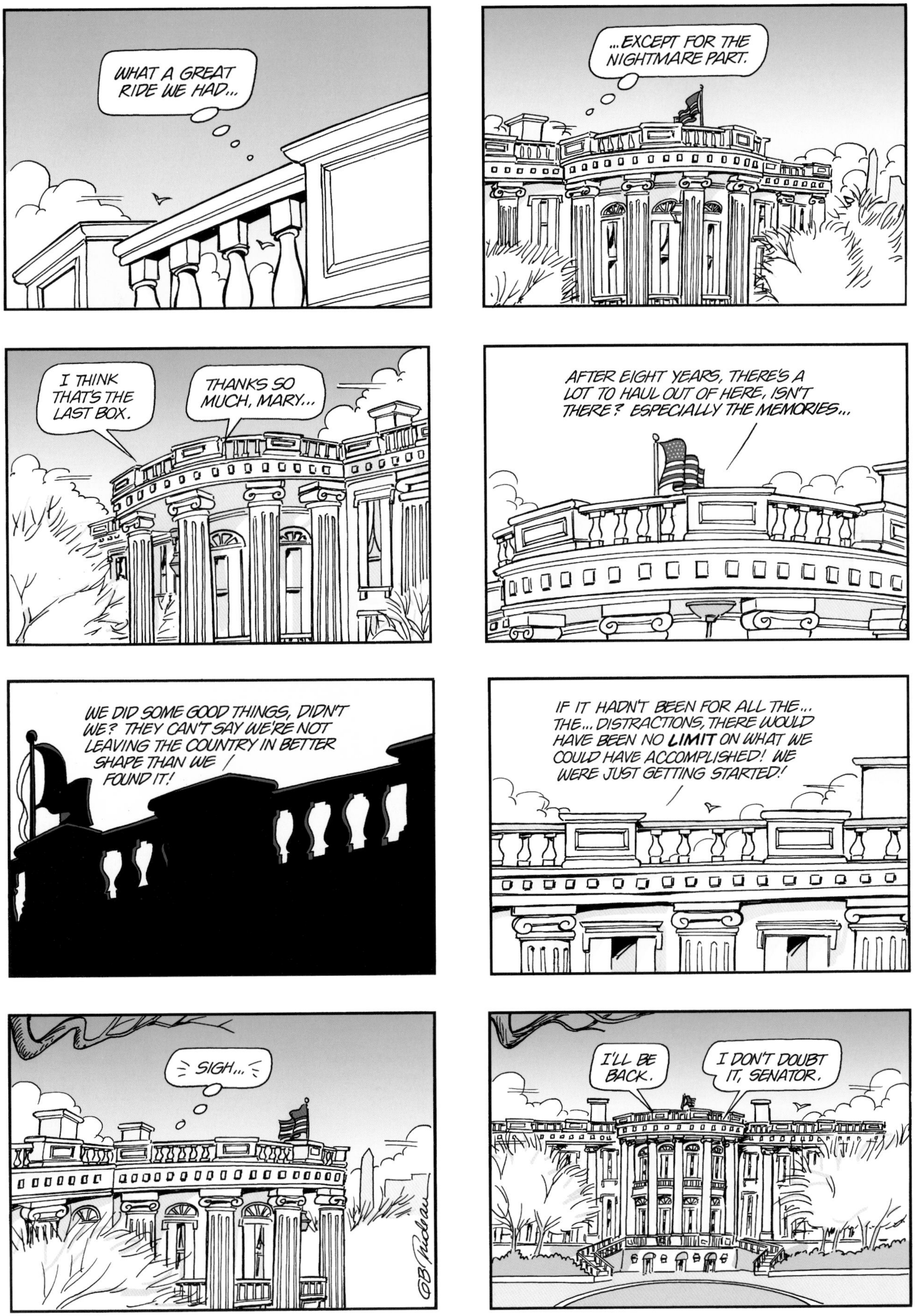
WHAT A GREAT RIDE WE HAD...
...EXCEPT FOR THE NIGHTMARE PART.
I THINK THAT'S THE LAST BOX.
THANKS SO MUCH, MARY...
AFTER EIGHT YEARS, THERE'S A LOT TO HAUL OUT OF HERE, ISN'T THERE? ESPECIALLY THE MEMORIES...
WE DID SOME GOOD THINGS, DIDN'T WE? THEY CAN'T SAY WE'RE NOT LEAVING THE COUNTRY IN BETTER SHAPE THAN WE FOUND IT!
IF IT HADN'T BEEN FOR ALL THE... THE... DISTRACTIONS, THERE WOULD HAVE BEEN NO LIMIT ON WHAT WE COULD HAVE ACCOMPLISHED! WE WERE JUST GETTING STARTED!
SIGH...
I'LL BE BACK.
I DON'T DOUBT IT, SENATOR.

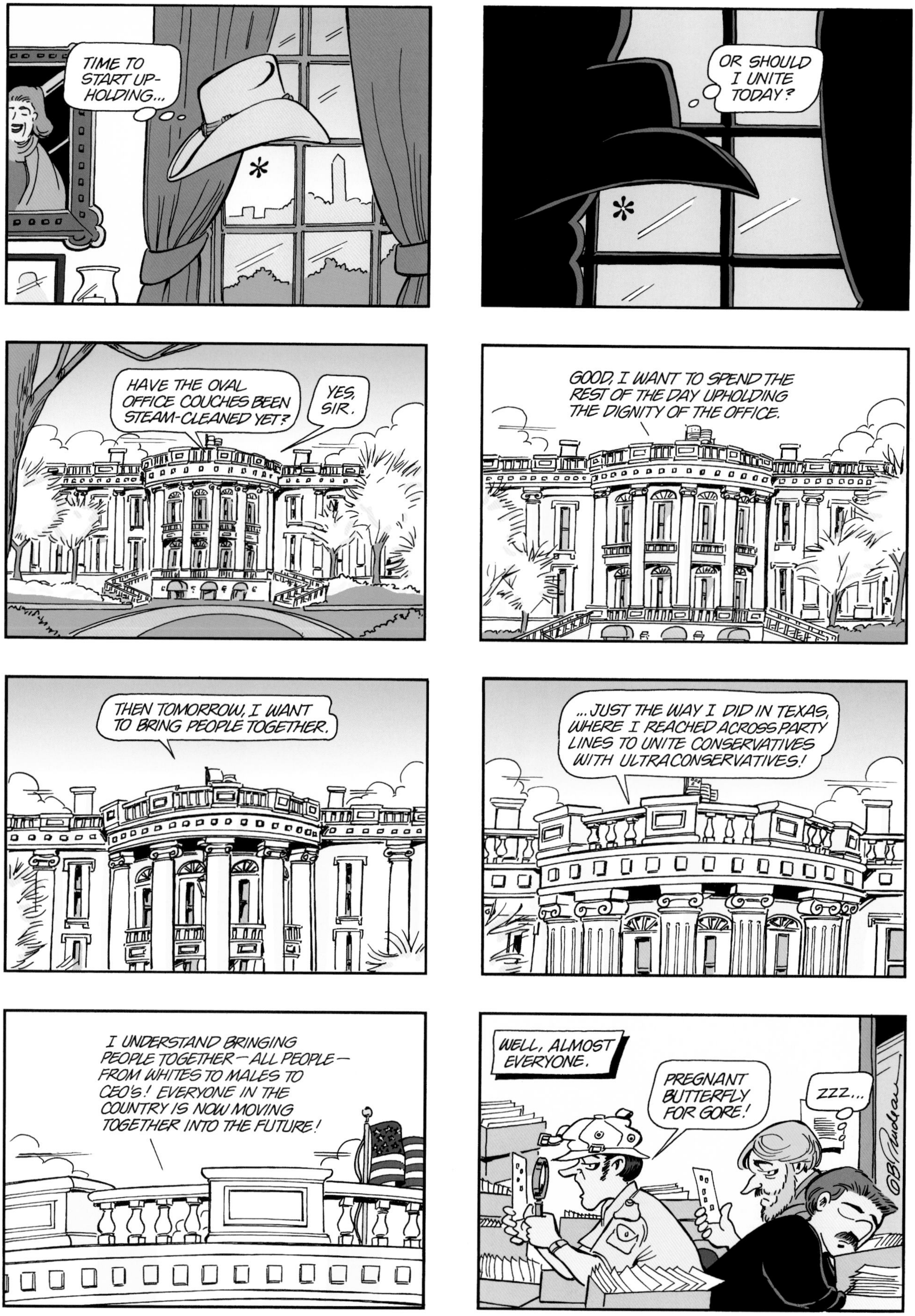
TIME TO START UP-HOLDING...
OR SHOULD I UNITE TODAY?
HAVE THE OVAL OFFICE COUCHES BEEN STEAM-CLEANED YET?
YES, SIR.
GOOD, I WANT TO SPEND THE REST OF THE DAY UPHOLDING THE DIGNITY OF THE OFFICE.
THEN TOMORROW, I WANT TO BRING PEOPLE TOGETHER.
...JUST THE WAY I DID IN TEXAS, WHERE I REACHED ACROSS PARTY LINES TO UNITE CONSERVATIVES WITH ULTRACONSERVATIVES!
I UNDERSTAND BRINGING PEOPLE TOGETHER—ALL PEOPLE—FROM WHITES TO MALES TO CEO'S! EVERYONE IN THE COUNTRY IS NOW MOVING TOGETHER INTO THE FUTURE!
WELL, ALMOST EVERYONE.
PREGNANT BUTTERFLY FOR GORE!
ZZZ...

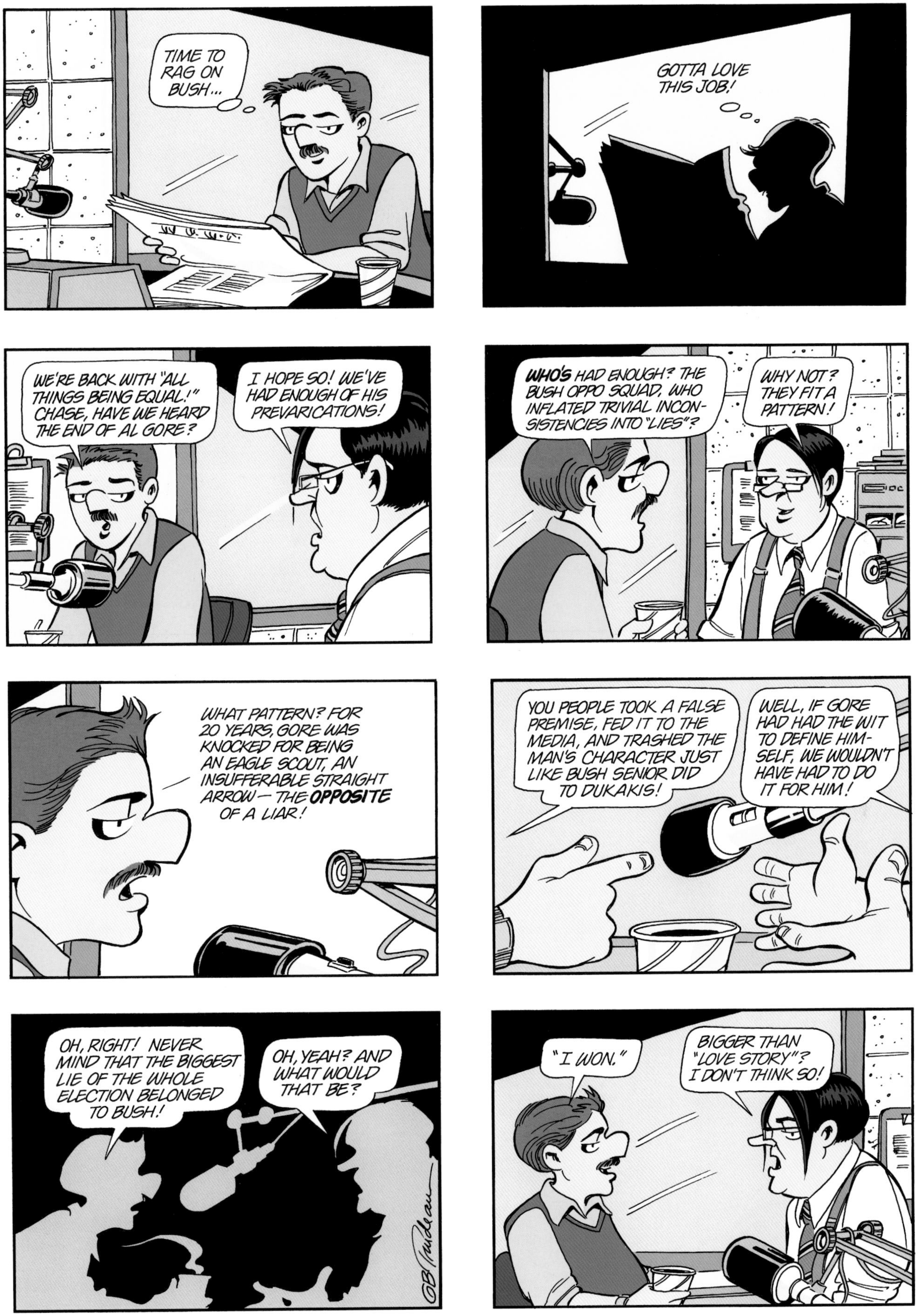
TIME TO RAG ON BUSH...
GOTTA LOVE THIS JOB!
WE'RE BACK WITH "ALL THINGS BEING EQUAL!" CHASE, HAVE WE HEARD THE END OF AL GORE?
I HOPE SO! WE'VE HAD ENOUGH OF HIS PREVARICATIONS!
WHO'S HAD ENOUGH? THE BUSH OPPO SQUAD, WHO INFLATED TRIVIAL INCONSISTENCIES INTO "LIES"?
WHY NOT? THEY FIT A PATTERN!
WHAT PATTERN? FOR 20 YEARS, GORE WAS KNOCKED FOR BEING AN EAGLE SCOUT, AN INSUFFERABLE STRAIGHT ARROW— THE OPPOSITE OF A LIAR!
YOU PEOPLE TOOK A FALSE PREMISE, FED IT TO THE MEDIA, AND TRASHED THE MAN'S CHARACTER JUST LIKE BUSH SENIOR DID TO DUKAKIS!
WELL, IF GORE HAD HAD THE WIT TO DEFINE HIMSELF, WE WOULDN'T HAVE HAD TO DO IT FOR HIM!
OH, RIGHT! NEVER MIND THAT THE BIGGEST LIE OF THE WHOLE ELECTION BELONGED TO BUSH!
OH, YEAH? AND WHAT WOULD THAT BE?
GBTrudeau
"I WON."
BIGGER THAN "LOVE STORY"? I DON'T THINK SO!

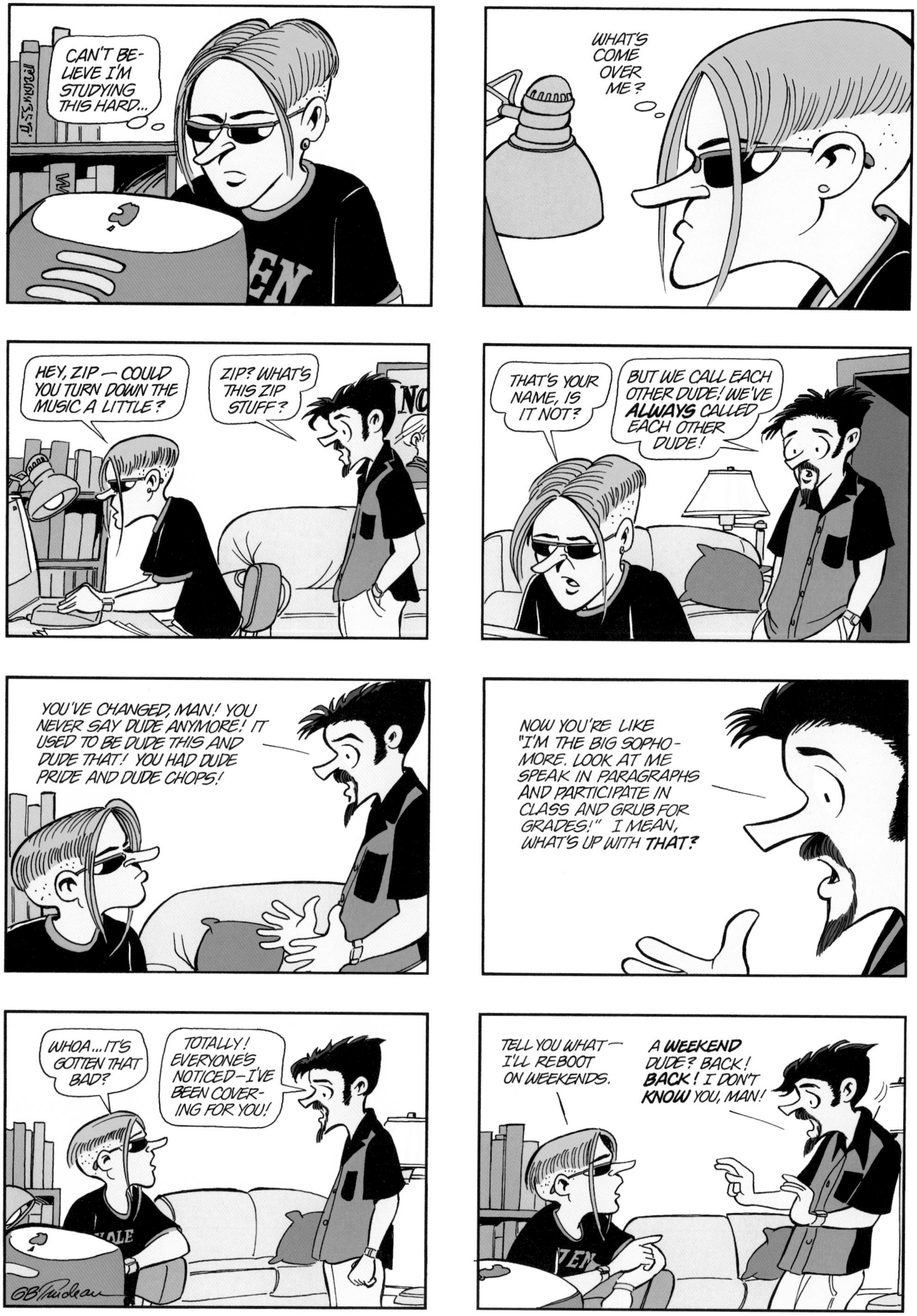
CAN'T BE-LIEVE I'M STUDYING THIS HARD...
WHAT'S COME OVER ME?
HEY, ZIP — COULD YOU TURN DOWN THE MUSIC A LITTLE?
ZIP? WHAT'S THIS ZIP STUFF?
THAT'S YOUR NAME, IS IT NOT?
BUT WE CALL EACH OTHER DUDE! WE'VE **ALWAYS** CALLED EACH OTHER DUDE!
YOU'VE CHANGED, MAN! YOU NEVER SAY DUDE ANYMORE! IT USED TO BE DUDE THIS AND DUDE THAT! YOU HAD DUDE PRIDE AND DUDE CHOPS!
NOW YOU'RE LIKE "I'M THE BIG SOPHO-MORE. LOOK AT ME SPEAK IN PARAGRAPHS AND PARTICIPATE IN CLASS AND GRUB FOR GRADES!" I MEAN, WHAT'S UP WITH **THAT?**
WHOA...IT'S GOTTEN THAT BAD?
TOTALLY! EVERYONE'S NOTICED—I'VE BEEN COVER-ING FOR YOU!
TELL YOU WHAT— I'LL REBOOT ON WEEKENDS.
A **WEEKEND** DUDE? BACK! **BACK!** I DON'T **KNOW** YOU, MAN!

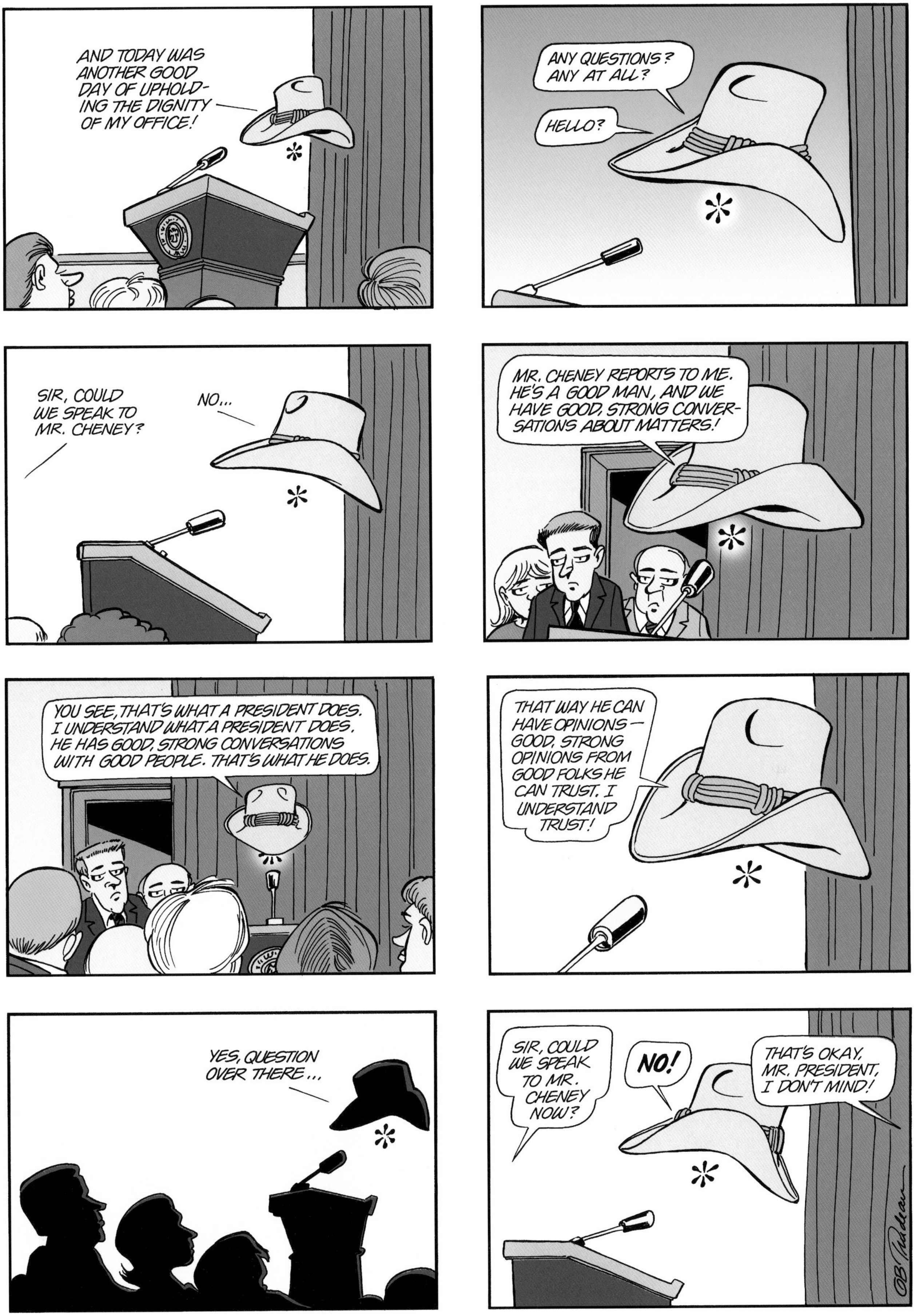

AND TODAY WAS ANOTHER GOOD DAY OF UPHOLDING THE DIGNITY OF MY OFFICE!
ANY QUESTIONS? ANY AT ALL?
HELLO?
SIR, COULD WE SPEAK TO MR. CHENEY?
NO...
MR. CHENEY REPORTS TO ME. HE'S A GOOD MAN, AND WE HAVE GOOD, STRONG CONVERSATIONS ABOUT MATTERS!
YOU SEE, THAT'S WHAT A PRESIDENT DOES. I UNDERSTAND WHAT A PRESIDENT DOES. HE HAS GOOD, STRONG CONVERSATIONS WITH GOOD PEOPLE. THAT'S WHAT HE DOES.
THAT WAY HE CAN HAVE OPINIONS — GOOD, STRONG OPINIONS FROM GOOD FOLKS HE CAN TRUST. I UNDERSTAND TRUST!
YES, QUESTION OVER THERE...
SIR, COULD WE SPEAK TO MR. CHENEY NOW?
NO!
THAT'S OKAY, MR. PRESIDENT, I DON'T MIND!

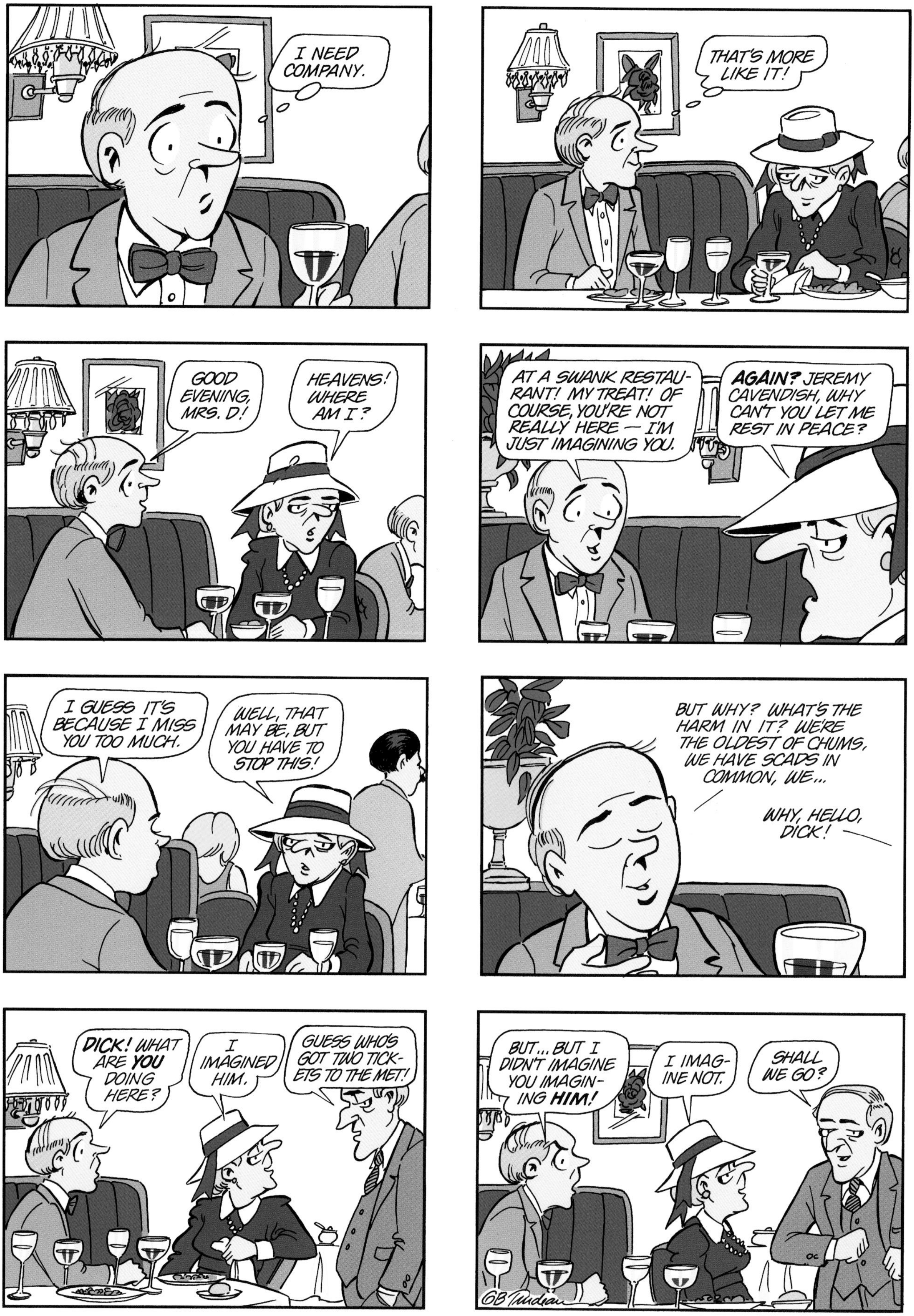
I NEED COMPANY.
THAT'S MORE LIKE IT!
GOOD EVENING, MRS. D!
HEAVENS! WHERE AM I?
AT A SWANK RESTAU-RANT! MY TREAT! OF COURSE, YOU'RE NOT REALLY HERE — I'M JUST IMAGINING YOU.
AGAIN? JEREMY CAVENDISH, WHY CAN'T YOU LET ME REST IN PEACE?
I GUESS IT'S BECAUSE I MISS YOU TOO MUCH.
WELL, THAT MAY BE, BUT YOU HAVE TO STOP THIS!
BUT WHY? WHAT'S THE HARM IN IT? WE'RE THE OLDEST OF CHUMS, WE HAVE SCADS IN COMMON, WE...
WHY, HELLO, DICK!
DICK! WHAT ARE **YOU** DOING HERE?
I IMAGINED HIM.
GUESS WHO'S GOT TWO TICK-ETS TO THE MET!
BUT... BUT I DIDN'T IMAGINE YOU IMAGIN-ING **HIM!**
I IMAG-INE NOT.
SHALL WE GO?
GB Trudeau

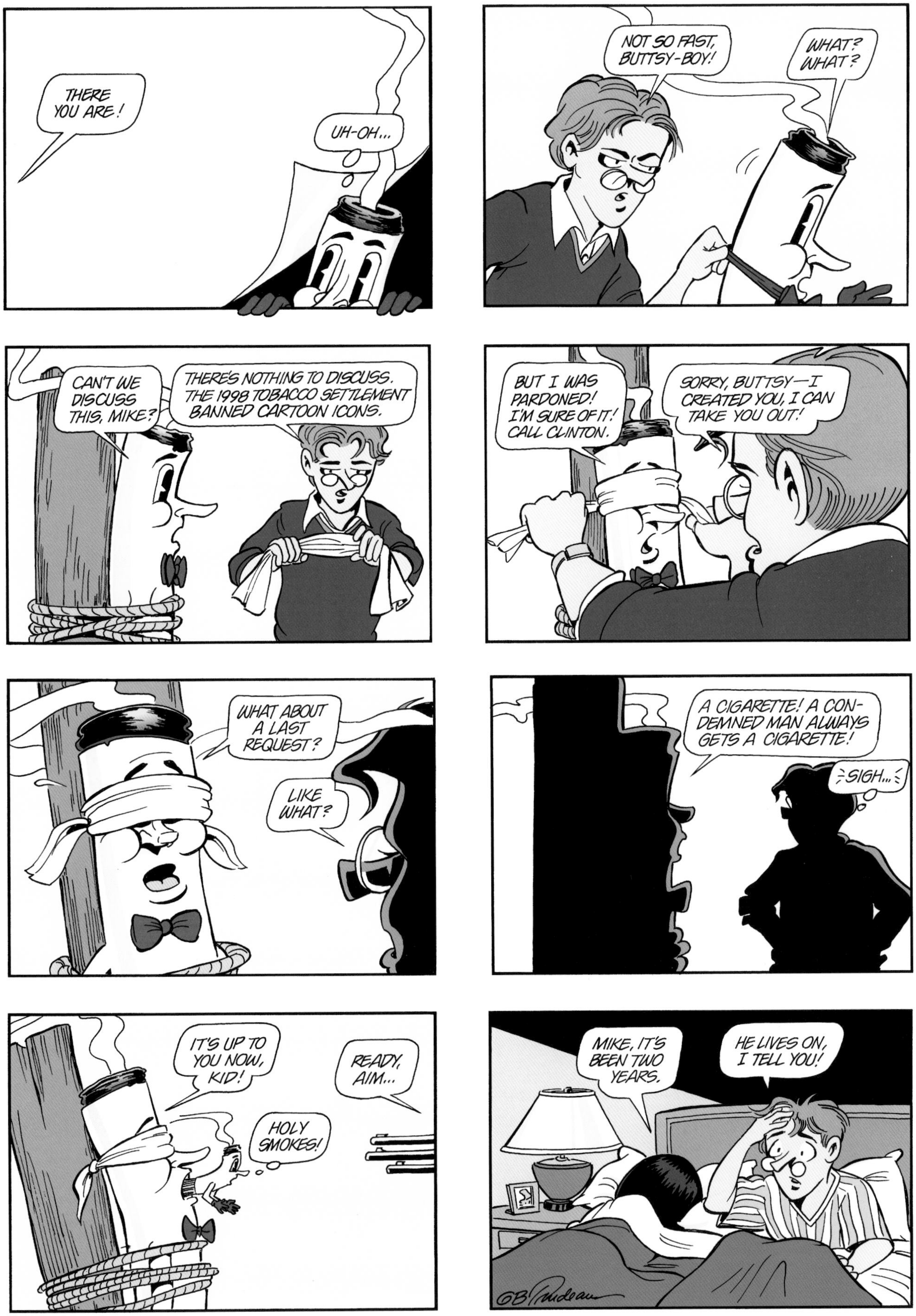
THERE YOU ARE!
UH-OH...
NOT SO FAST, BUTTSY-BOY!
WHAT? WHAT?
CAN'T WE DISCUSS THIS, MIKE?
THERE'S NOTHING TO DISCUSS. THE 1998 TOBACCO SETTLEMENT BANNED CARTOON ICONS.
BUT I WAS PARDONED! I'M SURE OF IT! CALL CLINTON.
SORRY, BUTTSY—I CREATED YOU, I CAN TAKE YOU OUT!
WHAT ABOUT A LAST REQUEST?
LIKE WHAT?
A CIGARETTE! A CON-DEMNED MAN ALWAYS GETS A CIGARETTE!
SIGH...
IT'S UP TO YOU NOW, KID!
READY, AIM...
HOLY SMOKES!
MIKE, IT'S BEEN TWO YEARS.
HE LIVES ON, I TELL YOU!

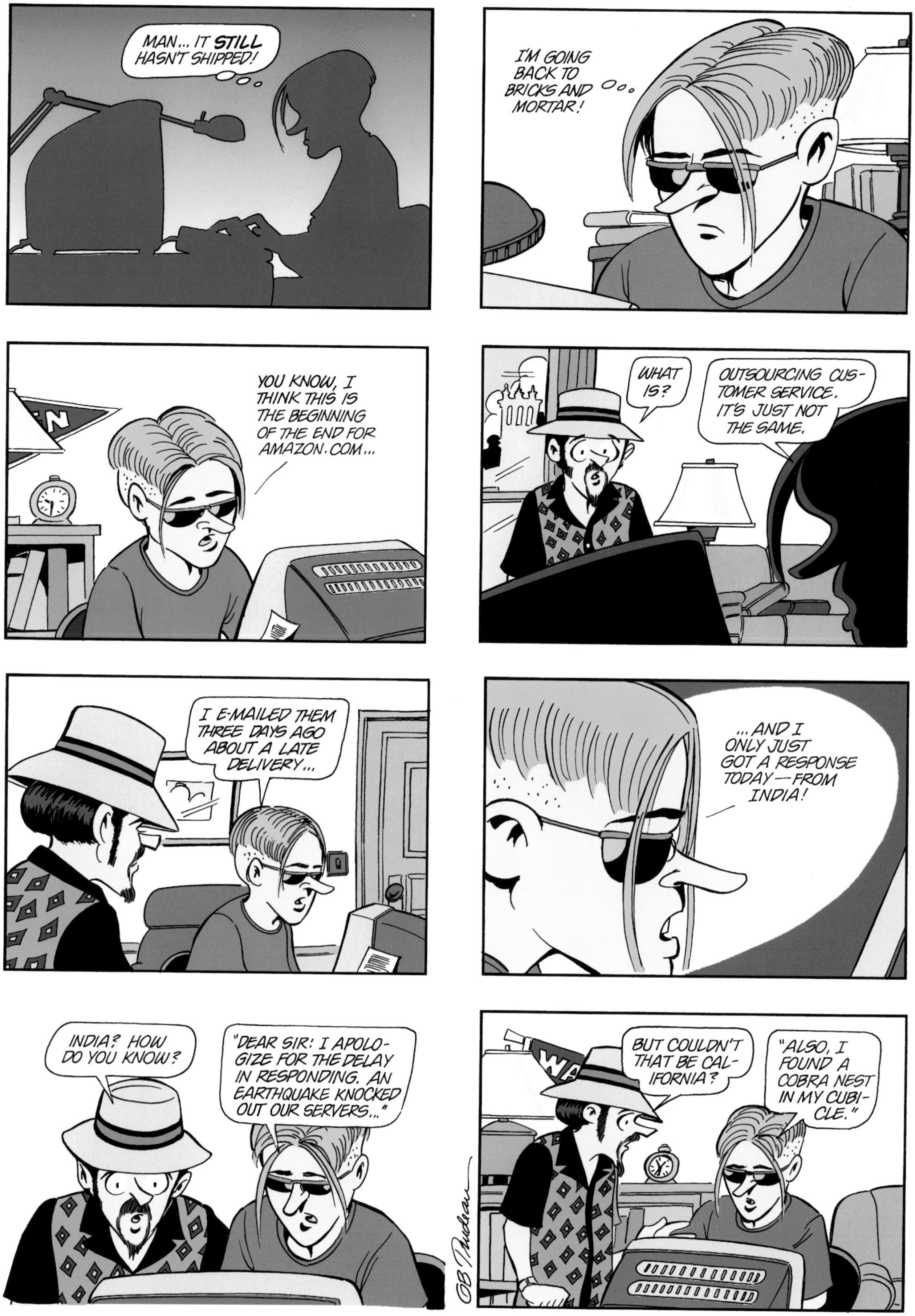
MAN... IT STILL HASN'T SHIPPED!
I'M GOING BACK TO BRICKS AND MORTAR!
YOU KNOW, I THINK THIS IS THE BEGINNING OF THE END FOR AMAZON.COM...
WHAT IS?
OUTSOURCING CUSTOMER SERVICE. IT'S JUST NOT THE SAME.
I E-MAILED THEM THREE DAYS AGO ABOUT A LATE DELIVERY...
...AND I ONLY JUST GOT A RESPONSE TODAY—FROM INDIA!
INDIA? HOW DO YOU KNOW?
"DEAR SIR: I APOLOGIZE FOR THE DELAY IN RESPONDING. AN EARTHQUAKE KNOCKED OUT OUR SERVERS..."
BUT COULDN'T THAT BE CALIFORNIA?
"ALSO, I FOUND A COBRA NEST IN MY CUBICLE."

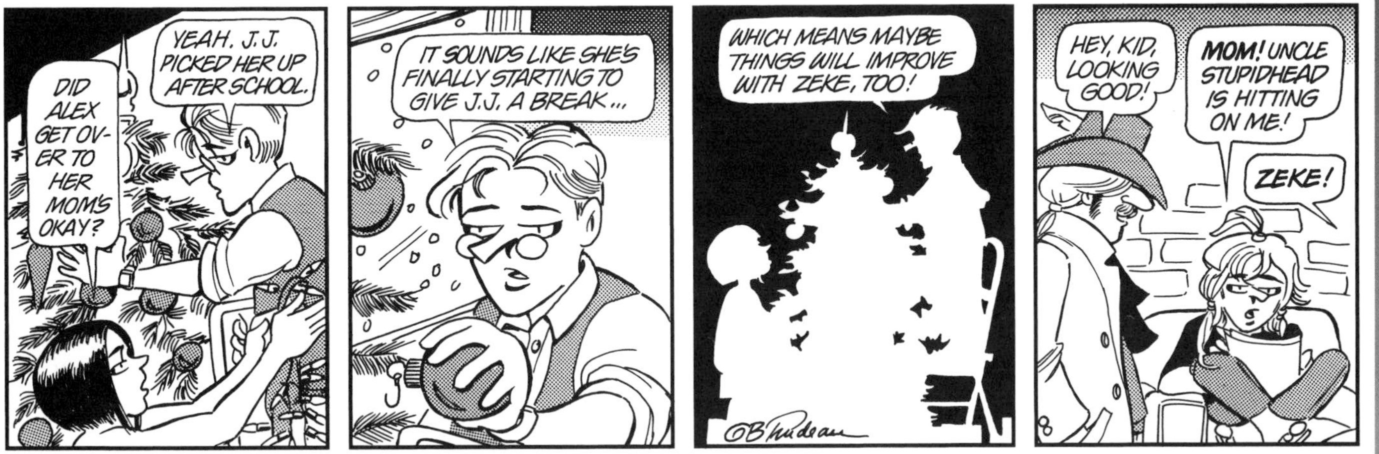
DID ALEX GET OVER TO HER MOM'S OKAY?
YEAH. J.J. PICKED HER UP AFTER SCHOOL.
IT SOUNDS LIKE SHE'S FINALLY STARTING TO GIVE J.J. A BREAK...
WHICH MEANS MAYBE THINGS WILL IMPROVE WITH ZEKE, TOO!
©B.Trudeau
HEY, KID, LOOKING GOOD!
MOM! UNCLE STUPIDHEAD IS HITTING ON ME!
ZEKE!

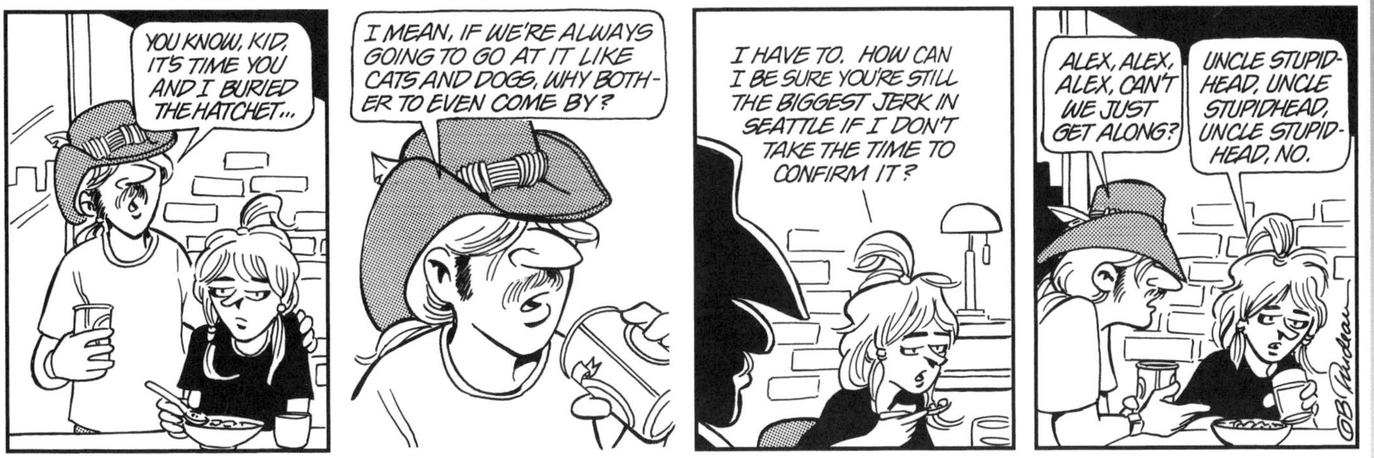
YOU KNOW, KID, IT'S TIME YOU AND I BURIED THE HATCHET...
I MEAN, IF WE'RE ALWAYS GOING TO GO AT IT LIKE CATS AND DOGS, WHY BOTHER TO EVEN COME BY?
I HAVE TO. HOW CAN I BE SURE YOU'RE STILL THE BIGGEST JERK IN SEATTLE IF I DON'T TAKE THE TIME TO CONFIRM IT?
ALEX, ALEX, ALEX, CAN'T WE JUST GET ALONG?
UNCLE STUPIDHEAD, UNCLE STUPIDHEAD, UNCLE STUPIDHEAD, NO.
©B.Trudeau

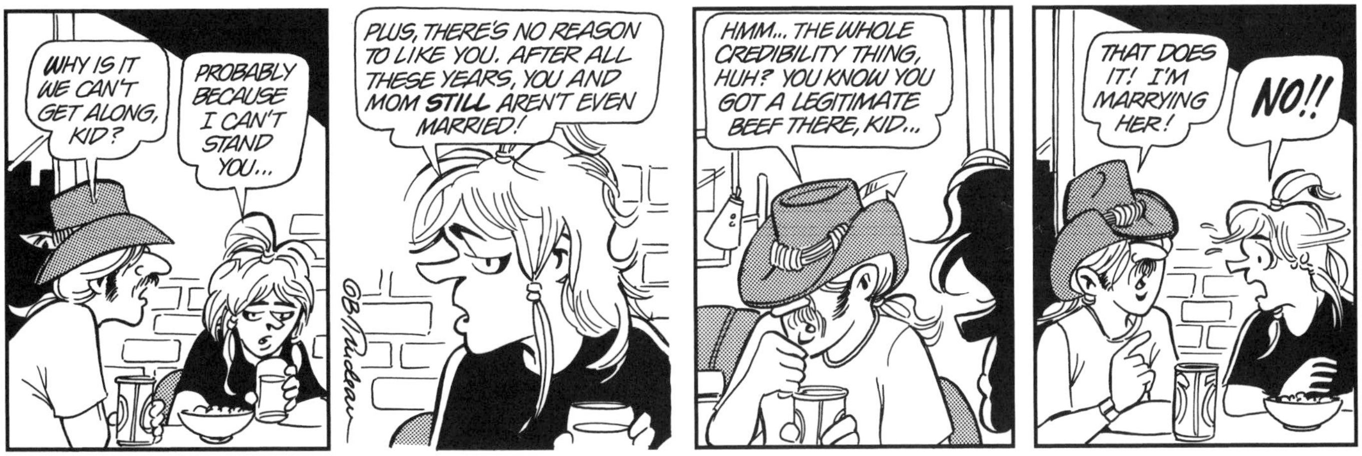
WHY IS IT WE CAN'T GET ALONG, KID?
PROBABLY BECAUSE I CAN'T STAND YOU...
PLUS, THERE'S NO REASON TO LIKE YOU. AFTER ALL THESE YEARS, YOU AND MOM STILL AREN'T EVEN MARRIED!
©B.Trudeau
HMM... THE WHOLE CREDIBILITY THING, HUH? YOU KNOW YOU GOT A LEGITIMATE BEEF THERE, KID...
THAT DOES IT! I'M MARRYING HER!
NO!!

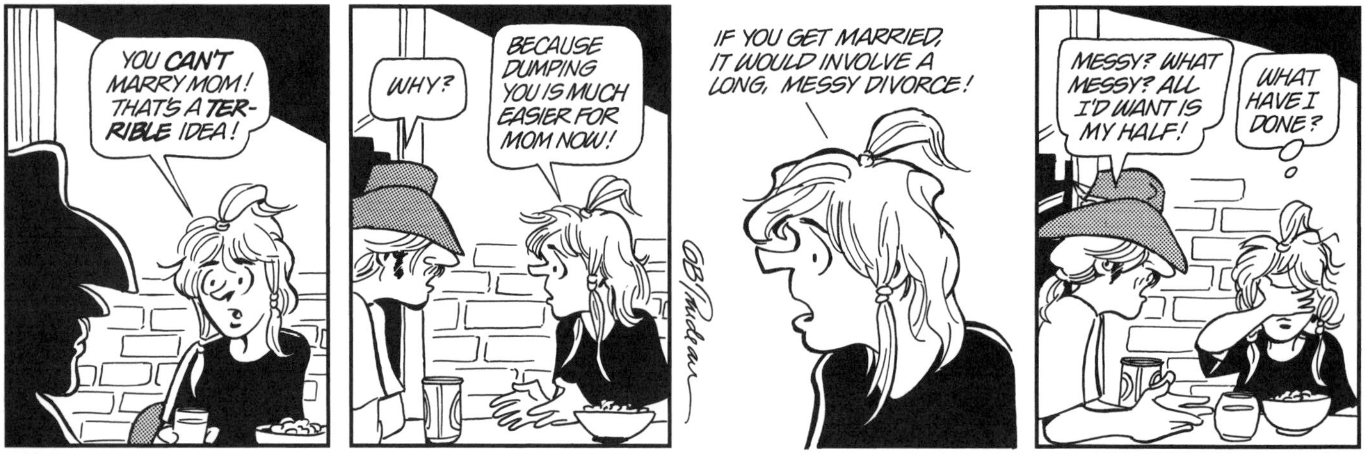
YOU CAN'T MARRY MOM! THAT'S A TERRIBLE IDEA!
WHY?
BECAUSE DUMPING YOU IS MUCH EASIER FOR MOM NOW!
IF YOU GET MARRIED, IT WOULD INVOLVE A LONG, MESSY DIVORCE!
MESSY? WHAT MESSY? ALL I'D WANT IS MY HALF!
WHAT HAVE I DONE?

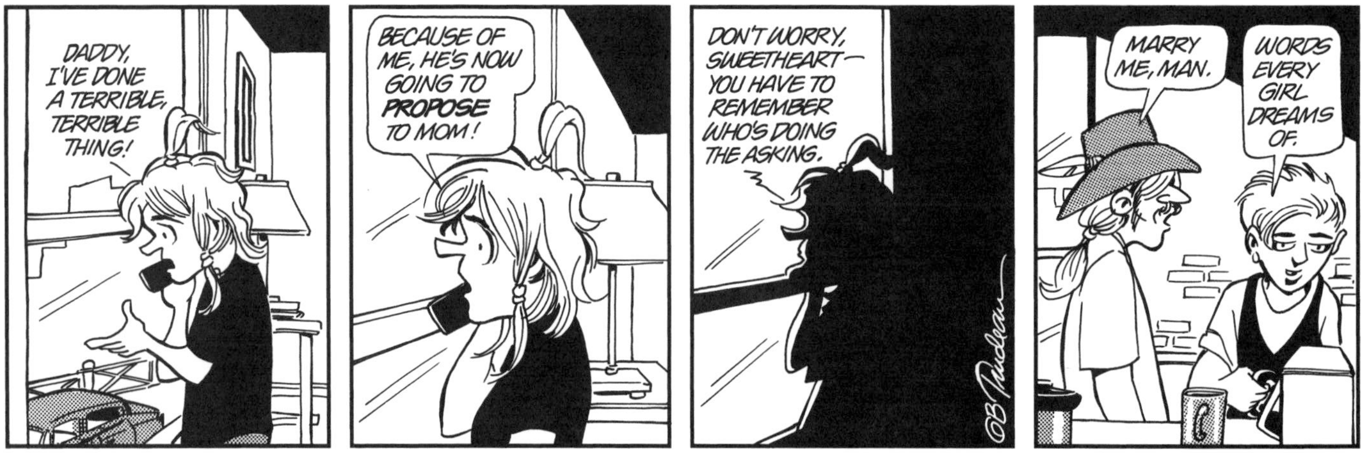
DADDY, I'VE DONE A TERRIBLE, TERRIBLE THING!
BECAUSE OF ME, HE'S NOW GOING TO PROPOSE TO MOM!
DON'T WORRY, SWEETHEART— YOU HAVE TO REMEMBER WHO'S DOING THE ASKING.
MARRY ME, MAN.
WORDS EVERY GIRL DREAMS OF.

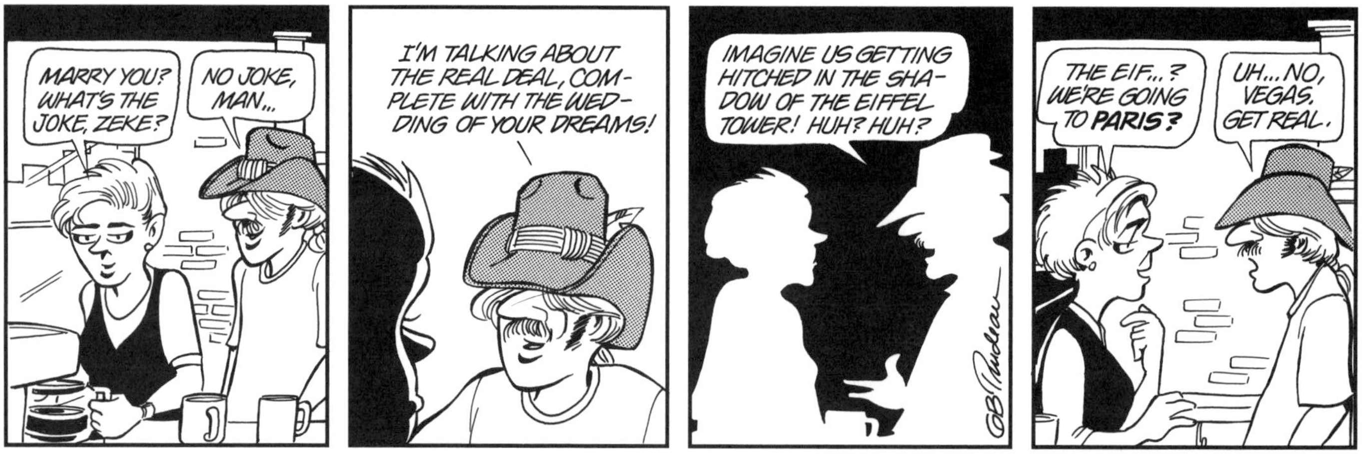
MARRY YOU? WHAT'S THE JOKE, ZEKE?
NO JOKE, MAN...
I'M TALKING ABOUT THE REAL DEAL, COMPLETE WITH THE WEDDING OF YOUR DREAMS!
IMAGINE US GETTING HITCHED IN THE SHADOW OF THE EIFFEL TOWER! HUH? HUH?
THE EIF...? WE'RE GOING TO PARIS?
UH... NO, VEGAS. GET REAL.

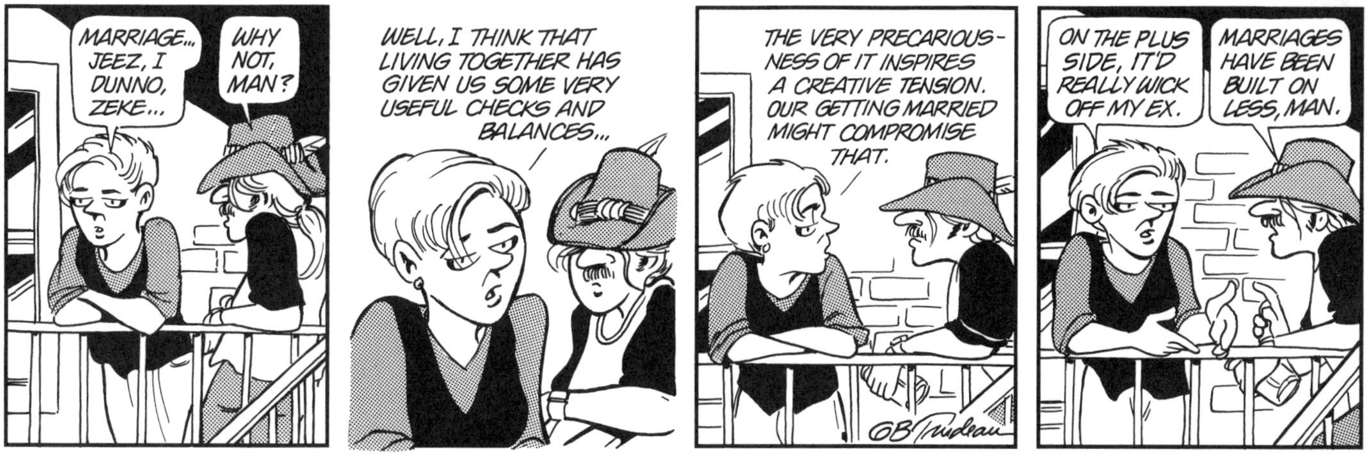
MARRIAGE... JEEZ, I DUNNO, ZEKE...
WHY NOT, MAN?
WELL, I THINK THAT LIVING TOGETHER HAS GIVEN US SOME VERY USEFUL CHECKS AND BALANCES...
THE VERY PRECARIOUSNESS OF IT INSPIRES A CREATIVE TENSION. OUR GETTING MARRIED MIGHT COMPROMISE THAT.
ON THE PLUS SIDE, IT'D REALLY WICK OFF MY EX.
MARRIAGES HAVE BEEN BUILT ON LESS, MAN.

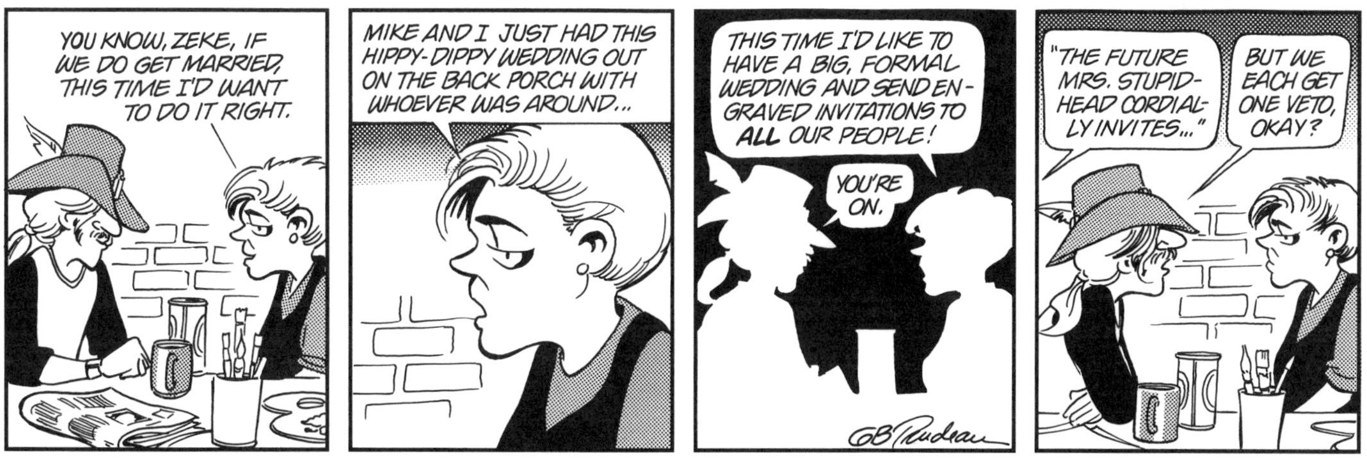
YOU KNOW, ZEKE, IF WE DO GET MARRIED, THIS TIME I'D WANT TO DO IT RIGHT.
MIKE AND I JUST HAD THIS HIPPY-DIPPY WEDDING OUT ON THE BACK PORCH WITH WHOEVER WAS AROUND...
THIS TIME I'D LIKE TO HAVE A BIG, FORMAL WEDDING AND SEND ENGRAVED INVITATIONS TO **ALL** OUR PEOPLE!
YOU'RE ON.
"THE FUTURE MRS. STUPIDHEAD CORDIALLY INVITES..."
BUT WE EACH GET ONE VETO, OKAY?

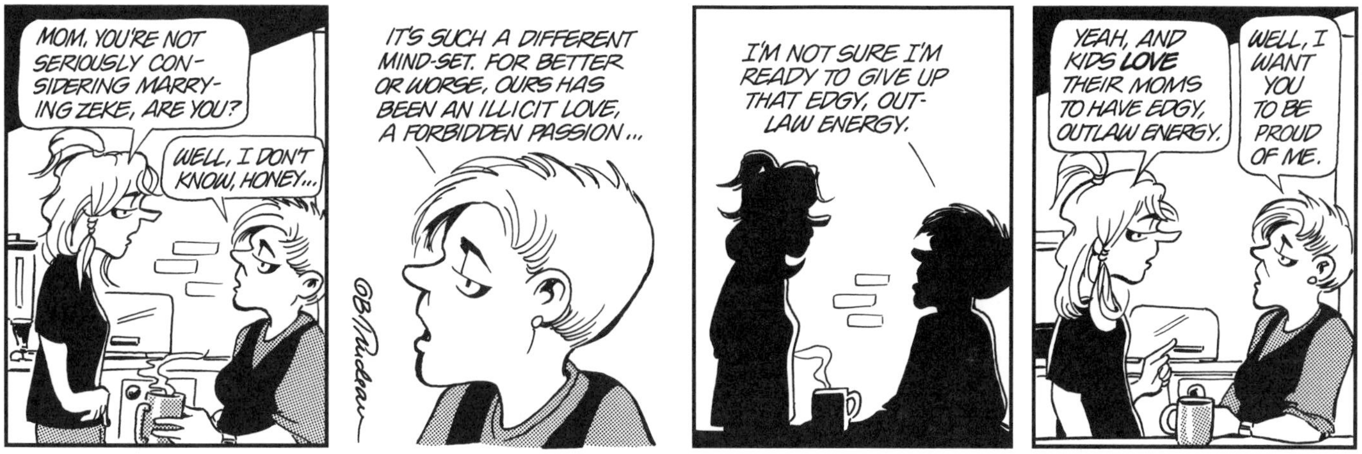
MOM, YOU'RE NOT SERIOUSLY CONSIDERING MARRYING ZEKE, ARE YOU?
WELL, I DON'T KNOW, HONEY...
IT'S SUCH A DIFFERENT MIND-SET. FOR BETTER OR WORSE, OURS HAS BEEN AN ILLICIT LOVE, A FORBIDDEN PASSION...
I'M NOT SURE I'M READY TO GIVE UP THAT EDGY, OUTLAW ENERGY.
YEAH, AND KIDS **LOVE** THEIR MOMS TO HAVE EDGY, OUTLAW ENERGY.
WELL, I WANT YOU TO BE PROUD OF ME.

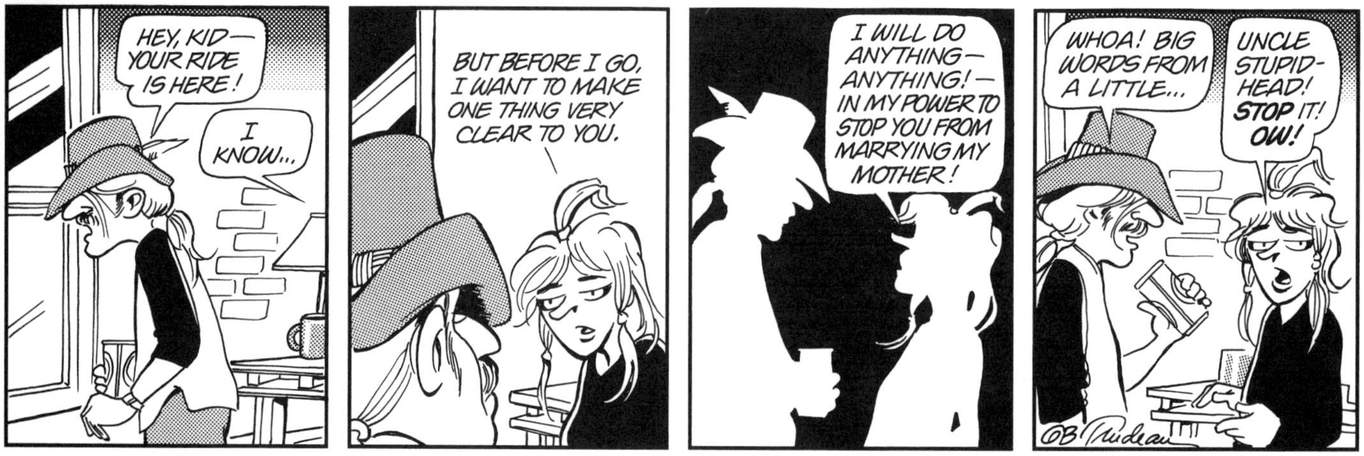
HEY, KID— YOUR RIDE IS HERE!
I KNOW...
BUT BEFORE I GO, I WANT TO MAKE ONE THING VERY CLEAR TO YOU.
I WILL DO ANYTHING— ANYTHING!— IN MY POWER TO STOP YOU FROM MARRYING MY MOTHER!
WHOA! BIG WORDS FROM A LITTLE...
UNCLE STUPID-HEAD! STOP IT! OW!
©B Trudeau

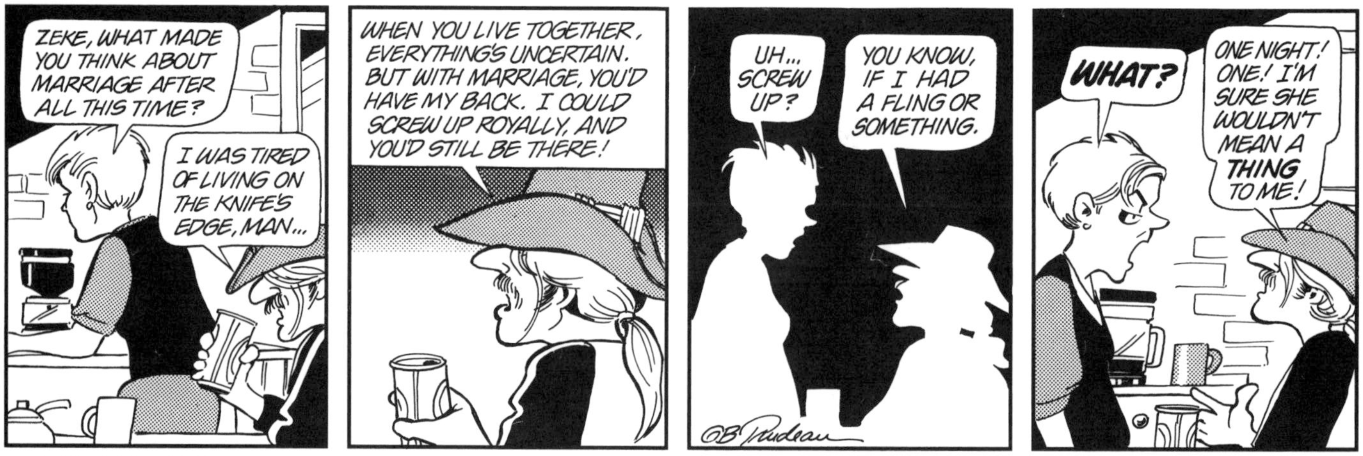
ZEKE, WHAT MADE YOU THINK ABOUT MARRIAGE AFTER ALL THIS TIME?
I WAS TIRED OF LIVING ON THE KNIFE'S EDGE, MAN...
WHEN YOU LIVE TOGETHER, EVERYTHING'S UNCERTAIN. BUT WITH MARRIAGE, YOU'D HAVE MY BACK. I COULD SCREW UP ROYALLY, AND YOU'D STILL BE THERE!
UH... SCREW UP?
YOU KNOW, IF I HAD A FLING OR SOMETHING.
©B Trudeau
WHAT?
ONE NIGHT! ONE! I'M SURE SHE WOULDN'T MEAN A THING TO ME!

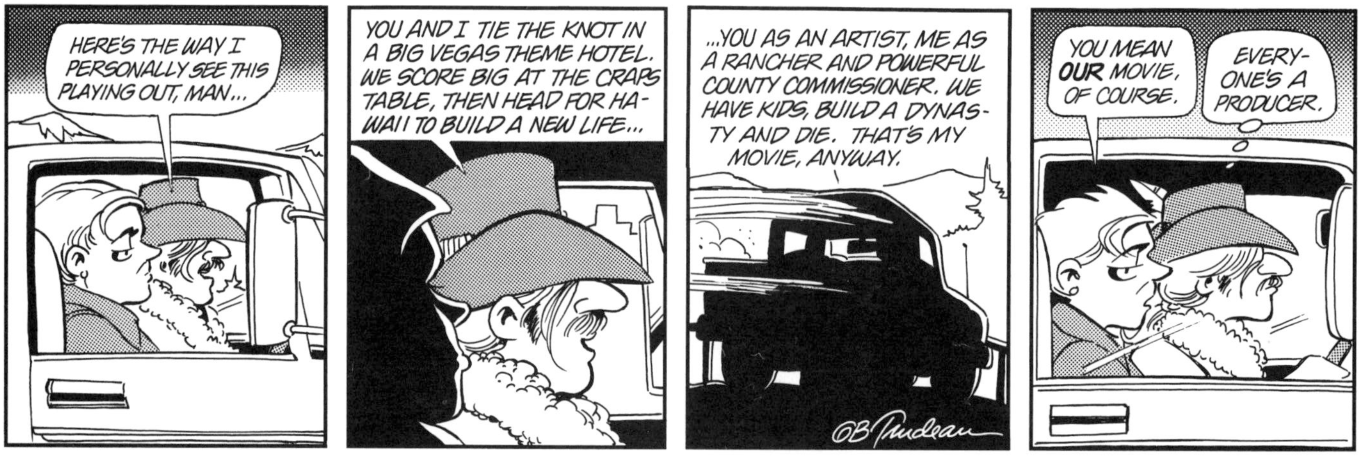
HERE'S THE WAY I PERSONALLY SEE THIS PLAYING OUT, MAN...
YOU AND I TIE THE KNOT IN A BIG VEGAS THEME HOTEL. WE SCORE BIG AT THE CRAPS TABLE, THEN HEAD FOR HAWAII TO BUILD A NEW LIFE...
...YOU AS AN ARTIST, ME AS A RANCHER AND POWERFUL COUNTY COMMISSIONER. WE HAVE KIDS, BUILD A DYNASTY AND DIE. THAT'S MY MOVIE, ANYWAY.
©B Trudeau
YOU MEAN OUR MOVIE, OF COURSE.
EVERYONE'S A PRODUCER.

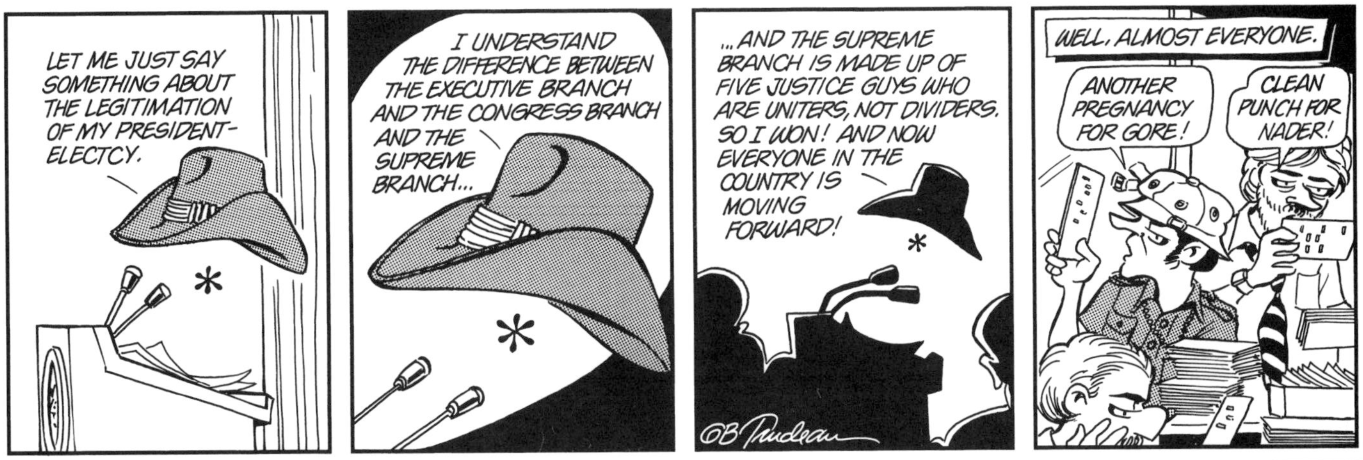
LET ME JUST SAY SOMETHING ABOUT THE LEGITIMATION OF MY PRESIDENT-ELECTCY.
I UNDERSTAND THE DIFFERENCE BETWEEN THE EXECUTIVE BRANCH AND THE CONGRESS BRANCH AND THE SUPREME BRANCH...
...AND THE SUPREME BRANCH IS MADE UP OF FIVE JUSTICE GUYS WHO ARE UNITERS, NOT DIVIDERS. SO I WON! AND NOW EVERYONE IN THE COUNTRY IS MOVING FORWARD!
WELL, ALMOST EVERYONE.
ANOTHER PREGNANCY FOR GORE!
CLEAN PUNCH FOR NADER!

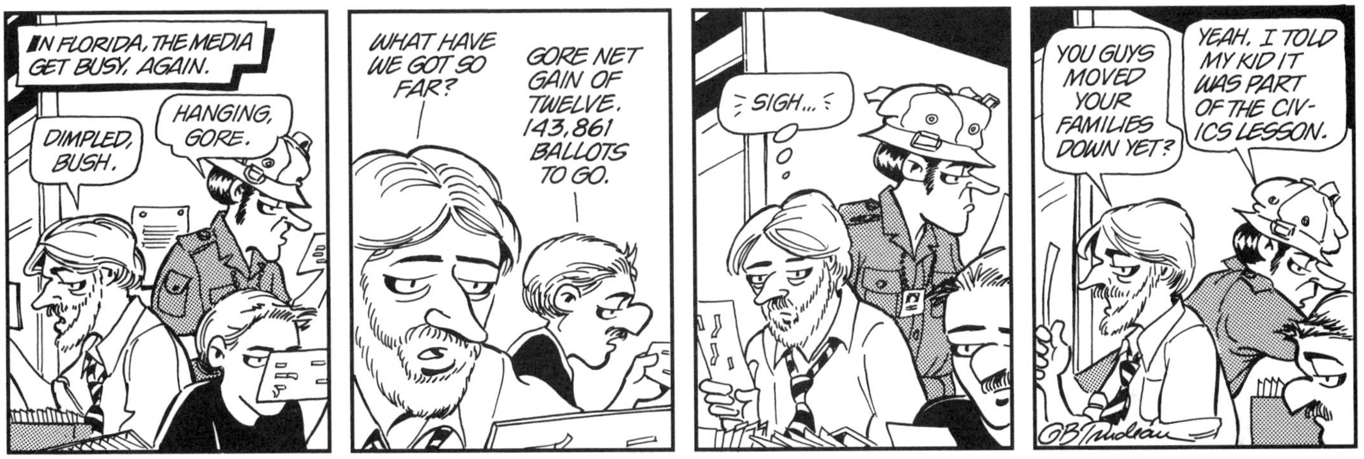
IN FLORIDA, THE MEDIA GET BUSY, AGAIN.
DIMPLED, BUSH.
HANGING, GORE.
WHAT HAVE WE GOT SO FAR?
GORE NET GAIN OF TWELVE. 143,861 BALLOTS TO GO.
SIGH...
YOU GUYS MOVED YOUR FAMILIES DOWN YET?
YEAH. I TOLD MY KID IT WAS PART OF THE CIVICS LESSON.

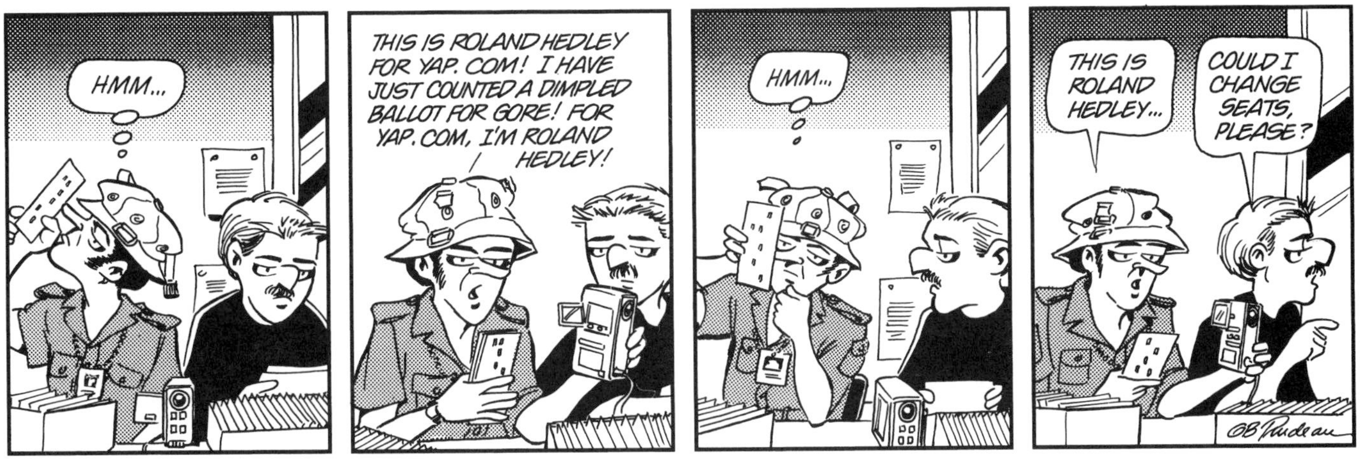
HMM...
THIS IS ROLAND HEDLEY FOR YAP.COM! I HAVE JUST COUNTED A DIMPLED BALLOT FOR GORE! FOR YAP.COM, I'M ROLAND HEDLEY!
HMM...
THIS IS ROLAND HEDLEY...
COULD I CHANGE SEATS, PLEASE?

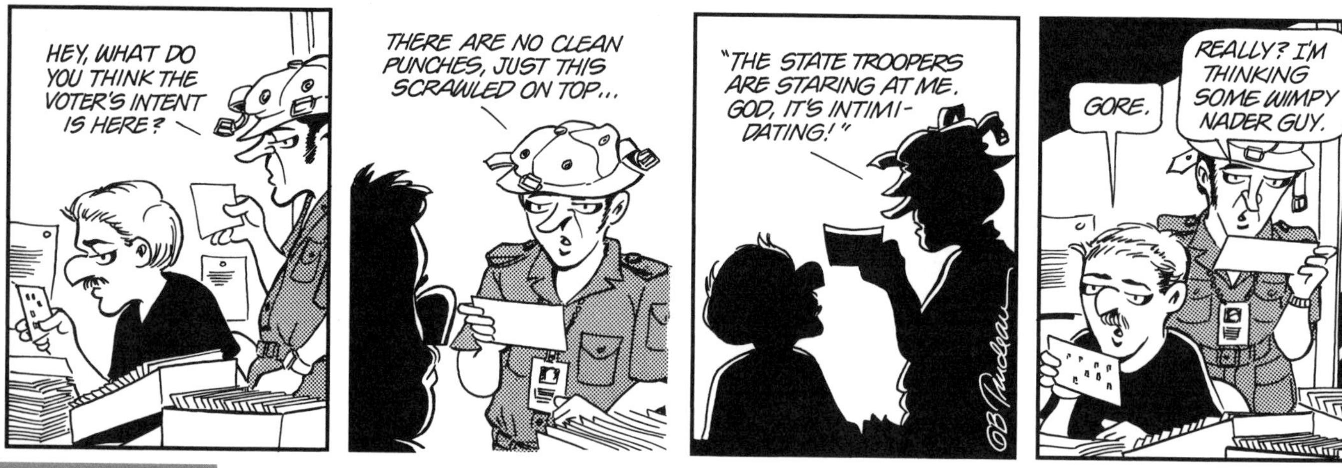
HEY, WHAT DO YOU THINK THE VOTER'S INTENT IS HERE?
THERE ARE NO CLEAN PUNCHES, JUST THIS SCRAWLED ON TOP...
"THE STATE TROOPERS ARE STARING AT ME. GOD, IT'S INTIMIDATING!"
GORE.
REALLY? I'M THINKING SOME WIMPY NADER GUY.

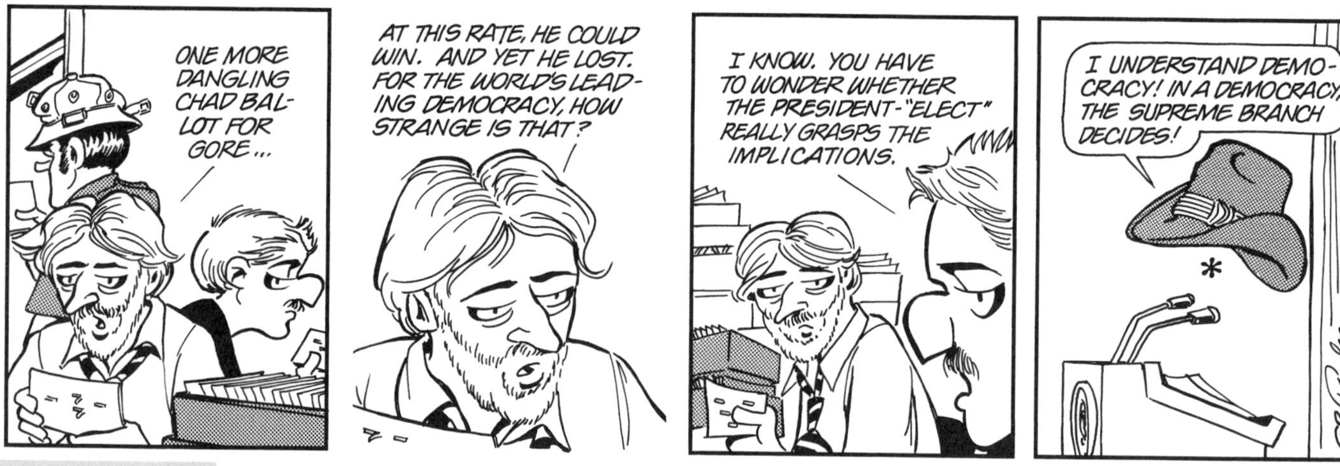
ONE MORE DANGLING CHAD BALLOT FOR GORE...
AT THIS RATE, HE COULD WIN. AND YET HE LOST. FOR THE WORLD'S LEADING DEMOCRACY, HOW STRANGE IS THAT?
I KNOW. YOU HAVE TO WONDER WHETHER THE PRESIDENT-"ELECT" REALLY GRASPS THE IMPLICATIONS.
I UNDERSTAND DEMOCRACY! IN A DEMOCRACY, THE SUPREME BRANCH DECIDES!

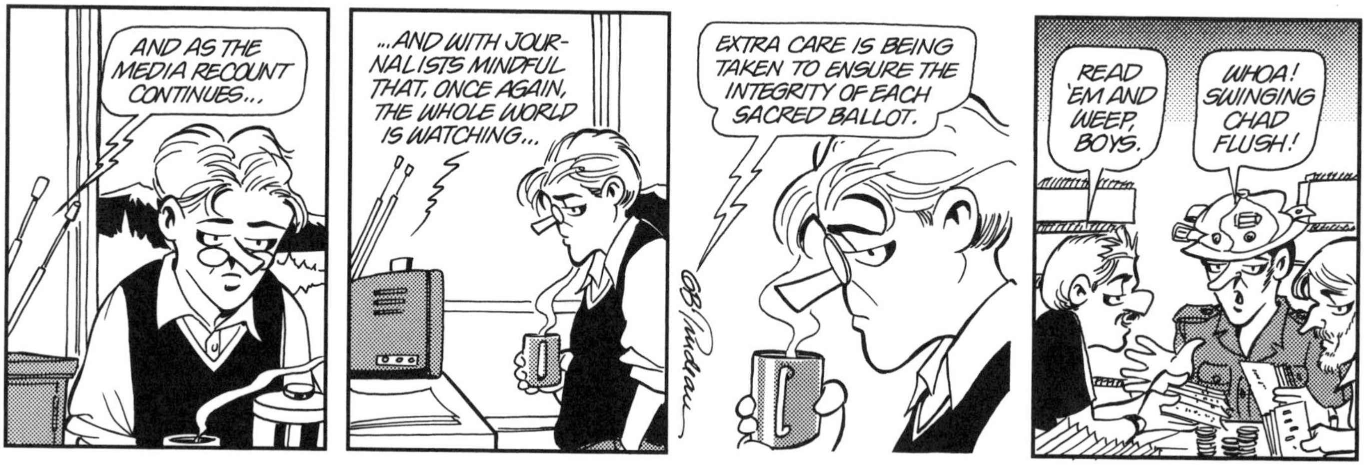
AND AS THE MEDIA RECOUNT CONTINUES...
...AND WITH JOURNALISTS MINDFUL THAT, ONCE AGAIN, THE WHOLE WORLD IS WATCHING...
EXTRA CARE IS BEING TAKEN TO ENSURE THE INTEGRITY OF EACH SACRED BALLOT.
READ 'EM AND WEEP, BOYS.
WHOA! SWINGING CHAD FLUSH!

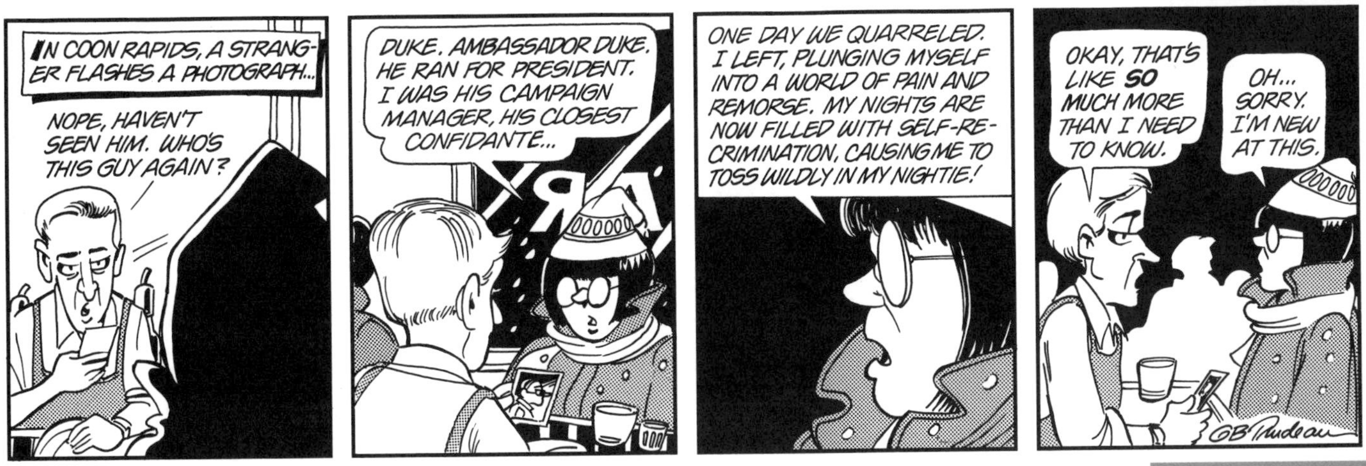
IN COON RAPIDS, A STRANGER FLASHES A PHOTOGRAPH...
NOPE, HAVEN'T SEEN HIM. WHO'S THIS GUY AGAIN?
DUKE. AMBASSADOR DUKE. HE RAN FOR PRESIDENT. I WAS HIS CAMPAIGN MANAGER, HIS CLOSEST CONFIDANTE...
ONE DAY WE QUARRELED. I LEFT, PLUNGING MYSELF INTO A WORLD OF PAIN AND REMORSE. MY NIGHTS ARE NOW FILLED WITH SELF-RECRIMINATION, CAUSING ME TO TOSS WILDLY IN MY NIGHTIE!
OKAY, THAT'S LIKE **SO** MUCH MORE THAN I NEED TO KNOW.
OH... SORRY. I'M NEW AT THIS.
GB Trudeau

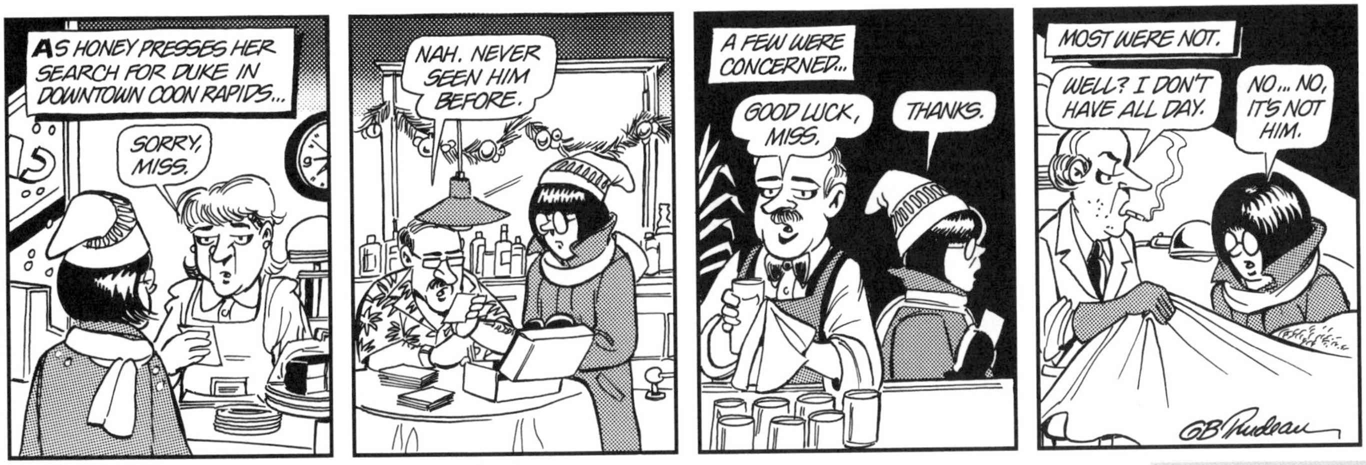
AS HONEY PRESSES HER SEARCH FOR DUKE IN DOWNTOWN COON RAPIDS...
SORRY, MISS.
NAH. NEVER SEEN HIM BEFORE.
A FEW WERE CONCERNED...
GOOD LUCK, MISS.
THANKS.
MOST WERE NOT.
WELL? I DON'T HAVE ALL DAY.
NO... NO, IT'S NOT HIM.
GB Trudeau

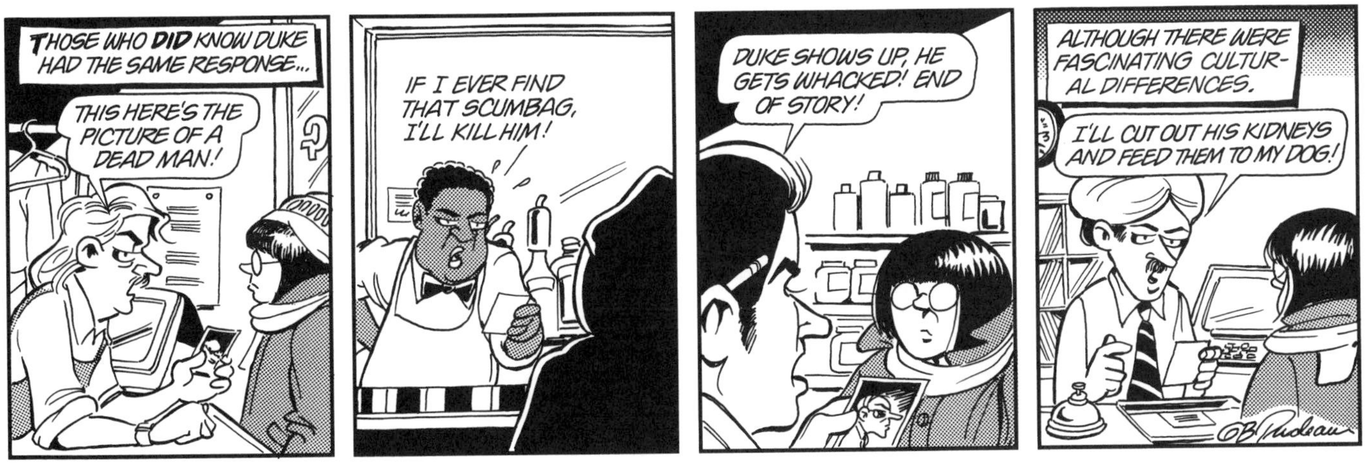
THOSE WHO **DID** KNOW DUKE HAD THE SAME RESPONSE...
THIS HERE'S THE PICTURE OF A DEAD MAN!
IF I EVER FIND THAT SCUMBAG, I'LL KILL HIM!
DUKE SHOWS UP, HE GETS WHACKED! END OF STORY!
ALTHOUGH THERE WERE FASCINATING CULTURAL DIFFERENCES.
I'LL CUT OUT HIS KIDNEYS AND FEED THEM TO MY DOG!
GB Trudeau

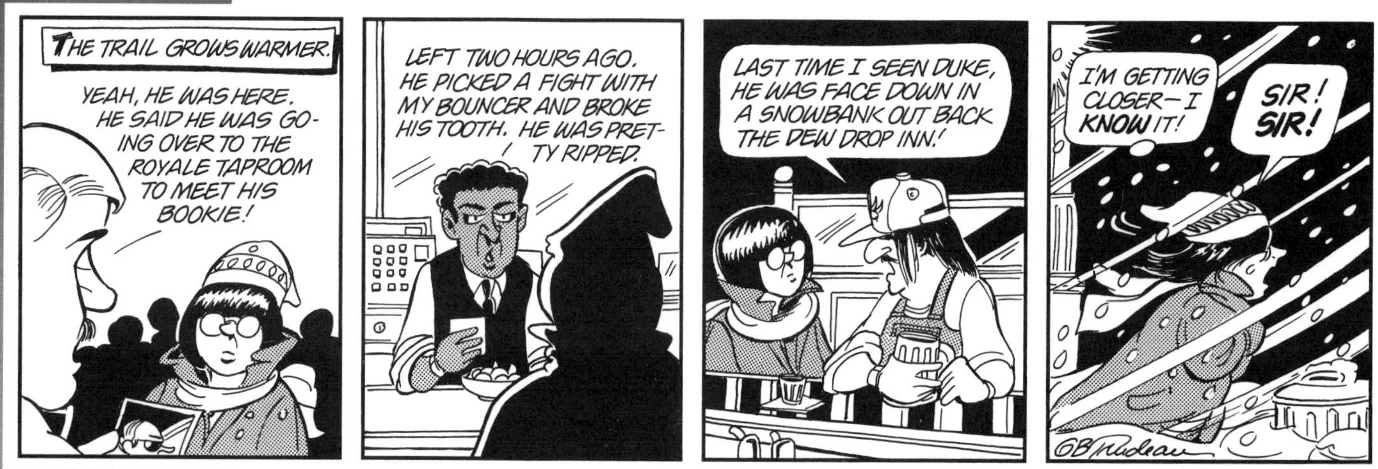
THE TRAIL GROWS WARMER.
YEAH, HE WAS HERE. HE SAID HE WAS GOING OVER TO THE ROYALE TAPROOM TO MEET HIS BOOKIE!
LEFT TWO HOURS AGO. HE PICKED A FIGHT WITH MY BOUNCER AND BROKE HIS TOOTH. HE WAS PRETTY RIPPED.
LAST TIME I SEEN DUKE, HE WAS FACE DOWN IN A SNOWBANK OUT BACK THE DEW DROP INN!
I'M GETTING CLOSER—I KNOW IT!
SIR! SIR!

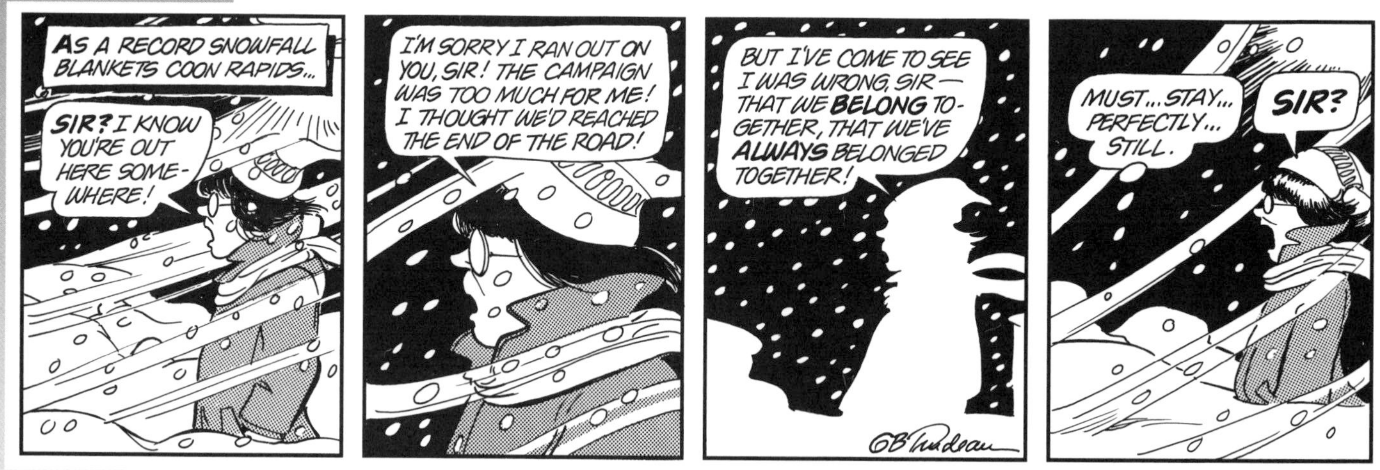
AS A RECORD SNOWFALL BLANKETS COON RAPIDS...
SIR? I KNOW YOU'RE OUT HERE SOMEWHERE!
I'M SORRY I RAN OUT ON YOU, SIR! THE CAMPAIGN WAS TOO MUCH FOR ME! I THOUGHT WE'D REACHED THE END OF THE ROAD!
BUT I'VE COME TO SEE I WAS WRONG, SIR—THAT WE BELONG TOGETHER, THAT WE'VE ALWAYS BELONGED TOGETHER!
MUST... STAY... PERFECTLY... STILL.
SIR?

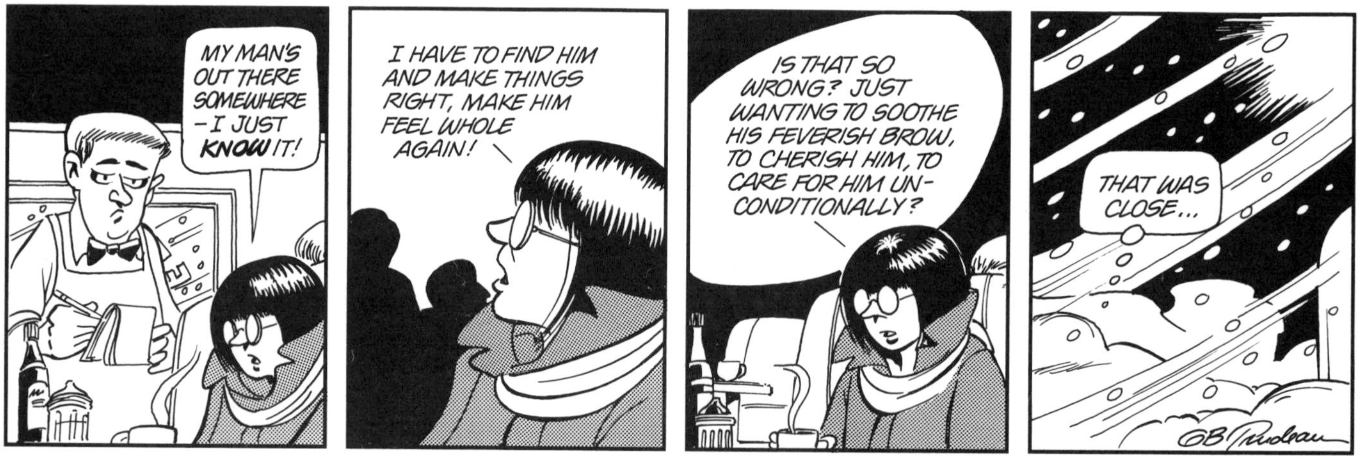
MY MAN'S OUT THERE SOMEWHERE —I JUST KNOW IT!
I HAVE TO FIND HIM AND MAKE THINGS RIGHT, MAKE HIM FEEL WHOLE AGAIN!
IS THAT SO WRONG? JUST WANTING TO SOOTHE HIS FEVERISH BROW, TO CHERISH HIM, TO CARE FOR HIM UNCONDITIONALLY?
THAT WAS CLOSE...

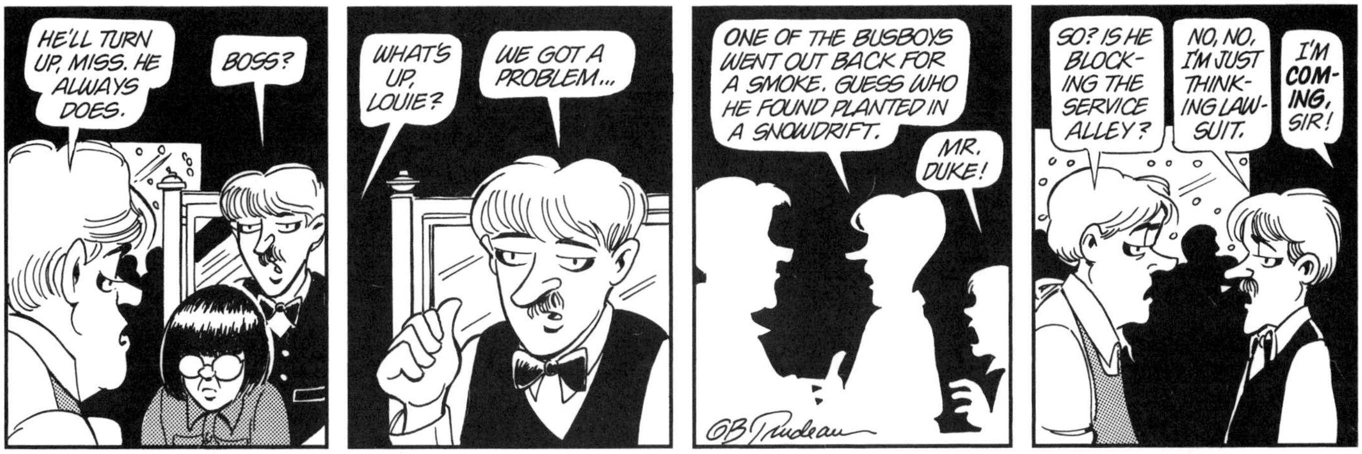
HE'LL TURN UP, MISS. HE ALWAYS DOES.
BOSS?
WHAT'S UP, LOUIE?
WE GOT A PROBLEM...
ONE OF THE BUSBOYS WENT OUT BACK FOR A SMOKE. GUESS WHO HE FOUND PLANTED IN A SNOWDRIFT.
MR. DUKE!
SO? IS HE BLOCKING THE SERVICE ALLEY?
NO, NO, I'M JUST THINKING LAWSUIT.
I'M COMING, SIR!

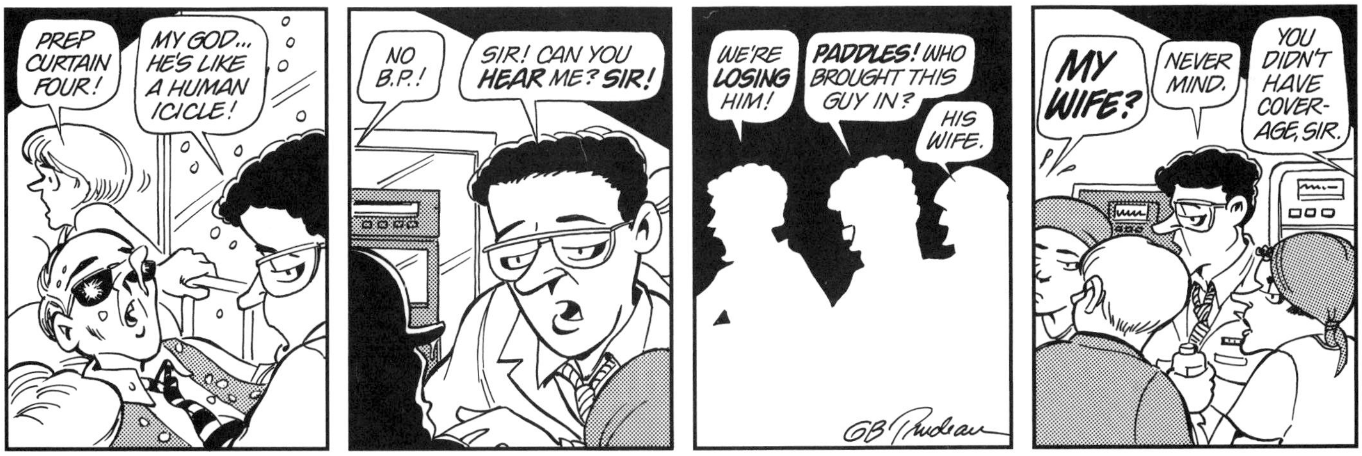
PREP CURTAIN FOUR!
MY GOD... HE'S LIKE A HUMAN ICICLE!
NO B.P.!
SIR! CAN YOU HEAR ME? SIR!
WE'RE LOSING HIM!
PADDLES! WHO BROUGHT THIS GUY IN?
HIS WIFE.
MY WIFE?
NEVER MIND.
YOU DIDN'T HAVE COVERAGE, SIR.

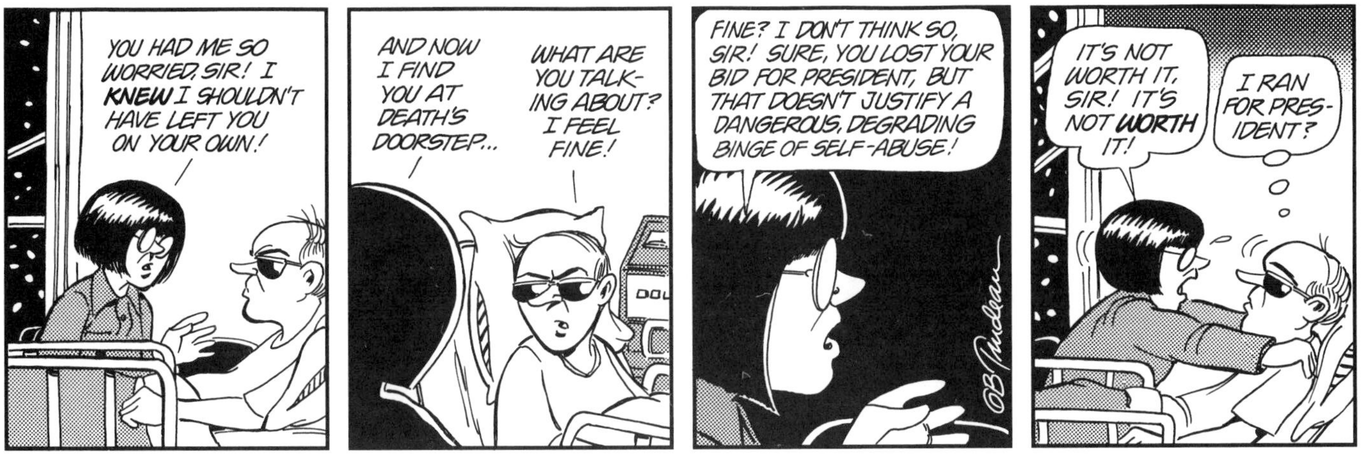
YOU HAD ME SO WORRIED, SIR! I KNEW I SHOULDN'T HAVE LEFT YOU ON YOUR OWN!
AND NOW I FIND YOU AT DEATH'S DOORSTEP...
WHAT ARE YOU TALKING ABOUT? I FEEL FINE!
FINE? I DON'T THINK SO, SIR! SURE, YOU LOST YOUR BID FOR PRESIDENT, BUT THAT DOESN'T JUSTIFY A DANGEROUS, DEGRADING BINGE OF SELF-ABUSE!
IT'S NOT WORTH IT, SIR! IT'S NOT WORTH IT!
I RAN FOR PRESIDENT?

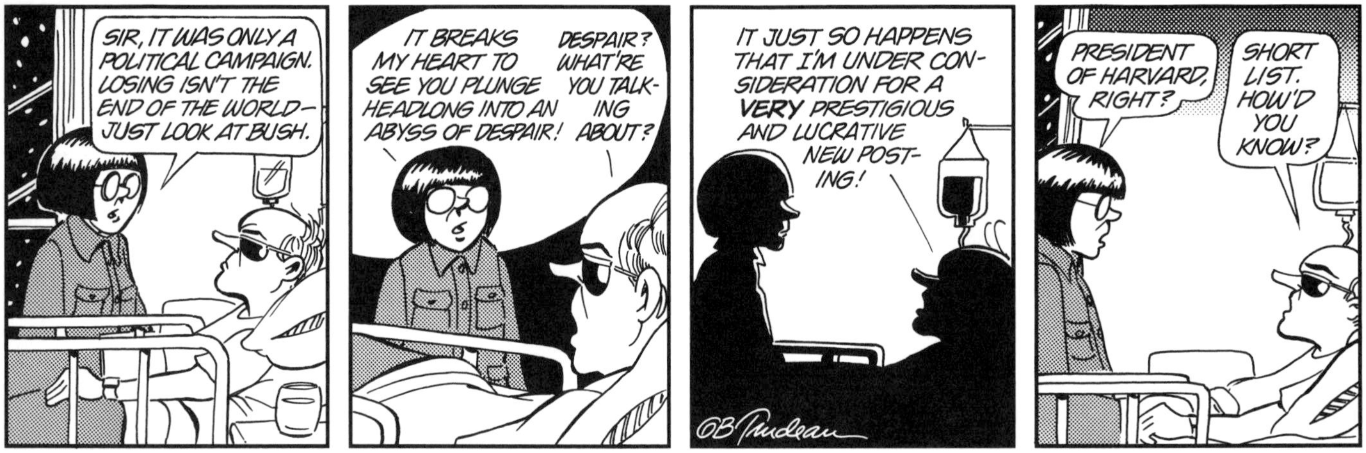
SIR, IT WAS ONLY A POLITICAL CAMPAIGN. LOSING ISN'T THE END OF THE WORLD— JUST LOOK AT BUSH.
IT BREAKS MY HEART TO SEE YOU PLUNGE HEADLONG INTO AN ABYSS OF DESPAIR!
DESPAIR? WHAT'RE YOU TALK-ING ABOUT?
IT JUST SO HAPPENS THAT I'M UNDER CON-SIDERATION FOR A **VERY** PRESTIGIOUS AND LUCRATIVE NEW POST-ING!
©B Trudeau
PRESIDENT OF HARVARD, RIGHT?
SHORT LIST. HOW'D YOU KNOW?

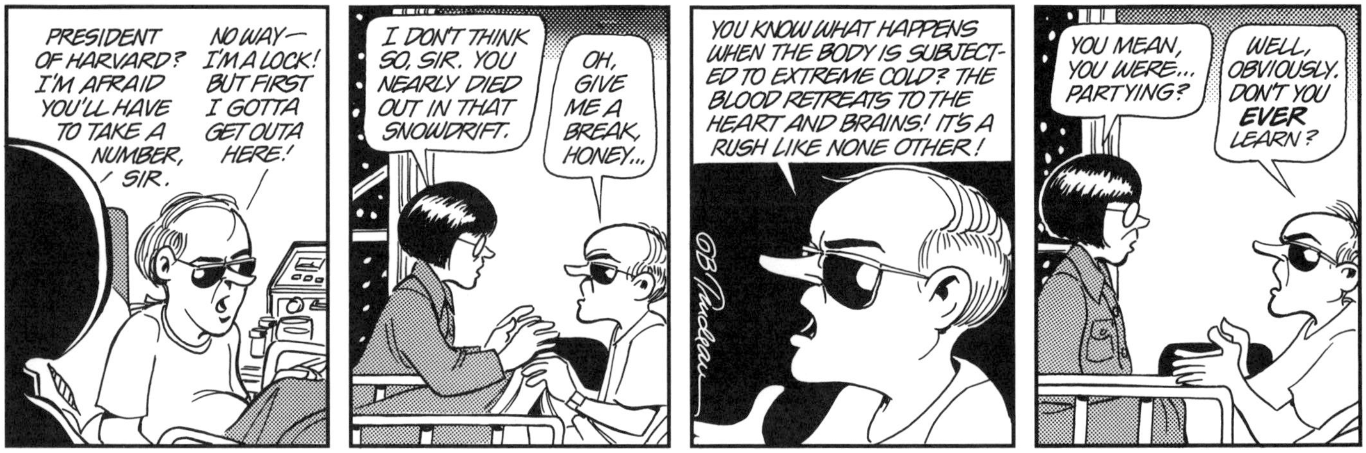
PRESIDENT OF HARVARD? I'M AFRAID YOU'LL HAVE TO TAKE A NUMBER, SIR.
NO WAY— I'M A LOCK! BUT FIRST I GOTTA GET OUTA HERE!
I DON'T THINK SO, SIR. YOU NEARLY DIED OUT IN THAT SNOWDRIFT.
OH, GIVE ME A BREAK, HONEY...
YOU KNOW WHAT HAPPENS WHEN THE BODY IS SUBJECT-ED TO EXTREME COLD? THE BLOOD RETREATS TO THE HEART AND BRAINS! IT'S A RUSH LIKE NONE OTHER!
©B Trudeau
YOU MEAN, YOU WERE... PARTYING?
WELL, OBVIOUSLY. DON'T YOU **EVER** LEARN?

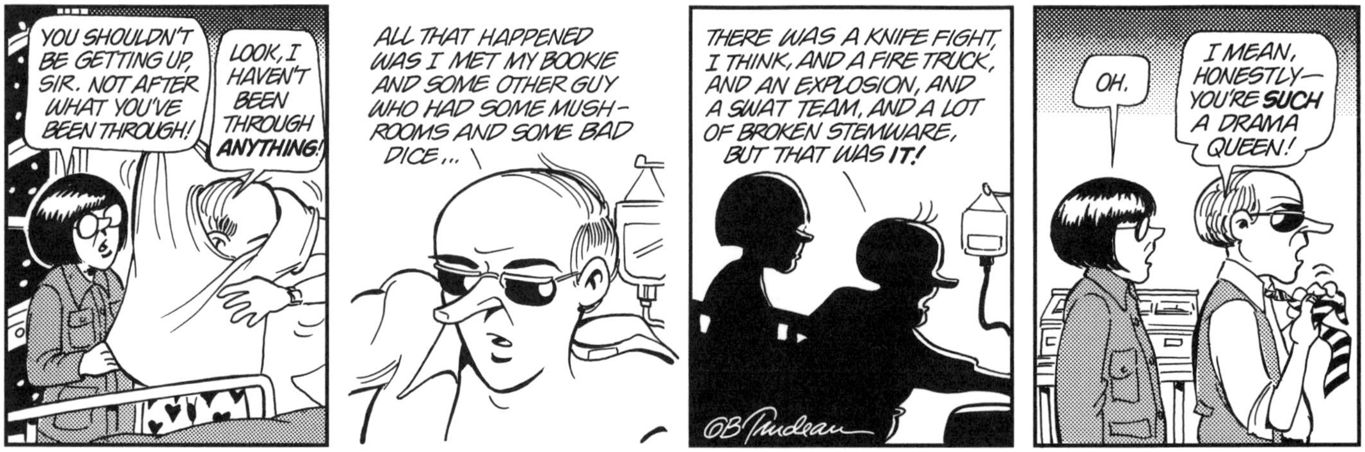
YOU SHOULDN'T BE GETTING UP, SIR. NOT AFTER WHAT YOU'VE BEEN THROUGH!
LOOK, I HAVEN'T BEEN THROUGH **ANYTHING!**
ALL THAT HAPPENED WAS I MET MY BOOKIE AND SOME OTHER GUY WHO HAD SOME MUSH-ROOMS AND SOME BAD DICE...
THERE WAS A KNIFE FIGHT, I THINK, AND A FIRE TRUCK, AND AN EXPLOSION, AND A SWAT TEAM, AND A LOT OF BROKEN STEMWARE, BUT THAT WAS **IT!**
©B Trudeau
OH.
I MEAN, HONESTLY— YOU'RE **SUCH** A DRAMA QUEEN!

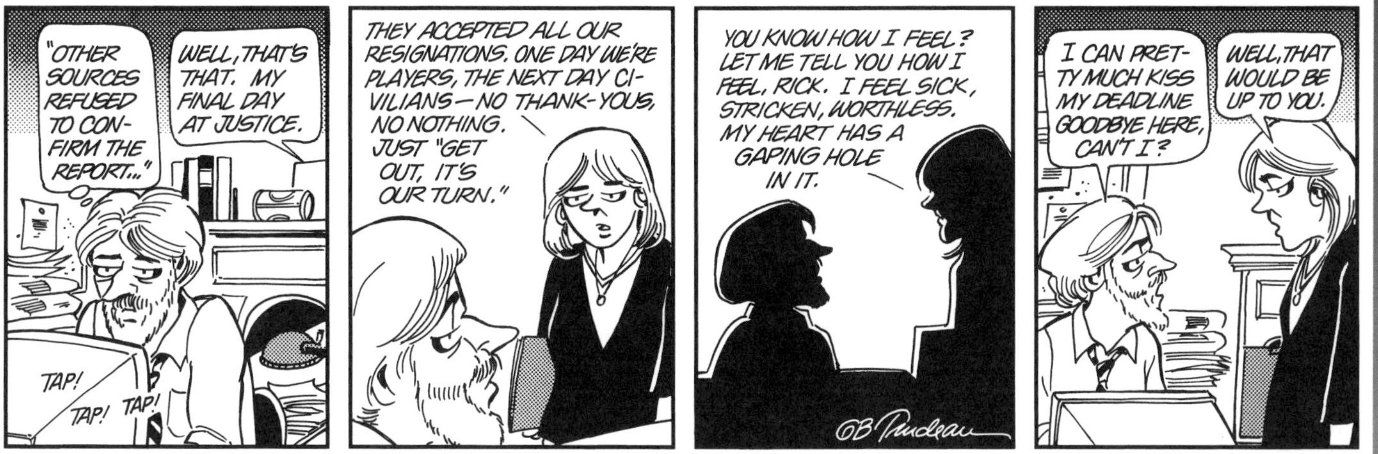
"OTHER SOURCES REFUSED TO CONFIRM THE REPORT..."
WELL, THAT'S THAT. MY FINAL DAY AT JUSTICE.
TAP! TAP! TAP!
THEY ACCEPTED ALL OUR RESIGNATIONS. ONE DAY WE'RE PLAYERS, THE NEXT DAY CIVILIANS — NO THANK-YOUS, NO NOTHING. JUST "GET OUT, IT'S OUR TURN."
YOU KNOW HOW I FEEL? LET ME TELL YOU HOW I FEEL, RICK. I FEEL SICK, STRICKEN, WORTHLESS. MY HEART HAS A GAPING HOLE IN IT.
©B Trudeau
I CAN PRETTY MUCH KISS MY DEADLINE GOODBYE HERE, CAN'T I?
WELL, THAT WOULD BE UP TO YOU.

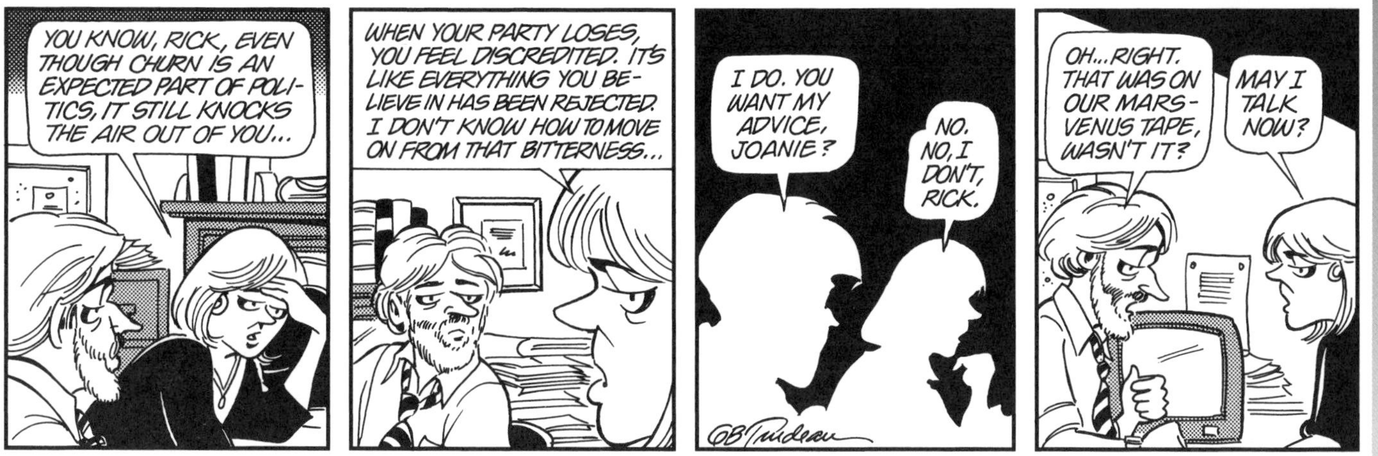
YOU KNOW, RICK, EVEN THOUGH CHURN IS AN EXPECTED PART OF POLITICS, IT STILL KNOCKS THE AIR OUT OF YOU...
WHEN YOUR PARTY LOSES, YOU FEEL DISCREDITED. IT'S LIKE EVERYTHING YOU BELIEVE IN HAS BEEN REJECTED. I DON'T KNOW HOW TO MOVE ON FROM THAT BITTERNESS...
I DO. YOU WANT MY ADVICE, JOANIE?
NO. NO, I DON'T, RICK.
©B Trudeau
OH... RIGHT. THAT WAS ON OUR MARS-VENUS TAPE, WASN'T IT?
MAY I TALK NOW?

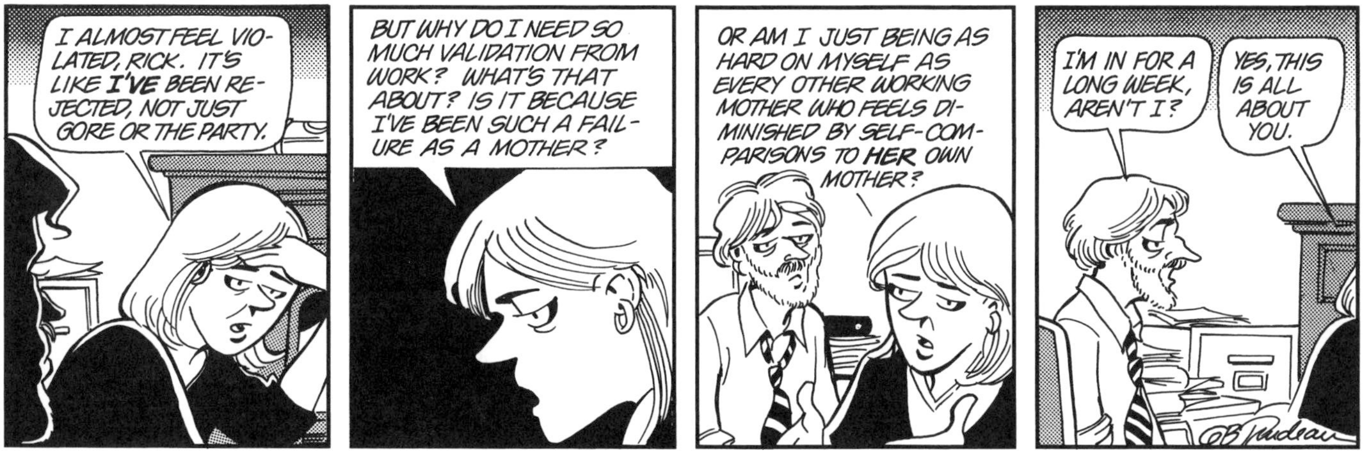
I ALMOST FEEL VIOLATED, RICK. IT'S LIKE I'VE BEEN REJECTED, NOT JUST GORE OR THE PARTY.
BUT WHY DO I NEED SO MUCH VALIDATION FROM WORK? WHAT'S THAT ABOUT? IS IT BECAUSE I'VE BEEN SUCH A FAILURE AS A MOTHER?
OR AM I JUST BEING AS HARD ON MYSELF AS EVERY OTHER WORKING MOTHER WHO FEELS DIMINISHED BY SELF-COMPARISONS TO HER OWN MOTHER?
I'M IN FOR A LONG WEEK, AREN'T I?
YES, THIS IS ALL ABOUT YOU.
©B Trudeau

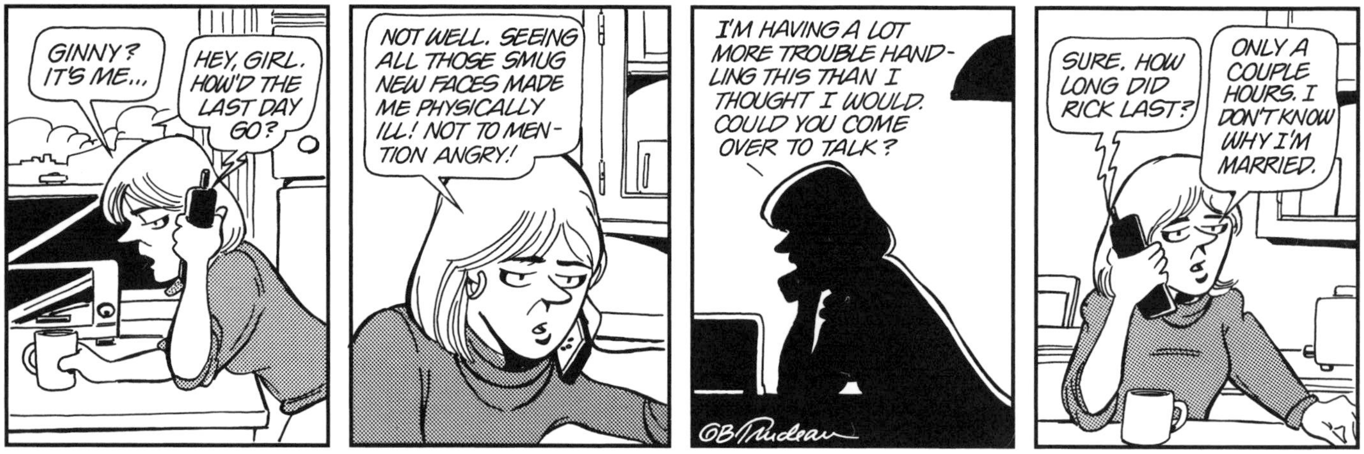
GINNY? IT'S ME...,
HEY, GIRL. HOW'D THE LAST DAY GO?
NOT WELL. SEEING ALL THOSE SMUG NEW FACES MADE ME PHYSICALLY ILL! NOT TO MENTION ANGRY!
I'M HAVING A LOT MORE TROUBLE HANDLING THIS THAN I THOUGHT I WOULD. COULD YOU COME OVER TO TALK?
SURE. HOW LONG DID RICK LAST?
ONLY A COUPLE HOURS. I DON'T KNOW WHY I'M MARRIED.
©B Trudeau

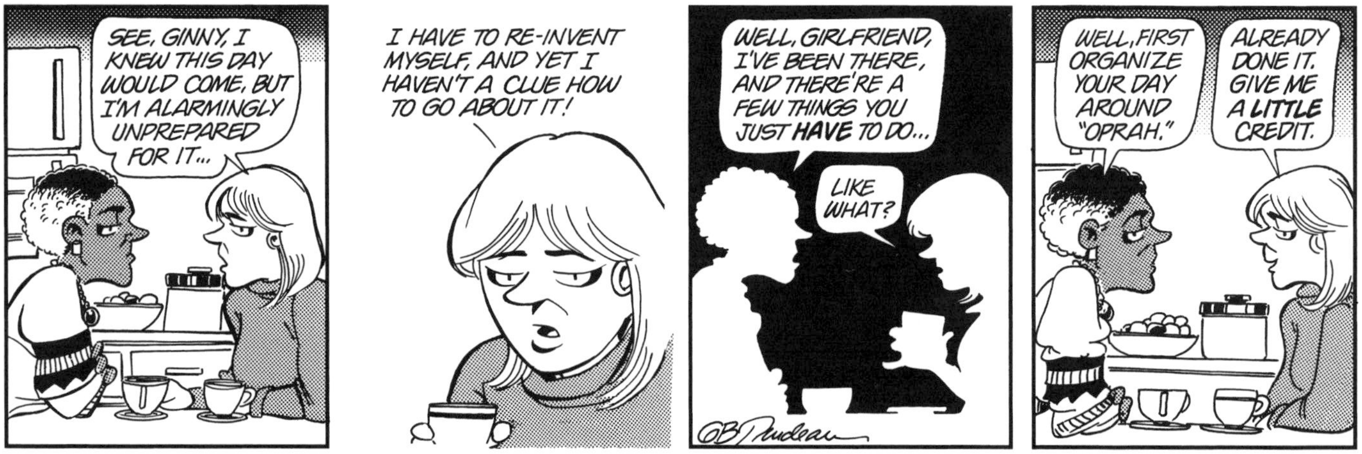
SEE, GINNY, I KNEW THIS DAY WOULD COME, BUT I'M ALARMINGLY UNPREPARED FOR IT...
I HAVE TO RE-INVENT MYSELF, AND YET I HAVEN'T A CLUE HOW TO GO ABOUT IT!
WELL, GIRLFRIEND, I'VE BEEN THERE, AND THERE'RE A FEW THINGS YOU JUST HAVE TO DO...
LIKE WHAT?
WELL, FIRST ORGANIZE YOUR DAY AROUND "OPRAH."
ALREADY DONE IT. GIVE ME A LITTLE CREDIT.
©B Trudeau

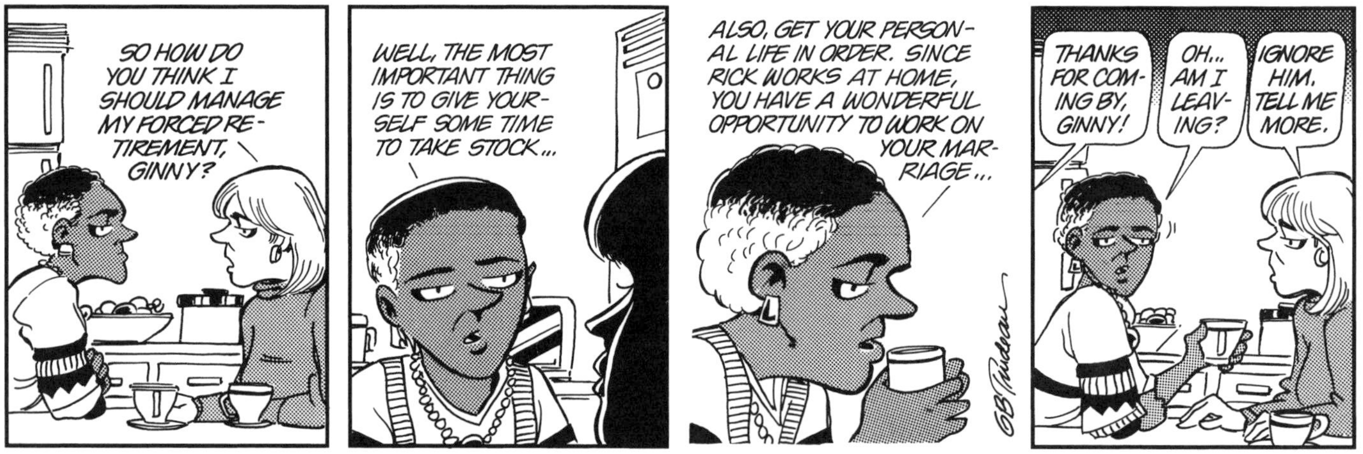
SO HOW DO YOU THINK I SHOULD MANAGE MY FORCED RETIREMENT, GINNY?
WELL, THE MOST IMPORTANT THING IS TO GIVE YOURSELF SOME TIME TO TAKE STOCK...
ALSO, GET YOUR PERSONAL LIFE IN ORDER. SINCE RICK WORKS AT HOME, YOU HAVE A WONDERFUL OPPORTUNITY TO WORK ON YOUR MARRIAGE...
THANKS FOR COMING BY, GINNY!
OH... AM I LEAVING?
IGNORE HIM. TELL ME MORE.
©B Trudeau

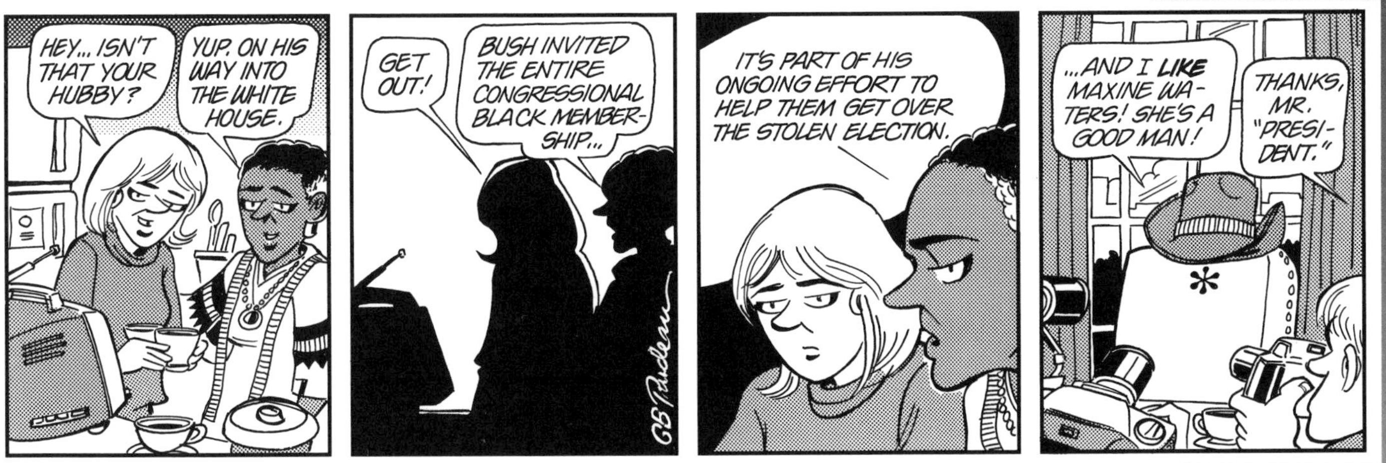
HEY... ISN'T THAT YOUR HUBBY?
YUP. ON HIS WAY INTO THE WHITE HOUSE.
GET OUT!
BUSH INVITED THE ENTIRE CONGRESSIONAL BLACK MEMBERSHIP...
IT'S PART OF HIS ONGOING EFFORT TO HELP THEM GET OVER THE STOLEN ELECTION.
...AND I LIKE MAXINE WATERS! SHE'S A GOOD MAN!
THANKS, MR. "PRESIDENT."

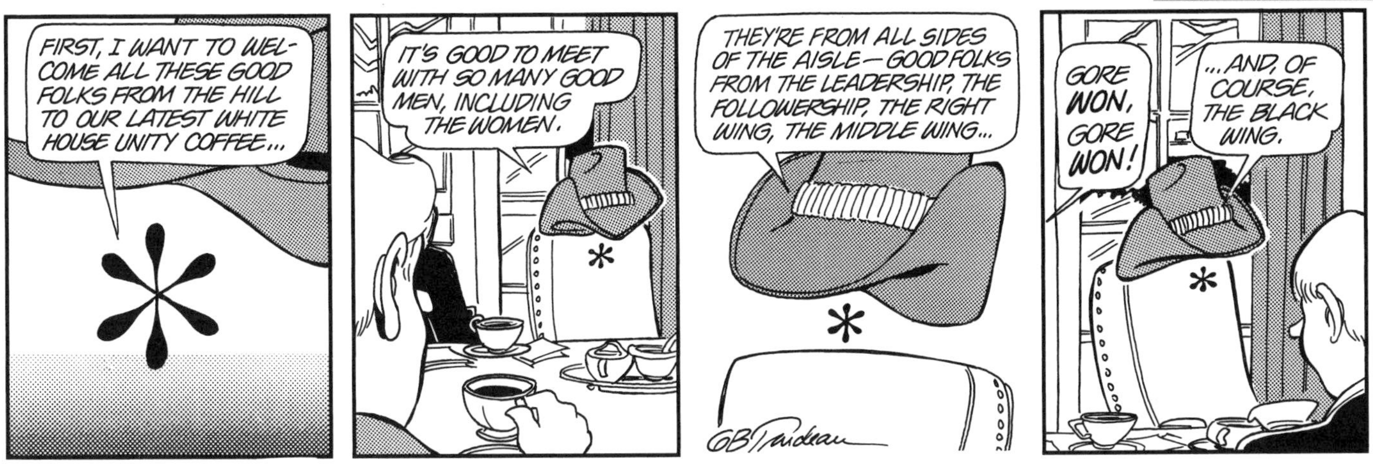
FIRST, I WANT TO WELCOME ALL THESE GOOD FOLKS FROM THE HILL TO OUR LATEST WHITE HOUSE UNITY COFFEE...
IT'S GOOD TO MEET WITH SO MANY GOOD MEN, INCLUDING THE WOMEN.
THEY'RE FROM ALL SIDES OF THE AISLE — GOOD FOLKS FROM THE LEADERSHIP, THE FOLLOWERSHIP, THE RIGHT WING, THE MIDDLE WING...
GORE WON, GORE WON!
...AND, OF COURSE, THE BLACK WING.

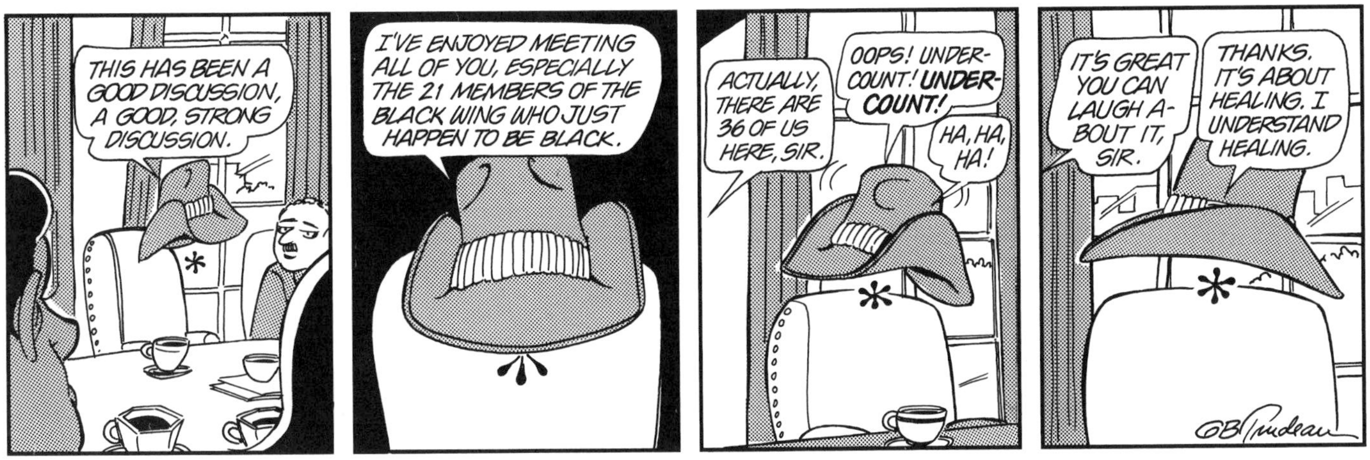
THIS HAS BEEN A GOOD DISCUSSION, A GOOD, STRONG DISCUSSION.
I'VE ENJOYED MEETING ALL OF YOU, ESPECIALLY THE 21 MEMBERS OF THE BLACK WING WHO JUST HAPPEN TO BE BLACK.
ACTUALLY, THERE ARE 36 OF US HERE, SIR.
OOPS! UNDERCOUNT! UNDERCOUNT!
HA, HA, HA!
IT'S GREAT YOU CAN LAUGH ABOUT IT, SIR.
THANKS. IT'S ABOUT HEALING. I UNDERSTAND HEALING.

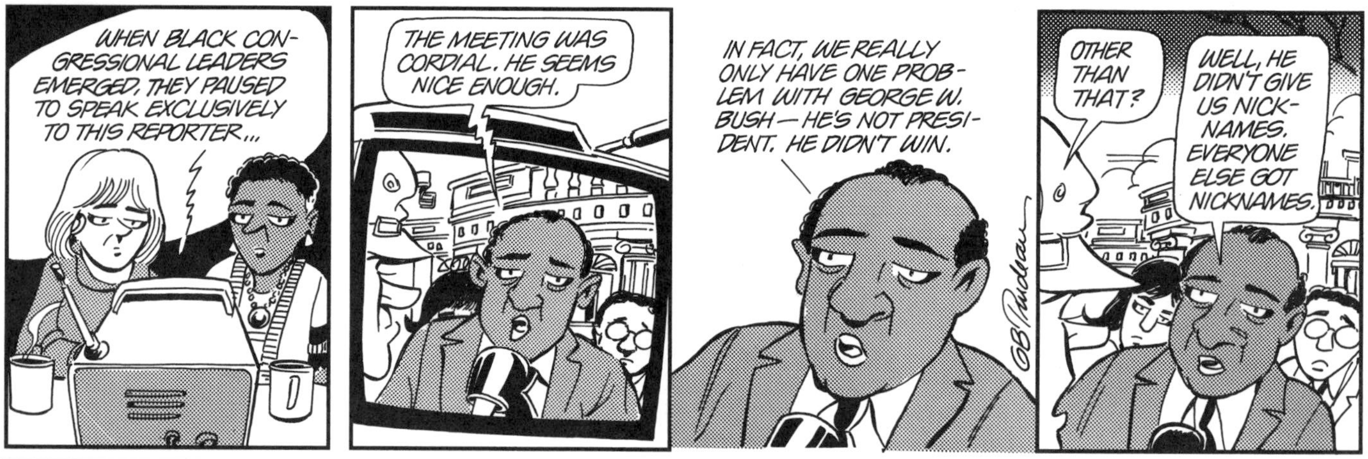
WHEN BLACK CON-GRESSIONAL LEADERS EMERGED, THEY PAUSED TO SPEAK EXCLUSIVELY TO THIS REPORTER...
THE MEETING WAS CORDIAL. HE SEEMS NICE ENOUGH.
IN FACT, WE REALLY ONLY HAVE ONE PROB-LEM WITH GEORGE W. BUSH — HE'S NOT PRESI-DENT. HE DIDN'T WIN.
OTHER THAN THAT?
WELL, HE DIDN'T GIVE US NICK-NAMES. EVERYONE ELSE GOT NICKNAMES.

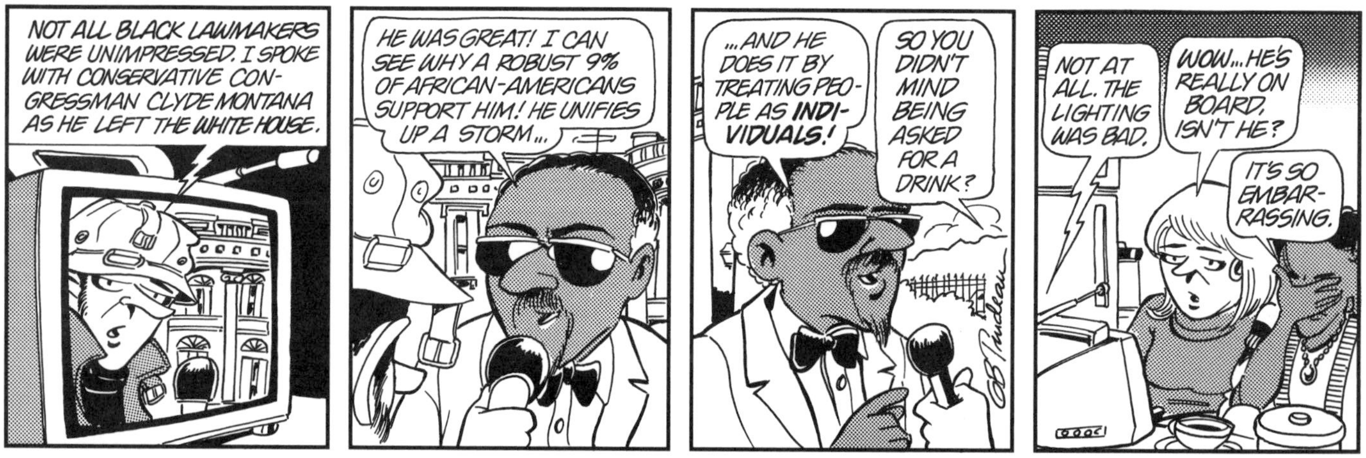
NOT ALL BLACK LAWMAKERS WERE UNIMPRESSED. I SPOKE WITH CONSERVATIVE CON-GRESSMAN CLYDE MONTANA AS HE LEFT THE WHITE HOUSE.
HE WAS GREAT! I CAN SEE WHY A ROBUST 9% OF AFRICAN-AMERICANS SUPPORT HIM! HE UNIFIES UP A STORM...
...AND HE DOES IT BY TREATING PEO-PLE AS INDI-VIDUALS!
SO YOU DIDN'T MIND BEING ASKED FOR A DRINK?
NOT AT ALL. THE LIGHTING WAS BAD.
WOW... HE'S REALLY ON BOARD, ISN'T HE?
IT'S SO EMBAR-RASSING.

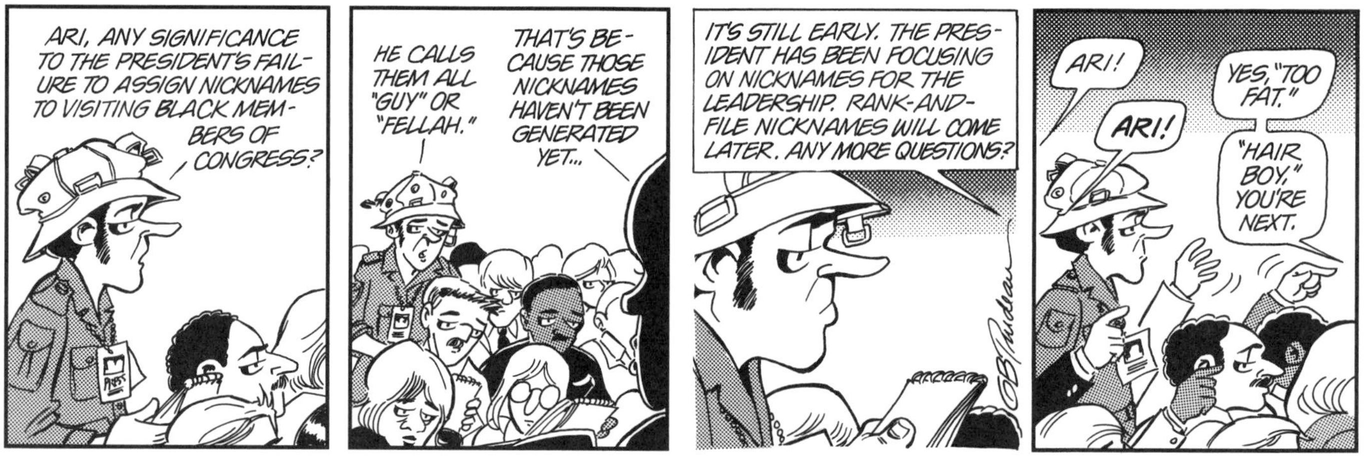
ARI, ANY SIGNIFICANCE TO THE PRESIDENT'S FAIL-URE TO ASSIGN NICKNAMES TO VISITING BLACK MEM-BERS OF CONGRESS?
HE CALLS THEM ALL "GUY" OR "FELLAH."
THAT'S BE-CAUSE THOSE NICKNAMES HAVEN'T BEEN GENERATED YET...
IT'S STILL EARLY. THE PRES-IDENT HAS BEEN FOCUSING ON NICKNAMES FOR THE LEADERSHIP. RANK-AND-FILE NICKNAMES WILL COME LATER. ANY MORE QUESTIONS?
ARI!
ARI!
YES, "TOO FAT."
"HAIR BOY," YOU'RE NEXT.

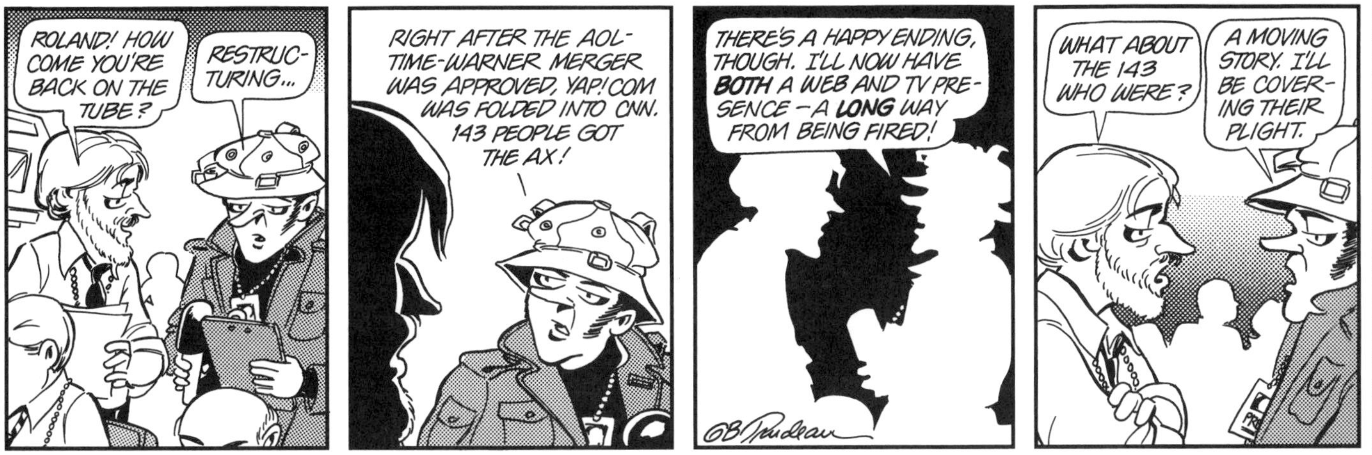
ROLAND! HOW COME YOU'RE BACK ON THE TUBE?
RESTRUC-TURING...
RIGHT AFTER THE AOL-TIME-WARNER MERGER WAS APPROVED, YAP!COM WAS FOLDED INTO CNN. 143 PEOPLE GOT THE AX!
THERE'S A HAPPY ENDING, THOUGH. I'LL NOW HAVE BOTH A WEB AND TV PRESENCE – A LONG WAY FROM BEING FIRED!
WHAT ABOUT THE 143 WHO WERE?
A MOVING STORY. I'LL BE COVERING THEIR PLIGHT.

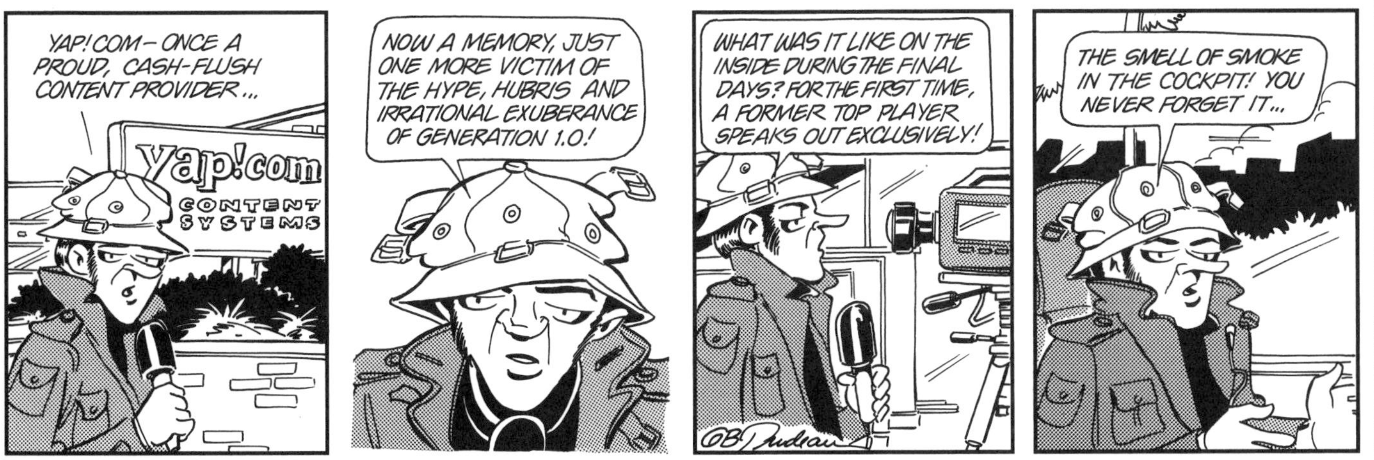
YAP!COM – ONCE A PROUD, CASH-FLUSH CONTENT PROVIDER...
yap!com
CONTENT SYSTEMS
NOW A MEMORY, JUST ONE MORE VICTIM OF THE HYPE, HUBRIS AND IRRATIONAL EXUBERANCE OF GENERATION 1.0!
WHAT WAS IT LIKE ON THE INSIDE DURING THE FINAL DAYS? FOR THE FIRST TIME, A FORMER TOP PLAYER SPEAKS OUT EXCLUSIVELY!
THE SMELL OF SMOKE IN THE COCKPIT! YOU NEVER FORGET IT...

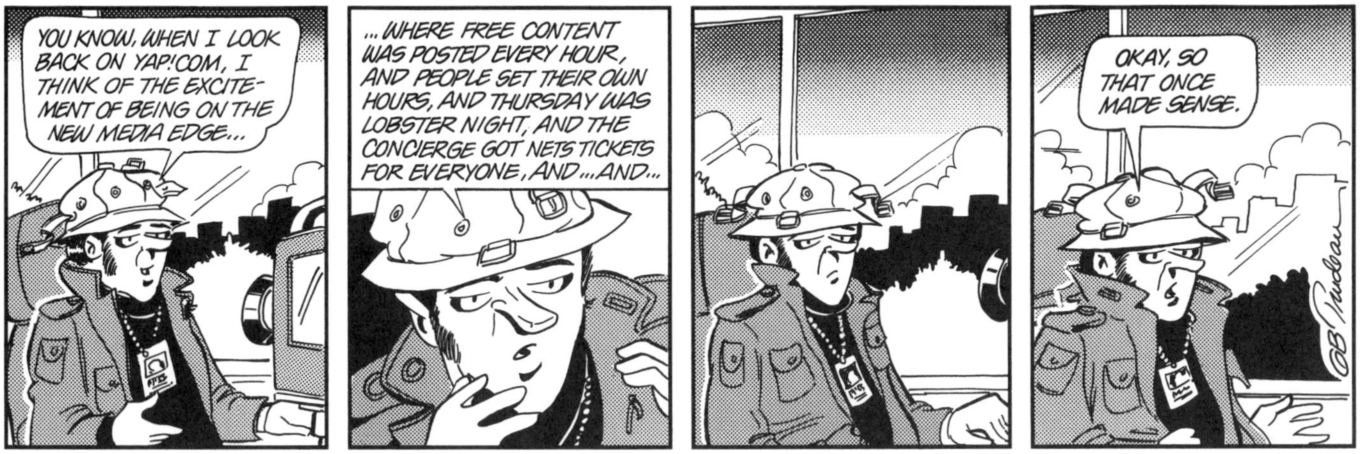
YOU KNOW, WHEN I LOOK BACK ON YAP!COM, I THINK OF THE EXCITEMENT OF BEING ON THE NEW MEDIA EDGE...
...WHERE FREE CONTENT WAS POSTED EVERY HOUR, AND PEOPLE SET THEIR OWN HOURS, AND THURSDAY WAS LOBSTER NIGHT, AND THE CONCIERGE GOT NETS TICKETS FOR EVERYONE, AND...AND...
OKAY, SO THAT ONCE MADE SENSE.

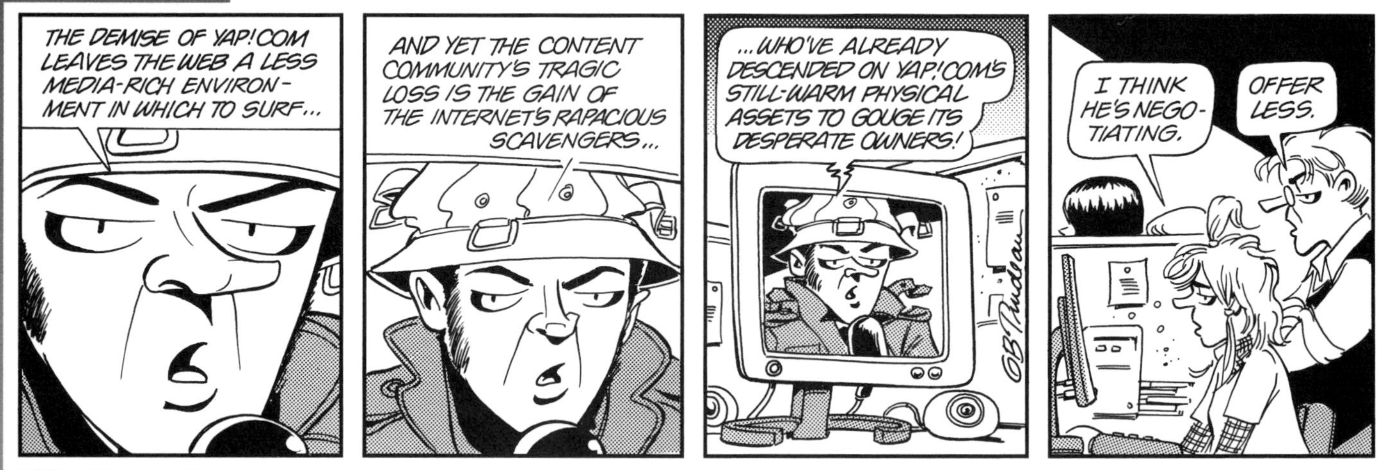
THE DEMISE OF YAP!COM LEAVES THE WEB A LESS MEDIA-RICH ENVIRON-MENT IN WHICH TO SURF...
AND YET THE CONTENT COMMUNITY'S TRAGIC LOSS IS THE GAIN OF THE INTERNET'S RAPACIOUS SCAVENGERS...
...WHO'VE ALREADY DESCENDED ON YAP!COM'S STILL-WARM PHYSICAL ASSETS TO GOUGE ITS DESPERATE OWNERS!
I THINK HE'S NEGO-TIATING.
OFFER LESS.

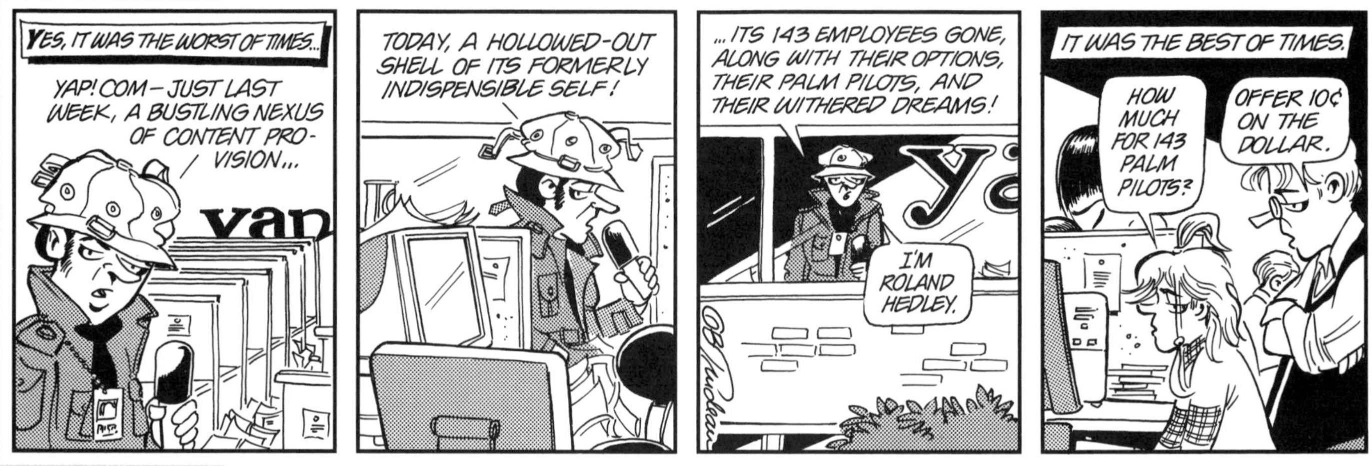
YES, IT WAS THE WORST OF TIMES...
YAP!COM — JUST LAST WEEK, A BUSTLING NEXUS OF CONTENT PRO-VISION...
TODAY, A HOLLOWED-OUT SHELL OF ITS FORMERLY INDISPENSIBLE SELF!
...ITS 143 EMPLOYEES GONE, ALONG WITH THEIR OPTIONS, THEIR PALM PILOTS, AND THEIR WITHERED DREAMS!
I'M ROLAND HEDLEY.
IT WAS THE BEST OF TIMES.
HOW MUCH FOR 143 PALM PILOTS?
OFFER 10¢ ON THE DOLLAR.

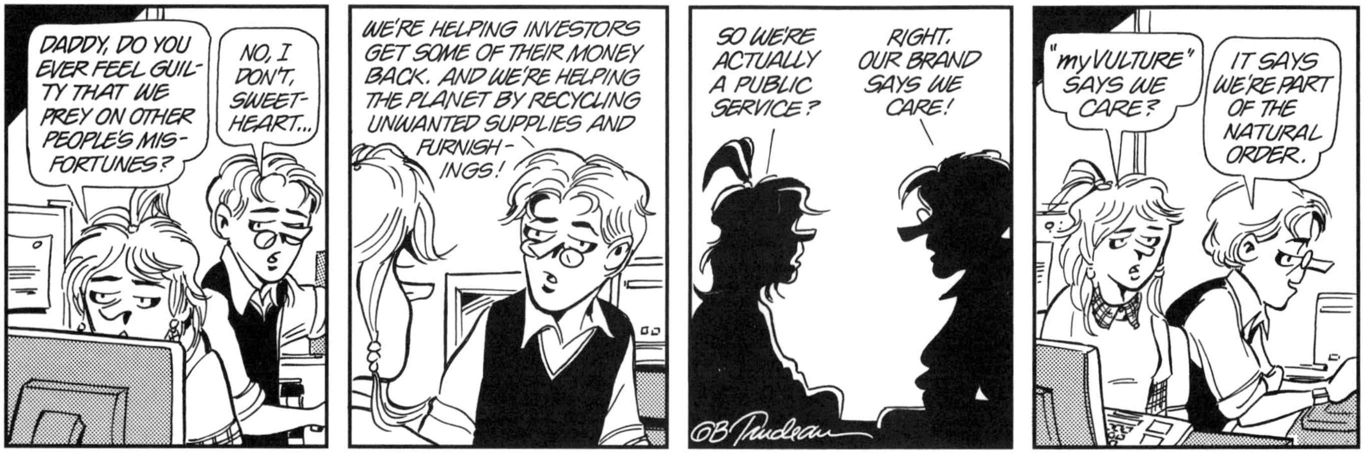
DADDY, DO YOU EVER FEEL GUIL-TY THAT WE PREY ON OTHER PEOPLE'S MIS-FORTUNES?
NO, I DON'T, SWEET-HEART...
WE'RE HELPING INVESTORS GET SOME OF THEIR MONEY BACK. AND WE'RE HELPING THE PLANET BY RECYCLING UNWANTED SUPPLIES AND FURNISH-INGS!
SO WE'RE ACTUALLY A PUBLIC SERVICE?
RIGHT. OUR BRAND SAYS WE CARE!
"myVULTURE" SAYS WE CARE?
IT SAYS WE'RE PART OF THE NATURAL ORDER.

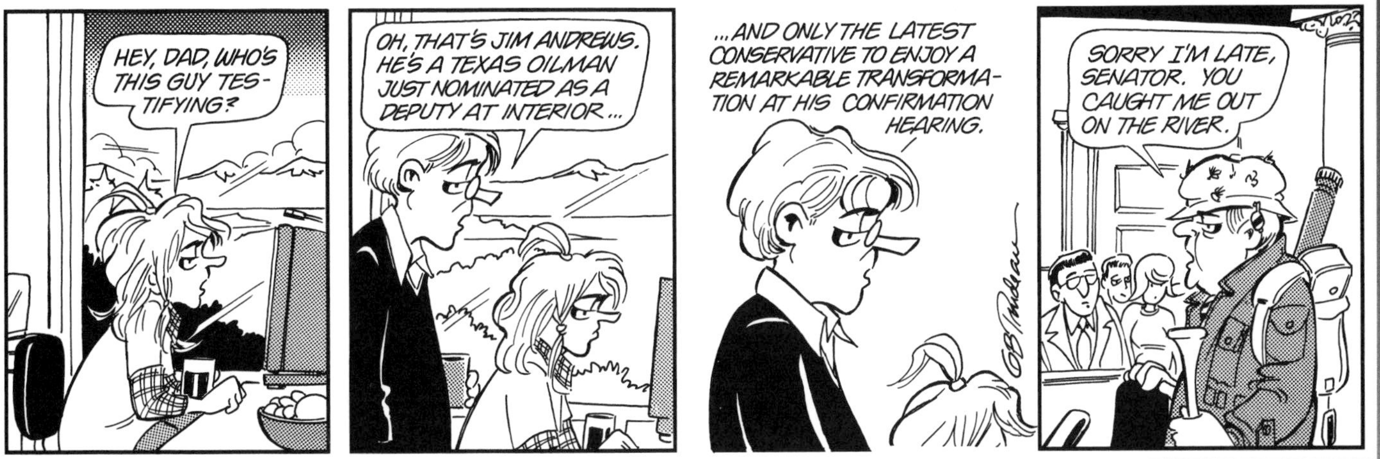
HEY, DAD, WHO'S THIS GUY TES-TIFYING?
OH, THAT'S JIM ANDREWS. HE'S A TEXAS OILMAN JUST NOMINATED AS A DEPUTY AT INTERIOR...
...AND ONLY THE LATEST CONSERVATIVE TO ENJOY A REMARKABLE TRANSFORMA-TION AT HIS CONFIRMATION HEARING.
SORRY I'M LATE, SENATOR. YOU CAUGHT ME OUT ON THE RIVER.

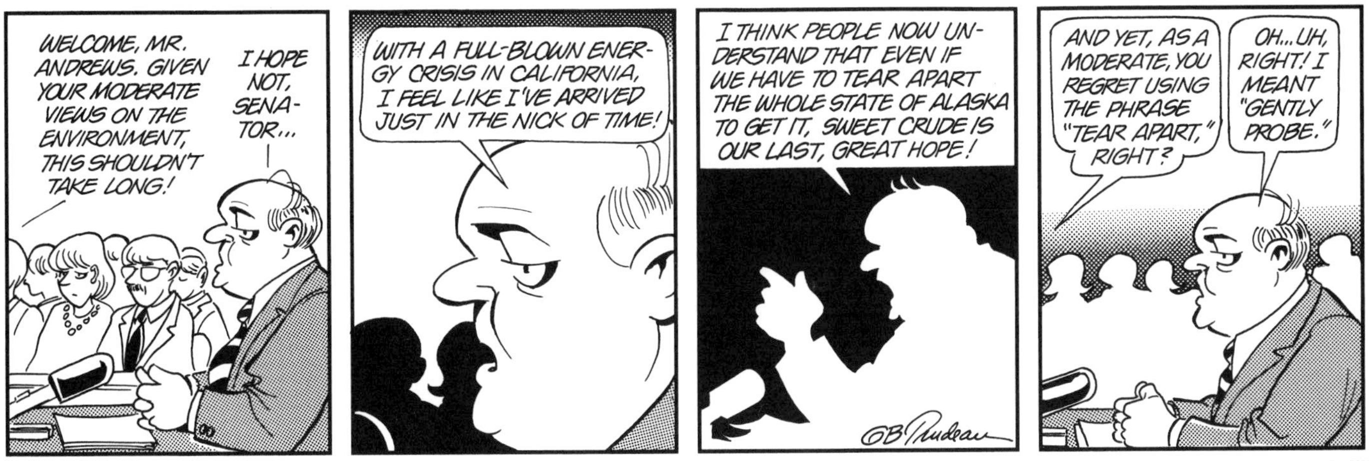
WELCOME, MR. ANDREWS. GIVEN YOUR MODERATE VIEWS ON THE ENVIRONMENT, THIS SHOULDN'T TAKE LONG!
I HOPE NOT, SENA-TOR...
WITH A FULL-BLOWN ENER-GY CRISIS IN CALIFORNIA, I FEEL LIKE I'VE ARRIVED JUST IN THE NICK OF TIME!
I THINK PEOPLE NOW UN-DERSTAND THAT EVEN IF WE HAVE TO TEAR APART THE WHOLE STATE OF ALASKA TO GET IT, SWEET CRUDE IS OUR LAST, GREAT HOPE!
AND YET, AS A MODERATE, YOU REGRET USING THE PHRASE "TEAR APART," RIGHT?
OH...UH, RIGHT! I MEANT "GENTLY PROBE."

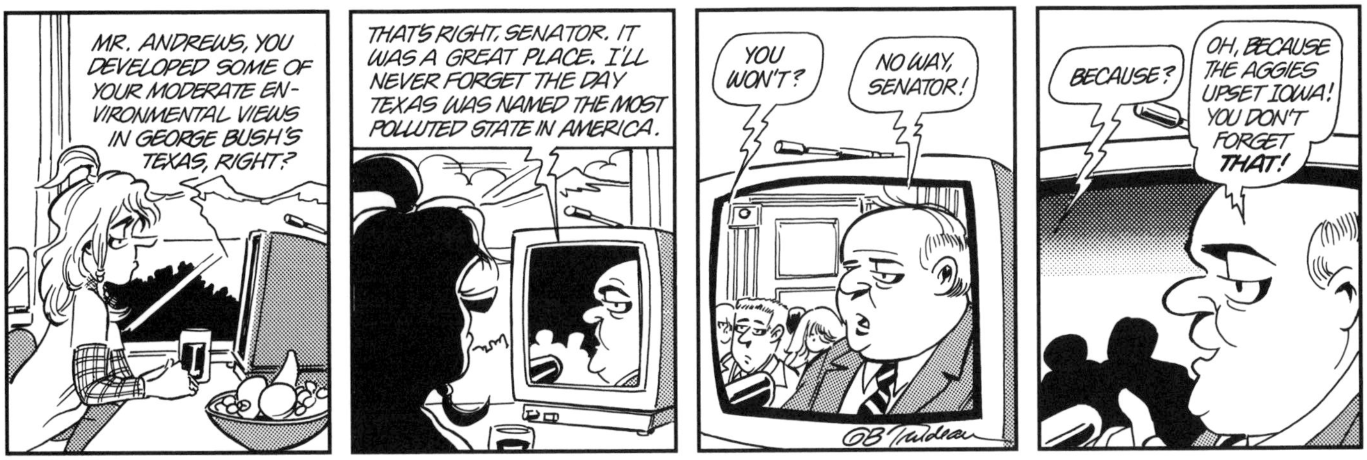
MR. ANDREWS, YOU DEVELOPED SOME OF YOUR MODERATE EN-VIRONMENTAL VIEWS IN GEORGE BUSH'S TEXAS, RIGHT?
THAT'S RIGHT, SENATOR. IT WAS A GREAT PLACE. I'LL NEVER FORGET THE DAY TEXAS WAS NAMED THE MOST POLLUTED STATE IN AMERICA.
YOU WON'T?
NO WAY, SENATOR!
BECAUSE?
OH, BECAUSE THE AGGIES UPSET IOWA! YOU DON'T FORGET THAT!

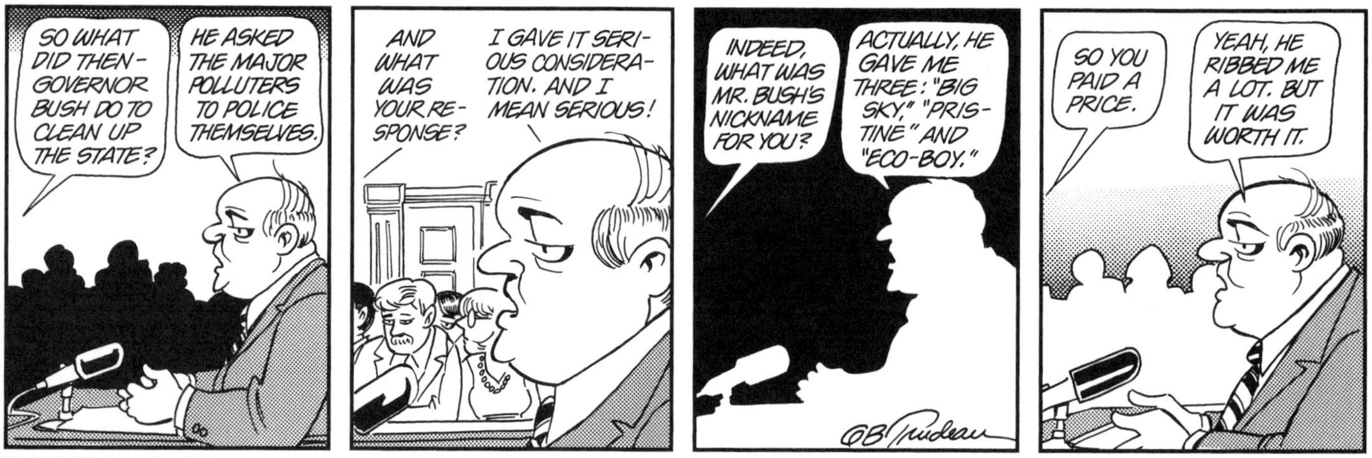
SO WHAT DID THEN-GOVERNOR BUSH DO TO CLEAN UP THE STATE?
HE ASKED THE MAJOR POLLUTERS TO POLICE THEMSELVES.
AND WHAT WAS YOUR RESPONSE?
I GAVE IT SERIOUS CONSIDERATION. AND I MEAN SERIOUS!
INDEED, WHAT WAS MR. BUSH'S NICKNAME FOR YOU?
ACTUALLY, HE GAVE ME THREE: "BIG SKY," "PRISTINE" AND "ECO-BOY."
SO YOU PAID A PRICE.
YEAH, HE RIBBED ME A LOT. BUT IT WAS WORTH IT.

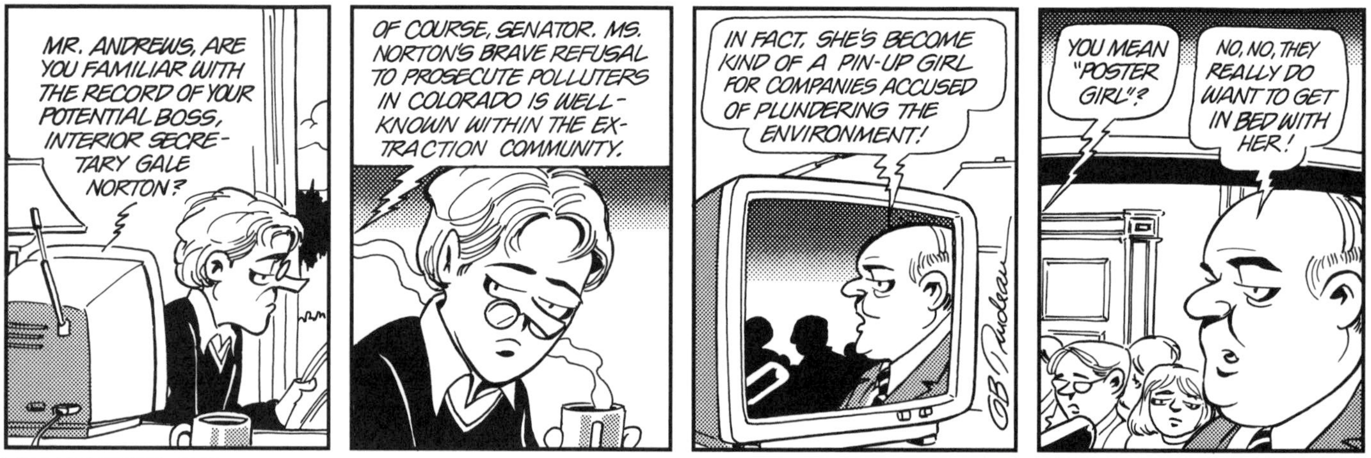
MR. ANDREWS, ARE YOU FAMILIAR WITH THE RECORD OF YOUR POTENTIAL BOSS, INTERIOR SECRETARY GALE NORTON?
OF COURSE, SENATOR. MS. NORTON'S BRAVE REFUSAL TO PROSECUTE POLLUTERS IN COLORADO IS WELL-KNOWN WITHIN THE EXTRACTION COMMUNITY.
IN FACT, SHE'S BECOME KIND OF A PIN-UP GIRL FOR COMPANIES ACCUSED OF PLUNDERING THE ENVIRONMENT!
YOU MEAN "POSTER GIRL"?
NO, NO, THEY REALLY DO WANT TO GET IN BED WITH HER!

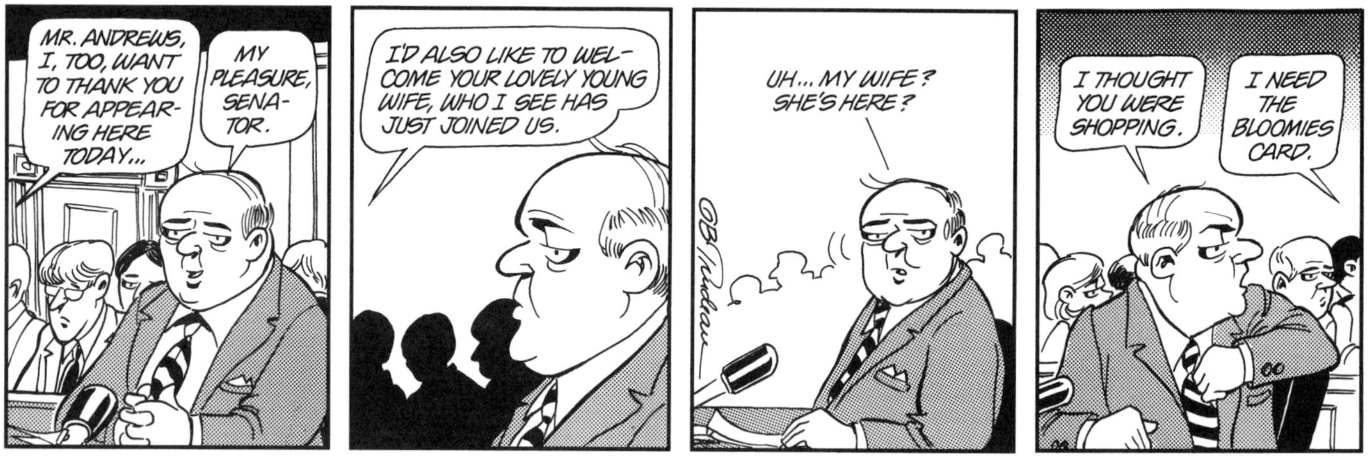
MR. ANDREWS, I, TOO, WANT TO THANK YOU FOR APPEARING HERE TODAY...
MY PLEASURE, SENATOR.
I'D ALSO LIKE TO WELCOME YOUR LOVELY YOUNG WIFE, WHO I SEE HAS JUST JOINED US.
UH... MY WIFE? SHE'S HERE?
I THOUGHT YOU WERE SHOPPING.
I NEED THE BLOOMIES CARD.

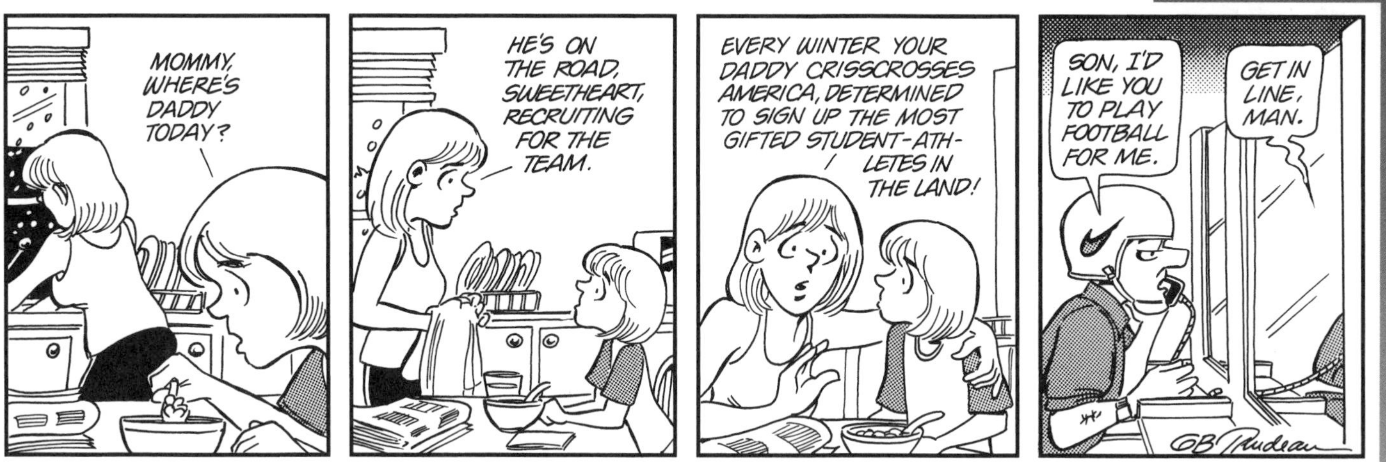
MOMMY, WHERE'S DADDY TODAY?
HE'S ON THE ROAD, SWEETHEART, RECRUITING FOR THE TEAM.
EVERY WINTER YOUR DADDY CRISSCROSSES AMERICA, DETERMINED TO SIGN UP THE MOST GIFTED STUDENT-ATHLETES IN THE LAND!
SON, I'D LIKE YOU TO PLAY FOOTBALL FOR ME.
GET IN LINE, MAN.
©B. Trudeau

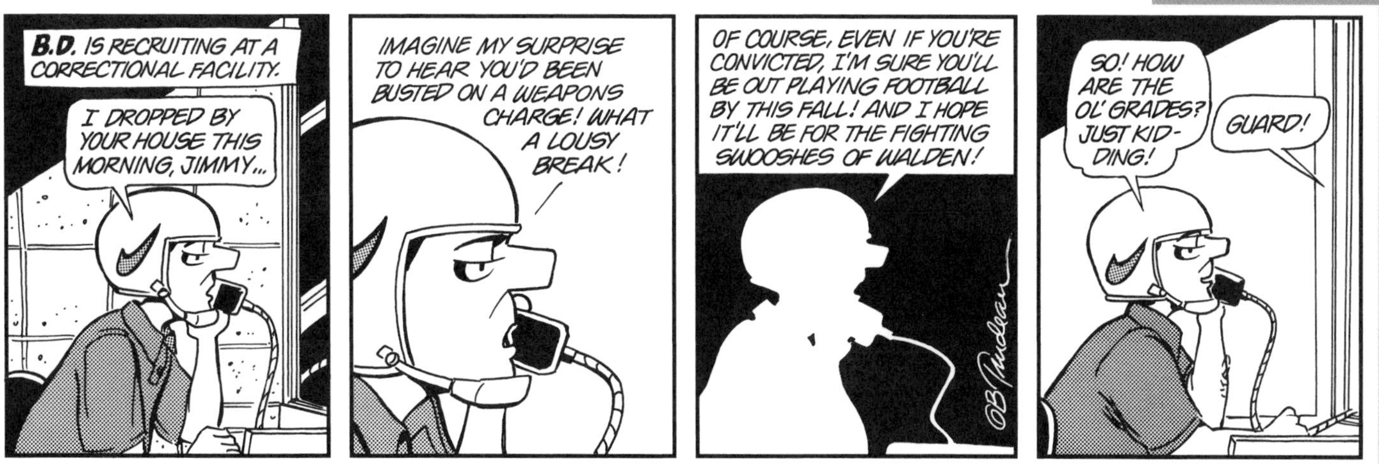
B.D. IS RECRUITING AT A CORRECTIONAL FACILITY.
I DROPPED BY YOUR HOUSE THIS MORNING, JIMMY...
IMAGINE MY SURPRISE TO HEAR YOU'D BEEN BUSTED ON A WEAPONS CHARGE! WHAT A LOUSY BREAK!
OF COURSE, EVEN IF YOU'RE CONVICTED, I'M SURE YOU'LL BE OUT PLAYING FOOTBALL BY THIS FALL! AND I HOPE IT'LL BE FOR THE FIGHTING SWOOSHES OF WALDEN!
©B. Trudeau
SO! HOW ARE THE OL' GRADES? JUST KIDDING!
GUARD!

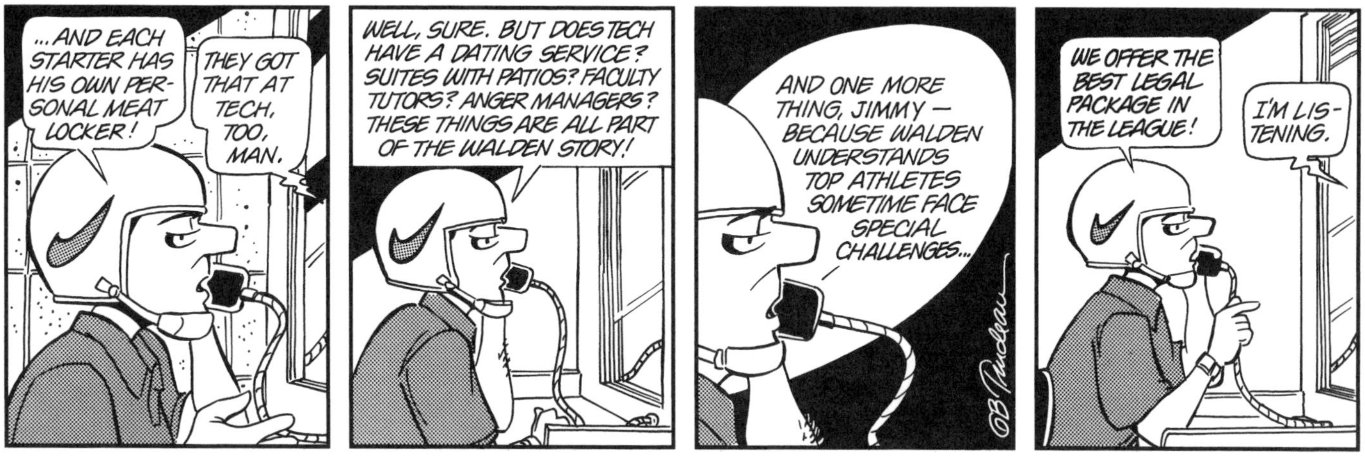
...AND EACH STARTER HAS HIS OWN PERSONAL MEAT LOCKER!
THEY GOT THAT AT TECH, TOO, MAN.
WELL, SURE. BUT DOES TECH HAVE A DATING SERVICE? SUITES WITH PATIOS? FACULTY TUTORS? ANGER MANAGERS? THESE THINGS ARE ALL PART OF THE WALDEN STORY!
AND ONE MORE THING, JIMMY — BECAUSE WALDEN UNDERSTANDS TOP ATHLETES SOMETIME FACE SPECIAL CHALLENGES...
©B. Trudeau
WE OFFER THE BEST LEGAL PACKAGE IN THE LEAGUE!
I'M LISTENING.

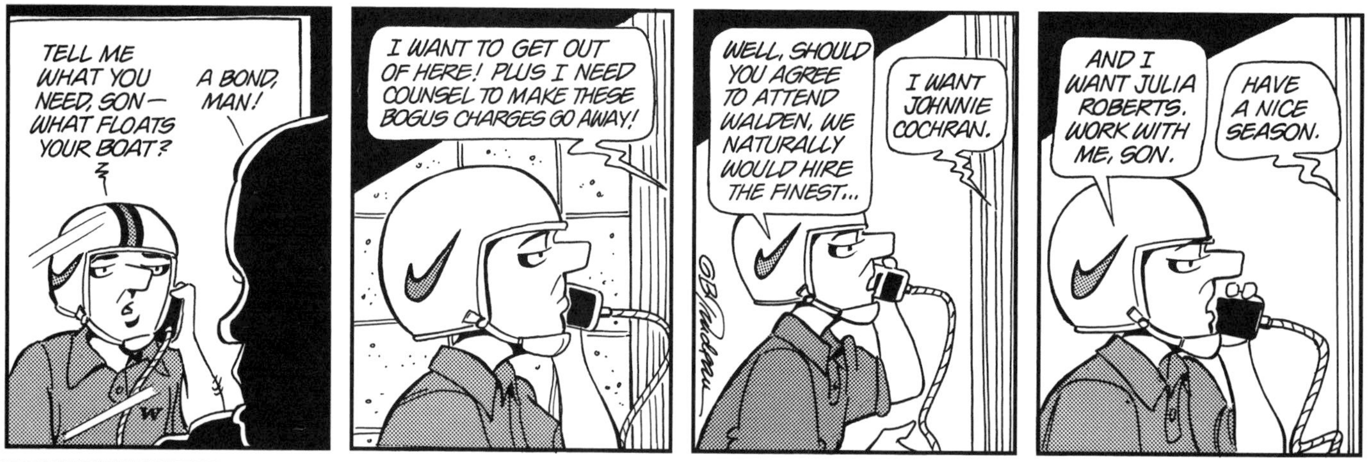
TELL ME WHAT YOU NEED, SON— WHAT FLOATS YOUR BOAT?
A BOND, MAN!
I WANT TO GET OUT OF HERE! PLUS I NEED COUNSEL TO MAKE THESE BOGUS CHARGES GO AWAY!
WELL, SHOULD YOU AGREE TO ATTEND WALDEN, WE NATURALLY WOULD HIRE THE FINEST...
I WANT JOHNNIE COCHRAN.
AND I WANT JULIA ROBERTS. WORK WITH ME, SON.
HAVE A NICE SEASON.

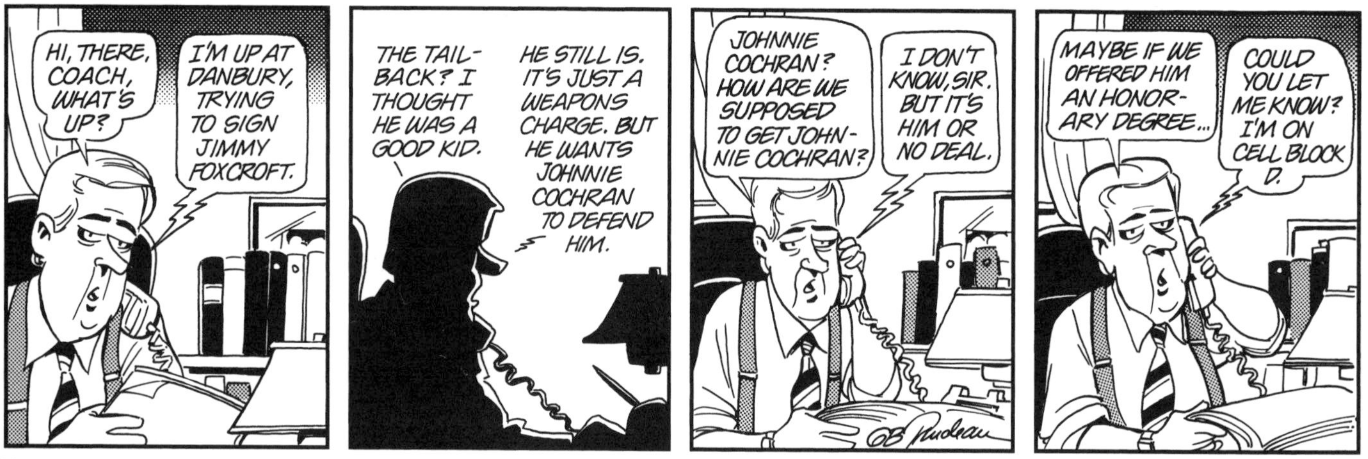
HI, THERE, COACH, WHAT'S UP?
I'M UP AT DANBURY, TRYING TO SIGN JIMMY FOXCROFT.
THE TAIL-BACK? I THOUGHT HE WAS A GOOD KID.
HE STILL IS. IT'S JUST A WEAPONS CHARGE. BUT HE WANTS JOHNNIE COCHRAN TO DEFEND HIM.
JOHNNIE COCHRAN? HOW ARE WE SUPPOSED TO GET JOHN-NIE COCHRAN?
I DON'T KNOW, SIR. BUT IT'S HIM OR NO DEAL.
MAYBE IF WE OFFERED HIM AN HONOR-ARY DEGREE...
COULD YOU LET ME KNOW? I'M ON CELL BLOCK D.

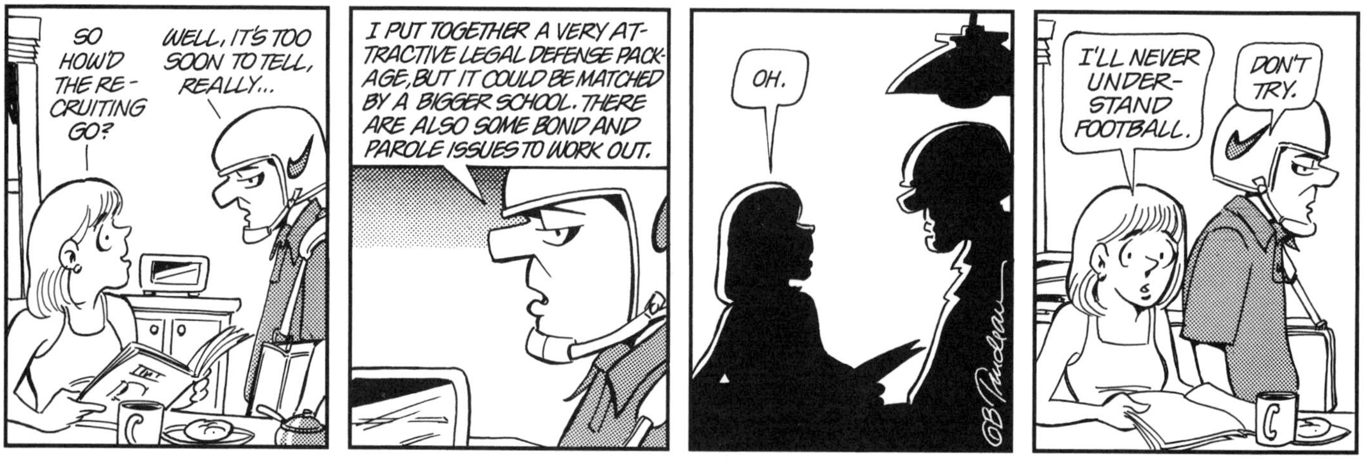
SO HOW'D THE RE-CRUITING GO?
WELL, IT'S TOO SOON TO TELL, REALLY...
I PUT TOGETHER A VERY AT-TRACTIVE LEGAL DEFENSE PACK-AGE, BUT IT COULD BE MATCHED BY A BIGGER SCHOOL. THERE ARE ALSO SOME BOND AND PAROLE ISSUES TO WORK OUT.
OH.
I'LL NEVER UNDER-STAND FOOTBALL.
DON'T TRY.

WE WANT TO PAY ATTENTION.
TAX CUTS!
WE REALLY DO.
VOUCHERS!
IT'S OUR CIVIC DUTY.
BI-PARTISANSHIP!
IF ONLY WE COULD STOP WATCHING BILL.
I DID NOT HAVE FINANCIAL RELATIONS WITH THAT WOMAN!

THE GREAT WAFFLER, STILL WITH US.
I DID NOT HAVE FINANCIAL RELATIONS WITH THAT WOMAN, MS. RICH!
THEN WHY IS THE RICH PARDON BEING INVESTIGATED BY THE FEDS?
AND WHAT ABOUT THE OTHER PARDONS TO CRONIES AND FAMILY?
WILL YOU TESTIFY BEFORE CONGRESS?
WILL RICH SEEK IMMUNITY?
WILL YOU BE RE-IMPEACHED?
THIS IS TOUGH ON THE MEDIA, ISN'T IT?
YES, SIR. REPORTERS ARE BEING CALLED OUT OF RETIREMENT.

HERE COME OL' FLIP-FLOP.
I KNOW THAT A LOT OF YOU ARE WONDERING...
...WHY SOMEONE WHO IS SO FOCUSED AND ATTUNED POLITICALLY IS SO UNDISCIPLINED AND TONE-DEAF WHEN IT COMES TO HIS PERSONAL BEHAVIOR.
WELL, LET ME TELL YOU WHY! I...
HEY... IS THAT A DONUT SHOP OVER THERE?
THIS WAY, PEOPLE!
LOOK OUT! HE'S LEADING US AGAIN!

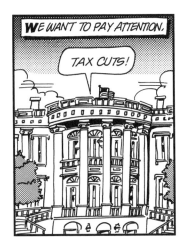

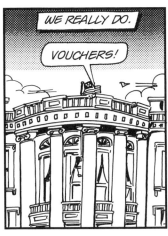

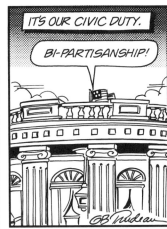

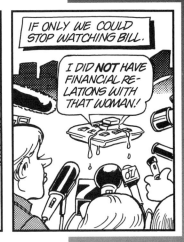

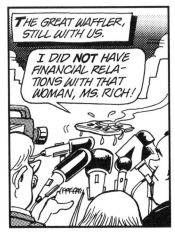

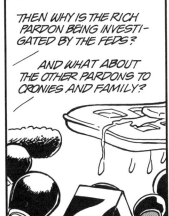

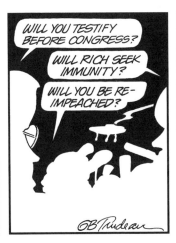

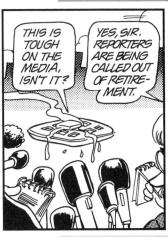

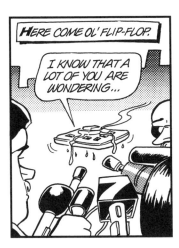

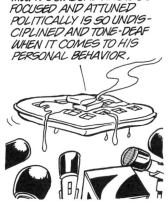

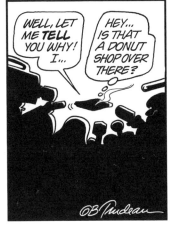

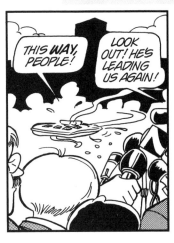

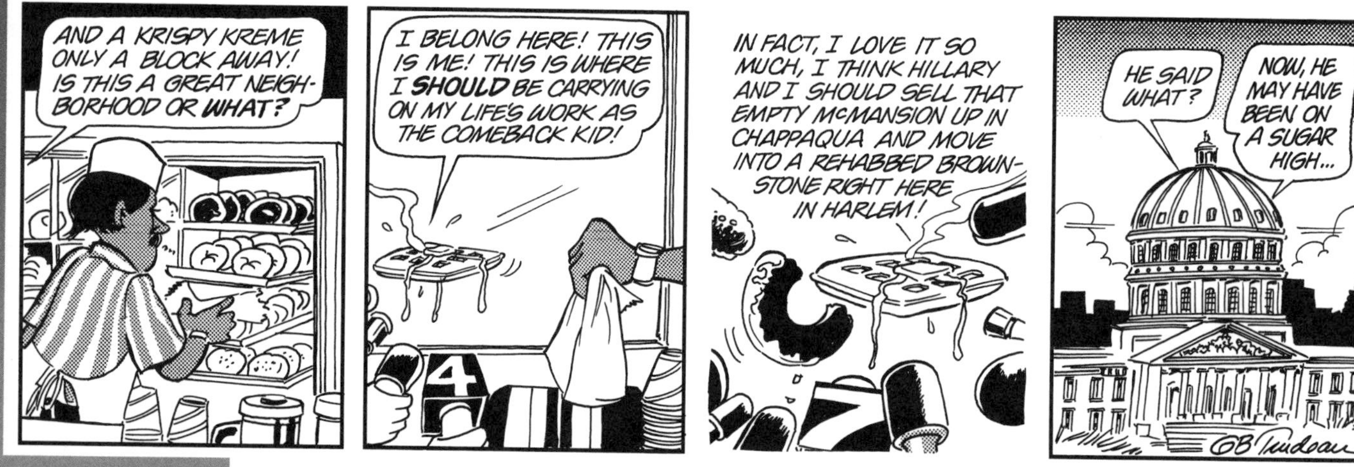
AND A KRISPY KREME ONLY A BLOCK AWAY! IS THIS A GREAT NEIGHBORHOOD OR **WHAT?**
I BELONG HERE! THIS IS ME! THIS IS WHERE I **SHOULD** BE CARRYING ON MY LIFE'S WORK AS THE COMEBACK KID!
4
IN FACT, I LOVE IT SO MUCH, I THINK HILLARY AND I SHOULD SELL THAT EMPTY McMANSION UP IN CHAPPAQUA AND MOVE INTO A REHABBED BROWNSTONE RIGHT HERE IN HARLEM!
7
HE SAID WHAT?
NOW, HE MAY HAVE BEEN ON A SUGAR HIGH...
GB Trudeau

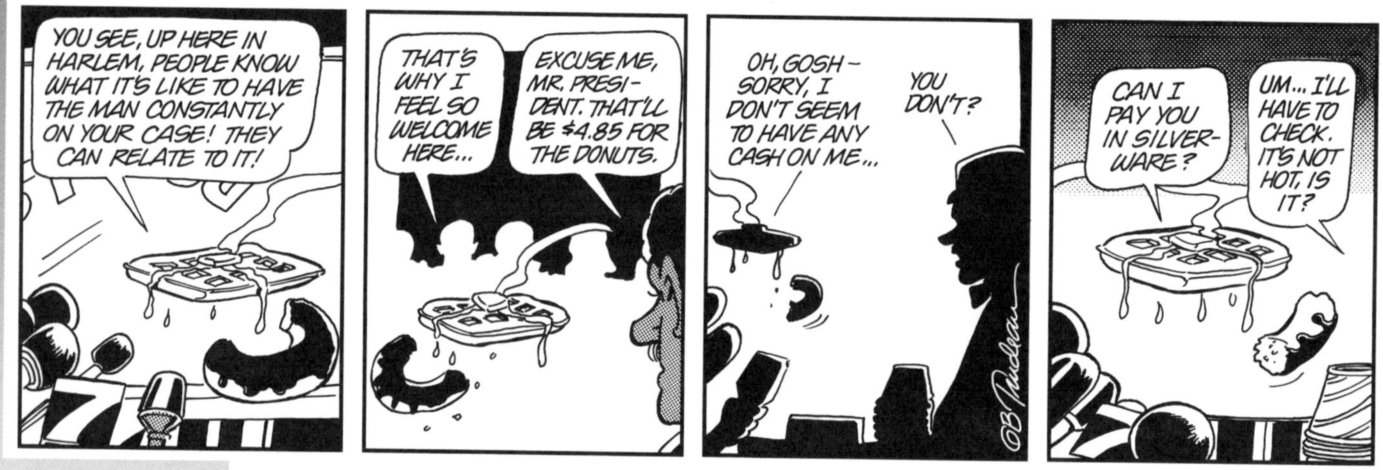
YOU SEE, UP HERE IN HARLEM, PEOPLE KNOW WHAT IT'S LIKE TO HAVE THE MAN CONSTANTLY ON YOUR CASE! THEY CAN RELATE TO IT!
7
THAT'S WHY I FEEL SO WELCOME HERE...
EXCUSE ME, MR. PRESIDENT. THAT'LL BE $4.85 FOR THE DONUTS.
OH, GOSH – SORRY, I DON'T SEEM TO HAVE ANY CASH ON ME...
YOU DON'T?
GB Trudeau
CAN I PAY YOU IN SILVERWARE?
UM... I'LL HAVE TO CHECK. IT'S NOT HOT, IS IT?
7

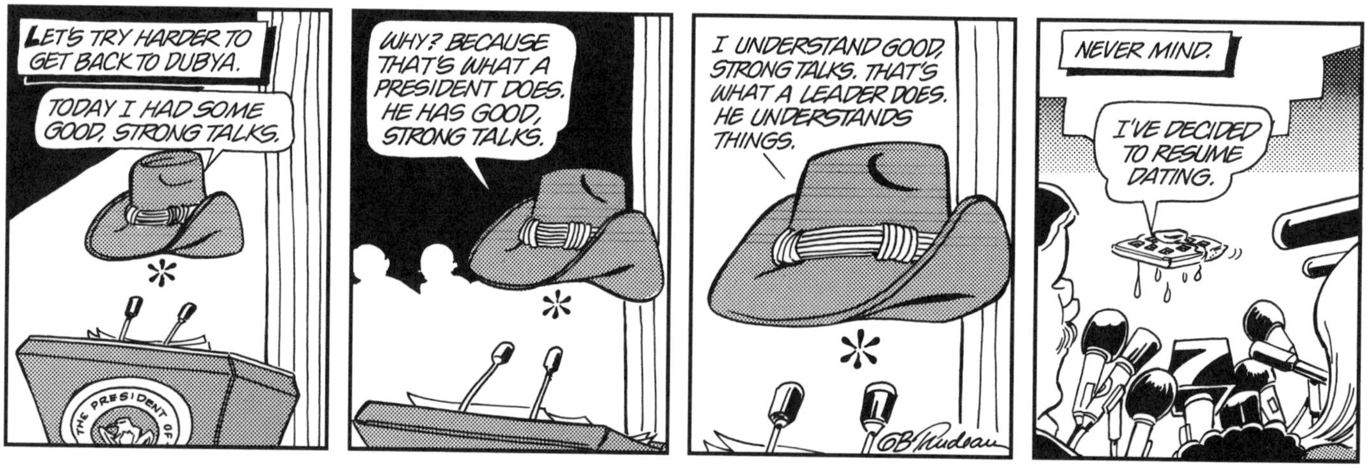
LET'S TRY HARDER TO GET BACK TO DUBYA.
TODAY I HAD SOME GOOD, STRONG TALKS.
THE PRESIDENT OF
WHY? BECAUSE THAT'S WHAT A PRESIDENT DOES. HE HAS GOOD, STRONG TALKS.
I UNDERSTAND GOOD, STRONG TALKS. THAT'S WHAT A LEADER DOES. HE UNDERSTANDS THINGS.
GB Trudeau
NEVER MIND.
I'VE DECIDED TO RESUME DATING.
7

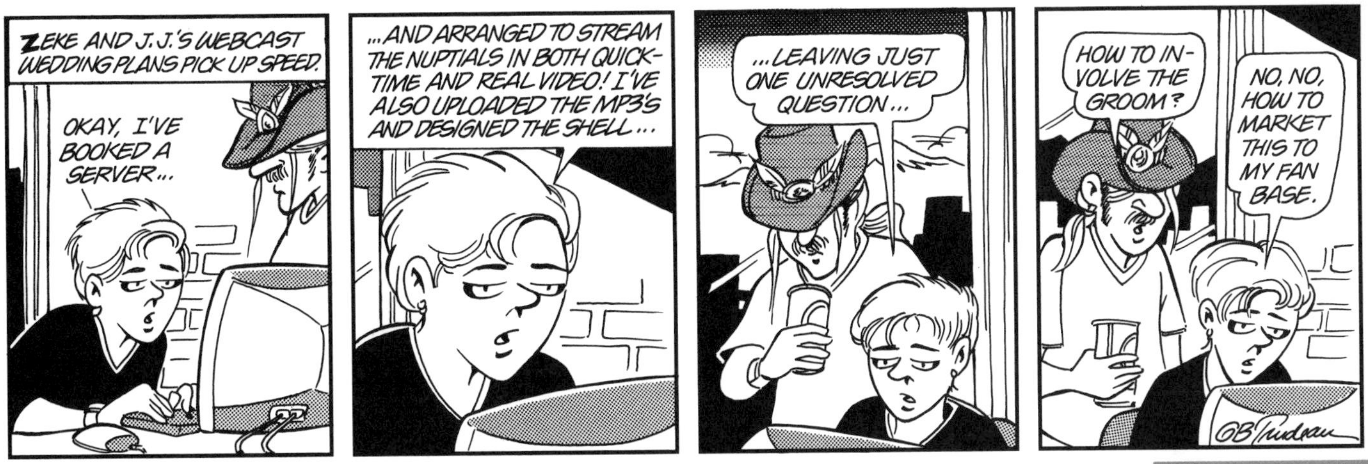
ZEKE AND J.J.'S WEBCAST WEDDING PLANS PICK UP SPEED.
OKAY, I'VE BOOKED A SERVER...
...AND ARRANGED TO STREAM THE NUPTIALS IN BOTH QUICK-TIME AND REAL VIDEO! I'VE ALSO UPLOADED THE MP3'S AND DESIGNED THE SHELL...
...LEAVING JUST ONE UNRESOLVED QUESTION...
HOW TO IN-VOLVE THE GROOM?
NO, NO, HOW TO MARKET THIS TO MY FAN BASE.

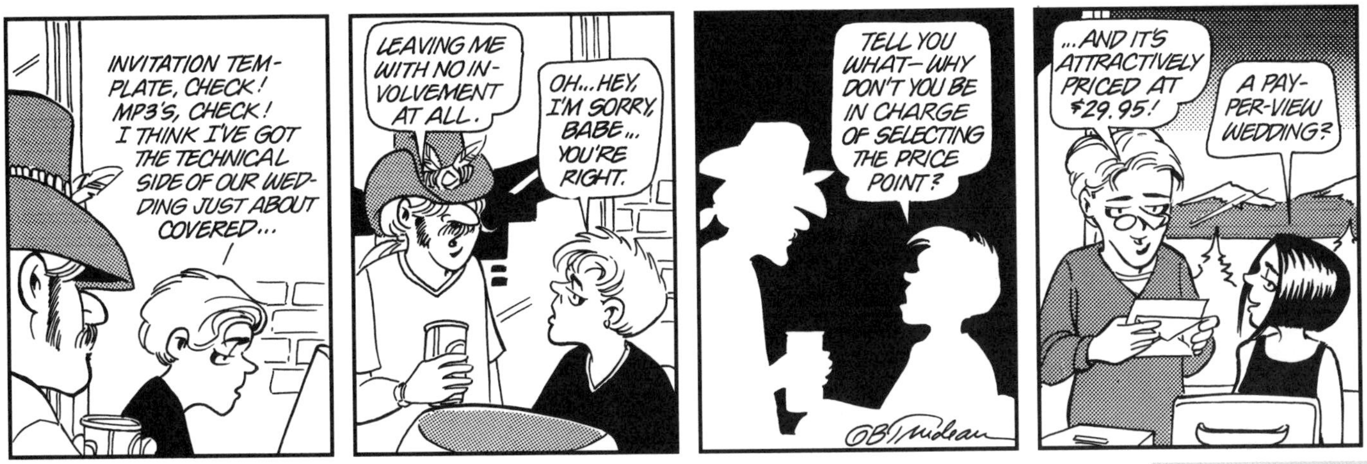
INVITATION TEM-PLATE, CHECK! MP3'S, CHECK! I THINK I'VE GOT THE TECHNICAL SIDE OF OUR WED-DING JUST ABOUT COVERED...
LEAVING ME WITH NO IN-VOLVEMENT AT ALL.
OH... HEY, I'M SORRY, BABE... YOU'RE RIGHT.
TELL YOU WHAT– WHY DON'T YOU BE IN CHARGE OF SELECTING THE PRICE POINT?
...AND IT'S ATTRACTIVELY PRICED AT $29.95!
A PAY-PER-VIEW WEDDING?

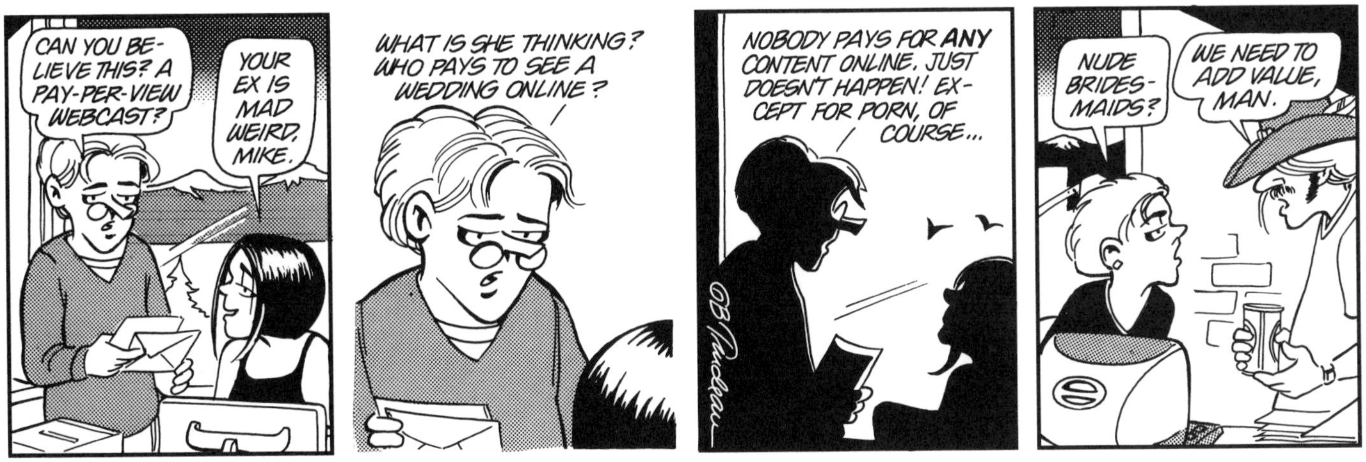
CAN YOU BE-LIEVE THIS? A PAY-PER-VIEW WEBCAST?
YOUR EX IS MAD WEIRD, MIKE.
WHAT IS SHE THINKING? WHO PAYS TO SEE A WEDDING ONLINE?
NOBODY PAYS FOR ANY CONTENT ONLINE. JUST DOESN'T HAPPEN! EX-CEPT FOR PORN, OF COURSE...
NUDE BRIDES-MAIDS?
WE NEED TO ADD VALUE, MAN.

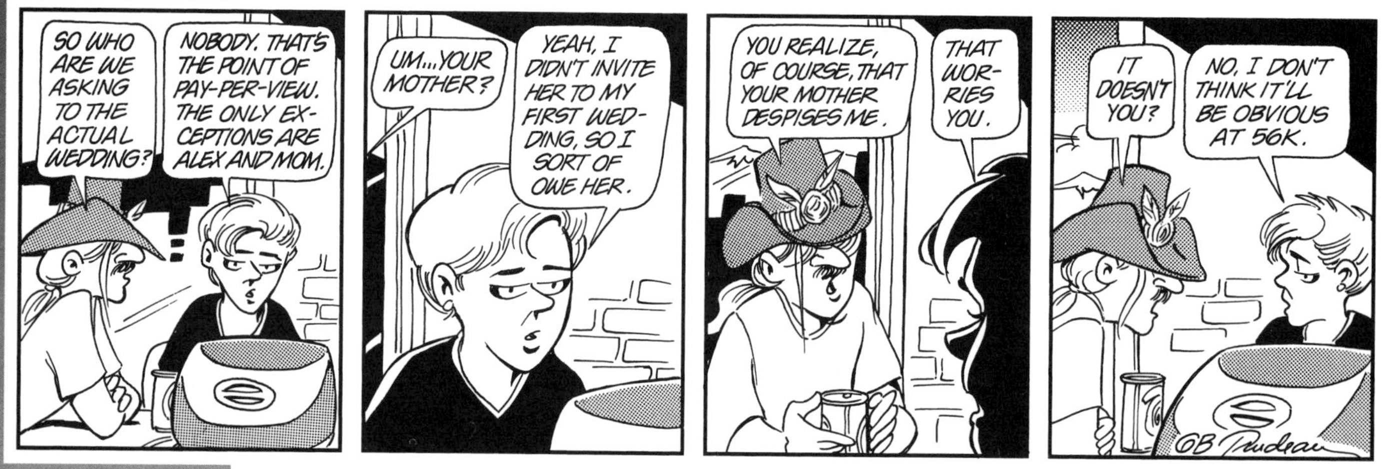
SO WHO ARE WE ASKING TO THE ACTUAL WEDDING?
NOBODY. THAT'S THE POINT OF PAY-PER-VIEW. THE ONLY EXCEPTIONS ARE ALEX AND MOM.
UM...YOUR MOTHER?
YEAH, I DIDN'T INVITE HER TO MY FIRST WEDDING, SO I SORT OF OWE HER.
YOU REALIZE, OF COURSE, THAT YOUR MOTHER DESPISES ME.
THAT WORRIES YOU.
IT DOESN'T YOU?
NO, I DON'T THINK IT'LL BE OBVIOUS AT 56K.
©B Trudeau

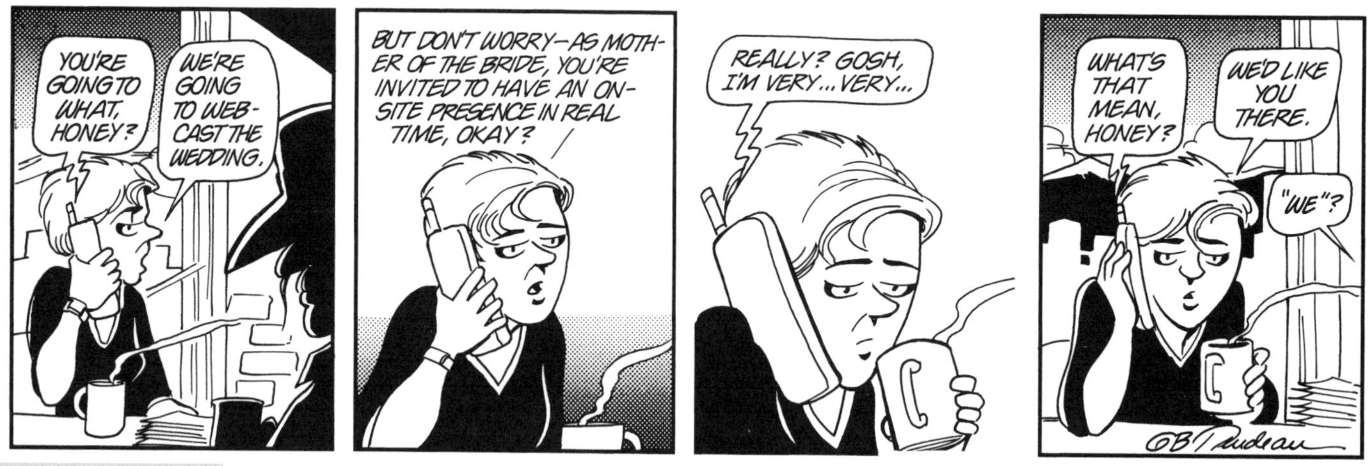
YOU'RE GOING TO WHAT, HONEY?
WE'RE GOING TO WEBCAST THE WEDDING.
BUT DON'T WORRY—AS MOTHER OF THE BRIDE, YOU'RE INVITED TO HAVE AN ON-SITE PRESENCE IN REAL TIME, OKAY?
REALLY? GOSH, I'M VERY... VERY...
WHAT'S THAT MEAN, HONEY?
WE'D LIKE YOU THERE.
"WE"?
©B Trudeau

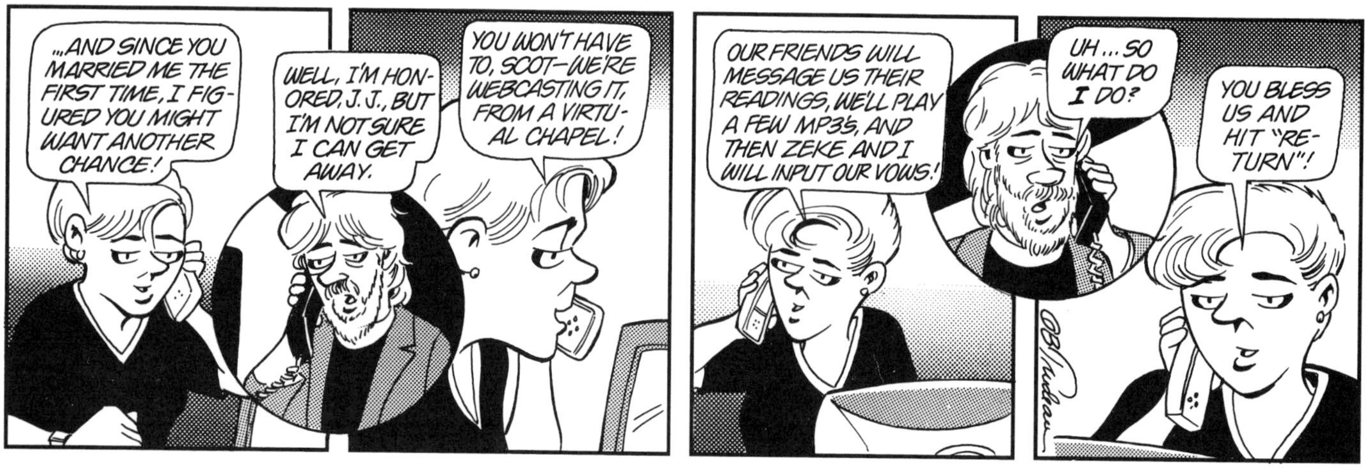
...AND SINCE YOU MARRIED ME THE FIRST TIME, I FIGURED YOU MIGHT WANT ANOTHER CHANCE!
WELL, I'M HONORED, J.J., BUT I'M NOT SURE I CAN GET AWAY.
YOU WON'T HAVE TO, SCOT—WE'RE WEBCASTING IT, FROM A VIRTUAL CHAPEL!
OUR FRIENDS WILL MESSAGE US THEIR READINGS, WE'LL PLAY A FEW MP3'S, AND THEN ZEKE AND I WILL INPUT OUR VOWS!
UH... SO WHAT DO I DO?
YOU BLESS US AND HIT "RETURN"!
©B Trudeau

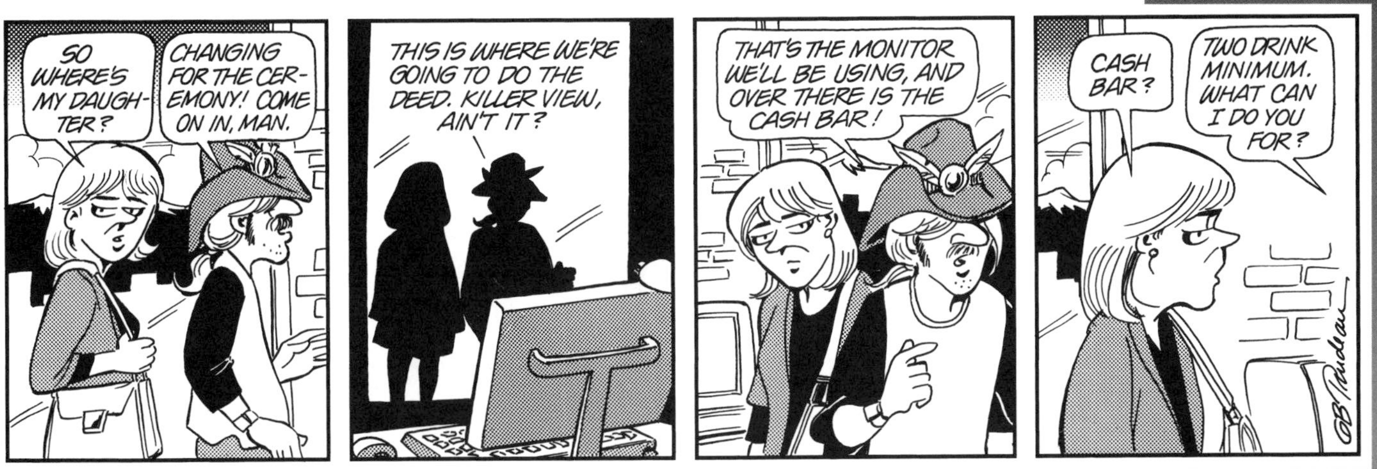
SO WHERE'S MY DAUGHTER?
CHANGING FOR THE CEREMONY! COME ON IN, MAN.
THIS IS WHERE WE'RE GOING TO DO THE DEED. KILLER VIEW, AIN'T IT?
THAT'S THE MONITOR WE'LL BE USING, AND OVER THERE IS THE CASH BAR!
CASH BAR?
TWO DRINK MINIMUM. WHAT CAN I DO YOU FOR?

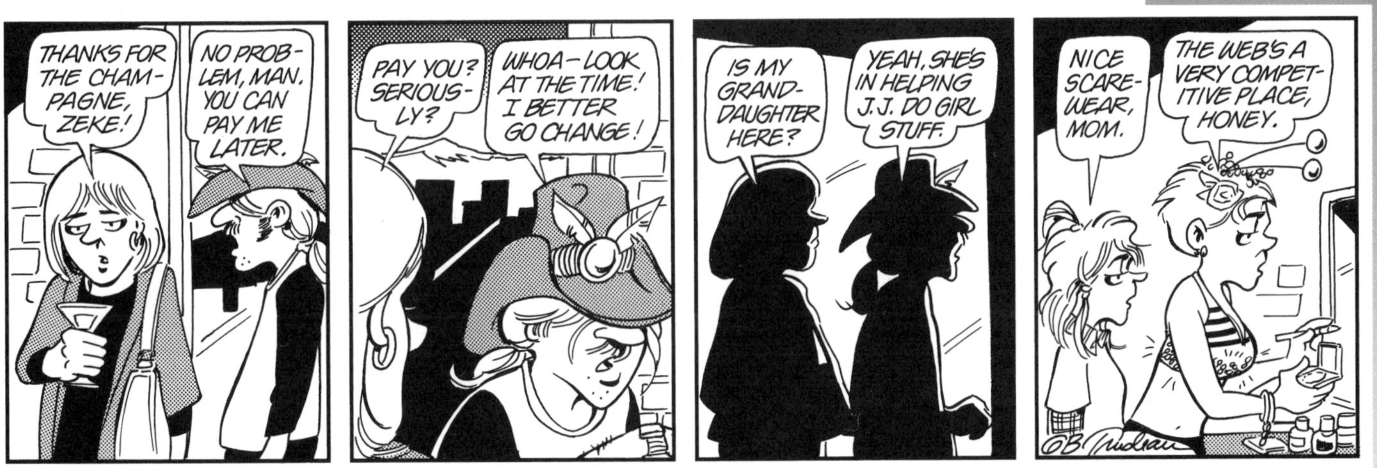
THANKS FOR THE CHAMPAGNE, ZEKE!
NO PROBLEM, MAN. YOU CAN PAY ME LATER.
PAY YOU? SERIOUSLY?
WHOA—LOOK AT THE TIME! I BETTER GO CHANGE!
IS MY GRAND-DAUGHTER HERE?
YEAH, SHE'S IN HELPING J.J. DO GIRL STUFF.
NICE SCARE-WEAR, MOM.
THE WEB'S A VERY COMPETITIVE PLACE, HONEY.

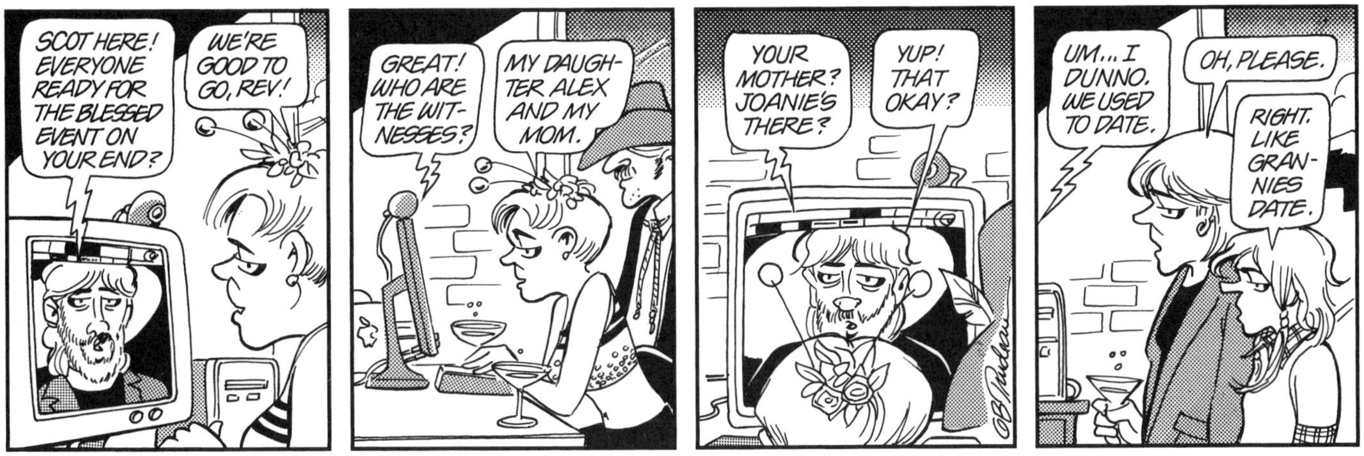
SCOT HERE! EVERYONE READY FOR THE BLESSED EVENT ON YOUR END?
WE'RE GOOD TO GO, REV!
GREAT! WHO ARE THE WITNESSES?
MY DAUGHTER ALEX AND MY MOM.
YOUR MOTHER? JOANIE'S THERE?
YUP! THAT OKAY?
UM... I DUNNO. WE USED TO DATE.
OH, PLEASE.
RIGHT. LIKE GRANNIES DATE.

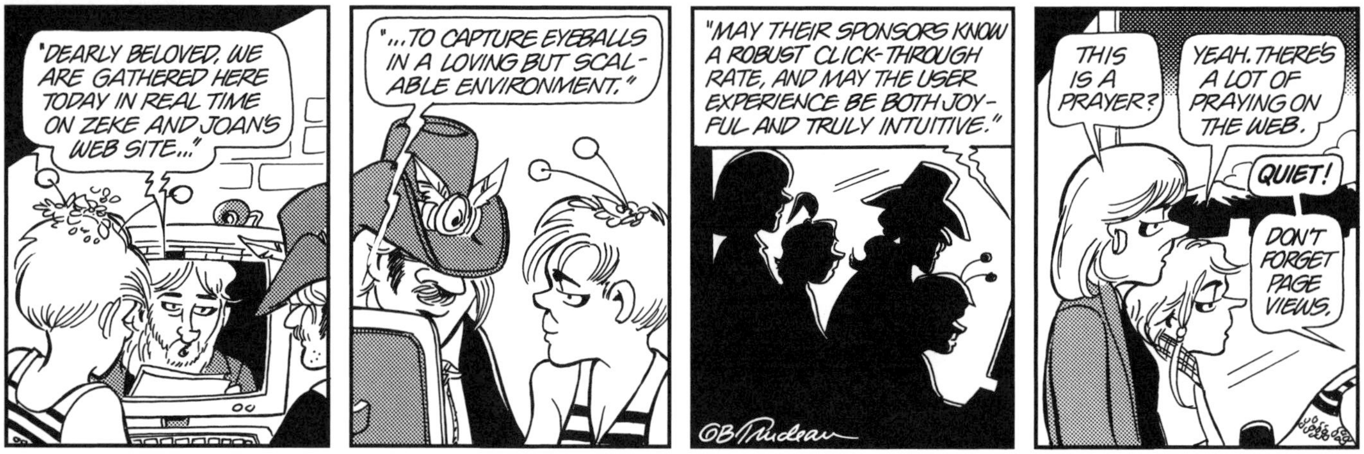
"DEARLY BELOVED, WE ARE GATHERED HERE TODAY IN REAL TIME ON ZEKE AND JOAN'S WEB SITE..."
"...TO CAPTURE EYEBALLS IN A LOVING BUT SCAL-ABLE ENVIRONMENT."
"MAY THEIR SPONSORS KNOW A ROBUST CLICK-THROUGH RATE, AND MAY THE USER EXPERIENCE BE BOTH JOY-FUL AND TRULY INTUITIVE."
©B Trudeau
THIS IS A PRAYER?
YEAH. THERE'S A LOT OF PRAYING ON THE WEB.
QUIET!
DON'T FORGET PAGE VIEWS.

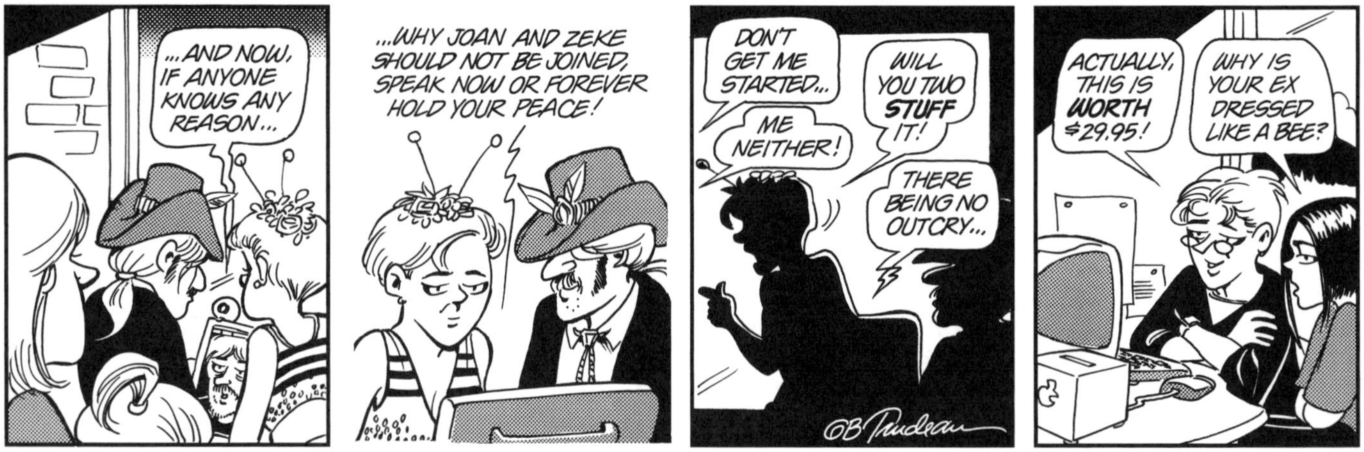
...AND NOW, IF ANYONE KNOWS ANY REASON...
...WHY JOAN AND ZEKE SHOULD NOT BE JOINED, SPEAK NOW OR FOREVER HOLD YOUR PEACE!
DON'T GET ME STARTED...
ME NEITHER!
WILL YOU TWO STUFF IT!
THERE BEING NO OUTCRY...
©B Trudeau
ACTUALLY, THIS IS WORTH $29.95!
WHY IS YOUR EX DRESSED LIKE A BEE?

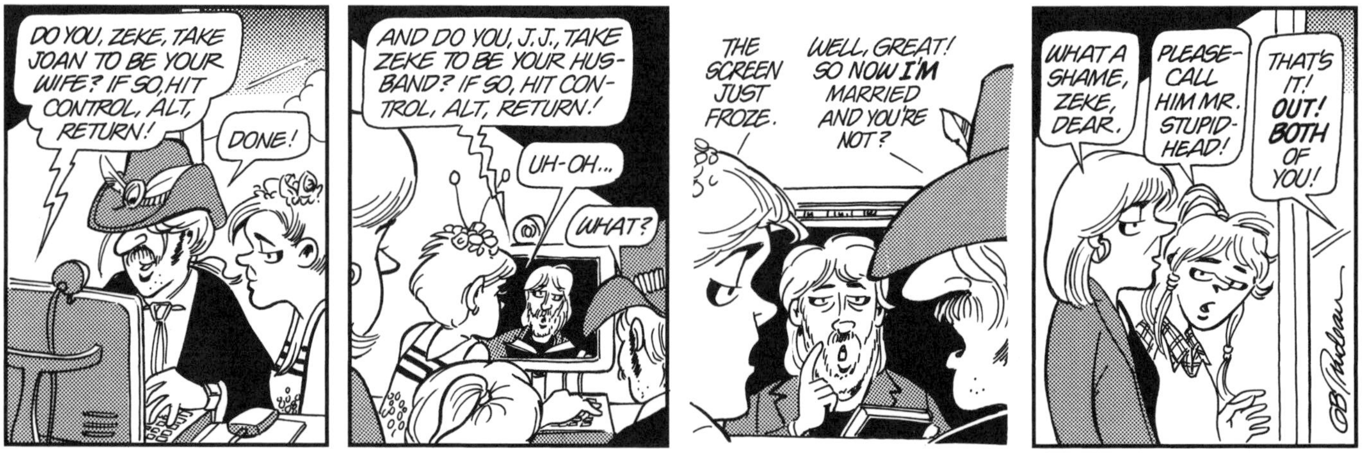
DO YOU, ZEKE, TAKE JOAN TO BE YOUR WIFE? IF SO, HIT CONTROL, ALT, RETURN!
DONE!
AND DO YOU, J.J., TAKE ZEKE TO BE YOUR HUS-BAND? IF SO, HIT CON-TROL, ALT, RETURN!
UH-OH...
WHAT?
THE SCREEN JUST FROZE.
WELL, GREAT! SO NOW I'M MARRIED AND YOU'RE NOT?
WHAT A SHAME, ZEKE, DEAR.
PLEASE-CALL HIM MR. STUPID-HEAD!
THAT'S IT! OUT! BOTH OF YOU!
©B Trudeau

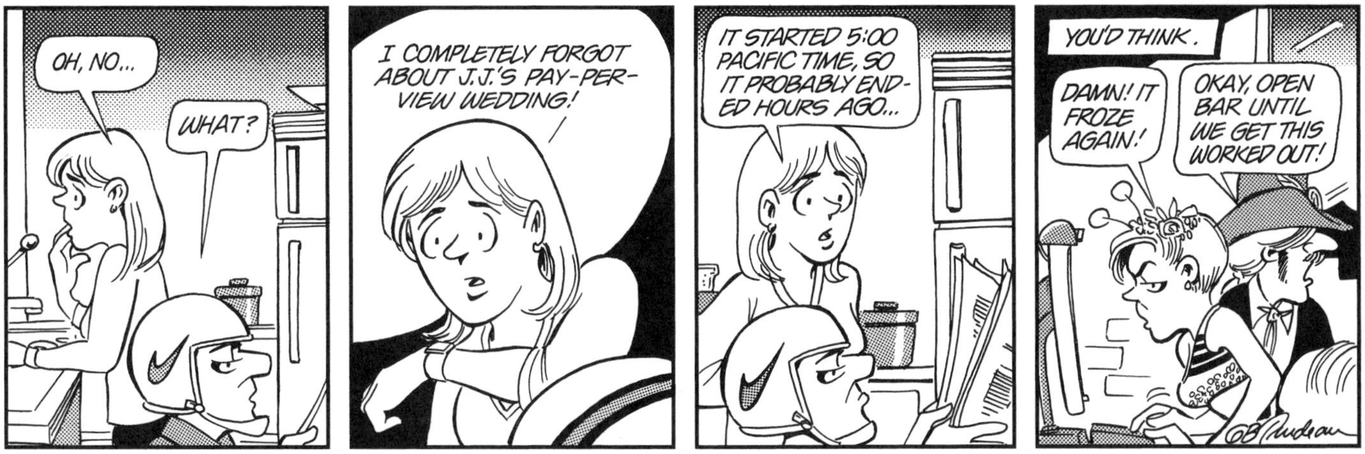
OH, NO...
WHAT?
I COMPLETELY FORGOT ABOUT J.J.'S PAY-PER-VIEW WEDDING!
IT STARTED 5:00 PACIFIC TIME, SO IT PROBABLY ENDED HOURS AGO...
YOU'D THINK.
DAMN! IT FROZE AGAIN!
OKAY, OPEN BAR UNTIL WE GET THIS WORKED OUT!
G.B. Trudeau

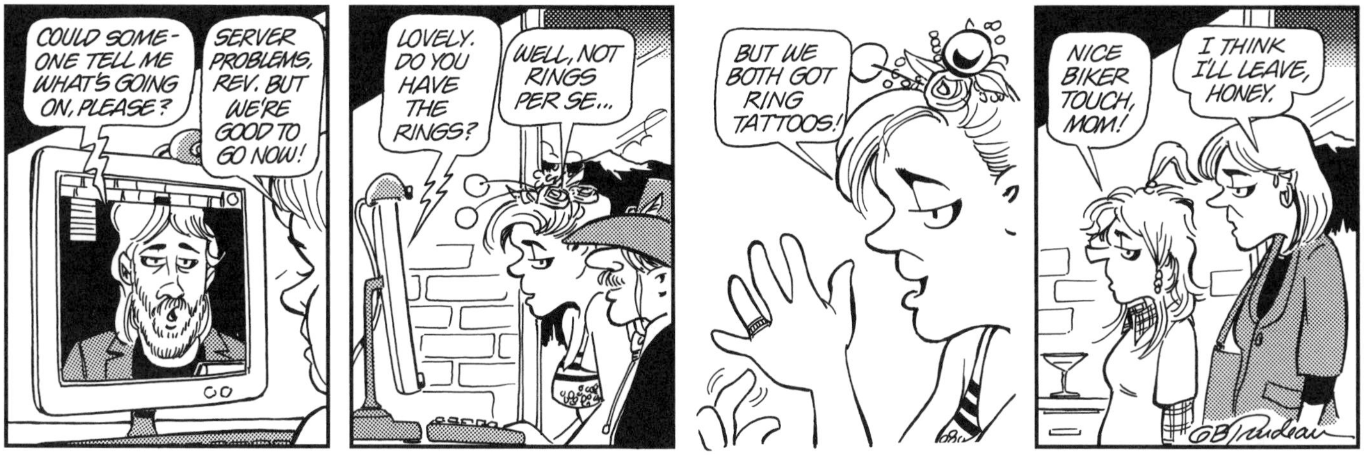
COULD SOMEONE TELL ME WHAT'S GOING ON, PLEASE?
SERVER PROBLEMS, REV. BUT WE'RE GOOD TO GO NOW!
LOVELY. DO YOU HAVE THE RINGS?
WELL, NOT RINGS PER SE...
BUT WE BOTH GOT RING TATTOOS!
NICE BIKER TOUCH, MOM!
I THINK I'LL LEAVE, HONEY.
G.B. Trudeau

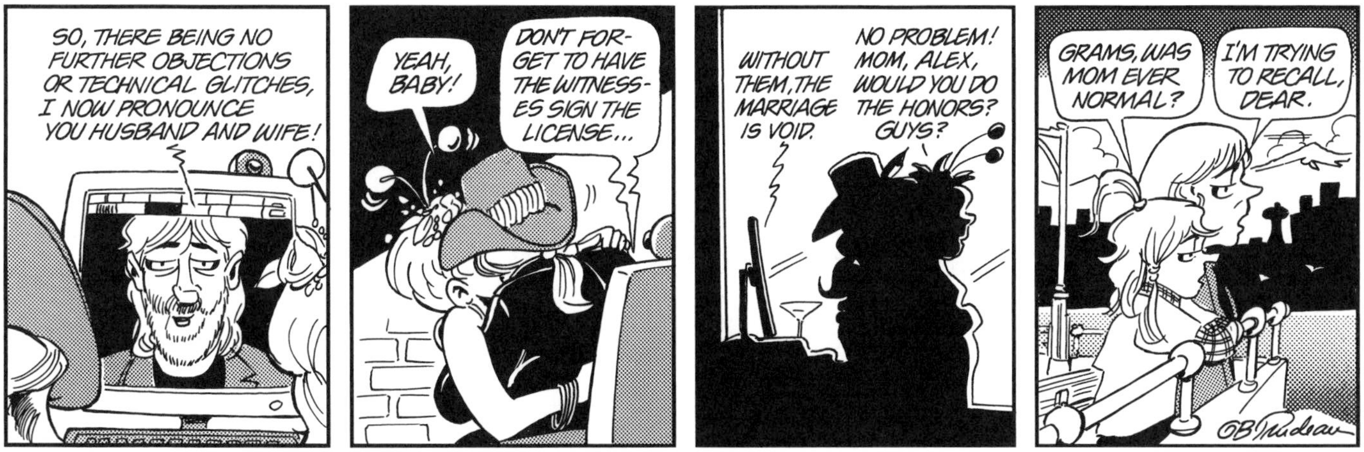
SO, THERE BEING NO FURTHER OBJECTIONS OR TECHNICAL GLITCHES, I NOW PRONOUNCE YOU HUSBAND AND WIFE!
YEAH, BABY!
DON'T FORGET TO HAVE THE WITNESSES SIGN THE LICENSE...
WITHOUT THEM, THE MARRIAGE IS VOID.
NO PROBLEM! MOM, ALEX, WOULD YOU DO THE HONORS? GUYS?
GRAMS, WAS MOM EVER NORMAL?
I'M TRYING TO RECALL, DEAR.
G.B. Trudeau

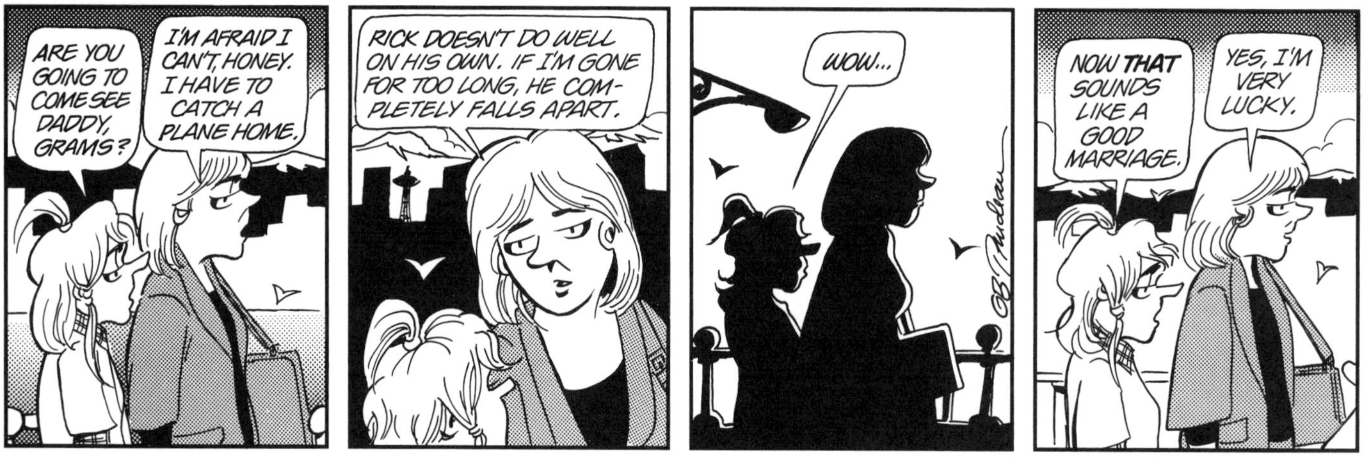
ARE YOU GOING TO COME SEE DADDY, GRAMS?
I'M AFRAID I CAN'T, HONEY. I HAVE TO CATCH A PLANE HOME.
RICK DOESN'T DO WELL ON HIS OWN. IF I'M GONE FOR TOO LONG, HE COMPLETELY FALLS APART.
WOW...
NOW **THAT** SOUNDS LIKE A GOOD MARRIAGE.
YES, I'M VERY LUCKY.

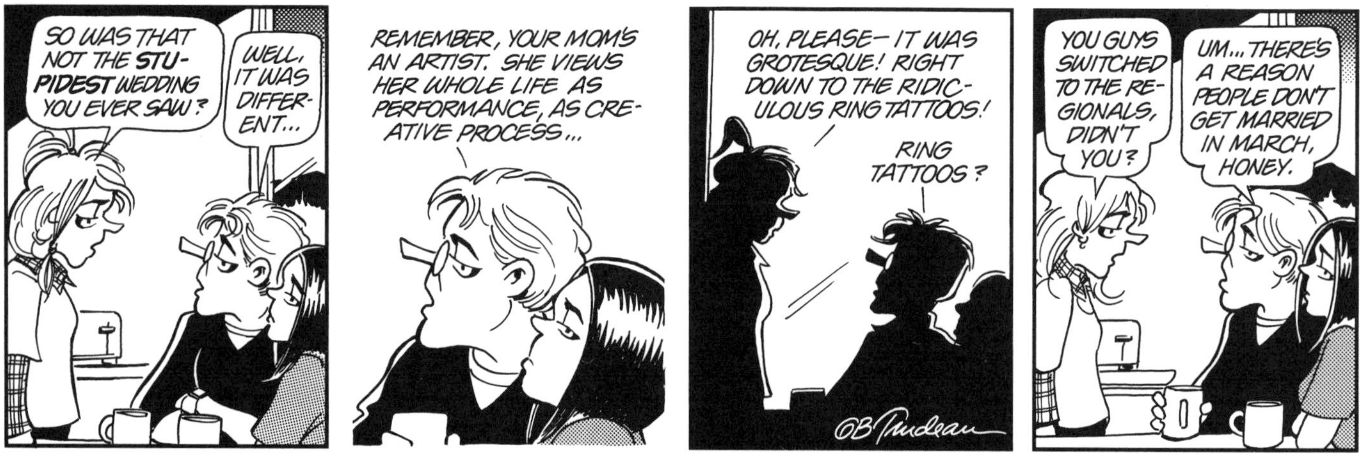
SO WAS THAT NOT THE **STUPIDEST** WEDDING YOU EVER SAW?
WELL, IT WAS DIFFERENT...
REMEMBER, YOUR MOM'S AN ARTIST. SHE VIEWS HER WHOLE LIFE AS PERFORMANCE, AS CREATIVE PROCESS...
OH, PLEASE— IT WAS GROTESQUE! RIGHT DOWN TO THE RIDICULOUS RING TATTOOS!
RING TATTOOS?
YOU GUYS SWITCHED TO THE REGIONALS, DIDN'T YOU?
UM... THERE'S A REASON PEOPLE DON'T GET MARRIED IN MARCH, HONEY.

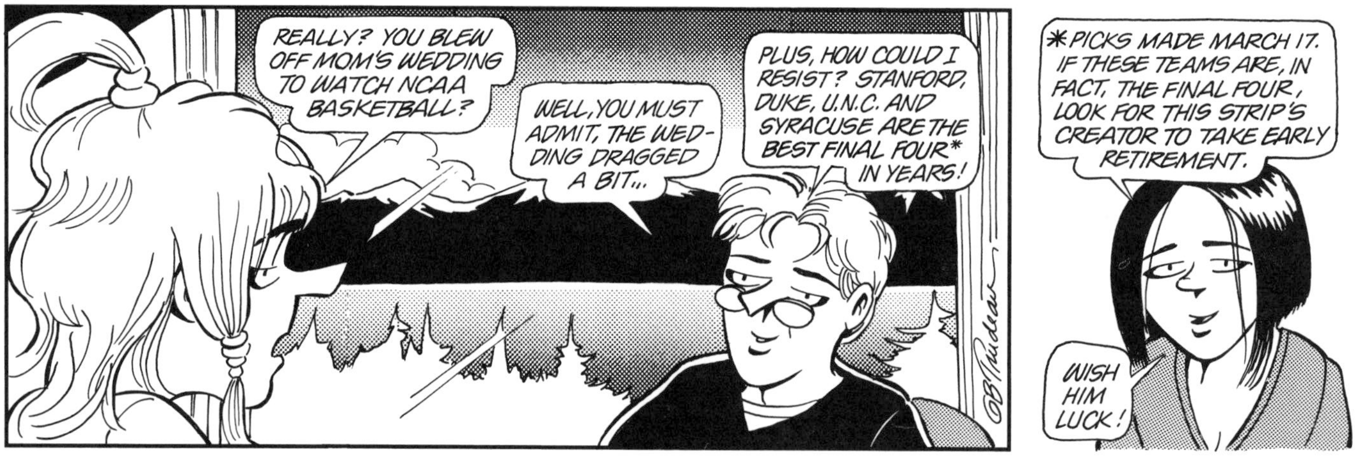
REALLY? YOU BLEW OFF MOM'S WEDDING TO WATCH NCAA BASKETBALL?
WELL, YOU MUST ADMIT, THE WEDDING DRAGGED A BIT...
PLUS, HOW COULD I RESIST? STANFORD, DUKE, U.N.C. AND SYRACUSE ARE THE BEST FINAL FOUR* IN YEARS!
*PICKS MADE MARCH 17. IF THESE TEAMS ARE, IN FACT, THE FINAL FOUR, LOOK FOR THIS STRIP'S CREATOR TO TAKE EARLY RETIREMENT.
WISH HIM LUCK!

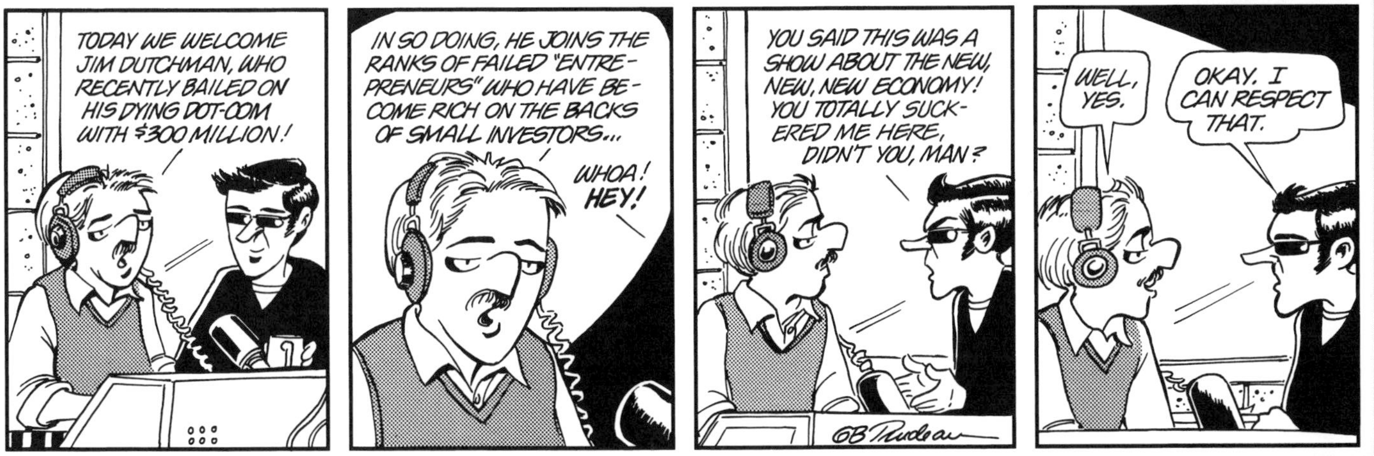
TODAY WE WELCOME JIM DUTCHMAN, WHO RECENTLY BAILED ON HIS DYING DOT-COM WITH $300 MILLION!
IN SO DOING, HE JOINS THE RANKS OF FAILED "ENTRE-PRENEURS" WHO HAVE BE-COME RICH ON THE BACKS OF SMALL INVESTORS...
WHOA! HEY!
YOU SAID THIS WAS A SHOW ABOUT THE NEW, NEW, NEW ECONOMY! YOU TOTALLY SUCK-ERED ME HERE, DIDN'T YOU, MAN?
WELL, YES.
OKAY. I CAN RESPECT THAT.

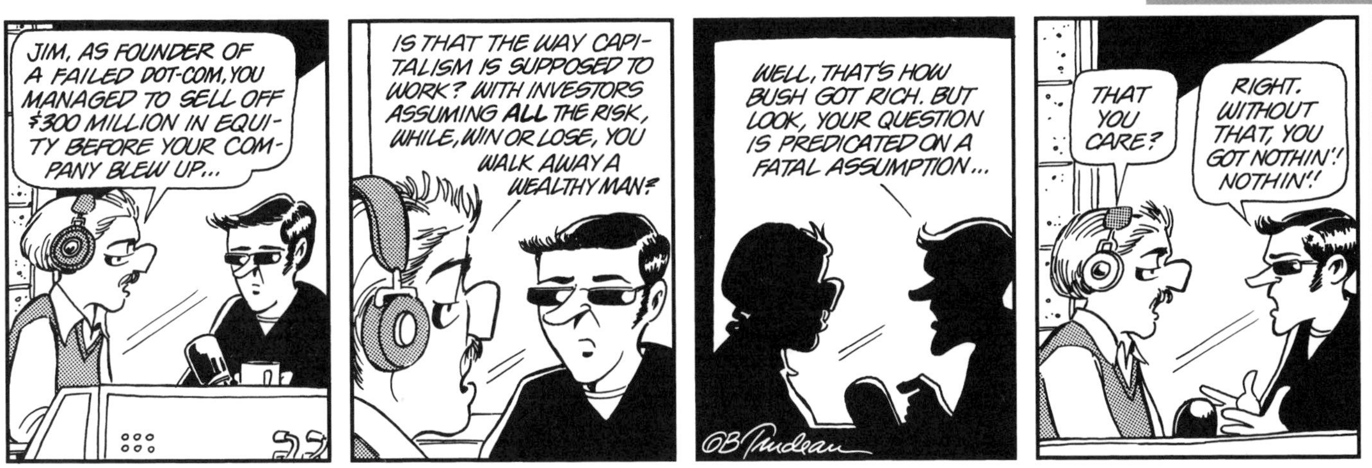
JIM, AS FOUNDER OF A FAILED DOT-COM, YOU MANAGED TO SELL OFF $300 MILLION IN EQUI-TY BEFORE YOUR COM-PANY BLEW UP...
IS THAT THE WAY CAPI-TALISM IS SUPPOSED TO WORK? WITH INVESTORS ASSUMING ALL THE RISK, WHILE, WIN OR LOSE, YOU WALK AWAY A WEALTHY MAN?
WELL, THAT'S HOW BUSH GOT RICH. BUT LOOK, YOUR QUESTION IS PREDICATED ON A FATAL ASSUMPTION...
THAT YOU CARE?
RIGHT. WITHOUT THAT, YOU GOT NOTHIN'! NOTHIN'!

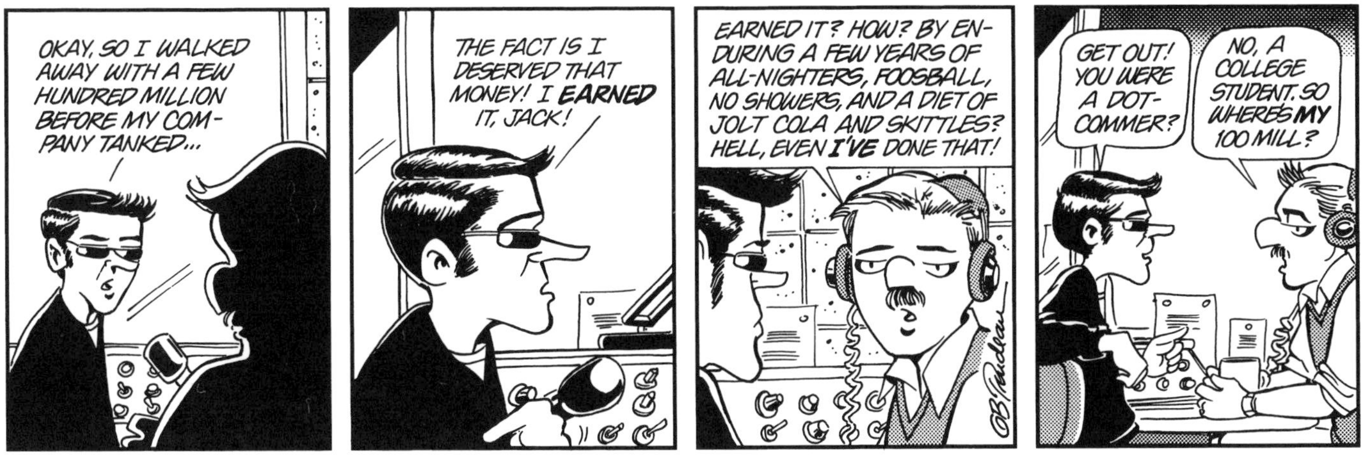
OKAY, SO I WALKED AWAY WITH A FEW HUNDRED MILLION BEFORE MY COM-PANY TANKED...
THE FACT IS I DESERVED THAT MONEY! I EARNED IT, JACK!
EARNED IT? HOW? BY EN-DURING A FEW YEARS OF ALL-NIGHTERS, FOOSBALL, NO SHOWERS, AND A DIET OF JOLT COLA AND SKITTLES? HELL, EVEN I'VE DONE THAT!
GET OUT! YOU WERE A DOT-COMMER?
NO, A COLLEGE STUDENT. SO WHERE'S MY 100 MILL?

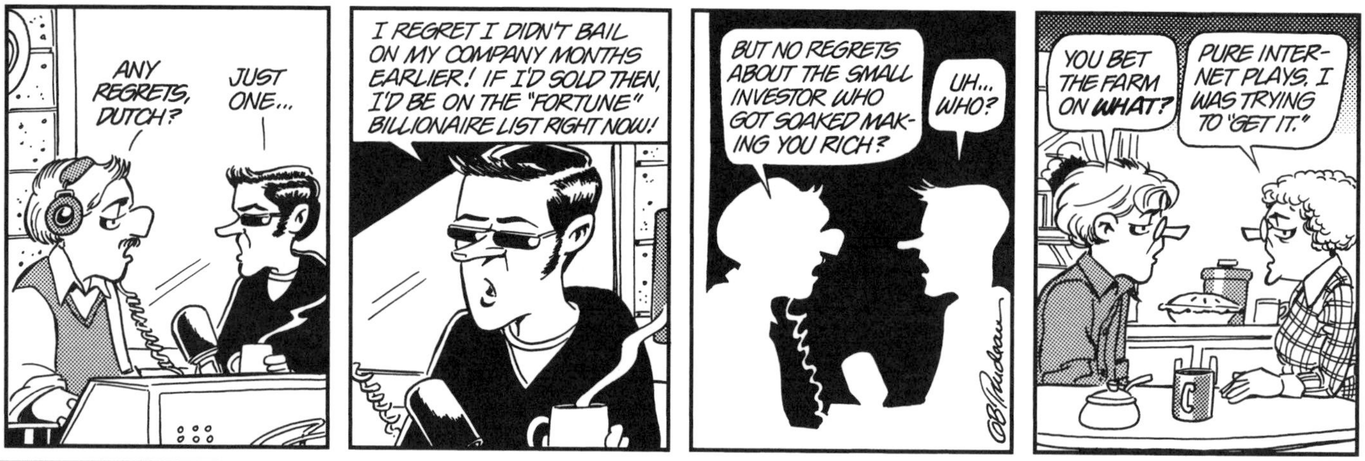
ANY REGRETS, DUTCH?
JUST ONE...
I REGRET I DIDN'T BAIL ON MY COMPANY MONTHS EARLIER! IF I'D SOLD THEN, I'D BE ON THE "FORTUNE" BILLIONAIRE LIST RIGHT NOW!
BUT NO REGRETS ABOUT THE SMALL INVESTOR WHO GOT SOAKED MAKING YOU RICH?
UH... WHO?
YOU BET THE FARM ON **WHAT?**
PURE INTERNET PLAYS. I WAS TRYING TO "GET IT."

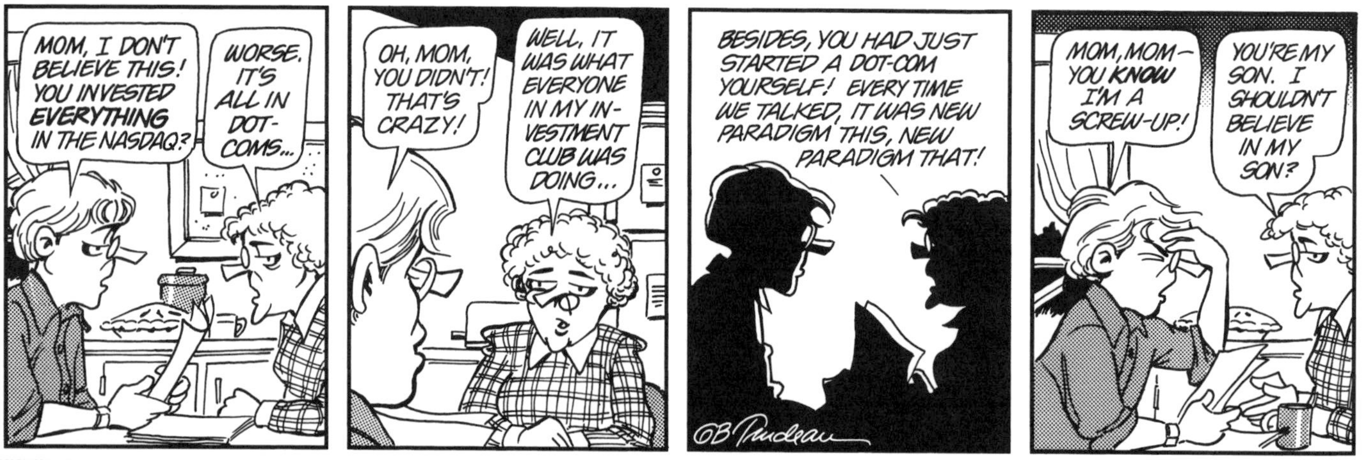
MOM, I DON'T BELIEVE THIS! YOU INVESTED **EVERYTHING** IN THE NASDAQ?
WORSE. IT'S ALL IN DOT-COMS...
OH, MOM, YOU DIDN'T! THAT'S CRAZY!
WELL, IT WAS WHAT EVERYONE IN MY INVESTMENT CLUB WAS DOING...
BESIDES, YOU HAD JUST STARTED A DOT-COM YOURSELF! EVERY TIME WE TALKED, IT WAS NEW PARADIGM THIS, NEW PARADIGM THAT!
MOM, MOM— YOU **KNOW** I'M A SCREW-UP!
YOU'RE MY SON. I SHOULDN'T BELIEVE IN MY SON?

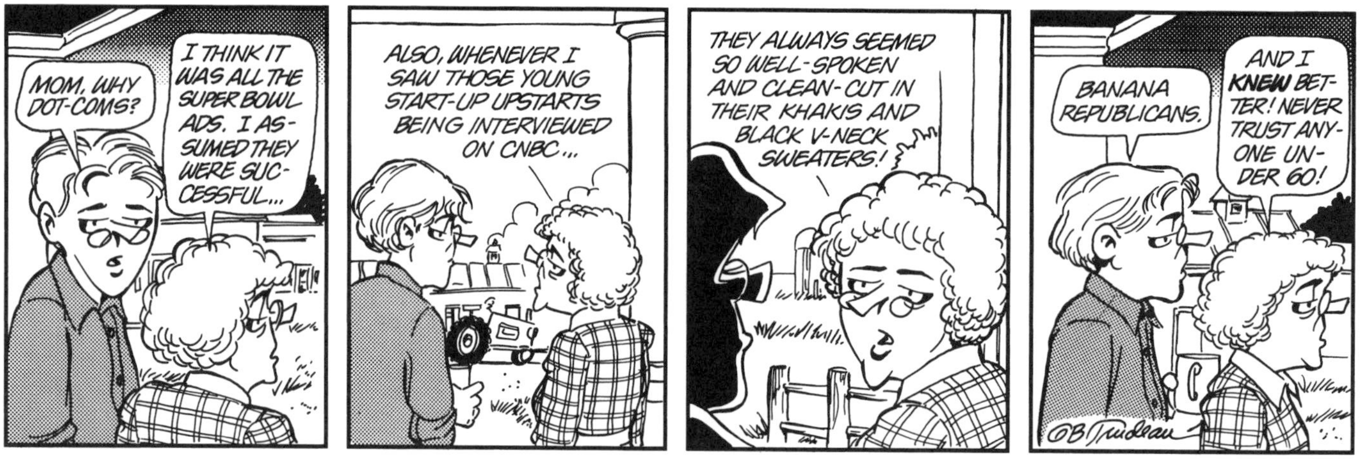
MOM, WHY DOT-COMS?
I THINK IT WAS ALL THE SUPER BOWL ADS. I ASSUMED THEY WERE SUCCESSFUL...
ALSO, WHENEVER I SAW THOSE YOUNG START-UP UPSTARTS BEING INTERVIEWED ON CNBC...
THEY ALWAYS SEEMED SO WELL-SPOKEN AND CLEAN-CUT IN THEIR KHAKIS AND BLACK V-NECK SWEATERS!
BANANA REPUBLICANS.
AND I **KNEW** BETTER! NEVER TRUST ANYONE UNDER 60!

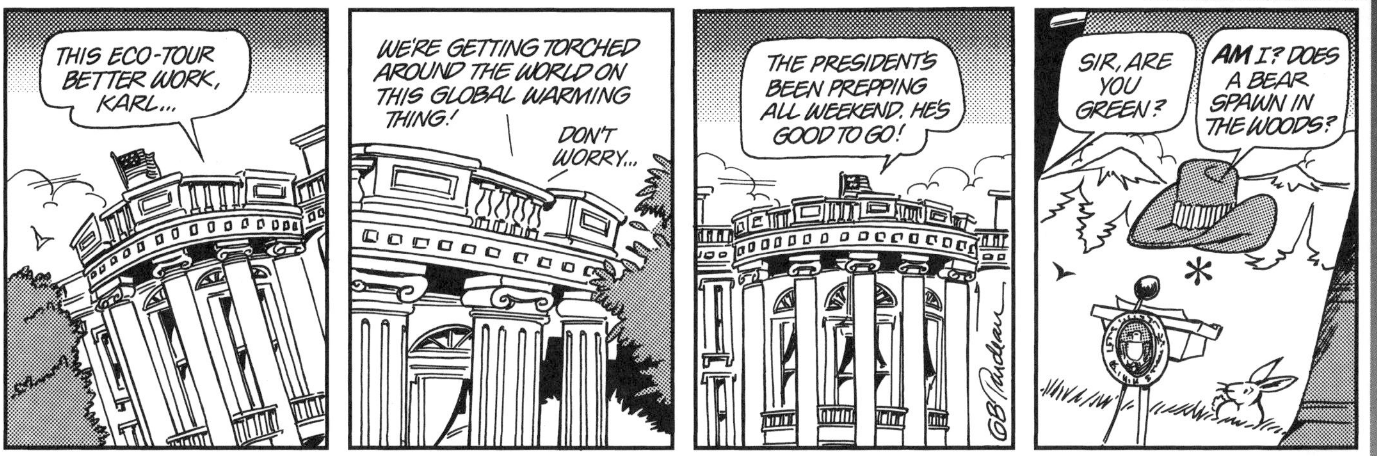
THIS ECO-TOUR BETTER WORK, KARL...
WE'RE GETTING TORCHED AROUND THE WORLD ON THIS GLOBAL WARMING THING!
DON'T WORRY...
THE PRESIDENT'S BEEN PREPPING ALL WEEKEND. HE'S GOOD TO GO!
SIR, ARE YOU GREEN?
AM I? DOES A BEAR SPAWN IN THE WOODS?

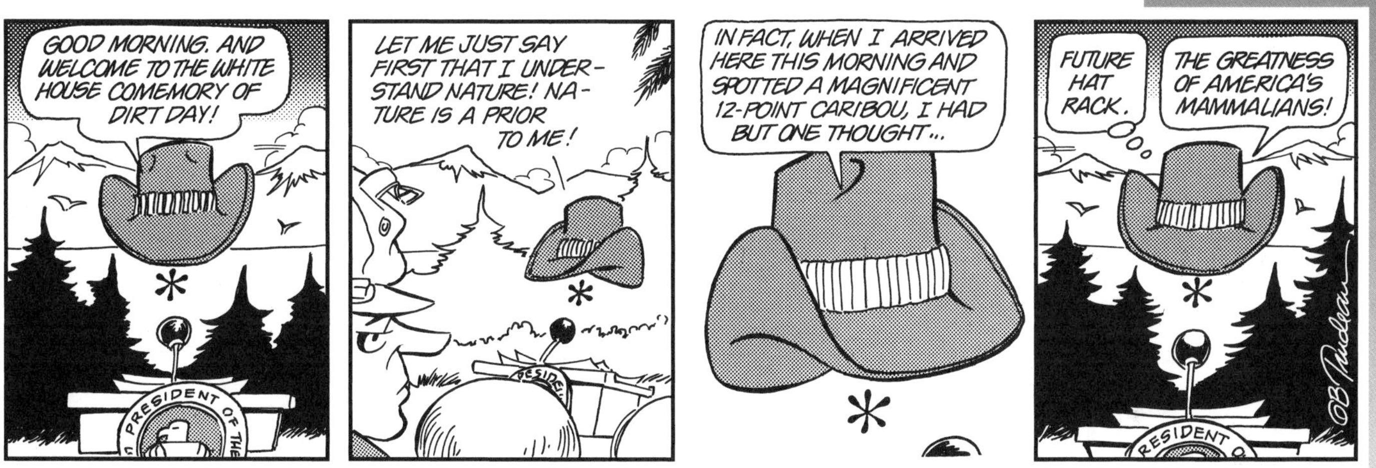
GOOD MORNING. AND WELCOME TO THE WHITE HOUSE COMEMORY OF DIRT DAY!
PRESIDENT OF THE
LET ME JUST SAY FIRST THAT I UNDERSTAND NATURE! NATURE IS A PRIOR TO ME!
IN FACT, WHEN I ARRIVED HERE THIS MORNING AND SPOTTED A MAGNIFICENT 12-POINT CARIBOU, I HAD BUT ONE THOUGHT...
FUTURE HAT RACK.
THE GREATNESS OF AMERICA'S MAMMALIANS!

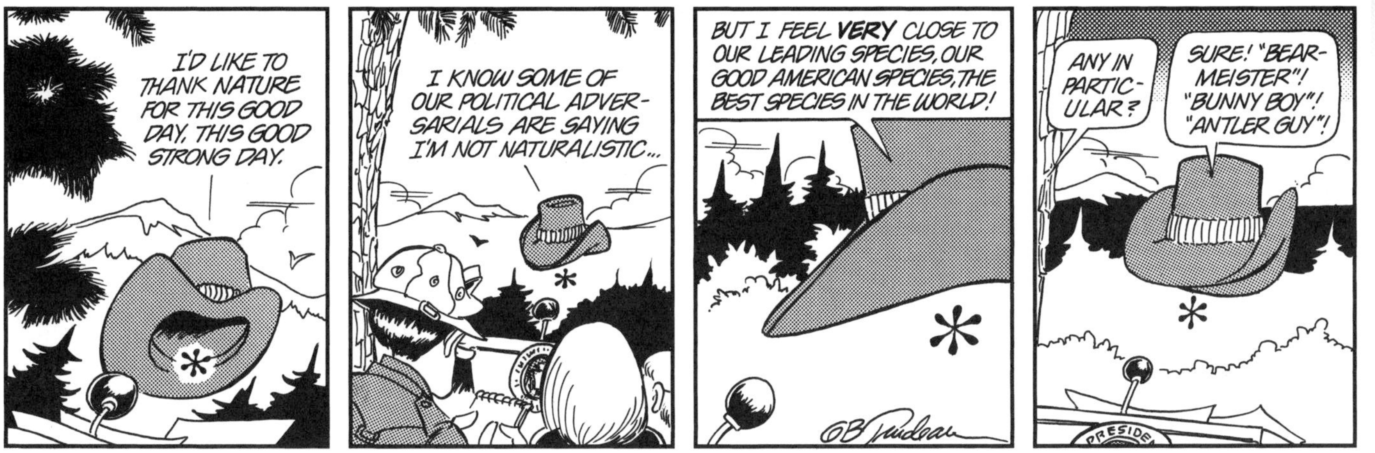
I'D LIKE TO THANK NATURE FOR THIS GOOD DAY, THIS GOOD STRONG DAY.
I KNOW SOME OF OUR POLITICAL ADVERSARIALS ARE SAYING I'M NOT NATURALISTIC...
BUT I FEEL VERY CLOSE TO OUR LEADING SPECIES, OUR GOOD AMERICAN SPECIES, THE BEST SPECIES IN THE WORLD!
ANY IN PARTICULAR?
SURE! "BEARMEISTER"! "BUNNY BOY"! "ANTLER GUY"!

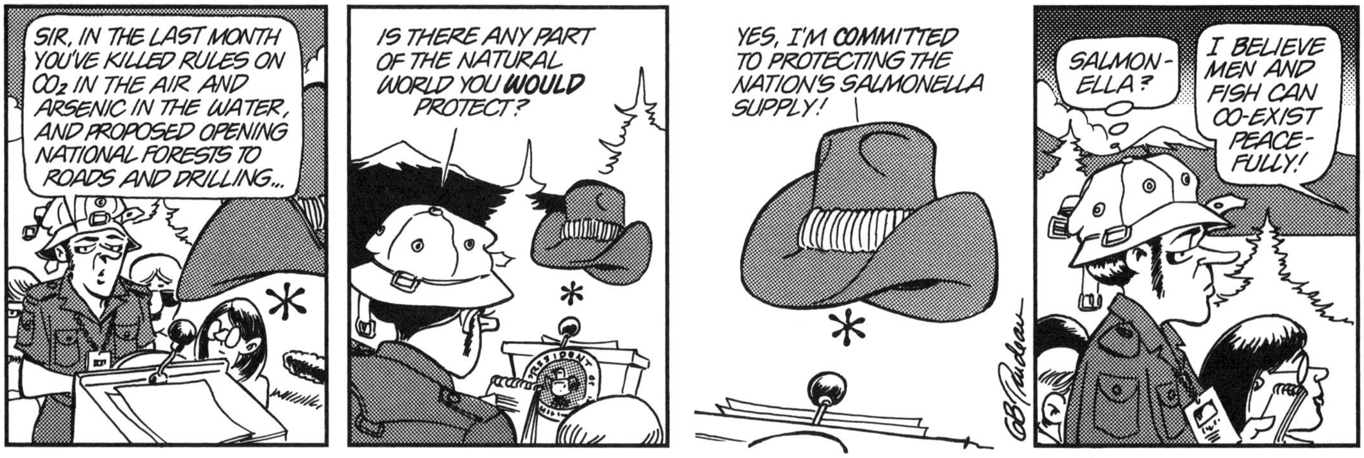
SIR, IN THE LAST MONTH YOU'VE KILLED RULES ON CO_2 IN THE AIR AND ARSENIC IN THE WATER, AND PROPOSED OPENING NATIONAL FORESTS TO ROADS AND DRILLING...
IS THERE ANY PART OF THE NATURAL WORLD YOU **WOULD** PROTECT?
YES, I'M **COMMITTED** TO PROTECTING THE NATION'S SALMONELLA SUPPLY!
SALMON-ELLA?
I BELIEVE MEN AND FISH CAN CO-EXIST PEACE-FULLY!

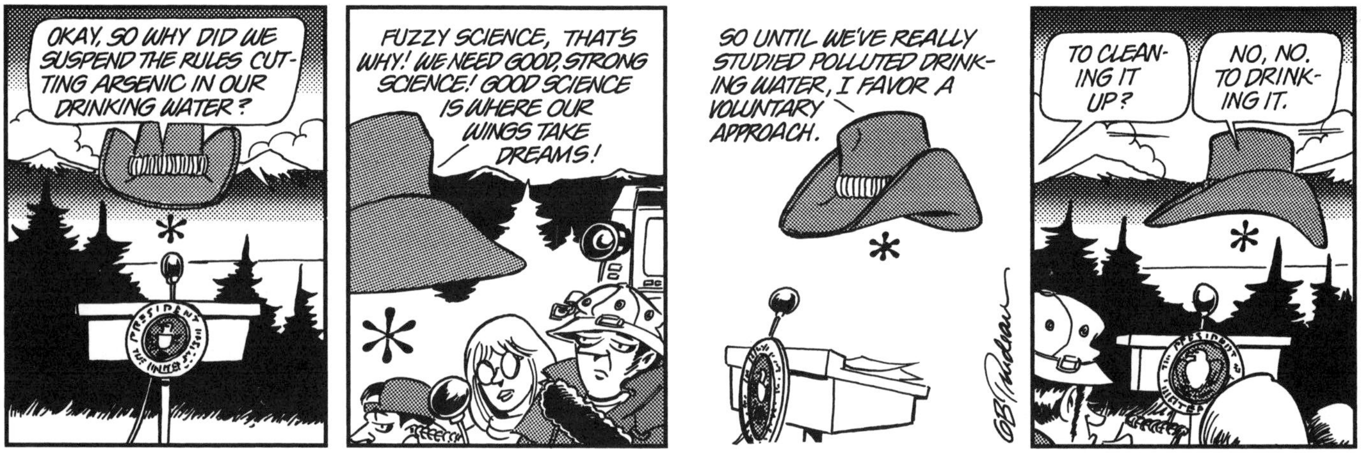
OKAY, SO WHY DID WE SUSPEND THE RULES CUTTING ARSENIC IN OUR DRINKING WATER?
FUZZY SCIENCE, THAT'S WHY! WE NEED GOOD, STRONG SCIENCE! GOOD SCIENCE IS WHERE OUR WINGS TAKE DREAMS!
SO UNTIL WE'VE REALLY STUDIED POLLUTED DRINKING WATER, I FAVOR A VOLUNTARY APPROACH.
TO CLEANING IT UP?
NO, NO. TO DRINKING IT.

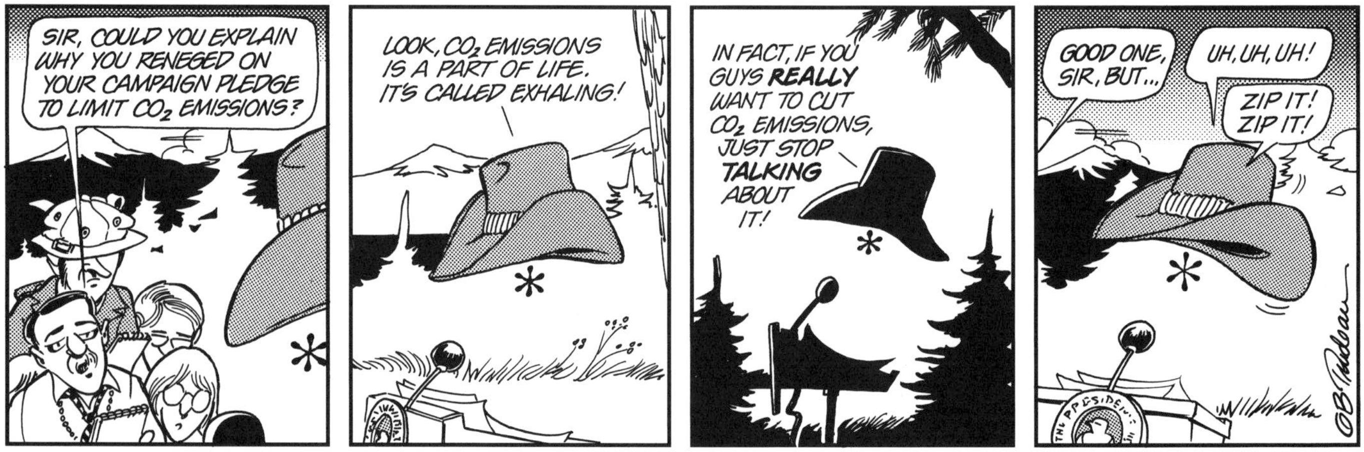
SIR, COULD YOU EXPLAIN WHY YOU RENEGED ON YOUR CAMPAIGN PLEDGE TO LIMIT CO_2 EMISSIONS?
LOOK, CO_2 EMISSIONS IS A PART OF LIFE. IT'S CALLED EXHALING!
IN FACT, IF YOU GUYS **REALLY** WANT TO CUT CO_2 EMISSIONS, JUST STOP **TALKING** ABOUT IT!
GOOD ONE, SIR, BUT...
UH, UH, UH!
ZIP IT! ZIP IT!

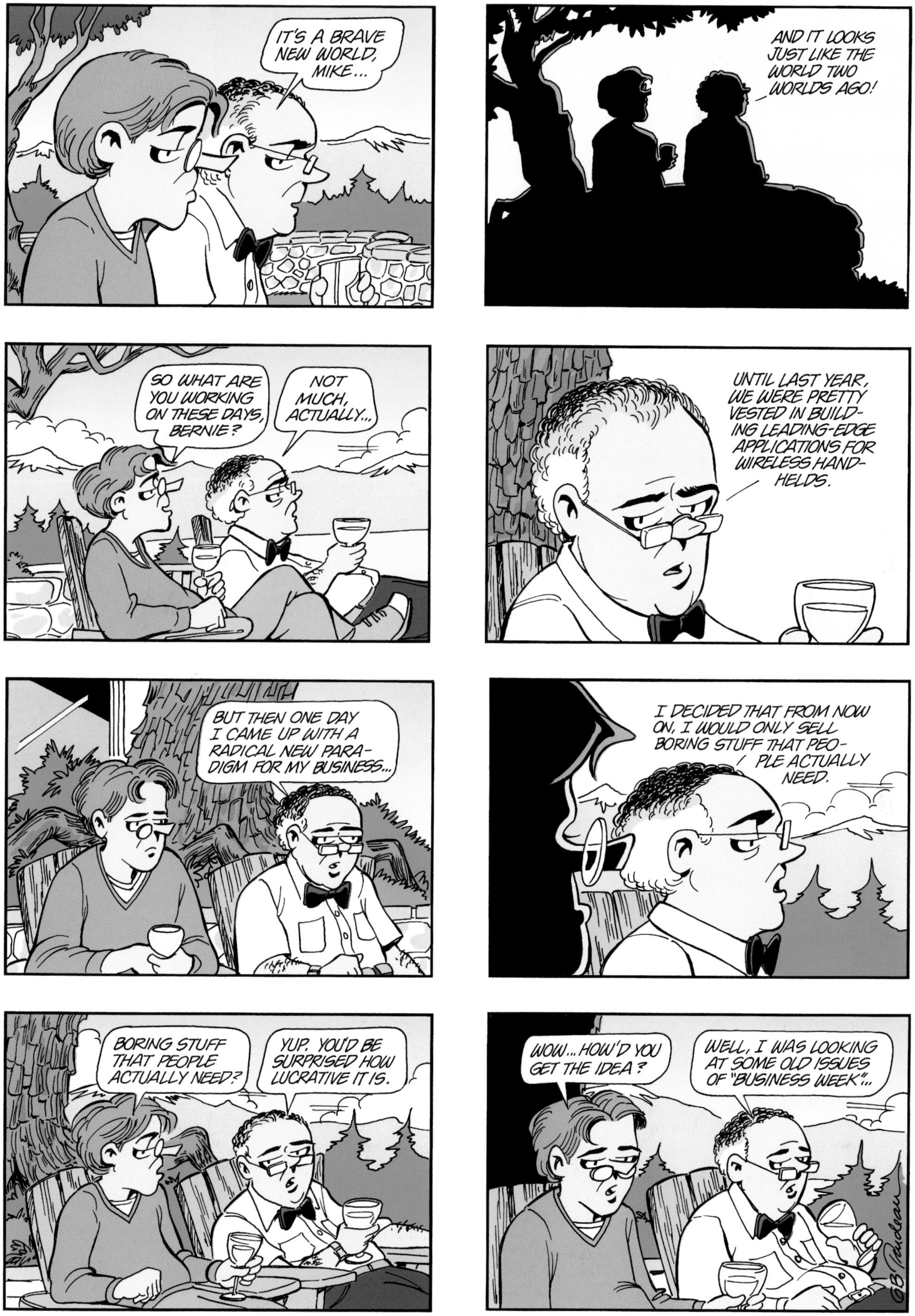
IT'S A BRAVE NEW WORLD, MIKE...
AND IT LOOKS JUST LIKE THE WORLD TWO WORLDS AGO!
SO WHAT ARE YOU WORKING ON THESE DAYS, BERNIE?
NOT MUCH, ACTUALLY...
UNTIL LAST YEAR, WE WERE PRETTY VESTED IN BUILDING LEADING-EDGE APPLICATIONS FOR WIRELESS HAND-HELDS.
BUT THEN ONE DAY I CAME UP WITH A RADICAL NEW PARA-DIGM FOR MY BUSINESS...
I DECIDED THAT FROM NOW ON, I WOULD ONLY SELL BORING STUFF THAT PEO-PLE ACTUALLY NEED.
BORING STUFF THAT PEOPLE ACTUALLY NEED?
YUP. YOU'D BE SURPRISED HOW LUCRATIVE IT IS.
WOW... HOW'D YOU GET THE IDEA?
WELL, I WAS LOOKING AT SOME OLD ISSUES OF "BUSINESS WEEK"...
GB Trudeau

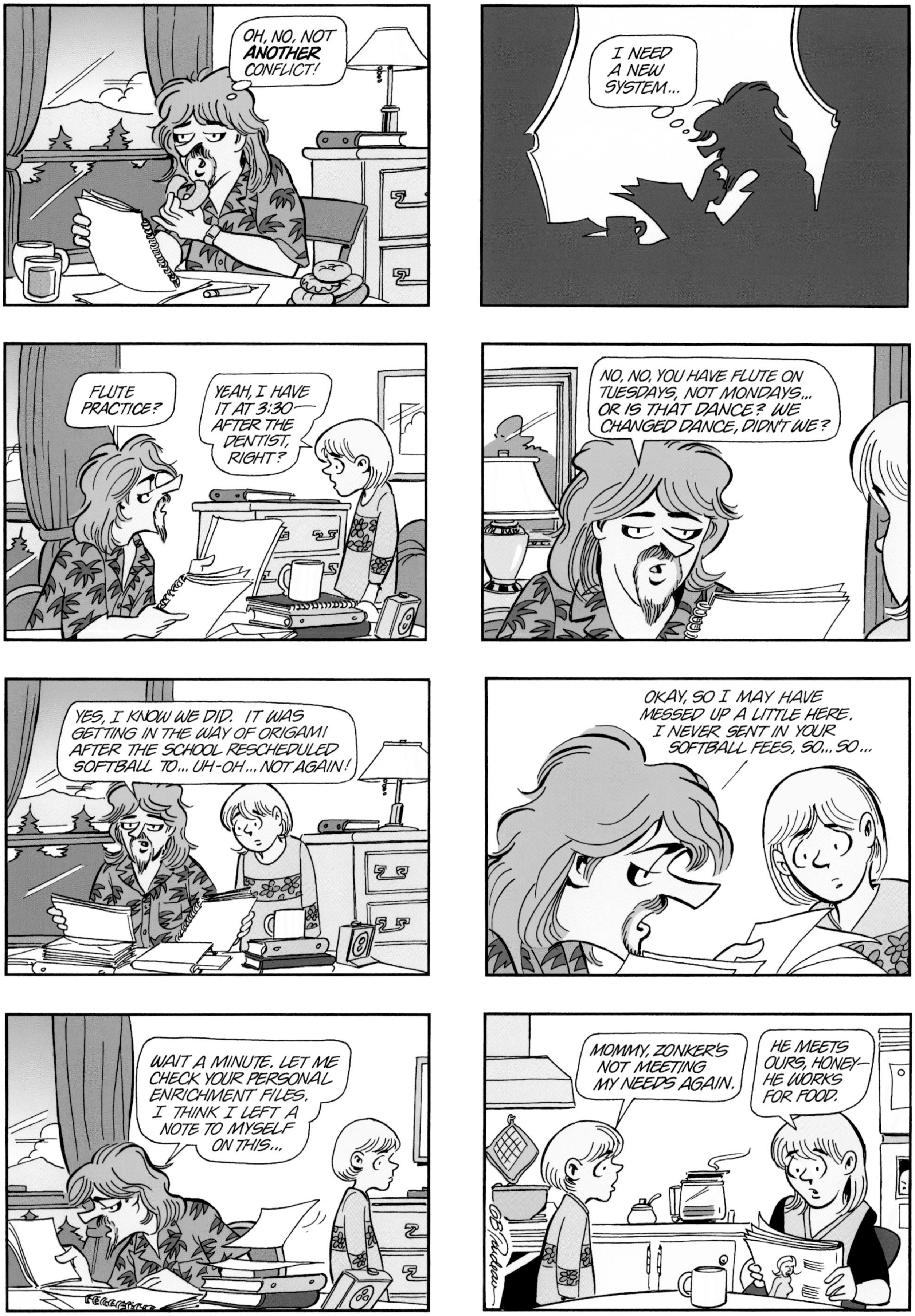
OH, NO, NOT **ANOTHER** CONFLICT!
I NEED A NEW SYSTEM...
FLUTE PRACTICE?
YEAH, I HAVE IT AT 3:30— AFTER THE DENTIST, RIGHT?
NO, NO, YOU HAVE FLUTE ON TUESDAYS, NOT MONDAYS... OR IS THAT DANCE? WE CHANGED DANCE, DIDN'T WE?
YES, I KNOW WE DID. IT WAS GETTING IN THE WAY OF ORIGAMI AFTER THE SCHOOL RESCHEDULED SOFTBALL TO... UH-OH... NOT AGAIN!
OKAY, SO I MAY HAVE MESSED UP A LITTLE HERE. I NEVER SENT IN YOUR SOFTBALL FEES, SO... SO...
WAIT A MINUTE. LET ME CHECK YOUR PERSONAL ENRICHMENT FILES. I THINK I LEFT A NOTE TO MYSELF ON THIS...
MOMMY, ZONKER'S NOT MEETING MY NEEDS AGAIN.
HE MEETS OURS, HONEY— HE WORKS FOR FOOD.
GB Trudeau

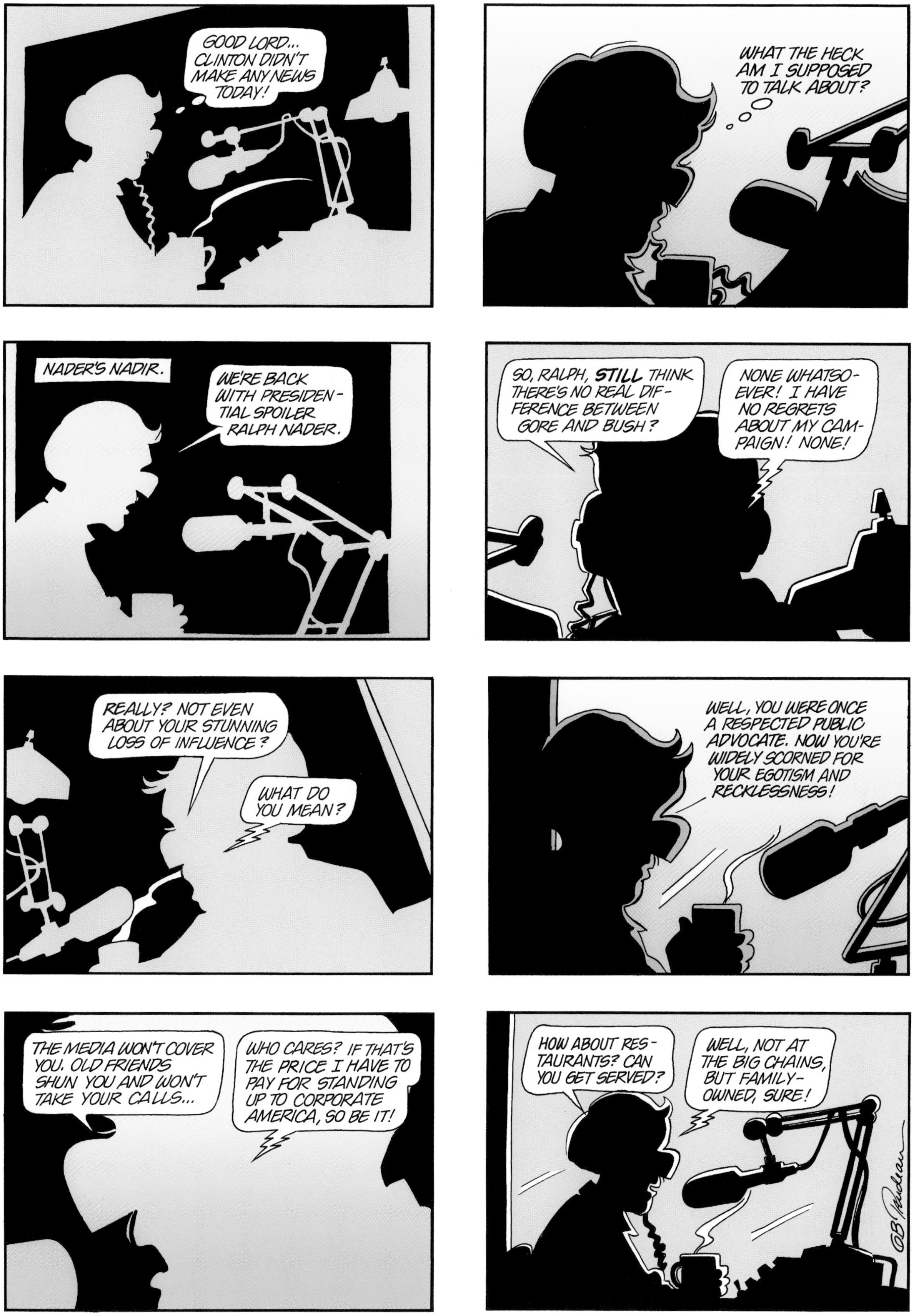
GOOD LORD... CLINTON DIDN'T MAKE ANY NEWS TODAY!
WHAT THE HECK AM I SUPPOSED TO TALK ABOUT?
NADER'S NADIR.
WE'RE BACK WITH PRESIDENTIAL SPOILER RALPH NADER.
SO, RALPH, STILL THINK THERE'S NO REAL DIFFERENCE BETWEEN GORE AND BUSH?
NONE WHATSOEVER! I HAVE NO REGRETS ABOUT MY CAMPAIGN! NONE!
REALLY? NOT EVEN ABOUT YOUR STUNNING LOSS OF INFLUENCE?
WHAT DO YOU MEAN?
WELL, YOU WERE ONCE A RESPECTED PUBLIC ADVOCATE. NOW YOU'RE WIDELY SCORNED FOR YOUR EGOTISM AND RECKLESSNESS!
THE MEDIA WON'T COVER YOU. OLD FRIENDS SHUN YOU AND WON'T TAKE YOUR CALLS...
WHO CARES? IF THAT'S THE PRICE I HAVE TO PAY FOR STANDING UP TO CORPORATE AMERICA, SO BE IT!
HOW ABOUT RESTAURANTS? CAN YOU GET SERVED?
WELL, NOT AT THE BIG CHAINS, BUT FAMILY-OWNED, SURE!

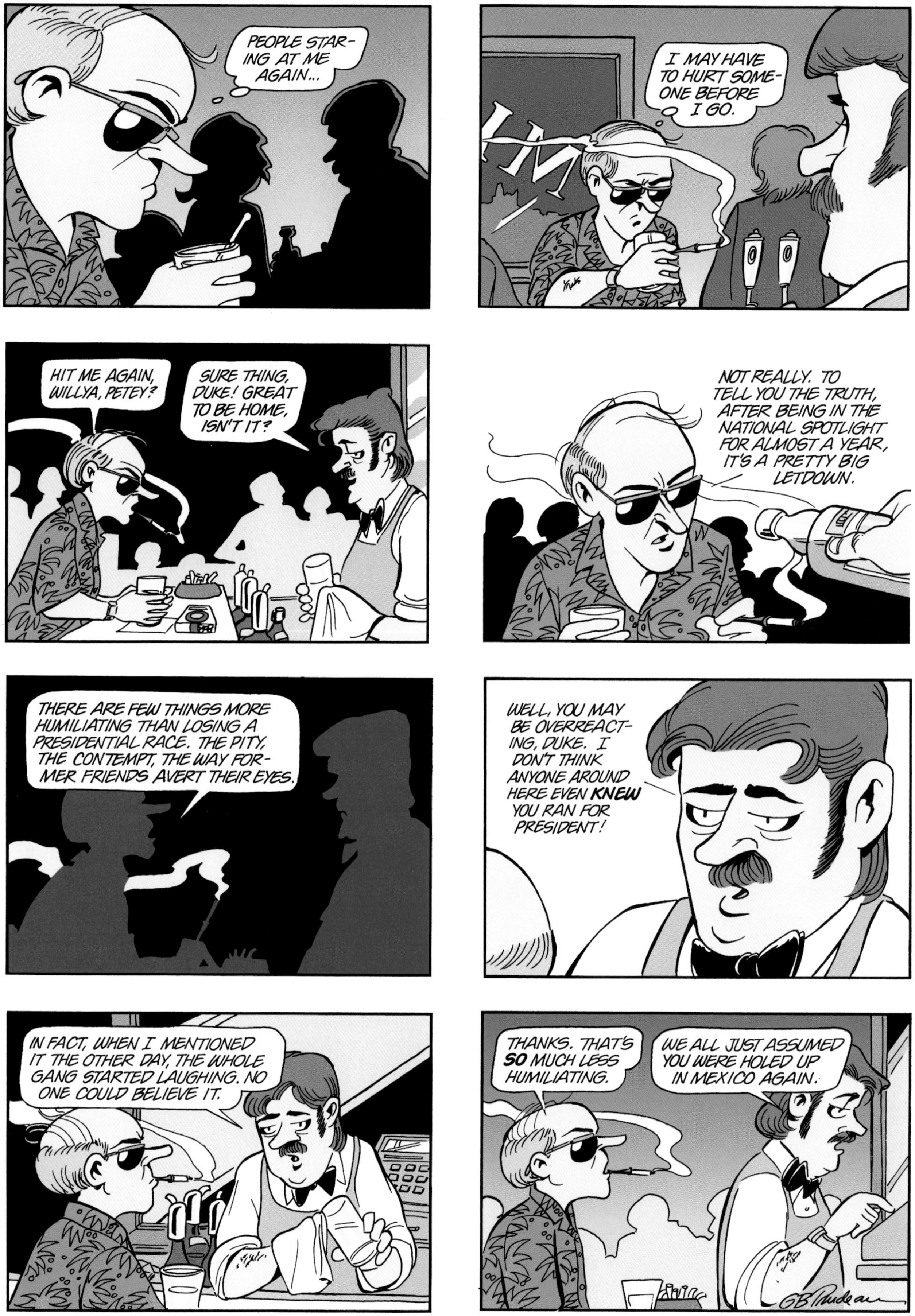
PEOPLE STARING AT ME AGAIN...
I MAY HAVE TO HURT SOMEONE BEFORE I GO.
HIT ME AGAIN, WILLYA, PETEY?
SURE THING, DUKE! GREAT TO BE HOME, ISN'T IT?
NOT REALLY. TO TELL YOU THE TRUTH, AFTER BEING IN THE NATIONAL SPOTLIGHT FOR ALMOST A YEAR, IT'S A PRETTY BIG LETDOWN.
THERE ARE FEW THINGS MORE HUMILIATING THAN LOSING A PRESIDENTIAL RACE. THE PITY, THE CONTEMPT, THE WAY FORMER FRIENDS AVERT THEIR EYES.
WELL, YOU MAY BE OVERREACTING, DUKE. I DON'T THINK ANYONE AROUND HERE EVEN **KNEW** YOU RAN FOR PRESIDENT!
IN FACT, WHEN I MENTIONED IT THE OTHER DAY, THE WHOLE GANG STARTED LAUGHING. NO ONE COULD BELIEVE IT.
THANKS. THAT'S **SO** MUCH LESS HUMILIATING.
WE ALL JUST ASSUMED YOU WERE HOLED UP IN MEXICO AGAIN.
GB Trudeau

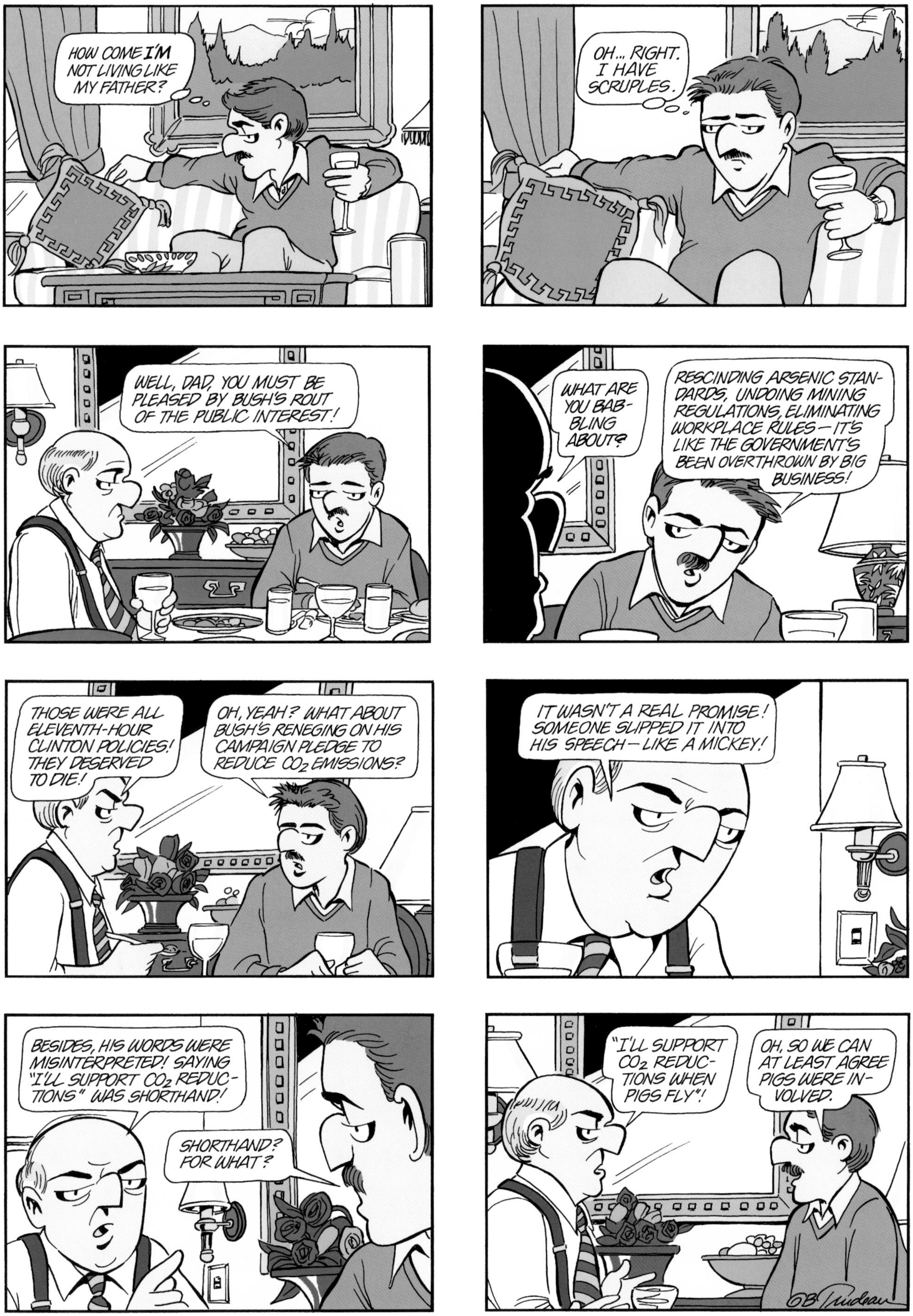
HOW COME I'M NOT LIVING LIKE MY FATHER?
OH... RIGHT. I HAVE SCRUPLES.
WELL, DAD, YOU MUST BE PLEASED BY BUSH'S ROUT OF THE PUBLIC INTEREST!
WHAT ARE YOU BAB-BLING ABOUT?
RESCINDING ARSENIC STAN-DARDS, UNDOING MINING REGULATIONS, ELIMINATING WORKPLACE RULES — IT'S LIKE THE GOVERNMENT'S BEEN OVERTHROWN BY BIG BUSINESS!
THOSE WERE ALL ELEVENTH-HOUR CLINTON POLICIES! THEY DESERVED TO DIE!
OH, YEAH? WHAT ABOUT BUSH'S RENEGING ON HIS CAMPAIGN PLEDGE TO REDUCE CO_2 EMISSIONS?
IT WASN'T A REAL PROMISE! SOMEONE SLIPPED IT INTO HIS SPEECH — LIKE A MICKEY!
BESIDES, HIS WORDS WERE MISINTERPRETED! SAYING "I'LL SUPPORT CO_2 REDUC-TIONS" WAS SHORTHAND!
SHORTHAND? FOR WHAT?
"I'LL SUPPORT CO_2 REDUC-TIONS WHEN PIGS FLY"!
OH, SO WE CAN AT LEAST AGREE PIGS WERE IN-VOLVED.
G.B. Trudeau

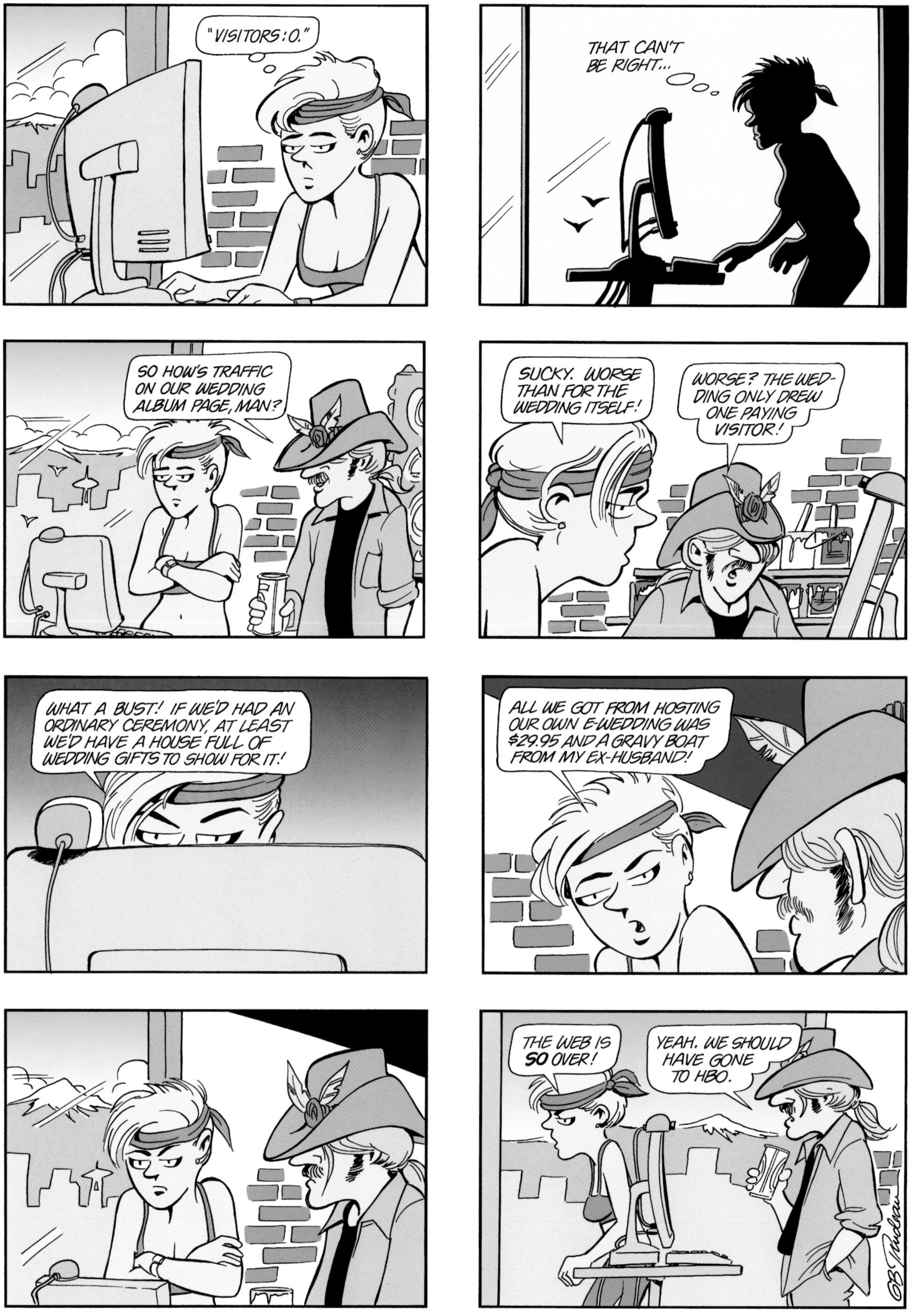
"VISITORS: 0."
THAT CAN'T BE RIGHT...
SO HOW'S TRAFFIC ON OUR WEDDING ALBUM PAGE, MAN?
SUCKY. WORSE THAN FOR THE WEDDING ITSELF!
WORSE? THE WEDDING ONLY DREW ONE PAYING VISITOR!
WHAT A BUST! IF WE'D HAD AN ORDINARY CEREMONY, AT LEAST WE'D HAVE A HOUSE FULL OF WEDDING GIFTS TO SHOW FOR IT!
ALL WE GOT FROM HOSTING OUR OWN E-WEDDING WAS $29.95 AND A GRAVY BOAT FROM MY EX-HUSBAND!
THE WEB IS **SO** OVER!
YEAH. WE SHOULD HAVE GONE TO HBO.
GBTrudeau

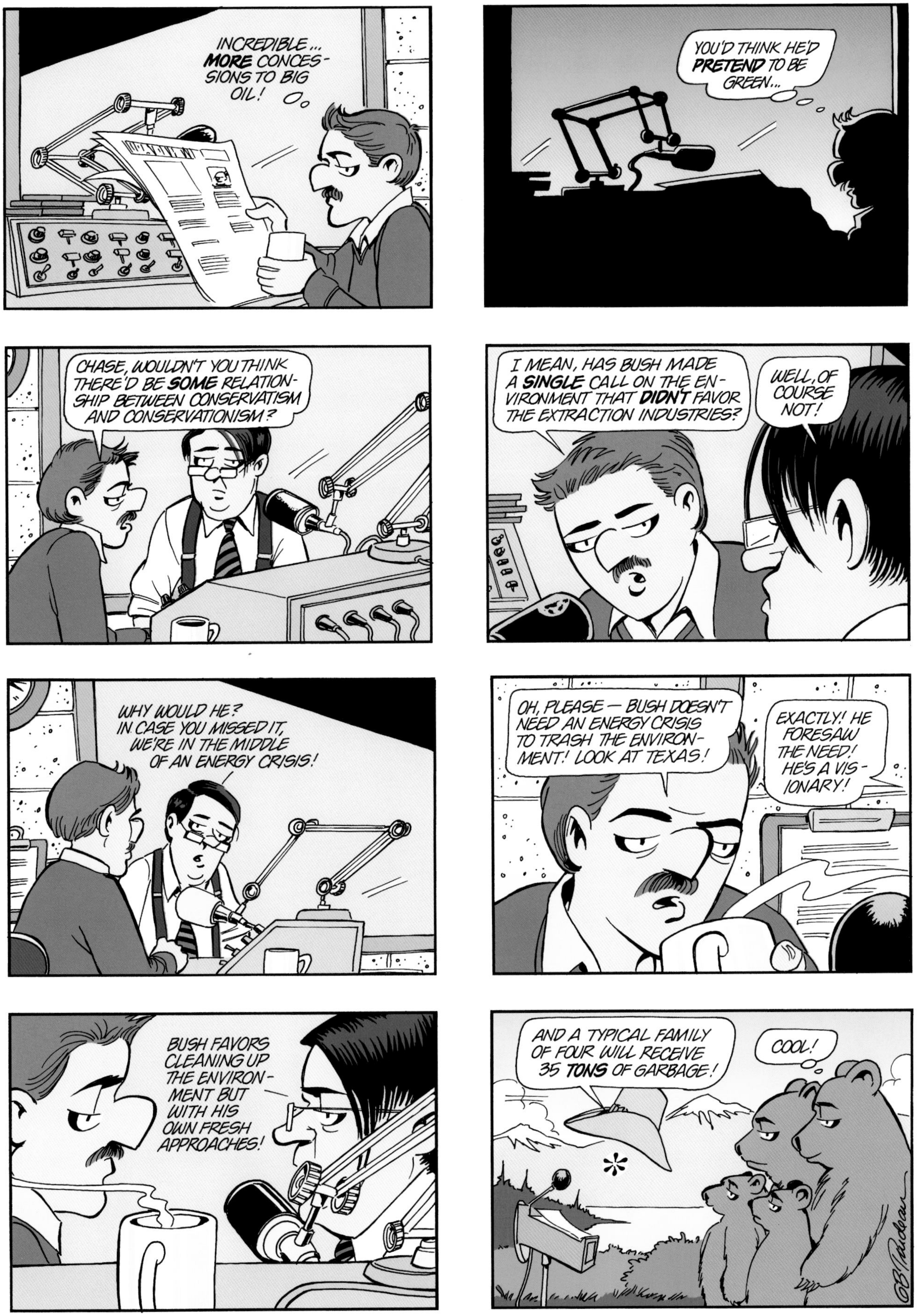
INCREDIBLE... MORE CONCESSIONS TO BIG OIL!
YOU'D THINK HE'D PRETEND TO BE GREEN...
CHASE, WOULDN'T YOU THINK THERE'D BE SOME RELATIONSHIP BETWEEN CONSERVATISM AND CONSERVATIONISM?
I MEAN, HAS BUSH MADE A SINGLE CALL ON THE ENVIRONMENT THAT DIDN'T FAVOR THE EXTRACTION INDUSTRIES?
WELL, OF COURSE NOT!
WHY WOULD HE? IN CASE YOU MISSED IT, WE'RE IN THE MIDDLE OF AN ENERGY CRISIS!
OH, PLEASE — BUSH DOESN'T NEED AN ENERGY CRISIS TO TRASH THE ENVIRONMENT! LOOK AT TEXAS!
EXACTLY! HE FORESAW THE NEED! HE'S A VISIONARY!
BUSH FAVORS CLEANING UP THE ENVIRONMENT BUT WITH HIS OWN FRESH APPROACHES!
AND A TYPICAL FAMILY OF FOUR WILL RECEIVE 35 TONS OF GARBAGE!
COOL!

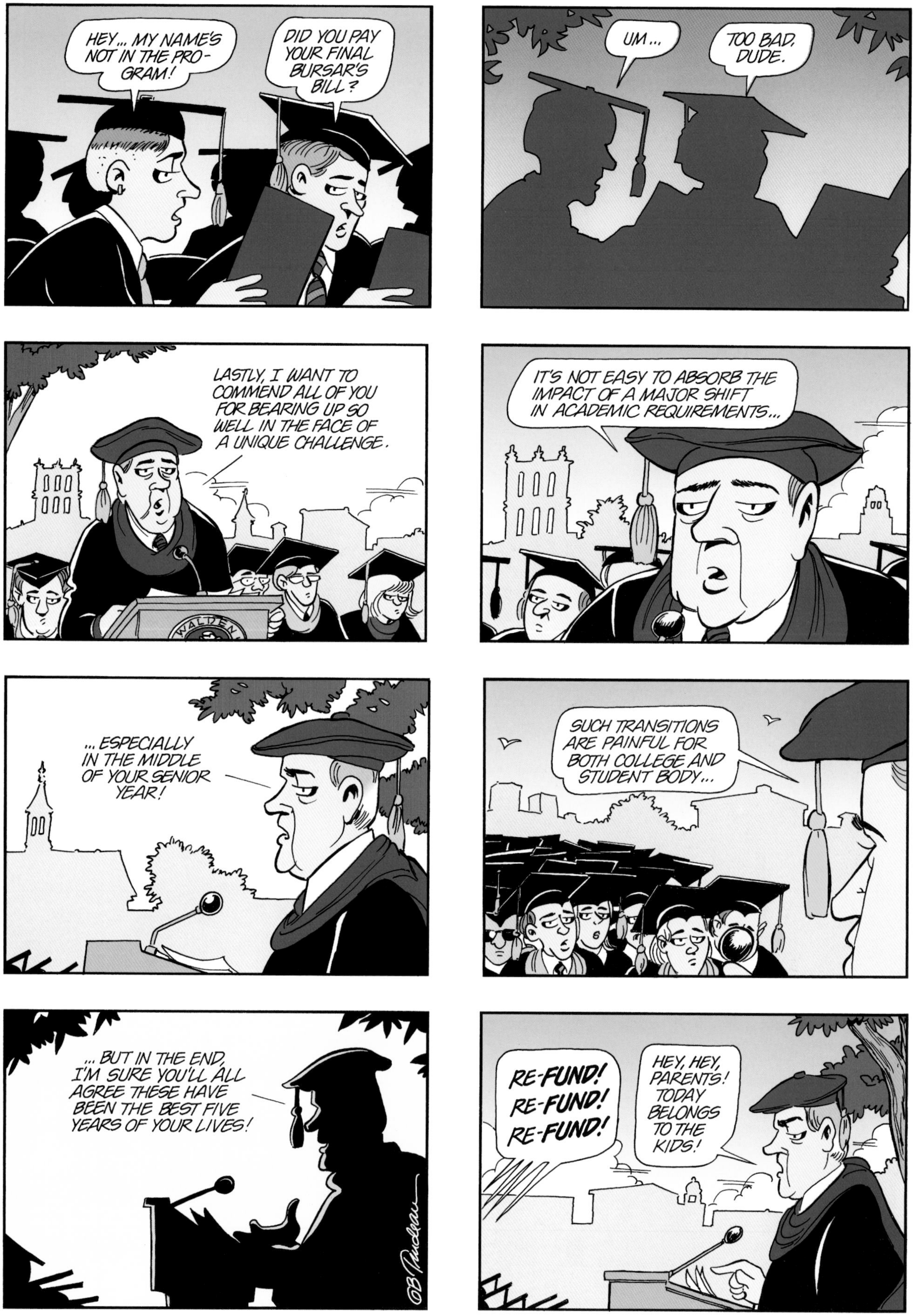
HEY... MY NAME'S NOT IN THE PRO-GRAM!
DID YOU PAY YOUR FINAL BURSAR'S BILL?
UM...
TOO BAD, DUDE.
LASTLY, I WANT TO COMMEND ALL OF YOU FOR BEARING UP SO WELL IN THE FACE OF A UNIQUE CHALLENGE.
IT'S NOT EASY TO ABSORB THE IMPACT OF A MAJOR SHIFT IN ACADEMIC REQUIREMENTS...
...ESPECIALLY IN THE MIDDLE OF YOUR SENIOR YEAR!
SUCH TRANSITIONS ARE PAINFUL FOR BOTH COLLEGE AND STUDENT BODY...
...BUT IN THE END, I'M SURE YOU'LL ALL AGREE THESE HAVE BEEN THE BEST FIVE YEARS OF YOUR LIVES!
RE-FUND! RE-FUND! RE-FUND!
HEY, HEY, PARENTS! TODAY BELONGS TO THE KIDS!

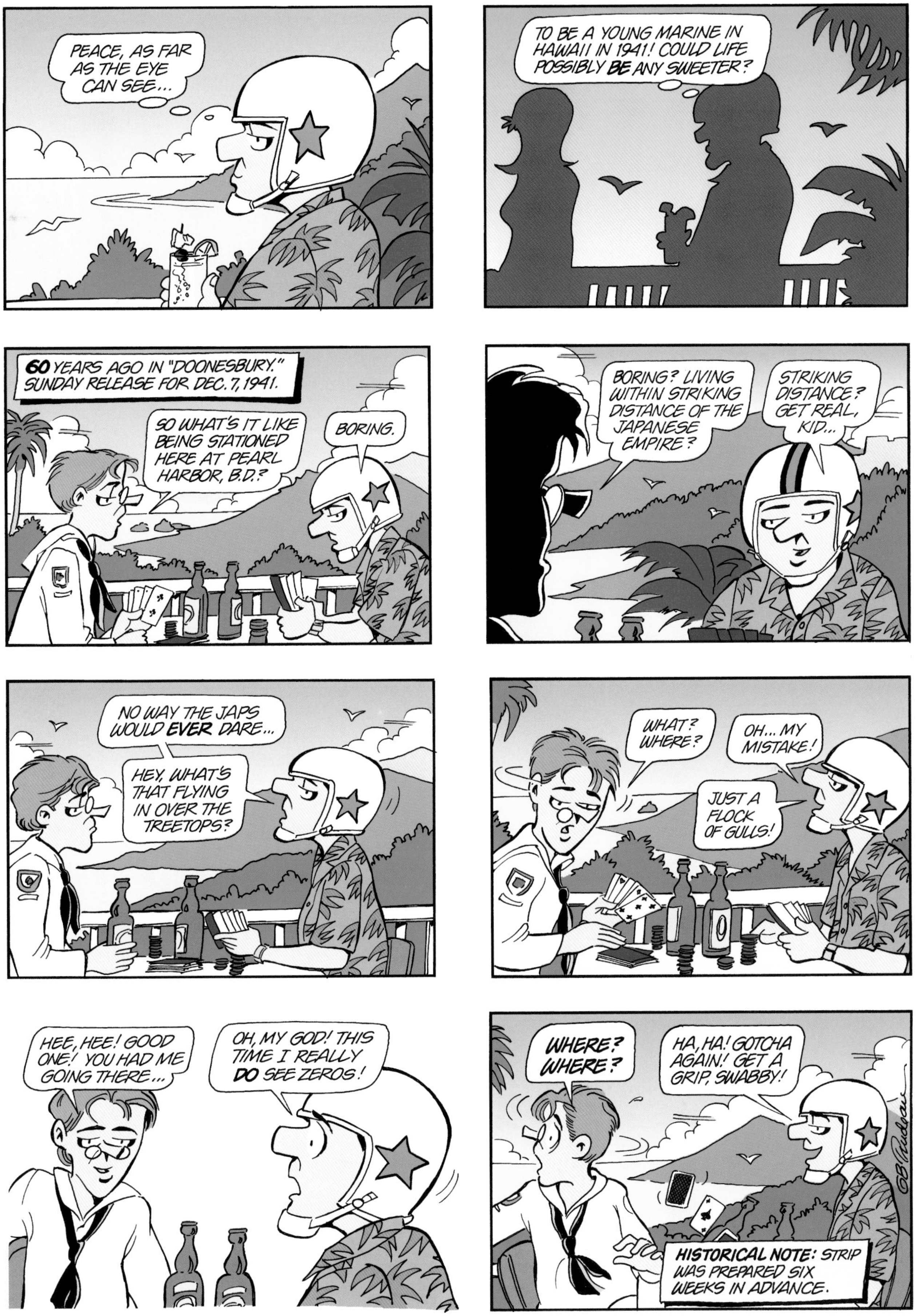
PEACE, AS FAR AS THE EYE CAN SEE...
TO BE A YOUNG MARINE IN HAWAII IN 1941! COULD LIFE POSSIBLY BE ANY SWEETER?
60 YEARS AGO IN "DOONESBURY." SUNDAY RELEASE FOR DEC. 7, 1941.
SO WHAT'S IT LIKE BEING STATIONED HERE AT PEARL HARBOR, B.D.?
BORING.
BORING? LIVING WITHIN STRIKING DISTANCE OF THE JAPANESE EMPIRE?
STRIKING DISTANCE? GET REAL, KID...
NO WAY THE JAPS WOULD EVER DARE...
HEY, WHAT'S THAT FLYING IN OVER THE TREETOPS?
WHAT? WHERE?
OH... MY MISTAKE!
JUST A FLOCK OF GULLS!
HEE, HEE! GOOD ONE! YOU HAD ME GOING THERE...
OH, MY GOD! THIS TIME I REALLY DO SEE ZEROS!
WHERE? WHERE?
HA, HA! GOTCHA AGAIN! GET A GRIP, SWABBY!
HISTORICAL NOTE: STRIP WAS PREPARED SIX WEEKS IN ADVANCE.

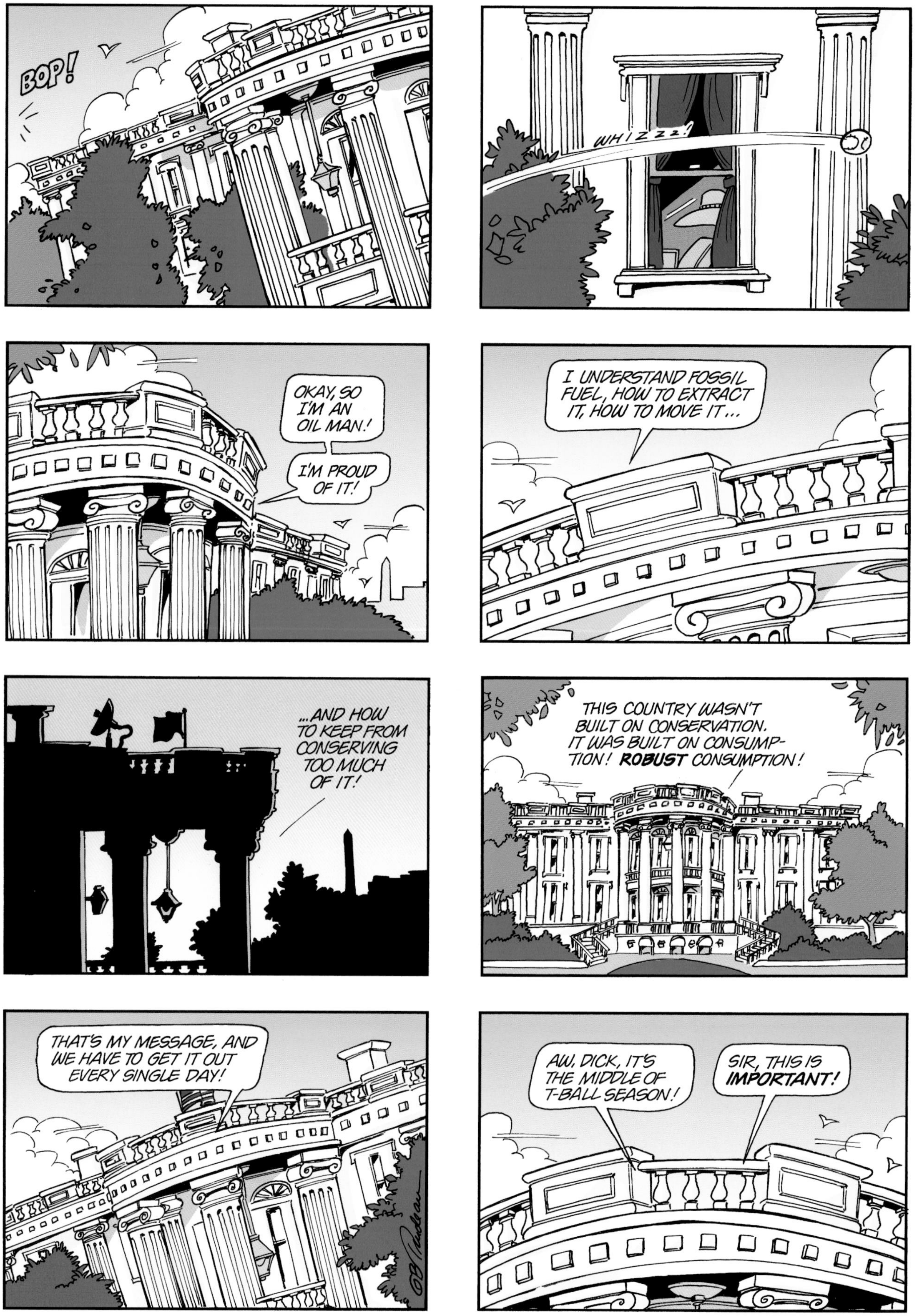
BOP!
WHIZZZ!
OKAY, SO I'M AN OIL MAN!
I'M PROUD OF IT!
I UNDERSTAND FOSSIL FUEL, HOW TO EXTRACT IT, HOW TO MOVE IT...
...AND HOW TO KEEP FROM CONSERVING TOO MUCH OF IT!
THIS COUNTRY WASN'T BUILT ON CONSERVATION. IT WAS BUILT ON CONSUMPTION! **ROBUST** CONSUMPTION!
THAT'S MY MESSAGE, AND WE HAVE TO GET IT OUT EVERY SINGLE DAY!
AW, DICK, IT'S THE MIDDLE OF T-BALL SEASON!
SIR, THIS IS **IMPORTANT!**

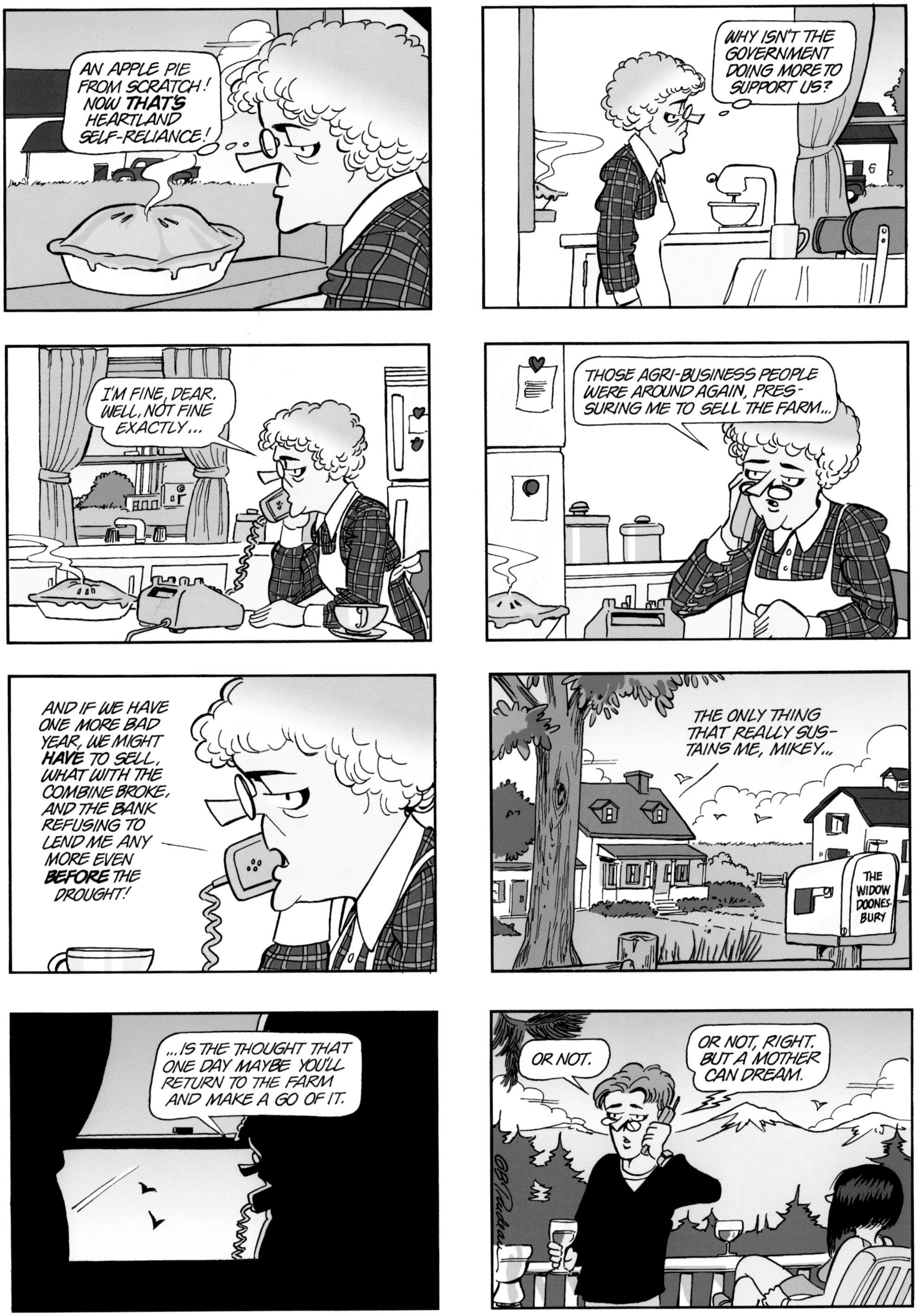
AN APPLE PIE FROM SCRATCH! NOW THAT'S HEARTLAND SELF-RELIANCE!
WHY ISN'T THE GOVERNMENT DOING MORE TO SUPPORT US?
I'M FINE, DEAR. WELL, NOT FINE EXACTLY...
THOSE AGRI-BUSINESS PEOPLE WERE AROUND AGAIN, PRESSURING ME TO SELL THE FARM...
AND IF WE HAVE ONE MORE BAD YEAR, WE MIGHT HAVE TO SELL, WHAT WITH THE COMBINE BROKE, AND THE BANK REFUSING TO LEND ME ANY MORE EVEN BEFORE THE DROUGHT!
THE ONLY THING THAT REALLY SUSTAINS ME, MIKEY...
THE WIDOW DOONESBURY
...IS THE THOUGHT THAT ONE DAY MAYBE YOU'LL RETURN TO THE FARM AND MAKE A GO OF IT.
OR NOT.
OR NOT, RIGHT. BUT A MOTHER CAN DREAM.

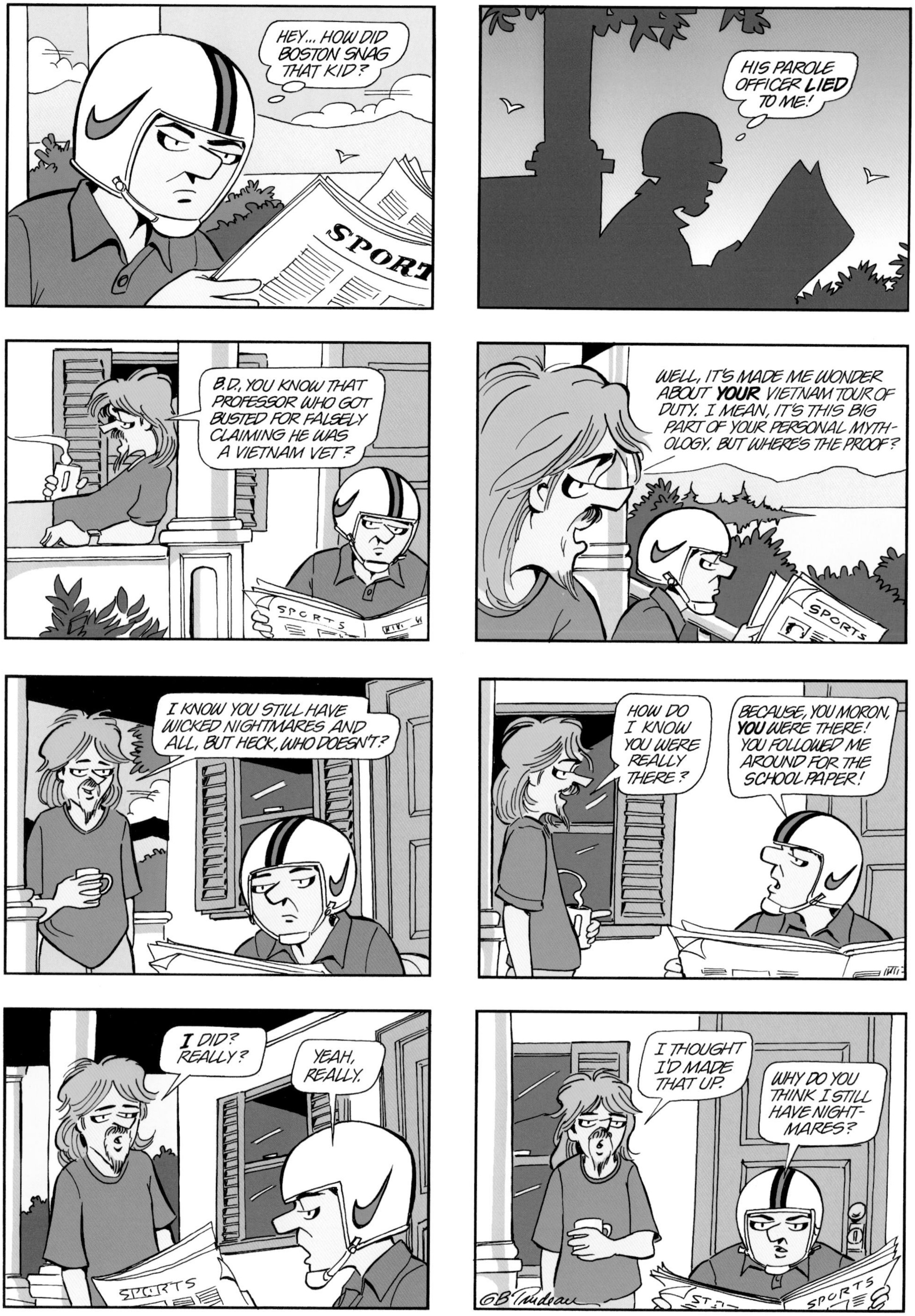
HEY... HOW DID BOSTON SNAG THAT KID?
SPORT
HIS PAROLE OFFICER **LIED** TO ME!
B.D., YOU KNOW THAT PROFESSOR WHO GOT BUSTED FOR FALSELY CLAIMING HE WAS A VIETNAM VET?
SPORTS
WELL, IT'S MADE ME WONDER ABOUT **YOUR** VIETNAM TOUR OF DUTY. I MEAN, IT'S THIS BIG PART OF YOUR PERSONAL MYTHOLOGY. BUT WHERE'S THE PROOF?
SPORTS
I KNOW YOU STILL HAVE WICKED NIGHTMARES AND ALL, BUT HECK, WHO DOESN'T?
HOW DO I KNOW YOU WERE REALLY THERE?
BECAUSE, YOU MORON, **YOU** WERE THERE! YOU FOLLOWED ME AROUND FOR THE SCHOOL PAPER!
I DID? REALLY?
YEAH, REALLY.
SPORTS
I THOUGHT I'D MADE THAT UP.
WHY DO YOU THINK I STILL HAVE NIGHTMARES?
SPORTS
©B Trudeau

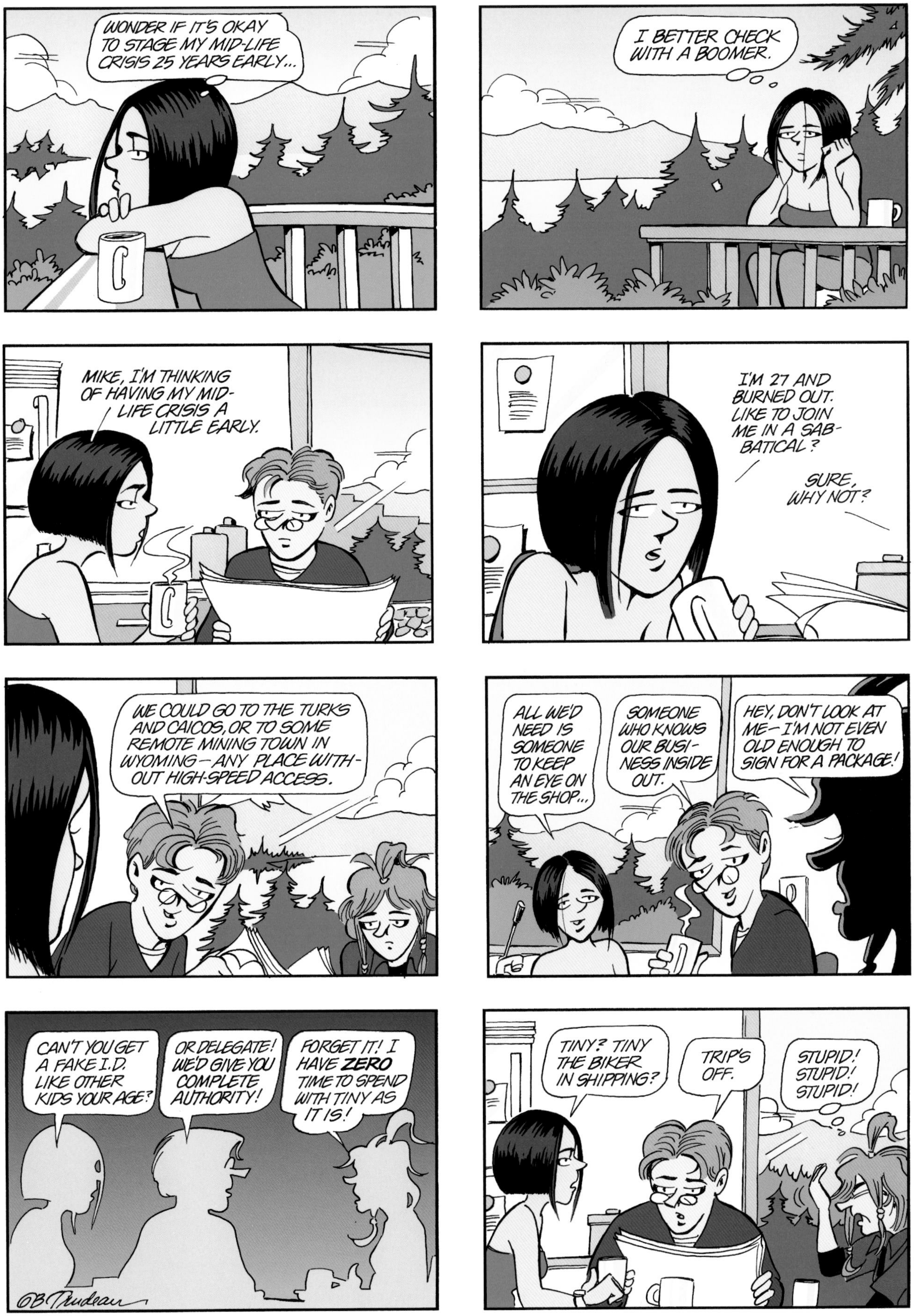
WONDER IF IT'S OKAY TO STAGE MY MID-LIFE CRISIS 25 YEARS EARLY...
I BETTER CHECK WITH A BOOMER.
MIKE, I'M THINKING OF HAVING MY MID-LIFE CRISIS A LITTLE EARLY.
I'M 27 AND BURNED OUT. LIKE TO JOIN ME IN A SAB-BATICAL?
SURE, WHY NOT?
WE COULD GO TO THE TURKS AND CAICOS, OR TO SOME REMOTE MINING TOWN IN WYOMING — ANY PLACE WITH-OUT HIGH-SPEED ACCESS.
ALL WE'D NEED IS SOMEONE TO KEEP AN EYE ON THE SHOP...
SOMEONE WHO KNOWS OUR BUSI-NESS INSIDE OUT.
HEY, DON'T LOOK AT ME — I'M NOT EVEN OLD ENOUGH TO SIGN FOR A PACKAGE!
CAN'T YOU GET A FAKE I.D. LIKE OTHER KIDS YOUR AGE?
OR DELEGATE! WE'D GIVE YOU COMPLETE AUTHORITY!
FORGET IT! I HAVE **ZERO** TIME TO SPEND WITH TINY AS IT IS!
©B. Trudeau
TINY? TINY THE BIKER IN SHIPPING?
TRIP'S OFF.
STUPID! STUPID! STUPID!

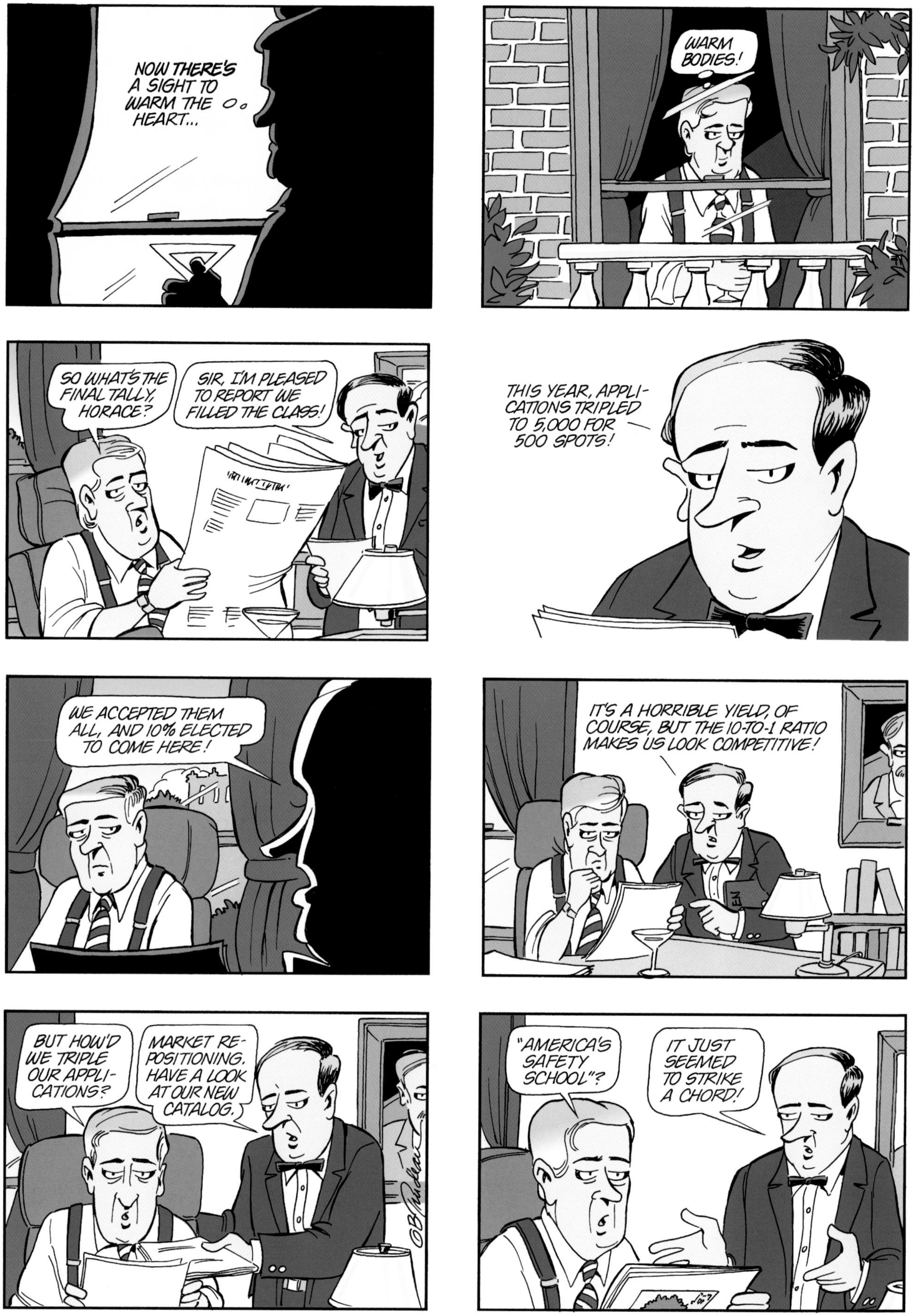
NOW THERE'S A SIGHT TO WARM THE HEART...
WARM BODIES!
SO WHAT'S THE FINAL TALLY, HORACE?
SIR, I'M PLEASED TO REPORT WE FILLED THE CLASS!
THIS YEAR, APPLICATIONS TRIPLED TO 5,000 FOR 500 SPOTS!
WE ACCEPTED THEM ALL, AND 10% ELECTED TO COME HERE!
IT'S A HORRIBLE YIELD, OF COURSE, BUT THE 10-TO-1 RATIO MAKES US LOOK COMPETITIVE!
BUT HOW'D WE TRIPLE OUR APPLICATIONS?
MARKET REPOSITIONING. HAVE A LOOK AT OUR NEW CATALOG.
"AMERICA'S SAFETY SCHOOL"?
IT JUST SEEMED TO STRIKE A CHORD!

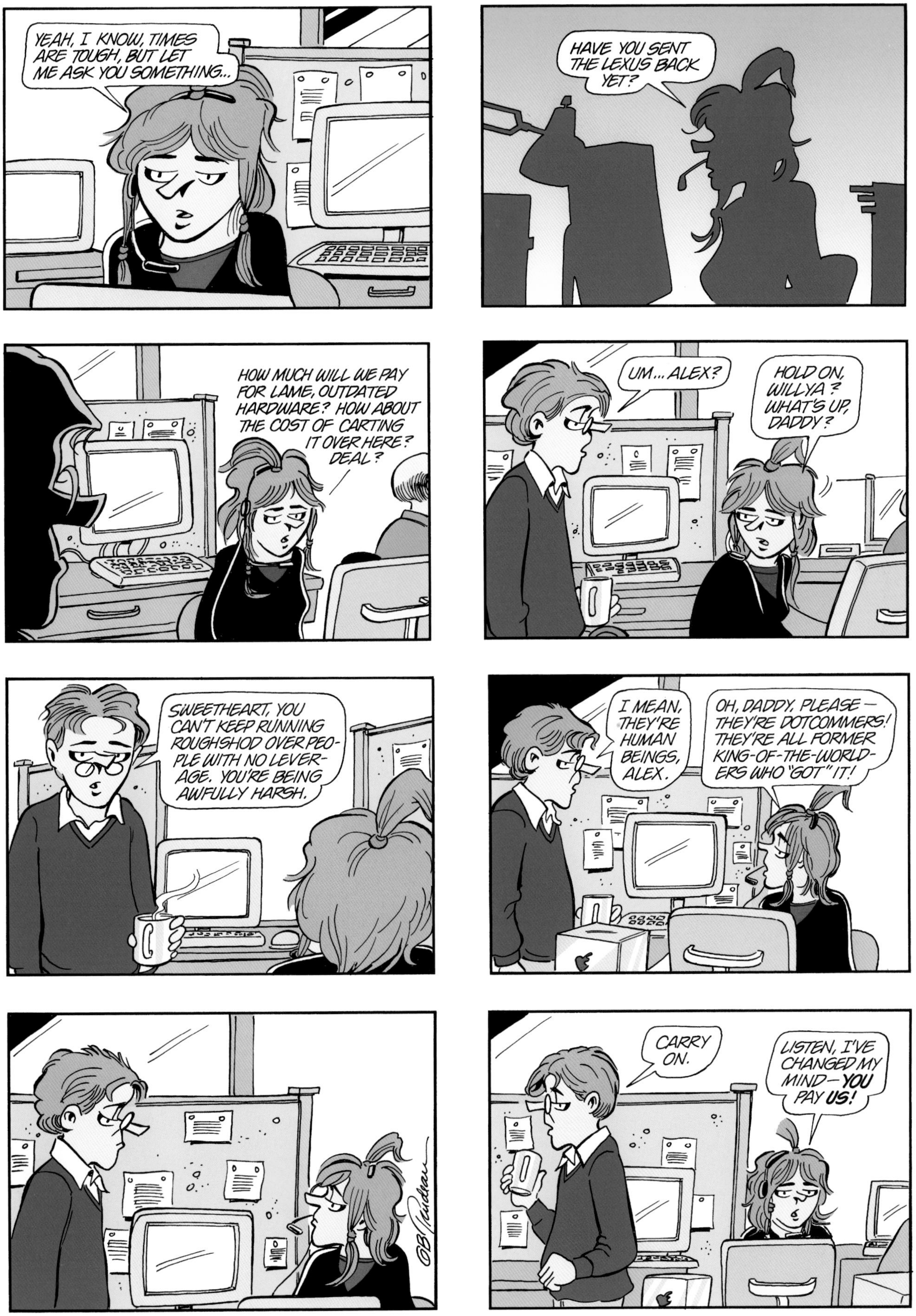
YEAH, I KNOW, TIMES ARE TOUGH, BUT LET ME ASK YOU SOMETHING...
HAVE YOU SENT THE LEXUS BACK YET?
HOW MUCH WILL WE PAY FOR LAME, OUTDATED HARDWARE? HOW ABOUT THE COST OF CARTING IT OVER HERE? DEAL?
UM... ALEX?
HOLD ON, WILLYA? WHAT'S UP, DADDY?
SWEETHEART, YOU CAN'T KEEP RUNNING ROUGHSHOD OVER PEOPLE WITH NO LEVERAGE. YOU'RE BEING AWFULLY HARSH.
I MEAN, THEY'RE HUMAN BEINGS, ALEX.
OH, DADDY, PLEASE — THEY'RE DOTCOMMERS! THEY'RE ALL FORMER KING-OF-THE-WORLDERS WHO "GOT" IT!
CARRY ON.
LISTEN, I'VE CHANGED MY MIND — **YOU** PAY **US**!

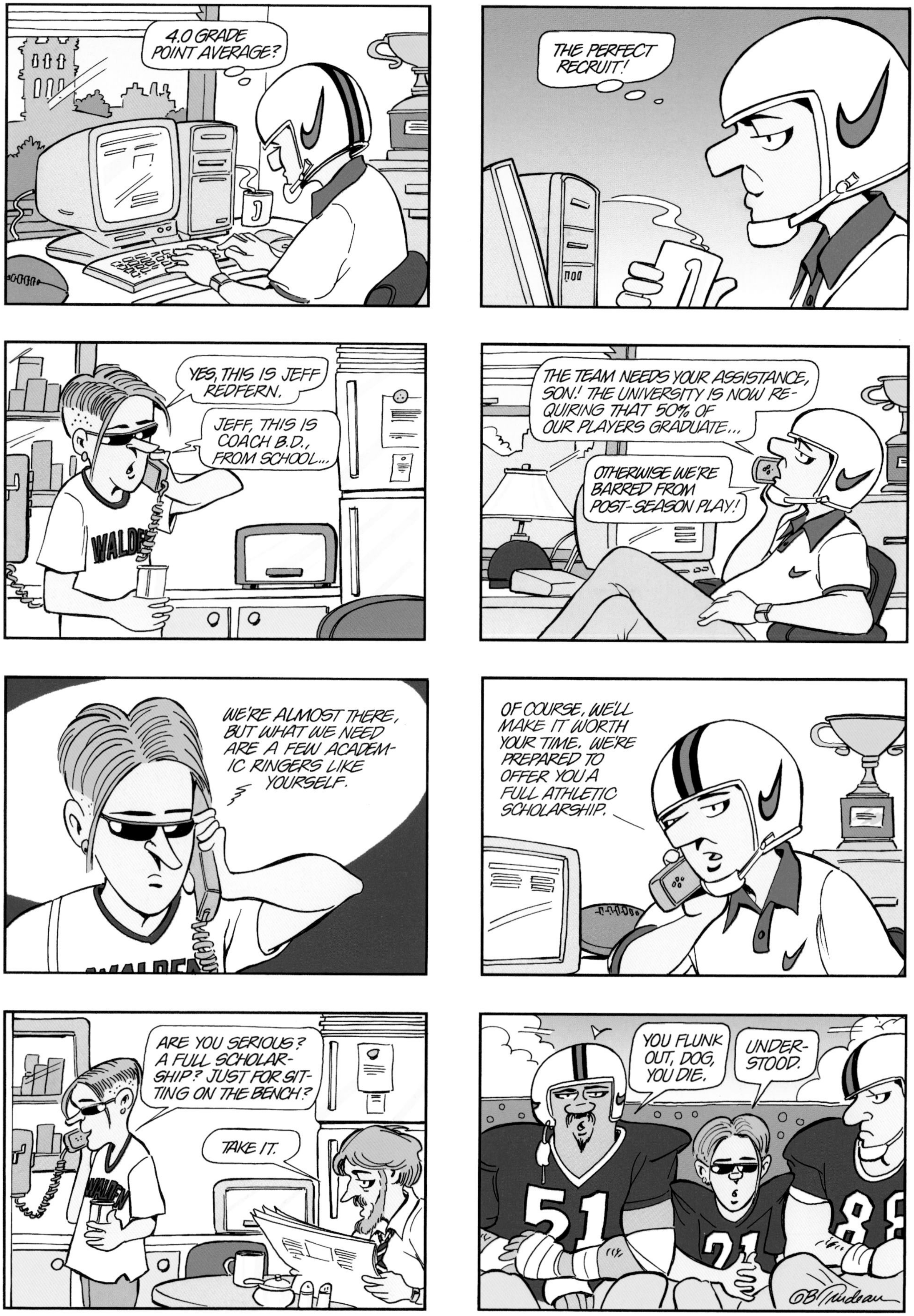
4.0 GRADE POINT AVERAGE?
THE PERFECT RECRUIT!
YES, THIS IS JEFF REDFERN.
JEFF, THIS IS COACH B.D., FROM SCHOOL...
THE TEAM NEEDS YOUR ASSISTANCE, SON! THE UNIVERSITY IS NOW REQUIRING THAT 50% OF OUR PLAYERS GRADUATE...
OTHERWISE WE'RE BARRED FROM POST-SEASON PLAY!
WE'RE ALMOST THERE, BUT WHAT WE NEED ARE A FEW ACADEMIC RINGERS LIKE YOURSELF.
OF COURSE, WE'LL MAKE IT WORTH YOUR TIME. WE'RE PREPARED TO OFFER YOU A FULL ATHLETIC SCHOLARSHIP.
ARE YOU SERIOUS? A FULL SCHOLARSHIP? JUST FOR SITTING ON THE BENCH?
TAKE IT.
YOU FLUNK OUT, DOG, YOU DIE.
UNDERSTOOD.
51
21
GBTrudeau

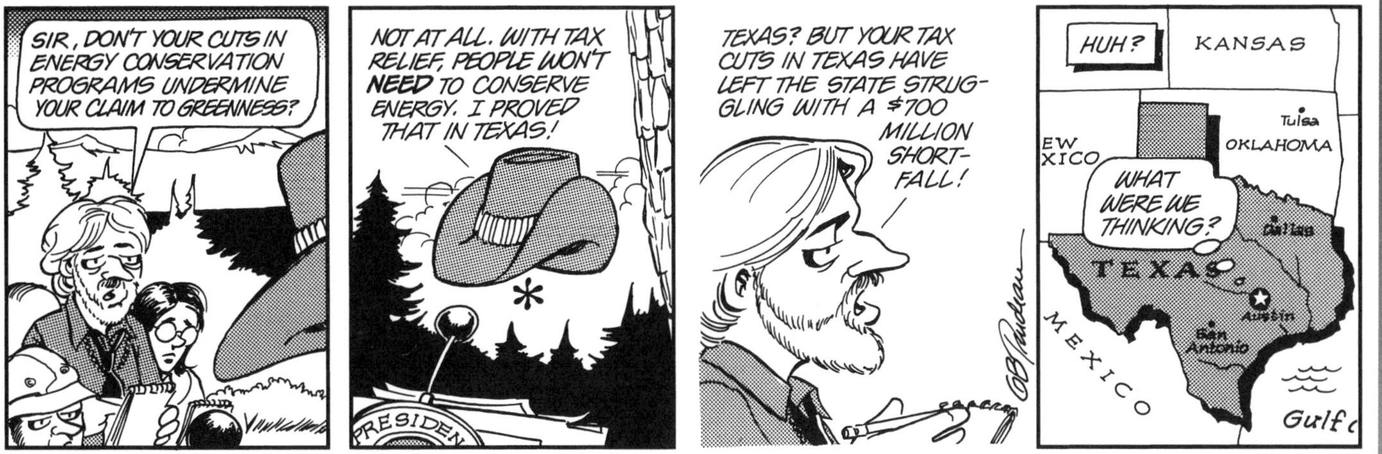
SIR, DON'T YOUR CUTS IN ENERGY CONSERVATION PROGRAMS UNDERMINE YOUR CLAIM TO GREENNESS?
NOT AT ALL. WITH TAX RELIEF, PEOPLE WON'T **NEED** TO CONSERVE ENERGY. I PROVED THAT IN TEXAS!
PRESIDEN
TEXAS? BUT YOUR TAX CUTS IN TEXAS HAVE LEFT THE STATE STRUGGLING WITH A $700 MILLION SHORTFALL!
GB Trudeau
HUH?
KANSAS
OKLAHOMA
Tulsa
EW XICO
WHAT WERE WE THINKING?
Dallas
TEXAS
Austin
San Antonio
MEXICO
Gulf

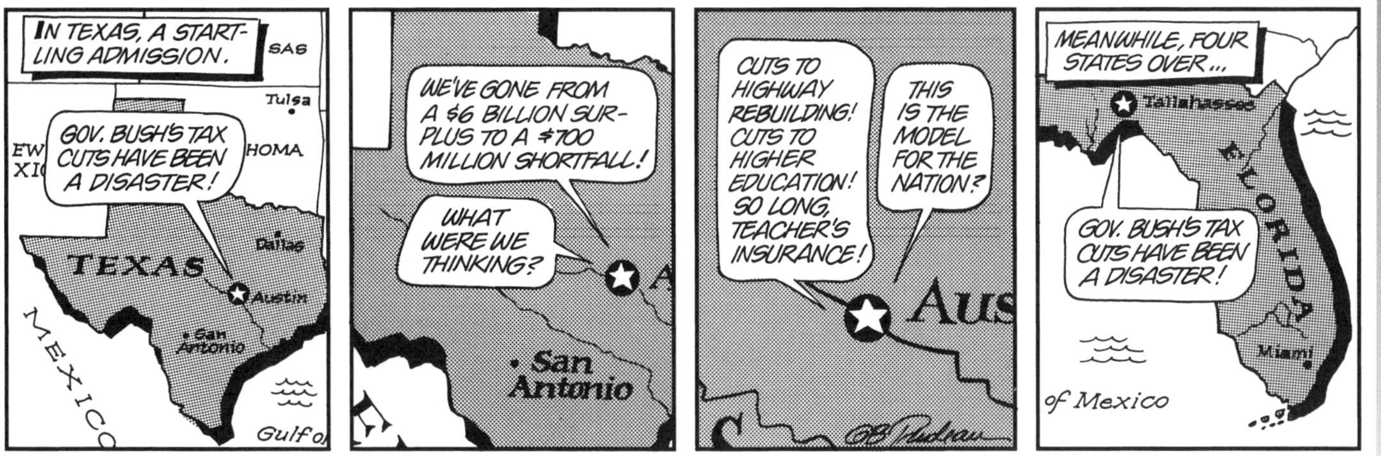
IN TEXAS, A STARTLING ADMISSION.
SAS
Tulsa
HOMA
GOV. BUSH'S TAX CUTS HAVE BEEN A DISASTER!
TEXAS
Dallas
Austin
San Antonio
MEXICO
Gulf of
WE'VE GONE FROM A $6 BILLION SURPLUS TO A $700 MILLION SHORTFALL!
WHAT WERE WE THINKING?
San Antonio
CUTS TO HIGHWAY REBUILDING! CUTS TO HIGHER EDUCATION! SO LONG, TEACHER'S INSURANCE!
THIS IS THE MODEL FOR THE NATION?
Aus
GB Trudeau
MEANWHILE, FOUR STATES OVER...
Tallahassee
FLORIDA
GOV. BUSH'S TAX CUTS HAVE BEEN A DISASTER!
Miami
of Mexico

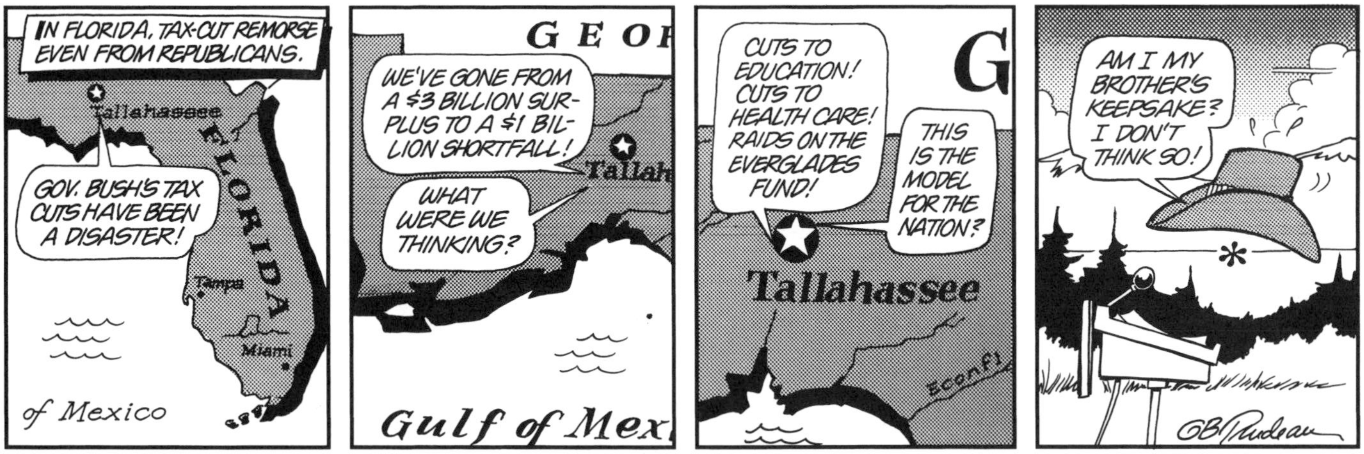
IN FLORIDA, TAX-CUT REMORSE EVEN FROM REPUBLICANS.
Tallahassee
FLORIDA
GOV. BUSH'S TAX CUTS HAVE BEEN A DISASTER!
Tampa
Miami
of Mexico
GEOR
WE'VE GONE FROM A $3 BILLION SURPLUS TO A $1 BILLION SHORTFALL!
Tallah
WHAT WERE WE THINKING?
Gulf of Mex
CUTS TO EDUCATION! CUTS TO HEALTH CARE! RAIDS ON THE EVERGLADES FUND!
THIS IS THE MODEL FOR THE NATION?
G
Tallahassee
Econfi
AM I MY BROTHER'S KEEPSAKE? I DON'T THINK SO!
GB Trudeau

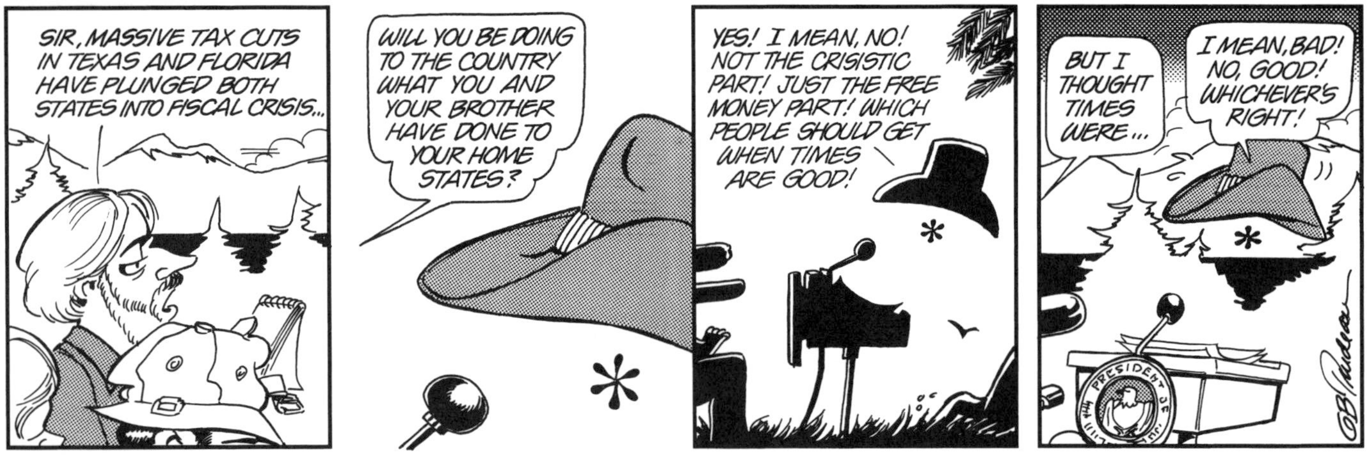
SIR, MASSIVE TAX CUTS IN TEXAS AND FLORIDA HAVE PLUNGED BOTH STATES INTO FISCAL CRISIS...
WILL YOU BE DOING TO THE COUNTRY WHAT YOU AND YOUR BROTHER HAVE DONE TO YOUR HOME STATES?
YES! I MEAN, NO! NOT THE CRISISTIC PART! JUST THE FREE MONEY PART! WHICH PEOPLE SHOULD GET WHEN TIMES ARE GOOD!
BUT I THOUGHT TIMES WERE...
I MEAN, BAD! NO, GOOD! WHICHEVER'S RIGHT!
©B Trudeau

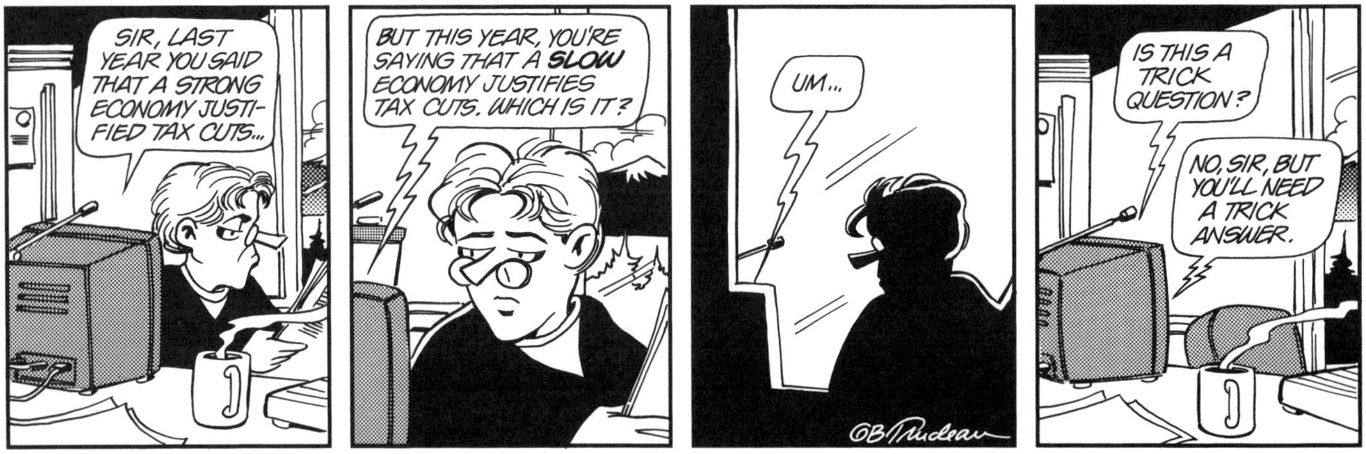
SIR, LAST YEAR YOU SAID THAT A STRONG ECONOMY JUSTIFIED TAX CUTS...
BUT THIS YEAR, YOU'RE SAYING THAT A **SLOW** ECONOMY JUSTIFIES TAX CUTS. WHICH IS IT?
UM...
©B Trudeau
IS THIS A TRICK QUESTION?
NO, SIR, BUT YOU'LL NEED A TRICK ANSWER.

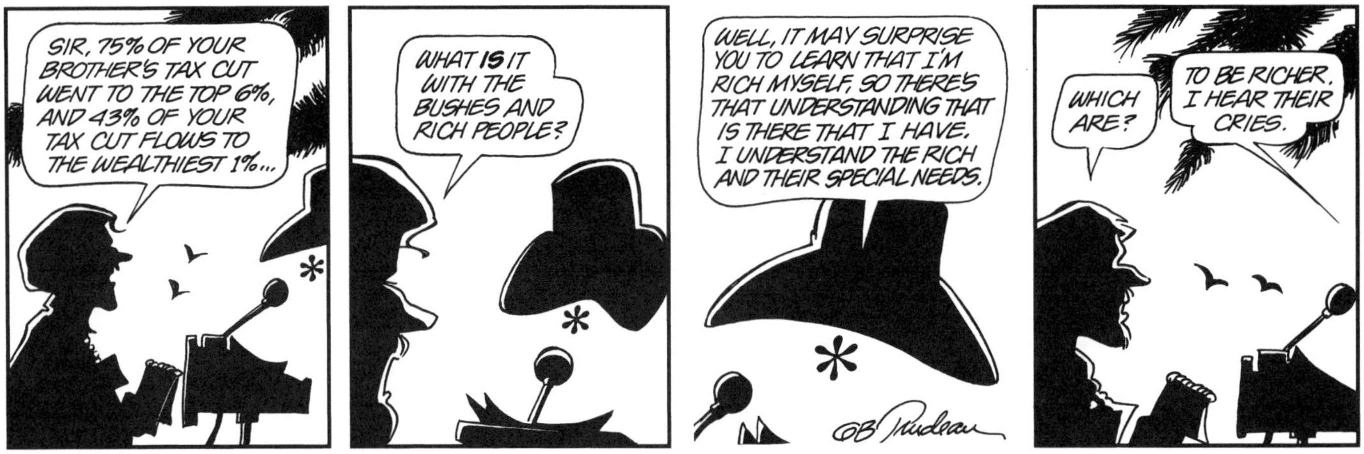
SIR, 75% OF YOUR BROTHER'S TAX CUT WENT TO THE TOP 6%, AND 43% OF YOUR TAX CUT FLOWS TO THE WEALTHIEST 1%...
WHAT **IS** IT WITH THE BUSHES AND RICH PEOPLE?
WELL, IT MAY SURPRISE YOU TO LEARN THAT I'M RICH MYSELF, SO THERE'S THAT UNDERSTANDING THAT IS THERE THAT I HAVE. I UNDERSTAND THE RICH AND THEIR SPECIAL NEEDS.
©B Trudeau
WHICH ARE?
TO BE RICHER. I HEAR THEIR CRIES.

WHEN DID YOU STOP USING THE DRYER, DAD?
RIGHT AFTER WE GOT OUR LATEST ELECTRICITY BILL. IT WAS INSANE!
THE DRYER'S THE BIGGEST ENERGY HOG, SO WE DECIDED TO SUN-DRY! WHAT COULD BE SIMPLER, RIGHT?
WRONG.
MY GOD... WHAT'RE THEY DOING?
I BETTER CALL IT IN...
GB Trudeau

Q. WHAT AMAZING ENERGY-SAVING DEVICE...
1435 BROADRIPPLE TERRACE!
... CHEAP, LOW-TECH, EASY TO INSTALL...
COPY THAT!
... IS BANNED BY NEARLY ALL OF CALIFORNIA'S 35,000 HOMEOWNERS ASSOCIATIONS?
THERE THEY ARE!
A. THE CLOTHESLINE.
SIR! STEP AWAY FROM THE LAUNDRY!
DAMN... BUSTED!
GB Trudeau

SIR! STEP AWAY FROM THE LAUNDRY!
WHY? I'M IN MY OWN YARD.
CLOTHESLINES ARE BANNED IN THIS NEIGHBORHOOD, SIR!
BUT I'M TRYING TO SAVE ENERGY.
SORRY, SIR, BUT OUTDOOR DRYING IS ASSOCIATED WITH POVERTY! IT REDUCES PROPERTY VALUES!
OH...
OKAY, NOW, DROP THE LINE! NICE 'N' EASY!
DO AS HE SAYS, SON.
YES, SIR.
GB Trudeau

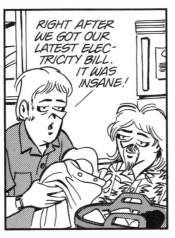

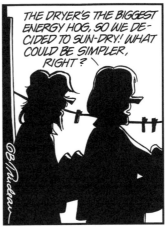

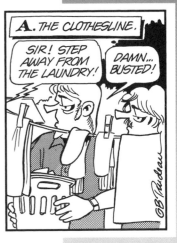

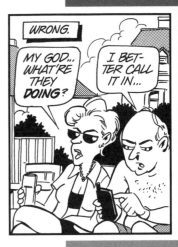

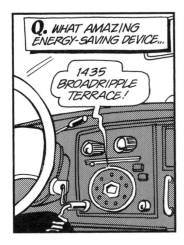

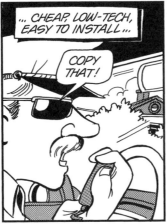

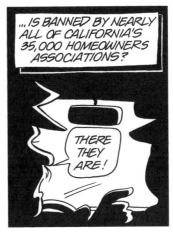

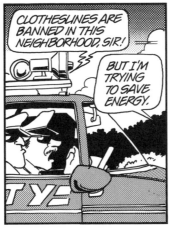

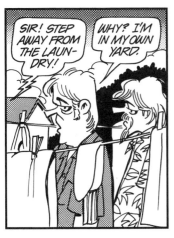

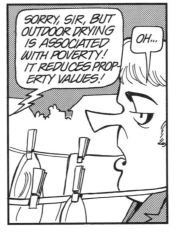

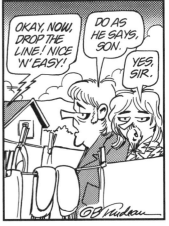

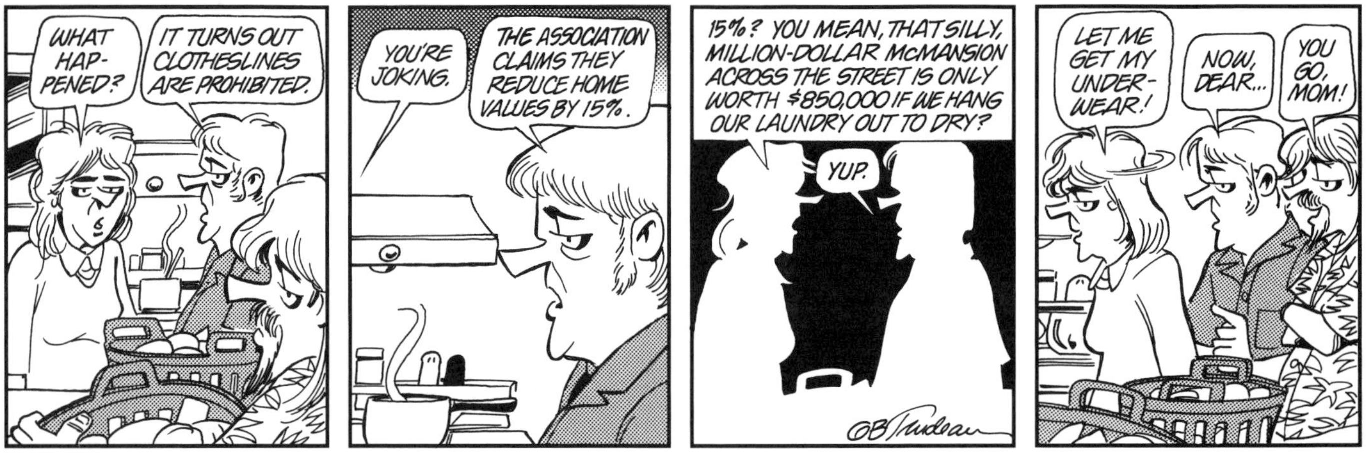
WHAT HAP-PENED?
IT TURNS OUT CLOTHESLINES ARE PROHIBITED.
YOU'RE JOKING.
THE ASSOCIATION CLAIMS THEY REDUCE HOME VALUES BY 15%.
15%? YOU MEAN, THAT SILLY, MILLION-DOLLAR McMANSION ACROSS THE STREET IS ONLY WORTH $850,000 IF WE HANG OUR LAUNDRY OUT TO DRY?
YUP.
GB Trudeau
LET ME GET MY UNDER-WEAR!
NOW, DEAR...
YOU GO, MOM!

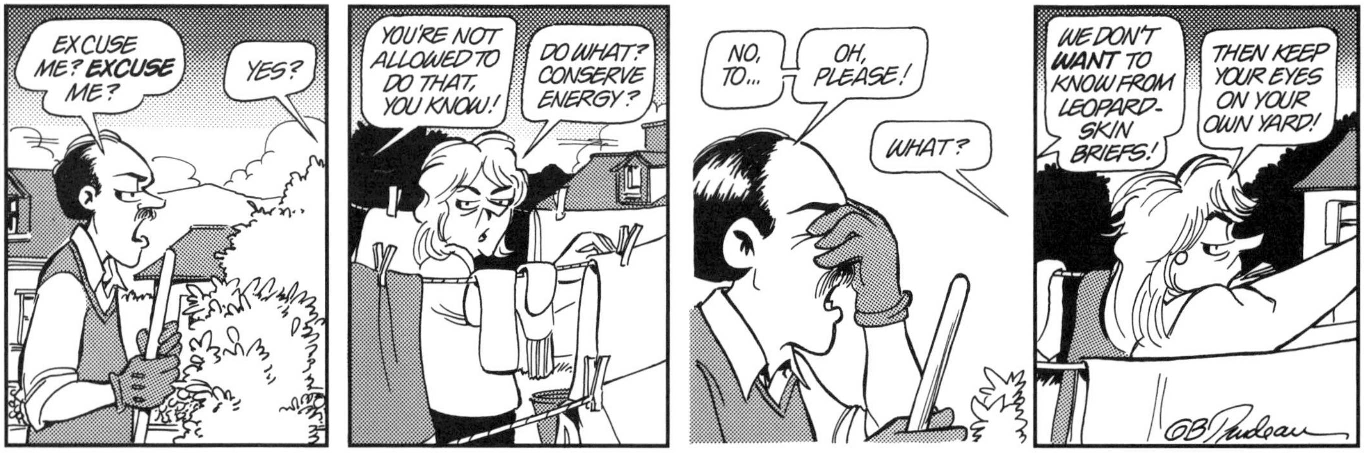
EXCUSE ME? EXCUSE ME?
YES?
YOU'RE NOT ALLOWED TO DO THAT, YOU KNOW!
DO WHAT? CONSERVE ENERGY?
NO, TO...
OH, PLEASE!
WHAT?
WE DON'T WANT TO KNOW FROM LEOPARD-SKIN BRIEFS!
THEN KEEP YOUR EYES ON YOUR OWN YARD!
GB Trudeau

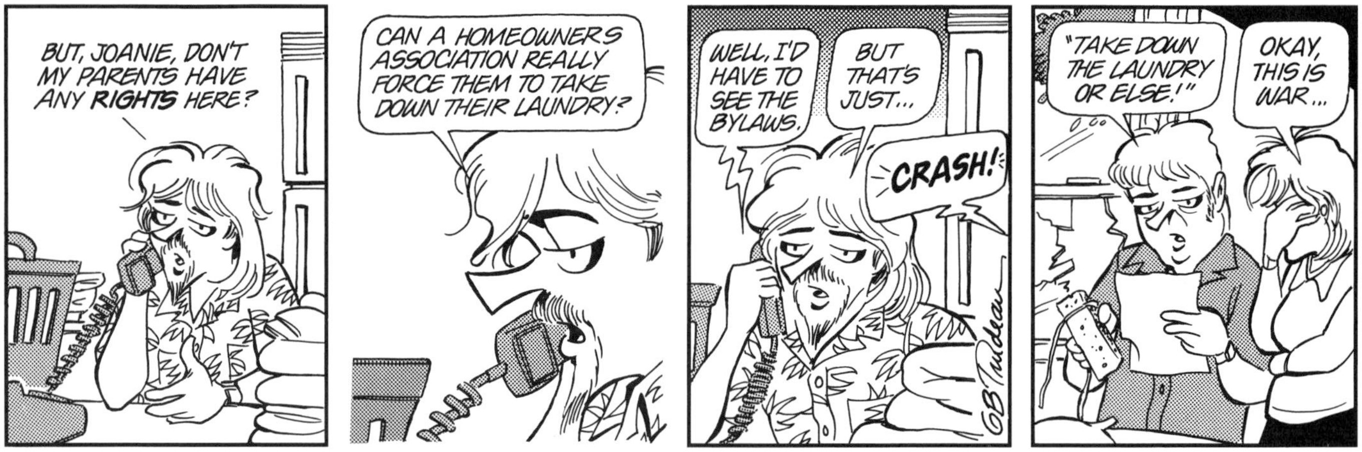
BUT, JOANIE, DON'T MY PARENTS HAVE ANY RIGHTS HERE?
CAN A HOMEOWNERS ASSOCIATION REALLY FORCE THEM TO TAKE DOWN THEIR LAUNDRY?
WELL, I'D HAVE TO SEE THE BYLAWS.
BUT THAT'S JUST...
CRASH!
GB Trudeau
"TAKE DOWN THE LAUNDRY OR ELSE!"
OKAY, THIS IS WAR...

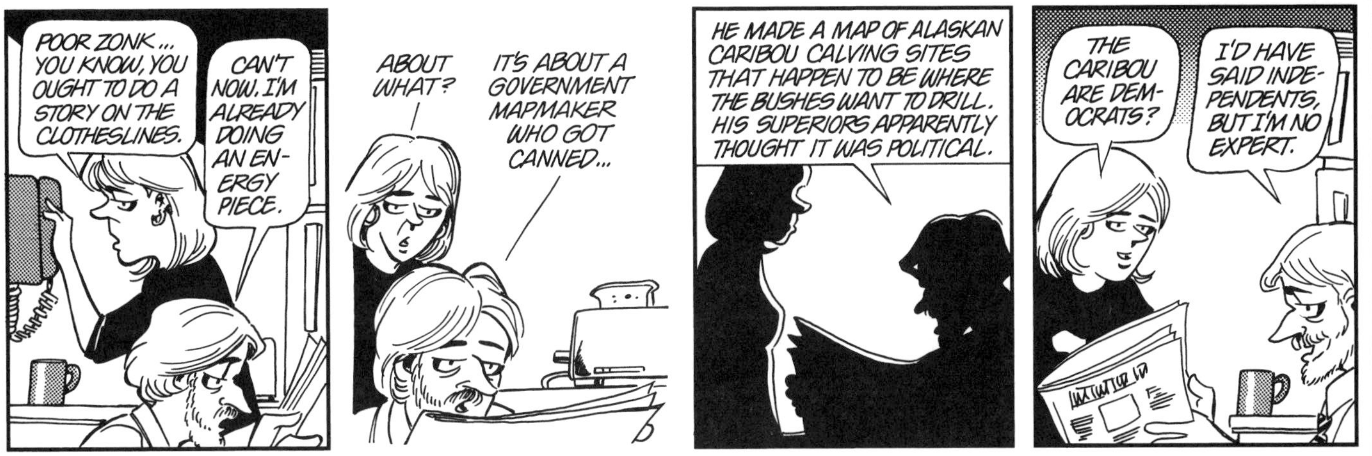
POOR ZONK... YOU KNOW, YOU OUGHT TO DO A STORY ON THE CLOTHESLINES.
CAN'T NOW. I'M ALREADY DOING AN ENERGY PIECE.
ABOUT WHAT?
IT'S ABOUT A GOVERNMENT MAPMAKER WHO GOT CANNED...
HE MADE A MAP OF ALASKAN CARIBOU CALVING SITES THAT HAPPEN TO BE WHERE THE BUSHES WANT TO DRILL. HIS SUPERIORS APPARENTLY THOUGHT IT WAS POLITICAL.
THE CARIBOU ARE DEMOCRATS?
I'D HAVE SAID INDEPENDENTS, BUT I'M NO EXPERT.

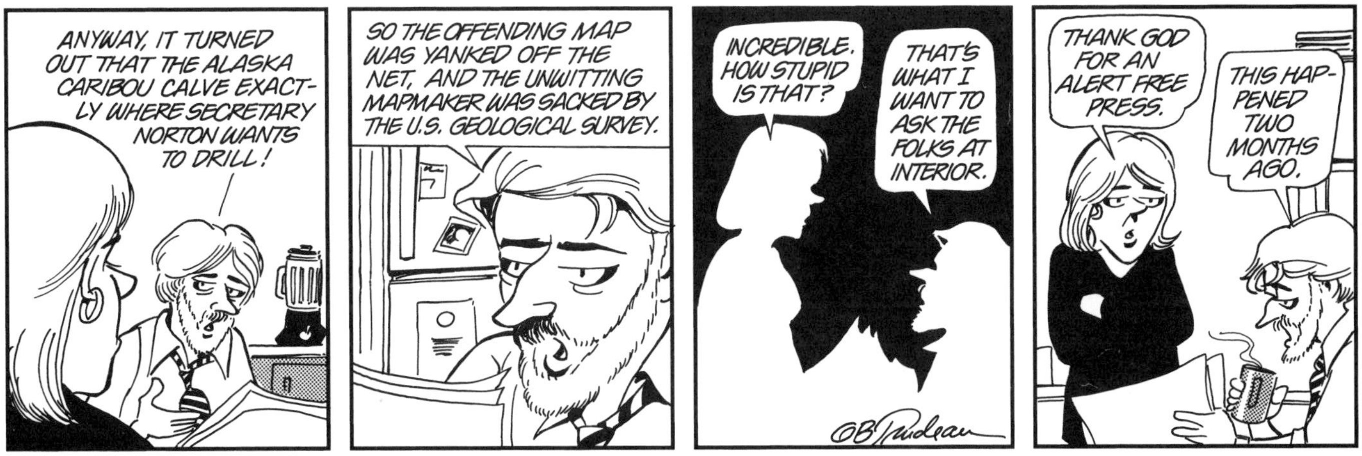
ANYWAY, IT TURNED OUT THAT THE ALASKA CARIBOU CALVE EXACTLY WHERE SECRETARY NORTON WANTS TO DRILL!
SO THE OFFENDING MAP WAS YANKED OFF THE NET, AND THE UNWITTING MAPMAKER WAS SACKED BY THE U.S. GEOLOGICAL SURVEY.
INCREDIBLE. HOW STUPID IS THAT?
THAT'S WHAT I WANT TO ASK THE FOLKS AT INTERIOR.
©B Trudeau
THANK GOD FOR AN ALERT FREE PRESS.
THIS HAPPENED TWO MONTHS AGO.

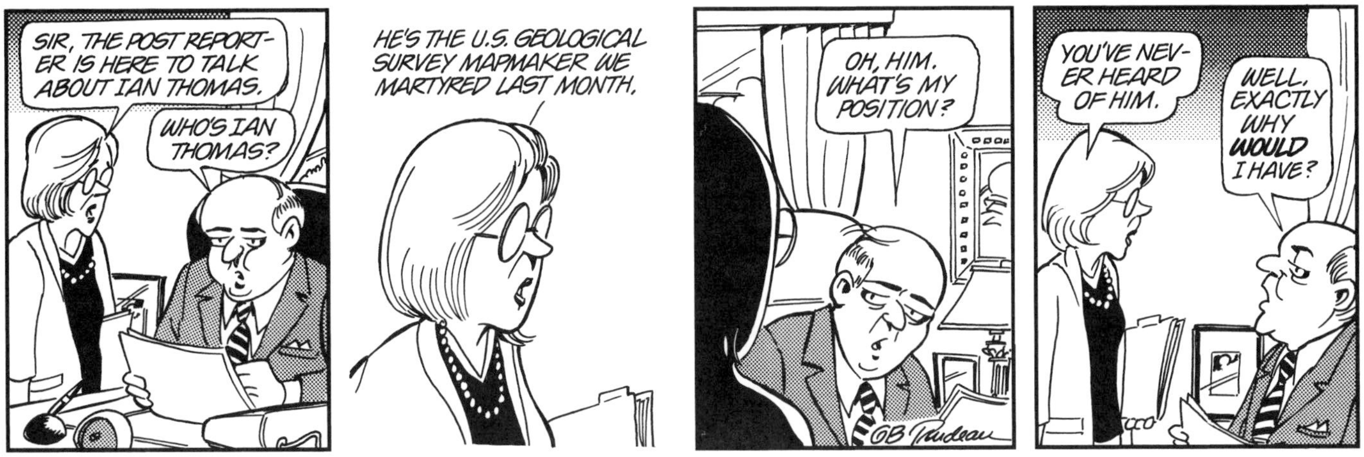
SIR, THE POST REPORTER IS HERE TO TALK ABOUT IAN THOMAS.
WHO'S IAN THOMAS?
HE'S THE U.S. GEOLOGICAL SURVEY MAPMAKER WE MARTYRED LAST MONTH.
OH, HIM. WHAT'S MY POSITION?
©B Trudeau
YOU'VE NEVER HEARD OF HIM.
WELL, EXACTLY WHY **WOULD** I HAVE?

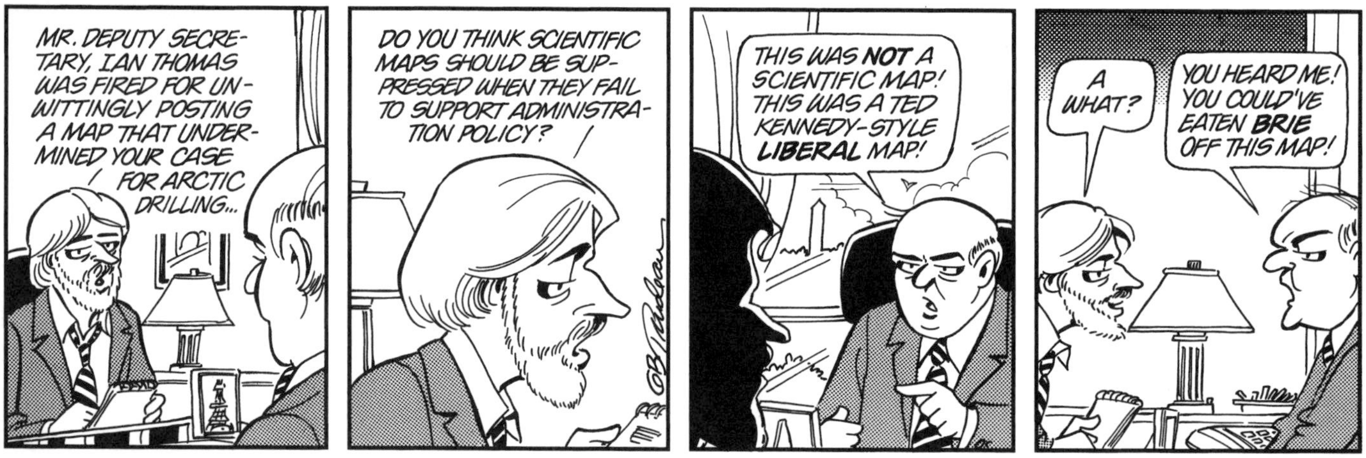
MR. DEPUTY SECRETARY, IAN THOMAS WAS FIRED FOR UNWITTINGLY POSTING A MAP THAT UNDERMINED YOUR CASE FOR ARCTIC DRILLING...
DO YOU THINK SCIENTIFIC MAPS SHOULD BE SUPPRESSED WHEN THEY FAIL TO SUPPORT ADMINISTRATION POLICY?
THIS WAS **NOT** A SCIENTIFIC MAP! THIS WAS A TED KENNEDY-STYLE **LIBERAL** MAP!
A WHAT?
YOU HEARD ME! YOU COULD'VE EATEN **BRIE** OFF THIS MAP!

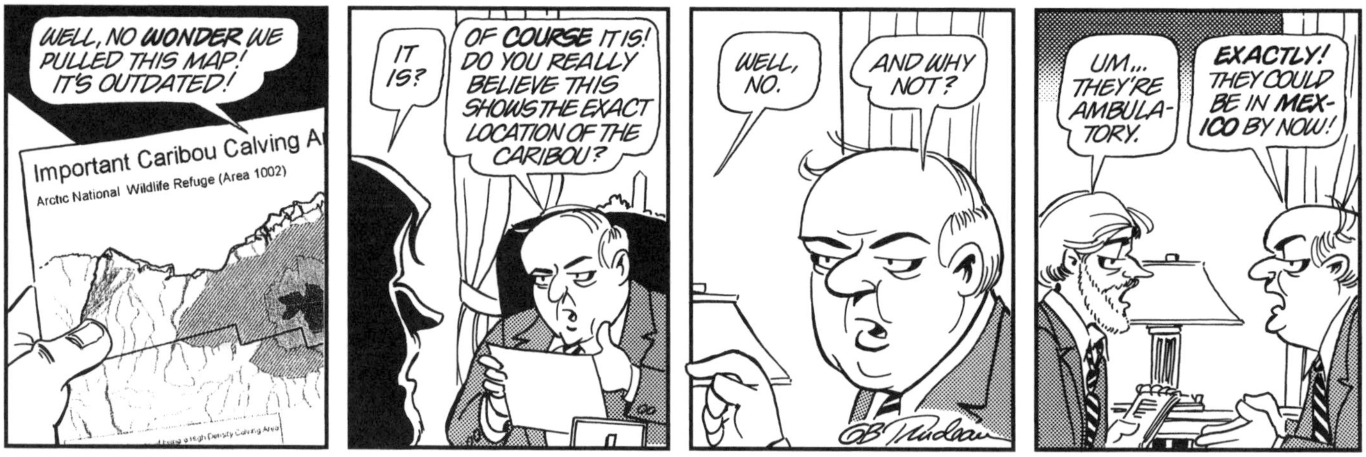
WELL, NO **WONDER** WE PULLED THIS MAP! IT'S OUTDATED!
Important Caribou Calving A
Arctic National Wildlife Refuge (Area 1002)
IT IS?
OF **COURSE** IT IS! DO YOU REALLY BELIEVE THIS SHOWS THE EXACT LOCATION OF THE CARIBOU?
WELL, NO.
AND WHY NOT?
UM... THEY'RE AMBULATORY.
EXACTLY! THEY COULD BE IN **MEXICO** BY NOW!

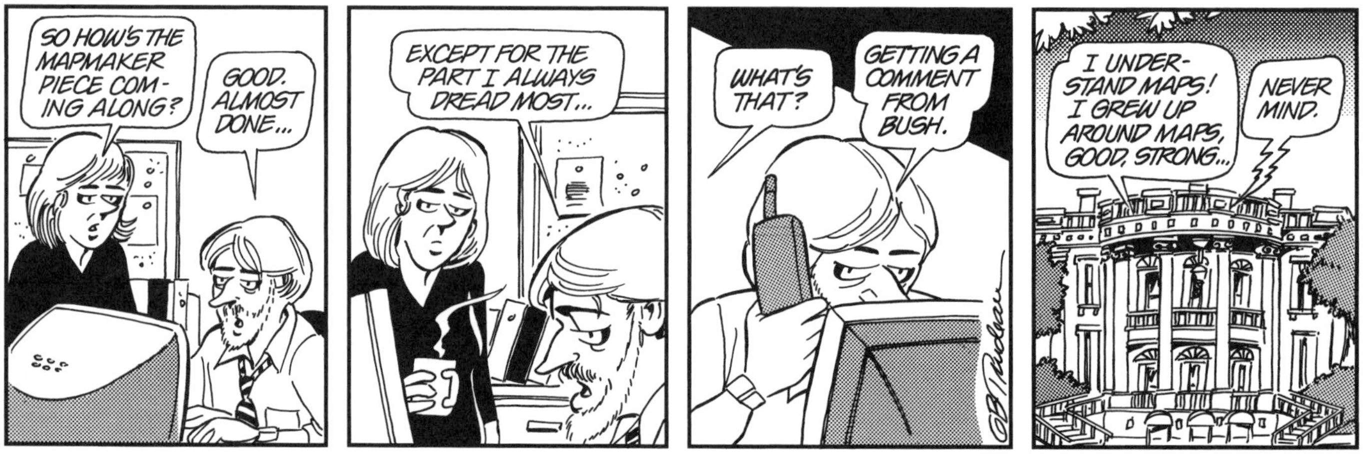
SO HOW'S THE MAPMAKER PIECE COMING ALONG?
GOOD. ALMOST DONE...
EXCEPT FOR THE PART I ALWAYS DREAD MOST...
WHAT'S THAT?
GETTING A COMMENT FROM BUSH.
I UNDERSTAND MAPS! I GREW UP AROUND MAPS, GOOD, STRONG...
NEVER MIND.

ON A WARM SPRING MORNING, YALE HONORS ONE OF ITS OWN.

GEORGE WALKER BUSH, CLASS OF '68...

MEDIOCRE STUDENT, FAILED OILMAN, PROBLEM DRINKER, YOU HAVE OVERCOME COUNTLESS PERSONAL LIMITATIONS...

TO DISTINGUISH YOURSELF... WELL, MAYBE "DISTINGUISH" ISN'T QUITE THE RIGHT WORD... NEVER MIND... TO DISTINGUISH YOURSELF BY WINNING THE PRESIDENCY...

AGAIN, "WINNING" MIGHT BE A LITTLE STRONG.

IT IS NOT! IT IS NOT!

GB Trudeau '70

AS YALE HONORS A RETURNING SON...

WHO'S THAT GETTING THE HONORARY DEGREE?

THE PRESIDENT OF THE UNITED STATES, YOU CHUCKLEHEAD!

WHOA... REALLY?

ARE YOU SURE? HE LOOKS SO MUCH SMALLER THAN LIFE.

GB Trudeau

AGAIN, MAYBE THE WORD "PROUD" IS OFF THE MARK...

JUST GIVE ME THE DAMN DECREE!

MEMBERS OF THE CLASS OF 2001— HOW SWEET IT IS, YOU KNOW?

WHEN I WAS HERE, RICH, WELL-CONNECTED KIDS FROM GREENWICH LOOKED DOWN ON A RICH, WELL-CONNECTED KID FROM TEXAS, EVEN IF HIS FAMILY WAS FROM GREENWICH!

YALE WAS A SMUG, ELITIST PLACE, WHERE INTELLECTUAL ARROGANCE WAS THE STATUS QUAD!

SEE? SEE?

QUO. QUO.

QUO. QUO, LOSER.

GB Trudeau

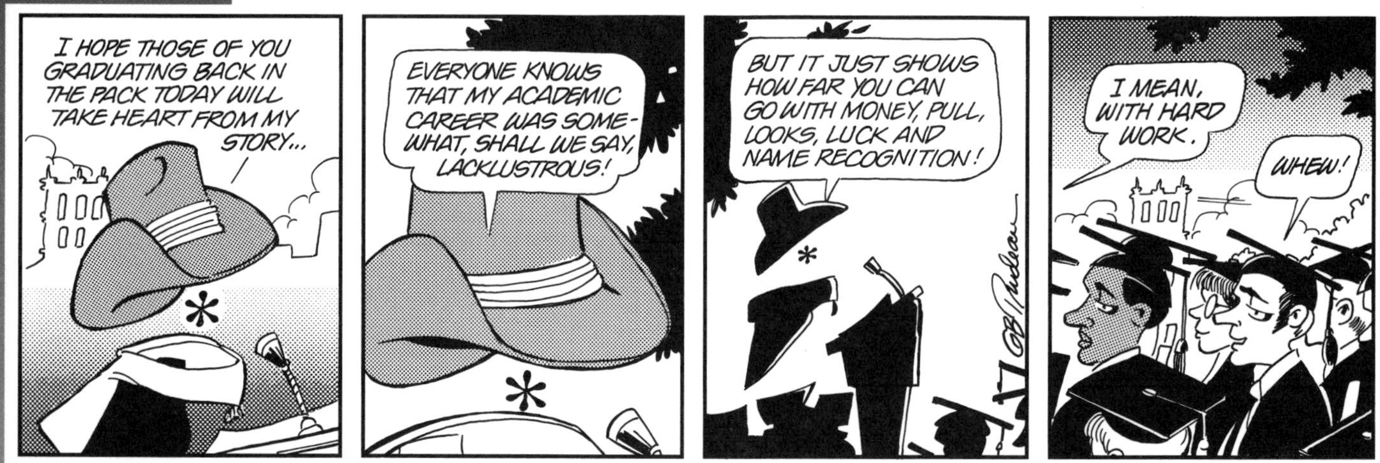
I HOPE THOSE OF YOU GRADUATING BACK IN THE PACK TODAY WILL TAKE HEART FROM MY STORY...
EVERYONE KNOWS THAT MY ACADEMIC CAREER WAS SOMEWHAT, SHALL WE SAY, LACKLUSTROUS!
BUT IT JUST SHOWS HOW FAR YOU CAN GO WITH MONEY, PULL, LOOKS, LUCK AND NAME RECOGNITION!
I MEAN, WITH HARD WORK.
WHEW!

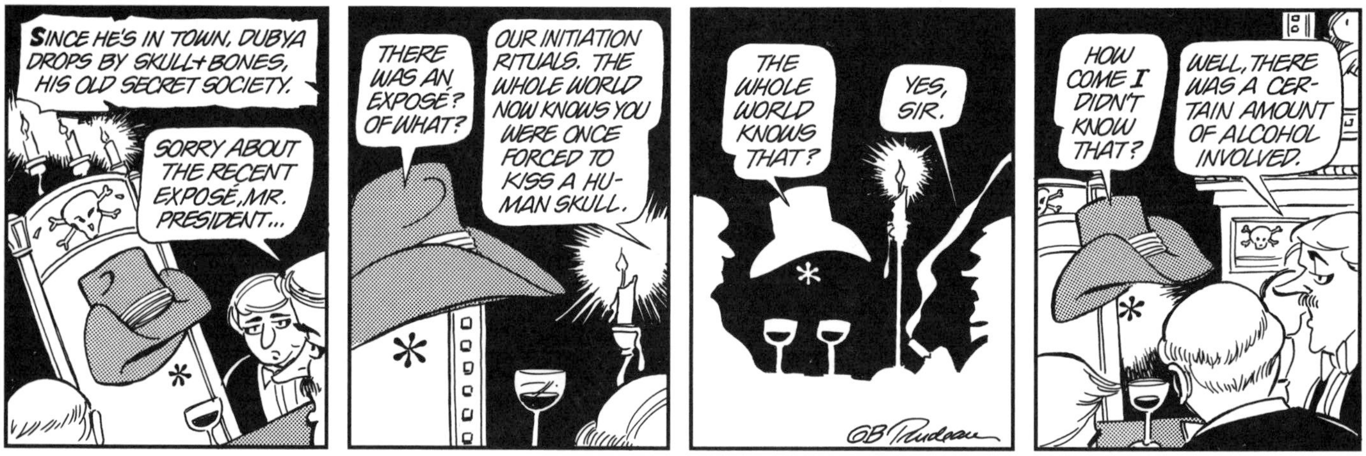
SINCE HE'S IN TOWN, DUBYA DROPS BY SKULL+BONES, HIS OLD SECRET SOCIETY.
SORRY ABOUT THE RECENT EXPOSÉ, MR. PRESIDENT...
THERE WAS AN EXPOSÉ? OF WHAT?
OUR INITIATION RITUALS. THE WHOLE WORLD NOW KNOWS YOU WERE ONCE FORCED TO KISS A HUMAN SKULL.
THE WHOLE WORLD KNOWS THAT?
YES, SIR.
HOW COME I DIDN'T KNOW THAT?
WELL, THERE WAS A CERTAIN AMOUNT OF ALCOHOL INVOLVED.

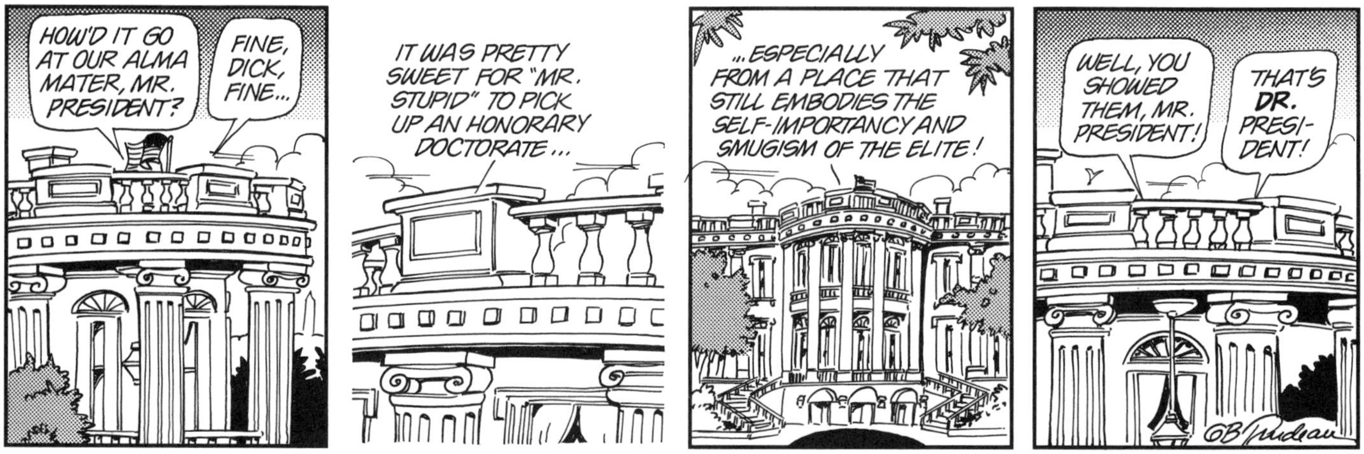
HOW'D IT GO AT OUR ALMA MATER, MR. PRESIDENT?
FINE, DICK, FINE...
IT WAS PRETTY SWEET FOR "MR. STUPID" TO PICK UP AN HONORARY DOCTORATE...
...ESPECIALLY FROM A PLACE THAT STILL EMBODIES THE SELF-IMPORTANCY AND SMUGISM OF THE ELITE!
WELL, YOU SHOWED THEM, MR. PRESIDENT!
THAT'S DR. PRESIDENT!